THE
CANADIAN
DICTIONARY
OF
BUSINESS
AND
ECONOMICS

DAVID CRANE

Published in 1993 by
Stoddart Publishing Co. Limited
34 Lesmill Road
Toronto, Canada
M3B 2T6
(416) 445-3333

Parts of this book originally appeared in *A Dictionary of Canadian Economics* published by Hurtig Publishers Ltd. in 1980.

Canadian Cataloguing in Publication Data

Crane, David.
The Canadian dictionary of business and economics

Previously published under title: A dictionary of Canadian economics.
ISBN 0-7737-2691-8

1. Economics — Dictionaries. 2. Canada — Economic conditions — 1945– — Dictionaries. I. Title. II. Title: A dictionary of Canadian economics.

HC112.C73 1993   330'.03   C93-093143-2

Cover Design: Brant Cowie/ArtPlus Limited

Printed and bound in the United States of America

To my parents, William and Mary Crane,
who brought me not only into the world but also to this
great country, which has so much to offer

Preface

This dictionary was born out of my own frustration at not being able to find the answers to questions when I wanted them. Whether it was a question of knowing what a budget deficit actually is, what leveraged buyout or junk bond really means, or how the Bank of Canada sets monetary policy, there was no single source to turn to. So, I decided to produce this dictionary, with a decidedly Canadian cast. In some respects this is an update of a similar dictionary I wrote in 1979, *A Dictionary of Canadian Economics*. But it is much more than that, for I found that in the space of barely a decade so much had changed in Canada. Not only did we have new terms, such as greenmail and porcupine, but much more significantly, most of the basic economic rules had changed. Laws dealing with competition policy, bankruptcy, all of our financial institutions, and intellectual property had been rewritten. We had the Goods and Services Tax, the Canada-United States Free Trade Agreement, Investment Canada, and now, the North American Free Trade Agreement. And we had new worries, such as trade-remedy laws, and new international commitments, such as Agenda 21, and new parameters for economics, such as sustainable development.

And it won't stop there. That's why I see a dictionary such as this as a project in need of continuous updating. This is where you, the reader and user, are so important: what terms are missing that you would like to see in future editions and what terms do you think could be better explained? Please let me know by sending your suggestions to me, care of the publisher.

In writing this dictionary, I needed and received a lot of help. My first thanks are to Mel Hurtig, who published my first dictionary and who agreed, as he was contemplating his new career, to let me take a proposal for this dictionary to Jack Stoddart at Stoddart Publishing. Everyone at Stoddart has been patient and positive as this project mushroomed. In particular, Donald G. Bastian and Elsha Leventis gave constant support. A special word of thanks is due to Heather Lang, who painstakingly edited the dictionary. Jane Tattersall of Carleton University also played a key role, as did many nameless people in government and private-sector bodies across the country.

And, of course, none of this would have been possible without the support, patience, and help of my wonderful wife, Françoise Hébert.

David Crane
Toronto, June, 1993

How to Use the Dictionary

The entries in this dictionary have been arranged alphabetically using the word-by-word system, in which headings are arranged according to the letters of the first word, with subsequent words used for determining order only when two or more headings begin with the same word. Entry titles appear in boldface type (e.g., **sustainable development**) and use capital letters only when the term is normally capped (e.g., **Prime Minister's Office**).

Wherever possible, the entries contain relevant Canadian information. Cross-references (marked in large capitals, e.g., CANADA-UNITED STATES FREE TRADE AGREEMENT) lead to other entries in the dictionary that will provide additional information on a subject or amplify an aspect of that subject.

Abbreviations

Following is a list of some common business and economics abbreviations:

AFL-CIO	American Federation of Labor-Congress of Industrial Organizations
AIB	Anti-Inflation Board
APEC	Asia Pacific Economic Co-operation Group
ASE	Alberta Stock Exchange
ASEAN	Association of South East Asian Nations
BCNI	Business Council on National Issues
BNA Act	British North America Act
BTU	British thermal unit
CA	certified accountant
CANSIM	Canadian Socioeconomic Information Management System
CBA	Canadian Bankers Association
CDC	Canada Development Corporation
CEO	chief executive officer
CESO	Canadian Executive Service Organization
CGA	certified general accountant
CIDA	Canadian International Development Agency
CLC	Canadian Labour Congress
CMA	Canadian Manufacturers' Association
CMHC	Canada Mortgage and Housing Corporation
COCOM	Co-ordinating Committee for Multilateral Export Controls
COMECON	Council for Mutual Economic Assistance
COO	chief operating officer
CPI	consumer price index
CPP	Canada Pension Plan
CRTC	Canadian Radio-television and Telecommunications Association
CSA	Canadian Standards Association
CSB	Canada Savings Bond
EC	European Community
ECC	Economic Council of Canada
ECU	European Currency Unit
EDC	Export Development Corporation
EFTA	European Free-Trade Association

EMS	European Monetary System
ERDA	Economic and Regional Development Agreements
FBDB	Federal Business Development Bank
FIFO	first in, first out
FIRA	Foreign Investment Review Agency
F.O.B.	free on board
FTA	Canada-United States Free Trade Agreement
GATT	General Agreement on Tariffs and Trade
GDP	gross domestic product
G-7	Group of Seven
GST	Goods and Services Tax
IATA	International Air Transport Association
IBRD	World Bank
ICAO	International Civil Aviation Organization
IDA	International Development Association
IDB	Inter-American Development Bank
ILO	International Labor Organization
IMF	International Monetary Fund
LAFTA	Latin-American Free-Trade Association
LIBOR	London Inter-Bank Offered Rate
LIFO	last in, first out
LME	London Metals Exchange
MBA	master of business administration
MLS	multiple-listing service
MSE	Montreal Stock Exchange
NAFTA	North American Free Trade Agreement
NAIRU	Non-accelerating Inflation Rate of Unemployment
NATO	North Atlantic Treaty Organization
NCI	National Commission on Inflation
NEB	National Energy Board
NEP	National Energy Program
NHA	National Housing Act
NRC	National Research Council
NYSE	New York Stock Exchange
OECD	Organization for Economic Co-operation and Development
OPEC	Organization of Oil Exporting Countries
OTC	over-the-counter
P/E	price/earnings ratio
PMO	Prime Minister's Office
R&D	research and development
RRIF	Registered Retirement Investment Fund
RRSP	Registered Retirement Savings Plan
SDR	Special Drawing Right
SIN	social insurance number
TQM	Total Quality Management
TSE	Toronto Stock Exchange
UN	United Nations
UNCTAD	United Nations Commission on Trade and Development
VAT	value-added tax
VSE	Vancouver Stock Exchange
WHO	World Health Organization
ZPG	zero population growth

ASEAN *See* ASSOCIATION OF SOUTH EAST ASIAN NATIONS.

ability-to-pay principle of taxation   The principle that the taxes paid by individual taxpayers should be based on their actual income and wealth, the idea being that Canadians who have high incomes have a greater ability to pay than Canadians with low incomes. This is the tax philosophy of most modern countries, including Canada, although the tax system in Canada has shifted to greater dependence on CONSUMPTION TAXES and to lower top marginal rates of PERSONAL INCOME TAX. The ability-to-pay principle assumes that one of the roles of the tax system is to redistribute income by making those with high incomes pay a proportionately greater share of the costs of government by taxing each $1,000 of additional income at a higher rate of tax. In 1992, the federal government applied a tax rate of 17 percent on taxable income up to $29,590, 26 percent on taxable income between $29,951 and $59,179, and 29 percent on taxable income of $59,180 or more; provincial tax rates are a percentage of the federal rate, ranging from 46 percent in Alberta to 64.5 percent in

Newfoundland, except in Quebec, which operates its own provincial tax system. The ROYAL COMMISSION ON TAXATION, which conducted the most sweeping review of the Canadian tax system in modern times, stressed in its 1967 report that "taxes are equitable when they are levied according to a defined tax capacity, or ability to pay, of individuals or groups." *See also* BENEFITS-RECEIVED PRINCIPLE OF TAXATION.

absenteeism   Improper absence from work by an employee. While there are legitimate reasons for an employee's absence, including a labour dispute, vacation, illness, or family death, employees will sometimes not show up for work simply because they don't feel like it. Companies or countries with high rates of absenteeism face higher costs and poorer productivity because missing workers slow down production or force companies to keep more workers on OVERTIME. Repeated absenteeism can be a cause for dismissal.

absolute advantage   The ability of a country or business enterprise to unilaterally set the price of a good or service without fear of competition because it possesses a unique resource or technology that allows it to produce more of that good or service than a second country or business with the same inputs. *See also* COMPARATIVE ADVANTAGE.

abstinence from consumption   The decision by an individual to save instead of spend. The saver forgoes consumption now in order to enjoy greater consumption in the future, which is made possible by the interest or capital gain resulting from saving and investing money instead of spending.

abuse of dominant position   Anti-competitive behaviour by dominant firms in an industry. Examples include: the acquisition of a customer who would otherwise be available as a market for a competing firm to impede a competitor's entry into the market; the purchase of products to prevent a reduction in existing price levels; the sale of products at a price lower than acquisition cost to eliminate or discipline a competitor. This type of behaviour is reviewable by the COMPETITION TRIBUNAL. For this provision to apply, one or a small number of firms must substantially control a class of business in Canada and have engaged in or be engaged in anti-competitive acts that prevent or lessen competition substantially. The tribunal may order a halt to certain business practices, order a partial divestment of assets, or take stronger remedial action in the most serious cases.

accelerated depreciation   A tax incentive to encourage business investment. The incentive, which is usually for a limited period, allows a business to depreciate a new investment against its tax liabilities at a faster rate than normal, although it does not permit a larger amount of depreciation over the life of the asset. By deducting larger amounts of depreciation in the early years of an asset, a business reduces its

immediate tax liabilities and, in effect, gets an interest-free loan. This incentive has been used a number of times by the federal government — in the 1963, 1965, 1972, 1973, and 1992 budgets, for example. *See* CAPITAL-COST ALLOWANCES.

accelerator principle   The process by which changes in national income determine the rate of capital investment by businesses in productive facilities. While business always has ongoing investment expenditures to maintain productive capacity, an increase in national income will result in increased consumption spending and, hence, the need for additional investment to meet this higher level of demand — in other words, to maintain a higher level of output, a higher level of capital stock is needed. This means that investment is tied to an increase in output and not the level of output. These changes in investment spending, working through the MULTIPLIER, in turn affect the rate of change in total income in the economy.

The accelerator helps to explain the BUSINESS CYCLE and is a factor in assessments of the economic outlook. For example, as the level of output rises during the recovery period of the cycle and business approaches the limits of its capacity to produce goods, further small increases in demand may generate significant new spending on plant, machinery, and equipment, so that business can meet rising demand. This additional capital spending will, through the multiplier, add to total income and thus to the rising level of consumer demand. Similarly, as consumer spending levels off and even stops growing, business will cease to add to its productive capacity. The absence of new capital spending, again working through the multiplier, will slow the economy down further by reducing the demand for machinery and equipment and new factories. Hence, a recession may occur even though consumer demand remains high because the economy has less business investment. At some point, though, the productive capacity of business will decline as machinery is removed from production through wear and tear, to the point where companies must begin to replace their machinery and equipment. When this happens, the economy begins to recover from the recession. As investment rises, the multiplier effect helps to boost consumer demand, thus generating new growth and the need for even greater capital investment. The accelerator, then, reinforces economic growth as the business cycle moves from recession to recovery, but has the opposite effect during the downswing into recession.

acceptance company A SALES-FINANCE COMPANY.

acceptance financing A technique to obtain short-term credit used by exporters in possession of a draft from an importer's bank authorizing payment on a pre-determined date. The exporter can take the draft to a bank that will pay the draft, less a percentage that is equivalent to the interest rate it would charge for a loan of the same amount and maturity. The draft, when accepted, is called a banker's acceptance. When the draft reaches its maturity date, the accepting bank presents it for payment to the importer's bank.

acceptance paper *See* COMMERCIAL PAPER.

account **1.** In bookkeeping, the record of expenses on the left side of the ledger and of income or revenue on the right side. **2.** In banks, trust companies, credit unions, and caisses populaires, the record of deposits and withdrawals of a customer. **3.** In a department store or other sales organization, or a credit card company, a statement of purchases and payments. **4.** In advertising, the

ongoing work for a client's particular product or service.

accountant A person who has met the admission requirements of a professional organization and who carries out bookkeeping, auditing, and other financial reporting and analysis. This is a generic term referring to a wide range of skills. CHARTERED ACCOUNTANTS are licensed to conduct public accounting or auditing across Canada while CERTIFIED GENERAL ACCOUNTANTS are licensed to do so in only some provinces. CERTIFIED MANAGEMENT ACCOUNTANTS work as in-house accountants in business and other organizations. *See also* AUDITOR.

accounting The profession of preparing and auditing reports on the financial transactions of businesses, government agencies and departments, charitable institutions, and other organizations. *See also* GENERALLY ACCEPTED ACCOUNTING PRINCIPLES.

accounting period The fiscal year of a corporation or other organization, or the period between the dates of two consecutive financial reports, as in quarterly reports. Corporations are required by law to produce an audited ANNUAL REPORT while publicly traded companies must also produce an unaudited QUARTERLY REPORT.

accounts payable The outstanding bills of a firm that are payable within 12 months; the money that a firm owes its suppliers for goods and services purchased for the normal operations of the business. Accounts payable are included on the BALANCE SHEET under CURRENT LIABILITIES.

accounts receivable The money that is owed to a firm by its customers for goods or services they have purchased from it and which must be paid within 12 months. Accounts receivable are included on the BALANCE SHEET under CURRENT ASSETS.

accrual-basis accounting   The standard method of business accounting, with revenues and expenses recorded at the time that transactions occur, rather than when payment is actually made or received. Thus, in a company annual report, the net earnings shown represent the profit or loss on the company's operations that occurred during the accounting period, rather than actual cash transactions. *See also* CASH-BASIS ACCOUNTING.

accrued interest   The interest that has built up on a loan or a security such as a BOND since the last interest payment was made. When someone buys a bond, the accrued interest will be taken into account in the price.

accumulated dividend   A dividend that is due on a preferred share but has not been paid. It becomes an obligation of the corporation; until it has been paid, no dividend can be paid to common shareholders.

Achnacarry Agreement   An agreement made by the world's three largest oil companies, Royal Dutch Shell, the Anglo-Persian Oil Company (later British Petroleum), and Standard Oil of New Jersey (later Exxon), at Achnacarry Castle in Scotland on September 17, 1928 to fix world oil prices and end a costly international price war in oil. Under the so called As-Is Agreement, the oil companies agreed to accept the existing shares each held in the world oil market, and to take other steps to achieve price stability and restrain oil production. Between 1928 and 1932, a number of other oil companies, including Texaco, Gulf, and Mobil, signed the agreement. By 1932, a number of other agreements had been signed to control prices and production in regional oil markets and to allow the larger oil companies to acquire control of smaller companies and thus prevent or limit competition. In 1938, Standard of New Jersey gave notice of its intention to withdraw from the agreement, and the following year the agreement was ended.

acid-test ratio   A measure of a company's ability to pay its bills and meet other obligations; it is also known as the liquid or quick ratio. The ratio is calculated by dividing the company's quick assets (current assets minus inventory) by its current liabilities. A ratio of, say, 1.5:1, means that there is $1.50 of quick assets for every $1 of current liabilities. If it were, say, 0.75:1, there would be just 75 cents of quick assets to meet every $1 of current liabilities. There is no general rule to say what the ratio should be, but if it is more than 1:1 then a company is considered to be in a good financial position. However, if a company has a rapid turnover of inventory, then a ratio of less than 1:1 might be acceptable.

acquisition   *See* TAKEOVER.

across the board   **1.** In a collective agreement, the same wage increase for all employees covered by the agreement. **2.** In pricing policy, a uniform price increase or reduction for all products in a producer's line or for all products on the shelves of a retailer. **3.** In trade policy, a uniform tariff reduction or increase.

act of God   A natural disaster that could not have been foreseen, or if foreseen, whose consequences could not have been prevented. The damage caused by a flood, earthquake, hurricane, or tornado, for example. Insurance companies do not include coverage for acts of God in normal policies; insurance can be purchased, but it is often prohibitively expensive.

active market A stock, commodity, or bond market in which there is a high volume of turnover generally, or for a particular share, commodity, or bond. The existence of an active market for an investment will make it more appealing since the investor can readily resell an investment without having to take a big discount.

active shares A daily listing compiled by a STOCK EXCHANGE and published on the financial pages of a newspaper, showing the shares traded the previous day, or in some instances the same day, by price and volume, along with their high and low prices during the previous 12 months.

actuary A person trained in mathematics and statistics who calculates the risks of insuring people for insurance companies. These calculations, depending on age, sex, occupation, and other factors, help to determine the premiums charged to particular individuals for insurance coverage. To practice as an actuary, a person must meet the professional standards and pass the requirements of the Canadian Institute of Actuaries.

ad valorem tax An indirect tax such as a tariff, excise tax, or duty that is levied as a percent of the value of the item taxed. The term is from the Latin, meaning "on the value of the item."

adjuster A person whose job it is to assess damage resulting from a fire, accident, theft, vandalism, or other cause of damage or loss against which an individual or organization is insured, and to arrive at an agreement with the insured individual or organization on the amount of compensation to be paid. The adjuster acts on behalf of an insurance company or broker.

adjustment assistance Programs to help workers and firms affected by reductions in tariffs or other trade liberalization measures. For workers, the policies can include retraining, payments to encourage early retirement, or mobility grants to help workers move to another community where the chances of obtaining a new job are higher. For companies, assistance can include grants or low-interest loans to modernize facilities or to develop new or improved products.

adjustment mechanism The process of correcting a balance of payments imbalance, such as a chronic CURRENT ACCOUNT deficit. A country can change its exchange rate, pursue domestic policies affecting prices and incomes, or alter policies on trade, travel, and currency transactions. A country with a deficit problem could devalue its currency to boost exports and discourage imports, adopt strict policies at home to curb inflation and cool domestic demand, and, under the Articles of Agreement of the INTERNATIONAL MONETARY FUND (IMF) for use in a serious crisis (under Article VIII), impose import, currency, and other controls affecting its trading partners provided there is IMF approval of the plan. A country with a continuing large current-account surplus could raise its exchange rate, making exports costlier and imports cheaper, or lower barriers to imports and boost domestic demand, or do both. The IMF compels countries seeking balance-of-payments assistance to pursue an adjustment program that must meet its approval as a condition of IMF assistance.

administered price A price that is set, usually in a monopolistic or oligopolistic industry, without great regard for the LAW OF SUPPLY AND DEMAND. Although prices in a competitive market would be expected to decline during a recession, when demand is weak, administered prices are unlikely to fall and may even be increased. Producers calculate their costs and add on a mark-up designed to yield a profit target regardless of short-term market conditions. Pharmaceutical companies, for example, may be in a position to extract high prices due to a lack of competing products and lengthy PATENT protection. Through regulatory processes, governments can also set prices or permit agencies to set prices — such as telephone and electricity rates, prices of products regulated by farm marketing boards, or prices charged through provincially controlled liquor boards.

administrative costs *See* OVERHEAD.

administrative law The law that governs the conduct of government regulatory agencies, tribunals, and other bodies to ensure that the rights of those who fall under the jurisdiction of these bodies are protected. The FEDERAL COURT OF CANADA hears appeals from those who believe that their legal rights have been overridden by such government bodies.

advance A payment to a business firm or crown corporation to tide it over until arrangements for long-term financing have been made. An advance is, in effect, a short-term loan.

advertising Methods of informing the public of the availability, quality, price, and distinctive features of goods and services, and of stimulating consumers to buy particular brands of goods or services. Most advertising is placed in newspapers and magazines, on radio or television, on billboards, or in direct mail.

Economists are divided over the role of advertising. Some argue that it is a vital means of informing consumers about the existence of and improvements in goods and services, leading to increased demand. Without such information, consumers would not benefit from the lower prices achieved through ECONOMIES OF SCALE, which are made possible by mass markets. Other economists argue that much advertising spending is wasted because it simply leads to people buying brand B of a product instead of brand A of the same product, or leads people to buy things they don't need or don't really want. They also argue that a large investment in advertising by a company is a form of product differentiation that acts as a barrier to the entry of would-be competitors into the market. *See also* ADVERTISING AGENCY, BRAND LOYALTY, MISLEADING ADVERTISING, PRODUCT DIFFERENTIATION. Advertising spending as a proportion of the selling price of a good or service varies widely, with advertising spending constituting a much higher proportion of the price of consumer goods and services than capital or intermediate goods and services. The Association of Canadian Advertisers represents major advertisers and is based in Toronto. Statistics Canada, in its annual survey, *Business Services,* provides some information on the advertising industry (publication 63-232).

advertising agency A firm that performs services for advertisers, including the creation and production of advertising campaigns, MARKET RESEARCH, and the purchase and placement of advertising in different media. The agency is either paid a commission of, say, 15 percent of the value of the advertising it places in the media for a client, or it bills the client for the work actually done. In some cases billing is split between the agency that creates the campaign and the firm that purchases the media space. The Institute of Canadian Advertising and the Canadian Advertising Research Foundation, both based in Toronto, are two industry associations.

Advisory Council on Adjustment A

five-person council, headed by then BCE Inc. chairman, Jean de Grandpré, appointed in 1988 by the federal government to examine how Canadian companies and workers should position themselves to benefit from the CANADA-UNITED STATES FREE TRADE AGREEMENT, identify specific adjustment issues arising from the trade agreement, and recommend changes in policies for labour adjustment and industrial competitiveness so that Canadians could take full advantage of the trade agreement. The council published its report, *Adjusting to Win*, in 1989. It rejected specific measures for workers affected by the free trade agreement, arguing that it was too difficult to identify the specific causes of plant shutdowns or corporate downsizing, and maintaining it would be unfair to have more generous programs for workers affected by the trade agreement than for workers affected by technological change or competition from other countries. It advocated a "trampoline" approach to labour adjustment, rather than simply reinforcing the social safety net, and advised that adjustment policies should be designed to help get workers back into the workplace as fast as possible. Education and training, along with a commitment to lifelong learning, were identified as the most critical needs. Canada's first ministers were urged to conduct a review of the education/training system, possibly through a royal commission. Industry training for employees should be mandated through a tax liability of 1 percent of payroll, with companies whose training spending fell below that level paying an equivalent tax that would go into a national training fund. The council also called for increased federal spending on training and adjustment, better advance notice of layoffs through changes to labour laws, assured severance pay equal to one week of pay for each year of employment to a maximum of 26 weeks, the immediate payment of unemploy-

ment-insurance benefits despite severance pay, improved benefits for workers 55 and older, and establishment of a special fund to compensate workers for back pay and benefits when companies go bankrupt.

The council report also outlined a number of measures to overcome the weakness of Canadian industry in research and development (R&D) and international competitiveness. It urged a greater effort to boost Canadian R&D, including setting R&D targets for individual industrial sectors and developing programs to achieve these targets; it also urged greater government-industry co-operation through government procurement and contracts to strengthen R&D. The report also called for strengthened technology-diffusion programs, more support by provincial governments for universities, especially in science and engineering, and consideration of improved R&D tax incentives. It called for reform of the manufacturers' sales tax, which discriminated against Canadian-made goods, an examination of the high cost of capital in Canada, removal of interprovincial barriers to trade and mobility, and a number of measures to strengthen the export efforts of Canadian companies. The report also addressed the problems of the food-processing industry. It called for a two-price system for dairy and poultry products, which would permit food processors to buy these products at the same price as their U.S. competitors. It urged other measures for the canola, flour milling, fruit and vegetable processing, and wine industries.

Advisory Council on the Status of Women An advisory body of up to 30 members established in 1973 in response to the report of the 1970 ROYAL COMMISSION ON THE STATUS OF WOMEN, to advise the minister responsible for the status of women in the federal cabinet. Its mandate is to bring before both the government and the public matters of concern to women and to advise the minister on matters relating to the status of women raised by the minister or by the advisory council's members. It acts as a research centre on women's issues and as a forum for different groups that want to address concerns such as employment equity, childcare facilities, women's and child poverty, and adequate workplace benefits.

affiliated company   A subsidiary company, or one that is related through common ownership by the same parent company. The parent company may own less than 50 percent of the voting shares of the subsidiary but still exercise effective control.

affirmative action   Federal or provincial measures to eliminate job discrimination and make up for the effects of past discrimination. For example, federally regulated companies are required to file reports showing what steps they are taking to increase the career opportunities for equity groups — women, aboriginals, the physically handicapped, and visible minorities. *See also* EMPLOYMENT EQUITY.

affluent society   The term made famous by economist John Kenneth GALBRAITH in his 1958 book of the same name. In it, he argued that scarcity was no longer a problem in the private sector, and economists should therefore encourage the allocation of additional resources to the public sector, where scarcity in the form of inadequate health care, schools, housing, parks, and other services and facilities still existed. An affluent society, Galbraith contended, produced more cars and trucks but neglected the construction of roads, highways, and public transit. Business was able, through advertising, to maintain the idea of scarcity or unfilled needs for consumer

goods, but no equivalent pressure existed for the production of more public goods and services, even though the need for them was much more urgent. This imbalance was a sign that the market economy by itself could not effectively allocate resources to meet the real needs of society. Increases in the general welfare and increases in GROSS DOMESTIC PRODUCT, he argued, were not necessarily the same thing.

African Development Bank (AfDB)   A regional development bank established in 1964 to help fund the economic development of the newly independent African states. The African Development Fund, an affiliated agency, was established in 1972 with membership open to non-African states. In 1982, membership in the African Development Bank itself was expanded to include non-African states, and Canada became a member. Canada's paid-in capital contribution at the end of 1992 was US$84.1 million, and Canada's total capital commitment of paid-in and collectible capital was US$1.4 billion. In addition, Canada helped organize the African Development Fund in 1973, as part of the bank, to provide low-cost financing; Canada's pledged capital at the end of 1992 was US$782 million. Canada has 3.32 percent of the bank's votes. Its headquarters are located in Abidjan, Ivory Coast. The bank provides commercial and concessional loans and technical assistance to member countries in Africa for economic development, transportation, energy, agriculture, and social infrastructure such as health and education.

agency shop   A unionized workplace where workers who are covered by a collective agreement do not have to belong to the union. Instead, the employer deducts an amount equal to union dues from non-members and turns over the money to the union. *See also* CLOSED SHOP, UNION SHOP.

Agenda 21 A report prepared by the UNITED NATIONS CONFERENCE ON ENVIRONMENT AND DEVELOPMENT (the "Earth Summit"), held in Rio de Janeiro, Brazil, in June, 1992, that represents a global consensus and political commitment at the heads of government level about what needs to be done to address world poverty and the continuing deterioration of the ecosystems that are essential for the well-being of all human life. The report recognizes that the present division in living standards between the rich and poor nations around the world is not sustainable and sets out an action plan on what is needed to bring human population and aspirations into some kind of environmental balance by the middle of the 21st century. Its goal is a "global partnership" for SUSTAINABLE DEVELOPMENT, including "a substantial flow of new and additional financial resources" to developing countries to assist their economic growth, based on sustainable development. The report estimates that US$125 billion a year, which is US$70 billion a year more than current aid financing, is needed to implement the action plan. The report also calls for the creation of a UNITED NATIONS (UN) COMMISSION ON SUSTAINABLE DEVELOPMENT to monitor the implementation of Agenda 21 by UN members and UN agencies, including the WORLD BANK and INTERNATIONAL MONETARY FUND The consensus on Agenda 21 at the Earth Summit in Rio marked the culmination of a process that began in December, 1983, when the UN General Assembly established the World Commission on Environ-ment and Development, chaired by Gro Harlem Bruntland, Prime Minister of Norway. One Canadian, Maurice Strong, served on the commission, and another, Jim MacNeill, served as secretary-general of the commission. Its report, *Our Com-*

mon Future, was published in 1987; it called for a new world order based on sustainable development. This led to the establishment of the UN Conference on Environment and Development, with four month-long meetings of the Preparatory Committee, starting in August, 1990, and concluding in April, 1992, which prepared the Agenda 21 report for the Earth Summit in June 1992. But while there was a consensus in favour of Agenda 21, no financial commitments were made by member countries to provide the additional US$70 billion a year in international aid to assure its implementation.

The Agenda 21 report consists of 40 chapters divided into four sections. Section 1 deals with the social and economic dimensions. In this section the preamble and the next seven chapters indicate the enormous challenges in adapting human and social behaviour to sustainable development in light of existing social and economic arrangements. This section calls for an acceleration of sustainable development, including an open world trading system, an expanded effort to combat poverty (including greater attention to health and education, safe water, sanitation, and land restoration), changes in consumption patterns (including greater energy efficiency and reduced wasteful packaging of new products), improved family planning to curb population growth, expanded programs for human health, investment in land-use planning and urban infrastructure, and research to integrate environmental protection, degradation, and restoration costs in environmental decision making.

Section 2 outlines resources for development and includes protection of the atmosphere, planning and management of land use, combatting of deforestation and desertification, mountain development, agriculture and rural development, conservation of biodiversity, sustainable biotechnology, protection of the oceans, protection and management of water resources, management of toxic chemicals, treatment of hazardous wastes, management of solid wastes and sewage, and treatment of radioactive wastes.

Section 3 sets out measures to strengthen major groups in the development process. These include programs for women, children and youth, indigenous people, support for nongovernmental organizations (NGOs), strengthening local institutions, assistance for workers and trade unions, promotion of responsible entrepreneurship and adaptation to sustainable development by business and industry, strengthening of international institutions in science and technology, and assistance for farmers.

Section 4 sets out the means of implementation. This includes financial resources of US$125 billion a year and achievement of the aid-assistance target for industrial countries, including Canada, of aid equal to 0.7 percent of GROSS NATIONAL PRODUCT as fast as possible, along with mechanisms to manage the flow of aid. Other measures include transfer of technology to developing countries, support for science for sustainable development, education and public awareness campaigns, capacity building in the developing countries to implement Agenda 21, the establishment of international institutions, including a UN Commission on Sustainable Development, development and strengthening of international law on environmental protection and trade policy, and improvement in the supply of data. *See also* EARTH COUNCIL, UNITED NATIONS CONFERENCE ON ENVIRONMENT AND DEVELOPMENT.

agent   Someone who acts for another person or group of persons in dealings with a third party. For example, a union officer acts on behalf of employees in dealing with their employer, a real-estate agent acts on behalf of a person trying to sell property, and an agent acts on behalf of athletes, entertainers, and artists in negotiating a contract. *See also* BROKER.

aggregate demand   The total demand for goods and services in the economy. It determines the overall level of activity in the economy, including the level of production and employment. Hence policies to change the level of production or employment are known as DEMAND MANAGEMENT policies. The level of aggregate demand is the total of GROSS DOMESTIC PRODUCT, published quarterly by Statistics Canada (publication 13-001). Its main components are consumer spending on goods and services; government spending on goods and services; capital investment spending by business and government; changes in inventories; and net exports of goods and services. The importance of aggregate demand in determining levels of output and employment, and hence the need for policies to stimulate aggregate demand when unemployment is high or restrain aggregate demand when inflation threatens, was first identified by John Maynard KEYNES.

aggregate supply   The total supply of goods and services produced in the economy, minus exports but plus imports.

agribusiness   A term originally used to describe the agricultural economy, ranging from the production of farm supplies, such as tractors, fertilizers, and pesticides, to the production, transportation, and distribution of farm products to food processors and grocery stores. Today, it is used to describe major farm corporations and food-processing companies that some farm groups fear plan to take over much of the country's farmland and squeeze out the family farm as the principal supplier of food.

Agricultural Products Co-operative Marketing Act A 1939 law passed by Parliament to help farmers establish marketing pools so that they could get better prices for their products. The passage of the act was an important step in the development of FARM MARKETING BOARDS in Canada. The federal government had first tried in the early 1930s to give farmers the power to establish marketing boards to control the sale of their products with the Natural Products Marketing Act of 1934. But this legislation was ruled unconstitutional by the courts. In 1936, British Columbia passed its Natural Products Marketing Act, which the courts found to be within provincial jurisdiction; other provinces then modelled their legislation on that of British Columbia. Under its 1939 legislation, the federal government guaranteed farmers an initial payment for their products at the time of delivery to the pool, usually a percentage of the estimated market price. The law thus made it easier for farmers to form national marketing organizations, which could get them better prices by negotiating from a position of strength with food processors and food-store chains. The legislation did not cover wheat and other grains, which came under the jurisdiction of the CANADIAN WHEAT BOARD.

Agricultural Products Marketing Act A federal law, passed in 1949, that allows the federal government to delegate powers to provincial marketing boards so that they can engage in interprovincial or export trade. Without such enabling legislation, provincial marketing boards would be restricted to activities within their own provincial boundaries. See also FARM PRODUCTS MARKETING AGENCIES ACT.

Agricultural Rehabilitation and Development Act (ARDA) A regional development program launched in 1961 to alleviate rural poverty and to finance water and land-use projects. In cost-sharing arrangements with the provinces, ARDA worked initially to keep farmers on the land through programs of farm consolidation and land reclamation. Its emphasis later shifted to land-use projects, including the conversion of low-productivity farmland for other purposes, such as recreation, woodlot, and timber, or for soil- and water-conservation projects. It was replaced by the Agricultural and Rural Development Act in 1967.

Agricultural Stabilization Board A federal crown corporation established in 1958 to stabilize or support farm prices. The initial commodities it was set up to help were slaughter capital, hogs, sheep, industrial milk, industrial cream, corn, soybeans, oats, and barley. Since then, other commodities have been added, including apples, tomatoes, potatoes, and wool. The board determines a prescribed price for a commodity, usually 90 percent of the five-year average of the market price, adjusted for the inflation in the costs of production. It made DEFICIENCY PAYMENTS when prices were below the prescribed price and purchases quantities of the surplus commodity to help raise the market price. The agency ensured farmers received a minimum price for their products. It was replaced in 1991 by the FARM INCOME PROTECTION ACT.

Agricultural Supplies Board A federal board established during the Second World War to ensure that agricultural production in Canada was high enough to meet Canadian and British fibre needs. The board allocated fertilizer and pesticide supplies and arranged the production of seeds normally imported from Europe. Working with the federal board were provincial production committees. Independent of the board but working with it were three other boards that purchased Canadian farm products for shipment to Britain. These were the Bacon Board (later the Meat Board), the Dairy Products Board, and the Special Products Board. This apparatus was dismantled at the end of the Second World War, in 1945.

Agriculture, Department of   The federal government department responsible for the well-being of the Canadian agricultural and food sector. It is responsible for food production and inspection, research and development, farm stabilization and relief measures, the pursuit of new markets, farm credit, compensation in the event of crop failure, emergency farm relief due to flooding or other natural disasters, and crop insurance. The department also provides technical and other services to improve farm productivity; it promotes the most effective ways to use fertilizers and improved crop- and livestock-production technologies. As well, the department inspects and grades farm products to maintain high quality. In addition, the department operates research laboratories and experimental farms to conduct research on crops, livestock, soil, and biotechnology, as well as other research. The CANADIAN WHEAT BOARD, the CANADIAN GRAIN COMMISSION, the NATIONAL FARM PRODUCTS MARKETING COUNCIL, the CANADIAN DAIRY COMMISSION, the FARM CREDIT CORPORATION, and the AGRICULTURAL STABILIZATION BOARD all report to the Minister of Agriculture. In addition, the department administers the PRAIRIE FARM REHABILITATION ACT. The department dates back to 1867. See also AGRICULTURAL PRODUCTS MARKETING ACT, CROP INSURANCE, LIVESTOCK FEED BOARD OF CANADA, FARM PRODUCTS MARKETING AGENCIES ACT, FARM IMPROVEMENT LOANS ACT, SUPPLY MANAGEMENT and FARM INCOME PROTECTION ACT.

Air Canada   A Canadian airline established by the federal government in 1937 as Trans-Canada Air Lines. The airline was founded to develop a transcontinental air service to all parts of the country, although its first commercial route was between Vancouver and Seattle. By 1939, the airline was offering cross-Canada service from Montreal to Vancouver, and this was soon extended to a coast-to-coast service. In 1943, the airline began transatlantic service. The airline expanded rapidly after the Second World War and either directly, or in association with other airlines, offered worldwide service — as well as service to Canada's smaller communities. Its name was changed to Air Canada in 1964. As a result of the Public Participation Act of 1988, about 43 percent of the airline was sold to the public; it was fully privatized the following year, when the remainder of the federal government's shares were sold to the public. Air Canada has its headquarters in Montreal.

air-transportation tax   A user-pay tax levied by the federal government since December 1, 1974. The tax is earmarked for TRANSPORT CANADA to help pay for the operating and construction costs of Canadian airports. There is a flat rate of $40 on overseas tickets and a sliding scale to a maximum of $40 on domestic flights. In the 1991-92 fiscal year, almost $490 million was raised by the tax.

Alberta Energy Company (AEC)   A crown corporation created by the Alberta government in 1973 as part of its industrial strategy to develop the resource base of Canada, though primarily in Alberta, and to provide Albertans with a new vehicle through which they could invest in the economic growth of Alberta and Canada. Shares were sold to residents of Alberta in 1975, thereby privatizing the company; by the end of 1992, 36.1 percent of AEC shares were still government-owned. Initially, shares could only be owned by Canadian citizens or residents and were traded on stock exchanges across the country. Under revised rules, no one may own more than 5 percent of AEC shares and total foreign ownership cannot exceed 10 percent. AEC is active in oil and gas, petrochemicals, forest-products, and pipeline industries. The head office of the AEC is in Calgary.

Alberta Energy Resources Conservation Board *See* ENERGY RESOURCES CONSERVATION BOARD.

Alberta Heritage Savings Trust Fund A special fund created by the Alberta government in 1976 to set aside a share of the province's oil and gas and other non-renewable natural resource revenues for the future benefit of Albertans, to strengthen and diversify the economy of Alberta, and to improve the quality of life for present and future generations of Albertans. Initially, the fund received 30 percent of provincial resource revenues each year and, in addition, reinvested its own investment income. But starting in fiscal 1982-83, the fund was required to pay its annual earnings into the provincial treasury. In fiscal 1983-84, the provincial government reduced its annual contribution to the fund to 15 percent of provincial revenues from non-renewable resources. Starting in fiscal 1987-88, the fund no longer received any infusion of provincial non-renewable resource revenues. The fund is divided into five divisions: the Alberta investment division, which invests in the debentures of Alberta crown corporations; the Canada investment division, which invests in the debt of federal and provincial governments; the capital projects division, which invests in projects providing long-term social and economic benefits to Albertans; the energy investment division, which invests in projects for the development, processing, and transportation of energy resources in Canada; the commercial investment division, which invests in shares of Canadian companies for a commercial rate of return; and the residual division, which invests in short-term financial paper. The fund produces a quarterly report on its investment activities, as well as an annual report, which must be reviewed by a committee of the Alberta legislature. The fund has its headquarters in Edmonton.

Alberta Oil Sands Technology and Research Authority (AOSTRA) An authority established in 1974 by the Alberta government to work with the oil and gas industry and other research bodies to develop the technologies to exploit the significant oil-sand bitumens found in the province; in 1975, its mandate was extended to heavy oils and in 1979, to enhanced recovery of conventional oil. In addition to pursuing the research necessary for economic and efficient recovery of oil, AOSTRA is also charged with conducting research into technologies to ensure an acceptable quality of the environment during and after recovery and processing operations. It is estimated that Alberta holds about two trillion barrels or 40 percent of the world's reserves of these heavy petroleum resources. AOSTRA and industry had invested about $1 billion in joint research ventures to the end of 1992.

Alberta Petroleum Marketing Commission A provincial agency created under the Petroleum Marketing Act of 1973 to sell the petroleum produced from Alberta crown leases. With the 1985 WESTERN ACCORD, the commission gave up its role in selling the oil companies share of Alberta oil production. The commission sells Alberta royalty oil belonging to the provincial government plus the Alberta government's share of oil production from the Syn-crude TAR SANDS project. In addition, it represents Alberta before regulating agencies, mainly on pipeline matters, provides various services under the National Gas Marketing Act (mainly pricing information to determine the average market price used in royalty cal-culations), and provides some private-sector services on contract, such as verifying costs in contracts between nat-ural-gas producers and groups that buy gas from many different producers for resale.

Alberta Stock Exchange (ASE)   The stock exchange founded as the Calgary Stock Exchange in 1913, which became important the following year when oil was discovered in Alberta's Turner Val-ley. Since then its growth has been closely tied to the performance of the oil and gas industry, although the diversification of the Alberta economy in recent years has helped give the exchange a broader role in raising capi-tal for a wide range of smaller compa-nies. Located in Calgary, it changed its name to the Alberta Stock Exchange in 1974.

allocation of resources   The use of a society's resources — its FACTORS OF PRODUCTION — to achieve the most efficient or lowest cost output of goods and services. In a world of PERFECT COMPETITION, this is assumed to be accomplished through the workings of MARKET FORCES and the LAW OF SUPPLY AND DEMAND. However, in the real world of IMPERFECT COMPE-TITION, the efficient allocation of resources is much more difficult to accomplish; MONOPOLY or OLIGOP-OLY leads to a misallocation of resources, the cost being the extra profit or ECONOMIC RENT earned by the monopoly or oligopoly producers. But there are many other barriers to the effi-cient allocation of resources, including poorly functioning labour markets, in

which it is hard to match workers seek-ing jobs with job vacancies; low levels of skills and knowledge; poorly functioning financial markets; resistance to change; laws, regulations, and red tape; empha-sis on non-economic goals; or excessive protection for the owners of patents and copyright.

allowance for credit losses   The amount set aside by a bank in its finan-cial statements to absorb anticipated credit-related losses from its portfolio of loans, acceptances, guarantees, let-ters of credit, and deposits with other banks. The allowance is increased by specific provisions for a major loan loss, country risk provisions for loans to developing countries, and general provisions. It is reduced by the write-off of net recoveries and losses realized in the sale and exchange of developing-country loans.

alloy   A metal, such as stainless steel, brass, or bronze, formed by the fusion of other metals.

amalgamation   The creation of a new corporation to take over the assets and liabilities of other existing businesses. *See also* MERGER, TAKEOVER, CON-SOLIDATION.

American Federation of Labor-Con-gress of Industrial Organizations (AFL-CIO)   A federation of the American Federation of Labor and the Congress of Industrial Organizations, formed in 1955, which is financed by per capita dues from member unions in the Unit-ed States and Canada. Approximately 40 percent of Canadian union members belong to unions affiliated with both the AFL-CIO and the CANADIAN LABOUR CONGRESS (CLC). There is, however, no formal connection between the AFL-CIO and the CLC, and the CLC has a strongly worded policy to support the autonomy of Canadian locals of international unions headquartered in the United States. *See also* CANADIAN STANDARDS OF SELF-GOVERNMENT.

amortization **1.** The reduction and retirement of a debt over a period of time by setting aside funds for the regular payment of interest and a part of the principal with each payment. Often a corporation will establish a SINKING FUND in which it sets aside money on a regular and pre-determined basis for the repayment of the debt. A MORTGAGE is an example of an amortized debt, since each payment includes interest and principal so that the loan may be paid off in a specified period of time through regular installments. **2.** The writing down of the costs of INTANGIBLE ASSETS, such as COPYRIGHT, PATENTS, TRADEMARKS, and GOODWILL, over a number of years instead of lumping them together in one year; each year a portion of the cost of the investment will be charged off as an expense. *See also* DEPRECIATION, DEPLETION.

amusement tax A tax on the price of admission to places of entertainment, such as movie theatres, sporting events, or other events where an admission is charged. Most provinces impose such a tax, although several of them, including Quebec, Manitoba, and Saskatchewan, have delegated the taxing power to their municipalities.

Andean Common Market A common market negotiated by Bolivia, Colombia, Ecuador, Peru, and Venezuela in 1990 and 1991 that was to establish a free-trade area by the end of 1992. A commission was set up to monitor the agreement and continue negotiations for a common external tariff by 1995 and the creation of a customs union, to pursue the harmonization of other policies in areas such as foreign investment, standards, and exchange-rate policy, and to seek ways to increase integration, trade, and investment. A dispute resolution system was also established, along with a council of ministers to give policy direction. The Andean Group, as it is called, faced certain conflicts; for example, some members were interested in joining the NORTH AMERICAN FREE TRADE AGREEMENT or in linking up with Mexico in a free trade agreement; these initiatives could weaken the cohesion that has been achieved among the Andean countries.

annual meeting The annual meeting for shareholders of a company, where they elect directors, approve the reappointment of auditors along with the auditor's report for the previous financial year, approve other company business, and question management on the company's affairs. All incorporated businesses in Canada, whether publicly traded or privately controlled, must by law hold an annual meeting. In the case of publicly traded companies, shareholders must receive adequate advance notice of an annual meeting, as well as other information on matters that management plans to present to shareholders at an annual meeting. Shareholders unable to attend can delegate their votes to someone else by signing a PROXY STATEMENT. The rules for annual meetings are set out in the CANADA BUSINESS CORPORATIONS ACT or, in the case of provincially incorporated companies, through similar provincial legislation. Companies may also be required to hold SPECIAL SHAREHOLDERS' MEETINGS to approve corporate transactions that represent a fundamental change for the business, such as the sale of substantially all of the assets, a major corporate reorganization, or changes in the articles of incorporation. The ONTARIO SECURITIES COMMISSION, under regulation 9.1, requires such a meeting to approve certain transactions between related companies in order to protect minority shareholders.

annual rate   The calculation of an annual rate from a daily, weekly, or monthly statistic, usually by simple multiplication; for example, taking a monthly increase in the rate of inflation and multiplying it by 12 to calculate an annual rate. Statisticians criticize this approach because the figure for a particular month may contain special or seasonal factors, an unusual development such as the impact of a strike, or other one-time factors. A more reliable measure is the calculation of the year-over-year increase, for example, the percentage increase in the inflation rate for a particular month from the same month a year earlier.

The annual rate of inflation or unemployment is the average of each of the monthly rates. In the case of the GROSS DOMESTIC PRODUCT (GDP), it is the average of each of the four quarterly rates of growth. If the GDP grew 1.3 percent in the first quarter, 1.7 percent in the second quarter, 2.1 percent in the third quarter, and 2.2 percent in the fourth quarter, then it grew 1.8 percent for the year.

annual report   The annual audited financial statement of a corporation, government department, or other agency or non-profit institution that contains an account of the financial results of the financial or fiscal year. All publicly traded corporations are required to publish an annual financial report that contains a BALANCE SHEET, EARNINGS STATEMENT, RETAINED-EARNINGS STATEMENT, and STATEMENT OF CHANGES IN FINANCIAL POSITION, verified in an independent AUDITOR'S REPORT, along with comparative financial information for the previous financial or fiscal year. Annual reports have to meet GENERALLY ACCEPTABLE ACCOUNTING PRINCIPLES, contain information required under federal and provincial corporation law and securities regula-

tions, and must be made available to shareholders of publicly traded companies within 140 days of the end of the financial year. Annual reports and accompanying information circulars for annual meetings must also contain the names of directors, details of aggregate compensation for officers and directors, details of share-purchase plans and options for employees and officers, a list of wholly and partly owned investments in other companies, information on transactions including lawsuits that could affect the company, and details of any special items requiring shareholders' approval. As well, annual reports typically contain a statement by the company's chief executive officer on the company's prospects and goals, along with an outline of the company's performance and activities during the past year. A copy of the annual report must be sent to all shareholders of record at a specified date in advance of the company's annual meeting.

Annual reports of federal government departments, agencies, and crown corporations are subject to the FINANCIAL ADMINISTRATION ACT and are reviewed by the AUDITOR-GENERAL. They do not contain the same information as a corporate annual report; for example, government departments do not provide balance-sheet information. Nor are government departments, agencies, and crown-corporation annual reports subject to the same requirement of timeliness. A government-department annual report provides details on how the department spent its funds during the fiscal year, program by program.

annual return   Financial information that must be filed with a government department each year. Non-profit charitable organizations must file a financial return each year with REVENUE CANADA if they wish to maintain their tax-exempt status and their right to issue tax-deductible receipts to financial supporters. Unions and corporations in Canada above a certain size are required to file information annually under the CORPORATIONS AND LABOUR UNIONS RETURNS ACT. Federally incorporated companies above a certain size must file an audited financial statement with the Department of CONSUMER AND CORPORATE AFFAIRS; provincially incorporated companies must also file some information with provincial government departments.

annuity The payment of a regular pension or similar benefit for a contracted number of years or for the lifetime of the beneficiary, paid out from an invested lump-sum of capital. The federal government at one time sold annuities to the public but stopped in 1975. When the government began selling annuities in 1908, before there were public pensions, they provided an important way for ordinary Canadians to set aside savings for their old age. Today, life annuities for the life of a beneficiary are sold by insurance companies, and term-certain annuities for a fixed number of years are sold by trust companies.

anti-dumping code *See* GENERAL AGREEMENT ON TARIFFS AND TRADE.

anti-dumping duty A duty or tax imposed by an importing country when imports are found to be selling below the price charged in the home market of the producer-country and also are causing injury or threatening to cause injury to local producers. In Canada, REVENUE CANADA investigates complaints, determines whether dumping has occurred, and assesses an anti-dumping duty. The CANADIAN INTERNATIONAL TRADE COMMISSION then holds a hearing to determine whether or not the dumping is injurious to the Canadian producers; if it is, the anti-dumping duty is applied.

Anti-Inflation Board (AIB) A federal board established by order-in-council on October 14, 1975, to administer wage and price controls in Canada; the AIB was confirmed in federal legislation on December 15, 1975. The controls were phased out between April 14 and December 31, 1978.

The role of the AIB was as follows: 1. Monitor price, pay, profit, and dividend changes to see that they stayed within government guidelines; 2. Identify changes in prices, pay, profits, and dividends that contravened the guidelines in fact or in spirit; 3. Identify wage or price behaviour that was likely to have an inflationary impact on the economy; 4. Ask the anti-inflation administrator to order a rollback or take other action where a negotiated rollback was impossible to achieve a reduction in prices, pay, profits, or dividends; 5. Educate Canadians on the dangers of continued inflation, its causes, and what action individuals could take to help reduce inflation.

The legislation established an anti-inflation administrator, whose job it was to enforce AIB guidelines with binding rollback orders and other measures. In cases of excessive price increases or profit levels, the administrator could order the excess revenues to be returned to consumers, to the market, in the form of price reductions, or to the Crown. Excessive pay increases could be recovered from employees, their employer, or both. An AIB appeal tribunal was created to hear appeals from companies, unions, and other affected groups against the decisions of the anti-inflation administrator.

The controls applied to about 1,500 companies, with about 2.3 million employees in the private sector, and to federal, provincial, and municipal governments and their agencies, with about two million employees.

The consumer price index rose 10.8 percent in 1975, the year controls were introduced. The basic wage guideline was 10 percent in the first year, 8 percent in the second year, and 6 percent in the third year. Businesses were required to hold prices to levels producing pre-tax profit margins no higher than the average profit margin of the previous five years. Price increases were restricted to cost increases and prices were expected to be cut if costs declined. Farmers and fishermen were exempt from the price guidelines, but the government said it would try to have farm marketing boards respect the guidelines. Regulated industries were also exempt from the guidelines. At the same time that the AIB came into being, the provinces also introduced rent controls or guidelines. The consumer price index rose 7.5 percent in 1976, 8.0 percent in 1977, and 9.0 percent in 1978.

The AIB guidelines were only one element of the government's anti-inflation program. Other measures promised included tighter monetary and fiscal policies, limits on the growth of government spending, and structural policies to increase the supply of energy, food, and housing, as well as to increase the competitiveness of the Canadian economy and improve labour-management relations. At the time AIB controls were introduced, a white paper on anti-inflation policies, The Way Ahead, was tabled by the Minister of Finance in Parliament.

anti-trust   *See* COMPETITION POLICY, COMBINES INVESTIGATION ACT, COMPETITION ACT.

apportionment   The attribution of costs and revenues within a company between different activities, departments, products, and services where it is not possible to clearly allocate costs or revenues. Examples include municipal or other taxes, office space, and corporate services such as human resource planning.

appraisal   The valuation of real estate, antiques, jewellery, and other assets for insurance, sale, or collateral purposes by qualified experts recognized by the insurance industry, banks, and antique, jewellery, and other dealers. The Appraisal Institute of Canada is the accreditation body for appraisers. The CRA designation is for real-estate appraisers and AACI is for business appraisers.

appreciation   An increase in the market value of an asset or security, such as real estate, shares, bonds, or antiques, or of a currency, such as the Canadian dollar. When the market pushes up the exchange rate of a currency under a floating exchange-rate system, that is known as appreciation; when the exchange rate is raised under a fixed exchange-rate system, that is known as a revaluation. An appreciation of the Canadian dollar means that the cost of foreign currencies is reduced.

apprenticeship   A formal process of job training to teach a person a specific skill or trade, and certification to show that an individual has met the skill requirements for a particular trade. Apprenticeship training typically takes place on the job, under the direction of a skilled worker; about 90 percent is on the job and 10 percent in a community college or other postsecondary institution. In some trades, apprenticeship training is necessary if a person is to join a union and gain a full-time job; this is especially true in the construction trades. In Canada, apprenticeship programs fall under provincial jurisdiction. Apprenticeship programs typically run three to five years; in the first year an apprentice earns about 50 percent of the journeyman rate, with the gap narrowing each year. Apprentices must get at least 50 percent in their exams; if they get at least 70 percent they receive a red seal, which qualifies them for recognition in the 40 trades recognized interprovincially. The value of a certificate is that it shows the holder has met a skill standard recognized by employers and unions.

appropriate technology Technology developed from local skills to meet the needs of a LESS-DEVELOPED COUNTRY, according to its own culture, level of expertise and requirements. Proponents of "appropriate technology" argue that it does not make sense for less-developed countries to import capital-intensive, costly, and energy-intensive technologies when those countries have high unemployment, lack the capital to pay for sophisticated technology that was not designed to meet their needs in the first place, and don't have the requisite level of education and skills in the population to use the technology effectively.

appropriation act An act of Parliament authorizing the spending of money for a specific purpose. Such an act must be passed each FISCAL YEAR for all government spending out of the CONSOLIDATED REVENUE FUND that is not authorized by some other act of Parliament; for example, spending for new military equipment would require an appropriation act, but cheques to senior citizens under the GUARANTEED-INCOME SUPPLEMENT would not, since Parliament has already authorized payment through separate legislation. In effect, appropriation acts cover spending for which there is no continuing statutory authority.

There are usually four appropriation acts in a fiscal year, but there could be fewer or more. Shortly after the government presents its spending ESTIMATES — usually by March 1 — for the new fiscal year that begins April 1,

it will introduce an interim Supply Bill in March, which is an appropriation act, to allow spending to take place while Parliament considers the spending estimates. In June, a second appropriation act is debated by Parliament after the consideration of the estimates by Parliamentary committees has been completed; this second act approves spending plans for the balance of the fiscal year, up to March 31 of the following calendar year. Later in the year, as spending plans change and new spending is undertaken, the government presents SUPPLEMENTARY ESTIMATES "A" and a later "B"; each of these must be accompanied by an appropriation act. Once each act has been passed by Parliament, an ORDER-IN-COUNCIL is sent to the governor-general asking him or her to send a warrant that authorizes spending out of the consolidated revenue fund. *See also* SPECIAL GOVERNOR-GENERAL'S WARRANTS.

Arab boycott of Israel An Arab embargo dating back to 1948 designed to penalize Israel by prohibiting trade between Israel and its Arab neighbours, blacklisting foreign companies with investments in Israel, and requiring companies doing business with Arab countries to sign an agreement that they will not do business with Israel or companies blacklisted because of their investments in Israel. There is no federal law prohibiting Canadian companies from complying with the Arab boycott, but in 1976, the government announced that federal support and services would be denied or withdrawn from any company, agency, or individual complying with any boycott that required them to engage in discrimination based on race, religion, or national or ethnic origin. Support and services that would be withdrawn include trade fairs and missions, the services of the EXPORT DEVELOPMENT CORPORATION, the CANADIAN COMMERCIAL

CORPORATION, and the Program for Export Market Development. Companies seeking government assistance in countries where the boycott was in effect were required to certify that the transaction did not contravene this policy. When the policy was announced, countries where the economic boycott existed included: Bahrain, Egypt, Iraq, Jordan, Kuwait, Lebanon, Libya, Oman, Qatar, Saudi Arabia, Syria, United Arab Emirates, Yemen Arab Republic, People's Democratic Republic of Yemen, Algeria, Morocco, Sudan, Tunisia, and Mauritania. In 1978, Ontario passed the Discriminatory Business Practices Act, which made any company or individual complying with a discriminatory boycott ineligible to provide goods or services to the Ontario government or any of its agencies for a period of five years.

arbitrage   A sophisticated form of investment in which shares, commodity futures, foreign exchange, or other securities are simultaneously purchased in one market and sold in another, with the investor realizing a profit on the difference in price between the two markets. When the price of a share listed on the Toronto and American stock exchanges is not identical, a fast investor can take advantage of the difference to make a profit by buying in the market where the price is lower and selling in the market where the price is higher. Arbitrageurs may be especially active if a stock is in play due to competing takeover bids.

arbitration   Third-party efforts to resolve disputes. The most common example is the use of arbitrators to resolve labour-management disputes in the negotiation of a new collective agreement, for example, to avoid a strike or lockout or to end a strike or lockout if one has occurred. Arbitration is also used to resolve grievances between management and labour over the implementation of a collective agreement. An arbitration board may consist of a single individual not connected with either party, or it may be a three-person board consisting of a representative from each of management and labour and a third person who is an independent. Federal and provincial labour departments supply arbitration assistance, including professional arbitrators, and can help in the selection of arbitrators. Arbitrators are also used to resolve domestic and international commercial disputes.

Arbitrators spend a great deal of time dealing with labour-management disputes over the interpretation of existing collective agreements — for example, in the right of management to reassign workers, change work procedures, or dismiss an employee. In binding or COMPULSORY ARBITRATION, the federal or provincial government will order striking or locked-out employees back to work and appoint an arbitrator to resolve the dispute by awarding a settlement with which management and labour must both live. Compulsory arbitration may be used to resolve public-sector disputes — for example, strikes by teachers, hospital workers, or transit workers — or disputes that if prolonged can cause widespread hardship, such as railway, postal, grain handling, or airline strikes. Before such a step is taken, Parliament or a provincial legislature must first pass legislation ordering the striking workers back to work.

Sometimes, management and labour will agree to voluntary arbitration to settle outstanding issues in the negotiation of a new collective agreement. Arbitrators may also be used to settle a stalemated labour-management negotiation through a process known as FINAL-OFFER SELECTION: each side makes a final offer dealing with all the unresolved issues in a negotiation, leaving it to the arbitrator to decide which offer should be accepted.

arm's length A transaction conducted between parties that have no corporate or other direct connections with each other, where each thus acts in its own interest. A foreign-based corporation and its Canadian subsidiary do not have an arm's length relationship with each other when the parent firm supplies parts, or charges for management, research, and other services. Tax authorities in REVENUE CANADA are supposed to make sure that charges by the foreign parent for head-office services, or TRANSFER PRICES, are set as if an arm's length relationship did exist, so that real market prices are charged on the transactions and the appropriate amount of corporate income tax and WITHHOLDING TAX is collected.

arrears ACCOUNTS PAYABLE that are overdue. The term also refers to overdue and unpaid interest and preferred-share dividends.

articles of incorporation *See* INCORPORATION.

Asia Pacific Economic Co-operation Group (APEC) An intergovernmental institution established in 1989 to increase consultation at the ministerial level on Asia-Pacific issues. The 15 members are Canada, the United States, Australia, New Zealand, Japan, South Korea, China, Hong Kong, Taiwan, Singapore, Thailand, Indonesia, the Philippines, Malaysia, and Brunei. A number of other countries, including Mexico, are seeking membership. APEC's technical work is carried out by 12 specialized working groups, while its political work is done by the Senior Officials' Meeting, which prepares the agenda for periodic ministerial meetings. Much of the work of APEC so far has focused on trade issues such as harmonization of standards, rules on intellectual property, co-ordination of rules on competition policy, and customs co-operation. In 1992, the APEC ministers established an Eminent Person's Group to develop a visionary trade-policy agenda for the region. Other work programs of special interest to Canada include marine-resources conservation, human-resources development, telecommunications, transportation, and energy. An annual ministerial meeting is held, with the 1994 meeting to take place in Indonesia, 1995 in Japan, 1996 in the Philippines, and 1997 in Canada. Periodic meetings of heads of governments may also be held. A small secretariat was opened in Singapore in 1993 to strengthen APEC's role as an important regional institution. The PACIFIC ECONOMIC CO-OPERATION CONFERENCE has observer status.

Asia Pacific Foundation of Canada A foundation established in 1984 by an act of Parliament. Its objectives are to heighten Canadian awareness that Canada is a Pacific country as well as an Atlantic one, raise Canada's profile in the Asia-Pacific region, increase Canadian participation in the Asia-Pacific economy, engage in policy research, assist business and other sectors to be better prepared to participate in the region, and educate and train young Canadians so that they will have the knowledge and skills to support Canada's future role in the Asia-Pacific region. The foundation has its headquarters in Vancouver and is supported by the federal and provincial governments and private industry.

Asian Development Bank (ADB) A regional development bank established in 1966 to stimulate economic growth and development in Asia and the Far East, modelled after the WORLD BANK. Canada was one of the original members. The bank promotes the investment of public and private capital in the region and also provides technical assistance to developing countries. About 60 percent of the capital of the bank, headquartered in Manila in the Philippines, has been provided by countries in the region, including Japan and Australia; Canada is one of the non-regional providers of capital to the bank, along with the United States, Britain, Germany, and Switzerland. The People's Republic of China became a member in 1986. Canada had contributed US$158.9 million to the bank to the end of 1992. Canada is also a contributor to the Asian Development Fund, a division of the bank that provides low-interest assistance to the poorest countries in the region; Canada had contributed US$919.6 million to the fund to the end of 1992. Canada had also contributed US$9.3 million to the bank's Technical Assistance Special Fund. Overall, Canada had contributed 6.6 percent of the bank's total funds to the end of 1992 and had 4.8 percent of the bank's votes. Membership consists of 36 countries in the Asia-Pacific region, including 32 developing countries; there are 16 member countries from Europe and North America.

ask price   The price sought by the would-be seller of a share, bond, or commodity contract. *See also* BID and CLOSE.

assay   The test carried out to determine the mineral content of samples of rock obtained from a mineral-exploration site. Mining companies that sell their shares to the public are required to get an independent assay report before making any comment on the mineral potential of a new mineral site.

assembly line   A method of industrial production in which the job of each worker has been reduced to its simplest routine, and various standardized parts are assembled by workers in a series of isolated steps into a finished product. In the production of an automobile, for example, a car will start on the assembly line as a bare frame and, step by step, have all of its parts — ranging from engine, transmission, axles, and body to wiring, wheels, windows, doors, seats, hubcaps, and headlights — added

to it by different workers or robots, each performing a single function, as it moves along the assembly line. *See also* FORDISM, LEAN PRODUCTION.

assessment   The value placed on land and buildings for the purpose of levying a PROPERTY TAX. Property may be taxed on the basis of FAIR MARKET VALUE, but many municipalities still employ other methods of assessment based on the historical cost or use of the property. As a result, properties of the same market value in the same community may be assessed quite differently for tax purposes depending on when they were built and how they are used. *See also* MILL RATE.

assessment work   The exploration and development work that a mining company is required to do on a property if it wishes to retain its rights to minerals that may exist on the land and obtain a LEASE to extract those minerals.

asset   Anything that can be sold and on which a money value can therefore be placed. On a BALANCE SHEET, everything that a company or any other organization owns that can be expressed as a dollar value is listed. Assets include land, buildings, machinery, inventories, mineral or oil and gas reserves, timber rights, patents, trademarks, copyrights, cash, securities, investments, and loans to other companies or affiliates, and money owed by customers. Assets are usually divided into CURRENT ASSETS and FIXED ASSETS. Current assets consist of cash and assets that are readily turned into cash within a normal operating year, such as inventories, accounts receivable, and short-term securities. Fixed assets include land and buildings, machinery, and other equipment. Other assets in the category include long-term investments in other companies and INTANGIBLE ASSETS, such as patents, trademarks, and copyrights.

asset stripper   A corporation or investor that acquires another company in order to make a profit by selling off all or many of its assets rather than continuing to operate the business. A corporation or investor can do this when the money realized from selling off the assets is significantly greater than the cost of buying the company.

asset value per share   The net value of a company's assets shown on its BALANCE SHEET, after deducting all its liabilities, divided by the total number of shares outstanding.

assignment   The transfer of a property or other specified rights by the owner of the property, in writing. A debtor may assign property to a trustee, who will dispose of it at the best possible price and use the proceeds to pay off creditors. The owner of a copyright, trademark, or patent may assign the rights generally, or for a specified market or use, to a manufacturer, distributor, film producer, or other possible user in return for a ROYALTY or other payment. Similarly, a retailer who sells a product to a consumer on credit may assign the debt to a sales-finance or other financial service company, which pays off the retailer and assumes the rights to the interest and repaid principal.

Association of South East Asian Nations (ASEAN)   A regional association for political, security, and economic co-operation established by Thailand, Indonesia, Malaysia, the Philippines, and Singapore on August 8, 1967. Brunei subsequently became a member. An annual ministerial meeting is held. In 1991, the ASEAN members declared their intention to form a free-trade area by 2008; the first steps to implementing a common effective preferential tariff took place on January 1, 1993. Tariff rates on a wide range of products are to be reduced to 20 percent by the year 2003 and 0 to 5 percent by 2008, when the ASEAN free-trade area — AFTA — is formally created.

assurance   The British word for INSURANCE.

Atlantic Acceptance Scandal   The 1965 bankruptcy of a major Toronto-based sales-finance company that, when put into receivership, had debts of $115 million and assets $32 million short of that. The company's shares fell from close to $21 to about $1 when it went into receivership; its collapse led to the collapse of the British Mortgage and Trust Co. of Stratford, Ontario, which lost more than $1 million in Atlantic shares and $4 million in Atlantic notes.
The Ontario government appointed Mr. Justice Samuel Hughes of the Supreme Court of Ontario to head an inquiry into the collapse. He found a serious lack of supervision over the operations of trust companies and other so-called near banks in his report, published four years later in 1969. It led, in 1970, to sweeping changes in Ontario's Loan and Trust Companies Act that gave the provincial government important new regulatory powers and the authority to intervene in the affairs of companies in difficulty, including taking over the administration of companies in trouble. The amendments also increased the obligations of companies to behave in a prudent manner.

Atlantic Accord   A 1985 agreement between the Canadian and Newfoundland governments on offshore oil and natural gas resource management and revenue sharing. The agreement established the Canada-Newfoundland Offshore Petroleum Board, consisting of six members, three appointed by each of the two governments and a chairman appointed jointly. The board is responsible for the declaration of discoveries, the granting of production licences, regulating good oil-field practice, the issuing of exploration rights, the approval of development plans, collecting royalties, and emergency powers. So that the board is responsive to both governments, the accord provides for joint policy direction on key issues such as industrial and employment benefits, public reviews, and decisions affecting the pace and mode of exploration and development. In addition, certain fundamental decisions of the board will be subject to review by the two governments. If the two governments cannot agree, the responsibility for approval rests with one of the two ministers: The federal minister has the power to make decisions related to the pace and mode of exploration and the pace of production when Canada has not attained or has lost self-sufficiency and security of supply. When these conditions are achieved, approval will rest with the provincial minister. The minister from Newfoundland has the responsibility for decisions on the mode of development, provided these decisions do not unreasonably delay the attainment of self-sufficiency and security of supply. The board can determine when public reviews are necessary and, where they are deemed to be necessary, require a project proponent to submit a preliminary development plan, and environmental and socio-economic statements, including a benefits plan. Benefits plans submitted by companies seeking approval for a project must include expenditures for research and development and education and training.

The principles of revenue-sharing between Canada and Newfoundland are the same as those between Canada and provinces with petroleum-related activities on land. The accord gives Newfoundland the jurisdiction to establish and collect royalties and other provincial-type resource revenues and taxes.

Newfoundland will receive the proceeds of royalties, provincial corporate income tax, sales tax, bonus payments, rentals and fees, and other forms of provincial-type petroleum revenue and taxes. An equalization offset payment formula will ensure that there will not be a dollar-for-dollar loss of EQUALIZATION PAYMENTS to Newfoundland as a result of offshore oil or gas revenues. Beginning in the first year of oil or gas production, Newfoundland will receive offset payments from the federal government equal to 90 percent of a year's reduction in equalization payments. Beginning in the fifth year, the offset rate will be reduced by 10 percent for each subsequent year.

The accord also established a Canada-Newfoundland Offshore Development Fund of $300 million, financed 75 percent by Canada and 25 percent by Newfoundland, to develop the infrastructure necessary for oil and gas development and to ensure Newfoundland can reap the benefits of offshore development. As well, the accord includes an Oil Pollution and Fisheries Compensation Regime to provide protection against oil-spill damages and debris. *See also* WESTERN ACCORD.

Atlantic Canada Opportunities Agency (ACOA)   A federal agency established in 1987 to manage federal regional-development funds and co-ordinate federal activities that contribute to regional economic growth in the Atlantic Provinces. Based in Moncton, the agency has an advisory board and works with the private sector, provincial and municipal governments, and other groups in the region to promote economic growth. The ACOA Action Program provides business development funding for small and medium enterprises.

Atlantic provinces   The provinces of New Brunswick, Newfoundland, Nova

Scotia, and Prince Edward Island. *See also* MARITIME PROVINCES.

Atlantic Provinces Economic Council (APEC)   An economic research organization established in 1954 to monitor the performance of the Atlantic economy and to develop policy proposals to improve economic performance. It has advocated a number of measures to narrow the gap between the region's per capita income and output and that of the rest of Canada, including regional development programs and a regional growth strategy based on key growth centres. It has also been a strong advocate of Maritime co-operation and even union. APEC is funded mainly by business but also receives support from the provincial governments. It is based in Halifax.

Atomic Energy Control Board (AECB)   A federal regulatory agency created under the Atomic Energy Control Act of 1946 to regulate the construction and operation of nuclear reactors, the transportation and disposal of nuclear wastes, the operation of uranium mines and uranium processing, and the export of uranium to countries that accept nuclear safeguards.

Atomic Energy of Canada Limited (AECL)   A federal crown corporation established under the Atomic Energy Control Act of 1946 to develop Canada's capacity to build its own nuclear-power and heavy-water production systems, to engage in nuclear research and development, to identify and develop other uses of nuclear technology in medicine and other areas, to develop an export market for Canadian nuclear technology, and to devise methods of disposing of nuclear wastes. It became a crown corporation in 1952 when it took over the Chalk River nuclear-research station from the NATIONAL RESEARCH COUNCIL. The crown corporation does most of the research and development and advanced engineering work on nuclear-power and heavy-water systems in Canada, but does not have its own manufacturing capacity; instead, actual manufacturing and construction is contracted out to private industry. It reports to Parliament through the Minister of ENERGY, MINES AND RESOURCES.

atomistic economy   An economy made up of many small, independent producers; the type of economy that pre-dated the Industrial Revolution and the shift to large industrial corporations and capital-intensive production facilities. An atomistic economy approximates the world of PERFECT COMPETITION found in conventional economic theory.

attrition   A method of reducing the number of employees in an organization by failing to fill vacancies when employees leave for a job in another organization or reach retirement age. It is one way of dealing with the need to eliminate jobs due to technological change or organizational restructuring; it is an alternative to laying off employees but achieves the same result over time.

auction   A sale in which goods are offered to competing buyers and in which the assets being sold go to the highest bidder. The auctioneer attempts to get the highest possible price for the seller and is paid a commission on the price he succeeds in obtaining for the seller. In some instances, the seller may set a reserve or minimum price below which the asset will not be sold. Auctions are often used to dispose of the assets of bankrupt firms or individuals or of firms that have not paid their taxes. Auctions are also used by governments to dispose of unclaimed, stolen, or lost property, or goods seized by customs officers, as well as to dispose of surplus assets. Livestock, oil and gas leases, and used cars at the wholesale level are sold by auction. The assets of an estate, such as furniture, jewellery, and works of art may also be sold at an auction to raise cash. *See also* DUTCH AUCTION.

audit   1. A review of the financial returns of a corporation or other organization to ensure that proper accounting procedures have been followed and that the financial information is accurate. All companies in Canada are required to maintain proper financial records and to have them audited by independent, professional accountants. The accountants are required to check the actual financial records of the company, to run whatever tests they feel are necessary to verify the accuracy of the records, to review the accounting system and internal audit controls, and to ensure that the current year's financial figures are fully comparable with the previous year's. A number of federal and provincial laws in Canada require auditors to follow the GENERALLY ACCEPTED ACCOUNTING PRINCIPLES and generally accepted auditing standards set out in the Canadian Institute of Chartered Accountants Handbook. *See also* AUDITOR'S REPORT. **2.** A review of the financial records of a company, individual, or charity by REVENUE CANADA to ensure that information filed by a taxpayer is accurate and complete.

auditor   1. An accountant in public practice who is retained to examine and report on the accuracy and soundness of the financial statements of a corporation or other organization. The auditor is an independent scrutineer whose verification and signature attach credibility to a financial statement and thus reassure investors, shareholders, and creditors. **2.** Employees within an organization who may or may not be trained accountants but who report to

management on whether the organization's policies, including financial controls, are being carried out by employees. In many cases, the internal auditors will report to the audit committee of a company's BOARD OF DIRECTORS.

Auditor-General   An officer of Parliament who, along with his staff, conducts an annual audit of government spending to see whether proper accounts are maintained, whether money is being spent for the purposes stipulated by Parliament, whether effective spending controls are being maintained, that money designated for one purpose is not being diverted to another, that all the money collected from the public is properly accounted for, that proper records are being kept on public property, and that generally accepted accounting procedures are being followed by government departments and agencies. Since 1985, the Auditor-General has also audited the financial statements of crown corporations, along with a private-sector auditor. The Auditor-General makes an annual report to Parliament that is then reviewed by the PUBLIC ACCOUNTS COMMITTEE of Parliament. The report itemizes instances of misspending or lack of adequate financial controls, and may contain recommendations on ways to improve financial procedures and accountability within the government and to ensure that the taxpaying public gets value for money. The office of auditor-general, which dates back to 1878, is one of the important checks or controls on the spending and accounting practices of government departments, agencies, and crown corporations. The Minister of FINANCE reports to Parliament for the Auditor-General.

auditors' report   The verification by independent auditors that the financial statements of a corporation or other organization are accurate and are based on GENERALLY ACCEPTED ACCOUNTING PRINCIPLES. Every PUBLIC COMPANY is required to appoint outside auditors to represent the shareholders and to verify, once a year, the accuracy and consistency of the company's financial statements. An audit includes examining evidence supporting the disclosures in the financial statements, assessing the accounting principles used and estimates made by management, as well as evaluating the overall financial statement presentation. However, the financial footnotes found in annual reports are the work of management, not the auditors.

Since the auditors are bound by the professional requirements of the accounting profession and their own ethical standards, as well as by various laws, their certification of a company's financial statements is an assurance to shareholders and others that a company's annual report gives an accurate description of its financial health. Quarterly reports of corporations are unaudited. In principle, the role of the auditors is to safeguard the interests of all the shareholders, not management or a controlling shareholder. At issue, though, is the extent to which an auditing firm will relax its standards to retain a lucrative auditing contract or the extent to which management will go to change auditors if its auditing firm seeks changes in the presentation of a company's financial statements before signing the auditors' report.

austerity program Government policies that deliberately and sharply reduce spending in the economy to deal with a balance-of-payments crisis, reduce a chronic and growing budget deficit, finance a war, or curb spiralling inflation. Canada embarked on a temporary austerity program in 1962 to improve its rapidly deteriorating balance-of-payments position. Import sur-

charges were imposed on about half of Canada's imports; duty-free exemptions for Canadians returning from foreign trips were sharply reduced; interest rates were raised; government spending was reduced; and the exchange rate of the Canadian dollar was raised to 92.5 U.S. cents, where it was pegged. The government began lifting some of the import surcharges in late 1962 and all were lifted by the end of 1963.

Australia-New Zealand Free Trade Agreement An agreement for free trade and closer economic relations between Australia and New Zealand. The agreement, which was signed in 1982 and took effect on January 1, 1983, provided a framework for the achievement of full free trade by 1995. It envisaged that closer economic relations would evolve over time but provided for a comprehensive review of the agreement in 1988. The 1988 review resulted in three protocols to the agreement: the first brought forward the timetable for the achievement of complete free trade from 1995 to 1990; a second protocol brought services within the trade agreement for the first time; and a third protocol provides for the harmonization of quarantine-administration procedures. From July 1, 1990, all remaining border restrictions to trade in goods that have at least 50 percent Australian or New Zealand content, such as tariffs, quantitative restrictions, import and export prohibitions, export incentives, and export bounties, were absolished. In addition, ANTI-DUMPING provisions were abolished between the two countries, and to facilitate the development of a single market, business law and trade practices legislation of the two countries were harmonized. The 1988 protocol on trade in services provided for full liberalization on July 1, 1990. However, each country was allowed to exempt certain services. New Zealand exempted certain aspects of its international aviation, telecommunications, shipping, and postal services, while Australia exempted certain areas of banking, airport services, domestic as well as international aviation, telecommunications, coastal shipping, broadcasting and television, construction, third-party and workmen's compensation, health insurance, and postal services. Service providers can operate in each other's market on the same basis as domestic service providers except that they are subject to the foreign investment policies of each government. The arrangement includes NATIONAL TREATMENT, commercial presence, and encouragement of acceptance of each other's licensing and certification requirements. The bilateral agreement also liberalized government procurement practices. But the agreement contains no provisions on investment, so that investors of each country are subject to the general foreign investment policies and requirements of the other country.

Austrian School A school of economic thought, dating back to the late 19th century and centred in Vienna, that adhered to the classical view of economics but added some important new insights. Its first chairman, Carl Menger, argued that the price of a good depended not on its cost of production but on its capability to deliver pleasure or UTILITY, which led to the MARGINAL UTILITY theory of value. A successor, Friedrich von Wieser, developed the concept of OPPORTUNITY COST. Eugen von Bohm-Bawerk developed a new theory on interest. Their efforts were continued by Ludwig von Mises and Friedrich von Hayek, both strong proponents of CLASSICAL ECONOMICS based on free markets and non-intervention by government.

autarky An economic and political system whose goal is economic self-sufficiency, in spite of the high costs of pursuing such a policy. To achieve self-sufficiency in food, machinery, technology, energy, and the other basics of economic life, a country would have to impose high import barriers and exchange controls, as well as heavily subsidize local industry and adopt regimented national planning; it might also have to conquer neighbouring countries to gain access to natural resources or agricultural land. Nazi Germany and Japan's Greater East Asia Co- Prosperity Sphere pursued autarky in the 1930s and into the 1940s before they were defeated by the Allied Powers, including Canada, in 1944 and 1945. The former Soviet Union and the Soviet-controlled states of Eastern Europe pursued a similar policy until the late 1980s and early 1990s, when their system collapsed due to its high costs and inefficiency. Autarky is sometimes spelled autarchy, although the latter word more properly refers to the rule of an absolute sovereign.

authorized capital The maximum number of shares and their par value, if any, that a corporation is permitted to issue under its articles of incorporation. The number of issued shares is the number the company has sold, while the outstanding shares are those that remain in public hands; PREFERRED SHARES may have been redeemed while COMMON SHARES may have been bought back by the company, thus reducing the number of outstanding shares from the original number issued. A company limits the number of shares it issues because the larger the number issued the more diluted the value; but if a company needs to reduce its debt or finance expansion it may issue additional shares to maintain a healthier DEBT/EQUITY RATIO. But if a company has issued all of its authorized capital, it can amend its articles of incorporation by SUPPLEMENTARY LETTERS PATENT and increase its authorized capital.

auto pact *See* CANADA-UNITED STATES AUTOMOTIVE PRODUCTS AGREEMENT.

automatic stabilizer *See* BUILT-IN STABILIZER.

automation The automatic and self-regulating control of all or part of a production process by machines, with the result that direct human activity in the production process is reduced. The use of computer and communications systems has brought about a new industrial revolution with automatic switching and process-control systems, along with feedback systems, permitting the complete control of industrial production, business services, and other tasks.

Computerized systems can direct the operation of machinery, including industrial robots, and control the entire process of a refinery or nuclear-power station. With the development of high-speed and low-cost semiconductors, automation will become even more advanced, permitting new levels of flexibility and customized production, as opposed to traditional mass production and standardized products. Computer-assisted design and computer-assisted manufacturing also have sharply reduced the time needed to upgrade products and design new products as well as reducing the down-time on machinery. Process-control systems, using highly sophisticated sensors and other monitoring equipment, can automatically adjust the industrial processes, such as refineries and boilers. But automation has extended far beyond the industrial floor to the office, hospital, telecommunications networks, financial services, airline reservation systems, and retailing. Inventory control in supermarkets, for example, can now be controlled through a bar-code system that records sales at the cash register and permits automatic reordering of high-volume products.

Automation has contributed to productivity growth and our standard of living. The productivity dividend should increase the overall wealth of society, creating the opportunity for new goods and services. But automation also means that society must pay more attention to retraining and adjustment programs for those displaced by automation.

average A single number that is intended to be typical of a series of numbers. For example, the average weekly wage is a figure that is representative of a wide range of individual weekly wages weighted according to the proportion of workers in each wage group; the average selling price of a new home is representative of the different prices being paid for many different new homes in different locations and of different size.

Averages are useful because they give a more accurate picture of performance over periods of time, a picture that can be used as a standard in assessing short-term performance. For example, current inflation, unemployment, and GROSS DOMESTIC PRODUCT growth rates are better understood if they are measured against past performance. Averages also give a truer picture of trends since they smooth out the impact of seasonal or one-time events, such as a railway strike or bad weather.

There are different ways of calculating averages. The most commonly used measure is the simple average, or arithmetic mean, which is derived by taking a series of numbers, adding them together, and then dividing the total by the number of numbers; for example, if Canada had in a five-year period inflation rates of 4.8, 4.4, 3.7, 2.9, and 3.1, then its average inflation rate would be 3.8 percent. A weighted average is calculated in the same way except that the relative importance of different components of the average are taken into account. For example, in calculating the CONSUMER-PRICE INDEX, which represents an average of a typical bundle of consumer purchases in a given month, more weight is given to percentage changes in food and housing costs than to recreational and insurance costs, since food and housing represent a much larger share of a family's monthly budget. *See also* MOVING AVERAGE, MODE, MEDIAN, MEAN AVERAGE.

average cost   The unit cost of production, which is determined by dividing the total costs of production over some period of time by the number of units produced. Average costing can help determine the optimal size of a production facility, such as a factory or refinery.

average-cost pricing   The pricing of a good or service based on average costs plus some additional margin for profits. *See also* MARGINAL-COST PRICING.

averaging down   The practice of buying additional shares or other securities at a lower price than the original cost in order to lower the average cost of the shares purchased.

average hourly earnings   The average hourly earnings of employees paid by the hour for all industries and for forestry, mining, manufacturing, construction, services, transportation and communications, trade, finance, and community, business, and personal services. The monthly Statistics Canada report, *Employment, Earnings and Hours* (publication 72-002), provides an indication of the trend of wage costs.

average propensity to consume   Total consumer spending divided by total personal disposable income.

average propensity to import   Total imports of goods and services divided by total national income.

average propensity to save   Total saving divided by total national income.

average rate of taxation   The amount of tax paid by an individual divided by the income on which the tax was paid. Each year the ORGANIZATION FOR ECONOMIC CO-OPERATION AND DEVELOPMENT publishes a report — *The Tax/Benefit Position of Production Workers* — that compares average tax rates in different countries.

B

baby boom The period of rapid population growth in the 1947-66 period when Canada's FERTILITY RATE averaged almost 4 percent a year, compared with a population replacement rate of 2.1 percent and a fertility rate of 1.66 percent a year in the early 1990s. The baby boom peaked in 1960, and the 20-year baby-boom generation accounted for nine million Canadians.

baby echo The increased number of babies born in the late 1980s and early 1990s, despite a low fertility rate, due to the fact that a large wave of baby-boom mothers were having children at approximately the same time.

backlog A build-up of orders that have yet to be filled; goods ordered by customers but not yet delivered. The volume of unfilled orders is an important business indicator for economic analysts trying to determine the short-term outlook for the economy. If the backlog of orders is on the rise, then factories will have plenty of work to keep them busy for some time — perhaps so much that they will need to hire more workers and expand their facilities. If the backlog is declining, factories will have a declining amount of work ahead, so they may lay off workers and delay expansion plans. Statistics Canada reports unfilled orders on a monthly basis in *Inventories, Shipments, and Orders in Manufacturing Industries* (publication 31-001).

bad debt A debt that is not expected to be repaid. Businesses make a provision in their accounts for such debts and write them off against profits, while banks and other financial institutions set aside reserves to cover such debts. In their annual reports, for example, banks will show an appropriation for losses in their EARNINGS STATEMENT; this figure is deducted from pre-tax profits. Interest rates charged by financial institutions also take into account the fact that not all debts will be repaid, just as retail prices take into account losses due to shoplifting and spoilage.

bad faith Negotiation of a collective agreement or contract when one of the parties either is not intent on reaching agreement or does not intend to honour the agreement when it is signed.

bait-and-switch selling The technique, illegal under the COMPETITION ACT, of luring customers into a store by advertising or promoting big-discount bargains without having the merchandise available and then trying to persuade the customers to buy other more expensive goods. It is a criminal offence.

Baker Plan A plan introduced by U.S. Secretary of the Treasury James Baker in October, 1985, to address the growing difficulties of heavily indebted developing countries due to the THIRD-WORLD DEBT CRISIS. The creditor nations, including Canada, opposed a negotiated reduction in the outstanding debt, in part because they believed the capital base of their own banks might not have been adequate to facilitate meaningful debt reduction. Instead, under the Baker Plan, the debtor countries would receive more assistance from the INTERNATIONAL MONETARY FUND (IMF) and the WORLD BANK in return for adopting long-term reforms, including adhering to free-market practices, bringing budget deficits under control, adopting more open trade and investment policies, and moving to greater deregulation and privatization. The commercial banks also made negotiations to restructure debts and stretch out repayment on the condition that countries first reach an agreement with the IMF on a domestic reform package. But the Baker Plan proved insufficient and was followed by the BRADY PLAN.

balance of payments A summary of all trade in goods and services, travel, financial, and investment transactions between Canadians and the rest of the world over a given period of time. The net inflow and outflow of money arising from Canada's economic dealings with other countries is a good indicator of its ability to pay its way in the world. The balance of payments is divided into two accounts: current and capital. The CURRENT ACCOUNT measures the current flow of goods and services between Canada and the rest of the world: merchandise imports and exports; service transactions including tourist spending, freight and shipping costs, business services, government transactions, and other services; and interest and dividend payments and receipts, along with other transfers such as the funds immigrants bring with them to Canada. Payments from corporate head offices by foreign-owned subsidiaries for management services, research and development, and copyrights, patent trademarks, and industrial-design royalties show up as non-merchandise payments. Canada usually has a surplus on merchandise trade and a larger deficit in both service and investment transactions, resulting in an overall current account deficit, which must be financed by the sale of Canadian assets to foreigners or by an increase in Canada's foreign debt. The CAPITAL ACCOUNT consists of long- and short-term capital flows between Canada and other countries. These flows include DIRECT and PORTFOLIO INVESTMENTS, short-term investments such as those in finance and commercial paper, bank term deposits and certificates of deposit for terms of one year or less, Canadian foreign aid and export credit financing, immigrants' remittances to relatives in their native countries and funds brought by immigrants to Canada, and movements of insurance funds. Canada usually imports more capital than it exports, both to finance its current-account deficit and to make up any shortfall on the capital account due to a net outflow of foreign direct investment, for example. Since the balance of payments must balance out at zero, the balancing item consists of a reduction in Canada's foreign-exchange reserves

— or, if Canada has a surplus on its current and capital accounts, an increase in its foreign-exchange reserves. In principle, the current account and the capital account should balance out, but they usually don't because STATISTICS CANADA is unable to capture all transactions. The difference is listed as a statistical discrepancy. If a country runs a persistent deficit on its balance of payments, international lenders at some point will force it to live within its means, since these lenders at some point will be less willing to lend, even if they are able to command high interest rates. To correct a balance-of-payments crisis a country must reduce its imports, usually through a domestic austerity program, and increase its exports. It may also need to bolster its foreign-exchange reserves or seek other assistance from the INTERNATIONAL MONETARY FUND. Statistics Canada publishes quarterly reports on Canada's balance of payments (publication 67-001) as part of the SYSTEM OF NATIONAL ACCOUNTS. Canada's NET INTERNATIONAL INVESTMENT POSITION is published annually by Statistics Canada (publication 67-202).

balance of trade The difference between the dollar or money value of a country's exports and imports of merchandise or of goods and services. If a country exports more than it imports, it has a trade surplus; if it imports more than it exports, it has a trade deficit. The balance of trade is an important part of a country's overall BALANCE OF PAYMENTS. Statistics Canada publishes a monthly report on Canada's merchandise trade (publication 65-001). Statistics on trade in goods and services are contained in the quarterly balance of payments report (publication 67-001).

balance sheet One of four basic financial statements in an annual report, the others being the EARNINGS STATEMENT, the RETAINED-EARNINGS STATEMENT, and the STATEMENT OF CHANGES IN FINANCIAL POSITION. The balance sheet shows the assets, liabilities, and shareholders' equity of a corporation on the last day of the financial year. Assets are what the company owns or is owed. They include current assets, such as cash, short-term securities, accounts receivable, inventories, and pre-paid taxes, and fixed assets, such as buildings, factories, machinery and equipment, minus depreciation. Liabilities are what the company owes others and include current liabilities such as accounts payable, income tax payable, and the portion of long-term debt paid off that year, and long-term debt. Shareholders' equity, which is calculated by deducting total liabilities from total assets, consists of equity capital invested by shareholders in the corporation, accumulated retained earnings, and the CONTRIBUTED SURPLUS, if any. A balance sheet must always balance: assets must be equal to the liabilities plus shareholders' equity.

balloon In some bond issues that are redeemed over a number of years, a disproportionately large amount may be paid out in the final year. This is the balloon payment.

bank A financial institution whose principal business is to accept deposits, pay interest on the deposits, honour cheques drawn on the deposits, and make loans using a proportion of the deposits not needed for chequing purposes and other daily transactions. The role of banks has been greatly expanded in Canada, particularly by the amendments to the BANK ACT that came into force in 1992. Banks had been able to own stock brokers, investment dealers, leasing companies, mutual fund companies, mortgage loan companies, factoring companies, and real-estate companies and to hold their own properties prior to 1992. But with the 1992 amendments, banks are able to own trust companies, insurance companies, merchant banks (called specialized financing corporations) that can hold equity in manufacturing and other non-related businesses for up to 10 years, information-service companies that can also manufacture and sell ancillary computer hardware and software, real-estate development companies, real-estate brokerages, and companies offering investment counselling and portfolio management. In Canada, a bank must be recognized as such under the Bank Act and by the BANK OF CANADA and is regulated by the OFFICE OF THE SUPERINTENDENT OF FINANCIAL INSTITUTIONS. There is no legal definition of a bank in Canada but there are two categories of banks in Canada: Schedule I banks and Schedule II banks. Schedule I banks must be widely held, with no one person owning more than 10 percent. Schedule II banks owned by Canadians can be closely held for their first 10 years but must be widely held after that. Foreign Schedule II banks can be wholly owned up to a certain size, but collectively are restricted to control of 12 percent of total Canadian banking assets. U.S.-owned banks are not subject to these restrictions as a result of the CANADA-UNITED STATES FREE TRADE AGREEMENT. The Bank Act restricts self-dealing so that a financial institution cannot enter into a transaction with related parties such as directors and officers of the financial institution or any companies in which they have a substantial interest. Boards of directors must have a conduct review committee to review permissible transactions entered into between the financial institution and related parties, while at least one-third of a bank's directors must be unaffiliated — which means they are neither major borrowers nor shareholders — and the majority of directors on both the audit committee and the conduct review committee must be unaffiliated. The 1992 Bank Act changes also eliminate the requirement for banks to maintain reserves at the Bank of Canada. *See also* CHARTERED BANK.

bank account   Money deposited in a bank by an individual, corporation, or other depositor. There are three basic types: 1. A chequing or current account, in which money is deposited and on which cheques are drawn, but on which no interest is earned; 2. A chequing-savings account, in which money is deposited, on which cheques are drawn, and in which interest is paid on a minimum credit balance; 3. A non-chequing-savings account, in which money is deposited and interest paid on the minimum credit balance, but on which no cheques can be written. This third type of account pays a higher rate of interest. A bank can legally refuse to release funds from an interest-bearing account unless it has been given seven days' notice of withdrawal, but normal practice is to honour withdrawals on demand.

Bank Act   The federal law, dating back to 1871, that regulates the chartered banks; it is revised approximately every 10 years to take into account changes in the economy and changes in the BANKING SYSTEM. It defines who may own and operate a bank and how a bank may be established; the system of corporate governance for a bank; what types of activities a bank may engage in; the types of investments that a bank may make; a bank's relationship with the government, the public, and the Bank of Canada; the types of directorships that a bank officer may hold; the qualifications for bank directors; the way banks maintain their books of account; procedures for banks to follow in reporting to the OFFICE OF THE SUPERINTENDENT OF FINANCIAL

INSTITUTIONS; the issuing of bank shares; and other matters affecting banks and the functioning of the banking system. Amendments to the Bank Act passed in 1991 and proclaimed in 1992 represented the 11th review of the legislation since it came into effect in the 19th century. The Bank Act will next be reviewed in 1997.

bank deposit   Money in banks that belongs to depositors but can be used by the banks to make loans and other investments; bank deposits are liabilities of the banks and assets of the depositors or customers. There are many different types of bank deposits; they include chequing accounts that pay no interest, chequing-savings accounts on which cheques can be written and on which interest is paid, non-chequing-savings accounts on which a higher rate of interest is paid, and term deposits, which are sums of money left with a bank for a fixed term in return for a higher rate of interest. Bank deposits are an important part of the MONEY SUPPLY.

bank draft   A cheque issued by a bank in its own name rather than in the name of the customer who has actually provided the funds for the cheque. It is used when a creditor does not want to accept a cheque from the bank customer, usually after previous cheques have been returned because insufficient funds were in the bank customer's account. A bank draft, on the other hand, bears the name of the bank itself and is equivalent to cash.

Bank for International Settlements (BIS)   An international financial institution that serves as a central bank for the central banks of individual nations and promotes co-operation between central banks. It was formed in 1930 to help co-ordinate international receipts and payments among central banks, notably from German war reparations, on the initiative of France, Germany, Belgium, Britain, and Italy. Since then it has been expanded to include all the central banks of Western Europe, along with those of Canada, Japan, and the United States. Although many of its earlier functions have been taken over by the INTERNATIONAL MONETARY FUND, the bank remains important because it acts as a settlement agent for central banks, makes short-term loans, provides a forum for monetary authorities from the Western world to monitor the international banking system, and enables members to make unofficial arrangements to deal with currency speculations and other problems. With the globalization of financial markets, the BIS in recent years has played an increasing role in developing minimum capital standards for banks and regulatory procedures to deal with banks operating in a number of different countries under different regulatory systems. The bank holds a monthly meeting at its headquarters in Basel, Switzerland. It also publishes its own assessment of world economic problems and monitors international lending through the EUROCURRENCY MARKET and other international financial markets.

bank loan   Credit extended by a bank to a borrower. A loan is an asset of the bank and a liability of the borrower. The loan may be SECURED or UNSECURED; if it is secured, the interest charged is lower. Banks may make consumer loans, which are used to finance consumer purchases; MORTGAGE loans to finance the purchase of real estate; DEMAND loans, which can be called in at any time; TERM LOANS, which are for a fixed term; call loans to INVESTMENT DEALERS; and various specialized forms of loans to finance exports and fluctuations in the WORKING CAPITAL of firms, to farmers, and to SALES-FINANCE and ACCEPTANCE

COMPANIES. Banks also provide lines of credit, that are equivalent to overdrafts and credit-card credit.

bank note   Paper currency issued by the BANK OF CANADA as part of the country's money supply. Bank notes are issued in denominations of $2, $5, $10, $20, $50, $100, and $1,000. Until June 30, 1989, Canada also issued a $1 bill but this was replaced by a coin in July, 1987. Bank notes were issued by Canada's chartered banks until 1935, when the Bank of Canada was established.

Bank of Canada   The central bank, that is responsible for Canada's monetary policy. It plays a vital role in determining the price level and overall rate of economic growth in the country by influencing the level of interest rates and the external value of the Canadian dollar. Its other responsibilities include the printing of money, the management of the national debt, the investment of funds for government agencies, and advising the Minister of Finance on appropriate economic policies. Under the Bank of Canada Act, its responsibility is to regulate "credit and currency in the best interest of the economic life of the nation." While the legislation instructs the bank to moderate fluctuations in economic growth, external trade, prices, and employment, the bank has since 1989 focused on targets for reducing inflation, arguing that the inflation rate is the variable over which it can have the greatest influence and maintaining that a stable value for the currency is a necessary pre-condition for sustained economic growth. The articulation and implementation of MONETARY POLICY is the most important role of the central bank. By influencing the level of short-term interest rates, the Bank of Canada influences the growth of the MONEY SUPPLY (narrowly defined to include currency and the public's holdings of chartered-bank demand deposits). The Bank of Canada can induce the level of short-term interest rates through its control over the supply of settlement balances available to financial institutions that are directly clearing members of the CANADIAN PAYMENTS ASSOCIATION, and through its OPEN-MARKET OPERATIONS, where it buys and sells government securities to signal its interest rate targets. The bank is also the lender of last resort to the banking system, making loans to solvent chartered banks and to MONEY-MARKET- DEALERS to help them meet extended liquidity needs. The bank influences the external value of the Canadian dollar by intervening in foreign-exchange markets, as well as by the monetary policies it pursues, and by managing the foreign-exchange reserves in the EXCHANGE-FUND ACCOUNT. As fiscal agent for the federal government, the Bank of Canada manages the government's deposit account through which flow most government receipts and expenditures. It also manages the national debt; it advises the government on the method of financing and the terms of new issues of bonds and treasury bills and also arranges the printing of these securities, their sale and distribution, and the payment of interest. The Bank of Canada also plays an important role in monitoring economic conditions and guards Canada's gold and currency reserves.

The Bank of Canada was established as a privately owned corporation in 1934 under the Bank of Canada Act, following a royal commission, the MacMillan Commission, which called for the establishment of a central bank, and began operations in March, 1935; but the Bank of Canada Act was amended in 1935 so that, by 1938, it was a government-owned operation. It is managed by a 14-person board of directors, including a governor and deputy-governor who each serve seven-year terms. The Deputy-Minister of FINANCE serves as an ex-officio but non-voting member of the board, thus providing a link between the bank and the government. At the same time, the Bank of Canada Act requires the governor of the bank to meet regularly with the Minister of Finance to discuss both monetary policy and its relationship to overall economic policy. While the Bank of Canada has considerable independence in pursuing its monetary-policy objectives, the government can overrule the bank. To do so, the Minister of Finance must issue written instructions to the bank; the instructions must be specific, for a specified period of time, and must be made public. Thus, the government has the ultimate responsibility for monetary policy.

bank rate The minimum rate of interest the BANK OF CANADA charges to the CHARTERED BANKS, to other members of the CANADIAN PAYMENTS ASSOCIATION, and to INVESTMENT DEALERS and MONEY-MARKET DEALERS for their infrequent loans. The bank rate is more important, though, as a signal to the banking system on the direction of MONETARY POLICY. An increase in the bank rate is normally a sign that the Bank of Canada plans to tighten the MONEY SUPPLY. This in turn will lead to an increase in interest rates charged by the chartered banks and other financial institutions to their customers, although it will normally take several weeks or even months of small changes in the bank rate before the effect is felt in most commercial rates. A drop in the bank rate is normally a signal that the Bank of Canada intends to relax monetary policy, and the banking system will respond by lowering interest rates. Although the bank rate has been formally fixed since 1980 at 1/4 of 1 percent, or 25 basis points, above the average yield on 91-day Government of Canada TREASURY BILLS at their auction each Tuesday, the bank influences the bank rate through its own tender price for treasury bills and its daily actions in influencing the supply of overnight settlement balances. The U.S. equivalent to the bank rate, set by the Federal Reserve Board in Washington, is the discount rate.

banker's acceptance A bill of exchange or negotiable instrument drawn by a borrower for payment at maturity and accepted by a bank. The acceptance constitutes a guarantee of payment by the bank and can be traded in the MONEY MARKET. Banks earn a "stamping fee" when they provide a guarantee.

banking group A group of investment firms that together manage and assume financial responsibility for a new issue of shares, bonds, or other securities. Each firm assumes part of the financial responsibility. *See also* UNDERWRITER.

banking system The activities of the CHARTERED BANKS, carried out in conjunction with the BANK OF CANADA, in accepting deposits and making loans.

bankrupt The legal status of an individual or company, under the Bankruptcy and Insolvency Act, that is unable to pay creditors and therefore has its assets administered by a Trustee in Bankruptcy.

bankruptcy The legal steps to protect creditors and provide relief for debtors through the federal Bankruptcy and Insolvency Act. Creditors can petition a company or individual into bankruptcy through the Bankruptcy Court, and if the court agrees, it will issue a receiving order. A debtor can go into voluntary bankruptcy by making an assignment in bankruptcy. In either case, a trustee — an accountant — is appointed, and in both cases, the trustee takes control of all the debtor's assets with a view to disposing of them so that creditors can be paid; in the case of individuals who are bankrupt, the law allows them to retain essential assets for daily living and to continue working. The act allows a corporation or individual to make a reorganization proposal, including pre-proposal stays against seizure of assets by both secured or unsecured creditors, to allow time for negotiation with creditors; secured creditors can also be made part of a reorganization plan. To facilitate reorganization, the act requires that a secured creditor give a company 10 days' notice of its intention to exercise its right to seize assets, giving the company time to file a notice in court of its plans to make a reorganization proposal. The purpose of a reorganization of a corporation is to attempt to save the business by stretching out and even reducing repayment; but a reorganization cannot be approved unless it provides for payment of wage claims and services rendered within six months preceding the bankruptcy up to an amount of $2,000 per employee. The law provides an automatic stay-of-proceedings period by secured and unsecured creditors that can be extended by court order for a period of up to six months, with extensions of 45 days at a time; the provision prevents creditors from taking action against the debtor company or from terminating agreements. But to get extensions, the debtor company must satisfy the court it is acting in good faith and that no creditor will be materially affected by the extension. The reorganization plan must be approved by 50 percent of creditors and two-thirds in value of both secured and unsecured creditors. When a company becomes bankrupt or is placed in receivership, suppliers have the right to reclaim products delivered within 30 days of the bankruptcy; farmers, fishermen, and aquaculturalists can recover products delivered within 15 days of bankruptcy. In the case of an individual who files a proposal for the orderly repayment of debts, a counsellor is provided to help reorganize finances and an administrator takes charge of money collected from the individual and distributes it to creditors at least once every three months. Consumer debtors are protected against lease terminations, loan accelerations, public utility shut-offs, and wage assignments, and they are given some protection against dismissal from employment during the negotiation of proposals with creditors. The Bankruptcy and Insolvency Act is administered by the Superintendent of Bankruptcy, an official of the Department of CONSUMER AND CORPORATE AFFAIRS. The department publishes monthly statistics on the number and size of corporate and individual bankruptcies.

bargaining agent   A union that has been chosen by a majority of employees in a BARGAINING UNIT and has been recognized by a federal or provincial LABOUR-RELATIONS BOARD as the legal representative of the employees in negotiating and implementing a COLLECTIVE AGREEMENT.

bargaining theory of wages   The theory that wage levels depend on the bargaining strength of unions and employers and not simply on the supply of and demand for labour.

bargaining unit   A group of employees in a firm, government agency, trade, or occupation, recognized as a unit for collective-bargaining purposes by a federal or provincial LABOUR-RELATIONS BOARD. A bargaining unit may consist of all the employees of a firm, of a particular group of employees in a firm, or of a particular trade or skill in all firms in an industry.

barriers to entry   Market obstacles

that inhibit or prevent the entry of new firms into an industry and thus restrict competition. Economies of scale in capital-intensive industries restrict entry; there are high start-up costs and a new competitor must have a high level of production to be price competitive. Unless the huge start-up costs can be justified by future projects, a would-be competitor in a capital-intensive industry will be reluctant to make the investment. Likewise, competitive advantages of existing producers — such as PRODUCT DIFFERENTIATION based on large investments in advertising, EXCLUSIVE DEALING contracts with retailers, and patent restrictions — can also make it difficult for a new firm to enter an industry. Other barriers to entry can include control of distribution systems and market outlets by existing producers, or control of essential raw materials or technology. Similarly, government regulation can be a barrier to entry; for example, farm marketing boards make it difficult for new agricultural producers to enter the market, while government licensing requirements restrict the entry of new radio, television, and airline services. Where there are significant barriers to entry, existing producers may be able to earn excess profits; but if there is relative ease of entry, then profit margins are likely to be lower. The barriers to entry represent the costs that would-be producers must overcome; their existence usually means, unless there is relative ease of entry, that new producers have higher costs, at least on first entering the industry, than do existing producers. A country that wants to increase competition has to find ways to reduce barriers to entry, for example, by changing patent laws, by outlawing exclusive dealing and other such arrangements, or by lowering tariffs.

barter A transaction in which goods or services are exchanged for other goods or services rather than money. Barter was common in primitive economies where trading took place for the most part in a single community and there were few goods or services exchanged. But in any economy where goods or services are traded over wide distances and where there is a large number of goods and services available, it is extremely difficult to bring buyers and sellers together or to determine fair exchanges.

Today, barter is sometimes used as a form of TAX EVASION and is a characteristic of the UNDERGROUND ECONOMY. A dentist, for example, may provide braces for a carpenter's child in exchange for new cupboards at home; the dentist avoids taxes, and the carpenter's dentistry bill is lower than it might have been. Barter is also used in trade between nations, with a country rich in resources but poor in manufacturing, for example, exchanging a fixed amount of a commodity for a TURN KEY OPERATION or major machinery and equipment. It is then up to the exporter receiving the bartered products to sell them for cash to other customers.

base period A selected month, year, or set of years used as the starting point in calculating an index number or growth rate. The base period always equals 100. Statistics Canada uses 1986 as its base year for most indexes and in calculating changes in CONSTANT DOLLARS or in real terms. If 1986 is the base year (1986 then = 100) and the consumer price index is 123.8, then consumer prices have risen 23.8 percent since 1986. Similarly, if 1986 is the base year and the GROSS DOMESTIC PRODUCT has risen by 29 percent in 1986 dollars (after inflation has been deducted for the period), then real growth or growth in physical output has been 29 percent.

base rate The lowest rate of pay in a

collective agreement. It is the pay that the lowest-paid class of worker would get. *See also* BASIC RATE.

basic rate   The rate of pay for doing a job during a normal shift; it does not include MERIT PAY, OVERTIME, bonuses, or night and other differentials or premiums.

basis point   One one-hundredth of a percentage point. If the prevailing short-term interest rate falls from 9.255 percent to 9.125 percent in the course of a week, for example, it is said to have fallen by 130 basis points, or one-eighth of a percentage point.

basis-point pricing   A method of pricing in which a producer sets a price by calculating the transportation costs from some fixed location to the customer and adding this to a fixed price; the fixed location may not be the location of the producer's plant, so the price arrived at may be higher than the fixed price plus the cost of transporting the product from the producer to the customer. It is as if a group of producers in Canada decided that the price of a product would be a fixed price plus a delivery transportation charge using Windsor as the fixed location; a buyer obtaining the product from a plant in Cornwall would pay the same price as if the product had come from Windsor.

basket clause   A clause in the Canadian and British Insurance Companies Act that limits higher risk investments outside prudent investments set out in the legislation to no more than 7 percent of the book value of a life insurance company's total assets.

Basle Accord   An agreement reached in 1988 through the BANK FOR INTERNATIONAL SETTLEMENTS to establish uniform minimum capital requirements for international commercial banks, including Canadian banks, by 1992.

Banks must have capital equivalent to 8 percent of risk-weighted assets. Commercial bank capital is divided into Tier-One Capital (the common shares and retained earnings of a commercial bank, that must be equivalent to 4 percent of risk-weighted assets) and Tier-Two Capital (other capital, that must make up the other 4 percent of assets).

Bay Street   The heart of Canada's financial markets, in downtown Toronto at the intersection of King Street and Bay Street, where the TORONTO STOCK EXCHANGE and Canada's MONEY MARKET, CAPITAL MARKET, and FOREIGN-EXCHANGE MARKET are based. The major banks, investment dealers, stockbrokers, and institutional investors are all located in this financial district.

bear   An investor who believes that the prices of shares, bonds, and commodities will decline. Thus, he or she may sell existing investments and also try to make a profit by selling, for future delivery, shares not owned, in the hope of buying them on the market at a lower price when he or she has to make delivery. This form of speculation is known as SELLING SHORT. *See also* BULL.

bear market   A market for shares, bonds, or commodities in which the trend of prices is down. *See also* BULL MARKET.

bearer security   A bond or share that is presumed to be legally owned by the person who physically possesses it; it is not registered in anyone's name in the books of the company issuing it or on the security. Interest is paid through coupons attached to the bond, each bearing the date on which it can be redeemed at a bank or elsewhere for cash. A bearer bond is as negotiable as cash at a bank or other financial institution.

Becker, Gary S. (b. 1930) The American economist awarded the Alfred Nobel Memorial Prize in Economic Sciences in 1992 "for having extended the domain of microeconomic analysis to a wide range of human behaviour and interaction, including non-market behaviour."

beggar-thy-neighbour policies Protectionist policies to reduce imports and increase exports, usually motivated by a country's desire to export its unemployment problems to its neighbours or to protect its local industries. Such policies include increased tariffs or other import barriers, export subsidies, and currency devaluations. These policies were employed by many different nations during the GREAT DEPRESSION as they scrambled to shift their unemployment to other countries by reducing imports and increasing exports. But the policies were self-defeating since they led to retaliation and shrinking export markets for everyone. In the end, everyone was worse off because everyone's exports were reduced.

Belanger-Campeau Commission *See* COMMISSION ON THE POLITICAL AND CONSTITUTIONAL FUTURE OF QUEBEC.

black knight An investor, including a corporation, that launches a hostile, or unwelcome, takeover of a company for another investor or firm.

beneficial owner The person who is the true owner of a business, shares in a company, or other asset. In some businesses the beneficial owner may be unknown, since he or she chooses to operate through an agent, trust officer, lawyer, or business partner. In other cases, shares and other securities may be registered in the name of a stockbroker or trust company simply to facilitate the sale of the securities. *See* *also* SILENT PARTNER.

beneficiary A person who is left an inheritance in a will or who is named to receive the proceeds of an insurance policy. Under Canadian law, an insurance company notifies a beneficiary at the last known address. If the beneficiary is not located, the insurance company holds the funds for five years. After that, the amount is written off and placed in an "unclaimed equity fund." If a claim is later received from a beneficiary or a descendent of a beneficiary after the five-year period, it is paid out of this fund.

benefits-received principle of taxation The principle that the taxes levied on a person or corporation should be related to the benefits that the person or corporation receives from these public services. While this approach can be used in some selective instances, such as an airport tax to cover the costs of building and operating airports, a gasoline tax to help pay for road construction and maintenance, or a charge for postal services or entry to public parks, museums and the like, it is difficult to apportion the costs of police, public health, social welfare, scientific research, and other such public services. Moreover, it would not make sense to tax social welfare recipients to pay for the social assistance they receive. *See* *also* ABILITY-TO-PAY PRINCIPLE OF TAXATION.

Bennett New Deal A series of measures by which Prime Minister R. B. Bennett in 1935 attempted to counter the GREAT DEPRESSION by reinvigorating the economy, cracking down on unfair business practices, providing better pay and working conditions, improving social assistance, and creating jobs. The measures were first outlined in a series of five radio talks to the country, starting on January 2, 1935, and were subsequently spelled out in the government's SPEECH FROM THE THRONE.

A number of measures were passed in mid-1935, but many were later declared to be unconstitutional.

The principal items of the legislation were as follows: 1. The Employment and Insurance Act, which provided UNEMPLOYMENT INSURANCE, a national employment service, and other measures to assist the jobless. It was later declared unconstitutional. 2. The Dominion Trade and Industry Commission Act, which established a commission to enforce the COMBINES INVESTIGATION ACT, investigate unfair business practices, recommend other measures to outlaw unfair business practices, and apply the national trademark "Canada Standard" to products meeting government specifications for quality. It was declared constitutional. 3. The Minimum Wages Act, which allowed the government to set MINIMUM WAGES in different industries across the country. It was declared unconstitutional. 4. The Weekly Day of Rest Act, which provided for one compulsory day of rest for workers each week, preferably Sunday. It was declared unconstitutional. 5. The Limitation of Hours of Work Act, which set out an eight-hour day and a 48-hour work week. It was declared unconstitutional. 6. Amendments to the Natural Products Marketing Act of 1934, which already permitted the establishment of MARKETING BOARDS for farm products such as milk and cheese. It was extended to include pulp and paper and other forest products. The act and its amendments were declared unconstitutional. 7. Amendments to the Criminal Code, imposing criminal penalties for MISLEADING ADVERTISING, failing to pay the minimum wage, or engaging in unfair business practices such as trade discrimination and price cutting to eliminate competition or a competitor. The amendments were upheld, except for the minimum-wage provision.

In all of these cases, the Supreme Court delivered its judgements on June 17, 1936. The decisions on appeals to the Judicial Committee of the Privy Council were made on January 28, 1937. Other New Deal measures proposed by Bennett included establishment of an ECONOMIC COUNCIL OF CANADA, tax reform to make the tax system more progressive or related to ability to pay, public works and monetary expansion to create jobs, health and sickness insurance, and other measures to protect the public and investors against unfair business practices. In spite of these measures, Bennett was defeated in the general election of 1935. Many Canadians believed that he had done far too little to fight the Great Depression in earlier years and that his New Deal was a last-minute election gimmick.

bequest   A gift of money, securities, real estate, works of art, and personal property left to relatives, friends, and other beneficiaries in the will of a deceased person.

Berne Convention   An international convention dating back to 1886 that provides protection to authors by requiring a signatory to grant the same protection to works of authors from other countries it grants to its own authors. Authors have the right to prohibit photocopying of their work or the unauthorized reproduction of their work in any form. Their rights are limited to their own lifetime plus another 50 years after their death.

beyond-economic-reach reserves   Proven oil or natural-gas reserves that cannot be included in the calculation of reserves because they are too far away from markets, or too small to be connected by pipeline or removed by tanker or liquefaction and tanker, or too expensive to extract. For example, oil and natural gas reserves in the far North cannot be included in NATIONAL ENERGY BOARD estimates of Canada reserves until a pipeline or other transportation link has been established.

bid The price a would-be buyer is willing to pay for a share, bond, or other security or asset. *See also* ASK PRICE. A bid is also an offer made to purchase at a stated price made by a prospective buyer at an auction, by a person making an offer to purchase a property, or by an investor or company for the shares of another company.

bid and asked quotations The bid is the highest price a buyer is willing to pay, while the asked price is the lowest a seller will accept; together they represent a quotation for a share on a stock market. These quotations, along with closing prices, are published in the financial pages of daily newspapers.

bid-rigging A criminal offence under the COMPETITION ACT, bid-rigging is an agreement by companies to refrain from competing on contracts in order to raise prices and profits. The companies agree in advance on which one is to win the contract and the others either make excessively high proposals or refrain from making a bid at all so that the designated company can win. Bid-rigging is designed to eliminate competition, especially on public contracts, leading to inflated bids and escalating costs that must be borne by the taxpayer. No effect on competition need be proven in pursuing a bid-rigging case.

big business The biggest corporations and financial institutions in the country; the top one hundred corporations in Canada. The *Financial Post* compiles an annual list of the country's top five hundred. The *Globe and Mail* compiles a similar annual list of the top one thousand publicly traded companies. Statistics Canada publishes an annual report on the ownership of corporations in Canada, *Inter-corporate*

ownership (61-517). Large corporations account for a disproportionately large share of economic activity in Canada and include the principal banking, transportation, energy, steel, forest products, mining, automotive, telecommunications, electrical, chemical, and food-processing corporations, as well as other corporations.

bilateral agreement An agreement on trade, investment, or other economic relations negotiated between just two countries as opposed to a multilateral agreement, which applies the same treatment to all of a country's normal trading partners under the principle of MOST-FAVOURED NATION. The CANADA-UNITED STATES FREE TRADE AGREEMENT, which came into effect in 1989, is a bilateral agreement. Prior to the Second World War, many of the economic dealings among nations were based on bilateral agreements. But after 1945 non-discriminatory multilateral agreements came to dominate trade, monetary, and other economic relations, although nations still negotiate bilateral arrangements such as the 1965 CANADA-UNITED STATES AUTOMOTIVE PRODUCTS AGREEMENT. More recently, though, there has been a greater trend to bilateral and regional arrangements. *See also* MULTILATERALISM.

bilateral monopoly A double MONOPOLY, in which there is one producer or supplier and one buyer or consumer of a particular good or service. Such situations are rare but can exist; for example, the government may be the only buyer for a sophisticated weapon, while there may be only one manufacturer of the weapon.

bill **1.** A statement to a buyer from a seller stating the amount owed for itemized goods or services. **2.** A financial document indicating a debt or payment that can be accepted as equivalent to cash in settling a business transaction.

bill of exchange   A note that commits the issuer to pay the beneficiary or bearer a specific amount on a specific date. The bill of exchange is often used in international trade and can be signed over to a financial institution, usually at a discount.

bill of lading   A document used in international trade indicating details of what is being shipped, the method of transportation, the name of the carrier, the date of delivery, and the recipient of the goods.

binding agreement   A formal treaty that requires each country to honour the terms of the agreement. For example, under the CANADA-UNITED STATES FREE TRADE AGREEMENT, each country is bound to accept the findings of a dispute-settlement panel.

binding arbitration   A method of resolving a dispute between two parties with both parties bound to accept the decision of an independent arbitrator. For example, binding arbitration is sometimes used to resolve a labour dispute.

birth rate   The number of people born in a country in a given year per 1,000 population. For example, Canada's crude birth rate in 1991 was 14 per 1,000 of the population compared with 21 per 1,000 in 1965. By way of comparison, the U.S. crude birth rate fell from 19 to 17 and the Mexican crude birth rate from 45 to 27 between 1965 and 1990. For the world as a whole, it fell from 35 to 26. The population growth rate is the difference between the birth rate and the DEATH RATE plus net migration. *See* CRUDE BIRTH RATE.

black economy   *See* UNDERGROUND ECONOMY.

black market   An illegal market established during conditions of war, military occupation, or economic crisis. Its purpose is to circumvent rationing and other restrictions such as price controls. Consumers making purchases in a black market pay excessive prices, reflecting the monopoly power of the sellers and the high risk of operating such a market.

blanket policy   An insurance policy covering damages or loss — resulting from theft, fire, accident, or other cause of harm — of all the possessions of a homeowner or tenant, without requiring an inventory of the possessions for the insurance company.

blind trust   A trust established to manage the assets of an individual, such as a cabinet minister or senior government official, so as to enable him or her to carry out his or her responsibilities without fear of a potential conflict of interest. While the trustee keeps the person informed of the value of the trust, he or she keeps confidential the actual securities bought and sold. Federal cabinet ministers are required to hold their assets in a blind trust.

block trade   The sale or purchase of an unusually large number of shares in a public company on a stock exchange, with the sale and purchase being made by a single seller and, often, a single buyer.

blocked currency   Foreign-exchange controls to prevent non-residents from acquiring, using, or repatriating a country's currency. Such controls may be invoked during a balance-of-payments crisis or during a war or political crisis.

blue chip   The common share of a

large, reputable, low-risk company that has a long record of regular dividend payments. In Canada, such companies would include BCE, Alcan, or the five major banks. Blue-chip stocks change over time; for example, the major steel stocks were once considered blue-chip investments but lost that status by the end of the 1980s due to large losses and uncertainty over their future.

blue-collar workers Workers who, generally speaking, are employed in an industrial plant, where conditions are dirty and where workers may change their clothes before leaving the plant. They are production and maintenance workers and may be unskilled, semi-skilled, or skilled workers; they either work with their hands or operate machines. *See also* WHITE-COLLAR WORKERS.

board lot The regular trading block of shares in a stock exchange, usually one hundred shares, which has been agreed to by a stock exchange.

board of directors The representatives of a company's shareholders, elected usually at a company's annual meeting, who are responsible to the shareholders for the proper management of the company. The board supervises the activities of the company and its senior officers and sets or approves company policies and objectives. The work of the board of directors usually includes the appointment and supervision of senior executives, the approval of budgets, financing plans, new products, takeovers and other business plans, the payment of dividends, and the approval of major contracts, including collective agreements. Most boards are divided into various committees, such as an executive committee and an audit committee. Members of boards of directors are usually paid an annual fee plus an additional payment for each board or board committee meeting attended. While directorships were once treated as largely a reward, laws and vulnerability to shareholder lawsuits now make the job much more demanding. Directors, for example, can be found financially liable for back wages to employees and other costs if a company goes bankrupt. Companies routinely purchase insurance for directors today.

board of trade A community association of businessmen, similar to a local chamber of commerce, usually formed to promote the interests of the local business community and to promote the economic development of the community. Montreal, Toronto, and Vancouver, for example, each have their own board of trade.

boiler room The place from which highly dubious stocks are sold by telephone. Promoters usually work with so-called sucker lists of individuals likely to have investment capital available; these are frequently doctors, lawyers, dentists, and people operating their own businesses. High-pressure sales tactics are applied, promising would-be investors fast profits if they purchase the stocks immediately. In the U.S., securities legislation in the 1930s made such swindles much harder to pull off, but such operations were relatively easy to run from Canada until the 1950s. Canadian promoters frequently applied boiler-room tactics to lists of U.S. investors, especially in the sale of dubious mining stocks. Such operations are now illegal in Canada.

bonanza Discovery of an extremely rich ore body.

bond A debt security in the form of a promissory note or certificate of indebtedness issued usually for a term running from at least five to seven years up to 20 years or longer. The bond certificate shows the name of the government or corporation issuing it, its face value, the annual rate of interest that will be paid and when, and the date on which the bond matures and the principal must be repaid in full. Although CANADA SAVINGS BONDS may be issued in denominations as small as $100, most bonds are issued in denominations of at least $1,000. Bonds are issued by federal, provincial, and municipal governments, crown corporations, business corporations, and financial institutions to raise long-term capital. Bond issues are subject to the regulations of the securities commission of the province in which they are issued. Their appeal to investors, especially INSTITUTIONAL INVESTORS, is that they have an assured return and are usually low risk. There is also a secondary market, the BOND MARKET, in which traders deal in already-issued bonds, hoping to earn capital gains on changes in the market value of the bonds due to changes in interest rates. Sometimes a bond is registered in the name of its owner, so that if it is stolen it is harder to dispose of. Coupon bonds have interest coupons attached, which can be cashed each year as they become payable. A first-mortgage bond is one that is secured by a mortgage against the corporation's assets. A DEBENTURE is a bond against which no assets of the corporation are pledged, and that represents a general claim against the corporation. A sinking-fund bond is one against which the company is setting aside funds each year for eventual repayment. A serial-bond issue is one in which a certain number of bonds mature each year. A callable bond is one that can be redeemed at any time. A convertible bond is one that the owner may convert into common or preferred shares. *See also* PERPETUAL BOND, PRIVATE PLACEMENT. The BANK OF CANADA uses the sale and purchase of bonds to help influence the MONEY SUPPLY; when it purchases bonds it increases the money supply by adding to the pool of funds in the banking system, and when it sells bonds it reduces the money supply by drawing on the pool of funds in the banking system.

bond market   The network of bond traders working in the banks, insurance companies, investment-dealer firms, and other financial institutions, who trade in bonds either on their own account or on behalf of their clients. There is no bond exchange, as there is a stock exchange with its own building, but there is a telecommunications network of bond traders. Investors buy and sell corporate, government, and hydro bonds for profit as interest rates — and hence, the market value of the bonds — change; a $10,000 bond with an interest rate of 8.875 percent, for example, would be worth more than $10,000 if average bond rates fell to 8.125 percent, and less if the average bond rate rose to 9.125 percent. The bond market consists of the primary market for new bond issues and the secondary market for the resale and purchase of bonds already in public hands. The bond market is regulated by the INVESTMENT DEALERS ASSOCIATION of Canada, along with the Toronto Bond Traders' Association and the Montreal Bond Traders' Association.

bond rating   The grading by an independent professional analyst of a corporate or government bond indicating the quality of the bond. The rating indicates the borrower's ability to pay the interest and repay the principal of the bond. The two top bond-rating firms, based in New York, are Moody's and Standard & Poor. The two principal Canadian firms are Dominion Bond Rating Service and Canadian Bond Rating Service. The top government rating from Canadian Bond Rating Service is AAA and the top corporate rating is A++. The top bond rating by Dominion Bond Rating Service and Standard & Poor is AAA while the top rating from

Moody's is Aaa.

bonded carrier A carrier that has posted a bond with the Department of NATIONAL REVENUE and is permitted to bring goods across Canada's borders to a final or other destination without having to complete the importing paperwork or to pay duties and taxes at the border. The paperwork is completed and the duties and taxes are paid at the carrier's destination. The bond required ranges from $5,000 for a truck to $80,000 for a plane, depending on size.

bonded good A good that is stored in a bonded warehouse so that taxes do not have to be paid on it until it actually leaves the warehouse. Liquor is often stored this way.

bonus bid The successful bid in a government auction of oil or natural-gas PERMITS or LEASES. The bonus bid is the highest bid.

book value The net value of a corporation or its individual assets, based on the value appearing in its balance sheet. Book value may or may not be market value; it may, for example, be the acquisition cost minus the depreciation to date or it may simply be the original purchase price. Hence, book value is not always a reliable guide to what a corporation or an asset is worth. It could significantly understate the value of land, mineral reserves, or patents, for example. Likewise, the stock of foreign direct investment in Canada is significantly understated because it is shown as book value and not market value.

bookkeeping Accounting records that show all transactions — that is, all expenses and all income. *See also* DOUBLE-ENTRY BOOKKEEPING.

boom A high and unsustainable level of business activity. It is usually characterized by high profits, soaring stock and commodity markets, full employment, and business operating at its full productive capacity; it is the high point in the BUSINESS CYCLE. However as that peak is reached, shortages in labour and goods develop, forcing up wages and prices. The ensuing inflation undermines the boom. A RECESSION normally follows. A boom is characterized not only by strong growth but by rapid growth. Its upper limit is reached when all the resources in the economy are fully utilized and shortages develop.

bootlegger A person who sells goods illegally; for example, someone who sells liquor to minors or who sells when provincially operated stores are closed: this is a contravention of provincial laws that forbid customers to resell liquor to others. The bootlegger makes his profit by charging a higher price per bottle than the price he has paid. A bootlegger may also sell an illegally made product, such as privately distilled liquor, or products such as cigarettes smuggled from the United States on which no Canadian taxes have been imposed.

bottom line A widely used term that means "what really counts." In accounting, the bottom line is the net profit remaining to the business and its shareholders after expenses, taxes, and interest have been paid.

bought deal The purchase of a new issue of shares from a company by an investment dealer for resale to the dealer's clients at a profit. The risk for the dealer is that the price may decline, meaning the dealer has to absorb the loss or hold onto the shares for longer than planned.

boycott The refusal by an individual, organization, or nation to deal with a firm or nation until it changes its policies or behaviour. It is a form of economic or political pressure. A union and its members may boycott the products of a firm if they or another union are engaged in a labour dispute with it. Similarly, consumers may boycott the products of a firm if they feel that it is overcharging, or they may boycott a particular store if they object to some of the merchandise it is selling. An example of a trade boycott is that of the Arab nations on economic dealings with Israel; it consists of a primary boycott by the Arab nations themselves against any direct dealings with Israel, and a secondary boycott in which Arab countries also refuse to have economic dealings with firms from non-Arab countries that have dealings with Israel.

Brady Plan   A plan introduced by the then U.S. Secretary of the Treasury in March, 1989, to address the problems caused by the THIRD-WORLD DEBT CRISIS following the failure of the BAKER PLAN. The Brady Plan recognized the need for a reduction of commercial bank debt owed by developing countries if the debt crisis was to be resolved. By 1989, it was clear that the heavily indebted developing countries could not manage their debt problems, even with new loans, unless they received some debt relief. The Brady Plan did not set out a formula or mechanism for debt relief. Instead, it left that to negotiations between the debtor countries and the banks, either by a reduction in interest rates or a reduction in the principal owed. Debtor countries were to present the banks with a "menu" of debt-reduction options, and the banks would be free to choose whatever best suited them. Banks could also provide new loans instead of negotiating a reduction in outstanding debt. Brady argued that the amount of debt outstanding was so large that the developing countries could not repay. But, he argued, by reducing the amount of debt owing, the commercial banks were much

more likely to see the remaining debt repaid. Mexico was one of the first debtor countries to restructure its debt after the Brady Plan was unveiled; it achieved a 35-percent reduction in its debt.

branch banking   A banking system in which there are only a few banks, with each one operating branches throughout the country. This enables each bank to acquire significant financial strength and to avoid being dependent on the economic health of a single region or community. This is the kind of banking system Canada has, as opposed to the regional banking system in the United States, where there are thousands of banks, most of them serving a relatively small area, perhaps a single community. While U.S. residents may benefit from a more competitive banking system in their biggest cities, Canadian residents are more likely to have a choice of banks if they live in smaller communities. Without the development of large national banks operating throughout the country, it is hard to see how Canada could have developed a banking system that is effectively Canadian owned and controlled.

branch-plant economy   An economy in which a large share of business activity is carried out by subsidiaries of foreign corporations. This means that important decisions on investment, jobs, research and development, new products, export markets, and financing are made in another country and not in the country where the activity may take place. Canada is an example. *See also* TRUNCATION, FOREIGN DIRECT INVESTMENT.

brand name   The name used by a firm to identify to consumers a product, line of products, or the firm itself, and thus to differentiate its goods and services from those of its competitors. Since the value of a brand name normally increases as a result of long-term investment in advertising and promotion to build customer loyalty, brand names can be worth a lot of money. Since they are also a form of product differentiation, brand names can become a powerful BARRIER TO ENTRY into an industry by would-be competitors. Brand names include those of manufacturers whose products are sold throughout the country; private brands are products that bear the name of the retailer or a name owned by the retailer, even though they may be manufactured by the same company that manufactures the national brand. Brand names are intangible assets — they are worth money and are registered as TRADEMARKS in Canada. Companies attempt to build up sales through brand loyalty.

Brandt Commission   An international commission of 16 persons appointed in September, 1977, by World Bank President Robert McNamara to seek out solutions to North-South problems and to respond to demands for a NEW INTERNATIONAL ECONOMIC ORDER. It was headed by former West German Chancellor Willy Brandt and its members included one Canadian, former Canadian Labour Congress President Joe Morris. The commission's report, *A Program for Survival*, was published in 1980 and called for the elimination of hunger and malnutrition by the end of the 1990s through the elimination of absolute poverty. It made a number of recommendations that were fundamental to the new international economic order, which entailed both a massive shift in resources to the developing world and a greater voice for developing countries in the world's major multilateral organizations such as the INTERNATIONAL MONETARY FUND and the WORLD BANK. It endorsed a COMMON FUND for key commodities of developing countries to assure more stable prices and export earnings; proposed better access for the exports of manufactured products from developing countries to the markets of the industrial world; urged a reform of the international monetary system, including a greater role for SPECIAL DRAWING RIGHTS (SDR) and the allocation of a greater share of SDRs to developing countries to reflect their needs; called for a new approach to development finance, including a form of international taxation under which all countries except the poorest would give a share of per capita national income to world development; and stressed that the needs of developing countries were so great that OFFICIAL DEVELOPMENT ASSISTANCE should be doubled, with all the industrial countries contributing 1 percent of GROSS NATIONAL PRODUCT by the year 2000. It also called for the establishment of a World Development Fund for program lending, as opposed to project lending, and for greater financial assistance to developing countries for energy and mineral development, along with greater lending by the commercial banks. The report called for a world summit of 25 top leaders to summon the political will to address global problems and to endorse a strategy for world economic development. The Brandt Commission also called for an emergency program for 1980-85 while long-term policies were designed and adopted. The emergency program called for the large-scale transfer of resources to developing countries, an international energy strategy, a global food program, and a start on major reforms to the international economic system. *See also* NORTH-SOUTH DIALOGUE.

break-even point   The level of sales needed by a company to recover both its fixed and variable costs. When income exceeds expenses, the firm makes a profit; when income fails to cover expenses, the firm suffers a loss. In planning a major investment, such as a new product, a company will take all of its costs into account, including research and development, prototypes, start-up manufacturing and marketing investments, and the COST OF CAPITAL, assess this against the market for the new product and the estimated price the market will be willing to pay, and calculate the point at which it can expect to break even. If the break-even point is beyond the estimated size of the market, the project should not go ahead. *See also* LEARNING CURVE.

break-up value   What the owners of a business would get if it were wound up and after its creditors had been paid.

Bretton Woods Agreement   An agreement reached among the governments of the United States, Britain, and Canada at a New Hampshire resort in 1944, to establish a multilateral and non-discriminatory monetary, trading, and investment order as the basis for post-war economic recovery. They wanted to prevent a return to the BEGGAR-THY-NEIGHBOUR POLICIES of the 1930s. The agreement was based on the deep-rooted belief that the citizens of individual nations would fare best in a global economy based on international specialization and comparative advantage and non-discriminatory policies among nations. The agreement led to the creation of the INTERNATIONAL MONETARY FUND (IMF), WORLD BANK, and the GENERAL AGREEMENT ON TARIFFS AND TRADE. At the heart of the post-war economic framework was a system of FIXED EXCHANGE RATES and convertible currencies, to be regulated by the strict rules of the IMF.

bridge financing   Short-term financing, particularly applicable to construction financing, until a mortgage or other long-term financing can be arranged.

British North America Act (BNA Act)   An act of the British Parliament that brought Canada into being as a nation on July 1, 1867, by joining together in a federation Ontario, Quebec, New Brunswick, and Nova Scotia. Since then, six other provinces have been created or have joined, the most recent being Newfoundland in 1949. The BNA Act has served as Canada's constitution. It sets out the federal and provincial spending and taxing powers, including concurrent powers, states the desire of the Fathers of Confederation that Canada be a single or common market, and spells out other details of the new nation, including the organization of political institutions. The act has been amended a number of times since Confederation; until 1982, any changes had to be made by the British Parliament since the BNA Act was an act of the British Parliament. In 1982, it was patriated to Canada and renamed the CONSTITUTION ACT, 1867. *See also* CONSTITUTION ACT, 1982, CANADIAN CHARTER OF RIGHTS AND FREEDOMS, FEDERAL SPENDING POWER, FEDERAL TAXING POWER, PROVINCIAL SPENDING POWER, PROVINCIAL TAXING POWER, DISTRIBUTION OF POWERS.

British preferential tariff   A tariff scheme that levied a lower or preferential tariff on goods traded among Commonwealth or former Commonwealth countries. The system originated in 1919 but took on greater importance with the Ottawa Conference of 1932, at which Britain, Canada, and other Commonwealth members signed reciprocal agreements instituting preferential tariff rates for each other's products. The Canada-United Kingdom agreement was phased out after 1973, when Britain entered the EUROPEAN COMMUNITY. But Canada still has reciprocal agreements with Australia and New Zealand and non-reciprocal agreements with other members of the Commonwealth. In

July, 1979, Canada gave South Africa six months' notice it was withdrawing from the Canada-South Africa Trade Agreement of 1932. The British preferential tariff rate is less than the MOST-FAVOURED NATION rate. But it is of declining importance and, for many less-developed Commonwealth countries, the GENERALIZED SYSTEM OF PREFERENCES results in lower tariffs than the so-called British preferential rate. The existence of the British preferential tariff was an important factor for a time in encouraging U.S.-owned companies to establish subsidiaries in Canada or to take over established Canadian firms. These Canadian branch plants gave the U.S. firms access to British and Commonwealth markets at the British preferential tariff, which for a time was much lower than the rate charged on goods shipped directly from the United States. *See also* OTTAWA AGREEMENTS.

British thermal unit (BTU) The amount of heat necessary to raise one pint of water one degree Fahrenheit. The measure is frequently used to compare the relative energy content of different sources of energy, such as oil, coal, natural gas, and uranium.

broker An independent agent who brings together a buyer and a seller so that a sale can be made. There are many different kinds of broker, each with a specialized knowledge of his market: in shares traded on the stock exchange, the stockbroker; in property (such as houses or commercial buildings), the real-estate broker; in commodities (such as wheat or porkbellies), the commodities broker; and in insurance, the insurance broker. For their services, brokers are paid a commission (BROKERAGE), which is usually related to the value of the transaction.

brokerage The fee or commission charged to a customer by a stockbroker, commodity dealer, real-estate agent, or other kind of broker.

Bruntland Commission *See* WORLD COMMISSION ON ENVIRONMENT AND DEVELOPMENT.

bubble A speculative commercial venture, common in the 18th and early 19th centuries, in which the value of shares would rise so high that they would bear no relationship whatever to the asset value or future earning power of the enterprise. Most such ventures were created to defraud investors; often, they succeeded. The psychological fever, usually for a company with land or mineral investments in another part of the world, would reach such a pitch that even normally rational investors would come to feel that they couldn't afford to stay out. At some point the bubble would burst; share prices would plummet, and investors would be left with worthless pieces of paper. Frequently their entire fortunes would be wiped out. The Bubble Act was passed in Britain in 1720 after the infamous South Sea Bubble, to control the sale of shares to the public. It was one of the first acts anywhere to protect investors.

Buchanan, James (b. 1919) The American-born economist who won the Alfred Nobel Memorial Prize in Economic Science in 1986 for "his development of the contractural and constitutional bases for the theory of economic and political decision-making." Just as economic man acted in his own self-interest, Buchanan contended that politicians and governments would behave the same way, which was not necessarily in the public interest. One consequence is that actions needed to serve the public interest will be delayed if unpopular because politicians will not want to bear the political cost. Buchanan, who rejected KEYNESIAN ECONOMICS, advocated a balanced budget because this would impose a discipline on politicians to behave responsibly.

bucket shop An illegal act by a stockbroker that consists of accepting an order to buy or sell a share without the intention of carrying out the transaction. The broker delays carrying out the transaction in the hope that the price of the share will change, thus enabling the broker to make a personal profit.

budget **1.** The annual statement, usually in February, by the federal Minister of FINANCE, setting out the government's expected revenues, spending, and resulting surplus or deficit for the fiscal year beginning April 1. The budget speech contains a review of the economy and an indication of expected economic performance for the year ahead, along with any proposed tax or tariff changes. It also includes a five-year economic forecast and a five-year fiscal plan showing how the government expects to manage its finances over the following five years. The budget also contains an estimate of the government's cash requirements, which is the amount of money it expects it will have to raise in financial markets in the next five fiscal years. The budget is followed by the presentation of the spending ESTIMATES on a department-by-department basis. The budget process begins in the preceding fall, when the Department of Finance determines the fiscal framework that sets the limits on government spending. Similar annual statements are made by each of the provincial finance ministers or treasurers. The federal government presents its budget as the BUDGETARY-ACCOUNTS BUDGET. Statistics Canada produces the NATIONAL-ACCOUNTS BUDGET; at the end of the FISCAL YEAR, STATISTICS CANADA presents the government's accounts in another form, the FINANCIAL-MAN-

AGEMENT SYSTEMS account. In addition, the government tables the PUBLIC ACCOUNTS, which set out actual revenues and expenditures, at the end of the fiscal year. The budgetary-accounts budget gives the best picture of department-by-department spending. The CASH-NEEDS BUDGET, which is part of the Minister of Finance's budget statement, shows the activities of the federal government in capital markets, and hence helps to analyze the impact of the budget on MONETARY POLICY and the availability of funds for private borrowers. The national-accounts budget measures the impact of government activity on the economy. And the financial-management system shows government spending by function, in areas such as health care, industrial development, and social welfare; it also details revenue by the type of tax and its base or by the kind of revenue from the sale of goods or services. Governments finance budget deficits by borrowing; they issue BONDS and TREASURY BILLS, which they sell to the public. **2.** A financial plan for any business or other organization showing expected sources of revenue, expected expenditures, and the resulting profit or loss. Budgets are usually drafted for the next fiscal year, but some organizations operate on five-year budgets, since this gives a better picture — and hence control — of revenue and expenditure trends and is more suited to strategic planning.

Budget Speech The speech made by the Minister of FINANCE, reviewing the state of the economy and setting out the FISCAL POLICY the government intends to follow in the ensuing 12 months. At the end of the speech setting out the budget, the Minister of Finance tables budget papers, which contain detailed information on the economy and the government's accounts, and moves formal WAYS AND MEANS MOTIONS that allow him or her to introduce legislation implementing the precise tax and tariff measures contained in his budget. The House of Commons has a six-day debate on these motions in what is known as the budget debate. At the end of the debate, a vote is taken that the government has to win; if it doesn't, it has lost the confidence of the House of Commons, and either a new cabinet must be installed or, more likely, a general election held. If the ways and means motions are adopted, the exact budget measures, usually in the form of amendments to the Income Tax Act or other existing legislation, are presented to the House of Commons for debate for clause-by-clause scrutiny and approval; the legislation must also be approved by the Senate. Although the budget measures must have the approval of Parliament, it is assumed that they will receive it, and the budget measures therefore usually come into effect the same evening the budget speech is read to the House of Commons. The speech is usually delivered at 4:30 P.M., Ottawa time, when domestic financial markets have closed.

budgetary-accounts budget   The revenue and spending program of the federal government, presented by the Minister of FINANCE each year, usually in the spring, for the coming fiscal year. The spending program is set out in the ESTIMATES, published in advance of the BUDGET SPEECH, while the budget gives the government's projection of revenues from taxes and other sources for the coming year. These budgetary accounts set out spending on a department-by-department basis that is approved by Parliament and paid out of the CONSOLIDATED-REVENUE FUND. The difference between spending and revenue is the budgetary deficit or surplus. The budgetary-accounts figures are one guide to the impact of the government's FISCAL POLICY on the econ-

omy, in particular to whether that policy is stimulative, restrictive, or neutral. Economists also use both the CASH-NEEDS BUDGET and the NATIONAL-ACCOUNTS BUDGET to assess the economic impact of government spending and taxing for the coming fiscal year. The budgetary-accounts budget is important as a system for parliamentary control of actual government spending, since it presents spending by department, on the basis of which members of Parliament can vote approval. It also shows the amount by which the federal net debt is raised or reduced. Its weakness for economic analysis is that it excludes significant areas of government spending and revenue, such as the operations of government pension plans for its own employees and the CANADA PENSION PLAN and government-owned crown corporations. It also makes no allowance for depreciation of government capital investment. *See also* FINANCIAL-MANAGEMENT SYSTEM. The PUBLIC ACCOUNTS, published at the end of the fiscal year, show the actual expenditures and revenues and can be compared with the earlier estimates and budget-speech projection of revenues. The Department of Finance publishes monthly statistics on the budgetary accounts.

budgetary control   A form of financial control in an organization in which senior and middle managers are expected to keep their costs and revenues in line with the budget that has been prepared for the financial year. If costs are out of line with those in the budget, then either new controls must be brought to bear to reduce them or the budget itself must be revised to reflect those added costs. In most organizations, monthly and cumulative performance can be compared with budgetary projections for the same periods.

buffer stocks   Stocks of commodities of international importance that are purchased by government agencies when prices are below an official price and supplies excessive, and sold when prices are high and supplies scarce, with the aim of stabilizing prices. In the late 1970s, the LESS-DEVELOPED COUNTRIES proposed that buffer stocks be established for a wide range of commodities through the creation of a COMMON FUND to finance the acquisition of such stocks. Agreement in principle on such a fund was reached between developed and less-developed countries in 1979 but it was not until 1988 that a modest Common Fund was established.

building permit   A permit issued by a municipality, granting permission for the construction of a particular type of building on a designated parcel of land. National and regional statistics on the value of building permits granted are a useful indicator of future economic activity, since these figures give an indication of the demand for construction labour, building materials, steel, and certain consumer durables such as furniture and appliances. Statistics Canada publishes a monthly report on the value and types of residential and non-residential building permits granted, using figures supplied by about 1,700 municipalities (publication 64-001). The statistics are broken down by province, municipality, and metropolitan area, and also indicate residential, industrial, commercial, government, and institutional spending. If the monthly value of building permits granted shows a series of increases, then construction activity, an important source of economic growth, is about to pick up. Conversely, a consistent decline in building permits issued indicates that economic activity may be heading for a decline or recession.

built-in stabilizer   A government program that automatically offsets fluctuations in the BUSINESS CYCLE and hence helps the economy to adjust to new conditions. For example, in a recession, unemployment-insurance and social-welfare payments help to sustain the overall level of demand in the economy. In a period of inflation, the income-tax system takes a bigger bite of rising incomes, even with indexation for inflation, thus relieving the pressure on demand in the economy. The existence of built-in stabilizers means that the economic system adjusts to some extent to changing economic conditions, without having to await new government initiatives. However, there may still be a need for additional government intervention as well — for example, through tax cuts or increases, through changes in MONETARY POLICY, or perhaps through the adoption of an INCOMES POLICY.

bull   In stock, bond, and commodity markets, a person who expects prices to go up and who backs up that belief by investing. The term itself dates back to the London Stock Exchange in the early part of the 18th century. *See also* BEAR.

bull market   A market in which the prevailing mood is one of optimism and in which prices are rising. *See also* BEAR MARKET.

bullion   Gold, silver, and other precious metals in the form of bars and ingots rather than coins, with a money value stamped on them. Part of Canada's foreign-exchange reserves are maintained in the form of bullion, and gold bullion is sometimes used, though less so now than in the past, by central banks to settle international payments. The price of gold bullion is determined in the GOLD MARKET. *See also* GOLD STANDARD.

Bureau of Competition Policy   A branch of the Department of CONSUMER AND CORPORATE AFFAIRS that enforces the COMPETITION ACT.

It is responsible for strengthening competition in the economy and halting unfair business practices that reduce competition or defraud the public. It deals with mergers, monopolies and combines, price-fixing and other restrictive business practices, and false or misleading advertising. The Director of Investigation and Research, who heads the Bureau of Competition Policy, conducts investigations or refers them to the COMPETITION TRIBUNAL, if the matter is one subject to civil review, and to the Attorney-General of Canada if criminal proceedings are warranted. The director can provide what is called an Advisory Opinion to a business proposing a plan or practice; the opinion is non-binding on the business and the director may revise his opinion if the facts change. The director can also issue Advance Ruling Certificates when he is satisfied a proposed merger is consistent with the Competition Act. The Director of Investigation and Research publishes an annual report outlining the activities of the Bureau of Competition Policy for the fiscal year.

Bureau of Consumer Affairs A branch of the Department of CONSUMER AND CORPORATE AFFAIRS that administers federal laws designed to protect consumers against fraudulent weights and measures, deceptive packaging, and hazardous or unsafe products. It also plays a role in consumer education.

Bureau of Corporate Affairs A branch of the Department of CONSUMER AND CORPORATE AFFAIRS that administers federal laws governing the operating of a business in Canada. These include the CANADA BUSINESS CORPORATIONS ACT, that sets out the requirements for incorporation and the filing of financial statements, as well as the various responsibilities of directors and officers of a corporation. The

bureau also administers the Bankruptcy and Insolvency Act and laws dealing with intellectual property, including the PATENT ACT, Industrial Design Act, Copyright Act, and Trade Marks Act. It has a special division that is responsible for federal activities in the regulation of securities markets in Canada. The bureau is also responsible for the registration of lobbyists.

business The production of goods or services for profit. The activity can be carried out by an individual, a family, a partnership, or an incorporated company.

business agent An employee of a union or union local whose job it is to look after the business affairs of a local, to help negotiate collective agreements, and to help union officers see that a collective agreement is implemented in the best interests of the union membership.

Business Council on National Issues (BCNI) A forum of chief executive officers of Canada's largest business corporations, organized in 1976 in the words of its founders to "help strengthen the country's economy, its social fabric, and its democratic institutions." The BCNI, as it is known, is made up of about 150 chief executive officers, with membership by invitation only and limited to executives with an interest in public policy. It has an executive committee, which leads the organization, and a president, who is the principle spokesperson for the organization. Overall direction is provided by a board of directors, also known as the policy committee, which meets at least four times a year. The board has 33 members, including three ex officio members — the elected heads of the Canadian Chamber of Commerce, the Canadian Manufacturers Association, and the Counseil du Patronat du Québec. The BCNI also has special task forces to deal with specific issues, such as free trade, the constitution, the environment, and the economy, and economic policy, and these may draw on the advice of member companies and independent consultants. For example, with the federal government the BCNI retained Michael Porter and The Monitor Co. to produce a special report on Canadian competitiveness, *Canada at the Crossroads*, which was published in 1991. The executive committee establishes the mandates for the task forces. The task forces then carry out the work and report back to the policy committee for discussion and approval. The president is then responsible for implementing the recommendations, for example, taking the findings to government, putting the proposals to a parliamentary committee, or making the findings public. The BCNI describes its philosophy as "anti-corporatist, liberal democratic, and supportive of organizational pluralism." It is based in Ottawa.

business cycle   The fluctuations in economic activity, alternating between recovery and fast growth toward FULL EMPLOYMENT and contraction and slower growth into RECESSION. While the sharp swings of the business cycle have been largely smoothed out since the introduction of KEYNESIAN ECONOMICS, which showed that increased government spending and tax cuts could bring an economy out of recession while reduced government spending and tax increases could cool inflation, many economists still believe that the business cycle is an important feature of economic life. The point of maximum output is called the peak; the point of lowest output is called the trough. A complete business cycle extends from trough to trough. The business cycle goes through five basic stages: 1. Recovery from the trough of the cycle, with economic growth stimulated by lower interest rates, a ready supply of investment capital and consumer credit, and government incentives such as a stimulative FISCAL POLICY, all working to make use of idle capacity in the economy. 2. A period of gathering steam as the pace of recovery gains momentum, increased demand leads to new investment, and the economy moves toward full employment. 3. Excess demand and the peak of the business cycle as growth pushes the economy beyond its full-employment potential, with shortages and inflation developing and government being forced to raise taxes and interest rates, reduce the growth rate of the money supply, and cut back on its own spending. 4. Contraction of economic growth, with industry pulling back new investment and cutting back production, employees being laid off, and tighter credit conditions taking effect. 5. The recession or trough, with business activities cut back, unemployment much higher, inventories sharply reduced, and inflation and costs under control. This last stage is the turning point in the down cycle, with government using monetary and fiscal policies to get economic recovery, or stage 1, underway again.

There is disagreement among economists on whether business cycles are an inevitable part of economic life or reflect the failure to refine economic policies to the point where EQUILIBRIUM can be maintained; economists also disagree on the causes of such business fluctuations, with some putting the blame on poor monetary management, others blaming fluctuations in investment in new productive facilities, others blaming underconsumption by consumers, and still others maintaining that fundamental changes are occurring, which are based on technological change, government regulatory and other policies that hamper market forces, and other such factors. *See also* ACCELERATOR PRINCIPLE.

business failures   Business firms that

go out of business either by going bankrupt or by being wound up because they cannot continue in operation. An increase in the number of business failures is usually a sign of worsening business conditions since, in a recession, with money tighter and demand weaker, marginal businesses have a harder time getting credit or finding new customers and orders. The Department of CONSUMER AND CORPORATE AFFAIRS reports business failures coming under the federal Bankruptcy and Insolvency Act and the Winding-up Act. Failures are reported by province, industry, and by dollar amount.

business game   *See* GAME THEORY.

bust   A sharp and severe drop in economic activity resulting in high unemployment, a sharp drop in prices, and a decline in investment. No major industrial country with a diversified economy and BUILT-IN STABILIZERS has experienced a bust since the GREAT DEPRESSION. But less-developed countries, which depend on a single commodity for much of their economic activity and most of their foreign-exchange earnings, can still experience dramatic declines in economic performance. So can individual industries in industrial countries — industries such as gold mining and agriculture — if world prices collapse in the face of oversupply or a sharp drop in demand. *See also* BOOM.

buyer's market   A market in which supply is greater than demand, and hence one in which there are more sellers than buyers. This means that buyers have market power that allows them to push down or hold down prices. *See also* SELLER'S MARKET.

buyer's strike   *See* CONSUMER BOYCOTT.

by-laws   **1.** The set of rules adopted by shareholders of a company, setting out the timing and date of shareholders' meetings, the role of directors' meetings, the election and qualification of directors, the number and duties of corporate officers to be appointed by the directors, the financial procedures of the company, and other such matters. Shareholders can amend their by-laws. **2.** Laws passed by municipalities dealing with such matters as land use, shopping hours, licensing of local businesses, and traffic controls.

by-product   A secondary product that is produced in the course of processing or manufacturing a principal product. It is not a waste because a use can be found for it. Sulphur, for example, is a by-product of the forest-products industry, produced during the processing of natural gas and wood chips to make wallboard.

Byrne Report   *See* NEW BRUNSWICK ROYAL COMMISSION ON FINANCE AND MUNICIPAL TAXATION.

C

CANSIM (Canadian Socioeconomic Information Management System) A fully computerized data bank of STATISTICS CANADA's current and historical information from its most widely used series of statistics. In addition to a full range of economics statistics, the data bank contains a considerable amount of social information, including statistics on health, education, science, culture, and the judicial system.

C.D. Howe Institute An economic-research organization that deals mainly in domestic public-policy issues and international economic issues. It was formed in 1973 through the merger of the C.D. Howe Memorial Foundation and the Private Planning Association of Canada. It has continued the work of three committees established by the Private Planning Association: the Canadian Economic Policy Committee, which concentrates on Canadian economic issues; the Canadian-American Committee, which deals with North American trade and other economic issues; and the British-North American Committee, which deals with international economic issues. The institute has its own research staff and also sponsors outside research. Among its publications is its annual *Policy Review and Outlook*, which reviews the economic outlook and suggests priorities for national economic policy. The institute is based in Toronto.

C.I.F. The charges of cost, insurance and freight in shipping exports and imports. *See* F.O.B.

COLA clause In a collective agreement, a cost-of-living allowance clause that automatically raises pay rates at specified periods during the life of the contract in line with increases in the CONSUMER PRICE INDEX. The clause may provide for complete indexation or put a limit on the percentage increase that will be paid.

COMECON *See* COUNCIL FOR MUTUAL ECONOMIC ASSISTANCE.

cabinet The prime minister and the various ministers who are appointed by him or her to head the different departments of government or to undertake special tasks. The cabinet meets together as a group to decide on government policy. There is also an inner cabinet, made up of a smaller number of key ministers and known as the planning and priorities committee. It is chaired by the prime minister and determines the government's basic goals, makes major policy decisions, and is the long-term planning arm of the government. In 1992, there were 16 cabinet committees, made up of key ministers in each of the relevant policy areas. In addition to priorities and planning, the main cabinet committees having an impact on economic policy including expenditure review; operations; communications; economic policy; environment; federal-provincial relations; human resources, income support, and health; privatization and regulatory affairs; trade; and treasury board.

Caisse de dépôt et placement du Québec An investment agency established by the Quebec government in 1965 to manage funds on behalf of the Quebec Pension Plan and various public sector pension plans and other public pools of capital. Its mandate is to invest subject to the normal risk-return considerations in its fiduciary responsibility to its future beneficiaries, to support the economic development of Quebec, and to broaden and improve the liquidity of the market for provincial securities and thereby to improve the management of the province's debt. The Caisse, which is based in Montreal, can hold up to 30 percent of the shares of an enterprise. It invests in bonds, shares, real estate, mortgage, short-term securities, and derivatives. At the end of 1992, it had assets of $41.3 billion. It is the largest investor in Canadian stock exchanges and held shares with a value of $14.3 billion at the end of 1992.

caisses populaires CREDIT UNIONS operated in Quebec; they are important financial institutions, providing many banking and other services. They are co-operatively owned by their members and in many cases are tied to churches. The first caisse populaire, or credit union, in North America was started by Alphonse Desjardins, a House of Commons shorthand reporter, in 1900 in Lévis, Quebec. A network of caisses populaires, La Confédération du Québec des Unions Régionales des Caisses Populaires Desjardins, has a number of important investments, including a share of the Provincial Bank of Canada and ownership of La Société Fiducie du Québec. Caisses populaires are regulated by the Quebec Minister of Finance responsible for financial institutions.

call A contract that gives the holder the right to buy from the existing owner of shares a specified number of shares in a particular company at a specified price during a specified period of time. The purchaser of this privilege pays the existing owner of the shares, the maker, a fee for this privilege. The purchaser of the call is under no obligation actually to buy the shares; what is purchased is the option of buying them. The purchase of calls instead of the shares themselves is a form of stock-market speculation. The investor is speculating that the price of the shares will rise above the call price by a certain date and is willing to pay a fee to buy a block of shares at the specified call price. The profit is the difference between the actual market price and the call price, minus the fee paid for the call. If the shares don't go up, the only loss is for the price of the call. The existing owner of the shares, the maker, gets money from the sale of the option and, if the option or call is exercised, still stands to make a profit, since the call price is higher than the existing market price. *See also* PUT, OPTION, STRADDLE.

call-back pay The extra pay due an employee who has completed a shift and is then called back to work before he or she is scheduled to return, either to fill in for an employee who has booked off sick or because some emergency or special need has arisen. The amount and conditions under which the employee is paid are specified in a COLLECTIVE AGREEMENT.

Cambridge School See NEOCLASSICAL ECONOMICS.

Canada Assistance Plan (CAP) A federal program introduced in 1966 to pay half the costs of provincial-municipal social assistance as defined under the program. It replaced a multitude of federal cost-sharing programs and extended federal assistance into new areas, such as assistance to needy mothers with dependent children, health-care costs of welfare recipients, and welfare services aimed at reducing the causes and effects of poverty, such as special training for people unable to retain jobs or programs to reduce child abuse. Aid is based on assessment of need rather than means. Assistance under the program includes aid to provide "basic requirements" such as food, shelter, clothing, fuel, and personal necessities; maintenance in a home for the aged, nursing home, or child-care institution; welfare services such as counselling, rehabilitation services, day-care, homemaker, and adoption services; and special needs for the rehabilitation, safety, and well-being of people in need. The provinces integrated their social-assistance programs under the Canada Assistance Plan. Quebec was the exception; it opted out and gets payments instead under the Federal-Provincial Fiscal Arrangements and Established Programs Financing Act, 1977. The February, 1990, budget placed a two-year ceiling of 5 percent on the growth of federal transfers under the plan to Ontario, British Columbia, and Alberta. The 1991 budget extended this for another three years.

Canada Business Corporations Act Federal legislation setting out the rules for establishing companies, along with a code of obligations and rights for management and shareholders. The act requires the public disclosure of audited financial statements by all companies with more than $10 million in annual revenues or assets of more than $5 million, including private companies; the financial statements are on file for public viewing at the Department of CONSUMER AND CORPORATE AFFAIRS in Ottawa. The legislation guarantees certain voting procedures to protect minority shareholder rights.

Canada Deposit Insurance Corporation (CDIC) An insurer of deposits and lender of last resort for banks and federally incorporated trust and loan companies. Provincially incorporated financial institutions may participate with the approval of their government. The CDIC is also a major creditor when financial institutions have to be liquidated and monitors the liquidation process to get the best return on claims due the insured depositors. The corporation was established in 1967 to protect Canadian depositors against the loss of their savings, following the failure of several financial institutions. See ATLANTIC ACCEPTANCE SCANDAL, PRUDENTIAL FINANCE CORPORATION AFFAIR. Depositors are protected against losses of up to $60,000 at a member institution. Premiums for member institutions have been one-tenth of 1 percent since 1986. Deposits insured including chequing and saving demand accounts, term deposits such as guaranteed-investment certificates with terms not exceeding five years, debentures issued by loan companies, money orders and certified cheques, provided these are payable in Canada and denominated in Canadian dollars. In its first 25 years, CDIC paid out $6.2 billion in liquidations or restructurings and subsequently recovered $3.4 billion in the same period. In 1991, it paid out $1.3 billion to insured depositors of Standard Trust and recovered $650 million in the following six months. Other major payouts included $318 million to the depositors of failed Northland Bank and $352 million to depositors of failed Canadian Commercial Bank, both in 1985, and $200 million for the restructuring of the Bank of British Columbia. Insurance is compulsory for the chartered banks, Quebec savings banks, federally incorporated trust and loan companies, and provincially incorporated trust and loan companies, and other institutions such as credit unions, where the provincial government consents (except Quebec — *see* QUEBEC DEPOSIT INSURANCE BOARD). In late 1992, a private-sector advisory committee was appointed by the Department of Finance to propose improvements to the CDIC system.

Canada Development Corporation (CDC)   A corporation created by the federal government in 1971 under the Canada Development Corporation Act. Its purposes were to help develop and maintain strong Canadian-controlled and Canadian-managed corporations in the private sector of the economy and to give Canadians greater opportunities to invest and participate in the economic development of their country. In introducing the act establishing the corporation, the Minister of FINANCE said that it should emphasize support for industries in which there are opportunities for the development and application of new technologies or for the exploitation and upgrading of Canadian natural resources, or those that have special relevance to the development of the North and in which Canada now has or can develop significant comparative advantages by international standards. The CDC was also expected to play a role in the RATIONALIZATION and improvement of various sectors of

industry in Canada. The CDC was not assigned the role of trying to buy back Canadian corporations from foreign owners, although it might do this in rationalization of an industry or in developing the base for an effective, Canadian-owned firm in an industry. The CDC was not to be a lender of last resort to firms in trouble; its investments were to meet the normal business test of profitability.

The CDC took control positions in firms in which it made investments; it selected six industries for investment: petrochemicals, mining, oil and gas, health care, pipelines, and VENTURE CAPITAL. Its major assets included Polysar Limited, 60 percent of Petrosar Limited, and 30 percent of Texasgulf Incorporated. It had authorized capitalization of 200 million shares of NO PAR VALUE and $1 billion of PREFERRED SHARES. As the CDC increased in size and profitability, the government's share of voting stock was to be reduced to 10 percent. CDC shares were sold to the public, with preferred shares also carrying a vote; the government's interest was reduced to two-thirds of the voting shares, the others being owned by private investors. The CDC was not a crown corporation or an agent of the Crown. CDC never achieved the goals set for it by government. It suffered both from weak management and the difficulty of operating as a mixed enterprise. Because CDC had some private shareholders, it could not pursue government objectives; nor could the government exercise its powers as the principal shareholder, since this would be seen as interference. However, no other shareholder could hold management accountable, leaving management free to pursue its own objectives. In the mid-1980s, the federal government began disposing of its shares and CDC began selling off its assets. By 1988, it was reduced to a single asset, Polysar Energy and Chemical Corporation, and its name was changed to reflect this.

Polysar was acquired by Nova, an Alberta corporation, and resold to a German petrochemical company.

Canada Development Investment Corporation A federal crown corporation established in 1982 to manage, prepare for privatization, and privatize commercial holdings of the federal government. Initial responsibilities included Canadair Ltd., de Havilland Aircraft of Canada, Teleglobe Canada, Eldorado Nuclear Ltd., the government's shares in the CANADA DEVELOPMENT CORPORATION (CDC), and the government's shares in Massey-Ferguson Ltd. The corporation subsequently organized, as the largest shareholder, the restructuring of the Newfoundland fisheries industry, leading to the establishment of Fishery Products International, and held the government's interest in National Sea Products during a restructuring of that company. By 1992, most of these holdings had been privatized, with the exception of CDC, which was wound up. Based in Toronto, the corporation continues to act as management and holding company for the federal government. When it was first established, the Canada Development Investment Corporation was also expected to play a role as an independent adviser to government in dealing with corporate restructurings and perhaps even to become a source of patient or long-term equity capital for the modernization of Canadian industry.

Canada Employment and Immigr-ation Commission (CEIC) A federal agency that administers federal manpower-training and assistance programs, unemployment insurance, and labour-market activities, including job-placement services in Canada Employment Centres. The agency also administers Canada's immigrant-recruiting and -processing services overseas and immigrant settlement services in Canada. It was created in 1977, merging the former UNEMPLOYMENT INSURANCE COMMISSION and the former Department of Manpower, which operated the Canada Manpower Centres, and taking over immigration recruiting and processing as well. It reports to Parliament through the Minister of EMPLOYMENT AND IMMIGRATION.

Canada-European Community Transatlantic Declaration A declaration signed by Canada and the EUROPEAN COMMUNITY (EC) in 1990 to increase consultation and co-operation between Canada and the EC. The declaration calls for regular meetings between the Prime Minister of Canada and the President of the European Council and President of the Commission of the European Communities, bi-annual meetings between Canada's Secretary of State for External Affairs and the President of the European Council and the President of the Commission of the European Communities, annual consultations between the Canadian government and the European Commission, and briefings by the President of the European Commission following semi-annual European Political Co-operation meetings of the EC's foreign ministers. The declaration, which is almost identical to a similar agreement signed between the EC and the United States at the same time, builds on the FRAMEWORK AGREEMENT FOR COMMERCIAL AND ECONOMIC CO-OPERATION signed by Canada and the EC in 1976. While much of the declaration deals with peace and security issues, it also sets out as common goals the pursuit of policies for a sound world economy, the promotion of market principles, improved assistance for developing countries, and adequate support for the former communist countries of Europe as they make the transition to democratic market systems. Canada and the EC pledge to work together to strengthen the multilateral trading system or GENERAL AGREEMENT ON TARIFFS AND TRADE, to promote liberalization of investment flows and trade in services, and to work together on other matters such as technical and non-tariff barriers to industrial and agricultural trade, services, competition policy, transportation policy, standards, telecommunications, high technology, and other areas. They promise increased exchanges and joint projects in science and technology, including space, research in medicine, environmental protection, energy conservation, and the safety of nuclear and other installations, and in communications, culture and education, including academic and youth exchanges.

Canada Gazette The official publication of the Government of Canada, which lists government appointments and publishes statutes, regulations, and orders in council. It is published weekly by the Department of SUPPLY AND SERVICES CANADA, and publication in the *Canada Gazette* constitutes official notification. The *Canada Gazette* began publication in 1841. Since 1974, it has been divided into three parts: Part I - general; Part II - regulations; and Part III - statutes.

Canada Grains Council A federal body created in 1969 to improve grain production, processing, handling, transportation, and marketing, including export sales. Its 32 member organizations are non-government representatives of the grain industry, including farmers, flour-milling companies, railways, terminal operators, wheat pools, and grain companies. The council meets twice a year. It has two basic purposes: to improve co-operation within the grain industry and to make recommendations on changes in government policy or industry practices to aid the development of the grain industry. The Council publishes an annual statistical handbook on Canadian and world grain

statistics and various reports on its research projects. It also operates a commercial database called Grainbase. It is based in Winnipeg.

Canada Health Act The legislation passed in 1984 to preserve the universality of Canada's health-care system by penalizing provinces that charge user fees for health services or allow doctors to engage in extra billing. The legislation replaced existing legislation that defined Canada's public health-care system — the Hospital Insurance and Diagnostic Services Act, the Medical Care Act, and the Extended Health Care Act. Under the 1984 legislation, a province would be penalized by a federal holdback of funds equivalent to what the province received from user charges and for the estimated income its doctors received through extra billing. The ban on extra billing led to a doctors' strike in Ontario in 1986, when that province introduced conforming legislation, and to a rotating strike by doctors in Saskatchewan in the same year.

Canada Labour Code The main body of federal labour law, which came into effect in July, 1971. It covers about 10 percent of the Canadian labour force, namely workers in industries that come under federal jurisdiction, such as railways, airlines, banks, and shipping companies. In addition, each province has its own labour laws. The Canada Labour Code was divided into five parts. Part I deals with fair-employment practices, such as a ban on job discrimination based on race, colour, religion, and national origin. Responsibility has since been transferred to the CANADIAN HUMAN RIGHTS COMMISSION. Part II has been consolidated with part III, which deals with labour standards such as the length of the work week, maximum hours of work, minimum wages, overtime layoffs, dismissal, and maternity leave. Part IV deals with job safety; and part V deals with the conduct of industrial relations and is administered by the Mediation and Conciliation Branch of the Department of LABOUR and the CANADA LABOUR RELATIONS BOARD.

The code deals with the organization of workers into unions, certification of bargaining units, and supervision of collective-bargaining procedures. It also gives unions a limited right to strike over technological change, even though a collective agreement is in effect. On any technological change likely to affect a significant number of employees, the employer must give 90 days' notice. The union may seek from the Canada Labour Relations Board the right to bargain or strike, but the board may grant permission only if there is no technological-change clause in a contract, or if the employer failed to give proper notice and the impact on the employees would be "substantial and adverse."

Canada Labour Relations Board (CLRB) An independent and quasi-judicial federal tribunal that deals with complaints from unions and employees concerning unfair practices under part V of the CANADA LABOUR CODE. Matters coming under its jurisdiction include certification and decertification of BARGAINING UNITS, illegal strikes and lockouts, applications by unions to reopen collective bargaining in the event of technological change, interference by employers with efforts of employees to organize and join unions, and complaints dealing with on-the-job safety. Prior to 1973, the tribunal was a branch of the Department of LABOUR.

Canada-Mexico Ministerial Committee Established in 1969 to improve Canada-Mexico ties and to deal with issues and opportunities facing the two countries. The committee consists of cabinet ministers from the two countries, who meet about once every 18 months.

The meetings are co-chaired by the foreign ministers of Canada and Mexico and alternate between the two countries. It last met in Ottawa in February, 1993. The committee also deals with activities arising under the 1990 Framework Agreement for Co-operation in Trade and Investment signed by the two countries, which sets out their intentions to expand trade and investment ties. In addition, more than 10 sub-agreements have been signed, dealing in such areas as tourism, forestry, the environment, agriculture, housing, customs procedures, narcotics, police co-operation, and financial arrangements leading to the signing of a Canada-Mexico tax treaty.

Canada Mortgage and Housing Corporation (CMHC) A federal crown corporation created in 1946 as part of the federal government's post-war reconstruction program to meet the housing needs of returning veterans from the Second World War. Its basic role today is to administer the NATIONAL HOUSING ACT and to help meet the housing needs of Canadians by insuring mortgage loans on new housing, to work with the provinces to provide housing for low-income Canadians who cannot find affordable housing, to support the special housing needs of the disabled, women in crisis, and aboriginals, to support prototypes of new forms of housing, and to conduct research and development into new construction methods, energy efficiency, and other means of improving housing for Canadians. Following the 1992 budget, a Canadian who can raise a 5 percent down payment for a new house, with an upper limit, can obtain CMHC insurance for a mortgage issued by a financial institution for the remaining 95 percent of the cost of the home. Canadians were also permitted to use up to $20,000 in their REGISTERED RETIREMENT SAVINGS PLANS toward a down payment. The social-housing programs of CMHC, often with provincial cost-sharing, include non-profit housing. It also carries out research on Canadian housing and mortgage markets. Its mortgage insurance business is profitable. Its headquarters are in Ottawa. The corporation also publishes monthly statistics in Canada on housing starts along with an annual compendium of housing statistics.

Canada-Newfoundland Offshore Petroleum Board *See* ATLANTIC ACCORD.

Canada Pension Plan (CPP) A national compulsory and contributory pension plan, which came into operation in January 1966 and began paying pensions a year later, after intensive negotiations and initial opposition from some provinces. All working Canadians between the ages of 18 and 69 were required to join. Quebec established its own parallel plan — the Quebec Pension Plan — which is fully integrated with the CPP so that all Canadians get benefits under one or the other of the plans and carry their benefits with them if they move to or out of Quebec. Initially, pensions were not paid until age 70, but by 1970, this had been reduced to age 65. Today, employed Canadians between the ages of 18 and 69 must contribute and nonretired workers may contribute to age 70. Employers and employees each pay 50 percent of the individual's premium, which is equivalent to 2.4 percent of pensionable earnings of $32,200, for a total premium of 4.8 percent of pensionable earnings. The 1986 federal legislation approved a formula to progressively increase the premium, so that it would reach 7.6 percent. The pension paid is equivalent to 25 percent of pensionable earnings, and the maximum benefit in 1992 was $636.11 a month. The CPP is indexed according to a Pensions Index. CPP benefits can start at age 60 on a reduced scale. In addition, CPP pays supplementary benefits to surviving spouses,

orphans, disabled contributors, and dependent children of disabled contributors. CPP also pays a lump-sum benefit equivalent to six months of pension benefit. Excess funds in the CPP Investment Fund are lent to the federal and provincial governments in proportion to the revenues that originated in the province that year. In Quebec, the QPP funds are deposited in the CAISSE DE DÉPOT ET PLACEMENT DU QUÉBEC to finance Quebec business, including direct shares in companies, as well as buying provincial and municipal bonds. The CPP is the single most important pension plan for most working Canadians since many private-sector employees have no company pension plan.

Canada Ports Corporation A federal crown corporation established in 1983 to replace the National Harbours Board as the agency responsible for managing the 15 ports under federal control.

Canada Savings Bond (CSB) A savings bond sold to the public each October, every year since 1946. CSBs are a popular form of savings, with most major companies offering payroll-deduction schemes so that employees can purchase them over the course of a year. They can also be purchased for cash. CSBs are attractive to investors because they can always be cashed in at any branch of a bank for their face value plus accrued interest.

The annual sale is handled by the Bank of Canada, working through the chartered banks, investment dealers, and other authorized sales agents, after the government has decided what the rate of interest will be and what special features, if any, should be attached to the bonds. CSBs are issued in denominations ranging from $100 to $10,000 and are of two types: regular-interest bonds, which pay interest each year, and compound-interest bonds, which accumulate interest and pay it when the bond matures. There are restrictions on who can buy CSBs — only individuals, some types of REGISTERED RETIREMENT SAVINGS PLANS, and estates — and there is usually a limit on how many can be purchased. There is no limit on the size of each year's issue, but the Minister of FINANCE can cut off sales at any time. CSBs were launched at the end of the Second World War after Canadians had developed the habit of this type of saving through the purchase of Victory Bonds to finance the war effort. Since then a wide range of alternative investment instruments have emerged through banks, trust companies, money market funds, and other sources, reducing the role of CSBs to a savings vehicle. In fiscal 1991-92, CSBs accounted for just 8 percent of the federal government's debt, compared with 15 percent in 1986-87.

Canada-United Kingdom Loan Agreement   A critical post-war loan by Canada to Britain of $1.25 billion, made in 1946 after the United States suddenly cut back its expected post-war assistance. The British had estimated that they needed $6 billion to avert a severe financial crisis, but the United States provided only $3.75 billion, and that under tough conditions. The Canadian loan to Britain, in relative terms, was a much greater level of assistance, as a percentage of the Canadian economy, than the subsequent U.S. Marshall Plan aid was as a percentage of the U.S. economy.

Canada-United States Air Quality Agreement   An agreement signed by Canada and the United States in 1991 to address the problems of transborder air pollution, including acid rain. The agreement recognized that each country was responsible for the effect of its air pollution on the other and committed each country to consult with the other in advance on any activities that might cause significant transboundary

air pollution, and states that each country must take steps to mitigate or avoid such risks. It also commits each country to develop the means to deal with transboundary air pollution problems, to report publicly on progress being made, to delegate to the INTERNATIONAL JOINT COMMISSION the holding of public hearings, provides a process for dispute settlement and requires that the accord be reviewed after five years. The first annex of the accord deals with acid rain, permanently capping sulphur dioxide emissions in the United States at 13.3 million tonnes and in Canada at 3.2 million tonnes. It requires scheduled reductions in emissions of nitrogen oxides from factories and power plants over 10 years, tighter emissions for motor vehicles, close monitoring of sulphur dioxide and nitrogen oxide emissions, and that specific actions be taken to protect both countries' wilderness areas from transboundary air pollution.

Canada-United States Automotive Products Agreement   An agreement signed by Canada and the United States on January 16, 1965, to create a North American market for motor-vehicle production, and, in the process, give Canadian workers more jobs and Canadian consumers lower prices for North American automobiles. The two countries hoped to create a broader market so that there would be greater specialization and hence greater efficiency, especially in Canada, and expected that conditional free trade in motor vehicles, original parts, and tires for original vehicles would make Canada more attractive as a location for motor-vehicle-industry plants. Canada agreed to allow eligible motor-vehicle manufacturers and auto-parts firms to import parts and finished vehicles duty-free. Motor-vehicle manufacturers in Canada had to meet three conditions: 1. To continue to manufacture motor vehicles in the same ratio as the motor-vehicle sales that existed in the 1964-model year. 2. To maintain Canadian VALUE-ADDED at least equal to that of the 1964-model year. 3. To meet specific capital-investment targets set out in letters of commitment to the Canadian government from each of the vehicle manufacturers. Canada hoped to increase production and employment, to boost its share of North American production to roughly the same as its consumption of North American motor vehicles, to reduce the gap between U.S. and Canadian motor-vehicle prices, to reduce its balance-of-payments deficit in the Canada-United States motor-vehicle and parts trade, and to obtain a share of research and development spending in the industry. Motor vehicle companies in Canada that met all the conditions of the Auto Pact could also import vehicles and parts duty-free from third countries.

For its part, the United States granted unconditional free entry of motor vehicles and original equipment parts from Canada. The agreement provided for a comprehensive review in 1968, and allowed either country to withdraw on one year's notice.

As a result of the CANADA-UNITED STATES FREE TRADE AGREEMENT (FTA), which came into force at the beginning of 1989, the rules of origin eliminated Canadian content and replaced it with North American content, with motor vehicles required to have 50 percent North American content to qualify for duty-free passage across the border. The FTA also barred any other companies from gaining autopact status, a move designed primarily to exclude the Japanese auto-makers' plants in Canada and the United States. Under the NORTH AMERICAN FREE TRADE AGREEMENT, Mexico becomes part of the North American motor-vehicle market, gaining duty-free access to the U.S. and Canadian markets for its motor-vehicle industry; the level of North American content necessary for

duty-free passage between the three countries was raised to 62.5 percent.

Canada-United States Defence Production Sharing Arrangement   An agreement between Canada and the United States to maintain a long-term rough balance in defence trade between the two countries. In 1959, after Canada cancelled plans to build its own military plane, the Arrow, officials of Canada and the United States reached an agreement under which Canada would rely on the United States for its major defence technology, while, in return, the United States would facilitate the development of a defence industry in Canada by permitting the duty-free entry of most military products and by making an exception to the Buy America Act, which required the U.S. Defense Department to purchase U.S.-made equipment. The agreement was reaffirmed in 1963, when the U.S. secretary of Defense, Robert McNamara, and the Canadian Minister of Defence Production, C.M. Drury, signed a memorandum of understanding that the two countries would aim for a general balance in defence procurement from each other. Once a year, officials from the two governments meet to review the level of procurement from each other's country.

Canada-United States Free Trade Agreement (FTA)   A free trade agreement that came into effect on January 1, 1989, that was designed to eliminate tariffs and other barriers to trade over a 10-year period, to harmonize certain standards and practices, to reduce barriers to trade in services, to impose constraints on various policy levers of the two governments, to harmonize certain standards and practices, to reduce barriers to trade in services, and to provide a means of dispute settlement. The negotiations began in May, 1986. In September, 1987, the negotiations broke off due to Canada's failure to gain

U.S. concessions on the application of U.S. anti-dumping and countervailing duties on Canadian exporters. The negotiations resumed shortly thereafter, and the two countries were able to reach agreement by October 3, 1987, the deadline under the U.S. "fast-track" approval process in the U.S. Congress. The text of the 214-page agreement was initialled by the two countries on December 10, 1987, signed by Prime Minister Brian Mulroney and President Ronald Reagan on January 2, 1988, and passed by the Canadian Parliament and the U.S. Congress late in 1988. The agreement is divided into 20 chapters

Chapter 1 sets out the objectives and scope of the agreement, maintaining it is consistent with Article XXIV of the GENERAL AGREEMENT ON TARIFFS AND TRADE (GATT), which sets out the conditions under which countries can enter into free-trade arrangements. The chapter sets the five objectives for the FTA — the elimination of barriers to trade in goods and services; the facilitation of fair competition within the free-trade area; the liberalization of conditions for cross-border takeovers and investments; the establishment of procedures for the administration of the agreement and the resolution of disputes; and laying the foundation for future bilateral and multilateral co-operation to expand and enhance the benefits of the agreement.

Chapter 2 sets out the definitions used in the agreement. For example, the word "measure" is used throughout the agreement. It is defined as "any law, regulation, procedure, requirement, or practice" of a government. Likewise, the chapter makes clear, "unless otherwise specified, a reference to province or state includes local governments."

Chapter 3 defines the rules of origin that apply in the agreement. The rules of origin define what products qualify for duty-free treatment when crossing the Canada-U.S. border. Goods containing imported raw materials or components from outside Canada or the United States qualify for duty-free treatment if they have been sufficiently changed — have VALUE-ADDED — in either country to be classified under a new tariff item. In some cases, such as automobiles, there is also a quantitative requirement that goods also achieve 50 percent Canadian or U.S. content. Special quotas exist limiting duty-free trade in clothing using offshore woven fabrics.

Chapter 4 sets out a 10-year period for the elimination of tariffs, tariff-related measures, quantitative restrictions, and other restrictive measures at the border by January 1, 1998. In some cases tariffs were completely eliminated on January 1, 1989; in a second category, tariffs were to be eliminated in five equal steps starting January 1, 1989; and in the remaining cases, tariffs were to be eliminated in 10 equal steps, starting on January 1, 1989. In the case of steel products covered by emergency United States trade restrictions, tariff cutting did not start until October 1, 1989. Canada and the United States also agreed to eliminate or regulate tariff-related programs that impeded trade. The United States agreed to eliminate the 0.17 percent customs user fee it charged on all imports by January 1, 1994. Likewise the agreement eliminates by January 1, 1994, the use of duty drawbacks on offshore imports by the United States and duty remission payments by Canada by January 1, 1998. Duty remission payments are repayments of duties to companies operating in Canada that meet certain performance requirements, such as production, employment, or export targets. Canada and the United States also agreed to eliminate quotas or other restrictions unless allowed by the agreement or GATT. This meant an end to Canadian embargoes on the import of used automobiles and aircraft; but it allowed both countries to control raw-log exports, and East Coast provincial governments to regulate the export of unprocessed fish. The agreement also allowed each country to retain existing import restrictions on agricultural products necessary to maintain SUPPLY MANAGEMENT systems, while permitting the duty-free entry of food products using these same agricultural raw materials. Each country agreed to give up its GATT right to impose export taxes; however Canada agreed to continue imposing an export tax on softwood lumber until Canadian provinces had adjusted STUMPAGE practices to the satisfaction of the United States. While either country could restrict exports, both were bound not to reduce the proportion of the good exported to the other country relative to the total supply compared to the proportion exported prior to the restriction, meaning that both countries would have to share a cutback in supply. At the same time, the agreement prohibited the use of licences, fees, or other measures to charge higher prices for exports than for domestic sales.

Chapter 5 sets out the commitment to national treatment by the two countries. National treatment means that once goods have entered from the other country, they will not be discriminated against, for example, through sales or excise taxes that are higher than for domestic goods, or environmental, health, safety or consumer-packaging rules that are different (and more onerous) than for the same products manufactured domestically. The commitment to national treatment applies to both federal and provincial state measures.

Chapter 6 deals with technical barriers to trade. The two countries agreed to avoid the use of standards, specifications, regulations, and rules for certification applying to goods, processes, and production methods so that each country's imports would not be restricted by the other. This does not prevent a country from having a higher standard or lower standard than the other; it does mean the same standard has to apply to products from both countries. It does not prevent Canada, for example, from requiring bilingual labelling, provided the same requirements apply to both Canadian and U.S. products. The two countries also agreed to make their standards more compatible, to recognize each other's laboratory certification systems, and to give advance notice of at least 60 days to each other of the full text of federal standards-related measures. They also agreed to further negotiations on achieving compatibility of standards-related measures.

Chapter 7 sets out the provisions in the agreement relating to agriculture. There is a prohibition on export subsidies in agricultural trade between the two countries, the elimination by Canada of rail-transport subsidies under the Canadian Western Grain Transportation program on exports to the United States through Canadian West Coast ports, and the elimination of all tariffs on agricultural products over 10 years, with a provision for Canada to snapback tariff protection for producers of fresh fruit and vegetables for a 20-year period if depressed prices and other conditions are met. The two countries agreed to mutual exemption from restrictions under meat-import laws to ensure free trade in beef and veal. Canada agreed to eliminate import licences for U.S. wheat, barley, and oats when U.S. grain support levels declined to Canadian grain-support price levels. Canadian global import quotas on chicken, turkey, and eggs were set at no less than 7.5 percent of the previous year's domestic production of chickens, 3.5 percent of the previous year's turkey production quota, and 1.647 percent of the previous year's production of shell eggs. The U.S. agreed not to restrict imports from Canada containing 10 percent or less of sugar. In addition, the two countries agreed to continue negotiations to harmonize technical regulations.

Chapter 8 deals with trade in wines and distilled spirits. Canada and the U.S. agreed not to discriminate, and to eliminate any discriminatory practices; for example, provincial liquor boards were required to end any listing, pricing, distribution practices, blending requirements, and standards and labelling practices that discriminated against U.S. products. Provincial liquor boards or any other public agency distributing wine or distilled products were allowed to charge the additional cost of selling an imported product, but differentials on wine that exceeded this amount were to be eliminated by 1995. Canadian whiskey and U.S. bourbon whiskey were recognized as distinct products.

Chapter 9 deals with trade in energy; it reaffirms provisions in chapter 4 that prohibit the imposition of taxes and charges on exports unless the same tax is applied to domestic consumers, as well as reiterating the chapter 4 requirement that any cutback in production must be shared proportionately between the two countries according to the proportions that existed prior to the reduction in supply. The United States agreed to end restrictions on the enrichment of Canadian uranium, and Canada agreed to eliminate the requirement that uranium be processed in Canada before export to the United States. The United States also agreed to end its embargo on the export of Alaska oil and allowed Canada to import up to 50,000 barrels a day. The two countries also agreed to allow existing and future incentives for oil and gas exploration and development to enhance the North American supply base. The two countries also agreed to negotiate a resolution of discrimination in cases where their respective energy regulatory agencies made rulings having such an effect.

Chapter 10 deals with trade in automotive products. While the CANADA-UNITED STATES AUTOMOTIVE AGREEMENT remained in place, two changes were made. First, the concept of Canadian content was eliminated, replaced by a requirement of 50 percent North American content for vehicles crossing the border duty free. Second, no additional auto companies operating in Canada were to be allowed to join the auto pact, which meant that the Japanese-owned auto companies were denied auto-pact benefits. In addition, duty-remission benefits for non-auto-pact companies in Canada were to be terminated by 1996, eliminating the incentive to Japanese and other non-auto-pact companies operating in Canada to increase their Canadian VALUE-ADDED. The embargo on importing used cars into Canada was ended in 1993. The two countries also agreed to establish a special panel to advise the Canadian and U.S. governments on auto-industry issues.

Chapter 11 sets out the rules governing the use of emergency measures to deal with a surge in imports. Until the end of 1998 either country is permitted to suspend duty reductions for a limited time or return to the tariff level that applies to third countries. No measure can last more than three years or extend beyond December 31, 1998. Moreover, the affected country is entitled to compensation through accelerated duty elimination on another product. After 1998, no action can be taken without the consent of the other country. In addition, Canada and the United States agreed to exempt each other from safeguard actions under the GATT where the Canadian or U.S. share of imports is not above 5 to 10 percent of total imports.

Chapter 12 outlines the exceptions to the overall provisions of the free trade agreement. Article XX of the GATT is incorporated into the trade agreement. This article allows import restrictions on pornographic material; allows restrictive measures, undertaken in compliance with international commodity agreements, on trade in gold and silver or to protect human, animal, or plant life (such as measures to protect endangered species), ensure compliance with domestic laws such as product and packaging standards, bar products made with prison labour, and protect cultural treasures. In addition, Canada and the United States are allowed to restrict the export of raw logs; eastern Canadian provinces are allowed to control the export of unprocessed fish, and the Canadian provinces are allowed to retain existing measures discriminating against U.S. beer. However, both countries were allowed to pursue their interests in GATT with respect to these provisions.

Chapter 13 deals with the rules on government procurement. Producers in either country have the right to bid on federal government contracts worth $33,000 or more unless they are reserved for small or minority business or excluded for national security reasons. Each country maintains a bid challenge procedure so that a supplier from the other country has a means of appeal if the company believes it has been discriminated against.

Chapter 14 sets out the provisions on trade in services. The two countries agreed to extend the principle of national treatment to most commercial services in any future laws and practices. While there was no rollback in laws and practices, future laws and practices had to be fully consistent with the principle of national treatment. The exceptions include transportation (marine, air, trucking, rail, and bus), basic telecommunications, doctors, dentists, lawyers, child-care, and government-provided services such as health, education, and social services. Sectoral annexes provided more detailed obligations for architecture, tourism, and enhanced telecommunications and provided scope for future additional annexes.

Chapter 15 facilitates the temporary entry of business travellers to the two markets to assist the sale of their goods and services and to provide after-sales

service to customers. Four categories of business traveller are set out: professional; trader; investor; or intracompany transferee. A business traveller must also state the specific purpose of the visit from one of seven categories: research and design; growth, manufacture, and production; marketing; sales; distribution; after-sales service; and general services.

Chapter 16 deals with the rules on foreign investment and takeovers. The principle of national treatment or non-discrimination on new businesses established by U.S. companies in Canada or vice versa is established. INVESTMENT CANADA's power to review U.S. takeovers of Canadian companies is reduced to Canadian companies with gross assets in excess of $150 million by 1992, compared with $25 million where the foreign bidder is from another country; in the case of indirect takeovers — the sale of a U.S.-owned company in Canada to another U.S.-owned company — Investment Canada's role was ended in 1992. Investment-related performance requirements, such as export sales, local content, and the use of domestic suppliers, are barred; however, product mandate, technology transfer, and research and development requirements are permitted in cases requiring Investment Canada approval. In the case of nationalization of an industry, the government of each country is obligated to provide fair and adequate compensation in the acquisition of foreign-controlled firms. Restrictions on the repatriation of profits or proceeds from a sale, other than those arising from the application of domestic laws with wide application or from balance-of-payments measures, are also prohibited. Nor can government compel a foreign-controlled subsidiary to sell any of its shares to the public or to sell an asset or enterprise. Existing limitations on U.S. investment in cultural industries, energy, and transportation were retained, but Canada could not introduce restrictions in new sectors.

Chapter 17 sets out the rules on financial services. U.S. banks and other financial institutions are treated the same as Canadian institutions, including the right to engage in all the same activities as a Canadian-controlled financial institution. In addition, the growth of U.S. financial institutions is not limited by the 16 percent ceiling on the overall size of the foreign-bank sector in Canada. Canadian banks operating in the United States are permitted to underwrite and deal in securities of the Canadian government and its agencies. In addition, Canadian financial institutions are guaranteed that in future reforms to the U.S. financial system, including changes to the restrictive Glass-Steagall Act, they will receive the same rights as U.S. financial institutions. Disputes on matters arising out of this chapter are to be dealt with by the Department of FINANCE and the U.S. Department of the Treasury.

Chapter 18 details how the agreement is to be administered and disputes resolved over interpretation of the agreement and possible future actions by either country that may conflict with the agreement. A Canada-United States Trade Commission is established to resolve disputes and deal with other issues arising out of the agreement; it is co-chaired by the cabinet minister from each country responsible for trade and is required to meet at least once a year. The commission can establish and delegate responsibilities to working groups of officials. Canada and the United States are required to give advance written notice of any measure that might materially affect the agreement. The other country has the right to consultations where there is a dispute over a practice or action of the other country, and if there is no resolution of the matter, either country may request a meeting of the commission. If the commission is unable to resolve the issue, a binding arbitration panel is to be established. If a country refuses to abide by the panel decision, the other country has the right to suspend some benefit of the trade agreement equivalent to the benefits it has lost as a result of the action of the offending country. Arbitration panels have five members, with each panel having at least two citizens from each country. Reports of the panels are made public and referred to the commission.

Chapter 19 provides processes to review disputes over anti-dumping and countervailing duty rulings in either country. Either country may seek the review of an anti-dumping or countervailing duty determination by a panel that determines whether existing trade laws in the country concerned have been applied correctly and fairly. Findings of the panels are binding on both countries. If a panel determines the law was properly applied, there is no further appeal. If the panel finds that the agency imposing the trade penalty in the United States or Canada erred on the basis of the same standards that would apply in a domestic court, it can require the agency to correct the error and make a new determination; the dispute settlement panel cannot, though, overturn the ruling or make a new determination of its own. Dispute panels have five members, with at least two from each country; final decisions are to be made within 315 days from the date on which a request for a panel is made. Either country is also entitled to the establishment of an extraordinary challenge panel of three members if there is evidence of gross misconduct, bias, or conflict of interest on the part of a binational panel member, evidence the panel seriously departed from a fundamental rule of procedure, or evidence the panel exceeded its powers or jurisdiction. The provisions of the chapter were to be in effect for five years, with a possible two-year extension, during which the two countries were to attempt to negotiate new rules on government subsidies, countervailing duties, and anti-dumping. If there was no agreement, either country could give six-months' notice of termination of the entire free trade agreement. This was the face-saving compromise reached in the 11th-hour negotiations to address Canada's priority goal of relief from U.S. trade laws. The two countries also agreed that any changes to their own anti-dumping and countervailing duty legislation would apply to each other only following consultation on the proposed changes and if this is specifically provided for in the new legislation. A bilateral panel may also be established to examine the proposed changes and propose modifications.

Chapter 20 contains a miscellaneous set of provisions. The two countries agree that nothing in the agreement affects their rights and obligations under the Canada-United States tax treaty, the GATT, and the INTERNATIONAL MONETARY FUND nor either country's right to protect its national security. The chapter grandfathers then-existing Canadian measures to protect its cultural industries and explicitly allows the United States to retaliate against any new measures. Canada was also required to provide copyright compensation for U.S. programs carried on Canadian cable TV systems by January 1, 1990, and to eliminate the requirement that Canadian publications be printed in Canada to qualify for tax treatment as a Canadian publication. The 1986 SOFTWOOD LUMBER AGREEMENT was also made a part of the free trade agreement. The agreement permits either country to maintain or create a monopoly, but only with prior notification and consultation and in a way that does not nullify or impair benefits for the other country under the agreement. The chapter also contains a general clause that permits either country to seek a dispute panel under chapter 18 where it considers that the application of any measure,

even if it does not conflict with the provisions of the agreement, causes nullification or impairment of any benefit "reasonably expected" directly or indirectly as a result of the agreement.

Canada-United States trade agreements   Trade agreements signed between the two countries in 1935 and 1938 to reverse protectionist trends in both countries, following the passage by the U.S. Congress of the Reciprocal Trade Agreements Act in 1934. In the 1935 treaty, the United States reduced its high tariffs to some extent, while Canada lifted some of its restrictions on the purchase of U.S. goods. The treaty made it easier for Canada to sell certain commodities, such as fish, lumber, cattle, dairy products, potatoes, and whiskey, to the United States, and improved access to the Canadian market for U.S. farm machinery, automobiles, electrical machinery and equipment, industrial machinery, and gasoline. However, the general level of tariffs remained higher than it had been at the start of the Depression. The 1938 treaty made much greater progress in reducing tariffs on both sides of the border, and remained in effect until the GENERAL AGREEMENT ON TARIFFS AND TRADE came into effect on January 1, 1948.

Canada-United States Trade Commission   *See* CANADA-UNITED STATES FREE TRADE AGREEMENT.

Canada West Foundation   A nonprofit research organization established in 1970 to conduct public policy and economic studies on western Canada concerns. Its objectives are to initiate and conduct research into the economic and social characteristics and potential of western and northern Canada in a national and international context; educate the public on the West's regional heritage and aspirations and its contribution to Canadian federalism; and act as a catalyst for informed debate. In 1991, the Canada West Foundation launched the Canada 2000: Alternatives for the Future project, a three-year research exercise to set out options for constitutional and economic reform. The Canada West Foundation is based in Calgary.

Canadian Advanced Technology Association (CATA)   A national association representing Canada's high-technology companies, founded in 1978 and based in Ottawa. The association serves as a network for its members, promotes the importance of high- technology for Canadian competitiveness and productivity, encourages innovation, and focuses on policies to increase workforce education and training, management skills, accessing global markets, adopting best practices, and attracting equity capital.

Canadian Arctic Resources Committee (CARC)   A public-interest organization founded in 1971 to conduct research into questions of northern-development policy, publish its research and recommendations, and participate in public hearings, such as those of the National Energy Board and environmental-assessment panels. It is funded by private individuals, foundations, corporations, and government. Its headquarters are in Ottawa.

Canadian Association of Oilwell Drilling Contractors   An association of oilwell drilling contractors established in Calgary in 1949 to deal with safety and training, accident prevention, workers' compensation, engineering, manpower, taxation, and other issues. Since 1972, the association has published monthly statistics on rig counts and drilling-rig utilization by province and depth category; these statistics are a useful indicator of activity in the oil and gas industry. The association has grown from 10 drilling-rig

contractors operating 52 rigs in Canada in 1949 to 92 drilling-rig contractors operating 505 rigs in 1992.

Canadian Association of Petroleum Producers   The principal organization representing the oil and gas industry in Canada, following the 1992 merger of the CANADIAN PETROLEUM ASSOCIATION and the Independent Petroleum Association of Canada. It is based in Calgary and will take over important functions of the Canadian Petroleum Association, including the annual publication on changes in the country's established oil and natural gas reserves and an annual statistical handbook on drilling exploration spending, oil and gas production, and other industry statistics. It also produces an annual business outlook.

Canadian Awards for Business Excellence   A series of federal awards to recognize outstanding achievements by Canadian companies for invention, innovation, industrial design, entrepreneurship, environment, marketing, small business, and quality. The program was announced in 1983 and the first awards made in 1984. Winners are permitted to use a special promotional logo on their products and promotional materials. In 1992, the federal government announced the awards would be co-managed with the National Quality Institute.

Canadian Bankers' Association (CBA)   An association representing the Canadian banking industry to which all Canadian chartered banks are required by law to belong. The association was created by an act of Parliament in 1900 and consists of all the chartered banks, which are represented by their chief general managers on the CBA executive council. One of its early responsibilities was to supervise the printing and distribution of paper money by the banks. It was only after Parliament created the BANK OF CANADA in 1934 that the role of the banks in printing money was reduced and eventually ended. The CBA also ran the clearing system for the Canadian banking system until 1980, when the CANADIAN PAYMENTS ASSOCIATION was established.

Today, the CBA's main functions are research on public policy affecting financial institutions, education, and public information about the banking system. It operates an educational program for banking-industry employees through its Institute of Canadian Bankers; in 1991, 27,000 bank employees took courses ranging from one week to one year. It also works with bank security departments and with police departments to improve bank security and prevent fraud. It makes representations to federal and provincial governments on behalf of the banking industry and helps the banks respond to government plans for new legislation affecting the banking industry. Its headquarters are in Toronto.

Canadian Business Hall of Fame   A system of recognition of the contributions by entrepreneurial men and women to the economic and social progress of Canada established by JUNIOR ACHIEVEMENT OF CANADA in 1979. Members are selected for "their outstanding contribution to improving the products, the processes, the efficiency, and the human relations of business," according to Junior Achievement. There is no Business Hall of Fame as such; instead, there is a system of awards marked by an annual banquet.

Canadian Centre for Occupational Health and Safety   A centre established by federal legislation in 1978 to promote health and safety in the workplace. The centre provides information to employers and workers and operates an on-line computer information system. It also produces training courses and databases on compact discs, which

it sells to users. Based in Hamilton, Ontario, it has a governing council consisting of federal and provincial government representatives and representatives from business and labour. Although established by federal legislation, the federal government is cutting back its funding; the provinces provide some funding and the centre earns revenues from the sale of its products.

Canadian Centre for Policy Alternatives
A research organization founded in 1980 to study economics and social issues from a left-wing perspective. Based in Ottawa, the Centre states that it "wants to demonstrate that there are thoughtful alternatives to the limited perspective of business research institutes and government agencies." Its mandate is to put forward research that reflects the concerns of women as well as men, labour as well as business, churches, cooperatives and voluntary agencies as well as government, and minorities and disadvantaged people as well as the more fortunate. It publishes research reports and sponsors conferences.

Canadian Chamber of Commerce   A national association of more than 500 community chambers and boards of trade along with more than 90 business and professional associations and additional corporate members that acts as an advocacy group on behalf of business. According to the chamber, it is dedicated to the promotion of entrepreneurship and a strong economy. It develops policy positions on major issues, monitors federal and international issues, solicits the views of its members and communicates these to the federal government and the public. The chamber, founded in 1929 to represent the interests of its members in national affairs, also delivers programs and services to its members to help improve their competitiveness in Canadian and export markets. Since 1945, it has been affiliated with the INTERNA-

TIONAL CHAMBER OF COMMERCE. The chamber also includes under its umbrella a number of affiliated business councils including the ASEAN-Canada, Canada-Arab, Canada-India, Canada-Korea business councils, and the Canada-Taiwan Business Association. Its offshore liaisons include the Canada-U.K. Chamber of Commerce, the Canadian Chamber of Commerce in Hong Kong, the Canadian Chamber of Commerce in Japan, and the Canadian Trade Office in Taiwan.

Canadian Commercial Corporation A crown corporation that acted as an agent of the federal government in dealing with foreign governments and state-owned companies, either to sell military and non-military goods and services or to purchase military and non-military goods and services. It helps Canadian firms to sell defence and non-defence goods and services to foreign governments and state-owned companies and to international agencies, as well as disposing of government surplus items, such as fighter aircraft, ships, and other used military hardware. It was created in 1946, originally for the purpose of procuring in Canada goods and services for U.N. relief agencies and foreign governments in need of food, motor vehicles, and other necessities. In 1992, the activities of the Corporation were integrated into the Department of SUPPLY AND SERVICES, although it retained its crown corporation status.

Canadian composite leading indicator A monthly composite indicator published by Statistics Canada that attempts to show the direction in which the economy is headed. It consists of ten key indicators: In retail trade, the latest furniture and appliance sales, the latest sales of other durable goods, and a housing index that is a composite of housing starts and Multiple Listing Service home sales; in manufacturing, it includes the latest new orders for durables, the shipments to inventory ratio for finished goods, and the length of the average work week in hours; its other indicators include business and personal services employment, the latest U.S. composite leading index, the Toronto Stock Exchange 300 stock price index, and growth in M-1 money supply in 1981 dollars. The indicator is based on 1981 = 100. Details are published in the *Canadian Economic Observer* (publication 11-010).

Canadian Construction Association A national association of construction companies, created in 1918, that represents more than 17,000 firms in commercial, industrial, institutional, highway, and engineering construction. Provincial construction associations are affiliates. The association has been a strong advocate of INDUSTRY-WIDE BARGAINING. It monitors and provides information to member firms on wage rates, collective agreements, arbitration awards, and working conditions in the construction industry. It also participates in the INTERNATIONAL LABOUR ORGANIZATION and provides the normal association services to members, such as representing their views to government and distributing information on tax and other government policy changes. The association's headquarters are located in Ottawa.

Canadian content Government rules to ensure that a minimum level of Canadian goods and services are employed in particular activities or projects. Examples include specified hours of Canadian programming on radio and television, the proportion of Canadian investments that must be held by insurance companies and pension funds, and the required level of Canadian goods and services, including labour, that must be employed on major resource projects in the North or on pipeline and tar-sands projects.

Canadian Council on Social Development A research organization for social-policy issues. It was founded in 1920 as the Child Welfare Council, later became the Canadian Welfare Council, and adopted its present name in 1970. It has five research groups, staffed by economists and social-policy experts: housing, citizen participation and social planning, health care, income maintenance and security, and personal social services. Its membership includes individuals, social agencies, federal, provincial, and municipal governments, and corporations. Its headquarters are in Ottawa.

Canadian Dairy Commission A federal agency created in 1966, becoming operative in 1967, to regulate milk and cream production in Canada so that farmers might receive what the commission considered to be a fair return on their labour and investment. The chairman of the commission chairs the Canadian Milk Supply Management Committee, which includes representatives of the provincial milk-MARKETING BOARDs and the provincial governments. The job of the committee is to manage the Milk Share Quota System, which allocates milk- and cream-production shares to each of the provinces under a federal milk-marketing plan. The Dairy Commission may help to stabilize milk and cream prices by purchasing excess supplies, and pays direct subsidies to dairy farmers to assure them of reasonable returns; about 37,000 dairy farmers receive direct subsidies each month. The commission also arranges export sales of skim-milk powder and other dairy products. It was the first national farm marketing agency to be created after the Canadian Wheat Board was set up in 1935.

Canadian dollar The official currency of the provinces of Canada, adopted in 1858 after Canadians indicated their preference for the decimal system over the British pound. The dollar was adopted in turn by the new nation of Canada with the passage of the Uniform Currency Act in 1871. Until 1910, the Canadian dollar was valued in terms of the British gold sovereign. However, with the Currency Act of 1910, it was redefined in terms of fine gold. From Confederation until the mid-1930s, the production of paper currency was largely in the hands of the chartered banks, with the government regulating the amount of dollars any bank could issue as legal tender. In 1934, the BANK OF CANADA was established as the country's central bank and it quickly took over the printing of Canadian dollars, although chartered-bank dollars were not fully withdrawn from circulation until about a decade later. The international value of the Canadian dollar is usually expressed either in terms of the U.S. dollar or of SPECIAL DRAWING RIGHTS.

Canadian Energy Research Institute An energy-research institute located at the University of Calgary and funded by the federal and Alberta governments and private industry. Established in 1975, it carries out independent economic and environmental research into Canadian energy needs and energy alternatives.

Canadian Environmental Assessment Act Legislation passed in 1992, replacing the 1984 Environmental Assessment and Review Process, that will apply to all federal government departments and agencies, crown corporations, harbour commissions, offshore petroleum exploration and production boards, and Indian band councils. Projects will be screened at an early stage into four levels of environmental risk: projects believed to pose little or no risk to the environment will be excluded from the assessment process; projects that are routine or repetitive in nature and which do not pose any significant environmental risk may be dealt with through class assessments; projects known to have a potentially significant risk require the responsible authority to assess the potential environmental impact and present a comprehensive report to the Minister of the Environment; other projects will be screened to determine potential environmental impacts, possible mitigation measures, and the need for additional assessment. The legislation increases the opportunity for public participation and gives the Minister of the Environment, rather than the minister of the initiating department, the authority to decide whether there is a need for additional public review. The Minister of the Environment can refer the project to a review panel or mediator. The panel is advisory rather than decision-making. The legislation provides for the establishment of joint federal-provincial review panels and a follow-up program, with final assessment reports required to include a follow-up plan to verify the accuracy of the environmental assessment predictions and to determine the effectiveness of any special measures or controls that were required.

Canadian Environmental Protection Act   Federal legislation that consolidated various federal environmental laws and which came into effect in 1988. The legislation empowers the federal government to take action against polluters and polluting activities and deals with the threats to human health and the environment from risks associated with the use of toxic substances. It created a list of priority substances to be assessed for health and environmental impacts in order to identify the need for regulatory controls, including waste-handling and -disposal procedures, and effluents and emissions. In addition, it set out notification requirements for organizations developing and manufacturing substances such as chemicals, polymers, and biotechnology products that are new to Canada.

Canadian Executive Service Organization (CESO)   An organization established in 1967 by the forerunner to the CANADIAN INTERNATIONAL DEVELOPMENT AGENCY and by a number of business executives to promote the economic and social growth of developing countries by providing technical, professional, and managerial expertise through the unpaid services of retired and semi-retired business executives. In 1969, its services were extended to Canada's aboriginal communities and in 1990, to the former Eastern European communist countries.

Canadian Export Association   An association of Canadian manufacturers, agricultural producers, construction companies, consulting engineers, and others interested in increasing export sales. Founded in 1943, the association provides information to members on changes in the trade policies and procedures of importing countries and of the Canadian government, occasionally makes representations to foreign governments on matters of concern, and represents the views of its members to the federal government. It is based in Ottawa.

Canadian Federation of Agriculture (CFA)   A national federation of provincial farm organizations and national or regional commodity organizations, formed to promote the interests of farmers and other agricultural interests, and to represent Canadian farmers in the International Federation of Agricultural Producers. The federation was originally set up in 1935 as the Canadian Chamber of Agriculture. Its headquarters are in Ottawa. The CFA believes the farm industry should be based in family-controlled and -operated enterprises and that the returns to farmers should be similar to the returns earned in other sectors of the economy. *See also* NATIONAL FARMERS UNION.

Canadian Grain Commission   A federal agency created in 1971 to administer the Canada Grain Act. It licenses all grain elevators in Canada used to store western-produced grain, and sets maximum tariffs that elevators may charge for storage. The commission is also responsible for grain-grading standards, as well as inspecting the quality of grain being delivered to storage, conducting surveys on the quality of each year's grain crop through its Grain Research Laboratory, studying new grain varieties, and conducting research into cereal grains and oil seeds. The commission replaced the Board of Grain Commissioners, which dated back to 1912, and is based in Winnipeg.

Canadian Human Rights Commission A federal agency created in 1977 to enforce the Canadian Human Rights Act. Among other areas of responsibility, it provides protection for EQUAL PAY and against job discrimination based on age, physical handicap, race, sex, marital status, national or ethnic origin, religion, or colour. Part I of the CANADA LABOUR CODE has been transferred to its jurisdiction.

Canadian Importers Association An association of companies, including manufacturers, agents, distributors, customs brokers, carriers, and others, with an interest in Canada's import trade. Much of the work of the association, created in 1932, consists of helping importers to meet Canada's import requirements and paperwork, or making representations to the federal government to simplify import procedures and reduce import barriers. It also helps to promote exports of Canadian manufactured goods. Its headquarters are in Toronto.

Canadian Industrial Renewal Board An agency established by the federal government in 1981 to help revitalize the textile, clothing, footwear, and tanning industries through a Sector Firms Program; to assist in the strengthening

and diversification of the economic base of the regions heavily dependent on these industries through its Business and Industrial Development Program; and to help textile, clothing, footwear, and tanning workers adapt to change through its Labour Adjustment Program. The board, which was based in Montreal, worked through a committee of private sector advisers. It was wound up in 1986, as originally planned. It invested about $240 million to help modernize about 400 plants at a total cost in excess of $1 billion, invested another $97 million to assist special areas, and spent about $50 million on labour adjustment.

Canadian Institute for Advanced Research A non-profit research institute established in 1982 to mobilize talented individuals in different institutions into networks to study major problems. It has programs in key areas affecting Canadians' economic, scientific, and social life. These include artificial intelligence and robotics; cosmology; superconductivity; population health; evolutionary biology; economic growth; law in society; earth system evolution; science of soft surfaces; and human development. It has created networks of researchers across Canada in leading universities as an alternative to the big research universities found in the United States, which Canada cannot afford to replicate. The economic-growth program is pursuing the role of ideas and innovation as the sources of wealth generation in a modern economy; it emphasizes the need for both government and the private sector to play a role in economic development and challenges the assumptions of NEOCLASSICAL ECONOMICS and the capacity of free markets on their own to generate future growth. Canada's future, the Toronto-based institute says, depends on its ability to encourage technological and institutional innovation and to create tradeable goods and services based on ideas. Without new sources of wealth, it argues, Canada will not be able to afford its social and other programs that define its quality of life. The institute also helped establish an industrial consortium, PRECARN, to interface with its work in artificial intelligence and robotics, and ensured that there were private-sector receptors for the results of research being done by institute fellows in universities.

Canadian Institute for Economic Policy An economic-policy research organization, formed in 1978 and funded by private citizens led by former Finance Minister Walter Gordon, to study and recommend fiscal, industrial, and other related policies to strengthen Canada in a rapidly changing international environment. It sponsored economic research and published its findings, with an emphasis on measures to increase Canadian economic, political, and cultural independence. It was wound up in 1984, when the sunset clause expiry date was reached.

Canadian International Development Agency (CIDA) A federal agency responsible for the administration of Canada's foreign-aid or official development-assistance program. It was originally established in 1960 as the External Aid Office, but in 1968 was reorganized as CIDA. The agency is responsible for carrying out Canada's foreign-aid policies and programs and handles about 75 percent of Canada's total international assistance. Its aid activities are divided into two programs: the Partnership Program, which is carried out in co-operation with international agencies such as the four regional development banks and the WORLD BANK, non-governmental and non-profit agencies, and business; and the National Initiatives Program, which consists of bilateral, government-to-government programs. The cabinet determines eligible coun-

tries to receive Canadian aid, based on each country's needs, human rights record, the quality of social, economic, and environmental policies, and Canada's political and economic relations with the country. In fiscal 1993-94, CIDA had a budget of $781 million for its Partnership program and $1.2 billion for its National Initiatives program. It handles about 80 percent of Canada's international assistance.

Canadian International Grains Institute A federal organization created in 1972 to work with the CANADIAN WHEAT BOARD and the CANADIAN GRAIN COMMISSION to help develop new markets for Canadian grains. Its efforts include developing new uses for grains and oilseeds within Canada, and helping less-developed countries to adapt grains to their diet, expand their grain-handling and transportation systems, and improve their skills in flour milling, bread baking, and the manufacture of macaroni and other pastas. Its headquarters are in Winnipeg.

Canadian Federation of Labour A national labour organization founded in 1982 as a non-partisan alternative to the CANADIAN LABOUR CONGRESS. It consists of 14 affiliated unions in construction, mining, manufacturing, communications, transportation, health care, and public service. It also operates an investment fund, the Working Ventures Canadian Fund Inc., which qualifies for tax incentives for investors. The federation says that "it is dedicated to promoting the interests of Canadian workers through direct, regular, non-partisan involvement in national affairs." It is based in Ottawa.

Canadian Film Development Corporation *See* TELEFILM CANADA.

Canadian International Trade Tribunal A federal tribunal established in 1988 to replace the Canadian Import Tribunal, the Tariff Board, and the Textile and Clothing Board. It determines whether injury to Canadian producers exists in cases where REVENUE CANADA has established that grounds for anti-dumping or countervailing duties exist; penalties can only be imposed if the tribunal is satisfied that there is injury or the threat of injury. It also conducts research and holds public hearings on economic, commercial, trade, and tariff matters referred to it by the Minister of FINANCE. In 1992, it was given the responsibilities of the Procurement Review Board, which had been set up under the CANADA-UNITED STATES FREE TRADE AGREEMENT, to hear bid challenges from U.S. or Canadian companies that contended they had been unfairly treated when bidding for a Canadian government contract.

Canadian Investor Protection Fund A fund established in 1969 by the Investment Dealers Association of Canada and the Montreal, Toronto, Alberta, and Vancouver stock exchanges to protect investors against losses due to the failure of a member firm. A limit of $500,000 has been placed on coverage provided for a customer's general account for losses related to securities and cash balances.

Canadian Labour Congress (CLC) A national labour federation representing about 58 percent of all union members in Canada through its roughly 115 affiliated unions. Altogether, it represents more than two million workers. The CLC was formed in 1956 through a merger of two rival labour federations, the Trades and Labour Congress of Canada and the Canadian Congress of Labour. The CLC is a voluntary organization and exercises no legal authority over its affiliated unions, although it acts as the country's principal spokesman for union members. Its activities, through a 45-member execu-

tive council and a national convention held every two years, include pressing for union interests in federal government policies, including budgets, legislation, and social-security benefits; establishing codes of behaviour to prevent conflicts over jurisdiction between unions, raiding, and other damaging practices; strengthening union democracy and ethics; researching pay, fringe benefits, and other questions for member unions; and improving public understanding of the role of unions through various educational and public-affairs programs. The CLC also represents Canada in international labour organizations, works to increase the autonomy of Canadian locals of U.S.-based international unions, and speaks for union members on questions of human and civil rights. Its international affiliations inlude the INTERNATIONAL LOBOUR ORGANIZATION, the INTERNATIONAL CONFEDERATION OF FREE TRADE UNIONS, the Trade Union Advisory Council to the ORGANIZATION FOR ECONOMIC CO-OPERATION AND DEVELOPMENT, and the Inter-American Regional Organization of Workers. *See also* CANADIAN STANDARDS OF SELF-GOVERNMENT, CHARTER OF LABOUR RIGHTS, CODE OF ETHICAL PRACTICES, CONFEDERATION OF NATIONAL TRADE UNIONS, CANADIAN FEDERATION OF LABOUR.

Canadian Labour Force Development Board An advisory board established by the federal government in 1991 as an independent board representing business, labour, the education-training community, and equity groups (women, visible minorities, aboriginal groups, and the disabled) with the purpose of addressing training and other labour-market issues. The mandate of the Ottawa-based board is to act as an advocate for more relevant, higher quality, and more accessible training, to advise the federal government on training and adjustment plans, and to make recommendations on training issues, such as occupational standards, apprenticeship systems, ways to improve access to training, how to co-ordinate income support and training, how to use training to improve equity, and how to allocate federal training funds. The board is co-chaired by representatives of business and labour.

Canadian Labour Market and Productivity Centre (CLMPC) A national organization established in 1984 with federal government funding to facilitate direct consultation between labour and business on key social and economic issues. Its establishment was recommended by the CANADIAN LABOUR CONGRESS (CLC) and the BUSINESS COUNCIL ON NATIONAL ISSUES following a series of consultations on industry sector strategies and industrial benefits from major resource and other projects organized by the federal government. The centre's mandate is to promote dialogue and to develop joint business-labour recommendations on ways to improve the operation of labour markets, facilitate adjustment, and raise Canada's productivity performance. The CLMPC has a board of directors, co-chaired by business and labour, with 12 representatives each from business and labour. Business members are recommended by the BCNI, the CANADIAN CHAMBER OF COMMERCE, and the CANADIAN MANUFACTURERS' ASSOCIATION. Labour representatives are proposed by the CLC and the Canadian Federation of Labour. The CLMPC is based in Ottawa and has a full-time executive director and staff. It publishes various economic reports and studies.

Canadian Life and Health Insurance Association An association established in 1894 to represent the life- and health-insurance companies doing business in Canada. In 1991, life insurance owned by Canadians amounted to $1.3 trillion, split almost 50:50 between group insurance and individual life insurance; assets held by Canadian life-insurance companies on behalf of Canadians amounted to $145.1 billion. The industry sells various forms of life insurance, health and disability insurance, annuities, REGISTERED RETIREMENT SAVINGS PLAN units, and Registered Retirement Investment Funds. The association, which sets business standards for member firms, is headquartered in Toronto.

Canadian Life and Health Insurance Compensation Corporation A consumer protection plan operated by the life- and health-insurance industry to protect policyholders up to certain limits.

Canadian Manufacturers' Association (CMA) A national association of roughly 9,500 manufacturers of all sizes from big to small. It represents the interests of Canadian manufacturers before federal and provincial governments and their agencies, and provides a range of services on industrial relations, exports, customs, and transportation, for example, for its members. It was founded in 1871 and its headquarters are in Toronto.

Canadian Network for Total Quality A private sector organization established in 1993 to promote TOTAL QUALITY MANAGEMENT in Canada. Its founding members included the CANADIAN MANUFACTURERS' ASSOCIATION, the CONFERENCE BOARD OF CANADA, and various educational and regional quality centres. The network will facilitate the availability and delivery of total quality information, services, and training. It is supported by a National Quality Institute, which coordinates the activities of the various members of the network. Based in Ottawa, the Canadian Network for Total Quality and the National Quality Institute are funded by the federal government. The National Quality Institute has also taken on the CANADA AWARDS FOR BUSINESS EXCELLENCE program.

Canadian Patents and Development Limited A federal crown corporation created in 1947 as a subsidiary of the NATIONAL RESEARCH COUNCIL to own and sell the right to use the patented inventions of the council and other government-financed research and development. All inventions by government employees are, under the Public Servants' Inventions Act of 1954, the property of the Canadian government. It was wound up in 1992.

Canadian Payments Association The financial network, established under amendments to the BANK ACT in 1980, that clears cheques, pre-authorized debits in savings and chequing accounts, and electronic transfers so that financial institutions accepting cheques and other transfers can get the money from financial institutions on which the cheques and other transfers are drawn. The system, which balances the books of the millions of daily financial transactions in Canada, is made up of the country's banks, trust and loan companies, major credit unions, and other financial institutions. It is chaired by an executive of the Bank of Canada. Every business day the members of the CPA send all of the cheques and other transfers they have cashed to one of eight regional clearing centres where the totals are calculated. To settle outstanding differences between financial institutions, credits or debits are made in the accounts these institutions maintain with the Bank of Canada. It is the speed of the clearing system that allows financial institutions to cash cheques and make other customer transfers without imposing waiting periods before the funds can be released. The system handles seven million transactions a day or 1.8 bil-

lion a year, totalling $12 trillion. The payments association also develops standards, for example, for electronic data interchange between financial institutions and corporations, and for DEBIT CARDS. Its headquarters are located in Ottawa.

Canadian Petroleum Association (CPA) An association of oil and natural-gas exploration, production, and pipeline companies and associated financing, engineering, geophysical, drilling, and other supplier industries, founded in 1952 and based in Calgary. In 1992, it merged with the Independent Petroleum Association of Canada to form the CANADIAN ASSOCIATION OF PETROLEUM PRODUCERS. Its members accounted for close to 80 percent of oil and natural-gas production in Canada.

Canadian Pulp and Paper Association An association of pulp, paper, and paperboard manufacturers, established in 1913 to carry out normal trade-association activities, such as presenting briefs to government and disseminating information to members on government policies and industry developments. It has two scientific groups, one dealing with the technology of pulp and paper mills and the other with woodlands. In addition, along with the federal government and McGill University, it funds the Pulp and Paper Research Institute. Its headquarters are in Montreal.

Canadian Radio-Television and Telecommunications Commission (CRTC) A federal regulatory agency created in 1968 as the Canadian Radio and Television Commission under the Broadcasting Act to supervise and regulate the Canadian broadcasting system, including radio and television stations, cable television, pay TV, and specialty services. It issues, renews, amends, suspends, or revokes broadcast licences, monitors the performance of licensees to see whether they meet Canadian-content and other programming requirements, and establishes Canadian broadcasting policies and regulations. It must approve changes of ownership of radio, television, and cable-TV companies. In 1976, the CRTC was also given the responsibility of regulating rates, business practices, and services of federally incorporated telephone and TELECOMMUNICATIONS companies, a responsibility previously exercised by the CANADIAN TRANSPORT COMMISSION; at the same time, to reflect its added responsibilities, its name was changed to the Canadian Radio-television and Telecommunications Commission. The CRTC must ensure that telecommunications rates are just and reasonable and that there is no unjust discrimination in providing services. The commission regulates the rates and tariffs of TELESAT CANADA and also regulates communications satellites through its jurisdiction over what may be carried by broadcasters and cable systems, including non-broadcast programming. The first regulatory agency for broadcasting was established in 1932 when the Canadian Radio Broadcasting Commission was established. It was replaced in 1958 by the Board of Broadcast Governors; it was replaced by the CRTC in 1968.

Canadian Securities Institute (CSI)
An organization established in 1970 by the Investment Dealers Association (IDA) and the Montreal, Toronto, Alberta, and Vancouver stock exchanges to improve the educational level of persons working in the securities industry, including financial analysts, securities salespeople, and mutual-fund salespeople. The CSI offers a number of courses on securities markets, including the Canadian Securities Course that dates back to 1964 and which must be passed by anyone wishing to sell securities, other than mutual funds, to the public. It also offers an advanced program, Canadian Investment Finance. Those

who complete the advanced program become Fellows of the Canadian Securities Institute (FCSI). The CSI also administers qualifying examinations for candidates to become new partners, directors, or officers of IDA-member firms. It is based in Toronto.

Canadian Space Agency A federal agency established in 1990 to co-ordinate Canada's missions in space, encourage the commercial exploitation of space capabilities, technology, facilities, and systems, and promote the transfer of space-derived technologies to other industries. The agency, based in Montreal, also advises the government on space policy. It is Canada's link to foreign partners in space: the National Aeronautics and Space Administration in the United States and the European Space Agency in Europe.

Canadian Standards Association (CSA) A non-profit association of manufacturers, government agencies, utilities, hospitals, retailers, consulting firms, and other groups, established to develop product safety, quality, and, in some cases, performance standards, and to test products to see whether they meet these standards. Those that do, bear a CSA trademark indicating that they have been tested and approved. CSA standards themselves are not legal, but they have, in many instances, been adopted by government agencies or departments. For example, under provincial laws, all household appliances sold in Canada must meet CSA standards and display a CSA trademark. The CSA has some 400 product committees, staffed by volunteers, which write product standards. When the CSA was founded in 1919, it concentrated on the fields of electrical and civil engineering, but today it writes standards and carries out testing for a wide range of products and technologies, ranging from solar-energy and health-care systems to hockey helmets and safety footwear. Its headquarters are in Toronto.

Canadian standards of self-government A set of principles adopted by the CANADIAN LABOUR CONGRESS in 1974 and included in its constitution to increase the autonomy of Canadian affiliates and locals of international unions. The standards support the election of Canadian officers in Canadian affiliates and locals, the principle that policies dealing with Canadian affairs are to be set by Canadian officers and members, and the concept that Canadian-elected representatives have the authority to speak for the union in Canada. In cases where an international union is affiliated with an international trade secretariat, the Canadian section of the union is supposed to be affiliated separately so that there is a separate Canadian presence and voice at the international level. The standards further state that international unions should do whatever is necessary so that constitutional requirements or policies of the international union do not prevent Canadian members "from participating in the social, cultural, economic, and political life of the Canadian community."

Canadian Tax Foundation A tax-research organization supported by the Canadian Bar Association, the Canadian Institute of Chartered Accountants, business corporations, and individuals. It conducts research into problems of taxation and public finance, ranging from technical taxation issues to questions of tax efficiency or fairness, the division of federal and provincial taxing and spending powers, and the revenue implications of tax changes. The foundation publishes an annual analysis of the revenues and spending of the federal government for the current fiscal year, along with a similar publication on provincial and municipal finances. It also publishes special studies and a jour-

nal, the *Canadian Tax Journal*. Founded in 1945, its headquarters are in Toronto.

Canadian Transport Commission (CTC) A federal regulatory agency created in 1967 under the National Transportation Act to supervise and regulate the activities of Canada's airlines, railways, shipping companies, interprovincial motor-vehicle transport, and commodity (except oil or natural gas) pipelines. It was replaced by the NATIONAL TRANSPORTATION AGENCY OF CANADA in 1988.

Canadian Wheat Board (CWB) A federal crown corporation, created in 1935, that has the exclusive responsibility for the sale of western-grown grains in export markets and in the Canadian market when used as a food. The CWB also sells feed-quality wheat and barley in the Canadian feed-grain market in competition with grain companies. The board either sells grains directly or through grains companies acting as its agents. As well as controlling the sale of western grains it also controls the amount of grains that farmers produce, the delivery of grains into elevators, the allocation of rail cars to move grain, and the shipping of grain by freighter to foreign markets.

Farmers deliver their grains to country elevators according to their quotas. From there, the board arranges shipment to large terminals in eastern Canada to Thunder Bay, Churchill, and various West-Coast ports. The board pays farmers in two stages. The first payment, the INITIAL PAYMENT, is guaranteed by the federal government before the start of the CROP YEAR and is a guaranteed floor price to farmers when they deliver their grain to elevators. If prices fall below initial payments, the federal government covers the project. The second payment, the FINAL PAYMENT, is made at the end of the crop year and depends on the amount of money the board has left over from selling the grain after paying its costs.

The board also administers the Prairie Grain Advance Payments Act, which provides interest-free cash advances to farmers for farm-stored grain.

capacity The maximum amount that can be produced by a factory, refinery, smelter, pipeline, or other industrial facility when it is operated in the most efficient manner.

capacity-utilization rate The actual output of an industry as a percentage of the output it potentially can produce with its existing plant, equipment, and workforce. It is an important economic indicator since by showing the level of activity in the industrial sector, it signals whether price pressures are emerging and whether new capital investment is likely to be needed. If industry is operating close to capacity, then price pressures are likely to increase in the economy. If industry is operating well below its capacity, it is unlikely that new capital investment will be made in the near future; conversely, if industry is operating at close to capacity and the economy is growing, then new investments to expand capacity are likely to be made. Statistics Canada publishes quarterly figures on capacity-utilization rates in manufacturing as a whole and on 22 different manufacturing sectors (publication 31-003) and has statistics dating back to 1961.

Cape Breton Development Corporation (Devco) An economic-development corporation created in 1967 by the federal government to take over and rehabilitate coal mines at Cape Breton, Nova Scotia, and to broaden the industrial base of the region. In 1988, its economic-development activities were spun off into a new entity, Enterprise Cape Breton Corporation. In 1992, Enterprise Cape Breton Corporation was absorbed into the ATLANTIC CANADA OPPORTUNITIES AGENCY. The government also announced it would investigate the possibility of privatizing the Cape Breton Development Corporation. It is based in Glace Bay, Nova Scotia.

capital **1.** In economics, one of the FACTORS OF PRODUCTION that contributes to economic growth. Investment in the physical capital of the economy — mines, smelters, paper mills, factories, machinery, tools, railways, trucking fleets, power stations, farm equipment, and other capital goods — expands the productive capacity of the economy. But increasingly, economists are recognizing that HUMAN CAPITAL, the investment in skills and experience, is also important. The stock of physical capital in an economy increases as new investments are made from the profits earned on existing capital. Capital is one of the factors of production, along with LABOUR and LAND and NATURAL RESOURCES. A growing number of economists regard knowledge or ideas as a fourth factor of production. **2.** In financial markets, the funds available for investment in financial assets, such as shares, bonds, CERTIFICATES OF DEPOSIT, or real property. *See* CAPITAL MARKET. **3.** In business, the total funds invested in the company to enable it to carry out its activities. These funds include long-term debt, common and preferred shares, and retained earnings.

capital account The section of the BALANCE OF PAYMENTS that details the inflow and outflow of funds between Canada and the rest of the world. A positive balance means that Canada has a positive capital inflow, but the capital inflow represents a future claim on Canada by foreigners and is actually a debt to the rest of the world that must be repaid at some future point. A positive capital account offsets a negative CURRENT ACCOUNT, with the capital inflows financing the current-account deficit each year. Theoretically, the current-account deficit and the capital-account surplus should be identical. However, because STATISTICS CANADA is unable to capture all the international transactions that take place, the difference between the current account and the capital account is reported as a statistical discrepancy in the capital account. The capital account includes inflows and outflows of direct investment, portfolio transactions representing the inflow and outflow of funds for the sale and purchase of shares and bonds, the international transactions of banks, the inflow and outflow of funds for the purchase of short-term money-market instruments such as TREASURY BILLS, other capital transactions, and changes in the government's holdings of international reserves. Direct foreign investment measures the actual cross-border flow of funds by corporations making investments or purchasing companies but does not include reinvested earnings of existing businesses by the foreign corporation nor funds raised in the local financial markets. Capital account statistics are reported quarterly by Statistics Canada (publication 67-001).

capital adequacy Rules setting out the minimum levels of capital for banks and investment dealers operating in securities markets. The International Organization of Securities Commissions, consisting of securities regulators from more than 50 countries including Canada, want banks and investment dealers to set aside 2 percent of their capital to cover risks on securities. *See also* BASLE ACCORD, which sets out minimum levels of capital for banks.

capital asset An asset that is to be used over a long period of time and therefore has a productive life of more than a year. Examples include factories, machinery, and equipment, and might also include PATENTS and other forms of INTELLECTUAL PROPERTY.

capital budget A budget that sets out planned investment in new facilities such as buildings, machinery, and equipment, along with details on how these are to be financed. Investment opportunities depend on the COST OF CAPITAL that new investments must meet if they are to be profitable. The cost of capital also determines the PAY-BACK PERIOD.

capital controls Formal restrictions on the ability of individuals to convert a domestic currency or assets into a foreign currency or asset. Capital controls may be imposed to preserve scarce foreign-exchange reserves; Canada imposed capital controls during the Second World War.

capital-cost allowances **1.** The term used in the Income Tax Act for DEPRECIATION. While companies have their own schedules of depreciation reflecting the rate at which different fixed assets wear out, the government can vary the rate at which companies may depreciate machinery, equipment, and other fixed assets to either encourage or discourage investment, depending on the stage of the BUSINESS CYCLE. Governments can also give richer levels of capital-cost allowance for targeted activities, such as investment in environmental technology or research-and-development facilities as an incentive for increased investment. **2.** An entry in the calculation of net domestic product or net domestic income, representing that portion of plant, machinery, and equipment that has worn out in the course of the year.

capital deepening An increase in the amount of capital invested per worker, thus making workers more productive and raising the capital-labour ratio. *See also* CAPITAL WIDENING.

capital flight The shift by residents of a country of their domestic assets into foreign-currency assets held outside the country. Capital flight usually occurs when investors fear a rapid increase in the rate of inflation, political instability, exchange-rate instability, and the possibility of capital controls. A contributing factor in the THIRD-WORLD DEBT CRISIS was the significant flight of capital from countries such as Mexico, Argentina, and Brazil, which put added pressure on these countries' abilities to service their debts. In the 1990s, as some of these countries, such as Mexico, stabilized their economies and opened up private-sector opportunities, they saw a repatriation of flight capital.

capital formation The net increase in a country's capital assets, such as factories, mines, machinery and equipment, buildings, highways, railways, and other assets. It is calculated from the GROSS DOMESTIC PRODUCT by adding together gross fixed-capital formation plus the value of change in physical inventories, and subtracting depreciation or capital-consumption allowances, which represent replacement of existing capital assets. The resulting figure is the net investment in the economy or the net capital formation.

capital gain An increase in the money value of an asset such as a share, bond, parcel of land, house, antique, or other asset, which results in a profit if the asset is sold. For example, if a share is bought at $26 and sold at $31, there is a capital gain of $5. See also CAPITAL-GAINS TAX.

capital-gains tax A tax levied on the profits from the sale of assets or the deemed sale of assets. Canada introduced a capital-gains tax on January 1, 1972, treating one-half of the capital gains as ordinary income in the hands of the taxpayer and subjecting it to the taxpayer's top marginal income-tax rate. The capital-gains tax applies to profits from the sale of shares, bonds, land, recreational and investment properties, and personal-use assets, such as jewellery, antiques, works of art, stamps, and coin collections, if they are worth more than $1,000. Capital losses may be deducted each year from capital gains. Capital-gain taxes are levied at the time of death, on certain gifts, and on the assets of Canadians who emigrate to other countries, although the assets themselves may not necessarily be sold; this provision was made in the Income Tax Act to replace the estate tax, which was abolished at the same time the capital-gains tax was introduced. Exemptions are allowed for personal residences and for property transfers to a spouse. In 1985, the government announced a $500,000 lifetime tax exemption for capital gains to be phased in over six years. This exemption was reduced to $100,000 in the 1987 White Paper on Tax Reform, and the $100,000 exemption was further limited by excluding real estate after the 1992 budget. See also VALUATION DAY.

capital goods Durable goods, such as machinery, buildings, or trucks that are used to produce other goods and expand economic output. An automobile is a capital good if it is used by a business. See also CONSUMER GOOD.

capital inflow The flow of funds into Canada from abroad, either in the form of direct investment (foreign companies purchasing Canadian companies or assets such as real estate, or foreign companies bringing in money to build new facilities or expand existing facilities), portfolio investment (the purchase of Canadian bonds and shares on Canadian bond and stock markets), or new debt (the purchase of new issues of Canadian bonds or short-term money-market instruments such as treasury bills). Canada requires a continuing capital inflow to finance its CURRENT ACCOUNT deficit. Capital inflows are reported in the quarterly balance of payments reports from Statistics Canada (publication 67-001). Canada's net status as a debtor or creditor nation is set out in the annual Statistics Canada report, *Canada's Net International Investment Position* (publication 67-202).

capital-intensive industry   An industry that makes heavy use of capital equipment, such as machinery, relative to its labour force and level of output. Examples of capital-intensive industries include oil refining, aluminum and nickel smelting, petrochemicals, electric power, steel production, tarsands oil production, and newsprint. However, a growing number of manufacturing industries, such as the assembly of automobiles, are also becoming more capital intensive. Capital-intensive industries usually show greater productivity gains than labour-intensive industries.

capital investment   The volume of spending in the economy each year on plant and equipment to replace worn-out and obsolete production facilities and on inventory investment (changes in the stocks of raw materials, unfinished goods, and finished goods in stock) and to increase the productive capacity of the economy. The quarterly *National Income and Expenditure Accounts* of Statistics Canada (publication 13-001) presents total investment spending. Capital investment is divided into government (subdivided into federal, provincial, and local) and business (subdivided into residential, non-residential, machinery and equipment, and physical change in inventories). Capital investment by crown corporations is included in the business sector. Capital investment by business depends on the level of corporate profits, the level of capacity utilization, and expectations about the future. Public capital investment can be used as a countercyclical tool, with governments increasing public infrastructure spending, for exam-

ple, during a recession to create jobs and speed up the recovery. Gross investment or total capital investment includes spending to replace worn-out capital; to get net investment, which shows the increase in productive capacity or capital stock, subtract capital consumption allowances from gross investment. Capital investment is an important source of economic growth and improved PRODUCTIVITY. Investment in HUMAN CAPITAL, such as training spending, is also important but is treated as consumption instead. *See also* ACCELERATOR PRINCIPLE. Statistics Canada publishes a review of public- and private-investment intentions of approximately 300 of the largest corporations, accounting for about 52 percent of business capital investment (publication 61-205). It follows up with a revised intentions survey (publication 61-206) as well as a detailed report on capital spending by manufacturing industries (publication 61-214) and exploration, development, and capital spending for the mining and oil and gas industries (publication 61-216). CANADA MORTGAGE AND HOUSING CORPORATION publishes monthly statistics on new housing starts.

capital-labour ratio   The ratio of capital to labour in the economy, which describes, in effect, the amount of machinery and equipment invested per worker. If industry is investing an increasing amount of capital per worker, the result is CAPITAL DEEPENING: workers have more machinery and tools and therefore the potential to become more productive. However, if industry investment grows simply to equip an increasing number of workers with an existing level of machinery per worker, the result is CAPITAL WIDENING. While the productive capacity of the economy has grown because there are more workers, the productivity of each worker has probably not been increased.

capital loss A decline in the money value of an asset such as a share, bond, parcel of land, house, antique, or other asset, which results in a loss if the asset is sold. For example, if a share is bought at $26 and sold at $21, there is a capital loss of $5. Capital losses can be deducted from capital gains in determining the taxable capital gains each year. *See also* CAPITAL-GAINS TAX.

capital market The various markets in which governments and corporations raise long-term capital in the form of bonds and shares. The sources of this capital include pension plans, insurance companies, trust companies, mutual funds, and individual investors. The intermediaries through which capital is moved from lenders to borrowers include investment dealers, stockbrokers, bond traders, underwriters, trust companies, and banks, while the principal institutions include the bond market and various stock exchanges. The bond and stock markets provide both new capital and a means of trading in these securities, thus improving their marketability. *See also* MONEY MARKETS, which provide short-term financing.

capital movements Flows of long-term and short-term capital between Canada and other countries. Capital movements are tracked quarterly by Statistics Canada in its report on the balance of payments, *Capital Account of the Balance of Payments* (publication 67-001). Capital movements include direct investment, portfolio investment (shares and bonds traded on stock and bond and money markets), the transactions of Canadian banks with non-residents, and foreign holdings of Canadian money-market instruments. While Canada's overall need for foreign capital is dictated by the size of the CURRENT ACCOUNT deficit, cross-border capital movements are heavily influenced in short-term markets by differences or spreads in short-term interest rates and the expectation of possible movements in the exchange rate. Longer term considerations include the possibility of political instability or uncertainty, which can force the central bank to pay an interest-rate premium or risk premium to attract the needed foreign funds. But uncertainty can also lead to CAPITAL FLIGHT. Much of the short-term money moved around daily in exchange markets consists of the surplus funds of corporations and other pools of capital. Short-term funds tend to seek out the highest interest rates in financial markets around the world.

capital outflow The movement of funds out of a country for the purpose of foreign direct investment, the purchase of foreign shares or financial securities, or lending money to other countries or their businesses. A country with a CURRENT ACCOUNT surplus will be a creditor to the rest of the world. However, capital outflows can also be driven by the fear of political uncertainty or instability. *See* CAPITAL FLIGHT. A current-account deficit country faced with a capital outflow, which runs down its foreign exchange reserves, may have to resort to currency controls — devalue its currency or raise interest rates to keep capital at home.

capital-output ratio The ratio between the capital employed in a business and the output of the business; it is also defined as the amount of capital needed to produce an additional unit of output. Capital-output ratios vary from industry to industry and from country to country. For example, the industrial countries have high capital-output ratios, since many of their industries are modern and CAPITAL INTENSIVE, whereas the less-developed countries tend to have low capital-output ratios, since they have abundant low-cost labour, less-advanced technologies, and LABOUR-INTENSIVE INDUSTRY.

capital rationing The situation that occurs when a company finds that the number of potential investment projects that meet or exceed its minimum rate of return exceeds the capital it has available for investment; the company is not in a position then to pursue the level of investment that it would in the profit maximizing model.

capital spending *See* CAPITAL INVESTMENT.

capital stock **1.** The equity capital invested in a business through the various classes of COMMON and PREFERRED SHARES. This capital may be contributed by the founder of the business and by other investors at the time the business is started, and it can be raised by the sale of new issues of common or preferred shares, depending on the authorized capital of the business. Owners of common shares have a say in the running of the business and have the ultimate claim on the assets of the business if it is wound up, after all creditors have been paid off. It is the money permanently invested in the business. **2.** The accumulated investment by society in productive physical assets at a point in time that consists of buildings, plant, machinery, and equipment that represents the productive power of the economy. Statistics Canada provides a measure of Canada's capital stock each year in its publication, *National Balance Sheet Accounts* (publication 13-214). However, the relevant value for an investor is the PRESENT VALUE of the income stream that the capital stock will generate in the future. Capital consumption or DEPRECIATION is the replacement value of the capital stock that is worn out or becomes obsolescent in the course of the year. The net accumulation in capital stock is the increase after deducting capital consumption or depreciation.

capital structure The sources of a company's long-term capital; it is the mix of EQUITY and long-term DEBT, along with RETAINED EARNINGS and CONTRIBUTED SURPLUS. One way to compare companies and assess their strengths is to review their debt/equity ratios. *See* INVESTED CAPITAL.

capital surplus *See* CONTRIBUTED SURPLUS.

capital tax A tax levied on wealth or assets rather than income. The federal government levies a tax on the capital of banks, trust and loan companies, and insurance companies to ensure they pay a minimum tax. The tax is assessed at 1 percent of capital between $200 and $300 million and 1.25 percent on any capital above $300 million. Some provinces, such as Quebec, Ontario, Manitoba, and British Columbia, levy a tax on the paid-up capital of corporations. *See also* WEALTH TAX.

capital widening Investment to equip new workers entering the workforce rather than investment to increase the amount of capital — such as tools and machinery — per worker. *See also* CAPITAL DEEPENING.

capitalism An economic and political system in which the means of production are largely privately owned and the rights of private property are respected by the state according to the RULE OF LAW and due process. Individuals are free to enter into contracts, to engage in entrepreneurial activity, and to consume or save and earn profits, while the role of the government is to protect individuals against abuses of power, to protect the public interest, and to maintain an economic climate in which private entrepreneurs can make a profit. Such a system relies on the energies and imagination of individuals acting in their own best interests and the unrelenting spur of competition to achieve economic and social progress for the community. Most capitalist societies have evolved into MIXED ECONOMIES, with governments playing a larger role in redistributing income, building and operating infrastructure, providing services such as education and health care, and correcting some of the ill effects of unrestrained market forces by providing a social safety net and enacting environmental protection laws. *See also* PRIVATE ENTERPRISE, MARKET ECONOMY. In most modern economies, the debate is over how to strike the right balance between the role of the private and public sectors in the trade-offs that have been made between equity and efficiency. In practice, the pendulum swings between the two.

capitalist A person who owns shares in a business enterprise.

capitalization *See* INVESTED CAPITAL.

capitalize An accounting rule that records the interest and related costs of a new project as an asset on the BALANCE SHEET until the project comes into production; then the interest and other costs must be treated as an expense in the INCOME STATEMENT.

captive market A market in which a firm faces little if any competition. One reason could be geographical location, for example, there may be only one cement manufacturer or sugar refinery in a particular region of the country, while transportation costs may discourage competition from outside producers. A firm may have a captive market because of vertical integration with another company, for example, a telephone-manufacturing company may be owned by a telephone company providing telephone service; it will have a captive market for its products if telephones made by other companies cannot be attached to its system. Or a firm may produce a unique product that other manufacturers use as a component in their products, or may be the sole source of a resource or commodity for which there are no readily available substitutes.

car loadings A weekly statistic published by Statistics Canada in its *Daily Bulletin* that shows the number of freight cars loaded in seven-day periods. The statistic is helpful in monitoring the general level of business activity in the country. Statistics Canada publishes a monthly report, *Railway Carloadings* (publication 52-001).

carat A method of weighing diamonds and other precious stones. One carat is equal to 0.200 grams.

carbon tax A tax on fossil fuels that is levied in proportion to their carbon content; the tax would fall most heavily on coal, next on oil, and the least on natural gas. The purpose of a carbon tax is to reduce emissions of carbon dioxide, which are one of the major greenhouse gases that restrict the escape of heat from the earth and contribute to global warming.

Caribbean-Canadian Economic Trade Development Assistance Program A program, also known as Caribcan, announced by Canada in 1986 that provides duty-free entry into Canada of goods from Commonwealth countries in the Caribbean. Some products, including clothing, textiles, lubricating oils, and methanol are excluded.

Caribbean Common Market (CARICOM) A grouping of 13 English-speaking nations in the Caribcan region, including Jamaica, Trinidad and Tobago, the Bahamas, Belize in Central America, and Guyana in South America, established in 1973 to strengthen the economy of its members through increased regional trade and a common approach to trade negotiations with third countries. All the members except for the Bahamas, which is not a signatory to the trading agreements, have agreed to implement a common external tariff and to reduce tariff levels by 1994 as part of the process of creating a common market. The CARICOM members are also reducing their common external tariff from 45 percent in 1992 to 30 to 35 percent in 1993, 25 to 30 percent by 1995, and 20 to 25 percent by 1997. Other members include Barbados, Antigua, Anguilla, Dominica, the Dominican Republic, Grenada, St. Lucia, and St. Vincent and the Grenadines. CARICOM was established as a successor to the Caribbean Free Trade Association, as a 12-nation effort launched in 1968 to create a free-trade area.

Caribbean Development Bank A regional development bank, established in 1970 and based in Bridgetown, Barbados, that operates under the United Nations Development Program. It grants loans and provides technical assistance. Canada was a founding member and has 10.27 percent of the votes. Canada has contributed $63 million in ordinary capital and $93 million to the Unified Special Development Fund, which provides concessional financing.

carrying charges The interest, insurance, warehouse, and other costs involved in maintaining an inventory.

carry-over stocks The amount of a crop that is still unsold at the end of a CROP YEAR or season, which therefore becomes part of the following year's supply. In the grain trade, for example, the carry over is the amount of wheat that remains in storage at the end of the crop year. While some carry over may be desirable if inventories or BUFFER STOCKS are low, a large carry over of a crop means that producers will have a harder time getting higher prices in the new crop year, since supplies will be high.

cartel An organization of producers — firms or nations — who band together in some kind of formal arrangement to set prices, determine production levels, and, sometimes, allocate markets. The goal of such an organization is to get higher prices and earn bigger profits by curbing competition and restricting output. Cartels of business firms are illegal in Canada and most other countries, as are cartel-like arrangements such as RIGGED BIDS and other restrictive practices. One example of a cartel is the ORGANIZATION OF PETROLEUM EXPORTING COUNTRIES (OPEC), which succeeded in raising the world price of oil from US$2.81 a barrel in 1973 to US$10.98 in 1974 and in enforcing its policies through a partial oil embargo and by persuading its members to restrain oil production to prevent any significant weakening of the cartel price. Further supply pressure raised the price to US$36.11 a barrel in 1980. However, the sharp rise in oil prices that it engineered brought on significant new non-OPEC discoveries, encouraged oil-substitution practices, and led to major investments in energy efficiency that reduced the amount of oil per unit of production in most industries. By 1992, the price had fallen to US$17.90 a barrel. Various efforts by producer nations to establish commodity cartels have generally failed. *See also* INTERNATIONAL BAUXITE ASSOCIATION. For a cartel to be successful, there has to be a small number of producers, no ready substitute for the commodity, and a willingness by the cartel members to accept limits on their production.

cash Paper money and coins. In accounting, cash on a company's books also includes the money it has in its bank accounts and other negotiable securities that are included in CURRENT ASSETS on a BALANCE SHEET.

cash-basis accounting   A system of accounting in which revenues and expenditures are recorded as they are received or paid out — as opposed to ACCRUAL-BASIS ACCOUNTING that records revenues and expenditures when transactions take place rather than when the money is received or paid out. Cash-basis accounting is rarely used in business.

cash flow   The funds available to a company to pay dividends and finance expansion. It is calculated by adding together net earnings or after-tax profits (before extraordinary items), all deductions that do not require an actual cash outlay, such as DEPRECIATION, and DEFERRED INCOME TAXES. Since it includes tax deductions that do not require an actual cash outlay, the cash-flow figure gives a more useful picture of a company's financial position and its ability to invest than net earnings or after-tax profits alone.

cash-needs budget   An estimate of the federal government's cash needs for the ensuing fiscal year and hence its impact on financial markets, interest and exchange rates, and monetary policy, as well as changes in the level of national debt. The estimate is contained in the Minister of FINANCE's annual BUDGET speech. It indicates the probable level of government borrowing in the year ahead and is used to assess the impact of the government's spending and taxing policies on financial markets, the availability of funds for private borrowers, monetary policy, money supply, and changes in the national debt. Cash needs are financed by increasing the level of government debt in public hands or by running down government cash balances, or both. If there is a surplus, then funds can be used to retire part of the national debt, to build up government cash balances in the chartered banks, or both.

The cash-needs budget includes government revenue and spending not included in the budgetary-accounts budget, even though it can have a significant impact on the cash needs of the government — revenue and spending that shows up in the annual budget document and the monthly Department of Finance Statement of Financial Transactions as non-budgetary items. Examples include payments under government pension plans for its own employees, receipts and payments under the unemployment-insurance program, or loans and advances to government agencies such as CANADA MORTGAGE AND HOUSING CORPORATION. Non-budgetary items can reduce the cash needs of the government and therefore the amount the government must borrow to finance the deficit. Excluded from the cash-needs budget are the operations of crown corporations, aside from transfers to or from the government.

cash squeeze   A shortage of cash in a corporation. Causes may include too many overdue accounts payable, a decline in sales, rising costs, the withdrawal of normal short-term credit, over-investment in non-liquid assets, and a large volume of long-term debt.

cash-surrender value   The value of a life-insurance policy should it be cancelled. It is the amount the owner of the policy would get and represents premiums paid and bonuses or interest earned on those premiums, minus administrative, sales, and other costs incurred by the insurance company.

casual workers   Workers employed only on a seasonal basis during peak periods. For example, department-store salesclerks at Christmas or food-processing workers in late summer. Casual workers do not have the same rights, such as severance pay and notice of layoff, as full-time employees.

casualty insurance   A general term usually used to describe all forms of insurance other than accident and life insurance. Examples include liability insurance and fire and theft insurance.

catch-up bargaining Efforts by a union in collective bargaining to obtain wage increases that take into account past losses in purchasing power due to inflation or the existence of wage and price controls. There may also be an effort to regain a wage position relative to other workers or trades that have won a big gain and altered previously existing wage relationships or differentials.

caveat emptor A Latin phrase that means "Let the buyer beware." In other words, it is up to the consumer to exercise caution when buying goods or services or signing a contract because the seller is not obliged to issue any cautions or provide information.

caveat venditor Latin phrase that means "Let the seller beware." This is the philosophy of modern consumer law, which obligates the seller to provide accurate information or face legal penalties.

census A nationwide survey of the population of a country to determine the number of people in the country, where they live, their age and sex, education, occupational status, type of residence, income, spending habits, religion, place of birth, language, and other details. In Canada, a census must be carried out every 10 years so that the boundaries and number of seats in the House of Commons can be redistributed in line with shifts in population. The last comprehensive census was taken in 1991 and the next will be taken in 2001. A more limited census is taken every fifth-year point; the last was taken in 1986 and the next will be taken in 1996.

Census data provides some of the most important information available to a country to determine such basic

trends as aging of the population, population movements among regions, levels of work skills and education, housing needs, school population, and other information necessary in determining government policies and spending priorities. The census data is also vital to business planning in determining the size and location of future markets, the demand for new products, and other effects on national markets.

The first census in Canada was taken in 1665 and 1666 by Jean Talon in what was then New France. The first census after Confederation was taken in 1871. Statistics Canada, which is responsible for the census, now takes a second census every five years, the last being in 1986, to revise the decennial census. It uses a household-sample technique, similar to that used in the decennial census but with a shorter list of questions, restricting itself to such matters as place of residence five years earlier, education, school attendance, and labour-force activity. Statistics Canada can obtain other information on population from income-tax returns, change of address for family-allowance cheques, and the number of pensioners applying for pension supplements.

census of manufacturers A detailed annual census of manufacturing in Canada showing the number and size of establishments, the number of production employees, the wage bill for production employees, spending on energy, cost of materials and supplies used, value of shipments of own manufacture, production VALUE-ADDED, the total number of employees, including those in non-production jobs, the total wage and salary bill, the total value-added, final value of shipments, and the location by province of manufacturing activity. An industry-wide series of statistics is published by Statistics Canada (publication 51-203) each year, along with separate reports on various manufacturing industries, such as automobiles, steel, food processing, chemicals, and electrical machinery.

central bank   An official institution that has the legal power to issue money and is responsible for the conduct of MONETARY POLICY, exchange-rate policy, management of the government's finances and debt, and the stability of the financial system. It also acts as a lender of last resort to the banking system. The central bank of a country usually has a high level of independence in conducting monetary policy but is ultimately responsible to elected officials. A central bank has varying goals: Germany's Deutsche Bundesbank, for example, has the single goal of pursuing low inflation (as will the proposed European Central bank), while the BANK OF CANADA's mandate is to regulate "credit and currency in the best interest of the economic life of the country." Central banks have their greatest impact on the monetary base or high-powered money, which consists of currency in circulation along with reserves held by chartered banks at the central bank. Other categories of MONEY SUPPLY are influenced by the way in which the public holds its savings and the types of financial instruments that the regulations governing the financial system permit. Other examples of central banks include the U.S. Federal Reserve Bank, the Bank of England, the Bank of Japan, and the Bank of France. Central banks work together through the BANK FOR INTERNATIONAL SETTLEMENTS.

central Canada   Ontario and Quebec.

centralization   **1.** In business, the tendency for decision making to be concentrated in the corporate head office instead of among subsidiaries, branches, and divisions. **2.** In Canada's federal system, the tendency for decision making to be concentrated in the national government in Ottawa instead of among the provincial governments.

The Canadian federal system is characterized by alternating centralizing and decentralizing pressures, although the Canadian federation is said to be the most decentralized in the world. *See also* DECENTRALIZATION.

Centre for the Study of Inflation and Productivity   An agency formed within the ECONOMIC COUNCIL OF CANADA in 1978 to monitor individual wage and price developments and general inflation trends in the economy, to alert the federal government to particular wage and price trends that deserved further attention, and generally to educate Canadians on the problem of inflation and the need for restraint. The centre was set up as a successor to the ANTI-INFLATION BOARD, but it had no special powers to obtain information from employers or unions, and had to rely on published information. Nor did it have wage and price guidelines within which to work. It was replaced in March, 1979, by the NATIONAL COMMISSION ON INFLATION.

certificate   A document establishing legal ownership to shares in a corporation, a bond, or other security.

certificate of deposit   An interest-bearing debt security of some multiple of $1,000, issued by a bank to a depositor, the deposit to be paid back at a stipulated date in the future. These certificates are usually for terms of one to six years; they are negotiable and allow a depositor to earn a higher rate of interest than otherwise. The depositor can sell the certificate of deposit to someone else if he or she needs the money.

certificate of origin   A document showing the country of origin of an imported product, which must be shown to customs officials from REVENUE CANADA when the product arrives in Canada.

certificate of public convenience and necessity A licence issued by the NATIONAL ENERGY BOARD authorizing a company or group of companies to build an oil or natural-gas pipeline. The certificate gives the applicant the power to expropriate land along the route approved by the Energy Board and sets out the terms and conditions under which the pipeline shall be built.

certification Recognition by a federal or provincial labour-relations board of a particular union as the official bargaining agent for a recognized BARGAINING UNIT. Recognition must be preceded by proof that a majority of employees in a bargaining unit have freely chosen to join the union.

certified cheque A cheque endorsed by a bank to certify that the funds have been set aside in the issuer's account to ensure payment.

certified general accountant (CGA) A person who has been trained in internal-management accounting and in public accounting in a program of training that meets the standards of the Canadian Certified General Accountants' Association and its provincial associates. CGAs are found more frequently in industry and government than in public practice, but in a growing number of provinces — British Columbia, Alberta, Saskatchewan, Manitoba, and New Brunswick — they have the same rights to public practice as a CHARTERED ACCOUNTANT. A decision by the Prince Edward Island Supreme Court in 1992 ordered the provincial government to extend the right to public practice to CGAs.

ceteris paribus A Latin phrase frequently used by economists meaning "all other things being equal." When it is said, for example, that ceteris paribus an increase in the price of French wine will lead to greater consumption of Italian, Spanish, and Californian wine, what's meant is that there will be greater consumption of these wines provided their prices are unchanged and there is no change in consumer desire for wine, while the demand for French wines will decline. Likewise, the promised gains from the CANADA-UNITED STATES FREE TRADE AGREEMENT were based on the assumption that other things, such as exchange rates and relative Canadian and U.S. interest rates would remain the same as they had been before the agreement came into effect.

chain store A retail network of stores owned and operated by the same company in the same region or province, across the nation, or even around different parts of the world. Chain stores usually specialize in some branch of retailing, such as food, clothing, shoes, automotive parts, books, hardware, drugs and cosmetics, or general merchandise, or operate as department stores. Chains operate under the general direction of a corporate head office and are able to achieve ECONOMIES OF SCALE through centralized advertising, purchasing, management training, and the use of computer facilities.

chairman of the board The senior officer in a company, who chairs the board of directors. He or she is not the most powerful single person in a company unless he or she also has the title of CHIEF EXECUTIVE OFFICER. In most companies, the role of the chairman is to direct the activities of the board of directors in monitoring the performance of the chief executive officer and senior management, approving the company's strategic direction along with the business plan and budget, and ensuring there is a plan of succession in the senior executive ranks. The chairman will also play a role in determining the compensation of the top management of the company, along with other board members. In some businesses, particularly the chartered banks, the chairman is also the chief executive officer.

Charlottetown Accord An agreement on constitutional reform reached by the federal government, the 10 provincial governments, the two territorial governments, and representatives of the aboriginal peoples on August 28, 1992, and defeated in a national referendum held on October 26, 1992. The key elements included a "Canada clause" that set out the fundamental characteristics of the country, providing guidance to the courts on the future interpretation of the entire constitution; a commitment to "social and economic union," expressed as a set of policy objectives to which governments would be committed but which would not be enforceable through the courts; a new Senate that would represent the provinces equally, with senators that could be appointed or elected according to the decision of each province and that, where there were differences between the House of Commons and Senate, could vote with the House of Commons as a single body, with the Senate holding about 15 percent of the total seats; adjustments to provincial representation in the House of Commons, with Quebec guaranteed 25 percent of the seats in perpetuity and with 42 new seats added to the House, including 18 each for Ontario and Quebec, four for British Columbia, and two for Alberta; the transfer of certain jurisdictional powers from the federal government to the provinces (labour market development and training, forestry, mining, tourism, and housing) and new constraints on the ability of the federal government to spend in areas of provincial jurisdiction along with new limitations on other federal prerogatives; a commitment to grant aboriginal peoples the inherent right to self-government, giving native

peoples a constitutional status equivalent to the federal and provincial governments; and changes to the rules on amending the constitution in the future, with any changes affecting the House of Commons or the Senate requiring the unanimous consent of the federal and provincial governments and any changes directly affecting the aboriginal people requiring their consent.

In the proposed social and economic union, the federal and provincial governments would be committed to maintaining a health care system that was universal, comprehensive, and publicly administered, to protecting the rights of workers to organize and bargain collectively, and to ensuring that all Canadians had a reasonable standard of living by providing adequate social services so that all Canadians had access to housing, food, and other basic necessities, as well as by providing quality primary and secondary education to all individuals and ensuring reasonable access to post-secondary education, and by protecting and sustaining the environment for future generations. The federal and provincial governments also agreed to work together to strengthen the economic union, including the free movement of persons, goods, services, and capital. A formal mechanism was to be set up to monitor adherence to the objectives of the social and economic union.

The federal government committed to making EQUALIZATION PAYMENTS (the current constitution commits it to the principle of equalization) so that all provincial and territorial governments have sufficient revenues to provide reasonably comparable levels of public service at reasonably comparable levels of taxation. The federal government would also be committed to ensuring a reasonably comparable economic infrastructure of a national nature in each province and territory. The provinces were also to be given the power to compel the federal government to negotiate a regional development within a reasonable period of time. The federal and provincial governments could also enter into agreements on cost-sharing programs that would be binding on future governments for five years. The Senate was to be given the power to ratify heads of regulatory bodies and government agencies, including the BANK OF CANADA, with a simple majority and would be able to veto bills relating to natural resource taxation, as well as those relating to French language and culture.

The federal spending power would be constrained, with the federal government being required to provide "reasonable compensation" to the government of a province that chose not to participate in a new Canada-wide shared-cost program established by the federal government in an area of exclusive provincial jurisdiction if the province chose to bring in a program or initiative that is "comparable to national objectives." Medicare is an example of a federal initiative in an area of exclusive provincial jurisdiction. Labour market development and training would be made an area of exclusive provincial jurisdiction. At the request of a provincial government, the federal government would be required to withdraw from all or any training or other labour market development, except for UNEMPLOYMENT INSURANCE, which would remain a federal responsibility. The federal government would be required to negotiate and conclude an agreement to provide reasonable compensation to provinces requesting the federal government to withdraw from certain fields or programs. But the federal government would also be required to retain and operate any program for any province that so requested. The federal training and labour market role would be limited to establishing national policy objectives for labour market development.

The federal government would also be obligated to negotiate and conclude

immigration agreements within a reasonable time at the request of any province, and federal responsibilities in the area of culture would be limited to grants and contributions by national cultural institutions while provinces would have exclusive jurisdiction over cultural matters within the province. The provinces would have exclusive jurisdiction in forestry, mining, tourism, housing, recreation, and urban affairs. The provinces could prohibit federal spending in these areas, and the federal government would be required to withdraw from existing activities in these areas — except when any province required it to continue a program. In telecommunications, the federal government would be required to negotiate an agreement with the provinces to coordinate and harmonize the procedures of their respective regulatory agencies in this field (in 1989, the Supreme Court of Canada declared the federal government had exclusive jurisdiction). The federal declaratory power (section 92 [10]{c} of the CONSTITUTION ACT, 1867, which allows the federal government to declare a work or undertaking to be in the national interest even if it invades an area of provincial jurisdiction, would not be permitted without the consent of the province in which the work or undertaking is to be located. The power was used to build the transcontinental railway across Canada, to establish the CANADIAN WHEAT BOARD, and to introduce wage and price controls.

The Charlottetown Accord did not contain any provisions to reduce interprovincial barriers to trade or to strengthen the Canadian common market. But an attached political accord, which did not have the status of a constitutional amendment, set out various principles and commitments, with implementation left to a future First Ministers' Conference. The accord pledged there would be no new barriers that "arbitrarily discriminate" on the basis of province of residence, origin, or destination. But this commitment would not apply to a provincial law aimed at reducing regional disparities within a province, marketing or supply management arrangements, laws relating to the provision of social services, the establishment and maintenance of monopolies, laws relating to labour practices, reasonable public sector investment practices or a subsidy or tax incentive program established for the purpose of encouraging investment, or the development and management of natural resources.

charter The document of incorporation of a company, setting out its AUTHORIZED CAPITAL, business purpose, and other such information.

Charter of Economic Rights and Duties of States A set of guidelines adopted by the United Nations General Assembly in December, 1974, for the conduct of international economic relations, similar to those adopted for a NEW INTERNATIONAL ECONOMIC ORDER by the United Nations in May, 1974. The charter, proposed originally by Mexico, asserted the right of states to absolute sovereignty over their natural resources, with compensation for nationalization of foreign business only according to domestic laws; the right of states to form natural-resource cartels; the right of less-developed countries to preferential and non-reciprocal trade treatment; and the right of less-developed countries to peg their export prices to import costs.

charter of labour rights A charter added to the CANADIAN LABOUR CONGRESS constitution in 1972 setting out union goals. They include the unfettered right to peaceful assembly and picketing; the right to bargain on technological changes and automation; the right to strike during the term of a collective agreement if bargaining cannot resolve a matter in dispute not covered by the

agreement; the right to a "meaningful say" on all economic and social questions affecting the vital interests of workers, along with union representation on government boards administering social programs; the right to training and retraining at the expense of the employer or the government; the right to take whatever steps may be necessary to protect the on-the-job safety and health of workers; the right to leisure through extended vacations and paid holidays; and the right to "a complete, secure retirement" at age 60, if so desired.

chartered accountant (CA) An accountant certified by a provincial institute of chartered accountants. CAs are trained to engage in public practice, which means setting up their own offices to act as AUDITORs and to provide tax, financial-management, and other such advice to clients, or to work in managerial positions in industry and government. Their national organization is the Canadian Institute of Chartered Accountants, based in Toronto.

chartered bank A financial institution that accepts deposits and makes loans and that plays an important role in the implementation of MONETARY POLICY. Chartered banks are regulated under the BANK ACT, which specifies their powers and regulates their methods of operation. The chartered banks are supervised by the Minister of FINANCE and the OFFICE OF THE SUPERINTENDENT OF FINANCIAL INSTITUTIONS; they also work closely with the BANK OF CANADA. There are two classes of banks in Canada: Schedule I banks, which must be widely held and in which no one person may hold more than 10 percent of the shares; and Schedule II banks, which if Canadian controlled can be owned by a Canadian on a closely held basis for 10 years — after that it must become widely held. Foreign-controlled banks are also Schedule II banks.

The banks accept a wide range of Canadian-dollar and foreign-currency deposits from Canadians and non-residents, including those against which cheques can be written. They also make a wide variety of Canadian-dollar and foreign-currency loans, ranging from mortgage and consumer loans to business, farm, construction, and MONEY MARKET loans. They are active in the money market, the capital market, and the foreign-exchange market. They can also own securities dealers, mortgage loan companies, trust companies, insurance companies, mutual-fund companies, real-estate companies, real-estate brokerages, information-service companies, investment counselling and portfolio-management companies, financial leasing companies, factoring corporations, and specialized financing corporations or merchant banks with the power to hold equity of up to $90 million for 10 years in a company in any line of business. Many of these new powers were the result of a sweeping financial reform package, including amendments to the Bank Act, which came into effect in 1992. The banks make their profits on the difference, or spread, between the interest rates they pay depositors and the interest they charge on loans, and, increasingly, on the fees for services they provide their customers. The Bank of Canada shapes monetary policy through the chartered banks by the sale and purchase of government securities, including TREASURY BILLS and manipulation of the level of the government's cash balances on deposit with the banks. The Bank of Canada can also use MORAL SUASION to try to direct bank lending to specific areas of the economy, such as small business or slow-growth areas. The banks act as agents for the government in the sale of CANADA SAVINGS BONDS. Because of their importance in the functioning of the economy, the banks have the right to borrow funds from the Bank of Canada.

Under the Bank Act, no individual or group of associated individuals is allowed to own more than 10 percent of the voting shares of a bank, while non-residents collectively may not own more than 25 percent of a bank's voting shares. For an exception, *see* MERCANTILE BANK AFFAIR. The banks carry compulsory deposit insurance for up to $60,000 on all Canadian-dollar accounts. *See also* CANADA DEPOSIT INSURANCE CORPORATION

chartist A financial analyst who attempts to determine the trend of future prices of individual shares by charting their past financial performance and volume of trading, and extrapolating into the future according to one of several patterns of movement of share prices based on patterns of investor behaviour.

chattel Personal property that is movable, such as an automobile, work of art, or coin collection.

chattel mortgage A loan that is secured by a chattel such as an automobile. If the borrower fails to repay the loan, then the lender can seize the chattel. Since chattel mortgages are registered in provincial registry offices, chattels being purchased by another party have to be checked to make sure that a chattel mortgage does not exist on the item being purchased; otherwise, the chattel could still be seized from the new owner if the earlier owner had failed to keep up his payments.

check-off A clause in a collective agreement requiring an employer to deduct union dues and assessments from employees in the BARGAINING UNIT who either belong to the union or have to pay dues even if they don't belong (*see* RAND FORMULA), and to turn these funds over to the union. This is the normal method of collecting union dues, and it relieves the union of the cost and time it would take to collect dues on its own. Although check-off is a standard clause in most collective agreements, it is still an arrangement that has to be negotiated in the first collective agreement between a union and an employer in most provinces.

cheque   A written order, usually on a standard cheque form printed by a bank or other deposit-taking financial institution, instructing the bank or other institution to pay the bearer or person named on the order either immediately, or on some future date written on the cheque, a sum of money specified on the order, and to deduct the amount from the cheque-writer's account. The person receiving the cheque can endorse it over to another party by signing it on the back. *See also* CERTIFIED CHEQUE, POST-DATED CHEQUE.

Chicago School   *See* MONETARISM.

chief executive officer (CEO)   The member of the board of directors of a firm, and officer in a corporation, who exercises the highest level of authority over the day-to-day activities and policies of the firm. He or she may be either the president or the chairman of the corporation and is responsible to the BOARD OF DIRECTORS and to the shareholders.

child benefit   A single monthly payment to lower-income parents that came into effect in 1993 to replace the family allowance, which had been available to all parents regardless of income, and the child tax credit, which had been income-related. All children under 18 are elegible. For a family with two children, the child benefit will be reduced at a rate of 5 percent of family net income over $25,921. There will be no payment to families with incomes of $75,000 or more.

child tax credit   A refundable TAX CREDIT introduced in 1978 for children eligible for family allowances. In 1992, the credit was $601, with a family income of $25,921 or less qualifying for the entire credit; there was also a supplement of $213 in 1992 for children under the age of seven. In 1993, family allowances, a child credit, and the refundable child credit were consolidated into one CHILD BENEFIT.

choice   The decisions that must be made in an economy or household due to a scarcity of resources about what goods and services are to be produced and consumed, in what quantities, and how they are to be distributed.

City   The square mile of London in which is based one of the world's most important financial and commercial centres. It is the location of the London Stock Exchange, the LONDON METALS EXCHANGE, major insurance organizations, including Lloyd's, the institutions that are responsible for much of the Eurocurrency investing and lending, the merchant banks, the foreign-exchange and gold markets, and a major short-term money market. It is Europe's largest financial centre and, after New York's Wall Street, the world's second-largest financial centre. *See also* BAY STREET, WALL STREET.

city-gate price   The price for natural gas delivered by a pipeline company to the collection point for a local gas distributor. For example, the Toronto city-gate price is the price charged by the gas-pipeline company shipping it from Western Canada to a delivery point at Toronto. It consists of the PLANT-GATE PRICE charged by the natural-gas producer, plus the transmission charge for delivering it to Toronto.

civil code   The system of civil law used in Quebec, dealing, among other things, with property, contracts, wills, trusts, sales, leases, partnerships, and debts. While the province has developed its own code, its system is based on the Napoleonic and Justinian codes. Cases are decided on the detailed principles set out in the code, unlike the COMMON LAW system inherited from Britain that the other provinces use, which relies heavily on precedents set in earlier cases. For more than one hundred years, Quebec relied mainly on the 1866 Civil Code of Lower Canada. In 1981, family laws were updated with the new Civil Code of Quebec. The 1866 code's provisions were drawn largely from the Custom of Paris brought to New France in 1663, the decisions of the Sovereign Council of New France up to 1763, and various laws passed between 1774 and 1866. In 1955, the Quebec legislature established the Civil Code Revision Office to make changes that would allow the code to better reflect changing Quebec society. In 1981, a new Civil Code of Quebec was proclaimed, replacing the 1866 code. There are two elements of the civil code: 1. The set of rules to be followed in all the different areas of civil law. 2. The rules of procedure to be followed in civil actions. If the code itself is not clear enough to allow a judge to decide a case, he or she has three forms of clarification that can be used. First, there are the Codifiers' Reports, documents prepared by the officials who drafted various sections of the code, which explain the intent of the relevant sections. Second, there is what is known as la doctrine, consisting of written opinions by legal experts specializing in various areas of law. And third, there is a body of written judgements, la jurisprudence, which shows how judges have interpreted various parts of the code in the past and which is similar to the use of precedents by common-law judges. While Quebec has its own civil code, it is governed by the same CRIMINAL CODE as the rest of

the country; criminal law falls under federal jurisdiction.

claim A portion of land containing mineral prospects that have been staked out, under federal or provincial law, by a prospector or mining company. The claim gives the holder the right to continue exploration and, if commercially feasible, to exploit the resources.

class action A legal action launched on behalf of most or all of the consumers of a product or victims of someone else's negligence. The costs of launching an action to recover damages may be too high for each individual, but are feasible if a large number of individuals file a joint suit and share the costs of the action. Class actions can be launched in Canadian courts, but their application is limited and they have not been widely used.

class struggle Karl MARX's economic interpretation of history. It is based on the theory that the different social classes — in particular, capitalists and workers — are locked in an inevitable conflict that will ultimately result in the revolution of the workers, or proletariat, and the overthrow of the capitalists, or bourgeoisie. The revolution will lead to the establishment of a socialist state, to be followed by its evolution into a COMMUNIST state.

classical economics The school of economic thought originating with Adam SMITH and further developed by Thomas Robert MALTHUS, David RICARDO, John Stuart MILL, and Jean Baptiste Say; see also SAY'S LAW. They believed in the wealth-creating power of competition and free markets and tended to oppose government intervention. Smith, however, feared that business interests had an instinctive desire to combine and restrict competition and warned of the offsetting needs for social institutions, including the family, the law, and religion to counter the forces unleashed by the pursuit of greed. Most, with the exception of Malthus, also believed that a free-market economy would naturally tend to FULL EMPLOYMENT. They also believed in FREE TRADE. Classical economists believed that the economy functioned through natural laws, much as the physical universe operates through the laws of nature; the LAW OF SUPPLY AND DEMAND in a free-market economy, for example, should yield full-employment conditions. In the classical model, each citizen pursued his or her own interests in a competitive market with the total of all those transactions and activities producing high levels of economic growth. The classical economists reacted against the earlier MERCANTILIST age, which emphasized a significant role for government in the economy. Classical economists provided the foundation for theories of free trade and COMPARATIVE ADVANTAGE, as well as the view that the least government is the best government. *See also* INVISIBLE HAND.

clear customs   The process of filing the necessary certificate of origin with customs officials, indicating the actual origin of the product so that customs duties can be assessed, and gaining the necessary evidence of customs approval, such as a certificate or stamp, that indicates the duties have been paid or that someone has accepted the obligation to pay the duties by a specified future date.

clearing system   1. A network of centres across Canada operated by the CANADIAN PAYMENTS ASSOCIATION to exchange cheques, electronic transactions, and other financial transactions and to settle any outstanding balances with one another on a daily basis. 2. Centres operated by STOCK EXCHANGES and member firms through the INVESTMENT DEALERS ASSOCIATION, to exchange share certificates and cheques for the thousands of transactions they handle on the floor of stock exchanges each day in buying and selling shares for customers. A similar arrangement exists to exchange traded bonds.

closed economy   An economy that has no external trade, or virtually no external trade. Post-war examples have included Albania after the post-1945 Communist takeover, China in the earlier years after the Communist takeover in 1949, and North Korea.

closed-end investment company   An investment company that owns major interests in other operating companies and whose shares are traded on a stock exchange. A closed-end investment company issues a fixed number of shares that are bought and sold by investors on the market, unlike a MUTUAL FUND, which redeems outstanding shares held by investors and regularly issues new shares as fast as it can sell them.

closed shop   A clause in a collective agreement that says that the only people who can be hired for jobs in a BARGAINING UNIT must be members of the union before being hired. This means that they are hired by the union. Closed shops are most common in the construction industry and on the docks, where union hiring halls allocate jobs among members in good standing. *See also* AGENCY SHOP, UNION SHOP.

closely held corporation   A corporation owned by a small number of individuals. Its shares are often not traded on a stock exchange or in the OVER-THE-COUNTER MARKET. *See also* PRIVATE COMPANY.

closing prices   The prices on a stock exchange, bond market, or commodities market at the end of the day's trading.

Club of Rome A private international association of businessmen, scientists, and scholars, founded in 1968 to study mankind's common problems, particularly problems of long-term resource supplies, environmental pressures, economic growth, and food supplies. The club has published several important studies that it financed. They include *The Limits to Growth* (1972), *Mankind at the Turning Point* (1974), and *RIO: Reshaping the International Order* (1976). While *The Limits to Growth* presented the stark and dramatic view that mankind would be doomed by environmental crises, a lack of natural resources, famine, and overpopulation, without a halt to economic and population growth, the *RIO* report said that economic growth should not be abandoned and that adoption of a NEW INTERNATIONAL ECONOMIC ORDER was a better approach to solving the problems of world poverty. The club was founded by Aurelio Peccei, an Italian industrialist, and is financed by the Agnelli Foundation and Volkswagon Foundation of Germany. *See also* LIMITS TO GROWTH, RIO PROJECT.

cluster A dynamic network of companies operating in the same industry and stimulating their mutual competitiveness by the nature of their synergy and interaction. The concept of clusters was developed by Harvard Business School professor Michael Porter in his 1990 study, *The Competitive Advantage of Nations*. Clusters provide a productive set of linkages, either vertical — between buyers and suppliers — or horizontal — with common customers, technology, and channels. According to Porter, one competitive industry will help develop another in a mutually reinforcing process. Such an industry will be one of the most sophisticated buyers of the products and services on which it depends, forcing the supplier industries to meet highly demanding standards. Its presence is crucial to developing competitive advantage in supplier industries. Porter cites Sweden's forest-products industry as one example of a successful cluster. Sweden is competitive not just in paper products but also in wood-handling machinery, sulphur boilers, conveyor systems, pulp-making machinery, control instruments, paper-making machinery, paper-drying machinery, and the chemicals used in making pulp and paper. Competitive supplier industries, Porter argues, can help encourage world-class downstream industries by providing technology, stimulating transferable skills, and becoming new entrants. A competitive cluster also creates new, related industries by providing ready access to transferable skills, by providing related entry by already established skills, and by stimulating spin-offs. Once a cluster is formed, the entire group of industries becomes mutually reinforcing, Porter argues. "Benefits flow forward, backward, and horizontally. Aggressive rivalry in one industry tends to spread to others in the cluster, through the exercise of bargaining power, spin-offs, and related diversification by established firms. Entry from other industries within the cluster spurs upgrading by stimulating diversity in R&D approaches and provides a means for introducing new strategies and skills. Information flows freely and innovations diffuse rapidly through the conduits of suppliers or customers who have contact with multiple competitors. Interconnections within the cluster, often unanticipated, lead to the perception of new ways of competing and entirely new opportunities." A cluster also builds up other dynamic institutions such as universities and community colleges that specialize in the research and skills of the industry cluster, basic research institutes, financial institutions and investors knowledgeable in the industry cluster, and other forms of supportive infrastructure. A cluster strategy is one approach to economic development.

Coase, Ronald H. (b. 1910) The British-born economist who was awarded the Alfred Nobel Memorial Prize in Economic Sciences in 1991 "for his discovery and clarification of the significance of transaction costs and property rights for the institutional structure and functioning of the economy."

code of ethical practices A code adopted by the CANADIAN LABOUR CONGRESS (CLC) in 1970 to strengthen union democracy, to encourage membership participation in union activities, and to prevent corrupt persons from holding union office. The code, which is part of the CLC constitution, gives the CLC and its affiliated unions the power to take disciplinary and corrective actions, including, if need be, the appointment of a TRUSTEE where union members have been deprived of their rights or union officers have been found to be corrupt. The code calls on all union members to exercise their union citizenship by participating in union meetings and affairs, and states the right of union members to vote for union officers, to be assured of honest elections, to be eligible for union office, and to be free to voice their views on union affairs without fear of punishment. It adds that, while a member has the right to criticize union policies and union officers, this does not include the right to undermine the union as an institution, to advocate dual unionism, to destroy or weaken the union as a collective-bargaining agency, or to engage in slander or libel. It states that union disciplinary actions must be carried out according to due process, with adequate notice, a hearing, and judgement on the basis of evidence. It calls for regular union conventions to elect officers freely.

code of liberalization of capital movements A code adopted by members of the ORGANIZATION FOR ECONOMIC CO-OPERATION AND DEVELOPMENT that binds member countries to policies favouring the free flow of capital, including an agreement not to enact new measures restricting foreign direct investment. The code, which dates back to 1974, has been revised several times. Canada had refused to sign the code, arguing that its high level of foreign ownership and the vulnerability of its industry to foreign takeovers made compliance a problem. However, in 1991, Canada agreed to sign the code but took advantage of its provision for sectoral reservations and listed the telecommunications, cultural, financial services, air and marine transportation, fishing, and energy as industries not included.

co-determination The participation by employees in the decision-making process of an enterprise by having employee representatives sit on the boards of directors of corporations, for example, or by setting up labour-management committees within a firm to address a range of workplace and production issues. The participation of workers on the boards of companies was made mandatory in West Germany in 1952, and has since been adopted as a goal for all countries within the EUROPEAN COMMUNITY. It is also required in Sweden. It has been discussed in Canada, but with little enthusiasm from either employers or unions. Employers fear interference with the rights of management, while unions fear that they will be co-opted, and hence their bargaining power in collective bargaining will be reduced.

codicil A document altering a will.

coin Pieces of metal bearing the imprint of the Canadian government that are recognized as legal tender or a medium of exchange. The metal used in smaller coins is usually worth less than the value stamped on them; however, they have the higher face value because they can be exchanged for paper money at their stated value. In Canada, coins are produced by the ROYAL CANADIAN MINT.

coincident indicator   A statistical measure of economic performance showing current economic conditions. Examples include real domestic product, the index of industrial production, and the seasonally adjusted unemployment rate. *See also* LAGGING INDICATOR, LEADING INDICATOR.

collateral   Various types of securities, such as shares, bonds, insurance policies, or other property, that are pledged by a borrower to a creditor to reduce the creditor's risk in case the loan is not repaid. If the borrower fails to repay the loan, the creditor can sell the collateral to recover the money. *See* BANKRUPTCY.

collective   An organization representing creators or owners of copyright works. The collective negotiates royalty rates with users and distributes the money to members of the collective. The Composers, Authors and Publishers Association of Canada and the Performing Rights Organization of Canada license the right to broadcast or perform musical works by Canadian and foreign composers. La Société pour l'avancement des droits en audio-visuel (SADA) manages copyright on behalf of Quebec companies engaged in producing and distributing audio-visual materials. Vis-Art, representing painters, photographers, designers, and sculptors, manages the sale of rights to commercial reproduction of members' works. The Canadian Reprography Collective collects royalties on behalf of authors for works photocopied in libraries, schools and universities, busi-

nesses, and other organizations. The COPYRIGHT ACT provides an exemption for collectives from the COMPETITION ACT, provided royalty agreements are filed with the COPYRIGHT BOARD.

collective agreement   A contract for a stated period of time, usually one to three years, between a union or group of unions and an employer or group of employers, that sets out the rates of pay, hours of work, vacations, fringe benefits, pension rights, working conditions, rights of workers, methods of dealing with technological change, check-off of union dues, procedures to be followed in settling grievances, and other terms and conditions of employment.

collective bargaining   The negotiation of a collective agreement between representatives of an employer or group of employers and representatives of a union or group of unions. Labour laws require that bargaining be conducted in good faith — that is, both sides are supposed to be sincere in their desire to reach an agreement. Collective bargaining is subject to rules and procedures set out in federal and provincial labour laws, which determine when and under what conditions a strike or lockout may occur, provide for conciliation and mediation, and may provide for compulsory arbitration.

collective goods   *See* PUBLIC GOODS.

collusion   An illegal written or unwritten agreement between companies to restrict competition in order to achieve higher profits. *See* COMPETITION POLICY, COMPETITION ACT.

Colombo Plan   A program adopted in 1950 by a group of donor countries, including originally Canada, Britain, Australia, and New Zealand, and later the United States and Japan, to assist the economic development of the nations of South-East Asia, including

India, Pakistan, Bangladesh, South Korea, Indonesia, Burma, Malaysia, the Philippines, Sri Lanka, Thailand, Afghanistan, and Singapore. Other countries that have received help under the plan include Iran, South Vietnam, and Cambodia. The Colombo Plan was one of Canada's first foreign-aid activities. It provides technical, educational, and economic assistance. Its consultive committee meets once a year. In 1974, it established a Colombo Plan Staff College for Technical Education, located in Singapore, that sends instructors to member countries and provides some training at its facilities in Singapore. The Colombo Plan, known officially as the Colombo Plan for Co-operative Economic and Social Development in Asia and the Pacific, is headquartered in Colombo, Sri Lanka. The plan was originally intended to run for six years only, but it has been extended a number of times since. But Canada withdrew in 1991, continuing only its interest in the Colombo Plan staff college.

Columbia River Treaty A treaty between Canada and the United States, signed on January 17, 1961, under which Canada agreed to build dams on the Columbia River in British Columbia that would substantially increase hydro-electric-power capacity south of the border and achieve flood-control benefits for both countries. Dams were to be built at the Arrow Lakes and the Duncan River within five years, while the Mica Dam was to be completed by 1970, with Canada and British Columbia bearing the costs. In return, Canada was to get half the power generated in the United States, plus payment for the flood-control benefits.

combination Temporary or on-going collusion by supposedly competing firms in an industry to reduce competition and to obtain higher profits by charging excessive prices, restraining production, and dividing the market.

Such collusion may be in the form of a written agreement, may result from secret meetings between representatives of the different members of the combination, or may be implicit, with firms in the industry following an acknowledged price leader. *See also* COMPETITION ACT, COMPETITION POLICY.

Combines Investigation Act The principal federal law that dealt with restrictive trade practices, mergers and monopolies, misleading advertising, or other practices that restricted competition. Because it operated through criminal law, a high burden of proof was required and the law, after many failed cases, was deemed ineffective in dealing with mergers and monopolies. It was replaced in 1986 by the COMPETITION ACT, which provides for civil procedures in dealing with mergers and monopolies while retaining criminal penalties for other offences.

command economy An economy in which government planners determine production, investment, and prices, and allocate resources, as opposed to a market economy in which countless individual decisions, shaped by government tax, spending, competition, and other policies largely determine production, investment, and prices. The Communist system is based on a command economy.

commerce A term sometimes used to describe the buying, storing, selling, and distribution of goods, as opposed to industry, which deals with the production of goods, and finance, which deals with the financing of industry and commerce.

commercial An advertisement broadcast on radio or television. Privately owned radio and television stations rely on the income from commercials to pay their costs and earn their profits. The CANADIAN RADIO-TELEVISION AND

TELECOMMUNICATIONS COMMISSION regulates the amount of broadcast time that may be taken up, in any consecutive 60 minutes, with commercials. Advertisers who make commercials that contain false or misleading claims are subject to penalty under the COMPETITION ACT.

commercial paper Short-term promissory notes and other negotiable securities issued by major corporations and repayable on a specified date. Commercial paper is normally purchased by other large corporations and is an important form of short-term investment for corporations and others with temporary cash surpluses. It is also an important method of short-term financing of trade or other business activities.

commercial policy Government policy that deals with foreign trade and investment, and that includes tariff and other trade agreements, export-financing facilities, rules to prevent dumping and other unfair trading practices, the establishment of trade-promotion offices in other countries, and export incentives.

commission 1. A government regulatory board or agency, such as the NATIONAL TRANSPORTION AGENCY OF CANADA and the CANADIAN RADIO-TELEVISION AND TELECOMMUNICATIONS COMMISSION. 2. A fee paid to a stockbroker, real-estate agent, customs broker, or other salesperson or agent in return for arranging a sale or purchase, or carrying out some other service.

commission of inquiry *See* ROYAL COMMISSION.

Commission on the Political and Constitutional Future of Quebec A 36-person commission appointed by the Quebec national assembly in 1990 to study and analyze the political and constitutional status of Quebec and to make recommendations following the failure by Manitoba and Newfoundland to ratify the MEECH LAKE AGREEMENT by the June 23, 1990, deadline. The commission was established unanimously by the assembly and included 18 members of the assembly, including the Premier of Quebec and the Leader of the Opposition, along wth 18 representatives of the Quebec public. It was co-chaired by Michel Belanger and Jean Campeau. The legislation establishing the commission stressed that "Quebecers are free to assume their own destiny, to determine their political status, and to assure their economic, social, and cultural development." The legislation argued that the CONSTITUTION ACT, 1982 was proclaimed over the objections of Quebec and that the Meech Lake Agreement would have made Quebec a party to the 1982 constitution, making it "necessary to redefine the political and constitutional status of Quebec." The commission report, adopted by 30 of its members on March 26, 1991, said that Quebec had only two choices: to negotiate a new deal with the rest of Canada or to choose independence as a separate state. It recommended that the Quebec national assembly adopt legislation authorizing a referendum on sovereignty to be held either between June 8 and 22 or October 12 and 26 in 1992. If the vote were affirmative, then Quebec would acquire the status of a soverign state exactly one year after the date of the referendum. In the meantime, the national assembly would establish a special parliamentary commission to study matters related to Quebec's accession to sovereignty. The same commission would be responsible for examining an offer of economic partnership from the federal government and making recommendations on such an offer to the national assembly. At the same time, a special parliamentary commission would be established to assess any offer of a new constitutional partnership made by the federal government and to make recommendations on it to the national assembly. However, the parliamentary commission would only consider an offer already formally binding upon the federal government and the other provinces. The Belanger-Campeau commission reiterated that "Quebecers are free to assume their economic, social, and cultural development."

Committee for an Independent Canada (CIC) A non-partisan committee of Canadians, formed in 1970, to campaign for greater Canadian ownership and control of the economy and to increase support for Canadian cultural expression. Its specific goals included the following: 1. Increased Canadian ownership of resources and industry, including efforts to regain ownership of foreign-owned enterprises in Canada. 2. A national development program that would allocate more resources to the underdeveloped parts of the country. 3. Canadian control, Canadian content, and adequate financing of Canada's communications media. 4. Greater autonomy for Canadian unions. 5. The Canadian design of the country's urban environment. 6. A greater Canadian orientation in education and foreign policy. In 1985, the organization was replaced by the COUNCIL OF CANADIANS.

commodity Although this can be used to refer to any product or good, the term is normally used to describe raw materials, or semifinished goods. The list of commodities that are traded internationally, and usually through commodity exchanges, include corn, wheat, soybeans, soybean meal, barley, flax seed, oats, canola, rye, rice, cottonseed oil, coconut oil, peanut oil, corn oil, soybean oil, beef, feeder cattle, hogs, pork bellies, cocoa, cocoa butter, coffee, orange juice, sugar, flour, gold, platinum, silver, palladium, aluminum, antimony, copper, lead, nickel, mercury, pig iron, scrap steel, tin, zinc,

Saudi Arabian light oil, North Sea Brent oil, West Texas Intermediate oil, Alaska North Slope oil, fuel oil, iron ore, bauxite, potash, lumber, cotton, wool, print cloth, rubber, cement, and coal.

commodity agreement An agreement between producer and consumer nations to stabilize prices and, usually, to provide for higher prices of a specific commodity. Agreements have been tried for sugar, tin, coffee, rubber, copper, and cocoa, but with limited success. The initiative for commodity agreements usually comes from producer nations, who seek protection against declining prices and excessive production, and who want to make sure that commodity prices at least stay even with inflation. Many less-developed countries rely heavily on a single commodity for a large share of their foreign-exchange earnings, and must sustain the income from commodity exports to pay for essential imports and the service costs of their foreign debt. With fluctuations in the business cycle of industrial nations, the price of basic commodities can also fluctuate widely, since most commodities are highly sensitive to the LAW OF SUPPLY AND DEMAND. Some commodity agreements provide for a BUFFER STOCK, built up through purchases of the commodity when there is excess supply, and sold off when there are shortages; some operate with maximum and minimum prices, with a top price at which the commodity will be sold and a minimum price at which consumers buy. Other features may include production restrictions, marketing quotas, or export controls. The International Jute Agreement, the International Rubber Agreement and the International Cocoa Agreement are examples. *See also* COMMON FUND.

commodity broker A broker who buys and sells COMMODITY FUTURES, COMMODITY OPTIONS, and SPOT contracts on COMMODITY MARKETS for customers. Like a stockbroker, a broker earns a commission that is a percentage of the value of the transaction.

commodity exchange A market in which commodities and FUTURES contracts for commodities are traded. The commodities themselves are not brought to the exchange; only contracts for immediate or SPOT delivery and future delivery are traded. There are commodity exchanges for grains, lumber, gold, silver, copper, soybeans, frozen orange juice, pork bellies, potatoes, coffee, tea, cotton, and other commodities. The WINNIPEG COMMODITY EXCHANGE is the principal exchange in Canada. Other major exchanges include the Chicago Board of Trade, the Chicago Mercantile Exchange, the London Metal Exchange, the New York Coffee and Sugar Exchange, and the New York Commodity Exchange, which includes the New York Cotton Exchange and the New York Mercantile Exchange. Contracts are purchased through COMMODITY BROKERS, who play a similar role to stockbrokers in arranging stock-exchange transactions.

commodity futures Contracts to deliver or to take delivery of a specified quantity of a commodity at a specified price on a specified date in the future. Such contracts are traded on COMMODITY EXCHANGES; their main role is to provide industries that trade in or use commodities with a means of HEDGING against sharp price fluctuations. *See also* FUTURES MARKET, SPOT MARKET.

commodity money Commodities that can be used as a medium of exchange and a store of value: through history, gold, silver, diamonds, cattle, wampum, and furs, have been used as money.

commodity option An OPTION that an investor can purchase, giving the right to purchase a futures contract at a specified price for a specified period of time. The investor pays a relatively low price for the option. If the futures contract does not rise above its value at the time the option was purchased plus the price of the option, then the option is not exercised. However, if the futures contract is, say, $14.75 at the time the option is purchased, the option price is 50 cents, and the futures contract rises to $15.75, then the option will be exercised, since $15.75 is greater than $14.75 plus 50 cents.

commodity theory of money The theory that the value of money is set by the value of the metal, such as gold or silver, of which it is made or upon which it is based. In the 19th century, a close relationship was maintained between the supply of gold in a nation's reserves and the supply of paper money in circulation.

common carrier A company or individual providing a service that must be available to everyone who wants to pay for it, and at the same price to all users. Examples include airlines, railways, trucking companies, bus and transit companies, taxicabs, telephone and telecommunications companies, and some pipelines. Common carriers are regulated by government at the federal, provincial, or municipal level, depending on the service. The federal government, for example, regulates airlines, pipelines, and telecommunications; the provincial governments regulate intercity bus services; and municipal governments regulate taxicabs.

common external tariff The adoption of an identical tariff by members of a free-trade area to be applied against imports from non-member countries. A free trade agreement that includes a common external tariff is a CUSTOMS UNION. The CANADA-UNITED STATES

FREE TRADE AGREEMENT and the NORTH AMERICAN FREE TRADE AGREEMENT do not provide for a common external tariff; Canada, the United States, and Mexico each maintain their own tariff schedules on imports from the rest of the world. However, the establishment of a free-trade area creates pressure for a common external tariff since producers in the country with the lowest tariff will have an advantage when importing raw materials, parts, and components from outside the free-trade area. *See also* COMMON MARKET.

common fund   A treaty signed in 1980 under the auspices of the United Nations by 101 developed and less-developed countries, including Canada, to establish a fund to be used to help finance BUFFER STOCKS of key commodities exported by developing countries, in order to help prevent sharp fluctuations in their prices and export earnings. The fund was established following a concerted campaign by less-developed countries, many of whom depend heavily on foreign-exchange earnings from a single commodity whose price fluctuates sharply, and who thus face periodic exchange crises, since the manufactured goods they must import do not show similar fluctuations in price. The managers of buffer stocks of selected commodities — tin, cocoa, coffee, rubber, and sugar are possible candidates — would sell stocks when prices are high and buy stocks when prices are low. The fund is divided into two parts, US $400 million put up by the participants, and a US $350 million second window, or special fund, to help poorer nations increase their commodity revenue by developing new markets, improving crop yields, and using research and development to improve crop varieties. Ratification was slow, however, and it was not until 1988 that sufficient countries had ratified the agreement, allowing it to come

into operation. In 1991, Canada withdrew from three international commodity organizations, for jute, coffee, and sugar. Canada withdrew from the international rubber agreement in 1988 and from the international cocoa organization in 1989. Canada was considering withdrawal from the common fund in 1992.

common law   A system of law in which the precedents and principles established in past court judgements are incorporated into current decisions by the courts. The system dates back to feudal days in Britain and has been transported to Canada, where it is the basis for civil law in all provinces except Quebec (*see* CIVIL CODE). Parliament or a provincial legislature can overturn common law by passing a new statute.

common market   An arrangement among a group of sovereign nations to eliminate tariffs and other barriers among them so as to permit the free movement of goods, services, people, and capital; a common market also has a common external tariff against imports from the rest of the world, unlike a FREE-TRADE AREA, which only has free movement of goods and services between the members of the free-trade area, but with each member country maintaining its own tariff and other barriers against the rest of the world. *See also* CUSTOMS UNION, EUROPEAN COMMUNITY.

common shares   Shares that represent an ownership interest in a company and usually, but not always, entitle the owners to vote at company annual and special meetings. Owners of common shares are entitled to receive any dividends declared, but a company has no legal obligation to pay dividends to the owners of common shares. The owners of common shares are entitled to all of the assets of the company after outstanding debts and taxes have been paid. SHAREHOLDERS' EQUITY in a company BALANCE SHEET is the interest of the owners of common shares.

Commonwealth An association of nearly 50 countries, including Canada, that were former colonies in the British Empire, along with Britain itself, and today representing about 25 percent of the world's population. The main role of the Commonwealth is to provide a means for leaders of developed countries such as Canada, Britain, and Australia to meet with leaders of countries in the developing world, such as India, Nigeria, Jamaica, Malaysia, Zimbabwe, Singapore, Bangladesh, and Sri Lanka. Based on a 1971 statement of principles, the members of the Commonwealth co-operate in advancing world peace, social understanding, racial equality, and economic development. The Commonwealth countries work together in international agencies, such as the United Nations Development Program. In addition, finance ministers from the Commonwealth usually meet in advance of the annual meetings of the INTERNATIONAL MONETARY FUND and WORLD BANK. The Commonwealth Fund for Technical Co-operation, established in 1971, provides aid to Commonwealth developing countries. The Commonwealth Secretariat, established in 1965, is located in London, England. *See also* FRANCOPHONIE.

Commonwealth preference *See* BRITISH PREFERENTIAL TARIFF.

Commonwealth Trade and Economic Conference A meeting of Commonwealth nations, chaired by Canada and held in Montreal in September, 1958, to foster "an expanding Commonwealth in an expanding world." Its purpose was to encourage trade and investment among Commonwealth members, to increase the flow of development assistance from the rich Commonwealth nations to poor Commonwealth nations, and to bring about the convertibility of British sterling and other currencies within the Commonwealth. Canada hoped that the conference would lead to a substantial reduction in its trade dependence on the United States by the rapid development of new markets in Britain and other Commonwealth members. Canada also hoped that Britain would reconsider its plans to gain membership in the EUROPEAN COMMUNITY in favour of this reinvigorated Commonwealth. The government of Prime Minister John Diefenbaker opposed British entry into the Community because it feared Canada would lose its preferential access to the British market, with Canada being forced into closer integration with the United States.

Communications Canada, Department of A federal government department established in 1969 to encourage and set policy for telecommunications services in Canada, and to protect Canadian interests in the allocation of airwaves and communications-satellite channels and in the development of international standards. The department funds research and development in telecommunications and operates the Communications Research Centre. The department tries to ensure that Canadians develop their own technologies and industries in the new world of telecommunications and information systems, and that consumers have access to such services at reasonable prices. The department also co-ordinates federal-provincial relations in communications policy and is responsible for the Canadian Workplace Automation Centre. In 1980, the department was also made responsible for Canadian CULTURAL INDUSTRIES, cultural heritage, and support for the arts. It is responsible for the Canada Council, Canadian Broadcasting Corporation, Canadian Film Development Corporation, the National Library of Canada, the National Archives, the National Film Board, the National Gallery, the PUBLIC LEND-ING RIGHT COMMISSION, and Canada's national museums. It also plays a key role in the development of COPYRIGHT policy.

Communism An economic and political system in which all private property, aside from some consumer goods, is abolished, and the state not only owns all the means of production but relies on central planning rather than on market forces to determine the allocation of resources, prices, new investments, and output. Communism traces its modern roots to Karl MARX (1818-1883), who saw it as the final and inevitable stage of social revolution, with the first stage being slavery, and moving from there through feudalism to CAPITALISM, and, with the collapse of capitalism, socialism. Communism would succeed socialism, with the withering away of the state, the elimination of all inequality and social classes, and the creation of a society based on the principle, "from each according to his ability, to each according to his needs." In such a society there would be no limit to the development of human potential. However, the Communist system collapsed during the 1980s, as centrally planned economies proved incapable of delivering an improved standard of living. Starting in Eastern Europe, the public rebelled against both the economic failure of Communism and the lack of political freedom. By the early 1990s, the Soviet Union had collapsed, to be replaced by the Commonwealth of Independent States, and, along with almost all of the former Communist states of Eastern and Central Europe, was moving to a market economy. While eschewing political freedom, China was also moving to a market economy, with Vietnam expected to

follow suit. The holdouts or hard-line Communist states remaining were North Korea and Cuba. By the time of the collapse of Communism, the administration of the Communist states bore little resemblance to the social and economic vision of Marx. *See also* MARXIST ECONOMICS.

company *See* CORPORATION.

company law *See* CORPORATION LAW.

Company of Young Canadians (CYC) A government program established in 1966 to provide innovative forms of employment for the growing number of young Canadians by training them to work with disadvantaged groups at the community level in the hope of providing both useful experience and employment for the young people and improving the quality of life for the community groups they assisted. While the CYC, as it was known, resulted in many positive accomplishments, the political radicalism of some of its young staffers proved highly embarrassing to the government. Its autonomy was curtailed in 1969, and the program wound up in 1976. Despite its problems, the program was viewed as an innovative way of providing jobs and experience for young people at a time when the entry of young people into the workforce exceeded the capacity of the economy to absorb them.

company seal The official seal of a company, which has to be used on certain corporate documents as required by law.

company secretary A company officer responsible for seeing that the company carries out its legal obligations, such as giving shareholders adequate notice of annual and special meetings, making sure that they get proxy documents and other corporate information, making sure that the share register of the company is kept up to date, filing corporate disclosure statements, and keeping proper minutes of meetings of the company's board of directors.

company town   A town in which there is only one significant employer and in which much of the housing and land and even the retail stores may also be owned by the company. Company towns may exist where there are big mining or pulp and paper operations; Ottawa has sometimes been called a company town because so many people who live there work for the federal government or its agencies.

company union   An organization of employees, all of whom work for the same company, that is not affiliated with a union that also represents employees in other firms. Company unions tend to be employee associations; often, they are organized by management as a way of keeping out of national or international unions. They rarely provide for the right to strike or the negotiation of a normal COLLECTIVE AGREEMENT.

comparative advantage   An important principle in international trade based on the assumption that each country is probably more efficient than others in producing some particular good or service, and that each country should concentrate on producing what it can produce most efficiently. Even if two countries can produce the same goods with equal efficiency, it still pays for each to specialize in just some of those goods and import the others, since specialization will lead to greater total production and lower costs for both. A country is said to have a comparative advantage in the goods that it can produce most efficiently. If every country concentrates on those goods in which

it has a comparative advantage, then trade between nations will benefit everyone, with consumers in all countries concerned buying the goods they need at the lowest prices. Each country gets the largest possible market for what it produces more efficiently, and benefits from lower-cost products it can't produce efficiently itself from countries that have a comparative advantage in those products. For example, it makes more sense for Canada to concentrate on growing wheat and raising livestock and to import citrus fruits and winter vegetables than to divert resources from wheat and livestock to produce, under costly hothouse conditions, much more expensive citrus fruits and winter vegetables. The notion of comparative advantage, developed by Adam SMITH, David RICARDO, and John Stuart MILL, is the basis of the FREE TRADE argument. However, the way in which economies create wealth today has changed fundamentally from the days in the 18th and 19th centuries when the theory was developed. In those days, comparative advantage was more likely to be based on some inherited advantage, such as climate or possession of natural resources or arable land. Today, wealth is created through ideas and innovation, so that countries can create a comparative or competitive advantage, rather than being forced to rely on climate, natural resources, or abundant labour. Japan, for example, has no natural resources, but by investing in ideas — through education, skills, research and development, and infrastructure — and by creating institutions to use and commercialize ideas — such as its corporate organization system, known as KEIRETSU, financing systems, and cooperation between the public and private sectors — Japan has created its comparative advantage in industries such as electronics, new materials, and automobiles.

compensatory fiscal policy The use of FISCAL POLICY to offset fluctuations in the BUSINESS CYCLE. In a recession, the government would incur or increase its deficit by cutting taxes or increasing spending or both, to raise the fever of demand in the economy. In a period of inflation caused by excess demand, it would raise taxes or reduce spending or both, in order to reduce the overall level of demand. *See* KEYNESIAN ECONOMICS.

competition A market system in which rival sellers try to gain sales at one another's expense, and, in the process, are forced to be as efficient as possible and to hold their prices down as much as possible. Competition is a sophisticated yet unco-ordinated mechanism that sorts out the actions of millions of buyers and sellers, and uses the resulting pattern of supply and demand to determine what shall be produced, in what quantities, and at what price. ADAM SMITH saw the market as an "invisible hand" that would ensure maximum efficiency and therefore the greatest benefits for consumers, as producers engaged in relentless competition to win the consumer's favour.

Insofar as competition exists, it is an effective way of achieving the efficient allocation of resources and the lowest cost for goods and services. Much of CLASSICAL and NEOCLASSICAL ECONOMICS is based on the notion of PERFECT COMPETITION, in which numerous firms sell identical goods and therefore have to hold down prices. However, the real world of the modern MIXED ECONOMY is one of IMPERFECT COMPETITION, where large firms are able to exercise a significant control over prices and over market share through brand loyalty and product differentiation, and where the BARRIERS TO ENTRY may prevent new firms from entering the industry and competing by selling at lower prices.

Competition laws exist to curb unfair business practices and to prevent mergers and acquisitions that would unduly lessen competition. In cases where a MONOPOLY exists, such as in the provision of electricity or local telephone service, a government regulatory agency may set rates to prevent market abuse. *See also* COMPETITION POLICY, COMPETITION ACT, COMPETITION TRIBUNAL.

Competition Act Federal legislation to promote competition in the Canadian economy, which came into effect in June, 1986, and replaced the COMBINES INVESTIGATION ACT. The act applies to almost all businesses in Canada and deals with both goods and services; it contains both criminal and non-criminal provisions. Criminal offences include conspiracy, bid-rigging, discriminatory and predatory pricing, price maintenance, and misleading advertising or deceptive marketing practices. Non-criminal matters subject to review and directive include mergers, abuse of dominant position, refusal to deal, consignment selling, exclusive dealing, tied selling, market restriction, and delivered pricing. These matters are referred to the COMPETITION TRIBUNAL by the DIRECTOR OF INVESTIGATION AND RESEARCH. When competitive issues arise affecting a regulated industry, the Director of Investigation and Research has the right to appear before any federal board, commission, or other tribunal, and may appear before provincial regulatory agencies if requested. Consumers can also sue to recover losses or damages resulting from anti-competitive behaviour where there has been a violation of the criminal provisions of the act or a failure to comply with a Competition Tribunal order.

Under the criminal provisions, which make up part VI of the act, conspiracy consists of any arrangement to lessen competition unduly, for example, by fixing prices; bid-rigging is defined as an agreement between parties in which one or more bidders will refrain from submitting bids on a contract or will submit bids based on pre-arranged prices; PRICE DISCRIMINATION is said to exist when a supplier charges different prices to competitors who purchase similar volumes of an article and resell in the same market; PREDATORY PRICING occurs when prices are sold at unreasonably low levels or at a lower level in one region of Canada than another, with the aim of lessening competition by eliminating a competitor; PRICE MAINTENANCE is an attempt by suppliers to force retailers to sell at high prices and eschew discounts or price reductions for customers; MISLEADING ADVERTISING consists of the making of false or misleading claims for a product or service, including unsubstantiated performance and durability claims, misleading warranties, and misrepresentations as to regular price; deceptive marketing practices include the misuse of promotional contests, such as failing to disclose the number and approximate value of prizes offered or other facts that affect the chances of winning, double ticketing where the higher of the two prices is charged, pyramid selling, sale above the advertised price, and bait-and-switch selling where a product is advertised at a bargain price but a reasonable supply is not available and customers attracted to a store by the bargain price are pressured to buy a higher-priced item.

Non-criminal reviewable matters, part VII of the act, include mergers — the acquisition of one or more businesses by another business. Companies have to notify the Bureau of Competition Policy when the parties together have total assets or gross annual revenues from sales in, from, or into Canada of over $400 million and value of the assets to be acquired or gross annual revenues from the sales of those assets exceed $35 million; in the case of an amalgamation, the second threshold is $70 million. The Competition Tribunal may prohibit or restructure any proposed merger for up to three years after the completion of the transaction, where the merger prevents or lessens competition substantially. *See* MERGER POLICY. In cases where one or two companies substantially control a type of business in Canada, they can be investigated for abuse of dominant position, for example, if they acquire a customer who would otherwise be available to a competitor, use product brands on a temporary basis to discipline or eliminate a competitor, or sell products at a price lower than the acquisition cost to discipline or eliminate a competitor. Other matters that can be reviewed and are subject to a Competition Tribunal order include refusal to deal, where a supplier will refuse to supply a customer who could provide competition, for example, a dairy refusing to sell milk to an independent ice-cream producer because the dairy also manufactures ice cream; consignment selling, where the supplier attempts to control the final selling price of the product or discriminates between consignees and other dealers; exclusive dealing, where a supplier requires or induces a customer to purchase primarily from him or to refrain from dealing in another product; tied selling, which is the practice of forcing a customer to acquire a second product from a supplier in order to obtain a supply of the first product, for example, a company renting photocopiers requiring that the photocopy paper be purchased from the same company; market restriction, where a supplier requires that a purchaser agree to limit the subsequent sale of the product to a limited geographic area; delivered pricing, where a supplier refuses to deliver an article to a customer on the same terms as other customers in the same area; and specialization agreements, where, for example, two companies each manufacturing the same two products agree to discontinue producing one of them in order to specialize in the other.

Each fiscal year, the Director of Investigation and Research publishes an annual report outlining his activities for the year. The report is available from the Bureau of Competition Policy in the Department of Consumer and Corporate Affairs, which is based in Hull, Quebec.

competition policy   Legislation that protects the consumer against unfair business practices and the exploitation by OLIGOPOLIES and MONOPOLIES, who could use their excessive market power to charge high prices and curb competition. The purpose of competition policy is to improve the efficiency of the market place and to promote COMPETITION. Among the specific practices covered by competition law are collusion among competitors to fix prices, to allocate markets, or to prevent the entry of new firms, or the takeovers of competitors, in order to reduce competition and achieve monopoly power. Other practices covered by competition law are PRICE MAINTENANCE, which prevents lower prices, MISLEADING ADVERTISING, and other restrictive practices. *See also* COMPETITION ACT.

Competition Tribunal   A federal tribunal established in 1986 under the Competition Tribunal Act, replacing the RESTRICTIVE TRADE PRACTICES COMMISSION. The role of the tribunal is to conduct reviews of cases referred to it by the DIRECTOR OF INVESTIGATION AND RESEARCH under the COMPETITION ACT and, where it finds an activity or proposed activity that would lessen competition substantially, to issue an order to cease and desist a practice, modify a practice, or, in the case of a merger, to order the dissolution of a merger or the sale of shares or assets on approval, only if certain conditions are first met. Reviewable matters, set out under part VII of the Competition Act, include, in addition to mergers, abuse of dominant position, refusal to deal, consignment selling, exclusive dealing, tied selling, market restriction, and delivered pricing. The implementation of foreign judgements, laws, and directives that could affect competition adversely in Canada, including refusals by foreign suppliers to supply a product, may also lead to hearings before the tribunal.

The tribunal is a court of record with all the powers of a superior court, including the attendance, swearing in, and examination of witnesses, production of and inspection of documents, and enforcement of its orders. The tribunal consists of up to four judges from the Federal Court of Canada and up to eight lay members, appointed by the cabinet for a fixed term of up to seven years. The cabinet designates a member of the tribunal as its chairman, who is responsible for and supervises the work of the tribunal. The tribunal is an adjudicative body operating independently of government. Unlike the former Restrictive Trade Practices Commission, it has no power to conduct inquiries or investigations of its own. As a rule, a tribunal panel typically has three members, including a judicial member who presides. Orders or decisions of the tribunal can be appealed to the Federal Court of Appeal.

competitiveness   The ability of a company to sell its products or services at a profit or of a country's industry in the aggregate to export goods and services to another country in order to pay for its imports. Competitiveness is usually taken to mean, for an advanced country such as Canada, the ability to sell goods and services to the rest of the world in arm's length transactions to yield both a profit for its enterprises and high wages for its workers.

complementary goods   Products that are not substitutes for one another, but for which demand is linked — if the demand for one rises, the demand for the other will automatically rise; similarly, a decline in the demand for one will result in a decline in demand for the other. This means that an increase in the price of one good will lead to a decline in the demand for the other. Examples include new housing and furniture and appliances, automobiles and snow tires, turkeys and bread used for stuffing.

compliance cost   The cost of complying with government regulations in areas such as the environment, health and safety, or pay equity.

composite demand   The total demand for a particular good or service, originating from a great many different users who may require it for many different purposes. For example, the total demand for steel will come from the automobile, machinery, construction, railway, electric-utility, farm-equipment, household-appliance, pipeline, refinery, ship-building, and many other different industries. *See also* INPUT-OUTPUT ANALYSIS.

compound interest   A rate of interest calculated by adding previous years' interest payments on to the original principal in calculating the current year's interest. For example, on a $100 bond paying 5 percent compound interest for five years, the first year's interest would be 5 percent of $100, or $5. The second year's interest would be 5 percent of $105, or $5.25. The third year's interest would be 5 percent of $110.25, or $5.51, and so forth, through to the fifth year when total interest would amount to $27.63 for the five-year period. If the 5 percent interest had been taken each year, the investor would have

received $25 in interest. Compound interest can produce large increases; for example, a $1,000 bond at 6 percent compound interest and a term of 12 years would pay out $2,012 at the end of 12 years, for total interest of $1,012. If the interest had been collected each year, the investor would have earned $720. *See also* SIMPLE INTEREST.

comptroller   *See* CONTROLLER.

Comptroller General of Canada   An office established by the federal government in 1978 to define policies and standards for internal auditing, program evaluation, and financial management within the federal government. Its job is to ensure that budgeting and financial control are integrated with program and operational controls so that Canadian taxpayers get value for their money. The office plays an important role in developing the financial officers, program evaluators, and internal auditors for the government and in improving the quality of financial management and control. It also monitors the quality of internal auditing in each government department and agency for the TREASURY BOARD.

compulsory arbitration   The intervention by government in a strike or lockout, where the government orders the two sides to abide by the decision of an arbitrator appointed to settle their dispute. Compulsory arbitration is usually used to resolve a strike that is hurting the economy or members of the public, such as a railway or dock-workers' strike, a strike by teachers, or by municipal or hospital workers.

compulsory check-off   *See* RAND FORMULA.

compulsory licensing   A provision in patent law that permitted another party to make, use, or sell a patented product against the wishes of the patent owner in order to prevent abuse, such as charging excessively high prices, that the patent owner could derive from his monopoly position. Canada had, since 1923, a policy that allowed the Commissioner of Patents to grant a compulsory licence for the production of a pharmaceutical product and to set the royalty rate to be paid to the patent owner. In 1969, the PATENT ACT was amended to permit compulsory licences to import pharmaceutical products or active ingredients used in the manufacture of pharmaceuticals and to sell the drug domestically, with a royalty payment for the use of the patent. This led to an increase in the production of patented pharmaceuticals in the form of generic equivalents, in Canada, providing increased price competition in the pharmaceutical industry — as well as the development and growth of Canadian companies producing under compulsory licence, known as the generic drug companies. In 1987, in response to strong pressure from the major international pharmaceutical companies and U.S. and European governments, the Patent Act was amended, tightening the use of compulsory licences. Compulsory licences for new pharmaceutical products could not be exercised for seven to 10 years after the drug had first been approved for sale by Health and Welfare Canada, depending on whether the active ingredients were manufactured in Canada or imported. In the case of new medicines invented and developed in Canada, the period of exclusivity may extend to the entire patent life of the product if the patent owner manufactures the medicine in Canada and completely or substantially supplies the Canadian market. A PATENTED MEDICINE PRICES REVIEW BOARD was also established to ensure that pharmaceutical companies did not take advantage of the weakening of the compulsory licensing system and raise their prices, and to monitor whether the pharmaceutical companies lived up to their promises to raise research and development spending in Canada in exchange for the amendments curbing the use of compulsory licences. In 1992, the federal government proposed further amendments to the Patent Act abolishing compulsory licensing and extending the exclusive patent protection for patented pharmaceuticals to 20 years, from 17 — the same level of patent protection provided for other products. The changes, passed by Parliament in 1993, were expected to have a strongly negative effect on the largely Canadian-owned generic-drug industry.

computer software   Computer programs, frequently designed and developed by independent software firms, to make possible the application of computer systems to a wide range of industrial, administrative, educational, health, and other uses. The software industry is one of the major new industries of the information or POST-INDUSTRIAL SOCIETY.

concentrate   A semiprocessed mineral ore from which almost all of the waste material has been extracted and which is ready for final processing into a refined product. Many of Canada's minerals are exported in this form, with the higher-value final processing and manufacturing use of the mineral being completed in the importing country.

concentration   The extent to which a small number of firms or establishments account for the major proportion of output, assets, employment, and profits in a particular industry. An industry is said to be highly concentrated when a small number of firms account for a significant proportion of output, employment, assets, or profits. The Department of CONSUMER AND CORPORATE AFFAIRS, in a 1971 study, *Concentration in the Manufacturing Industries of Canada,* said, "Where an industry consists of a number of firms such that no single one or single small group can exert a dominant influence on pricing, then the structural basis for a reasonably competitive market mechanism exists. On the other hand, where a small group of firms, such as the largest four or the largest eight in the industry, account for a dominant share of output, then the possibility of serious restrictions on the competitive process must be taken into account." The study found the degree of concentration in Canada to be higher than that in the United States. *See also* MONOPOLY, OLIGOPOLY, PERFECT COMPETITION, IMPERFECT COMPETITION, CONCENTRATION RATIO.

concentration ratio   The percentage of shipments, employment, assets, or profits accounted for by the four largest enterprises within a group of competing firms. Three common measures are used: 1. The inverse index, which shows the number of firms or establishments that account for 80 percent of factory shipments or employment in a particular industry. 2. Industry concentration ratios, which show the percentage of the value of shipments accounted for by the largest 4, 8, 12, 16, 20, and 50 enterprises or establishments in a particular industry. 3. The HERFINDAHL INDEX, which measures the total number of companies in the market and their relative market shares. The Herfindahl index is the sum of the squared company market shares; if the index is 1, then a single company exercises a monopoly; if there are 10 companies of equal size, then the index is 0.1. The closer the index to 1, the greater the concentration; the closer the index to zero, the greater the level of competition.

concentrator   A mineral-processing plant that removes much of the waste material from a mineral ore and produces a CONCENTRATE or semi-processed metal. The concentrate must then be further processed, in a smelter, for example, to produce a fully refined metal.

concession   The granting, usually by a government, of the right to do something — for example, to search for and extract oil, gas, or other minerals, to cut timber, or to construct a railway. In return, the government agency will normally levy a charge or royalty and, in the case of mineral and timber rights, may also impose various conditions, such as a minimum level of exploration spending per year or replacement tree planting.

concessional financing   Loans made to developing countries by industrial countries or international agencies at below-market rates; in many instances these loans are made to countries that would not be considered creditworthy by commercial lenders, such as banks. In addition to obtaining loans at below-market rates, the developing countries also benefit from extended repayment periods that can run from 30 to 50 years and grace periods in the early life of the loan that require no interest payments. These "soft loans" are usually reserved for the poorer developing countries. The WORLD BANK has established a special agency, the INTERNATIONAL DEVELOPMENT ASSOCIATION, to provide concessional financing or "soft loans" to the poorer developing countries. *See also* CANADIAN INTERNATIONAL DEVELOPMENT AGENCY. The Export Development Association provides concessional financing through the CANADA ACCOUNT, which it manages on behalf of the federal government. Concessional financing or "soft loans" are sometimes used to win export contracts for major contracts in the developing world, sometimes through a CREDIT MIXTE, or mixed credit, which is part commercial loan and part concessional financing. Industrial countries are supposed to follow guidelines from the ORGANIZATION FOR ECONOMIC CO-OPERATION AND DEVELOPMENT, which set limits on the use of concessional financing as a competitive tool to win export contracts.

conciliation The use of a third party, usually a federal or provincial labour-department official, to avert a strike or lockout or to end one during COLLECTIVE BARGAINING negotiations. A conciliator attempts to come up with a compromise solution through intensive discussions with both sides in a dispute, but neither side is under any legal obligation to accept a conciliator's recommendations.

conciliation report A further stage in the conciliation process during COLLECTIVE BARGAINING negotiations. It is the recommendation of a conciliation board, consisting of management and union representatives and a government official, for the settlement of a dispute over a new contract. A conciliation officer from a federal or provincial department of labour makes a preliminary effort at conciliation and, depending on progress or lack of progress, recommends to the federal or provincial Minister of Labour that a conciliation board be appointed or not be appointed, depending on whether the officer thinks anything can be accomplished. The minister then decides whether or not to appoint such a board. If the decision is that there should be a further conciliation effort, the formal conciliation board is set up and given the task of hearing the arguments of both sides and trying to resolve their differences. The conciliation report that is produced is not binding on either side and may not be a unanimous report.

Generally speaking, a strike or lockout cannot occur until after a week-long cooling-off period following the presentation of the conciliation-board report, or two weeks after the decision by a federal or provincial labour minister that no conciliation board will be appointed. Failure of a conciliation board to reach a unanimous agreement does not mean that there will be a strike or lockout. The employer and the union may decide to call in a mediator. *See also* MEDIATION

concurrent powers Under the CONSTITUTION ACT, 1867, taxing or spending powers that may be exercised by either the federal or provincial governments, or both. For example, both levels of government can impose DIRECT TAXES, establish pension plans, legislate consumer protection and environmental standards, and implement agricultural development and assistance programs.

condition of entry *See* BARRIERS TO ENTRY.

conditional discharge The freeing of a bankrupt firm, or person, from its liabilities, provided it carries out certain steps specified in the conditional discharge order.

conditional grant The payment of a grant from one level of government to another for a specific purpose, as set out in law. Examples would be payments from the federal government to the provincial governments under the CANADA ASSISTANCE PLAN or other such programs, or payments by provincial governments to municipalities for transit, education, or other specified purposes. The money cannot be used by the receiving level of government for anything other than the purpose specified by the donor level of government. *See also* SHARED-COST PROGRAMS.

conditional sale   A sale that is not completed and transfer of title is not made until agreed-on conditions have been met. For example, the sale of a building may be conditional on the vendor's making certain repairs or alterations or on winding up an existing mortgage on the property, or on the purchaser's being able to arrange a new mortgage.

conditionality   The requirements for economic reform or restructuring set by the INTERNATIONAL MONETARY FUND (IMF) as a condition for obtaining financial help. Typically, the IMF sets out, with the borrowing country, a package of economic reforms, such as measures to reduce the budget deficit, lower inflation, and improve the functioning of markets, which the country then pledges to implement; in return, the IMF provides the financial help necessary to achieve the reforms, while monitoring the adherence of the country to its reform program. In recent years, the IMF has been criticized for the harshness of its adjustment programs forced on developing countries, especially the poorer countries, and today anti-poverty programs are included in adjustment and restructuring policies.

condominium   The ownership of a specific dwelling unit, an apartment or town house, for example, in a multiunit building, along with a share of the ownership of the land and of the common areas of the building, such as the lobby, recreation and service areas, and hallways. The cost of maintenance and repair of the project is shared among all the owners. Individual owners are taxed separately by the municipality. Condominiums are governed by provincial legislation, which requires that each condominium have an administrative structure for the condominium corporation, including a board of directors elected from among the owners. While most condominiums consist of housing units, the same structure can be used for the ownership of office units, factory space, vacation residences, and even land. *See also* CO-OPERATIVE, where owners have shares in the project instead of title to a specific dwelling unit.

Confederation of National Trade Unions (CNTU)   A labour federation based largely in Quebec that grew out of the Canadian Catholic Federation of Labour, established in 1921 with the active encouragement and support of the Roman Catholic Church. In 1960, the labour federation changed its name to the CNTU and eliminated all religious references or connections from its charter of organization. The CNTU exercises significant power over its affiliated unions and has its own strike fund. It strongly favours a social-democratic system and supports the establishment of a separate Quebec. It represents less than 10 percent of Canadian union membership. Its name in French is Confédération des syndicats nationaux, or CSN.

Conference Board of Canada   A private non-profit research organization, which is funded by business, government, and labour. It studies management policies and practices, public-policy issues, the economic environment, and international business. It has an economic-research group that publishes quarterly reports on the national and provincial economic outlook, along with two quarterly surveys, one on business confidence and investment-spending intentions, and the other on consumer confidence and spending intentions. Its compensation-research centre conducts research into pay scales, industrial relations, and fringe benefits. It has a market-research division, which studies market-research applications, and a public-affairs division, which publishes reports on such issues as the responsibilities of corporate directors. Its National Business and Education Centre helps business and education leaders work together to improve Canada's educational system, and it provides National Awards for Excellence to recognize business-education partnerships. It also conducts extensive research on employer training in Canada. The board was established in the United States in 1916. In 1954, a Canadian office was established in Montreal as a division of the U.S. organization. The institute became more of a Canadian organization after 1970, when its headquarters were moved to Ottawa. In 1981, it acquired a separate legal identity in Canada.

conference of first ministers A meeting of the prime minister and the 10 provincial premiers. The conferences have become annual events and are held for usually three purposes: 1. To deal with constitutional reform. 2. To discuss economic policies. 3. To work out agreements on SHARED-COST PROGRAMS and changes in fiscal arrangements. A small secretariat exists in Ottawa to provide various ongoing services for such conferences. The first conference was held in 1906, but they did not become annual events until the late 1960s. *See also* FEDERAL-PROVINCIAL CONFERENCE, PREMIERS' CONFERENCE, FEDERAL PROVINCIAL RELATIONS OFFICE.

conference of ministers of finance and provincial treasurers Regular meetings of the federal and provincial ministers and their senior advisers, which have been taking place at least once a year since 1964 to discuss economic and fiscal policies and to co-ordinate fiscal policies in the preparation of annual budgets. The ministers also meet to discuss tax-sharing and changes in fiscal arrangements, special economic problems such as inflation,

and co-ordination of such matters as foreign borrowing. The federal Minister of FINANCE chairs the meetings.

Conference on International Economic Co-operation (CIEC) A conference, co-chaired by Canada and Venezuela, held to negotiate agreement on a NEW INTERNATIONAL ECONOMIC ORDER; the conference was made up of eight developed countries, seven members of the ORGANIZATION OF PETROLEUM EXPORTING COUNTRIES (OPEC), and 12 LESS-DEVELOPED COUNTRIES. The conference first met in Paris in December, 1975, to deal with the work of four commissions that had been established beforehand to deal with energy, raw materials and commodity agreements, foreign aid, and the problem of foreign debts. Canada was a member of the commissions dealing with energy and foreign aid. During 1976, the four commissions attempted to work out specific recommendations, but the subsequent ministerial conference in Paris at the end of the year failed to reach agreement on major issues. The less-developed countries wanted relief from the burden of their foreign debts and a new system of pricing raw materials; the developed countries wanted OPEC members to agree to restrain energy-price increases. The conference was terminated in June, 1977, without much progress. Since then, agreement has been reached on a COMMON FUND for certain commodities that are important to the less-developed countries.

confidence factor The level of optimism or pessimism among consumers, businesspeople, and investors. While difficult to measure, the outlook of consumers, businesspeople, and investors has an important effect on their decisions concerning whether or not to spend or invest. Consumers will postpone purchases of homes or major consumer products if they think that economic conditions will worsen, for example. Similarly, businesspeople will delay hiring workers or expanding their production capacity if the economic outlook is uncertain. The CONFERENCE BOARD OF CANADA publishes quarterly consumer- and business-confidence surveys.

confirmation A printed statement from a stockbroker or investment dealer to a customer setting out the details of the purchase or sale of a security. The confirmation is usually mailed out at the time that the sale or purchase is executed.

conflict of interest The situation that can arise when a person in a position of trust offers advice or acts in a way that benefits himself or herself rather than the person on whose behalf he or she is supposed to be acting. Examples of conflict of interest include a stockbroker advising a client to buy shares in a company from which his or her own firm is making a fee as an underwriter, a company awarding a contract to another company because the owner of the winning company is related to the president of the awarding company, or an officer or director of a financial institution making a loan to a company in which he or she has a financial interest. The stockbroker is supposed to act on behalf of the client and not his or her employer; the company president is supposed to act in the best interests of the company, not relatives; and the officer or director of a financial institution is supposed to act on behalf of depositors and shareholders, not himself or herself. *See also* SELF-DEALING. Provincial securities legislation imposes penalties on INSIDERS in publicly traded companies to prevent them from using corporate information not available to other shareholders to make a profit or avoid a loss.

conglomerate A corporation that grows by acquiring control of various companies in unrelated industries. The purpose is not to increase VERTICAL or HORIZONTAL INTEGRATION but to exercise control over a large number of diversified companies by becoming the largest but not the sole shareholder in each of the underlying companies. A conglomerate company can exercise a great deal of control through LEVERAGE; for example, Conglomerate ABC may own 51 percent of company D, which in turn is the largest shareholder of company E, which in turn is the largest shareholder in company F. This means the conglomerate is the principal shareholder voice in companies D, E, and F. Such acquisitions are usually financed in part by cash and in part by an exchange of shares, or by issuing new preferred or convertible shares. A conglomerate with a rapid acquisition record can show significant gains in earnings from year to year. However, some investors, influenced by the experience of the 1980s, have cooled on conglomerates, because too high a price may be paid for acquisitions, the acquisitions may not have been carefully checked out, or the conglomerate itself may have built up a large debt obligation that depends on steadily rising earnings for repayment and maintenance of dividends. If the economy moves into recession, the conglomerate may find itself faced with inadequate revenues to service its debt or, alternatively, it may force the underlying companies to continue paying dividends even when these are not justified by earnings, to the detriment of other shareholders in these companies. There are also benefits to diversification: it may represent the best way of investing excess funds, and such diversification may also be necessary to maintain the life of the firm.

Conseil du Patronat A federation of more than 130 employer associations in

Quebec; it also has some 435 corporations as members. Its principal role is to represent the views of private industry to the Quebec government, unions, and the public. It has a mandate as well to work with Quebec unions and government to resolve problems facing Quebec. It provides information and analysis on the economy, government actions, and proposed legislation in Quebec. It is also active in the field of industrial relations, although it does not itself intervene in COLLECTIVE BARGAINING. The conseil was established in 1969 and is based in Montreal.

conservation   The careful use of renewable and non-renewable natural resources to ensure their greatest long-term benefit to society and to prevent them from being wasted or damaged through environmental carelessness. Conservation of renewable resources includes sustained-yield policies to limit the catch of species of fish or species of wildlife as well as reforestation programs to replace harvested trees, along with measures to protect the fertility of the soil, and laws to prevent the pollution of air and water. Conservation of non-renewable resources includes policies to prevent the waste of these resources by pricing them to reflect their real value, the use of technology to find more efficient uses or substitutes, the recycling of materials and direct limits on production or end-use.

conserver society   A term originating with the SCIENCE COUNCIL OF CANADA to describe an economic system that puts less emphasis on increases in per capita consumption of resources and greater emphasis on the careful use of resources and technology. The conserver society, an early version of SUSTAINABLE DEVELOPMENT, assumes that the supply of natural resources is limited and that more attention should be paid to the needs of future generations.

It also assumes that the process of industrialization often leads to unanticipated results, such as pollution, so that growth is not an unmixed blessing, and that, too often, man seems to be an afterthought to technology, rather than the master of technology. The conserver society does not mean a no-growth society; it anticipates new industries and new technologies, but with more emphasis on product durability and efficiency. It puts emphasis on a much more careful use of energy and other resources, and on stronger efforts to anticipate and reduce waste and pollution. It emphasizes economy in design, doing more with less, and favours greater efforts at recycling. In a conserver society, the pricing mechanism would reflect not only the private production costs of a product but also, as far as possible, the total cost to society, such as the ecological and social impact, so the market system would allocate resources more efficiently. The Science Council first used the term in 1973, and spelled out the concept of a conserver society in detail in a 1977 report entitled *Canada as a Conserver Society*. The conserver society, the Science Council said, was based on concern for the future; economy of design; diversity, flexibility, and responsibility; recognition of total costs; and respect for the biosphere.

consignment   The shipment of goods to another person or firm who acts as the seller; until the goods are sold, the shipper remains the owner of the goods. For example, a manufacturer in Winnipeg, who sends goods on consignment to an agent in Toronto to sell to other firms or individuals, retains ownership of the unsold goods and pays the agent a fee or commission on the goods that have been sold. The seller or agent can return unsold goods to the manufacturer.

consignment selling   1. A reviewable practice by the COMPETITION TRI-

BUNAL under the COMPETITION ACT if a supplier attempts to control the price at which a dealer sells the product or attempts to discriminate between consignees or other dealers. **2.** A system of distribution in which stores take delivery of merchandise for sale, but with the right to return unsold merchandise to the manufacturer or wholesaler.

consolidated financial statement A financial statement, such as a company annual report, that presents the financial reports of a parent company and of its subsidiaries together. If the parent company has only a part interest in one of the subsidiaries, say 60 percent, then the financial statements are adjusted to reflect this; 40 percent of the earnings would be deducted for this subsidiary and allocated to minority interests.

consolidated revenue fund The general pool of all revenues of the federal government, such as tax, tariff, and licence-fee income, and profits from crown corporations. All money received by the federal government must be credited to this fund and be properly accounted for. THE RECEIVER-GENERAL OF CANADA, normally the Minister of SUPPLY AND SERVICES, is the official recipient. The money does not actually sit in one big fund: it is divided among the chartered banks and their branches across Canada, or is on deposit to the receiver-general at the BANK OF CANADA. Not only does the TREASURY BOARD strictly control the deposit of all government income, but also, none of the money can be spent unless there is a specific law passed by Parliament authorizing uses for the money. APPROPRIATION ACTS, for example, must be passed by Parliament each year authorizing the payment of civil-service salaries and other administrative costs. Other spending, such as interest on the public debt or old-age pensions, is authorized by individual acts of Parlia-

ment. Each provincial and municipal government has a similar fund.

consolidation The merger of two or more existing companies into an entirely new company, as opposed to a takeover or merger, where one of the firms becomes a subsidiary of another, or is absorbed into the other.

consortium A group of independent companies that have joined together to undertake a specific project. The COMPETITION ACT imposes restraints on the role of consortiums in domestic projects so that their activities do not lessen competition, but permits groups of companies to join together for export sales. There are different types of consortiums. One example is that of a group of companies in related industries banding together to bid on a domestic or export sale of, say, a nuclear reactor, an airport, or a transit system. Since the prospective customer wants to deal with one supplier and to have firm total-price bids, it makes more sense for a company, bidding to build an airport for example, to create a consortium of suppliers, engineers, architects, and so forth so that a complete bid can be made. Another kind of consortium is that of a group of companies in the same industry joining together for a common purpose, such as lumber companies joining together to promote sales in another country and sharing the promotion costs; a group of companies forming a research-and-development consortium to undertake pre-competitive research and development in some specific area; or a group of companies joining together to build a project that is too large for any one on them to undertake, such as a tar-sands oil plant or a pipeline.

conspicuous consumption The purchase of goods and services to impress other people rather than from any intrinsic use of the good or service itself; the pleasure of the purchase comes from its perceived impact on others. The American economist and social thinker Thorstein Veblen explored the psychological dimensions of consumer spending in his book, *The Theory of the Leisure Class* (1899). He argued that all income groups spend at least part of their income for conspicuous consumption, or the need to impress others, and identified such spending by its contribution to the "comfort" or "fullness" of life.

conspiracy   An agreement or arrangement to reduce competition unduly by fixing prices, thereby preventing new competitors from entering the market, or in any other way limiting competition. Conspiracy has been a criminal offence in Canada since 1889, and penalties under the COMPETITION ACT include a fine of up to $10 million or up to five years in prison, or both. There is no necessity to show the existence of direct communication between companies to prove that there is a conspiracy: evidence can be inferred from behaviour. However, it is necessary to prove that the parties intended to and did enter into an agreement, though it is not necessary to prove that the intent of the conspiracy was to lessen competition unduly or to show that the conspiracy, if implemented, would eliminate all competition in the market. Agreements between companies to export products are generally exempt from the Competition Act.

constant costs   Unit costs that remain unchanged in spite of increases in total output if the price of all the variable inputs remain unchanged; there are no gains from ECONOMIES OF SCALE. Examples include custom-made jewellery or handmade clothes, which require the time and skills of highly specialized workers.

constant dollars   A statistical term designed to show physical changes in output, income, profits, or sales by adjusting dollar values for a year, or a series of years, for inflation. By eliminating changes due to inflation, meaningful comparisons of economic performance can be made for different periods of time. For example, the GROSS DOMESTIC PRODUCT (GDP) for 1993 can be expressed either in current 1993 dollars or in constant dollars with, say, 1986 as the base year. The constant-dollar figure will deduct all the inflation of the period from 1986 to 1993 and show the 1993 GDP in terms of 1986 purchasing power, allowing a direct comparison of real economic performance and showing the real changes taking place in output, income, and other economic statistics. The expression of economic data in constant dollars is especially useful in times of high inflation; it shows the real changes that have occurred, as opposed to the changes that simply reflect inflation.

constitutional law   The body of law that deals with the respective powers of each level of government and their agencies or with the powers of the state to legislate or regulate private behaviour or activities. This body of law interprets the CONSTITUTION ACT, 1867 and the CONSTITUTION ACT, 1982, including the CANADIAN CHARTER OF RIGHTS AND FREEDOMS, along with a large number of other conventions, laws, agreements, and COMMON LAW precedents that collectively make up the Canadian constitution. These include the British Bill of Rights of 1689, the Act of Settlement of 1701, the past decisions of the Judicial Committee of the Privy Council and the Supreme Court of Canada, and various federal and provincial laws relating to the constitution. The central issues include the respective SPENDING and TAXING POWERS of each level of government, and jurisdictional questions. The courts have had to adjudicate important cases clarifying the respective powers of the federal and provincial governments. For example, in 1937, the courts affirmed that Canada could sign treaties with other countries but that a treaty could not force a change in the law of a province where provincial jurisdiction existed; the provinces alone could change their own laws. In a 1976 case, the Supreme Court of Canada ruled that rapidly rising inflation was a valid reason for the federal government to unilaterally impose its ANTI-INFLATION BOARD controls under section 91 of the Constitution Act, 1867, which allows the federal government to make laws for the "peace, order, and good government" of Canada. A number of provinces argued that controls fell under section 92, which allocates to them control over "property and civil rights." In 1990, the Supreme Court ruled that the CANADIAN RADIO-TELEVISION AND TELECOMMUNICATIONS COMMISSION had the jurisdiction to regulate telephone companies that had been regulated by provincial agencies.

constrained-share company A Canadian company that has restrictions or constraints on the number of its shares that can be sold to non-Canadians or non-residents. Bank, trust-company, broadcasting, telephone, and insurance-company shares are examples. Any company can impose restrictions on the sale of its shares to non-residents through its charter of incorporation or through company by-laws.

Constitution Act, 1867 Formerly the BRITISH NORTH AMERICA ACT of 1867, this is the legislation setting out the basic constitution of Canada and, in particular, the federal system of government and the distribution of federal and provincial government powers.

Section 91 sets out the federal powers. The federal government was given exclusive jurisdiction over: the postal service, defence, navigation, shipping, money and banking, census and statistics, criminal law, and a number of other areas. The federal government was also given the power to raise money "by any mode or system of taxation." And in addition it was given a general authority to legislate for the "peace, order, and good government of Canada." Section 92 sets out the corresponding provincial powers. The provincial governments were given responsibility for the management and sale of public lands and the forests on them, which the provinces subsequently argued also meant the natural resources found on those lands; the establishment of hospitals, municipalities, and local works; and property and civil rights. Provinces were restricted to direct taxation within the province. Section 93 spelled out provincial powers in the field of education and section 94 gave both the federal and provincial governments powers in the fields of agriculture and immigration. Subsequently, the provinces turned over some areas of jurisdiction to the federal government, such as unemployment insurance in 1940 and old-age pensions in 1952.

Constitution Act, 1982 Legislation approved by the federal Parliament and all the provinces except for Quebec giving Canadians the power to amend their own constitution, creating a CANADIAN CHARTER OF RIGHTS AND FREEDOMS, setting out an amending formula, giving constitutional recognition to regional development and equalization payments as Canadian commitments, promising future negotiations with Canada's aboriginal peoples, renaming the BRITISH NORTH AMERICA ACT the CONSTITUTION ACT, 1867, and amending provincial powers over non-renewable natural resources and forestry resources in that legislation. Under the amending formula, most amendments would require the approval of the federal Parliament and of at least two-thirds of the provinces having at least 50 percent of Canada's population; in some instances, such as amendments affecting the Crown, the right of each province to have at least the same number of members of Parliament as it had senators in 1982, the use of the English or French language, or the composition of the SUPREME COURT OF CANADA, unanimity is required. The federal and provincial governments commit themselves to promoting "equal opportunities" for the well-being of all Canadians, to "furthering economic development to reduce disparity in opportunities," and to "providing essential public services of reasonable quality to all Canadians." The federal and provincial governments also commit themselves to "the principle of making equalization payments to ensure that provincial governments have sufficient revenues to provide reasonably comparable levels of public services at reasonably comparable levels of taxation." In amendments to section 92 of the Constitution Act, 1867, the power of the provinces with respect to non-renewable natural resources and forestry resources was expanded. Provinces were given exclusive jurisdiction in exploration, development, conservation, and management of these resources, including primary production and the development, conservation, and management of electric power; in the export of these resources and electricity to the other provinces, provided there is no price discrimination or discrimination in shipments; and to impose any system of taxation on these resources and electricity production. *See also* MEECH LAKE AGREEMENT, CHARLOTTETOWN ACCORD.

consumer The ultimate user of all goods and services. The GROSS DOMESTIC PRODUCT, for example, measures national output as it reaches final consumers, and does not count intermediate and semifinished goods. According to CLASSICAL ECONOMIC theory, consumers are sovereign in the economy because they decide, through their purchases and the prices they are willing to pay, what goods and services shall be produced. *See also* CONSUMER SOVEREIGNTY.

Consumer and Corporate Affairs, Department of The federal government department charged with protecting consumers against unfair business practices and promoting economic efficiency through competition, thus working to ensure the market system functions to the benefit of the consumer. Set up in 1967, the department enforces laws dealing with consumer packaging, labelling, product safety, misleading advertising, weights and measures, and standards of performance for consumer products, including warranties. It deals with PATENTS, COPYRIGHT, TRADEMARKS, and industrial design, along with BANKRUPTCY. It enforces the COMPETITION ACT and deals with mergers, takeovers, monopolies, and restraint of trade. It also administers federal business laws governing the incorporation and governance of business firms under the Canada Business Corporations Act. The department is divided into three key divisions: the BUREAU OF CONSUMER AFFAIRS, the BUREAU OF CORPORATE AFFAIRS, and the BUREAU OF COMPETITION POLICY.

consumer boycott A decision by consumers, often the result of organized efforts by consumer or other interest groups, to refrain from purchasing a product or service because of a price increase, poor environmental practices, or unfair labour practices, for example.

consumer credit Credit available to consumers in the form of cash loans, lines of credit, installment buying, or credit cards, to purchase consumer goods and services. Changes in the level of consumer credit are published quarterly by Statistics Canada in its FINANCIAL FLOW ACCOUNTS (publication 13-014). The statistics include department-store credit, credit-card credit, personal loans, and installment purchases. The stock of outstanding consumer credit is published by the BANK OF CANADA. The main sources of consumer credit are banks, finance companies, trust companies, credit unions, caisses populaires, acceptance companies, and department stores. Changes in the volume of outstanding consumer credit can be an indicator of consumer confidence and therefore broader economic trends. If credit balances are rising, that may be a sign that consumers are optimistic about the economy and their jobs and therefore their ability to repay their increased debt; conversely, if balances decline, this may be a sign consumers are getting worried about their jobs or the cost of living, and want to reduce their existing debts and build up their savings.

consumer demand The total volume of consumer purchases of goods and services. Consumer demand typically represents close to 60 percent of total spending in the economy. Statistics Canada measures consumer demand quarterly and annually in its NATIONAL INCOME AND EXPENDITURE ACCOUNTS (publication 13-001). Consumer spending is divided into durable goods such as motor vehicles and furniture and appliances; semidurable goods such as clothing and footwear; non-durable goods such as food and beverages, gasoline and energy; and services, including restaurant and hotel spending, foreign travel, and paid and IMPUTED RENT. Normally, rent should be excluded and when it is, consumer demand is closer to 50 percent of total spending in the economy. While consumer demand for necessities shows little fluctuation, consumer demand for durable goods such as cars, appliances, and furniture is sensitive to economic conditions and interest rates. The fluctuation in demand for consumer durables has an important impact on the overall level of economic activity. For example, a decline in consumer demand for durables not only affects employment and production in auto, appliance, and furniture companies, but also affects many ancillary industries, such as steel, plastics, rubber, aluminum, copper, nickel, and forest products. Likewise, an upsurge in consumer demand can have a dramatic effect on employment and investment, as industries expand to meet the growth in consumer purchases. One of the most direct ways to stimulate economic activity during periods of economic sluggishness is to cut personal income taxes, and thus boost the purchasing power of consumers. The increased consumer spending should result in more jobs and investment, which also increases government tax revenues and reduces government spending on social assistance and unemployment insurance. Similarly, in periods of excess demand and rising inflation, a tax increase can cool off consumer spending and thus slow down the economy.

consumer good A good that is produced to satisfy the need of a person, as opposed to a CAPITAL GOOD, which is used to further the production and distribution of other goods or services. A washing machine purchased by an individual is a consumer good; if purchased by a hotel, it is a capital good. Consumer goods consist of durables, such as automobiles, appliances, or furniture, which have a fairly long life; semidurables, such as clothing, which have a relatively short life; and non-durables, such as food and soap, which are consumed almost as soon as they are purchased.

consumer law Law that is designed to protect consumers against dangerous products, or deceptive or fraudulent business practices. Federal laws, for example, protect consumers against misleading advertising, false packaging and labelling, dangerous foods and drugs, hazardous products, and various forms of price manipulation. Provincial laws provide protection against unfair contracts, regulate door-to-door sales-people, and permit municipalities to inspect restaurants and other facilities for health infractions, to control taxi-cab rates, to license many forms of commercial activity, and to implement other measures to protect consumers. Some of the earliest examples of con-sumer law, dating back to the 19th century, include the Interest Act, to protect consumers against usury, and the Food and Drug Act, to protect con-sumers against unsafe products. Today, consumer protection laws include — in addition to the Food and Drug Act — the Hazardous Products Act, the Motor Vehicle Safety Act, the Weights and Measures Act, the Bills of Exchange Act, the Consumer Packaging and Labelling Act, and parts of the Bank Act. *See* COMPETITION ACT, BUREAU OF CONSUMER AFFAIRS.

consumer price index (CPI) A monthly measure of changes in the retail prices of goods and services pur-chased by Canadians living in 82 com-munities, in all parts of the country, with a population of 30,000 people or more; price indexes are available for the 18 largest communities and the 10 provinces. The index is based on the shopping basket of about 300 goods and services that families of from two to six people, with annual incomes of $38,925 would normally have bought in 1986.

The basket is revised periodically to reflect changes in the buying habits of Canadians. It is a weighted index, which attributes greater importance to price changes for food and housing, for exam-ple, than to price changes for bus tickets and movie-theatre admissions. The CPI uses a base year, for example, 1986 = 100. In its basket of goods and services, Statistics Canada gives food a 17.59 per-cent weight, housing a 36.67 percent weight, clothing an 8.72 percent weight, transportation a 17.87 percent weight, personal and health care a 4.21 percent weight, recreation, reading, and educa-tion a 9.04 percent weight, and tobacco and alcohol a 5.91 percent weight. Each of these general categories is, in turn, broken down into subcategories. A sea-sonally adjusted, monthly consumer price index is also produced, showing underlying inflation trends. Economists sometimes use a three-month rolling average rate, reflecting the inflation per-formance of the most recent three months, to get a clearer picture of infla-tion trends. Others look at what is called the core rate of inflation, which is every-thing in the consumer price index except for its two most volatile ele-ments: food and energy. Statistics Cana-da also publishes price indexes that exclude indirect taxes and subsidies and give a clearer measure of market changes; these are published as the Net Price Indices and are included in the monthly *Consumer Price Index* publica-tion. It is the CPI that is used in COST-OF-LIVING ALLOWANCE (COLA) CLAUSES and in INDEXATION of the income-tax system, and in social bene-fits such as the old-age pension. The monthly measure is published by Statis-tics Canada (publication 62-001).

consumer sovereignty The free-mar-ket assumption that it is the consumer who, through his or her power to choose how to spend his or her money, determines what shall be produced and in what quantity. The price a consumer is willing to pay and the changes in his or her tastes are said to make the consumer the dominant player in the economy, with producers simply responding to what consumers demand in a competitive market. If a price is too high, the consumer will signal the economic system that he or she is unwilling to pay, and either prices will decline or production will decline. Similarly, if consumers no longer derive satisfaction from a particular product, they will stop buying it and the producer may go out of business. While consumers undoubtedly can exercise enormous power in the economic system, economists also note that there are other forces shaping economic output, such as the exercise of monopoly power, the use of advertising to shape consumer wants and tastes, and the absence of full product and price information. *See also* POST-KEYNESIAN ECONOMICS.

consumer surplus The difference between the total satisfaction a consumer obtains from a good or service (and hence, the maximum price the consumer would be willing to pay) and the actual price the consumer has to pay. Alfred MARSHALL developed the concept; it assumes that consumers generally would be willing to pay more for many goods and services than they actually pay, the difference being the consumer surplus. Hence, the total utility of a good or service for a consumer is the price he or she pays plus the consumer surplus.

Consumers' Association of Canada (CAC) A voluntary organization formed in 1947 as the Canadian Association of Consumers by women who had served in the women's section of the WARTIME PRICES AND TRADE BOARD; its name was changed in 1961 to the Consumers' Association of Canada. The national association and its provincial counterparts are financed largely by government and act as a voice for consumers, making representations to government, industry, producers, and retailers. CAC campaigns for improvements in consumer-protection laws and consumer interests before regulatory boards and in standards-setting organizations, marketing agencies, and other advisory and consultative bodies. It researches and tests consumer goods and services and publishes the magazines *Canadian Consumer* and *le consommateur canadien*. Its headquarters are in Ottawa.

consumption Spending by consumers, individually or in the aggregate, on goods and services to meet current needs. Consumption consists of private spending on goods and services such as food, furniture, and clothing, and public spending on such services as health, education, and welfare. Spending on investment goods and services, such as factories, machinery, engineering, and geological services, is not usually included. Roughly 80 percent of the gross domestic product (GDP) is spent on consumption, depending on the stage of the business cycle in any particular year and the bunching of major investment projects. The remaining portion of GDP is spent on capital investment. A good argument can be made that part of the spending that is treated as consumption, such as spending on education or on consumer durables such as dishwashers and cars, has an important element of investment, since the spending is expected to yield future benefits and not just meet current needs.

consumption function The relationship between CONSUMPTION spending and the variables that influence consumption such as PERSONAL DISPOSABLE INCOME and SAVINGS.

consumption tax A sales tax that is applied to the goods and services that people buy. In recent years, there has been a shift away from a progressive income tax system, based on ability to pay, to consumption or sales taxes that are more regressive in that the same rate of tax applies regardless of the income of the purchaser. *See* GOODS AND SERVICES TAX.

contestability The ability to enter or leave a market with ease, which means there are no BARRIERS TO ENTRY.

continental shelf The offshore area, under water, marking the transition from the continent to the sharp drop to the ocean depths; it is believed to be rich in minerals and oil and natural-gas reserves. Along the Nova Scotia coast, it varies from 60 to 100 nautical miles from shore, and from Newfoundland it varies from 100 to 280 nautical miles, before dropping to between 183 and 366 metres at the outer edge. On the Pacific coast, it extends 50 to 100 nautical miles from shore, and drops to 366 metres below the water surface at its outer edge. In the Arctic, it ranges through most of the region, with the Arctic islands perched on top. It extends past Greenland on the east and 50 to 300 nautical miles west from the outermost Arctic islands.

continentalist A political term sometimes used to describe those who advocate the closer integration of the Canadian and U.S. economies through free trade, energy-sharing, or other such policies that constrain or eliminate Canadian safeguards for cultural identity, Canadian ownership, or other levers of Canadian-based decision-making. *See also* NATIONALIST.

contingency fund Money set aside in a corporation or other organization to meet an unforeseen expenditure.

contingency protection *See* TRADE-REMEDY LAWS.

continuous disclosure The requirement that a publicly traded company report any material change that is likely to have a significant impact on the company, and therefore its stock-market value, within 10 days of the event. Examples could include the firing of the CHIEF EXECUTIVE OFFICER, the loss of a major contract, or the discovery of internal fraud or other developments that would require a restatement of past earnings.

contract An agreement between two or more parties to do something or not to do something, usually in exchange for money or some other consideration, which is enforceable under law. If one of the parties fails to live up to his or her obligations under a contract, he or she can be sued by the other party or parties. Usually a contract is in writing, but it does not have to be. For example, a sale of a good in which money changes hands, and hence a transaction takes place, is a contract in which the seller is assumed to have supplied a good or service that is what it was represented to be and that can do what the seller claimed it would. A contract made under duress or undue influence, or made as a result of misrepresentation, can be overturned by the courts.

contract law The body of law that defines contracts and sets out the conditions under which contracts must be made if they are to be legally binding. For example, a contract must be entered into freely, must be made by parties legally competent to enter into contracts, and must not be made as a result of misrepresentation or force. Contracts must also have a purpose and represent an exchange of obligations between the parties. When one of the parties to a contract fails to live up to his or her obligations, the other party can go to court to obtain an order requiring him or her to live up to his or her obligations.

contract proposals   Proposals made by an employer or a union for a new COLLECTIVE AGREEMENT during COLLECTIVE BARGAINING. Such proposals are the subject of negotiation between representatives of the employer and the union.

contracting out   The practice of hiring another company to perform a function previously carried out internally by a corporation, government, or other agency's own staff. The main purpose of contracting out is to lower costs, but contracting out is sometimes done because an organization may find it lacks the skills it needs to perform a function, such as managing a computer system.

contraction   A stage in the BUSINESS CYCLE; it is the decline in economic activity that occurs after the peak in the cycle has been reached and before the trough of the recession has been reached.

contractual link   *See* FRAMEWORK AGREEMENT FOR COMMERCIAL AND ECONOMIC CO-OPERATION.

contributed surplus   That part of the SHAREHOLDERS' EQUITY in a firm that results from the firm's being able to sell new shares for more than PAR VALUE or, if NO PAR VALUE, their stated price at the time they were offered to the public. The difference between the par value or stated price and the price obtained is the contributed surplus. Thus, if a company issues 100,000 new shares at $10 a share and is able to sell them at $12 a share, the extra $2 a share, or $200,000 in total, is listed as contributed surplus on the company's books.

contributory pension plan   A pension plan where costs are shared, usually equally, by the employees and the employer, with weekly premium deduc-tions being made from the pay cheques of employees. Under Canadian pension laws, an employee loses the share paid by the employer if he or she changes jobs before completing at least two years of consecutive employment. *See* VESTING.

controller   An executive within a corporation or other organization who is responsible for designing the system of financial controls and financial reporting, and for seeing that these systems are carried out properly. The controller is usually an accountant. A controller's functions should not be confused with those of the treasurer or the vice-president of finance of an organization, who are responsible for financial planning, budgeting, management of the organization's cash, arranging bank and other credit, and generally determining profit and other targets.

controlling interest   The block of shares in a company that is sufficient to allow the holder to appoint the management and choose the directors. In a widely held company, a shareholder may need only 10 percent of the shares to have a dominant voice in the company. Usually, however, 51 percent of the voting shares are needed to ensure control.

conventional areas   Those parts of Canada that have a long history of oil or natural-gas production: essentially, Alberta, Saskatchewan, and British Columbia.

conventional mortgage   A mortgage on a home that has been obtained from a financial institution or other investor without being insured under the NATIONAL HOUSING ACT or other government program.

conventional recovery   The production of crude oil from oil reservoirs through traditional recovery techniques, including water-flooding and infill drilling.

conventional reserves   Oil or natural-gas reserves that can be exploited with normal recovery technologies.

conversion loan of 1958   A major refinancing of government bonds in 1958. Holders of wartime Victory Loan Bonds of $6.4 billion that were to mature between 1959 and 1966 were offered a conversion-loan issue maturing in 1961 at 3 percent, in 1965 at 3.75 percent, in 1971 at 4.5 percent, and in 1983 at 4.5 percent. Victory Loan Bonds totalling $5.8 billion, or about 90 percent of the outstanding bonds, were turned in for the new bonds. At the time, it was a major government financing exercise, since it equalled roughly half of the federal government's marketable debt. It had unforeseen results, however, since it decreased the liquidity of the Canadian financial markets and forced many borrowers, such as the provinces and corporations, to turn to the U.S. market. This, in turn, put upward pressure on the Canadian dollar and hurt Canadian efforts to recover from a recession.

convertibility   The ability to convert one currency into another with few, if any, restrictions. The Canadian dollar is freely convertible into other major currencies. However, some countries maintain foreign-exchange controls and restrict the convertibility of their currency to essential purposes, such as the financing of necessary imports. During the Second World War, Canada imposed strict controls on the convertibility of the Canadian dollar.

convertible   A corporate BOND, DEBENTURE, or PREFERRED SHARE that can be exchanged for a stated number of common shares in the same corporation, usually at the option of the purchaser of the security. In some

instances, a company can force conversion. Convertible bonds and preferred shares are a device to attract investors during periods of inflation. Investors who fear that future inflation will reduce the value of their securities may be reassured by knowing that they can exchange them for common shares, which are more likely to keep up with inflation; they also have appeal because they allow investors to capture some of the gains if a company's shares increase significantly in value. The convertibility feature may also allow corporations to raise money at somewhat lower interest rates.

conveyance   The transfer of the title of ownership from the seller of land or buildings to the purchaser, and the registration of this transfer in a registry office.

cooling-off period   **1.** In collective bargaining, the period of time after CONCILIATION before a strike or lockout can legally take place — usually one to two weeks. **2.** In consumer-protection law, the period of time a consumer has to change his or her mind after signing a contract with a door-to-door or similar salesperson.

co-operative   A business organized for the mutual benefit of all its members. They own the enterprise, use its services, run it, and share in its profits or surplus at the end of the financial year. Co-operatives are common in many parts of Canada and include credit unions, caisses populaires, housing projects, farm-marketing organizations, and stores selling consumer goods. Co-operatives were widely used by farmers in the late 19th century to develop the dairy industry and to establish mutual insurance companies to provide lower-cost insurance. In the early 20th century, western grain farmers organized co-operatives to own and operate grain elevators and wheat pools to sell their grains. Co-operatives were also organized to provide financial services, in the form of the CAISSE POPULAIRE system in Quebec and CREDIT UNIONS in other parts of Canada. The greatest use of co-operatives is made in Quebec and Saskatchewan. St. Francis Xavier University of Antigonish, Nova Scotia, developed many of the ideas on the role of co-operatives.

Co-ordinating Committee for Multilateral Export Controls (COCOM)   A committee of representatives of NORTH ATLANTIC TREATY ORGANIZATION (NATO) countries, including Canada, and other industrial countries such as Japan, that compiles lists of strategic goods NATO members agree to deny countries that could pose a military threat either directly or in a region such as the Middle East. Therefore, the goods on these lists will not be sold by committee members to denied countries. It surveys both military technology and civilian products, such as computers and telecommunications equipment, that may have military applications. COCOM was originally established to prevent the sale of militarily sensitive equipment to the communist countries, but with the collapse of communism COCOM it is now paying more attention to military developments in countries such as Iran, Iraq, India, Pakistan, and China. The members of COCOM are Belgium, Britain, Canada, Denmark, France, Germany, Greece, Italy, Japan, the Netherlands, Norway, Portugal, Turkey, and the United States.

co-production   An arrangement between film or television program producers in Canada and other countries recognized by the Canadian government that allows the production to qualify for Canadian tax incentives, direct funding, and Canadian content on television.

copyright   Legal protection for creators — writers, computer software writers, sculptors, architects, painters, movie producers, recording and performing artists and companies, dance choreographers, and others — against the production, performance, publication, or conversion of their work into another form (for example, a book into a movie) without their express permission. The original Copyright Act, proclaimed in 1924, was substantially revised in 1987, with further reforms promised. The act confers on creators the exclusive right to ownership of their works. Creators are able to derive income from their intellectual property by selling rights of reproduction for royalty or other income. They are also able to control the uses to which their works may be put. In Canada, a creator has copyright protection for his lifetime and for another 50 years after his death. In other cases, such as photographs or phonograph records, the protection is for a straight 50 years. It is not necessary to register ownership of copyright in Canada. Canadian copyrights are protected in other countries through international reciprocal arrangements. These are the 1928 Berne Convention and the 1952 Universal Copyright Convention.

Copyright Board of Canada   A board established in 1989, replacing the Copyright Appeal Board that had been founded in 1936 to review and approve royalties paid for musical works in Canada. In 1992, the federal government announced that the activities of the board would be transferred to a new INTELLECTUAL PROPERTY BOARD.

core   A sample of mineral rock obtained for ASSAY purposes, generally to help determine the location of valuable minerals. A core is obtained by drilling and is usually about two centimetres (one inch) in diameter.

corner the market　The purchase by a single buyer, or a small group of buyers acting together, of a large part of the available supply of a particular commodity or shares in a particular company. The buyers are thus in a position to control the price and resell at a much higher price than they paid.

corporate bond　A bond that has been issued by a corporation.

Corporate Higher-Education Forum
An organization established in 1983 to improve collaboration between business and universities. Membership is by invitation, and members are the top executives in their organizations — university presidents and corporate chief executive officers. The forum conducts research into education policy issues and publishes reports. Its research reports include university-business collaboration in research, international business studies, business funding for university projects, competency development in business for working life, and lifelong learning. The forum has also published a report on the public education system, from kindergarten to grade 12, including a set of learning objectives. It is based in Montreal.

corporate income tax　Tax levied on the income of a corporation after business expenses and other permitted deductions. Canadian corporations must pay tax on income earned anywhere in the world, while Canadian subsidiaries of foreign corporations must also pay tax on their Canadian income. Corporations are permitted to deduct all of their operating expenses, local property taxes, interest payments, and bad debts, along with DEPRECIATION and any other provisions under the Income Tax Act. Mining companies are allowed to deduct exploration spending as it is made, and they are also permitted to write off capital equipment for new mines in the year

the spending is done; but provincial oil and gas, or mineral royalties, and provincial mining taxes, cannot be deducted as expenses in calculating federal taxable income. In addition, corporations are permitted to claim various INVESTMENT TAX CREDITS for specific purposes, such as research and development.

Both the federal and provincial governments are allowed, under the CONSTITUTION ACT, 1867, to levy corporate income taxes. The basic federal rate is 28 percent, with a 22 percent rate on manufacturing and processing profits, and a 12 percent rate on Canadian-controlled private corporations on the first $200,000 of profits. A special 3 percent surtax on federal corporate income tax payable was introduced in 1987. Provincial corporate income tax rates vary but range between 15 and 17 percent. Three provinces — Quebec, Ontario, and Alberta — operate their own corporate-income-tax systems while the other provinces and territories have corporate income taxes collected on their behalf by the federal government. Federal corporate income taxes were introduced in Canada in 1917 to help finance the costs of the First World War and to reduce the high profits of wartime industries; they had been levied by the provinces since the turn of the century, although the rates were quite low.

corporate state　A form of political and economic system in which decision making is in the hands of the major power groups, usually business, labour, and governments. This reduces the role of democratically elected members of Parliament, and power, perhaps even statutory power, is allocated to non-elected groups such as business and union leaders. While there is a need for co-operation among such groups — in the evolution of consensus policies, for example, to get agreement on fair pay, profit, and price standards, or on economic priorities — there is the danger that such TRIPARTISM could lead to a diminution of the role of the ordinary citizen, who does not have a say through membership in a power group. The principle of government accountability to the public may also be reduced.

corporate strategy The long-range plans of a corporation, looking five years or longer into the future. A corporate strategy sets out plans for new or improved products, new methods of marketing or the pursuit of new markets, research and development, investments in new methods of production or in expanded capacity, the withdrawal from low-profit products, training and skills needs, and takeovers to diversify into new lines of business. Major corporations usually plan research and development projects, investment plans for new facilities, diversification, acquisitions (to increase their market share, or to extend the business backward into raw materials or forward into further processing or distribution), and profit targets several years in advance. Once overall corporate strategy has been devised, individual sectors of the business, such as corporate finance, engineering, marketing, or research, can then develop their own strategies to help reach corporate goals. A good corporate strategy must also take into account what competitor firms are also likely to do.

corporation A legal entity, created under federal or provincial corporation law, with an existence or life of its own, quite separate from those who created it. A corporation has the rights and obligations, under law, of a person, but differs from a person in that its life is infinite, unless it goes bankrupt or its owners decide to wind it up. Corporations can issue shares to the public to raise money for growth. The assets of a corporation belong to the corporation and not to the owners; the owners are entitled to a share of the assets if the corporation is wound up and to their share of the profits, in the form of dividends, that are not reinvested in the corporation. Corporations represent a major institutional innovation. Under the LIMITED LIABILITY of a corporation, the owners are not liable for its debts if it goes bankrupt; their loss is restricted to the investments they have made in the corporation so that shareholders do not have to fear any additional obligation. This has made it possible for corporations to raise money and for the economy to benefit from the risk taking necessary for innovation and growth. *See also* INCORPORATION, PRIVATE COMPANY, PUBLIC COMPANY, CANADA BUSINESS CORPORATIONS ACT. Some corporations have been created by an act of Parliament, such as Bell Canada and the CHARTERED BANKS.

corporation law The body of federal and provincial law that governs the incorporation of companies, sets out the rules under which they will operate, controls takeovers and deals with restrictive trade practices, regulates the financial structure of corporations, and deals with the rights of shareholders and responsibilities of company directors and officers. *See* CANADA BUSINESS CORPORATIONS ACT, COMPETITION ACT, SECURITIES LEGISLATION. Corporations may be either incorporated at the provincial level, if their objectives are provincial, or at the federal level if their objectives are national. Like the federal government, the provinces each have their own version of the Canada Business Corporations Act.

Corporations and Labour Unions Returns Act (CALURA) Legislation passed by Parliament in 1962, and effective January 1, 1963, to help document and assess the extent and relative importance of foreign-controlled corporations in the Canadian economy, and to provide information on the internal administrative practices and financial operations of unions whose headquarters are in the United States. The information on foreign-controlled corporations includes spending on research and development, charitable donations, and tax payments to federal and provincial governments, as well as broader statistics on balance-sheet details and income and expense statements. Details are provided on Canadian-controlled corporations as well, so that the relative significance of foreign-controlled firms can be determined. Separate annual reports are published by Statistics Canada on corporations (publication 61-210) and unions (71-202).

correspondent bank A bank in another country that handles the affairs in that country on behalf of a Canadian bank; in some smaller countries a Canadian bank with an office there may act on behalf of another Canadian bank as well. Canadian banks also act as correspondent banks for many foreign banks in Canada.

cost All the expenses incurred in producing a good or service. There are different categories of costs: 1. Total cost is the sum of all the expenses for all the factors of production used in producing a given level of goods or services. 2. A fixed cost is the basic expense or overhead of an enterprise, and exists regardless of the level of production — mortgage payments or rental costs for productive facilities, for example, or maintenance expenditures and management salaries. 3. A variable cost is the expense for the parts and components, raw materials, energy, and production-worker wages in producing goods and services. 4. A marginal cost is the cost of producing one extra unit of output. 5. The average cost is the total cost of the enterprise's output divided by the number of units of output. *See also* OPPORTUNITY COST.

cost accounting A specialized system of accounting to help businesses identify and allocate the true costs of producing a given unit of output. Among other things, the enterprise is broken down into cost centres or departments where individual stages of production take place; a portion of the overhead or FIXED COSTS is allocated to each of the cost centres, depending on floor space, number of workers, energy use, or some other factor or set of factors. Cost accounting is an important technique, since it allows a business to analyze precisely its true costs and allocate them among different operations in the business. The company can then implement more effective cost controls, or consider alternative ways of undertaking a particular part of the production process.

cost-benefit analysis The method used to determine the overall costs and benefits of undertaking a particular project, such as a new highway, hospital, subway system, or airport. Business investment decisions are usually made on the basis of expected rate of return on capital, or DISCOUNTED CASH FLOW. However, in the absence of such a measurement for many public projects, analysts calculate the net public welfare or the social rate of return. With growing concern over external costs such as congestion and pollution, cost-benefit analysis is widely used in public-project analysis and in government review of industrial projects such as pipelines and refineries. Applying cost-benefit analysis, planners looking at a proposed new expressway, for example, would include among the benefits the reduced travelling time of motorists and the advantages this brings to individuals and businesses, the value of the construction work in the local economy, and the possibility that the new expressway would lead to the creation of new businesses along the route, hence, to new jobs and tax revenues. Among the costs would be included the permanent loss of the land for alternative purposes, the cost of the land, the cost of access roads, the possibility that the new expressway will bring extra traffic into the community and thus cause traffic congestion, the pollution arising from any increased traffic flow, and the possibility that the new expressway would lead to a reduction in the use of transit systems. The calculations of costs and benefits contain some degree of uncertainty, not only because unforeseen factors in the future could alter the expected outcomes, but also because there can be disagreement over what costs and benefits to include and how they should be valued. There are also uncertainties over how to calculate the social rate of return, or the social cost, which includes both private costs and EXTERNALITIES.

cost centre A distinct department or production point in an enterprise whose costs can be separately identified and to which a measurable part of the firm's overhead or FIXED COSTS can be allocated. It is an important part of COST ACCOUNTING, designed to help businesses allocate their total costs to the different stages of production and distribution.

cost of capital The average cost to a company of all of its funds, such as the interest it must pay on its debt and the dividends it pays its common and preferred shareholders, less the economic depreciation of the investment and tax treatment of that depreciation, and the taxation of corporate profits and whatever tax incentives are available. The cost, expressed as a percentage, is weighted to reflect the relative shares of the different forms of capital. The cost of capital is one tool used by a company in making an investment decision; it is usually the minimum rate of return that a company will seek on a new

investment for the project. The lower the cost of capital, the longer the period before payback is required and the lower the rate of return a project must generate. Countries with a high cost of capital are unable to undertake investments that are possible in countries with a low cost of capital.

cost of living *See* CONSUMER PRICE INDEX

cost-of-living allowance clause (COLA) The indexation of wage rates, pensions, and social benefits to increases in the rate of inflation. Wage contracts sometimes contain clauses providing for partial or full indexation of wages. Government social benefits also make some provision for indexation so that benefits do not erode as a result of inflation.

cost-of-service principle of taxation See USER-PAY PRINCIPLE OF TAXATION.

cost-plus contract A contract that allows the contractor to charge for all the costs of completing the contract, and to add a percentage of the cost or a fixed fee as profit, as opposed to a contract that sets a fixed amount of money the contractor may charge to supply goods and services or to complete a certain type of work, such as construction of a building. A cost-plus contract is often used when it is difficult to calculate the total cost of a project, such as the design and production of a new military aircraft or weapon. Its disadvantage is that it provides no incentive to the contractor to control his costs.

cost-push inflation Inflation said to be caused by excessive wage and price increases, reflecting the market power of particular unions and corporations, rather than by excess demand or spending in the economy. In such a situation, wage increases rise faster than productivity, thus raising business operating costs. Businesses grant wage increases because they believe that they can pass them along to consumers through higher prices, without suffering a loss of sales or a drop in profits. Cost-push inflation may also be caused by a sharp increase in commodity prices. While business leaders put the blame on unions for rising costs, union leaders contend that they are merely responding to earlier price increases and argue that price increases are not related to wage increases. Whatever the cause, it would seem the case that, when the total of wage increases in the economy is higher than productivity gains in the economy, either profits will fall significantly, or the excess of additional wages over national output will have to represent inflation. During cost-push inflation, wages and prices may be moving up at a fast rate, even if there is considerable unemployment and slow economic growth. Some economists argue that some form of INCOMES POLICY is also necessary to deal with cost-push inflation. *See also* STAGFLATION, DEMAND-PULL INFLATION, WAGE-PRICE SPIRAL.

Council for Mutual Economic Assistance (COMECON) A council created in 1949 by the Soviet Union, in response to the Marshall Plan in Western Europe, with the goal of developing an integrated economy among the communist countries with the Soviet Union as the dominant member. It was formally dissolved in 1991, with the collapse of the communist system and the shift by most member countries to market economies. Its members included, in addition to the Soviet Union, Czechoslovakia, East Germany, Poland, Hungary, Romania, Bulgaria, Outer Mongolia, Cuba, and Vietnam. Albania had been a member but withdrew in 1961. At its 33rd annual conference, in June, 1979, North Yemen, Afghanistan, Angola, Ethiopia, Finland, Iraq, Laos, Mexico, Mozambique, and Yugoslavia attended as official observers.

The council was originally established as a means of integrating the economies of Eastern Europe and Outer Mongolia with that of the Soviet Union. In its early days, the COMECON countries attempted to develop a self-sufficient economy and discouraged trade with the West. The Soviet Union, through COMECON, also attempted to make other members specialize in particular economic sectors, and thus integrate their economies into that of the Soviet Union.

Council of Canadians A national organization established in 1985 to protect and strengthen Canadian identity and political, cultural, social, and economic sovereignty so that Canada can play a constructive, respected, and independent role in the world community. The council advocates greater Canadian ownership and control in the Canadian economy, greater effort to preserve Canadian cultural identity, and greater support for public enterprise. The council was formed to replace the COMMITTEE FOR AN INDEPENDENT CANADA, in response to growing concern over the erosion of Canadian sovereignty with the dismantling of the FOREIGN INVESTMENT REVIEW AGENCY and the NATIONAL ENERGY PROGRAM, as well as government efforts to establish much closer relations with the United States. In 1987, the Council of Canadians organized the Pro-Canada Network, an alliance of some 30 national organizations that shared a basic concern over the future direction of Canada and a fear that Canada was in danger of losing its distinctiveness and sovereignty under the weight of American pressure. The council played a vigorous role in opposing the CANADA-UNITED STATES FREE TRADE AGREEMENT and the NORTH AMERICAN FREE TRADE AGREEMENT.

Council of Maritime Premiers A cooperative arrangement among the three Maritime provinces of Nova Scotia, New Brunswick, and Prince Edward Island, signed in 1971, following the MARITIME UNION STUDY published the previous year. The three provinces agreed to meet quarterly to discuss common problems and to co-ordinate activities, to establish a secretariat to serve the council, to create a Maritime Provinces Commission for long-term planning, to examine the feasibility of a joint legislature, and to discuss ways to make legislation uniform throughout the region. The three provinces hoped to initiate studies on common economic, social, and cultural policies, to co-ordinate activities that affected all three provinces, and to make joint submissions to the federal government. The commission was not activated, and consideration of a joint legislature was quietly dropped. However, their efforts took on new life after the 1989 report on the council and its future direction by Charles McMillan of York University. In May, 1991, the council issued a discussion paper on Maritime economic integration, setting out a vision for much closer economic co-operation among the three provinces. In 1992, the provinces each passed a Maritime Economic Co-operation Act.

counter-cyclical policies   Government policies to offset the trend of the business cycle. During a recession, for example, government can relax monetary, fiscal, and other policies to increase aggregate demand and create jobs, or tighten these same policies to curtail economic growth and check inflation pressures as the economy moves toward its peak in the business cycle.

counter-cyclical spending   Government spending that increases during an economic downturn or recession and decreases during an economic recovery. Examples include transfer payments to households, such as unemployment insurance and social-welfare payments.

But governments may also introduce additional spending, such as spending on public works or infrastructure, to offset the impact of recession; likewise, governments may scale back such spending during the recovery phases of the business cycle.

countertrade   International trade in which an export sale is paid for in other products rather than currency.

countervailing duty   A duty imposed to offset the effect of an alleged subsidy in the country of origin. The United States has imposed or threatened to impose countervailing duties on goods shipped by Canadian firms that have received regional development grants or research and development assistance, or which have operated under licensing or marketing systems different from those in the United States, such as the STUMPAGE FEE system to manage crown forests or FARM-MARKETING BOARDS that regulate production of farm products such as pork. Under the U.S. system, any company can file a complaint with the U.S. Department of Commerce, which makes a preliminary finding of a subsidy, with an estimate of its value. If favourable, the U.S. International Trade Commission makes a preliminary finding of injury. The U.S. Commerce Department then conducts hearings and comes up with a final determination of a penalty. Next, the International Trade Commission holds hearings to make a final determination that there is injury to U.S. producers. If it finds injury, the Commerce penalty is applied to the exports to the United States. The U.S. use of its trade laws to harass Canadian exporters has long been a source of friction between the two countries. Canadian industry complains that the law allows U.S. companies to launch trade actions that, even if they are known to be ill-founded, cost Canadian companies considerable time and money to defend in Washington, through Washington law firms, and often cost sales because of the uncertainty such actions create in the minds of would-be U.S. importers. One of Canada's most important goals in the CANADA-UNITED STATES FREE TRADE AGREEMENT was to eliminate the ability of U.S. companies to harass Canadian exporters in this way, by developing a code of permitted subsidies and imposing greater discipline on the use of U.S. trade law. But the United States refused to negotiate and Canada was forced to give in; instead, it settled for a DISPUTE SETTLEMENT MECHANISM in which a binational panel will hear Canadian complaints that the U.S. countervailing duty was unfairly imposed. The panel's role is to ensure that U.S. agencies conformed to U.S. due process when imposing the penalty; if the panel finds that some mistake in process was made, it can order the U.S. agency to redo the case or reassess the calculation of injury or penalty. Canada also imposes countervailing duties on imports, as it did in 1987 on U.S. corn. The duty lapsed in 1992. REVENUE CANADA assesses whether there are grounds for such a duty and what the duty should be. The CANADIAN INTERNATIONAL TRADE TRIBUNAL then holds a hearing to determine whether the subsidy is causing injury to Canadian producers. If it is, then the duty is applied.

countervailing power   Checks and balances in the economy to prevent powerful groups from freely exercising their power. Examples include the ability of strong unions to challenge large corporations, the bargaining power of big retail chains in negotiating prices with large manufacturers, and the use of government regulation and competition laws to check oligopolistic practices by labour, business, and the professions. The existence of such countervailing power is a characteristic feature of the MIXED ECONOMY. See also John Kenneth GALBRAITH.

coupon   An attachment to a bond certificate that entitles the owner to a specified amount of interest on a particular date. When that date is reached, the bond owner clips the coupon from the bond certificate and presents it at a bank for payment. Hence the term coupon clipper to describe wealthy individuals who live off the income they receive by clipping bond coupons.

coupon rate   The annual interest paid on the face value of a BOND.

covenant   A binding condition included in a contract or other legal agreement.

Coyne Affair   A major confrontation between the government of John Diefenbaker and the BANK OF CANADA over the conduct of monetary policy. In 1960 and 1961, a major disagreement brewed up between the Diefenbaker government, which wanted an easier monetary policy to stimulate economic growth, and Bank of Canada Governor James Coyne, who insisted on a tighter monetary policy. The government wanted Coyne to resign but he refused; confronted by legislation forcing him to resign, Coyne stepped down in July, 1961, after having his "day in court" before a committee of the Senate. Coyne's successor, Louis Rasminsky, only accepted the post after an agreement with the government clarifying the responsibility for monetary policy. In subsequent amendments to the Bank of Canada Act, it was made clear that while the governor of the Bank of Canada was responsible for the conduct of monetary policy on a day-to-day basis, the government had the power to issue directives to the governor for a change in policy that the governor would have to implement, or resign. Thus the ultimate responsibility for monetary policy rested with the government of the day. For his part, Coyne was an outspoken governor during his term, which ran from 1955 to 1961. He was especially outspoken on the dangers to Canada of growing foreign ownership of the economy.

craft union   A union whose membership is restricted to workers with a particular skill. Examples include unions representing different types of construction workers such as plumbers, electricians, bricklayers, carpenters, and labourers, or such workers as truck drivers. But as skills have changed, and even disappeared in the economy, craft unions have broadened their membership to include other types of workers. *See also* INDUSTRIAL UNION.

Crane's law   There's no such thing as a free lunch.

crawling peg   A modification of the fixed-exchange-rate system, which would allow a wider fluctuation up and down from the par value than the 1 percent either way that was permitted when the fixed-exchange-rate system of the INTERNATIONAL MONETARY FUND was in effect. It would allow more movement in a country's exchange rate, before monetary authorities had to intervene to maintain its value, than the PAR-VALUE system did until its demise in 1971, but less flexibility than the FLOATING-EXCHANGE-RATE system. The crawling peg was advocated by some economists, but not adopted, following the breakdown of the fixed-exchange-rate system in 1971. The floating-exchange-rate system was adopted instead.

credit   **1.** Obtaining the use of goods or services now with a promise to pay for them later. Consumer credit permits a consumer, for example, to acquire goods immediately and to pay for them over several months or years; it also provides loans to consumers so that they can buy goods or services now. Similarly, trade credit allows retailers, wholesalers, and manufacturers to obtain goods and services without paying for them immediately. **2.** Loans by banks, trust companies, credit unions, caisses populaires, and other lenders, to enable individuals, corporations, and governments to buy goods and services now, on the promise of future repayment plus interest. **3.** In double-entry bookkeeping, an entry signifying an increase in liabilities or income or a decrease in assets or expenses. *See also* DEBIT.

credit bureau   A company that keeps records of the credit history of individuals, such as their repayment of debts and whether or not they tend to make payments on time, and supplies information for a fee to financial institutions that are considering making loans, giving a credit card, or granting a line of credit for an installment-purchase account in a department store. The practices of credit bureaus fall under provincial jurisdiction and, in response to consumer concern over the accuracy of information in credit-bureau files and the injustice that can arise if a person is denied a loan because a credit-bureau file contains false information, provinces have passed legislation requiring credit-granting institutions to inform a consumer seeking a loan that credit-bureau files may be checked and allowing consumers the right to see the contents of their credit-bureau files. The Associated Credit Bureaus of Canada, established in 1939, is the national industry association. It is based in Toronto.

credit card   A plastic card issued by a department store, bank, credit-card company, airline, car-rental agency, gasoline company, or other business, that entitles the holder to credit. Billings are normally monthly, and interest is usually only charged on the balance outstanding at the end of 30 days. Credit-card companies and banks issuing credit cards usually charge stores, restaurants, airlines, and others a percentage of the bill as a handling charge. The profits from credit cards come from handling charges and from the interest earned on outstanding balances of card users. *See also* DEBIT CARD.

credit controls   Policies of the BANK OF CANADA or the government to expand or reduce the availability of credit or to restrict credit to certain uses. Aside from the normal techniques used in setting MONETARY POLICY to determine the overall supply of credit, a government can be selective and legislate high down-payments for consumer purchases on credit, require stock exchanges to increase the MARGIN requirements on the purchase of shares, or require higher down-payments on the purchase of houses if, for example, it wants to slow economic growth.

credit line   Approval by a bank or other financial institution of a level or line of credit that can be drawn on as needed. The advantage to the borrower is that the funds are there whenever needed and don't have to be negotiated at the time they are needed. Credit lines are widely used in business and normally are renegotiated each year; credit lines are also available to consumers in the form of overdraft limits.

Credit mixte   A combination of market rates and concessional rates to finance an export sale; the effect is to lower the overall interest rate on the financing. The ORGANIZATION FOR ECONOMIC CO-OPERATION AND DEVELOPMENT attempts to impose some discipline on the use of credit mixte.

credit squeeze   Measures by the central bank to tighten the amount of credit available in the economy, thus forcing up interest rates. The purpose is to reduce the level of activity in the economy and bring about a lower rate of inflation.

credit union   A co-operative financial institution that is owned by its members and that operates for the benefit of its members by accepting savings deposits and making loans, including mortgage loans, and providing other services, such as chequing and credit-card services. Most credit unions are one-branch organizations associated with a place of employment; however, in Quebec, where they are known as CAISSES POPULAIRES, there are multibranch systems. Credit unions date back to 1900 in Canada. In all the provinces except Quebec, credit unions organized themselves into provincial centrals or sociétés and in 1953 many of them joined together in a national organization, the Canadian Co-operative Credit Society to enable the transfer of funds across provincial boundaries. Credit unions are subject to provincial regulation, Nova Scotia having introduced the first regulatory laws in 1932. Credit unions enjoyed strong growth in western Canada in the 1930s and 1940s. Outside of Quebec, the Vancouver City Savings Credit Union is the largest in Canada.

creditor   A person, bank, supplier, or other business, to whom money is owed. For example, ACCOUNTS PAYABLE listed under current liabilities on a firm's balance sheet are the claims of creditors against the firm. Other creditors would include the holders of long-term debt notes, such as banks or the owners of the firm's outstanding bonds, mortgages, and other such instruments.

creditor nation   A nation that has a balance-of-payments surplus in its trade and other economic transactions with other countries, and therefore is in a position to lend money or to make investments in other countries.

According to some economists, a country should evolve, as its economy develops, from a DEBTOR NATION with infant industries to a mature creditor nation. Some economists worry that that has not happened in Canada's case, and that Canada has moved from being a young debtor nation to the status of a mature debtor nation. The CURRENT ACCOUNT measures the flow of transactions with the rest of the world while Canada's NET INTERNATIONAL INVESTMENT POSITION measures the stock or its outstanding level of net foreign debt.

creeping inflation A small but steady increase in the rate of inflation. While the individual increases may seem quite small, over time they can be significant.

critical-path method (CPM) A technique to find the shortest and lowest-cost way to complete a major project, such as the construction of a nuclear-power station, a tar-sands or heavy-oil plant, a mining smelter, pipeline, assembly line, or subway system. Using this technique, each sequence of activities that must be carried out consecutively is set down as a "path." In any project, there are many such paths. The "critical path" is the one that will take the longest to complete, and therefore determines the length of time it will take to complete the project. The other paths are scheduled around the critical path so that no time is lost in completing the project. At the same time, every effort is made to reduce the time needed to complete the critical path. The great benefit of this technique is that it identifies the various paths of the project and enables the most efficient scheduling of work to take place.

crop insurance A form of insurance to protect farmers against heavy financial losses due to the loss of crops caused by bad weather, floods, and other such threats. In 1959, Parliament passed the Crop Insurance Act, to permit the federal government, with the provinces, to make crop insurance available to farmers across the country. In 1991, this was replaced by the FARM INCOME PROTECTION ACT, which introduced the gross-revenue insurance program. It provides both crop insurance, with farmers paying 50 percent of the premiums and federal and provincial governments 25 percent each, and market-revenue protection, with farmers paying one-third of the premium, the provincial government 25 percent, and the federal government the remainder.

crop year In the grain industry, the year that starts at August 1 with harvesting, and runs to July 31 of the following year. The 1992-93 crop year began August 1, 1992, and ended July 31, 1993.

crop yield A measure of the productivity of the land; it is the amount of a crop produced per acre of land in production. It is calculated by dividing the total production of a crop for afarm, region, or country by the number of acres planted. In Canada from 1966 to 1970, wheat yields averaged 24.3 bushels per acre; from 1971 to 1975, wheat yields averaged 25.3 bushels per acre. In 1991 wheat yields averaged 33.6 bushels per acre.

cross-elasticity of demand A measure of the impact of a price change in one good on the demand for another good. If the price of coffee goes up and leads to an increase in demand for tea, then the two are substitutes. However, if the price of tea goes up and this leads to a fall in the demand for lemons, then the two are COMPLEMENTARY GOODS. The cross-elasticity of demand is calculated by taking the percentage change in the demand for the second good and dividing it by the percentage change in the price of the first good. If there is a positive result, the goods are substitutes; if negative, they are complements.

cross on the board   A stock-exchange transaction that occurs when the same broker has both a buy and sell order on a particular stock at the same price.

cross-subsidization   The financing of one activity by a company through the profits earned in another activity. For example, telephone companies historically maintained low local-service rates by charging high rates for long-distance calls. The same situation can occur in an airline, where more profitable long-haul flights help cover the costs of short-haul service.

crowding out   The decline in savings available to private-sector borrowers when high government deficits absorb a major share of national savings. The absorption of savings by the public sector can be offset by increased foreign borrowing. However, over time, foreign obligations can become a burden on the economy as the cost of external debt servicing can draw a growing share of domestic output. Crowding out usually leads to an increase in interest rates as borrowers compete for funds.

Crow's Nest Pass Agreement   An agreement between the federal government and the Canadian Pacific Railway Company, made in 1897, in which the railway agreed to maintain in perpetuity a fixed schedule of freight rates in western Canada for wheat and flour, in exchange for large land grants, including mineral rights, and a $3.3 million subsidy toward the construction of the railway. The railway has charged the maximum permitted since the First World War, when it actually suspended the agreement and exceeded the rates. With some modifications, the rates

were restored from 1925 to 1927. However, with the prescribed rates representing an increasingly smaller portion of the railway costs over time in transporting grain, there was increased pressure from the railway to find a way to recover more of its costs and abolish the agreement. Western farmers vigorously resisted any change, however, arguing that the railway made a deal and should live with it. After vigorous debate in the early 1980s the federal government narrowed the choices down to a few options, including one that would have paid a rail subsidy to western farmers and allowed freight rates to rise to their true costs. In the end, however, the government introduced the WESTERN GRAIN TRANSPORTATION ACT, which, effective January 1, 1984, allowed rates to rise to 10 percent of the world price for grain, with the federal government paying the remainder of the grain transportation cost; however, points have not risen to that extent. In return, the railways agreed to invest in new equipment and improved service.

crown corporation   A federal or provincial, publicly owned enterprise, established to carry out a regulatory, advisory, administrative, financial, or other service for the government, or to produce goods or services for the public. Federal examples include the EXPORT DEVELOPMENT CORPORATION, ATOMIC ENERGY OF CANADA LIMITED, and the BANK OF CANADA. Until they were privatized, AIR CANADA and PETRO-CANADA were also crown corporations. Provincial examples include Ontario Hydro, B.C. Hydro, Hydro Quebec, B.C Rail, and the Saskatchewan Telephone System. Federal crown corporations are designated as such under the FINANCIAL ADMINISTRATION ACT and are subject to government and parliamentary controls under extensive 1984 amendments to the act. Crown corporations have played a dynamic role in the development of the Canadian economy and in meeting important public needs efficiently where Canadian private investors were unwilling or unable to meet Canadian needs; they are a unique response to the needs of a country with a relatively small and spread-out population. Crown corporations pre-date Confederation. For example, in 1841 a crown corporation was established to build a canal system for the United Provinces of Canada. The oldest existing crown corporation is the National Battlefields Commission, established in 1908. The establishment of Canadian National Railways in 1919, when a number of private sector railroads went bankrupt, represented a major step in the evolution of the crown corporation toward the operation of a public enterprise. Others that followed included the Canadian Broadcasting Corporation (1932), the CANADIAN WHEAT BOARD (1935), and Air Canada (1937).

The federal government, under the Financial Administration Act, identifies three different types of crown corporations: 1. Agency corporations, which are responsible for various trading or service activities of the government, or for the handling of various government procurement, construction, or disposal activities, usually on a quasi-commercial basis. Examples include Atomic Energy of Canada Ltd., CANADIAN COMMERCIAL CORPORATION, the CANADIAN DAIRY COMMISSION, the Export Development Corporation, FARM CREDIT CORPORATION, THE FEDERAL BUSINESS DEVELOPMENT BANK, CANADA DEPOSIT INSURANCE CORPORATION, CANADA MORTGAGE AND HOUSING CORPORATION, and VIA RAIL CANADA. Their operating and capital spending budgets must be approved by the TREASURY BOARD and their annual corporate plans approved by the CABINET. 2. Proprietary corporations, which provide financial services or produce other goods or services for the public, and which operate on their own in a commercial manner without annual funding from Parliament. Examples include the CANADA PORTS CORPORATION, and Canadian National Railways. Eldorado Nuclear, Air Canada, and Petro-Canada were also in this category until they were privatized. The operating budgets of proprietary corporations require no government approval but capital budgets must be approved by the Treasury Board and annual corporate plans approved by cabinet. Some of these corporations pay corporate income taxes just as private corporations do. 3. Exempt corporations, which operate under their own enabling legislation but which are classified as crown corporations under the Financial Administration Act. Examples include the Bank of Canada, the Canadian Broadcasting Corporation, the CANADIAN FILM DEVELOPMENT CORPORATION, and the Canadian Wheat Board. In 1991, Statistics Canada published a special report, *Compendium of Public Sector Statistics,* which provided financial information on crown corporations. All crown corporations report to Parliament through a designated cabinet minister. The federal government has participated in other businesses as a shareholder, but these businesses — for example, the CANADA DEVELOPMENT CORPORATION, Canadair Ltd., and PANARCTIC OILS LIMITED — were never crown corporations since they had other shareholders or because they were never designated as a crown corporation under the Financial Administration Act.

crown forest Forest lands owned by the federal government or a provincial government, and which may be harvested by lumber or pulp and paper companies operating under a federal or provincial timber licence or other such arrangement.

crown land   All federally and provincially owned lands, including national and provincial parks, crown forests, historic sites, and undeveloped land not owned by a private individual or entity.

crude birth rate   The number of live births, per year, for each thousand of population at the middle of that year. The rate of natural increase in population is the difference between the crude birth rate and the CRUDE DEATH RATE, and is usually expressed as a percentage rate of change. While the crude birth rate is useful in making international comparisons of population change, its weakness is that it depends very much on the age composition of the population, as well as on the number of children that women of childbearing age are actually having. Hence, population experts also look at the FERTILITY RATE and the INFANT-MORTALITY RATE of different countries in analyzing population trends. In 1991, Canada's crude birth rate was 14.9, compared with 16.3 in the United States, 11.3 in Germany, 9.9 in Japan, 13.8 in Britain, 14.3 in Sweden, 13.3 in France, 12.6 in Switzerland, and 9.8 in Italy. Canada's crude birth rate has been in long-term decline over the past 50 years. In the 1940s and 1950s, it was about 28, declining sharply through the 1960s and into the 1970s. In 1991, the Northwest Territories had a crude birth rate of 29.9, the highest in Canada. Among the provinces, Alberta had the highest crude birth rate, 17.0, while Newfoundland had the lowest, 12.5. The Canadian Centre for Health Information at Statistics Canada publishes data on birth and fertility rates. It also publishes historical reports, such as *Selected Birth and Fertility Statistics, Canada 1921-1990* (publication 82-553).

crude death rate   The number of deaths per year for each thousand of population at the middle of that year.

The rate of natural increase in population is the difference between the CRUDE BIRTH RATE and the crude death rate, expressed as a percentage rate of change. The crude death rate depends on the age composition of the population, life expectancy, and the INFANT-MORTALITY RATE.

crude oil and equivalent   A term used to describe total oil production from conventional oil reservoirs, synthetic-oil production from tar-sands plants, and pentanes plus, a by-product of natural-gas production.

cultural industries   Industries that reflect and express Canadian cultural experience and ideas; the cultural industries include newspapers, magazine and book publishing, sound recordings, film production and distribution, radio and television broadcasting and programming, and cable television and pay-TV services. Canada has a number of programs to enhance its cultural industries. These include Canadian ownership regulations and restrictions on foreign investment in Canadian cultural industries; regulatory provisions requiring minimum levels of Canadian content on radio and television; tax rules under Bill C-58, which limit advertising-expenditure tax deductions to Canadians advertising in Canadian media; and various grants and subsidies for book publishing, magazines, TV and film production, and sound recordings. Under the CANADA-UNITED STATES FREE TRADE AGREEMENT, Canada was allowed to retain existing arrangements for cultural industries, but the United States was allowed to retaliate if Canada introduced any new laws or arrangements that U.S. companies opposed.

Cultural Property Export and Import Act   Federal legislation passed in June, 1975, which came into force in

September, 1977, to control the export of national cultural treasures and to police the illegal importation of foreign cultural treasures. It is administered by the Department of the Secretary of State, through the Canadian Cultural Property Export Review Board.

cum dividend   With dividend. The purchaser of a share cum dividend will receive the next dividend payable, because the transaction takes place before the date of record when the next dividend is declared. Shareholders on the company's books on the date of record are the ones who will receive the dividend. The price of a share sold just before the next dividend takes into account the fact that the new owner will get the dividend. *See also* EX DIVI-DEND.

cumulative preferred share   A PRE-FERRED SHARE whose owners are entitled to an annual dividend; if the dividend is not paid in a particular year, the unpaid dividend becomes a liability of the corporation and must be paid before any more dividends are paid to the owners of COMMON SHARES.

currency   The various notes and coins used in a country as a medium of exchange. In Canada, this consists of paper money issued by the BANK OF CANADA and coins produced by the Royal Canadian Mint. The Bank of Canada took over the responsibility for producing paper money when it was created in 1934. Until then, paper money was produced by the CHARTERED BANKS; their role was phased out between 1935 and 1945. In 1950, the remaining chartered-bank notes became a liability of the Bank of Canada.

currency area   An area in which a number of smaller countries peg or tie their currency to the dominant currency in the region or the currency of their most important trading partner.

The most important currency area is the EUROPEAN COMMUNITY, where a number of countries have tied their exchange rate effectively to the German mark through the EUROPEAN MONE-TARY SYSTEM. Mexico has tied its exchange rate to the U.S. dollar, and while Canada maintains an independent exchange rate, there are suggestions that Canada and Mexico could some day form a currency area with the United States, following on the NORTH AMERICAN FREE TRADE AGREE-MENT. The main support would come from Canadian exporters and investors seeking greater certainty in trade and investment. In the past, the British maintained a strong sterling bloc, with former colonies tying their currency to the British pound. A similar franc zone was formed between the French franc and former French colonies.

currency swap   A transaction in which two parties exchange a specified amount of currencies for a specified period of time.

current account   A measure of a country's transactions with the rest of the world. The current account includes merchandise trade; trade in services such as tourism and travel, freight and shipping costs (including oil and gas pipelines), business services (including payments to foreign head offices for service charges, licensing and royalty payments, as well as trade in management consulting, engineering, and other tradeable services, and payments for film distribution and franchises), and other service transactions; and investment income and transfers, including dividend and interest payments, foreign-aid flows, the money immigrants bring with them, and remittances of immigrants. The current-account balance is determined by adding together the net balances with the rest of the world in merchandise trade, trade in services, and investment income and transfers. Canada has run a current-account deficit through much of its history, with a surplus in merchandise trade too small to offset a deficit in services and a deficit in investment income and transfers. The current-account flows are reported quarterly by Statistics Canada as part of the BALANCE OF PAYMENTS (publication 67-001). A current account is usually financed by an increase in foreign debt, which is set out in the CAPITAL ACCOUNT. When a country runs a current-account deficit it is borrowing funds from the rest of the world; when it is running a surplus it is lending funds to the rest of the world. The net outstanding stock of obligations or assets is set out in the NET INTERNATIONAL INVESTMENT POSITION (publication 67-202). Another way of looking at a country's current-account position is that when a country has a current-account deficit its national investment exceeds its national savings, so it has to borrow the difference from the rest of the world; likewise, when a country has a current-account surplus, it has an excess of national savings over national investment, so it lends the surplus to the rest of the world. A key factor in the gap between national savings and national investment is the size of government fiscal deficits; national saving is the combination of private saving and public saving, so that the current-account deficit can approximate the difference between private savings and the budget deficits of the various levels of government. The current-account position can also be expressed as the difference between income and absorption, with absorption consisting of consumption and investment. When a country has a persistent current-account deficit it can be said to be living beyond its means. While a current-account deficit can be financed by foreign investment or borrowing, these represent obligations that must be repaid. Repayment is usually made

through increasing a country's trade surplus — either by rapidly expanding exports or, alternatively, by imposing measures to reduce imports. A country cannot run a current-account deficit indefinitely; at some point, international financial markets or agencies such as the INTERNATIONAL MONETARY FUND will require a country to live within its means. A current-account deficit is not necessarily good or bad; it depends on whether the increase in foreign debt is for investment purposes or to finance consumption; it also depends on the stage of development of a country, with countries at an early stage of development expected to be deficit countries and countries at a mature stage of development to be surplus countries.

current asset   An asset that, during the course of the year, will either be used in the production of goods or services, or be converted into cash. Examples include cash and short-term securities, ACCOUNTS RECEIVABLE, inventories, and work in progress. These are the liquid assets of a firm and, after CURRENT LIABILITIES are deducted, represent its WORKING CAPITAL and hence its capacity to finance its on-going operations. Current assets are listed in a firm's BALANCE SHEET.

current liability   A liability of a firm that must be paid within the next 12 months. The most common examples are ACCOUNTS PAYABLE to suppliers, the current year's interest on long-term debt, taxes, and dividends payable within the year. Current liabilities are listed on a firm's BALANCE SHEET. *See also* CURRENT ASSET.

current ratio   The ratio of a firm's CURRENT ASSETS to its CURRENT LIABILITIES. It is one measure of a firm's liquidity, and hence its ability to meet current costs out of current income. It is calculated by dividing current assets by current liabilities. *See also* ACID-TEST RATIO, QUICK RATIO.

current return The annual return or yield on an investment as calculated at any point in time. In the case of a company share, it is the current annual dividend divided by the current market price. In the case of a corporate or government bond, it is the annual interest paid on the bond divided by its current market price.

curriculum vitae An outline of a person's age, education, work experience, awards, and other interests and activities. A curriculum vitae, or resume, is often sought by employers to help screen applicants for a job.

customs broker A broker or agent who does the paperwork and manages other steps in clearing imports through the customs officers of REVENUE CANADA at the lowest possible rate on behalf of an importer or, in the case of an exporter, through the customs officials of the destination country.

Customs Tariff Act Federal legislation that sets out the different classes of tariffs that are applied to imports from other countries. There are five different classes of tariffs: the British preferential tariff, which is the lowest tariff rate and is applied to imports from Commonwealth countries that are not members of the European Community; the general preferential tariff, the next lowest tariff level, which applies to imports from less-developed countries and some Eastern European countries and which, unless it is renewed, expires June 30, 1994; the Britain and Ireland tariff, which applies to Commonwealth countries in the European Community but which is being gradually changed to match the most-favoured-nation tariff; the most-favoured-nation tariff, which applies to Canada's 110 trading partners in the GENERAL AGREEMENT ON TARIFFS AND TRADE (GATT); and the general tariff, the highest tariff level, which applies to countries with which Canada has no trading agreement. Canada is reducing to zero by January 1, 1998, tariffs on products from the United States under the CANADA-UNITED STATES FREE TRADE AGREEMENT; in addition, Canada will reduce to zero tariffs on goods from Mexico by January 1, 2008, under the NORTH AMERICAN FREE TRADE AGREEMENT. Canada also provides duty-free entry for a wide range of products from the Commonwealth Caribbean countries under the Carribbean-Canadian Economic Trade Develpment Assistance Program. Tariffs to all of Canada's GATT trading partners will also be lowered by about one-third in the URUGUAY ROUND of GATT trade negotiations.

customs union A free trade agreement among two or more nations who also impose a common external tariff on imports from nations outside the customs union. The EUROPEAN COMMUNITY, when it was created in 1957, was a customs union. Since then it has evolved into a COMMON MARKET, in which the free movement of workers, capital, and business operations are also permitted. A customs union differs from a FREE-TRADE AREA in that it has a common external tariff, whereas individual nations in a free-trade area each apply their own tariff schedule on imports from nations that do not belong to the free-trade area.

customs valuation The determination by a country's customs officials of the tariff category of an import and therefore the tariff rate that will apply.

cut-throat competition Price-slashing by competitive firms to gain a larger share of market or to drive a competitor out of business. Since price-slashing can mean operating at a loss, there must be an opportunity at some point in the future for a successful firm to recoup those losses by establishing a strong enough market position to raise prices to a higher level than existed before. Otherwise, in cases of excess supply, cut-throat competition may lead to losses for all the firms. While COMPETITION POLICY encourages competition among firms, the law prohibits PREDATORY PRICING where a powerful firm uses deep price discounts to drive other firms, with fewer financial resources and therefore lower staying power, out of business or out of a particular product line or service.

cyclical fluctuation   Short-term changes in the pace of economic activity that reflect changes in the phase of the business cycle or shocks to the system, such as a significant increase or decline in the price of oil, that deviate from the long-term trend of economic growth.

cyclical industry   An industry whose sales and profits fluctuate with changes in the business cycle. A cyclical industry differs from a stable industry whose performance is largely unaffected by changes in the business cycle because its products or services are needed at roughly the same level, regardless of the state of the economy. A cyclical industry should not be confused with a seasonal industry, whose goods or services have a peak level of demand in a particular season or seasons each year; a seasonal industry may also be a stable industry. Examples of cyclical industries include the steel, lumber, newsprint, machinery, and automotive industries.

cyclical stock   A share in an industry that is highly vulnerable to changes in the BUSINESS CYCLE. For example, forest products and mining-company stocks are likely to decline during a recession and rise during a recovery. In a recession, the demand for their prod-ucts falls, as do prices for their products. In a recovery, the volume of sales increases while the prices obtained for their products also rises.

cyclical unemployment   Changes in the unemployment rate resulting from changes in the pace of economic activity; increases in unemployment resulting from a downturn in the BUSINESS CYCLE. Governments resort to COUNTER-CYCLICAL POLICIES, such as increased public spending, tax cuts, or an easier monetary policy to reduce such unemployment.

damages Money that must be paid to indemnify someone for a loss or an added cost resulting from some action or failure to act by the person required to make this payment.

date of record The date by which a shareholder must own a share so that he or she is entitled to a dividend.

days of grace Extra time that is normally allowed beyond the stated payment date, during which payment can usually still be made without penalty. The time is usually three days.

dead time Time when an employee is being paid but is not working because machinery is not functioning or needed parts or materials are not available. *See also* DOWN-TIME.

deadheading The movement of empty freight cars or other railway rolling stock, trucks, aircraft, and buses. This may occur in the movement of grain and mineral ores, for example, where large shipments are made from grain elevators or mines to customer delivery points such as ports or steel plants, and where there are no major shipments of products to be carried back to the grain-producing areas or mining communities. Interprovincial barriers have also led to deadheading in the trucking industry, thereby raising the cost of transportation in Canada. However, a number of steps have been taken to open trucking markets within Canada, but there are still some barriers.

deadweight The cargo weight, along with fuel oil, water and food, that a ship is capable of carrying when fully loaded.

deadweight loss The loss attributable to taxes. Taxes affect choices made in the economy — the choice of whether to work or pursue leisure, the choice of whether to consume or invest — and the distortions in decisions caused by taxes have a direct impact on the economy. In effect, taxes change the prices of a multitude of decisions made in the economy so that companies may end up underinvesting and workers declining to work overtime. However, since taxes cannot be avoided, one goal of tax policy should be to hold to a minimum the distortions or deadweight losses of the tax system for any given revenue target.

dealer   Someone who buys goods from a manufacturer or distributor for resale; if the manufacturer or distributor agrees not to sell to a competing dealer in the same area, then the dealer has an exclusive dealership.

death rate   The number of deaths per 1,000 population in a year. *See* CRUDE DEATH RATE.

death taxes   Taxes on the estates of individuals when they die, often known as ESTATE TAXES or SUCCESSION DUTIES. Provincial governments first levied estate and inheritance taxes before the First World War. The federal government began levying similar taxes in 1941. In 1949, Ottawa doubled the rate and offered half to the provinces, who then dropped their own taxes; all but British Columbia, Ontario, and Quebec agreed. In 1964, the federal government raised the provincial share to 75 percent. In 1972, the federal government gave up the field of estate taxes or succession duties, along with GIFT TAXES, and instead introduced DEEMED REALIZATION at death under its new system of CAPITAL-GAINS TAX. The provinces now had complete jurisdiction, but one after another, the provinces dropped the tax. By 1975, only British Columbia, Manitoba, Ontario, and Quebec imposed succession duties or estate taxes. By 1980, Quebec was the only province left levying such taxes and it stopped in 1985. In 1968, the federal tax had exempted the first $50,000 of an estate, then imposed a graduated tax rate as the value of the estate rose, from 15 percent on the first $20,000 to 50 percent on any amount in excess of $300,000.

debasement   The reduction of the metallic value of a coin below its face value.

debenture   A corporate or government bond or promissory note that is not secured by a mortgage or a claim on any specific asset of the borrower, but is based simply on the general creditworthiness of the borrower. Because of this, holders of debentures have a lesser claim on a corporation's assets should it fail than holders of secured debt such as first-mortgage bonds. Sometimes debentures are CONVERTIBLE into common shares or carry WARRANTS permitting the owner to pay for common shares at some specified price that is expected to be below the future market price; the purpose is to increase the attractiveness of the issue to would-be investors. Sinking-fund debentures require the borrower to pay a fixed amount toward redemption to a trustee each year. A subordinated debenture is one that is designated as junior to the other securities or debts issued by the borrower.

debit   An entry on the left side of the books of account in double-entry bookkeeping. A debit is a payment to someone else, and represents a reduction in liabilities or income or an increase in expenses or assets. On the other side of the ledger, the debit is represented as an increase in assets, indicating the receipt of goods in return for the payment. A debit balance exists if total debits are greater than total credits.

debit card   A card, similar to a credit card, that allows the cost of a purchase to be deducted automatically from a customer's bank account. To complete the transaction at the point of sale, a customer punches his or her confidential personel identification number into a terminal. The eventual widespread use of debit cards could eliminate much of the need for individuals to carry cash.

Debreau, Gérard   The French-born American economist who won the Alfred Nobel Memorial Prize in Economic Science in 1983 for "having incorporated new analytical methods into economic theory and for his rigorous reformulation of the theory of general equilibrium."

debt   Money or property that is owed to another person or corporate or government lender, and that must be repaid, normally with interest. Debt can take many forms, including bank loans, BONDS, DEBENTURES, and PROMISSORY NOTES. The borrower pays interest for the use of the money and normally must repay the debt by a specified date.

debt buyback   The purchase by a foreign country of some or all of its foreign debt at a discount and for cash. This was one of the techniques used to lower debts as a result of the THIRD-WORLD DEBT CRISIS.

debt capacity   The ability of a borrower to take on a new debt. The upper limit is determined by the total volume of interest that the borrower can reasonably bear. As a firm's debt increases, the burden of debt costs may become too great, forcing the firm to pay even higher interest rates on new debt, to resort to EQUITY financing for new capital, or to curtail expansion plans and cut back on its existing operations. Individuals and even countries are subject to similar constraints to borrow, based on their debt capacity.

debt capital   Investment capital that consists of long-term bonds and, to some extent, preferred shares, which hence does not represent ownership. Many critics of Canada's high level of foreign ownership of industry argue that the country should have relied much more on foreign debt capital than on foreign EQUITY CAPITAL, which consists of common shares and, hence, ownership of industrial assets. Others argue that reliance on debt capital is more costly, since owners of debt capital must be paid interest each year, regardless of the performance of the business, whereas owners of the equity capital of a business may collect no dividends until many years after the business has been established.

debt-capital ratio   The total debt of a company as a percentage of total debt and SHAREHOLDERS' EQUITY at year-end. The lower the percentage, the greater the financial strength of the company.

debt-equity ratio   A ratio used by financial analysts and lending institutions to determine whether a company's outstanding long-term debt should be further increased, or whether the company should raise additional capital through a new issue of COMMON or PREFERRED SHARES. There are two ways of determining the DEBT-EQUITY RATIO. One is by dividing the outstanding long-term debt by the market value of all outstanding preferred and common shares; the other is to divide all outstanding long-term debt by the book value of SHAREHOLDERS' EQUITY, as listed in the company's annual report. In either case, as a general rule, the total outstanding long-term debt should not be greater than the market value of outstanding common and preferred shares or the book value of the shareholders' equity.

debt-equity swaps   A method of reducing a country's foreign debt by exchanging it for shares in domestic private enterprises. An investment banker buys government debt of a LESS-DEVELOPED COUNTRY from a bank at a discount, presents the debt certificate to the country's central bank for the face value in local currency, and invests the funds directly in the shares of a local company or sells the currency to another corporation planning to invest in the less-developed country. At the same time, the process allows the country to retire a portion of its foreign debt. Debt-equity swaps began in Chile in 1985; by 1989, some 13 highly-indebted less-developed countries, mostly in Latin America, had used debt-equity swaps to reduce about US$32 billion of foreign debt to commercial banks. There is an inflation risk if the debt is not swapped for shares in local companies; if the foreign currency debt is swapped for local currency, the central bank must issue local currency that investors can use to purchase shares. A high volume of debt-equity swaps can lead to an inflationary increase in a country's domestic money supply. Debt-equity swaps emerged as one approach to deal with the THIRD-WORLD DEBT CRISIS.

debt-for-nature swap   A method of reducing a LESS-DEVELOPED COUNTRY's foreign debt that is designed to also help protect the environment. A private environmental group, for example, may purchase part of a country's foreign-currency debt at a discount and then exchange it for that country's commitment to preserve and protect an environmentally sensitive area, such as a tropical rain forest. The first debt-for-nature swap occurred in Bolivia in 1987 when Conservation International bought US$650,000 of Bolivian debt owed Citicorp of New York for US$100,000 and used it to buy the Beni reserve of 330,000 acres, which is home to nomadic Indians and a habitat for some 13 endangered species. According to the World Resources Institute, by August, 1992, 12 countries (Bolivia, Costa Rica, Dominican Republic, Ecuador, Ghana, Guatemala, Jamaica, Madagascar, Mexico, Philippines, Poland, and Zambia) had negotiated debt-for-nature swaps. The face value of the debt involved in these

swaps was just over US$100 million.

debt forgiveness   The writing off of loans, usually by a government or multilateral creditor to a poor country. *See also* THIRD-WORLD DEBT CRISIS, PARIS CLUB, BAKER PLAN, BRADY PLAN.

debt management   The raising of funds by the BANK OF CANADA for the federal government to make sure it has sufficient money to pay its bills and meet its various obligations. This role also entails advising the government on the total level of debt, its composition, its term to maturity, its cost, and its influence on overall credit conditions. The bank, acting as the federal government's banker, thus assists the government in carrying out its FISCAL POLICY by helping to finance its budget deficit. The bank, as fiscal agent for the government, issues new bonds on its behalf; depending on the government's needs, the issue could be sold to replace or roll over existing bonds, or to raise new money. The bank also discusses with the government the upper limits it believes are appropriate for the government's cash demands from money markets, and the dangers to the economy of an excessively large budget deficit. The bank may indicate to the government that it is not prepared to accommodate a rising deficit in time of high inflation, thus forcing the government to reduce spending, delay planned programs, increase taxes, or order the bank to meet its demands. A rising government deficit can always be accommodated in the market at rising interest rates; if the government deficit replaces other forms of borrowing that are declining, interest rates need not increase.

debt relief   Measures to reduce the debt burden of the poorest less-developed countries. The debts of these countries have risen significantly since the 1973-74 period, when the ORGANIZATION OF PETROLEUM EXPORTING COUNTRIES (OPEC) quadrupled the world price of oil. The UNITED NATIONS CONFERENCE ON TRADE AND DEVELOPMENT, representing the less-developed countries, has sought the cancellation of debts owed by the poorest nations. Debt relief was a major demand of the NEW INTERNATIONAL ECONOMIC ORDER. The subject was discussed at the CONFERENCE ON INTERNATIONAL ECONOMIC CO-OPERATION from 1975 to 1977, and Canada, a participant, cancelled $232 million in debts owed by a number of the poorest countries in 1978. With the THIRD-WORLD DEBT CRISIS that was precipitated in 1982, and the decline in world commodity prices, pressure was renewed for debt relief for the poorest developing countries. In 1987, Canada cancelled another $672 million in debts owed by the poorest countries, followed by $181 million in 1990, for a total of $1.2 billion. In 1992, Canada announced it would be willing to convert $145 million owed by Latin American countries into local currencies to be used for local environmental projects. Since 1978, Canada has cancelled an additional US$730 million of debt owed by the poorest countries. At the Toronto economic summit in 1990, the GROUP OF SEVEN agreed on new measures to reduce the debt of the poorest countries. *See also* PARIS CLUB.

debt rescheduling Techniques to either change the length of time and perhaps the rate of interest on outstanding debt or to reduce the amount of debt owed. The term is usually applied to the restructuring of debt owed by developing countries but debt rescheduling can also be a key element in restructuring a company in financial difficulty. In all cases, the agreement of creditors is essential. *See also* THIRD-WORLD DEBT CRISIS, PARIS CLUB, BAKER PLAN, BRADY PLAN.

debt service The interest and other costs of a debt.

debt service ratio The total debt servicing costs of a country as a percentage of its exports of goods and services.

debt servicing Interest payments and scheduled repayments of principal on a loan, along with any administrative costs in managing the loan, that must be made by a borrower to creditors in a financial or fiscal year.

Debt Servicing and Reduction Account A special fund established in 1991 by the federal government to receive money to be used for the sole purpose of paying interest on the public debt and, if possible, to pay down the debt. The account receives the net revenues from the GOODS AND SERVICES TAX, net proceeds from the sale of CROWN CORPORATIONS, and gifts to the Crown from the public.

debt-to-GDP ratio A measure of the burden of public debt and a target for fiscal policy. The goal in deficit reduction is to stabilize and then reduce the debt-to-GDP ratio so that the burden of accumulated debt on the economy is reduced. However, as long as government deficits exceed the growth of the economy, the debt-to-GDP ratio will increase, so that government debt will represent a growing burden on the economy.

debtor A person, company, government, or other institution that owes money to someone else. *See also* CREDITOR.

debtor nation A nation that runs a recurring BALANCE-OF-PAYMENTS deficit and therefore accumulates a growing obligation to the rest of the world. It must attract foreign capital — either DEBT CAPITAL in the form of loans or EQUITY CAPITAL in the form of foreign ownership — to meet its international obligations, since it cannot pay its way in the world through the export of goods and services or from its income from its own overseas investments and other sources.

In the early stages of development, a country is expected to run a chronic balance-of-payments deficit, since it is busy building up its industry and INFRASTRUCTURE such as railways, power stations, universities, water and sewer systems, and highways. But it is expected to graduate, first into a mature debtor, with interest and dividend payments to foreigners still so high as to prevent a current-account surplus, then, as interest payments decline and exports of goods and services expand, into a CREDITOR NATION, exporting debt and equity capital and helping younger nations to build up their economies. Canada has not followed this pattern; it has a mature industrial economy in many respects, and yet still runs a chronic balance-of-payments deficit. One of the roles of the INTERNATIONAL MONETARY FUND is to help debtor nations to manage their external debt and bring their balance of payments into better balance.

decentralization   1. In corporate organization, a system that gives decision-making authority to individual divisions or subsidiaries of the firm, with head office setting only major policies and approving new expenditures above those required for the routine operation of the division or subsidiary. **2.** In production planning, locating manufacturing plants and other facilities close to markets, instead of concentrating manufacturing in one or a few large centralized plants. **3.** In a system of federalism, such as Canada's, the granting of considerable autonomy in taxing and spending to the provinces, as opposed to the central or national government. *See also* CENTRALIZATION.

decertification   The loss of the right by a union to represent a group of workers in a BARGAINING UNIT in COLLECTIVE BARGAINING with their employer. This right is lost if the majority of members of the bargaining unit vote to apply to a federal or provincial LABOUR-RELATIONS BOARD to take away the union's right to be their representative.

decreasing costs   The decrease in production costs per unit of output as production increases. *See also* ECONOMIES OF SCALE, MASS PRODUCTION.

decreasing term insurance   A form of TERM INSURANCE in which the amount payable to beneficiaries in the event of death declines each year. This form of insurance is often used in conjunction with major debts, such as a mortgage on a house or a loan obtained by a partnership. Thus, payment of the debt is assured if the borrower dies, so that, in the case of the house, the family can pay off the mortgage, or, in the case of the partnership, the remaining partner can continue the business without being burdened by repayment of the late partner's share of the debt.

dedicated reserves   Natural gas reserves that are committed by a natural gas production company to a specific purchaser through a long-term contract.

deductible clause   A clause in an insurance policy that requires the insured person to pay the first part of the cost of damages covered. For example, automobile insurance policies require the automobile owner to pay the first say, $100 of the repairs. This saves insurance companies from having to handle large numbers of small claims where the administrative and handling costs would probably exceed the repair costs.

deed   A document transferring ownership of land, buildings, or other property from one party to another.

deemed realization   The assumption that an asset has been sold, even though it hasn't been, so that a CAPITAL-GAINS TAX can be levied. For example, in Canada there is deemed realization of the shares and other assets left in the estate of an individual who dies, so that a capital-gains tax is collected from the estate, even though the assets themselves may not be sold. Similarly, a Canadian who gives up residence in this country pays a capital-gains tax on his or her assets — if they are not sold, there is deemed realization.

defalcation   The misuse or theft of money by someone holding it in trust for others — for example, a lawyer holding trust funds for his or her client.

default   The failure by a person, corporation, or government to live up to obligations under a contract. The obligations may include completing work, delivering goods, making payments on a loan, or redeeming bonds or preferred shares by a certain date. For example, if a borrower fails to pay the interest on a loan or the principal due on a loan, he or she is in default. Similarly, when a party to a futures contract fails to make or take delivery of the commodity in the futures market, he or she is in default.

Defence Research Board (DRB)   An advisory board, created in 1947, to give the Minister of National Defence advice on how science and technology can be used to help national defence. The board has a full-time chairman and vice-chairman, and 12 appointed members. The president of the NATIONAL RESEARCH COUNCIL, the Minister of National Defence, and three senior military officers also sit on the board.

defensive stock   The stock of a company that generates relatively stable earnings and maintains dividend payments even during a severe recession. A telephone company is an example.

deferred annuity   An ANNUITY whose payments don't begin until some time in the future — for example, on reaching the age of 65 — although the premiums have to be paid a number of years in advance. Such annuities are sold by life-insurance and trust companies.

deferred demand   Demand for goods and services that can be postponed into the future if there are shortages. While the demand for food cannot be deferred, the demand for cars, appliances, furniture, and other consumer goods and services, such as house-painting, can be deferred.

deferred income taxes   The difference between income taxes owed if assets are depreciated according to generally accepted accounting principles and the taxes actually paid as a result of CAPITAL-COST ALLOWANCES under the Income Tax Act. The difference arises because deductions for depreciation are recognized for different time periods for accounting and tax purposes. The Income Tax Act permits a company to use the declining-balance method of calculating DEPRECIATION in its tax return, which results in larger depreciation deductions in the early life of an asset than those obtained through the straight-line method of calculating depreciation used in the company's annual report to shareholders. This extra depreciation in the early life of the asset is accounted for in the company's EARNINGS STATEMENT as deferred income taxes, and it is added on the liability side of the BALANCE SHEET to the reserve for deferred income taxes. In later years, the tax deduction for depreciation of the asset will be less than that claimed in the company's annual report, and the extra payment will have to come from the reserve. However, in the meantime, the company has the use of the money, interest free. An individual's tax liability may also be deferred by certain types of investments, for example, by investments in REGISTERED RETIREMENT SAVINGS PLANS, CONTRIBUTORY PENSION PLANS, and various TAX SHELTERS.

deficiency letter A letter to the issuer of a preliminary PROSPECTUS for a new issue of company stock that sets out questions that must be properly answered before the prospectus is approved and the sale of stock proceeds.

deficiency payment A government subsidy to farmers for the difference between market prices and those guaranteed under an agricultural support program.

deficit The situation that exists when spending exceeds revenues; the opposite is a SURPLUS. *See also* BUDGET.

deficit financing The policy decision of a government to spend more than it raises by taxation and other means, with the BUDGET deficit being financed by government borrowing. Deficit financing is common during periods of high unemployment and slow economic growth, and is a means of raising purchasing power or the overall level of DEMAND in the economy. But deficit-financing can also occur during periods of strong economic growth if a government has failed to bring spending under control or raise taxes. Likewise, the accumulation of debt can bring debt servicing costs to such a high level that continued deficits are inevitable without harsh measures. *See also* BUDGETARY-

ACCOUNTS BUDGET, CASH-NEEDS BUDGET, NATIONAL-ACCOUNTS BUDGET.

deflation **1.** An actual decline in the general level of prices in the economy. The cause is usually a protracted slowdown in economic activity brought about by a contractionary or restrictive MONETARY POLICY. Deflationary policies may be pursued to bring down the rate of inflation or improve the BALANCE OF PAYMENTS by tightening up monetary policy and FISCAL POLICY. Demand falls, interest rates rise, and credit is harder to obtain, and the resulting decline in economic activity, if long enough, will lead to an actual fall in real estate, commodity and other prices. *See also* DISINFLATION. **2.** The adjustment of the GROSS DOMESTIC PRODUCT (GDP) and its various components, expressed in current dollars, by the overall rate of inflation in the economy, to show the change in gross domestic product or its components in real or volume terms. The inflation index used is called the GDP deflator.

deflation trap The risk to an economy in which deflation is taking place that declining prices will generate pressures for further declines in prices, creating a downward spiral into a depression as the equity disappears from real estate and other assets and companies are forced to shed more workers to lower their operating costs.

deflationary gap The gap between the level of spending, including investment, needed in an economy to maintain full employment, and the actual level of spending and investment taking place. Full employment can only be achieved if the level of aggregate demand is increased to use idle capacity in the economy. To restore full employment, governments can increase their own spending or provide new incentives through FISCAL POLI-CY, or ease monetary conditions through MONETARY POLICY. *See also* KEYNESIAN ECONOMICS.

deindustrialization   A contraction in manufacturing activity in a country due to its lack of competitiveness and the ability of investors to earn a better return from manufacturing in other parts of the world. While there is a long-term trend to increased service-sector activity in the industrial countries, deindustrialization is still a matter of concern when it is caused by a decline in competitiveness, compared with other industrial nations, and jeopardizes the ability of a country to pay for the imports it needs. This lack of competitiveness may stem from low productivity and rising unit-labour costs, an overvalued exchange rate, or a lack of investment in research and development, worker skills, or new production technologies. A country that deindustrializes can face serious BALANCE OF PAYMENTS problems.

delisted stock   COMMON or PRE-FERRED SHARE that is no longer traded on a stock exchange. The reasons for delisting include the repeated failure by a company to abide by stock-exchange rules, the bankruptcy of a business, the redemption of the share — usually a preferred share — and the withdrawal of so many shares from distribution that the number still outstanding for trading is far too low.

deliverability   The maximum amount of natural gas that can be delivered from a natural-gas reservoir at any particular point in its life without jeopardizing the size or long-term production capability of the reservoir.

delivered pricing   The practice of refusing a customer delivery of an article on the same trade terms as other customers in the same area. It is a reviewable practice under the COMPE-TITION ACT. However, the COMPETI-TION TRIBUNAL will not make an order against a supplier when it finds that the supplier is unable to accommodate an additional customer without first making a significant capital investment.

delivery   The delivery by sellers of shares on or before the fifth business day following the sale.

Delphi Technique   A method of technological and social forecasting developed in the early 1960s. A group of experts are asked, individually, to give their opinion on some future event. The responses are then assembled and circulated to the same group of experts, who thus have the chance to revise their own views or respond to other forecasts. These revised forecasts are again assembled and recirculated. The process may be repeated several more times, until some kind of group forecast or consensus is reached.

demand   The combined desire, ability, and willingness on the part of consumers to buy a good or service. Aggregate demand or market demand is the total of the demands of all consumers in the economy. Demand is determined by income and by price, which is, in part, determined by SUPPLY. Government can raise the level of aggregate demand by lowering taxes or increasing its own spending, or both. *See* LAW OF SUPPLY AND DEMAND.

demand and supply curves   The representation of the DEMAND and SUPPLY SCHEDULES for a particular good or service. Their intersection is the meeting point of producers and consumers and, other things being equal, shows the likely price and volume of production, or the EQUILIBRIUM point, for the particular good or service. The demand curve, in effect, shows how much of a product or service a consumer would buy at various possible prices.

demand deposit   A bank deposit that can be withdrawn at any time without prior notice to the bank or other deposit-taking institution. Demand deposits include funds in chequing-non-savings accounts, and do not earn interest; they are part of the most narrowly defined MONEY SUPPLY (M-1).

demand for money   The amount of assets or wealth that individuals and firms desire to hold in the form of money.

demand loan   A loan that must be repaid whenever the lender calls it in, as opposed to an installment loan, which has to be paid by a pre-determined date, usually in monthly or weekly amounts. Because demand loans can be called at any time, they usually carry a lower rate of interest.

demand management   1. The use of government-spending, monetary, and tax policies to control the level of demand in the economy, and hence the rate of economic growth and level of unemployment. Demand-management policies are used to moderate fluctuations in the BUSINESS CYCLE. *See also* KEYNESIAN ECONOMICS, FISCAL POLICY, MONETARY POLICY. **2.** The use of energy efficiency and conservation measures to reduce the demand for energy. By the encouragement of energy efficiency and conservation, utilities can reduce the need to invest in new sources of energy, such as electric power plants or hydrocarbon megaprojects. Demand management can be a more cost-effective way of meeting future energy needs, particularly when environmental costs are also taken into account.

demand-pull inflation   Inflation caused by too much demand or purchasing power in the economy, with too much money chasing too few goods. When there is excess purchasing power relative to the physical supply of goods and services, the only outcome can be rising prices. Too much money available for spending when there is a limited supply of goods and services, plus full employment, leads consumers to bid up the prices of available goods and services, and leads firms to bid up available supplies of labour. The GROSS DOMESTIC PRODUCT (GDP) will go up because prices go up, but the real GDP cannot rise faster than a country's ability to produce goods and services at full-employment levels, which is why demand-pull inflation is often described as too much money chasing too few goods.

Monetary and fiscal policies can be used to avoid demand-pull inflation, by cutting back on demand in the economy before the BUSINESS CYCLE hits its peak; the same policies can also be used to curb demand if demand-pull inflation already exists. Raising interest rates, reducing the growth rate of the money supply, raising taxes, and freezing government spending will all help to reduce demand and thus cool off demand-pull inflation. MONETARISTS blame demand-pull inflation on increases in MONEY SUPPLY in excess of the long-term growth rate of the economy. *See also* COST-PUSH INFLATION.

demand schedule (curve)   A curve that shows the quantity of a good or service that consumers will buy at different prices. As prices rise, demand tends to fall, while a decline in prices will tend to raise demand. Hence, there is always a relationship between the demand for a good and its price; a demand curve shows this relationship. Price is usually shown on the vertical axis and demand along the horizontal axis, so that the curve rises upward to the left and downward to the right.

demographic transition   The change-over in the rate of population growth of a country, from a high rate of growth to a low rate of growth, with both the BIRTH and DEATH RATES moving from a high rate of growth to a low rate of growth. Usually, the death rate of a population declines first, with birth rates continuing at a high level. The result is rapid population growth. Birth rates begin to decline until birth and death rates are about equal, and both are significantly lower than they were earlier. The demographic transi-tion is related to the stage of economic development of a country: a poor country typically has high birth and death rates, but with rising income its death rate falls as nutrition and health care improve and, subsequently, its birth rate falls as people become more affluent and tend to have smaller fami-lies.

demography   The scientific study of human populations, including their size, composition by age and sex, and distribution and growth, along with the factors determining population growth, such as BIRTH and DEATH RATES and migration.

demurrage   Extra charges made by railways, trucking and shipping compa-nies, and airlines, to load, unload, or store goods if there is a delay or if extra time is required. For example, if a grain terminal is backed up due to conges-tion in a port, the railways may charge a demurrage fee to compensate them for the extra time needed to unload the wheat, and ships will do likewise.

Dene Nation proposal   A proposal pre-sented to the federal government in 1976 by the Indian Brotherhood of the Northwest Territories for a "Dene gov-ernment with jurisdiction over a geo-graphical area and over subject matters now within the jurisdiction of either the Government of Canada or the Gov-ernment of the Northwest Territories." The Indian Brotherhood sought land ownership, control over non-renewable resource development, protection of hunting, fishing, and trapping rights, preservation of the Dene language and culture, and compensation for "past use of Dene land by non-Dene." The Dene said they wanted to replace Treaty Eight of 1899 and Treaty Eleven of 1921 with a new arrangement that would allow them to make their own decisions about their educational sys-tem, political institutions, and other matters, as well as to develop their own economy. In 1977, the prime minister rejected the concept of a separate Dene Nation, and in 1978, the Indian Broth-erhood was renamed the Dene Nation. The Dene and Métis subsequently agreed to joint negotiations with the federal government, and in 1981, for-mal negotiations on land claims were launched although the Dene were informed that constitutional and politi-cal development could not be resolved in the claims forum. The negotiations led to an interim agreement in 1986, which identified areas for negotiation and included $350 million of compen-sation and 181,300 square kilometres (70,000 square miles) of land. In 1988, the negotiators initialled an agreement in principle, and after approval by the Dene and Métis, it was signed on Sep-tember 5, 1988, by the leaders of the Dene and Métis, the prime minister, and the government leader of the Northwest Territories. Implementation negotiations, including negotiations over allocations of land, continued into 1990. But the agreed deadline of March 31, 1990, for completion passed because of Dene-Métis concerns over treaty rights, aboriginal rights, and the entrenchment of self-government. In April, 1990, the Minister of INDIAN

AFFAIRS AND NORTHERN DEVELOP-MENT met with Dene and Métis leaders, and the parties initialled the agreement as final and agreed to recommend it for ratification, to be held before March 31, 1991. But before ratification could take place, new disagreements broke out in the Dene-Métis community, and the final efforts to establish a Dene Nation were suspended. *See also* NUNAVUT.

density **1.** The amount of building that can be done on a given parcel of land. It is usually expressed as the number of housing units or as the coverage or gross floor space permitted. If a piece of land is zoned at 3.2 times coverage, the gross floor area can be no greater than 3.2 times the area of the lot. Municipal zoning by-laws are usually expressed in terms of the type of building permitted in an area and the density of construction. Some municipalities also impose height restrictions. **2.** The number of people per acre or hectare.

Department-store Sales A monthly report from Statistics Canada on department-store sales at the national and provincial levels (publication 63-002). Department-store sales can be a useful indicator of consumer confidence. *See also* RETAIL TRADE.

departure tax A tax charged by some countries, including many of the less-developed countries, on travellers departing from an airport or port.

depletion The entry in a natural-resource company's books to recognize the running down of the natural resources that form part of its assets, since these resources cannot be replenished. The "wasting" of these resources is similar to the DEPRECIATION entry used in a company's books to mark the deterioration of physical machinery and equipment.

depletion allowance A tax deduction, similar to depreciation, that used to be granted to oil, natural-gas, mining, forest-products, and other natural-resource industries. The depletion allowance for exploration and development was abolished on July 1, 1989, as part of the federal government's shift to a neutral corporate-tax system. The principal assets of natural-resource companies consist of their natural resources, which are reduced over time as they are exploited and hence are known as wasting assets. Companies were permitted a deduction for depletion, based on the cost of finding and developing the natural resource, so that they could recover these costs and find new natural resources. In Canada, depletion had to be earned and was equivalent to one-third of the expenditure in finding new natural resources. Like depreciation, depletion is not a cash outlay. It reduces a company's tax liability, and hence increases its after-tax profits. The federal government, in abolishing depletion allowances, argued that a reduction in overall rates of corporate taxation would compensate for the loss of the depletion allowance.

deposit **1.** A small downpayment on a product or property made by a would-be buyer that signifies his or her probable intention of purchasing it and retaining an exclusive right to purchase for a specified period of time. **2.** Funds placed in a savings or other financial-institution account.

deposit institution A bank, trust company, credit union, caisse populaire, or other financial institution that accepts deposits of money from the public, manages accounts on which cheques can be written, sells guaranteed-investment and other savings certificates, and makes loans. A deposit is an asset of the depositor and a liability of the financial institution taking the deposit. The activities of deposit institutions are regulated by federal or provincial legislation, depending on the type of financial institution and whether they are federally or provincially incorporated. *See also* FINANCIAL INTERMEDIARY.

deposit insurance Insurance to protect depositors against the complete loss of their savings deposited in a bank, trust company, major credit union, caisse populaire, or other deposit institution, if the financial institution fails. The CANADA DEPOSIT INSURANCE CORPORATION and the QUEBEC DEPOSIT INSURANCE BOARD provide protection for all Canadian-dollar deposits up to $60,000 at insured institutions, with the institutions legally required to obtain and pay for such insurance. The existence of deposit insurance adds to the stability of the financial system and makes it easier for a small and new deposit institution to compete in the market for savings dollars. Canada has had deposit insurance since 1967, following the failure of several financial institutions, including the ATLANTIC ACCEPTANCE Company, British Mortgage and Trust Corporation, and PRUDENTIAL FINANCE Corporation.

depreciation **1.** A method of calculating and writing off the costs to a firm of its various ASSETs, such as machinery, buildings, trucks, and equipment, over their useful life, reflecting wear and tear or technological obsolescence. It is an accounting exercise, and no actual cash transaction takes place. However, depreciation reduces taxable income. Investment in such fixed assets, which wear out or become obsolete over time, is a normal expense of business. However, since such assets have a reasonably long life — buildings longer than machinery and machinery longer than vehicles — it makes more sense, in determining the real costs of operating the business, to allocate a share of the total cost to each year of the normal life of the asset, rather than to deduct the total cost as an expense in the year of purchase. The cost of the asset is divided by the number of years of useful life as calculated for accounting or tax purposes, and the resulting amount is deducted for each of the years as an ordinary business expense, before calculating the company's profit. The amount claimed is not actually paid out as an expense each year when it is claimed for tax purposes, but it is deducted from taxable income and reduces the firm's tax liability. Hence, it increases profits and represents money available to the firm for the replacement of machinery and equipment, expansion, retirement of debt, diversification, or payment of a higher dividend to shareholders.

The depreciation claimed by a firm is included in the EARNINGS STATEMENT under expenses. Depreciation claimed by all Canadian businesses is identified in the GROSS DOMESTIC PRODUCT statistics as capital-cost allowances. When the government wishes to encourage business investment, it can bring in ACCELERATED DEPRECIATION provisions for a short period. In 1987, capital-cost allowance rates were lowered to bring them into line with economic depreciation, thereby reducing the role of capital-cost allowances as an incentive for investment; in 1992, the capital-cost allowance was improved slightly to encourage investment. If the government wishes to encourage a particular form of activity, such as RESEARCH AND DEVELOPMENT, REGIONAL DEVELOPMENT, or environmental cleanup, it may allow firms to claim, say, 150 percent of the capital costs for depreciation purposes. Depreciation is thus an important contribution to a firm's cash flow.

There are two basic methods of calculating depreciation: (i) Straight-line depreciation, where the cost of the asset is divided by the number of years of its useful life and the same amount is deducted each year. This is usually used in a company's annual report. (ii) Declining-balance depreciation, which provides a greater write-off in the early years of life of the asset. The depreciation each year is calculated as a percentage of the cost of the asset after the depreciation of the previous year is deducted. This is the usual method used in a company's tax return. Depreciation is a bookkeeping entry; it does not entail a cash expenditure, but it is part of the CASH FLOW of a business. However, funds from depreciation are not set aside to finance replacement equipment but are used for whatever purpose the company sees fit. *See also* DEFERRED INCOME TAXES. **2.** A rise in the cost of a foreign currency, or conversely a fall in the value of the Canadian dollar, as a result of market pressures in a FLOATING-EXCHANGE-RATE SYSTEM. A depreciation of the Canadian dollar makes its exports cheaper in foreign markets, thereby boosting exports, but increases the cost of imports and the cost of servicing foreign debt denominated in foreign currencies. While a currency depreciation has a stimulative impact on export industries, it is usually equated with a weak economy and a declining standard of living since a country has to produce more to pay for what it imports. *See also* DEVALUATION.

depressed area An area whose level of unemployment and personal income is significantly below the national average. *See* REGIONAL DEVELOPMENT.

depression An extended period of sharply reduced economic activity, with widespread unemployment, declining prices, little capital investment, and a large number of business failures. A depression is much more severe than a recession, lasts for a much longer period of time, and tends to be global in impact. Depressions hit the Canadian economy from 1873 to 1879 and from 1929 to 1939. To restore AGGREGATE DEMAND, governments can increase spending and cut taxes. *See* GREAT DEPRESSION.

deputy-minister The highest ranking official in a federal or provincial government department. Deputy-ministers are appointed by the prime minister or a provincial premier. While deputy-ministers for the most part rise through the ranks of the public service, and as such are non-partisan and there to serve whatever political party is elected to office, there has been a tendency in recent years to politicize the upper ranks of the public service and to introduce an element of partisanship to its most senior ranks. A deputy-minister is the interface between his or her government department and the relevant cabinet minister. While the responsibility for decision making rests with the cabinet, deputy-ministers are supposed to provide advice to cabinet ministers in making decisions and to implement decisions of the cabinet, as well as managing their departments and the on-going programs of their departments.

deregulation A reduction in government regulation of business activities, including approval for new investment projects. The purpose is usually to reduce business operating costs created by complying with government regulations, and to speed up new investment.

derivatives Various types of financial contracts that identify and cover against specific forms of market risk, such as swaps and options. Since the mid-1980s, this has been the fastest growth area in the financial services market, growing from about US$1,000 billion in the mid-1980s to US$8,000 billion in 1991.

derived demand The demand for a factor of production, such as land, labour, or capital, or for another commodity, that results from the demand for a good or service that it helps to produce or that is used in association with the good or service being produced. For example, demand for a house or apartment leads to a demand for construction workers, mortgage financing, and building materials, as well as a demand for appliances, furniture, and carpeting when it is finished.

deterrent fee An extra fee charged to discourage the unnecessary use of a service. For example, provincial governments used to be able to permit doctors to charge patients an extra fee, in addition to the payment they got from the provincial health service, to discourage people from making unnecessary visits to a doctor until the practice was effectively banned under the CANADA HEALTH ACT. A problem with a deterrent fee in such cases is that it is also levied on necessary visits, and is a burden for people with low incomes. Another example is the fee charged by a telephone company for personal directory assistance, if the desired number is already listed in the phone directory.

devaluation The deliberate reduction by a government of the par or official value of its currency in terms of the value of the currencies of other nations. Although devaluations are normally associated with a regime of FIXED EXCHANGE RATES, a devaluation can also occur as a result of deliberate policy steps under a system of FLOATING EXCHANGE RATES. On May 2, 1962, when exchange rates were fixed, Canada devalued its exchange rate to 92.5 U.S. cents; it had been floating at 95 U.S. cents shortly before. Devaluation can serve as an economic stimulus, since it reduces the price of exports and makes them easier to sell, while raising the price of imports, making it easier for domestic producers to compete against imports. It also has an inflationary impact, since it raises the price of essential imports. For that part of Canada's foreign debt denominated in foreign currencies, devaluation means higher debt-servicing costs. *See also* DEPRECIATION.

developed country A country that has a high per capita income, high standards of health care, education, and housing, an advanced industrial economy, a capacity in leading-edge technology, and high levels of agricultural productivity. The developed countries include Canada, the members of the EUROPEAN COMMUNITY, the United States, Japan, Australia, and New Zealand. The developed countries are also known as the North in the NORTH-SOUTH DIALOGUE. *See also* DEVELOPING COUNTRIES.

developer A company or individual who undertakes projects to build housing subdivisions, commercial office buildings and shopping centres, and apartment complexes.

developing country A country with a low per capita income and inadequate savings to finance economic development, in particular industrialization. Developing countries are usually characterized by higher rates of population growth, lower levels of life expectancy and literacy, and a dependency on agriculture and natural resources. *See also* DEVELOPED COUNTRY

development 1. The modernization of a country's economy, including investment in INFRASTRUCTURE such as power stations, schools, telecommunications, airports, and railways, and in technologically advanced industries. 2. The work that is carried out to bring an oil or natural-gas reservoir into production or to open up and extract a mineral-ore deposit. **3.** The design and refining of a new invention to turn it into a commercially acceptable product.

development assistance *See* OFFICIAL DEVELOPMENT ASSISTANCE.

Development Assistance Committee (DAC) A special committee within the ORGANIZATION FOR ECONOMIC CO-OPERATION AND DEVELOPMENT, set up to monitor, co-ordinate, and assess OFFICIAL DEVELOPMENT ASSISTANCE of member countries, including Canada. The goal of DAC is to increase the volume of resources made available to developing countries and to improve the effectiveness of aid. DAC publishes an annual assessment of each member's aid activities and reports on the progress each member nation is making toward the PEARSON COMMISSION target of official development assistance, which is equal to 0.7 percent of each member's gross national product. DAC also assesses the needs and problems of the LESS-DEVELOPED COUNTRIES. DAC publishes an annual report, *Development Co-operation*, every year that reports on the aid programs of the industrial countries and addresses key issues in development.

development decades Ten-year plans by the United Nations (UN) to strengthen the economies of the LESS-DEVELOPED COUNTRIES. The first development decade, proclaimed in 1961, set a goal of at least 5 percent annual growth in national income in the less-developed countries by the end of the decade. Developed countries, such as Canada, were asked to provide 1 percent of their gross national product (GNP) as aid to the developing countries. On December 21, 1990, the UN General Assembly designated 1991 to 2000 as the Fourth UN Development Decade and adopted an International Development Strategy for the decade. The principal aim is to make the 1990s a decade of accelerated development for the DEVELOPING COUNTRIES through strengthened international co-operation resulting in a significant improvement in the human condition in these countries and a narrowing of the gap between rich and poor countries. Six goals were set out: A surge in growth in the developing countries; a development process that is responsive to social needs, seeks a significant reduction in extreme poverty, promotes the development of human resources and skills, and is environmentally sound and sustainable; improvement of the international monetary and trade systems; a stronger and more stable world economy and sound macroeconomic management; strengthened international development co-operation; and special efforts to deal with the problems of the least developed countries.

development economics The branch of economics concerned with how LESS-DEVELOPED COUNTRIES can evolve into more affluent industrial societies with higher per capita incomes. It deals with different types of development strategies open to poor countries.

development phase The phase when a proven oil or gas field is brought into production through the drilling of the necessary production wells or an ore body is brought into production through the construction of the extraction process for the ore body.

differentiated product Techniques employed, such as brand names, design differences, and technical differences, to distinguish a company's products from those of its competitors.

dilution   The reduction in a company's EARNINGS PER SHARE caused by an increase in the number of outstanding shares in the company. This can result from the conversion of CONVERTIBLE bonds or convertible preferred shares into COMMON SHARES, from the issue of new common shares, or from the exercising of WARRANTS to acquire new common shares.

diminishing marginal productivity An economic proposition stating that the larger the quantity of one factor when it is combined with fixed quantities of the other FACTORS OF PRODUCTION, the progressively lower the gain in productivity from that factor. For example, in a factory with fixed space and fixed numbers of machines, the use of additional workers will increase output. However, each extra worker will add less to the total output than the previous worker as long as the factory space and number of machines remain unchanged.

diminishing marginal utility An economic proposition stating that each extra unit consumed yields less utility or satisfaction than the previous unit consumed. For example, while one chocolate bar may yield enormous satisfaction and a second one almost as much, the seventh, eighth, and ninth chocolate bars will yield less and less satisfaction. The same is true with rising money income; proponents of the ABILITY-TO-PAY PRINCIPLE OF TAXATION argue that a dollar taxed away from a wealthy individual is much less likely to be missed than a dollar taxed away from a low-income individual, since the wealthier individual gains less satisfaction with each additional dollar of income.

diminishing returns   *See* LAW OF DIMINISHING RETURNS.

direct cost   A cost that is related directly to the volume of output — for example, costs of the raw materials or parts used to manufacture a product, along with the cost of the labour required to make the product. Such costs are also known as variable costs. *See also* INDIRECT COST, FIXED COSTS.

direct investment   Investment made in physical assets, such as a new factory or shopping centre, or to acquire effective control of another corporation by purchasing sufficient shares in the company to exercise control, as opposed to PORTFOLIO INVESTMENT, which is made simply for the yield in interest, dividends, and capital gains that can be obtained. Direct investment consists of investment made to expand an existing business by providing new EQUITY CAPITAL, to start up a new business, or to take over an existing business. FOREIGN DIRECT INVESTMENT consists of direct investments made by corporations or individuals from one country in the business sector of another country. Statistics Canada reports on foreign direct-investment flows in its quarterly BALANCE-OF-PAYMENTS reports (publication 67-001).

direct placement   The placing of a new issue of shares or bonds directly with a small group of purchasers, such as pension funds or other institutional investors, instead of through a widely distributed public underwriting of the issue.

direct selling   A sales campaign aimed directly at the final consumer of a good or service, organized usually by the producer. This type of sales effort bypasses retailers and other sales organizations; it includes, for example, door-to-door sales and direct-mail sales.

direct tax A tax that is paid directly by the person or firm on which it is levied and that, generally speaking, is hard to shift to another person. Examples include personal and corporate income tax, and capital-gains tax. Indirect taxes are taxes levied on expenditures, such as sales taxes, gasoline taxes, alcohol and tobacco taxes, and customs duties. Under the CONSTITUTION ACT, 1867, both the federal government and the provincial governments have the power to levy direct taxes. The federal power is in section 91 (3) and section 122, while the provincial power is in section 92 (2).

director A person who is elected by a company's shareholders or appointed by a company's owners to serve on the company's BOARD OF DIRECTORS. Directors supervise the work of the company's officers and set company policy. They must own at least one share in the company and are expected to act in the best interests of the shareholders and not management. Under federal and provincial CORPORATION LAWS, directors are required to make it their business to know what is going on in the company on whose board they serve. They may be liable for illegal acts committed by the company if those acts are committed with their knowledge or consent, and they are liable for gross negligence if they are delinquent in their role as supervisors of the company's activities and policies. They are, under law, expected to exercise, as Ontario's legislation puts it, "the degree of care, diligence, and skill that a reasonably prudent person would exercise in comparable circumstances." Thus, the position of company director is no longer the honorary post it used to be. Today, the law imposes important responsibilities on directors to protect the interests of shareholders and the company. Directors may be held personally responsible for some corporate problems, such as unpaid wages of employees, so corporations usually provide insurance for their directors. Compensation is paid in the form of directors' fees.

Director of Investigation and Research Under the COMPETITION ACT, the person responsible for enforcing the act in a fair, effective, and timely manner. The director heads the BUREAU OF COMPETITION POLICY and is the only person who can refer mergers and unfair business-practice cases to the COMPETITION TRIBUNAL for review. The director also investigates illegal activities under the Competition Act, such as misleading advertising, bid-rigging, and price discrimination. The director may also appear before federal regulatory agencies, such as the NATIONAL ENERGY BOARD, if a competition issue arises. The director has sweeping powers to investigate, such as the right to seek a search warrant before a judge, search premises, and seize records. A search warrant can also be extended to computer systems.

dirty float The intervention by a country's central bank in FOREIGN-EXCHANGE MARKETS to assist its export or other industries by helping to move the currency up or down or stabilize it in the face of intense market pressures, even though it claims it is letting its currency float freely in a FLOATING-EXCHANGE-RATE SYSTEM. This differs from modest intervention to smooth out day-to-day fluctuations in the rate, and thus to maintain an orderly market.

disability benefits Payments through WORKER'S COMPENSATION and various insurance programs to employees who are no longer able to work, or who can only work at a lesser-paying job, as a result of injuries or ill health suffered on the job.

disallowance The power of the federal government under the CONSTITUTION ACT, 1867, to disallow a provincial law. This power must be exercised within one year of enactment of the provincial law and may be used if a provincial law is declared unconstitutional, contrary to "Dominion policy" or "Dominion interest," or to "reason, justice, and natural equity." Some 112 provincial laws have been disallowed. However, the power is largely inoperative today: it was last exercised in 1943.

disclosure A requirement that information be made available to the public at large or to specific individuals who may be affected by a specific action. For example, publicly traded corporations are required to publish extensive financial information, verified by an AUDITOR according to GENERALLY ACCEPTED ACCOUNTING PRINCIPLES, each year. Similarly, a bank, finance company, credit union, or other financial institution lending money to someone must disclose the interest rate and the cost of the loan, while someone in a position of public trust — an elected representative, for example — must disclose whether he or she has a financial or other interest in the outcome of a decision, determining, for example, who should get a contract. Securities commissions require comparative audited financial statements of publicly traded companies, including a statement of profit and loss, a statement of surplus, a balance sheet, and a statement of changes in financial position within 170 days (140 in Ontario) of the end of the financial year, and unaudited quarterly statements within 60 days from the end of each of the first three quarters of the financial year, including an income statement. Most provinces also require disclosure of a material change in a company's affairs — any change that could be expected to have an important impact on the market price of its securities. This could

include the firing of the chief executive officer, negotiation of a merger or takeover, the discovery of discrepancies in financial accounts, a major lawsuit, the loss of a major contract, a change in the nature of the business, or the resignation of members of the board of directors. The BANK ACT requires not only the disclosure of the cost of borrowing and interest rates, but also requires the disclosure of service charges for deposits and other normal banking services.

discomfort index An index designed by U.S. economist Arthur Okun to show the combined effect of inflation and unemployment at any point in time. It is obtained by adding the unemployment rate and the rate of increase in the consumer price index for the same period.

discount 1. A reduction in the price of a good or service from its list or market price in return for prompt payment, a large-volume purchase, or other similar reason. 2. The amount by which a preferred share or bond sells below its face or par value. 3. The charge made for cashing in a promissory note, investment certificate, or other debt before it matures.

discount market *See* MONEY MARKET.

discount rate The rate of interest used to determine whether a proposed investment project is viable. *See* DISCOUNTED CASH FLOW.

discounted When a factor that affects the price of a share or other security, such as a drop in profits, a market glut of a company's product, or a change in tax policy, has already been taken into account in determining the security's price before the announcement actually occurs, and, therefore, has already been discounted by investors.

discounted cash flow An analytical tool that helps corporations to determine the true profitability of a project or to value certain kinds of assets such as oil and gas reserves by discounting the expected future cash flow from the project against its net present value. Since money received in the future is worth less than money in hand today — due both to the erosion of its value from inflation and to the lost income that could be earned if it were available to invest at some interest rate such as the long-term corporate or government-bond rate — the profitability of a project cannot be determined by simply adding together the profits from each future year. Using the DISCOUNTED CASH FLOW method, the value of future earnings is discounted by an anticipated future rate of inflation and the number of years before the profit is earned. The discounted values of profits from each future year are added together to produce a true rate of return. In effect, a firm can calculate what level of future cash flow would be required to justify an investment; it would have to earn a return at least equal to the cost of money as represented by, for example, a long-term bond rate or its own cost of capital. A firm can then decide, based on its calculation of risk and its normal discounted-cash-flow rate of return, whether to make the investment. *See also* NET PRESENT VALUE, TIME VALUE OF MONEY.

discounted value In the process of making an investment decision, the value of the future profits that producers expect to get from a new plant or piece of machinery or equipment, as opposed to what they would get if they lent the same money out at prevailing rates of interest.

discouraged worker An unemployed person who has given up looking for a new job and who therefore is unlikely to be counted as unemployed in the official LABOUR-FORCE SURVEY. This person may be an older and unskilled worker in a declining industry or a resident of a slow-growth area. Statistics Canada estimates the number of discouraged workers in its monthly labour-force survey (publication 71-001).

discovery rate The rate at which net new additions are added to oil and natural-gas reserves in a 12-month period. For a country's oil or natural-gas reserves to increase, the discovery of new reserves must be greater than the consumption of oil or natural gas in the same period. The ASSOCIATION OF CANADIAN PETROLEUM PRODUCERS publishes an annual report on net changes in Canada's oil and gas reserves.

discretionary income The after-tax income of individuals that is not needed to pay for essentials such as food, shelter, and clothing. It can either be saved or spent on alternative goods or services, depending on the tastes, interests, or wants of the consumer.

diseconomies of scale An increase in the average cost per unit of production, as production rises, because of the exceedingly large scale on which the producer operates. This can be due to internal factors: for example, the firm may become so big that it becomes increasingly costly and difficult to manage and operate. Or it can be due to external factors, such as increased pollution clean-up costs due to the concentration of major industries along the same river or lake system. *See also* ECONOMIES OF SCALE.

disequilibrium A state of imbalance among the various forces within a system so that there is a tendency for change among the variables. For example, an imbalance or international payments that, to be correct-

ed, may require changes in MONE-
TARY POLICY and the exchange rate
of the currency.

disguised unemployment Forms of
unemployment that do not show up in
official unemployment statistics. There
are two principal types: **1.** Persons
engaged in activities well below their
skills or talents, or activities that provide
little useful employment, such as subsistence farming. **2.** Persons who would
like to work but see little opportunity,
and decide not to seek employment.
Examples include women who want to
enter the labour force but instead
remain at home because they believe
they lack the skills for employment, or
students who decide to continue their
education because jobs aren't available.

disinflation A reduction in the rate of
inflation either as a result of government policy or of declining economic
activity. *See also* DEFLATION.

disintermediation The flow of funds
outside of the financial system; for
example, companies lending or borrowing surplus funds directly instead of
passing the funds through a financial
intermediary such as a bank.

disinvestment The decision not to
make new investment to replace plants,
machinery, and equipment that is
wearing out. The result is a decline in
the productive capacity of the economy. In a company, it can also be a decision to get out of certain activities by
selling off or closing down operations.

disposable income The money available to individuals for spending and
saving after taxes and social insurance
premiums, such as unemployment
insurance and Canada Pension Plan
premiums, have been deducted. Total
personal disposable income in the
economy can be obtained from GROSS
DOMESTIC PRODUCT statistics (Statis-

tics Canada publication 13-001) by
deducting current transfers to government from personal income. These
transfers include income tax, employee
contributions to social insurance and
government pension funds, and other
transfers to government. Personal disposable income is the principal source
of savings and spending in the economy.

dispute settlement mechanism A
procedure in international trade to permit one country to challenge a trade
ruling or practice by another. Under
the GENERAL AGREEMENT ON TAR-
IFFS AND TRADE (GATT), a country
that has a trade dispute with another
and believes that a trade practice or
ruling is contrary to that country's
obligations under GATT can seek a dispute settlement panel to adjudicate the
dispute. If the finding of the GATT
panel rules in favour of the country
making the complaint, and the panel
report is adopted by the GATT Council,
then the country in default of its GATT
obligations must either change its policy or ruling or face GATT-sanctioned
retaliation. Under the CANADA-UNIT-
ED STATES FREE TRADE AGREE-
MENT, there are two forms of dispute
settlement. Chapter 18 provides for a
binational panel to be established when
one country takes an action that the
other believes is contrary to the free
trade agreement or nullifies an expected benefit. If a country fails to respond
to a panel finding by reversing a policy
or trade action, the other country has
the right to retaliate.The panel finding
is binding. In chapter 19, a dispute
panel can be established to review an
ANTI-DUMPING or COUNTERVAILING
DUTY action by one country where the
other country believes the law has been
misapplied or important evidence
excluded. The panel cannot overturn a
trade action but can require the relevant agency to reconsider its decision
based on the findings of the panel.

Under the NORTH AMERICAN FREE TRADE AGREEMENT (NAFTA), a similar system of panels to review final dumping and countervailing duty determinations by the national authorities in each country. The binational panels will be composed of five individuals, drawn from a roster maintained by the three countries. A panel must apply the domestic law of the importing country in reviewing a determination. The panel will either confirm the decision of the importing country's trade authority or send the decision back for a fresh hearing or review by the authority if it finds that the domestic law has been improperly applied. NAFTA provides each country with the unilateral right to retain and amend its anti-dumping and countervailing duty laws. But any amendment that affects the imports from the other NAFTA parties may be subject to a panel review to determine its consistency with the goals of NAFTA and GATT. If there is an inconsistency and it cannot be resolved, then the country or countries requesting the review may take comparable legislative action or terminate the agreement. NAFTA also provides for an extraordinary challenge procedure; following a panel decision either country may request the establishment of an extraordinary challenge committe, consisting of judges or former judges. If it determines that one of the grounds for the extraordinary challenge has been met, the original panel decision is voided and a new panel established. An additional safeguard mechanism ensures that the panel process functions as intended. A NAFTA country may request a "special committee" to determine whether the application of another country's domestic law has prevented the establishment of a panel, prevented a panel from rendering a final decision, or prevented the implementation of a panel decision. If the special committee makes an affirmative finding and the matter cannot be resolved, the complaining country may suspend the binational panel system with respect to the other country or suspend other NAFTA benefits. For disputes other than those arising from anti-dumping and countervailing duty actions, a more general dispute settlement mechanism is established. Whenever a matter arises that could affect a country's rights under NAFTA, it may request consultations on the matter, with speedy consultations promised under NAFTA. If the matter cannot be resolved in 30 to 45 days, any country may call a meeting of the NAFTA Trade Commission of cabinet-level officials. If the countries are unable to resolve the matter, then an arbitral panel can be established. The third country may also join as a complaining party or limit its participation to oral and written submissions. The panel will be charged with making findings of facts and with determining whether the action taken by the offending country is consistent with NAFTA. The panel may also make recommnedations to resolve the dispute. The panel will have five members, chosen from a trilaterally agreed roster of experts. The panel will have 90 days in which to make an initial report to the disputing countries; they will have 14 days to respond and the panel no more than 30 days to present a final report, which will be made public. If a panel finds in favour of the complaining country, the offending country has 30 days or another mutually agreed period of time to conform to the recommendations of the panel. If it does not, the complaining country may suspend the application of equivalent benefits until the issue is resolved. In the event of disputes between a foreign investor and a host government, a separate dispute settlement process is available.

dissaving The level of spending that is greater than disposable income for the same period. It means that an individual, or all individuals together, are either dipping into past savings or taking on debts that will have to be repaid from future earnings. The result is a decline in NET WORTH.

distribution 1. In economics, the study of how the total income in the economy is shared among workers, landlords, investors, and others. The question of who gets what and how the total flow of goods and services is allocated is one of the principal concerns of modern economics. This branch of economics includes the study of market forces, competition, and the role of market forces and supply and demand in determining prices, wages, profits, rents, and interest rates. **2.** In the economic system, the physical and financial means of moving goods from factories, through wholesalers and retailers, to the ultimate consumers.

distribution costs The various costs of advertising, marketing, warehousing, selling, and delivering goods and services.

distribution of powers The division of spending, taxing, and regulatory powers between the federal and provincial governments under the CONSTITUTION ACT, 1867. *See also* FEDERAL SPENDING POWER, FEDERAL TAXING POWER, PROVINCIAL SPENDING POWER, PROVINCIAL TAXING POWER. The federal government, through Parliament, has jurisdiction over defence and foreign relations; monetary policy and banking; interprovincial and international trade; tariffs; patents; copyright; weights and measures; interprovincial and international transport and communications, including railways, airlines, telephones, telecommunications, broadcasting, and pipelines; incorporation of companies with extra-provincial objectives, along with competition policy, bankruptcy, and laws dealing with business practices; labour relations in areas under federal jurisdiction, such as banking and transportation; and postal services and navigation. The federal government also has jurisdiction over lands, mines, and minerals in the Northwest Territories and Yukon and in the offshore areas of Canada. It may also regulate the intraprovincial and international movement of resources and levy taxes on them. In an emergency, the federal government may set energy-resource prices and allocate supplies.

The provincial governments, according to the CONSTITUTION ACT, 1867, have jurisdiction over economic matters having to do with "property and civil rights," such as contracts, regulation of selling securities, and insurance; intraprovincial production, trade, and marketing; intraprovincial transport and communications (except for aeronautics); labour relations covering all workers and employees under provincial jurisdiction, and regulation of the professions; and the incorporation and practice of businesses operating within the province. The provinces own and regulate mineral, oil, and natural-gas, land, and water rights, including timber and hydro-electric rights. Agriculture and consumer protection are both areas of concurrent jurisdiction. While in fisheries the federal government has clear jurisdiction over the negotiation of INTERNATIONAL FISHERIES CONVENTIONS, along with international and interprovincial trade, navigation, and pollution controls, the provinces control the catch and marketing of fish within their boundaries. In 1967, the Supreme Court of Canada ruled that the federal government had jurisdiction over offshore resources along the Pacific coast. In 1976, it ruled that the federal government could impose wage and price controls. In 1978, it ruled that cable television also came under federal jurisdiction. And in 1990, it ruled that the CANADI-

AN RADIO-TELEVISION AND TELE-COMMUNICATIONS COMMISSION had the power to regulate telephone companies regulated by provincial governments.

distributive justice   The form of justice that is concerned with fairness in the distribution of wealth and income, economic opportunity, and political and civil rights.

distributor   Someone who arranges to sell products on behalf of a manufacturer. The distributor may act as a wholesaler but may also take on other responsibilities, such as advertising, the establishment of dealerships, and servicing.

disutility   The opposite of utility or satisfaction; the ability of a good or service to cause inconvenience, discomfort, and even pain. Once a person has more of something than he or she can consume or store, the good stops providing even a diminishing marginal utility and yields disutility instead. The same is true of work. A person wants to work in order to earn enough money to meet various wants. However, after a certain number of hours of work, disutility or inconvenience replaces utility or satisfaction; this is one reason why workers may be reluctant to work overtime.

diversification   **1.** As applied to the investment portfolio of an individual or institution, the spreading of risk by purchasing shares of various companies in different industries, or a variety of securities, such as BONDS, PREFERRED SHARES, COMMON SHARES or MUTUAL FUNDS. **2.** As applied to corporations, the entry into new types of businesses or product lines, so as to reduce the risk of becoming too dependent on a single or restricted product line that could become obsolete, or to expand opportunities for higher profits.

A company may diversify into related or unrelated areas of business. For example, a sugar company could diversify into convenience foods, soft drinks, fast-food restaurants, and other related areas; or it could diversify into property development, cable television, and other unrelated areas. Diversification is often the most rapid means of business growth; in the case of the sugar company, for example, there is little it can do to increase sugar consumption directly once per capita consumption reaches a high level, so it uses its profits to diversify. **3.** In the case of a city, region, or country, the effort to develop new types of economic activity so as to reduce the risk of being too dependent on a single industry for employment and income, or to develop new export markets to reduce the risk of being excessively dependent upon a single market.

divestment   The sale or winding up of assets or part of its business by a company, often to get rid of unprofitable or low-profit activities and to concentrate on the most productive parts of the business.

dividend   A payment made out of profits by a corporation to its COMMON and PREFERRED shareholders. While the payment is usually in cash, it can also be made in the form of new shares. When the dividend is in the form of new shares, it is not treated as income but is taxed for capital gains when the shares are sold. The advantage to a company of issuing shares or stock dividends is that it retains more of its profits for reinvestment. Canadian companies tend to pay out about half of their after-tax profits as dividends, although this varies widely from company to company. The amount of dividend paid to owners of common shares usually depends a great deal on the level of profits, although companies frequently pay out dividends in excess of their profits during the downside of the BUSINESS CYCLE. However, preferred shareholders are entitled to a fixed annual dividend.

dividend tax credit A tax incentive to encourage Canadians to invest in Canadian corporations, first introduced in a 1949 federal budget, with taxpayers permitted a 10 percent dividend tax credit. In 1972, this was raised to a 20 percent credit, and taxpayers were also permitted a "gross-up" of 33.3 percent. By 1975, the incentive was raised again, to a 25 percent tax credit and 50 percent gross up. Taxpayers, in their tax returns, added together their dividends from Canadian corporations, grossed this income up by 50 percent, calculated the federal tax, then deducted a federal tax credit equal to 75 percent of the gross-up. This resulted in a lower tax rate on dividend income for Canadian taxpayers who invested in Canadian shares. Corresponding reductions are also available for the provincial portion of the income tax. If a taxpayer received $2,000 in dividends, he or she would gross this up by 50 percent, or $1,000, creating a taxable amount of $3,000. Federal tax would be calculated on this amount, but the taxpayer would also be able to deduct from the tax payable a federal tax credit of 75 percent of the gross amount, in this case $1,000, yielding a tax credit of $750. Thus, the tax liability could be reduced to zero, depending on the taxpayer's income bracket. Since 1975, the dividend tax credit has been reduced; in 1988 it was lowered to a 16.7 percent dividend tax credit and gross-up of 25 percent.

dividend yield The annual rate of return on COMMON SHARES, obtained by dividing the annual DIVIDEND by the current market price of the share.

division of labour Specialization in an economy, so that individual workers perform a single task in the production process and use their particular talents or skills to the best advantage. It was the key to increased output, higher productivity, and the application of ECONOMIES OF SCALE in the age of industrial mass production. ADAM SMITH was probably the first economist to write about the benefits accruing from the division of labour. He used the model of a pin factory, noting that one worker could only make a few complete pins each day but if each worker made only a part of each pin, then the same number of workers could produce thousands of pins in a day. Smith also emphasized that the opportunity to realize the greatest benefits from the division of labour depended on having access to a large market. Hence, just as a domestic economy could benefit from specialization or the division of labour, a world economy with free trade would lead to international specialization and even greater benefits from the international division of labour. While it is still relevant to talk of an international division of labour — for example, clothing and shoe industries have moved from high-wage developed countries to lower-wage developing countries — computerized systems have forced a change in the workplace away from single-task mass production to multi-skilling of workers who function in work teams where they share and exchange tasks.

division of powers In the CONSTITUTION ACT, 1867, the division of spending and taxing power between the federal and provincial governments. *See also* FEDERAL SPENDING POWER, FEDERAL TAXING POWER, PROVINCIAL SPENDING POWER, PROVINCIAL TAXING POWER, DISTRIBUTION OF POWERS.

documentary credit A written line of credit from a bank, on behalf of an importer, to an exporter authorizing the exporter to draw drafts on the bank up to a specified amount and subject to certain conditions.

dole Social assistance in the form of cash, food, shelter, and clothing to families and individuals in need. Prime Minister R.B. Bennett, in the depths of the Great Depression in 1935, said that the dole "was a condemnation of our economic system. If we cannot abolish the dole, we should abolish the system."

dollar The currency in use in Canada since Confederation in 1867; in fact, the dollar became the official currency unit of the Province of Canada in 1858. The Canadian dollar was issued by Canada's major banks until 1935. Today, the BANK OF CANADA has had the exclusive power to issue dollars. The Bank of Canada issues $2, $5, $10, $20, $50, $100, and $1,000 notes. The central bank last issued $1 bills in 1989; since 1987, they have been issued as coins known as LOONIES. Other countries using a dollar currency include Australia, Bahamas, Barbados, Bermuda, Hong Kong, Jamaica, New Zealand, Singapore, Taiwan, Trinidad and Tobago, and the United States. From 1879 to 1914, the Canadian dollar was on the gold standard and it could be converted to gold. It returned to the gold standard briefly in the mid-1920s but has either floated or been pegged to the U.S. dollar since the end of the First World War.

domestic-content requirements A requirement that a product contain a minimum amount of local content. Through the FOREIGN INVESTMENT REVIEW AGENCY, Canada tried to impose domestic-content requirements as a condition for approving the foreign takeover of a Canadian-based business or for the establishment of a new investment by a foreign corporation. However, the GENERAL AGREEMENT ON TARIFFS AND TRADE (GATT), in a 1984 decision, ruled that written undertakings by investors purchasing goods of Canadian origin or goods from Canadian sources was inconsistent with the national treatment obligations under GATT article III, part 4 since it would tip the commercial balance in favour of the Canadian product and against imported goods. Under both the CANADA-UNITED STATES FREE TRADE AGREEMENT and the NORTH AMERICAN FREE TRADE AGREEMENT, some products, notably automobiles, have to have a minimum level of North American content to pass across borders in the free-trade areas on a duty-free basis. But Canadian content rules for autos have been largely eliminated.

Dominion Lands Policy The policy pursued by the federal government between 1870 and 1930 in settling the prairie provinces, following the transfer by the British government of Rupert's Land and the Northwest Territories from the Hudson's Bay Company to the new dominion. The federal government, under the Dominion Lands Acts of 1872 and 1908, disposed of crown lands and granted exploitation rights for natural resources such as minerals, timber, and water, a power that, under the CONSTITUTION ACT, 1867, would normally have belonged to the provinces. These lands and their natural resources, known as Dominion Lands, were used to stimulate the construction of railways and the settlement of the region, in a race to prevent rapid U.S. westward expansion from spilling north into the Prairies, and thus to prevent the region from becoming part of the United States. The federal government made railway land grants, including 25 million acres to the Canadian Pacific Railway Company, provided free homesteads for settlers, set aside land for schools and townsites, created the great Rocky Mountain national parks, granted mineral, water, and timber rights, and designated land for cattle grazing. The program of western settlement, lasting 60 years, was probably one of the most important activities of the federal government in the first hundred years of Confederation. In 1930, the federal government turned over remaining crown lands and mineral rights to Alberta, Saskatchewan, and Manitoba.

dormant company An incorporated company that is no longer active but files annual returns and meets other obligations to retain its legal status.

double-entry bookkeeping The standard system of accounting or financial recordkeeping. Every transaction results in a credit on one side of the ledger and a debit on the other side, so that total credits on one side of the ledger should equal total debits on the other side so that the books should balance. Credits represent money owed the firm or assets owned by the firm, while debits represent debts of the firm owed to others. If, for example, a firm borrows $1 million dollars to buy new machinery, the borrowed funds represent a credit, while the machinery represents a debit. To put it another way, the credits represent the funds available to the business while the debits represent the ways in which those funds are used.

double taxation The taxation of the same taxable income more than once. This can happen in two different ways: 1. The same taxable income may be taxed more than once within the same jurisdiction. For example, corporate profits are taxed as they are earned by a business enterprise and then taxed again when they are received by shareholders in the form of dividends. The Income Tax Act offsets this to some extent through a GROSS-UP AND CREDIT system; see also DIVIDEND TAX CREDIT. 2. Double taxation can occur when competing tax authorities each tax the same tax base. For exam-

ple, in the absence of federal-provincial agreements, Canadians could find the federal and provincial governments each trying to raise revenue by operating competing income-tax systems. Similarly, in the absence of TAX TREATIES, foreign-controlled corporations could find themselves taxed both by Canada and by the tax authorities of the parent firm's country on the profits earned by the Canadian subsidiary or by the foreign subsidiary of a Canadian company.

double ticketing Selling a product that has two different price stickers or tags on it at the higher of the two prices. This is illegal under the COMPETITION POLICY. The lower price must always prevail.

Dow Jones Average A daily index of prices on the New York Stock Exchange, based on the average of the prices of 30 major stocks listed on the exchange. The current index dates back to 1928.

down-time The period of time in which machinery and other equipment is not in operation so that repairs, adjustments, and maintenance can be carried out. During this period of time, workers are idle.

downpayment A real-estate term for the amount of EQUITY CAPITAL a purchaser invests in a new house or other property. The difference between the price of the property and the downpayment is usually covered by a mortgage or mortgages.

downstream The transportation, refining, marketing, and distribution of products made from crude oil, such as gasoline and aviation fuel, after it has been extracted from the ground. *See also* UPSTREAM.

draft A written order to pay, such as a cheque, but written by the person to whom money is owed, and addressed to the debtor, instructing the debtor to pay the funds to the bank. The order is sent by the creditor to the bank, which presents it to the debtor for payment.

draft prospectus A draft or early version of a preliminary PROSPECTUS for internal use by a company and its underwriters. It has no legal standing.

drilling rig A mobile drilling system used to drill oil and gas wells. The number of drilling rigs in use is a good indicator of drilling activity in the oil and gas industry. The CANADIAN ASSOCIATION OF OILWELL DRILLING CONTRACTORS in Calgary publishes monthly statistics on the number of drilling rigs in use.

dry hole An oil or natural-gas well that has been drilled but is not productive because the quantity of oil or gas found is below the commercial level necessary for production.

dual listing The listing of the shares of a company on more than one stock exchange. There is a growing tendency for the largest companies to list in each of the major stock markets around the world. But even small- or medium-size Canadian companies may list on NASDAQ and other U.S. exchanges. Dual listing increases the number of potential investors and can result in a higher trading price for the shares.

due diligence 1. A detailed investigation of a company issuing new shares or bonds or of a company that is being purchased. Among the areas investigated are the company's corporate charter, by-laws, and corporate minutes for the previous five years; the company's audited and unaudited financial statements for the past five years; any changes in the company's auditors in that period; the company's principal products, major customers, and suppliers; any patents, copyrights, and other arrangements that are material to the business; the company's past and current relationships with its banks, creditors, and suppliers; the nature and conduct of the business through communication with the company's key officials; and the quality of the company's property, plant, and equipment. **2.** A requirement, set out by the INVESTMENT DEALERS ASSOCIATION OF CANADA, that stockbrokers investigate individuals opening new accounts for the trading of shares and other financial assets, ensure that any trading order for any account is within the bounds of good business practice, and ensure that any recommendations made for an account are appropriate for the client and in keeping with the customer's investment objectives.

dumping The sale of a product in a foreign market at a price less than that charged in the country of origin. It is subject to anti-dumping duties under the GENERAL AGREEMENT ON TARIFFS AND TRADE (GATT) when the practice injures or threatens to cause injury to producers in the importing country. GATT adopted an anti-dumping code in 1967, and Canada implemented the code the following year. Charges of anti-dumping are investigated by REVENUE CANADA, which determines the level of dumping and the penalty that should be imposed in the form of an anti-dumping duty. Determinations of injury are made by the CANADIAN INTERNATIONAL TRADE TRIBUNAL.

Dumping may take place to get rid of excess production — it means that the extra production can be sold without having to cut prices in normal markets — or it may occur as part of a corporate strategy, either to discourage the entry of a new firm into the business, to enlarge a producer's share of the market, or to gain entry to a market. Sometimes dumping is assisted by the government of the producer's country, through hidden subsidies and other devices, to increase exports and thus to create jobs at home.

Dumping is difficult to identify. In Canada, not only must dumping be proven, but it must also be shown that the dumping is causing injury or inhibiting industrial growth. Dumping is the international price equivalent of PRICE DISCRIMINATION by domestic producers. According to GATT, dumping can be subject to penalty if "it causes or threatens material injury to an established industry," or if it "materially retards the establishment of a domestic industry."

duopoly A market in which there are only two producers or suppliers of a particular good or service. Neither producer can behave as if it had a complete MONOPOLY because it has to take the other's pricing and production policies into account. However, the opportunity is there for an understanding between the two producers to limit production, divide markets, and charge monopoly prices. *See also* OLIGOPOLY.

duopsony A market in which there are only two purchasers or consumers and many producers of a particular good or service. The market power of the two consumers may be such that they can force producers to sell at unprofitable or barely profitable prices.

durable goods Producer or consumer goods with a life expectancy of more than three years. Examples include production machinery, trucks, railway rolling stock, and consumer durables such as household appliances and automobiles. The purchase of durable goods can be postponed, so the demand for durable goods can be subject to wide swings, depending on the state of the economy.

Durable-Goods Orders A monthly report from Statistics Canada on increases in orders for durable goods (publication 31-001). Durable-goods orders are an important economic indicator.

Dutch auction An auction in which the auctioneer sets a high opening price and then lowers the bids until a buyer is found.

Dutch disease The distortions that occur in a country's economy as a result of major resource discoveries or a sharp increase in the price obtained for resource exports. The high value of the resource exports raises the exchange rate and reduces the competitiveness of other industries, especially manufacturing. As a result, the country can end up with an underdeveloped manufacturing sector and face serious problems if resource prices fall sharply or its resource reserves become uneconomic. The term came into being in the 1960s, reflecting the experience of the Dutch after huge discoveries of natural gas in the Netherlands.

duty A TAX or TARIFF levied on goods when they are imported, exported, or consumed.

duty drawback The return to an importer of the duty paid when the importer brings certain products into the country for additional processing and then re-exports the product. The duty is repaid at the time of re-exporting on the proportion of the imported parts or components that are actually re-exported.

duty remission A government incentive to encourage domestic investment by paying back to a company the import duties it pays on machinery, parts, and components; in many instances, a benefiting company must be engaged in production for export markets. The

FINANCIAL ADMINISTRATION ACT gives the government the power to remit duties when it is "in the national interest." In 1968, the federal government introduced a plan to remit duties paid on imported machinery when the machinery was not manufactured in Canada. The federal government has used duty-remission schemes to encourage auto and auto-parts companies to locate in Canada, remitting duties for companies making specific commitments to locate or expand in Canada and to increase Canadian VALUE-ADDED in the vehicles and parts produced in Canada. Under the CANADA-UNITED STATES FREE TRADE AGREEMENT, Canada must end duty-remission schemes for auto companies by January 1, 1996. However, the NORTH AMERICAN FREE TRADE AGREEMENT extended the deadline to 2001 for Canada-Mexico trade.

dwelling unit   A separate living quarter that has a private entrance from the outside or from a common hall or stairway inside the building. Thus, a dwelling unit can be a separate house, apartment, flat, townhouse, or other such premises. The term is used in census surveys. In the 1971 census, STATISTICS CANADA found 6,034,510 dwelling units, 59.5 percent of which were single-family residences. Some 60.3 percent were owner-occupied and 39.7 percent were rented. In the 1991 census, Statistics Canada found 10,018,265 dwelling units, of which 56.9 percent were single-family residences. Some 62.2 percent of the dwelling units were owner-occupied, 37.1 percent rented, and the remainder band housing.

ECU *See* EUROPEAN CURRENCY UNIT.

earmarked tax   A tax designated for a particular purpose. Education taxes are earmarked for the school system and gasoline taxes can be designated for road and highway construction and maintenance. The federal AIR TRANS-PORTATION TAX is earmarked for TRANSPORT CANADA to help finance Canada's airport system, so revenues from the tax do not go into the CON-SOLIDATED REVENUE FUND. The problem with earmarked taxes is that they can lead to underspending or overspending in particular public sectors; that's why policy makers generally prefer to see all tax revenues go into consolidated government funds, with spending based on demonstrated need.

earnings   The returns to labour, capital, and ideas or intellectual property. Earnings include wages, salaries, commissions, profits, interest, dividends, royalty and licensing payments for intellectual property, and rents.

earnings per share   The net earnings of a firm, before extraordinary items and minus preferred dividends, divided by the 12-month average of the monthly averages of outstanding COMMON SHARES. Financial analysts monitor trends over time in earnings per share. A company with a rising earnings-per-share record will hold more appeal than one whose earnings per share, though perhaps higher, remain stagnant or are declining. The figure shows individual shareholders how well they are doing on their investment, since these earnings per share belong to them, regardless of whether they are paid out in dividends or reinvested in the business to build up SHAREHOLD-ERS' EQUITY. The earnings-per-share figure forms the denominator for the PRICE-EARNINGS RATIO, another important figure used by investors in trying to determine the future price of shares in a company.

earnings statement   That part of an ANNUAL or QUARTERLY REPORT issued by a company that shows the sources of its revenues and how they have been spent. What is left over is the net earnings or profit of the company, the money that can be used to pay dividends to shareholders and to reinvest in the business. An earnings statement is divided into four sections: 1. The operating section outlines total income from the sale of the firm's goods or services, minus the cost of sales, which includes labour, parts, raw materials, and energy used to produce the firm's goods or services. This yields the gross operating profit. From this are deducted the selling and administrative costs of the firm, depreciation, and various other costs, such as contributions to employee pension plans or payments for directors' fees. All of these costs are deducted from the gross operating profit to give the net operating profit, or loss. 2. The non-operating section of the earnings statement adds non-operating income such as interest and dividends from company investments, royalty payments on its patents, and rents from surplus property the firm owns, to the net operating profit. To this is added something called extraordinary items. These are unusual additions to income or losses and can include a big profit on the sale of a piece of company land or subsidiary, an unusual loss from a bad investment, or a loss of part of the business due to a flood or other disaster. The resulting figure is the company's remaining income from all sources. 3. The creditors' section of the earnings statement shows payments to creditors, who have to get their money before the owners can get their profits. Payments to creditors include interest on bank loans or outstanding bonds or mortgages, and income taxes. These are deducted from the income of the company. 4. The owners' section of the earnings statement shows the net earnings (profit) or deficit (loss). The net earnings are transferred to the RETAINED-EARNINGS STATEMENT, which shows how much of the profits may be reinvested in the business and how much is paid out to shareholders in the form of dividends. The earnings statement is also known as the income statement. *See also* BALANCE SHEET, STATEMENT OF CHANGES IN FINANCIAL POSITION.

Earth Council   A non-governmental international body, based in Costa Rica, formed in 1993 following the 1992 UNITED NATIONS CONFERENCE ON ECONOMY AND DEVELOPMENT, or "Earth Summit," to promote and monitor the follow-up and implementation of agreements reached at the Earth Summit. Its initial sponsors included the International Council of Science Unions, the World Conservation Union, and the Society for International Development. Canada's INTERNATIONAL DEVELOPMENT RESEARCH CENTRE provided assistance in launching the council. Working with non-governmental organizations from around the world, it also collects and disseminates information and promotes programs to advance SUSTAINABLE DEVELOPMENT. *See also* AGENDA 21.

easement   The right of the owner of a particular piece of land in an adjoining piece of land. The right may be for access to his land through a neighbour's property — a right-of-way — or it may be to prevent his neighbour from building in such a way as to interfere with the enjoyment of his own property — by interfering with light reaching windows, for example.

East Asian Economic Grouping   A 1990 proposal by the Prime Minister of Malaysia, Mahathir Mohammed, to create a new trading bloc of Asian countries. Its members would have included the six members of the ASSOCIATION OF SOUTHEAST ASIAN NATIONS (ASEAN), along with China, Taiwan, Hong Kong, South Korea, Vietnam, Myanmar, and Japan. The idea was strongly opposed by the United States, which applied pressure to Japan to also oppose it even though the United States was creating its own North American trading bloc. Since then, the ASEAN members have announced plans to form a free-trade area.

eastern Canada   New Brunswick, Nova Scotia, Prince Edward Island, and Newfoundland.

easy money   The condition in financial markets when interest rates are low and credit can be easily obtained. *See also* TIGHT MONEY.

econometrics   The application of mathematics and statistics, usually with the aid of computers, to identify and measure relationships between different economic activities or variables. Econometric models are used to help understand economic behaviour and to measure the impact of various economic policies on future economic performance. The equations identify, for example, relationships between prices and wages, disposable income and consumer spending, and investment and the cost of capital. *See also* ECONOMIC MODELS.

Economic and Regional Development Agreements (ERDA)   Bilateral framework agreements between the federal government and each of the provinces that set out overall objectives for joint economic and regional development, along with a statement on the implementation of each agreement, including annual meetings of the relevant federal and provincial ministers. Subsidiary agreements commit both levels of government to certain expenditures and actions on a cost-sharing basis. The agreements run until 1994. In 1992, the federal government announced they would not be renewed.

economic convergence   The belief that lower-income countries will grow faster than high-income countries and, as a result, catch up in living standards but that as they do, their own growth rates will inevitably slow to those in the richest countries. Capital flows from the rich countries to the poor countries while technology also flows from technology-rich countries to technology-poor countries. As poorer countries catch up, their growth rates are expected to slow to those of the richest countries. Some economists, for example, argue that the more rapid economic and productivity growth rates of Japan and Germany must inevitably slow to rates found in the United States and Canada as these countries reach U.S. and Canadian levels of income and wealth.

Economic Council of Canada (ECC)   An advisory body created in 1963 to develop a national consensus on medium- and long-term policy needs and to help the country to improve its economic performance. The council was abolished by the federal government as a cost-cutting measure in 1992, but the decision was also seen as a move to stifle independent economic research that was sometimes critical of government. While it existed, the council was the principal economic research organization in Canada. It consisted of a full-time chairman and two directors who were professional economists, along with 25 other members who were drawn from the business, labour, farm, academic, and other communities; they were appointed by the prime minister. The council was backed up by its own staff of professional economists. The council held its first meeting in January, 1964. It published an annual review on the economy, special studies on economic issues, staff research reports, and special studies carried out at the request of the government.

The council's role, as defined in the legislation setting it up, was to suggest "how Canada can achieve the highest possible level of employment and efficient production, in order that the country may enjoy a high and consistent rate of economic growth and that all Canadians share in rising living standards. "Specifically, its role is as follows: 1. To assess regularly the medium- and long-term prospects of the economy and compare them with the country's potential for economic growth. 2. To recommend government policies that would help Canada achieve its economic potential. 3. To consider ways to strengthen and improve Canada's international financial and trade position. 4. To study ways to increase Canadian ownership, control, and management of industries in Canada. 5. To study how growth, technological change, automation, and changing international conditions may affect employment in Canada."

The council has had a number of special studies referred to it by the government, including studies on how to reform competition policy and laws dealing with intellectual property, including copyright and patent laws, and how to reduce both government regulation and instability in the construction industry. The council staff also developed an econometric model of the Canadian economy, known as CANDIDE. For a brief period in 1979, it was charged with the responsibility of monitoring wage and price changes in the economy following the phasing out of the ANTI-INFLATION BOARD; it created the CENTRE FOR THE STUDY OF INFLATION AND PRODUCTIVITY to carry out this function. The council was the largest single economic-research body in Canada but was unpopular with federal government officials and ministers because it could be critical of government policy and offer alternatives. See also ONTARIO ECONOMIC COUNCIL, ATLANTIC PROVINCES ECONOMIC COUNCIL, FRASER INSTITUTE, C.D. HOWE INSTITUTE, INSTITUTE FOR RESEARCH ON PUBLIC POLICY, the CANADIAN CENTRE FOR POLICY ALTERNATIVES, and the CANADIAN INSTITUTE FOR ECONOMIC POLICY.

economic determinism In Marxist terms, the belief that our political, cultural, and social attitudes are determined by ownership of the means of production; attitudes will differ significantly among feudal, capitalist, and communist societies because the economic relationships among people differ in each. Since Karl MARX and his followers also believed that economic systems evolved according to immutable laws of history, they took public attitudes to be pre-determined and granted that capitalists couldn't be personally blamed for their behaviour. In a broader sense, it is the view that social, cultural, and political progress is shaped mainly by economic forces.

economic development The progress of an economy from primary production to industrialization and from a capital-deficient to a capital-surplus position. The goal of economic development is to raise per capita incomes through increased investment and productivity. While external capital can help finance investment, economic development also depends on generating adequate domestic savings to finance investment so that a country can move from agriculture to industry. In his 1960 book, *The Stages of Economic Growth*, the American economist W.W. Rostow identified five stages of economic development: 1. The traditional society, which is based on long-standing traditions or customs and experiences little growth. 2. A transitional period, in which the conditions for economic take-off are established by discarding past customs and traditions. 3. The take-off period, in which past customs no longer curb innovation and the application of technology — so that the economy achieves investment levels that make growth and technological progress self-sustaining. 4. The drive to maturity, with the economy becoming more export oriented and diversifying away from the industries that contributed to its take-off. 5. The move to a consumer society, with an increasingly affluent consumer demand leading to the production of innovative new products and services.

economic efficiency   The ultimate goal of economic policy; it is achieved by producing, allocating, and distributing goods and services at the lowest possible economic cost and according to what consumers most desire. However, in setting policy, policy makers also have to take into account other costs, such as social costs and environmental costs. *See also* EXTERNALITIES, PERFECT COMPETITION.

economic good   Anything that is relatively scarce; unlike a FREE GOOD, it is only available at a cost or sacrifice of some other good. Anything that can be bought or sold is an economic good. Thus, the definition also includes the services of a person, as well as something a person produces.

economic growth   The increase over a period of time in the production of goods and services. Economic growth is usually measured as the percentage increase in GROSS DOMESTIC PRODUCT over a specified period of time, after adjusting for inflation; since population is constantly changing, a more precise measure is the rate of growth of real per capita income. Economic growth is one of the principal goals of virtually all modern societies, since it is considered necessary to increase the size of the economic pie if the standard of living of most people in the world is to be raised. Even the CONSERVER SOCIETY and SUSTAINABLE DEVELOPMENT allow for economic growth. But economic growth does not reflect all the gains and losses in a modern economy. It does not show the leisure-time gains from the shorter work week made possible by improved productivity; nor does it adequately reflect the costs to society of dealing with pollu-

tion, industrial disease, and similar problems.

Many factors affect the rate of growth in a country, and not all countries need the same rate of economic growth to achieve full employment. Among the factors are growth in the size of the labour force, the level of capital stock, the rate of innovation or technological progress, investment in research and development, the level of education and skills of the work force, cultural attitudes toward business and growth, the possession of natural resources, the level of managerial know-how, the level of savings, and the sophistication of financial markets. Economic growth is the consequence of the accumulation of inputs or an increase in productivity from a given set of resources. The main sources of economic growth are consumer spending, residential investment, business investment, government spending on goods and services, government investment, exports, and increases in inventories. In the growth accounting framework, the rate of growth of output in the economy depends on the rate of technological progress, the rate of increase in labour inputs, and the rate of growth of capital.

economic history   An account of past events and forces that have influenced the growth of a nation, region, or institution, or the study of past events and institutions to develop a theory of economic growth or development in a particular society. Harold INNIS is Canada's best-known economic historian. See W.T. Easterbrook and M.H. Watkins, eds., *Approaches to Canadian Economic History* (Toronto, 1967). *See also* STAPLE THEORY.

economic imperialism   The use of economic power by a nation or corporations to exploit another part of the world. Marxists argued that economic imperialism was the inevitable result of capitalism and represented its final stage before its collapse. The accumulation of capital at home would lead to declining profit rates, forcing capitalists to seek higher profits through investments abroad. Because of their control over governments, capitalists would use the power of the state, including its armies and navies, to help them to secure raw materials and markets. However, according to Marxists, such empire building was bound to lead to international conflict among competing capitalist states, with the resulting wars bringing on revolution by the workers and the overthrow of capitalism. By this definition, only capitalists can be imperialists.

economic indicators   Economic statistics that give important clues to changing economic conditions. There are three types: LEADING INDICATORS, COINCIDENT INDICATORS, and LAGGING INDICATORS.

economic integration   The reduction or elimination of trade and investment barriers and the harmonization of laws, standards, and business practices so that the economies of different countries function almost as though they were a single economy. Many observers point to the increasing ties between the Canadian and U.S. economies as an example, with free trade hastening this process.

economic law   A proposition that expresses a precise relationship among different economic phenomena, and that may be used to predict the outcome of economic events. Two of the best-known economic laws are the LAW OF SUPPLY AND DEMAND and the LAW OF DIMINISHING RETURNS.

economic life   The useful life of a machine, pipeline building, smelter, or other asset. After a period of time it

makes more sense to replace an asset than to pay the rising costs of maintenance and repair.

economic man   The theoretical view of man developed by CLASSICAL economists. According to this view, each individual possesses full knowledge of the market and is motivated solely by rational economic considerations. The classical school used this view of man to develop its model of PERFECT COMPETITION. The theory overlooked other motivations, such as family, religion, nation, envy, and revenge, as well as the fact that many individuals lacked full knowledge of the market.

economic model   A scientific approach to economic forecasting and analysis that became even more widespread with the availability of computers. Economic models use series of mathematical equations that define numerically the relationships among different sectors of the economy. Most economic or econometric models contain more than one thousand equations. The best-known economic models are those of the BANK OF CANADA, and the University of Toronto's Institute of Policy Analysis.

Economic models depict the economy in several different ways. A macroeconomic model will try to show how the Canadian economy — or some major part of it — functions through simultaneous equations that explain relationships among key elements in the economy, such as the relationship between changes in personal income and consumer spending, between output and demand, between prices and wages, or between production and raw materials, energy, labour, and capital. A macroeconomic model deals with the economy as a whole but within a social setting, so it must include demographic and social behaviour. According to Lawrence Klein, a leading U.S. economic model builder, the economy is viewed "as one large establishment with three main accounting statements." These are a national income statement, an operating statement of inputs and outputs, and a national balance sheet. The national income statement shows the receipt and disposition of income in the economy, such as household spending, business investment, government spending, foreign trade, tax revenues, wages and interest, and profits. The input-output system traces intermediate goods and services through the production process. For example, trees, a primary forestry output, are delivered to pulp mills as an input, then to paper mills as an input, then as newsprint to newspapers as an input, and sold to final consumers as a newspaper. The input-output system shows the flow from one stage of production to the next, with transportation added at each stage, along with electricity and other energy demands, as well as the consequences for marketing, distribution, and retail establishments. Models are kept up to date with the latest statistical data, and are used to forecast economic performance and to test the effects of different policies or assumptions, such as budget plans, on future economic performance. While economic models are increasingly sophisticated, they underestimate change and are not equipped to anticipate events such as the Persian Gulf war, a constitutional crisis, or a major strike in a key industry.

economic nationalism The desire of a country to control as much of its own economic future as possible. Economic nationalism can range from a concern over the high level of foreign control of the economy to a desire to be almost completely self-sufficient in everything the country consumes. Economic nationalism is a reaction to the power of TRANSNATIONAL or MULTINATIONAL CORPORATIONS over national governments and the loss of capacity by individual countries to foster institutions or pursue policies that differ to any great extent from those of the United States or other major economic powers that are the home to most international corporations. Economic nationalists are concerned, for example, that with the growth of global media conglomerates the Canadian cultural identity, and the cultural industries that reflect that identity, will be subsumed in the absence of Canadian policies to ensure the viability of Canadian cultural industries. Moderate economic nationalism is not opposed to foreign ownership as such but regards the high levels of foreign ownership and control in the Canadian economy as excessive, since it puts too much investment decision-making power, as well as the location of core activities and high-value jobs outside of Canada, into the hands of foreign corporations. Therefore, economic nationalists favour policies to constrain the foreign takeover of Canadian companies as well as other policies to foster the growth of healthy Canadian-controlled companies in the private and public sectors. Economic nationalists also fear that without sufficient economic independence, Canadian social, health care, and workplace safety and equity policies will also be threatened. *See* COMMITTEE FOR AN INDEPENDENT CANADA, COUNCIL OF CANADIANS.

economic planning Government intervention in investment and spending decisions. There are various types of economic planning: 1. Consensus planning, where the government attempts to bring in business and labour as partners in an effort to reach agreement on economic goals and investment priorities. *See also* TRIPARTISM. 2. INDICATIVE PLANNING, in which the government sets out investment and other targets for the economy and tries to get business and labour support. 3. Socialist planning, in which the government nationalizes certain key industries or has a stake in them and directs their investment and other activities, influencing activity throughout the economy in the process. 4. Total state planning, as was practised in communist countries, where the government owns all the industries and sets economic targets that the managers of its own industries must meet. In the MIXED ECONOMIES of most Western nations, the government engages in some kind of economic planning, however informal. Governments have many tools at their disposal to direct economic growth. These include not only the broad levers of fiscal and monetary policy, but a wide range of incentives and grants. One of the functions of the ECONOMIC COUNCIL OF CANADA was to set performance indicators for the country, indicating desired targets for economic growth, investment, employment, and inflation, for example. Economic planning is not confined to governments; most major corporations engage in long-term planning. *See also* CORPORATE STRATEGY.

economic policy The measures adopted by the government to achieve its economic goals. Those goals will typically include economic growth, increased employment, low inflation, a current-account surplus, improved productivity performance, and improved international competitiveness. However, depending on circumstances, the goals could put more emphasis on reducing inflation than on sustaining employment, or vice versa. Government goals may also include increased research and development, a greater capacity for innovation, increased exports, or any number of such objectives. The main tools available to a government to implement its policies are the use of spending and taxing powers, or FISCAL POLICY, the availability of credit, interest rates, and the exchange rate, or MONETARY POL-

ICY. Government can also use its ability to legislate and regulate to implement economic policy.

economic rent In the case of natural resources, the surplus value that is generated from the sale of the resource, above and beyond the price needed to satisfy the normal profit requirements necessary to justify the original investment. It is the surplus value of the resource itself. For example, when oil was priced at $2 a barrel in the early 1970s, this was sufficient to meet the profit requirements of the industry. The quadrupling of the price of oil after 1973 represented the economic rent of the oil. A key question when economic rent is produced is who should get it; in the case of the oil, it is shared among the shareholders of the oil industry, the producing-province governments, and the federal government. Economic rent is also the reward an inventor or innovator gains from being the first to market with a new product or service where the price received yields a high profit. Likewise, a performing artist or other talented individual is able to earn an economic rent when his or her income exceeds that of the only other occupation that same individual could pursue. *See also* RENT.

economic sanctions Measures to halt or restrict trade, investment, and other economic relations with a country or group of countries, as punishment for particular domestic or international behaviour. By imposing an economic cost on a country for its behaviour, it is hoped the country will change its behaviour. For example, in 1965, the United Nations adopted economic sanctions against Rhodesia, to force it to change its policies of racial discrimination. Likewise, the United States imposed economic sanctions on the Soviet Union following its invasion of Afghanistan by barring exports of American grain. In 1935, the League of Nations voted sanctions against Italy after it invaded Ethiopia. More recently, economic sanctions have been used against South Africa to pressure it to end its policy of apartheid, against Libya to discourage its support for international terrorism, and against Iraq as punishment for its invasion of Kuwait. At the beginning of 1993, export permits were required under the Export and Import Permits Act for all goods shipped to Bosnia-Herzegovina, Croatia, Haiti, Libya, South Africa, and Yugoslavia.

economic scarcity   *See* SCARCITY.

economic self-sufficiency   *See* SELF-SUFFICIENCY.

economic summit   The annual meeting of the leaders of the GROUP OF SEVEN (G-7) countries — the United States, Japan, Germany, France, Italy, Britain, and Canada — along with the president of the EUROPEAN COMMUNITY. The first summit was held in 1975, but Canada did not join the group until 1976. The first summit was held in 1975, but Canada did not join the group until 1976. Economic summits have been held in Canada twice, in 1981 in Ottawa-Montebello, and in 1988 in Toronto. The next G-7 summit in Canada will be held in 1995.

economic system   The way in which economic life is organized; in particular, the way in which wealth and income are distributed, the means of production are owned, and the public and private sectors influence consumption, investment, and savings. In a LAISSEZ-FAIRE economy, the allocation of resources is left to market forces and the means of production are in private hands. In a MIXED ECONOMY, both government and private citizens determine the allocation of resources and own the

means of production. In a totally planned economy, the government alone determines the allocation of resources and owns the means of production.

economic theory   A descriptive statement about how the economic system or some part of it functions, and how economic performance, however defined, can be improved. Economic theories include both broad MACROECONOMIC theories — dealing with growth, consumption, investment, saving, prices, trade, money, and employment — and MICROECONOMIC theories — dealing with particular industries, labour markets, competition, and the firm. Many economic theories are identified with particular schools of economic thought, such as MERCANTILISM, CLASSICAL ECONOMICS, MARXIST ECONOMICS, NEOCLASSICAL ECONOMICS, KEYNESIAN ECONOMICS, POST-KEYNESIAN ECONOMICS, and MONETARISM.

economic union   An agreement among a group of states to eliminate all barriers to the free movement of trade in goods and services as well as labour and capital, and to harmonize monetary and other economic policies. The EUROPEAN COMMUNITY is one example of an economic union; the United States is an example of an economic union within a federal system. INTERPROVINCIAL BARRIERS in Canada mean this country has yet to attain all the benefits of economic union.

economic warfare   **1.** Actions to hinder the ability of an enemy to wage war. Methods can include the dumping of forged currency in the territory of an enemy to create confusion; the blockading of an enemy's ports to prevent the entry of vital materials; and the bombing or sabotage of the enemy's vital industrial, communications, and transportation centres, or

reserves of essential supplies such as oil.
2. An escalation in economic conflict between nations, usually arising from a trade dispute, in which the two countries adopt increasingly restrictive or punitive measures, such as tariff escalation or other trade penalties, to reduce the level of imports from each other.

economics   The study of choice in a world of scarcity. Economics examines how individuals, firms, and societies decide what to produce, how it should be priced, how output should be distributed, and how all of these various activities are interrelated. It is concerned with finding ways to maximize welfare through the most efficient means of allocating scarce resources. Economists both develop economic principles or laws, and apply economic laws to achieve such goals as full employment and stable prices. *See* MACROECONOMICS, MICROECONOMICS, WELFARE ECONOMICS. Although economics is treated as a science, most theories of economics contain values or assumptions about a desirable society.

economies of scale   Reductions in the average cost of a product, achieved by increasing the volume of output and in that way using labour, machinery, and other factors of production more efficiently. For a smaller country, such as Canada, achieving economies of scale may depend on having access to larger foreign markets, since the Canadian market by itself may be too small to support the most efficient volume of production in many industries. A firm should be able to produce a product more efficiently by making use of modern machinery and equipment, skilled and specialized labour, interchangeable parts, automation and large-scale distribution, and be able as a result to fund on-going research and development. However, these economies can only be achieved when the volume of production is high enough to justify the capital investment and extensive division of labour; when production is high enough, a capital-intensive, highly specialized plant can produce at a much lower average cost than a similar but smaller plant.

This explains why, in many modern industries such as petrochemicals, mineral processing, automobile assembly, and telecommunications, small companies find it hard to survive, and why it is important to have access to large markets. In many instances, where the costs of innovation and of capital equipment are so high, access to large markets is essential if the benefits of economies of scale are to be achieved — or indeed, the investment in a new plant made. At some point, when MARGINAL COST equals AVERAGE COST, a plant will stop yielding economies of scale; it will then be at a point where DISECONOMIES OF SCALE begin, with each extra unit of output costing more than the average cost and thus being unprofitable. In other words, a plant can produce both too little and too much. At the same time, modern production technologies, especially those based on microelectronics, permit highly specialized niche production that is much less dependent on large economies of scale.

economist   Someone who has been trained in economics and who makes his or her living by applying economic analysis to the problems of the real world, or who teaches and studies economics with the object of adding to human knowledge and understanding of how economic systems really work. Economists are found in business, governments, universities, or other organizations.

economize   To produce a product or service more efficiently than before.

effective demand   The actual consumption and investment that takes place in the economy as a result of existing purchasing power. It is the principal determinant of output and employment.

effective rate of interest 1. The true rate of interest that is paid, at an annual rate, for a sum of money that is repaid in regular installments. For example, $1,000 borrowed at a monthly interest rate of 1.5 percent and repaid in 12 equal installments carries a nominal rate of 18 percent. However, since the borrower does not have the full use of the $1,000 for the entire 12 months, but only the use of the declining unpaid balance, the effective interest rate turns out to be 19.86 percent. **2.** The actual yield on a bond, based on the actual price paid for the bond. If a $1,000 bond carries a 9 percent rate of interest, yielding an annual interest coupon of $90, but a purchaser is able to buy it for 90 percent of the face value, or $900, then the purchaser will receive $90 interest on a $900 purchase, for an effective rate of interest, or yield, of 10 percent.

effective rate of protection The real degree of tariff protection afforded a domestic producer, as opposed to the tariff rate listed in the tariff schedule. Effective tariff rates are normally higher than the listed tariff schedule would suggest. For example, most countries charge low or zero tariffs on imported raw materials but higher tariffs on imported finished products; this means that the effective tariff on the VALUE-ADDED in the finished product is higher than the listed tariff for the product. In the case of a simple product that is half labour and half a raw material, if there is a 15 percent tariff on the product itself and no tariff on the raw material, then the effective tariff rate on the labour half of the product is 30 percent. This is the effective rate of protection.

effective tax rate The percentage of income paid out in tax. In the progressive-income-tax schedule, the marginal tax rate rises as taxable income rises; to determine the effective tax rate, the total income tax payable is divided by the total income on which it was paid. In a sales tax, the effective rate and the nominal tax rate are identical.

efficiency The most effective use or allocation of resources to yield the maximum benefits or welfare — for example, the lowest possible costs, or the satisfaction of the greatest number of people. It is the elimination of waste. Efficiency in the first sense — the effective use of resources — is often applied to individual firms in comparing how well they organize the productive process (labour, management, machinery, new technology) to achieve the lowest possible production cost for their products. But efficiency has a much broader meaning as well, referring to the way in which all of the various FACTORS OF PRODUCTION are used to achieve maximum output throughout the economy at the lowest cost, or to achieve a distribution of the output of society that results in the greatest degree of satisfaction *See* PARETO OPTIMUM, WELFARE ECONOMICS, MONOPOLY, IMPERFECT COMPETITION. An economy with a high level of monopoly power held by some factor or factors of production will have a lower level of economic efficiency. PERFECT COMPETITION in theory should yield the highest level of economic efficiency.

efficient market hypothesis The assumption that share prices reflect all the information available to all market participants so that no one can secure an unfair advantage over the market as a whole. This assumes perfect competition and implies that a share price will only change when new information is available.

egalitarianism   The reduction or elimination of great disparities between wealth and poverty in a society. Reducing these disparities is one of the basic aims of civilized societies, though there are great differences over how far they should be reduced. It is argued, for example, that near equality of incomes would reduce the incentive to work, leading to a less innovative or entrepreneurial society and a lower standard of living for everyone. Some experts maintain that the emphasis should be on equality of opportunity rather than on equality of result. Most societies aim for some kind of middle ground, with some emphasizing egalitarianism and others emphasizing incentives and opportunity. However, experience shows that equality of opportunity by itself is insufficient to achieve a balanced distribution of wealth, since there are basic differences in the aptitudes of people. Moreover, those who inherit wealth start off in life well ahead of those who come from needy backgrounds, and even a person's earliest childhood can affect his ability to recognize and take advantage of opportunity in later life. Some techniques to achieve egalitarianism include free elementary and high-school education and subsidized university education, a PROGRESSIVE TAX system, a CAPITAL-GAINS TAX, INCOME-MAINTENANCE PROGRAMS, and a WEALTH TAX. *See* John Porter, *The Vertical Mosaic* (Toronto, 1965); John Rawls, *A Theory of Justice* (Cambridge, MA, 1971); and Arthur Okun, *Equality and Efficiency: The Big Tradeoff* (Washington, 1975).

elasticity   The responsiveness in the supply or demand for a particular good or service to a change in its price. A particular good or service is said to be highly elastic if changes in price produce significant changes in its consumption or production; conversely, a product is said to be inelastic if its consumption or production shows little change, even with a significant price change. The consumption of French wines or chocolate bars may increase sharply if prices fall significantly, and vice versa. However, if the price of electricity or bread rises or falls, it may have only a modest impact on consumption. Elasticity is usually measured as the percentage change in supply or demand for each 1 percent of change in price.

elasticity of demand   The change in demand that results from a change in price. Usually, if the price of a good or service goes up, demand will fall, but the degree to which this happens varies widely among goods and services. Elasticity of demand attempts to measure the extent to which increases or decreases in price produce decreases or increases in consumption. Generally speaking, price changes for essentials will result in little change in demand; demand in such cases is said to be inelastic. Price changes for luxury goods, on the other hand, may have a large impact on demand; demand is then said to be highly elastic.

elasticity of substitution   The increase in one factor of production, say capital, that is required to offset a reduction in another factor, say labour, while maintaining a constant rate of output for a product or service. While it is possible to achieve some degree of substitution, at some point substitution will no longer be possible.

elasticity of supply   The change in supply that results from a change in price. Usually, if the price of a good or service goes up, supply will increase, and vice versa. However, the degree to which this happens varies widely among goods and services and depends, among other things, on how fast producers can respond to price changes. For example, there may be a long delay between a sharp increase in the price of wheat or beef cattle and an increase in the supply of wheat or beef cattle. However, if an industry is operating below capacity and there is an increase in demand for its product, it should be able to respond quickly. If producers are earning high profits, they can absorb lower prices; if they are producing at low profits, a lower price may lead to reduced production, and hence reduced supply.

electric power Electricity generated principally from three sources: hydro-electric power, generated by installing dams and turbines on major rivers; thermal power, generated in power stations by burning oil, natural gas, or coal; and nuclear power, generated by using uranium in nuclear-power reactors. New sources of electricity include solar energy and the use of modern windmills.

electronic data interchange (EDI) A system employed by corporations and financial institutions to conduct business transactions, such as the payment of bills or the placing of orders, electronically. The system speeds transactions and eliminates paperwork.

electronic funds transfer A system used by Canadian corporations and financial institutions to transfer funds electronically instead of by writing cheques.

electronic mail The transmission of information electronically via a message storing and switching centre, to addresses with facsimile receivers or computer terminals.

electronic payments system The use of computers and telecommunications systems to largely eliminate the need for cash, cheques, and credit cards and, in the process, reduce substantially the paperwork in handling the payment of bills, mailing of pension and other

cheques, and processing of customer accounts. Corporations already make significant use of ELECTRONIC FUNDS TRANSFER. The next step would be to bring this more fully to the consumer. Automatic teller machines already permit the electronic payment of bill and bank credit-card accounts. DEBIT CARDS will permit cashless transactions in the retail sector. Pay cheques are already electronically deposited in bank accounts for many workers. The next step will be to deposit government social welfare and old-age security cheques directly into client bank or trust-company accounts.

embargo A government-imposed ban on the import or export of certain goods for health, national-security, political, or other reasons. An embargo may be imposed on cattle and beef imports from a country where cattle disease has broken out; similarly, Canada may restrict the export of technologically advanced products to countries that represent a threat to world peace or security if the products have an important military application. *See* EXPORT AND IMPORT PERMITS ACT, ECONOMIC SANCTIONS.

embezzlement A form of WHITE-COLLAR CRIME; an embezzler, through fraudulent accounting methods and other techniques, steals money or other assets from his or her employer. Embezzlement is an offence under the Criminal Code.

emergency power The power of the federal government to exercise, in times of emergency, powers that would normally belong to the provinces. This power — the "Peace, Order, and Good Government" clause in section 91 of the CONSTITUTION ACT, 1867 — has been used not only in wartime but, in 1975, for the first time, in peacetime. In 1975, the federal government established the ANTI-INFLATION BOARD to implement a nation-wide system of wage and price controls, although the power to control wages and prices to a large extent falls under provincial jurisdiction. In 1976, the SUPREME COURT OF CANADA ruled that this power could be invoked in "very exceptional" economic circumstances, such as sharply rising inflation during a period of high unemployment.

eminent domain   A government's right to expropriate private property for public use. In return, it is required to pay fair compensation. The government may exercise its right of eminent domain, for example, if it needs land for a highway, airport, public housing, or park. Usually, a government will try to buy the land it needs without having to resort to the exercise of its expropriating powers. However, in cases where a large number of properties have to be acquired or where property owners either refuse to sell or are demanding unreasonable prices, the right of eminent domain is exercised. It is an example of the limitations that exist on the rights of private property.

employed person   As defined in the monthly LABOUR-FORCE SURVEY produced by Statistics Canada, a person who, during the survey week, did any work at all, full- or part-time, or who had a job but was not at work due to illness, disability, personal or family responsibilities, bad weather, a labour dispute, or vacation. Work, as defined in the survey, includes any kind of work for pay or profit, including unpaid family work that contributes directly to the operation of a farm, business, or professional practice owned or operated by a related member of the same household.

employee ownership   The full or part ownership of an enterprise by its employees. Many companies offer stock-purchase plans to their employees, sometimes as a company benefit and sometimes as a substitute for a company pension plan. Employees sometimes become significant or complete owners of an enterprise facing closure, with the belief that they can operate the facility more efficiently than the previous owner.

employer   An individual or organization that hires a person for the production of goods or services. Employers include companies, governments, public institutions such as schools and hospitals, or non-profit organizations such as religious, charitable, or public advocacy organizations. Some employers can be individuals — a doctor or dentist hiring a nurse, a household hiring a gardener, or a farmer hiring help, for example. Employers are governed by various laws and labour codes in their treatment of employees.

employer association   An organization of employers formed mainly to engage in joint bargaining with labour unions, either in a metropolitan area or in a province. Employer associations are necessary, so that industry-wide bargaining can take place. *See,* for example, CANADIAN CONSTRUCTION ASSOCIATION.

employer of last resort   The idea that government should employ anyone who is able and willing to work but who cannot get a job in private industry due to an insufficient number of jobs. This could include payments by government to charitable agencies and similar groups to hire unemployed people to do socially useful tasks. The federal government's 1973 *Working Paper on Social Security in Canada* recommended that community employment programs be established to provide useful local jobs in areas of chronic unemployment, or for people who, due to handicaps or for other reasons, had a hard time finding jobs. *See also* GUARANTEED ANNUAL INCOME.

employment agency A middleman who recruits full- and part-time workers for employers and helps people to find jobs. Some deal exclusively in the placement of executive or professional staff and others specialize in providing temporary workers. The largest employment agency is the CANADA EMPLOYMENT AND IMMIGRATION COMMISSION, operated by the federal government. Most agencies are privately operated.

Employment and Immigration, Department of A federal government department created in 1976 with responsibility for unemployment insurance, job-training, labour-market adjustment, and immigration policies. It is also responsible for Canada's SOCIAL INSURANCE NUMBER system and for the enforcement of the EMPLOYMENT EQUITY ACT and the Federal Contractor's Act. The department acts as a strategic policy and program evaluation body. The actual delivery of programs is carried out by the CANADA EMPLOYMENT AND IMMIGRATION COMMISSION. The commission assists unemployed Canadians looking for work through counselling, training, job creation, employment services, and labour market programs. It works with the provinces to provide training and administers the payment of unemployment insurance benefits. The commission operates about five hundred Canada Employment Centres that maintain an inventory of available jobs in the local labour market. Its labour-market adjustment program includes human-resource planning, workplace training, work sharing, industrial adjustment, and employment equity. The commission also works with communities facing serious unemployment problems. The commission also enforces the Immigration Act within Canada and deals with programs for immigrant settlement and adjustment in Canada.

Employment and Income, White Paper on See WHITE PAPER ON EMPLOYMENT AND INCOME.

employment contract A contract between an employee and an employer, setting out the work an employee is expected to perform and the compensation that will be received. Employment contracts are for fixed periods of time, subject to renewal.

employment equity Measures to eliminate discrimination in the workplace due to gender, age, handicaps, race, or religion. Employment-equity laws may also call for AFFIRMATIVE ACTION to increase the number of designated disadvantaged groups in a workplace. The federal government and most provinces have some kind of employment-equity provisions. See also PAY EQUITY.

Employment Equity Act Federal legislation, passed in 1986, that requires all employers coming under federal jurisdiction, such as banks, airlines, and railways, as well as federal crown corporations with one hundred or more employees, to eliminate any workplace discrimination, including pay levels, hiring, and promotion, against four groups that traditionally have been disadvantaged: women, visible minorities, aboriginal peoples, and persons with disabilities. The act requires that affected companies implement employment equity plans, identify and eliminate barriers to employment equity, achieve a representative workforce and report annually on their results. Employers must consult with persons designated by their employees to act as their representatives, or with a bargaining agent in cases where a union represents employees. To achieve targets employers must implement special measures to improve employment prospects for designated groups by increasing their participation in all occupational groups within the company.

employment index A monthly index published by Statistics Canada that measures changes in employment in different industries and regions. The publication is *Employment, Earnings and Hours* (publication 72-002).

employment standards Laws governing basic conditions of work, such as minimum wages, overtime pay, public holidays, vacations with pay, pregnancy leave, occupational health and safety, wrongful dismissal, notice of layoffs, severance pay, and payment of wages. Each province and the federal government has a labour-standards code or an equivalent body of law. *See also* CANADA LABOUR CODE.

end product A manufactured product ready for use by a consumer or by a producer of consumer goods and services.

endogenous change A change in economic activity resulting from the change in another economic variable — inflation caused by excessive demand, for instance. *See also* EXOGENOUS CHANGE.

endogenous growth The result of deliberate investments in industrial research and development by profit-seeking enterprises. *See also* EXOGENOUS GROWTH.

endorsement The signature on the back of a cheque or other bill of exchange that transfers ownership to another person.

endowment A gift of revenue-producing assets to a charitable, religious, or educational institution. Only the revenue is spent; the assets, which may consist of shares, bonds, mortgages,

real estate, or even rights to a patent, are kept intact.

endowment insurance A form of life insurance under which the person insured receives the insurance benefit, provided he or she lives to a certain age. If he or she dies before then, the beneficiaries get the money.

energy-conversion efficiency A measure of how much energy is needed to convert a primary source of energy into energy for use by consumers — how much energy it takes, for example, to convert the bitumen from tar sands into crude oil, or how much coal has to be burned to create so much electricity.

Energy Council of Canada A coalition of about 120 public and private energy organizations that represents Canada in the World Energy Council, an international organization that brings together energy industry leaders from about 100 different countries. Council members include federal and provincial government departments; oil, natural gas, and electric power companies; pipeline and engineering companies; engineering and energy industry associations; and a number of universities as affiliate members. The council has a small secretariat in Ottawa. Activities in Canada include annual conferences on energy issues, the preparation of a Canadian energy-assessment report and an assessment of the role of energy in competitiveness. The World Energy Council holds an international gathering every three years; the last was held in Madrid in 1992 and the next will be held in Tokyo in 1995.

energy efficiency The amount of energy required to operate an automobile, machine, appliance, or other product. One of the most important ways of conserving energy is to reduce the amount of energy needed to achieve a given level of output — to reduce the amount of gasoline needed to carry an automobile a kilometre, for example.

Energy, Mines and Resources, Department of   The federal government department responsible for energy and mineral policies in Canada. The existing department was established in 1966; its predecessors included the Department of the Interior, established in 1873 to manage the acquisition of Rupert's Land from the Hudson's Bay Co.; the Department of Mines, established in 1907; the Department of Mines and Resources, established in 1936; and the Department of Mines and Technical Surveys, established in 1949. The department's energy branch formulates energy policy for Canada, including monitoring of supply and demand trends. It negotiates and finances federal participation in energy megaprojects, such as the Hibernia offshore oil project, and heavy-oil and tarsands projects in Alberta and Saskatchewan. It is also responsible for energy conservation programs and the fostering of renewable energy sources. The minerals branch monitors national and international mineral developments and advises the federal government on mineral policy. The department also manages research-and-development programs for the energy and mining industries, including direct funding and several laboratories. The Canada Centre for Mineral and Energy Technology (CANMET) is responsible for the science and technology activities. In addition, the department is responsible for the Geological Survey of Canada, including surveys, mapping, and remote sensing. In 1992, the department was given responsibility for the PETROLEUM MONITORING AGENCY, a federal body established to monitor the performance of the oil and gas industry and trends in Canadian and foreign ownership and control. It is also responsible

for the NATIONAL ENERGY BOARD. It works with The Department of INDIAN AFFAIRS AND NORTHERN DEVELOPMENT on resource projects and policies in the Northwest Territories and Arctic and with ENVIRONMENT CANADA in formulating Canadian policies on global warming. It represents Canada at the INTERNATIONAL ENERGY AGENCY and in international negotiations on energy and mineral policy. It is also responsible to Parliament for the ATOMIC ENERGY CONTROL BOARD OF CANADA and ATOMIC ENERGY OF CANADA LIMITED.

energy policy   The policy to match energy supply and demand and to reduce demand by improving energy conservation and efficiency. Measures can include policies to increase energy supplies, such as tax incentives for exploration and development of oil and gas, negotiation of supply agreements with foreign countries, subsidies for the construction of energy projects, funding of research and development, and direct government investment in and ownership of energy companies, such as electric utilities or oil and gas companies. See PETRO-CANADA. However, energy policy can also target DEMAND MANAGEMENT, pursuing pricing, tax, regulatory, subsidy, and research and development measures to reduce energy demand. Under Canada's federal system, both the federal and provincial governments have responsibilities for energy policy. See also NATIONAL ENERGY POLICY, SOFT-ENERGY PATH, SUSTAINABLE DEVELOPMENT.

Energy Resources Conservation Board   Alberta's energy regulatory agency; it regulates the activities of the oil, gas, coal, and electric-power industries. Its specific functions include the determination of Alberta's natural-gas reserves and Alberta's own future needs, and the level of reserves available for export to other parts of Canada or the United States; the issuing of permits to drill oil and gas wells; the approval of construction plans for oil or gas pipelines to be built within the province; the approval of new tar-sands and heavy-oil projects; the approval of exploration and development plans for coal mining; the approval of new electricity-transmission lines in the province; and the responsibility for reviewing the need for new electric-power plants. The board was established in 1938 as the Petroleum and Natural Gas Conservation Board; it was given new powers and its name was changed in 1971. It is based in Calgary.

Energy Supplies Emergency Act   A law passed by Parliament in 1979 giving the federal government sweeping powers to allocate oil, natural gas, and coal in the event of shortages caused by international events, natural disasters, technical failures, strikes, embargoes, or other emergencies. With the declaration of an emergency by the government, an Energy Supplies Allocation Board can be created to implement emergency plans, allocate supplies, set prices, and, on instruction from the government, introduce a system of rationing, including gasoline rationing. The law replaced a similar 1974 law that lapsed in 1976. Its passage in 1979 also implemented a Canadian promise to the INTERNATIONAL ENERGY AGENCY to put in place a law permitting the government to control the allocation of oil supplies in an emergency.

Engel's law   As a family's income increases, it spends a declining proportion of that income on food and other necessities; in other words, poor families spend a much greater share of their income on food and necessities than do rich families. The law was formulated by Ernst Engel, a German statistician, in the 19th century. It led to the notion of DISCRETIONARY INCOME.

enhanced recovery   The additional oil or natural gas recovered, in addition to that which can be recovered through standard production processes, through SECONDARY and TERTIARY RECOVERY.

Enterprise Development Program   A federal program established in 1977 to provide last-resort loan guarantees for companies attempting to modernize or reorganize their facilities to meet import competition, and to provide grants to companies developing new technology in Canada. The program was administered by a 16-person Enterprise Development Board, half of whose members are from the public sector, half from the private sector; the board approved loan guarantees and grants. The Minister of INDUSTRY, SCIENCE AND TECHNOLOGY was responsible to Parliament for the program. It was wound up in 1984.

Enterprise for the Americas Initiative   A proposal by U.S. President George Bush made in June, 1990, for a hemispheric free-trade area linking all of North America and South America. No timetable was set, but the first step was to complete the NORTH AMERICAN FREE TRADE AGREEMENT (NAFTA), forming a free-trade area between Canada, the United States, and Mexico. NAFTA contains an accession clause, permitting other countries to join. Early candidates include Chile and Venezuela.

entrepôt   An international trading centre that re-exports goods shipped from elsewhere. For example, Hong Kong is an entrepôt because it is a re-export centre for goods shipped from China.

entrepreneur   A person who either starts a business or aggressively expands an existing one. An entrepreneur is normally identified with risk taking and new ideas, as opposed to a businessman or corporate executive, who keeps an existing business going. The entrepreneur is considered vital in a dynamic economy, since he or she is often in the forefront of innovation, new technology, and new products and services. The entrepreneur frequently assumes all of the early financial and other risks, and the failure rate among entrepreneurs is high. But the entrepreneurial spirit may be essential if new ideas and products are to be introduced; in fact, it is sometimes regarded as a FACTOR OF PRODUCTION. Traditional or NEOCLASSICAL ECONOMICS does not include a role for entrepreneurs.

entry and exit   The ease with which firms are able to enter or leave an industry. In a world of PERFECT COMPETITION there should be no BARRIERS TO ENTRY for new firms; in a world of IMPERFECT COMPETITION, there are, by definition, barriers to entry.

Environment Canada   The federal government department, created in 1971, that is responsible for the administration of Canada's environmental laws that protect air, water, and soil; the administration of laws for the protection of the country's renewable resources (such as forests, wildlife, and birds); the operation of Canada's weather services; the administration of Canada's national parks and historic sites; the implementation of rules and regulations set down by the INTERNATIONAL JOINT COMMISSION; the negotiation and administration of international environmental agreements and conventions; and the implementation of the government's GREEN PLAN, which proposes to spend $3 billion between fiscal 1990-91 and 1996-97. Key laws include the Canadian Environmental

Protection Act, the Canada Water Act, the Environmental Contaminants Act, the National Parks Act, the Migratory Birds Convention Act, and the Canada Wildlife Act.

Renewable-resource programs include the Canadian Wildlife Service. In addition, an Inland Waters Directorate manages water-resources programs within Canada or with the United States, and carries out river-basin studies under the Canada Water Act. The Lands Directorate carries out land-use planning and has completed a Canada Land Inventory. The department's Environmental Protection Service deals with air and water pollution, under the Canadian Environmental Protection Act and the Canada Water Act, and with solid wastes and environmental contaminants, under the Canadian Environmental Protection Act. The department operates a number of research facilities. The department plays a growing international role, not just in implementing the GREAT LAKES WATER QUALITY AGREEMENT and the CANADA-UNITED STATES AIR QUALITY ACCORD, but also in implementing the MONTREAL ACCORD ON THE OZONE LAYER and conventions arising from the UNITED NATIONS CONFERENCE ON ENVIRONMENT AND DEVELOPMENT dealing with global warming and biodiversity. Together with the Department of ENERGY, MINES AND RESOURCES, Environment Canada is responsible for developing a global-warming strategy for Canada.

environmental impact statement   A document that spells out the impact on the environment of a proposed project. It is a form of cost-benefit analysis, dealing with the physical and ecological impact of a project. Most provinces and the federal government have an environmental impact process. The Canada Environmental Protection Act, for example, sets out the environmental-impact-statement requirement and hearing process for projects falling under federal jurisdiction. The NATIONAL ENERGY BOARD requires an environmental impact statement for proposed pipelines. Alberta requires a statement on projects where the surface of the land is to be disturbed — for surface coal mines and tar-sands plants, for example — or for major pulp and paper projects. Ontario's Environmental Assessment Board has wide powers to hold hearings on most major projects with environmental implications, although the cabinet can grant exemptions from hearings and overturn the board's decisions.

equal opportunity Workplace provisions banning job or pay discrimination based on gender, race, religion, language, age, or physical handicap.

equal pay As set out in the federal Human Rights Code, the principle that men and women should receive equal pay for work of equal value. Pay equity bans an employer from paying male and female workers different rates of pay for, essentially, the same work performed in the same establishment, when performing the work requires essentially the same skills, effort, and responsibility, and when it is performed under similar working conditions. The federal law is enforced through the CANADIAN HUMAN RIGHTS COMMISSION; provincial laws tend to be enforced through the employment-standards branches of their labour departments.

equalization payments Unconditional transfer payments, through the federal government, from the rich provinces to the poorer provinces to help equalize per capita tax revenues from coast to coast. They are based on the principle that every Canadian, regardless of where he or she lives, should enjoy a basic level of public services, such as health care, education,

and social assistance, and infrastructure, such as roads, sewer systems, and water supplies, at reasonably comparable levels of taxation. Without equalization payments, Canadians living in the poorer provinces would either have to accept a much lower level of basic public services, or have much higher levels of taxation imposed on them by the provinces, something that would only contribute to a more rapid exodus of people and even greater difficulties for those who remained. Equalization payments, which date back formally to 1957 but have antecedents from the start of Confederation in 1867, were enshrined in the CONSTITUTION ACT, 1982. Section 36 states that "Parliament and the legislatures, together with the government of Canada and the provincial governments, are committed to the principle of making equalization payments to ensure that provincial governments have sufficient revenues to provide reasonably comparable levels of public service and reasonably comparable levels of taxation."

Equalization payments are of great importance to some provinces; they account for about 25 percent of provincial revenues in Atlantic Canada, 20 percent in Manitoba, 15 percent in Saskatchewan, and 10 percent in Quebec. Equalization agreements are normally renewed every five years, but the current agreement runs for just two years, to March 31, 1994. Equalization agreements are included as part of the Federal-Provincial Fiscal Arrangements and Federal Post-Secondary Education and Health Contributions Act, 1977. Under the act, provincial taxing capacity is measured in 32 different categories such as personal income tax, general sales tax, gasoline tax, tobacco tax, capital tax, non-commercial-vehicle licences, revenue from the sale of beer, wine, and spirits, corporate income tax, lottery revenues, remittances from provincially owned crown corporations, local property taxes, and a wide range of resource revenues. For each of these sources a national average rate of tax is determined. In the case of each province, the per capita yield for each revenue source is obtained by multiplying the province's tax base by the national average tax rate, and dividing this by the province's population. The equalization entitlement for each revenue source is the difference between the average per capita yield in five representative provinces (Quebec, Ontario, Manitoba, Saskatchewan, and British Columbia) and the per capita yield in each province. The same calculation is made for all 32 revenue sources and per capita deficiencies and excesses are added together. If a province has a net per capita deficiency, the deficiency is multiplied by the province's population to calculate the equalization payment it should receive. Equalization payments are limited by a cap that holds increases to the annual rate of growth of GROSS DOMESTIC PRODUCT beyond the level for the period from 1992 to 1993.

equilibrium   1. The state of the economy when supply and demand are equal or in balance. Equilibrium is rarely, if ever, achieved because of constant changes in technology, products, prices, and tastes. But economic forces are assumed to be moving toward or away from equilibrium at any point in time. Until the time of John Maynard KEYNES, economists believed that equilibrium would result in FULL EMPLOYMENT, but Keynes showed that it was possible to have both equilibrium and high unemployment. Equilibrium is assumed to represent a balance in which there is no tendency for economic variables to change. **2.** An approximate balance in a country's BALANCE OF PAYMENTS with the rest of the world.

equilibrium price   The sustainable price in a competitive market; the intersection of the DEMAND AND SUP-PLY CURVES; the point at which the amount that producers will readily supply and the amount that consumers will readily buy is equal. Higher prices will lead to a reduction in the amount that consumers will buy; lower prices will lead to a reduction in the amount that producers will supply. *See also* Alfred MARSHALL.

equity   1. Fairness, as in the tax system. The best way to achieve equity or fairness in the tax system is to base it on the ABILITY-TO-PAY PRINCIPLE OF TAXATION. Economic policy in a modern society tries to balance the goals of equity, which is concerned with dealing with those left behind by the market, and efficiency, which is concerned with the least wasteful means of production. **2.** *See* EQUITY CAPITAL.

equity accounting   An accounting convention that allows a company with an investment in another company that is less than a controlling interest to attribute its share of that company's annual profit or less into its own financial results. For example, if a company held 15 percent of another company, it would attribute 15 percent of its annual profit or loss into its own financial results.

equity capital   The capital in a firm that represents ownership and risk. The owners of the equity capital — the firm's preferred and common shareholders — are entitled to all the assets and income of the firm after all the claims of creditors have been paid. SHAREHOLDERS' EQUITY consists of all assets minus all liabilities; it is represented on a firm's balance sheet, and consists of the original capital put into the firm by its backers, subsequent issues of common shares sold to the public, and RETAINED EARNINGS. While equity capital represents ownership and is only entitled to a return after creditors have been paid, DEBT CAPITAL consists of loans that must be repaid with interest but represent no permanent claim on the firm's assets. DIRECT INVESTMENT is equity investment.

equity earnings A company's share of earnings from an unconsolidated subsidiary or other company in which it holds 50 percent or less of the equity.

erosion The loss of land caused by the removal of rock and soil, through flooding, or by the action of the wind, rain, or rivers and other bodies of water. During the 1930s, drought and strong winds combined to sweep away large areas of topsoil in the prairie provinces. The PRAIRIE FARM REHABILITATION ADMINISTRATION was established by the federal government in 1935 to restore prairie farmlands and to prevent a recurrence of the 1930s dustbowls.

escalation clause A clause in a contract providing for an increase in the price of goods or services if costs rise above a specified level. In a construction project, the contractor may require a clause that relates the final price of the project to changes in the cost of labour or building materials. Some union collective agreements give union members an automatic wage increase if the rate of inflation rises above a certain level. *See also* COLA CLAUSE.

escape clause **1.** A clause in a contract that permits one of the parties to withdraw or alter his obligations without penalty under certain specified circumstances. *See also* FORCE MAJEURE. **2.** In trade agreements, a clause that permits the importing country to suspend a preferential tariff on a particular product if imports of the product reach such a level that they cause severe problems for a domestic industry. Article XIX of the GENERAL AGREEMENT ON TARIFFS AND TRADE permits the suspension of tariff concessions when a surge of imports causes or threatens to cause serious injury to domestic producers. There are similar provisions in the CANADA-UNITED STATES FREE TRADE AGREEMENT and the NORTH AMERICAN FREE TRADE AGREEMENT to deal with important surges. *See also* SAFEGUARDS.

escrowed shares Shares of a corporation that cannot be sold by the owner until certain conditions have been met, or without the approval of a regulatory authority, such as a stock exchange or provincial securities commission. In the meantime, the owner is entitled to receive dividends, if any, and to vote the shares at company annual meetings. Escrow arrangements are often made when a small mining or oil and gas company buys exploration properties, paying the vendors with TREASURY SHARES. The vendors have to deposit their shares with a trustee until a specified amount of exploration work has been done or a specified length of time has passed. This is to prevent the sale of the shares on the market before exploration has been carried out. Similarly, the founders of a new company who have issued shares to the public may be required to hold their shares in escrow for a period of time to ensure that the founders do not abandon the business once they have sold shares to the public.

Established Programs Financing (EPF) The system under which the federal government shares in the cost of hospital insurance, medicare, and post-secondary education in Canada. The current system dates back to 1977 and the Federal-Provincial Arrangements and Established Programs Financing Act, 1977, under which the federal government's contribution consisted of a combination of tax points transferred to the provinces and cash payments. In the 1992-93 fiscal year, federal cash transfers amounted to $8.1 billion, while the transfer of tax points yielded $11.6 billion. In 1983, the legislation was renamed the Federal-Provincial Fiscal Arrangements and Federal Post-Secondary Education and Health Contributions Act, 1977, and limits were introduced on the growth in such transfer payments. Total compensation was set at the national average per capita contribution in the 1975-76 period, escalated by the growth in per capita GROSS NATIONAL PRODUCT and multiplied by the population of each province. Through the 1980s and into the 1990s, the federal government continued to tighten EPF payments, leading the provinces to charge that the federal government, having induced the provinces to introduce programs such as hospital insurance and medicare by providing 50 percent of the costs in the beginning, was now leaving the provinces to cope with rising costs. In 1990, the federal government announced that EPF payments would be frozen for two years at 1989-90 levels. In 1991, it announced the freeze would extend to the end of the 1994-95 fiscal year. In 1992, the EPF arrangements were extended for just two years, until March 31, 1994, instead of the normal five, pending a federal review of all of its transfer programs.

established reserves Oil or natural-gas reserves that can be recovered under current technology and present and anticipated economic conditions, and are already specifically proved by drilling, testing, or production, plus contiguous recoverable reserves that are interpreted to exist, based on geological, geophysical, or similar information, with reasonable certainty. *See also* ULTIMATE POTENTIAL RESERVES.

estate The real and personal property owned by an individual after debts have been deducted. The word is normally used to describe the net worth of an individual at the time of death.

estate tax A tax imposed on an estate before its proceeds are distributed to the beneficiaries of the estate. The federal estate tax, which dated back to 1959 when it replaced federal SUCCESSION DUTIES, was abolished at the end of 1971. It was replaced by the CAPITAL-GAINS TAX, with deemed realization of capital gains included in the tax return of the individual in the year of his or her death. An exception is made for those assets in the estate transferred to the spouse. Although Alberta and Saskatchewan had withdrawn from the estate-tax field by then, other provinces continued to impose an estate tax. But the provinces gradually withdrew from the field, with Quebec being the last to withdraw, in 1985. *See also* GIFT TAX.

Estey Commission *See* INQUIRY INTO THE COLLAPSE OF THE CANADIAN COMMERCIAL BANK AND THE NORTHLAND BANK.

estimates The document submitted to Parliament each year by the president of the TREASURY BOARD, spelling out in detail the spending plans of the government, for each department, agency, and crown corporation, for the new fiscal year that begins on April 1. The process begins in July of the previous year when the Treasury Board requests each organization that requires funding from Parliament to update its individual Multi-Year Operational Plan, covering the next three fiscal years. During October and November, the Treasury Board reviews these documents in the context of overall spending plans contained within the FISCAL FRAMEWORK, the overall limits on government spending set by the Minister of FINANCE. The framework provides for the on-going costs of government initiatives as well as reserves that provide limited funding for the government's priorities as determined by cabinet and reserves for work-load adjustments to existing programs and for demographic and inflation changes to the major social programs. By the end of November, departments, agencies, and crown corporations that are to receive funding are aware of the results of the Treasury Board review and are then required to convert the first updated year into their individual Main Estimates. This work must be completed by February, when the estimates documents are tabled in Parliament. The estimates, which must be referred to Parliamentary committees on or before March 1 of each fiscal year, consist of three distinct parts: Part I — the Government Expenditure Plan, which serves as a link between the BUDGET as presented by the Minister of Finance and the actual financial requirements that will be placed before Parliament; Part II — The Main Estimates, which details by individual vote the precise spending requirements of each organization contained in the estimates, and supports the Appropriation Bill that Parliament will be asked to approve; and Part III — the departmental spending plans provide details on the objectives and results of individual programs, including linkages between resource requirements, results (both planned and actual), and objectives. The individual standing committees of the House of Commons and the Senate Committee on National Finance examine the various spending plans during the next four months, and during the various reviews, ministers and senior officials may be called to explain and defend their spending activities and respond to questions from members of Parliament. The standing committees of the House of Commons must report the estimates back to the House of Commons by May 31. If not they are deemed to have reported estimates without change.

In late March, Parliament normally approves an APPROPRIATION ACT (Interim Supply) that will provide each vote in the estimates with sufficient cash authority to cover its forecast expenditures during the first three months of the new fiscal year; Appropriation Acts authorize the payment of funds for specific purposes out of the CONSOLIDATED REVENUE FUND. Normally this amount is three-twelfths of the amount in the estimates, but more funding may be requested in the case where expenditures are seasonal in nature, for example, the summer employment of students. Once the committees have reported the estimates, Parliament will approve a second Appropriation in June that will provide the balance of the spending authority contained in Main Estimates.

Some of the spending in the estimates does not require approval each year because Parliament has previously approved legislation that allows certain expenditures to continue from year to year without renewing annual spending authoirty — these are known as STATUTORY expenditures. Examples of statutory spending authorities are old-age security pension, EQUALIZATION PAYMENTS to the provinces, and payments under the Canada Assistance Plan. Statutory expenditures are included in the Main Estimates for the information of Parliament and to give a more complete picture of government spending requirements.

In addition to the main estimates, Supplementary Estimates are tabled in Parliament normally twice each fiscal year in November and March. Supplementary estimates provide additional funding for new spending progams that could not be included in the Main Estmates because the final details of the plans were not finalized at the time of tabling the Main Estimates; they also provide additional funding for existing programs that have experienced unusual changes to their individual forecast spending requirements. The FINANCIAL ADMINISTRATION ACT permits the government to spend money in an emergency through SPECIAL GOVERNOR-GENERAL'S WARRANTS. These warrants must be published in the *Canada Gazette* within 30 days, so that the public has been given notice, and they must be reported to Parliament within 15 days of the opening of the next session.

Eurobond market That part of the EUROCURRENCY MARKET that deals in government and corporation bonds. A Eurobond is a bond denominated in a Western European currency issued to a corporation or government outside the country in which the security is denominated. For example, a bond issued by a Canadian corporation or government agency in Deutsche marks or British pounds. Canadian corporations, provincial utilities, and governments, including municipalities and school boards, borrow in the Eurobond market. Canadian banks and investment dealers are active in helping to place issues of Eurobonds.

Eurocurrency market The international market for bank and other deposits and loans outside the jurisdiction of the national economies issuing the currencies, and hence outside any national currency controls and other regulations. Eurodollars are U.S. dollars loaned and borrowed in financial markets outside the United States; Euromarks are German marks loaned and borrowed outside Germany; Euroyen are Japanese yen loaned and borrowed outside Japan. Depositors in the Eurocurrency market include banks, corporations, and central banks; borrowers include corporations, governments, and government agencies. Eurobonds are the principal long-term investment instrument. The substantial portion of Eurocurrency funds is loaned and borrowed in Europe, although there are smaller Eurocurrency markets in other parts of the world. The Eurocurrency market today is the largest and least-regulated money market in the world. It includes Canadian dollars on deposit in banks in London and elsewhere outside Canada. The Eurocurrency markets are closely linked by electronic communications among such centres as New York, London, Frankfurt, Brussels, Toronto, Zurich, Tokyo, Hong Kong, and Singapore. Funds flow into the Eurocurrency market seeking short-term investments and money-market instruments, including overnight loans and the purchase of short-term TREASURY BILLS, as well as longer-term bonds. The pace of activity in the Eurocurrency market can have a significant impact on a country's exchange rate since traders will sell off bonds and other securities denominated in a currency they believe is overvalued, or buy up securities denominated in a currency they believe is undervalued, creating additional pressure on a currency.

There is concern on the part of some monetary authorities about the lack of regulation of Eurocurrency markets, which, according to some estimates, amount to more than $1 trillion in financial assets. While Eurocurrency markets today represent a pool of many different currencies, the market began with the pool of surplus U.S. dollars held outside the United States. Starting in the late 1950s, U.S. banks and corporations began borrowing U.S. dollars held by Europeans to bypass U.S. government regulations. The U.S. dollar remains the most significant currency traded in Eurocurrency markets.

Eurodollars U.S. dollars loaned and borrowed outside the United States, and hence outside the control of U.S. monetary and securities authorities. Eurodollars are U.S. dollars deposited in a bank outside the United States, including foreign branches of U.S. banks. *See* EUROCURRENCY MARKET, EUROMARKET.

European Bank for Reconstruction and Development (EBRD)   A multilateral development bank established in 1990 that began lending in 1991. Based in London, its main purpose is to assist the former Communist countries of Eastern and Central Europe, including the states of the former Soviet Union, make the transition to market-based economies. Unlike other multilateral development banks, the EBRD's principal focus is on the private sector; its charter states that 60 percent of its funding must be directed either to private-sector companies or state-owned enterprises that are to be privatized. The remaining 40 percent of EBRD funding can be used for loans to governments of the qualifying recipient countries. The EBRD provides loans, equity, debt guarantees, and underwriting for the private sector, all on commercial terms. In private-sector projects, the bank normally limits its participation to 35 percent of the total capital required for the project; the smallest loan it will make is for ECU 5 million. Funds for small and medium businesses will be made available through local financial intermediaries. Loans to governments may be made at various rates. Initial capitalization of the EBRD was ECU 10 billion or US$12 billion; Canada was one of the founders, contributing 3.4 percent of the initial capital. The EUROPEAN COMMUNITY holds 51 percent of the shares, the United States 10 percent, and Japan 8.75 percent.

Euromarket   The international capital market that deals in EUROBONDS, EURODOLLAR, and other international securities.

European Commission   A body of 17 members, appointed by the 12 nations in the EUROPEAN COMMUNITY (EC), that administers the treaties, laws, and directives of the EC and proposes and implements measures to advance the interests of the EC. It also prepares the EC budget. Each EC commissioner heads at least one department of the EC administration, such as energy, competition, industrial policy, trade or foreign affairs. There are 20 such departments or directorates. The commissioners are appointed by the member governments (two each from France, Germany, Italy, Spain, and Britain, and one each from Luxembourg, the Netherlands, Belgium, Denmark, Greece, Portugal, and Ireland) for renewable four-year terms. The president and five vice-presidents of the European Commission are appointed from among the commission members, for renewable two-year terms. While appointed by member state-governments, the commission members are there to act on behalf of the EC as a whole, rather than for the countries from which individual members come. The EUROPEAN PARLIAMENT has the power, by a two-thirds vote, to fire the commission, and also controls the spending budget of the commission. The European Commission has three essential functions: 1. To ensure that EC rules and principles of the common market are respected and that the provisions of the European treaties and decrees of EC institutions are properly implemented; 2. To prepare for the EUROPEAN COUNCIL OF MINISTERS, the principal political body of the EC, measures to advance the development of EC policies in fields such as agriculture, technology, the environment, social policy, research and development, and trade — only the European Commission may propose new laws and directives; 3. To implement EC policies based on decisions or treaty provisions made by the European Council of Ministers. In some areas, such as competition policy, the European Commission has extensive powers to act on its own; in others, such as trade policy, it must operate under the direction of the European Council of Ministers. The European Commission also manages certain funds or programs, including those for the support and management of agriculture (the European Agricultural Guidance and Control Fund), the promotion of science and technology (the Framework Program for Research and Technology Development), the encouragement of regional development (the European Regional Development Fund), the employment of young people (the Social Fund), or the management of EC relations with developing countries (the European Development Fund). Based mainly in Brussels, but with offices in Luxembourg as well, the European Commission has about 15,000 officials, of whom about 20 percent are translators for the nine languages used in the EC.

European Community (EC)   A common market agreed to by six Western European countries (France, West Germany, Italy, the Netherlands, Belgium, and Luxembourg) in March, 1957, under the Treaty of Rome, and which came into being on January 1, 1958. Since then, the EC has been expanded to include, as of January 1, 1973, Britain, Ireland, and Denmark; as of January 1, 1981, Greece; and as of January 1, 1986, Spain and Portugal. A number of other countries, including Sweden and Austria, have indicated their desire to join at an early date. In 1992, the EC and the EUROPEAN FREE-TRADE ASSOCIATION negotiated a new agreement, the European Economic Area, for the free movement of goods, services, capital, and people, but it did not come into effect as planned at the start of 1993 because Switzerland, in a 1992 referendum, voted against it. The EC also has free trade agreements covering a wide range of products with Turkey and a number of developing countries; the EC has also negotiated trade agreements with several former Communist countries in Eastern Europe.

The origin of the EC dates back to the efforts by Jean Monnet, the French economist and diplomat who devised France's post-war economic recovery plan, and French Foreign Minister Robert Schuman in 1950 to establish a French-German common market for coal, iron, and steel; other countries were invited to join, and in 1951, Belgium, France, Germany, Italy, Luxembourg, and the Netherlands signed a treaty establishing the European Coal and Steel Community (ECSC). Their coal, iron, and steel industries were placed under a supranational authority, and a council of ministers was set up to make major decisions. A parliamentary assembly was added and a EUROPEAN COURT OF JUSTICE established to ensure compliance with decisions and to adjudicate disputes. An ECSC committee, under Belgian Foreign Minister Paul-Henri Spaak, investigated the potential for further integration, and in 1956, his committee's recommendations were adopted, leading to two Treaties of Rome in 1957 — one creating the European Community and the other, the European Atomic Energy Commission. The original purpose of the EC was to achieve free trade among its members, which was accomplished by January 1, 1968, 18 months ahead of schedule, with a common external tariff levied on all imports from outside the EC. But the broader goal of the EC was to achieve a high level of economic, social, and political integration, with widespread co-operation on industrial, scientific, and regional development policies; the free movement of labour and capital within the EC; and agreement on EC-wide policies on agriculture, competition policy, transportation, communications, international economic policy, monetary arrangements, and foreign policy. In 1979, the EC adopted the EUROPEAN MONE-

TARY SYSTEM to provide a more stable exchange-rate environment within the EC; a EUROPEAN CURRENCY UNIT was also created as a unit of account for the EC. The next step was taken with the adoption in 1986 of the Single European Act, ratified by all member states by the July 1, 1987, deadline, which provided for the creation of a single, internal market without frontiers and the free movement of labour, capital, and goods and services by December 31, 1992. More than three hundred measures had to be adopted by all 12 members to implement the Single European Act. The Single European Act also moved the EC to a much broader system of European-wide rules and policies, strengthening the capacity of the EUROPEAN COMMISSION to make rules affecting business, consumers, and governments. It included EC-wide policies and programs on technology and industry, progress toward economic and monetary union, the strengthening of social and economic cohesion in Europe, new measures on the environment and the workplace, mutual recognition of diplomas, an EC-wide competition policy, including new rules on mergers and acquisitions, and greater harmonization of some tax rates. It also included a social charter, covering industrial relations and dealing with, among other things, support measures for the unemployed, health protection and safety in the workplace, the promotion of equality of access for women in training and employment, the free movement of workers, and mutual recognition of occupational qualifications. In 1992, the members of the EC signed the Maastricht Treaty, taking the EC even further along the road to monetary and political integration. If ratified by its members, the Maastricht Treaty will create a European Union, with a European citizenship. In effect, the Maastricht Treaty establishes a European Union based on the three pillars of a common foreign and security policy, an economic and monetary union, and a greater co-ordination of justice and home affairs. Under the proposed European citizenship, a resident would have the right to work and live anywhere in the EC and to stand for and vote in local elections and the EUROPEAN PARLIAMENT elections anywhere in the EC. The treaty reaffirms the EC's commitment to reducing regional disparities and provides for a cohesion fund to finance projects in member countries where the per capita GROSS DOMESTIC PRODUCT (GDP) is less than 90 percent of the EC average. A new chapter on industrial policy allows the EC to adopt measures to aid small and medium businesses, help industries cope with structural change, and promote industrial innovation and competitiveness, including research and development projects with industry, provided this does not distort competition. Other changes would allow the EC to propose trans-European networks in transportation, telecommunications, and energy, make proposals on consumer protection, and play a more active role in the environment. All member states but Britain agreed to new provisions on a social charter, allowing for EC-wide rules, for example, on working conditions, the consultation of workers, and equal employment rights for men and women.

Under proposals for economic and monetary union, the first step would be taken in January, 1994, with the creation of the European Monetary Institute, the forerunner of the planned European Central Bank. The institute will co-ordinate the monetary policy of member countries, oversee the preparations for the transfer to a single European currency, and create the conditions for economic and monetary union. The EC will move to economic and monetary union in 1997 if the European Council of Ministers decides, by a qualified majority, that a majority of EC members meets five conditions: 1. An inflation rate within 1.5 percentage points of the three best-performing countries; 2. Interest rates within 2 percentage points of the three best-performing countries; 3. A budget deficit of less than 3 percent of GDP; 4. A national debt of less than 60 percent of GDP; and 5. No devaluation within the exchange-rate mechanism of the EUROPEAN MONETARY SYSTEM for the past two years. If not enough countries meet these criteria, then economic and monetary union will commence in 1999 with as many members as can meet the criteria. Britain has reserved its right to opt out. With economic and monetary union, a single European currency will replace national currencies and a European Central Bank will replace national central banks in setting interest rates and conducting monetary and exchange-rate policy. The finance ministers of the participating countries will meet regularly in a body to be known as Eurofin. It will supervise the European Central Bank. It will also issue broad guidelines for fiscal policy and, if it determines a country's policy is inconsistent with economic and monetary union, can recommend changes. If it judges a country's budget deficit to be excessive, it may call for cuts. If, after a public warning from Ecofin, a country disregards calls for fiscal action, Ecofin ministers may insist that all bonds issued by that country carry a notice that its budget deficit has been judged to be too high, may cut off credit to that country from the European Investment Bank, and may even impose a fine. Moreover, no government in financial difficulty has the right to be bailed out by the EC. In foreign and security policy, the EC ministers will determine what areas call for "joint action." In justice and home affairs, EC ministers will co-operate on refugee asylum, immigration, frontier rules, crime, customs, and terrorism and drugs. The Maastricht Treaty also introduces the principle of subsidiarity, with the EC promising to act "only if and in so far as the objectives of the proposed action cannot be sufficiently achieved by the member states and can therefore by reason of scale or the effect of the proposed action, be better achieved by the Community." The Maastricht Treaty would also give some additional powers to the EUROPEAN PARLIAMENT. If the Maastricht Treaty is ratified by the member states, a conference would be held in 1996 to review the treaty arrangements, in particular, those dealing with defence policy and the powers of the European Parliament.

The EC is managed by a EUROPEAN COMMISSION made up of appointed representatives of EC members, plus a supporting bureaucracy, based in Brussels, which reports to a EUROPEAN COUNCIL OF MINISTERS, consisting of one cabinet minister from each EC state. The European Parliament, whose members were directly elected for the first time in 1979, is expected to strengthen the evolution of political union within the EC, although the powers of the parliament are strictly limited. It cannot initiate EC-wide legislation, or even reject it, but it does control the EC budget. EC agricultural policy is administered through the COMMON AGRICULTURAL POLICY, which guarantees minimum prices to farmers and finances them through levies on member states and agricultural imports. A European Investment Bank was created within the EC in 1958 to assist regional development. A number of former colonies of EC members have associate membership in the EC, which entitles them to preferential tariff treatment. In 1976, Canada signed a trade and investment agreement with the EC. See FRAMEWORK AGREEMENT FOR COMMERCIAL AND ECONOMIC CO-OPERATION.

European Council of Ministers The main political decision-making body of the EUROPEAN COMMUNITY (EC), the European Council of Ministers consists of the leaders of the EC member governments, who meet at periodic summits held two to three times a year. In addition to the leaders of the 12 member states, the leaders' foreign ministers also attend summits, along with the president of the European Commission. But on other occasions, the participants change as the agenda changes; for example, agriculture ministers from the 12 EC nations attend meetings regarding agriculture, environment ministers attend meetings dealing with the environment, and so forth. The job of each minister is to represent the interests of his or her own country. The presidency of the council rotates every six months among the various members of the EC, giving each member the opportunity once every six years to set the agenda and introduce issues of concern to that country. The council meets several times a month, with the subject under discussion determining the ministers who attend. Most decisions are made by a qualified majority vote of 54 votes out of a possible 76; Germany, France, Italy, and Britain have 10 votes each; Spain eight votes; Belgium, the Netherlands, Greece, and Portugal, five votes each; Denmark and Ireland, three votes each; and Luxembourg, two votes. A member can seek a unanimous vote on a matter that it considers to be of national interest; some broader questions, such as the admission of new members to the EC, also need a unanimous vote. The council has an advisory committee of permanent representatives, which consists of the ambassadors accredited by the member states to the EC and their staffs, known as the Committee of Permanent Representatives, or COREPER. While it is the body with ultimate political responsibility for the EC, the main functions of the European Council of Ministers are to set the direction and general policy guidelines for the EC. However, it cannot initiate proposals of its own. Instead, it must respond to proposals from the European Commission. Its decisions go to the European Parliament, where they can be accepted, amended, or rejected. The European Council of Ministers then needs an unanimous vote to override the Parliament; however, if the European Commission sides with the European Council of Minsters, only a qualified majority is needed. *See also* EUROPEAN COMMISSION, EUROPEAN PARLIAMENT.

European Court of Justice A special court based in Luxembourg that provides binding interpretations of the European treaties, directives, and laws of the EUROPEAN COMMUNITY (EC). With 13 judges and six advocates-general appointed for six-year terms, the court can quash at the request of an EC country, company, or individual any measures adopted by the EUROPEAN COMMISSION and EUROPEAN COUNCIL OF MINISTERS that are incompatible with the European treaties; likewise, the court can quash at the request of the EC a measure of a member country that is incompatible with the European issues. The court can also render at the request of a national government an interpretation on the validity of an EC law.

European Currency Unit (ECU) A central bankers' currency, based on a basket of EUROPEAN COMMUNITY (EC) members' currencies, and introduced in 1979 as part of the EUROPEAN MONETARY SYSTEM (EMS). It is the unit of account within the European Community. The ECU is being used to settle debts among central banks of EUROPEAN COMMUNITY (EC) members participating in the EMS, and it also plays an important role in determining the need for currency intervention and in funding credit facilities in the EMS. It may become an important reserve asset, not only for EC members but for other nations as well. Each country's share in the ECU basket is weighted, based on each country's share of total EC output, with an ECU central rate established for each currency.

European Free-Trade Association (EFTA)   A free-trade area established by seven European nations in 1959 under the Stockholm Agreement as an alternative to the EUROPEAN COMMUNITY (EC). Its members were Britain, Sweden, Norway, Denmark, Switzerland, Portugal, and Austria. While the members agreed to the eventual elimination of tariffs on trade among themselves (this was achieved by the end of 1966), they did not establish a common external tariff, as the European Community had, on trade with other countries. Each member of EFTA was left free to make whatever kind of commercial arrangements it wished with non-EFTA nations. Nor did EFTA members adopt other policies to integrate their economies, as the European Community had. In 1961, Finland became a member, and in 1970, Iceland joined; membership of Finland and Austria in the European Community was out of the question at that time, due to conditions of neutrality imposed on them by the Soviets. EFTA was weakened in 1973, when Britain and Denmark became members of the European Community. In 1979, Portugal was accepted for membership in the European Community, and became a full member in 1986. The EC has negotiated free trade agreements with EFTA members who decided not to seek membership in the community. Thus, the 18 nations of the EC and EFTA are joined together in a free-trade arrangement. In 1992, the EC and EFTA negotiated the European Economic Area, which would have led to the free movement of goods, services, capital, and

people. But it did not come into effect in 1993, as planned, because Switzerland, in a referendum, voted against it. But five EFTA countries — Austria, Finland, Norway, Sweden, and Switzerland — have applied for full EC membership. The other EFTA members are Iceland and Liechtenstein.

European Investment Bank (EIB)   A development bank established by the European Community (EC) in 1958 under the TREATY OF ROME to make loans or provide loan guarantees for regional development projects in the EC, developing countries associated with the EC through the Lome Convention, and Turkey and former Communist states in Eastern Europe. It also provides loans or loan guarantees for modernization or development projects necessary for the achievement of the common market, or for projects linking different countries in the EC. The bank is based in Luxembourg and its board consists of EC finance ministers. The bank raises funds on financial markets and re-lends them on a non-profit basis for regional development, infrastructure, protection of the environment, a reduction in energy dependence, and the strengthening of the international competitiveness of industry, in particular by developing advanced technologies or through restructuring; since 1979, the EIB has also provided loans for the New Community Instrument, which in turn funds small and medium enterprises in manufacturing and directly related services, in particular in innovation and new technologies.

European Monetary Agreement   An arrangement made by European countries to facilitate the settlement of outstanding payments imbalances among them and to provide short-term balance-of-payments assistance, through a European Fund, to European nations participating in the agreement. It came into effect in December. 1958, with the

BANK FOR INTERNATIONAL SETTLE-MENTS acting as its agent. The European Monetary Agreement was a further step in the post-war restoration of currency convertibility and the establishment of common procedures for European countries in dealing with balance-of-payments problems. After the Second World War, when Europe was economically shattered and currency transactions rigidly controlled, the Intra-European Payments Agreement was set up under the EUROPEAN RECOVERY PROGRAM (Marshall Plan) to facilitate trade among European nations. This was replaced in 1950 by the European Payments Union, organized by the ORGANIZATION FOR EUROPEAN ECONOMIC CO-OPERATION, later called the Organization for Economic Co-operation and Development (OECD). The purpose of the European Payments Union was to act as a clearinghouse to settle balances among members, to provide short-term balance-of-payments assistance to members, and to encourage the European nations to pursue a multilateral approach to balance-of-payments arrangements, rather than a network of bilateral arrangements. In 1958, the European Payments Union was replaced by the European Monetary Agreement.

European Monetary System (EMS) A system of FIXED EXCHANGE RATES within the EUROPEAN COMMUNITY (EC), agreed to in July, 1978, and implemented in March, 1979. It created an exchange-rate mechanism for participating countries, established the EUROPEAN CURRENCY UNIT (ECU) as a unit of account within the EC, and established a pool of reserves for the settlement of payments imbalances. A European Monetary Co-operation Fund was established to manage the system. Britain did not join the exchange-rate mechanism until October, 1990, withdrawing on what it said was a temporary basis in 1992 following unacceptable

exchange-rate speculation. Italy entered only after it had negotiated special treatment. At the end of 1992, Britain, Italy, and Greece were not actively participating in the exchage-rate mechanism. The purpose of the EMS is to stabilize currency rates among EC members and thereby encourage trade and investment within the community. Fluctuating international exchange rates in the 1970s caused constant changes in exchange rates between different EC members and discouraged investment decisions, since businesses could never be sure of how different EC-member exchange rates would relate to one another. Under the exchange-rate mechanism, each nation set its exchange rate in relation to the ECU at a fixed level. Each currency could move up or down by 2.25 percent against the others (in Italy's case, 6 percent). If a country's currency moves to the outer bound of the exchange-rate mechanism, its central bank is required to intervene to bring its currency back in line. The European Monetary Co-operation Fund must approve a currency revaluation or devaluation by a member of the exchange-rate mechanism. In 1992, the exchange-rate mechanism came under intense pressure from financial markets. After failing to strengthen the pound despite significant interest-rate increases, Britain withdrew from the system, although it had joined just two years earlier. Spain imposed some foreign-exchange controls and Italy suspended its participation temporarily. The French franc also came under intense pressure. Critics pointed to the event as evidence that EC plans for a single currency were either premature or misguided; others suggested that the EC might adopt a two-speed approach to monetary union, with the strong-currency countries moving first, to be followed by the weaker countries much later, when their economies were in better shape.

European Parliament A chamber of 518 deputies or MPs elected from the 12 member states of the EUROPEAN COMMUNITY (EC). The European Parliament, located in Strasbourg, has limited powers, but is of growing importance. In 1979, the members of the European Parliament were directly elected for the first time. About 175 million people were qualified to vote. Prior to this, a smaller chamber of 198 members had been appointed from the parliaments of member countries. Members of the European Parliament do not form a government and opposition; instead, they sit as members of different trans-European political parties rather than as representatives of their respective countries. Nor can they pass laws. However, they review all EC-wide laws drafted by the EUROPEAN COMMISSION for approval by the EUROPEAN COUNCIL OF MINISTERS, and they can pass resolutions concerning these laws, either endorsing, amending, or rejecting them. The European Commission frequently incorporates such resolutions into its revised draft laws. If a law is rejected or amended, the European Council of Ministers can only overrule the European Parliament by a unanimous vote; however, if the European Commission sides with the European Council of Ministers, then only a qualified majority is needed. Similarly, the European Parliament can initiate new policies by passing resolutions calling for EC action. It also controls the EC budget, mainly by setting the spending budget of the community; it has no say over the raising of revenue. It can also fire the European Commission, investigate some forms of spending, establish investigating committees that can summon EC officials and commissioners, extract and publish information on the way the community is run, and take other EC institutions to the EUROPEAN COURT OF JUSTICE for an infringement of EC treaties. Under the proposed Maastricht Treaty, signed in 1992 but also requiring ratification by all EC members, the European Parliament would gain an effective veto over EC legislation. If the parliament's MPs rejected a draft law of the European Council of Ministers or if the European Council of Ministers rejected the European Parliament amendments, a conciliation committee would be formed. If the committee could not find a compromise, then the law would not pass. This would apply to measures on the single-market, education, culture, health, and consumer policies as well as programs for the environment, research and development, and trans-European networks for transportation, telecommunications, and energy. The European Parliament would also have to approve an EC international agreement with budgetary implications or other implications that touched on areas where the European Parliament had a right of veto. In addition, the Maastricht Treaty promised a 1996 conference to further review the powers of the European Parliament.

European Recovery Program The program named after U.S. Secretary of State General George C. Marshall as the MARSHALL PLAN. It followed a speech made by Marshall at Harvard University in June, 1947, in which he proposed generous U.S. aid for the recovery of Europe, provided that the Europeans agreed to work together and developed specific plans for their economic recovery. The offer was extended to all European nations, including the Soviet Union and Eastern Europe, but was taken up only by the nations of Western Europe.

Sixteen European nations met in Paris in 1947 at a meeting that led to the formation of the Organization for European Economic Co-operation the following year; it subsequently became the ORGANIZATION FOR ECONOMIC

CO-OPERATION AND DEVELOPMENT. Its task was to co-ordinate the use of Marshall Plan assistance and to ensure that the aid was being employed properly. In 1948, the U.S. Congress passed the Economic Co-operation Act, authorizing the spending of money under the Marshall Plan. Between 1948 and 1951, when the program was terminated, the U.S. provided about US$12 billion of assistance to Europe.

The Marshall Plan was also important to Canada, which was experiencing severe balance-of-payments problems following the Second World War. Following lengthy negotiations with the United States, the U.S. government agreed that Marshall Plan funds could be used by European countries to purchase goods and services from Canada. As a result, more than $1 billion was spent on Canadian goods and services by European nations using Marshall Plan funds; these purchases played an important role in improving Canada's balance-of-payments situation in the period before the Korean War.

ex ante   Expected before the event; in economics the term incorporates expectations about future events. *See also* EX POST.

ex dividend   Without dividend. DIVIDENDS are payable to owners of COMMON SHARES registered on a particular date. If the share is sold after that date and before the dividend is mailed out, the seller and not the new owner will receive the dividend cheque.

ex interest   Without interest. A purchaser or seller of bonds would take into account the date of the next interest payment in setting the price. If a bond is sold, say, three months before the next annual interest payment is due, the seller's price will include a calculation for a share of the interest (three-quarters, in this case). The purchaser will get this back, since he or she will receive the full year's interest when it is paid.

ex officio   A position held by an individual by virtue of another post he or she holds, rather than because of personal aptitudes. For example, the Deputy Minister of ENERGY, MINES AND RESOURCES was an ex officio member of the board of directors of PETRO-CANADA until it was privatized in 1991; the Deputy Minister of FINANCE is an ex officio member of the board of directors of the BANK OF CANADA. The president of a corporation is usually an ex officio member of all senior corporate committees.

excess capacity   The situation that exists when the actual output of a firm or industry is less than that needed to utilize fully all the resources or factors of production employed in the firm or industry. In economic terms, it means that a firm or industry is operating at a level from which it is still possible to decrease its average cost; its MARGINAL COST is still lower than its average cost. By producing more, it is possible to make marginal cost and average cost equal, which results in the production level that achieves the lowest possible price for the consumer. Excess capacity may be caused by fluctuations in the business cycle or the existence of too many firms in an industry. It is the second situation that concerns economists, because the presence of too many firms means that ECONOMIES OF SCALE cannot be achieved, and the consumer must pay the cost of chronic excess capacity through higher prices until the weaker firms have left the industry or the industry has restructured or rationalized. Statistics Canada publishes quarterly figures showing capacity utilization in manufacturing industries (publication 31-003).

excess demand   The situation that exists when the demand for goods and services in the economy is greater than the supply available to meet the demand. As a result, consumers bid up prices to pay for the same goods and services, and inflation results. *See* DEMAND-PULL INFLATION. The normal response of government authorities is to check the growth of demand by raising taxes, cutting spending, slowing the growth of money-supply, and raising interest rates.

excess-profits tax   A tax to reduce profits arising from unusual and temporary business conditions. For example, countries usually impose such a tax during wartime when demand is abnormally high and most industries are operating at full capacity. Canada imposed the Business Profits War Tax in 1916 and introduced an excess-profits tax in 1939, which was made much more severe in 1940. Such a tax is usually levied at an extremely high rate, up to 100 percent, on profits in excess of a normal or base period.

excess supply   The situation in which the quantity of goods or services available from suppliers at a particular price is greater than the demand from consumers. This should cause producers to reduce prices so that consumers will increase their purchases.

exchange   **1.** One of the principal activities studied in economics; the process in which one good or service is accepted for another. In a world of increased specialization, the need for an efficient means of exchange is vital. The use of money as a medium of exchange enables a wide variety of goods and services to be produced and the benefits of COMPARATIVE ADVANTAGE to be widely pursued. **2.** A place where trading occurs. For example, a stock exchange is a place where buyers and sellers of shares can negotiate prices and carry out transactions. Similarly, a commodity exchange is a place

where buyers and sellers of commodities, such as agricultural and mineral products, can negotiate prices and carry out transactions.

exchange controls   Any restriction by a government on the sale or purchase of foreign currencies by its own citizens. The restrictions may range from a ban on the export of the country's currency or restrictions on the repatriation of profits from a subsidiary to its foreign parent, to restrictions on the convertibility of a currency into other currencies and government regulation of the amounts of foreign exchange that can be obtained and the purposes for which it can be used. During the Second World War, for example, Canada limited the purchase of U.S. dollars by Canadians to essential imports and essential travel under the Foreign Exchange Conservation Act. See also FOREIGN EXCHANGE CONTROL BOARD. Similar controls were reintroduced in November, 1947, to save scarce U.S. dollars; legislation — the Emergency Foreign Exchange Conservation Act — was passed in 1948. The measures included high domestic excise taxes on products with a high import content along with quotas or prohibitions on other imports from dollar countries. The program was highly unpopular since Canadians had an enormous pent-up demand for new products after the long stretch of unmet consumer demand through the GREAT DEPRESSION and the Second World War. By July 31, 1948, the taxes and duties were withdrawn, with remaining import quotas being phased out not long after. The purposes of foreign-exchange controls are to discourage imports and foreign travel, to prevent the outflow of capital or otherwise to solve balance-of-payments problems, to preserve scarce foreign-exchange reserves, and to boost domestic employment opportunities.

exchange-fund account   Canada's FOREIGN-EXCHANGE RESERVES of U.S. dollars, gold, SPECIAL DRAWING RIGHTS, and other reserve assets, maintained by the BANK OF CANADA on behalf of the Canadian government. The bank's transactions in foreign-exchange markets are made from this account. The Department of FINANCE publishes monthly statistics showing changes in foreign-exchange reserves, thus enabling analysts to monitor the intervention activities of the bank, and hence its policy on Canada's exchange rate.

exchange of shares   A method of financing the takeover of one company by another; instead of paying cash, the acquiring company may offer to the shareholders of the acquired company an exchange of its shares for theirs, so that the shareholders of the acquired company become shareholders in the merged and larger enterprise.

exchange rate   The number of units of the Canadian dollar that are needed to buy one U.S. dollar or one unit of another foreign currency; it is the price of a national currency, such as the Canadian dollar, expressed in terms of another currency. For example, if the Canadian dollar is trading at 80 U.S. cents, it will take C$1.25 to buy US$1; if the U.S. dollar is trading at 90 U.S. cents, it will take C$1.11 to buy US$1. To calculate the exchange rate for the Canadian dollar, divide the foreign currency — for example, the U.S. dollar — by the exchange rate in that currency for the Canadian dollar; if the U.S. exchange rate for the Canadian dollar is 80 U.S. cents, divide US$1 by 80 U.S. cents. The result is C$1.25. Likewise, to get the U.S. exchange rate for the Canadian dollar, divide the Canadian dollar by the Canadian exchange rate — in this case, C$1.25; the result is 80 U.S. cents. Changes in the exchange rate of a country's currency change the

prices of its imports and exports, the cost of foreign travel, the cost of servicing foreign-debt denominated in foreign currencies, and the attractiveness of foreign direct investment. An increase in the exchange rate of the Canadian dollar will make imports, foreign travel, foreign debt-servicing costs, and foreign investment cheaper but exports more expensive; a decline in the exchange rate of the Canadian dollar will have the opposite effect. After 1945, with the creation of the INTERNATIONAL MONETARY FUND, and until 1971, the world operated on a system of fixed exchange rates, although the Canadian dollar floated between 1952 and 1960 and from 1970 onwards; since 1971, the world has operated on a system of floating exchange rates, although there have been periodic efforts to set target zones. See PLAZA ACCORD, LOUVRE ACCORD. In a floating-exchange-rate system, changes in a country's exchange rate can be influenced by its inflation rate, its level of economic growth, changes in its terms of trade (in Canada's case an increase or decline in resource prices), political stability or uncertainty, its level of interest rates, its accumulation of foreign-denominated foreign-currency debt, or the changing status of another currency (a weakening U.S. dollar, for example, will tend to push up the Canadian exchange rate as money traders flee the U.S. dollar; the reverse is true if the U.S. dollar strengthens). *See also* FIXED EXCHANGE RATE, FLOATING EXCHANGE RATE, VALUE OF THE CANADIAN DOLLAR, INTERNATIONAL MONETARY FUND.

excise duty   A tax imposed as a fixed amount on domestic beer, distilled spirits, raw leaf tobacco, and tobacco products, and levied in addition to EXCISE TAXES. Imports are excluded because they are subject to customs duties or tariffs. In the case of cigarettes, the combined excise tax and excise duty has risen, depending on the type of cigarette, from $11 to $12 per 1,000 in 1976 to $48.85 to $50.75 in 1989, and $79.25 to $81.15 in 1992.

excise tax An indirect tax levied on a specified list of products and services; it is levied on the manufacturer in the case of domestically made goods, or on the duty-paid value of imported goods either as an AD VALOREM TAX or as a fixed amount. The Excise Tax Act levies the tax on domestic and imported wine, tobacco products, jewellery, large automobiles, passenger-vehicle air conditioners, clocks, watches, airline tickets, and auto and aviation gasoline. Exported goods are exempt. Although the tax is levied on manufacturers and importers, the tax itself is shifted on to the consumer, who pays it in the retail price of the product. The tax was originally introduced as a luxury tax on items such as jewellery. The tax has been used to discourage smoking through sharp increases in the rate of tax. In the case of cigarettes, the tax on five cigarettes increased from 3 cents in 1976 to 10.7 cents in 1981 and 25.5 cents in 1992. The AIR TRANSPORTATION TAX is an excise tax.

exclusive dealing An agreement between a supplier and a customer under which the customer agrees to purchase products from the supplier and not to deal in other products sold by the supplier's competitors. Such agreements are common in FRANCHISE contracts. However, the practice can be subject to abuse if it is used to keep small or new suppliers out of the market and is reviewable by the COMPETITION TRIBUNAL.

exclusive economic zone The right of a coastal state to control the living resources, such as fisheries, and non-living resources, such as oil, natural gas, and seabed minerals, of the sea for two hundred miles off its coast, while allowing freedom of navigation to other states beyond 12 miles. The coastal state also has the responsibility to manage the conservation of all natural resources within the 200-mile limit. This was the position adopted at the third session of the Third U.N. Conference on the Law of the Sea, in 1975. Canada declared its adoption of a 200-mile fishing zone, but not an exclusive economic zone, effective January 1, 1977.

exclusive listing An agreement between a real-estate agent and the owner of a house or other property, that guarantees the real-estate agent a specified commission if the property is sold during a specified period, whether or not the real-estate agent actually brings about the sale. *See also* MULTIPLE-LISTING SERVICE.

executive A person in a business corporation, government agency, or any other institution, who is responsible for setting or implementing assigned tasks or policies and who has the decision-making authority to carry out his or her responsibilities. The amount of authority is related to the responsibilities of the executive. As responsibilities increase, so does the decision-making authority.

executive federalism The use of conferences between the prime minister and the provincial premiers, known as First Ministers' Conferences, to make policies affecting Canada where constitutional jurisdiction is shared or unclear or where co-operation is needed to overcome constitutional impediments.

executor The person named in a WILL to see that its instructions are carried out. The most important responsibility of an executor is to see that the ESTATE of a deceased person is properly distributed to beneficiaries.

exempt market   An unregulated market for large-scale investors, such as financial institutions, pension funds, and major corporations, in government and corporate bonds and commercial paper.

exercise price   The price at which an option may be exercised.

exogenous change   A change in economic activity resulting from a non-economic cause — for instance, a sharp increase in food prices resulting from widespread flooding. *See also* ENDOGENOUS CHANGE.

exogenous growth   A model of economic growth in which innovation is treated as only a by-product of investments in machinery and equipment rather than as a direct outcome of investing in ideas or innovation, such as through spending on research and development. *See also* ENDOGENOUS GROWTH.

expectations   Attitudes or beliefs about future economic activity. While expectations are hard to measure, they can have a significant impact on future trends. Consumers who expect interest rates to rise may delay the purchase of homes or major consumer products, thus slowing down business activity. Wage-earners who expect inflation to continue or to get worse may demand even bigger wage increases in collective bargaining, thus adding to inflation pressures. Businesspeople who are gloomy about future profits because they expect costs to rise sharply or because they see few signs of future market growth will delay investment plans, thus slowing down economic growth. Economists now use business- and consumer-confidence surveys to help measure changes in expectations. But this remains a crude tool. Business- and consumer-confidence surveys are published quarterly by the CON-FERENCE BOARD IN CANADA. Each month in its *Daily Bulletin* (publication 11-001) since April, 1990, Statistics Canada has published the short-term expectations of a group of about 23 economic analysts on month-ahead forecasts of key indicators such as year-over-year changes in the CONSUMER PRICE INDEX, growth of the GROSS DOMESTIC PRODUCT, the UNEMPLOYMENT RATE, and merchandise exports and imports. Expectations also have a more substantive role in that households and firms have to make long-term decisions based on expectations of future incomes and rates of return. Economists distinguish between static expectations, which assume next year will be like this year, adaptive expectations, where households and firms alter their expectations based on experience, and rational expectations, in which households and firms make use of all available information along with their judgements on how the economy works to determine their expectations of the future.

expense   **1.** Any form of business spending. **2.** In accounting, the requirement that a company include all interest costs associated with a major investment as an operating expense once it comes into production; prior to that, the interest costs are capitalized.

expense account   Money spent by business, union, government, or other officials for travel, entertainment, information, and other such items to help them carry out their jobs. These expenses are tax deductible, but the organization claiming them must be able to show REVENUE CANADA that the expenses are related to business, and must be able to provide receipts if they are requested. In some instances, the Income Tax Act permits only a partial deduction: for example, 80 percent of the claimed expenses for meals and entertainment.

exponential growth   A continuous, compound rate of growth — for example, compound interest in a bank account, unrestrained population growth, or continuous economic growth. Exponential growth is often expressed in terms of doubling. For example, if savings, population, or the economy grow by 1 percent a year, they will double in 72 years, but if they grow at 4 percent a year, they will double in 18 years, and if they grow at 10 percent a year, they will double in 7.2 years. The doubling time is equal to 72 divided by the growth rate.

export   A product or service sent from one country to another. Statistics Canada produces a monthly report on Canada's merchandise exports (publication 65-001). Statistics on Canada's exports of goods and services are contained in the quarterly balance of payments data (publication 67-001).

Export and Import Permits Act   Legislation giving the federal government the power to control the volume and destination of exports and to regulate imports. Its underlying purpose is to ensure sufficient essential commodities or products to meet essential Canadian needs, and to protect domestic industries against damaging imports through the maintenance of an import-control list that sets limits on imports — for example, on textiles from different countries. Through export controls, the government can also prevent the sale of strategic products where that sale might be detrimental to the security of Canada and its allies, restrict the sale of Canadian products or commodities at a time of international shortages by requiring that Canadian needs be met first, require the processing of natural resources before they are exported, and prevent the excessive export of Canadian natural resources during a period of depressed prices. Canada's capacity to constrain exports of raw materials to the United States during a period of shortage was sharply reduced as a result of the CANADA-UNITED STATES FREE TRADE AGREEMENT.

Under the legislation, exporters shipping products from Canada must obtain an export permit if they are shipping any of the roughly 150 items on the government's Export Control List of strategic materials or products or endangered flora and fauna, or if they are shipping to countries on the government's Area Control List — countries that are subject to various economic sanctions for political or security reasons. Importers must obtain an import licence to bring into Canada items on the government's Import Control List that, in addition to certain types of firearms, also includes products from endangered species.

export consortium   A group of companies submitting a common bid on a foreign project or acting together to promote the sale of a product, such as lumber, that they all make. Canada's COMPETITION ACT restricts the ways in which companies in related industries can act together, but permits them to work together to promote exports. Consortiums are often organized for a bid on a major foreign project, such as an airport, power station, pulp and paper plant, and other such projects, or generally to promote the export sale of Canadian commodities.

export controls   Any kind of limitation on exports, either by quantity, destination, or level of processing. Uranium exports can only be exported after Canada's own needs have been ensured, and after the importing nation has satisfied Canada that it will meet certain safeguard conditions to prevent the uranium from being used to make nuclear weapons. Nuclear reactors can only be exported to countries that agree to similar safeguard conditions. Militarily significant products cannot be exported to South Africa, Cuba, North Korea, or some Middle Eastern countries or may only be permitted to others, such as China, under certain conditions. *See also* EXPORT AND IMPORT PERMITS ACT, TRADE EMBARGO.

export credit   Financing provided either to domestic exporters or foreign purchasers to generate sales of Canadian goods and services.

Export Development Corporation (EDC)   A crown corporation established to help expand Canada's export trade. It provides various kinds of assistance to Canadian corporations, such as: **1.** Export-credit insurance, which provides Canadian firms with payment of up to 90 percent if foreign buyers fail to pay for purchases of Canadian goods and services; this includes fees to engineering companies, and payments for patent rights and advertising for auditors, design companies, and technological services. **2.** Long-term loans to foreign buyers, usually foreign governments, of Canadian capital equipment, such as nuclear power stations or hydro-electric equipment, rail and transit systems, airports, hospitals, pulp and paper plants, or telecommunications systems, or for the purchase of Canadian services, such as engineering or feasibility studies. **3.** Guarantees to Canadian corporations investing abroad against up to 85 percent of losses caused by nationalization or political upheaval. **4.** Guarantees to financial institutions against losses in financing a Canadian exporter or a foreign importer of Canadian goods and services. In 1993, EDC's legislation was amended to allow it to borrow 15 times its capital instead of 10 times, to make equity investment in overseas projects, to help Canadian companies

with contracts on major projects, and other changes reflecting the globalization of competition.

The EDC also manages the CANADA ACCOUNT, which provides concessional financing for exports to high-risk countries, usually in the developing world. It usually requires 60 percent Canadian content in exports it finances. The EDC plays a significant role in the financing of Canadian trade, even though Canada has a large banking system. The corporation was established in 1969, replacing its predecessor, Export Credits Insurance Corporation, a crown corporation established in 1944 as part of Canada's post-war RECONSTRUCTION program. The EDC is expected to operate in a commercial manner, charging premiums on its insurance programs, charging fees for its loan guarantees, and requiring the repaying of export loans, with market rates of interest, except in the case of the Canada Account, which is financed directly by the government. The EDC raises its funds in domestic and foreign markets. It reports to Parliament through the Minister of EXTERNAL AFFAIRS AND INTERNATIONAL TRADE.

export incentive   Any form of government assistance to increase exports. Incentives may range from government help in developing foreign markets to subsidized export financing, tax rebates or concessions, or special grants for export marketing, transportation, or other costs. The GENERAL AGREEMENT ON TARIFFS AND TRADE bans the use of export subsidies in items coming under its jurisdiction; since many agricultural items are not covered, countries have been able to provide direct subsidies for the export of grains, for example. The ORGANIZATION FOR ECONOMIC CO-OPERATION AND DEVELOPMENT has set limits on the use of subsidized or concessional interest rates in export financing.

export insurance   Insurance taken out by an exporter to provide protection against non-payment. *See also* EXPORT DEVELOPMENT CORPORATION.

export-led growth   The strategy of promoting economic development through investing in industries that will supply products to world markets. South Korea and Taiwan are examples of economies that have pursued an export-led growth strategy — a strategy that Mexico is now also pursuing. It is the opposite of an import-replacement strategy, in which high trade barriers are used to discourage imports and savings are invested in industries to serve the domestic market. India and Mexico up to the mid-1980s are examples of countries that have pursued an import-replacement strategy.

export licence   A government permit to export a particular commodity or product to a particular country or to any country. An export licence is needed in Canada to export strategic goods of possible military value to countries that could pose a threat to Canada or to regional stability. An export licence is also required in Canada to export uranium or nuclear-reactor systems or natural gas. In the event of a shortage of a particular commodity, the federal government may invoke the EXPORT AND IMPORT PERMITS ACT to ensure that exports do not deprive Canadians of a needed commodity because non-residents are willing to pay much higher prices.

export multiplier   The total increase in a country's GROSS DOMESTIC PRODUCT that results from an increase in exports. *See also* MULTIPLIER.

export-price index   A monthly index of changes in the level of export prices, published by Statistics Canada in its report on merchandise trade (publication 65-001). *See also* TERMS OF TRADE.

export quota   A restriction on the level of exports from a producer country. A quota may be imposed by the exporting country to protect domestic consumers from shortages. But in international trade, importing countries sometimes negotiate export quotas with exporting countries to protect their own domestic industries — for example, in the steel, television-set, and textile industries. Canada has negotiated a number of such "voluntary" export-quota agreements or EXPORT-RESTRAINT AGREEMENTS with Asian and other developing countries to limit textile shipments. Within the GENERAL AGREEMENT ON TARIFFS AND TRADE, exporters and importers have negotiated the MULTIFIBRE ARRANGEMENT, which provides for bilateral quotas on wool, synthetic, and cotton products.

export-restraint agreement   An agreement negotiated by Canada with countries that are exporting to Canada, in which the exporting countries agree to limit their exports of specified products to specified ceilings. Although these agreements are called "voluntary," they are usually forced on exporting nations. However, because they are described as "voluntary," even though they constitute a NON-TARIFF TRADE BARRIER, they have been beyond the reach of the GENERAL AGREEMENT ON TARIFFS AND TRADE.

export subsidy   *See* EXPORT INCENTIVE.

export tax   A tax or duty on an exported commodity. While export taxes are rare, they are permitted under the GENERAL AGREEMENT ON TARIFFS AND TRADE. However, under the CANADA-UNITED STATES FREE TRADE AGREEMENT, Canada surrendered its right to apply export taxes on products destined for the United States, with one exception: an export tax on softwood-lumber shipments to the United States. *See* SOFTWOOD-LUMBER DISPUTE. In this instance, the purpose of the tax was to reduce the competitive advantage enjoyed by Canadian softwood-lumber producers in the United States, by making its products more expensive. For a brief period in 1992, Canada imposed an export tax on cigarettes to discourage smuggling; cigarettes were being shipped out of Canada without federal excise taxes and duties being imposed and then smuggled back into Canada. The tax was introduced in February, 1992, and repealed in April, 1992. An export tax on unprocessed commodities can be used to encourage greater processing in Canada — for example, fishery products — or to conserve a scarce commodity without penalizing domestic consumers. Canada levied an export tax on oil, under the PETROLEUM ADMINISTRATION ACT, from 1974 until 1985. The price of oil in Canada had been controlled and held below the world price since 1973. The purpose of the tax was to recover on export sales the difference between the price charged Canadians for oil and the higher world price U.S. refineries would pay to get the same grade and quantity of oil, and to use the revenues to subsidize the price paid for oil imports at world prices in Eastern Canada.

exports Goods and services produced in one country that are sold and shipped to another. Merchandise exports — sometimes called visibles — consist of products or commodities. Statistics Canada publishes a monthly report on merchandise trade (publication 65-001). Service exports — sometimes called invisibles — consist of banking and insurance services, transportation, travel and tourism, technol-

ogy and know-how, and the receipts from foreign investment, such as interest and dividends. Statistics Canada publishes quarterly reports on Canada's exports of goods and services in its balance of payments data (publication 67-001). Merchandise exports account for just over 20 percent of the Canadian GROSS NATIONAL PRODUCT (GNP). Merchandise and service exports together account for just over 25 percent of the GNP.

exposure The risk when an asset or liability is denominated in a foreign currency and is not covered or HEDGED or when a financial institution has a large portion of its portfolio in the assets of a single country or industry.

expropriation The forced sale of one's property to the government or a government agency. The power to expropriate may be exercised by government or its agencies and, where provided by law, by private companies, such as railways and pipeline companies. A government may expropriate a corporation — for example, Saskatchewan's expropriation of potash-mining companies, Quebec's expropriation of a private asbestos-mining company, or the expropriation by Quebec and British Columbia of private power companies — or it may expropriate land — for an airport, for public housing, for expansion of a university, for a right-of-way for a new highway, for a power-transmission line, or for a park.

The principal federal law is the 1970 Expropriation Act, which sets out the procedures that must be followed and provides certain protections to those whose property is being acquired. The act includes procedures for pre-expropriation notice and hearings to deal with objections to the planned acquisition, for the actual expropriation and possession, and for compensation, including the arbitration of disputes over price. The compensation code is based on FAIR MARKET VALUE. Generally speaking, governments use expropriation as a last resort when property owners refuse to sell or hold out for excessive prices. Sometimes governments resort to expropriation when they need to acquire a very large area of land that may be owned by several hundred property owners. There are also provincial laws dealing with expropriation.

extendible bond or debenture   A bond or debenture that allows the holder to extend the term or maturity date by a number of years.

External Affairs and International Trade, Department of   The federal government department that is responsible for looking after Canada's interests abroad and responding to foreign nations that have interests in Canada, promoting Canadian exports and formulating and implementing Canadian trade policy, and directing Canada's overseas aid programs. It also manages Canada's immigration policy overseas. The department has three cabinet ministers: the Secretary of State for External Affairs, the Minister for International Trade, and the Minister for External Relations and International Development. Its economic activities include an Ambassador for Multilateral Trade Negotiations and the Trade Negotiations Office, the Chief Air Negotiator, and the Prime Minister's Personal Representative for the Economic Summit, who organizes Canada's participation in the annual GROUP OF SEVEN summit. The trade functions of the department include the responsibility for negotiating trade agreements with other countries, dealing with trade disputes through the GENERAL AGREEMENT ON TARIFFS AND TRADE (GATT), and promoting Canadian trade through programs such as the Program for Export Market Development. Trade and invest-

ment officials are stationed in Canadian embassies abroad and in major consular posts. While many aspects of Canada's foreign commercial relations and trade promotion are in the hands of the Department of FINANCE or the Department of INDUSTRY, TRADE AND COMMERCE, the Department of External Affairs also plays a role in setting trade, investment, and other such policies, and takes part in negotiations on energy, communications, transportation, and science. It is responsible for Canada's participation in the United Nations and for Canada's relations with the WORLD BANK, the GATT, and the ORGANIZATION FOR ECONOMIC CO-OPERATION AND DEVELOPMENT. The Secretary of State for External Affairs is responsible to Parliament for the INTERNATIONAL JOINT COMMISSION and the CANADIAN INTERNATIONAL DEVELOPMENT AGENCY. In 1992, the INTERNATIONAL DEVELOPMENT RESEARCH CENTRE lost its independent status and was made a departmental corporation. The department was set up in 1909.

external diseconomies of scale   The harmful effect that one person's or firm's actions can have on others. These damages can be widespread, or may affect some quite specific group. Examples of external diseconomies affecting the public at large are traffic congestion and air pollution as more people acquire cars, air and water pollution from factories, the radioactive fallout from above-ground nuclear testing, and global warming as the use of carbon-based fuels increases. An example of an external diseconomy affecting a specific group is the loss of livelihood by fishermen due to over-fishing as more fishermen exploit a fishing ground.

In recent years, economists and policy makers have tried to find ways of identifying such external diseconomies and attributing the cost as much as possible to those who do the damage.

For example, pollution-control requirements in the pulp and paper, mineral-smelting, and steel-making industries are an attempt to make the polluter pay; in economic terms, the cost of an external diseconomy has thus been attributed to its source, so that it appears in the price system. But some examples cannot be costed in this way. For example, while it is possible to legislate fuel-efficient cars, with the car companies recovering the costs in the price they charge to consumers, it is more difficult to attribute other costs of the automobile. In street congestion, for example, it might be unfair to levy a charge against every user of the road, since this would impose a heavier burden on those with low incomes using a public facility.

external economies of scale The beneficial effect that one person's or firm's actions can have on others. Research and development that results in inventions that help everyone is an example. The external economies resulting from the invention of electricity, the telephone, petrochemical fertilizers, modern pharmaceuticals, and the computer are enormous. Smaller but still important examples might include the decision by one farmer to plant a long line of trees to prevent soil erosion; the farmer's neighbours would also benefit. A firm may carry out a skill-training program for new workers; other firms can benefit, since they can hire workers away once they have been trained. Because of the external economies they produce for the public at large or for particular industries or groups, governments can justify spending on research and development, universities, and other such activities.

externalities Costs that may not show up in the price system or the GROSS DOMESTIC PRODUCT but which affect the welfare of individuals and firms. They can be harmful (*see* EXTERNAL DISECONOMIES OF SCALE) or they can be beneficial (*see* EXTERNAL ECONOMIES OF SCALE). The study of externalities, or social costs and benefits, has become an increasingly important area of economics in recent years. In particular, there has been a strong effort to identify external diseconomies and recover their costs — through taxes or pollution-control laws, for example. At the same time, there has been much more effort to identify social benefits resulting from investments in research and development, health care, and education.

extra dividend An additional cash or stock dividend paid by a company to its shareholders, in addition to its normal dividend.

extractive industry A natural-resource industry that exploits oil, gas, and other minerals from the earth or from underneath bodies of water.

extraordinary item In a corporate annual report, an unusual gain or loss that affects net profits. It can be a one-time gain from the sale of an asset, or a write-off of the loss on an unsuccessful business venture; in a corporate EARNINGS STATEMENT, it is added to (a gain) or deducted from (a loss) net operating profit.

extrapolation A technique of economic forecasting that consists of projecting past trends forward in time. For example, if per capita consumption of refined-oil products has averaged 5 percent a year for the past 25 years, a forecaster might calculate the demand in the year 2000 by assuming that the same rate of growth will continue. The danger in this technique is that it does not take account of factors that could affect per capita consumption — in this case, a sharp rise in oil prices or major initiatives to address the threat of global warming that might lead to significant energy-conservation measures, smaller and fuel-efficient cars, or a switch to electric power or natural gas.

extraterritoriality   The attempt by one country to extend its laws to cover activities taking place in another country. This has been a major source of contention between Canada and the United States, because the United States has tried to apply its anti-trust, securities, and international trade laws to the Canadian subsidiaries of U.S. corporations. For example, the United States has used its Trading with the Enemy Act to ban U.S. exports to Cuba and China; in the process, it has also tried to stop Canadian subsidiaries of U.S. firms from trading with Cuba, China, or other countries on its embargo list. Similarly, the United States has extended its anti-trust laws to the activities of its firms abroad, including those in Canada, while the U.S. Securities and Exchange Commission has claimed the right to require registration of any corporation in which 30 percent of the stock is owned by U.S. citizens. Canada and the United States have had a long series of discussions on this issue. In January, 1959, Canadian Justice Minister E. Davie Fulton and U.S. Attorney General William Rogers agreed that in future the two countries would consult with each other whenever it appeared that the interests of one would be affected by action taken under the other's competition laws dealing with mergers and acquisitions. In November, 1969, Canadian Justice Minister Ron Basford and U.S. Attorney General John Mitchell extended the Fulton-Rogers understanding to Canada-U.S. co-operation in the prosecution of international restrictive business practices, such as cartel activities and restrictive practices of MULTINATIONAL CORPORATIONS. New efforts to improve Canada-U.S. co-operation and to avoid conflict over extraterritoriality were initiated with the visit to Canada,

in January, 1978, of U.S. Vice-President Walter Mondale. But the United States has not given up the right to apply its laws beyond its borders despite its agreement to deal with some issues case by case, and to work through the Canadian government. In 1984, Canada passed legislation — the FOREIGN EXTRATERRITORIAL MEASURES ACT — compelling foreign-owned subsidiaries in Canada to abide by Canadian laws rather than foreign laws that would prevent trade between Canada and another country, or face penalties. Canada is also an active member of the Committee of Experts on Restrictive Business Practices in the ORGANIZATION FOR ECONOMIC CO-OPERATION AND DEVELOPMENT. The committee works on international agreements dealing with restrictive business practices.

F.O.B. (free on board) The delivery of goods without insurance or transportation charges to a specified location, where the buyer obtains actual ownership. For example, a truckload of light bulbs delivered from Toronto to Winnipeg F.O.B would be delivered without transportation or insurance charges to the buyer in Winnipeg. The F.O.B. price would be the value of the goods as delivered to the customer.

face value The value that appears on a bond or debenture; it is the amount the issuer will pay to redeem the security at maturity. The face value or PAR VALUE is not necessarily the market value.

factor 1. A financial institution that takes over the ACCOUNTS RECEIVABLE of a firm, at a discount, and collects the money owing. This saves small manufacturers the trouble of operating their own credit departments, and keeps them supplied with WORKING CAPITAL. The firm using the factor may have to get the factor's approval if credit passes a specified limit for certain customers or before granting credit to a new customer. Factors are usually equipped to run credit checks. The chartered banks are among the financial institutions offering factoring services. There is a trade association, the Factors and Commercial Financing Conference of Canada. 2. An input — labour, capital, land (including natural resources), or ideas — used in the production of goods and services.

factor cost The pre-tax value of goods and services produced, based on the costs of the FACTOR inputs plus subsidies, used in the system of NATIONAL ACCOUNTS. Each month, Statistics Canada publishes *The Real Gross Domestic Product at Factor Cost by Industry* (publication 15-001).

factor endowment The relative availability of the various FACTORS OF PRODUCTION in each country. A country's relative supply of factors can be a critical determinant of its COMPARATIVE ADVANTAGE in world trade. For example, a large supply of unskilled labour can give a developing country an advantage in some maufacturing industries; the availability of natural resources, the supply of advanced manufacturing infrastructure, a high level of education, and climate can also be sources of advantage.

factors of production   Productive resources used in a variety of combinations to create additional goods or services; sometimes called inputs. The three traditional factors of production are as follows: 1. Land, which includes not only land but also the quality of the soil, water, natural resources, and forests. 2. Capital, which includes the accumulated stock of factories, transportation systems, commercial buildings, computers, and other machinery and equipment. 3. Labour, which includes not only physical capacity but all the accumulated knowledge and skills of people. Some economists take the view that entrepreneurial or management ability and innovation should be considered additional factors of production. U.S. economist Robert Solow, for example, has argued that technological progress should be treated as a separate factor of production; continuing Solow's work, U.S. economist Paul Romer (also a fellow of the Canadian Institute for Advanced Research) argues that ideas and innovation are separate factors of production. In any enterprise, production results from the combination of factors of production; managerial know-how should lead to the most efficient mix. Rent is the income earned by land, interest the income earned by capital, wages and salaries the income earned by labour, and profit the income earned by entrepreneurial effort and innovation.

fair-employment laws   Laws designed to protect workers against discrimination based on race, colour, religion, or national origin. The federal and provincial governments have various laws to provide such protection. The federal law is contained in the Canadian Human Rights Code. It prohibits discrimination by employers, unions, or employment agencies in any place of employment under federal jurisdiction. It bans the use of any form or application for employment, any job advertising, or any written or oral statement that suggests any discrimination or preference based on race, colour, religion, or national origin. The CANADIAN HUMAN RIGHTS COMMISSION provides protection against job discrimination. *See also* EMPLOYMENT EQUITY, EMPLOYMENT EQUITY ACT, PAY EQUITY.

fair market value   The amount that a buyer would readily pay for something and at which a seller would readily sell it in a free market. It is a price freely arrived at without pressure or obligation on either side.

fair market-value assessment   *See* MARKET-VALUE ASSESSMENT.

fallacy of composition   A fallacy based on the assumption that something that is good for each person alone is therefore good for the entire community. It may be good for each individual to save more and spend less and it is certainly important that some people save so there are funds available for investment; but if everyone did this, economic growth might slow down, unemployment would increase, and everyone could end up worse off.

family   STATISTICS CANADA has three definitions: 1. For census purposes, a family is a husband and wife with or without children, or a parent with one or more unmarried children, living together in the same dwelling. 2. In surveys on family income and income distribution, a family is considered to be an economic unit, or a group of individuals sharing a common dwelling and related by blood, marriage, or adoption — a definition that includes all relatives. 3. In family-spending surveys, a family is defined as a group of people who depend on a common or pooled income for all major expenses in the same dwelling — a definition that includes students sharing an apartment, for example.

family allowance A monthly allowance paid from 1945 to 1992 to families with children to help cover the costs of child maintenance. The program was started on July 1, 1945, but underwent a number of changes. Originally, all families received the same tax-free benefits for children under the age of 16. In 1964, the federal government expanded the program with a Youth Allowance for youngsters aged 16 and 17 if they were still in school or physically disabled. In 1974, the family allowance age limits were raised to include children under the age of 18, indexed to the CONSUMER PRICE INDEX, and made taxable. In 1979, the level of family allowances was frozen but a refundable child tax credit of $200 was introduced that was payable to parents with incomes below the tax-exempt level and that could be claimed as a credit against taxable income for taxpayers above the threshold level. In 1987, the child tax deduction for income tax was converted to a credit. And in 1992, the federal government announced it would consolidate the family allowance, refundable tax credit, and the child tax credit into a new CHILD BENEFIT, effective January 1, 1993. Quebec and Alberta operate their own family allowance systems; in addition, Quebec provides a special payment for newborn babies, to encourage a higher rate of population growth. The payment in 1992 was $500 for the first child, $1,000 for the second child, and $7,500 for each additional child.

family business A business owned and operated by a family — usually, a small business. In most instances the various members of the family all work in the business. Many of today's largest corporations started off as family businesses.

farm A holding of land on which agricultural products are raised or grown with the purpose of selling this output to others. For census purposes in Canada, a farm is defined as a holding that produced at least one of the following products for sale: crops, livestock, poultry, animal products, greenhouse or nursery products, mushrooms, sod, honey, and maple syrup products. There are four main types of farms, according to Statistics Canada. They are as follows: 1. Livestock farms, where cattle, hogs, dairy products, and poultry for eggs and meats are raised. 2. Grain farms, which produce wheat, oats, barley, flax, and rapeseed. 3. Special-crop farms, which produce vegetables, fruits, potatoes, and various root crops. 4. Other farms, including those that combine livestock and grain production. Statistics Canada publishes *Farming Facts* each year (publication 21-522) and *Agricultural Financial Statistics* (publication 21-205).

farm-assistance programs The range of federal and provincial programs to sustain farm income, modernize and expand farms, finance irrigation and drainage, develop better farming methods and improved seeds and livestock through research and development, promote the sale of farm products, and assist farm ownership. The programs are designed to ensure that the country has a productive agricultural industry, and to make sure that individual farmers get a fair share of national income. Many farm-assistance programs deal with specific problems such as crop failure, drought, depressed prices, farm credit, transportation, and rural poverty. *See also* AGRICULTURAL STABILIZATION BOARD, CANADIAN DAIRY COMMISSION, CANADIAN WHEAT

BOARD, CROP INSURANCE, FARM CREDIT CORPORATION, FARM MARKETING BOARDS, FARM INCOME STABILIZATION ACT, FARM PRODUCTS MARKETING AGENCIES ACT, PRAIRIE FARM REHABILITATION ADMINISTRATION.

farm cash receipts The gross cash income of farmers from the sale of farm products, advance payments for grain, and payments from various farm-assistance programs. Farmers must pay all their costs out of these receipts. The figure is published quarterly by Statistics Canada in its *Agricultural Economic Statistics* (publication 21-603). *See also* FARM NET INCOME.

Farm Credit Corporation (FCC) A crown corporation set up in 1959 to replace the Canadian Farm Loan Board that had been established in 1929. It provides long-term mortgage credit to farmers to acquire land, seed, fertilizer, livestock, and machinery and equipment, to construct farm buildings, and to make other improvements. Other functions include financial and management services for farmers. From 1972 until 1980, it administered the federal government's Small Farm Development Program, which helped marginal farmers to retire early or to stop farming, by buying up their land. Where possible, the land was sold to other farmers who could use the land to improve their productivity. Its headquarters are in Regina.

Farm Improvement Loans Act A federal program to help farmers get loans from banks and other financial institutions for new machinery, livestock, the installation of farm electrical systems, major repairs, fencing and drainage, the repair and construction of farm buildings, and for the acquisition of additional land. The act, administered through AGRICULTURE CANADA, provides guarantees to financial institu-

tions making such loans.

Farm Income Protection Act Legislation designed to provide greater certainty of income for farmers by providing insurance and a farm income fund for farmers in poor years. The act, which came into effect in 1991, replaced provisions of the Agricultural Stabilization Act, the Crop Insurance Act, and the Western Grain Stabilization Act. It provided a gross-revenue insurance plan (GRIP) and a net-income stabilization account (NISA). The purpose of GRIP is to provide farmers with financial assistance in the event of losses due to production and market risks over which they have no control. It includes a crop insurance program in which farmers pay 50 percent of the premium, with the federal government and the provincial governments paying 25 percent each. It also includes market revenue protection, with farmers paying 33.3 percent of the premium, the federal government 41.7 percent, and the provincial governments 25 percent. NISA is a fund in which farmers set aside money in good years to be drawn on in poor years. As well, the fund receives payments by the federal government and participating provincial governments. The program is voluntary; participating farmers put 2 percent of their net eligible sales into the account, with federal and participating provincial governments matching the amount. Almost all provinces belong; however, Quebec has opted out.

farm-machinery arrangement A free-trade arrangement between Canada and the United States permitting the duty-free movement of farm machinery between the two countries. In 1913, at the urging of its farmers, the United States removed its tariff on most farm machinery produced in Canada. In 1944, Canada granted duty-free access for U.S.-made farm machinery. The purpose of the tariff elimination was to help farmers get farm machinery at lower prices.

farm marketing boards Boards established under federal or provincial law to set or negotiate prices of farm products, to market farm products and collect levies from farmers to pay marketing-board costs, and to maintain reserve stocks for some commodities. In some cases, the boards operate systems of SUPPLY MANAGEMENT, which includes setting production quotas for individual farmers. Membership is compulsory for farmers. Individual provinces operate their own marketing boards, but a number of national marketing agencies have been formed for commodities in which there is considerable interprovincial or international trade. Important national marketing boards include the CANADIAN WHEAT BOARD (1935), the CANADIAN DAIRY COMMISSION (1966), the Canadian Egg Marketing Agency (1973), the Canadian Turkey Marketing Agency (1974), and the Canadian Chicken Marketing Agency (1979).

Both Ottawa and the provinces acted in the 1930s to set up producer marketing boards, but initial efforts were turned back by the courts. British Columbia passed a Produce Marketing Act to set up marketing boards for certain fruits and vegetables, but this was ruled unconstitutional in 1931 on the grounds that it affected interprovincial trade and that the levy on producers was an INDIRECT TAX. The federal Natural Products Marketing Act of 1934 tried to establish a system of national marketing boards, but it was ruled unconstitutional on the grounds that it interfered with provincial powers. Finally, the British Columbia Natural Products Marketing Act of 1936 was upheld by the courts and became the model legislation for all of the provinces. It permitted provincial marketing boards to regulate and control, within provincial boundaries, the pricing, production, transportation, storage, and marketing of farm products, and to collect levies from farmers to pay the costs. In 1956, Parliament passed the Agricultural Products Marketing Act, which allowed it to delegate to provincial marketing boards the power to regulate interprovincial and export trade and to collect levies for such purposes. This allowed the provinces to use a federal law to raise money for a provincial purpose. In 1960, the Supreme Court upheld the federal law, and declared that marketing-board levies on producers were not an indirect tax but a contractual payment.

In 1972, Parliament passed the FARM PRODUCTS MARKETING AGENCIES ACT, which permitted the provinces and Ottawa to work together to form national farm marketing boards. Since then, national marketing boards have been formed for eggs, turkeys, and chickens. Today, about 60 percent of farm cash income is earned through marketing boards, with the products controlled ranging from poultry, eggs, honey, and hogs, to milk, fruit, grains, tobacco, soybeans, and maple syrup. Farmers maintain that marketing boards lead to more stable prices and protect them against boom-bust cycles. In the long run, they argue, this benefits the consumer, because it ensures adequate production at reasonable prices. Consumer critics contend that marketing boards lead to higher prices by subsidizing inefficient farmers through quotas, thus preventing efficient farmers from producing more at less cost. *See also* SUPPLY MANAGEMENT.

farm net income The annual income that farmers have left over for family income, personal taxes, and new investments, after paying their farm expenses. It includes an estimate for the value of farm products consumed on the farm. Farm net income is calculated by adding together the cash receipts farmers get for the sale of their products, supplementary payments from various farm-assistance programs, and income in kind, which includes not only farm products consumed on the farm but an imputed rental value for the farm dwelling, and then deducting farm expenses, such as fuel, electricity, fertilizer, commercial feed, interest on farm loans, machinery, wages to farm labour, and depreciation. In calculating the role of agriculture in the GROSS DOMESTIC PRODUCT, Statistics Canada calculates a second version of farm net income, which includes changes in the value of livestock and crop inventories. Statistics Canada publishes quarterly estimates of farm net income (publication 21-603).

Farm Products Marketing Agencies Act   A federal law passed in 1972 that permits the establishment of national farm marketing agencies and boards for specific agricultural products when provincial governments see a need. Such a need may occur if it is difficult to market a farm product effectively within the jurisdiction of individual provincial marketing boards because of extensive interprovincial trade. Under the act, national farm marketing agencies with supply control have been established for eggs, turkeys, and chickens. These are the Canadian Egg Marketing Agency, the Canadian Turkey Marketing Agency, the Canadian Chicken Marketing Agency, and the Canadian Broiler Hatching Egg Marketing Agency. In addition, the legislation permits the establishment of farm marketing agencies that do not control supply or production. In 1993, the legislation was amended to permit commodity groups to impose levies on farm products to fund market research, new product development, and other mar-

ket development activities. The federal agencies work with their provincial counterparts; they have no direct dealings with local farmers. The act also established a National Farm Products Marketing Council, which monitors the performance of national agencies and assists the provinces to establish new marketing agencies when they wish. *See also* SUPPLY MANAGEMENT.

fast track   Procedures under U.S. trade law that allow the U.S. administration to enter into international trade negotiations and that set specific deadlines by which the U.S. Congress must vote a trade agreement up or down; while the U.S. Congress is regularly consulted during the course of trade negotiations, once an agreement is submitted to Congress it can only vote in favour or against and cannot amend an agreement negotiated with other countries. The Tokyo and Uruguay Rounds of the GENERAL AGREEMENT ON TARIFFS AND TRADE, the CANADA-UNITED STATES FREE TRADE AGREEMENT, and the NORTH AMERICAN FREE TRADE AGREEMENT were all negotiated under fast-track authority. If the U.S. administration desires to pursue a trade negotiation, it must give written notice to the House of Representatives Ways and Means Committee and the Senate Finance Committee, and each must affirm or deny permission within 60 legislative days. The process sets a deadline by which a proposed trade agreement must subsequently be presented to the Congress. Once the U.S. president has signed a trade treaty, this sets in motion the fast-track process for approval. Once the president has presented the trade agreement to Congress it must vote in favour or against the agreement within 90 sitting days. If the president needs an extension of the fast-track authority, he or she must submit a request at least 90 days before the deadline for otherwise submitting the trade package to Congress. Extensions can only be made for two years.

fast write-off   A tax incentive to encourage new investment by business by allowing a rapid depreciation over, for example, one or two years instead of the normal five to 10 years. This lowers the cost of capital for business by permitting higher depreciation deductions for tax purposes, thus lowering the amount of tax that must be paid by the business.

feasibility study   The examination of a proposed project to see whether it makes technical and financial sense. This type of review should be made before any major capital project is undertaken.

featherbedding   A rule imposed by a union in a collective agreement to artificially increase the number of jobs needed in an organization or the amount of time and labour to complete a project. Such rules may limit the number of bricks a bricklayer may lay in a day, break a job down into many different segments, each requiring a different worker, or require workers to repeat the work already performed automatically by a machine.

fecundity   The capacity of a woman to bear children, as opposed to fertility, which is the actual bearing of children. *See also* FERTILITY RATE.

Federal Business Development Bank (FBDB)   A crown corporation established in 1975 to replace the Industrial Development Bank, which had been established in 1944 under the supervision of the BANK OF CANADA. Its purpose is to assist the growth of small and medium businesses in Canada. It provides loans, loan guarantees, and export-receivable financing. It also operates a venture-capital division that can make equity investments as a minority shareholder in small and medium businesses. The FBDB also provides various counselling and other services to small and medium businesses, including its Counselling Assistance to Small Enterprise, or CASE, which uses the services of retired businesspeople. It reports to Parliament through the Minister of INDUSTRY, SCIENCE AND TECHNOLOGY. Its headquarters are in Montreal.

Federal Court of Canada   A federal court created in 1971 to hear appeals by citizens against the rulings or actions of federal government agencies and departments, including claims against the Crown, and appeals on the actions of federal boards, tribunals, and other commissions. This includes appeals from assessments under the Income Tax Act and the Citizenship Act. The Federal Court also hears claims by the Crown and adjudicates disputes between citizens over intellectual property violations, such as the infringement of copyright, trademarks, or patents. As well, the Federal Court can review decisions of federal boards, commissions, or tribunals where it can be shown that a tribunal has failed to observe a principle of natural justice, has acted beyond its jurisdiction, or has conducted its hearings in a capricious manner. It succeeded the Exchequer Court of Canada, originally established to deal with admiralty matters, intellectual property disputes, and tax matters.

Federal Environmental Assessment and Review Office   A federal review agency established in 1973 to assess the environmental impact of federal projects. When a federal department finds that a project could have significant environmental impact, the minister refers the project to the review office, which appoints a panel of experts to make an assessment. The project cannot proceed until the Minister of the ENVIRONMENT has reached a decision on the panel's report. The originator of the project must prepare an ENVIRONMENTAL IMPACT STATEMENT.

federal-provincial conference An important institution in the Canadian federal system that brings the federal and provincial governments together to deal with important issues that concern them both. Although there is no reference to federal-provincial conferences in the CONSTITUTION ACT, 1867, or the CONSTITUTION ACT 1982 the MEECH LAKE ACCORD, if it had been ratified, would have constitutionalized federal-provincial conferences by requiring an annual First Ministers' Conference on the economy and the constitution. They have come to play an important negotiating and co-ordinating role in setting economic, trade, training, and many other policies. In addition to First Ministers' Conferences on the constitution, the economy, or other matters of concern, there are federal-provincial conferences on a regular basis on finance, energy, mining, forestry, training, consumer laws, communications, industrial development, trade, health, social policy, law, and other issues attended by the relevant federal and provincial ministers or their officials. These conferences have increased in importance as the actions and policies of the federal and provincial governments have come increasingly to affect each other.

There are two types of federal-provincial conferences: continuing conferences, which meet regularly to discuss common problems in such areas as labour relations, consumer laws, finance and social policy; and ad hoc conferences, which are called to deal with specific problems. The continuing conferences are supported by working committees of officials from the federal and provincial governments; if the meetings of the officials are included, there are more than 500 federal-provincial meetings a year. To facilitate such meetings, the federal government, in 1973, established the Canadian Intergovernmental Conference Secretariat, to provide staff support for the organization of federal-provincial conferences. The important role of federal-provincial conferences in making the Canadian federal system work has led to the term "executive federalism." *See also* CONFERENCE OF FIRST MINISTERS, FEDERALISM.

federal-provincial fiscal arrangements The agreements negotiated between the federal and provincial governments through which federal taxing power is used to help provincial governments meet their responsibilities, to finance areas of shared jurisdiction, to achieve national standards, and to ensure that low-income provinces can maintain services similar to the national average without unreasonably high taxes compared with other provinces, while avoiding a balkanization of the tax system or a tax jungle. These arrangements became increasingly important after the Second World War as education, health, and social programs expanded; the delivery of programs in these areas is largely under provincial jurisdiction, but much of the taxing power is in federal hands. Between 1947 and 1961, the federal government negotiated tax-rental agreements with most provinces in personal and corporate income taxes and death duties; in return for not implementing their own personal and corporate income-tax systems, participating provinces were assured of a certain percent of federal tax collections in these fields. In 1954, Quebec introduced its own personal income-tax system. Quebec had its own corporate income-tax system from 1947; Ontario introduced its own corporate income-tax system in 1957 and Alberta did the same in 1981.

The tax-rental agreements ended in 1961, followed by a new system in 1962. Instead of compensating provinces that suspended their right to operate their own personal and corporate income-tax systems, the federal government said the provinces henceforth would have to enact their own income-tax legislation; the federal government would collect the taxes on their behalf, if the legislation was consistent with the federal legislation. There were three other developments in this period. One was the introduction of opting out, which allowed a province to withdraw from a program and receive tax points instead; in 1960, Quebec received 1 percentage point of corporate income tax in place of university cash grants from the federal government, and, in 1964, Quebec got 3 percentage points of personal income tax in lieu of the Youth Allowance for 16- and 17-year-olds. A second development was the build-up of tax abatement or transfer of tax points to the provinces as a method of transferring funds to the provinces. In 1965, with the Established Programs Financing (Interim Arrangements) Act of 1965, the provinces were offered 14 percentage points of personal income tax in exchange for cash payments for hospital insurance, 4 percentage points for CANADA ASSISTANCE PLAN payments, and 1 percentage point for vocational training and health grants. Quebec opted for all, and by 1965, its abatement was 44 percent compared with 21 percent for the other provinces. The third development was the move to more formal arrangements for EQUALIZATION PAYMENTS to the provinces with per capita tax revenues from a variety of provincial revenue sources, at comparable rates of taxation, that were below the national average for all provinces, or a representative group of provinces, so that the provinces

below the national average could provide roughly comparable levels of service at roughly comparable levels of taxation.

During the 1970s, the costs of established programs — equalization payments, hospital insurance, medicare, and post-secondary education — continued to climb. In the Federal-Provincial Fiscal Arrangements and Established Programs Financing Act, 1977, the federal government reduced its basic income tax to free up more room for the provinces and amended the method of paying its contribution for established-programs financing by providing an additional 9.143 points of personal income tax along with per capita cash payments not specifically tied to provincial spending in these areas — so-called block funds that could be used by the provinces in any way they chose. The cash contribution was equal to 50 percent of the national average per capita payment for the three programs in the years 1975 and 1976, was increased with the growth rate of the GROSS NATIONAL PRODUCT (GNP), and was multiplied by the population of each province. In 1982 and subsequent years, the formula was amended again for the established programs in the renamed Federal-Provincial Fiscal Arrangements and Federal Post-Secondary Education and Health Contributions Act, 1977, so that the combined tax point and cash payments were, on a per capita basis, equal for each province. Total compensation was the national average per capita federal contribution in fiscal 1975 and 1976, escalated with per capita GNP growth, and multiplied by the population of each province. The estimated value of the tax points is then deducted and the cash payment is the difference between the two.

Starting in 1986, the federal government began to limit payments under established-programs financing by reducing the GNP escalator by two percentage points for 1986 and 1987 and subsequent years. In its 1989 budget, the federal government announced that, effective in the 1990-1991 period, the annual growth in established-programs financing would be reduced by a further 1 percentage point; the legislation also promised that the rate of growth would not be less than the inflation rate. In its 1990 budget, the federal government announced that established-programs financing would be frozen at the 1990-1991 per capita level for two years; the 1991 budget extended the freeze on per capita established-programs financing until the end of the 1994-1995 fiscal year. In 1992, the federal-provincial fiscal arrangements were extended for just two years, to March 31, 1994, instead of the traditional five-year extension, pending a federal review of all its transfers.

In addition, the federal government transfers funds to the provinces under the CANADA ASSISTANCE PLAN (CAP), which came into effect in 1966, with the federal government paying 50 percent of eligible costs. In its 1990 budget, the federal government announced that provinces not receiving equalization payments — Ontario, British Columbia, and Alberta — were limited to 5 percent annual growth for two years. The B.C. government, joined by Ontario, took the federal government to court on the issue. The B.C. Court of Appeals ruled in 1990 that the federal government had to contribute 50 percent of the cost of social welfare services in B.C. and that the B.C. government had a "legitimate expectation" that the federal government would not impose limits on CAP payments without provincial consent. In 1991, the Supreme Court of Canada affirmed the right of the federal government to unilaterally change the funding formula. In the meantime, the 1991 federal budget had extended the 5 percent growth limit on CAP payments to provinces not receiving equalization to the end of

the 1994-1995 fiscal year. In 1992 and 1993, total federal cash transfers to the provinces were $26.2 billion, while total tax transfers amounted to $12.8 billion, for total transfers of $39 billion. For established-programs financing, cash payments were $8.1 billion, while tax transfers were $11.6 billion. Details on federal fiscal arrangements are published by the Department of FINANCE and by Statistics Canada in the annual publication, *Federal Government Finance* (publication 68-211).

federal-provincial relations The negotiations and arrangements that are essential to the working of the Canadian FEDERAL SYSTEM. With shared or overlapping spending, taxing, and regulatory powers, changing demands on both levels of government, and regional disparities in the ability of some provinces to provide comparable public services at comparable rates of taxation, a highly interdependent system has evolved. Many of the decisions affecting Canadians are made at federal-provincial conferences or through other forms of federal-provincial negotiation, leading to what is known as "executive federalism" in which Parliament and the provincial legislatures play a secondary role of enacting what has already been agreed to. First Ministers' Conferences, chaired by the prime minister, deal with major issues, while federal-provincial meetings of agency department ministers (such as Finance) or line department ministers (such as trade, health care, or training) or their senior officials deal with more specific and often technical issues. A Canadian Intergovernmental Secretariat provides support services and both federal and provincial governments maintain a staff of officials responsible for intergovernmental relations. Since 1960, the provincial premiers have held an annual conference to discuss relations with the federal government (which sends an observer) and to look at areas where they can harmonize policies and reduce interprovincial barriers. The four Western premiers and the Council of Maritime Premiers also meet at least once a year. Under the MEECH LAKE ACCORD, if it had been ratified, Canada's revised constitution would have required an annual First Ministers' Conference on the economy and the constitution.

Federal-Provincial Relations Office An office responsible to the prime minister, created in 1975 to assist the prime minister and the cabinet in their responsibilities for federal-provincial affairs, including constitutional reform, to help individual government departments to deal with federal-provincial issues, and to increase federal-provincial consultation on a wide range of issues. It also advises on aboriginal constitutional matters. The office organizes CONFERENCES OF FIRST MINISTERS and monitors provincial views of federal programs and provincial policies that affect federal responsibilities. Its responsibilities, then, include both the on-going conduct of intergovernmental relations and longer-term issues dealing with constitutional change, as well as the on-going management of the federation and national unity.

Federal Reserve System The central bank system of the United States. It was created in 1913. There are 12 regional Federal Reserve banks in the United States and a national board of governors, operating under the chairman of the Federal Reserve Board, based in Washington. The Federal Reserve Board sets reserve requirements for U.S. banks, supervises the banking system, sets interest rates, reviews the activities of district reserve banks, controls the production of currency, and takes part in the Open Market Committee (which also includes the presidents of five federal reserve banks, including always the president of the Federal Reserve Bank of New York). The Open Market Committee determines monetary policy and exchange-rate policy. The Federal Reserve System operates in the open market through the Federal Reserve Bank of New York. The chairman of the Federal Reserve is appointed by the U.S. president for a fixed term of four years; this appointment must be approved by the U.S. Senate. The other members of the Federal Reserve's Board of Governors are also appointed by the president.

federal spending power The power of the federal government to spend or lend money, as set out in the CONSTITUTION ACT, 1867. The federal government has wide jurisdiction over matters of general or national concern. Section 91 of the Constitution Act, 1867, gives the federal government the general power to make laws "for the Peace, Order, and Good Government of Canada," and lists the areas in which the federal government, through Parliament, has exclusive authority. This list of 31 classes of federal power — ranging from trade and commerce, defence and postal services to shipping, navigation, and weights and measures — illustrates but does not restrict the federal spending power. The federal government can spend directly in any field; there is no constitutional barrier, for example, to its establishing a CROWN CORPORATION to engage in any kind of business. In such cases, it is exercising its power to legislate and spend on public property under section 91 (1A) of the Constitution Act. The federal government can also spend in areas normally falling under provincial jurisdiction by introducing SHARED-COST PROGRAMS, which make federal grants to the provinces conditional on the provinces abiding by federal legislation that sets out the terms under which conditional grants can be made.

In this way, for example, the federal government introduced shared-cost programs for health insurance and the Trans-Canada Highway system. Similarly, the federal government can use its power to lend money, for example, for housing and urban development through the CANADA MORTGAGE AND HOUSING CORPORATION. Section 95 gives the federal and provincial governments concurrent power over agriculture and immigration, with federal law paramount in cases of conflict. Similar concurrent powers exist for old-age pensions and various supplemental benefits, but, in these areas, federal law cannot override provincial law. The federal government has significant and powerful spending — and taxing — powers; it has been able to act in such areas as health, education, and housing, and to fund cultural programs, such as the Canada Council, where there is a clear provincial responsibility as well. The greatest restraint on federal power may be its limited power to regulate. *See also* FEDERAL TAXING POWER, PROVINCIAL SPENDING POWER, PROVINCIAL TAXING POWER.

federal system   A sharing by the federal and provincial governments of spending, taxing, and regulatory powers, based on on-going consultation and compromise. Section 91 of the CONSTITUTION ACT, 1867, (formerly the British North America Act) gives the federal government exclusive jurisdiction over postal services, census and statistics, defence, navigation, shipping, money and banking, and criminal law, as well as the authority to make laws for the "Peace, Order, and Good Government of Canada." The federal government is also given sweeping powers to raise money "by any Mode or System of Taxation." Provincial powers are set out under Section 92, which gives the provinces the right to make laws respecting "Property and Civil

Rights in the Province," in addition to the management and sale of public lands belonging to them (interpreted to include natural resources), and the establishment and management of hospitals, municipal governments, local works and undertakings. Provincial taxing powers were limited to "Direct Taxation within the Province in order to the Raising of a Revenue for Provincial Purposes." Section 93 sets out provincial rights in education, and Section 94 sets out areas of shared jurisdiction, such as immigration and agriculture. But the operating of the federal system has also depended on interpretation by the courts of the provisions of the Constitution Act, 1867. Until 1949, the Privy Council in Britain was responsible for interpretation of the Canadian constitution, and it heavily favoured the provinces. In a critical 1896 decision, for example, it declared that provincial powers over property and civil rights had paramountcy over the authority of the federal government to enact laws for the "Peace, Order, and Good Government of Canada." It subsequently nullified the capacity of the federal government to act in the "regulation of trade and commerce," and it heavily favoured the provinces in the field of social policy, as seen in the fate of the 1930s BENNETT NEW DEAL. As a result, the federal and provincial governments have been forced to co-operate closely in making the Canadian federal system work. In 1927, for example, the federal and provincial governments jointly funded a means-tested system of old-age pensions. In 1940, the provinces transferred control of UNEMPLOYMENT INSURANCE to the federal government, and did the same with old-age security in 1952. For its part, the federal government stayed out of personal and corporate income-tax fields until the First World War, and out of DEATH DUTIES until the Second World War. But since 1945, the federal and provincial governments have had to rely on a wide range of intergovernmental arrangements, including cost-sharing and fiscal arrangements, resulting in a growing level of federal transfer payments to the provinces. The system has had its share of tensions, as federal and provincial governments competed over their areas of jurisdiction and Canadians debated whether they wanted a stronger federal government or a more decentralized federation. Provinces objected, for example, to the federal ability to launch spending programs in areas of provincial jurisdiction, such as health care, by offering to fund 50 percent of such programs to provinces agreeing to meet federal or national standards, and to subsequent federal cutbacks in cost sharing once provinces joined such programs. Likewise, provincial governments have jealously guarded their rights with respect to natural resources, which were reinforced in the CONSTITUTION ACT, 1982. (*See also* NATIONAL ENERGY PROGRAM.) For its part, the federal government has struggled to reduce INTERPROVINCIAL BARRIERS in Canada to achieve the economic benefits of a single market. Attempts to redefine areas of jurisdiction and federal spending powers in the MEECH LAKE ACCORD and the CHARLOTTE-TOWN AGREEMENT were defeated. *See also* EQUALIZATION PAYMENTS, FEDERAL-PROVINCIAL FISCAL ARRANGEMENTS.

federal taxing power The federal government, under section 91 (3) of the CONSTITUTION ACT, 1867, is given the power to "Raise Money by any Mode or System of Taxation." This allows it to levy DIRECT TAXES such as income tax, and INDIRECT TAXES such as customs and excise duties. The federal government can also use its powers of taxation to regulate the economy, under its general power under section 91 to

make laws for "the Peace, Order, and Good Government of Canada." It is much less clear how far the federal government can go in using its taxing power to regulate activities that otherwise fall under provincial jurisdiction. *See also* FEDERAL SPENDING POWER, PROVINCIAL SPENDING POWER, PROVINCIAL TAXING POWER.

federal transfers to the provinces Cash or tax transfers to the provinces to ensure all provinces can provide essential public services in areas of provincial responsibility such as education, health care, and social services, to reduce regional disparities, promote national economic management by helping stabilize provincial revenues, and develop and maintain national standards. The three most important programs are ESTABLISHED PROGRAMS FINANCING, EQUALIZATION PAYMENTS and the CANADA ASSIST-ANCE PLAN.

federalism A form of political and economic union in which the national and provincial governments are each sovereign within their own areas of jurisdiction and in which there is a wide range of interdependence, since the actions of one level of government will frequently affect the other level. This means that, in any working federal system, there has to be a great deal of co-operation between the two levels of government if the citizens of the country, who frequently are not concerned about the fine print of a constitution, are to have the economic, social, and other policies that bring them maximum benefits. In Canada, a great many formal and informal arrangements exist to achieve co-operation. *See*, for example, FEDERAL-PROVINCIAL CONFERENCE. But no matter how carefully the division of spending, taxing, and other powers is defined, there are bound to be arguments and confrontations from time to time when important issues are at stake. *See also* DISTRIBUTION OF POWERS.

federation of labour A province-wide association of union locals and community labour councils set up to deal with their provincial and municipal governments on provincial labour laws and other matters of interest or concern. Provincial labour federations are chartered by the CANADIAN LABOUR CONGRESS.

fee The payment made for a professional service or for the right to do something — for example, a payment for legal or medical services, for a hunting or fishing licence, or for entry to a government campsite or a cultural institution such as an art gallery or museum.

feedstock The raw material — crude oil or natural gas — used in an oil refinery or petrochemicals plant.

fertility rate The number of live births per year, per 1,000 women of child-bearing age, at mid-year. The definition of child-bearing age varies; it usually starts at age 15 and extends to either age 44, 45, or 49, depending on the statistical agency. Statistics Canada uses age 45, while the United Nations uses age 49. The total fertility rate is the number of children, on average, that a woman would bear if her child-bearing experience were the same as that of a cross-section of women of different age groups in a given year. It is sometimes used to estimate the average number of children per completed family. Demographers also calculate age-specific fertility rates for women in different age groups. Throughout the world, the fertility rate is falling below family-fecundity or biological-reproductive capacity. Statistics Canada produces an annual estimate of the fertility rate in Canada, *Report on the Demographic Situation in Canada*

(publication 91-209E). *See also* ZERO POPULATION GROWTH.

fiat money Paper money that has the value stated on it, but which is not backed by or convertible into gold or silver. Because the government has declared it to be legal tender and the public accepts it as such, it functions without gold or silver backing. All currency in circulation in Canada is fiat money; it cannot be converted into gold or silver and there are no gold or silver reserves to back its face value. The Bank of Canada Act of 1934 called for the maintenance of a gold reserve of at least 25 percent of the Bank of Canada's note and deposit liabilities. This requirement was withdrawn in 1940, when Canada's gold reserves became part of the country's foreign-exchange reserves, where they have remained ever since.

fiduciary A person — for example, a trust-company officer — who holds and manages assets in trust for someone else. Trust companies in Canada are the only financial institutions empowered to play a fiduciary role.

fifo *See* FIRST IN, FIRST OUT.

film distribution A key profit centre in the film industry, it is the intermediary role between film producers and film exhibitors such as theatres, TV stations, and other markets. Film distribution is the single most important source of funding for the making of films. In Canada, the film-distribution industry is tightly controlled by the major U.S. film producers in Hollywood, collectively known as the Motion Picture Export Association of America; as a result, almost all the profits from film distribution in Canada are reinvested in new U.S. films; in addition, Canada is not treated as a separate market but as part of the U.S. market. Major U.S. studios have also controlled Canada's main movie-theatre chains. This has meant that Canadian film producers have lacked access to film distribution revenues for investment in Canadian films and also have had difficulty accessing exhibition space in Canadian theatres. Canada indicated in 1987 that it planned legislation to force the treatment of Canada as a separate market, with Canadian film companies allowed to bid for distribution rights of independent studio films in Canada. This was strongly opposed by the U.S. government and the U.S. film industry, and legislation was not proceeded with. In addition, the CANADA-UNITED STATES FREE TRADE AGREEMENT allows the U.S. government to retaliate against any new Canadian cultural industry policies that affect U.S. interests in the Canadian market.

final good Goods or services purchased by the final or ultimate consumer or user. These are the only kinds of goods and services included in the GROSS DOMESTIC PRODUCT. Purchases of writing paper are included in final demand in the economy, but not the purchases of the pulp used to make the paper. *See also* INTERMEDIATE GOOD, RAW MATERIAL.

final-offer selection A method of resolving a labour or other dispute in which an arbitrator picks the entire final offer of one of the parties to the dispute rather than seeking to construct a compromise from among the various offers.

final payment In the western grains industry, the payment the federal cabinet authorizes the CANADIAN WHEAT BOARD to make to farmers at the end of the CROP YEAR. Whether or not there is a final payment, and how large it is, depends on the funds the Wheat Board has left over after the year's crop is sold and its marketing and other costs are met. *See also* INITIAL PAYMENT.

final prospectus The prospectus that is accepted by provincial securities commissions for filing and that meets all the requirements for information that must be made to initial buyers of a new BOND, share, or other security issue. *See also* PRELIMINARY PROSPECTUS.

final-utility theory of value The theory that value depends on final or MARGINAL UTILITY. Thus, necessities of life, such as air and water, are cheap because additional units are freely available, while diamonds and gold, while of limited practical use, are costly because of the difficulty in obtaining additional units.

Finance, Department of The principal economic-policy-making department of the federal government. The department dates back to Confederation and at one point included the TREASURY BOARD, responsibility for the ROYAL CANADIAN MINT, management of OLD-AGE SECURITY PENSIONS, and the Comptroller of the Treasury. Today, its functions are focused on economic analysis, advice and policy making. It produces the BUDGET each year and sets FISCAL POLICY, is in charge of tax policy, and manages Canada's international monetary and economic relations, including Canada's relationship with the INTERNATIONAL MONETARY FUND and the GROUP OF SEVEN (G-7) finance ministers. It has six key branches. The tax policy and legislation branch does not collect taxes, but it monitors the economic and social impact of the tax system and sets tax policy; in 1970-71 and 1987-88, it handled two major revisions to personal and corporate income taxes in Canada. In 1990, it set up the GOODS AND SERVICES TAX, which came into effect in 1991. The

Economic Development Policy Branch monitors and analyzes the performance of Canada's various industry sectors and provides advice; it also includes a Crown Corporations Division that, with the Treasury Board, reviews the corporate plans and capital budgets of crown corporations. The Fiscal Policy and Economic Analysis Branch monitors the economic performance of the country as well as the fiscal situation; it analyzes the major foreign economies as well as the Canadian economy and tracks government revenues and spending to determine whether fiscal policy is on target. It also conducts economic and financial forecasts for the government and publishes a quarterly economic assessment, *The Quarterly Economic Review*. The International Trade and Finance Branch monitors and analyzes international financial markets and the performance of the international financial system; it also advises on tariffs and trade policy and on Canada's relations with developing countries. The Financial Sector Policy Branch deals with the functioning and health of the Canadian financial system and the development of policies affecting the financial system and financial markets. Its other activities include management of the PUBLIC DEBT, the foreign-exchange market, and Canada's balance of payments, including the accumulation of foreign debt. The Federal-Provincial Relations and Social Policy Branch advises on fiscal arrangements with the provinces, including federal transfers, and advises on social policy and spending. The Finance department is responsible for the BANK ACT, the Bretton Woods Act, the CANADA DEPOSIT INSURANCE CORPORATION, the CANADIAN INTERNATIONAL TRADE TRIBUNAL, the CANADIAN PAYMENTS ASSOCIATION Act, the Export Credits Insurance Act, the INCOME TAX ACT, the Investment Companies Act, the Loan Companies Act, the OFFICE OF THE SUPERINTENDENT OF FINANCIAL INSTITUTIONS, the SMALL LOANS ACT, the Tariff Board Act, and the Trust Companies Act.

Financial Administration Act   Federal legislation, dating back to Confederation but frequently amended since then, that establishes the rules and regulations for the handling of public funds. It sets out what is to be done with monies that are collected, the rules on how these monies are to be spent, and what kind of financial-reporting system is to be used. It provides for the system of PUBLIC ACCOUNTS, the operation of the CONSOLIDATED REVENUE FUND, and the establishment of the Department of FINANCE and the TREASURY BOARD, and of such offices as the OFFICE OF THE COMPTROLLER GENERAL OF CANADA. It also sets out the reporting and other rules governing the conduct and accountability of crown corporations.

financial asset   On a balance sheet, either cash or an investment that can be converted into cash — for example, bonds, shares, and short-term notes. For an individual, a financial asset is a financial security with the individual having a contractual right to receive future payment in the form of interest.

Financial-Flow Accounts   Part of the system of NATIONAL ACCOUNTS produced quarterly by Statistics Canada, showing the source and disposition of savings in the economy, including savings flowing into or out of Canada. The economy is divided into 14 sectors and 25 subsectors including different levels of government, monetary authorities, private households, unincorporated businesses, private-sector industrial corporations, crown corporations, financial intermediaries such as banks and trust companies, pension funds and insurance companies, and the rest of the world. The accounts give the lending and borrowing for each sector by type of financial asset (shares, bonds, loans, trade receivables, and mortgages, for example). The movement of funds among the different sectors is also shown, giving an overall view of where savings have originated in the economy and where they have been used. The flow of funds out of one sector becomes its financial asset; the receipt of those funds in another sector becomes its liability. The acquisition of assets by each sector are set out under 27 different headings while the increase in liabilities from other sectors is set out under 22 different headings. Each sector normally is both a borrower and a lender; when a sector borrows more than it lends it is a net borrower, while if it lends more than it borrows it is a net lender. The personal sector tends to be a net lender while the corporate and government sectors tend to be net borrowers. Collectively, Canada's domestic sector is a net borrower, so the rest of the world is a net lender to Canada. Financial assets and liabilities in the economy are balanced out. Statistics are published quarterly by Statistics Canada (publication 13-014). While the *Financial-Flow Accounts* measure the flow of savings in the economy, the NATIONAL BALANCE-SHEET ACCOUNTS attempt to measure the stock of savings and debt at the end of each year. In addition, the BANK OF CANADA publishes details of outstanding government and corporate bonds and shares each October.

financial futures   Contracts in which a buyer and a seller agree, through a futures broker, to purchase or deliver a specified dollar volume of a particular financial security such as a TREASURY BILL at a price and on a date agreed to at the time of the sale of the contract. Most securities to be delivered under a financial-futures contract have a specified coupon rate. While the futures market is used for HEDGING, the existence of a financial-futures market also allows investors to speculate on changing interest rates. Changes in rates will change the price of the financial securities.

financial institution   A bank, trust company, credit union, caisse populaire, or provincial savings office that accepts deposits and makes loans, or an insurance company, mutual fund, stockbroker, or pension fund that accepts savings and uses them to make investments on behalf of its clients.

financial intermediary   A financial institution that accepts savings as deposits and re-lends the money to borrowers, earning a profit on the difference between the interest rate it pays savers and the interest rate it charges borrowers. Financial intermediaries play a vital role in the economy, channelling the funds of millions of savers, with a wide variety of saving needs, into the hands of borrowers with widely different borrowing needs. In effect, such institutions are the middlemen between savers and borrowers. Examples of financial intermediaries include chartered banks, trust companies, credit unions, caisses populaires, life-insurance companies, investment dealers, and stockbrokers. Many intermediaries are highly specialized, and, in sophisticated financial markets, many transactions may be between different financial intermediaries. *See also* CAPITAL MARKET, MONEY MARKET.

financial-management system   The method of presenting government revenues and expenditures according to function instead of department. It provides the best outline of government spending by function and is the only system that permits an examination of how much is actually spent by governments in Canada each year —

either collectively or separately by federal, provincial, and local government — in areas such as health, education, social welfare, regional development, transportation, law enforcement, or industrial development. The financial-management system details revenues by type and spending by function. All social-welfare spending is lumped together, for example, unlike the BUDGETARY-ACCOUNTS BUDGET, which lists spending by department; the problem with the latter system is that identification of total spending in a particular area such as social-welfare spending is difficult if not impossible to ascertain. In the case of social-welfare spending, for example, some spending comes under the budget of the Department of HEALTH AND WELFARE CANADA, some comes under the budget of the Department of EMPLOYMENT AND IMMIGRATION CANADA, and some may come under other departments. Historical details have been published by Statistics Canada for all three levels of government — federal, provincial, and local — for the period from 1965-66 to 1991-92 (publication 68-512). *See also* NATIONAL ACCOUNTS SYSTEM, PUBLIC-ACCOUNTS SYSTEM.

financial markets   The intermediaries that get savings to those who want to invest either in a country or, increasingly, between countries.

financial ratio   A benchmark to determine the creditworthiness of a company. The most frequently used ratios include the CURRENT RATIO (the ratio of current asssets to current liabilities), the DEBT-TO-EQUITY RADIO, and the DIVIDEND cover (the number of times net profits exceed dividends). The purpose of these ratios is to calculate the income or assets available to cover lenders of capital to the business.

financial sector   The sector of the economy that encompasses the activities of financial institutions. Along with non-financial corporations and households it makes up the private sector.

financial statement   The annual accounting statement of a business. It includes the BALANCE SHEET, the EARNINGS STATEMENT, and the statement of RETAINED EARNINGS or surplus. *See also* ANNUAL REPORT.

financial year   *See* FISCAL YEAR.

finder   An agent who succeeds in finding a buyer or a seller and thereby enables a transaction to take place. The agent is paid a fee or commission, known as a finder's fee.

fine-tuning   Using the levers of economic policy — monetary and fiscal policy, for example — to smooth out short-term fluctuations in the economy. Experience has led economists to reconsider hopes they once had of being able to moderate short-term fluctuations in the economy quickly. Not only does it take time for changes in economic policy to make themselves felt, but statistics may be slow in picking up the direction and magnitude of economic changes and alerting policy-makers to the need for policy fine-tuning.

fire and casualty insurance   Insurance purchased to provide protection against losses caused by a fire and other perils. Fire and casualty insurance policies often provide protection against other forms of property damage, such as burst pipes, explosions, lightning, riots, vandalism, windstorms, hail, theft, and collapse due to the weight of ice, snow, or sleet.

firm   A business organization, large or small, that produces goods or services for a profit. It can be an owner-operated business, a partnership, or a limited liability or incorporated firm that ranges in size from a small company with a handful of employees to a global or transnational firm. In addition to the profit motive, all firms have certain common characteristics: they employ various FACTORS OF PRODUCTION, add value, and sell what they produce to someone else.

first in, first out (FIFO)   The most widely used method in Canada of determining the value, in a company's books, of INVENTORY. It assumes that the first goods purchased or produced for the company's inventory are the first ones used up or sold from the company's inventory, so that inventory is valued at acquisition cost and not replacement cost. In periods of rapid inflation, this method of inventory valuation tends to undervalue inventories and lead to higher taxable income. *See also* LAST IN, FIRST OUT, and INVENTORY.

first ministers' conference   *See* CONFERENCE OF FIRST MINISTERS.

first mortgage   The mortgage that has first claim on a property; the mortgage that is paid off first in the event of foreclosure.

first world   The rich, highly industrialized nations of the world, including Canada, the United States, Japan, the European Economic Community, Australia, and New Zealand. These countries are also called the developed countries, and the North (in the NORTH-SOUTH DIALOGUE), and are the members of the ORGANIZATION FOR ECONOMIC CO-OPERATION AND DEVELOPMENT.

fiscal agent   An investment dealer appointed by a government or corporation to give it financial advice on the management of its debt and the planning of its future financial needs, and

to manage new issues of its bonds, shares, or other securities.

fiscal drag   The reduction of purchasing power or demand in the economy that occurs during a period of high inflation because tax revenues in a progressive-income-tax system rise faster than government spending. The effect is to weaken the economy's capacity for future growth unless something is done — taxes cut or government spending increased — to get that purchasing power back into the economy. The marginal tax rate in the income-tax system takes a greater tax bite with each income increase, so government revenues can rise sharply in a period of rapid inflation, while government spending shows less of an increase. Indeed, government spending may even be reduced in a period of rapid growth, because unemployment-insurance, welfare, and other such payments will be reduced, adding to the fiscal drag. To some extent, the fiscal drag caused by inflation is offset in Canada, because the income-tax rates are adjusted each year to take inflation into account. *See* INDEXATION.

fiscal framework   The economic parameters developed each year by the Department of FINANCE as the critical first step in preparing the BUDGET and the spending ESTIMATES. The department projects expected revenues and spending, based on existing tax rates and government programs, and economic conditions and legal obligations, and, if there is a projected deficit, it shows the various ways in which the deficit might be financed (through tax increases, borrowing, spending cuts, or some combination of such measures). It shows the cabinet how much elbow room there is for new spending programs and/or tax cuts, or how much need there is for spending cuts and/or tax increases.

fiscal indicators Measures of the direction of fiscal policy and benchmarks of the success of fiscal policy. Indicators include the ratio of public debt to GROSS DOMESTIC PRODUCT (GDP) — whether it is increasing, stabilizing, or declining. While an increase in the debt-to-GDP ratio can be expected during times of emergency, such as a war, or during an extended recession, a long-term upward trend spells trouble for policy makers since it means that servicing the debt burden will take a growing share of government revenues, leaving little flexibility to fine-tune fiscal policy in a recession or to embark on new spending programs. Thus, the long-term goal of fiscal policy is to stabilize and reduce the debt-to-GDP ratio. Other fiscal indicators include, as a percent of GDP, the budget deficit or surplus, government financial requirements, public debt charges, budgetary revenues, and budgetary expenditures. Fiscal indicators are available for the federal government, provincial governments, and federal and provincial governments combined. Fiscal indicators for both levels of government can be compared with the fiscal performance of other countries. Comparable data is included in the INTERNATIONAL MONETARY FUND's *World Economic Outlook* and in statistical reports from the ORGANIZATION FOR ECONOMIC CO-OPERATION AND DEVELOPMENT.

fiscal policy The use of the government's taxing and spending powers to achieve a full-employment economy with stable prices and to smooth out sharp swings in the business cycle. The role of fiscal policy in maintaining economic growth and employment has been one of the great lessons of KEYNESIAN ECONOMICS. Through its taxing and spending powers, the government can run deficits to boost aggregate demand and create jobs; or it can increase taxes and reduce spending to hold back the level of demand and check inflation, and, in the process, achieve a budget surplus. Ideally, over the life of the business cycle, government spending and revenues should balance out. In each year's federal budget, a five-year fiscal plan is included, which sets out targets for government revenue, spending, and deficit (or surplus) and the DEBT-TO-GDP RATIO.

There are many different ways in which the use of the tax system can affect the performance of the economy: tax increases reduce consumption and hence the purchasing power of consumers, and discourage investment by business; tax cuts can add to purchasing power and encourage economic growth; tax incentives to business can accelerate business investment; a tax surcharge on corporate income tax will slow down investment; cuts in tariffs and sales taxes will reduce prices for consumers. Similarly, government spending can have an important effect on economic behaviour: a reduction in government spending on goods and services will reduce the overall level of demand in the economy and slow economic growth, while an increase will boost demand and growth; government spending on public works can give an extra boost to job creation, while a cutback on public works can quickly reduce employment in the construction industry; a government increase in transfer payments, such as pension supplements to the needy, can quickly boost consumer spending and hence the overall level of demand in the economy.

In 1945, as the Second World War ended, the federal government committed itself to using fiscal policy "to maintain a high and stable level of employment." Fiscal policy worked reasonably well from 1945 to the mid-1970s, but an inflation overhang from the Vietnam War, and supply shocks, especially in oil but also in other raw materials, led to a period of stagflation

— a combination of high unemployment and high inflation — into the early 1980s. During this period, fiscal policy came under strong criticism by MONETARISTS who argued that targeting money supply was the most appropriate means of achieving steady economic growth, high levels of employment, and low inflation. During the 1980s and into the 1990s, fiscal policy was also handicapped in Canada by a growing level of public debt; servicing the cost of that debt emerged as the biggest single expenditure of government and as it grew, as a share of GDP, governments faced budget deficits even in periods of strong economic growth in the mid-to-late 1980s. As a result, fiscal policy has been weakened as an economic tool in the 1990s, with governments preoccupied by the goal of stabilizing and then reducing the debt-to-GDP ratio. Because of the division of spending and taxing powers in the Canadian form of FEDERALISM, the fiscal impact of the provinces is significant, but the federal and provincial governments have yet to find a way of co-operating so there is a strong degree of co-ordination in fiscal policy. *See also* MONETARY POLICY, FULL-EMPLOYMENT BUDGET, BUILT-IN STABILIZER, POTENTIAL OUTPUT.

fiscal year   The financial or accounting year for any government, corporation, or other organization. It is any consecutive 12 months; for most corporations and other organizations, it coincides with the calendar year of January 1 to December 31. But for the federal government and provincial governments, it runs from April 1 to March 31. The U.S. fiscal year runs from October 1; the Japanese fiscal year from April 1; the Mexican fiscal year from January 1; and the European Community fiscal year from January 1. However, while the German and French fiscal years begin on January 1, the British fiscal year begins on April 1.

Fisher equation   An equation devised by U.S. economist Irving Fisher demonstrating that the inflation rate on a bond must include both a real rate of interest and an inflation premium, based on the expected rate of inflation over the life of the bond, to compensate lenders for the decline in the principal of the bond over time as a result of inflation.

Fisheries and Oceans, Department of   The federal government department responsible for the management and conservation of fishery resources in Canada's coastal waters and inland waters; the original department, the Department of Marine and Fisheries, was established in 1868. The department's role has increased significantly since January, 1977, when Canada proclaimed jurisdiction over a 200-mile fishing zone along its coasts. The department manages Canada's participation in INTERNATIONAL FISHERIES CONVENTIONS, the inspection of fishing practices and gear, adherence to fishing quotas, programs to modernize fishing fleets, programs to market fishery products, and the negotiation of federal-provincial fishing agreements. The department also carries out fisheries and oceans research. Under the CONSTITUTION ACT, 1867, the federal government has jurisdiction over coastal and inland waters; however, most provinces manage their own inland waters under agreements with the federal government. The department is responsible for the FRESHWATER FISH MARKETING CORPORATION.

Fisheries Prices Support Board   A federal agency established in 1947 that provides price support for fishery products when prices are in serious decline. It can purchase and stockpile fishery products and pay DEFICIENCY PAYMENTS to the fishing industry. It reports to the minister of FISHERIES AND OCEANS.

Fisheries Research Board   A federal research organization that advises the Minister of FISHERIES AND OCEANS on needed fisheries and marine research. The board members include scientists from provincial agencies and universities, and executives from the fishing industry.

fishing zones   The zones along Canada's east and west coasts where Canada has full control over fishing rights and activities. Since January 1, 1977, Canada has claimed jurisdiction for 200 miles (370 kilometres) from its coastline. This means that fishermen from other countries who wish to fish in these waters have to have Canada's permission and have to follow Canadian fisheries-conservation and -management regulations. Foreign fishermen are allowed to catch fish declared surplus to Canada's fishing capacity and within total fishing-catch quotas. As Canadian fishing capacity increases, the role of foreign fishermen will be reduced. A number of foreign countries have signed fishing agreements with Canada, so that they can fish in Canada's fishing zones. *See also* INTERNATIONAL FISHING CONVENTIONS.

fixed asset   An asset of a more or less permanent nature that is essential to the operation of a business and that is used to produce goods and services. Fixed assets include the land, building, machinery, furniture, and other equipment owned or leased by a business. They have a reasonably long life and, for accounting and tax purposes, their declining value, due to wear and tear or eventual obsolescence, is written off through DEPRECIATION. *See also* CURRENT ASSET.

fixed cost   Expenses that must be paid and that do not change irrespective of the level of revenue or output of a business. Costs that do not change in a business, at least in the short run, regardless of the level of production are often described as overhead. They include rent, maintenance, interest payments on outstanding debt, property taxes, insurance, and administrative salaries. Even if production fell by 50 percent, these costs would remain the same. However, if it appeared that production would remain much lower for a long time, then some of these costs could be reduced. Some administrative staff might be fired, or the firm could move to a smaller building and save on rent, maintenance, insurance, and property taxes.

fixed-exchange-rate system   A system under which individual countries are required to maintain the exchange rate of their currency, with some fluctuation within a band on either side of its fixed rate or par value. The exchange rate is fixed between the domestic currency and a key foreign currency or basket of currencies; in Canada's case, when it operated on a fixed exchange rate, the rate was fixed in terms of U.S. dollars. This was the monetary system agreed on at BRETTON WOODS in 1944, and which the world used, through the INTERNATIONAL MONETARY FUND (IMF), from 1945 to 1971. It was replaced by a system of FLOATING EXCHANGE RATES.

Under the fixed-exchange-rate system, countries had to intervene in foreign-exchange markets to maintain the value of their currencies and to raise or lower their official exchange rates when their balances of payment were in FUNDAMENTAL DISEQUILIBRIUM. They had to follow international rules set out in the articles of agreement of the IMF. By the late 1960s, as international conditions became unsettled due to the big U.S. balance-of-payments deficit, continued global inflation, and shifts in the balance of economic power among nations, fixed exchange rates became increasingly difficult to maintain. After the United States abandoned the gold standard and its fixed exchange rate in 1971, other major nations soon followed suit. In March, 1973, the IMF officially ended the fixed-exchange-rate system, though there are periodic proposals from international economists and bankers for its reintroduction.

Canada had a fixed exchange rate through most of its history to 1950, and from 1962 to 1970. Its dollar floated between 1950 and 1962, and was floated again in 1970 with permission from the IMF. Some analysts suggest that with the elimination of the NORTH AMERICAN FREE TRADE AGREEMENT that Canada and Mexico could someday peg their currencies to the U.S. dollar. *See also* EUROPEAN MONETARY SYSTEM.

fixed-income securities Any security whose yield is fixed. Corporate and government bonds (including Canada Savings Bonds), guaranteed-investment certificates, treasury bills, guaranteed-investment certificates, and preferred shares all fall into this category. COMMON SHARES, whose dividend rate may vary from year to year, are not fixed-income securities.

fixed investment An investment in plant, machinery, and equipment. Government fixed investment includes schools, hospitals, roads, bridges, transit systems, airports, ports, and computer systems for government operations. Private fixed investment includes housing, pipelines, telecommunications systems, mines and smelters, oil and chemical refineries, railways, factories, commercial office projects, shopping centres, and computer systems.

fixed-price contract A contract someone has agreed to fulfill for a specified price, regardless of any increase in costs. *See also* COST-PLUS CONTRACT, ESCALATION CLAUSE.

fixed shift The policy of keeping the same workers on the same shift in a business or other organization that has several shifts of workers and operates 24 hours a day. This means that a worker will always work the same shift. *See also* SPLIT SHIFT.

flag of convenience The flag flown by a ship, indicating the country where it has been registered, as opposed to the country in which it is owned. Usually the flag of convenience represents a country that offers low taxation, has lax laws on minimum wages and working benefits, and has only modest safety regulations, all of which reduce the costs of operating the ship. While a ship may be owned in Canada, the United States, or Western Europe, it is likely to be registered in Liberia, Panama, Honduras, or other states that offer such flags of convenience.

flat tax A simplified form of personal income tax in which all forms of income, including capital gains, would be taxed at the same rate, with a single rate to apply to all tax filers, and basic deductions eliminating the tax liability for lower-income filers. The purpose of a flat tax is to simplify the tax system and eliminate the extensive use of tax shelters and other schemes, as well as the cost of accountants and other tax advisers in filing tax returns and arranging personal finances.

flexwork The practice of letting employees set their own starting and finishing times each day, provided that they work a stipulated number of hours.

floating-exchange-rate system A system in which the exchange rates of currencies are set by the market forces of supply and demand in international foreign-exchange markets. Unlike the FIXED-EXCHANGE-RATE system, the monetary authorities have no commitment to a particular exchange rate. The central bank manages monetary policy without a commitment to a particular exchange rate, and lets the exchange rate fluctuate in line with changing economic circumstances, such as changes in the rate of domestic inflation, interest rates and interest-rate spreads between the domestic currency and those of other countries, productivity, economic growth, commodity prices and terms of trade, and balance-of-payments surpluses or deficits. By using the price mechanism of supply and demand to set exchange rates, individual nations need not intervene in foreign-exchange markets to protect the value of their currency. Nonetheless, countries do intervene to smooth out fluctuations in their exchange rates or to counter speculators. Occasional intervention of this sort is known as a clean float. Intervention by a country deliberately to change the value of its currency, or to prevent market forces from changing the value, is known as a dirty float. Floating exchange rates became the rule rather than the exception after 1971, when the U.S. government took the U.S. dollar off the gold standard. In March, 1973, the INTERNATIONAL MONETARY FUND officially ended the regime of fixed exchange rates that had been adopted in 1944 as part of the BRETTON WOODS AGREEMENT. Exchange rates thus can float on the market in response to supply and demand, central-bank interventions, or changes in interest rates, which draw in or drive out capital and thus affect the demand for particular currencies.

The floating-exchange-rate system has its drawbacks, as the fixed-exchange-rate system did. Speculators can still cause an exchange crisis, and the existence of floating rates adds an element of uncertainty to international trade and investment. Nor are floating exchange rates a substitute for domestic policies that deal with the problems of inflation, excessive foreign borrowing, and uncompetitive industry. Canada has had more experience with the floating dollar than any other Western nation. The Canadian dollar floated from 1950 to 1962, and has floated again since 1970.

floor trader   An employee of a stockbroker or commodity dealer who is qualified to buy and sell shares, contracts, or other securities on the floor of a stock exchange or commodities exchange on behalf of his firm and its clients.

flow   An economic magnitude measured over a period of time; for example, the level of savings flowing into mortgages over the course of a month, quarter, or year; the weekly volume of steel production; the quarterly output of the economy; and the current account deficit for the year. *See also* STOCK.

flow-through shares   Shares that allow shareholders to capture tax deductions and credits that would otherwise be claimed by the corporation. Canadian mining companies have been allowed to issue flow-through shares at a premium price because the investors are able to take advantage of tax deductions and credit for exploration against their other taxable income. The purpose of flow-through shares is to reduce the cost of capital for mining companies.

flurry   A surge of buying in a foreign-exchange, stock, or commodity market, usually by speculators anticipating an announcement of some sort that will lead to high prices.

Fonds de solidarité des travailleurs du Québec   *See* QUEBEC SOLIDARITY FUND.

Food and Agriculture Organization (FAO)   An important United Nations agency headquartered in Rome. It was founded by a special conference held in Quebec City in October, 1945, to help deal with the food problems of countries whose economies had been devastated by the Second World War. However, it quickly assumed a much broader role, helping to solve worldwide problems of food supply and distribution. It provides a wide range of technical and other assistance to the LESS-DEVELOPED COUNTRIES to improve their production and distribution of agricultural, fisheries, and forest products. It is also responsible for monitoring the balance between world food supply and demand, for handling emergency food-aid programs, and for preparing emergency relief planning. It has been responsible for the 1960 Freedom from Hunger Campaign, the 1969 World Agricultural Development Program for 1985, and the 1974 WORLD FOOD CONFERENCE. Canada has been a member from the start, and, because of its agricultural, fisheries, and forestry expertise, is a member of the FAO Council and many specialized FAO bodies. *See also* WORLD FOOD COUNCIL.

Food and Drug Act   A federal law, dating back to 1920 and administered by the Department of HEALTH AND WELFARE CANADA, designed to protect consumers against risk to health, or against fraud or deception in the foods, drugs, cosmetics, and medical devices they buy. The law's scope ranges from protection against harmful and unsanitary food, controls over the types of food additives that can be used, and the levels of pesticides and agricultural chemicals that can be found in foods, to protection against misleading or deceptive claims for medicines.

Food Prices Review Board   A federal board established in April, 1973, to report quarterly on the reasons for food-price changes by product group, and to make policy recommendations when appropriate. It was subsequently empowered to investigate any price increase in any food product by any producer or firm where such an increase appeared unwarranted, to publish a report, and to make recommendations, if any, to correct the situation or to prevent it from recurring in the future. Thus, it monitored food prices, handled public complaints, investigated price increases, and advocated food- and agriculture-industry policy changes. It was replaced by the much broader ANTI-INFLATION BOARD in October, 1975.

fool's gold   A piece of rock that, superficially, appears to contain gold. In reality, it is pyrite, a shiny yellow mineral that is known as sulphide of iron.

force majeure   A clause in a contract that permits the supplier of a commodity such as oil or natural gas to deliver less than promised, due to an act of God such as a flood, or an act of war, an act of a government, or other causes, such as a strike.

forced sale   A sale instigated by creditors who want their money, rather than a sale willingly made by the owner of the property.

forced saving   Unwilling savings by consumers who have no choice, either because goods are not available or the government is taking their income through taxation to prevent consumption. Governments can use tax increases or compulsory savings plans in times of war to cool consumer demand and to finance wartime investments, forcing consumers to reduce their spending in the process. Governments can also impose credit controls to restrict consumer spending and force consumer saving.

Fordism A system of manufacturing based on the use of interchangeable parts and a moving assembly line, introduced by Henry Ford in the 1920s to mass produce automobiles. Fordism separated intellectual from manual work; engineers designed the product while workers assembled it. In addition, work was divided into easily learned, repetitive steps, administered through a hierarchal, authoritarian system of management. Fordism eliminated the need for skilled workers or craftsmanship. While the system was geared to mass production of a limited number of products or models, it also was prone to quality problems since defects were identifed by inspectors at the end of the assembly line. Quality control was not the responsibility of assembly-line workers. The system was based on economies of scale but also required large inventories of parts and components. Fordism became the dominant manufacturing system until the emergence of LEAN MANUFAC-TUTING in Japan in the 1960s and in North America in the 1980s.

forecasting The projection or estimation of future economic or technological performance. Forecasts can be short-term, medium-term, or long-term. They can be for a country or group of countries, or they can be for a firm, industry, or community. Techniques can range from simple projection forward from past trends or calculations from an analysis of LEADING INDICATORS, to the use of computer ECONOMETRIC models of the economy that use thousands of equations to describe a vast multitude of relationships. Banks, investment dealers, and independent economic-research organizations such as the CONFERENCE BOARD OF CANADA, all publish annual economic forecasts, and many of them publish quarterly or semiannual changes in their forecasts based on more up-to-date statistics.

The federal government publishes some figures from its array of internal economic forecasts in the annual BUD-GET; provinces do likewise in their annual budgets. The ORGANIZATION FOR ECONOMIC CO-OPERATION AND DEVELOPMENT (OECD) publishes forecasts twice a year for the Western world and for individual OECD members, including Canada, and the INTERNATIONAL MONETARY FUND publishes its *World Economic Outlook* each May, along with an update each September; its reports also include separate forecasts for major economies, including Canada.

Forecasts rarely turn out to be exactly right, but they represent the best available information at the time they are made and can give some reasonably clear indications of economic trends. *See also* DELPHI TECHNIQUE.

foreclose To bring about the sale of a property because the owner has failed to make payments on the mortgage, taxes, or other debts. Foreclosure has to be approved through a court order before a sale can take place.

foreign aid Assistance by DEVEL-OPED COUNTRIES to help the LESS-DEVELOPED COUNTRIES to reduce poverty and carry out programs of economic development to raise their standard of living; foreign aid may also be provided as emergency relief in the case of famine, flooding, earthquakes, or other natural disasters. Foreign aid began in earnest after the Second World War, with the breakup of the old colonial empires, the experience of reconstruction in Western Europe through Marshall Plan aid, and the creation of the WORLD BANK. With the emergence of the Cold War, and the competition between the Western World and the Communist World for the allegiance of the emerging new nations, an additional and increasingly important reason emerged: foreign aid was launched both for reasons of morality and reasons of geopolitical self-interest. More recently, additional arguments for foreign aid have included the potential of developing countries as markets for Western products once these countries are launched on a growth path. There is also the argument that, since virtually all population increase over the next several decades will take place in developing countries, the Western nations will face an increasingly hostile world, and the pressures of mass migration if living conditions do not improve in the developing world. Another argument is that unless the rich Western nations assist the developing world to reduce population growth and achieve economic growth through sustainable development, the biosphere will become inhospitable for everyone. Canada provides different forms of foreign aid, including financial, technical, and food aid. Part of the foreign-aid budget is channelled through international agencies, such as the WORLD BANK, the United Nations Development Program, or regional development banks; part of it is handled on a bilateral basis through the CANADIAN INTERNATIONAL DEVELOPMENT AGENCY, and part of it is handled through non-governmental organizations and the INTERNATIONAL DEVELOPMENT RESEARCH CENTRE.

Foreign Claims Commission A federal commission created in 1970 to help Canadian citizens to settle outstanding claims against foreign governments. The bulk of the commission's work has been to deal with claims of Canadians against the governments of Hungary, Romania, Poland, and Czechoslovakia, for payments that pre-date the forced establishment of Communist governments in those countries.

foreign direct investment Investment by a foreign corporation or indi-

vidual for the purposes of owning, controlling, and operating a business in another country. MULTINATIONAL CORPORATIONS account for much of the foreign direct investment that takes place, operating through their FOREIGN SUBSIDIARIES. There are many different motives for foreign direct investment, though they are all related to the profits of the parent company. A multinational corporation may establish a foreign subsidiary to secure supplies of raw materials, to take advantage of low-cost labour or low taxes, to establish a strong enough presence in a foreign market to discourage the creation of local competitors, to buy out foreign firms that could become competitors, to increase its market share and profits, to develop new markets, or because this is the cheapest way to serve a foreign market. Foreign direct investment does not include purchases by non-residents of BONDS or of SHARES purchased strictly for DIVIDENDS and potential CAPITAL GAINS; this is known as PORTFOLIO INVESTMENT.

Statistics Canada measures foreign direct investment in terms of the proportion of foreign-owned capital to total long-term capital employed in different industries, and in terms of the total capital employed in non-resident-controlled businesses. Three regular Statistics Canada reports are published: an annual report on foreign direct investment, published under the CORPORATIONS AND LABOUR UNIONS RETURNS ACT (publication 61-210); an annual report on Canada's INTERNATIONAL INVESTMENT POSITION (publication 67-202) and BALANCE OF PAYMENTS statistics, published each quarter (publication 67-001), which show the amount of new foreign direct investment in Canada by non-residents and the amount of new foreign direct investment abroad by Canadians. Foreign-controlled corporations in Canada today depend more on the reinvestment of their RETAINED EARNINGS than on fresh flows of direct investment capital for their growth. Statistics Canada will start publishing retained earnings data in 1994; an approximate measure can be calculated by taking the stock of foreign direct investment in *Canada's International Investment Position* (publication 67-202) and deducting the flow of foreign direct investment each year.

Foreign Direct Investment in Canada A federal report, published in 1972, usually known as the Gray Report, since the study into ways to increase Canadian ownership and control was headed by Revenue Minister Herb Gray. The report outlined the implications for Canada of a high level of foreign control of manufacturing and resource industries, and concluded that foreign direct investment was very much a cost-benefit issue. As the report put it: "Foreign direct investment is a complex combination of costs and benefits: easy access to foreign entrepreneurial talent, technology, capital, and markets must be offset against TRUNCATION; the competitive stimulation in certain cases must be counterbalanced by the restrictions on competition in others; the provision of export markets in certain cases must be counterbalanced by export restrictions in other cases; increased economic growth, jobs, tax revenues, etc., must be offset against the long-term effects of foreign direct investment on our industrial structure."

The report considered a number of alternatives to increase the benefits and reduce the costs. It rejected a policy of requiring 51 percent Canadian ownership in all business enterprises as too costly. It found some value in policies to require Canadian ownership in key sectors of the economy, such as banking, broadcasting, and transportation, but only as a supplement to other national policies. It further recommended creation of a review agency,

either in the form of an independent tribunal or as an administrative agency responsible to a cabinet minister.

The agency was to review six aspects of foreign investment: foreign takeovers of Canadian firms; the establishment of new business enterprises in Canada by foreign investors; new licensing and franchise arrangements by Canadians with foreign interests; major new investments by existing foreign-controlled enterprises in Canada; existing foreign-controlled enterprises in Canada, even if they were not planning new investment; and major new investments abroad by Canadian-owned multinational corporations. However the review process was handled, the report said, the criteria for approving, rejecting, or otherwise dealing with foreign direct investments should be set out in legislation. Each proposal received should be reviewed according to its contribution to productivity and industrial efficiency, its compatibility with the government's own industrial strategy, the contribution it made to economic growth and new employment, its geographic location within Canada, its effect on competition within the industry in question, and its other economic benefits. The report also said that the proposed agency should be the central agency dealing with foreign direct investment in Canada, and that it should gather data on foreign investment, engage in research on the effects of foreign investment and policies to deal with it, and serve as a registry of the activities of Canadian-controlled multinationals. The report led to the establishment of the FOREIGN INVESTMENT REVIEW AGENCY.

foreign exchange The currencies of other countries used to pay for imported goods and services and foreign travel, and to service foreign-denominated foreign debts and other obligations. The ownership of foreign exchange gives the residents of one country financial claims on another. The convertibility of major currencies means that hundreds of thousands of individuals, firms, and governments can buy and sell from one another, invest in each other's countries, travel abroad, and engage in a wide range of economic relationships. If a Canadian firm needs U.S. dollars, Japanese yen, or Italian lira to pay for imports, it can obtain them from a FOREIGN-EXCHANGE MARKET through a bank or other financial institution; similarly, if a German or British importer needs Canadian dollars to pay for imports from Canada, these can also be obtained on foreign-exchange markets, as can Canadian dollars for a U.S. investor buying a Canadian company, or a Canadian going to Florida or Hawaii in the winter.

Foreign exchange allows individuals, corporations, or governments to settle foreign debts. In settlements between countries, a central bank can use or accept its own currency, other currencies, or SPECIAL DRAWING RIGHTS issued by the INTERNATIONAL MONETARY FUND. Individual countries maintain foreign-exchange reserves to settle international debts arising from financial claims held by foreigners, and to use on foreign-exchange markets to smooth out fluctuations in the value of their own currencies. Foreign exchange is also a claim on another country in the form of currency.

Foreign Exchange Control Board   A board created in 1939 under the Foreign Exchange Control Act to restrict capital flows from Canada and to limit the use of Canada's scarce foreign-exchange reserves to essential purposes. The board had the power to license imports and exports of goods, currency, and capital, including stocks and bonds. It regulated all transactions with residents of other countries. In April, 1940, all Canadians were required, under the foreign-exchange-acquisition order, to sell their holdings of foreign exchange to the foreign-exchange board; at the same time, the BANK OF CANADA turned over its gold holdings to the board, so that all of Canada's foreign-exchange reserves were under the control of a single body. In July, 1940, the board ceased selling foreign exchange to Canadians for pleasure travel. In the latter days of the Second World War, the board began to lift its controls. However, it was not until December, 1951, that the government revoked its foreign-exchange regulations. The Foreign Exchange Control Act was repealed in 1952.

foreign-exchange dealer   Banks and other institutions that buy and sell foreign currencies on the FOREIGN-EXCHANGE MARKET. Most of the trading in Canada is done by the banks on behalf of customers, on their own account, or on behalf of the Bank of Canada.

foreign-exchange market   A market where foreign currencies are traded, and the daily, or spot, and future prices of currencies are decided. The Canadian market is centred in Toronto and consists of an electronic communications network linking the chartered banks, the BANK OF CANADA, currency dealers, and other traders. This market, in turn, is linked to other financial centres, such as New York and London, so that, for most currencies, there is a global market. It is on the foreign-exchange market that companies buy and sell the currencies that they need for trade and investment or have earned for trade and investment. It is also the market in which a central bank intervenes to defend its country's exchange rate, by buying or selling its own currency or the currencies of others, and thus affecting supply and demand.

foreign-exchange operations The purchase and sale of assets denominated in various currencies by a central bank to stabilize a currency's exchange rate. In the process, however, the sale and purchase of foreign-denominated assets affects the money supply. If a central bank is the net purchaser of foreign exchange, this will result in an increase in the domestic money supply; if the central bank is a net seller, this will result in a decline in the monetary base.

foreign-exchange reserves Currencies and liquid assets held by a country that can be used to settle its international BALANCE OF PAYMENTS or to intervene in FOREIGN-EXCHANGE MARKETS to defend its exchange rate. In Canada's case, foreign-exchange reserves consist mainly of U.S. dollars and U.S. treasury bills, gold, and SPECIAL DRAWING RIGHTS. These reserves are held in the EXCHANGE-FUND ACCOUNT; the Department of FINANCE publishes a monthly report on changes in the account, which can be a useful guide to the scale of intervention by the BANK OF CANADA in exchange markets to ensure a stable float of the Canadian dollar.

Foreign Extraterritorial Measures Act Legislation passed in 1984 by Parliament prohibiting a Canadian-domiciled company, regardless of country of ownership, from complying with a foreign law. The legislation was motivated by a need on the part of Canada to curb the U.S. practice of trying to apply U.S. laws, such as the U.S. Trading with the Enemy Act, to U.S.-owned subsidiaries in Canada — in this case an attempt by the United States to prevent U.S. subsidiaries from trading with prohibited countries such as Cuba, even though Canada had an open trading relationship with Cuba. In 1990, for example, the U.S. Congress passed legislation containing the so-called Mack Amendment, which would have made it illegal for a U.S.-owned subsidiary to trade with Cuba. Canada invoked the Foreign Extraterritorial Measures Act, although in this instance the U.S. legislation was vetoed by the U.S. president.

foreign investment The purchase by non-residents of business enterprises, mineral deposits or rights, timber or fishing licences, buildings, land, shares, bonds, futures contracts, certificates of deposit, short-term money-market instruments, bank deposits, or other assets capable of yielding a return. Foreign investment is classified as short-term or long-term, and as debt investment (investment in financial assets) or equity investment (investment in the ownership of physical assets). Equity investment may consist of PORTFOLIO INVESTMENT in shares and bonds for capital gain, interest, and dividends, or DIRECT INVESTMENT in shares or productive assets to own or operate a business. *See also* FOREIGN DIRECT INVESTMENT. The various types of foreign-investment flows are shown each quarter in the BALANCE-OF-PAYMENTS report of Statistics Canada (publication 67-001). The stock of foreign investment is reported annually as Canada's international investment position (publication 67-202).

Foreign Investment Review Agency (FIRA) A federal agency created to screen foreign takeovers of Canadian firms and the establishment of new foreign-owned businesses in order to determine whether they result in "significant benefit" for Canadians. The agency was approved by Parliament in 1973 in the Foreign Investment Review Act, following publication in 1972 of the government report, FOREIGN DIRECT INVESTMENT IN CANADA (the Gray Report). The agency began screening foreign takeovers in April, 1974, and new foreign businesses in October, 1975.

The agency made a recommendation to cabinet through the minister responsible, while the cabinet made the final decision to allow or disallow. The task of the agency was not to block foreign investment, but to make sure that the significant-benefit test was met; this meant that the agency could negotiate with a foreign corporation to get it to agree to do certain things to meet the significant-benefit test. Agreements between foreign companies and the agency were not made public; but the agency was supposed to police the agreements, to make sure that commitments were met. If a foreign corporation refused to carry out agreements it made earlier, then the agency could force divestiture through the courts.

The significant-benefit test considered the impact of a takeover or new investment on employment, research and development, exports, Canadian participation in management and ownership, the purchase of Canadian goods and services, and capital investment. The agency was also required to seek out provincial government views on proposed takeovers and new businesses. The criteria of significant benefit spelled out in the Foreign Investment Review Act were as follows: 1. The effect of the investment on the level and nature of economic activity in Canada, including the effect on employment, on resource processing, on the utilization of parts, components, and services produced in Canada, and on exports from Canada. 2. The degree and significance of participation by Canadians in the business enterprise and in the industry sector to which the enterprise belongs. 3. The effect on productivity, industrial efficiency, technological development, innovation, and product variety in Canada. 4. The effect on competition within any industry or industries in Canada. 5. The compatibility of the investment with national industrial and economic policies, taking into consideration industrial and economic-policy objectives enunciated by a province likely to be significantly affected by the proposed investment. Effective October, 1975, existing foreign-owned businesses in Canada also had to obtain FIRA approval if they expanded into an unrelated business. A related business was defined to include vertical integration, both backward toward raw materials or forward toward distribution; manufacturing of a substitute product for an old line; a new business providing new products with essentially the same technology and production processes used in the old business; the marketing of new products resulting from research and development carried out by private companies in Canada; and a new business that is classified in a special list issued by the federal government as being in the same field as the old business. FIRA published an annual report of its activities. In 1985, it was replaced by INVESTMENT CANADA, whose mandate was to attract foreign investment to Canada.

foreign ownership   *See* FOREIGN DIRECT INVESTMENT.

foreign sector   Economic activities conducted with non-residents. Thus, the foreign sector of the economy includes exports and imports, travel, interest and dividend payments to or from non-residents, income and payments for international banking services, international payments for management fees, patent rights, franchises, transportation services, and long- and short-term capital flows.

foreign subsidiary   A company that is controlled by a foreign corporation. Many foreign corporations have subsidiaries in Canada, while a number of Canadian firms have subsidiaries abroad. Most foreign subsidiaries established in Canada were set up to develop the Canadian market for the foreign parent or to exploit Canadian natural resources. A few carry out specialized manufacturing activities for world-wide markets on behalf of the foreign parent. *See also* TRUNCATION, FOREIGN-SUBSIDIARY GUIDELINES.

foreign-subsidiary guidelines Federal government guidelines for good corporate behaviour by foreign subsidiaries in Canada. *See* NEW PRINCIPLES FOR INTERNATIONAL BUSINESS and GUIDING PRINCIPLES OF GOOD CORPORATE BEHAVIOUR.

Forestry Canada The federal department set up in 1989 to help develop a Canadian forestry policy, conduct forest research and development, and provide forest protection and management in forests under federal jurisdiction, such as those in the Northwest Territories and Yukon. The federal government has had a role in forest policy since 1899 when a Chief Inspector of Timber and Forestry was appointed — at the time the then Department of the Interior was responsible for vast tracts of forest land in Western Canada that came with the acquisition of Rupert's Land from the Hudson's Bay Company. In 1960, a separate Department of Forestry was established, but it eventually became the Canadian Forestry Service, first in AGRICULTURE CANADA and later in ENVIRONMENT CANADA until 1989. The department negotiates federal-provincial forest resource-development projects, pursues new methods of dealing with insects and disease, conducts research into new areas such as biotechnology and value-added wood products, and encourages industry research and development.

forgery A WHITE-COLLAR CRIME in which a false document, such as a cheque, is made, or in which a legal document is altered. A cheque may have a false signature; or the amount on the cheque may be altered.

forward exchange A foreign currency that is bought or sold at a specified price for delivery at some specified future date. For example, an importer who is to take delivery of products in three months and who wants insurance against higher prices caused by a decline in his or her own country's exchange rate, will buy a three-month futures contract, enabling him or her to take delivery of the foreign currency that will be needed at a price that protects against a loss on the import transaction. Exporters who are being paid in foreign currencies will do the same thing. *See also* FUTURES MARKET.

forward exchange rate The exchange rate being quoted for a currency for delivery 30 or 90 days into the future. The rate for immediate transactions is the SPOT PRICE.

forward integration A merger or takeover by a business enterprise of another business enterprise that takes the acquiring firm one step further up the ladder in the production-distribution process, or an investment in a new facility for the same purpose. A mining company, for example, may take over a processing or manufacturing firm to add value to resources or build a facility for the same purpose; an oil company may buy a chain of independent gasoline stations or build new gasoline stations as a market for its oil; likewise, a manufacturer of auto parts may acquire a chain of auto-repair shops. The purpose is to acquire a market for the firm's production.

forward market A market in which traders buy and sell futures contracts, such as commodities or foreign currencies, for delivery at prices fixed when the contract is originally made. *See also* FUTURES MARKET.

forwarding agent A business firm that collects merchandise from factories, warehouses, and other locations and delivers it to a dock, railway station, or airport for shipment to its ultimate destination. Forwarding agents carry out a specialized role in the transportation industry, acting as middlemen between the transportation companies and firms that need products shipped. Forwarding agents make all the arrangements necessary for their customers, including booking space with the railways, ship companies, and airlines.

fossil fuel Hydrocarbon fuels formed over millions of years through the heat and pressure exerted on decaying vegetable matter. Oil, natural gas, and coal are examples. The burning of fossil fuels is the single biggest man-made source of greenhouse gases, which cause global warming.

four pillars The four types of financial institutions in Canada: chartered banks, trust and loan companies, insurance companies, and investment dealers. In a sweeping reform process that began in 1985 with the release of a federal government green paper, The Regulation of Financial Institutions, and culminated in 1992 with the proclamation of new legislation, banks, trust and loan companies, and life insurance companies were permitted to enter many of each other's forms of business directly or to own subsidiaries that could do this. All three could, under the new rules, engage in consumer-credit and mortgage lending, provide business loans, issue credit cards, engage in leasing and factoring, issue travellers' cheques, deal in foreign exchange, engage in portfolio and money mangement, provide investment counselling, own securities dealer or investment dealer subsidiaries and engage in stock trading and corporate underwriting through these subsidiaries, operate real-estate and mortgage-brokerage services and engage in real-estate development and management, engage in asset securitization, deal in gold and silver, participate in export and import financing, administer pension plans, and provide certain information-processing services. Banks and trust companies can own insurance companies and insurance companies can own banks or trust companies. However, life-insurance companies cannot take deposits, while banks and trust companies cannot use their branch networks to distribute insurance products or issue life annuities. Following the 1985 green paper, the federal government in 1986 issued a blue paper, New Directions for the Financial Sector. In June, 1987, the rules were changed to permit banks to own securities dealers and the OFFICE OF THE SUPERINTENDENT OF FINANCIAL INSTITUTIONS was established. In December, 1987, the discussion draft of the Trust and Loan Companies Act was released; it was intended to serve as the model for federal financial institutions legislation. In September, 1990, the government tabled a white paper, Overview of Legislative Proposals, and the first of four bills of the federal financial institutions legislation. In December, 1991, the financial services reform package received royal assent and was proclaimed in the spring of the following year. The legislative package includes a SUNSET CLAUSE of five years from the date of proclamation, requiring the BANK ACT and other financial services legislation to be reviewed in 1997.

fourth world The poorest of the LESS-DEVELOPED COUNTRIES, with the lowest per capita incomes, few prospects for economic growth without massive outside assistance, and few if any natural resources. Countries in this group include most of those in central Africa, India, Pakistan, and Bangladesh, and have a per capita GROSS DOMESTIC PRODUCT of $200 or less.

Framework Agreement for Commercial and Economic Co-operation A formal treaty signed by Canada and the members of the EUROPEAN COMMUNITY (EC) in July, 1976, following the enunciation by Canada of its new foreign-economic policy, the so-called THIRD OPTION, in 1972. Under the treaty, Canada and members of the EC agreed to develop closer economic relations and to consult regularly on ways to increase trade and investment ties. A Joint Co-operation Committee was established, consisting of cabinet ministers from Canada and the EC, to monitor progress under the agreement and to suggest ways of increasing economic co-operation. The first such meeting was held in Brussels in December, 1976.

Subcommittees of officials were established to pursue progress in particular areas — for example, non-ferrous metals, forest products, aerospace products, nuclear equipment, and construction and information equipment. The agreement is intended to increase joint ventures by Canadian and EC industries, to increase two-way investment, to encourage licensing agreements, to facilitate joint research and development, and to boost joint activities in third-world countries. One area of disagreement between Canada and the EC has been over the treatment of natural resources. The EC members wanted secure supplies of raw materials; Canada wanted greater processing of resources before they were exported. Failure to agree on accessibility to resources led to the exclusion of commitments on resources from the treaty. Following the signing of the treaty, Canada tried, with limited success, to persuade Canadian business to follow up with direct discussions with European industries on technology transfer and strategic alliances, and with more vigorous sales efforts in Europe. In November, 1990, a Transatlantic Accord was issued, institutionalizing annual meetings between the prime minister and the head of the country holding the European presidency plus the President of the Commission of the European Communities. *See also* CANADA-EUROPEAN COMMUNITY TRANSATLANTIC DECLARATION.

franchise A licence or privilege granted by a corporation or government to sell a particular product or to offer a service in a given area; often an advertised trade name is part of the franchise. Governments grant franchises to operate radio or television stations on a certain part of the airwaves, or to provide transportation services between particular communities. Many small businesses are operated as franchises — fast-food outlets, for example, or auto-parts and repair shops. In a business-franchise contract, the franchisor (the person who grants the franchise) will sell the use of a trade name, and usually certain equipment and supplies, to the franchisee (the person obtaining the franchise) in exchange for a one-time payment, royalties based on sales, and an agreement to meet all the standards for product or service quality, such as staffing and decor, imposed by the franchisor.

Francophonie An association of French-speaking countries founded in 1970 to promote economic development and pursue cultural, educational, scientific, and technological ties. The first full ministerial meeting was held in Paris in 1986. In 1987, a ministerial conference was held in Quebec City, attended by, in addition to Canada, France, Belgium, and Luxembourg, as well as Vietnam and more than 20 other French-speaking former French colonies from Africa. At the 1987 meeting, Canada announced $17 million in aid for French-speaking African nations and forgave these nations $325 million in outstanding loans. There are currently 34 members, including Canada; Quebec and New Brunswick are part of the Canadian delegation.

Fraser Institute   An economic research and educational organization founded in 1974 to identify the benefits to Canadians of a FREE-MARKET ECONOMY, and to identify ways to strengthen competitive forces within the economy. The institute also analyzes the impact of government controls and regulations on the well-being of Canadians. It is funded by its corporate and individual supporters and by the sale of its studies. It is based in Vancouver.

fraud   A WHITE-COLLAR CRIME in which an individual, using false information or documents, cheats another person or organization out of money or other assets, or deceives a person or organization into signing a disadvantageous contract. Fraud is a criminal offence, and the offended party can sue for damages.

fraudulent bankruptcy   A deliberate bankruptcy designed to cheat creditors or suppliers of money, goods, or services. A person may, for example, establish a store, obtain goods on credit, sell them, and not pay suppliers; the money is diverted out of the business so that it cannot be recovered by creditors, whereupon the retailer declares bankruptcy. It is a criminal offence.

free and clear   A statement signifying that there are no outstanding claims or liens on a property. Thus, a vendor is free to sell a property and a purchaser can buy it, without fear that a third party will appear with a claim on the property.

free enterprise   *See* PRIVATE ENTERPRISE.

free good   Goods that are available in such abundance that they can be obtained without cost to the consumer — fresh air, sunshine, and a climate favourable to high agricultural productivity are examples — as opposed to an ECONOMIC GOOD, which is scarce and requires cost and effort to obtain. With the development of the concept of EXTERNALITIES, economists are re-examining the idea of free goods. With air pollution in cities, for example, it is questionable whether clean air is a free good; someone has to pay to keep it clean. *See also* FINAL-UTILITY THEORY OF VALUE.

free list   A list of goods that are not subject to import duties.

free-market economy   An economy in which prices and production are largely determined by private ownership and the unrestricted play of market forces through the LAW OF SUPPLY AND DEMAND. However, many of the virtues of efficiency, consumer choice, and low prices claimed for a free-market economy exist only under conditions of PERFECT COMPETITION. In the real world of IMPERFECT COMPETITION, market forces have a major role to play, but they may need to be reinforced by government intervention in the form of COMPETITION POLICY to deal with MONOPOLY or OLIGOPOLY, modified, for example through tax and regulatory policies, to deal with EXTERNALITIES such as pollution, or to encourage desirable activities such as research and development, and constrained by laws and policies to ensure social stability through social policy and measures to achieve a more equitable distribution of income. *See also* MIXED ECONOMY.

free port   A port at which goods are accepted without the payment of customs duties. A free port is usually used to attract tourists or to assemble products for reshipment.

free trade   International trade that takes place without the imposition of any tariffs or other barriers, such as quotas, government procurement rules, or import or export licences, to the free movement of goods and services. Proponents of free trade cite the doctrine of COMPARATIVE ADVANTAGE. They argue that free trade would lead to the most advantageous international division of labour and specialization, increase the potential output of all nations, and improve the standard of living of everyone. However, opponents fear that, like LAISSEZ-FAIRE conditions in domestic markets, free trade could lead to monopoly power and worsen rather than reduce disparities in income, while reducing the political sovereignty of individual nations. Since the end of the Second World War, however, there has been a gradual reduction in international tariff and other trade barriers, and the establishment of a number of FREE-TRADE AREAS around the world. *See also* CANADA-UNITED STATES FREE TRADE AGREEMENT, NORTH AMERICAN FREE TRADE AGREEMENT, AUSTRALIA-NEW ZEALAND FREE TRADE AGREEMENT, GENERAL AGREEMENT ON TARIFFS AND TRADE, EUROPEAN COMMUNITY, CUSTOMS UNION, COMMON MARKET, MERCANTILISM, NEO-MERCANTILISM.

free-trade area   An agreement between two or more countries to abolish TARIFF and NON-TARIFF BARRIERS on some or all goods and services moving between them. They may agree to apply a common external tariff on imports from other countries, or to let each member set its own tariff policy. Article XXIV of the GENERAL AGREEMENT ON TARIFFS AND TRADE permits groups of countries to form free-trade areas. Examples include the EUROPEAN COMMUNITY, the EUROPEAN FREE TRADE ASSOCIATION, the CANADA-UNITED STATES FREE TRADE AGREEMENT, the NORTH AMERICAN FREE TRADE AGREEMENT, and the CANADA-UNITED STATES AUTOMOTIVE PRODUCTS AGREEMENT.

free-trade zone   A duty-free area near a port or airport where goods are imported and re-exported duty free, sometimes with some assembly or other manufacturing activity taking place. *See also* MAQUILADORA.

Freedman Report   A major report by Mr. Justice Freedman of the Manitoba Court of Appeal, under the Industrial Relations and Disputes Investigations Act, which dealt with the rights of management and labour in the introduction of technological and other changes not covered in a collective agreement. The investigation was initiated in November, 1964, after railway trainmen, conductors, firemen, and engineers launched a WILDCAT STRIKE when the Canadian National Railway Company (CNR) tried to eliminate crew changes at several divisional points.

Mr. Justice Freedman found that the CNR had acted legally in reducing crew changes when technological improvements made this possible. However, he said that the issue none the less should have been a matter of negotiation: "The present situation which permits management to make unilateral changes in working conditions during the contract period is a manifest inequity which clamours for correction," he said. Either party should have the right to refer the issue to an arbitrator, picked either by the affected unions and their employer or by the Minister of LABOUR, to determine whether the proposed change would cause a material change in the working conditions of the employees. If it didn't, Mr. Justice Freedman said, the change would be permitted to be carried out immediately. If it did, the employer should be required to delay the change until the next collective-bargaining period, unless the union agreed to the changes. Mr. Justice Freedman dealt only with the CNR case, but said that the procedures and policies he recommended for that case could be applied to similar situations in other instances of technological change: "The old concept of labour as a commodity simply will not suffice; it is at once wrong and dangerous. Hence there is a responsibility upon the entrepreneur who introduces technological change to see that it is not effected at the expense of his work force." Mr. Justice Freedman also said that communities affected by technological change were entitled to a hearing on the reasonableness of the CNR's proposals, and that the federal and provincial governments had a responsibility to compensate them for the economic loss. The CNR, he said, also had a responsibility to compensate affected workers and to pay their expenses in moving to jobs in other communities. Federal and provincial labour codes were subsequently amended to require advance notice of technological change.

freedom of entry The ability of new firms to enter the market freely. In a world of PERFECT COMPETITION, no one firm has any particular advantage over any other, so that new firms can enter with ease; the consumer benefits because new firms will eliminate the excess profits that existing firms in the industry may have earned. In the real world of IMPERFECT COMPETITION, existing firms may enjoy an advantage, such as recognized brand names, supe-

rior technology, or ECONOMIES OF SCALE, so that freedom of entry does not exist and established firms are able to earn higher profits. Freedom of entry implies an absence of BARRIERS TO ENTRY.

freight rates The rates charged by railways, airlines, and trucking firms to move goods and commodities. Freight rates are not subsidized and, in Canada, except for air-cargo rates, they are unregulated. *See* CROW'S NEST PASS AGREEMENT.

frequency distribution A statistical technique used to organize a large volume of data into understandable groups. For example, the income of Canada's several million families can be organized by broad classification: under $19,999, $20,000 to $29,999, $30,000 to $39,999, $40,000 to $49,999, and so on. This technique greatly simplifies analysis of statistics.

Freshwater Fish Marketing Corporation A federal agency established in 1969, to help rejuvenate the freshwater fishing industry of the Prairie provinces, parts of northern Ontario, and the Northwest Territories. It operates a processing plant in Winnipeg and a smaller plant in LaRonge, Saskatchewan. It promotes the domestic and export sales of freshwater fish and also provides some working capital loans. It is based in Winnipeg.

frictional unemployment Unemployment due to lags between the time people leave old jobs and the time they take new ones. Even when there is FULL EMPLOYMENT, there is always some frictional unemployment. People may not be sure which new job they want, or they may lack information about the jobs available, and therefore have to spend time getting that information. Frictional unemployment can be reduced to some extent by improving labour markets, so that more information is available about job vacancies and skills that are needed, or by providing labour-mobility assistance so that people can move more easily to new jobs in other communities. *See also* CYCLICAL UNEMPLOYMENT, STRUCTURAL UNEMPLOYMENT, SEASONAL UNEMPLOYMENT.

Friedman, Milton (b.1912) The American economist who was awarded the Alfred Nobel Memorial Prize in Economic Science in 1976 for his "achievements in the fields of consumption analysis, monetary history and theory and for his demonstration of the complexity of stabilization policy." Friedman has won recognition for his development of the PERMANENT-INCOME THEORY. He is closely associated with MONETARISM, which challenged KEYNESIAN ECONOMICS and argued that a stable growth rate in money supply in a free-market economy was the best assurance of sustained economic growth and low inflation.

fringe benefits Benefits, other than wages or salary, provided by an employer for an employee. They include paid vacations, group life and disability insurance, dental and supplementary hospital and drug insurance, reimbursement for educational courses, a share of pension costs, and share purchase plans. In Canada, fringe benefits account for about one-third of payroll costs, with wages and salaries accounting for the other two-thirds. Fringe benefits can also include the cost of subsidizing staff cafeterias, employee recreation programs, and similar activities.

Frisch, Ragnar (1895-1973) A Norwegian economist who was awarded the Alfred Nobel Memorial Prize in Economic Science in 1969 jointly with the Dutch economist J. TINBER-

GEN for "having developed and applied dynamic models for the analysis of economic proccesses." Frisch is the originator of the word "econometrics."

front-end loading The practice of insurance companies, mutual funds, and sellers of registered retirement savings plans, of claiming the initial premiums or payments for administrative, interest, and other costs. If a person cancels a policy or takes early redemption, much of the investment may have been claimed by the financial institution to cover its costs and risk. *See also* NO-LOAD.

frontage The measurement of a parcel of land where it fronts on a street, highway, or body of water.

frontier reserves Reserves of crude oil and natural gas that may have great potential but which, at present, cannot be shipped to market at competitive prices and for which no physical distribution system, such as a pipeline, exists. Canada's frontier areas include the Mackenzie delta, the Beaufort Sea, the Arctic islands, and parts of the offshore areas of Eastern Canada.

frozen asset An asset that cannot readily be converted into cash or used for the owner's personal benefit. Assets of enemy nationals may be frozen in wartime; similarly, in legal, business, or nationalization disputes, assets may be frozen until disagreements have been resolved.

full-cost pricing The standard method of pricing a product or service used by a company; it includes a share of corporate overheads, the average unit cost of producing a good or service, and a profit margin.

full employment The condition existing when everyone who is able and willing to work can find a job. It can also be defined as the level of utilization of labour and capital existing when an economy is operating at its POTEN-TIAL OUTPUT or POTENTIAL GROSS DOMESTIC PRODUCT. This does not mean that there will be zero unemployment because there is always some FRICTIONAL UNEMPLOYMENT, due to people who are in the process of changing jobs or people who turn down available jobs because they are confident that something better is imminent; there is also always some SEASONAL UNEMPLOYMENT. Full employment has traditionally been a fundamental goal of economic policy; the condition of full employment should mean that the economy is operating at its full capacity. However, in a number of countries, pursuit of ZERO INFLATION has become the principal economic objective, the assumption being that zero or low and stable inflation will create the conditions leading to full employment. Economists today differ on what constitutes full employment. For a long time, it was held to be 4 percent unemployment. Some economists and policy makers have argued in recent years that, with more generous unemployment-insurance benefits and with more families having more than one income, people take longer to choose new jobs, and that full employment should therefore be considered an unemployment rate of 7.5 percent or even higher. As part of the post-war reconstruction, the federal government in 1945 committed itself to "maintain a high and stable level of employment."

full-employment budget   A calculation that measures what the country's fiscal position would be if the economy were operating at full employment and existing tax policies and spending programs were in place; the country could have a full-employment surplus or full-employment

deficit. The full-employment budget is a useful analytical tool, for it may show, for example, that a government could afford to increase its deficit to fight unemployment, since FISCAL POLICY, in full-employment conditions, would yield a surplus or balance — or it may show that the deficit is so large that, even with full employment, there would still be a deficit. Economic growth yields tax revenues at a rate faster than the growth of the economy, due to the progressive nature of the income-tax system; similarly, a growing economy has a declining need for unemployment assistance and welfare benefits. Hence, using the full-employment budget, policy makers can see not only how much room they have for economic stimulus, but whether or not they should be planning a tax cut or new spending programs to counter the FISCAL DRAG that could prevent the economy from reaching full-employment output.

fully diluted earnings per share   The earnings per common share if all outstanding rights, warrants, and options were exercised and all convertible securities converted into COMMON SHARES.

functions of money   The different uses of money in a modern economy. Money is a medium of exchange, a standard of value, a store of value, and a standard of deferred payments when a debt is to be repaid.

fund   Money and other financial assets that are held in reserve for a specified purpose. Examples include a trust fund for heirs, an endowment fund for a charity, a stabilization fund for commodities, a contingency fund for emergencies, or a sinking fund for the repayment of debts.

Fund for Rural Economic Development (FRED)   A federal regional development program introduced in 1966 to promote the social and economic growth of low-income, high-unemployment, and predominantly rural areas. A total of five agreements with four provinces were signed to aid the Manitoba Inter-Lake region, Prince Edward Island, the Gaspé region of Quebec, and the Mactaquac and northeastern regions of New Brunswick. By 1979, the program had expired, with only the P.E.I. agreement still in effect.

fundamental disequilibrium 1. The situation that exists when a country runs a large and persistent CURRENT ACCOUNT surplus or deficit that at some point will require corrective action. **2.** The condition described in the articles of agreement of the INTERNATIONAL MONETARY FUND when the system of FIXED EXCHANGE RATES operated, indicating the need for a country to revalue or devalue its exchange rate and to take other measures to correct its BALANCE OF PAYMENTS problems. It meant that the actual exchange rate of a country should be much higher or lower than the official exchange rate, and that the official exchange rate or par value had to be changed and other economic policies adopted to improve economic performance. The condition of fundamental disequilibrium does not technically exist in a system of FLOATING EXCHANGE RATES, but balance-of-payments problems and the need for changes in domestic economic policies have not disappeared.

funded debt The outstanding debt of a company, in the form of bonds, debentures, and other securities, that is not due to at least anther 12 months.

futures market A market in which investors buy and sell commodities and foreign exchange for future delivery. While the market is speculative in nature, it performs the important economic function of spreading risk, and provides a year-round market for commodities. There is also a growing market in financial futures. Commodity dealers are able to protect themselves against wide swings in prices by HEDGING. There are two prices quoted — the spot, or actual price, and the futures price, for delivery, say, three months ahead. Futures markets also trade in OPTIONS: the right to buy or sell a commodity at a set price at some future date. Futures traders are speculating on the difference between the futures price and the spot price three months later or longer. Futures markets trade in a wide range of commodities including wheat, canola, corn, coffee, cocoa, hogs, cattle, gold, copper, silver, lumber, plywood, a number of currencies including the Canadian dollar, heating oil, some financial instruments such as treasury bills, bankers' acceptances, long-term government bonds, interest-rate futures, and stock-market indices. The WINNIPEG COMMODITY EXCHANGE is the Canadian futures market for various grains and canola. The MONTREAL STOCK EXCHANGE trades futures contracts in Canadian bankers' acceptances and Canadian government long-term bonds. The TORONTO FUTURES EXCHANGE trades in stock-indices futures, based on the TSE 35 Index. Other major futures exchanges include the Chicago Board of Trade, the Chicago Mercantile Exchange, the Commodity Exchange in New York, the New York Mercantile Exchange, the New York Futures Exchange, and the London Metals Exchange. The futures market includes hedgers, who use the market as a form of insurance; by selling futures contracts a producer can recover some of the losses that may be incurred on a commodity if prices fall, while, by buying futures contracts, a purchaser can ensure existing prices in a commodity that will be acquired at a future date. Speculators trade in the market to make a profit by buying and selling contracts to take advantage of price fluctuations.

G

GATT *See* GENERAL AGREEMENT ON TARIFFS AND TRADE.

gains from trade The additional income that a country can enjoy by participating in international trade. By exporting to world markets, a country can specialize in the products and services in which it is most competitive, and by importing, a country can acquire a wider selection of goods and services, and it can acquire them at lower prices than if it tried to produce all those same goods and services itself.

Galbraith, John Kenneth (b. 1908) A leading POST-KEYNESIAN economist born in Canada but for most of his life a U.S. citizen and professor of economics at Harvard University. He has been a strong advocate of a permanent INCOMES POLICY to control inflation. In his book *American Capitalism: The Concept of Countervailing Power* (1952), Galbraith argued that equilibrium is achieved in the economy not by intensive competition but by the checks and balances of big units. Big labour acts as a check on big corporations; big retail chains as a check on big manufacturers; big government, by its purchasing power, acts as a check on other big units. Throughout the economy, the countervailing power of big buyers and big sellers serves as the main form of restraint on OLIGOPOLY.

In *The Affluent Society* (1958), Galbraith argued that sufficient abundance existed to allow all members of industrial countries to enjoy a comfortable standard of living; scarcity was not the problem. However, the emphasis on private-sector production had led to a distortion in the distribution of society's resources, so that private affluence was accompanied by public squalor. This was why there was an abundance of television sets and fast-food restaurants, but a shortage of parks and decent schools. Mass-market advertising and widespread consumer credit only served to increase the demand for private consumer goods at a time when the real need was to increase spending on public goods, Galbraith argued. This meant gross domestic product was not an adequate measure of economic progress. While it showed steadily rising output, this did not necessarily signify improvements in human welfare if public goods such as hospitals, libraries, schools, parks, transit, public housing, and other needs were being neglected.

In *The New Industrial State* (1967), Galbraith depicted the mature corporation as the strategic planning unit of society, desiring social stability and stable growth. Entrepreneurs were replaced by corporate bureaucrats, who used scientific techniques, ranging from engineering to social psychology, to shape demand and set long-term goals. These scientific and bureaucratic corporate managers, Galbraith argued, had their like-minded counterparts in government; together, they formed modern society's technostructure or planning apparatus. Galbraith predicted a world-wide trend toward a uniform technostructure and value system. In *Economics and the Public Purpose* (1973), Galbraith pointed to the unequal development of modern economies; on one side is the planned economy of the large corporation, while on the other is the market economy of farmers, small businesses, and entrepreneurs. The modern state, according to Galbraith, serves the interest of the powerful planning sector, while neglecting the market sector. He proposed major changes in economic policy making: a reallocation of public spending to meet public needs rather than the needs of major corporations; a comprehensive tax reform — to tax alike all increases in the command over resources; the use of public spending on needed projects rather than tax cuts to stimulate the economy during a recession; a sharply reduced role for monetary policy; a guaranteed annual income; permanent wage and price controls to deal with big corporations and big unions; and the creation of a public planning authority to meet public needs in the economy.

galloping inflation   *See* HYPERINFLATION.

gambling   Betting on the outcome of an event, usually based either on a game of chance or skill, or on a contest. In 1970, Canada's Criminal Code was amended, giving the provinces the authority to license, operate, or regulate most forms of gambling. This led to a surge in provincially run lotteries and legalized casinos in Alberta and Manitoba; in 1992, Ontario announced it would also license casinos. Sports betting, aside from betting at race tracks, is still illegal.

game theory   A technique used in business education to give students experience in devising competitive corporate strategies. Game theory deals with conflicts; players are given a simulated business situation and then handed the task of achieving certain objectives in competition with other players who represent other firms. A player has to calculate how another player — a "business competitor" — will react if he or she cuts prices, changes product mix, boosts advertising, or makes other decisions that corporate managers make in real life. Computers are used so that the results of decisions can be quickly seen. *See also* ZERO-SUM GAME.

garnishment   A court judgement that allows a creditor to go to an employer and have part of an employee's pay deducted each week until an overdue loan or debt has been paid off. The employer transfers the money to the creditor before the employee gets his pay cheque or pay deposit.

gasoline tax   Federal and provincial taxes imposed on gasoline. The provinces began levying a gasoline tax in the 1920s to pay for the construction of roads with the advent of widespread use of automobiles. The federal government later brought in an excise tax on gasoline. Today, gasoline taxes are used both as a source of revenue and as a means of encouraging consumers to purchase fuel-efficient automobiles.

gearing The ability of a company to borrow against its equity base. The EXPORT DEVELOPMENT CORPORATION, for example, can borrow 15 time its shareholder's equity. Gearing permits a company to increase its overall capital for business expansion.

General Agreement on Tariffs and Trade (GATT) An international trade agreement whose objective is the liberalization of world trade. It includes a set of international rules on trade practices that all its signatories are pledged to respect, provides a place to resolve trade disputes, and provides a forum for the negotiation of further trade liberalization. It has a secretariat in Geneva to monitor trade practices and to see that the GATT rules are followed.

GATT was one of several multilateral institutions formed in the aftermath of the Second World War to prevent a return to the protectionism and discriminatory policies of the GREAT DEPRESSION, and to promote instead international trade and investment in a world economy governed by non-discriminatory policies and international agreements on codes of conduct. Expanding world trade, it was argued, would benefit all nations by encouraging efficient production based on comparative advantage; international specialization, it was expected, would raise the standard of living of people throughout the world.

GATT initially was signed by 23 countries, including Canada, in 1947, and came into effect on January 1, 1948. By May, 1993, some 111 countries subscribed to the trade rules. GATT emerged following the failure by the U.S. Congress to endorse creation of a much more ambitious International Trade Organization (ITO). When it was first set up, it was planned as a temporary agreement until the International Trade Organization came into being; but in 1950, the U.S. Senate rejected the ITO, and GATT became the permanent institution.

GATT emphasized non-discriminatory trade policies — that is, trade policies in which a country would treat all of its trading partners alike — arguing that discriminatory trade agreements could lead to trade wars, retaliation, further protectionism, and reduced volumes of international trade. The fundamental principle of MOST-FAVOURED NATION that lies at the heart of the GATT says that all GATT members must extend the same trade privileges to all GATT partners; preferential treatment can be extended to some under free-trade agreements provided they meet the conditions of free-trade areas set out under Article XXIV of the GATT. It has pressed for the use of tariffs as the only acceptable method of protecting local industry and has tried to curb the use of quotas and to prescribe rules where they are used. This has led to the tariffication of trade barriers, which is the replacement of quotas and similar barriers with high tariffs that are reduced over time. GATT has tried to make the trading environment more stable by emphasizing the binding of tariff reductions negotiated in successive rounds of trade negotiations; once a country binds its tariffs at the new, lower levels it cannot raise them again without penalty. It has established rules and procedures that individual nations should follow in dealing with DUMPING and other improper trade practices and in resolving trade disputes through its dispute settlement system. It has also achieved a system of generalized trade preferences for the less-developed countries.

GATT rules permit the formation of free-trade areas, such as the EUROPEAN COMMUNITY or the CANADA-UNITED STATES FREE TRADE AGREEMENT, provided the free-trade area, as set out under Article XXIV, eliminates trade barriers on virtually all trade within the region and does not raise barriers against other GATT members. Its three basic objectives are the multilateral reduction of tariffs by negotiation; the non-discriminatory application of tariffs to all trading partners; and the gradual elimination of non-tariff barriers such as quotas, subsidies, and the use of health and other regulations to block imports. Further reductions of trade barriers were negotiated in the Annecy Round of 1949, the Torquay Round of 1950-51, the Geneva Round of 1955-56, the Dillon Round of 1961-62, the Kennedy Round of 1964-67, and the Tokyo Round of 1974-79. The URUGUAY ROUND was launched in 1986.

General Arrangements to Borrow (GAB)   An on-going line of credit provided by the GROUP OF TEN (G-10) nations, including Canada, to the INTERNATIONAL MONETARY FUND (IMF) since 1962. The purpose is to provide additional financing to the IMF, when needed, to protect currencies against speculative attacks and to finance programs to restore exchange-rate stability. The G-10 countries — Canada, the United States, Britain, France, Germany, Japan, the Netherlands, Belgium, Italy, and Sweden — have to give prior approval before the IMF could make use of the credit. In 1992, the GAB line of credit was 18.5 billion SPECIAL DRAWING RIGHTS or US$26.6 billion. *See also* GROUP OF TEN.

general equilibrium   The existence in an economy of an equilibrium or balance between supply and demand in all industries and markets. General equilibrium is achieved when the competing demands for scarce goods and services and factors of production have been allocated through the price system in an on-going and interdependent process. For example, in labour markets, differences in wages will encourage workers to move among firms and among industries. However, the labour market will evolve into a stable struc-

ture of wage differences that reflects a matching of supply and demand for labour; when this is achieved, wage differences will tend to stabilize, and equilibrium is achieved. When equilibrium exists in all markets for factors of production and supply of goods and services, then general equilibrium has been achieved.

General equilibrium analysis is the study of the conditions necessary to achieve general equilibrium and of the impact on general equilibrium of changes in one sector of the economy. It is a useful tool in helping to analyze the interdependence of different sectors of the economy; however, general equilibrium is never achieved in real life, since any economic system is always in a state of change. Technological innovation, new consumer tastes, oil-price increases, and changes in tax laws, for example, all affect general equilibrium.

General Investment Corporation   A Quebec government corporation established in 1962 to invest in industrial enterprises and to help develop Quebec's industrial base under local ownership. It was intended that the ownership would be shared equally among the Quebec government, the CAISSES POPULAIRES, and the public. Shares were sold to the public in 1963, but the Quebec government repurchased them in 1972 because of the corporation's poor financial performance. The corporation can be both a majority owner of a subsidiary enterprise and a partner in a joint venture. Its most important holdings include interests in two aluminium smelters with U.S., European, and Japanese partners, a 24.4 percent stake in the forest products company Domtar, and control of Le Groupe MIL, which is active in shipbuilding, naval design and engineering, and offshore oil and gas technologies. In 1979, the corporation formed a joint venture with Gulf Canada and Union Carbide to establish a new petrochemical company, Petromont Inc. It is now a GIC-Union Carbide venture. The headquarters of General Investment Corporation are in Montreal. Its name in French is the Société générale de financement du Québec (SGF).

general strike   A general work stoppage by union members in an attempt to paralyze the economy, either throughout a nation or in a particular region, in a bid to win their demands. In 1976, Canadian unions organized a "day of protest" against the federal government's wage- and price-controls program; they did not call it a strike, since a strike would have been illegal under their collective agreements. *See also* WINNIPEG GENERAL STRIKE.

generalized system of preferences (GSP)   A system of preferential or lower tariffs for LESS-DEVELOPED COUNTRIES, adopted by the GENERAL AGREEMENT ON TARIFFS AND TRADE in 1971 to help stimulate the economic growth of developing countries. Canada and the United States implemented the system in 1974. The purpose of GSP is to help developing countries increase their exports of manufactured products.

generally accepted accounting principles (GAAP)   The guidelines and techniques used by auditors to verify the financial statements and annual reports of a company. The guidelines are prepared by the Canadian Institute of Chartered Accountants. The AUDITOR'S REPORT in a company's financial statement must indicate whether or not the statements are based on generally accepted accounting principles; if there is any discrepancy, it must be indicated by the auditors.

Geological Survey of Canada (GSC)   A branch of the Department of ENERGY, MINES AND RESOURCES that carries out geological research and survey work to determine Canada's oil, natural-gas, uranium, and other mineral-resource reserves. It also carries out research into geological and geophysical techniques. GSC operates the Institute of Sedimentary and Petroleum Geology in Calgary and the Atlantic Geoscience Centre in Dartmouth, Nova Scotia. GSC publishes occasional assessments of Canada's oil and natural-gas reserves, including assessments of the country's ULTIMATE POTENTIAL RESERVES. It is one of the earliest government institutions; it was established in 1842 by the Province of Canada.

geophysics   Prospecting for minerals using scientific methods — in particular, geophysicists trying to detect the presence and size of mineral ores. Different minerals have different levels of magnetism, radioactivity, or electrical conductivity, for example, which can be detected by instruments above ground.

gift tax   A tax levied on a donor when he makes a gift to another person. The federal government imposed a gift tax until the beginning of 1972, when the CAPITAL-GAINS TAX came into effect. The gift tax was turned over to the provinces, but no province imposes such a tax today. The federal government assumes deemed realization of the capital gain when a person makes a gift to someone else except when the gift is to the spouse, or consists of a farm or small business given to other members of the family. In the case of farms and small businesses, the recipient has to pay the capital gain that would have been paid by the donor, if the recipient ever sells the farm or business. Quebec imposes a 20 percent tax on the donor of any gift of more than $3,000 per person, and imposes an annual maximum on all tax-free gifts of $15,000 given by an individual. Quebec provides an exemption for family farms and businesses.

Glassco Commission   *See* ROYAL COMMISSION ON GOVERNMENT ORGANIZATION.

global alliance   An agreement by two or more companies in the same industry to share the risks and costs of developing products and markets globally. In many industries, the research and development costs and risks as well as the market-development costs are so high that co-operative ventures are sought between companies that might otherwise be competitors. While one motive is to reduce risk, the other is to share markets. Few global alliances entail exchanges of equity or cross-ownership, but there is a sharing of the results of research and development and technology; in some cases a new company may be established in which the various members of the strategic or global alliance each has an equity share.

Global Environment Facility (GEF) A three-year pilot project launched in 1990 to fund environmental projects in developing countries that would benefit the global environment. Four areas of environmental concern were targeted for investment grants, technical assistance, or, in some instances, research assistance. These four areas were global warming, biodiversity, international waters, and ozone depletion. The initiative for the facility came from France and Germany, and agreement was reached among 24 countries, including Canada, to launch the facility in 1990. It is a joint project of the WORLD BANK, the UNITED NATIONS DEVELOPMENT PROGRAM, and the UNITED NATIONS ENVIRONMENT PROGRAM. Its initial funding amounted to US$1.3 billion, including a US$800 million Trust Fund (Canada contributed US$8 million), US$300 million in co-financing (Canada's share was US$12 million), and US$200 million under the MONTREAL PROTOCOL

to help developing countries phase out ozone-depleting substances. The pilot phase of the GEF ends in mid-1994. However, the UNITED NATIONS CONFERENCE ON ENVIRONMENT AND DEVELOPMENT in 1992 called for new international arrangements to help developing countries finance investments and programs to protect the world environment and the GEF was expected to play an on-going role. The GEF may also be expanded to cover other areas of global concern, such as land degradation (desertification and deforestation).

globalization   The shift in investment, production, and trade decisions from serving national markets to serving world markets. With the continuing decline in trade barriers, the shift by most countries to market economies, the shrinking of communications and transportation time and costs, and the increasing rapidity with which technologies can be transferred, businesses now face competition from almost every part of the world as well as enjoying market opportunities in every part of the world. However, globalization significantly increases the pressure on companies to remain competitive and to develop specialized niches in the world market or develop global alliances with other companies to share the risks and rewards of the new global economy. Globalization also increases the pressure on countries, through their economic policies, to keep their costs under control and to take into account the attitude of corporations, which can invest almost anywhere in the world, to new regulatory, tax, or social measures. Globalization will force the rich industrial nations, such as Canada, to increase investments in education, training, research and development, technology diffusion, and other elements of INDUSTRIAL STRATEGY so that they can develop and sustain specialized niches in world markets based on unique high-value goods and services.

go public   A term used to describe a privately owned company's decision to get its shares listed on a stock exchange and to sell its shares to the public. A company going public in Canada has to get the approval of a provincial SECURITIES COMMISSION and file a PROSPECTUS. It must also be accepted for listing by a STOCK EXCHANGE.

gold-exchange standard   The system under which countries expressed their exchange rates in gold but, instead of keeping gold in their foreign-exchange reserves, kept a stable currency that was freely convertible into gold. India was on the gold-exchange standard in the early part of the 20th century; it kept its reserves in the British pound sterling, which could be converted into gold.

gold fix   The daily practice by five participating London bullion houses of fixing the free-market gold price by matching the bid and offer prices. The practice takes place twice daily, at 1030 hours and 1500 hours.

gold market   In Canada, gold can be purchased from banks, and gold futures can be traded on the WINNIPEG COMMODITY EXCHANGE. The international price of gold, which affects trading in gold and gold futures around the world, is set daily in two different centres — London and Zurich. In London, the international price is set as a result of daily trades among five bullion dealers, and, in Zurich, it is set by three major banks that operate a gold pool.

gold pool   An agreement among eight central banks, which lasted from 1961 to 1968, to maintain the price of gold at $35.19875 (U.S. currency) by buying and selling gold out of their exchange reserves on the London market. The pool originally consisted of the United States, Britain, France, Germany, Italy, Belgium, the Netherlands, and Switzerland, and operated through the BANK FOR INTERNATIONAL SETTLEMENTS. France withdrew early in 1968, and with the price of gold soaring, the arrangement was replaced by the even shorter-lived TWO-TIER GOLD PRICE.

gold reserves   Gold held by individual countries as part of their foreign-exchange reserves. While gold is no longer used to back up paper money or as an official part of the international monetary system, it is still an important part of many countries' foreign-exchange reserves. *See also* GOLD STANDARD.

gold standard   The use of a fixed amount of gold as the basic standard of value of a currency. Before the First World War, Britain was the leading country on the gold standard. Many other nations found it just as convenient to hold British pounds as to hold gold in their reserves, not only to settle their international balances of payment, but also to back their domestic currencies. Britain went off the gold standard during the First World War, returned to it briefly in the 1920s, and went off it permanently in 1931. The United States, in a monetary agreement with Britain and France in 1934, fixed the price of gold at US$35 an ounce, a rate that was adopted by the INTERNATIONAL MONETARY FUND (IMF) in 1947 under its FIXED EXCHANGE-RATE SYSTEM. Gold was the numeraire in the IMF in setting the exchange rate for individual countries. Other countries pegged their currencies to the U.S. dollar, while the U.S. dollar was fixed at US$35 an ounce of gold. The system collapsed in 1971, when world gold prices soared; troubles had already emerged in 1961 when eight countries set up a GOLD POOL to try to maintain, through market intervention, a US$35 gold price. That system failed, and, in 1968, a TWO-TIER GOLD PRICE SYSTEM was established with one price of US$35 for transactions between central banks and another market-driven price for commercial transactions. But the United States, in 1971, abandoned the gold standard. The IMF moved to a FLOATING-EXCHANGE-RATE SYSTEM and replaced gold as the IMF's numeraire with SPECIAL DRAWING RIGHTS. Canada was on the gold standard at the time of Confederation. However, at the start of the First World War, under the Finance Act of 1914, Canada went off the gold standard, along with Britain. After the war, under a new Finance Act of 1923, Canada returned briefly to the gold standard between July, 1926, and January, 1929, but withdrew after a run of the Canadian dollar led to a shortage of gold; an emergency was declared and the gold standard was suspended, though Canada was not officially declared off the gold standard until September, 1931.

Under the gold standard, a country's currency is defined in terms of a specific weight and fineness of gold. The appeal of the gold standard was that it imposed a strict discipline on governments, who were anxious to retain their gold reserves and were thus disposed to take harsh measures to keep their inflation rate down and international creditors happy. Investors also liked gold because it was international and had a relatively stable value. But the standard also had great flaws. It tied world economic growth and the expansion of trade and investment to the supply of a metal dug out of the ground in just a few countries.

golden handcuff An enriched package of compensation for a senior executive in a company that makes it expensive for that executive to leave and work for a competitor. For example, to qualify for certain benefits, an executive may have to stay with an employer for a specified number of years.

golden parachute An enriched package of compensation paid to senior executives leaving a company or government organization. Senior executives in a corporation that is a potential takeover target may try to discourage takeovers by committing the company, through employment contracts, to pay them enormous severance payments should company ownership change.

good Any commodity, product, or service that serves a human want. Economists talk of two types of good, an ECONOMIC GOOD, which is a scarce good and therefore bears a price, and a FREE GOOD, which is so abundant that it cannot command a price. A distinction can also be made between private goods and PUBLIC GOODS, such as parks and museums, which can be shared by all.

good faith The assumption in business and in collective bargaining that the parties to a transaction or agreement are sincere in their actions, want to reach an agreement, and will honour it when it is made.

Goods and Services Tax (GST) A federal sales tax that came into effect on January 1, 1991, and that replaced the MANUFACTURERS' SALES TAX. A form of VALUE-ADDED TAX, the GST is applied at a rate of 7 percent to almost every sale of a product or service made or imported into Canada. Sellers of goods and services must register with REVENUE CANADA and collect the taxes on behalf of the government. The net revenues from the tax, after administrative costs and the payment of a sales tax credit to low-income consumers, go into the federal government's DEBT SERVICING AND REDUCTION ACCOUNT to service and reduce the public debt. While initial plans called for no exemptions, a number of exemptions from the tax or reduced rates were implemented. Exemptions were made for basic groceries, prescription drugs, medical devices, residential rents, health and dental services, financial services, daycare services, local transit services, and most educational services. The resale of old houses was also exempt, but new house sales were subject to the tax: at 7 percent for new houses costing $450,000 or more, 4.5 percent for houses costing less than $350,000, and a phased-in rate for houses in between those prices, rising to 7 percent. Exports were also exempt, as were sales by small businesses with annual revenues of less than $30,000 and occasional sales by private individuals, such as the sale of furniture, appliances, or a car. Federal government departments and agencies pay the tax but provinces and territorial governments do not since the federal government cannot tax them. Municipal governments, universities, schools, and hospitals pay but also get part of the tax credited back; the effective tax rates are 3.0 percent for municipalities, 2.31 percent for universities, 2.24 percent for schools, and 1.19 percent for public hospitals. Registered charities and designated nonprofit organizations pay an effective rate of 3.5 percent. Tourists can apply for a full rebate on accommodation costs and most consumer goods they purchase. Farmers also receive special treatment. Treaty Indians on reserves who purchase goods and services for use on the reserve are also exempt. A refundable sales tax credit is paid to lower-income Canadians to offset the GST. Businesses collect the tax for the government. They can deduct the GST already paid on goods and services they purchase in calculating their own tax liabilities. However, the final consumer cannot do this.

goodwill The value placed on the reputation, know-how, and trademarks of a company. Goodwill is the difference between what one company pays for another and the value of the acquired company's TANGIBLE ASSETS. It is an INTANGIBLE ASSET and represents earning power, just as machines and buildings do. A company with a good reputation has usually invested in that reputation through the quality of its product or service, its willingness to deal with customer problems, the non-business role it plays in the community (for example, through its support of charities), and the advertising and promotion money it has spent to make sure that the public is aware of its name, product, and reputation. Goodwill is the money value of a firm's reputation and the premium the public is willing to pay for products or services bearing its name or brand names.

Gordon Commission *See* ROYAL COMMISSION ON CANADA'S ECONOMIC PROSPECTS.

government bond A bond issued by a federal, provincial, or municipal government, school board, or other government agency.

government cash balances The daily cash balances maintained by the federal government, consisting of term balances and demand balances. In fiscal 1991-92, the federal government maintained an average cash balance of $2.3 billion. At the end of each business day the government decides, based on its forecast of daily cash balances, how much of the next day's balance will be auctioned in term balances to direct clearers (financial institutions), with the remainder held as demand balances with the clearers. The goal is to keep the demand balance at the minimum level necessary and to allocate as much as possible to interest-earning term deposits. While both term and demand balances pay interest, term balances pay a higher rate.

Government of Canada bonds   Bonds sold by the federal government in denominations ranging from $1,000 to $1 million and available in registered or bearer form. Interest is paid semi-annually. New issues are sold through public tender, with the BANK OF CANADA acting as the government's fiscal agent, through a syndicate of primary distributors made up of Canadian securities dealers and the principal Canadian banks. The price is set by auction. The bonds are bought and sold in the domestic secondary market. At the end of fiscal 1991-92, foreigners held 38 percent of the federal government's marketable bonds. *See also* CANADA SAVINGS BONDS.

government procurement   Purchases by governments and government agencies of goods and services, including goods and services for its own use, such as computers, computer terminals, trucks, and consulting advice, as well as goods and services to provide a public service, such as airports, nuclear-power stations, telecommunications services, and military equipment. Some policy makers argue that government procurement should be used as a tool of INDUSTRIAL STRATEGY, by giving a preference to domestic firms and thus assuring them of a market if they develop new technologies or products. Others argue that there is a limit to such a policy, because other countries would retaliate and because it can be considered a NON-TARIFF BARRIER. Some provincial governments give their own firms a preference when awarding contracts to encourage their growth and development. Within Canada, use of preferential government procurement by provincial governments has forced companies to create inefficient plants in different provinces instead of build-

ing strong national firms. The Tokyo Round of the GENERAL AGREEMENT ON TARIFFS AND TRADE included a government procurement code that opened national government procurement markets to foreign producers. Under the CANADA-UNITED STATES FREE TRADE AGREEMENT each country has expanded access to the other's national government procurement market. The same arrangement exists under the NORTH AMERICAN FREE TRADE AGREEMENT. The agreements provide for the establishing of an appeals office in each country to determine whether a foreign supplier, say, from the United States or Mexico was unfairly treated by the Canadian government in the awarding of a contract. *See also* PROCUREMENT REVIEW BOARD OF CANADA.

government revenues   All income received by a government. It includes tax and tariff revenues, royalty income from natural resources, proceeds from the sale of crown lands or licences for the use of crown lands for forest or mineral exploitation, profits from crown corporations, fee and licence revenues, direct charges to users of government services, investment income, the sale of government assets, and the proceeds from the sale of government bonds and treasury bills. *See also* FEDERAL TAXING POWER, PROVINCIAL TAXING POWER.

government spending   The total spending by the federal, provincial, and municipal governments and their agencies, such as local school boards and universities. Government spending can take several forms: direct spending on goods and services; capital investment in housing, airports, power stations, and the like; transfer payments to individuals, other levels of government, or corporations; interest on the public debt; and TAX EXPENDITURES, the forgone revenue or value of all the tax incentives and write-offs that governments give to industry and individuals. Government spending is an important part of AGGREGATE DEMAND in the economy and through FISCAL POLICY governments can influence economic performance by contracting or expanding spending.

governor-in-council Decisions of a federal or provincial government made by the Crown — the governor-general or a lieutenant-governor — on the advice of the Privy Council, which, in practice, is the cabinet. Confirmation of a cabinet decision by the governor-in-council gives the decision the force of law; these confirmations are known as orders-in-council, and federal orders-in-council are published in the *Canada Gazette*. In the early days of Confederation, the governor-general exercised considerable discretion: between 1867 and 1878, he refused to give royal assent to 21 bills passed by Parliament, and would attend cabinet meetings. Today, he or she plays only a ceremonial role.

grace period A short period of time after an interest payment or debt payment falls due in which the debtor can still meet the obligation without penalty. The period is usually three days, and covers such contingencies as a cheque being delayed in the mail.

grain growers' associations Organizations formed by Prairie grain farmers in the early part of the 20th century to increase their bargaining power with the railways and grain-elevator companies. The associations became effective lobbyists for reforms in the grain-handling system, but over time their effectiveness waned and they disappeared.

grain-handling system The system that handles the storing, grading, cleaning, and movement of western Canada's grain from the farms to final destinations. It includes primary or country elevators, terminal and transfer elevators, mill elevators, the railways that move grain, grain inspection, the weighing and cleaning services, and the loading facilities at ports where grain ships pick up their cargoes. It is a large network of different companies, co-operatives, and government agencies and departments engaged in assembling, storing, processing, and transporting grains. It also includes the CANADIAN WHEAT BOARD, which acts as the principal marketing agency for Prairie grain producers, and the CANADIAN GRAIN COMMISSION, which is responsible for establishing and maintaining quality standards for Canadian grain to satisfy domestic and export markets, and for the efficient functioning of the grain-handling system. Typically, grain is trucked by a farmer to a primary or country elevator, where the grain is weighed and graded. From there, the grain is shipped to a port terminal where it is cleaned and dried, and then stored and shipped to final customers. A strike in any one part of the grain-handling system can close the entire system down.

grain trade The international traders who sell Canadian grains. In addition to the CANADIAN WHEAT BOARD, the grain trade includes a number of firms that act as selling agents on behalf of the board.

Grains Group A federal body created in 1970 to advise the cabinet minister responsible for the CANADIAN WHEAT BOARD. The minister served as chairman of the group, which was made up of advisers from the Department of AGRICULTURE, Department of INTERNATIONAL TRADE, and the Ministry of TRANSPORT. It reviews problems in grain handling and marketing, transportation, and production. In 1986 it was replaced by the Grains and Oil Seeds Branch of the Department of

Agriculture, which manages grain policies and programmes.

grandfather clause A clause inserted in new legislation when the new legislation prohibits or restricts certain activities that had been permitted until then; the purpose of the grandfather clause is to exempt all existing persons or firms that had already been engaged in the now-prohibited or restricted activity before the legislation was introduced.

grant A government payment intended as an incentive to an individual, organization, or corporation, to perform a certain task. For example, governments give grants to individuals and firms to carry out research and development, and to firms to make investment in areas with chronically high unemployment.

gratuity A tip, given in return for a service rendered.

Gray Report *See* FOREIGN DIRECT INVESTMENT IN CANADA.

Great Depression A worldwide economic collapse that lasted for most of the 1930s and that was precipitated by bank failures in Europe and a stock-market collapse in the United States. Industrial production worldwide fell nearly 50 percent between 1929 and 1932. There was also widespread deflation as prices fell about 30 percent. The Great Depression led to political upheaval in many countries, resulting in dictatorships in Germany and Italy that set the stage for the Second World War. The collapse was so severe that between 1929 and 1933, the trough in the depression, Canada's GROSS NATIONAL PRODUCT fell 42 percent, and by 1933 the unemployment rate was about 30 percent. Between 1929 and 1933 the consumer price index fell 23 percent; for some items the fall was much sharper — 37 percent for food and 31 percent for clothing. In many industries, those workers who held their jobs suffered major wage cuts; for example, in the transportation-equipment industry, the number of workers fell 43 percent between 1929 and 1933, while average wages fell 36 percent. Across Canada, average annual earnings for production workers fell 25 percent in this period. Total wages and salaries fell 72 percent in the construction industry, 64 percent in forestry, 53 percent in fishing, 47 percent in agriculture, and 44 percent in mining and manufacturing. Federal government tax revenues fell nearly 30 percent while personal disposable income fell 40 percent. Trade came to a near halt; exports fell 55 percent between 1929 and 1933, while imports fell 71 percent. Gross fixed investment fell 78 percent; the value of residential construction fell 69 percent and total construction, 77 percent. Many businesses were wiped out and many families saw all their assets disappear. While all parts of Canada suffered greatly, the Great Depression's effects were especially felt in regions and communities dependent on primary products as world commodity prices plummeted with the sharp decline in international trade and investment. For example, the price Canadians received for copper exports fell 60 percent between 1929 and 1933. In western Canada, the combination of the virtual disappearance of export markets for grains, a collapse of world grain prices, and sharp reductions in production due to a drought that turned the Prairies into a dust-bowl, led to economic collapse. Saskatchewan personal income fell 70 percent between 1928, a peak year for wheat exports, and 1933; in Alberta, the drop was 55 percent and in Manitoba, 45 percent. The three Prairie provinces were effectively bankrupt, as were thousands of municipalities across Canada. The numbers of unemployed

Canadians, mainly men in that era, became so large that from 1933 to 1936 the federal government operated unemployment relief camps. However, conditions were so severe in many of these camps that unemployed men rebelled. One riot in Regina resulted in many injuries and the death of one policeman. Through most of the 1930s, most economists and business leaders urged the government to pursue a balanced budget and conservative economic policies. In 1935, though, then Conservative Prime Minister R.B. Bennett brought in his own New Deal to provide greater relief for the unemployed. (*See* BENNETT NEW DEAL.) However, he was defeated in the 1935 election, and his successor, William Lyon Mackenzie King and his Liberal government, dismantled most of Bennett's measures after seeking to have them declared unconstitutional. Earlier, in 1932, Bennett had hosted a British Commonwealth trade conference in Ottawa that led to higher tariffs against the rest of the world by Commonwealth countries and lower tariffs among Commonwealth countries. *See* OTTAWA AGREEMENTS. The Great Depression led to the emergence of several new political parties in Canada, including the Social Credit Party, the Co-operative Commonwealth Federation (the predecessor to the New Democratic Party), the Union Nationale Party in Quebec, and the short-lived Reconstruction Party, formed by a Bennett cabinet minister, H.H. Stevens.

The Great Depression spread from the industrial countries to the developing countries, with economies in Latin America, Asia, and Africa collapsing in the wake of plummeting commodity prices. Economic problems were compounded by the response of industrial countries, which raised trade barriers in the belief that by pursuing protectionist policies they would create more demand for domestically produced goods and thereby generate more employment. However, this kind of beggar-thy-neighbour policy created a vicious circle because it led to unemployment in trading partners and a decline in international trade, so that in the end unemployment increased worldwide.

There are a number of different explanations for the Great Depression. John Maynard KEYNES blamed its onset on a loss of investor confidence and its deepening on the failure of governments to boost AGGREGATE DEMAND to restore investor confidence. Milton FRIEDMAN, a monetarist, blamed the Great Depression on excessively tight monetary policy that led a normal business cycle downturn to become a depression. Charles Kindelberger, another American economist, blamed it on the failure of the United States to exercise world economic leadership, at a time when Britain was no longer able to do so. Instead, the United States adopted the harsh Smoot-Hawley tariff increases in 1930 that made the international situation worse. Other economists have blamed the Great Depression on delayed consequences of the First World War, including the onerous reparations imposed on Germany and the burden of war debts, and on the GOLD STANDARD, which prevented countries from pursuing more flexible and expansionary monetary policies.

Great Lakes Water Quality Agreement
An agreement signed by Canada and the United States in April, 1972, to achieve specified clean-up targets for the Great Lakes and the international section of the St. Lawrence River, with specific programs to be in place by 1975. The agreement followed the report of the INTERNATIONAL JOINT COMMISSION in 1970, which pointed to the urgent need to halt the deterioration of the Great Lakes, which resulted from the presence of phosphates, mercury, lead, DDT, and bacteria. Pollution had

severely damaged the Great Lakes fishing industry and spoiled recreational beaches, and, through eutrophication, oxygen was being consumed, thus destroying life in the water.

Canada and the United States agreed on a set of water-quality standards; on measures to deal with municipal and industrial waste disposal, including pollution from the pulp and paper, petrochemicals, base-metal-mining, and food-processing industries; on a 50 percent reduction in the amount of phosphates dumped into the Great Lakes each year; and on contingency plans to deal with oil spills and other wastes from Great Lakes shipping. The agreement was revised and signed in November, 1978; the 1978 agreement was re-negotiated and further revised by an amending protocol in 1987. Objectives included tighter controls to deal with oil wastes from Great Lakes shipping, new objectives on the control of wastes from municipalities and industry, tougher curbs on toxic pollutants, the identification of airborne pollutants entering the Great Lakes, the identification and control of pollution from agriculture, forestry, and other land-use activities, further reductions on phosphates entering the Great Lakes, and new limits on radioactivity. The International Joint Commission monitors the agreement's progress. The Canadian costs are shared by the federal and Ontario governments under a federal-provincial agreement. Two binational boards, the Great Lakes Water Quality Board and the Great Lakes Science Advisory Board, were established to advise the International Joint Commission.

green paper   A document published by the government that contains proposals for change. The proposals do not represent government policies or intentions, but are put forward to generate public discussion and debate. *See also* WHITE PAPER.

Green Plan   A program to spend $3 billion on environmental projects between the periods of 1990-91 and 1996-97, unveiled by the federal government in December, 1990. It addressed a number of major areas of concern: environmental stresses such as toxic or hazardous wastes and their implications for human health; waste management, and emergencies such as toxic waste or oil spills; atmospheric change, including acid rain, global warming, and ozone depletion; an improved system of managing renewable resources such as soil, forests, and fisheries; the preservation and protection of wildlife and parks; action to protect and restore the quality of Canadian water, the protection of the arctic environment; the preservation of Canada's historical heritage; and improved environmental reporting. The Green Plan also promised new efforts to improve scientific knowledge of the threats to the environment, new effort to use science and technology to protect the environment, and measures to help Canadian environmental opportunities.

green revolution   The introduction of new, high-yielding wheat and rice seeds especially suited to the conditions of the DEVELOPING COUNTRIES, along with scientific methods of agricultural production that were introduced in the 1960s. The use of new hybrid seeds, along with irrigation, chemical fertilizers, pesticides, and modern farming techniques, gave less-developed countries the potential to raise their food output significantly.

greenmail   The accumulation of shares in a company by an investor or corporation for a potential takeover which are then purchased by the targetted company at a premium price in order to head off a takeover. The investor or corporation threatening the takeover ends up with a big profit on the shares it had purchased, while the targetted company has had to pay a premium price, and perhaps incur debt, to buy off the takeover threat.

Gresham's law Bad money drives out good; when two moneys of equal legal-tender value but different real value are in circulation, the more valuable of the two will be hoarded rather than spent. If gold and silver coins are in circulation, with equal legal-tender value but with the gold coins actually worth more than the silver, then the gold coins will be hoarded and the silver ones used for commerce. It could be argued that the law also applied to international exchange markets in the late 1960s: the U.S. dollar and gold had fixed legal-tender values, but the real value of gold was so much higher than its U.S. dollar value that some countries and investors hoarded gold and cashed in their U.S. dollars for gold. The law is named after Sir Thomas Gresham (1519-1579), an adviser to Queen Elizabeth I.

grey market A market in which a scarce commodity is sold at above-market prices for immediate delivery. Unlike a BLACK MARKET, which is illegal, a grey market is legal, but prices are much higher than those prevailing in the normal market.

grievance A formal complaint against an employer by an employee or group of employees, or by a union contending that there has been a breach of the COLLECTIVE AGREEMENT. It can also consist of a formal complaint by an employer against a union or an employee, also on the grounds that the collective agreement has been broken, although such grievances by employers are rarer. Once a grievance has been filed, a number of steps must be followed — steps that are usually spelled out in the collective agreement. Normally, the union and the employer will try to settle the grievance in the department where it happened. If this fails, then higher levels of both management and the union will try to reach a settlement. Should they fail, the grievance goes to ARBITRATION, where a ruling is made that is binding on the employer, the union, and the employees concerned.

gross domestic product (GDP) The most comprehensive measure of the value of goods and services produced in the economy. It includes the value of physical production of goods and services as well as the value of changes in physical inventories over the period measured. The GDP is published quarterly and annually by Statistics Canada as the *National Income and Expenditure Accounts* (publication 13-001). The GDP is available in current dollars or in constant dollars, which show real growth after deducting inflation. Real GDP, which is the most widely used measure of economic growth, is derived from a base year, currently 1986. The GDP is presented in two different ways: the expenditure method, which is the total of all the forms of final demand in the economy (such as consumer spending and business investment) and is known as the gross domestic expenditure; and the income method, which adds together all the forms of income in the economy, such as wages and salaries, government transfers, and business profits.

The gross domestic expenditure is calculated by adding the following: 1. consumer spending on goods (durables, semidurables and nondurables) and services, including imputed rent on owner-occupied housing; 2. government spending on goods and services by the federal, provincial, and local governments, and hospitals and the Canada Pension Plan and Quebec Pension Plan (but not including government transfer payments or interest payments on the public debt); 3. total investment by all levels of government, including physical change in inventories, and by business, including residential construction, non-residential construction, and machinery and equipment, along with physical changes in farm and non-farm inventories; 4. exports of goods and services; 5. imports of goods and services; and 6. any statistical discrepancy. The total of all of these is the gross domestic expenditure, which is identical to the gross domestic product.

The gross domestic product is calculated by adding together the following: 1. wages, salaries, and supplementary income; 2. corporate profits before taxes; 3. interest and miscellaneous investment income; 4. net income of farmers; 5. net income of non-farm unincorporated businesses, which includes imputed rent for owner-occupied housing; and 6. an inventory valuation adjustment. The total of these is the net domestic product at factor cost. Capital-cost allowances are added yielding GDP at factor cost. Subsidies are subtracted along with indirect taxes and any statistical discrepancy, to give the GDP, which is equal to the gross domestic expenditure.

The GDP data also provide a breakdown of personal income and spending and the source and disposition of savings in the economy. Personal income is the combination of the following: 1. wages, salaries, and supplementary labour income; 2. farm operators' income; 3. net income of non-farm unincorporated businesses (including rent); 4. interest, dividends, and miscellaneous investment income; and 5. current transfers from governments, corporations, and non-residents. Personal disposable income is personal income minus current transfers to government, such as taxes and pension contributions. Personal consumption of goods and services consists of personal disposable income minus current transfers to corporations or non-residents and personal savings.

Gross savings in the economy available for investment consist of the following: 1. net domestic savings by persons and unincorporated businesses, business enterprises, and government; 2. capital-consumption allowances of persons and unincorporated businesses, business enterprises, and governments; 3. the surplus or deficit on current account (a current-account deficit is a source of savings in the economy provided by non-residents); and 4. any statistical discrepancy. Total investment equals gross savings less the statistical discrepancy.

The gross domestic product differs from the GROSS NATIONAL PRODUCT (GNP) in that it only measures the output of goods and services within Canada. The GNP includes the GDP plus investment income received from the rest of the world minus investment income paid to non-residents. In other words, GDP measures the income of the factors of production within a nation's boundaries while the GNP measures the income of the residents of a country no matter where it is owned. Because Canada has a high level of foreign investment within its borders and a lower level of its own investment outside Canada, its GDP is larger than its GNP.

gross domestic product at factor cost A monthly measure of the GROSS DOMESTIC PRODUCT (GDP) based on incomes paid to the factors of production. The Statistics Canada report (publication 15-001) does not include indirect taxes less subsidies and depreciation. It is a useful monthly tracking of GDP growth.

gross domestic product deflator An overall measure of inflation in the economy that is more comprehensive than the CONSUMER PRICE INDEX because it covers all price changes in the economy and not just those for consumer goods and services. It measures the proportion of growth in the GROSS DOMESTIC PRODUCT (GDP) that is due to inflation and is published quarterly by Statistics Canada in the *National Income and Expenditure Accounts* (publication 13-001). When the inflation is deducted from the growth rate, the resulting figure is the real rate of economic growth or real output, expressed in 1986 dollars. The implicit price index, as the GDP deflator is also called, is based on 1986, and in addition to an overall index for the total economy, deflators are also produced for personal and government spending, business investment, and exports of goods and services.

gross domestic product (GDP) per capita A measure of economic well-being that is often used to compare the standard of living of different countries. But it has limitations both as an international benchmark and as a measure of economic progress. For example, the market prices of goods and services in two different countries could be quite different even though their per capita GDP might be the same, so that the standard of living as measured by what an individual can buy could be quite different. In addition, per capita GDP does not reflect differences in the distribution of income between countries or activities outside the money economy such as housework and barter. Increases in per capita GDP within a country can also give a misleading impression of a rising standard of living; instead of reflecting rising productivity, an increasing per capita GDP may simply reflect an increase in the proportion of the population in the workforce. *See also* PURCHASING-POWER PARITY EXCHANGE RATE, HUMAN DEVELOPMENT INDEX

gross-fixed-capital formation The total capital investment in the economy by government and industry, including spending on new housing, before deducting DEPRECIATION or capital-consumption allowances for the normal wear and tear or obsolescence of capital stock. Gross-fixed-capital formation minus depreciation or capital-cost allowances equals net new capital formation, or the addition to the nation's capital stock.

gross income The total income of an individual or enterprise before expenses and taxes have been deducted. In some business enterprises it may be the total income after deducting the cost of goods sold, but before deducting other expenses and taxes.

gross investment The sum of gross domestic investment and net foreign investment in the economy. It includes investment spending on new facilities, machinery and equipment, new housing, and changes in business and government inventories. Net investment, which represents the addition to capital stock, is gross investment minus depreciation or capital consumption allowances.

gross national product (GNP) A nation's total output of goods and services or GROSS DOMESTIC PRODUCT (GDP) plus the net income received by its residents from the rest of the world and minus the investment income, such as interest and dividends, earned by non-residents. Since Canada has a large part of its economy owned by non-residents and a high level of foreign debt, there is a significant outflow of interest and dividends which is far greater than the foreign income of Canadians, so Canada's GNP is smaller than its GDP.

gross-domestic-product gap The difference between an economy's GROSS DOMESTIC PRODUCT at FULL EMPLOYMENT and its actual output when it is operating below full-employment rates. Calculations can be made of the lost output of the economy for each percentage point of unemployment above the full-employment rate. *See also* POTENTIAL OUPUT, POTENTIAL GROSS DOMESTIC PRODUCT.

gross profit   An accounting term, meaning sales revenue left over after deducting the cost of producing the goods sold, but before deducting sales, administrative, and other indirect business costs. It consists of net sales minus the cost of the goods sold.

gross provincial product (GPP)   The value of goods and services produced within the geographic boundaries of each province; the provincial equivalent of the GROSS DOMESTIC PRODUCT. Statistics are produced annually for each province by Statistics Canada (publication 13-213), and date back to 1961.

gross-up and credit system   An incentive for Canadians to invest in the shares of Canadian companies; the taxpayer adds 25 percent to the amount of the dividends received from Canadian companies and pays taxes on this higher amount. However, at the same time, the taxpayer receives a credit of 16.7 percent of the cash amount of the dividends against federal and provincial tax owed based on this grossed-up amount. For example, if a top-bracket taxpayer received $1,000 in dividends he or she would gross this up by 25 percent or $250 and pay income tax on $1,250. But a dividend tax credit of 16.7 percent or $167 would be deducted from the tax owed, so that the actual tax paid is less than it would be on other sources of income. *See* DIVIDEND TAX CREDIT.

group insurance   A single life and disability insurance policy covering all members of an organization; it is often used by an employer to provide relatively low-cost life and disability insurance for all of his or her employees. The cost is low because the administrative costs are low. The contract is between the insurance company and the employer; individuals enter and leave the plan as they enter and leave employment with the firm.

Group of Seven (G-7)   The seven major industrial nations that have met at formal summits since 1975. The group includes the United States, Canada, Britain, Germany, Japan, France, and Italy. The President of the European Community also attends. Canada was excluded from the first economic summit at Rambouillet, France, in November, 1975, but has attended subsequent summits; the 1981 summit was held in Ottawa and the 1988 summit in Toronto. Although the original intent was to hold small meetings at a personal level between the leaders of the major industrial nations so that they could gain a better understanding of one another's economic problems and goals, the meetings have become highly structured, and each country's delegation now includes a number of other ministers, including those dealing with foreign affairs, finance, and trade, and a large staff of officials. At the same time, the agenda has been broadened to include almost any issue on the political agenda of the G-7 countries, from defence and the environment to AIDS and counterterrorist co-operation. There is also pressure to expand the membership. The President of the Soviet Union met with the G-7 at the 1991 summit and the Russian president met with the G-7 at the 1992 summit. There is also a G-7 of finance ministers that meets several times a year, including the annual and mid-year meetings of the International Monetary Fund, to co-ordinate economic policy. The G-7 finance ministers initially consisted of the Group of Five, whose currencies constituted the basket for SPECIAL DRAWING RIGHTS: Britain, France, Germany, Japan, and the United States.

Following the 1985 Plaza Accord, in which the G-5 ministers agreed to devalue the U.S. dollar, Canada protested its exclusion; the members at the 1986 summit in Tokyo agreed to allow the Canadian and Italian finance ministers to join. Initially, the G-5 ministers met, then invited Canada and Italy to join their meetings. After the LOUVRE ACCORD in 1987, which led to a new agreement on exchange-rate targets, at which Canada and Italy were excluded from the initial discussions and brought in after the key decisions had been made, the practice was changed, and all seven finance ministers now participate in all meetings. The central bank governors of the G-7 countries also attend. In addition, the managing director of the INTERNATIONAL MONETARY FUND (IMF) frequently attends since the IMF monitors the economic performance of the G-7 countries.

Group of Seventy-seven (G-77)   A group of developing countries that, starting in 1967, meet as a caucus and also negotiate on behalf of the developing countries on international development issues, especially in United Nations agencies. By 1992, the G-77 membership had increased to 127 countries. *See* UNITED NATIONS CONFERENCE ON TRADE AND DEVELOPMENT (UNCTAD).

Group of Ten (G-10)   The finance ministers and central bank governors, or their officials, of the leading industrial countries, who meet on a regular basis to discuss problems of the international monetary system and ways to make the system function more effectively. The group came into being after the GENERAL ARRANGEMENTS TO BORROW fund was created in 1962 by the same 10 nations, to help the INTERNATIONAL MONETARY FUND (IMF) to deal with balance-of-payments problems; the member countries have a commitment to lend their currencies

up to a specified amount to the IMF when additional resources are needed. Switzerland joined in 1984 but the group continues to be called the G-10. The Group of Ten's influence has declined since the emergence of the GROUP OF SEVEN as the principal forum in which the Western nations attempt to co-ordinate their economic and monetary policies. However, it still has some role to play in policy co-ordination. Its members are Canada, the United States, Britain, Germany, France, Italy, Belgium, Japan, the Netherlands, Sweden, and Switzerland. Chairmanship rotates among members of the group.

Group of Thirty   A group of 30 leading bankers, businessmen, economists, and finance officials from developed and developing countries organized in 1979 by a former managing director of the INTERNATIONAL MONETARY FUND, Johannes Witteveen. The group meets several times a year to discuss the world economic situation and publishes periodic reports. Its offices are located in New York and London. Canadian banks all belong through the CANADIAN BANKERS ASSOCIATION.

Group of Twenty (G-20)   The Interim Committee of Finance Ministers of the INTERNATIONAL MONETARY FUND (IMF), created in 1974 to advise the fund on improvements to the structure of the world financial system. Members include the finance ministers of the United States, Germany, Japan, Britain, Canada, and France, plus 15 others elected from the fund's members. The Interim Committee of Finance Ministers plays an important role in setting direction and identifying priority issues for the IMF. *See also* DEVELOPMENT COMMITTEE.

Group of Twenty-four (G-24)   A group formed by the GROUP OF SEVENTY-SEVEN at its Lima, Peru, meeting in 1972 to negotiate on behalf of developing countries on international monetary and development matters. The G-24 has eight members each from Africa, Asia, and Latin America. Its members are Algeria, Argentina, Brazil, Colombia, Cote d'Ivoire, Egypt, Ethiopia, Gabon, Ghana, Guatemala, India, Iran, Lebanon, Mexico, Nigeria, Pakistan, Peru, Philippines, Sri Lanka, Syria, Trinidad and Tobago, Venezuela, and Zaire; Yugoslavia had also been a member when it was a united nation. The Group of 24 usually meets at the same time as the mid-year and annual meetings of the INTERIM COMMITTEE of the INTERNATIONAL MONETARY FUND and the Development Committee of the WORLD BANK.

growth stock   Shares of a company that is expected to have exceptionally good prospects for growth in dividends and capital gain.

grubstake   Financial assistance, or supplies of equipment, food, and clothing, provided to a prospector, in exchange for a share in any discovery the prospector may make.

guarantee   1. The promise by a third party to a lender to pay back a loan if the borrower fails to do so. Sometimes a bank is unwilling to make a loan to an individual without a promise by a third party to pay back the debt if need be. The person providing such an assurance is a guarantor. **2.** A synonym for an expressed WARRANTY that comes with certain consumer products such as electrical appliances.

guaranteed annual income   A social welfare system that is designed to ensure a minimum level of income to all individuals and families. While a guaranteed annual income is often portrayed as a more efficient method of delivering social assistance, it also raises some difficult issues of implementation, including how to define income,

where to set the minimum income level, how outside earnings would be treated, how it would deal with abuse, and what existing social programs would be eliminated as a result. One way of delivering a guaranteed annual income could be through a NEGATIVE INCOME TAX, with payments to individuals or families whose income fell below the value of their income-tax exemptions or some defined level of minimum income. If a family or individual had no outside income, then the federal government would guarantee a minimum payment; if the individual or family had additional income, the government supplement could decline by, say, one-third so that of every $1 earned, the income guarantee would be reduced by 33 cents. At some point, as outside income grew, the income guarantee would decline to zero. The design of a negative income tax would require setting the guaranteed minimum level of income, determining the tax rate at which additional income would be taxed, and setting the break-even level at which the income supplement would equal zero. In 1970, a federal white paper, Income Security for Canadians, rejected a guaranteed-income plan for Canadians; however, from 1975 to 1978, the federal and Manitoba governments conducted a joint experiment in a negative income tax, with mixed results. In 1985, the ROYAL COMMISSION ON THE ECONOMIC UNION AND DEVELOPMENT PROSPECTS FOR CANADA proposed a guaranteed annual income, which it called a Universal Income Security Program. A universally available income guarantee, it would replace the GUARANTEED-INCOME SUPPLEMENT, FAMILY ALLOWANCES, the CHILD TAX CREDIT, married exemptions, child exemptions, the federal share of CANADA ASSISTANCE PLAN social-assistance programs, and federal contributions to social housing; the old-age security pension would have remained in place.

However, the level of income security proposed by the commission was relatively low — depending on whether the personal income-tax exemption was left in place or eliminated. The guaranteed annual income proposed by the royal commission would have ranged between $2,750 and $3,825, compared with the 1985 rate of $3,904.92 for the guaranteed-income supplement with the personal income-tax exemption in place. Supporters of a guaranteed annual income argue that the difference between existing income-maintenance schemes and a guaranteed annual income is that existing schemes discourage recipients from trying to supplement their income, while a guaranteed annual income could be designed to include a strong work incentive by letting recipients keep part of their earnings. They also argue that a guaranteed-annual-income system would be cheaper to administer and would eliminate the need for the great variety of assistance programs that now exist, each of them designed to deal with a particular kind of income need. Canada has a form of guaranteed annual income for senior citizens; it is the guaranteed-income supplement, a payment that is made in addition to the old-age pension to senior citizens whose total income is below a certain level.

guaranteed-income supplement (GIS) A federal social program introduced in 1967 to ensure a minimum monthly income to all recipients of the old-age security — with the minimum in 1967 of $105 a month, consisting of a basic pension of $75 and a guaranteed-income supplement of $30. Initially, senior citizens were assured of a cost-of-living adjustment to a maximum of 2 percent a year. Full adjustment for the CONSUMER PRICE INDEX (CPI) began in 1972 and quarterly CPI adjustments in 1973. At April 1, 1992, the maximum monthly GIS had risen

to $444.98 for single seniors and $289.84 for a married person whose spouse also received the old-age security pension, to ensure a minimum annual income for seniors, from all sources, of $10,679.99 for single seniors and $13,919.99 for couples. The amount of the GIS is the difference between the old-age security pension plus whatever other income the senior citizen has and the minimum income target of the program.

guaranteed-investment certificate (GIC) A debt security, usually issued by a trust company or bank, that pays a fixed rate of interest, generally at least one percentage point higher than can be earned on a savings account at the time the security is purchased, for a fixed term or period of time. These investment certificates are issued in denominations of $1,000 or more for terms of one to five years; they are issued in denominations of $5,000 or more for terms of 364 days or less.

guideline A government attempt to influence behaviour by setting out a standard of desired behaviour that lacks the force of law. Guidelines may be used, for example, to restrain pay and price increases, to persuade foreign-owned subsidiaries to do more research and development, to encourage companies to reduce industrial pollution to a certain level, to foster affirmative action or employment equity within an organization, or to discourage corporations from doing certain things, such as borrowing abroad. *See also* MORAL SUASION.

Guiding Principles of Good Corporate Behaviour Guidelines issued by the federal government on March 31, 1966, to define good corporate citizenship for foreign-controlled subsidiaries operating in Canada. The objectives encouraged were as follows: 1. Pursuit of sound growth and full realization of the company's productive potential, thereby sharing the national objective of full and effective use of the nation's resources. 2. Realization of maximum competitiveness through the most effective use of the company's own resources while recognizing the desirability of achieving appropriate specialization of productive operations within the internationally affiliated group of companies. 3. Maximum development of market opportunities in other countries as well as Canada. 4. Where applicable, the extension of processing of natural-resource products to the degree practicable on an economic basis. 5. Pursuit of a pricing policy designed to assure a fair and reasonable return to the company and to Canada for all goods and services sold abroad, including sales to the parent company and other foreign affiliates. 6. In matters of procurement, the search for and development of economic sources of supply in Canada. 7. The development, as an integral part of the Canadian operation wherever practicable, of the technological research and design capability necessary to enable the company to pursue appropriate product-development programs, so as to take full advantage of market opportunities domestically and abroad. 8. Retention of a sufficient share of earnings to give appropriate financial support to the growth requirements of the Canadian operation, having in mind a fair return to shareholders on capital invested. 9. The development of a Canadian outlook within management, through purposeful training programs, promotion of qualified Canadian personnel, and inclusion of a major proportion of Canadian citizens on the company's board of directors. 10. The development of a financial structure that provides opportunity for equity participation in the Canadian enterprise by the Canadian public. 11. Periodic publication of information on the financial position and operations of the company. 12. Appropriate attention to and support for recognized national objectives and established government programs designed to further Canada's economic development, and encouragement and support for Canadian institutions directed toward the intellectual, social, and cultural advancement of the community. Large and medium-sized subsidiary companies were also asked to provide confidential information on their operations from time to time. In 1975, the guidelines were replaced by the NEW PRINCIPLES FOR INTERNATIONAL BUSINESS.

guns and butter   A metaphor used to illustrate the point that economics is about choice, and to illustrate how resources are allocated to achieve the maximum welfare for the community. No country can have all the guns it wants and all the butter it wants; economics helps society to determine the combinations of both that can be produced, with the knowledge that in choosing more of one, society is sacrificing some of the other. In a FULL EMPLOYMENT economy, extra production of one product means less production of another.

Halibut Treaty The first treaty negotiated by Canada on its own with a foreign power; it was signed in 1923 with the United States to settle fishing rights in the North Pacific Ocean. Britain's efforts to sign with Canada were rejected by the Canadian government.

Harbour Commission A semiautonomous federal body, which includes local as well as federal appointees, that is responsible for the administration of a local port. Each commission reports to the Minister of TRANSPORT. The ports operated by commissions include Toronto, Hamilton, Windsor, the Lakehead, Oshawa, Belleville, and a number of West Coast ports, including Westminster, Nanaimo, and Port Alberni. *See also* PORTS CANADA.

hard currency A currency that is freely convertible, that enjoys a stable exchange rate, and for which demand is consistently high relative to its supply; it may be used as a currency held as a foreign-exchange reserve. The U.S. dollar, German mark, Japanese yen, and

Swiss franc are examples of hard currencies; the Canadian dollar can also be considered a hard currency although it is rarely held in other countries' foreign-exchange reserves. Nations of the industrialized world tend to have hard currencies, while the LESS-DEVELOPED COUNTRIES have SOFT CURRENCIES. Developing countries find that they have to pay for the products of industrial countries in hard currencies; no one wants their currencies since there may be nothing to buy with soft currencies, or there are no profitable investments to be made. This means that the developing countries may find it difficult to earn the hard currencies they need for essential imports.

hard sell An intensive sales effort that puts considerable pressure on consumers to buy. Increasingly, consumer laws are including a cooling-off period to allow consumers to reconsider decisions they may have made under pressure.

harmonization The process of bringing different countries' standards or laws (for example, in areas such as technical or performance standards, product safety or environmental requirements) into closer alignment with each other.

Harrod-Domar growth model   A theory of economic growth, developed in 1939, that supported the conclusion of John Maynard KEYNES that an economy would not necessarily return to full employment and steady growth after sliding into recession. It was developed almost simultaneously by the British economists Roy Forbes Harrod and Evsey David Domar.

haulage   The term used to describe the rates charged by trucking companies to carry goods.

Hayek, Friedrich August von (1899-1992)   The Austrian-born economist who was awarded the Alfred Nobel Memorial Prize in Economic Science in 1974, along with Gunnar Karl MYRDAL, "for their pioneering work in the theory of money and economic fluctuations and for their penetrating analysis of the interdependence of economic, social, and institutional phenomena." An ardent advocate of free-market economics and a strict opponent of government intervention, Hayek believed that governments should give priority to low inflation by tightly controlling the growth in MONEY SUPPLY, even if this meant extremely high unemployment.

Health and Welfare Canada, Department of   The federal government department responsible for meeting Canada's health-care, social-welfare, and old-age security needs. Formed in 1919 as the Department of Health, it became the Department of National Health and Welfare in 1944. Its health-care responsibilities include the administration of the CANADA HEALTH ACT, which provides federal funding and sets national standards for medicare, the provision of medical services to Canada's Native people, the administration of the FOOD AND DRUG ACT, and the approval of new drugs. The department's income-security responsibilities include the CANADA PENSION PLAN, the GUARANTEED-INCOME SUPPLEMENT, and the OLD-AGE SECURITY. The CANADA ASSISTANCE PLAN is its principal social-welfare program. The department is also responsible for federal programs in fitness and amateur sport, the research and education campaigns on AIDS and smoking, and the Medical Research Council.

health insurance   Canada's system of public health insurance, which is jointly funded by the federal and provincial governments. To receive federal funding under the terms of the CANADA HEALTH ACT, a provincial health plan must be: comprehensive and cover essentially all physician services; universal and therefore available to everyone; accessible; portable, so that provinces will treat newcomers from another province without long residency requirements; and non-profit and publicly administered. Saskatchewan was the first province to offer a system of medicare, with its program coming into effect on July 1, 1961; it was bitterly opposed by the medical profession there and led to a 23-day medical strike. In 1961, the federal government appointed a Royal Commission on Health Services, chaired by Mr. Justice Emmett Hall. Its report, presented in June, 1964, came out unanimously in favour of federal support for "comprehensive, universal programs of provincial health services." These programs, the Hall report said, should cover medical services; dental services for children, expectant mothers, and social-welfare recipients; prescription drugs; optical services for children and social-welfare recipients; prosthetic services; and home-care services. In December,

1966, Parliament passed the Medical Care Act, which was to come into effect July 1, 1967, but was then delayed for one year. On July 1, 1968, only two provinces had programs that met federal conditions for cost sharing: Saskatchewan and British Columbia. In 1969, Newfoundland, Nova Scotia, Manitoba, Alberta, and Ontario joined. They were followed by Quebec and Prince Edward Island in 1970, New Brunswick and the Northwest Territories in 1971, and the Yukon in 1972. During the 1970s, concerns arose that a number of provinces were effectively undermining the principles of universal public health care by allowing doctors to extra bill, that is to add an additional charge to payments on top of the amount they received from provincial health insurance agencies. A follow-up report on Canada's health-care system by Mr. Justice Emmett Hall, in 1981, called for a ban on extra billing, declaring it contrary to the Canadian health-care system; if doctors and provincial governments were unable to agree on medical fees, Hall's report said, the issue should be resolved through binding arbitration. In 1984, Parliament passed the Canada Health Act, which banned extra billing and penalized provinces that permitted extra billing by deducting $1 in federal grants for every $1 of extra billing in a province.

heavily-indebted middle-income countries A group of better-off developing countries whose serious debt problems led to the THIRD-WORLD DEBT CRISIS in 1982. Most of these countries were in Latin America and were candidates for various initiatives, including the BAKER PLAN and the BRADY PLAN. Under the 1989 Brady Plan, for example, countries pursuing economic reforms qualified for additional loans from the WORLD BANK and regional development banks and received help in reducing debt and debt-service obligations to commercial banks. Uruguay, Mexico, the Philippines, Costa Rica, and Venezuela were among the first to reduce their commercial bank debt through Brady negotiations.

heavy crude oil Thick crude oil that requires special techniques, such as steam injection, for extraction. Sizeable quantities of heavy oil can be found in southern Saskatchewan and Alberta.

Heckscher-Ohlin principle An explanation for the law of COMPARATIVE ADVANTAGE that says the advantage is based on different factor endowments. A country that has an abundance of natural resources will gain its comparative advantage in international trade from its natural resources. Likewise, a country with abundant cheap labour will find its advantage in labour-intensive industries, while a country rich in capital will find its advantage in capital-intensive production. The resource-rich country will import labour-intensive and capital-intensive products; the labour-rich country will import natural resources and capital-intensive products; the capital-rich country will import natural resources and labour-intensive products. While the principle may have had validity in an earlier era, in today's competitive global economy, countries invest in creating comparative advantage, for example, by fostering education, training, and research and development; technological progress is a new factor of production.

hedging Action to reduce, and perhaps even eliminate, the risk of a loss from changes in the price of commodities or foreign exchange. The risk is covered by buying futures on the FUTURES MARKET; a profit on the futures will cover a loss on the commodity or foreign exchange, while a loss on the futures can be covered by a profit on the commodity or foreign exchange. In effect, rather than waiting to find out what a commodity price or exchange rate will be a year from now, an investor can buy a contract today, at today's prices, to sell the commodity or currency at today's prices. The investor uses a forward contract — an agreement to buy or sell a commodity or currency at a future date for a specified price — to reduce exposure to commodity or currency changes. For example, a flour company may buy wheat at, say, $4 a bushel to be milled into flour for delivery in three months' time. To protect itself against a sudden drop in wheat prices, which would also reduce flour prices, the flour company will contract to deliver an equal amount of wheat at $4 a bushel in three months. If the price of wheat has dropped to $3 a bushel in three months, the flour company will have lost money on its flour; however, it can buy wheat in the market for $3 a bushel, which it can instantly resell, through its futures contract, at a profit. The profit on the futures contract should cancel out the loss on the flour, so that the flour company will end up with the rate of profit it had expected from its normal processing of wheat. If the price of wheat shoots up to $5 a bushel, the flour company would make an extra profit on its flour, but that extra profit would be used to cover the loss on the futures contract, since the company has to buy the wheat at $5 a bushel and deliver it to someone who will only pay $4 a bushel.

An importer who has to pay a bill in a foreign currency will go through the same exercise, with a futures contract on a foreign currency, if he feels there is any likelihood that the exchange rate will change before the delivery and billing dates. Hedging protects normal profits but eliminates the opportunity for windfall profits, since any big gain in the value of the commodity or foreign exchange will be offset by the loss on the futures contract.

hedonistic principle The notion that individuals are motivated in their actions by the pursuit of pleasure, self-interest, or the avoidance of pain or discomfort. This principle is the basis of the theory of UTILITY as an economic concept.

Heeney-Merchant Report A report on principles for partnership between Canada and the United States, written by Arnold Heeney, twice Canadian ambassador to the United States, and Livingstone Merchant, twice U.S. ambassador to Canada. In January, 1964, Prime Minister Lester B. Pearson and U.S. President Lyndon Johnson asked the two men to produce guidelines "to make it easier to avoid divergences in economic and other policies of the two countries." Heeney and Merchant investigated a number of recent causes of friction, including Canadian trade with Cuba, union disputes in Great Lakes shipping, U.S. magazines in Canada, and oil and gas export and import policies, and asked the officials involved in both countries how these disputes might have been better handled. In their July, 1965, report, *Principles for Partnership*, Heeney and Merchant recommended an on-going committee of Canadian and U.S. government officials to back up the work of the JOINT MINISTERIAL COMMITTEE ON TRADE AND ECONOMIC AFFAIRS, a wider role for the INTERNATIONAL JOINT COMMISSION, more effective use of the Permanent Joint Board on Defence, and a joint study of Canada-U.S. energy policies. Canadian authorities, the report said, "must have confidence that the practice of quiet diplomacy is not only neighbourly and convenient to the United States but that it is in fact more effective than the alternative of raising a row and being unpleasant in Canada." The report caused controversy in Canada, both for its advocacy of quiet diplomacy in dealing with Canada-U.S.

disputes, and because of its recommendation that Canada strive to avoid public disagreement with the United States on international questions, "especially upon critical issues." This was taken to mean that Canada should not express itself publicly on U.S. foreign policy; at the time, the United States was engaged in the war in Vietnam.

help-wanted index   A monthly index of the volume of help-wanted advertising in 20 metropolitan areas compiled by Statistics Canada (publication 71-204) since 1981. The index is a useful indicator of changes in the unemployment rate.

Herfindahl index   A measure of corporate concentration or competition in a market for a particular good or service. The index is the sum of the squared company sizes, each measured as a proportion of the size of the market. The closer the index to 1, the greater the degree of concentration; 1 equals a complete monopoly by one company. For example, if the top company in the notepad market has 40 percent of the sales, the next company 10 percent, the next company 9 percent, and the next two companies 8 percent each, then the top 5 companies have 75 percent of the market; the remaining 25 percent of the market is held by five companies with a 5 percent share each. The Herfindahl index is the sum of the squares of $0.40 + 0.10 + 0.09 + 0.08 \times 2 + 0.05 \times 5$, or 0.203. However, if each of the five top notepad companies had a 15 percent market share, then the Herfindahl index would be 0.125 and the concentration ratio would be nearly half that of the first case, where one company had a 40 percent market share.

Hicks, Sir John Richard (1904-1989)   The British economist who was awarded the Alfred Nobel Memorial Prize in Economic Science in 1972, jointly with Kenneth Arrow, "for their pioneering contributions to general economic equilibrium theory and welfare theory."

hidden inflation   Inflation that does not show up in the form of price increases, but in a decline in the size or quality of a product or service. For example, the size of a chocolate bar may be reduced instead of its price being raised so that the consumer gets less chocolate bar for the same price.

hidden tax   A tax that is included in the price of goods or services, but is not separately identified to the consumer; it is usually an INDIRECT TAX such as a tariff or excise tax that raises the price of the product or service. While it is paid in the first instance by the importer, manufacturer, or other business firm, the tax is added into the price of the product or service and shifted on to the consumer.

hidden unemployment   People who are unemployed but who don't show up in the unemployment statistics compiled by Statistics Canada in its monthly LABOUR-FORCE SURVEY (publication 71-001). The hidden unemployed include discouraged workers who have stopped looking for work because of their age, health, or lack of skills, or because they live in an area of chronic unemployment, as well as people who would like to work but don't try to find a job because they don't think they have a chance to find one. Aboriginals living on reservations who don't have jobs are also among the hidden unemployed. The term can also be applied to workers with part-time jobs who really want full-time jobs. Every March, the *Labour Force Survey* reports on the number of Canadians who have not been in the labour force for at least one year, who would like a job, but have not been looking because they believe no suitable job is available. Each month, the survey reports the number of Canadians who have not looked for work in the previous six months, though they would like to work, because they believed no suitable work was available.

historical cost   An asset in a balance sheet whose value is expressed as the actual cost at the time it was acquired and not its current market value; in today's dollars, it might cost much more to replace. Historical cost is the acquisition cost. It also means that property and other assets may be worth considerably more than the BALANCE SHEET shows. BOOK VALUE is based on historical cost rather than market value.

hoarding   The accumulation of goods or money far in excess of normal everyday needs, by a business or individual. The main motive for hoarding is the belief that there will be a shortage so that prices will rise significantly or supplies will be unavailable.

hog fuel   A by-product fuel made from the scraps of pulp mills, plywood mills, and sawmills — scraps such as bark, shavings, sawdust, and rejected lumber scraps.

holding company   A company set up to own controlling blocks of shares of other companies, and to run those companies; a holding company does not need to own all the shares of the companies in its portfolio but just enough to control them. From a relatively small financial base, an investor or group of investors in a holding company can end up controlling a large corporate empire. The shares of a holding company are sometimes traded on a STOCK EXCHANGE.

home country   The country of origin of a multinational or transnational company with investments in other parts of the world. *See also* HOST COUNTRY.

homesteading   A federal program under the DOMINION LANDS POLICY set up to attract settlers to western Canada in the late 19th century and early 20th century. For $10, a family received 160 acres of land, but the settler had to build a home and cultivate a specified amount of land in three years to keep the property.

homogeneous products   Goods that are seen to be identical to one another by consumers and are therefore perfect substitutes, so that all suppliers have to charge the same price. *See also* PRODUCT DIFFERENTIATION.

horizontal expansion   The expansion of a firm within the industry in which it is already active; the purpose is to increase its share of the market for a particular product or service. An example would be a truck manufacturer who expands by taking over another truck manufacturer.

horizontal integration   The decision of a company to specialize at one level of the production and distribution system. *See also* VERTICAL INTEGRATION.

host country   The country in which a multinational or transnational company invests. *See also* HOME COUNTRY.

hostile takeover   An attempt by an investor or firm to acquire control of another firm when the key shareholders and top management of the targeted firm are opposed to such a takeover.

hospital insurance   A program of universal access to hospital care for all Canadians. Introduced by Saskatchewan in 1947 and in British Columbia in 1949, it subsequently became a national shared-cost program after Parliament passed the Hospital Insurance and Diagnostic Services Act in April, 1957, and came into effect on July 1, 1958, in qualifying provinces. The five provinces that were ready to participate on July 1 were Newfoundland, Manitoba, Saskatchewan, Alberta, and British Columbia. On January 1, 1959, Nova Scotia, New Brunswick, and Ontario joined; on October 1, 1959, Prince Edward Island joined. Quebec was the last province to participate, on January 1, 1961. In 1984, the hospital-insurance legislation was absorbed into the CANADA HEALTH ACT. *See also* HEALTH INSURANCE.

hot money   Funds flowing out of a country for speculative reasons. These can range from anticipated exchange controls or increased taxation to changes in monetary policy. Expectations of a change in the country's exchange rate can also be a reason for money to flee to another financial centre.

household   A person or group of persons occupying the same dwelling. Usually a household is a family, but it may consist of a group of unrelated persons, of two or more unrelated families living together, or of one person living alone. Statistics Canada measures households in several ways: by average size; by type — that is, family or non-family; and by age and marital status of the head of the household. A household is a decision-making unit and in economics is often the basic unit of analysis; much of the economic data that is collected, for example, is collected for households rather than individuals. *See also* FAMILY.

household formation   An important statistic that shows the net increase in a year of new households. The rate of household formation is used to estimate the demand for new homes and CONSUMER GOODS. The rate can increase faster than overall population growth if there is a large number of young people in their late teens and

early 20s who expect to leave home and live on their own. Statistics Canada publishes details of household formation following each census in the publication *Dwellings and Households* (publication number 93-311).

household survey   A survey by a market-research firm or by STATISTICS CANADA to obtain information from the various members of households. Household surveys are often used in MARKET RESEARCH; they are also widely used by Statistics Canada to calculate statistics on unemployment, family income, eating habits, and spending, for example.

housing co-operative   1. A form of social housing in which residents have the right to occupy the building in which they live and pay a monthly charge for the use of the property. They are responsible for the administration of the building in which they live. 2. A form of home ownership in which individual homeowners own shares in a common property. A co-operative differs from a CONDOMINIUM in that while condominium owners actually hold titles to the housing unit in which they live, co-operative owners own shares in a building corporation and have the use of a particular housing unit.

housing starts   A monthly statistic compiled by CANADA MORTGAGE AND HOUSING CORPORATION (CMHC) showing the number of new housing units on which construction has begun. The statistic is often expressed in terms of an annual rate and is based mainly on the number of building permits issued by Canadian municipalities, with some adjustment made for the length of time it normally takes before excavation work begins. The figure includes single-family homes, duplexes, townhouses, and rental and condominium apartments. CMHC publishes the *Housing Information Monthly* and the annual

Canadian Housing Statistics. A housing start is usually defined as the time when the concrete is poured into the ground for the foundation.

human capital The accumulated knowledge, skills, and experience of the workforce that contribute to the productivity and growth of an economy. Investments in the health, education, and skills of the workforce can increase human capital. The assumption is that a healthy, well-educated, and skilled workforce will have a higher rate of productivity and thus contribute to stronger economic growth. The concept of human capital is used to help justify public spending on health and education.

human-development index A measure of the quality of life of a country, it measures the life expectancy, educational attainment, and per capita income of the population of each country to give a composite picture of human development. It defines human development as the enlargement of people's choices. The index was developed by the UNITED NATIONS DEVELOPMENT PROGRAM in 1990 and is published as part of its *Human Development Report* each year. In 1993, Canada ranked second, behind Japan; however, when adjusted for gender differences, Sweden and Norway ranked at the top and Canada number 11, and when adjusted for distribution of income, Japan ranked number one and Canada ranked number six. The index gives a broader measure of standard of living than per capita GROSS DOMESTIC PRODUCT.

Hyde Park Agreement An agreement between Canada and the United States, signed April 20, 1941, in which the two countries agreed to share their industrial capacity and resources in the defence of the North American continent. The agreement was of more immediate importance to Canada, which was already heavily involved in the Second World War and seriously short of U.S. dollars to buy strategic materials and parts; the United States agreed to accelerate its purchases of defence materials and supplies from Canada, and to broaden its lend-lease arrangements, so that U.S. parts obtained for weapons assembled in Canada for British use could be included under U.S. lend-lease financing of the British war effort. The agreement paved the way for close economic cooperation and joint production planning once the United States entered the Second World War, following the Japanese attack on Pearl Harbour on December 7, 1941.

hydro-electric power Electricity created by the exploitation of Canada's major rivers through the use of power dams and power-generating facilities. The electricity is carried to market by long-distance transmission lines. About 58 percent of Canada's electrical-generating capacity was derived from hydro-electric facilities in 1991.

hydrocarbons Natural resources consisting of hydrogen and carbon. They exist in solid (coal), liquid (oil), and gaseous (natural gas) forms. Hydrocarbons are a major source of energy, but they are also a serious source of greenhouse gases, which contribute to global warming.

hyperinflation Sharp and escalating increases in prices, usually of 50 percent or more a month; an inflation rate of 50 percent a month is a 12,875 percent inflation rate for the year. These increases can be so immense that they lead to the collapse of ordinary commercial dealings, the disorganization of production, and social breakdown. The wealth of large groups may be wiped out in a matter of weeks. Money becomes worthless and the monetary system ceases to function. Such economic collapses usually take only a few months to run their course; fortunately, there are few cases in modern history. The best known was in Germany in the 1920 to 1923 period; inflation soared 2,500 percent in one month. Hyperinflation also created anarchy in China, Hungary, and Greece after the Second World War, with Hungary setting a record 19,300 percent in one month. During the 1980s, Argentina, Bolivia, Brazil, Nicaragua, Peru, Poland, and Yugoslavia all experienced hyperinflation and in the early 1990s, Russia also found itself faced with the threat of hyperinflation.

hypothecate   To pledge real property or securities as collateral for a loan.

hypothesis   A theoretical explanation, usually based on deductive thinking or logic, that is tested by the collection of economic data and statistical analysis.

hysteresis   An increase in the natural rate of unemployment resulting from a prolonged period of high unemployment; as a result, part of the rise in unemployment becomes permanent. One reason is that unemployed workers, after a long period of unemployment, suffer a decline in their human capital so that they remain unemployable even after the shock that caused the high unemployment is over. In other cases, workers never develop the early work experience and skills necessary to become permanent members of the labour force because of the prolonged period of unemployment, so that they are condemned to a working life of part-time or temporary jobs. With a large number of hard-to-place workers, efforts to reduce unemployment without rekindling inflation became more difficult, so that the NON-ACCELERATING INFLATION RATE OF UNEMPLOYMENT increases.

I

IS/LM model An economic model that is used to assess the impact of various macroeconomic policies on aggregate demand. It was developed by the Nobel Prize-winning British economist Sir John HICKS in 1937. The IS schedule shows the relationship between the level of aggregate demand and the interest rate, while holding all other variables such as government spending and tax rates fixed. An increase in interest rates slows both investment and consumption, thus depressing aggregate demand; a reduction in interest rates has the opposite effect. The LM schedule shows what combination of interest rate and aggregate demand consistent with money market equilibrium is necessary for a given level of real-money balances. An increase in interest rates reduces the demand for money, and for monetary equilibrium to be restored, an increase in aggregate demand is necessary. The level of aggregate demand in the economy is determined by the intersection of the IS and LM curves. The IS/LM model can be used to determine what combination of fiscal and monetary policies will be most effective in restoring equilibrium to the economy. For example, an increase in government spending or a cut in taxes will increase aggregate demand, though part of the benefit will be lost due to the rise in interest rates and prices resulting from an increase in aggregate demand. Likewise, an increase in money supply will increase aggregate demand, though part of the benefit again will be lost to higher prices.

idle capacity The unused productive capacity of a firm, an industry sector, or an economy due to a lack of demand for its products. Statistics Canada publishes statistics on excess or idle capacity in the manufacturing industry and for 22 different sectors in its quarterly report, *Capacity Utilization Rates in Canadian Manufacturing* (publication 31-003).

illegal strike Any work stoppage by union members in violation of labour laws or a COLLECTIVE AGREEMENT. In Canada, strikes may not take place during the life of a collective agreement. An illegal strike is sometimes called a WILDCAT STRIKE.

illiquidity A circumstance where assets are not readily convertible into cash, except at a significant loss.

immigrant remittances Money sent by immigrants to their families in their country of origin. These remittances are an important source of income for families in less-developed countries and an important source of foreign exchange for their governments. Statistics Canada measures the outflow of such remittances in its BALANCE-OF-PAYMENTS accounts (publication 67-001). Immigrants to Canada also bring capital with them, especially under the Business Immigrataion program, which is aimed at entrpreneurs, investors, are self-employed (including sports and artistic personalities). Entepreneurs who wish to establish businesses in Canada or invest in businesses in Canada are given preference by immigration officials. The remittances contribute to a balance-of-payments deficit for the country from which they are sent and to a surplus for the country to which they are sent.

immigration The movement of people into one country, such as Canada, from another country, for permanent residence. Immigrants usually come to a new country to seek a better economic life, to seek political freedom, or to escape persecution. For the recipient country, immigrants contribute to economic growth and bring needed skills, and they also contribute to the social, political, and cultural life of their new country. Canada's immigration regulations favour newcomers who already have family members in Canada, have needed skills, bring entrepreneurial plans, and capital to start new businesses, or who are political refugees. Canada's current target is 250,000 immigrants per year; in the five-year period 1987-91, Canada averaged 190,000 immigrants per year.

imperfect competition The condition that prevails in a market when one producer is able to increase prices charged without the loss of a significant volume of sales; this may be due to PRODUCT DIFFERENTIATION, BRAND LOYALTY or other BARRIERS TO ENTRY for would-be competitors, anti-competitive practices, or the possession of various OLIGOPOLY powers. This differs from a market in which perfect competition prevails and no single producer has sufficient market power to affect prices. The notion of perfect competition is built on the assumption that products are homogeneous and interchangeable. However, in the world of imperfect competition, producers invest heavily in advertising, packaging, design, and other forms of product differentiation, along with spending on research and development, so that products are no longer homogeneous. These investments can effectively act as barriers to entry for new firms wishing to enter an industry, and thereby protect a MONOPOLY or oligopoly from new competition. Imperfect competition may also exist because consumers are unable to obtain all the market information they need about alternative products, or are unable to obtain it without going to a great deal of trouble. Most major industries operate in a world of imperfect competition. However, perfect competition is assumed in the free-market model of CLASSICAL and NEOCLASSICAL ECONOMICS. Imperfect competition is said to exist between perfect competition and monopoly market power.

imperial preference *See* BRITISH PREFERENTIAL TARIFF.

import controls Various measures to restrict the flow of all imports, of imports of specific items, or of imports from specific countries. Controls range from the imposition of IMPORT SURCHARGES and TRADE EMBARGOES to IMPORT QUOTAS imposed on the recommendation of agencies such as the CANADIAN INTERNATIONAL TRADE TRIBUNAL or negotiated in the form of so-called voluntary export-restraint agreements with exporting countries. Specific controls can also be imposed under the EXPORT AND IMPORT PERMITS ACT or on agricultural products under other trade legislation. In 1947 and in 1962, Canada imposed temporary import controls on a wide range of products to deal with temporary balance-of-payments problems. Canada has imposed quotas on imports of clothing and textiles from developing countries since 1962 under the Long-Term Cotton Agreement and its 1974 successor, the MULTIFIBRE AGREEMENT. The GENERAL AGREEMENT ON TARIFFS AND TRADE permits a country to impose temporary restrictions on imports under its safeguards arrangements; the CANADA-UNITED STATES FREE TRADE AGREEMENT and the NORTH AMERICAN FREE TRADE AGREEMENT also permit some import restrictions on a temporary basis to deal with a surge in imports. Canada's SUPPLY MANAGEMENT system restricts the import of chickens, turkeys, eggs, and milk and dairy products.

import duty   See TARIFF.

import leakage   The proportion of purchasing power in a country that is spent on imports rather than on domestically made goods and services. When a government implements tax cuts or adopts other measures to boost domestic purchasing power and create more jobs, the extent to which the extra income is spent on imports — the leakage — will reduce the full impact of the tax cuts or other measures designed to increase domestic demand.

import licence   A licence issued by the federal government to allow an importer to bring into the country a specified quantity of goods that meet specified standards. Normally, an import licence is not required, but it may be if the imported good is subject to an import quota, strict health standards, or some other restriction. See also EXPORT AND IMPORT PERMITS ACT.

import penetration   The extent to which imports supply the domestic market.

import-price index   A Statistics Canada monthly index of changes in import prices published as part of the *Summary of Canadian International Trade* (publication number 65-001). See also TERMS OF TRADE.

import quota   A limit on the amount of a commodity, product, or class of product that can be imported during a specified period of time. Canada, for example, imposes quotas or negotiates export-restraint agreements for imports of textiles, clothing, shoes, electronic products, and other goods. See also MULTIFIBRE ARRANGEMENT, SUPPLY MANAGEMENT. Import quotas raise prices for consumers; they are designed to encourage domestic production by guaranteeing domestic firms protection against strong import competition and ensuring domestic producers of a fixed portion of the total market.

import restrictions   Any kind of measure that limits imports. Examples include artificially high import valuations by customs officials, import quotas, government purchasing policies that favour domestic companies, or health, engineering, safety, and other standards designed to limit imports. See also NON-TARIFF BARRIERS.

import substitution   A strategy for economic development in which a country attempts to develop its industrial base by erecting high barriers against imports to encourage domestic companies to produce the products previously imported. Canada's NATIONAL POLICY was in large part a policy of import substitution. This is the development path chosen by some developing countries, such as India and, until the late 1980s, by many Latin American countries such as Mexico and Brazil. Other countries, such as South Korea and China, have pursued export-led growth; Mexico has now shifted to this strategy.

import surcharge An additional, temporary tariff imposed on top of existing tariffs to reduce imports and thus help correct a major BALANCE OF PAYMENTS deficit. The INTERNATIONAL MONETARY FUND permits member-countries to impose a surcharge on a temporary basis for that purpose. Canada imposed import surcharges during its 1947 and 1962 foreign-exchange crises, as did the United States in its 1971 balance-of-payments crisis. In November, 1947, under the Emergency Foreign Exchange Conservation Act, Canada imposed high excise taxes on a wide range of goods from the United States, including autos, cameras, appliances, bicycles, motorcycles, outboard motors, and cosmetics; the taxes were lifted at the end of July, 1948. In June 1962, Canada imposed temporary surcharges ranging from 5 to 15 percent on about one-half of Canada's imports; the surcharges were lifted by April 1, 1963. During the same period, Canada also reduced the duty-free allowance for travellers overseas by two-thirds and for travellers to the United States by three-quarters.

import valuation The estimated value of a product for import-duty purposes. Import valuation can be a matter of dispute. A foreign subsidiary in Canada importing parts and components from its parent firm may be charged a TRANSFER PRICE by its parent that is lower than its market value so as to avoid full payment of customs duties. Import valuation can also be used as a NON-TARIFF BARRIER when a country imposes an artificially high value on imports for import-duty purposes.

imports Goods and services that are produced in one country but consumed in another. Canada, for example, imports many of the products and services it uses from the United States or other countries. Imports increase the range of choice available to consumers and lead to lower prices by increasing competition. However, a country must also export in order to pay for its imports, otherwise, it either is forced to sell off its assets to pay for the imports or it accumulates a foreign debt that must be repaid. Figures on Canada's merchandise imports are published monthly by Statistics Canada (publication 65-001); figures on Canada's imports of goods and services are published in Statistics Canada's quarterly reports on the balance of payments (publication 67-001).

impulse buying A spur-of-the-moment purchase, usually motivated by packaging or design, resulting from a consumer seeing the product on display. This kind of consumer purchase helps to explain the large investments some consumer-goods companies make in appealing packaging and design.

imputed cost The cost to an owner of using an asset instead of deriving income from it. For example, the owner of a business that owns its own commercial or factory space could earn rent if it did not use the space itself. That income is imputed income and is the OPPORTUNITY COST to the business of using the commercial or factory space itself.

imputed income   The estimated value of non-money income, such as the food a farmer grows and consumes directly, free board and meals for employees, the personal use of a company car, or other employee non-money benefits. Some forms of imputed income are taxed; they are treated as TAXABLE BENE-FITS. Some forms of imputed income, such as IMPUTED RENT, are also included in the GROSS DOMESTIC PRODUCT.

imputed rent   An estimate of the benefits a homeowner receives, after allowing for maintenance, financing, and other costs, from living in his or her own home; it is similar to the rent a landlord would receive if the landlord owned and rented out the building, though no actual cash outlay occurs. In its calculation of GROSS DOMESTIC EXPENDITURE, Statistics Canada makes a calculation for imputed rent in its estimate of consumer spending on services; in its calculation of GROSS DOMESTIC PRODUCT, it includes an estimate of imputed rent in the net income of non-farm unincorporated businesses.

in kind   Payment in goods or services, as opposed to money.

in situ recovery   When used in reference to the OIL SANDS, the recovery of the oil without having to engage in open-pit mining of the sands. Heat techniques and steam pressure are used to extract the oil.

incentive   A reward system to encourage someone to do something. For example, if the government wants the public to save more, it can make interest on savings income-tax free; if it wants people to conserve energy by buying smaller cars or insulating their homes, it can reduce the sales tax on smaller cars or raise it on larger cars or let people deduct the cost of insulation from their income tax; if it wants industry to speed up investment plans, it can introduce an INVESTMENT TAX CREDIT; if it wants industry to increase research and development, it can let industry write off the costs at a faster rate. There are many different ways the tax system can be used, as a carrot or a stick, to provide incentives. Direct grants can also be used as incentives. Likewise, companies can provide an incentive for employees through pay increases based on merit, rewards for employee suggestions, commissions on sales, and profit sharing. In marketing, companies may offer consumers an incentive to purchase through, for example, reduced or zero interest for a temporary period or if a payment is made before a certain date, a discount, a chance to win a prize, or an extended warranty.

incidence of taxation   The person who ultimately pays a particular tax. Many taxes can be shifted from the person or corporation on whom they are levied — backward on to suppliers or forward on to consumers. For example, corporate income taxes are passed forward to consumers in the prices that corporations charge. Similarly, the excise tax and duty on tobacco products are included in consumer prices, as are alcohol taxes. However, if competition is intense, then a corporation may have to bear the tax itself, squeezing its own profit margin.

income   **1.** The money and other benefits flowing to individuals, firms, and other groups in the economy from the various FACTORS OF PRODUCTION. Income accrues from the returns to labour in the form of wages and salaries, from the returns to capital in the form of INTEREST and dividends, from the returns to land and intellectual property in the form of RENT or ROYALTIES, and from the returns to entrepreneurship in the form of PROFIT. Income also includes TRANSFER PAYMENTS to individuals from government. *See also* PERSONAL INCOME. **2.** For an individual, money income and taxable benefits, such as the use of a company car, from all sources before the payment of taxes. In a corporation, net income is a synonym for profits. **3.** In tax theory, any increase in the command of an individual over goods and services. Thus income would include spending on goods and services and increases in net worth arising from all sources, including CAPITAL GAINS, BEQUESTS, and LOTTERY winnings. *See also* PERSONAL INCOME TAX, CORPORATE INCOME TAX.

income averaging A method of reducing the income-tax liability for lump-sum or windfall payments by spreading out the tax liability over a number of years. Otherwise, the taxpayer would have to pay a higher share of this income in taxes in the tax year in which it was received, leaving less of the money for personel use in subsequent years, even though the taxpayer might be counting on this income for use over several years. Since 1972, athletes, entertainers, film producers, and musicians receiving a large payment; individuals getting lump-sum payments from pension plans or stock-option benefits; or others getting large payments from profits on the sale of a private business or from other sources, have been able to reduce their tax liability by buying an income-averaging annuity. All the money is paid into the annuity, and the individual is taxed only on the money received from the annuity each year. The amount of money must be the same each year; the annuity can be for a fixed number of years or for life.

income distribution 1. The share of total income in society that goes to each fifth or quintile of the population. Between 1981 and 1991, the share of the top 20 percent or quintile of the Canadian population rose from 41.7 percent of total income to 43.8 percent, while the share of the bottom 20 percent or quintile rose from 4.6 percent to 4.7 percent of total income in Canada; the share of the bottom two quintiles, representing 40 percent of Canadians, fell from 15.5 percent in 1981 to 15 percent in 1991. Statistics Canada publishes an annual review of income distribution in its report, *Income Distributions by Size in Canada* (publication 13-207), which is based on a survey of about 41,000 households — either economic family units consisting of groups of individuals related by marriage, blood, or adoption or unattached individuals. Total income includes wages and salaries, net income from self-employment, investment income, pensions, miscellaneous income such as alimony, and government transfer payments such as unemployment insurance, social welfare, and payments to seniors. Transfer payments from government accounted for 63.4 percent of the income of the lowest quintile in 1991 and 13.4 percent of total income of all Canadians. Total income does not include income in kind, such as assisted housing or free health and dental care. *See also* INCOME INEQUALITY, INCOME REDISTRIBUTION. **2.** The distribution of national income between the various FACTORS OF PRODUCTION; for example, the share of national income represented by wages and salaries or by corporate profits. *See also* POVERTY LINE.

income effect The change in a person's purchasing power, resulting from a change in the price a person has to pay for a good or service. If, for example, a consumer has to pay a higher price for a particular good, this has the effect of reducing that consumer's total purchasing power or income available for other goods and services. This change will affect the range of goods and services the person can buy. The effect will depend on whether there are substitutes, the size of the price increase or decrease, and how essential certain goods or services may be. Likewise, if the price of a particular good falls, the consumer now has additional purchasing power that can be used to acquire other goods or services. A tax increase or reduction has the same income effects as the change in the price of another good or service. A similar effect occurs with an increase in real wages: the higher the real wage, the greater the amount of leisure that can be afforded.

income elasticity of demand The extent to which the demand for a product responds to a change in income. Demand is income inelastic when the demand for a product increases at a lower rate than an increase in income; most necessities of life are income inelastic. Demand is income elastic when demand for the product increases at a higher rate than an increase in income; many consumer products are income elastic. To determine the income elasticity of demand, divide the percentage increase in demand by the percentage increase in income. If the result is less than one, demand is inelastic; if the result is greater than one, demand is elastic.

income inequality Differences in income among individuals, groups of individuals, or regions. Differences may be due to differences in property wealth, including inherited wealth; in personal ability; in education and training; in opportunity, including social connection; in family support; or in age and health, or may simply be the result of bad luck. One of the purposes of the income-tax system, based on ability to

pay, is to redistribute income and thus to reduce inequality. *See also* INCOME REDISTRIBUTION.

income-maintenance   programs Programs that provide cash payments to individuals to raise their income to some minimum level — above the POVERTY LINE, for example, or to a minimum subsistence level, or up to a minimum comfort level. Examples include UNEMPLOYMENT INSUR-ANCE, social assistance from provincial and municipal governments, the GUARANTEED-INCOME SUPPLE-MENT for senior citizens, OLD-AGE SECURITY PENSION, the spouse's allowance, the CHILD BENEFIT, and WORKER'S COMPENSATION.

income redistribution Policies to reduce INCOME INEQUALITY. The income-tax system is one means of redistributing income, since it collects proportionately more taxes from those with higher incomes and enables society to provide social assistance and free or low-cost public services, such as health care, education, and subsidized housing, to those with low incomes. Taxes on wealth or capital, including inherited wealth, can also help to redistribute income and reduce great inequalities in wealth in society. Tax policies, the provision of essential services such as housing and health care at little or no cost, and transfer payments to individuals, all help to redistribute income. *See also* NEGATIVE INCOME TAX.

income security programs Federal and provincial programs to ensure Canadians receive a minimum level of income; some programs provide temporary support until recipients can obtain employment or upgrade their skills for better-paying jobs, while others are permanent, such as those for seniors. Examples include the OLD-AGE SECURITY PENSION, GUARAN-

TEED INCOME SUPPLEMENT, and spouse's allowance for seniors; the CHILD BENEFIT for children in low-income families; the CANADA ASSISTANCE PLAN and provincial add-ons for families and individuals; and unemployment insurance for unemployed workers.

income statement *See* EARNINGS STATEMENT.

income tax A tax levied on the income of individuals and corporations. The tax is levied on taxable income — that is, on the income remaining after allowable tax deductions. Under the CONSTITUTION ACT, 1867, both the federal and provincial governments can levy an income tax. In the case of PERSONAL INCOME TAX, all the provinces except Quebec have a tax rate that is a percentage of the basic federal tax, and that is collected for them by the federal government; Quebec has its own personal income-tax system and collects the tax directly from Quebec residents. In the case of CORPORATE INCOME TAX, the provinces levy a tax that is a percent of taxable corporate income as established under the federal Income Tax Act, and that is collected by the federal government for all of the provinces except Ontario, Quebec, and Alberta, which collect their own corporate income taxes. Federal income tax was introduced in Canada in 1917, through the Income War Tax Act, as what was expected to be a temporary tax to help finance the costs of the First World War; some provinces, though, had imposed a corporate income tax at the turn of the century. The word "war" was not dropped from the title of the legislation until 1947, when it became simply the Income Tax Act. Income-tax revenues today account for close to 60 percent of budgetary revenues: about 50 percent from personal income taxes, and about 7 percent from corporate income tax. Canada's income-tax system underwent major revisions in 1972 and 1988, but perhaps the most far-reaching change, in terms of revenues, was the 1974 move to index personal income-tax deductions and rates. One of the most controversial questions in personal income-tax systems is the definition of income. Ideally, the definition might include actual spending by an individual during the course of a year on goods and services, and increases in net worth. However, the income-tax system deals largely with current income. *See also* ROYAL COMMISSION ON TAXATION, TAX EXPENDITURES. Income-tax rates or the value of various deductions or credits can be changed as part of fiscal policy to raise or lower the level of AGGREGATE DEMAND in the economy. A reduction of income taxes increases personal spending power in the economy, for example. The income-tax system can also be used to encourage certain types of behaviour or activity; for example, the deduction for investments in REGISTERED RETIREMENT SAVINGS PLANS (RRSP) encourages Canadians to save for retirement, while tax incentives for research and development encourage Canadian companies to invest in the development of new products. Likewise, the tax system can be used to deliver social benefits, such as the CHILD BENEFIT.

Personal taxable income is defined in the Income Tax Act and the tax levied is based on the rate schedule also set out in the legislation. Provinces, aside from Quebec, levy their personal income tax as a percentage of the basic federal tax. Income includes wages and salaries and certain taxable benefits, such as the use of a company car or the subsidy element of a low-interest company loan; income of self-employed and unincorporated businesses; interest and dividends; capital gains on the sale of shares or property; and other sources of income, such as the federal OLD-AGE SECURITY PENSION, which is subject to a special tax or clawback.

Lottery winnings, gifts, and inheritances are not counted as income, nor are social-assistance and workmen's compensation payments, although they must be reported. Some income taxes can be deferred; for example, taxes on income saved through registered pension plans, RRSPs and deferred profit-sharing plans. The principal deductions from income, aside from those permitted for pension plan and RRSP contributions, include child-care expenses, union dues, and professional association fees. Each taxpayer receives a non-refundable tax credit and, in addition, there is a non-refundable tax credit for a spouse, for children, for seniors over the age of 65, and for disabled Canadians. There is also a DIVIDEND TAX CREDIT for investors in shares of Canadian companies. In the 1992 tax year, the federal marginal tax rate róse from 17 percent on the first $29,590 of taxable income to 29 percent on taxable income in excess of $59,179. The federal tax payable is subject to a 3 percent surcharge. In 1992, the provincial income tax ranged from 64.5 percent of the basic federal tax in Newfoundland to 46 percent in Alberta. Since 1973, both the marginal tax rate and the basic exemptions and credits have been indexed to the CONSUMER PRICE INDEX. Since 1986, the indexation has been limited to increases in the consumer price index above three percentage points. See also CAPITAL GAINS TAX. The federal corporate income tax is levied much the same way as the personal income tax. Corporations report all sources of income, deduct permitted expenses, defer some taxes under provisions for CAPITAL-COST ALLOWANCES or depreciation, include capital gains and losses, calculate earned tax credits for activities such as research and development, and pay taxes on taxable corporate income. In 1992, the basic federal corporate income-tax rate was 28 percent for general business, 22 percent for profits from manufacturing and processing, and 12 percent on the first $200,000 of active business income of Canadian-controlled private corporations. A 3 percent surtax was levied on federal corporate income tax payable. The federal government provides a tax credit of 10 percent of corporate taxable income earned in each province or territory to make room for the provinces or territories to levy their own corporate income tax.

incomes policy Government policies to limit the growth of income, such as wages, salaries, profits, dividends, and rents, in order to help reduce or restrain the rate of inflation. Examples of incomes policies include wage and price controls, a wage and price freeze, voluntary wage and price guidelines, tax-based incomes policies that tax away excessive wage or profit increases or reward workers and companies abiding by guidelines, and consensus agreements by government, business, and labour on wage and price restraints. Incomes policies are used to deal with COST-PUSH INFLATION rather than DEMAND-PULL INFLATION. They have two effects: they can curb actual income increases, and they can alter expectations of future inflation, reducing the demand for big wage, price, and rent' increases. Proponents of incomes policies argue that they can reduce the cost of fighting inflation, in the form of higher unemployment and increased business failures, by ameliorating the need for extended monetary and fiscal restraint.

Canada imposed an incomes policy in the Second World War (see WARTIME PRICES AND TRADE BOARD). Since the mid-1960s, Canada has reviewed and implemented various forms of incomes policy. In its third annual review in 1966, the Economic Council of Canada concluded that "a formal incomes policy would not be an effective way of meeting the problem in Canada, except possibly under rare emergency conditions and then only on a temporary basis." In its 1966 annual report, the Bank of Canada hinted at the need for an incomes policy. A 1968 federal government white paper, Policies for Price Stability, recommended the creation of a commission on prices and incomes to "discover the facts, analyze the causes, processes, and consequences of inflation, and to inform the public and the government on how price stability might be achieved." In 1969, the PRICES AND INCOMES COMMISSION was established, and in 1970, it implemented a program of voluntary price and profit guidelines, including a 6 percent wage and salary target. The commission was wound up in 1972. In its concluding report, *Summary Report: Inflation, Unemployment and Incomes Policy*, the commission blamed Canada's inflation problems on inflationary expectations resulting from a prolonged period of inflation running through the 1960s. "In effect, an 'inflation factor' appears to be incorporated, implicitly if not explicitly, in the setting of wages and prices and in the level of interest rates." In 1973, the federal government created the FOOD PRICES REVIEW BOARD. In 1975, full wage and price controls were imposed through the ANTI-INFLATION BOARD (AIB). The controls ran until the end of 1978 and the AIB was succeeded by the CENTRE FOR THE STUDY OF INFLATION AND PRODUCTIVITY. In March, 1979, the centre was replaced by the NATIONAL COMMISSION ON INFLATION; it was abolished in July, 1979. In 1982, another exercise in incomes policy was introduced with the SIX AND FIVE PROGRAM, which limited federal government pay and all indexation except for the guaranteed-income supplement and veterans' pensions to six percent through to the end of July, 1982, and to five percent in the following year. The Six and Five Program was wound up on January 1, 1985.

incorporation The legal steps taken by an individual or group of individuals to obtain a charter from the federal or provincial government to establish and operate a LIMITED-LIABILITY company. If the application is granted, a charter is issued in the form of LETTERS PATENT or articles of incorporation. Some companies have been created by a special act of Parliament or a provincial legislature — telephone companies, for example, some railways, and, for many years, chartered banks. The rules governing incorporation of companies are set out in federal and provincial CORPORATION LAW.

increasing costs Costs that rise for each unit of output as the volume of production increases. At some point in the production process, the average cost per unit of output begins to rise instead of continuing to decline. This can be due to production putting additional strain on the assembly line, the increased costs of overtime for labour, or the increased difficulty in extracting a natural resource. As pressure in a natural-gas or oilfield declines after much production, for example, more expensive recovery methods become necessary. *See also* LAW OF DIMINISHING RETURNS.

increasing returns The circumstances in which the application of an additional FACTOR OF PRODUCTION yields progressively greater increases in output. At some point in production, DIMINISHING RETURNS set in. *See also* ECONOMIES OF SCALE. In new theories of economic growth, however, investment in ideas (research and development, scientific knowledge, intellectual property) are believed to yield ever-increasing returns.

increment A small increase either in costs or in income.

indemnity Payment for damages. Some life-insurance policies carry a double-indemnity clause, which doubles the insurance paid in the event of death in certain types of accidents, such as an air crash.

independent union A union that has no affiliation with a national or international labour congress or organization.

index A figure used in statistics to show average values and their percentage change over a period of time, with the change being measured from a base period. For example, if the CONSUMER PRICE INDEX is 130.5 and the base year is 1986, then 1986 equals 100 and consumer prices are 30.5 percent higher than they were in 1986. Any year, month, or week can be a base period; it is made equal to 100 and the percentage change in whatever is being measured is calculated from that point. The consumer price index is an average value of consumer prices for many different products, with the different products being weighted according to their importance in the household budget. Statistics Canada produces many useful indexes, such as an employment index. And a price index for new housing, in addition to the monthly consumer price index. Major stock exchanges also produce indexes showing the average change of prices on a daily basis. *See also* TORONTO STOCK-EXCHANGE INDICES.

index of industrial production A monthly index published by the ORGANIZATION FOR ECONOMIC CO-OPERATION AND DEVELOPMENT (OECD) in its publication *Main Economic Indicators* for OECD member countries, including Canada. It shows changes in the volume of output by the mining, oil and gas, manufacturing, and utility industries.

index of leading indicators A monthly composite index of leading indicators published by Statistics Canada in the *Canadian Economic Observer* (publication 11-010). The 10 components are retail sales of furniture and appliances; retail sales of other durable goods; the housing-outlays index; the U.S. composite leading index; the shipments to inventory ratio for finished goods in manufacturing industries; new orders for durable goods; the average number of hours worked per week in manufacturing; employment in business and personal services; the TSE 300 composite stock-price index; and changes in M-1 money supply.

indexation The automatic adjustment of pensions, wages, social-assistance benefits, and income-tax rates for the full or partial effects of inflation to ensure that there is no — or only partial — decline in the real purchasing power of these payments as a result of inflation. Canada's income-tax system has been indexed since January 1, 1974; the basic exemptions and the rate schedule are adjusted for inflation so that taxpayers are not pushed into higher tax brackets as their pay goes up, unless they have had a real increase in their income. From 1974 to 1982, indexation of the tax system was based on the average inflation rate for the 12 months ending in October of the previous year. In 1983 and 1984, it was subject to the Six and Five Program under federal INCOMES POLICY. In 1985, the system reverted to full indexation. Since 1986, indexation has been allowed only for inflation in excess of 3 percent. Many social benefits have also been indexed, including OLD AGE SECURITY PENSION, the GUARANTEED-INCOME SUPPLEMENT, and various tax and social benefits for children. *See also* COLA CLAUSE.

Indian Act The principal federal legislation setting out the federal government's relationship with the Indian and Inuit peoples of Canada, and in particular the management of reserve lands and funds; its relationship with aboriginal local government; and the status of Indians. The CONSTITUTION ACT, 1867, gives the federal government legal jurisdiction over "Indians and Lands reserved for the Indians." In 1939, the Supreme Court of Canada extended this to include Canada's Inuit population. Aboriginal legislation pre-dates Confederation; the first Indian Act was passed in 1876; the present law dates back to 1951, but it was amended in 1985 to restore the status of Indian women who had married non-Indian men and of their children.

Indian Affairs and Northern Development, Department of   The federal department responsible for the federal government's relationships with Indian and Inuit citizens; northern economic development, including oil, gas, and other mineral development; the environmental protection of the land and waters north of the 60th parallel; and the federal government's responsibilities in the Yukon and Northwest Territories. The current department was established in 1966. It administers the Indian Act, which sets out its legal obligations to Canada's aboriginal peoples; assists the economic development of aboriginal communities, including skills development and the formation of new businesses; negotiates the settlement of Indian and Inuit land claims; and assists the evolution of aboriginal self-government. In Calgary, the department operates Indian Oil and Gas Canada, which is responsible for promoting oil and gas exploration, development, and production on reserves. The department also administers the lands and the natural resources of lands and waters north of the 60th parallel, funds scientific research in the northern environment, supports the economic development of

northern communities, and is in charge of transfer payments to the Yukon and Northwest Territories. In addition to the Indian Act, it administers the Arctic Waters Pollution Prevention Act and the Canada Petroleum Resources Act, as well as other legislation.

Indian Claims Commission   An independent body established by the federal government in 1991 to inquire into and report on disputes between the First Nations and the federal government over claims based on treaties, agreements, or administrative actions. The commission, which is based in Ottawa, is mandated to conduct impartial inquiries where a First Nation disputes the federal government's rejection of a specific claim or where a First Nation disagrees with the compensation criteria used by the federal government in negotiating settlement of a claim. Claims arising from alleged violations of treaties or other aboriginal rights are divided into two categories: specific and comprehensive. Specific claims are those arising from existing government obligations under treaties, agreements, or statutes, while comprehensive claims are those based on aboriginal land claims where there is no existing treaty. The Indian Claims Commission deals only with disputes arising out of specific claims. Before the creation of the Commission, First Nations could not challenge government decisions about specific claims without going to court.

indicative planning   A form of government planning in which targets are set for the economy and for individual industries and economic sectors. These targets may be set by the government alone, or by the government in consultation with industry and labour. Indicative planning is usually voluntary, but it may include fairly strong pressure by government, along with incentives, to see that the targets are met. French industrial recovery and modernization after the Second World War was aided by extremely detailed indicative planning.

indicators Economic statistics that are used for economic analysis and forecasts. STATISTICS CANADA, the BANK OF CANADA, and some specialized government departments are the principal sources of economic indicators. Statistics Canada publishes a wide range of LEADING, LAGGING, and COINCIDENT INDICATORS. It also publishes monthly the CANADIAN COMPOSITE LEADING INDICATOR, an index based on 1981 = 100, which is based on furniture and appliance sales, other durable goods sales, a housing index, new manufacturing orders for durables, a shipment to manufacturing ratio for finished goods, the length in hours of the average manufacturing work week, business and personal services employment, the U.S. composite leading index, the TSE 300 stock-price index, and changes in the M-1 money supply in 1981 dollars (published in *The Daily Bulletin*, publication 11-001, and *The Canadian Economic Observer*, publication 11-010).

indifference curve The representation on a graph of all the various combinations of goods and services that yield a consumer the same degree of satisfaction. It is used with a budget line, which shows the various combinations of goods and services that can be purchased by a consumer with a given amount of income and prices.

indirect cost Any expense in a business that cannot be identified with a specific part of the production process. The cost is divided by the number of units produced and an equal portion is added to the price of each unit of output. It includes property taxes, rent, property maintenance, and administrative costs; it is a synonym for overhead.

indirect tax A tax that is levied on goods and services and not on the final consumer of a good or service, and which is collected and forwarded to the government by the seller. However, indirect taxes are almost always ultimately paid by the final consumer in the price of the good or service; in other words, it is a tax that can be shifted on to someone else. Indirect taxes include customs duties and excise taxes. Under the CONSTITUTION ACT, 1867, indirect taxation is the exclusive preserve of the federal government. One reason for this is that the Fathers of Confederation wanted Canada to be a single market; they feared that, if the provinces were allowed to impose indirect taxes, they would use them as barriers to trade from other provinces. Indirect taxes are not the major source of revenue today, but, until the First World War, they provided almost all of federal revenues. *See also* DIRECT TAX.

induced consumption The increase in consumer spending that results from new capital investment. An increase in capital investment leads to a rise in employment and incomes earned in the construction, machinery, and related industries, which in turn has a MULTIPLIER effect on other industries, including consumer goods and services. Thus, an investment-led recovery can stimulate consumer spending.

induced investment The increase in capital investment that results from an increase in spending by consumers. As consumer spending rises, industry approaches its productive capacity or sees the opportunity to introduce new products. A consumer-spending-led recovery can stimulate additional capital investment.

industrial assistance programs Federal and provincial programs to assist industrial growth, aid industries that need to modernize, or promote research and development. Examples of these programs include loan guarantees or subsidized financing, managerial counselling and assistance, export financing, trade missions, and direct grants. The shipbuilding and textile industries, for example, have benefited from industrial assistance programs.

Industrial Defence Board An advisory body created by the federal government in April, 1948, to advise the cabinet on the industrial war potential of Canada, to maintain a plan for wartime industrial production, and to work with the Canadian armed forces and defence and resource industries. It included senior government officials and business executives, and worked closely with its U.S. counterpart, the National Security Resources Board. Its activities were absorbed into the CANADA-UNITED STATES DEFENCE PRODUCTION SHARING ARRANGEMENT and other Canada-U.S. liason activities including the North America Industrial Base Organization, led by the Department of National Defence, and coordinated within Canada by the Industrial Coordination Committee in The Department of INDUSTRY, SCIENCE, AND TECHNOLOGY.

industrial democracy The participation by employees in the management and decision making of the firm or organization for which they work. It can include anything from job-safety councils to freedom for employees to organize their working hours or patterns, so long as they maintain a specified production level, to the compulsory establishment of labour-management committees within an organization and the seating of employee representatives on the boards of directors of a firm; in Germany and Sweden, for example, employees are entitled to membership on the boards of directors of companies. While industrial democracy is well advanced in some European countries, such as Germany and Sweden, for the most part, Canadian unions have resisted forms of industrial democracy, and have emphasized collective bargaining instead, while Canadian business has also resisted the notion of giving its employees much voice in the affairs of companies, citing the threat to what it calls the rights of management. However, the growing interest in TOTAL QUALITY MANAGEMENT is forcing business to give more freedom to employees to organize their work and to make decisions when dealing with customers.

industrial development corporations Public corporations established by the federal and provincial governments to assist industrial development. They provide low-interest loans, direct grants, equity participation, industrial parks, negotiated energy rates, local tax concessions, leaseback, and other assistance, to attract industry and thus to create jobs. Examples include Alberta Opportunity Company, the B.C. Development Corporation, the New Brunswick Industrial Development Board, Newfoundland and Labrador Enterprise, the Ontario Development Corporation, Prince Edward Island's Business Development Agency, the Quebec Industrial Development Corporation, Manitoba's Communities Economic Development Fund, the Saskatchewan Economic Development Corporation, the Nova-Scotia Business Development Corporation, and the CAPE BRETON DEVELOPMENT CORPORATION.

industrial dispute A STRIKE, LOCKOUT, slowdown, WORK-TO-RULE, or any other quarrel between a union and employer that results in a reduction or stoppage of work. The Department of LABOUR publishes monthly statistics on strikes and lockouts in Canada.

industrial espionage Underhanded efforts by one company to learn the commercial secrets, such as design changes, investment plans, marketing strategies, or new product plans, of a competitor. These efforts range from the hiring away of key employees and wiretapping, to flying over drilling sights, theft, and bribery. Many of these techniques are illegal.

industrial organization A specialized area of economics that deals with the structure of an industry and the behaviour of individual firms within that industry. It studies factors affecting the ownership of the industry, industrial performance, mergers, pricing policy, innovation, oligopoly and monopoly, trade practices, and profits.

industrial policy Programs adopted by government to promote the growth and competitiveness of companies and workers. In a modern economy in which ideas, innovation, and knowledge are the driving forces, governments can play an important role by, for example, providing strong incentives for research and development, building up the knowledge and human-resource base through investments in education and basic research, facilitating the diffusion of technology to industry, sharing the risk with industry in developing pre-competitive or generic technologies and in commercializing new technologies, spurring competition, finding ways to encourage private-sector lending and investment for industrial upgrading and new technologies, opening foreign markets and supporting exports, encouraging training in industry and retraining of unemployed workers, stimulating the growth of small and medium-size companies that produce tradeable goods and services, creating market-launch opportunities through government procurement, establishing crown corporations or entering into joint ventures as equity partners with private-sector companies to pursue new opportunities, and promoting a culture based on innovation and partnerships within the economy.

industrial products price index A monthly price index produced by Statistics Canada (publication 62-011), with 1986 = 100; it measures the prices of manufactured goods as they leave the factory, and represents about a quarter of the prices in the economy.

industrial psychology The field of psychology concerned with the management of people, on-the-job relations among people or between people and machines, the psychological needs of workers and their career objectives, personnel policies — including hiring, training, and appraisal — and work practices and productivity.

industrial relations *See* LABOUR RELATIONS.

industrial strategy A set of policies to strengthen the competitive position of a country's manufacturing and tradeable service industries. An industrial strategy may target certain industrial sectors or critical technologies as vital to a country's economic future. Although the term is often greeted with horror by economists, almost every country has an explicit or implicit industrial strategy, even if the strategy is simply to rely on free markets, free trade, and competition. The real debate is over what kind of industrial strategy to pursue. *See also* INDUSTRIAL POLICY.

industrial targeting A selective industrial strategy of picking certain key industries for development.

industrial union A union that represents all or almost all of the employees in a particular firm or industry, regardless of job or level of skill; it is sometimes called a vertical union. Examples include the unions in the steel and pulp and paper industries and in the public service. *See also* CRAFT UNION.

industrialization   The process of transforming an agricultural and cottage-industry economy into one in which production is centred on manufacturing and organized in factories by utilizing new technology and mechanization to achieve ECONOMIES OF SCALE. Industrialization brings with it major changes in the way society is organized and in the relations among different groups in society. It gives new importance to managers and engineers and creates a large class of wage-earners. *See also* POST-INDUSTRIAL SOCIETY. Many of the world's LESS-DEVELOPED COUNTRIES are currently pursuing industrialization in order to raise their standard of living, thereby creating new competition for the industries of Canada and other advanced industrial countries, many of which are responding through INDUSTRIAL POLICY to create new high-value industries as they are displaced from clothing, auto parts, consumer electronics, and light manufacturing. Industrialization today also has to cope with environmental constraints and the demands of SUSTAINABLE DEVELOPMENT.

industry   A producer of tradeable goods or services. The term can refer to a single firm, or collectively to all producers in a nation, or all producers of a particular product or service (for example, the oil industry, the trucking industry, the mining industry, the manufacturing industry, the steel industry, the auto industry, or the aviation industry). A separate term, "commerce," is sometimes used to describe banking, retailing, and other financial and retail or wholesale activities. *See*

STANDARD INDUSTRIAL CLASSIFICATION.

Industry, Science and Technology, Department of (ISTC)   The federal government department responsible for improving Canada's international competitiveness through industrial policies, and strengthening the research base of Canadian universities and the support of Canadian small business; it is also responsible for tourism promotion. The department has three ministers: the Minister of Industry, Science and Technology, the Minister of Science, and the Minister of State for Small Business and Tourism. The department was reorganized into its present structure in 1990; until 1982, when it was known as the Department of Industry, Trade and Commerce, it also had responsibility for international trade. From 1982 until 1990, it was the Department of Regional Industrial Expansion; the Ministry of State for Science and Technology was a separate department. Its mandate since 1990 has included the development and use of science and technology; the elimination of interprovincial barriers within Canada; entrepreneurship and the growth of small business; tourism; investment in Canadian industry; and economic development programs for Canada's aboriginal population. Its divisions include a policy division that formulates policy in trade, entrepreneurship, small business, and industrial competitiveness; Tourism Canada, which promotes tourism from other countries and tourism by Canadians within their own country; a capital goods and service industries division, which works with the auto, urban transit, rail, industrial and electrical equipment, services and construction, aeronautics, defence electronics, space, shipbuilding, and marine and land defence-system industries; the industry, technology and regional operations division, which works with the environmental, information, forest, materials, chemicals, biotechnology, forest-products and consumer-products industries; the science and technology division, which is responsible for science and technology strategy and strengthening the university research base; the aboriginal economic programs division; and the Prosperity Secretariat, a federal consultative task force appointed by the federal government in 1991 to advise on competitiveness policies. The department is responsible for the CANADIAN SPACE AGENCY, the NATIONAL RESEARCH COUNCIL, the FEDERAL BUSINESS DEVELOPMENT BANK, INVESTMENT CANADA, the NATURAL SCIENCE AND ENGINEERING RESEARCH COUNCIL, the NATIONAL ADVISORY BOARD ON SCIENCE AND TECHNOLOGY, the SMALL BUSINESS LOANS ACT, STATISTICS CANADA, ECONOMIC AND REGIONAL DEVELOPMENT AGREEMENTS with Ontario and Quebec, and the CAPE BRETON DEVELOPMENT CORPORATION.

industry-wide bargaining   Collective bargaining in which all the unions and employers in an industry negotiate a uniform contract. It can be nation-wide or province-wide, or it can cover only a metropolitan area. The goal is to avoid a multiplicity of strikes occurring in different parts of the year in the same industry. In Canada, the various railway unions negotiate at the same time with the railway companies. Industry-wide bargaining also occurs in the pulp and paper industry and in the construction industry in some regions or provinces.

inedible end product   A term used by STATISTICS CANADA in export and import statistics to describe non-food manufactured products.

inelastic demand   Demand that shows little change as a result of a price change. An increase in price will not reduce demand by much; a reduction in price will not increase demand by much. The demand for life's necessities is inelastic: for example, no matter how much producers lower the price of sugar or bread, it is unlikely that they can increase the demand very much; even with an increase in price, consumers will continue to buy the product unless the price rise is significant and persistant and there is a ready and acceptable substitute (tea instead of coffee or chicken instead of beef, for example). *See also* ELASTICITY OF DEMAND.

inelastic supply   Supply that shows little change as a result of a price change. An increase in the price will not increase the supply by very much; a reduction in the price will not reduce the supply by very much.

infant industry   A new and underdeveloped industry that is said to be capable of establishing itself and becoming competitive against international corporations if given the chance to develop to a size sufficient to achieve ECONOMIES OF SCALE and its own technology. Temporary protection through high tariffs, government procurement or other barriers, and subsidies or incentives to keep out foreign competition are sometimes used to help develop an infant industry. Initially, this forces consumers to pay higher prices, but, in theory, once the industry becomes efficient, the high-tariff protection will no longer be necessary and consumers will benefit through lower prices, while the country will benefit through the creation of a new competitive industry and the wealth and employment it brings. The view that new industries should be protected by high tariffs until they have established themselves in their own market was popular in the 19th century. Sir John A. Macdonald used the argument of infant industries to justify high tariffs as part of his NATIONAL POLICY following Confederation. Countries such as Japan and South Korea have developed their high-technology industries by pursuing infant-industry strategies.

infant-mortality rate The number of infant deaths per thousand live births in a given year.

inferior good A good whose consumption falls as the income of consumers rises. As their incomes rise, consumers will switch from bologna and macaroni to ham and steaks. *See also* INCOME ELASTICITY OF DEMAND.

inflation A persistent rise in the price of goods, services, and factors of production over an extended period of time, as measured by a price index such as the CONSUMER PRICE INDEX or the GROSS-DOMESTIC-PRODUCT DEFLATOR; it is the percentage change in the price index. Inflation reduces the purchasing power of the dollar or any other unit of money, and tends to redistribute income from those with savings or those on fixed incomes to those who owe money or have sufficient bargaining power in the economy to raise their prices, wages, or professional fees above the rate of inflation. A high inflation rate can also lead to speculative investments rather than investments in new productive capacity and lead to a loss of competitiveness in international markets as UNIT LABOUR COSTS rise faster than those of competitors. Monetary authorities give a high priority to achieving low inflation and price stability, arguing that protecting the value of money is the best contribution they can make to economic growth. Inflation can come from a price shock, such as a sudden increase in oil or other commodity prices, or can be of a more persistent nature, resulting from budgetary deficits and excess demand in the economy, monopoly power, structural barriers or bottlenecks, and inflationary expectations. There are various types of inflation. In its 1991 budget, the federal government and the Bank of Canada jointly set inflation targets of year-over-year increases in the consumer price index at 3 percent at the end of 1992, 2.5 percent at mid-1994, and 2 percent at the end of 1995, with the goal of lowering inflation expectations and providing greater confidence in stable prices for investment. *See also* COST-PUSH INFLATION, DEMAND-PULL INFLATION, STRUCTURAL INFLATION, ZERO INFLATION, HYPERINFLATION, PRICE INDEXES, and INCOMES POLICY.

inflation accounting The recalculation of a company's financial statements to show the effects of inflation on the company's assets and earnings. In a period of prolonged and high inflation, real profits are overstated, while the replacement costs of plant, of machinery and equipment, and of inventories are understated; this also means that depreciation deductions, based on historic costs, are too low to replace assets as they wear out. The result is a misleading presentation of a company's real financial performance. This is particularly true in the case of CAPITAL-INTENSIVE INDUSTRIES such as steel, petrochemicals, and pulp and paper. In inflation accounting, BALANCE SHEET items such as plant, machinery and equipment, and inventories, which are carried at historical cost, are adjusted either for the general rate of inflation since they were acquired or are revalued in terms of their current replacement cost. This means that on the INCOME STATEMENT, figures for both the cost of goods sold and depreciation must also be increased to reflect the changes made in the balance sheet.

The result is either a smaller profit or perhaps even a loss. Rising profits in a period of strong inflation are often called paper profits.

inflation tax The capital losses suffered by investors in money and money-based assets such as bonds as a result of inflation.

inflationary expectations The belief that inflation is going to continue and will probably get worse; if this belief becomes entrenched it leads firms and unions to reflect it in their behaviour and build future inflation into their prices and wage demands. One of the goals of anti-inflation policy is to change expectations and behaviour.

inflationary gap The extent to which planned investment in the economy exceeds the savings available under full-employment conditions. The result is inflation, since the demand for goods and services will exceed the available supply, thus bidding up prices for the available goods and services. The government response usually is to curb consumption through tax and interest-rate increases and other dampening measures.

inflationary spiral A persistent increase in the rate of inflation resulting from efforts by labour, business, and investors to gain higher returns in response to rising prices, thereby creating a vicious circle of rising prices and rising wages and other input costs. This rivalry among different groups leads to a self-reinforcing upward push on prices. Business seeks to raise or maintain its share of the GROSS DOMESTIC PRODUCT by raising prices to boost profits; labour responds by demanding higher wages, which in turn are passed on in the form of still higher prices. As the inflation spiral takes root, expectations of increased inflation lead various groups in the economy to build these expectations into their price and wage demands, thus accelerating the inflation process. *See also* COST-PUSH INFLATION, INCOMES POLICY.

information circular A report distributed to shareholders of a corporation in advance of a shareholders' meeting that sets out the matters to be dealt with at the meeting.

infrastructure The basic capital assets of a country; these assets are important to industrial development and economic growth. Infrastructure includes roads and highways, electric-power systems, airports, water-supply systems, railways, telecommunications systems, serviced land for industry and housing, sewage systems, urban transit, and other such facilities. Since the health and education of the workforce is important in economic development, investment in hospitals, schools, universities, and the like are also a part of infrastructure. Infrastructure investment facilitates economic growth in a variety of ways: airports connect a region to the rest of the world; competitive telecommunications systems lower the communications costs and allow new services for companies operating in national and international markets; efficient highways reduce the time needed to transport goods and lower the wear and tear on truck fleets; urban transit systems allow greater mobility of workers; adequate water supplies permit the growth of food-processing and other industries; and reliable power supplies allow industries to operate without having to worry about sudden power outages.

inheritance tax *See* SUCCESSION DUTY, GIFT TAX.

injury A benchmark used by domestic trade agencies, such as the CANADIAN INTERNATIONAL TRADE TRIBUNAL, to determine whether ANTI-DUMPING or COUNTERVAILING DUTIES should be levied on imports. Proof of injury or the threat of injury is required if trade penalties are to be levied. Indicators of injury include a fall in output or sales, a loss of market share, falling profits, increased unemployment, plant shutdowns, and a declining return on investment.

initial established reserves Reserves of oil or natural gas that can be produced with current technology and at current prices prior to the start of production. *See also* ESTABLISHED RESERVES.

initial payment In the western grains industry, the payment the federal cabinet authorizes the CANADIAN WHEAT BOARD to make at the start of the CROP YEAR to grain farmers. Handling costs at local grain elevators and transportation costs to Thunder Bay or to West Coast ports are deducted, which gives farmers their guaranteed floor price. If the wheat board is unable to recover this price in world grain markets, the deficit is paid by the federal government. *See also* FINAL PAYMENT.

initial volume in place The total volume of crude oil, tar sands, heavy oil, and raw natural gas calculated to exist in a reservoir before any volume has been produced.

injunction A court order that requires certain things either to be done or not to be done. In labour relations, it is a court order telling an employer or union to do or not to do something. An employer in a strike, for example, may seek an injunction ordering a union to reduce the scale of its picketing. An ex parte injunction is one in which the party affected is absent during the application hearing. An interim injunction is one that prohibits something

from happening until another action has been completed — the sale of goods whose ownership is in dispute in a trial, for example.

Innis, Harold A. (1894-1952) Canada's leading economic historian. Innis explained the growth and settlement of Canada and the development of its political, cultural, and financial institutions in terms of the exploitation of successive commodities or staples for export markets. This is the so-called STAPLE THEORY of Canadian development. In Innis's view, a new country — New France and, later, Canada — had to grow by serving as a supplier of commodities to the much more highly specialized and developed economies of older nations. This emphasis on commodities, in turn, determined where communities would be located, the role of government in maintaining the economic system (through support for transportation, for example), the types of jobs that would exist, the nature of social relationships, and many other aspects of life.

Innis first outlined his theory of Canadian development in 1930 in his book *The Fur Trade in Canada: An Introduction to Canadian Economic History*. He showed how the fur trade, based on the demand of Europeans for beaver fur and the need of Indians for manufactured goods, spread settlements and transportation links through the interconnected lakes and rivers of central Canada. Innis demonstrated that through the fur trade and through the economic development of fish, timber, wheat, and minerals, Canada grew as a country because of its geography and not in spite of it, as so many economic and political historians had maintained. In other words, there was an east-west unity to the country, as development spread from the St. Lawrence system westward, along the Canadian Pacific Railway to the wheat economy. This development, especially its importance in ensuing transportation links, helped to account for the active role of government in the Canadian economy.

Other works by Innis expanded on or reinforced the staple theory. See, for example, *Problems of Staple Production in Canada* (1933), *Settlement and the Mining Frontier* (1936), and *The Cod Fisheries* (1940). Later in his career, Innis became fascinated by the role of communications in developing and shaping civilization. He wrote *Political Economy in the Modern State* (1946), *Empire and Communications* (1950), *The Bias of Communication* (1951), and *Changing Concepts of Time* (1952). Innis was a major figure in Canadian intellectual history, and spent most of his career at the University of Toronto.

innovation   The use of a new idea, material, or technology by an industry or company to produce new goods or services or to change the way in which goods or services are produced or distributed. *See also* INVENTION, which is the actual discovery of something new; innovation is the application of something new. Innovation can include improved managerial systems, new production techniques, new technology, the industrial results of research and development, or the application of information technologies to a business. Joseph Schumpeter (1883-1950), who wrote *The Theory of Economic Development* (1934) and *Capitalism, Socialism, and Democracy* (1942), regarded the innovator as the crucial figure in capitalism. He also argued that only big corporations could afford to bear the risks and make the capital investments necessary for innovation. Since the emergence of the information economy however, based on information technologies, it has become evident that small and medium-size businesses have a key role to play in innovation. Some economists, such as Paul Romer, an American economist who is also a fellow of the CANADIAN INSTITUTE FOR ADVANCED RESEARCH, argue that economic growth depends primarily on a society's ability to generate ideas, or to innovate, and that economic progress depends not only on technological innovation but also institutional innovation. Therefore, innovation is vital in a dynamic economy and raises the standard of living through constant gains in productivity. *See also* RESEARCH AND DEVELOPMENT.

input   A factor — land, labour, capital, know-how — used in the production process to obtain output in the form of goods and services.

input-output analysis   The branch of economics that analyzes the relationships between changes in output in particular industries and the effect those changes have on the output of other industries. Input-output tables are composed with horizontal columns listing inputs and vertical tables listing outputs. In Canada, the flow of goods and services between different industries is published annually by Statistics Canada in *The Input-Output Structure of the Canadian Economy* (publication 15-201).

Input-output analysis is an important tool for economists because it itemizes the production of an industry or the economy and analyzes the raw materials, parts, and components that production will require from other industries. By developing descriptions of such relationships, it is possible to calculate in detail the industrial impact of an increase or a reduction in demand for a product, such as motor vehicles. Input-output analysis for the automobile industry will show, for example, how much steel, plastics, glass, carpeting, or electrical wiring is needed to produce a specific number of cars. Similarly, it is possible to determine how much steel will be needed in a given year by adding up the steel demand of key users, assuming certain levels of output, such as the auto, construction, aircraft, pipeline, electrical, and other industries. In turn, it is possible to calculate how much iron ore, coal, and energy will be needed to produce the estimated level of steel required. Input-output analysis is also part of the system of NATIONAL ACCOUNTS. The total of all the inputs must equal the total of all the outputs. Input-output analysis was developed by the U.S. economist WASSILY LEONTIEF. It is a highly refined tool of analysis today because computer systems can be used to collect and manipulate data.

Inquiry into the Collapse of the Canadian Commercial Bank and the Northland Bank An inquiry ordered by the federal government in 1985 to look into the causes of the collapse of two chartered banks and the role played by regulators. The inquiry was headed by Supreme Court of Canada Justice Willard Estey, who was also asked to make recommendations on ways to improve the regulation of Canadian banks to prevent a recurrence of bank failures. In its 1986 report, the Estey Commission blamed bank management, directors, and auditors, along with regulators, for the bank failures, charging that all had failed to adequately carry out their responsibilities. It charged that bank management, in addition to reckless lending policies, issued false financial statements that overstated the value of its loans and bank profitability. The auditors were criticized for accepting financial statements that did not meet banking-industry standards or accurately portray the true financial position of the two banks. The directors of the two banks were criticized for failing to carry out their responsibilities of monitoring the performance of management; instead, they left all policy direction and decision

making to the senior management of the two banks. The regulators also came under criticism for failing to assess the loan portfolio and for failing to support the banks' auditors when they finally did challenge management. The Estey Commission was particularly critical of the Inspector-General of Banks; it charged he had complete knowledge of the situation but, despite this, had failed to intervene. The Estey Commission recommended that the regulatory process be tightened, with the Office of the Inspector-General of Banks merged with the CANADA DEPOSIT INSURANCE CORPORATION to improve supervision of the banking system. Instead, in 1987, the federal government established the OFFICE OF THE SUPERINTENDENT OF FINANCIAL INSTITUTIONS. Depositors in the two banks were compensated for their losses but shareholders lost their equity.

insider Any senior company officer, director, or shareholder owning more than 10 percent of the shares of a company, or any other person who may have access to information about a company's affairs or prospects that is not generally available to ordinary shareholders or to members of the public. The possession of inside information may permit an insider, for example, to sell a company's shares before an unexpected loss is announced to the public, or to buy additional shares before the announcement of an exceptional profit or a takeover bid. For this reason, federal and provincial laws restrict the right of insiders to buy and sell shares, either directly or indirectly, through a relative, partner, or associate company, and require insiders to report regularly all changes in their holdings of a company's shares. Insiders are usually defined as all directors of a corporation, all senior officers (including the chairman, vice-chairman, president, vice-presidents, secretary, treasurer, and general manager), the five highest paid officers of the company, and anyone owning or controlling more than 10 percent of the voting shares of the company. Insiders may also include directors and senior officers of another company that has more than 10 percent of the voting shares of the company concerned. Federal law also includes directors and senior officers of subsidiary companies as insiders.

insider report A report, published monthly by provincial securities commissions, of any changes in total holdings of shares in a company by an INSIDER. Initial filings must be made by anyone within 10 days of becoming an insider, showing direct and indirect ownership of shares in the company. Any subsequent changes in those holdings must be reported as they occur. The purpose of such reports is to inform shareholders and the public of the trading activities in the company by its directors and senior officers. Failure by an insider to make a timely or accurate report is an offence punishable by provincial law.

insider trading The buying and selling of shares by INSIDERS of a company by making illegal use of confidential or privileged information. An insider who makes use of confidential information to trade in shares directly or through relatives or partners before the information is made public can be sued and forced to compensate anyone for direct losses suffered, as well as being forced to return the profit to the company. There are also restrictions on insider trading during takeover bids.

insolvency The inability of a company, individual, or government to repay debts when they become due. This does not mean the company is necessarily bankrupt. Insolvency occurs when liabilities exceed assets. *See also* BANKRUPTCY.

Inspector-General of Banks The federal office that, until 1987, monitored the activities of the chartered banks incorporated under the BANK ACT, and other banks incorporated under the Quebec Savings Bank Act, to ensure that they were in a sound financial position and that they were acting within the terms and conditions set out under banking laws. The office was created after the failure of the Home Bank in 1923; a total of nine banks had failed or had their charters repealed between 1900 and 1923. In 1987, following the report of the INQUIRY INTO THE COLLAPSE OF THE CANADIAN COMMERCIAL BANK AND THE NORTHLAND BANK, a new OFFICE OF THE SUPERINTENDENT OF FINANCIAL INSTITUTIONS was created.

installment credit A form of consumer credit in which the consumer makes regular repayments of equal amounts on specified dates, where each payment includes interest and principal. This form of credit is used to purchase automobiles, electrical appliances, furniture, and other major CONSUMER GOODS, with a downpayment frequently being required as part of the agreement.

installment receipts A new issue of stock purchased by investors through a series of payments instead of a single or lump-sum payment.

Institute for Research on Public Policy (IRPP) A national non-profit research institute incorporated in 1972 that began operation in 1974. It is funded by the federal government, the provincial governments, and private industry. The institute sponsors research studies on a wide range of public-policy issues. In 1993, its main areas of research included social policy reform, the effectiveness of Canada's system of governance, a reassessment of learning, the emergence of new city-regions, and the environment and SUSTAINABLE DEVELOPMENT. Its headquarters are in Montreal.

institutional investor   A financial organization, such as a PENSION FUND, INSURANCE company, or MUTUAL FUND, that manages a portfolio of bonds, shares and other securities, and other assets such as real estate, and has a steady flow of money to invest. Institutional investors are another form of financial intermediary: insurance companies invest premiums they receive from policy holders, pension fund organizations invest the contributions they receive from employers and employees, and mutual fund organizations invest the savings they receive from investors. Banks and trust companies are also institutional investors since they operate mutual funds and sell REGISTERED RETIREMENT SAVINGS PLAN units to the public. The role of institutional investors is to invest these funds to generate future flows of income. Institutional investors have become the main buyers and sellers on stock exchanges and are major buyers and sellers in bond and mortgage markets as well. While such investors can influence prices on a stock exchange, they tend not to exercise any direct influence in the companies whose shares they buy; instead, they act as passive investors.

instrument   A document: for example, a PROMISSORY NOTE, or the legal document incorporating a company. A negotiable instrument is a promissory note or other debt instrument that can be signed over to another party.

insurance   A contractual arrangement under which an insurer will provide protection against risk in return for payment of a premium. Insurance is a way of spreading risk since, for most

forms of insurance aside from life, most of those insured never have cause to collect, so that their premiums pay for those who do suffer losses. Premiums are based on risk so that they are sufficient to pay future claims, cover the operating profit of an insurance company, and yield a profit. Almost any kind of risk can be protected against by an insurance company. The most common forms of insurance policy are those for the loss of life, disability, theft, accident and sickness, fire, and automobile accidents. The insurance company provides compensation to make up for the loss or damages. Insurance companies use the premium income as investment capital from which future claims are paid; the types of investments they can make are regulated — for example, under the Canadian and British Insurance Companies Act. The OFFICE OF THE SUPERINTENDENT OF FINANCIAL INSTITUTIONS regulates the activities of insurance companies and reports to Parliament through the Minister of Finance. *See also* LIFE INSURANCE, CASUALTY INSURANCE, NO-FAULT AUTOMOBILE INSURANCE.

insurance agent   A person who arranges insurance coverage by acting as a middleman or intermediary between clients who have a great variety of insurance needs and different insurance companies who offer a range of specialized coverage. This person either acts as an agent on behalf of particular insurance companies or seeks out the best available price and policy for clients. The agent is paid commissions by the insurance companies. Agents also handle claims arising from the insurance contracts they have arranged.

Insurance, Department of   The federal government department that, until 1987, administered laws applying to federally incorporated insurance, trust, loan, and investment companies; foreign insurance companies operating in Canada; certain pension funds; small loan companies; licensed moneylenders; co-operative credit societies operating under the Co-operative Credit Associations Act; and provincially incorporated insurance companies registered with the department. One of the most important roles of the department was to ensure that the financial institutions it monitored complied with federal regulations intended to ensure their financial soundness. The department was set up in 1910; for the previous 25 years, it had been a branch of the Department of Finance. In 1987, it was replaced by the OFFICE OF THE SUPERINTENDENT OF FINANCIAL INSTITUTIONS.

intangible assets   Assets that are nonphysical, which means they cannot be touched or measured. They include patents, trademarks, franchises, goodwill, and copyright. They are essential to the operation of a business and, while they have a money value, they are hard to value, and are usually included as miscellaneous items on a BALANCE SHEET at only nominal value — say, at one dollar.

integrated oil company   An oil company that is active in all the different areas of the oil industry, from oil exploration and development, production, and refining to distribution and marketing, including the operation of gasoline stations. It participates in both UPSTREAM and DOWNSTREAM activities.

integration   **1.** Increasing ties that bind the economies of different countries together. For example, the integration of the Canadian and U.S. economies can result from growing trade and the progressive reduction of tariffs, the construction of energy-supply systems that cross the border, the tendency to harmonize economic policies, and the increasing linkages between the banking systems and the financial markets of the two countries, along with special bilateral arrangements worked out in tax treaties, trade agreements, exemptions (such as Canada's exemption from the U.S. INTEREST-EQUALIZATION TAX), and a dependence on each other for travel and tourism business. See also CANADA-UNITED STATES FREE TRADE AGREEMENT, the NORTH AMERICAN FREE TRADE AGREEMENT. **2.** The extent to which a company organizes the different stages of production either internally or at ARM'S LENGTH. See also VERTICAL INTEGRATION, HORIZONTAL INTEGRATION.

intellectual property   The ownership of ideas, creations, inventions, designs, and trade names. Intellectual property consists of PATENTS, TRADEMARKS, and industrial designs, or of creations, such as literary, musical, and artistic works or computer software, which are protected by COPYRIGHT. Laws governing intellectual property can have an important impact on the rate of innovation in an economy; inventors, designers, authors, film makers, and entrepreneurs are likely to be more active if the economic benefits of what they create are protected and adequately rewarded with royalties or other payments. In Canada, laws dealing with intellectual property are the responsibility of the Department of CONSUMER AND CORPORATE AFFAIRS. International protection is co-ordinated through the WORLD INTELLECTUAL PROPERTY ORGANIZATION. In addition, protection of intellectual property rights is becoming an important part of trade agreements, including the NORTH AMERICAN FREE TRADE AGREEMENT and the URUGUAY ROUND.

Intellectual Property Board (IPT)   A board established to replace the COPYRIGHT BOARD and the Trademarks

Opposition Board, announced in the 1992 federal budget and passed in 1993. The IPT will fix royalties, which performing rights societies or collectives may collect in return for granting licences for the performance of dramatic or musical works. It will also decide how royalties should be divided, including royalties on the retransmission of TV and radio signals. In addition, the IPT will adjudicate disputes over the copyright royalties to be paid. It will decide opposition and cancellation proceedings arising under the Trademarks Act. The IPT has a chairperson, vice-chairperson, and up to six members.

intensive cultivation The use of modern agricultural methods to increase yields from land. These methods include the application of chemical fertilizers and pesticides, mechanized agricultural equipment, new seed varieties, and highly trained farm labour.

Inter-American Development Bank (IDB) A regional development bank established in 1959 that provides loans and other assistance to countries in Latin America and the Caribbean. The bank has its headquarters in Washington. Canada became a member in 1972 and at the end of 1992, had 4.39 percent of the votes. It had contributed US$142.1 million in ordinary capital and committed for US$2.24 billion of callable capital. It has also contributed US$262 million to the Fund for Special Operations, the soft window of the bank. In 1986, the IDB established an affiliate, the Inter-American Investment Corporation, to encourage the growth of private-sector corporations in Latin America and the Caribbean. Canada is not a participant.

interbank market The money market serving the banking industry, in which banks borrow or lend to one another. The interest charged is the interbank

offer rate and the rate for deposits is the intermarket bid rate.

Intergovernmental Council of Copper-Exporting Countries A commodity group established in 1968 to co-operate in raising prices for copper producers. Canada is not a member though it is an important copper exporter. Members include Chile, Indonesia, Peru, Zaire, and Zambia; Australia is an associate member. The organization is based in France.

Inter-Governmental Maritime Consultative Organization A United Nations organization formed in 1959 to combat ocean and coastline pollution and to promote safety at sea. Canada, with its long coastline, has been an active member from the start. One of the organization's major concerns is the intentional or accidental discharge of oil and other pollutants at sea.

interindustry competition Competition among companies in different industries where there is a high degree of substitution for their products. For example, the steel, plastics, and aluminum industries compete with one another as suppliers of materials for auto bodies. Soft-drink, mineral-water, iced-tea, and wine and beer companies compete for summertime beverage sales. Poured-concrete, steel, brick, and glass companies compete in providing building materials for apartment and office towers. Interindustry competition can also occur in the pursuit of consumer sales — the travel industry, the summer-cottage industry, stockbrokers, financial institutions selling investment certificates and retirement plans, and encyclopedia salespeople, are all competing with one another for discretionary consumer spending.

interdependence The mutual dependence that exists among individuals, communities, and regions of a country, or among different countries in the world. For example, in the world economy, the MACROECONOMIC policies adopted in a large country, such as the United States, Germany, or Japan, will almost inevitably have an impact on the economies of the other countries. Trade and investment also lead to greater interdependence. No nation makes everything its consumers consume; indeed, with increasing specialization, nations are becoming even more dependent on one another. Canada, for example, depends on semiconductor production in other countries for key inputs into its own manufactured products, which it in turn may export. Likewise, investment decisions by multinational corporations link economies together as different subsidiaries around the world fulfill specialized functions. Similarly, events in one part of the world can have a major impact on countries that are far away; for example, a crop failure or crop surplus in Russia or China has quite different implications for the prices Western farmers receive for their grain and the volume of grain shipments, while a military confrontation in the Middle East will influence prices and profits of oil and gas companies in Alberta. Citizens in a country or nations around the world have a common stake in the functioning of their economic systems. Industrial countries are dependent on Saudi Arabia for their oil, for example, but the Saudis are dependent on a stable Western economy, so they can safely invest their PETRODOLLARS, and on Western industry to supply the industrial goods they need to modernize their economy and meet their health and INFRASTRUCTURE needs. Similarly, Quebec is dependent on a healthy economy in Ontario, while Ontario manufacturers need a growing market in Quebec. Canadian prosperity, in turn, depends on economic growth in the United States, Europe,

and Japan, and on the smooth functioning of the world monetary system. Interdependence is a characteristic of modern economic life. *See also* GLOBALIZATION.

interest The price paid by a borrower for the temporary use of someone else's money or, conversely, the price charged by a lender for the temporary use by someone else of his money. It is expressed as a percentage of the amount borrowed or lent; this is the INTEREST RATE. Individuals pay interest on their mortgages and consumer loans, and on the unpaid balances on their credit cards; they earn interest on their savings bonds, bank accounts, GUARANTEED-INVESTMENT CERTIFICATES, and REGISTERED RETIREMENT SAVINGS PLANS. Businesses pay interest on their corporate bonds, INVENTORY, working-capital loans, MORTGAGES, sales financing, and other debts, while earning interest on their cash balances and other financial assets. Governments pay interest on their BONDS and TREASURY BILLS. *See also* BANK RATE, PRIME RATE.

interest arbitrage The purchase of foreign short-term financial assets, such as TREASURY BILLS, in order to earn a higher rate of interest.

interest capitalization The conversion of unpaid interest on a loan to the principal that must be repaid when the loan matures.

interest cover The number of times that the earnings of a company exceed the interest costs on its outstanding long-term debt. This indicates the extent to which a company could experience a fall in earnings and still be able to meet its interest obligations.

interest futures A means of speculating or HEDGING on short-term and long-term interest rates. Investors can buy futures contracts on the Chicago Board of Trade and Mercantile Exchange for U.S. treasury bills and U.S. government mortgages. *See also* FUTURES MARKET.

interest-equalization tax   A U.S. tax levied from 1963 to 1974 on the interest and dividends earned by U.S. citizens, financial institutions, and corporations on foreign bonds, shares, short-term financial paper, and other such investments. Its purpose was to halt the flow of U.S. funds abroad because U.S. interest rates were lower than foreign interest rates. The tax, which was announced on July 18, 1963, underlined Canada's strong dependence on U.S. capital markets when it sparked a crisis in Canadian financial markets. Canada obtained an exemption, announced on July 23, but there was the implied threat that, if Canadian borrowing increased over traditional levels, the exemption would be lifted. Canada also had to agree not to increase the level of its foreign-exchange reserves through the proceeds of new U.S. borrowing. This ceiling imposed a strong need on the BANK OF CANADA to monitor Canadian foreign borrowing, and, in some cases, to ask would-be borrowers to use the Canadian market instead.

The interest-equalization tax consisted of a 15 percent tax on purchases by Americans of shares in foreign corporations, and a tax, ranging from 2.75 percent on short-term securities to 15 percent on long-term bonds, on interest paid to Americans on new loans they made to non-residents. New FOREIGN DIRECT INVESTMENT by U.S. corporations was excluded. The new tax led to a plunge in Canadian financial markets and a sharp decline in the Canadian dollar when it was first announced, since it would have almost completely barred Canadian borrowers from using U.S. financial markets. The U.S. government agreed to a condition-al exemption for Canada, which turned the market around; the U.S. Congress made a number of other changes in the tax to benefit Canada, before passing it in 1964.

In 1966, Canada announced co-operation with new U.S. controls on foreign investment by U.S. corporations, which had been announced late in 1965, in order to maintain exemption from the interest-equalization tax. Canadian investors were asked not to buy securities issued by U.S. corporations or their non-Canadian subsidiaries that would be subject to the tax if purchased by Americans; this was to prevent Canada from being used as a pass-through by Americans trying to avoid the tax. It was feared, for example, that Canadians might buy such securities and then turn to U.S. capital markets for additional borrowing. A more serious problem with the U.S. guidelines, however, was that U.S. multinationals were asked to reduce the funds they transferred to their foreign subsidiaries, including their Canadian subsidiaries. Depending on decisions made by U.S. parent companies, funds for Canadian subsidiaries could be cut back much more than the overall global reduction, thus shifting the subsidiaries' requirements to Canadian financial institutions. Such a shift, in turn, could crowd out higher-risk Canadian borrowers on Canadian financial markets.

In 1968, the U.S. guidelines were made mandatory, and U.S. multinationals were also ordered to increase the repatriation of earnings from their foreign subsidiaries, including those in Canada. With such a high level of U.S. ownership of Canadian industry, such policies could have caused serious damage to the Canadian economy. This was reflected in the Canadian-dollar crisis in early 1968; eventually, Canada obtained an exemption from the U.S. guidelines for non-financial corporations, and, at the end of 1968, the

United States lifted its ceiling on Canada's foreign-exchange reserves, which had been imposed in 1963 in exchange for an exemption for the interest-equalization tax.

One result of the U.S. policies was that Canadian borrowers began to make more use of the EUROCURRENCY MARKET. On January 29, 1974, the United States announced that it was terminating its guidelines on foreign investment and the interest-equalization tax. The next day, Canada discontinued the guidelines it had imposed to prevent Canada being used as a pass-through by U.S. investors.

interest rate The price charged for the use of someone else's money. The interest rate, in effect, reflects the terms and conditions under which money or goods today are traded off for money or goods at some future date. According to classical economic theory, the interest rate is influenced both by the supply of loanable funds and the demand for loanable funds. If interest rates are high, the supply will increase and the demand fall; likewise, if interest rates are low, the demand will increase but the supply may fall. But there are other factors, so that the demand for loanable funds is also influenced by the expectations of business for future sales and profits, while the supply of loanable funds is also influenced by the willingness of individuals to defer consumption today for future consumption. Other economists argue that the interest rate is based largely on monetary conditions. Monetary authorities can influence SHORT-TERM INTEREST RATES through MONEY SUPPLY and the conduct of monetary policy. See BANK RATE. However, long-term interest rates are more dependent on the market, where investors make assessments about levels of risk having to do with a borrower's creditworthiness and the currency in which a loan is made, as well as the extent to which their portfolio is already invested in a particular borrower's debt. *see also* BOND MARKET. The key interest rates in Canada are the bank rate, the PRIME RATE, and the yield on long-term Government of Canada bonds.

interest-rate spread In a financial institution, the difference between the interest paid on deposits and the interest charged on loans. The term also refers to the difference in the level of interest rates between two countries — for example, the difference between interest rates in Canada and in the United States.

interest rate swap An exchange between two parties of interest-bearing securities, one of which has a fixed rate of interest and the other a floating rate that may be pegged to the PRIME RATE or to LIBOR.

Interim Committee A committee of 22 finance ministers established in 1974 to advise the INTERNATIONAL MONETARY FUND (IMF) on the management and evolution of the international monetary system, and to deal with problems in the system. The committee meets twice a year, in advance of the annual meeting of the IMF, usually in September, and at a mid-year point, usually in April. The membership reflects the membership of the IMF's Executive Board. Canada has been a member from the start, and the first chairman of the Interim Committee was a Canadian, then-Finance Minister John Turner. The chairmanship of the committee always goes to an industrial nation.

interim statement A financial statement published by a public company for its shareholders, showing semiannual or quarterly financial results, including earnings per share. Such statements, unlike a company's annual report, are not usually audited by the company's outside auditors. Its purpose is to give shareholders a progress report on how the company is doing; it is not intended as a complete financial accounting.

interlisted share A share in a company that is listed on more than one stock exchange. Many important Canadian companies are listed on the Toronto, Vancouver, and Montreal stock exchanges. Some large Canadian companies are also listed on U.S. stock exchanges, such as the New York or American Stock Exchanges, or on NASDAQ, and some blue-chip American corporations are listed on the TORONTO STOCK EXCHANGE. A few Canadian companies are also listed on overseas stock markets such as the London Stock Exchange and the Tokyo Stock Exchange. When a share is listed on more than one exchange, there is sometimes an opportunity to make a profit through ARBITRAGE.

interlocking directorate The situation that exists when a person sits on the board of directors of two or more companies that may compete with one another, or have a business relationship with one another that can give rise to a conflict of interest. The public concern is that interlocking directorates may reduce competition or lead to a conflict of interest. The BANK ACT also has provisions to deal with SELF-DEALING.

intermediate good A good used in the production of another good, as opposed to a final good, which is ready for consumption by a consumer. All the parts and components that go into the production of a television set, along with the machinery used in the manufacture of the television set, are intermediate goods; the television set is a final good. Intermediate goods are not counted in the calculation of the GROSS DOMES-

TIC PRODUCT; their value is accounted for in the value of final goods.

intermediation The vital role in the economy of financial institutions that serve as middlemen between savers and borrowers. Intermediation is the act of accepting deposits, on which interest is paid, and making loans, on which interest is charged. The key financial intermediaries are banks, trust companies, credit unions, and caisses populaires. However, INSTITUTIONAL INVESTORS are also intermediaries in that they take insurance premiums, pension-plan contributions, and mutual-fund sales and invest these to generate future flows of income for their clients.

internal audit A review or audit of the financial accounts of a company or other organization by its own accounting staff, as opposed to an annual audit conducted by an outside accounting firm to verify the accuracy of the accounts. Boards of directors of corporations usually establish an internal audit committee of the board to monitor the activities of a company.

internal financing The financing of a company's investments from its RETAINED EARNINGS instead of from increased borrowing or the issue of new shares.

internal migration The movement of people from one region of Canada to another, from one province to another, or from rural to urban society. Statistics Canada publishes a variety of figures showing internal migration in Canada in the annual publication, *Report on the Demographic Situation in Canada* (publication 91-209E).

internal rate of return The inflation-adjusted real rate of interest earned on a proposed investment. To proceed, the proposal should at least earn the COST

OF CAPITAL plus a minimum level of profit commensurate with the risk.

International Air Transport Association (IATA) The international organization that represents scheduled airline companies. Based in Geneva today, it was established in 1945 by an Act of the Canadian Parliament; it still maintains an office in Montreal. The two main functions of IATA are to co-ordinate tariffs, to act as a clearinghouse for international flights to determine what portion of an airfare goes to each airline, and to accredit travel agencies that meet IATA standards. Air Canada and Canadian Airlines International are members.

International Atomic Energy Agency (IAEA) An international organization affiliated with the United Nations, set up in 1957 in Vienna to promote the peaceful use of atomic energy, in particular the use of nuclear power, under controlled and safe conditions. Canada has been a member of its board of governors from the start, due to its important role in the world nuclear industry. Under the terms of the 1968 Treaty for the Non-Proliferation of Nuclear Weapons, the IAEA inspects nuclear-sales agreements to individual nations to make sure that the facilities cannot be used for possible military purposes. It inspects individual nuclear facilities to make sure that the safeguards set out under the treaty are being complied with. The IAEA also conducts research into the peaceful uses of atomic energy and into nuclear safety and the disposal of nuclear wastes.

International Bank for Reconstruction and Development (IBRD) *See* WORLD BANK.

international banking The operation of bank branches and subsidiaries by Canadian banks outside of Canada for trading in foreign exchange, providing finance for international trade, and managing correspondent banking relationships between Canadian and foreign banks.

International Bauxite Association (IBA) A cartel of bauxite-producing nations set up in 1974 to get higher prices for bauxite-alumina, and to discourage competitive price-cutting by members. The founding members were Australia, Guinea, Guyana, Jamaica, Sierra Leone, Surinam, and the former Yugoslavia. Since then, the Dominican Republic, Ghana, Haiti, and Indonesia have joined. IBA members account for about 65 percent of world bauxite production. The principal activity of member-nations has been to increase state ownership of bauxite reserves and to raise substantially the tax and royalty revenues from bauxite production. The members have also explored methods of increasing processing and manufacturing in the resource countries. The secretariat is in Kingston, Jamaica.

International Chamber of Commerce A Paris-based association of chambers of commerce from many different countries, including Canada, which promotes international trade in goods and services and the free flow of investment. It also promotes the free-market economy system, based on competitive private enterprise, and fosters the economic growth of developing and developed countries. The chamber represents the private sector internationally, for example, at the United Nations and its agencies, and other specialized agencies such as the GENERAL AGREEMENT ON TARIFFS AND TRADE. The chamber also is active in a number of technical areas to facilitate international trade, such as standardizing documentation used in international trade. The chamber was established in 1919, and Canada has been a long-time member. Canadian business is represented through the CANADIAN COUNCIL FOR INTERNATIONAL BUSINESS. The International Bureau of Chambers of Commerce is an adjunct to the International Chamber of Commerce, and the CANADIAN CHAMBER OF COMMERCE is a member.

International Civil Aviation Organization (ICAO) A United Nations agency, with headquarters in Montreal, concerned with the growth and safety of international civil aviation. Its activities include international agreements on the conditions under which aircraft fly over another nation's territory, safety standards and procedures, arrangements under which all nations can share in the growth of civil aviation, and the compilation of statistics on civil aviation. The agency was formally established in 1947 after 26 nations, including Canada, approved a Convention on International Civil Aviation. It has about 130 members today, with a governing council of 30 nations, including Canada.

international commodity agreement *See* COMMODITY AGREEMENT.

international competitiveness The extent to which a country such as Canada can compete in international trade while also achieving a rising standard of living. Countries compete through specialization, by controlling costs and using the best available systems of production to be price competitive, and by investing in innovation to produce new or distinctive products or services. *See also* UNIT LABOUR COSTS. Each year the World Economic Forum publishes a World Competitiveness Report, assessing the competitiveness of industrial and key developing nations in a variety of areas, from political and financial stability to the quality of labour and management relations, the capacity for innovation, and the quality of education.

International Confederation of Free Trade Unions (ICFTU) An international association of trade unions formed in 1949 by a number of national trade-union congresses, including the CANADIAN LABOUR CONGRESS (CLC). It was formed as an alternative to the World Federation of Trade Unions, a largely Communist organization formed in 1945. ICFTU supports efforts to strengthen free unions in countries where they are weak or almost non-existent, and also attempts to achieve some co-operation among unions from different countries in dealing with the spread of MULTINATIONAL CORPORATIONS. In particular, it is concerned about efforts by multinationals to move out of countries with strong unions and labour laws to countries with weak unions and weak labour laws. Canada has played an important role in the organization; in 1972, a CLC president, Donald Macdonald, became the organization's first president from outside Europe. The AMERICAN FEDERATION OF LABOUR-CONGRESS ON INDUSTRIAL ORGANIZATION (AFL-CIO) of the United States withdrew in 1969 because it objected to the number of contacts by British and German unions with unions in Communist nations. The AFL-C1O returned to the ICFTU over the objections of the CLC, which charged the U.S. body with being an agent for U.S. foreign policy. The headquarters of the ICFTU are in Brussels.

International Convention for the High Seas Fisheries of the North Pacific Ocean An agreement between Canada, the United States, and Japan, to manage the fisheries of the high seas of the North Pacific to get the maximum sustainable production, and to implement conservation procedures that will ensure the long-term availability of fish. The agreement is also important to Canada because the practices followed in the high seas affect the level of salmon and other fish within Canadian coastal waters. The International North Pacific Fisheries Commission, which administers the convention, is located in New Westminster, British Columbia. Canada signed the convention in 1952.

International Convention on Dumping Wastes at Sea   An international agreement to help protect the oceans by regulating the manner in which ships may dispose of garbage and other wastes at sea. It was negotiated in 1972, following the United Nations Conference on the Environment in Stockholm. Canada has signed the convention and is an active supporter of measures to enforce it.

International Court of Justice   An international court organized within the United Nations System in 1945, replacing the Permanent Court of International Justice that was established by the League of Nations in 1920. It deals with disputes arising from the United Nations charter or treaties or other agreements between nations. Litigants before the court are sovereign nations.

International Development Association (IDA)   An affiliate of the WORLD BANK, formed in 1960, which gives loans at little or no interest to the poorest of the LESS-DEVELOPED COUNTRIES, mainly those with annual per capita incomes of less than US$400. The IDA loans are long-term loans and are usually made for INFRASTRUC-TURE projects, such as roads, hospitals, and schools, as well as for water supplies, agricultural development, education, health, population measures, technical assistance, and public administration. IDA funds are obtained through replenishments, normally every three years, with contributions coming from 34 countries, including some of the more successful developing countries. Canada has been one of IDA's financial supporters from the

start and has been one of the largest sources of capital. In the period from 1960 to 1992, Canada was the sixth largest supporter and providing 5.5 percent of IDA funds, which in turn had extended US$75 billion in credits to 90 countries through June 30, 1992. In the tenth replenishment of IDA, running from 1993 to 1996, Canada was one of 34 donors who agreed to supply about US$18 billion; Canada supplied about 4 percent of the new funding. The IDA is based in Washington.

International Development Research Centre (IDRC)   A Canadian centre created to help the LESS-DEVELOPED COUNTRIES solve their problems through research and development. The centre was established in 1970 by the Canadian government to help less-developed countries build up their research facilities, scientific skills, and specialized institutions, and to solve their problems in such areas as agriculture, the food and nutrition sciences, the population and health sciences, and the information sciences. The centre is now funding research and training programs in many different parts of the less-developed world. It has a board of 21 of whom 11, including the chairman and the vice-chairman, are Canadians; the remaining nine are from other countries. The IDRC's headquarters are in Ottawa. In 1992, the centre lost its independent status and was made a department corporation of the Department of EXTERNAL AFFAIRS.

international economics   The area of economics concerned with international trade and investment, including the role of international economic institutions, the problems of the world monetary system, capital flows, the role of multinational corporations, commodity agreements, economic development, and co-ordination of economic policy among the major nations.

International Energy Agency (IEA) An international forum coordinating the energy policies of 22 industrial nations, including Canada. It is associated with the ORGANIZATION FOR ECONOMIC CO-OPERATION AND DEVELOPMENT, and was originally set up in 1974 to deal with problems of oil supplies and prices after the 1973 embargo by Arab oil-exporting nations against the United States and the Netherlands. It started with 16 members, including Canada, and now has 23. It promotes plans to reduce the growth of oil consumption and has devised emergency measures to share oil in a shortage, and has also co-ordinated a number of energy research and development projects to find future alternatives to oil. The IEA objectives also include the promotion of cooperative relations between oil-producting and oil-consuming nations. An increasing part of its activity today consists of analyzing future energy supply and demand patterns, assessing the energy policies of individual IEA member countries to determine the effectiveness of energy conservation and efficiency measures, and examining ways in which industrial countries can develop alternative sources of energy and reduce their consumption of hydrocarbons in order to reduce the future level of greenhouse gases that contribute to global warming.

The IEA set up an emergency management system in 1974 under an agreement on an international energy program. It commits the IEA countries to reducing demand and sharing available oil in the event of a major oil supply disruption. It also requires participating countries to hold oil stocks equivalent to at least 90 days of net oil imports. The program is supervised by the Standing Group on Emergency Questions, which is advised by an industry advisory board composed of senior supply experts from international oil companies. The emergency oil-sharing system could be activated if one or more of the participating countries are deprived of at least 7 percent of normal oil supply; under the system, available oil is shared among member countries according to a formula based on past consumption. In a supply emergency, the international allocation of oil would be managed by the executive director of the IEA. In each country, a National Emergency Sharing Organization would supervise the internal distribution of oil supplies. The IEA has also developed additional measures to respond to oil-supply disruptions. These could include: early and co-ordinated use of stocks; measures to reduce oil consumption; short-term fuel switching; increased domestic production; and discouragement of unusually large spot-market purchases by governments or private companies. Procedures have been established to enable governments to agree quickly on a co-ordinated stock draw and other measures early in any significant disruption, if this is judged necessary to calm the oil market. The emergency oil-sharing system was not triggered during the oil-supply disruptions of the 1970s and early 1980s because the shortfalls were less than 7 percent of normal supplies. But the emergency oil-sharing system is kept in readiness through periodic operational tests, known as Allocation Systems Tests, which are carried out approximately every two years. They stimulate a major oil supply disruption.

The IEA also co-ordinates the energy policies of member countries to avert a major future oil shortage. IEA members agreed to adopt policies of energy conservation and alternative energy sources, so that, in 1985, their total oil imports were limited to 26 million barrels a day, compared with 22 million barrels a day in 1977. Each country set its own import target, at which the 26-million-barrel target can be reached while economic growth is still maintained. Canada's share was originally to restrict net oil imports to 800,000 barrels a day, or one-third of consumption, whichever was lower, by 1985. This was subsequently reduced to 600,000 barrels a day. The IEA members are Australia, Austria, Belgium, Britain, Canada, Denmark, Finland, France, Germany, Greece, Ireland, Italy, Japan, Luxembourg, the Netherlands, New Zealand, Norway, Portugal, Spain, Sweden, Switzerland, Turkey, and the United States. The IEA is based in Paris.

International Finance Corporation (IFC) An affiliate of the WORLD BANK, created in 1956 to promote the development of a strong private sector in developing countries. It provides both equity and loans. It can invest directly in up to 25 percent of the ownership of a business, provide direct loans or loan guarantees to private lenders, and provide loan capital to foreign-development banks for private-industry projects. The IFC obtains its funds from the paid-up capital of its member nations, including Canada; from the sale of shares or notes it holds in existing projects; or in the form of loans from the World Bank. It is based in Washington.

International Fisheries Convention An agreement among Canada and other nations on the maximum level of catch, on the type of gear that can be used, and on conservation and scientific-research programs in the fishing area and for the species covered by individual conventions. Each convention is implemented by a commission set up under the agreement. Canada's first fisheries convention, signed in 1923, was the Canada-U.S. Convention for the Preservation of the Halibut Fishery of the North Pacific Ocean and Bering Sea. There are now about 10 such conventions, the most recent being the 1979 Canada-U.S. East Coast Fishery Resources Agreement, covering fishing on George's

Bank off Eastern Canada. Fishing conventions exist for seals, tuna, whales, Great Lakes fisheries, and salmon. *See also* NORTHWEST ATLANTIC FISHERIES ORGANIZATION and the INTERNATIONAL CONVENTION FOR THE HIGH SEAS FISHERIES OF THE NORTH PACIFIC OCEAN.

International Fund for Agricultural Development (IFAD) A specialized United Nations agency created in 1976 to help the LESS-DEVELOPED COUNTRIES raise their food production and improve nutrition by providing low-interest loans. The fund was proposed by the United Nation's 1974 WORLD FOOD CONFERENCE, and more than US$1 billion was provided by DEVELOPED COUNTRIES and less-developed countries, including US$33 million from Canada during the fund's first three years. By mid-1989, IFAD had invested US$2.7 billion in 247 projects in 91 countries. Decisions regarding the fund are shared equally among developed countries, less-developed countries, and members of the ORGANIZATION OF PETROLEUM EXPORTING COUNTRIES (OPEC), which has supplied close to one-third of the funds from the OPEC Special Fund. The fund, which is based in Rome, began operating in December, 1977, and made its first loan in April, 1978. *See also* WORLD FOOD COUNCIL.

international indebtedness The amount of money that countries owe to foreign lenders, in particular to foreign governments, international agencies, foreign banks and other financial institutions and investors, and foreign corporations. Canada's international indebtedness is reported annually by Statistics Canada in its publication *Canada's International Investment Position* (publication 67-202). Canada is a net debtor, which means that the amount of money it owes to foreign lenders and investors is greater than the amount owed to Canadians by foreign borrowers. The level of Canada's net foreign debt has been rising strongly in recent years and was about $300 billion at the end of 1992. As a country's foreign debt rises, it must allocate a growing share of its GROSS DOMESTIC PRODUCT each year to service the debt; at the same time, a growing level of foreign debt, relative to gross domestic product, makes a country's domestic macroeconomic policies subject to the growing influence of foreign creditors. Canada's international obligations include bonds, bank deposits, shares, various short-term financial instruments, the retained earnings in foreign-controlled firms here, and FOREIGN DIRECT INVESTMENT in Canadian industry. But it is the level of foreign debt, represented by bonds and short-term money-market instruments, that represents the most serious obligation, since interest payments must be made no matter what the state of the economy, whereas dividend payments on foreign-owned equity can be suspended. A country is expected to be a net debtor as its economy is being developed and a net creditor once its economy has been developed. However, Canada has remained a net debtor, with the increase in its international obligations creating future claims by non-residents for interest and dividends from Canada.

International Institute for Sustainable Development   A research institute based in Winnipeg and established in 1990 by the Canadian and Manitoba governments to promote sustainable development in decision making. It was part of Canada's response to the report of the World Commission on Environment and Development. The institute has an international board of directors and engages in both policy research and communications. Its research program includes studies on sustainable development and indigenous people, studies on the role of

business in sustainable development, and an examination of international trade and sustainable development. The institute is working with national and international environmental groups around the world.

international investment position   See NET INTERNATIONAL INVESTMENT POSITION.

International Joint Commission (IJC)   A Canada-United States agency set up in 1911, following the Boundary Waters Treaty of 1909, to settle disputes between the two countries over the use of the thousands of different waterways that cross their common border. A set of principles on the use of these waterways for transportation, hydro-electric power, and irrigation is set out in the Boundary Waters Act, and these principles are, in effect, terms of reference for the IJC. Canada and the United States each have three members, and the IJC's approval is required for any use of, construction on, or diversion of a body of water that crosses the border where it would affect the natural level or flow in the other country, or that would raise the level of water on the other side of the border.

The IJC has a long record of dealing with Canada-U.S. problems in the past, including problems with power developments such as the Columbia power project, and with transportation and agricultural disputes. In recent years, it has taken an increasingly active role in reviewing water-pollution problems on the Great Lakes and along other parts of the Canada-U.S. border. It is responsible for monitoring progress under the GREAT LAKES WATER QUALITY AGREEMENT. It has also dealt with some problems of air pollution and monitors progress under the Air Quality Accord. In Canada, it reports to the Secretary of State for EXTERNAL AFFAIRS, and in the United States, to the Secretary of State.

International Labour Organization (ILO) An international organization representing governments, unions, and employers, formed under the Treaty of Versailles in 1919 to set international labour standards, such as limitations on child labour, minimum wages, the right to organize unions freely, vacations with pay, maximum hours of work, non-discrimination, job safety, and the provision of social assistance. Canada has been a member from the start; Prime Minister R.B. Bennett, introducing his "New Deal" in 1935, justified his legislating in areas of provincial jurisdiction on the grounds that he was implementing ILO standards. In 1946, the ILO became a United Nations agency headquartered in Geneva; it was based in Montreal during the Second World War.

In recent years, the ILO has paid increasing attention to job needs, particularly in the LESS-DEVELOPED COUNTRIES, and to improving social security. It also disseminates a great deal of labour information and provides technical help to less-developed countries in setting up collective-bargaining, job-safety, and other labour-law provisions. Canada has ratified 24 of the ILO's more than 135 conventions. Each country's delegation consists of four members, one an employer, one from a union, and two from government. In 1977, the former president of the CANADIAN LABOUR CONGRESS, Joe Morris, served as chairman of the ILO's governing body.

International Maritime Organization (IMO) A UNITED NATIONS agency established in 1948 to enforce international rules of navigation, support research into safe and efficient port operation and navigation aids, design systems to reduce maritime pollution, and help countries develop their own merchant-marine service. Canada was one of the founding members. The agency is based in London.

international migration The movement of people from a country or group of countries to another country or countries.

International Monetary Fund (IMF) A specialized UNITED NATIONS agency, created as a result of the BRETTON WOODS AGREEMENT in 1944 and which began operations in 1947 to maintain and enforce a world monetary system based on fixed exchange rates and to provide financial and technical assistance to countries with temporary balance-of-payments problems; following the collapse of the fixed-exchange-rate system in 1971 and its replacement by a floating-exchange-rate system, the role of the IMF has been to promote exchange-rate stability and orderly exchange arrangements among its members, to serve as a source of liquidity for the international monetary system, and to help both developing countries and the former Communist states of Eastern Europe and the former Soviet Union develop economic strategies to develop market-based economies. The IMF provides temporary credits to members to help them correct their balance-of-payments difficulties, usually in conjunction with a structural adjustment program that sets out economic targets, such as reduced fiscal deficits and lower inflation, that a recipient country must pursue. The IMF also provides financing to assist medium-term economic restructuring. The IMF's resources come from the quotas or capital subscriptions of member countries, its capacity to borrow from official lenders, and its ability to draw on a line of credit from various countries under the GENERAL ARRANGEMENTS TO BORROW (GAB). Each country's quota determines its voting power in the IMF, its share of IMF-issued SPECIAL DRAWING RIGHTS (SDR), and its capacity to access IMF resources. Quotas are based on the size of a country's economy, on its current-account performance, and on its official reserves and other economic criteria. IMF quotas, as a result of the Ninth General Review of Quotas, totalled SDR 146 billion, while the GAB totalled SDR 18.5 billion. The original concern of the IMF, formed at the United Nations' Monetary and Financial Conference at Bretton Woods, New Hampshire, in July, 1944, as one of the post-war agencies formed to assist the orderly growth of an international economy, was to facilitate the expansion of international trade and investment and thereby raise world living standards by avoiding a return by the industrial nations to the destructive policies of exchange controls, competitive devaluations, and bilateral arrangements that had sprung up during the Depression of the 1930s. The IMF created a system of convertible currencies with fixed exchange rates and various provisions to help countries within the system to solve their balance-of-payments problems, with rules to ensure compliance. Without a system of FIXED EXCHANGE RATES, strict conditions under which they could be changed, and the ability to convert different currencies into other currencies, post-war planners believed that it would not be feasible for international trade, borrowing, investment, and travel to take place, especially on the enlarged scale envisaged by the post-war world.

Under the original IMF system, each country had a fixed exchange rate, with fluctuations permitted only within a very narrow range; each country was also committed to make its currency fully convertible into the currencies of other IMF members as soon as possible. If an individual nation's currency fluctuated beyond the permitted narrow range, due to its own economic mismanagement or to structural difficulties, it was required to correct its internal economic policies — for example, by bringing down inflation or by stimulating growth. Changes in the exchange rate were permitted only in conditions of "fundamental disequilibrium" — that is, when a country could no longer afford to defend its existing exchange rate without imposing unacceptably high costs, such as extreme unemployment, on its people. The IMF also had financial reserves of foreign currencies and gold to help individual countries to get over balance-of-payments difficulties, which it backed up with the GAB, an agreement of standby credit from leading industrial nations, plus swap arrangements with the BANK FOR INTERNATIONAL SETTLEMENTS. Although Canada had an exemption, permitted under IMF rules for "exceptional circumstances," which allowed its dollar to float between 1950 and 1962 and again starting in 1970, the fixed-exchange-rate system worked fairly well until the late 1960s, when growing international concern over the huge surplus of U.S. dollars, and the inability of the U.S. government to solve its balance-of-payments problems led to the breakdown of the fixed-exchange-rate system. In 1969, the IMF created a new form of international money, Special Drawing Rights (SDR), which was intended eventually to replace gold and the U.S. dollar as the principal reserve asset of the system used to settle balances of payment among nations, and which became the unit of account for the IMF. However, the pressures on a U.S. dollar pegged to a heavily undervalued gold standard, and a fixed-exchange-rate system, with the U.S. dollar as its linchpin, led to further pressure for change, and to the 1971 decision by the U.S. to unpeg the U.S. dollar from gold and let it float in international currency markets.

At the end of 1972, the fixed-exchange-rate system had been replaced by a FLOATING-EXCHANGE-RATE SYSTEM. IMF members began negotiation of a new monetary system to preserve the international framework of rules and measures to help individual nations to deal with balance-of-payments problems, and also to permit a more flexible method of determining exchange rates. In January, 1976, agreement was reached at a conference in Jamaica. Changes were subsequently made in the IMF's articles of agreement, formalizing the replacement of the system of fixed exchange rates by a system of floating exchange rates, subject to IMF surveillance so that individual nations would not artificially manipulate the value of their currencies for competitive reasons. The surveillance system, in which the IMF monitors the economic performance of policies of each of its member countries, is one of its most important functions today. At the same time, the IMF further reduced the role of gold in the world monetary system. The IMF retained its power to police the system, since nations needing IMF assistance to solve their balance-of-payments and international debt problems had to agree to economic policies worked out in consultation with the IMF.

IMF assistance is important for two reasons: the fund is able to provide significant credit assistance, and its participation in helping a country to solve its balance-of-payments problems makes it easier for the country to raise capital from other sources, including banks. With the sharp rise in world oil prices in 1973, the IMF strengthened its ability to help developing countries solve their balance-of-payments problems and to reform their economies, based on market principles, for long-term economic growth. In 1974, it created an Oil Facility to help poor nations finance balance-of-payments deficits caused by the sharp increase in oil prices. Its subsequent structural adjustment and enhanced structural adjustment facilities have access to about US$11.5 billion to provide concessional credits to low-income member countries, giving the IMF a larger role in helping low-income countries

achieve economic progress. The IMF also played a key role in addressing the THIRD-WORLD DEBT CRISIS, which started in 1982, when the IMF held its annual meeting in Toronto. The IMF helped heavily indebted nations restructure their economies and helped implement the BAKER PLAN and the BRADY PLAN to deal with the third-world debt crisis. The IMF took on additional responsibilities at the start of the 1990s, with the break-up of the Communist bloc of nations in Eastern Europe and the former Soviet Union; it has the responsibility for working with these nations to develop economic strategies to convert their economies to market systems, co-ordinating the aid efforts of the industrial nations, and providing direct assistance from its own resources.

For countries with balance-of-payments problems, the IMF has a series of lending facilities. An IMF member has access to a Reserve Tranche to the extent that its IMF quota exceeds the IMF's holdings of its currency in its General Resources Account. An IMF member may purchase up to the full amount of its Reserve Tranche at any time, provided there is a balance-of-payments need; credit is made available in four tranches. The first credit tranche of 25 percent is made available, provided a member country can show it is making a reasonable effort to deal with its balance-of-payments problems; additional upper credit tranches are available to a member country if it adopts policies that provide appropriate grounds for believing its balance-of-payments problems will be resolved within a reasonable period. This Reserve-Tranche access constitutes the IMF's standby lending facility. In addition, there are a number of other lending facilities. The Extended Fund Facility provides medium-term loans to address balance-of-payments problems; to qualify, a country must accept IMF conditions set out in explicit policies and achievement targets that are monitored by the IMF. Other IMF facilities include the Enlarged Access Policy, which provides additional financing to members whose payments imbalances are large in relation to their quotas. The access limits on standby and extended arrangements are from 90 to 110 percent of quota annually, from 270 to 330 percent over three years, and from 400 to 440 percent on a cumulative basis. The IMF has also introduced a number of specialized facilities, designed mainly to help developing countries. These include the Compensatory and Contingency Funding Facility for countries experiencing unexpected shocks to their economic programs, such as a drop in commodity prices or unanticipated increases in cereal-grain import prices, or an unexpected event such as a major earthquake or cyclone; a Buffer Stock Financing Facility, to help a country finance its contribution to an IMF-approved international buffer stock; the Structural Adjustment Facility, which provides additional assistance to low per capita income developing countries with severe balance-of-payments problems who are attempting to comply with IMF conditions; and the Enhanced Structural Adjustment Facility, which augments the Structural Adjustment Facility. In 1993, the IMF established the Systemic Transformation Facility to provide short-term assistance to economies in transition, such as the republics of the former Soviet Union. However, access to these various facilities depends on countries following and continuing to follow policies and rules laid down by the IMF. Canada exercised access to IMF facilities in 1962 and 1968.

The IMF publishes its annual *World Economic Outlook* in May, and a subsequent revision in September and is moving to a third revision at the end of the year. It conducts annual, confidential reviews of the economic performance and policies of individual member countries and advises member countries on their economic and monetary policies. In addition, the IMF promotes policy co-ordination among the GROUP OF SEVEN industrial countries. It also provides technical assistance to member countries, notably developing countries and the former members of the Soviet Union, in central banking, balance of payments, taxation, and other matters.

Canada was one of the original members of the IMF, its participation being authorized under the BRETTON WOODS AGREEMENT Act. Initially, there were only 45 IMF members; in September, 1992, there were 173 member countries. Each member has a quota of exchange reserves or capital subscription it must deposit with the IMF, depending on its economic size. With the most recent quota increase, agreed to in 1992, Canada's share has shrunk to 2.99 percent, reflecting the growth in economic power of countries such as Germany and Japan and the growing importance of developing countries. The IMF has a formal committee of 22 executive directors, who represent their own countries and, in some cases, a group of countries; these executive directors constitute the Executive Board and are responsible for the day-to-day operations of the IMF. Canada is an executive director and represents the Bahamas, Barbados, Grenada, Jamaica, and Ireland. Approval of changes in the IMF rules requires approval from 60 percent of its members and 85 percent of the votes as represented by quotas. *See also* INTERIM COMMITTEE. The headquarters of the IMF are located in Washington.

international oil price The price charged for crude oil in world markets. For Canada, the price is the price for which oil would sell in Chicago, known as the Chicago parity price, less the pipeline or other distribution cost back to the Canadian refinery, such as Edmonton. Oil prices for four crudes — Brent North Sea, West Texas Intermediate, Dhubai, and Alaska North Slope — are all tracked through futures markets. From 1973 until 1980-81, the ORGANIZATION OF PETROLEUM EXPORTING COUNTRIES (OPEC) attempted to control world oil prices at periodic price-setting meetings. However, the OPEC price in the 1990s has became a national price, reflecting what the OPEC members would like to get for their oil.

International Standards Organization (ISO) A nongovernment body established in 1947 to develop worldwide standards to ensure product quality, compatibility, safety, and reliability. Agreed standards are also important for the smooth functioning of international trade. A primary objective of the ISO is to replace the divergent standards of individual countries with international standards. One result has been the Standards Code of the GENERAL AGREEMENT ON TARIFFS AND TRADE signed by more than 30 countries, including Canada. The ISO is supported by the national standards organizations of 90 countries representing more than 95 percent of world industrial production, including the CANADIAN STANDARDS ASSOCIATION.

International Telecommunications Union (ITU) An international agency, founded in 1865 but now a United Nations agency, that establishes and monitors international conventions and standards on telecommunications services, including the allocation and use of radio frequencies, standardization of equipment, the improvement of international telecommunications services, and the delineation of policy issues on new technologies, such as broadcasting satellites. Canada is a member of the 36-nation ITU council, which is headquartered in Geneva and

now has about 140 nations as members.

International Tin Agreements A series of international commodity agreements between tin-exporting and tin-importing nations, designed to provide stable and reasonable prices, ensure adequate supplies, and promote export earnings through new uses for tin. There were six agreements, 1956-61, 1961-66, 1966-71, 1971-76, 1976-81, and a one-year extension in 1982. The International Tin Agreement was wound up in 1983 with the collapse of the world tin market. Membership had been open to all exporting and importing countries, and Canada was a signatory. The agreements were administered by the International Tin Council, which was made up of both exporting and importing nations. The International Tin Council is now inactive but has not been formally wound up. The main tin exporters are Malaysia, Bolivia, Thailand, and Indonesia.

international trade The flow of goods and services between countries. Countries export the goods and services in which they are most competitive and import the goods and services in which they are uncompetitive, with the welfare of all countries increasing as a result. In CLASSICAL ECONOMICS theory, countries export those goods and services in which they have a COMPARATIVE ADVANTAGE, which was assumed to be a reflection of a country's natural advantages; but in today's global economy, a country can create its comparative advantage, for example through INDUSTRIAL POLICY. Canada's balance-of-merchandise trade is reported monthly by Statistics Canada (publication 65-001), and its balance of trade in goods and services, quarterly (publication 67-001). The international rules for world trade are set out in the GENERAL AGREEMENT

ON TARIFFS AND TRADE, which publishes annual statistics on world trade. *See also* CANADA-UNITED STATES FREE TRADE AGREEMENT, the NORTH AMERICAN FREE TRADE AGREEMENT.

International Trade Advisory Committee (ITAC) An advisory committee of 45 representatives of the business, labour, consumer, academic, and research communities who report to the Minister of International Trade. It is a permanent advisory committee that was started up in 1986, as Canada entered into free-trade negotiations with the United States, for the purpose of an ongoing, confidential, and two-way flow of information and advice between the government and the private sector on international trade issues dealing with trade policy, market access, and trade development. Members must be Canadian citizens and are appointed for two years (they can be reappointed). All members are required to sign a security declaration undertaking to respect the confidentiality of classified information given to them by the government. In addition, the Minister of International Trade appoints members to 13 different Sectoral Advisory Groups in International Trade, known as SAGITs; the role of these groups is to ensure that sectoral views are taken into account on international trade matters. The chairpersons of SAGITs sit as members of ITAC. The 13 SAGITs deal with the following industry sectors: agriculture, food and beverages; apparel and fur; arts and cultural industries; communications, computer equipment and services; consumer and household products; energy, chemicals, and petrochemicals; financial services; fish and fish products; forest products; general services; industrial and transportation equipment; minerals and metals; and textiles, footwear, and leather. Additional SAGITs can be created as needed.

International Trade, Department of *See* EXTERNAL AFFAIRS AND INTERNATIONAL TRADE.

international transit Free and uninterrupted passage through another country's territory, waters, or airspace, by ships, planes, trains, trucks, or pipelines. For the most part, the passage through territorial waters or airspace is covered by international agreement or law; for example, the INTERNATIONAL CIVIL AVIATION ORGANIZATION has helped to develop the transit rules for civil aviation. Canada has treaty agreements with the United States that provide for the free and uninterrupted passage of oil and natural-gas pipelines through each other's territory; each pipeline project requires a separate treaty. In 1977, Canada and the United States signed two pipeline treaties, one concerning transit pipelines and the other concerning the pipeline to carry Alaska natural gas through western Canada to the United States. The purpose of such treaties is to make sure that at some date after the pipeline is built, the other country doesn't impose new conditions or taxes, or interfere with the project.

international union In Canada, a union with members in both Canada and the United States, whose headquarters is almost certain to be in the United States. About half of all Canadian union members belong to international unions; a much higher percentage of industrial and construction workers belong to international unions, since the principal Canadian unions tend to be those representing public-sector employees. The autonomy of Canadian locals in international unions has been an issue, and, in 1970, the CANADIAN LABOUR CONGRESS (CLC) adopted a resolution to strengthen autonomy. The resolution urged the election of Canadian union officers by Canadian members, that elected Canadian representatives be the ones authorized to speak for the union in Canada, and that elected Canadian officers and Canadian union members determine policy positions in dealing with Canadian issues and the Canadian government. The bigger international unions have tended to encourage Canadian autonomy, but some international unions are more rigid. In 1974, the CLC passed another resolution calling for stiffer enforcement of its 1970 policy. *See also* CANADIAN STANDARDS OF SELF-GOVERNMENT.

International Wheat Council (IWC)　An international organization of major wheat-exporting and -importing countries, established in 1949 to promote international wheat trade, to stabilize world prices for wheat when this is in the interest of exporters and importers, to resolve world wheat problems, to keep close records of crop forecasts and importer needs, and to negotiate international agreements on minimum and maximum prices, when this is possible. The council maintains a secretariat in London, which collects up-to-date information on world wheat supply and demand, and publishes an annual review of the world wheat situation. The council has administered successive international wheat agreements that attempted to regulate world wheat prices, and it has also held food-aid conventions that provided the opportunity for wheat-exporting and wealthy industrial nations to allocate a portion of their crops or cash equivalents to buy wheat to give as a gift to the LESS-DEVELOPED COUNTRIES. The last international wheat agreement was signed in 1971 and extended to 1983, when it collapsed because of a subsidy war between the United States and the European Community. A new international wheat agreement was negotiated in 1986.

interpolation　The calculation of a figure from within a known range of figures, as opposed to EXTRAPOLATION. For example, Canada carries out a full census once every 10 years; taking the census figures for 1961, 1971, 1981, and 1991, it would be possible to make fairly detailed interpolations for, say, the year 1988.

interprovincial barriers　Provincial laws or policies restricting the movement of goods or services from one province to another to favour local businesses, professions, and workers and to force companies to locate facilities there. Provincial government procurement policies that restrict tendering to local companies, require the presence of a local facility to qualify as a supplier, or price discriminate in favour of local suppliers, are one example. Other barriers include, in construction and services, a requirement to use local materials and labour, policies that restrict building to provincial companies, and policies that restrict the mobility of labour, such as professional licensing and trades certification. In addition, provincial crown corporations, municipalities, hospitals, universities, colleges, and schools have a lack of open tendering. Provincial restrictions on the sale of beer and wine have also impeded national distribution; policies have included listing restrictions, provincial mark-ups, and restrictions on distribution and marketing. Barriers in labour markets include different provincial licensing or certification requirements for professionals and skilled trades, and provincial residency requirements associated with licensing and work. In agriculture, restrictions on provincial production and imports of products from other provinces, associated with SUPPLY MANAGEMENT, also serve as barriers to trade. Other barriers are found in other industries, such as trucking. Section 121 of the CONSTITUTION

ACT, 1867, was intended to create a single internal market in Canada. It states that: "All articles of the growth, produce, or manufacture of any one of the provinces shall, from and after the Union, be admitted free into each of the other provinces." However, judicial interpretation rendered the clause almost unusable, except in emergencies. In 1993, however, after many false starts, the Council of Ministers on Internal Trade representing the federal and provincial ministers responsible for trade, agreed in principle to a comprehensive process for the elimination of the remaining barriers to internal trade by March 31, 1995. The ministers embraced a set of principles to enhance internal trade, agreed to apply the principles to their own jurisdictions, and committed to report back on how they would implement these principles so as to ensure the free flow of goods, services, people, and capital across Canada. They also planned to establish a dispute settlement mechanism to enforce their agreement on the internal market. Their intention was to reach an agreement by June 30, 1994, to be in effect by March 31, 1995, and ratified by all governments by June 30, 1995.

interprovincial conferences Meetings of representatives of provincial governments without the participation of the federal government. *See also* PREMIERS' CONFERENCE, WESTERN PREMIERS' CONFERENCE, COUNCIL OF MARITIME PREMIERS, FEDERAL-PROVINCIAL CONFERENCE, CONFERENCE OF FIRST MINISTERS.

interprovincial trade Trade that crosses provincial boundaries and thus falls under federal regulation. It includes the movement of farm products and energy. Section 91 of the BRITISH NORTH AMERICA ACT gives the federal government general powers over trade and commerce in Canada, but these powers were significantly reduced through judicial interpretation of the Constitution Act, 1867. As a result, Canada has failed, through the persistence of INTERPROVINCIAL BARRIERS, to gain the economic benefits of a single internal market. Statistics Canada publishes periodic information on the volume of trade between the provinces in its occasional publication, *The Destination of Shipments of Manufacturers* (31-530). It was published in 1979 and 1984 and is to be published again using 1992 statistics.

intertemporal choice The decision by a household as to whether to consume now and spend or to consume later and save. By saving now, a household is deferring consumption until some future date and is thus making an intertemporal choice. Households balance out their consumption and savings to maximize their UTILITY. The decision by a firm on how much to invest in a particular year also represents an intertemporal choice.

intervention currency A strong, stable currency used by different nations to settle their balances of payments, and employed by a nation in foreign-exchange markets when controlling fluctuations in its own currency's exchange rate. For most of the post-war period, it was the U.S. dollar alone, but today it may include the German mark and the Japanese yen. Canada, for example, uses these intervention currencies to influence the value of the Canadian dollar in foreign-exchange markets. But the Canadian dollar is not used as an intervention currency by other countries — one reason being that there are not enough in circulation outside Canada; Canada lacks the strength and size of economy to justify the use of its dollar as an intervention currency.

intestate The circumstance in which someone dies without leaving a will.

intrinsic value   The underlying usefulness of a commodity or product; for example, the ability of an item of food to satisfy a person's hunger. In a modern economy, it is the supply and demand of the food product, rather than its intrinsic value, that determines its price.

invention   The origination of a new technology, product, service, or production or distribution process through research and development, as opposed to its application. *See also* INNOVATION, PATENT.

inventory   The raw materials and parts, work-in-progress, and finished goods held by a firm, and their total value. Inventory in raw materials and parts is held in order to meet the future production needs of a firm, while an inventory of finished products is held to meet new orders. A manufacturing company, for example, must have sufficient materials and parts available so that its production lines can operate efficiently and will not have to slow down or halt production temporarily due to insufficient raw materials or parts. If a manufacturer fears a strike in one of its suppliers or in a transportation industry, it will build up its inventory to tide it over the expected strike; otherwise, the firm may have to shut down while its competitors keep working and gain some of its customers. Similarly, a retailer wants to make sure that it has enough winter coats on hand to supply its customers. If the retail establishment underorders, it loses sales; by the time it can get delivery on a new order, the season may be over. Likewise, a supplier wants to be able to quickly fill new orders, which means it will want to maintain some inventory of finished products; it may also be more efficient to produce at a given rate rather than to vary production according to fluctuations in demand. Excessive inventories, however, are costly; a manufacturer may find itself stuck with a supply of outdated products, or a retailer may find itself, at the end of the winter season, with too many coats that may be out of style the following winter. In order to improve their competitiveness, manufacturers are reducing the inventories they carry and are requiring their suppliers to maintain a flow of parts and materials as needed, on a daily or even half-daily basis. *See* LEAN PRODUCTION.

Changes in the physical volume of inventories are a factor in the rate of economic growth and level of GROSS DOMESTIC PRODUCT (GDP). If inventories are low and business expectations are for economic growth, then businesses are likely to rebuild their inventories to more satisfactory levels, contributing to increased AGGREGATE DEMAND in the economy. Therefore, the size of inventories can be a barometer of business confidence. The two principal forms of inventory monitored in the GDP are physical changes in the inventories of non-farm businesses and changes in farm inventories, which include farm-stored grain and livestock and farm products in commercial channels. The value of these changes represents the change in the average value of the units held in inventory. Since companies measure their inventories in a variety of different ways, an adjustment must be made for capital gains or losses in presenting GDP accounts. This is reported as the INVENTORY-VALUATION ADJUSTMENT.

inventory control   Since inventories represent tied-up capital and can also spoil or become obsolete, businesses try to maintain inventories that are as low as possible but sufficient to meet business needs. This is an important element of management, and has become more scientific with the use of computerized control systems and financial management techniques. *See* LEAN PRODUCTION.

inventory cost The costs incurred by companies in holding inventories of raw materials and components or of finished products. These costs include the interest cost to finance the inventory, along with the costs of warehousing or storage, the costs of insurance, and the risk that the inventory will deteriorate or become obsolete. *See* LEAN PRODUCTION.

inventory profit The profits of a firm resulting from the fact that it had large inventories in stock during a period of rapid inflation, and increased the price of its products accordingly.

inventory turnover The number of times a firm's average inventory is replaced during the course of a year. The turnover rate is determined by dividing the cost of goods sold during the year by the average inventory.

inventory valuation The method used in a company's BALANCE SHEET, under current assets, to determine the value of inventories. The most widely used method is FIRST IN, FIRST OUT (fifo), which assumes that the items acquired earliest for the inventory are the first used or sold, so that the value of inventory represents the cost of the most recently acquired inventory. Two other methods of valuation are as follows: 1. LAST IN, FIRST OUT (lifo), which assumes that the most recently acquired inventory items are the first to be used or sold, so that the value of inventory represents the cost of the oldest materials and goods; and 2. the average-cost method, in which an average value is determined for all items in the inventory. The method of inventory valuation used is a factor in calculating the cost of goods sold and therefore helps to determine the profitability of a firm. A large profit made on inventories due to inflation may be illusory, since the inventory will have to be replaced at much higher prices, and part of the profit just earned will have to finance the cost of inventory replacement.

inventory-valuation adjustment A figure used by STATISTICS CANADA in its GROSS DOMESTIC PRODUCT calculation, to show the change in the value of inventories due to price changes. This enables Statistics Canada to separate out the physical change in inventories from changes due simply to inflation; the resulting figure is important in analyzing economic performance and in calculating future business performance and economic growth.

invested capital The total of SHAREHOLDERS' EQUITY in a corporation, plus outstanding long-term debt, minus the portion of long-term debt to be paid off in the following 12-month period. In other words, invested capital consists of the total assets of a business minus its current liabilities. It represents the capital at work in a corporation. One useful way of measuring the profitability of a corporation is to calculate profits as a percent of invested capital — this is known as return on invested capital, and shows how well management is using the resources of the corporation, including its credit.

investment 1. Spending on CAPITAL STOCK such as factories, commercial property, housing, mines, and machinery, or on public or private INFRASTRUCTURE, so as to increase the productive capacity of the economy. The GROSS DOMESTIC PRODUCT distinguishes between residential and non-residential investment. New investment is an important source of economic growth and PRODUCTIVITY improvement; it is undertaken to increase profits. It depends on the expected level of demand in the economy and the existing level of productive capacity, the need to replace obsolete equipment so as to remain competitive, and the anticipated growth in population and income, new inventions, changes in public tastes, new export markets, and other such factors. Economic policy makers have to find ways of encouraging investment so that enough of it takes place, but in an orderly way, so that it will not contribute to inflation. Gross investment in the economy is the total amount of investment spending; net investment is the actual addition to the nation's productive capacity or capital stock, and is obtained by deducting depreciation or capital-consumption allowances from gross investment. In this sense, investment refers to new capital in the economy, such as a new factory, and not to the sale of shares by one investor to another. **2.** In its broader meaning, investment is any purchase of an asset to increase future income or capital, or both. It represents savings, as opposed to consumption, and includes purchases of shares, bonds, property, works of art, and a wide range of short-term financial securities, such as certificates of deposit, guaranteed-investment certificates, treasury bills, and finance-company paper. **3.** Spending on inventory is also an investment.

investment banking **1.** In a chartered bank, the operations that manage a bank's funding position and its holdings of treasury bills, bonds, and preferred and common shares. **2.** A more generic term used to describe the raising of capital for industry. *See* INVESTMENT DEALER, UNDERWRITER.

Investment Canada A federal agency that, since June 30, 1985, has been responsible for reviewing foreign takeovers of Canadian companies. The agency, which replaced the FOREIGN INVESTMENT REVIEW AGENCY, has a three-part mandate: to promote investment in Canada by Canadians and non-

Canadians; to conduct research and advise the government on investment issues; and to review foreign acquisitions of Canadian companies to see whether they are likely to be of "net benefit" to Canada. The Minister of INDUSTRY, SCIENCE AND TECHNOLOGY approves or rejects acquisitions, based on a report and recommendation from Investment Canada. The agency has two sets of rules for reviewable takeovers of Canadian companies, one for takeovers by U.S. corporations, and another for corporations from the rest of the world. As a result of the CANADA-UNITED STATES FREE TRADE AGREEMENT, Investment Canada reviews direct acquisitions of Canadian companies by U.S. investors where assets of the Canadian company are $150 million or higher; a review of an indirect acquisition, in which control of a foreign subsidiary in Canada changes as a result of an international transaction, is not required unless the assets of the Canadian company represent more than 50 percent of the value of the total assets acquired in the international transaction. However, U.S. investments in the uranium, financial services (except insurance), cultural industries, and transportation services are subject to the same threshold levels as investors from the rest of the world. This preferential treatment is being extended to Mexican investors under the NORTH AMERICAN FREE TRADE AGREEMENT. In the case of takeovers by investors from other countries, a review is required for all direct acquisitions of Canadian businesses with assets of $5 million or more, all indirect acquisitions of $50 million or more, and indirect acquisitions of Canadian businesses with assets of $5 million or more where the Canadian business represents more than 50 percent of the value of the total international transaction. In 1992, the federal government announced that it was abandoning the Oil and Gas Acquisitions Policy that had prohibited the sale of financially sound Canadian-controlled oil and gas companies to non-Canadians; the same threshold levels would apply for U.S. and non-U.S. investors in the oil and gas sector as in other industry sectors. The government also relaxed its policy on the foreign takeover of Canadian book-publishing companies; the previous policy of forcing divestiture within two years of an indirect acquisition was abandoned and, instead, indirect acquisitions of Canadian book-publishing companies will be reviewed to determine whether they are of net benefit to Canada. Direct acquisition of Canadian-owned book-publishing companies will be allowed where the companies are in serious financial difficulty and no Canadian investor is interested in acquiring the company. Non-Canadian investors are not permitted to start a new business in book publishing or distribution. All acquisitions and new businesses under the threshold levels must still be reported to Investment Canada, with a filing setting out the nature and size of the investment. Even small investments below the threshold levels may be reviewed under Section 15 of the Investment Canada Act, which deals with Canada's cultural heritage and national identity. These cultural industries include book, magazine, and newspaper publishing; film and video production, distribution, sale, and exhibition; audio or video music production, distribution, sale, and exhibition; and music publishing, distribution, and sale.

When a foreign investor files an application to take over a Canadian company, Investment Canada is required to consult with the province in which the business is located and the BUREAU OF COMPETITION POLICY. It then discusses with the investor the plans for the proposed acquisition and may negotiate changes to make the takeover more acceptable. Investment Canada then makes a report and recommendation to the Minister of Industry,

Science, and Technology, who makes the final decision on whether the proposed takeover is of net benefit to Canada. In determining net benefit, the minister takes the following criteria into account: the effect of the takeover on economic activity in Canada, including the effect on employment, resource processing, the use of Canadian parts, components, and services, and on exports from Canada; the degree and significance of participation by Canadians in the Canadian business and in any industry in Canada of which it forms a part; the effect of the investment on productivity, industrial efficiency, technological development, product innovation, and product variety in Canada; the effect of the investment on competition within any industry or industries in Canada; the compatibility of the investment with national industrial, economic, and cultural policies, taking into consideration industrial, economic, and cultural policy objectives enunciated by the government or legislature of any province likely to be significantly affected by the investment; and the contribution of the investment to Canada's ability to compete in world markets. Within 45 days of an application, the minister must either approve the takeover, seek a 30-day extension, or longer if the applicant agrees, or reject the takeover. If there is no notification by the minister after 45 days, or after an additional 30 days if an extension had been made, the minister is deemed to have approved the acquisition.

investment club A group of individuals who pool their savings together into one investment fund, usually adding an agreed-on amount to it on a monthly basis, and invest the money in shares and other securities as a single investor. In this way they are able to invest in a variety of securities and to spread their risk. Some clubs make their own investment decisions while others retain an investment analyst to make recommendations on investments or to manage the funds directly.

investment company A company that invests its capital in the shares and other securities of other companies. There are two types: 1. CLOSED-END INVESTMENT COMPANIES have fixed capitalization; their shares may be listed on stock exchanges, where they can be bought or sold. 2. OPEN-END INVESTMENT COMPANIES, or MUTUAL FUNDS, which have unlimited capitalization, with shares being issued as they are sold and shares redeemed when shareholders wish to liquidate their holdings. Mutual funds are not listed on stock exchanges.

investment counsellor An individual who advises clients on how to invest their funds. Investment counsellors must be registered, under provincial securities laws, with a SECURITIES COMMISSION.

investment dealer A financial firm that has two principal functions: 1. To help corporations and industries who need investment capital to raise it on the best possible terms, and to help pension funds, insurance companies' trust funds, corporations, and individuals with investment capital to get the best return on their funds. 2. To help provide a secondary market for outstanding BONDS, COMMERCIAL PAPER, finance paper, TREASURY BILLS, and UNLISTED SHARES. Investment dealers play an important role in advising governments and corporations on the size, type, and timing of new offerings, including such questions as whether to issue bonds, PREFERRED SHARES, or COMMON SHARES, and whether there should be a PRIVATE PLACEMENT to PUBLIC ISSUE, along with advice on whether a company should go public, how to prepare a PROSPECTUS, how to handle mergers, and the like. Investment dealers also buy and sell new and outstanding debt and other invested securities on their own account, maintaining an inventory so that there is always a ready market. They UNDERWRITE new issues, and buy and sell outstanding issues. Some of them also operate the MONEY MARKET, dealing in short-term funds and thus playing an important role in the BANK OF CANADA's implementation of MONETARY POLICY through OPEN-MARKET OPERATIONS. Most investment dealers are part of a securities firm that is a STOCKBROKER as well, which acts as an agent for clients in buying and selling SHARES on recognized STOCK EXCHANGES.

Investment Dealers Association (IDA) An association of INVESTMENT DEALERS and STOCKBROKERS, both individuals and firms, established to encourage saving and investment by providing safe financial markets for investors through self-regulation of the securities industry, the adoption of high standards of behaviour by members, and the provision of training courses for those working in the industry. The present non-profit body was created in 1916 as the Bond Dealers Association of Canada; it adopted its present name in 1934. Members of the IDA must meet a set of standards before they are accepted and must continue to meet those standards if they wish to remain as members; the most important standards have to do with the safety of client funds, and the maintenance of a minimum amount of net free capital to meet emergencies. The IDA is to a large extent responsible for the rules governing the operation of the MONEY MARKET and the OVER-THE-COUNTER MARKET in Canada. It works closely with provincial SECURITIES COMMISSIONS and operates a number of programs to protect the investing public. It administers, with the Toronto, Montreal, and Vancouver stock exchanges, a national contingency fund of $1.5 million, to provide assistance to clients in the event of a collapse of a member's firm. It is based in Toronto. *See also* CANADIAN SECURITIES INSTITUTE.

investment guarantee   A government program to encourage corporations to invest in LESS-DEVELOPED COUNTRIES; the government promises to reimburse the corporation for all or most of its investment costs in a less-developed country if an investment is expropriated with little or no compensation. Guarantees are provided to Canadian firms through the EXPORT DEVELOPMENT CORPORATION. *See also* MULTILATERAL INVESTMENT GUARANTEE AGENCY.

investment incentives   Government measures to encourage business firms to invest in new facilities, to undertake a particular type of investment, such as new spending on research and development or on pollution-control equipment, or to invest in areas of chronic unemployment and slow economic growth. There are many types of subsidy or incentive. They range from direct grants, such as those offered by the Department of INDUSTRY, SCIENCE AND TECHNOLOGY, the ATLANTIC OPPORTUNITIES AGENCY, or the Western Diversification Fund, low-interest loans, and loan guarantees, to various tax measures, such as an INVESTMENT TAX CREDIT, ACCELERATED DEPRECIATION (sometimes called accelerated capital-cost allowances), and special write-off provisions for investing in certain areas, such as research and development or a slow-growth region of the country. An investment incentive can also consist of low-cost power supplies, direct government spending on INFRASTRUCTURE that would normally be part of a corporation's costs, or reduced royalty payments on natural-resource extraction.

investment income   The investment received by an individual, corporation, or pension or endowment fund, trust, or other organization, from its holdings in securities and property. It includes rent from property, dividends from shares in corporations, and interest from bonds, guaranteed-investment certificates, bank accounts, certificates of deposit, treasury bills, and other financial securities.

investment portfolio   The list of investments held by an individual, pension fund, or other investor. The portfolio should reflect the investment strategy of the owner; the emphasis may be on income or on capital gain, or on some particular combination, depending on the needs of the investor.

investment schedule   The schedule that displays the way in which investment rises as national income grows. Investment will increase faster than income due to the necessity to replace aging capital stock and to raise productive capacity.

investment tax credit   A subsidy from the government to corporations to encourage them to expand their operations generally or to undertake a specific kind of investment, such as more investment in research and development facilities, in pollution equipment, or investments in areas of chronic unemployment. It reduces the cost of capital and takes the form of a credit, equal to a percentage of investment spending, that can be deducted by a corporation from the income tax it owes to the government. An investment tax credit thus reduces the tax liability of a corporation making an investment. In its 1986 budget, the federal government eliminated the investment tax credit, except for investments in regions of high unemployment and in research and development. In December, 1992, the federal government introduced a temporary small-business investment tax credit for the purchase of eligible machinery and equipment made after December 2, 1992, and before 1994.

invisible hand   A concept developed by Adam SMITH; the theory that, although each individual pursues his own selfish interests, the welfare of society is achieved through the competing interplay of the resulting market forces. The competing forces of supply and demand, acted out through millions of individual transactions, achieve an EQUILIBRIUM that represents the best interests of society through the most efficient allocation of resources. Smith put it this way in *An Inquiry into the Nature and Causes of the Wealth of Nations* in 1776: "every individual, therefore, endeavours ... to employ his capital ... that its produce may be of the greatest value ... He generally, indeed, neither intends to promote the public interest, nor knows how much he is promoting it ... he intends only his own security; ... only his own gain, and he is in this, as in many other cases, led by an invisible hand to promote an end which was no part of his intention... By pursuing his own interest he frequently promotes that of the society more effectually than when he really intends to promote it." This concept is at the core of LAISSEZ-FAIRE economics, and is used by advocates of the FREE-MARKET ECONOMY to argue against government interference. However, the invisible hand assumes PERFECT COMPETITION. If there is IMPERFECT COMPETITION, then there is no invisible hand to ensure that the economy functions in the best interests of society. Government intervention is needed to deal with MONOPOLY or OLIGOPOLY, with EXTERNAL DISECONOMIES such as pollution, and to make sure that public wants ignored by monopolists or oligopolists are met.

invisibles   The non-merchandise part of a country's current account in its BALANCE OF PAYMENTS. It includes the wide range of payments and receipts for all kinds of services, including interest and dividends; travel; patent and royalty payments; management and other fees between subsidiaries and head offices; insurance and banking services; transportation, including shipping; various gifts; and the funds immigrants bring to a country or remit to their homelands. The balance in trade or VISIBLES plus the balance in invisibles equals the current-account surplus or deficit. Canada usually has a visibles surplus and an invisibles deficit, and tends to run an overall current-account deficit that is offset by inflows of foreign capital.

inward orientation   The behaviour of a country that attempts to foster economic development by raising trade barriers and focusing on the development of local industries to serve the domestic market. This is the import substitution model of development. *See also* OUTWARD ORIENTATION.

iron law of wages   The theory that wages can never be sustained above the level necessary for minimal subsistence. If wages rise above that level, the number of workers will increase, and families will be able to afford to have more children. This, in turn, will increase the supply of workers, and force wage rates below the subsistence level. As workers stop working because wages do not even provide subsistence, production will fall. Employers will then offer higher wages to attract workers, with wages once more temporarily rising above the subsistence level. However, soon they will slip below subsistence levels again, as the cycle repeats itself.

This gloomy 19th century view was an outgrowth of the Malthusian (*See* Thomas Robert MALTHUS) view of the world, and its conviction that man's limited ability to increase the food supply was a great constraint on all human activity. Experience tells a different story. The reserve army of the unemployed, which was supposed to be available to replace workers wanting more money, does not exist. It ignores, as well, the fact that employers have a need for an enormous variety of skills that are not interchangeable, and in competitive labour markets have to bid for these skills. It also ignores the role of unions in negotiating wages and protecting jobs and the role of government in setting minimum wages. By the middle of the 19th century, a new wage theory, the WAGE-FUND THEORY, had been developed to explain how wages were set. It has been replaced, in this century, by the MARGINAL-PRODUCTIVITY THEORY OF WAGES.

irrigation   Methods of bringing water to agricultural land to increase output or to make farming possible; techniques include the use of pipes or ditches. *See* PRAIRIE FARM REHABILITATION ADMINISTRATION.

isoquant   A graph that shows the different combinations of FACTORS OF PRODUCTION that can be used to produce a product. Assuming a given level of technology, various combinations of labour and capital can be used in the production of the product, the one substituting for the other. A shoe company, for example, might be able to produce 1,000 pairs of shoes by employing either 50 workers and 10 machines or 100 workers and five machines. An isoquant could then be constructed, with one axis of a graph showing the number of employees and the other axis the number of machines; different points of the graph would show the different combinations of workers and machines that could produce the 1,000 pairs of shoes.

issue   The distribution of a company's securities. *See* NEW ISSUE.

issued capital   The proportion of AUTHORIZED CAPITAL that has been sold to the public in the form of PREFERRED and COMMON SHARES. Issued capital is usually less than authorized capital; a company anxious to raise new investment capital will, if stock-market conditions are good, issue new shares if the company hasn't reached its authorized limit, instead of borrowing money, which increases its future interest costs

issuer bid   An offer by a company to buy back its shares or other securities convertible into its own shares.

J-curve The curve followed by a country's BALANCE OF PAYMENTS after its currency has been devalued. Initially, the balance of payments will worsen because of the flow of goods already in inventory and transit and contracts signed before the devaluation occurred. But as importers and exporters adjust to the price impact of the devaluation, the country's balance of payments will turn around and begin to improve. There is nothing automatic about this; there may be other factors that militate against the J-curve to some extent, in addition to the time it takes for firms to adjust. For example, in spite of price reductions for exports, industry's capacity to produce more may be too low to take advantage of new market opportunities, or there may not be an increase in demand for these products in other countries, even with lower export prices. But the J-curve expresses what should happen and usually does happen following a devaluation.

jawbone economics Efforts by government to restrain price and wage increases by talking up the need for restraint to fight inflation. This talk may be accompanied by suggested price and wage guidelines and by singling out individual firms and unions for public attention if they disregard the guidelines or need for restraint. Sometimes a government may threaten action, in public or behind closed doors, against a firm or union that ignores the need for restraint. *See also* MORAL SUASION. Jawbone economics may be successful for a short period, but it may be a prelude to an INCOMES POLICY that eventually includes some kind of legal controls or punishment for misbehaving firms and unions.

job description An outline of the various duties of a person doing a particular job, along with a description of his authority and the authority to whom he reports. A job description is used to determine the qualifications needed for a job and as a benchmark to assess how well a person is doing it.

job enrichment Attempts to increase personal satisfaction and motivation on the job. Techniques include giving workers more say in how they organize their activities, the adoption of the so-called open office and generally more open work environment, opportunities for workers to discuss how their jobs should be performed, and efforts to increase challenges and worker responsibilities. The purpose is to reduce absenteeism and dissatisfaction, and to increase productivity.

job evaluation An organized assessment of the skills needed to perform a particular job; it is used as the basis for differential rates of pay in an industry or firm.

job-safety laws Federal and provincial laws to protect the health and safety of workers. They cover such items as heating, lighting, ventilation, tunnelling, the protection of dangerous machinery, electrical installations, boiler pressure, toxic chemicals, and sanitation. There may be special laws dealing with more dangerous industries, such as construction and excavation, mining, and forestry.

job security Various provisions in a collective agreement that give workers protection in the event of automation or of new production methods or products.

jobber A middleman or local wholesaler who buys from manufacturers, importers, and national wholesalers, and sells to local retailers.

Johnson, Harry (1923-1977) Canada's best-known international economist, Johnson was a prodigious writer and synthesizer of economic ideas covering an enormous range of issues. He was most highly recognized for his work in international trade, macroeconomic policy, international monetary policy, and issues in political economy. Johnson was highly critical of Keynesian economics for what he saw as its failure to deal with the problem of inflation; his

essay "The Keynesian Revolution and the Monetarist Counter-Revolution" was published in his 1972 book, *Further Essays in Monetary Policy.* He was also critical of sociological theories of inflation. He regarded inflation as a global monetary phenomenon which had to be understood in the context of world money supply. Not surprisingly, then, he rejected the use of incomes policies to deal with inflation. Johnson did pioneering work in the monetary approach to balance of payments, showing that balance of payments problems had a monetary explanation. this was set out in his 1958 book, *International Trade and Economic Growth.* Johnson was also critical of many programs designed to aid less developed countries, contending that they were not based on rigorous economic analysis but on a desire to do good. Many of his ideas were set out in his 1967 book, *Economic Policies Toward Less Developed Countries.* Illustrating the wide range of his interests, Johnson also wrote about the development of knowledge and technological progress and their role in economic development and welfare; see for example his 1975 book, *Technology and Economic Interdependence.* Johnson also became a strong advocate of free trade and wrote on the costs of protectionism and the contributions of trade to economic welfare; many of his ideas are contained in his 1971 book, *Aspects of the Theory of Tariffs.* Although Johnson spent much of his university teaching career at the University of Chicago, which he joined in 1959, along with a period from 1966 to 1974 when he held chairs simultaneously at Chicago and the London School of Economics, he retained a strong interest in Canada. In 1962, in his Allan B. Plaunt Memorial Lecture at Carleton University, he blamed the unemployment and inflation problems of the 1958-1961 period on "Canadian government policy (or lack of policy) and specifically the policy of the central bank." He called for a monetarist policy with "some simple rule of monetary management, for example, to increase the money supply at a constant rate corresponding to the long-run rate of growth." The lecture was published in the book *Canada in a Changing World Economy*. In 1963, Johnson wrote *The Canadian Quandry: Economic Problems and Policies*, and in 1965, addressed Canadian issues again in *The World Economy at the Crossroads*. Johnson supported Canada's move to a floating exchange rate in the late 1960s, when most of the world still operated on a fixed-exchange-rate system. In 1978, the year after his death, *The Canadian Journal of Economics* ran a special issue on his work, as did the *Journal of Political Economy* in 1984.

joint account   A bank account in which two or more persons have signing authority and therefore can write cheques and make deposits. The account may require at least two signatures on a cheque or only one, depending on the arrangement made. But each party to the account is liable for any overdraft. Joint accounts are widely used by husbands and wives to manage their household budgets.

joint agreement   In labour relations, a collective agreement among three or more parties. It may consist of an industry-wide contract between many different employers and a single union or several unions. Or it may consist of an agreement between one employer and several different unions representing different groups of workers in the firm.

joint costs   The costs incurred in producing two or more products simultaneously. For example, in petroleum refining, gasoline, fuel oil, kerosene, and naphtha are all produced at the same time. In flour milling, different types of flour and wheat germ are produced simultaneously. In meat packing, various meat products, hides, and

shortening are produced simultaneously. The problem for accountants is to allocate these joint costs in the early, simultaneous stage of production. At a more advanced level of production, costing becomes easier because the products reach a stage at which they require separate types of processing.

joint demand   The demand for two or more products that normally must be used together — in the auto industry, for example, the demand for steel, glass, rubber, carpeting, paint, plastics, electrical wiring, and other products used in the manufacture of a car. A change in the demand for cars will also result in a change in demand for tires and other products used in autos, such as car radios. An understanding of joint demand is important in understanding the economic impact of, say, a major price increase or decrease for one commodity on the demand for other products.

Joint Ministerial Committee on Trade and Economic Affairs   A forum for cabinet-level consultation between Canada and the United States that began in 1953 and continued until 1970. The committee met almost every year, under the chairmanship of the Canadian Secretary of State for EXTERNAL AFFAIRS and the U.S. Secretary of State, and included cabinet ministers from both countries concerned with finance, trade, agriculture, energy, industrial development, balances of payment, mining, and other such matters of joint concern. The governor of the BANK OF CANADA and the chairman of the U.S. FEDERAL RESERVE Board also attended these meetings, which alternated between Ottawa and Washington.

joint tenancy   A form of ownership of land and the buildings on it, in which two or more persons have a common interest and equal rights and in which there is a right of survivorship. This means that, upon the death of one of the owners, the surviving owners automatically own the portion held by the deceased partner. *See also* TENANTS IN COMMON.

joint venture A specific project carried out by two or more firms or by industry and government together. The Syncrude TAR SANDS plant in Alberta was a joint venture of oil companies and of the federal, Ontario, and Alberta governments. Joint ventures are often undertaken if one firm is too small to carry out a project by itself or if the various partners have complementary skills or technologies. It is a way to share the risks of developing a new technology or to tap the expertise of different specialized partners in the joint venture. If the joint venture is successful, the partners also share the rewards. Some countries try to encourage multinational corporations to form joint ventures with local enterprise rather than creating wholly-owned subsidiaries.

journeyman A skilled worker — for example, a carpenter or electrician — who has completed his or her apprenticeship program.

Junior Achievement of Canada The Canadian branch of an international organization founded in the United States in 1919 whose purpose is to teach young Canadians the virtues of free enterprise, the workings of business, and applied economics. Business volunteers work with young Canadians in high school to help them set up and run their own businesses during the school year, as well as teaching the basics of business. Junior Achievement was introduced in Vancouver in 1955 by an American businessman as an extention of the Junior Acheivement in the United States. In 1967, as a centennial project, the CANADIAN CHAMBER OF COMMERCE established Junior Achievement of Canada. Based in Toronto, Junior Achievement also manages the CANADIAN BUSINESS HALL OF FAME.

junior bond A corporate bond with limited collateral; the collateral has been committed as security for more senior debt and is therefore subject to these more senior claims.

junior company A company that, from an investment point of view, does not have an established earnings or dividend record.

junk bond A high-yield bond issued by a high-risk borrower with a poor bond rating. Junk bonds were used extensively in the 1980s to finance LEVERAGED BUYOUTS and other takeovers.

jurisdictional dispute A conflict between two or more unions over who shall represent workers in a particular firm or industry, or over which union members should work on a particular job. It may also be a conflict between two different levels of government over taxing, spending, or regulatory powers, or between different countries over who controls the resources in a disputed body of water.

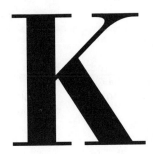

Keidanren The powerful Japanese Federation of Economic Organizations that represents all the leading industrial associations in Japan. It is the most influential private-sector association and plays a major role in developing, with the Japanese government, that country's industrial and trade policies.

keiretsu A Japanese system of business organization built around the model of a family. In a Japanese keiretsu, companies that form a network are organized around a core bank and own shares in each other. This not only protects members of the keiretsu from the threat of unfriendly takeovers, but it also protects them from stock-market pressures based on quarterly financial results, so that companies are able to concentrate on long-term strategic objectives. A typical keiretsu consists of about 20 companies whose industries can range from banking, trading, consumer electronics, and machinery to chemicals, automobiles and parts, semiconductors, and computers, and whose top executives meet on a regular basis to exchange ideas, information, and plans. Underneath this top tier, there is often a second tier of 50 or more

companies that are similarly linked. This process can extend further down the chain. Members of a keiretsu frequently act as customers or suppliers to one another, and the intimate knowledge that the core bank gains from its cross-holdings in the other keiretsu members can allow it to provide lower-cost capital and reinforce long-term strategic investing by the other keiretsu members. Much of the industrial restructuring that takes place within the Japanese economy takes place within the keiretsu structure.

key sector An industry that is considered strategically important to the economic or cultural life of the country. The Canadian government has identified certain sectors of the economy that must be under complete or near-complete control of Canadian-owned companies. These include transportation, banking, broadcasting, and publishing. This doesn't guarantee that the Canadian-controlled firms will meet Canadian objectives. For example, the government has had to impose Canadian-content requirements on the broadcasting industry, as well as requiring Canadian ownership, to get broadcasters to devote sufficient time to Canadian programming. Industrial strategy often focuses on the development of key technology sectors; the United States, for example, targets what it calls critical technologies.

Keynes, John Maynard (1883-1946)
The British economist who provided the theoretical basis for government intervention in the economy through FISCAL POLICY to achieve FULL EMPLOYMENT. In the process, he pointed economic policy in a new direction. Keynes developed his main economic theory on the importance of AGGREGATE DEMAND in the economy during the GREAT DEPRESSION in *The General Theory of Employment, Interest, and Money*, published in 1936. *See also* KEYNESIAN ECONOMICS. Keynes rejected the view of the NEOCLASSICAL ECONOMISTS, who believed that the economy was self-correcting and could be expected to sustain low unemployment and high economic growth on a regular basis. Keynes believed, instead, that the economy was subject to wide swings due to changing attitudes by business to investment; when optimistic, business would invest, and when pessimistic, it would cut back investment. This would quickly spill over into a fall in production and a rise in unemployment. Keynes did not believe that business investment decisions were made according to some rational, mathematical analysis but were based on what he called the "animal spirits" of businessmen. As he wrote in *The General Theory of Employment, Interest, and Money*, "most, probably, our decisions to do something positive, the full consequences of which will be drawn out over many days to come, can only be taken as a result of animal spirits — of a spontaneous urge to action rather than inaction, and not the weighted average of quantitative benefits multiplied by quantitative probabilities."

Keynes did not believe that the free-market economy, on its own, had the capacity to achieve sufficient economic growth to restore full employment. One reason was what he called the stickiness of wages and prices: wages and prices do not automatically decline, so the economy does not adjust to changing market conditions. Therefore, Keynes argued, government should use macroeconomic policy, especially fiscal policy, to stimulate aggregate demand and encourage an increase in production and investment, thus restoring full employment.

Keynes spent most of his life working for the British Treasury or teaching economics at Cambridge University. He was a British delegate to the Versailles Peace Conference in 1919 but opposed allied demands for huge reparations from Germany. He wrote a book that year, *The Economic Consequences of the Peace*, in which he argued that the reparations demanded from Germany were not only immoral, but placed an impossible burden on the country.

In 1936, he published his *General Theory*, after the economists of his day had failed to find a cure for the Great Depression. During the Second World War, he worked as an adviser in the British Treasury and was one of the architects of the post-war multilateral institutions, based on the 1944 BRETTON WOODS AGREEMENT. However, the resulting INTERNATIONAL MONETARY FUND, built around a central role for gold and the U.S. dollar, fell far short of his own ideas of how to reform the world monetary system.

Keynes called for a world clearing bank and an international currency, to be called the bancor. The clearing bank would finance balance-of-payments deficits. If a country's balance of payments fell into a chronic and unsustainable deficit, then surplus countries and the deficit country would all have to take corrective steps. Keynes argued that this would give all countries a stake in achieving equilibrium in the international economy, instead of placing most of the burden on deficit countries.

Keynesian economics The school of economics based on the ideas developed by John Maynard KEYNES and his followers, and based largely on Keynes' major work published in 1936, *The General Theory of Employment, Interest, and Money*, which revolutionized the theory and practice of economics in the 20th century. Keynesian economists rejected the NEOCLASSICAL view that the economy, left to its own devices, tended to operate at full-employment levels. They argued that it was possible for the economy to achieve an equilibrium level at less than full employment, and hence for high unemployment to continue for lengthy periods of time. Neoclassical economists had assumed that all national income would be spent on either consumption or investment goods, and that monetary policy could be used, by adjusting interest rates, to determine the levels of consumption, savings, and investment. Keynes and his followers showed that not all income would necessarily be spent, and that, if it was not, the level of demand in the economy would be insufficient to maintain full employment.

Keynesian economists also rejected the view that the level of interest rates could determine how much people would spend, save, and invest. They argued that the level of saving and spending depended not on interest rates but on how much income a person had; as a person's income rose, the proportion of income spent tended to decline, and the proportion saved tended to rise (*see also* MARGINAL PROPENSITY TO CONSUME). The decision to invest would depend not simply on the cost of borrowed goods but also on the expected rate of return on the investment, something affected very much by an investor's confidence in the future. However, as investment increased, the rate of return would decline (*see also* MARGINAL EFFICIENCY OF CAPITAL). This meant, according to Keynesian economists, that a rich industrial economy would have to find new opportunities for investment to achieve and maintain full employment. Hence, the role of government in running a deficit, to make sure that the level of spending on consumption or investment goods in the economy matched the full-employment level of savings. The MULTIPLIER would then ensure that this additional government spending would generate higher levels of income and employment, and hence, new opportunities for private investment.

Keynes and his followers thus put considerably less emphasis on MONETARY POLICY, and introduced a much bigger role for fiscal policy in achieving full employment. They also paved the way for a more significant role for government in economic management, and therefore reduced reliance on free-market forces. They believed that a free-market, capitalist economy, left to its own devices, would fail to achieve long-term full employment, and that any kind of private-enterprise system could only be maintained through government intervention in a MIXED ECONOMY. Keynesian economics flourished until the 1970s, when first INFLATION and then STAGFLATION came to be seen as the principal challenges for economic policy makers. As a result, some economists embraced MONETARISM and its reliance on an anti-inflationary monetary policy, and rejected the notion that governments, through fiscal and other policies, could effectively manage economic performance. The result was a shift back to neoclassical economics, with its emphasis on less government intervention and a greater role for market forces. This led in turn to policies favouring deregulation, privatization, and SUPPLY-SIDE ECONOMICS. However, in the late 1980s, as economies stagnated under the burden of slow growth, high unemployment, and a widening disparity between rich and poor, economists turned their attention to refining Keynesian economics. *See also* POST-KEYNESIAN ECONOMICS.

kickback An illegal or improper payment by a supplier to a retailer: for example, by a contractor to a government or private builder, or by a worker to a union official to get a job.

Kirby report *See* TASK FORCE ON ATLANTIC FISHERIES.

kiting The practice, sometimes with fraudulent intent, of juggling bank accounts by depositing cheques back and forth between different accounts to make it look as though there is more money on hand than there really is, or to cover a temporary cash shortage. While kiting was a widespread practice in the days before computerized banking, when the CLEARING of cheques was slower, it is harder today because of much speedier clearing by computers.

Klein, Lawrence (b. 1920) The American economist who won the 1980 Alfred Nobel Memorial Prize in Economic Science for "the creation of ECONOMETRIC MODELS and the application to the analysis of economic fluctuations and economic policies."

knowledge industry A broad term describing an industry that produces information goods and services, and whose employees are scientists, technicians, and skilled knowledge workers and managers. Examples include the telecommunications industry, research and development organizations, the mass media, accounting, education, and banking.

Kondratieff wave The theory that business cycles run for long periods of 50 to 60 years, named after a Russian economist, Nikolai Kondratieff, who made important studies of long-term cycles during the 1920s. He argued that these long cycles are due to fundamental changes in investment, production techniques, technology, and new markets, and were part of the rhythm of long waves inherent in the capitalist system; several decades of prosperity are followed by several decades of slump. According to Kondratieff, the start of a new wave or cycle brings with it great changes in society and expansion into new markets, which in turn can provoke revolution and war. Examples of his cycles include the Industrial Revolution of the late 18th and early 19th centuries; and the new steel-making technology and use of steam at sea in the last half of the 19th century; and the introduction of electricity, the internal-combustion engine, and chemicals in the first half of the 20th century. The computer, telecommunications, and microelectronic technologies of the late 20th century, the information revolution, could be another example.

Koopmans, Tjalling (1921-1985) The Dutch-born economist who, along with Leonid Kantorovich, won the 1975 Alfred Nobel Memorial Price in Economic Science for "their contributions to the theory of optimum allocation of resources." Koopmans, who became an American, applied linear programming, or what he called activity analysis, to economics, using it to solve problems in transportation, investment, and economic performance.

Kuznets, Simon (1901-1985) The Russian-born economist who won the 1971 Alfred Nobel Memorial Prize in Economic Science for "his empirically founded interpretation of economic growth which has led to new and deepened insight into the economic and social structure and process of development." Kuznets, who became an American citizen, expanded the application of ECONOMETRICS and also made an important contribution to the study of income distribution.

labour One of the FACTORS OF PRODUCTION, labour is the human effort employed in the production of goods and services. It consists not only of the number of workers and the hours they have worked, but also of their physical and mental effort, skills, and initiative. This effort is rewarded by salaries, wages, professional fees, commissions, bonuses, and other payments.

labour agreement A contract between a union on behalf of employees in a workplace and an employer setting out pay and various conditions of work for a specified period — one, two, or three years. It is usually called a COLLECTIVE AGREEMENT.

labour council An association of union locals in a metropolitan area or district that works to represent union interests and concerns in local matters. The locals usually belong to CANADIAN LABOUR CONGRESS-affiliated unions.

Labour, Department of Also known as Labour Canada, the federal government department, established in 1900, that is responsible for labour laws and policies affecting unions, management, and workers under federal jurisdiction. It assists in the mediation and resolution of labour disputes, sets standards for wages and conditions of employment and occupational health and safety, promotes workplace programs to encourage co-operation and adjustment, and promotes Canada's interests in improved labour conditions in international bodies. About 10 percent of the labour force comes under its jurisdiction, including the banking, rail, airline, and shipping industries, and the employees of the federal government and its agencies, and crown corporations. The department influences provincial labour laws indirectly, since reforms at the federal level can encourage provincial reforms. The department is responsible for the CANADA LABOUR CODE and the CANADA LABOUR RELATIONS BOARD, which deal with the basic administration of federal labour law. The department also publishes nation-wide statistics on wage settlements and time lost due to strikes and lockouts, investigates labour-management questions to reduce the incidence of strikes and lockouts, publishes detailed data on wage rates for communities across Canada, and works with union leaders to represent their concerns and interests in the formulation of government policy. The department is also Canada's liaison with the INTERNATIONAL LABOUR ORGANIZATION.

labour dispute   A dispute between an employer and employees belonging to a union, which may lead to a STRIKE in which workers stop working and mount a picket line at the place of work to prevent or discourage others from dealing with the employer, or which may lead to a LOCKOUT of the workers by the employer. Employees can also pressure an employer by working to rule, which means that they follow every step in the formal labour contract in carrying out their duties, by refusing to work overtime, which has the practical effect of slowing down the pace of activity, or by engaging in rotating strikes to interrupt the provision of service in targeted locations, which are changed from day to day.

labour force   As defined in the LABOUR-FORCE SURVEY of Statistics Canada (publication 71-001), all Canadians 15 years and over who are employed or unemployed. It does not include members of the Canadian armed forces, inmates in penitentiaries, or residents of Indian reservations, the Yukon, and the Northwest Territories. Included among the employed are people who, during the survey week, did any kind of work, full or part time, including people who weren't paid but who contributed to a family-owned business, and people who had jobs but weren't working due to illness, a strike or lockout, bad weather, or vacation. Included among the unemployed are those who are actively looking for work, were laid off, or were unemployed but had a new job to start in four weeks or less. The size of the labour force is calculated from a

monthly survey of 62,000 households across Canada.

labour-force survey   A monthly survey by Statistics Canada to determine the actual and SEASONALLY ADJUSTED UNEMPLOYMENT RATES, as well as growth in employment and in the size of the labour force, which are broken down by sex, age, level of education, and province; some information is also available for major cities. The survey also measures the participation rate of Canadians of labour-force age in the labour force and gives a detailed picture of employment changes in major industries, information on numbers of workers not working due to labour disputes, and other labour-force data. It is based on a survey of 62,000 households with a total of about 115,000 respondents, across Canada, taken during a reference week each month, usually in the week containing the 15th of the month. It started in 1946 as a quarterly survey but became a monthly survey in 1952. The monthly survey is published by Statistics Canada (publication 71-001). Historical statistics are found in publication 71-201. *See also* UNEMPLOYMENT RATE, EMPLOYMENT INDEX, LABOUR FORCE.

labour hoarding   The practice followed in some companies of retaining skilled employees during a recession even though not all workers will be fully employed and unit costs will thus rise. The reason for this policy is that management has an investment in the employees in the form of their on-the-job training and experience. If a firm has to hire new employees at the time of the next economic recovery, it will have to invest in training new workers. Retaining employees during a recession means that the firm avoids the problems and costs of attracting new workers during the next recovery. Labour hoarding occurs mainly during short-lived recessions. If a recession is prolonged, an employer will lay off workers, starting with the least experienced and least skilled.

labour income The most important measure of demand in the economy, since labour income accounts for roughly 70 percent of income in the economy. As measured by STATISTICS CANADA, it includes wages and salaries paid to employees, along with payments by employers for the future benefits of employees, such as pension-plan contributions and unemployment-insurance and workmen's-compensation premiums for 18 industries, by province. So labour income is also an important measure of labour costs in the economy. Wages and salaries include bonuses, commissions, taxable allowances and benefits, and directors' fees. Labour income does not include the salaries of the armed forces or the self-employed. The monthly data are contained in Statistics Canada publication 72-005.

labour-intensive industry An industry that uses a high proportion of labour per unit of output and a relatively low proportion of capital, compared with the average for all industries. This means wages will form a disproportionately large part of the industry's or firm's total costs. Examples include clothing, footwear, and retailing industries. Labour-intensive industries in high-wage industrial countries such as Canada are highly vulnerable to competition from low-wage countries. Some industries have shifted from labour intensive to CAPITAL INTENSIVE; these include the automobile, steel, and food-processing industries.

labour legislation Federal and provincial laws that spell out the rights of labour and management, how labour relations are to be conducted, and the procedures for union certification and decertification, collective bargaining,

mediation, and strikes and lockouts. Such laws also deal with minimum wages, job safety, accident prevention, job discrimination, maternity protection, layoffs and termination of employment, vacations with pay, public holidays, hours of work, technological change, the use of replacement workers during a strike, and overtime. Labour laws guarantee workers the right to organize; they establish labour-relations boards to certify unions as bargaining agents, and compel employers to bargain in good faith with a certified union. These laws also prohibit employers from interfering in union efforts to organize and guard against other unfair labour practices. They set out strict rules on collective bargaining, and the steps, including CONCILIATION and MEDIATION, that must be followed before a strike or lockout can legally take place. Strikes and lockouts are prohibited during the life of the contract. *See also* CANADA LABOUR CODE.

labour market The market in which wages and the quantity of labour employed are determined based on the supply of and demand for labour. It includes many submarkets for particular skills and industries; but these many submarkets affect one another, since relative-pay relationships are important and since there may also be a high or low degree of labour mobility between one skill or industry and another. Economists often talk of the efficiency of labour markets — the speed with which news on job vacancies reaches workers seeking jobs, the mobility of workers from one job to another, the skills-training available, and the impact of unions as a barrier to entry. The FRICTIONAL UNEMPLOYMENT rate can be reduced somewhat if labour markets are efficient in matching job vacancies with workers, encouraging mobility to better jobs, and making skills-training available. The supply side of the market consists of the number of workers available and their level of skills, while the demand side of the market consists of the requirements of employers for additional labour, at different levels of skills, to meet their production targets.

labour market institutions   Arrangements that affect the speed at which labour markets adapt to new economic conditions or which affect the level and composition of employment. Factors include the costs of laying off workers and the payroll taxes incurred in hiring new workers, both of which may discourage employers from hiring; the benefits available under unemployment insurance, which may deter workers from accepting new jobs; the flexibility or rigidity of wages; and the availability of training or retraining for workers.

labour mobility   The ability of workers to change jobs or move into new careers. Government can aid labour mobility by providing up-to-date information about available jobs, grants for workers to move to new communities where jobs exist, or skills training so that workers can move up the occupational ladder to better-paying jobs. A high degree of labour mobility shows that labour markets are working well, and that the social system is open and does not put barriers in the way of people who have the talents or skills to move into better jobs. The main barriers to labour mobility are lack of knowledge of job vacancies, lack of money to move out of an area of chronic unemployment into one where jobs are available, lack of access to education and skills training, or union and professional restrictions that make it hard for newcomers to enter the skill or profession. A high degree of labour mobility can lead to lower rates of unemployment.

labour productivity   A measure of PRODUCTIVITY calculated by dividing total output in the economy, or in the business sector, by the labour used to produce it. What is measured is output per unit of labour.

labour relations   A specialized field that deals with the relations between employers and employees, including COLLECTIVE BARGAINING. Most employers have a labour-relations staff, while some universities designate the field as a special area of study. Increasingly, the field of labour relations is subject to regulation under federal and provincial labour laws. The term INDUSTRIAL RELATIONS is sometimes used in manufacturing companies.

labour-relations board   A federal or provincial board that administers labour laws and deals with some forms of labour-management grievances. Such boards, among other things, monitor the certification of unions as bargaining agents, adjudicate complaints of unfair labour practices, and grant or revoke collective-bargaining rights. *See also* CANADA LABOUR RELATIONS BOARD.

labour slowdown   A form of labour protest that falls short of a complete work stoppage but is designed to put pressure on an employer to resolve an outstanding dispute with the union or to settle a contract. The advantage to the union members is that the employer must continue to pay them, even though they are producing less than they normally would. *See also* WORK TO RULE.

labour theory of value   The theory that labour is the source of all value. The idea was first expressed by David RICARDO, who argued that all costs of production were embodied or stored in labour costs. But the idea is usually associated with Karl MARX, who argued that the surplus between the subsistence wages paid by employers and the revenues gained from the sale of what the workers produced properly belonged to the workers, but was appropriated by capitalists as the inevitable exploitation of workers under the capitalist system. According to the theory, only labour — the amount of labour needed to produce something — gives a good or service value. No account is taken of the part played by CAPITAL or LAND in the production process; no provision is made for rent or profits. The theory also disregards such sources of value as SCARCITY or UTILITY. Thus, if a product requires five hours of labour to make, it is worth five times as much as a product that takes one hour to make. Marx used the theory to argue that workers were exploited by capitalists. He complained that a product that took, say, five hours of labour to make, might require 10 hours of labour to buy — the difference between the wages paid the workers and the value of the goods produced, the profit, being the extent to which capitalists exploited labour.

labour turnover The number of employees who leave a company or other place of employment in the course of a year as a percent of the total number of employees.

labour union *See* UNION.

Laffer curve A representation purporting to show the optimal rate of taxation, developed by U.S. economist Arthur Laffer in the 1980s. He argued that governments could end up collecting less in revenues if tax rates were high than they would if tax rates were low since high tax rates would create a disincentive to generate additional income on the part of individuals. A lower tax rate, on the other hand, would encourage more investment and lead to additional growth, providing governments with a bigger tax base. Laffer developed a curve that he claimed would show the point at which increases in the tax rate would cease to produce additional tax revenues. The Laffer curve, and its assumption of the benefits of lower tax rates, became one of the main planks of the SUPPLY-SIDE economists during the Reagan administration in the United States from 1980 to 1988, and the justification for major tax cuts in that period. The Laffer curve was dismissed by many economists as unfounded in economic theory and a misguided leap of faith that turned the United States from a creditor nation to a debtor nation.

lagging indicator A statistical series that follows on the heels of changes in economic conditions to provide evidence of changes in the economy — statistics on business investment, for example, are a lagging indicator because business tends to delay investment until the economy has grown sufficiently to justify additional investment. LEADING INDICATOR, COINCIDENT INDICATOR.

laissez-faire An economic doctrine (from the French, meaning "let it be") that asserts that the best way to achieve strong economic growth and a high standard of living is to limit government intervention in the economy to maintaining the value of the currency and protecting private property. Competition, open markets, and untrammelled private enterprise are seen as the key sources of economic progress. The belief in unrestricted private enterprise emerged in the 18th century as a reaction against government interference and MERCANTILISM. Laissez-faire economists argued that self-interest should be allowed a free rein, since this would result in the optimal allocation of resources and provide the surest protection of political liberties in the process. Laissez-faire began to lose its appeal in the late 19th century because it led to the growth of MONOPOLY and OLIGOPOLY and a socially unacceptable inequality of income. Government intervention was needed to deal with harsh social conditions, such as the use of child labour and the arbitrary treatment of workers, as well as to break up monopolies and to provide human and physical infrastructure, from education to clean water and roads. *See also* MIXED ECONOMY.

land   One of the classical FACTORS OF PRODUCTION, which includes all of the limited natural resources found on land, such as minerals, oil and gas, forests, and the fertility of the soil; it also includes the resources of the sea, such as fish and offshore minerals. RENT is the return on land; it may consist of a royalty paid on mineral resources, a direct payment or rent for the use of the land, or a tax or fee.

land assembly   The acquisition of adjoining parcels of land from different owners, often through middlemen or brokers, for a major commercial or housing project. Land assembly is usually carried out by private developers, but the federal and provincial governments sometimes work together to assemble land for a public-housing project, airport, or other such facility.

land reform   The break-up of large landholdings in less-developed countries or of collective farms in former Communist countries and the distribution of this land to individual farmers in smaller holdings, so that they can retain the income they earn through their own effort. Such reform is carried out not only for reasons of equity: it is also argued that land reform should lead to higher agricultural output, since individual farmers will have a greater incentive to work hard and increase their output.

land registry   A provincial office where the titles to all individual parcels of land and buildings are registered. Titles are searched at such offices whenever a property is bought or sold, to ensure that there are no outstanding claims against the property.

land-transfer tax   A tax levied on the sale of land or real estate. It is a percentage of the sale price.

land-use planning   The designation of land for specific purposes or the banning of certain types of activity on particular parcels of land. For example, municipalities designate which land can be used for low- or high-density housing, industry, office buildings, and stores, through zoning by-laws. Provincial governments may restrict the conversion of prime agricultural land into other uses such as housing projects, shopping centres, and industrial parks. Federal and provincial parks are a form of land-use planning: land is set aside for recreational use. In some cases, provision is made for mixed use — for example, in a municipality land may be used for apartments or offices; federal or provincial land may be used for forestry and as recreational parkland.

landlord   The owner of a property who leases out the use of his property to others in return for payment or rent.

landlord and tenant laws   Provincial laws that set out the rights of landlords or property owners and tenants, the people who rent the property. These laws set out the conditions under which a tenant may be evicted, the responsibilities of the landlord and tenant for the care of the property, lease rights, and other such matters. Such laws may also cover rent controls or procedures for tenants to appeal large rent increases.

language of work   The language used by an employee on the job. In most parts of Canada it is English; in Quebec, it is French, with some government-approved exceptions for head-office activities. In federal government activities, the general principle is that public employees should be able to work in the language in which they feel most at home, although this does not always apply. This reflects the spirit of the Official Languages Act, passed by Parliament in 1969, which said that English and French "possess and enjoy equality of status and equal rights and privileges as to their use in all the institutions of the Parliament and Government of Canada."

last in, first out (lifo)   A method of determining the value, in a company's books, of its INVENTORY. It assumes that the first items removed or sold from inventory were the last ones to be placed in the inventory, so the cost of goods sold is based on the cost of the most recently purchased parts and components in inventory, even though these may not be the ones actually used. But it also values the items remaining in inventory according to the cost of the last lot received. This approach is favoured during periods of high inflation, since it results in a more accurate assessment of the replacement value of the inventory. It results in higher expenses being reported in a company's books and hence, lower reported profits. *See also* FIRST IN, FIRST OUT.

Latin American Economic System (SELA)   A regional organization established in 1975 to promote the trade and development interests of 26 Latin American and Caribbean nations, based in Caracas, Venezuela. SELA stands for Sistema Economico Latino-Americano.

Latin American Free Trade Association (LAFTA)   An early attempt to achieve a free trade area in Latin America. The agreement was signed in 1960 by Argentina, Brazil, Chile, Mexico, Paraguay, Peru, and Uruguay. Ecuador, Colombia, and Venezuela joined later. Only modest progress was made in reducing tariffs among the LAFTA members. In 1968, LAFTA agreed in principle with the members of the Central American Common Market to establish a single common market for Latin America by 1985. But a year later, in 1969, Bolivia, Chile, Colombia, and Ecuador formed a new free trade group, the ANDEAN PACT. The remaining LAFTA members wound up the association in 1981 and replaced it with the Latin American Integration Association, which achieved only modest progress in eliminating or reducing some tariffs between its members, which were Argentina, Bolivia, Brazil, Chile, Colombia, Ecuador, Mexico, Paraguay, Peru, Uruguay, and Venezuela. Instead Latin American nations are moving toward a series of regional free trade agreements, including the Andean Pact and MERCOSUR, with Mexico negotiating a separate NORTH AMERICAN FREE TRADE AGREEMENT with Canada and the United States, which could be expanded to include other Latin American nations. *See also* ENTERPRISE FOR THE AMERICAS INITIATIVE.

Latin American Integration Association (LAIA)   A successor organization to the LATIN AMERICAN FREE TRADE ASSOCIATION, set up in 1981 to help integrate the economies of Latin America. Its members are Argentina, Bolivia, Brazil, Chile, Colombia, Ecuador, Mexico, Paraguay, Peru, Uruguay, and Venezuela.

laundering   *See* MONEY LAUNDERING.

law of diminishing marginal utility   An economic law stating that, as a consumer buys more of a good, the satisfaction derived from each extra unit is less and less, even though his total satisfaction may increase with additional consumption. For example, a steak-lover may want to eat a good many steaks in a week, but at some point each additional steak yields less and less satisfaction, although each one continues to add some satisfaction. The first steak in the week will yield a great deal of satisfaction, but the fourth, while still yielding some satisfaction, will yield less, and the fifth less still. The ability of the consumer to appreciate more steaks declines, although it does not disappear. This law can be used to justify a tax system based on the ability to pay. Since each dollar of income yields some but less and less satisfaction, taxing away from those with high incomes to help those with low incomes adds to the total utility or satisfaction in the community.

law of diminishing returns   An economic law stating that, although an increase in one of the factors of production while the other factors remain fixed will cause total output to increase, at some point each extra unit of that factor of production will yield successively smaller increases in output. This is because the extra units of that factor of production have less and less of the other factors of production, which are fixed, to work with. For example, in a factory with a fixed amount of machinery and space, the addition of extra workers will at some point add less and less output, because there will be less and less space and machinery for each worker to use.

law of downward-sloping demand   If the price of one good is raised while all other prices are unchanged, less of the good will be demanded. Similarly, if the supply of a good is increased, the extra supply can only be sold if the price is reduced.

law of one price   If there are no barriers to trade between a domestic and a foreign market, then the prices of commodities should be the same in both

markets. The ability to make a profit if the prices were to be different in the two countries by buying in the low-price country and selling in the high-price country — what is known as ARBITRAGE — helps ensure that the prices do in fact converge in the two markets.

law of supply and demand   The basic law determining what is produced and in what quantity and at what price in a free-market economy. If the demand for a product is greater than the supply, the price will rise; in this way, a scarce resource will be allocated to those willing to pay a higher price. At the same time, rising prices will encourage new producers to enter the market, so that supply will increase and prices will decline. Similarly, if supply rises, prices will fall, unless demand increases at the same time. If supply rises and the demand remains constant, prices will fall. Through the market mechanism, the equilibrium price is the price at which goods are willingly produced and willingly purchased. The law of supply and demand thus operates to allocate scarce resources in society, assuming that conditions of PERFECT COMPETITION exist, by determining stable prices based on the intersection of supply and demand forces.

law of the sea   *See* UNITED NATIONS CONFERENCE ON THE LAW OF THE SEA.

Law Reform Commission of Canada A federal commission created in 1970 to study the country's laws and legal procedures, including laws affecting business, administrative law, and the legal powers of regulatory agencies, and to recommend improvements and reforms. The commission, which reported to Parliament through the Minister of Justice, was abolished in 1992, along with a number of other government-funded research bodies.

layoff The temporary or permanent loss of a job. An employer may temporarily lay off workers, for example, if there is a strike at a supplier or because inventories of the finished product are too high. But if the economy is in recession and the prospects for recovery are distant, then an employer will be more inclined to announce permanent layoffs. In the latter case, the workers laid off may have first chance at jobs when the company begins rehiring; but that may not be for 18 months or longer, so it is more likely that the workers will seek out jobs elsewhere. Under the CANADA LABOUR CODE, workers must receive advance notice of layoffs, with the length of notice depending on the number of workers affected. Provincial labour laws have similar provisions.

lead manager The underwriting company that leads a new issue of shares or bonds. The lead manager is responsible for all dealings with the issuer, as well as the preparation of the prospectus and the planning and organization of the issue, including how it will be sold and distributed. The lead manager organizes the syndicate and selling group for the new issue.

lead time The amount of time it takes for an economic action to be completed. The term is used in several senses: It can describe the amount of time that elapses before a change in economic policy, such as a tax cut for instance, starts to have any effect, which in this case would be an increase in consumer spending. It can refer to the amount of time it takes to build a major project, such as a nuclear-power plant or natural-gas pipeline; in such a case it might be 10 years before engineering design, regulatory hearings, financing, and construction are all completed. Or it may refer to the time that elapses between the ordering of goods or parts and the date they are actually delivered.

Knowledge of lead times is important in economic and business planning.

leading indicator A statistical series that provides advance signal of changes in economic activity. Leading indicators represent decisions already made that will affect the future performance of the economy, or reflect expectations by investors and others about future economic prospects. Examples include statistics on the deflated value of building permits, indicating future construction activity; primary steel production, indicating orders by auto, construction, and other industries; the deflated value of pre-tax profits, indicating the resources available for business expansion; the deflated value of the money supply, indicating credit conditions; the Toronto Stock Exchange composite index, indicating investors' expectations of future profits and dividends; the average hours worked in manufacturing, indicating the intensity with which labour is being used and the likelihood of new hiring; and the ratio of selling prices to unit labour costs, indicating profit margins. Two Canadian banks publish their own leading-indicator indexes: the Royal Bank of Canada and the Canadian Imperial Bank of Commerce. Statistics Canada publishes its own CANADIAN COMPOSITE LEADING INDICATOR in its monthly *Economic Observer* (publication 11-010). *See also* LAGGING INDICATOR, COINCIDENT INDICATOR.

leads and lags 1. The speed-up or delay in the payment of trade and other international debts that may occur when there is uncertainty about a country's future exchange rate. If the Canadian dollar is expected to rise in value, then Canadian importers will delay paying (a lag) until the change takes place, since the expected rise means that they will need fewer Canadian dollars to pay the bill. But if the

Canadian dollar is expected to decline in value, a Canadian importer will speed up (a lead) payment to a foreign supplier because, if payment is delayed, extra Canadian dollars will be needed to pay the bill. International corporations and active importers and exporters are always watching for possible exchange-rate changes, and try to time their payments and billings to earn an extra profit or to avoid an unnecessary cost if they can. This can have an unsettling effect on a country's balance of payments and may add to the need for exchange-rate adjustment. 2. The difference in timing between the peaks and troughs of the BUSINESS CYCLE and the peaks and troughs of leading and lagging indicators. For example, machine-tool orders, a leading indicator, may peak a year before the business cycle peaks, while consumer spending, a lagging indicator, may peak after the business cycle has peaked.

leakage The extent to which efforts by a country to influence economic conditions are diluted by external forces. For example, a tax cut to stimulate the economy by increasing consumer spending may not have the impact anticipated, because much of the increased purchasing power may simply be spent on imports instead of on domestic-made goods and services. This means the increased demand for domestic-made goods and services is not sufficient to generate the level of new business investment that had been expected. Leakage may also occur if consumers decide to pay off old debts instead of increasing their spending, or if an accelerating rate of inflation offsets the higher purchasing power from a tax cut.

lean manufacturing A manufacturing system based on teams of workers that are each capable of doing multiple of tasks, including maintenance, inspection, and machine setup. Developed in the Japanese automobile industry in the 1950s and 1960s, and transferred to other manufacturing industries, the system allows teams of workers to turn out products using less inventory, less investment, and with fewer mistakes than the mass production techniques of FORDISM. Lean manufacturing is based on worker participation rather than managerial authoritarianism. It gives top priority to quality control, continuous improvement of manufacturing and other operations, worker skills and training, and cooperative management. With employee participation in teams, quality problems are identified and corrected during the manufacturing process instead of only at the end of the assembly line. Inventories are regarded as costs, so suppliers are required to be flexible and adapt to just-in-time inventory systems; this means that relationships between manufacturers and suppliers become much more important. Under lean manufacturing, suppliers must adopt the same techniques to meet the quality demands of manufacturers and to be able to contribute to continuous improvement of parts and components. Because of the cell or team approach used in lean manufacturing, companies also have more flexibility in producing small batches of customized products.

learning curve The process by which unit costs of production are reduced over time as management and workers acquire experience with a system of production and learn to use it with increasing efficiency.

lease 1. A contractual agreement between the owner of a property and someone who pays for its exclusive use for a specified period of time; the owner is the lessor and the user is the lessee. A lease may be for a house, apartment, commercial building, piece of land, automobile, aircraft, oil tanker, or other major capital good. A lease sets out the terms and conditions under which the contract is made, including the rights and responsibilities of both the lessor and lessee. **2.** A contract between an oil, natural-gas, or mining company and the federal or a provincial government; it gives the company the right to extract resources in return for a royalty payment. *See also* PERMIT.

leaseback A method of business financing in which a firm sells a plant, office building, or other capital asset to a financial institution or other private investor, on condition that the firm can lease the plant, building, or other asset back for a specified number of years at a negotiated rent. There are many advantages to such an arrangement. For the firm, it means that the business is assured of the facilities it needs; in the meantime, it can also obtain the proceeds from the sale to use as working capital to expand, while writing off the leaseback costs as a business expense. For the investor, the arrangement represents a reasonably safe investment with an assured rate of return.

leasehold land Land on which a person or firm may build a property but which is owned by someone else; the person or firm building the property has a long-term lease for the land.

leasing A method of business financing in which a firm determines its need for major capital goods — say, oil tankers, aircraft, or heavy machinery — and approaches a financial institution or private investors and arranges to lease the capital goods from them, instead of buying them itself. There may be a tax advantage to the financial institution or private investors, and the firm thus does not have to tie up its working capital or use its line of credit at the bank. Another form of leasing is that in which a business firm acquires capital goods —

say, cars and trucks — and leases them to a variety of users for short periods of time.

least-developed countries Countries with a per capita gross national product of US$600 or less, according to the WORLD BANK. In 1992, it listed 43 countries, including China and India, that fell into this category. Collectively, these countries, with their 3.1 billion people, accounted for about 60 percent of the world's population. A narrower definition, which consists of countries with a per capita GROSS NATIONAL PRODUCT of US$100 or less, with manufacturing representing less than 10 percent of GROSS DOMESTIC PRODUCT and a literacy rate of 20 percent or less, was adopted by the UNITED NATIONS CONFERENCE ON TRADE AND DEVELOPMENT in 1971. Under this definition there were in 1989 a total of 41 countries, which accounted for 12 percent of the world's population but barely 1 percent of the world's gross domestic product. *See also* FOURTH WORLD.

ledger The computer file or book in which the accounts of a firm or other organization are initially recorded. Separate ledgers may be maintained for different activities of the firm or other organization, such as ACCOUNTS PAYABLE and ACCOUNTS RECEIVABLE.

legacy *See* BEQUEST.

legal tender Money that, under a country's laws, must be accepted in the settlement of any obligation or debt. In Canada, the Canadian dollar is the legal medium of exchange and cannot be refused when offered in payment of a debt.

leisure A form of non-monetary income that is not measured in national income and other statistics that are designed to illustrate improvements in the standard of living. Leisure is earned when workers get a shorter work week with no cut in pay and is purchased when workers refuse overtime. It is reflected in many practices — in shorter work weeks, longer vacations with pay, more public holidays, and less discretionary overtime. It is made possible by improved productivity, which raises total output in the economy at a faster rate than the growth in population.

lend-lease A U.S. program of assistance to its Second World War allies, introduced in 1941, which did not require repayment as such but which expected the equipment to be returned after the war. The United States also expected the recipients to agree to an open, multilateral trade and investment environment after the war. The program was important to Canada because, under the HYDE PARK AGREEMENT, British lend-lease assistance could be used for material and components from the United States that Canada needed for inclusion in military equipment it was supplying to Britain. This relieved the drain on Canada's low supply of U.S. dollars to pay for such material and components.

lender of last resort An important function of the BANK OF CANADA and other central banks: they lend funds to the chartered banks when the chartered banks have temporary shortages of funds. This happens only rarely, and the funds are usually not needed for more than a few days, but the presence of the central bank as a lender of last resort adds an important element of strength to the banking system, and is one reason why a repeat of the GREAT DEPRESSION of the 1930s would be unlikely. The term is sometimes applied to government development corporations if they take on the function of assisting private firms that cannot obtain financing from any private source, such as a chartered bank or venture-capital firm.

Leontief, Wassily (b. 1906) An American economist (but born in Leningrad) who won the Alfred Nobel Memorial Prize for Economic Science in 1973 for "the development of the INPUT-OUTPUT method and for its application to important economic problems."

less-developed country (LDC) A term that is applied to about one hundred countries at varying stages of economic development, all of which have a per capita income relatively well below that of Canada and other industrial countries. In 1990, Canadians had a per capita GROSS NATIONAL PRODUCT of US$20,470, compared with an average of US$350 for the lowest-income developing countries and US$2,220 for middle- income developing countries. Many less-developed countries have a low rate of domestic savings, a large part of the population engaged in agriculture, a low level of industrialization, inadequate infrastructure, large segments of the population living near the subsistence level, a dependence on foreign capital and development assistance, and considerable disguised unemployment. But others have managed to achieve high savings and investment levels and sharply rising living standards. LDCs range from countries with strong economic prospects whose main needs are capital, education, infrastructure, and markets, such as Mexico, South Korea, Thailand, Turkey, and Brazil to those with serious but surmountable difficulties, such as India, Egypt, Jamaica, and Nigeria, and those with scarce resources, a strong poverty cycle, burdensome population problems, and extremely low per capita incomes, such as Bangladesh, Ethiopia, and Afghanistan. The LDCs include most of Central and South America, all of Asia except Japan, most of Africa except for South Africa, southeast Europe, and the Caribbean Islands, and account for more than 70 percent of the world's population. *See also* THIRD WORLD, FOURTH WORLD, NEW INTERNATIONAL ECONOMIC ORDER, UNITED NATIONS CONFERENCE ON TRADE AND DEVELOPMENT, CANADIAN INTERNATIONAL DEVELOPMENT AGENCY, NORTH-SOUTH DIALOGUE, DEVELOPMENT ASSISTANCE, FOREIGN AID, INTERNATIONAL BANK FOR RECONSTRUCTION AND DEVELOPMENT.

letter of credit An instruction from one bank to a bank in another country to pay the bearer a specified sum, provided that the attached conditions are met. The issuing bank guarantees repayment to the correspondent bank. Letters of credit are important in foreign trade, since they give exporters an assurance of payment. A Canadian exporter shipping goods to, say, Mexico, will get a letter of credit through the Mexican customer in which the customer's Mexican bank instructs its Canadian correspondent bank to pay the Canadian exporter a certain sum, with the Mexican bank guaranteeing the Canadian bank repayment. If the Mexican customer defaults, this becomes a problem for the Mexican bank.

letters patent A synonym for articles of incorporation; the charter granted to a company when it is incorporated under federal or provincial law. The document sets out the company's proposed name, the purposes of the company, its AUTHORIZED CAPITAL, and the number of directors.

leverage The ability of a firm to raise an increasing amount of debt relative to its equity and reinvest it in the hope of earning a higher return than the interest payments that have to be made or the debt. A firm may borrow large sums of money in the form, say, of corporate bonds, preferred shares, and medium-term bank financing, thus relying heavily on DEBT CAPITAL, as opposed to another firm that may obtain more of its financing through the issue of COMMON SHARES, thus relying heavily on EQUITY CAPITAL. If the firm relying heavily on debt capital earns a higher rate of return on this capital than it must pay in interest and preferred dividends, then the extra earnings are attributed to the common shares, thus boosting their value and, in all likelihood, their dividends. In a company relying heavily on equity capital, the profits would have to be spread among a larger number of common shares, so that earnings per share would be lower even if total profits were identical. A company may succeed in significantly improving the position of its common shareholders by borrowing large sums of money and using them profitably. But, if the market turns and a tighter monetary policy leads to higher interest rates and a recession, then a firm may find much greater difficulty in earning the cash flow to finance its debt-servicing costs; this will reduce earnings and lower the value of the firm's shares. At the same time, the value of the asset for which the debt was raised in the first place may decline in value, forcing lenders to call in loans or force the sale of assets, and also leading to a plunge in the value of the firm's common shares. If the firm finds that it is no longer able to earn a profit on its borrowed capital, it may have to halt dividends to common shareholders and sell off assets. Leverage can be a risky method of raising common-share earnings, as many real-estate and other firms found in the early 1990s. Individuals also seek gains from leverage by investing through margin accounts or options that only require the payment of a fraction of the value of the security's value.

leveraged buyout The takeover, of a company, that is financed by debt — bank loans and JUNK BONDS, that pay extremely high rates of interest — instead of by cash, or by exchanging shares, where the acquiring company pays the shareholders of the takeover target with shares in the acquiring company, or the sale of new shares. As a consequence, the resulting firm is saddled with a large amount of debt at high interest rates. In a leveraged buyout, the successful acquirer often plans to pay down the debt by the sale of assets and through increases in cash flow in the acquired company from lowering costs, such as cancelling research and development or other long-term activities and by laying off workers. Leveraged buyouts are highly vulnerable to rising interest rates and a recessionary economy.

Lewis, Sir Arthur (b. 1915) Winner of the Nobel Memorial Prize in 1979, along with Theodore SCHULTZ, for "their pioneering research into economic development research with particular consideration of the problems of developing countries." The St. Lucia-born economist stressed the importance of physical and social infrastructure, from roads and water to education and communications, as a precondition of economic growth. He also pointed to the dual economies of many developing countries where a large supply of agricultural workers meant that wages in urban centres were depressed until urban growth absorbed the supply of agricultural labour. In 1955, he wrote his groundbreaking book *The Theory of Economic Growth*.

liabilities All the debts of a corporation, partnership, or individual; one part of the BALANCE SHEET. Liabilities include 1. short-term or current liabilities such as accounts payable, short-term debts, income and other taxes due, and the amount of long-term debt that must be paid within twelve months; and 2. long-term liabilities, which include long-term debts and deferred income taxes. Liabilities are the contributions by creditors to a business, and increase as a result of increases in assets financed through borrowing or as a result of incurring other new expenses. On a balance sheet, liabilities are subtracted from assets — what remains is the SHAREHOLDERS' EQUITY, or ownership in the business. Thus, assets always equal liabilities plus shareholders' equity.

liability insurance A form of insurance that protects the holder by paying legal claims, usually up to a specified maximum, arising from injury, death, or other damage to a third party resulting from negligence in the care of property or manufacturing of a product, or from mistakes made by an employee.

LIBOR *See* LONDON INTER-BANK OFFERED RATE.

licence A certificate permitting a person, firm, or organization to do something legally. Licences are widely used by governments, for example, to permit someone to operate a radio or television station or a cable-television system, to export uranium, to import certain agricultural products, to work in a certain occupation or profession, to hunt or fish, or to sell hot dogs from a stand on the main street of a city or town. Owners of PATENTS and COPYRIGHTS grant others a licence to use their works in return for a fee or royalty. For example, a manufacturer may grant a licence to another company to manufacture or distribute its products in a specified market. *See also* COMPULSORY LICENCING.

lien The right of a creditor to attach a claim to someone else's property or to take possession of that property until a debt is repaid. It means that the actual owner of the property cannot sell it to a third party until he has first paid off his creditor. But the creditor cannot sell the property without the permission of the courts after all other efforts have failed to secure payment of the debt. There are various types of liens. A bank or mortgage company, for example, may attach a claim to a property if the owner is behind in his payments. A builder-repairman may attach a mechanic's lien to a property if he has performed repair, renovation, or other such work and has not been paid. A landlord may seize the possessions of a tenant who is behind in his rent, while a hotel owner may seize the baggage of a hotel guest who has not paid his bill. And a government may attach a claim to property if taxes are unpaid.

life-cycle theory of consumption and saving   The pattern of saving and consumption over the lifetime of a household, with current consumption not related to current disposable income but to the expected lifetime earnings and changing needs of the household over the lifetime. Since households want a smooth consumption path they dissave or borrow when they are young and have low incomes, save during their working years to accumulate assets for their old age, and dissave when they are old.

life insurance   A contract between an individual and an insurance company in which the insurance company promises to pay a sum to the family or other beneficiaries of the individual if the individual should die while the contract is in force; in return, the insured person agrees to pay a regular and specified premium. Sometimes the insurance is paid by a third party, who is usually the beneficiary; for example, a partnership may place an insurance policy on the life of each partner, with the surviving partners the beneficiaries. Employers may also provide life insurance for their employees, with their families as beneficiaries, as a fringe benefit. In endowment life-insurance policies, the insured person collects a cash sum if he reaches a certain age.

The most common forms of life insurance are: 1. Term insurance, in which insurance is provided for short periods of time, ranging from a trip, in the case of air travel, to, say, five years, in the case of normal term insurance. Premiums may increase with age and the insured has no claim for cash once the term is up. This form of insurance is popular with people who want considerable protection when their families are young and they have few other assets, but who expect to accumulate other assets, such as their own home, shares, and a valuable pension plan as they grow older. 2. Whole life insurance, in which the person whose life is insured continues to pay premiums for life or until a certain age, say, 65.

life table   A calculation of life expectancy that shows how many people would survive out of, say, 100,000 persons born in a particular year, based on past death rates prevailing over a certain period of time. Successive calculations are made for all those in the same group who reach two years of age, three years, and so on, all the way through the lifespan. Thus, a life expectancy is calculated, for example, for all those born in 1941 who reach the age of 40. The life table is an important demographic tool used to calculate the future size of the population and has important specific-use applications — in the life-insurance industry, for example, in pension and labour-force planning, and in the calculation of future school and university populations. Life tables may understate the lifespans of a generation because they do not always take into account medical progress.

lifo   *See* LAST IN, FIRST OUT.

limit order   An instruction from a client to a broker to sell a share at a specified price or above.

limit pricing   The practice of a MONOPOLIST in holding down prices so as to discourage the entry of a competitor into a particular industry or product line.

limited company   A private or public company with LIMITED LIABILITY. It is designated as such by the use of the word "Limited" or "Ltd." in its name.

limited liability   The limitation of a shareholder's liability for losses incurred in a business to the money invested in the business; creditors cannot attach a claim to the shareholder's other possessions, such as the family house and savings, as they could before the days of the limited-liability company. If a limited-liability company has a big debt, its creditors can demand that its assets be sold; if these do not meet the creditors' claims, the creditors are out of luck — they cannot sue the shareholders. The legal distinction between a company and its shareholders was developed in the 19th century and paved the way for a rapid growth not only in business enterprise but also in the capacity of companies to raise capital from investors for high-risk activities. As an institutional change, the emergence of the limited-liability company had a profound impact on countries that adopted this form of business organization. Without limited liability, it would not be possible to organize large corporations and persuade individuals to invest in them. It is an important legal concept that makes modern corporations, large pools of savings, and dynamic economic growth possible, and encourages individuals to risk their money without fear of losing all they own in the event of the failure of a company they invest in. In particular, its absence would prevent pension funds and insurance companies from investing in shares; it would expose even the small investor to the loss of all he owned, even if he bought just a few shares in a company that failed.

limited parnership   A business owned and operated by more than one person and in which the various partners have only a limited liability for the debts of the business — usually up to the level of their investment commitment should the business fail. Limited partnerships are found most often in real-estate ventures, where tax incentives are a key element of the investment package. The partnership is operated by a general manager, and investors in effect assume a responsibility for their share of the mortgage. Tax considerations allow for a low up-front contribution, and the rental income stream of the property is expected to cover the mortgage payment obligations of each partner. See also SOLE PROPRIETOR-SHIP, PARTNERSHIP, and CORPORA-TION.

limits to growth   A view of the world's future that sees the combination of population growth and rising standards of living creating an unsustainable pressure on the world's supply of natural resources, its ability to produce food, and the functioning of the ecological system. Unless the world reverts to ZERO POPULATION GROWTH, undertakes large-scale recycling of resources, practises conservation, and aims for zero economic growth, it faces famine, the collapse of the environmental support systems, drastic declines in standards of living, and exhaustion of energy and mineral resources within the next hundred years. This gloomy view of man's future, which resurrects some of the fears of Thomas Robert MALTHUS, is based on two studies: Jay Forrester's *World Dynamics* in 1971 and the CLUB OF ROME's 1972 study

The Limits to Growth by Dennis Meadows and others. While many economists accepted the need for population control, the careful use of resources, and measures to safeguard the environment, they rejected the computer model of man's future devised by Forrester, Meadows, and others. They pointed out that the pricing system can ration the use of resources and encourage the development of substitutes, and noted that man's history is one of adapting technology to raise productivity and overcome natural barriers to growth. There is no reason, they argued, to believe that man will be any less inventive in the future. Since these earlier criticisms, however, there has been renewed concern over the tension between a rising world population, the aspiration of people in LESS-DEVELOPED COUNTRIES for a higher standard of living, and the pressures on the world's carrying system or biosphere. *See also* RIO PROJECT, SUSTAINABLE DEVELOPMENT.

line of credit The agreement by a bank or other lender to make credit up to a certain upper limit available to a borrower that the borrower can draw on when necessary. The financial institution may require notice that a drawing on the credit is to be made. All businesses establish a line of credit with their bankers, with the amount of such lines being renegotiated from time to time. Lines of credit are negotiated in advance of the need for credit. Banks usually retain the right to revise a company's line of credit if its financial circumstances should change.

linear programming A mathematical technique used to solve certain business and economic problems, usually those in which the best course of action has to be chosen from among several alternatives. The technique may be used, for example, to help firms to choose their most profitable product mix, the best location of a plant site, or the most economic cattle-feed mix that meets a specified nutritional standard.

linkage **1.** The effect that the growth of one industry has on the growth of others. The growth of the petrochemicals industry can stimulate the growth of the oil and natural-gas industries as suppliers, and the growth of the plastics, fertilizer, and synthetic-fabrics industries as users of its output. Similarly, the basic steel industry influences the growth of supplier industries such as iron ore and coking coal, and user industries such as those making finished steel products. **2.** In trade and other international negotiations, the linking of agreement on one issue with settlement of a disagreement on another issue. For example, in the late 1960s, when the United States had oil-import quotas, Canada told the United States that it could only get more Canadian natural gas, which the United States wanted, if it also agreed to buy more Canadian oil, which the United States was refusing to do.

liquid asset Cash, plus any assets that can be quickly converted to cash. These include CANADA SAVINGS BONDS, certificates of deposit, bank term deposits, and guaranteed-investment certificates. Other assets that are also liquid but, depending on the market, may lead to a loss if they are sold to investors, include government and corporate bonds and shares.

liquid market A market in which there are sufficient buyers and sellers so that individual sales and purchases can be made with ease.

liquidation The termination of a business, either by a company's creditors seeking repayment of their loans or by shareholders who want to realize the value of their holdings, a process also known as winding up a business. An intermediary — a liquidator — is usually appointed to sell the company and get the best price possible for the assets, to pay off the creditors, and to distribute the remaining cash to the eligible shareholders or owners. If the proceeds are not sufficient to pay off all creditors, then collateralized creditors such as banks, which have lent with first claim on specific assets of the company, along with federal and provincial tax departments, are paid first. The remaining funds are distributed on a pro rata basis to the remaining creditors.

liquidator   The person appointed by creditors who takes over the affairs of a company when it is being wound up to make sure that the creditors are paid off before the owners or shareholders get their proceeds.

liquidity   **1.** The capacity of a firm to meet its obligations or to handle unanticipated costs. There are two ways of measuring this. The first is the CURRENT RATIO test, which is the ratio of current assets to current liabilities. The second is the QUICK RATIO or acid-test ratio, which is the ratio of current assets minus inventories to current liabilities. The second method is preferred, because inventories may not always be readily saleable. **2.** The availability of money to meet the obligations of a particular industry or the private sector generally, or the capacity of individual nations to obtain hard currencies, SPECIAL DRAWING RIGHTS, or gold, to settle their international balances of payments and thus to finance their trade and investment. **3.** The ability to convert an asset into cash quickly with little or no loss in its value. A person is said to be highly liquid if he has considerable cash, or assets that can be quickly converted to cash at little cost. Currency is the most liquid asset of all, but most bank- and trust-company deposits are also highly

liquid, as are CANADA SAVINGS BONDS. **4.** The capacity of a market for a particular share or other security to absorb normal levels of buying and selling without wide fluctuations in price.

liquidity constraint   The inability of individuals or firms to borrow against future income because lenders believe they will be unable or unlikely repay any loans they obtain.

liquidity preference   The desire by savers to hold their money in cash or bank accounts rather than to invest it in shares, bonds, mortgages, and other such investments, which are less easy to convert back to cash. A high liquidity preference represents an unwillingness to save. People have a variety of motives for preferring to hold their money in highly liquid forms. These include the normal-transactions desire to have enough money on hand to meet everyday needs, the precautionary desire to have money readily available to meet an emergency, and the speculative desire to hold on to highly liquid assets in the belief that stock-market conditions will improve or interest rates go up. Thus, the demand for money on hand is influenced by many factors, including the level of income a person has, his expectations about investment opportunities, the current level of interest rates, and cultural attitudes. Because savers value liquidity, they must be compensated by a relatively high return for holding less liquid assets.

liquidity trap   Circumstances in which interest rates are so low there is no incentive to save and households therefore prefer to hold highly liquid assets. Under these conditions a government cannot stimulate the economy by further reductions in interest rates; instead it must use increased government spending or lower taxes if it wants to boost AGGREGATE DEMAND in the economy.

list price   The published price of a product before any markdown has been made for high-volume purchases, dealer discounts, or other trade rebates.

listed company   A company whose shares meet the listing requirements of a STOCK EXCHANGE and are traded on the exchange. Each stock exchange has its own listing requirements. The required level of earnings, net working capital, and minimum net tangible assets for a company to be listed depends on the size and importance of the exchange. The TORONTO STOCK EXCHANGE has the most demanding requirements and the VANCOUVER STOCK EXCHANGE and ALBERTA STOCK EXCHANGE the least demanding.

Companies must meet a number of requirements to maintain their listed status on a stock exchange; if they fail to meet these requirements or break stock-exchange rules, they may be suspended from trading or lose their listed status altogether. Listing requirements range from engraving company share certificates so that they cannot be forged and filing quarterly financial statements to filing an annual report in response to a standard stock-exchange questionnaire on general corporate information and reporting any changes in dividends and in other financial arrangements, including sale of new shares and any proposed material change in the company's business or affairs. This last requirement is important and covers such matters as the speedy reporting of takeover bids, the acquisition or sale of a major block of shares or such assets as a mining or oil property, any change in ownership that may affect control, any change in the directors or principal officers of the firm, and any change in the nature of the business.

listing statement   A stock-exchange report providing basic information on a company when its shares are listed.

livestock   Agricultural production of cattle, sheep, hogs, and chickens for consumption.

Livestock Feed Board of Canada   A federal crown corporation established in 1966 to deal with feed-grain shortages in eastern Canada and British Columbia. Headquartered in Montreal, the agency mandate is to ensure the availability of feed grain in eastern Canada and British Columbia at stable prices and to ensure the availability of adequate storage space in eastern Canada. The agency also administers the Feed Freight Assistance Program, which subsidizes transportation costs and carries out market monitoring and research activities.

load   The charges in an insurance contract, mutual-fund contract, registered retirement savings plan, and other such investments to cover administration and selling costs, including a salesperson's commission. *See also* FRONT-END LOADING.

loan   A sum of money borrowed by a government, firm, small businessman, individual, or other organization from a lender at an agreed rate of interest, for a specific purpose and usually for a specified period of time. There are many different types of loans — for example, SECURED LOANS and UNSECURED LOANS, VENTURE-CAPITAL loans, BRIDGE FINANCING, and MARGIN loans. Loans are made by many institutions, including banks, trust companies, sales-finance companies, acceptance companies, stockbrokers, and mortgage-loan companies.

loan guarantee   An assurance to a lender by government, a government agency, a corporation or an individual that a loan to a third party will be repaid by the entity giving the guarantee. Loan guarantees are used by governments to help companies obtain capital for growth or to finance export sales to riskier markets.

loan insurance   Insurance that is available for consumers on consumer and mortgage loans. Consumers pay a premium and, in the event of their death, the lender is paid off so that there is no claim against the estate.

loan shark   An unlicensed moneylender who lends money at unconscionable rates of interest and who may resort to violence and other illegal means to force repayment. The federal government has legislated a "criminal rate of interest," which is an effective annual rate in excess of 60 per cent, to help prosecute loan sharks.

loanable funds   The potential supply of money available to be lent to governments, business, other organizations, and individuals. It consists of current savings (including retained earnings in business firms and a reduction in business cash balances) or a transfer of funds from bank chequing accounts to non-chequing accounts, investment certificates, and the like, and increases by the central bank in the money supply. These are the funds available for use by government, business, other organizations, and consumers.

lobby   An organized attempt by a corporation, industry, union, or any special-interest group to persuade government to do something or not to do something. Lobbying is not illegal in Canada, and there are many types of lobbying and lobbyists. Under the Lobbyists Registration Act, which came into effect in 1989, lobbyists are required to register with the Lobbyists Registration Branch of Consumer and Corporate Affairs. Failure to do so or the filing of false information can lead to penalties of up to two years in jail and a fine of $100,000. Professional lobbyists who arrange meetings or communicate with MPs, senators, or members of the executive branch of the public service to influence future legislation; to defeat, pass, or amend legislation once it is before Parliament; to seek a change in any regulation under the Statutory Instruments Act; to influence the development of any policy or program of the federal government; to seek the award of a monetary grant, contribution, or financial benefit from the federal government; or to seek the award of a contract, must register their names and other details, give the names of clients, and indicate what area of public policy they are seeking to influence. A separate registry is maintained of employees of companies or other organizations whose jobs include government relations, with much more limited reporting requirements.

local   The smallest unit in a UNION. A union usually consists of a national or international body made up of dozens or hundreds of locals, depending on its size; sometimes, for administrative convenience, locals are organized into regional bodies. Each local elects its own officers, handles its own negotiations with employers, and administers local union matters.

local taxes   Taxes levied and collected by municipalities for municipal purposes, including, in most provinces, local school boards. Since they are creations of the provinces, under the CONSTITUTION ACT, 1867, municipalities are limited to imposing DIRECT TAXES to raise revenue. The main types of local taxation are PROPERTY TAXES on land and buildings; business taxes that are levied on the operators of local businesses; and water taxes, which are designed to recover all or part of the cost of providing residents with clean, drinkable water.

location theory   The branch of economics that attempts to determine the factors that influence where a firm will locate a plant or other activity. Depending on the nature of the industry, the factors range from straight economic considerations, such as access to resources or a university, or closeness to markets, to less-quantifiable considerations, such as political stability and the desire of professional employees to live in or near a city that has a wide range of cultural and social activities.

The factors affecting the location of a firm differ for individual industries. For example, a smelter would be expected to locate near a mineral ore-body because the costs of transporting a heavy ore with considerable waste would be high; but if the transportation cost is low, for oil moved by pipeline, for example, then the oil may be refined close to market, since it is easier to refine the oil into many different oil products close to market than to arrange the transportation of each product separately over a long distance. Although aluminum or nickel are processed in remote areas, finished aluminum and nickel products tend to be produced close to where they are consumed. For high-technology industries, closeness to a university with high-quality science and engineering departments will be important, while for a high-value manufacturing company, proximity to good skills-training institutions will be important. For labour-intensive industries, access to low-cost labour is critical. Closeness to markets, costs of transportation, availability of skilled labour, local labour and environmental laws, the chance of a complementary industry, tax and government incentives, the availability of cheap energy in energy-intensive industries, and the need for supporting service industries and local infrastructure, are all factors affecting the location of industry. *See also* REGIONAL DEVELOPMENT.

locked in   A situation where an investor cannot get out of an investment except by incurring a loss or sacrificing a part of his or her profit.

lockout   A labour dispute in which the employer closes his establishment so that the employees cannot work and are not paid. Like a STRIKE, a lockout can only follow certain other legal steps after a COLLECTIVE AGREEMENT has expired. While lockouts are much less frequent than strikes, they are sometimes resorted to by employers, either to force a settlement or to weaken the power of the union. In some industries, such as meat packing, where a number of contracts in major firms expire at about the same time, some meat packers may bring on a lockout if one firm has been struck. The purpose is to reduce the pressure on the struck packer to agree to a high settlement, which he might have to do if the other firms stayed open and picked up part of his business.

locomotive principle   The expectation that in the face of a worldwide slowdown one of the major economies (the United States, Germany, or Japan), will stimulate its own economy and in the process benefit other parts of the world economy; when a major country, such as the United States, stimulates its own economy, it also increases the demand for imports, thus pulling along its trading partners as well, hence the analogy to a locomotive. The United States, Germany, and Japan are the only economies that are big enough to act as locomotives for the world economy. One of the purposes of policy co-ordination among the GROUP OF SEVEN nations is to determine when the need for a locomotive arises and to assess whether one of the major economic powers is able and willing to play that role.

lode   A mineral deposit that is found in a body of soil or rock.

logical fallacy of composition The mistaken conclusion that because something is good for each individual, it is therefore good for the community as a whole. For example, it may be a good idea for individuals to save more and borrow less, but if everyone did this the economy would suffer from a fall in consumer demand; workers would be laid off, and people would end up having less to save or having to dip into their savings to get by.

Lome Agreement An agreement signed by the EUROPEAN COMMUNITY (EC) and 46 countries from Africa, the Caribbean, and the Pacific in the capital of Togo, Lome, in 1975, giving duty-free access to the EC for most exports from these countries, which are mainly former colonies of EC nations. The EC also provides financial aid through the European Development Fund and helps stabilize the agricultural export income of these countries, which now number about 60, through a program called Stabex. Since 1975, the Lome Agreement has been renewed three times.

London Interbank Offer Rate (LIBOR) The reference point for many international syndicated loans, especially those made in EUROCURRENCY MARKETS. The rate is not set by the central bank but is determined by the leading banks in much the same way that they set rates for CERTIFICATE OF DEPOSIT rates in individual countries. It is the interest rate at which banks offer to lend funds in the international interbank market. Just as domestic loans are often made in relation to the PRIME RATE, international loans are often made at a specified number of BASIS POINTS above LIBOR, depending on the risk. The rate is the rate available to the most creditworthy banks operating in the London market.

London Metals Exchange (LME) The world's principal spot and futures market for metals such as copper, lead, zinc, nickel, tin, and silver. Although much of the output of the world's metal mines is sold through negotiated contracts between producers and consumers, the LME plays an important role in the pricing of metals. The exchange dates back to 1881.

long-range planning Planning for a decade ahead or longer. Long-range planning by governments or business attempts to take account of the major changes taking place in technology, the supply and demand for natural resources and fuels, the changing social and political attitudes, demographic changes, and the evolution of new international relationships. It is strategic planning.

long selling The selling of shares that the seller already owns, as opposed to SELLING SHORT.

long term A period of time that is long enough so that all the factors of production in a firm or the economy can be varied to achieve a more efficient level of output. This means long enough to retool industrial plants, to install new methods of production, to train workers in new skills, to adapt new technologies, and to build new production facilities. In the long run, such fundamental changes can be made; but in the short run, a firm or economy has to work with its existing facilities and methods and can only increase output by making better use of its existing factors of production or by adding inputs, such as more labour.

long-term asset Sometimes called a fixed asset. Long-term assets may consist of buildings, plant and equipment, land, and other assets of a relatively permanent nature or assets that at least have a long life. Long-term assets are listed on the BALANCE SHEET below CURRENT ASSETS.

long-term debt A bond, debenture, or other form of debt maturing after 10 years.

long-term forecast An economic forecast that looks five years or longer ahead.

long-term liability A debt that does not have to be repaid within the next 12 months. As a long-term debt, or a portion of it, approaches the repayment date, it will cease to be a long-term liability and will become a short-term liability instead. Long-term liabilities are listed on the BALANCE SHEET after short-term or current liabilities.

loon The brass-copper coin that replaced Canada's paper $1 bill in 1989. Also known as the "loonie," the coin depicts the loon bird on one side.

loophole An unexpected interpretation of a law or contract, usually a tax law, resulting from it being badly or vaguely worded, that allows someone to do something that was not intended — to evade taxes, for example, or to get out of an onerous requirement in a contract.

Lorenz curve A curve that can be used to show the degree of inequality of distribution of wealth, income, or some other variable in a country.

loss **1.** In a corporation's financial year, the failure to earn sufficient revenues to cover costs. **2.** In an investment, the sale of an asset for less than the sum paid for it.

loss leader A product sold by a retailer at a loss to attract customers into his store. The expectation is that, once the consumer is in the store, he will decide to buy a better-quality product or to buy other products in addition to the loss-leader item.

lottery A game of chance designed to raise money. Participants buy tickets that have a series of numbers printed on them; a sequence of numbers is selected, and the winners, the people holding tickets containing those numbers, get the prizes. Lotteries are operated in Canada by the provincial governments and by charitable organizations. An amendment to the Criminal Code in 1969 legalized lotteries in Canada by making it no longer an offence to organize and operate a lottery. In 1970, Loto Québec was set up as the first government-operated lottery. In 1973, Parliament created the Olympic Lottery to help finance the 1976 Olympic Games in Montreal. In 1975 to 1976, Ontario and the Western provinces launched their lottery schemes. Also in 1976, the federal government created Lotto Canada, a crown corporation, to operate a national lottery to reduce the debt of the 1976 Olympics; funds have also been used to help finance the 1978 Commonwealth Games in Edmonton, the 1979 Canada Games, and amateur sport and fitness programs across Canada. In 1979, the federal government announced its intention to get out of the lottery business and leave it to the provinces; Lotto Canada was subsequently wound up.

Louvre Accord An agreement reached by the GROUP OF FIVE (G-5) finance ministers plus Canada at the Louvre, in Paris in February, 1987, to confirm that the U.S. dollar had fallen enough since the PLAZA ACCORD in 1985. The ministers agreed to try to maintain their respective exchange rates within secret target zones. The G-5 ministers met by themselves and then invited Canada and Italy to join them as the GROUP OF SEVEN finance ministers; Italy refused to participate, maintaining it was simply being asked to rubber-stamp the G-5 agreement but Canada did attend.

Luddite A term used today to describe those opposed to technological change. It was originally applied to British workers who, in the early 19th century, destroyed labour-saving machinery, which they said was contributing to unemployment. The term is said to come from a Ned Lud who, late in the 18th century, was reputed to have destroyed machinery in anger over the loss of jobs it caused.

lump-of-labour fallacy The belief that there is only so much useful work to be done in society so that technological progress can only lead to higher unemployment; as a consequence, the supporters of this belief resist the introduction of technological change, seek shorter working hours, and justify various work rules that lead to FEATHER BEDDING. It is a static view of economics and ignores the possibilities for new consumer wants and new industries, as well as the role of government in stimulating economic growth and creating more jobs.

lump-sum payment An unusual or one-time payment, for example, the payout from a REGISTERED RETIREMENT SAVINGS PLAN, the receipt by an author of a large payment for the film rights to a book, the payment to a beneficiary of an insurance policy, or the receipt by an individual of all his past payments into a pension plan when he changes jobs. Income-tax authorities allow taxpayers to lessen the tax load on such payments, which otherwise would be treated as ordinary income in the year received and thus be subject to the top marginal tax rate. Registered retirement savings plans are converted into annuities, for example, and taxed as the annuity pays out an annual sum to the recipient. *See also* INCOME AVERAGING.

luxury tax A tax on articles not considered essential to everyday life. Canada, for example, imposes at the federal level an excise tax on alcohol, cigarettes, perfume, jewellery, and other luxury items.

M-1, M-2, M-3   *See* MONEY SUPPLY.

Macdonald Commission   *See* ROYAL COMMISSION ON THE ECONOMIC UNIONS AND DEVELOPMENT PROSPECTS FOR CANADA.

Machinery and Equipment Advisory Board   A federal board created in 1968 to consider applications for duty remission on imported machinery and equipment. The board, consisting of a chairman and the deputy-ministers of the then departments of Finance, National Revenue, and Industry, Trade, and Commerce, could grant the remission of duty on imported machinery and equipment if they were not available from a Canadian source and if it was in the public interest to do so. Under Canada's import policy on machinery and equipment, tariffs were remitted on imports to reduce the cost of business investment, unless there was a Canadian producer of the machinery. The board was also in a position to identify types of machinery for which demand was high enough to justify production in Canada. In 1985, it was transferred to REVENUE CANADA.

MacPherson Commission on Transportation   *See* ROYAL COMMISSION ON TRANSPORTATION.

macroeconomic policy   The use of MONETARY and FISCAL policies to manage the economy and achieve economic goals such as FULL EMPLOYMENT, low INFLATION, ECONOMIC GROWTH, or a more stable BALANCE OF PAYMENTS.

macroeconomics   The study of the behaviour and performance of the economy as a whole, as opposed to MICROECONOMICS, which concerns itself with the study of sectors of the economy. Macroeconomics concerns itself with the big picture, the overall level of consumption, investment, and government spending in the economy; in other words, macroeconomics is concerned with the combined results of the millions of individual decisions that routinely take place in the economy. It looks at the aggregate of demand, the workings of monetary and fiscal policy, the banking system, prices, savings, trade, and the balance of payments. It is concerned with the gross domestic product, total employment, inflation, savings rates, the balance of payments, investment, and trade. Macroeconomists deal with policies to achieve full employment and stable prices. Macroeconomics tries at the theoretical level to understand how and why firms and households make the decisions they do and how they will behave in differing circumstances. It also tries to understand the behaviour of the economy by extrapolating the behaviour of typical firms or households to predict the behaviour of key variables and to establish relationships among these variables.

maintenance of membership A clause in a collective agreement that requires all union members to remain in good standing in their union for the life of the contract if they wish to keep their jobs. A union member who breaks union rules and is no longer a member in good standing would have to be fired by his or her employer.

make-work project A method of increasing jobs without necessarily accomplishing anything of great usefulness. For example, a union may insist on certain unnecessary job practices to inflate the number of employees and, therefore, its membership. *See also* FEATHERBEDDING. In times of high unemployment, government sometimes pays unemployed workers to carry out miscellaneous jobs, such as cleaning out culverts alongside highways, washing windows in senior citizens' homes, or other such tasks, simply to get purchasing power into the economy and to help speed up economic recovery.

Malthus, Thomas Robert (1766-1834) A British clergyman and professor of political economy, best remembered for his pessimistic warning about population growth, which was contained in his *Essay on the Principle of Population as It Affects the Future Improvement of Society*. The essay was first published anonymously in 1798 and was revised six times, with the final edition published in 1826. Population, Malthus said, could not exceed food supply. However, there was a tendency for population to grow at a geometric rate (1, 2, 4, 8, 16, 32), while food production could only be increased at an arithmetic rate (1, 2, 3, 4, 5, 6, 7). This meant an expanding population would put enormous and increasing pressures on the prevailing standard of living. Efforts to increase the productivity of the land, Malthus argued, would be thwarted by the LAW OF DIMINISHING RETURNS; in other words, the earth was limited in its capacity to provide the basic needs of a growing population. At the same time, the costs of producing extra food would rise, so that real wage rates would decline and the growth of population would reduce mankind to the margin of subsistence. Malthus refrained from advocating population controls, but campaigned for late marriages and sexual abstinence.

It was Malthus's gloomy view of humans being doomed to a subsistence existence and periodic bouts of famine or other natural disasters that would hold population growth in check, that led Thomas Carlyle to call economics the "dismal science." What Malthus failed to foresee were the great gains in agricultural productivity achieved in the 19th and 20th centuries as a result of science. Nor did he anticipate the decline in FERTILITY RATES. Nonetheless, the Malthusian view of population pressures on food supplies may have some relevance to some LESS-DEVELOPED COUNTRIES. *See also* NEO-MALTHUSIANISM.

man-hour The amount of work done by one employee in an hour. It is a unit used to measure productivity and to calculate labour and other costs.

man-year *See* PERSON-YEAR.

managed float A floating-exchange-rate system in which the central bank intervenes in foreign-exchange markets to moderate sharp fluctuations in the nation's exchange rate or to push the exchange rate, over time, either up or down. While some intervention is accepted by the major nations to moderate unusual fluctuations, interventions to push a currency up or down deliberately are regarded as improper. The former is considered a clean float, the latter a dirty float.

managed trade Trade that is subject to quotas or other restrictions that effectively control the volume of trade. The purpose is to control the level of exports or imports of certain products or to keep a trade surplus or deficit within a specified limit. Trade in clothing and textiles, for example, has been managed under a quota system that limits exports under the MULTIFIBRE AGREEMENT. Countries also negotiate VOLUNTARY EXPORT AGREEMENTS. The purpose of managed trade is to regulate the flow of trade between countries, as opposed to free trade, which accepts the market outcome of competition.

management **1.** The people in a firm or other organization who have authority and make decisions, as opposed to labour, which carries out the decisions so that the tasks set by management are fulfilled. **2.** The running of a firm or other organization, including the setting of objectives, the planning of new products and services, the co-ordination of all the different activities of the organization, the setting of policies for employees, customer relations, sales, and other practices, and the utilization of the various factors of production to achieve the most efficient level of output or provision of services. In a typical organization, there is senior management, which sets policies and objectives, middle management, which takes charge of various functions such as sales or accounting, and on-the-floor or supervisory management, which is at the level of foreman or office manager.

management buy-out The purchase of the entire business or a division of the business by the management in a company. Management usually obtains its financing from outside sources, and may resort to a LEVERAGED BUYOUT.

management by exception A form of management control in which higher-level management intervenes only when actual performance deviates significantly from planned performance. It means that management has only to concern itself with details of an operation when something is going wrong.

management by objectives A form of management control in which employees are motivated, and their performance assessed, through personal job goals that are defined by the employee and his or her supervisor, or senior executive, together. Firms can also set corporate objectives that are agreed to by the board of directors and become the performance targets for senior executives.

management consultant A person or firm that specializes in helping businesses and other organizations to improve their managerial efficiency or to solve particular management problems, such as poor inventory control, sour employee relations, or the failure of a production line to function effectively. A management consultant may be called in to help reorganize a company, to introduce a computer system, to help find new top executives, to train senior employees in management skills, or to reorganize lines of command, for example. Canadian management consultants have provincial accreditation bodies and a national trade association, the Canadian Association of Management Consultants.

management fee   A fee charged by an INVESTMENT COMPANY to a mutual fund or pension plan for advice on investments or management of the investment portfolio.

management science   The application of modern mathematical and computer techniques to management. For example, the use of OPERATIONS RESEARCH, GAME THEORY, or LINEAR PROGRAMMING to make investment or pricing decisions.

management services   The charge made by a parent company to its foreign subsidiaries, to cover head-office costs in administering the subsidiary or to recover costs for the use of head-office know-how by the subsidiary. Up to a point, such charges are legitimate, but they can be abused to get profits out of a Canadian subsidiary without paying corporate income tax or withholding tax. REVENUE CANADA has strict rules on charges that can be deducted as management services. Statistics Canada publishes information on the charges made by foreign parent companies to their Canadian subsidiaries in Canada's International Trade in Services (publication 67-203).

manifest   An itemized inventory of the cargo of a ship, plane, freight car, long-distance truck, or of the contents of a warehouse.

manipulation   Buying or selling the shares of a company to falsely create the impression of active trading and, in the process, deliberately seeking to raise or lower the price of the shares so that other shareholders will buy or sell, depending on the objective of those doing the manipulating.

manpower planning   Planning that assesses the future demand for labour within a firm, including types of skills needed, and develops a strategy to recruit and train future employees or to upgrade the skills of existing employees. Manpower planning can also be done at the provincial or national level to identify the future supply and demand for labour, changing job skills in the economy, and the types and numbers of immigrants necessary to fill skill gaps. This means that manpower planning is an important element in setting education policy, immigration levels, and skills-training needs. Unless the necessary skills training is carried out, an inflation-generating bottleneck can occur in labour markets as an economy expands. The Department of EMPLOYMENT AND IMMIGRATION CANADA publishes periodic estimates of future manpower needs for many different job categories.

manpower policy   Any policy that deals with labour supply. Manpower policies include programs to facilitate the mobility of labour to jobs, placement services for the unemployed, job training and retraining, policies to help workers adapt to technological change, and improved methods of letting workers know where job vacancies exist.

manufacturers' new orders, shipments, and inventories   An important monthly indicator published by Statistics Canada that helps to identify economic trends (publication 31-001). It shows, by province and for 22 industries, the dollar value of shipments, new orders, unfilled orders, inventories held by manufacturers, and the inventory-to-shipments ratio. A coming recession could be signalled by a decline in the growth of new orders and a build-up in inventories. Conversely, an upsurge in new orders and a decline in manufacturers' inventories could be a sign of economic recovery.

manufacturers sales tax   A federal sales tax introduced in 1924 and imposed on the sale price on goods manufactured or produced in Canada, or imported into Canada, unless specifically exempted from the tax. Because manufacturers sold their products in different ways and through different types of distribution systems, customers ended up paying different amounts of tax. In 1930, the tax had declined to just 1 per cent, but the need for revenues pushed it up to 8 percent by 1936, and by 1986, it was up to 12 percent. The tax gave importers an advantage over domestic producers since the sales tax base on imports was the value for customs duty, and not the transportation, marketing, advertising, and other costs included in the price and tax base of Canadian-produced goods. The tax also put Canadian exporters at a disadvantage. The 1967 ROYAL COMMISSION ON TAXATION proposed that the tax be replaced by a retail sales tax, to be jointly administered by the federal and provincial governments; as an alternative, it proposed a VALUE-ADDED TAX. In 1975, the Minister of Finance tabled a discussion paper proposing a sales tax at the wholesale level. In 1977, a Commodity Tax Review Committee reversed support for a wholesale sales tax, opposed a value-added tax, and called for a joint federal-provincial retail sales tax. In the 1981 budget, the government announced it would replace the tax with a wholesale sales tax to come into effect on June 1, 1982, but this did not go ahead. In 1983, the Minister of FINANCE appointed a committee to review the manufacturers sales tax and to propose alternatives. The committee rejected a wholesale sales tax and proposed instead that the federal government negotiate with the provinces to shift the tax to the retail level, including a federal-provincial value-added tax. In 1987, the Minister of Finance published a white paper on tax reform that promised an end to the manufacturers sales tax and its replacement by "a broadly based multi-stage tax that extends to the retail level. This multi-stage tax would be a form of value-added tax. It would be levied on and collected from all businesses, in stages, as goods move from primary producers and processors to wholesalers, retailers, and finally consumers. Under this multi-stage tax, businesses will pay tax on their sales and claim a credit for any tax paid on their purchases." The tax would treat all businesses the same way, eliminate the favourable treatment enjoyed by importers, help Canadian exporters, and treat all goods and services alike. The Minister of Finance proposed three options: a national sales tax jointly administered by the federal and provincial governments; a goods and services tax to be applied at a uniform rate on virtually all goods and services in Canada; or a value-added tax. In 1991, the manufacturers sales tax was replaced by the GOODS AND SERVICES TAX.

manufacturing industry   An industry that takes raw materials, semifinished products, or finished parts and components, and uses them to produce final goods or intermediate goods used in the production of final goods.

maquiladora   A foreign trade zone in Mexico. The system was established in Mexico in 1965.

margin   1. The amount an investor pays toward the total cost of shares when the shares are bought on credit; in margin accounts with stockbrokers, the unpaid balance is a loan from the broker. The loan must be backed by collateral. Stock exchanges strictly regulate the margin — the difference between the market value of the shares and the loan the broker will make against it — and the total amount of credit extended to investors. Investors in the Toronto

Stock Exchange are required to put up 100 percent of the price of shares trading for less than $1.50, 80 percent for shares in the $1.50 to $1.74 range, 60 percent for shares trading at $1.75 to $1.99, and 50 percent of shares trading at $2 or more. Margin buying is not permitted on shares selling for less than $1.50. If the price of a share purchased on margin falls, then the investor has to supply additional funds to the broker since the broker has to reduce the credit available; alternatively, the investor can sell his shares and take a loss. One reason for the Great Crash on stock markets in 1929 was that investors at that time had been able to buy shares on margin with very low downpayments. This encouraged speculation. However, when margin loans were called once prices began to fall, investors panicked and dumped their shares in a futile attempt to cut their losses, thereby adding to the sharp fall in prices. One of the lessons of the Crash was the need for strict margin rules and significant up-front money from investors. **2.** The difference or spread between the interest paid by a bank or other financial institution on the funds of depositors and the interest rate the same financial institution charges to its borrowers.

marginal borrower   A borrower who will not borrow if the rate of interest is raised any further; either the higher rate will exceed the return that can be expected from the use of the borrowed money, or he will be unable to afford the loan if the rate is raised. As interest rates rise, businesspeople will be deterred from expanding their facilities, and would-be home buyers may postpone a decision to buy a house. Conversely, as interest rates fall, business will find a greater incentive to invest and families to buy houses.

marginal buyer   A consumer who decides not to make a purchase if the price of the product or service rises any higher. Thus, a corporation has to assess the impact of price increases on the volume of sales it can expect to make as a result.

marginal cost   An important concept in determining the price of goods, the quantity produced, and hence the allocation of resources in society. At a given level of output, the marginal cost is the extra cost incurred by a firm in producing one additional unit of output. Marginal cost tends to decline at first, due to ECONOMIES OF SCALE, level out, and then rise again, due to the LAW OF DIMINISHING RETURNS. The optimal level of production will be the optimal profit level, which is reached when the marginal cost is equal to the average selling price. All production in excess of that level will be made at a loss; all production up to that level is made at a profit. If a firm wants to expand production and profits, it has to reduce its marginal cost through improved managerial know-how, a more highly skilled labour force, or technological change.

marginal-cost pricing   A pricing strategy that sets prices at the marginal cost of producing one extra unit of the good in question. For marginal-cost pricing to be profitable, the marginal cost cannot be higher than the average cost of production.

marginal efficiency of investment The rate of return from an extra one dollar of investment. While increases in investment can be expected to yield additional profits, returns will start to decline at some point, eventually falling below the rate of interest that has to be paid on the additional one dollar of investment, so that investments are no longer profitable. This is because the first investments will be the most profitable investments; but as additional investments are made, those that are left will yield lower and lower returns. The rate of interest or COST OF CAPITAL will also determine the marginal efficiency of capital: the higher the cost of capital, the fewer the profitable investments that can be made. New technology can also affect the return from an investment.

marginal land   Land whose productivity is such that its output will only just recover the cost of production. Whether land is marginal or not depends on prevailing prices for the commodities produced. If prices rise, the amount of land considered marginal declines, whereas if prices fall, the amount of land considered marginal goes up.

marginal mine   A mine whose quality of ore or accessibility of ore is such that its output just recovers the cost of production. Whether or not a mine is marginal depends on existing prices. If the price of, say, copper or nickel rises, then mines that were marginal, and hence not worth operating, become profitable, and hence worth operating. Similarly, if mineral prices decline, then the mine will have to be closed down if a loss is to be avoided. The rise or fall in mineral prices also determines, in an economic sense, the level of available mineral reserves.

marginal producer   A producer who is just able to recover production costs at the existing price for a product — for example, a farmer who just recovers production cost at the prevailing price of, say, corn or milk. *See also* MARGINAL MINE.

marginal product   The increase in output that results from the addition of one unit of input — an extra worker, an extra machine, or an extra acre of land for example — while the other factors of production are held constant. The marginal product of labour is the extra output achieved by a worker in a factory when all other factors, such as machinery, are held constant. The marginal product of land is the extra output of a farm, achieved when the number of acres farmed is increased but the number of workers and amount of farm machinery remains unchanged. The concept of marginal product helps to determine the distribution of income in a society; the different factors of production are arranged to achieve maximum profit. Since wages are the marginal product of labour, interest or profits the marginal product of capital, and rent the marginal product of land, the way in which society arranges the use of these factors will determine the way in which national income is distributed.

marginal product of labour   The additional output created by hiring an additional worker, with all the other FACTORS OF PRODUCTION held constant or fixed. Initially, an increase in workers may lead to a corresponding rise in the marginal product of labour as jobs become more specialized, but at some point the marginal product will decline since the firm will no longer be able to productively employ the additional workers.

marginal-productivity theory of wages   The theory that wages are determined by the value of the extra product that an additional worker can produce. If, in a factory employing 100 workers, the number is reduced to 99, the reduction in the value of output is equal to the marginal output of that worker, and is the basis for determining the wages of all the workers. The number of workers increases to the point where marginal productivity reduces the wage level to the point where it is no longer attractive to work. If the wage level is negotiated, the number of workers will be increased until the wage level is equal to the marginal product. Once the marginal product becomes less than the wage rate, it no longer pays an employer to hire additional workers. According to this theory, wages can only be increased if the marginal productivity of the workers is increased or, up to a point, if the number of workers is reduced. It establishes the relationship between wage increases and productivity increases. An increase in marginal productivity not only results from workers working harder or getting additional skills, but also can result from technological change, larger markets, and hence, economies of scale or improved managerial know-how.

marginal propensity to consume   The amount of extra consumption that will result from an increase in income. When a person gets an increase in income — for example, a pay raise or a tax cut — that person is likely to spend some of the additional money and save some. The behaviour will differ from individual to individual, depending on existing disposable income and consumer tastes. The ratio is determined by dividing the increase in spending by the increase in income. Suppose someone gets a raise of $400 and spends $300 of it; the marginal propensity to consume equals 300 divided by 400, or 0.75. It is an important consideration in determining whether an across-the-board tax cut will stimulate new consumer spending, or whether it is better to concentrate the tax cut among low-income earners with a higher marginal propensity to consume. The average propensity to consume measures the proportion of national income that is consumed as opposed to saved.

marginal propensity to import   The proportion of any increase in income that will be spent on imports.

marginal propensity to save   The amount of extra saving that will result from an increase in income. When a person gets an increase in income — for example, a pay raise or tax cut — that person is likely to save some of the money and spend some of it. The behaviour will differ from individual to individual, depending on existing disposable income and consumer tastes. The ratio is determined by dividing the increase in saving by the increase in income. Suppose someone gets an increase of $400 and saves $100 of it; the marginal propensity to save equals 100 divided by 400, or 0.25. If the government wants to encourage consumer spending through a tax cut and the marginal propensity to save is high among those with high incomes and low among those with low incomes, the government will likely give the greatest tax-cut benefit to those with lower incomes, since it knows that the money is more likely to be spent and spent quickly.

marginal rate of substitution   The rate at which a consumer will substitute one product for another to maintain total satisfaction or utility from the two combined. It is the ratio of the MARGINAL UTILITY of two items; graphically, it is shown as the INDIFFERENCE CURVE.

marginal revenue   The extra revenue that a seller gets from the sale of one extra unit of output. To realize its maximum profit, a firm will keep producing until its marginal revenue is equal to its MARGINAL COST. After that, it will lose money on additional products sold. A producer tries to reach the point where the extra revenue from the last unit sold equals the extra cost of making it.

marginal-revenue product   The additional revenue resulting from the employment of one additional FACTOR OF PRODUCTION to produce additional output; it is calculated by multiplying the marginal product and the price charged for that product.

marginal tax rate   In the income-tax system, the rate of tax levied on each additional dollar of taxable income. In a progressive income-tax system, the marginal tax rate rises as taxable income rises. In the 1992 income-tax schedule, the federal rate ranged from 17 percent on the first $29,590 of taxable income and 26 percent on taxable income between $29,591 to $59,179, to 29 percent on all taxable income of $59,180 or more. In 1949, the combined federal and provincial tax rate ranged from 15 percent on the first $1 of taxable income to 84 percent on taxable income of $400,001 and more; by 1987, the tax rate had declined to 9 percent on the first $1 of income and to 51 percent on taxable income of $63,347 or more. In 1992, the combined rate was 26.61 percent on the first $1 of taxable income, 40.69 percent on taxable income between $29,591 and $59,179, and 46.84 percent on taxable income of $59,180 or more.

marginal utility   The extra satisfaction that a consumer derives from consuming an extra unit of a particular good or service. As consumption increases, the utility or satisfaction yielded by each extra unit declines, although the total utility continues to increase. The price a consumer is said to be willing to pay is the price he or she is willing to pay for the last unit consumed. This means that to increase sales, the price of the good will have to be lowered. In economic theory, the intersection of marginal utility with MARGINAL COST determines the kind and volume of goods a society should produce and at what price. *See also* LAW OF DIMINISHING MARGINAL UTILITY, PARADOX OF VALUE.

Maritime provinces   The provinces of New Brunswick, Nova Scotia, and Prince Edward Island. *See also* ATLANTIC PROVINCES.

Maritime Union Study   A study sponsored by the three Maritime provinces of New Brunswick, Nova Scotia, and Prince Edward Island, and carried out under the supervision of John Deutsch, principal of Queen's University, to investigate the opportunities for economic and other forms of regional co-ordination and co-operation. Begun in March, 1968, the study was completed and published in October, 1970. It recommended creation of the COUNCIL OF MARITIME PREMIERS, a Maritime Provinces Commission to carry out regional economic planning, and a joint legislative assembly. The assembly would meet once a year and carry out regional economic planning and regional negotiation with the federal government, establish common administrative services and uniform legislation, and co-ordinate existing provincial policies. The assembly would also prepare a constitution for a single Maritime government and implement the various steps necessary to achieve political union. The assembly would review its activities at the end of five years and, if the prospects for union were not encouraging, review the entire program. Political union was rejected by the Maritime premiers, but the Council of Maritime Premiers was established.

mark-up   The difference between what it costs to make or buy a product and the price charged when it is sold to someone else. Many corporations and stores price their products by marking up the product by a fixed percentage, so that whenever costs rise, these are passed along to the consumer. The mark-up, normally a percentage of the cost, covers the seller's costs of production, selling costs, and profit.

market   1. The place or process that brings buyers and sellers together to exchange goods for money or for other goods, at a price that is arrived at through an implied auction in which buyers and sellers negotiate price. A typical market offers consumers a wide range of substitutable products. However, while the concept of a single market is often used in economics to explain the workings of PERFECT COMPETITION, in which there are many buyers and sellers, the way the law of SUPPLY AND DEMAND determines prices, and the allocation of resources, real-world markets usually suffer from IMPERFECT COMPETITION, where there may be few buyers or few sellers. *See also* MONOPOLY, MONOPSONY, OLIGOPOLY, OLIGOPSONY, DUOPOLY, DUOPSONY. For examples of real-life markets, *see* STOCK EXCHANGE, COMMODITY MARKETS, AUCTION. **2.** The demand, actual or potential, for a product or service.

market access   The extent to which an exporter has access to a foreign market. One of the goals of any trade negotiation is to improve market access, by achieving lower tariffs or eliminating them altogether, by reducing customs inspections, documentation, and other barriers at the border, and by reducing or eliminating non-tariff barriers such as quotas, discriminatory technical standards, or government procurement policies that favour local industry.

market capitalization   **1.** The total value of a company's shares, which is obtained by multiplying the current market price by the number of shares outstanding. **2.** The total value of all shares listed on a stock exchange, which is obtained by adding together the market capitalization of all of the companies listed on the exchange.

market economy   An economy in which the setting of prices and the allocating of resources are determined largely by the competitive forces of supply and demand. The greater part of economic activity results from the actions of these private corporations and individuals. Most economies in the world are either market economies or are moving to a market economy, and the world's principal economic organizations, such as the INTERNATIONAL MONETARY FUND, GENERAL AGREEMENT ON TARIFFS AND TRADE, ORGANIZATION FOR ECONOMIC COOPERATION AND DEVELOPMENT, and WORLD BANK, promote the strengthening of market economies. But market economies can still have widely varying degrees of public-sector activity, in which market forces are promoted, for example, through COMPETITION POLICY, PRIVATIZATION, AND DEREGULATION, or in which market forces are contained by INCOME REDISTRIBUTION, government regulation, public-sector investment, and INDUSTRIAL POLICY. Most market economies represent some degree of balance between the private and public sectors. *See also* MIXED ECONOMY.

market entry   The ability of a firm to enter an industry and in the process establish itself as a new supplier in the market. Firms are attracted into a market when they see existing suppliers earning high rates of return. However, market entry may be impeded by BARRIERS TO ENTRY.

market failure   Circumstances where the efficiency of the market place fails to deliver a desired outcome due to imperfections in the market. These circumstances include: a failure to provide certain goods that are wanted, such as low-cost housing; a failure to invest enough where the private returns are inadequate but the social returns are higher, such as in basic research and development; or a failure to include certain costs, such as pollution costs, in the price of a product; as well as in situations where a MONOPOLY or OLI-GOPOLY emerges, which forces consumers to pay a higher price than they would if real competition existed. Economic theory assumes PERFECT COMPETITION, but economists also accept that there will be cases of market failure. In those situations, government intervention may be necessary to correct the results of the market failure.

market forces The competitive forces of supply and demand, which, in a market economy, determine prices, output, and the method of production. Market forces play a significant role in many industries, such as consumer products and services, but only a limited role in industries with administered or regulated prices, such as electric power, basic telephone service, and beer, wine, and spirits, which are distributed and sold through provincially operated or regulated retail outlets.

market imperfection Imperfections in a market that lead to wage or price rigidities. Imperfections include a lack of competition due to MONOPOLY or OLIGOPOLY power, for example, or other BARRIERS TO ENTRY. But market imperfection can also result from flaws in LABOUR MARKETS, such as impediments to labour mobility, labour laws that allow workers to resist market forces, or restrictive entry requirements for professions or skilled trades.

market maker A securities trader who makes firm bids or offers for designated securities in order to maintain liquidity in the market. These traders, employed by securities firms, are known as registered traders on the Toronto Stock Exchange and specialists on the Montreal Stock Exchange.

market order An order to buy or sell a security at the best current price that can be immediately obtained.

market penetration *See* MARKET SATURATION, MARKET SHARE.

market power The ability of a firm or workers to gain an increase in prices or compensation without losing sales or jobs.

market price The most recent price at which a security traded.

market research Research, including consumer surveys, to determine consumer attitudes to existing products and those of competitors, or to a possible new product; or research to determine the size of a domestic or export market for an existing or planned product. Market research examines consumer buying habits or behaviour, use of leisure time, consumer needs or wants, criticisms of existing products, perceptions of competitors' products, and other competitive information. Market research is used by MANAGEMENT to determine MARKETING strategies, including product changes, new packaging, changes in product design, or revisions in advertising and promotion. It is also used to help decide whether a new product should be launched, and may include test marketing in a small number of communities, to see what the consumer reaction is likely to be.

market restriction A restriction imposed by the supplier of a product, as a condition of supplying the product, that requires the customer to offer the product only in a defined geographic area; the supplier imposes a penalty if the customer breaks this condition. It is a reviewable business practice by the COMPETITION TRIBUNAL. However, for an order to be issued against the supplier, it must be shown that the practice substantially lessens competition.

market saturation The extent to which a potential market for a particular product has been filled. If, for example, 95 percent of households have a colour television set, then there is much less growth available in the market, without a technological or design breakthrough, than if only 25 percent of households had a colour television set. As market saturation increases, a business is forced to rely more heavily on replacement sales or on product changes that enlarge the market — in this case, the development of a smaller and cheaper colour television that could be sold as a second set, or a colour television with improved picture or sound quality.

market share The company's sales for a particular product as a percentage of total industry sales for that product. A basic aim of a corporation's strategy is either to retain its market share or to expand its market share. It is used as an indicator of COMPETITION or CONCENTRATION in an industry; where no firm has more than, say, 5 percent of the market, there is considerable competition, but where one or two firms control, say, 80 percent of the market, there is little competition. See HERFINDAHL INDEX, CONCENTRATION RATIO. Market share can also refer to the share of a domestic market enjoyed by imports or by domestic producers.

market structure The basic characteristics of a market, indicating the degree of competition or concentration among sellers and their ability to administer prices, or the degree of competition or concentration among buyers and their ability to control prices. Among the factors affecting the power of sellers are the size of market share held by the largest firms, the BARRIERS TO ENTRY for new firms, and the degree of product differentiation. But not all the market power is on the side of the sellers. If there is a small number of large buyers — say, department-store chains — and a large number of sellers — say, clothing manufacturers — and significant barriers to entry for new department-store chains, then the buyers will have a big say in determining prices. See also MONOPOLY, MONOPSONY, OLIGOPOLY, OLIGOPSONY, COMPETITION POLICY, VERTICAL INTEGRATION, HORIZONTAL INTEGRATION.

market value The going or current trading price, or the price at which security can be purchased or sold. See also FAIR MARKET VALUE.

market-value assessment A method of assessing land and buildings for property-tax purposes based on market value as opposed to historical value. The tax or MILL RATE is levied on the periodically redetermined fair market value of the property. The advantage is that all assessment is based on the same standard, as opposed to methods of assessment based on historic value or special use, where the same-sized properties just a few blocks apart may end up paying much different property taxes because of different assessment formulae.

marketable A security that can easily be traded because a ready group of buyers exists and because there are no legal or other impediments to the sale.

marketing The planning and implementation of a strategy for the sale, distribution, and servicing of a product or service. Marketing starts with MARKET RESEARCH, in which consumer needs and attitudes and competitors' products are assessed, and continues through into ADVERTISING, promotion, distribution, and, where applicable, customer services, repair services, packaging, and sales and distribution. In the case of consumer durables, marketing often includes servicing, repair, and WARRANTY policies. Marketing is an important responsibility of corporate management, especially in consumer-goods industries. Marketing plans form an important part of corporate strategy for new products and business expansion. Marketing can be viewed as an investment since a company has to spend money to establish a sales base for a product, just as it has to invest in production facilities; for example, a Canadian company planning to expand its markets to Japan may have to accept several years of losses in Japan in order to establish a profitable marketing position there.

marketing board   A board of producers operating under legal authority that is empowered to control the production, and distribution of agricultural products, and in some cases prices, in order to provide more stable incomes for farmers. *See also* FARM MARKETING BOARD, SUPPLY MANAGEMENT.

Markowitz, Harry (b. 1927)   The American economist who, along with Metron MILLER and William SHARPE, was awarded the Alfred Nobel Memorial Prize in Economic Sciences in 1990 for his "pioneering work in the theory of financial economics."

Marshall, Alfred (1842-1924)   A leading British economist and exponent of the CLASSICAL school of economics. Marshall helped to develop MICROECONOMICS as an important part of economic analysis. He argued that the entire economic system was too complicated to be studied as one huge activity, and urged that it be examined "a bit at a time"; from these separate studies, a picture of the total economic system would emerge.

Marshall developed a new theory of value, as well as the concept of equilibrium price. He argued that demand was related to the additional satisfaction or utility that each unit of a good purchased would yield, and recognized that there would be declining utility with each additional unit purchased — diminishing marginal utility. This meant that at some point a consumer will decide to hold on to his or her money rather than purchase additional units. However, if the price is reduced, then demand should increase again — the so-called ELASTICITY OF DEMAND; it was Marshall who introduced the word "elasticity" into economics. From this model, Marshall was able to construct a DEMAND CURVE. Similarly, a supply curve could be constructed, showing the quantity of units that suppliers would be willing to produce at different price levels. The intersection point of the two curves — what Marshall called the bite of the scissors — represented the equilibrium price, the point at which consumers would willingly buy and suppliers would willingly produce. If the price was higher, there would be over-production; if it was under, there would be shortages.

Marshall believed that competition was effective in allocating resources in society, and, while he saw the danger that firms in areas of new technology would become large entities with great market power with which to achieve economies of scale, he was skeptical about the dangers of OLIGOPOLY or MONOPOLY. He believed that a number of restraints existed on bigness, not the least of them being the natural lifespan that he believed a corporation followed, from birth and expansion to decline and death. Marshall was also confident that full employment was the natural state of the economy; market forces, left to adjust for market fluctuations, would always return the economy to full employment.

Marshall introduced a number of other ideas into economics, in addition to his concepts of equilibrium, prices, and the relationship between demand and value, or satisfaction. For example, he introduced the idea of short-run and long-run considerations, so that the time element became important in considering changes in supply and demand and the effect on prices. Marshall also rejected the idea held by CLASSICAL and MARXIST economists that labour was the only source of value in production and that all income in excess of payment to labour represented profits. He included in the income of labour, salaries paid to management and wages imputed to management in owner-operated business. He also argued that much of what was called profit was really interest that was due to owners of capital in return for abstaining from consumption. Profits in excess of management income, and interest paid to the owners of capital and reinvested in the business, were a temporary phenomenon or the sign of a monopoly, he said.

Marshall spent most of his academic life at Cambridge University; his major contributions to the study of economics are contained in his most important book, published in 1890, *Principles of Economics*.

Marshall-Lerner criterion   The extent to which imports will fall and exports increase as a result of the currency DEVALUATION, or imports increase and exports decline as a result of a currency REVALUATION; without PRICE ELASTICITY in import and export demand, currency devaluations or revaluations will fail to correct a large BALANCE-OF-PAYMENTS deficit or surplus. The success of a currency change in addressing a balance-of-payments problem, then, depends on the extent to which consumers respond to the currency-induced price changes.

Marshall Plan   *See* EUROPEAN RECOVERY PROGRAM.

maturity   The date on which a bond, debenture, or other loan becomes due and payable.

Marx, Karl (1818-1883)   A German-born economist, sociologist, historian, and revolutionary. Marx is one of the most important thinkers in modern political and economic history. He was born in Germany in 1818 and spent much of his early life in radical activities in Germany and France. In 1849, he moved to Britain with the help of his friend Friedrich Engels, and settled in London, where he lived until his death in 1883.

Marx's grim views on industrial society and the crisis of capitalism were elaborated in a period when many workers were confined to slums and were paid subsistence wages, while capitalists lived lives of ostentatious luxury, exploited workers, including children, and used the limited powers of the state to protect their own privilege. Economic instability was chronic; workers had no protection, and were doomed to miserable and often short lives. For Marx, this type of society could not survive. However, he rejected the possibility of reform, and said that, by the scientific laws of history, capitalist society would collapse, to be replaced by a new and better society first as a socialist state and then under a system of communism. He and Engels published the *Communist Manifesto* in 1848. In 1859, Marx published the first part of his *Contribution to the Critique of Political Economy*, and in 1867 the first volume of his monumental work, *Das Kapital*. It and the two subsequent volumes published posthumously, in 1885 and 1894, provided the foundation for MARXIST ECONOMICS and COMMUNISM.

Marxist economics   The school of economics originating with Karl MARX (1818-1883) and developed by his followers. Marxism asserts the scientific inevitability of a historical evolution of society from primitive agriculture to industrial capitalism to socialism and then to Communism, but most of its analysis is concerned with the collapse of capitalism rather than the workings of post-capitalist societies. The basis for Marxist thought was set out in Marx's monumental work in three volumes, *Das Kapital*. In it, Marx claimed to have discovered the laws governing the unfolding of history and their inevitability, asserting that no degree of reforming zeal could prevent the collapse of capitalism, although it could delay it. Marx also made the important sociological connection between the nature of the economic system and the social behaviour, attitudes, and roles of people in it. The economic system, he said, determined the way that people thought and the types of social relationships they had with one another. Likewise, the system of production determined the class structure of a society.

Marx argued that capitalism was inherently unstable and doomed because it was based on conflicts and tensions that were fixed in the capitalist system, and that could only be eliminated by destruction of the system. These conflicts were rooted in the fact that the means of production were privately owned, thus making workers dependent on capitalists for their jobs and creating two distinct classes in society: capitalists and workers. Marx argued that all value came from labour and that capital in the form of machinery merely represented stored-up labour. But, by their control over the means of production, capitalists were able to exploit workers. According to Marx, workers might need to work only six hours a day to acquire the necessities of life; capitalists were able to force them to work 12 hours a day, with the product or surplus from the other six hours of work going to the capitalist. This surplus value of labour led to the accumulation of additional capital (machinery) by the capitalists, reducing the need for labour per unit of output and making workers even more depen-

dent on capitalists. At the same time, growing mechanization reduced the need for skills and allowed employers to use the lower-priced labour of women and children.

However, Marx argued, capitalists were simultaneously caught up in their own competitive struggle with one another, with their declining rate of profit (resulting from intense competition), which forced them to mechanize faster and faster, and with the problems of big firms increasing in size and small and medium firms being driven out of business. Thus, the drive of capitalists to accumulate would lead to the demise of competition and the growth of monopoly power, which in turn would widen even further the inequalities of income in society. Moreover, the drive for mechanization would increase the "reserve army of the unemployed," so that capitalists could depress wages by threatening to replace workers who were dissatisfied with others who were unemployed.

As capitalism moved toward its inevitable crisis, the misery of the growing number of unemployed and the chronic instability of the system would worsen. Finally, a cataclysmic depression would result in revolution, with the workers overturning the huge combine of capitalist power in a violent upheaval. Thus, according to Marx, "the expropriators [of surplus labour value] are expropriated," paving the way for socialism, from there to Communism, which emancipates mankind, eliminates the class struggle and division resulting from the private ownership of the means of production, ends exploitation, and produces a new society based on the withering away of the state and on the ethic, from each according to his abilities, to each according to his needs. Subsequent Marxist thinkers have attributed the failure of the capitalist system to collapse to the growth of great colonial empires, which delayed the fall in the rate of profit and slowed down the growth of mass unemployment at home. Capitalist prosperity, according to Marxists, has thus come to depend on exploiting third-world countries for their natural resources and their markets. At the same time, Marxists believe that imperialism has only delayed capitalism's collapse, while internationalizing the class struggle and inevitable revolution, and sowing the seeds of conflict among the great imperial powers as they struggle for markets.

Other economists question not only Marx's assumptions about the inevitable laws of historical change based on economic determinism, but also his analysis of capitalism and the inevitability of a falling rate of profit, declining real wages for workers, mass unemployment, and a falling wage share of the GROSS DOMESTIC PRODUCT. KEYNESIAN ECONOMICS, which uses fiscal policy to maintain domestic demand, along with new techniques and rising productivity, which support new industries and new investment opportunities, has led to the MIXED ECONOMY, with rising real per capita incomes, that Marx did not foresee.

mass market   The market for a widely used consumer product that is sold to many different income and age groups. Typical mass-market products include soaps, cosmetics and detergents, food products, cigarettes, alcohol, automobiles, and cameras. They are promoted heavily through advertising during prime-time television viewing, through mass-circulation newspapers, and other media that reach large audiences. Mass-market products tend to have high advertising and promotion budgets.

mass production   The production of large quantities of identical goods using standardized parts and modern machinery, while limiting the role of labour to the performance of the simplest tasks in an assembly line, where work has been broken down into the greatest possible division of labour. By using modern machinery and computerized production controls, along with standardized parts, and by limiting workers to routine, repetitive tasks, management is able to achieve great savings in production costs and to benefit from ECONOMIES OF SCALE. However, mass production is being replaced by FLEXIBLE PRODUCTION that, using information-technologies-based production systems, allows producers to provide specialized or customized goods and services and to diversify and change production lines much more frequently. *See* LEAN PRODUCTION.

master of business administration (MBA)   A graduate degree earned for passing a university program designed to train managers or executives. Business-management skills taught include finance, marketing, personnel management, corporate planning, business ethics, computer science, accounting, business-government relations, corporate law, mergers and takeovers, management of research and development, and the role of business in modern society.

material fact   A fact — a decision, development, or result — that significantly affects, or could be reasonably expected to have a significant effect on, the market price or value of a company's shares or bonds. Under Canadian securities laws, companies are required to provide timely disclosure of material facts. Examples include the loss of a major contract, the firing of the chief executive officer, the launching of a major lawsuit against the company, the resignation of the company's auditors, or a restatement of financial results.

mature economy   A stage of economic development in which the rate of population growth slows to the replacement rate and perhaps declines, leading to a fall in the proportion of gross domestic product going to new domestic capital investment and an increase going to investment abroad, and in which the largest share of employment and output is found in the service sector. One of the risks in a mature economy is that economic activity is focused on financial activities that recirculate existing wealth rather than investing in innovation to ensure the ability to generate new wealth.

maturity The date when a bond, preferred share, or other security or debt becomes due and the principal must be repaid.

Meade, Sir James Edward (b. 1907) The British economist who was awarded the Alfred Nobel Memorial Prize in Economic Science in 1977, jointly with Bertil OHLIN of Sweden, for "their path-breaking contribution to the theory of international trade and international capital movements." Meade was recognized for his work in international trade theory; he has also been an advocate of INCOMES POLICY and is concerned with issues of inequality and income distribution.

mean average The mathematical or simple average that is obtained by adding together a series of numbers and dividing the resulting figure by the number of figures that have been added together. For example, if the rate of economic growth in the Canadian economy were 4.2 percent in 1987, 5.0 in 1988, 2.3 in 1989, -0.5 in 1990, and -1.7 in 1991, the mean average, or simply the annual average increase, from 1987 to 1991, would be 1.9 percent a year — the sum of the five years divided by five. *See also* MEDIAN, MODE.

means test A test to determine whether a person qualifies for a welfare grant or other social benefit. It typically consists of an effort to determine the income of the applicant, along with other information, such as number of dependents, personal health, employability, age, and household size. Means tests were for a long time considered degrading, but with the rising cost of universal social-welfare programs, which are said to give too much money to those who don't need help and too little to those who do, there is a move back to wider use of the means test. Now, the emphasis is on using a person's income-tax form to determine need. *See also* NEGATIVE INCOME TAX, CHILD BENEFIT, GUARANTEED-INCOME SUPPLEMENT.

mechanic's lien *See* LIEN.

mechanization The use of machinery to replace human labour in agriculture and industry. While the term is still used to describe the changes taking place in less-developed countries, in the major industrial countries the word AUTOMATION is more frequently used; it includes the use by industry of computerized control systems with self-adjusting feedback.

median An average calculated by taking the middle number in a range of values. For example, in determining median income, the numbers are arranged by size and the middle number is picked as the median number, assuming that there is an odd set of numbers. If there is an even set of numbers, then the two central numbers (the second and third if there are four numbers, or the 13th and 14th if there are 26) are added together and divided by two. Suppose there are 400 families and that 110 have an annual income of $10,000; 100 get $12,500; 100 get $13,750; 50 get $15,000; and 40 get $15,500. The median income is $13,750. Suppose, instead, that there are 360 families and that 110 get an annual income of $10,000; 100 get an annual income of $12,500; 100 get an income of $13,750; and 50 get an annual income of $15,000. Since there is no middle number, the second and third numbers ($12,500 and $13,750) are added together and divided by 2, yielding a median income of $13,125. *See also* MEAN AVERAGE, MODE.

mediation   A final effort to prevent a strike or lockout in a labour dispute, using a third party to help find a compromise solution. Mediation follows the collapse of CONCILIATION, with the mediator meeting separately with each side in an effort to avert a strike or lockout, or to end one that has already started. *See also* ARBITRATION, COMPULSORY ARBITRATION.

medium-term bond   A bond or other security maturing in three to 10 years.

medium-term forecast   An economic forecast that looks three to five years ahead. This is usually long enough to determine when recovery from a recession should begin, or when a current period of economic expansion will start to weaken and turn downward toward a recession.

Meech Lake Agreement   A constitutional accord reached by the federal and provincial governments in 1987 but which failed to achieve the necessary approval from all 10 provincial legislatures, along with the federal Parliament, by the June 23, 1990, deadline; Manitoba and Newfoundland did not meet the deadline for the required unanimous approval, and the agreement died. The purpose of the Meech Lake Agreement was to bring about the full participation of Quebec in Canada's revised constitution of 1982, which it had not accepted at the time, to recognize the principle of the equality of all provinces, to provide new arrangements for federal-provincial cooperation, and to require that annual first ministers' conferences on the state of the economy and on the constitution

be held, commencing no later than December 31, 1988. It gave Quebec a greater role in immigrant selection and allowed for similar arrangements with other provinces; recognized Quebec as a distinct society; allowed for the provincial selection of senators; defined the role of the federal Parliament and provincial legislatures in promoting the fundamental characteristics of Canada (the existence of French-speaking Canadians concentrated in Quebec but also present elsewhere in Canada, and the existence of English-speaking Canadians concentrated outside Quebec but also present in Quebec); and allowed the provinces to nominate judges to fill Supreme Court vacancies, with Quebec guaranteed at least three of the judges. On shared-cost programs, the federal government would provide reasonable compensation to the government of a province that chose not to participate in a national shared-cost program established by the federal government in an area of exclusive provincial jurisdiction "if the province carries on a program or initiative that is compatible with the national objectives." Also it provided for an annual constitutional conference of first ministers, with the agenda always to include Senate reform and the role and responsibilities of the provinces in relation to fisheries. The proposed amending formula for future constitutional change required the unanimous approval of the federal and provincial parliaments and legislatures on matters affecting the Crown, Governor-General and Lieutenant Governors, the powers of the Senate and the manner of selecting Senators, the number of Senators from each province and their residence requirements, the right of a province to a number of members of Parliament not less than the number of Senators by which the province was entitled to be represented on April 17, 1982, the principle of proportional representation in the House of Commons, the use of the French or English language, the Supreme Court of Canada, the extension of existing provinces into the territories, the establishment of new provinces, or the amendment of this pact.

menu costs   All the various expenses incurred when nominal prices change; for example, restaurants must revise and reprint their menus, catalogue companies must revise and reprint their catalogues, and vending machines must be recalibrated.

Mercantile Bank Affair   A dispute between the Canadian government and the First National City Bank of New York (Citibank) over the sale of the Mercantile Bank of Canada. In 1963, Citibank told the Bank of Canada and Finance Minister Walter Gordon that it proposed to buy the Mercantile Bank of Canada, the only foreign-controlled bank in Canada, from its Dutch owners. Mr. Gordon told the U.S. bank that he opposed the sale, that the charter of the Mercantile Bank would be up for renewal in 1964, and that it would not necessarily be renewed. He said that the government viewed the banking industry as a vital part of the economy and that, if Mercantile fell under aggressive U.S. control, it would become a significant participant in the Canadian banking system and would lead to a flood of applications from other foreign banks to establish themselves in Canada. Mr. Gordon advised Citibank against completing the transaction indicating that, if it did, it would do so at its peril. He pointed out that the Bank Act was about to be reviewed. Citibank went ahead with the takeover anyway.

In 1965, amendments to the Bank Act were proposed by the government that would have frozen the growth of any bank if more than 25 percent of its voting shares were owned by non-residents; Mercantile was 100 percent owned by Citibank. Following intensive negotiations, Citibank was given five years in the eventual 1967 amendments to the Bank Act to reduce its ownership to 25 percent or to cut back its liabilities (deposits) to 20 times its authorized capital. If it did not, it would be subject to a fine of $1,000 a day. In 1971, Mercantile and the government agreed to plans for the sale of new shares to Canadians that would lead to 75 percent Canadian ownership by 1980. Disappointed by the Mercantile Bank's financial performance, Citibank sold it to the National Bank of Canada, in November, 1985.

mercantilism   The economic doctrine of the 17th and early 18th centuries that stressed the importance of gold, obtained by running a trade surplus, as the benchmark of a nation's prestige and power. By obtaining gold from other nations in return for its trade surplus, according to the mercantilists, a country increased its own capacity to expand its domestic economy and finance military activities. Hence, mercantilist economic policies stressed the importance of obtaining a surplus of exports over imports, and justified government intervention in the form of tariffs, subsidies for domestic industries, monopolistic privileges for trading companies, and quotas. However, at the same time that a trade surplus strengthened some countries, trade deficits weakened others, since they had to give up gold reserves. The mercantilists were challenged on this score by the CLASSICAL economists, led by Adam SMITH, who rejected international trade as a ZERO-SUM GAME in which one country's growth had to lead to another country's decline. The classical economists contended that consumers suffered as a result of mercantilist protectionism and subsidies for industry; they argued that everyone would be better off in a world without restrictions, and advocated

FREE TRADE. NEO-MERCANTILISTS today argue that a liberal world-trading and -investment order benefits mainly the stronger nations and corporations; the neo-mercantilists support state intervention to obtain greater benefits for their own countries. Free traders see neo-mercantilism simply as old-fashioned protectionism, dressed up in a new vocabulary of INDUSTRIAL STRATEGY.

merchandise trade Exports and imports of raw materials, semi-processed or fabricated materials, and manufactured goods. Statistics Canada publishes monthly data in its *Summary of Canadian International Trade* (publication 65-001). The information provides details on exports and imports by country of destination or origin and by commodity group. The principal commodity groups are live animals; food, feed, beverages, and tobacco; inedible crude materials; inedible fabricated materials; and inedible end products. The report also provides information on changes in Canada's TERMS OF TRADE and gives trade data on both a customs basis and balance-of-payments basis. The customs basis is derived from information filed with Canadian Customs officials by exporters and importers and, in the case of trade with the United States, with the records of U.S. Customs as well. Imports are valued according to the Valuation Code of the GENERAL AGREEMENT ON TARIFFS AND TRADE, which requires that the value for duty of imported goods be equivalent to the transaction value or the price actually paid; if the transaction is not ARM'S LENGTH, for example, between a Canadian subsidiary and its foreign parent, then the Valuation Code sets out a number of steps that must be followed. The value of imports excludes the freight and insurance costs in bringing the goods to Canada. To countries other than the United States, Canadian exports are recorded at the value set out on export documents, which is the actual selling price or the transfer price in the case of exports to affiliated companies, including freight and insurance to the port or point of exit. Canada's imports and exports are classified under the Harmonized System (the Harmonized Commodity Description and Coding System), which is used by almost all countries and classifies goods according to what they are and not by their stage of fabrication, their use, or other criteria. The balance-of-payments basis adjusts the customs-basis data to make it compatible with Canada's SYSTEM OF NATIONAL ACCOUNTS. Customs-basis trade statistics are based on customs documents. Balance-of-payments adjusted data take into account cross-border shipments where there is no change of ownership, such as in parent-subsidiary trade, and other changes to better reflect all economic transactions between residents and non-residents.

merchant bank A specialized financial institution that deals in corporate finance and, more particularly, in corporate takeovers, mergers, and corporate reorganization. It is itself a source of equity capital, holding shares in companies or its own account. A merchant bank has industry and finance experts who can analyze the resources and prospects of individual firms, advise them on how to grow, and find acquisitions for them as part of their growth strategy. Amendments to federal legislation governing banks, trust and loan companies, and life-insurance companies allows them to form merchant banks or SPECIALIZED FINANCING INSTITUTIONS. These institutions can hold up to $90 million in equity for up to 10 years in industrial and other non-financial corporations. Merchant banks can play a vital role in assisting the growth of industry.

merchant marine   Ocean-going freighters, tankers, and other commercial ships. Canada has, for all intents and purposes, no merchant marine of its own. Its exports and imports are carried almost entirely in the merchant marines of other nations.

Mercosur Agreement   A 1991 agreement between Argentina, Brazil, Paraguay, and Uruguay to establish a common market. The four countries signed the Assuncion Treaty, which set out the parameters for the common market. The common market was to proceed in two stages, with Argentina and Brazil achieving a common market by December 31, 1994, and all four countries achieving a common market by December 31, 1995. Under the proposal, there would be a free movement of goods, services, and capital, and harmonized systems to deal with foreign trade. The agreement also proposed the co-ordination of sectoral and macroeconomic policy in foreign trade, agriculture, industrial development, monetary policy, financial services, customs, and transportation. In addition, in 1992, the Mercosur countries signed a trade and investment framework agreement with the United States.

merger   The combining together of the assets of two or more companies into a larger, single firm. Most mergers result from one company taking over another company and absorbing the acquired corporate assets into its own corporate structure; in such mergers, the acquired company loses its separate corporate identity. A horizontal merger is one in which competitive companies in the same industry are merged. A vertical merger is one in which companies at different stages of production or distribution in the same industry are merged. A conglomerate merger is one in which companies in totally unrelated businesses are merged. While mergers can sometimes make an industry more efficient, or may be necessary to enable any of the firms in the industry to survive, they can also lead to increased CONCENTRATION and OLIGOPOLY, so they are subject to review under the COMPETITION ACT.

The Competition Act applies to every merger in Canada. Companies are obliged to notify the BUREAU OF COMPETITION POLICY, where two thresholds are set: 1. The companies and their affiliates must have total assets in Canada or gross annual revenues from sales in, from, and into Canada of more than $400 million; and 2. The value of the asset to be acquired or gross revenues from the sales generated by those assets must exceed $35 million. Following notification, the companies must wait seven to 21 days before completing the transaction. The Director of Investigation and Research uses this time to study the proposed merger to determine whether it raises any competition concerns. If the director believes a merger will prevent or lessen competition, it can be taken to the COMPETITION TRIBUNAL for review any time up to three years after the completion of the transaction. A decision of the tribunal is not just based on concentration or market share. The tribunal must also consider the amount of foreign competition, whether a party to the merger has failed or is likely to fail, the availability of substitute products, barriers preventing new competition from entering the market, the extent to which effective competition remains in the market, the likelihood of the removal of a vigorous and effective competitor, and the nature and extent of change and innovation in a relevant market. The tribunal can order the dissolution of a merger or proposed merger, or the disposition of certain assets or shares. In the case of a proposed merger, the tribunal may allow the merger to proceed, order it not to proceed, or make the approval conditional on the parties not engaging in certain activities that prevent or substantially lessen competition. The tribunal will not make an order if it finds that the merger is likely to bring about gains in efficiency, though these gains must clearly offset the effects of any reduction in competition.

merit goods   Goods that are produced in greater quantity by government than would be produced if people were left to choose to consume by themselves. National parks and museums are examples.

merit pay   The additional pay in excess of the base rate that an employee gets for superior performance on the job.

merit rating   An evaluation of an employee's work to determine whether that employee should be promoted to a higher job, or be given MERIT PAY for performing an existing job in a superior manner.

Metric Commission of Canada   A commission created in 1971, with a full-time chairperson and 20 part-time commissioners, to develop a plan to convert some 100 different sectors of the economy to the metric system and to monitor their progress. It reported to the then minister of INDUSTRY, TRADE AND COMMERCE. The commission was wound up in 1985.

metric conversion   The program of the federal government to convert from the imperial to the metric system of measurement. Although the metric system had been legal in Canada since 1871, it was not widely used. After the British decision in 1965 to convert to the metric system, the Canadian government considered similar action in Canada; in 1970, a white paper on metric conversion that urged adoption of the metric system was published. The following year, the METRIC COMMISSION OF CANADA was appointed to achieve conversion by 1980. The national program of guideline dates was approved by the government, which affirmed 1980 as the target for the completion of conversion to the metric system. The principal reasons given for conversion were that the metric system is the system used by most of Canada's trading partners and that the system itself is a simpler one, since everything is a multiple or division of 10. The main reasons many Canadians opposed the conversion were the large costs of converting, the inconvenience to the public caused by having to learn a new system, and the fact that the United States, Canada's largest trading partner, found conversion to the metric system too difficult and postponed plans for conversion. In 1985 the federal government relaxed the metric rules, announcing that companies had the choice of using metric alone or imperial units along with metric units in three retail sectors: gasoline and diesel fuels, home furnishings, and individually measured foods.

metropolitan area   For census purposes in Canada, the main labour market of a large built-up area with a population of 100,000 or more. There are 25 such areas, accounting for about 60 percent of the country's population. They are Calgary; Chicoutimi-Fonquière; Edmonton; Halifax; Hamilton; Kitchener; London; Montreal; Oshawa; Ottawa-Hull; Quebec; Regina; St. John; St. Catharines-Niagara; St. John's; Saskatoon; Sudbury; Thunder Bay; Toronto; Vancouver; Victoria; Windsor; and Winnipeg. Metropolitan areas define not only labour markets, but trading markets for stores, newspapers, and various other producers of goods and services.

microeconomics   That part of economics concerned with individual economic sectors or groups of decision makers, such as households and firms, as opposed to MACROECONOMICS, which studies the economy as a whole. Microeconomics puts the economy under a microscope, examining it at a disaggregated level, and studies the allocation of resources and distribution of income in competitive markets where the price mechanism is allowed to work. It investigates such questions as how prices are set in particular industries, how labour markets work, the factors contributing to increased demand for a particular commodity, the theory of the firm, the distribution of income, and the consequences of IMPERFECT COMPETITION.

middle distillates   Refined products made from crude oil, including diesel fuel, light fuel oil, kerosene, and stove oil.

middleman   A person or firm serving as an intermediary between producers and consumers, sellers and buyers. A middleman may be a WHOLESALER, a BROKER, or a JOBBER.

migration   The movement of people in or out of a country, a province or a region. Statistics Canada publishes an annual survey, *Immigration and Citizenship* (publication 93-316), which presents data on immigrant and non-immigrant populations. It also publishes an annual survey, *Mobility and Migration* (publication 93-322) that shows migration patterns in Canada.

mill   A production facility where an ore is treated to recover metals from it, or where wheat or other grains are processed to produce flour.

Mill, John Stuart (1806-1873)   A British economist in the CLASSICAL school of economics. He is best known, though, for his break from classical orthodoxy, and in particular for his view that the state could play an important role in improving the well-being of the people. He noted, for example, the failure of economic progress under free-market forces to improve the standard of living of the needy.

Mill spent most of his life as an employee of the East India Company, his work there giving him considerable spare time to develop his ideas in political economics. His most important work, *Principles of Political Economy with Some of Their Applications to Social Philosophy*, was published in 1848. Mill helped to develop the theory of COMPARATIVE ADVANTAGE, but he turned his attention largely to the optimistic view that education and improved economic security for the people would lead to reduced population growth and higher aspirations.

Mill maintained that there was nothing inevitable about the unfair distribution of income in society, and said that it could and should be altered. The state, he said, could play a much more significant role than was usually assumed in classical economics. It could be a civilizing influence by spreading education and introducing decent facilities, such as parks and museums. It could also levy taxes to pay for socially useful projects. He also regarded the economic system of his day as one step along the road to socialism, but a form of socialism in which the state would not play a dominant role. Mill was also a supporter of trade unions, maintaining they were necessary to offset the power of employers.

Mill was also a sharp-tongued social critic. While he was aware of the rapid economic growth of the United States, he noted that this was mainly to the benefit of white males: "All that these advantages seem to have done for them is that the life of the whole of one sex is devoted to dollar hunting, and of the other to breeding dollar hunters." Mill, who campaigned for an extension of the vote to working people and women, was defeated in his bid for re-election to Britain's parliament after serving one term.

mill rate   The property-tax rate, expressed usually as a percent rate per $1,000 of the assessed value of a property.

Miller, Merton (b. 1918)   The American economist who, along with Harry MARKOWITZ and William SHARPE, was awarded the Alfred Nobel Memorial Prize in Economic Sciences in 1990 for his "pioneering work in the theory of financial economics."

mineral reserves   Mineral-ore reserves that are known, physically, to exist, or are considered likely to exist and that may or may not be economically exploited. Such reserves fall into four categories: proven ore reserves; probable ore reserves; possible ore reserves; and indicated ore reserves.

minibudget   A term used to describe an economic statement by the Minister of FINANCE in the House of Commons, in which tax, tariff, spending or other economic policy changes are announced; the minibudget is an update or revision to the full BUDGET that reflects changing economic conditions. It does not include the full range of information and budget papers contained in a formal budget, and is not treated in the House of Commons rules as a budget. Minibudgets are usually brought in by a government to deal with new economic circumstances that have occurred since the full budget was introduced earlier in the year, or because the levels of output, employment, or inflation set out in the official budget have not been met. A minibudget is also called a baby budget. The

most recent minibudget was in December, 1992.

minimax principle   A cautious approach to decision making in which the best decision among several choices is the one that would produce the least harmful results if something went wrong.

minimum efficient scale   The production point for a firm when the AVERAGE COST ceases to decline, so that there are no more gains to be realized from ECONOMIES OF SCALE; it is the lowest level of production required to achieve economies of scale. In some industries, constant returns to scale start at this point. This is usually the case in industries in which the minimum efficient scale represents a significant share of the total market. In other industries, once the average cost curve ceases to decline it begins to increase or turn upward, reflecting DISECONOMIES OF SCALE.

minimum wage   The lowest wage, expressed as so much an hour, that an employer may legally pay an employee. The purpose of the minimum wage is to protect employees against exploitation and to ensure that they are able to earn at least a subsistence level of income. There are separate federal and provincial minimum wages, each applying to workers under their own jurisdiction. Minimum-wage laws also differentiate for some industries or according to age, and, in some sectors, may exempt workers altogether. Ontario minimum-wage laws, for example, provide a lower minimum wage for those working in the tourist industry. People working as maids are excluded from minimum-wage protection in some provinces, and farm labour is also excluded in some provinces. Quebec, under its Collective Agreement Decrees Act, may order that the wages agreed on in a collective agreement for a particularly large firm in an industry also be paid by the other firms in the same industry.

The full effect of minimum wages is still a matter of dispute among economists. Some argue that minimum wages are essential to prevent exploitation. Others contend that high minimum wages result in fewer jobs, since employers cannot afford to hire as many people; as a result, the people who are supposed to be helped by minimum wages actually suffer through higher unemployment. A federal minimum wage was introduced in Canada in 1965; it was $1.25 an hour; in 1993, it was $4 per hour. But most people covered by minimum-wage legislation fall under provincial jurisdiction where there are wide differences in minimum-wage levels. The first minimum wage, for women, was introduced in Manitoba in 1918, while the first minimum wage for men was introduced in British Columbia in 1925. Minimum-wage rates are usually changed every 12 to 18 months.

Mining Association of Canada   An association of producing mining companies, exploration companies, and mineral refineries and smelters, that presents the views of the mining industry to the federal government on matters of mining, exploration, development, and exports. It deals with policies ranging from taxation to environmental protection. The association also has a research and environmental co-ordinator, who keeps track of improvements in mining techniques and environmental safeguards. It has about 100 mining-company members who account for about 95 percent of mining production in Canada, excluding coal. It was founded in 1935 as the Canadian Metal Mining Association, but changed its name in 1965. It is based in Ottawa.

minority interest   1. The shareholders in a company who do not own enough shares to control the enterprise alone or in concert with a small number of other shareholders; all the shareholders other than those who have a controlling or majority interest. Securities commissions have a special responsibility to safeguard the interest of minority shareholders. Policies on disclosure and INSIDER TRADING are examples. In addition, in a takeover bid for less than 100 percent of a company, the bidder is required to purchase shares, on a pro ratio basis, from all shareholders who have tendered their shares. The Ontario Securities Commisssion has other requirements, including independent valuations, in cases of related company transactions or decisions to make a company private by buying out minority shareholders, for example. **2.** In the financial statements of a corporation, an item representing the shares of a subsidiary owned by other shareholders. This is reflected both on the balance sheet where the minority interest held by other shareholders is noted and on the earnings statement where the portion of the subsidiary's earnings accruing to the minority shareholders is noted. *See also* EQUITY ACCOUNTING.

mint   The government-controlled enterprise that produces metal coins for everyday use and gold and silver for commemorative purposes. In Canada it is the ROYAL CANADIAN MINT.

misleading advertising   Advertising that makes a false or misleading claim, such as unsubstantiated performance or durability, misleading warranties, false health claims, or misrepresentation as to regular price. Misleading advertising is a criminal offence under the COMPETITION ACT.

mismatch   An imbalance between the terms on loans or assets in the portfolio of a financial institution and the terms on deposits and other funds or liabilities to customers. For example, a financial institution will try to balance the volume of three-year fixed-rate mortgages with the volume of three-year GUARANTEED INVESTMENT CERTIFICATES or other term deposits. A mismatch can expose a financial institution to significant losses if, for example, it is financing medium-term mortgages at fixed interest rates with short-term deposits on which it suddenly has to pay much higher rates of interest to depositors.

misrepresentation A false statement intended to deceive a person into buying a good or service, or entering into a contract. The harmed party may sue for damages and have the contract rescinded. Consumer-protection laws provide some protection for the public. *See*, for example, MISLEADING ADVERTISING, which is a criminal offence, and product labelling and packaging laws.

mixed credit The combination of commercial and concessional financing made by an industrial country to a developing country to finance an export sale, or by a multilateral development bank to finance a development project. Part of the loan is repaid at commercial or market rates and part at below-market rates. The use of mixed credits by industrial countries is regulated by the ORGANIZATION FOR ECONOMIC CO-OPERATION AND DEVELOPMENT to prevent excessive competition through interest-rate subsidies.

mixed economy An economic system in which both government and the private sector have important roles to play and in which both make decisions affecting the allocation of resources; Canada is an example. Private corporations operate alongside public corporations, while the government, through tax, competition, corporate, labour, environmental, contract and other

laws, regulatory agencies, moral suasion, income redistribution, industrial policy, social policy, and its purchasing power, modifies the workings of market forces to protect the public and to achieve public goals that are not necessarily the goals of private corporations. The mixed economy is a compromise between capitalism and socialism that has evolved during the 20th century to retain the dynamics and innovation of the profit motive of private initiative, while also seeking to limit the powers of private corporations and individuals where they act against the perceived public interest or where market failures exist. The mixed economy uses the resources of the economy to achieve social goals, including greater opportunity for those on the lowest rungs of the economic ladder and a minimum income for all of its citizens. While most countries, including Canada, recognize the important role of market forces, competition, and the price mechanism in allocating resources, these same countries also pursue interventionist public policies where needed and function as mixed economies.

mixed enterprise A business that has both public-sector and private-sector shareholders. The CANADA DEVELOPMENT CORPORATION was established to become a mixed enterprise. PETRO-CANADA is a current example. Government equity can be an important source of capital but a mixed enterprise cannot pursue public-sector goals that are inconsistent with commercial goals, since this would be unfair to private-sector shareholders who have invested in the enterprise for commercial reasons.

mobility of labour *See* LABOUR MOBILITY.

mode The number in a series of numbers that occurs most frequently. Where 300 cars are for sale and the price for 65 of them is $6,000, for 80 is

$8,820, for 40 is $11,975, for 75 is $14,085, and for 40 is $15,880, the mode is $8,820, since there are more cars marked at this price than at any other.

model *See* ECONOMIC MODEL.

modified union shop A workplace where a union has been recognized as the BARGAINING AGENT, but in which existing non-union employees are not required to join the union. However, new employees and those who joined the union during or after CERTIFICATION proceedings must remain union members.

Modigliani, Franco (b. 1918) The Italian-born American economist who won the Nobel Memorial Prize in Economic Science in 1985 "for his pioneering analyses of saving and of financial markets." He developed the life-cycle model of savings, which relates the changing savings and investment behaviour of households to their changing needs based on their age.

monetarism The macroeconomic theory that maintains that economic performance depends solely on the rate of growth of the MONEY SUPPLY. Monetarists believe the market is self-regulating so that economies will return to full employment without government intervention. In fact, monetarists contend that activist macroeconomic policies contribute to economic difficulties rather than solving them. Monetarists hold that a stable growth in money supply is the essential pre-condition for low inflation and price stability, and that this policy will lead to sustained economic growth and high levels of employment. Monetarism is identified with the University of Chicago economist and Nobel Prize winner Milton FRIEDMAN and his followers, who argue that the optimal economic performance is achieved by having the central bank set a long-term growth rate in money supply consistent with the ability of the economy to produce a growing volume of goods and services, and then letting the free market allocate resources within society. Monetarists reject short-term manipulation of money-supply growth to influence AGGREGATE DEMAND, contending that it is ineffective and will do more harm than good because changes in the rate of growth of money supply are disruptive. A temporary increase in the rate of growth of money supply is ultimately inflationary, monetarists contend. They also reject the use of FISCAL POLICY as an important instrument of economic policy, and argue that it has little or no impact on the level of economic growth, the rate of inflation, or the creation of jobs; fiscal policy decides how the GROSS DOMESTIC PRODUCT (GDP) is divided between the public and private sectors, but not the size of GDP.

Monetarists see inflation as a DEMAND-PULL phenomenon that occurs when governments run fiscal deficits and increase the money supply to finance these deficits. With too much money chasing too few goods, inflation results. Monetarists also contend that as long as money-supply growth is stable and consistent with long-term growth potential in the economy, then labour and business will not be able to generate COST-PUSH inflation by passing on wage and price increases to the public without suffering a loss in sales. Unlike KEYNESIANS, who believe government should use fiscal policy to manage AGGREGATE DEMAND to sustain growth and employment, MONETARISTS believe that controlling the growth rate of the money supply is the only policy that matters. Monetarists are strong believers in the free market, competition, and non-intervention by government. From November, 1975 to

1982, the BANK OF CANADA pursued a policy of setting monetary targets each year, but the policy was abandoned, in part because of the difficulties in defining money supply. In November, 1975, the Governor of the Bank of Canada announced a target range for the growth of the MONETARY AGGREGATE M-1 (currency in circulation plus the public's holdings of chartered-bank demand deposits) of not less than 10 percent but well below 15 percent, measured from the average level of money holdings over the three months centred on May, 1975. The target range had been slowly reduced to a range of 4 to 8 percent when it was dropped in 1982.

monetary accommodation The policy of maintaining full employment by an expansionary monetary policy.

monetary aggregates A synonym for MONEY SUPPLY, however defined.

monetary base The portion of the MONEY SUPPLY that represents the balance-sheet liabilities of the BANK OF CANADA to the private sector, and that can be defined to include Bank of Canada notes or paper currency in circulation, plus Canadian dollar deposits held by the chartered banks and other members of the CANADIAN PAYMENTS ASSOCIATION to facilitate the settlement of the exchanges of cheques and other payment items within the Canadian Payments System. This is sometimes called "high-powered money." MONETARISTS argue that its control over the monetary base should allow the central bank to effectively control money supply. The Bank of Canada does not use this approach to control the rate of monetary expansion; instead, it adjusts short-term interest rates to influence the level of transaction balances held by the private sector. *See also* MONETARY POLICY.

monetary policy The money-supply and credit policies of the BANK OF CANADA that determine the availability and cost of credit in the economy and, thereby, the rate of economic growth, the level of employment, and the rate of inflation. Monetary policy also plays a key role in determining the exchange rate of the currency, which in turn affects the level of output by affecting the prices of exports and imports. The goals of monetary policy have varied over time, but since 1988, the goal of monetary policy has been to achieve low and stable rates of inflation, with the Bank of Canada arguing that price stability is the most important contribution it can make to long-term economic growth in Canada. *See* ZERO INFLATION. The Bank of Canada controls the rate of growth of the money supply through the control of interest rates. The policy objective of the central bank is to achieve rates of monetary growth consistent with a satisfactory rate of real economic growth and price stability. In the February, 1991, budget, the Bank of Canada announced a medium-term monetary policy designed to lower year-over-year increases in the CONSUMER PRICE INDEX (excluding food and energy) to 3 percent by the end of 1992, 2.5 percent by the end of 1994, and 2 percent by the end of 1995, with the goal of further reductions after that until price stability at 0 to 1 percent inflation was achieved. The Bank of Canada allowed itself leeway of plus or minus 1 percentage point to accommodate price shocks and did not include inflation increases due to one-time increases in federal or provincial sales or excise taxes.

Controlling the growth of the money supply tends to stabilize total spending on goods and services in the economy. For example, if the rate of spending exceeds the rate of monetary expansion, interest rates tend to rise, which in turn induces firms and individuals to moderate their spending; in this way, it is argued, inflationary pressures arising from excess demand are curbed. Monetary policy is also influenced by other developments, such as changes in the BALANCE OF PAYMENTS and the EXCHANGE RATE. This can lead to conflicting pressures. For example, even if the economy is weak, if interest rates are not increased, an outflow of Canadian capital to other countries may occur, thus reducing the exchange rate of the Canadian dollar and adding to inflation.

The Bank of Canada has two basic ways to influence interest rates: 1. Through its control of the supply of settlement balances, it can, on a day-to-day basis, influence the level of government deposits in the chartered banks, and thus control the level of settlement balances of the chartered banks available for lending and to meet the current cash or other needs of their customers. The Bank of Canada always knows promptly whether there will be a significant change in these cash balances of the chartered banks; these changes can result from large flows of government receipts or disbursements. It can decide to let existing cash balances in the chartered banks cover the net disbursements, thus running down the level of settlement balances held by the chartered banks. This forces the chartered banks and other direct clearers to seek new funds; they will usually do this by raising short-term interest rates. Thus, if the Bank of Canada wants to raise short-term rates, it can reduce government cash balances with the direct clearers. Conversely, if it wants to reduce short-term rates, it can increase settlement balances in these institutions, thus increasing the level of the settlement balances and, hence, the supply of loanable funds.

2. The Bank of Canada can also alter interest rates through OPEN MARKET OPERATIONS, that is its sale and purchase of government securities. It holds a large portfolio of TREASURY BILLS and government bonds. By selling from its portfolio, it can increase the supply of government securities in the market. This has the paradoxical result of reducing the market value of government treasury bills and bonds, and thus increasing their effective yield or interest rate. Similarly, if the Bank of Canada wants to reduce short-term rates, it can buy government treasury bills and bonds, thus raising the demand for such securities and, hence, their market value. This, in turn, reduces their effective yield or interest rate. Interest rates are also influenced by the changes the Bank of Canada makes in the BANK RATE. This is a signal that the bank wants interest rates to be raised or lowered. *See also* BANK OF CANADA, MONEY SUPPLY. The Bank of Canada publishes weekly statistics that show changes in money supply, the level of government cash balances, Bank of Canada balance-sheet items, and a variety of interest rates. These statistics indicate the direction of monetary policy.

monetary union   An agreement between a group of countries to either adopt a common currency or to maintain fixed exchange rates between their currencies, along with full freedom of movement of capital and, where there is more than one currency, full convertibility of currency. It also implies a common monetary policy. The EUROPEAN COMMUNITY is moving to monetary union. Some analysts have suggested that the NORTH AMERICAN FREE TRADE AGREEMENT will some day lead to monetary union in North America, with both the Canadian dollar and the Mexican peso pegged to the U.S. dollar. The advantage would be greater certainty for investors and exporters; the cost would be a loss of any independent monetary control by the Canadian and Mexican central banks.

monetization of the public debt The sale of bonds by the government directly to the BANK OF CANADA that effectively allows the government to finance the public debt by printing money. As a country's debt rises, investors become more concerned that the government will monetize the debt, which would be inflationary and reduce the value of outstanding government bonds and other securities held by investors, causing them to take a capital loss on their portfolios. RATING AGENCIES differentiate between public debt denominated in a domestic currency and public debt denominated in a foreign currency. While a government can always pay its domestic-currency debt by monetizing the debt, it cannot print the money of another country.

money A financial asset that gives the holder a command over resources and that is also a medium of exchange for goods and services; it is legal tender for the settlement of debts or purchase of goods or services. Money has a variety of functions. The first is as a medium of exchange that allows an economic system based on the division of labour to function; the alternative would be a BARTER system. Second, money is a unit of account, or a yardstick in which prices, debts, and wages are expressed. Third, it is a means of storing value or holding one's wealth for future consumption. As legal tender, money must be accepted as payment for an obligation. Without money, it is hard to see how an economy could function at anything more than the most primitive level.

money illusion The failure of a person to appreciate that, although he or she has more money than before — due, for example, to a pay raise — he or she may be no better off, and could be worse off, than before because inflation means that the purchasing power of a dollar is less than it was before. For example, someone whose annual income has risen from $28,500 a year to $37,050 a year over a five-year period might think that he or she has made a real gain in earning power. But if inflation has risen 35 percent over those same five years, he or she is actually worse off; the person would need an annual income of $38,475 to have the same purchasing power he or she had five years earlier.

money laundering The use of the banking system to give the proceeds from criminal activity legitimacy by depositing cash and then, through a series of transactions, eliminating its identity and making it possible for the money to end up in legitimate investments. One way is for the initial deposit to be made in a TAX HAVEN where the identity of depositors is concealed and then returned to Canada in the form of investments in real estate or legitimate businesses. Another way is to deposit money through small businesses established for that purpose, such as a restaurant, trucking company, or dry-cleaning establishment. Since 1989, money laundering has been a crime in Canada. The Canadian banks and trust companies co-operate with the law-enforcement agencies by reporting any suspicious cash deposits; according to the Canadian Bankers Association, on average about 100 suspected money-laundering transactions are reported by banks to law-enforcement officers every month.

money market The sector of the CAPITAL MARKET in which short-term capital is raised and invested and in which short-term securities, such as treasury bills, commercial paper, bankers' acceptances, guaranteed-investment certificates, and other securities maturing in three years or less are traded. The money market as a national, organized market came into being in 1953 to assist the BANK OF CANADA in carrying out its responsibility for MONETARY POLICY and to increase the opportunities for investment of short-term funds in the economy. The principal participants in the money market are the federal, provincial, and municipal governments, the chartered banks, the Bank of Canada, and major corporations and non-profit organizations. The market is operated through a telephone network organized by 10 investment dealers known as MONEY-MARKET DEALERS. Since these dealers also hold large inventories of short-term securities, which are essential for the smooth operation of the market, they qualify for day-to-day loans from the banks and, if needed, short-term credit from the Bank of Canada (update).

money-market dealers Investment dealers who trade in and hold inventories of government short-term bonds and treasury bills, and who thus, as jobbers, form the heart of the MONEY MARKET. Because these 10 dealers hold inventories, they are able to meet the various needs of the Bank of Canada, the chartered banks, and other institutions participating in the money market. To help finance their activities they can get day-to-day loans from the chartered banks or short-term loans from the Bank of Canada. The money-market dealers operate the money market through a telephone network connecting their various offices.

money-market fund A mutual fund that invests in domestic and foreign money-market instruments such as commercial paper and treasury bills. *See also* MUTUAL FUND.

money order A cheque issued by a post office, bank, or other institution, that can be cashed on demand. It is purchased for a fee plus the face value and made out to a person, company, or organization designated by the purchaser. The recipient can instantly convert it to cash.

money supply The total amount of money in an economy at any given time that is available to make payments to others. Money supply includes not only cash, but bank deposits, deposits in financial institutions, certain types of short-term notes, and, in its broadest definition, could include Canada Savings Bonds and even credit-card credit lines. The data used to calculate money supply are published weekly by the Bank of Canada. There are several definitions of the money supply, from a narrow definition to a broad one. The main definitions used in Canada are M-1, M-2, and M-3.

M-1 is the MONETARY BASE (Bank of Canada notes or paper in circulation, along with Canadian-dollar deposits with the Bank of Canada held by the chartered banks and other members of the CANADIAN PAYMENTS SYSTEM) plus coins in circulation and all Canadian-dollar demand deposits, which can be withdrawn by depositors at any time without prior notice, minus a private-sector float and demand deposits at investment-dealer subsidiaries or interbank demand deposits. M-1 is about 75 percent larger than the monetary base. This definition is not the same as the U.S. definition of M-1. In Canada, M-1b is equivalent to the U.S. M-1. The U.S. M-1 consists of the Canadian M-1 plus chequable savings deposits, which usually can be withdrawn at any time, even though formally they can require advance notice of withdrawal.

M-2 consists of M-1 plus personal savings deposits (which consist of personal notice deposits such as daily interest chequable and non-chequable accounts, non-daily interest chequable and non-chequable accounts, and personal fixed-term accounts) plus chequable and non-chequable non-personal or corporate notice deposits minus notice deposits at investment-dealer subsidiaries and interbank notice deposits. Canadian M-2 corresponds to U.S. M-2. M-2 is about 11 times greater than the monetary base and about 6.5 times greater than M-1. The Bank also calculates what it calls M-2 plus. This consists of M-2 plus deposits at trust companies; deposits and shares at caisses populaires, credit unions, and provincial savings banks; money-market mutual funds; and annuities purchased from life-insurance companies. M-2 plus is about 75 percent larger than M-1.

M-3 consists of M-2 along with all non-personal term deposits in financial institutions, including certificates of deposit and other fixed-term deposits held by business corporations, plus foreign-currency deposits of Canadian residents booked in Canada, such as U.S. dollar accounts in Canadian financial institutions, minus fixed-term deposits at investment-dealer subsidiaries, fixed-term interbank deposits, and an exchange-rate adjustment. M-3 is about 13.3 times as large as the monetary base, 7.7 times as large as M-1, and about 20 percent greater than M-2.

The Bank of Canada tries to maintain a growth rate of money supply consistent with its ZERO-INFLATION TARGETS. As announced in the February, 1991, budget, these are to reduce year-over-year increases in the CONSUMER PRICE INDEX (minus food and energy) to 3 percent by the end of 1992, 2.5 percent by the end of 1994, and 2 percent by the end of 1995, with the goal of further reductions after that until sustained low inflation or price stability is achieved. The central bank uses its ability to manipulate the growth rate of the money supply to influence market interest rates and thereby influence wage and price behaviour, output, and employment. Its primary tool is through OPEN-MARKET OPERATIONS through which it buys and sells government securities to increase or decrease money supply, and, through that process, influence interest rates. *See also* MONETARY POLICY.

money wage   The wages paid in money to an employee. The current or nominal money value does not necessarily indicate the real value or purchasing power, since price increases may have reduced the actual purchasing power of the money wages. So long as money wages keep pace with inflation, there is no decline in real wages. But if money wages rise more slowly than prices, then real wages have declined. Thus, stating an increase in a money wage by itself, without reference to price changes, does not indicate much about the real value of the wage increase. A person might get a money-wage increase and still suffer a real-wage loss. *See* MONEY ILLUSION.

monopolistic competition   A market characterized by a large number of producers and low barriers to entry. However, while the products in this market are close substitutes, they are sufficiently differentiated to allow a producer some influence over their price; in this way, the producer has some small degree of monopoly power. *See also* PERFECT COMPETITION.

monopoly   A market in which there is only one producer but many buyers and no substitute for that producer's product or service, which enables the single producer to exercise considerable power over the price, quantity, and quality of the product. This situation makes the produer a monopolist. The absence of competition usually means that the consumer has to pay higher prices than would prevail with competition. The goal of a monopolist is to maximize profits. Fewer of the products are available, since one way to maintain high prices is to create artificial scarcity by withholding products from the market. The extent of a monopolist's power depends on the ability of consumers to substitute other products.

Governments can regulate monopolists by reducing tariffs, so that imports provide competition, or governments can regulate prices or the rate of return through a regulatory agency, threaten to break up a monopolist, impose an excess-profits tax to take away the monopoly profit, introduce more liberal patent or other laws, which give would-be competitors access to the technology of the monopolist, or threaten to nationalize the monopolist. In some cases, a monopoly is unavoidable — for example, in the provision of local telephone or cable-television services, although new technologies are beginning to provide alternatives such as cellular phones and satellite receivers for TV. However, in cases where a monopoly is unavoidable, such is in supplying electricity to the home, government can regulate the rate of return for the utility. *See also* COMPETITION ACT, UTILITY RATE OF RETURN, OLIGOPOLY.

monopsony A market in which there is only a single buyer for a product, service, or commodity; this enables the buyer to exercise considerable power over the price that the producer is able to charge. It is the opposite of MONOPOLY. Monopsony occurs only rarely — for example, in a one-company town, where there is only one employer who is able to check demands for higher wages. A monopsony-type situation can arise in other industries — for example, wherever the retail market is dominated by two or three major department-store or supermarket chains who buy from a multitude of suppliers. A similar situation would arise for competing shopping-centre developers, who would need a supermarket to anchor the centre but would have only two or three chains with which to negotiate.

Montreal Protocol on Substances that Deplete the Ozone Layer An international agreement signed in Montreal in September, 1987, to protect the ozone layer by reducing the consumption and production of chlorofluorocarbons (CFCs), halons, and other dangerous substances. The protocol, which came into effect on January 1, 1989, required each signatory to freeze its production and consumption of CFCs at 1986 levels by July 1, 1989, to reduce them by 20 percent by 1993, and to achieve a further reduction to 50 percent of 1986 levels by 1998. Each nation was also required to limit its production and consumption of halons to 1986 levels by 1992. Concern over the growing threat to the ozone layer, with its consequences for human, animal, and plant health, led a meeting of the signatories in Helsinki in 1989 to agree to phase out CFC production altogether by 2000. A 1990 meeting of the signatories in London in 1990 led to further tightening of the targets, including controls on the use of carbon tetrachloride and methyl chloroform. At a 1992 meeting of the signatories in Copenhagen, new targets were set for each country: a 75 percent reduction in the production and consumption of CFCs by January 1, 1994, and 100 percent elimination by January 1, 1998; a 100 percent elimination of halons by Janury 1, 1994; an 85 percent reduction in the producton and consumption of carbon tetrachloride by Janurary 1, 1995, and 100 percent elimination by January 1, 1998; and a 50 percent reduction and consumption of methyl chloroform by January 1, 1994, and 100 percent elimination by January 1, 1996. LESS-DEVELOPED COUNTRIES were given an extra 10 years to meet the targets, and an interim fund of US$240 million was established to help DEVELOPING COUNTRIES meet the costs of implementing the protocol. In addition, the protocol sanctions the use of trade penalties against countries that defy the Montreal Protocol.

Montreal Stock Exchange (MSE) A stock exchange that was created in Montreal in 1874 after 11 years of operation as an informal exchange. In 1926, the Montreal Cash Exchange was founded so that shares not listed on the MSE could be traded; in 1953 this became the Canadian Stock Exchange, which reached an agreement with the MSE to share trading facilities. In 1974, the Canadian Stock Exchange merged with the MSE.

moonlighting The holding of two or more paying jobs at the same time by a single individual. A person who works during the day, for example, may get a second job during the evening or on weekends.

Moore Report A report on the implications of foreign ownership of brokerage and investment houses and on alternative methods of financing the securities industry, published in June, 1970. It recommended a freeze on the foreign ownership of Canadian securities firms. "Canada has recognized that the national interest requires the retention of Canadian control over banks, loan companies, life-insurance companies, and finance companies. The same conclusion should apply to securities firms," it said. The report also opposed allowing securities firms to go public. Instead, it proposed that up to 40 percent of a securities firm's invested capital could be owned by approved outside investors, including up to 25 percent of the voting shares; no single approved outside investor would be allowed to own more than 10 percent of a firm's total equity. The study was sponsored by the INVESTMENT DEALERS ASSOCIATION and the Toronto, Montreal, and Vancouver stock exchanges in May, 1969, following the takeover of Royal Securities Corporation, a Canadian-owned MONEY-MARKET DEALER, by the U.S.-owned brokerage firm of Merrill, Lynch. Trevor Moore, the senior vice-president of Imperial Oil Limited, chaired the study. In July, 1971, the Ontario government announced that the ONTARIO SECURITIES COMMISSION would require that all new entrants into the securities industry be limited to 25 percent non-resident ownership; however, the commission could grant exemptions, while a GRANDFATHER CLAUSE exempted all existing firms with greater than 25 percent foreign ownership. Similar rules were adopted by the TORONTO STOCK EXCHANGE. In 1987, the Ontario Securities Commission removed most of the foreign ownership requirements and in 1988, eliminated them entirely.

moose pasture A term for worthless land.

moral hazard The risk that individuals will behave in a way that raises cost to society. They behave this way because they are insured against personal loss.

moral suasion Efforts by the government or the BANK OF CANADA to persuade companies, including financial institutions, either to do something or not to do something. These efforts lack the weight of laws to back them up and are based on the moral authority of government or the implied threat of legislation. The federal government, for example, may want the provinces, municipalities, and corporations to limit their foreign borrowing; to accomplish this, the Minister of FINANCE may appeal to these groups not to borrow abroad unless absolutely necessary, arguing that such restraint is necessary for the economic welfare of the country. Similarly, the Bank of Canada may appeal to the banks to increase their loans to small business or to regions with chronic unemployment, arguing that the banks and other institutions have a moral obligation to the country to do this. Moral suasion is also used when governments try to persuade business and unions to restrain price and wage increases in order to prevent inflation and protect other workers from a loss of jobs, or pensioners from hardship caused by the erosion in the value of their pensions.

moratorium   A period of time during which debtors are freed from an obligation to pay their debts. A moratorium may be declared on the debts of a developing country that is undergoing a balance-of-payments crisis, the moratorium being one of the remedies to help the country bring its balance-of-payments problems under control. Similarly, a moratorium may be declared on certain types of debts, for example, mortgages on farms and personal residences during a domestic economic crisis.

morbidity   The extent of sickness and disease in a population. It is one way of measuring the health of a population.

mortality table   *See* LIFE TABLE.

mortgage   A loan to buy land, a building, or other major piece of property. The property is pledged as security for the loan. If the borrower defaults, the mortgagor has the right to seize and sell the property to recover the amount of the loan that is still outstanding; however, he or she has to get court permission first. There are various types of mortgages, depending on the priority of claim they have on the property. The holder of the first mortgage has first claim, the second mortgage has second claim, and so on. For this reason, the interest rate for the second mortgage is higher than the interest on the first, since the holder of the second mortgage incurs somewhat greater risk. Banks and trust companies are

the major providers of mortgage financing for residential property, but life-insurance companies are a major provider of funds for commercial projects.

mortgage-backed securities   Securities traded in the bond market that are backed by residential mortgages insured under the NATIONAL HOUSING ACT. The securities are sold to investors in $5,000 units and pay a combination of interest and principal each month. Like bonds, their prices fluctuate depending on the level of interest rates.

mortgage broker   A person or firm whose business it is to bring mortgagors and mortgagees together in return for a commission or fee. A mortgage broker arranges mortgages for people seeking such loans, places funds in mortgages for investors, and borrows on his or her own account to finance mortgages; a broker may also buy and sell mortgages.

mortgage debenture   A fixed-interest loan, obtained by a company or other organization, in which the loan is secured by real property of the company or organization.

mortgage insurance   Insurance obtained to pay off the outstanding balance of a mortgage should the mortgagee die. Since the outstanding balance of a mortgage declines over time, homeowners often obtain a form of TERM INSURANCE to cover the mortgage.

mortgage-loan company   A federally or provincially incorporated company that borrows money, usually for terms of one to five years, and relends it in the form of mortgage loans. Most such companies are subsidiaries of chartered banks or trust companies. Hence, the borrowed funds can be obtained by the guaranteed-investment certificates and other term deposits of the trust companies and banks.

most-favoured nation (MFN) A fundamental principle of the world multilateral trading system under the GENERAL AGREEMENT ON TARIFFS AND TRADE (GATT), which requires that a country extend the same tariff rate to all of its GATT trading partners. Although the goal of GATT is non-discrimination in international trade, the GATT also permits free-trade areas provided that members of the free-trade area eliminate all or virtually all trade barriers among themselves and do not raise barriers against their other GATT partners. The GATT also permits a preferential tariff for developing countries, the GENERALIZED SYSTEM OF PREFERENCES (GSP), in which industrial countries adopt lower tariffs on imports from developing countries than they would apply to the same products from industrial countries; however, these GSP tariffs must be available to all developing countries and not applied on a discriminatory basis that favours some developing countries over others. Countries that are not members of the GATT, such as China and the former Soviet states, can negotiate MFN status with individual GATT countries.

motivational research Psychological research into consumer behaviour, attitudes, and preferences. Motivational research is an important marketing tool used in the preparation of advertising, promotional, and packaging plans. It may, for example, be used to determine why consumers prefer brand A instant coffee over brand B, or how consumers would react to a change in a product.

moving average An average calculated from a changing series of figures, so that, as the latest figure is added, the earliest is dropped. This type of average is useful in measuring changing economic conditions, such as unemployment and inflation, since it is more current than year-over-year comparisons and more accurate in identifying trends than annualized data for a single month, which can be influenced by unusual developments or one-time shocks. STATISTICS CANADA calculates three-month moving averages for some economic data, such as employment and unemployment levels and rates. When the three-month moving average for March is published, it averages the statistics for January, February, and March; when the April data are published, they will be added, and January dropped. The process repeats itself each month through the year.

Multifibre Arrangement (MFA) An international agreement that came into effect in 1974, and is now extended to the end of 1993, that sets out bilateral quotas for exports of clothing and textile products from DEVELOPING COUNTRIES to industrial countries. It covers about 50 percent of world trade in clothing and textiles. Its purpose is to control the growth of clothing and textile exports from developing countries to the industrial countries through the use of quotas. It is a NON-TARIFF BARRIER. Canada is a signatory and had bilateral agreements with 28 low-cost countries and unilateral agreements with five others. In 1992, Canada imported 348 million units of garments; of these, 310 million units came from low-cost, or MFA, producers, and 222 million units, or 72 percent of the total imports, were controlled under MFA agreements. One of the objectives in the URUGUAY ROUND is to end the MFA, replacing quotas with tariffs that would be steadily lowered over time. The MFA was extended 12 months to December 31, 1993, after the failure to conclude the Uruguay Round in 1992. It was the fifth extension of the MFA.

Multilateral Investment Guarantee Agency An agency of the WORLD BANK established to promote foreign investment in developing countries by providing insurance against non-commercial risks such as nationalization and by providing promotional and advisory services to help developing countries create an attractive climate for foreign direct investment. The agency began operations in June, 1988, with initial capitalization of SDR 1 billion, and by June 30, 1992, some 115 nations had signed up, including Canada on June 30, 1992. Canada had 3.38 percent of the votes. A developing country that seeks insurance coverage must be a member of both the INTERNATIONAL MONETARY FUND and the World Bank.

multilateralism The negotiation of trade, investment, and other international agreements that apply to virtually all countries, as opposed to BILATERAL AGREEMENTS or PLURILATERAL AGREEMENTS, which define trade and other relationships between just two or more countries, to the exclusion of others. Since the end of the Second World War, the major nations have attempted to develop and strengthen multilateral arrangements and to curb discriminatory or bilateral agreements among small numbers of countries. Examples of such arrangements include the INTERNATIONAL MONETARY FUND and the GENERAL AGREEMENT ON TARIFFS AND TRADE. The underlying philosophy is that multilateralism will lead to a greater expansion of world trade and economic growth. Bilateralism and plurilateralism, it is argued, can encourage restrictive trade blocs, protectionism, and beggar-thy-neighbour policies, which restrict the growth of trade and investment as well as weakening the commitment of countries to maintain and strengthen multilateralism.

Canada was a strong advocate of the multilateral approach after the Second World War, in large part because it was felt that this would give the country some chance to curb the unilateral exercise of economic power by the United States. In the absence of strong multilateral institutions and arrangements, it was also feared that Canada would be forced into closer bilateral arrangements with the United States, in which Canada would be by far the weaker partner and would hence lose much of its independence in economic and foreign policy. In 1986, Canada weakened its commitment to multilateralism by embarking on negotiations leading to the CANADA-UNITED STATES FREE TRADE AGREEMENT, followed by the NORTH AMERICAN FREE TRADE AGREEMENT.

multinational corporation A corporation that has subsidiaries in more than one other country, and that operates from an international or global perspective. Multinational corporations are able to use their financial resources, technology, managerial know-how, established systems of distribution, product identity, and economies of scale to set up subsidiaries in countries around the world and to allocate production according to local labour costs and skills, tax policies and incentives, distribution costs, and other such factors. They have become an important means of TECHNOLOGY TRANSFER and job creation, but they also have a number of significant drawbacks: 1. A real transfer of technology may not occur, since research and development for the most part remain in the country of the parent company; this means host countries may get less technological knowledge than they would if they tried other arrangements, such as joint ventures and technology licensing. 2. The existence of a large number of multinationals in a host country can mean that local residents do not develop top-level management skills, since these may be left to the parent-company head office. 3. The entry of multinational corporations into a nation can prevent the creation of local companies in the same industry, since multinationals can quickly and more cheaply establish local subsidiaries. In particular, multinationals may pre-empt the development of high-technology industries, while leaving the less profitable, declining industries to local business. 4. The existence of a large number of foreign subsidiaries weakens the ability of the government to control its economy, since many decisions on investment, research, product lines, exports, wage policies, and corporate practices are made in foreign parent-company head offices. 5. The existence of many subsidiaries of multinationals leads to a fragmented industrial structure that is weak in research and development and that lacks the capacity to meet the challenge of changing technology and growing third-world imports on its own. 6. Foreign subsidiaries may have an unwelcome effect on local cultures, shaping consumer tastes and values away from local traditions and values. 7. Multinationals may deprive local treasuries of taxes to which they are entitled by overpaying their head offices for management services and research and by manipulating transfer prices between the local subsidiary and the multinational's companies elsewhere in the world. 8. Since multinationals tend to seek a higher rate of return on capital invested abroad, consumers in countries where the multinational has established affiliate operations may pay higher prices. 9. Multinationals can frustrate local aspirations, by refusing to sell shares in a subsidiary to local investors and by refusing to place local citizens in positions of top management. 10. Multinationals may increase foreign domination, by bringing with them their own bankers, insurers, marketing and advertising agencies and by using the same machinery and equipment suppliers, engineering companies, and suppliers of parts and components as they use in their home countries. Multinationals are also called transnational corporations. *See* UNITED NATIONS CENTRE ON TRANSNATIONAL CORPORATIONS, INVESTMENT CANADA.

multiple-listing service (MLS) The listing of a property for sale or rent with all members of a local real-estate board; whichever firm arranges the sale or lease, collects the commission. *See also* EXCLUSIVE LISTING.

multiplier The increase or decrease in AGGREGATE DEMAND resulting from an increase or decrease in some form of spending, such as business investment, government spending, or consumer spending. The total increase or decrease will always be greater than the initial spending increase or decrease. The decision of a firm to build a new factory, for example, sets off a long chain of spending and employment. If a firm decides to build a $10 million factory, for example, it will pay out $10 million to the contractor, building-materials suppliers, machinery and equipment suppliers, and others. These, in turn, will spend at least some of the $10 million; if their MARGINAL PROPENSITY TO CONSUME is 80 percent, then they will spend $8 million. If the people and firms who get the $8 million have a marginal propensity to consume of 75 percent, they will spend $6 million. So without tracing the initial investment very far, it is possible to see how a $10 million investment decision has already resulted in the spending of $14 million more than the cost of the original project. The size of the multiplier effect will depend not only on the marginal propensity to consume but also on the MARGINAL PROPENSITY TO IMPORT. The same kinds of calculations can be made to measure the multiplier effect of a tax cut that increases purchasing power, since the direct cost of the tax cut to government will lead to an increase in aggregate demand that is much larger than the cost of providing the tax cut, or a government decision to accelerate public-works spending to create jobs. And the multiplier effect amplifies reductions in investment or aggregate demand as well as increases; a $1 billion decline in investment will have a much larger multiplier effect on TOTAL GROSS DOMESTIC PRODUCT and employment. The multiplier has become an important tool of economic management and analysis since John Maynard KEYNES used it in the 1930s. It allows government, for example, to calculate the resulting investment from a tax cut, the total growth in national income resulting from the increased investment, and the additional tax revenue that, in turn, will be generated through the multiplier effect as it increases the gross domestic product.

municipal debenture A debt security that is issued by a municipality and is much the same as a bond, except that it is not secured by any municipal assets but is based on the general creditworthiness of the municipality. There are two types of municipal debenture: serial debentures, in which a percentage of the principal is repaid each year, and term debentures, which mature on a specified date.

Municipal Development and Loan Fund A special fund established by the federal government in 1963 to help create jobs by making low-cost loans available to municipalities to carry out needed public works. The fund was launched with $400 million to finance loans covering two-thirds of the cost of eligible projects that were approved by the provinces; 25 percent of the loan would be forgiven if the projects were

completed by March 31, 1966, the terminal date of the program. Eligible projects included hospital and school construction, transit projects, and water and sewer projects. *See also* WINTER-WORKS PROGRAM.

Munitions and Supply, Deparment of A federal government department established in 1940 to handle all purchasing for the armed forces, to control the allocation of commodities and products essential to the war effort, such as coal, rubber, oil, timber, steel, machine tools, motor vehicles, ships, chemicals, and electric power, and to help set up new industries for war production. Many wartime plants were built and equipped with government money, but these facilities were for the most part operated by private industry under government supervision. In some instances, CROWN CORPORATIONS were created to manufacture, for example, synthetic rubber, precision instruments, small arms, and ships. Federal government procurement today is carried out by the Department of SUPPLY AND SERVICES.

mutual company A company that has no shareholders and that is owned by its customers. Many life-insurance companies in Canada are mutual companies. Profits are shared among policyholders.

mutual fund A fund that raises money from small investors through the sale of units and uses the proceeds to invest in a wide portfolio of shares, bonds, or other securities. Mutual funds provide an opportunity for investors to spread the risk of investing across a wider range of securities than they could do on their own as well as eliminating the necessity of choosing from among individual securities. But as is the case with individual securities, the performance of mutual funds varies widely, depending on the quality of the fund managers; the performance of various mutual funds can be tracked on the financial pages of daily newspapers, which list the value of the fund portfolios divided by the number of units outstanding. Some mutual funds charge an up-front commission or front-end load; others charge a redemption fee, while others charge no commissions, and hence are called NO-LOAD FUNDS. Most mutual funds are open ended, which means that the number of shares outstanding is always changing as investors buy and sell shares; some, though, are closed-end funds, with no additional shares being sold and the outstanding shares traded on a stock exchange. The fund managers earn a fee for their management of the funds. Mutual funds are available for investment in Canadian or foreign equities, including equities in developing countries, in Canadian or foreign bonds, in specialized sectors such as gold or oil and gas, or in Canadian and foreign short-term funds, known as money-market funds. Other funds offer a combination of equities and shares and are known as balanced funds. Funds investing in equities are growth funds and those investing in bonds or other financial assets are income funds. Many mutual funds are eligible for REGISTERED RETIREMENT SAVINGS PLANS. The Investment Funds Institute of Canada, based in Toronto, is the association representing the mutual-fund industry. Mutual funds have to be registered with provincial securities commissions.

Myrdal, Gunnar (1898-1987) The Swedish economist who won the Nobel Memorial Prize in Economic Science in 1974, along with Friedrich von HAYEK, for "their pioneering work in the theory of money and economic fluctuations and for their penetrating analysis of the interdependence of economic, social, and institutional phenomena."

NAIRU *See* NON-ACCELERATING INFLATION RATE OF UNEMPLOYMENT.

NASDAQ The principal U.S. over-the-counter stock market; its full name is the National Association of Securities Dealers Automated Quotations system. The computerized trading system is operated by the National Association of Securities Dealers as a market for small and medium enterprises. A number of Canadian companies are also listed.

narrow market *See* THIN MARKET.

national accounts *See* SYSTEM OF NATIONAL ACCOUNTS.

national-accounts budget A method of presenting the federal government's budget so that its full impact on the economy can be assessed, including government investment; the government sector is treated as just another sector in the economy, along with households and corporations, to reflect its contribution to national output. The national-accounts budget measures only the government revenue and spending that has an immediate effect on the flow of income in the economy in the year that it occurs, with the exception of corporate-income-tax revenue, which is reported on an accrual basis. It does not provide a good basis for analyzing fiscal policy, aside from giving an overall indication of the direction of fiscal policy and its overall contribution to economic growth. It includes, in addition to government spending on goods and services and transfer payments, all the expenditures and income of the unemployment-insurance program, all the expenditures and income of the government's pension funds for its own employees, an allowance for depreciation of capital assets, and the net profit or loss of government business enterprises. This method of budget presentation also shows revenues as they are earned or become due, and expenditures when the liabilities are incurred, rather than when the money is actually received or paid out, as is the case in the BUDGETARY-ACCOUNTS BUDGET. That means, for example, that corporation tax revenues are credited to the government's revenue accounts when the taxable income is earned, instead of when it is paid to the government several months later. The national-accounts budget can be extended to include provincial and municipal data as well, making it possible to assess the total economic impact of activities of all three levels of government. It is also the budget that can be compared with those of other countries, since the national-accounts system is the only one that is comparable to the public finance systems of other countries.

The national-accounts-budget forecast has been included in the annual BUDGET SPEECH since 1964. Details have been published quarterly by Statistics Canada since 1926 in its NATIONAL INCOME AND EXPENDITURE ACCOUNTS (publication 13-001) and government finance statistics. *See also* FINANCIAL-MANAGEMENT SYSTEM, PUBLIC ACCOUNTS, CASH-NEEDS BUDGET. Revenues and expenditures in the federal budget are presented on a public-accounts basis.

National Advisory Board on Science and Technology (NABST)   A board of Canadian scientists, business leaders, and others concerned with science and technology policy; it was created in 1986 to advise the prime minister. It is also chaired by the prime minister. The board advises on domestic and international developments in science, technology, and innovation; on how to co-ordinate the science and technology efforts of governments, universities, and business; and generally, on how to respond to international competition. The board also reviews federal science and technology programs and publishes various reports. Its secretariat is located in the Department of INDUSTRY, SCIENCE AND TECHNOLOGY.

National Balance-Sheet Accounts   An annual estimate of the net worth of each sector of the economy and for the country as a whole, published by Statis-

tics Canada (publication 13-214). The report provides year-end estimates of the assets and liabilities for each sector and for all of Canada, based on estimated market values. For each sector — persons and unincorporated businesses, non-financial corporations, governments, and financial institutions — the net worth is the sum of tangible and financial assets minus liabilities. The sum of all the resident sector's tangible assets — such as housing, commercial properties, mines, railways, pipelines, power plants, other non-residential structures, machinery and equipment, inventories, consumer durables, and land — is the national wealth. Canada's net national wealth is calculated by subtracting Canada's net international investment position from the national wealth estimate. If the value of land is deducted, national wealth is a measure of the country's stock of capital. The same report also shows credit-market debt for persons and unincorporated businesses, non-financial private corporations, the federal government, and other levels of government. It also shows outstanding bank loans, other loans, Canada short-term paper, other short-term paper, mortgages, and bonds. The national balance-sheet accounts do not take into account the deterioration of the environment or the consumption of stocks of non-renewable resources.

National Commission on Inflation (NCI)   An agency established in March, 1979, after Canada's program of wage and price controls was ended, to monitor prices, profits, costs, and compensation, and to make reports to the federal cabinet on any increases that appeared prejudicial to efforts to reduce inflation or to maintain or improve the competitiveness of Canadian industry. It was given broad powers to obtain company and other records. It was not given rollback powers, but could make reports to the government on out-of-line increases and recommend steps that could be taken against firms, professional associations, or unions that made inflationary gains. The commission replaced the CENTRE FOR THE STUDY OF INFLATION AND PRODUCTIVITY; its mandate was to expire June 30, 1980, but it was abolished in July, 1979.

National Council on Welfare   A citizen advisory council established in 1969 by the federal government to advise the Minister of NATIONAL HEALTH AND WELFARE on the problems of low-income Canadians, and the policies and programs affecting their well-being. It has 21 members and includes past and present welfare recipients, as well as social-work professionals and experts from universities and private and public social agencies. The council publishes several reports a year dealing with issues such as income security, retirement income, health care, poverty statistics, tax reform, the working poor, children in poverty, single-parent families, community economic development, and child welfare.

national debt   The outstanding debt of all levels of government and their agencies resulting from cumulative budget deficits. It consists of outstanding government bonds, including CANADA SAVINGS BONDS, TREASURY BILLS, the debts of crown corporations, and Canadian drawings if any, from foreign central banks and from the INTERNATIONAL MONETARY FUND. The Department of FINANCE publishes an annual report on the federal debt, its *Debt Operations Report*. While the nominal level of the debt has soared through the 1980s and into the 1990s, the best measure of the burden of the debt is the debt-GDP ratio; this ratio is one of the fiscal indicators included in the federal budget each year. For the federal and provincial governments combined, the debt-GDP ratio rose from about 43 percent in fiscal 1982-83 to almost 90 percent in 1992-93. However, when all the debt is owned by Canadians, it is not a burden to Canada since the interest is a transfer from taxpayers to debt holders, who are all within the country. However, if a growing portion of the debt is held by non-residents, then it is a burden to the country because a share of GROSS DOMESTIC PRODUCT must be transferred out of the country to non-residents each year. Statistics Canada, in its *Financial Management System*, provides the most comprehensive annual data, on a comparable basis, of the debt position of all levels of government (publication 68-512).

National Design Council   A federal advisory body created in 1961 to encourage Canadian industry to pay more attention to the distinctive design of its products, and to encourage the development of a strong industrial-design industry in Canada in order to make Canada more competitive. The council believed that distinctive Canadian designs would lead to a more competitive Canadian manufacturing industry, and thereby boost output and employment. It was wound up in 1985.

National Energy Board (NEB)   A federal regulatory agency created in 1959 primarily to oversee the oil and gas industry; it also regulates interprovincial and international trade in electricity. Since its establishment, the board's role has changed significantly, reflecting the shift from a highly regulated oil and gas industry to a largely deregulated industry. The board today licenses oil, gas, and electricity exports, approves interprovincial and international oil or gas pipelines and power lines, and sets tolls and tariffs for oil and gas pipelines that fall under federal jurisdiction. In addition, the board conducts periodic reviews of energy supply and demand in Canada, including long-term projections. The board also addresses environmental concerns in the approval of pipelines and power lines. The board was responsible for the administration of the NATIONAL OIL POLICY from 1961 to 1974, for the administration of Canada's export-price policy for oil and gas under the PETRO- LEUM ADMINISTRATION ACT of 1975, and for the administration of parts of the NATIONAL ENERGY PROGRAM intro- duced in 1980. Until 1987, the board was also responsible for implementing gov- ernment policy that only permitted nat- ural gas exports after it was satisfied sufficient Canadian reserves had been set aside to meet Canadian needs for the future. Under the policy, which is to let market forces operate as freely as possi- ble, as long as they serve Canadian needs adequately and fairly, the board only intervenes where it finds that increased exports could cause the market difficulty in meeting Canadian gas requirements. In 1991, the National Energy Board's head office was moved from Ottawa to Calgary. The energy board also main- tains a close working relationship with its U.S. counterpart, the Federal Energy Regulatory Commission.

National Energy Program (NEP) A major federal initiative in 1980 to restructure Canada's oil and gas indus- try, following the doubling of world oil prices in 1979; the initiative was based on the expectation that world oil prices would continue to increase in real terms. A continued increase in world oil prices would have resulted in huge windfall gains for the oil and gas indus- try, which was largely foreign con- trolled, and for the oil-producing provinces, with serious implications for fiscal policy and the system of EQUAL- IZATION PAYMENTS in Canada. The NEP, as it was known, significantly increased the role of the federal govern- ment in the oil and gas industry. Its main objectives were to increase federal energy revenues; to shield Canadian

consumers from an immediate price shock due to sharp increases in world oil prices through a made-in-Canada oil price; to increase Canadian control of the oil and gas industry to 50 percent by 1990, from the 1981 level of 36.5 percent (the actual level achieved in 1990 was 40.9 percent); to ensure ener- gy security by offering higher prices for high-cost oil production and by provid- ing incentives for consumers to switch from oil to natural gas or electricity; and to encourage long-term energy effi- ciency by providing incentives for home insulation and other energy-efficiency practices, and by providing research and development support for renewable forms of energy. In its efforts to achieve a more appropriate sharing of windfall oil and gas revenues, the federal gov- ernment introduced a number of new taxes. These included the Petroleum- and Gas-Revenue Tax, the Oil-Export Charge, the Incremental Oil-Revenue Tax, the Natural-Gas and Gas-Liquids Tax, and the Petroleum Compensation charge.

The Petroleum and Gas Revenue Tax was applied to the net operating revenues of oil and gas companies before the deduction of exploration and development costs, interest, and capi- tal-cost allowances, and allowed the federal government to capture a share of the ECONOMIC RENT accruing to oil and gas companies as a result of the sharp increase in world oil and gas prices. The Oil Export Charge was an export tax equal to the difference between the world and domestic well- head price of oil; it was designed to ensure that oil producers continued to ship oil to Canadian consumers despite the fact that Canada's oil price was below the international price. The Nat- ural Gas and Gas Liquids Tax was imposed on domestic and export sales of natural gas and, like the Petroleum and Gas Revenue Tax, was designed to increase revenues for the federal gov- ernment. The Petroleum Compensation

Charge was imposed on domestic oil consumption, with the proceeds used to equalize the prices of domestic and imported oil so that consumers using more costly imported oil would pay the same domestic price as consumers using cheaper Canadian oil. In addition, the federal government imposed a Canadian-ownership special charge, which was a flat tax on all domestically consumed oil and gas, to finance the takeovers of foreign-controlled energy firms by federal crown corporations such as Petro-Canada.

While synthetic-oil production from Canada's tar sands was brought up to world price levels, the price of all other Canadian oil production was to increase by a set dollar amount each year. The NEP also replaced the special corporate income-tax treatment of exploration and development incentives, which it said favoured the foreign-owned oil and gas companies that possessed the high levels of cash flow against which to utilize the incentives, with a system of cash grants called the Petroleum Incentives Program (PIP). The program provided more generous grants for Canadian-controlled oil and gas companies than for foreign-controlled companies. The grants were also more generous for activities in Canada's frontiers or the Canada Lands areas situated within Canada but outside the boundaries of any Canadian province — the North and the Atlantic offshore. Combined with a requirement under the CANADA OIL AND GAS LANDS ADMINISTRATION that at least 50 percent of any Canada Lands project for oil and gas development be 50 percent Canadian-owned, the PIP grants were designed to ensure a strong Canadian presence in the frontier regions. The NEP also led to the establishment of the PETROLEUM MONITORING AGENCY, which tracked the ownership and control levels of the oil and gas industry and the performance of the industry.

The NEP sparked a bitter confrontation between the federal and Alberta governments that, in 1981, led to significant modifications and an energy-pricing and -taxation agreement between the federal government and the western producing provinces of Alberta, British Columbia, and Saskatchewan. The federal government modified its oil-pricing regime, agreeing that conventional oil discovered after 1981, known as new oil, and all synthetic or tar-sands oil were to receive the equivalent of the world oil price; this was known as the New Oil Reference Price (NORP). Also, the price of old oil discovered earlier would increase more rapidly than proposed under the NEP, until it reached 75 percent of NORP. Also, while the rate of the Petroleum and Gas Revenue Tax was increased 50 percent, the Natural Gas and Gas Liquids Tax was dropped for exported natural gas. Domestic natural gas was to be priced at 65 percent of the British-thermal-unit-equivalent oil price at the TORONTO CITY GATE in order to accelerate the shifting of consumers away from oil. The federal government agreed to set the rate of the Petroleum Compensation Charge so that it would be sufficient to finance the on-going subsidy on imported oil and the higher prices of oil eligible for NORP. For its part, the Alberta government agreed to finance Petroleum Incentive Payments for activities within Alberta. The agreement also introduced a new federal tax, the Incremental Oil Revenue Tax, to capture a share of the windfall gains from allowing the price of old oil to rise faster than originally planned under the NEP. The agreement with the western provinces forced the federal government to modify its made-in-Canada pricing plans but resulted in provincial recognition of the federal government's right to impose energy taxes.

While the NEP was based on the assumption — widely held by the oil and gas industry and the producing provinces, as well as by the federal government — that real oil and gas prices would continue to rise through the 1980s, the reverse happened. As world oil prices declined, various elements of the pricing and taxing regime of the 1980 NEP and the 1981 agreement with the western provinces were amended or dropped, culminating in the WESTERN ACCORD of 1985. By 1992, the federal government had also abandoned the NEP goal of 50 percent Canadian control of the oil and gas industry, when it announced that foreign takeovers of Canadian oil and gas companies were no longer prohibited and that INVESTMENT CANADA should treat takeover bids in the same way as it would treat bids to take over other Canadian-controlled companies. At the same time, the federal government announced that it was dropping the requirement that oil and gas projects in Canada Lands have at least 50 percent Canadian participation.

National Farm Products Marketing Council An advisory body created in 1972, under the FARM PRODUCTS MARKETING AGENCIES ACT, to advise the federal Minister of AGRICULTURE on the establishment and operation of FARM MARKETING BOARDS to ensure that the interests of both producers and consumers are protected, and to work with the marketing boards to promote Canadian farm products in interprovincial and export trade. It consults with farmers, consumer groups, provincial and national marketing boards, and the federal and provincial governments, on the operation of marketing boards and the identification of possible new marketing boards.

National Farmers Union A national organization of farmers established in 1969 through a merger of provincial organizations, some of which dated back to the late 19th century. Unlike the

CANADIAN FEDERATION OF AGRICULTURE, the National Farmers Union restricts its membership to farmers and does not permit other agricultural interests to become members. It acts as a spokesperson for farmers. Its headquarters are in Saskatoon.

National Harbours Board A federal board created in 1935 to administer most of Canada's major ports. In 1983, it was replaced by PORTS CANADA.

National Health and Welfare, Department of *See* HEALTH AND WELFARE CANADA.

National Housing Act (NHA) The principal housing legislation of the federal government, the purposes of which are to maintain an adequate flow of mortgage funds into housing at reasonable rates by insuring mortgages on new housing; to help finance rental housing for low-income Canadians who cannot find affordable housing in the private housing market; and to provide government assistance, in the form of loans and grants, to meet specialized housing needs such as those of the physically disabled, women in crisis, and aboriginal peoples. The act is administered by CANADA MORTGAGE AND HOUSING CORPORATION. The original housing legislation was contained in the Dominion Housing Act of 1935. The first National Housing Act was passed in 1938. It has been completely revised and amended many times since then.

national income The total money income received by all residents in the economy after deducting capital-consumption allowances. It includes wages, salaries, and supplementary labour income; corporation profits before taxes; interest and miscellaneous investment income; the net income of farm operators; the net income of nonfarm unincorporated business; and inventory valuation adjustments. It is equal to the NET DOMESTIC PRODUCT at FACTOR COST or the GROSS DOMESTIC PRODUCT minus indirect taxes, capital-consumption allowances, and any statistical discrepancy plus subsidies as reported in the NATIONAL INCOME AND EXPENDITURE ACCOUNTS (Statistics Canada publication 13-001).

national income and expenditure accounts The overall record of Canada's economic activity each year, these accounts measure the total value of goods and services produced and the allocation of income derived from the sale of these goods and services. The key set of accounts is the GROSS DOMESTIC PRODUCT (GDP), the measure of the value of goods and services produced within Canada. Another measure, the GROSS NATIONAL PRODUCT (GNP), measures the value of output accruing to residents of Canada for the output occurring within Canada or elsewhere. Canada's GDP is bigger than its GNP because the high level of net foreign investment in Canada leads to a net outflow of funds each year. There are two sides to the accounts: the GDP is the income side of the accounts, showing the distribution of income among wage and salary earners, corporations, farmers, unincorporated businesses, governments, and inventory; the gross domestic expenditure (GDE), or expenditure side, shows consumer spending, government spending on goods and services, government and business investment, inventory, exports and imports. GDP and GDE are equal. Statistics Canada publishes *The National Income and Expenditure Accounts* on a quarterly basis (publication 13-001).

National Oil Policy Canada's oil policy that designated which parts of the country should be served by domestic oil and which parts by imported oil. The policy, announced on February 1,

1961, set production targets of 625,000 barrels a day by mid-1961, rising to 800,000 barrels a day by 1963. This original policy rejected proposals for extending the oil-pipeline system from western Canada, beyond the Ontario border, to Montreal. Instead, it drew a line down the Ottawa River valley, banning the sale of foreign oil west of the line in Ontario, and reserving oil markets east of the line in Quebec and the Atlantic provinces for foreign oil. Since the price of foreign oil was low, it was felt that Eastern Canada should not have to buy more costly oil from Alberta and Saskatchewan; it was left to Ontario and the United States to help develop western Canada's oil industry by providing a market. Instead of a pipeline to Montreal, increased sales of western Canadian oil would have to be made through increased exports to the United States. This oil policy continued until 1973. On December 6, 1973, a new national oil policy was announced, which included a plan to extend Canada's oil pipeline into Montreal and, eventually, to Halifax. The line was only extended to Montreal, and plans to extend it as far as Halifax were dropped. Under the new policy, Canada was to have a single-price oil policy, with the Canadian oil price below the international price; a tax on oil exported to the United States and general federal tax revenues were to be used to subsidize the cost of imported oil in eastern Canada. Plans were also announced to establish a Canadian company in the oil and gas industry to operate in all phases of the industry, from exploration to refining and marketing. *See* PETRO-CANADA. With the introduction of the NATIONAL ENERGY PROGRAM in 1980, a made-in-Canada oil price was adopted that subsidized the price of imported oil for Canadians so that the domestic price was lower than the world price. In 1985, the National Oil Policy was abandoned, with no restrictions on where imported oil could be used in Canada and with pricing left to the international marketplace. *See also* ROYAL COMMISSION ON ENERGY.

National Policy   The nation-building policies of the Canadian government following Confederation in 1867. The government's purpose was to create an east-west transcontinental economy that could counter the north-south pull of the much stronger U.S. economy, and could develop the economic basis for a separate Canadian nation. The National Policy implied an active role for government in creating the conditions under which a separate Canadian nation and economy could develop. The three principal elements of the National Policy were as follows: 1. The construction of the Canadian Pacific Railway, under Canadian control, across the Prairies to the Pacific coast. 2. Mass settlement of the Prairies, made possible by generous land grants and an open-door policy on immigration, to ensure Canadian sovereignty and to provide an economic reason for the railway to exist. 3. The Protective Tariff of 1879, introduced after the 1876-79 depression, to foster the growth of the Canadian manufacturing industry and, by discouraging imports from the United States, to encourage east-west trade in Canada. *See also* DOMINION LANDS POLICY.

National Research Council (NRC)   A federal agency created in 1916 to carry out scientific research and development and to finance and encourage scientific activities in Canadian universities and industry. In addition to basic research in its own science laboratories across Canada, the council carries out research into problems of national concern and develops scientific standards — for building codes and durability of basic materials, for example. The NRC also has important responsibilities in standards and measurements in Canada, for example in

construction materials, electrical resistance, and luminous intensity for lighting. Since the late 1980s, the NRC has been under growing pressure to shift from basic research to applied research that is more immediately useful to industry. The council also plays a major role in disseminating scientific information; one of its activities is the Canadian Institute for Scientific and Technical Information (CISTI), which provides online access to an extensive collection of scientific and technical data. It also manages the Industrial Research Assistance Program that is designed to help small and medium businesses use advanced technologies. That makes council inventions available to would-be users. It is based in Ottawa. Its research facilities include the Institute for Marine Biosciences (Halifax); the Institute for Biological Sciences (Ottawa); the Biotechnology Research Institute (Montreal); the Canadian Institute of Industrial Technology (Winnipeg); the Institute for Environmental Chemistry (Ottawa); the Herzberg Institute of Astrophysics (Ottawa); the Industrial Materials Institute (Boucherville, Quebec); the Institute for Marine Dynamics (St. John's, Newfoundland); the Institute for Research in Construction (Ottawa); the Institute for Mechanical Engineering (Ottawa); the Institute for Aerospace Research (Ottawa); the Plant Biotechnology Institute (Saskatoon); the Steacie Institute for Molecular Sciences (Ottawa); the Institute for Basic Measurement Standards (Ottawa); the Institute for Microstructural Sciences (Ottawa); and the Institute for Information Technology (Ottawa).

National Revenue, Department of   See REVENUE CANADA.

National Roundtable on the Environment and the Economy   An advisory body established in 1989 to promote SUNSTAINABLE DEVELOPMENT by consensus decision making. Membership is drawn from government, industry, labour, academia, environmental groups, and aboriginal peoples. Legislation giving the national roundtable permanent status describes its mandate as to "play the role of catalyst in identifying, explaining, and promoting, in all sectors of Canadian society and in all regions of Canada, principles and practices of sustainable development." It conducts research and analysis, advises government, industry and other groups on sustainable development, and increases public awareness of the cultural, social, economic, and policy changes necessary to achieve sustainable development. It reports to the prime minister and includes in its membership the ministers of finance, environment, energy, and industry. It is based in Ottawa and has a small full-time staff. Each of the provinces also operates a similar roundtable, with the provincial roundtables reporting to their respective premiers.

National Transportation Agency of Canada An independent agency established under the National Transportation Act in 1987; it came into effect at the start of 1988 and is responsible for the economic regulation of Canada's transportation system. The agency replaced the Canadian Transport Commission. The agency licenses Canadian and foreign air carriers operating in Canada, Canadian air carriers operating in other countries, and northern marine resupply services. It issues rail certificates of fitness or public convenience and necessity, and waivers for coastal carriers. It is also responsible for the rail infrastructure programs, the approval of mergers and acquisitions in the transportation industry, pilotage tariffs, the regulation of international air tariffs and northern marine tariffs, the administration of the Shipping Conferences Exemption Act, 1987, and the regulation of transportation facilities and services for travellers with disabilities. In addition, it administers subsidies and rates for various services provided by transportation companies, evaluates proposals from railways to rationalize and close rail lines, and monitors railway investments in the Western grain-transportation system. The agency is based in Hull, Quebec. In addition to the Shipping Conferences Exemption Act and the National Transportation Act, it administers the Railway Act, the Aeronautics Act, the Motor Vehicle Transportation Act, the Pilotage Act, the Railway Relocation and Crossing Act, the Western Grain Transportation Act, the Maritime Freight Rates Act, and the Atlantic Region Freight Assistance Act. Under the legislation, the agency consists of a chairman, vice-chairman, and six permanent members; at least one member must represent each region of Canada — the Pacific, the Prairies, Ontario, Quebec, and the Atlantic.

national treatment A provision in international trade agreements in which a country pledges to treat the firms and citizens of other countries in the agreement in the same way that it treats its own firms and citizens under its laws and regulations. There is no distinction based on country of origin.

national union A union that operates only in Canada, as opposed to an INTERNATIONAL UNION, which recruits members on both sides of the border. The major national unions in Canada are the Canadian Union of Public Employees, the Public Service Alliance, the Canadian Auto Workers, and the Canadian Paperworkers' Union. Most national unions are affiliated with the CANADIAN LABOUR CONGRESS, but some are affiliated with the CONFEDERATION OF NATIONAL TRADE UNIONS or the CANADIAN FEDERATION OF LABOUR.

nationalization The takeover of a privately owned corporation by the government so that it can be operated as a publicly owned corporation. Compensation is normally, although not always, paid. In most countries it is paid at FAIR MARKET VALUE, but in some countries it may be set artificially low. Examples in Canada include the takeover of private power companies in Quebec and British Columbia during the 1960s, and the takeover of potash mines by Saskatchewan in the 1970s and asbestos mines by Quebec in the 1980s. Nationalization does not include all sales of private companies to a government; it consists only of those cases in which the government identifies a company that it wants and acquires it, even though the owner may not want to sell. Governments may nationalize companies because the companies are a NATURAL MONOPOLY, such as a power provider. Government ownership of natural resources will allow the government to collect ECONOMIC RENT, while ownership of major individual enterprises will allow government to play an active role in a key or strategic sector of the economy.

native claims Claims by native groups for recognition of rights to and interests in lands across Canada, including the North. Their claims are based on their traditional use and occupancy of the land, or are made for renegotiation of their rights under treaties already negotiated with the Crown. Aboriginal claims are based on the traditional use and occupancy of lands by native groups, such as the Inuit in the North, as opposed to claims based on treaties signed by native groups and the Crown before or after Confederation where there is disagreement over the meaning of the terms. Natives argue that many of the treaties were signed under duress. Native peoples have a number of issues they want settled, including clarification of treaty rights, some form of self-government on the lands claimed, along with recognition of limited sovereignty, the recognition of traditional hunting and fishing rights, the ownership of land, a share of mineral rights, and cash payments. In 1974, the Department of INDIAN AFFAIRS AND NORTHERN DEVELOPMENT formed the Office of Native Claims to represent the government of Canada in negotiations with native groups. In 1975, a settlement with the Cree and Inuit people of the James Bay area was signed. Other claims negotiated with the native peoples, Inuit, and Métis of the Yukon and the Northwest Territories include the establishment of NUNAVUT in the Northwest Territories. In 1991, the INDIAN CLAIMS COMMISSION was established as an independent body to inquire into and report on disputes between First Nations and the federal government where the First Nation either disputes the government's rejection of a specific claim based on a treaty or agreement, or disagrees with the compensation criteria used by the government in negotiating settlement of a claim. The native peoples represent less than 2 percent of Canada's population: about 300,000 Indians and 18,000 Inuit. However, it represents about 10 percent of Saskatchewans' population and 11 percent of Manitoba's population. *See also* DENE NATION.

natural-gas reserves *See* ESTABLISHED RESERVES, INITIAL ESTABLISHED RESERVES, REMAINING ESTABLISHED RESERVES, ULTIMATE POTENTIAL RESERVES.

natural increase The difference between the CRUDE BIRTH RATE and the CRUDE DEATH RATE.

natural monopoly An industry in which the basic investment costs are so high that it does not pay for more than one firm to supply the product or service — for example, a telephone company supplying local service, an electricity utility, a cable-TV company, or a natural gas pipeline. It is much cheaper for the existing firm to increase its output or to lower its prices slightly than for a second firm to make the capital investment necessary to compete. Natural monopolies tend to be regulated in order to protect the public against excessively high prices, although the role of regulatory agencies was relaxed starting in the 1980s.

natural rate of unemployment   *See* NON-ACCELERATING INFLATION RATE OF UNEMPLOYMENT.

natural resources   The living and non-living elements of the environment that can be used to sustain life and to produce goods and services. These include mineral deposits, fish and wildlife, fertile soil, forests, and water for electric power, agriculture, and transportation. Natural resources are usually classified as renewable resources (examples include timber, fish, and water), since they reproduce themselves, or as non-renewable resources (such as mineral deposits), which means that, once used, they cannot readily be replaced. A natural resource is of no value if there is no known use for it; if a use is discovered, it has utility, or value. Similarly, the value of reserves of various natural resources depends on the costs of exploitation and their use; if the cost of iron ore is, say, $100 a ton, and it would cost $150 a ton to mine a particular ore-body, then the ore-body is of no use; but if the reverse were true and the iron ore cost $100 to produce but could be sold for $150, then the iron-ore body would have value. A decline in the supply of one natural resource can be offset by developing a natural or synthetic substitute; during the Second World War, for example, synthetic rubber was developed as a replacement for natural rubber.

Natural Science and Engineering Research Council (NSERC)   A federal council established in 1978 to promote and fund research in Canada's universities and to finance graduate students in science and engineering in Canadian or foreign universities. Its mandate is to ensure that Canada has an adequate supply of scientists and engineers. In addition to funding research grants and scholarships, NSERC manages Canada's Centres of Excellence, which are joint university-industry research centres engaged in pre-competitive research and development. It is based in Ottawa.

near money   An asset that can be used to settle a debt or complete a transaction but is not legal tender. However it can be readily converted into a medium of exchange or legal money. Examples include CANADA SAVINGS BONDS and TREASURY BILLS.

negative income tax   The use of the income-tax system to determine and deliver the social assistance an individual should receive as a GUARANTEED ANNUAL INCOME. The negative income tax can be used to replace income-maintenance and other social-welfare programs and to provide benefits to special groups, such as the working poor. The tax return is used as a form of means test. Just as the progressive tax system imposes an increasing marginal rate of taxation on increasing levels of taxable income, so a negative income tax would include a negative marginal tax rate below a defined poverty line, so that people with income below that line would be given money to raise their income to the poverty-line level. The amount would depend on the gap between their incomes and the defined poverty line. A person with no income would get 100 percent of the poverty-line amount.

Two of the advantages of the negative income tax are as follows: 1. It provides a single system of assistance and therefore is much easier and cheaper to administer; 2. It includes, unlike many direct forms of social assistance, an incentive for a person with a low income to work, since the income a person earns just above the poverty line would be taxed at a low marginal rate. This would leave that person with most of his earned income and, therefore, better off than if he did not work. A key question in such a system would be the level chosen for the poverty line. If it were quite low, it would provide little assistance to the working poor and other groups. If it were fairly high, then it would be a major exercise in income redistribution and could be quite costly; it could also be a disincentive to work.

negligence   A TORT or civil action to recover damages from someone who has failed to carry out his or her legal responsibility to take reasonable care to prevent another person's death, injury, or financial loss. For example, a building owner who fails to put salt or sand on ice outside his building during winter is liable in a negligence action if a passerby slips and is injured.

negotiability   The ability to transfer ownership of a cheque, promissory note, bond, or other financial paper by endorsing it over or delivering it directly to another person. The new owner acquires full legal title to the money that the financial paper represents.

neoclassical economics   The school of economics that emerged in the late 19th century, replacing CLASSICAL ECONOMICS, and that dominated economics until it was challenged by KEYNESIAN ECONOMICS in the 1930s. The neoclassical school assumed that the economy would normally operate at full employment, and that any deviation would be temporary because the economic system was self-adjusting. It assumed that full employment was the normal condition because it assumed that all national income would be spent; hence, on-going unemployment was impossible. It also assumed that, if economic activity declined and unemployment increased, wage rates would fall, thus raising the demand for workers and reducing unemployment. It assumed as well conditions of PERFECT COMPETITION and that government, by adjusting interest rates through its monetary policy, could always ensure an adequate flow of savings and investment. Neoclassical economists introduced mathematics into the study of economics and began the study of what is today known as MICROECONOMICS. While they emphasized, as the classical economists had done, the role of market forces in allocating resources and setting prices, the neoclassical school acknowledged that market imperfections could exist, and studied small groups, such as firms and households, to understand the decision-making process and to find ways to correct market imperfections. Neoclassical economists also studied the relationships among different sectors of the economy, and how resources were allocated in the free-market economy. While the neoclassicists were right to emphasize the role of markets and competition, they have paid too little attention to the reality of IMPERFECT COMPETITION, the role of technological change, and market failures, as well as exaggerating the tendency of individuals to act in their best economic interests to the exclusion of family, religions, or other interests, critics say. The leading economists in the neoclassical school included Alfred MARSHALL of Britain, Leon Walras of Switzerland, John Bates Clark of the United States, Eugen von Bohm-Bawerk of Austria, and Knut Wicksell of Sweden.

neo-Keynesian economics   *See* POST-KEYNESIAN ECONOMICS.

neo-Malthusianism The view that, while Thomas Robert MALTHUS (1766-1834) was correct in his belief that population growth would outpace increases in food production, he was wrong in his belief that moral restraint and later marriages were the only acceptable means to counter rising population. Neo-Malthusians advocate policies of birth control to check population growth.

neo-mercantilism A term used by free-market economists who see in proposals for INDUSTRIAL POLICY a revival of mercantilist policies. The term was coined by Canadian economist Harry JOHNSON, who argued that modern industrial policies to strengthen industries based on new technologies through various forms of government support were simply old-fashioned protectionism in new clothes.

net asset value The value of total assets of a corporation remaining after total liabilities have been deducted. *See* SHAREHOLDERS' EQUITY. It is sometimes used as the basis for determining profitability or rate of return.

net asset worth A method of determining the underlying value of shares in a company by dividing the company's net assets by the number of outstanding shares.

net book value The value of a fixed asset on a balance sheet; it is the original cost of the asset minus any depreciation taken to date.

net cash flow The money available to a company for reinvestment, consisting of retained earnings for the year plus depreciation.

net change 1. The change in the price of a share or other security from the closing price on one day to the closing

price on the next trading day. 2. The change in a flow or stock after adding together changes in both directions. For example, the net change in foreign direct investment in Canada is obtained by adding together gross outflows from Canada to other countries and gross inflows into Canada from other countries. Likewise, the net addition to Canada's foreign debt is obtained by adding together the gross increase in Canadian holdings of the debt from other countries and the gross increase in foreign holdings of Canadian debt.

net domestic product The GROSS DOMESTIC PRODUCT minus capital-consumption allowances; this reflects the fact that a part of the country's capital stock is worn out or used up in producing annual economic output.

net economic welfare A measure developed by two U.S. economists, James Tobin and William Nordhaus, to give a better estimate of standard of living than the usual measure of per capita GROSS DOMESTIC PRODUCT (GDP). They add to the GDP an estimate for the value of leisure, represented by the decline in the work week, and for the value of work performed by people in the home (such as parents who have stayed home to look after their children). At the same time, certain parts of the GDP, such as the costs of fighting pollution or crime, are deducted from the GDP. The GDP by itself fails to measure such non-monetary gains as more leisure time; it also treats the costs of dealing with such social problems as prisons, for example, as contributions to economic growth.

net farm income Farm cash receipts less farm operating costs and depreciation. Statistics Canada publishes an annual report on net farm income in its *Agricultural and Economic Statistics* (publication 21-603, series 92-002) The report, which provides the best indicators of the economic performance of the agricultural sector, details farm-cash receipts, livestock- and animal-production receipts, crop receipts, direct program payments, detailed farm-operating costs, depreciation, and the value-of-inventory change. The same report also provides a balance sheet of the agricultural sector and details the contribution of the agricultural sector to the GROSS DOMESTIC PRODUCT.

net foreign debt The net amount owed by a country to its foreign creditors. The net foreign debt includes all debt of both the private and public sectors. The stock of Canada's net foreign debt is published annually by Statistics Canada in *Canada's International Investment Position* (publication 67-202). The flow of foreign debt is contained in the CAPITAL ACCOUNT of Canada's BALANCE OF PAYMENTS, published quarterly (publication 67-001). The BANK OF CANADA, once a year, publishes information on Canadian bonds outstanding, including the currency of denomination.

net income The profit of a company after all of its expenses, including taxes, depreciation, and interest on long-term debt, have been deducted. It is the money available to pay dividends to shareholders and to reinvest in the expansion of the firm.

net interest margin The difference between what a financial institution earns on loans and securities and what it pays out on deposits and various debentures, expressed as a percentage of average total assets.

net international investment position The net stock of outstanding loans, direct investment, portfolio investment, and other investment between a country and the rest of the world. When a country's net international

investment position is positive, its residents hold a stock of net claims against the rest of the world — for example, through direct ownership of businesses in other countries or through portfolios of foreign bonds — which makes that country a net creditor to the rest of the world. When the net international investment position of a country is negative, its residents hold a stock of net debts to the rest of the world — for example, non-residents own many of its businesses or hold many of its bonds — which makes that country a net debtor to the rest of the world. Canada has been a net debtor to the rest of the world since Confederation. Statistics Canada publishes *Canada's International Investment Position* annually (publication 67-202). The key Canadian foreign assets are direct investment; stocks, bonds, and other debt; official international reserves; Government of Canada loans and subscriptions; and non-bank deposits. The main Canadian foreign liabilities include direct investment; stocks, bonds, and other debt; the net foreign-currency position of Canadian banks; and money-market securities. Direct investment includes all long-term capital (equity and debt) provided by an investor, along with retained earnings.

net investment The net addition to a country's or firm's productive capacity. Net investment indicates whether the productive resources of the economy or firm have increased or declined after the cost of replacing obsolete or worn-out equipment has been taken into account. It is calculated for Canada in GROSS DOMESTIC PRODUCT statistics by subtracting capital-cost allowances or depreciation from gross-fixed-capital formation or capital investment. For a firm, it consists of capital spending minus depreciation.

net loss A company's loss after all of its expenses, including taxes, depreciation, and interest on long-term debt, have been deducted from its revenues.

net national income   The total flow of income earned in the economy by labour, capital, and land. Net national income consists of wages, salaries, and other labour income; military pay and allowances; corporation profits before taxes but minus dividends paid to non-residents; interest and other investment income; accrued net income of farmers from farm operations; and the net income of non-farm unincorporated businesses, including rent and changes in the value of inventories. If INDIRECT TAXES and depreciation (capital-cost allowances) are added to net national income the result is GROSS DOMESTIC PRODUCT. Net national income statistics, produced quarterly by Statistics Canada, are sometimes used to analyze changes in the distribution of income among labour, business, and other groups in the economy (publication 13-001).

net present value   A method of calculating the present value of an investment by measuring its future income stream against the costs of the investment. In the calculation the total costs and revenues expected for an investment project over the life of the project are adjusted or discounted so that future cash inflows and outflows are expressed in their PRESENT VALUE. For example, future revenue from a project, to be expressed in terms of its present value, is discounted to reflect current interest rates and risk: at a 10 percent interest rate, a dollar will yield $1.10 next year, so that to have $1 next year requires 91 cents today ($1 divided by $1.10). This means the present value of $1 next year is 91 cents today. Net present value is an important analytical tool for corporations and others in making investment choices; faced with several possible projects, investors will choose the one with the highest net

present value or reject all the projects if the rate of return is less than the prevailing interest rates. In such a situation, they would be better off to invest their money in government bonds or other financial securities. *See also* DISCOUNTED CASH FLOW.

net price   The price paid after all discounts have been deducted.

net price index   A modification of the CONSUMER PRICE INDEX published by Statistics Canada on a quarterly basis as the net price index of the consumer price index in table 32 and 33 of the NATIONAL INCOME AND EXPENDITURE ACCOUNTS (publication 13-001). The net price index eliminates tax changes and government subsidies from the measure of inflation, showing instead the inflation caused by the factors of production.

net profit   *See* NET INCOME.

net reproduction rate   A measure of population change; it is the number of daughters, expressed per 1,000 women, that the current generation of women in their child-bearing years will have during those years, based on current age-specific fertility and mortality rates. It is thus a projection of the number of women there will be in the next generation, or the female reproduction rate. A net reproduction rate greater than 1:1 means that the population should increase; of less than 1:1, that it should decline; and at unity, or 1:1, that it should remain stationary.

net worth   The value of the remaining assets after a firm's or a person's liabilities have been deducted from total assets. In a company, the net worth of the firm is calculated on the balance sheet by deducting total liabilities from total assets, to yield what is known as SHAREHOLDERS' EQUITY, or net worth. This is what the shareholders would get if the company was wound up. A similar calculation can be made for an individual by adding together such assets as a family home, pension-plan contributions, savings, assets such as furniture, car, and cottage, and any other assets, and then deducting liabilities, such as the unpaid balance on a mortgage and outstanding loans and consumer debt.

netback   The value of crude oil after it has been refined into various products such as gasoline, aviation fuel, and petrochemical feedstocks and these products have been sold, after deducting transportation and refining costs.

New Brunswick Royal Commission on Finance and Municipal Taxation   A royal commission appointed in 1962, headed by E.G. Byrne, that reported its recommendations in 1964. It proposed sweeping changes to municipal finance in the province, including having the province take over all the costs of education, public health, hospital services, social assistance, and justice, and the adoption of a uniform tax code throughout the province. The proposed province-wide tax code included a provincial property tax for education, greater reliance by the province on the retail-sales tax to finance local responsibilities, a new automobile tax, and the complete renegotiation of tax concessions to industry. Money for local purposes was to be raised in a property-tax system based on MARKET-VALUE ASSESSMENT. The commission also proposed a substantial consolidation of local governments and school boards, reducing their number by more than half. The provincial government followed up on many of the recommendations. New Brunswick became the first province to completely reorganize its system of municipal finance and taxation in the post-war period.

new classical economics   See RATIONAL EXPECTATIONS THEORY.

New Deal   See BENNETT NEW DEAL.

New International Economic Order (NIEO)   Proposals advocated strongly in the late 1970s and early 1980s, in particular by the LESS-DEVELOPED COUNTRIES, for a substantial change in their economic relations with the industrialized world, including Canada. The less-developed countries maintain that significant changes are necessary if they are to achieve a rate of economic growth sufficient to solve their problems of poverty and to improve the standard of living of their people. They complain that the world is divided into exporters of commodities (the less-developed countries) and exporters of manufactured goods (the developed countries); that the terms of trade work against them; that they are too dependent on the industrial world for the finance needed for development, a fact that they say is burdening them with an excessive load of debt and a need to earn increasing amounts of foreign exchange simply to pay interest; and that they are forced to depend on the growth rate of the industrial world for their own economic growth. In their view, the political colonialism of the past has been replaced by economic colonialism, with the industrial countries holding down the price of raw materials while charging increasingly higher prices for manufactured goods. They further complain that the trade policies of the industrial countries restrict their ability to export, because industrial countries have low tariffs on raw materials but higher tariffs and quotas on manufactured imports from the less-developed countries. They want much better access for their manufactured products, sharply increased flows of foreign aid, full control over their natural resources, including prices that at least keep pace with the rising costs of manufactured imports, renegotiation or elimination of much of their outstanding debt, and a greater role in determining the policies of the INTERNATIONAL MONETARY FUND, the GENERAL AGREEMENT ON TARIFFS AND TRADE, and other international bodies. The formation of the UNITED NATIONS CONFERENCE ON TRADE AND DEVELOPMENT (UNCTAD) was an early effort by the less-developed countries to get a better economic deal. It was followed, in 1974, by the United Nations General Assembly's adoption of two resolutions that set out new principles for economic co-operation on trade, aid, debt management, and other concerns, and that were enshrined in the Declaration and Program of Action on the Establishment of a New International Economic Order. Key goals included commodity agreements to sustain higher prices for the raw-material exports of developing countries, expanded access to industrial world markets for the products of developing countries (including preferential access), increased official development assistance or foreign aid, and a greater voice for developing countries in the major multilateral institutions. *See also* CONFERENCE ON INTERNATIONAL ECONOMIC CO-OPERATION, CHARTER OF ECONOMIC RIGHTS AND DUTIES OF STATES.

new issue   The raising of new long-term capital by the sale to investors of common shares, preferred shares, or bonds. The sale may be made directly to the public or through a PRIVATE PLACEMENT to institutional investors. If it is to be sold to the public, the issue must first be approved by a provincial SECURITIES COMMISSION. *See also* PRIMARY DISTRIBUTION. New issues are offered both by corporations and governments and their agencies.

new orders   *See* MANUFACTURERS' NEW ORDERS, SHIPMENTS, AND INVENTORIES.

New Principles for International Business   Federal government guidelines for good corporate behaviour by foreign-controlled subsidiaries in Canada, tabled in the House of Commons on July 18, 1975. They replaced the 1966 guidelines, the GUIDING PRINCIPLES OF GOOD CORPORATE BEHAVIOUR. The new guidelines, like the ones they replaced, represented government policy and had been approved by cabinet. According to the new guidelines, foreign-controlled firms doing business in Canada should do the following: 1. Pursue a high degree of autonomy in decision-making and risk-taking functions, including innovative activity in the marketing of resulting new products. 2. Develop as an integral part of the Canadian operation an autonomous capability for technological innovation, including research and development, engineering, and industrial design and pre-production activities. 3. Retain in Canada a sufficient share of earnings to give strong financial support to the growth and entrepreneurial potential of the Canadian operation. 4. Strive for a full international mandate for innovation in market development, when it would enable the Canadian company to improve its efficiency by specializing collective operations. 5. Aggressively pursue and develop market opportunities throughout international markets. 6. Extend the processing in Canada of natural resource products to the maximum extent feasible on an economic basis. 7. Search out and develop economic sources of supply in Canada for domestically produced goods and for professional and other services. 8. Foster a Canadian outlook among management, as well as larger career opportunities within Canada. 9. Create a financial structure that provides opportunity for substantial equity participation in Canadian enterprise by the Canadian public. 10. Pursue a pricing policy designed to ensure a fair and reasonable return to the company and to Canada for all goods and services sold abroad, including sales to parent companies and other affiliates. 11. Regularly publish information on the operations and financial position of the firm. 12. Give appropriate support to recognized national objectives and established government programs, while resisting any direct or indirect pressures from foreign governments or associated companies to act in a contrary manner. 13. Participate in Canadian social and cultural life, and support those institutions that are concerned with the intellectual, social, and cultural advancement of the Canadian community. 14. Endeavour to ensure that access to foreign resources, including technology and know-how, is not associated with terms and conditions that restrain the firm from observing these principles.

new trade theory The theory that in oligopolistic industries government intervention can reshape the existing structure of global competition to the benefit of national welfare. This means that countries specialize not only because of the advantages gained from their differences, but also because of the increasing returns to large-scale production that make specialization itself a competitive advantage. This then is an argument for government intervention in the form of industrial policy. A country benefits in two different ways. First, since oligopolistic industries tend to earn higher returns or economic rents than industries operating under perfect competition, policies that help domestic firms win a larger market share of the global market will increase national welfare. Second, since certain industries generate greater external economies or social returns, government policies to promote these industries can improve national welfare by fostering these spillages. Expanding high-technology industries or others where there may

also be increasing returns, for example, lead to demands for highly skilled and educated labour, and specialized supply and service industries. A dollar will yield, then, a different return depending on which industry it is invested in. One of the leading economists in new trade theory is Paul Krugman, an American.

New York Stock Exchange (NYSE) The world's leading stock exchange, based on Wall Street in New York.

newly industrialized countries (NIC) A DEVELOPING COUNTRY in the process of rapid industrialization but whose per capita income is still too low to include it among the DEVELOPED COUNTRIES. A large portion of the exports of the newly industrialized countries consists of industrial products such as electrical machinery, consumer goods, and steel and wood products. Examples include South Korea, Taiwan, Hong Kong, and Singapore, with the list expanding now to include Thailand, Malaysia, Mexico, and the southern provinces of China.

niche market A highly specialized market for an intermediate or consumer product. It is argued that Canadian industry, instead of attempting to compete head on with large U.S., European, or Japanese corporations in mass markets, should specialize in high-value products for niche markets.

Nikkei 225 average The Japanese equivalent of the Toronto Stock Exchange 300 Composite Index; it measures the performance of the Tokyo Stock Exchange's 225 most important shares and treats their performance as representative of the performance of the market as a whole.

no-fault automobile insurance A system of automobile insurance in which there is, in the courts, no determination of blame for an automobile accident before payments for bodily harm and, perhaps, automobile damages are made by insurance companies. In most provinces, the courts, under the TORT system, have to determine who is responsible for an accident before damages can be paid. Under a no-fault system, the court hearing is not needed, so there are significant savings in legal and other costs. Each person in the accident is recompensed according to the bodily damages suffered, with payment for each injury determined by a set of schedules — for example, $250 for a broken wrist. Everyone is treated in the same way regardless of income, wealth, or occupation, and the courts are used to seek damages only in cases of death or serious injury. The elimination of fault has to be voted on by a provincial legislature before a no-fault scheme can be introduced. Saskatchewan brought in the world's first form no-fault system of automobile insurance in 1946. Today, three provinces have full no-fault insurance: Quebec, Ontario, and Manitoba (planned). Under no-fault, payments for economic loss are based on scheduled benefits, as opposed to the tort system where parties can be sued.

no par value   Common shares that have no face value. When they are first sold to the public, a price is set by the underwriters in line with what investors are believed to be willing to pay. The value of the shares depends on total SHAREHOLDERS' EQUITY divided by the number of common shares outstanding.

Nobel Prize in Economics   A prize awarded annually since 1969 to an economist or economists who, according to the statute establishing the prize, have "carried out a work in economic science of the eminent significance expressed in the Will of Alfred Nobel drawn up on November 27, 1895." The prize is sponsored by the Swedish central bank but is awarded by the Royal Swedish Academy of Sciences. The award is for specific achievements rather than to an "outstanding person."

nominal national product   The total output of the economy measured in current prices instead of constant or real prices that have been adjusted to eliminate growth due only to inflation.

nominal price   1. The estimated price of a commodity or product for which there is no recent price. **2.** The face value of a bond or preferred share, which may differ from the market price.

nominal rate of protection   The amount by which a domestic producer can raise prices while still remaining price competitive with an imported product. If an imported product worth, say, $1,000, is subject to a 7.5 percent tariff, then its selling price will be $1,075. If a domestic producer can produce the same product for $1,025, then the producer can raise the price to $1,075 without becoming uncompetitive. The extra $50 — 5 percent of the cost of the import — is the nominal rate of protection.

nominal yield   The interest or dividends received on a bond or preferred share, expressed as a percentage of its face or par value. The nominal yield may differ from its actual yield, which is a percentage of the market value. A $1,000 bond with a 7 percent interest rate has a nominal yield of $70. But if the bond is trading at $980, then its actual yield is 7.14 percent.

nominee holding   The purchase and holding of shares, land, or other assets in the name of a stockbroker, bank, or trust company, rather than in the name of the actual owner. Sometimes nominee holdings are established to conceal the identity of the true owner. For example, developers trying to assemble a large parcel of land from a variety of different owners may use this approach, employing several real-estate brokers, to avoid speculation and a sharp increase in price.

non-accelerating inflation rate of unemployment (NAIRU)   The level to which unemployment can be reduced without rekindling inflation; it is also known as the natural rate of unemployment. It is the rate of unemployment to which the economy can be expected to return as it recovers from a recession. Any attempt to lower the unemployment rate below this rate, it is argued, will lead to higher inflation. Canada's non-accelerating inflation rate of unemployment is estimated to be between 7 and 8 percent and has been rising for more than 15 years. However, some economists believe a country's NAIRU can be lowered through various labour-market policies, such as measures to provide training to unemployed workers, improve labour mobility, and increase access to skilled trades where the number of apprentices is restricted.

non-cumulative   The dividend on a preferred share that does not accumulate if it is unpaid.

non-durable goods   Consumer goods that have only a limited life, such as food products, clothing, drugs, toiletries, and the like. They are goods that are quickly used up.

non-negotiable   A bond, debenture, or other security whose ownership cannot be changed simply by an endorsement on the back of the certificate or by delivery to the would-be buyer.

non-market sector   Those sectors of the economy that do not operate in a normal commercial manner and that do not depend on sales revenue to cover any or all of their costs. Examples include the education system, health care, most museums and art galleries, and national and provincial parks.

non-performing assets   Loans on which the payment of interest or repayment of principal are not being made.

non-performing loan   A loan that is in arrears or that has been renegotiated with reduced interest rates. When a bank or other financial institution doubts that the interest or principal of a loan will be paid, it is placed on a cash or non-accrual basis, which means that interest is only recognized when it is received in cash. Financial institutions place loans on a cash basis when payments are 90 days in arrears, unless the loan is well secured and the loan is in the process of being collected. All loans are classified as non-accrual and therefore non-performing when a payment is 180 days in arrears. A renegotiated reduced-rate loan is a loan whose interest rate has been reduced, because of the weak condition of the borrower, below the market rate that would be charged new borrowers for similar loans.

non-price competition   The type of competition that occurs in an oligopolistic industry. Competition is not based on price cutting but on advertising, contests, packaging, giveaways, design, and various other techniques of product differentiation. Sometimes this kind of competition can lead to improved products or services, but it may mean that consumers end up paying more than they would if there were price competition.

non-profit corporation   A corporation formed to carry out a charitable, educational, religious, social, environmental, or other activity for the benefit of its members or of the public at large; it is not expected to operate at a profit. REVENUE CANADA rules define the nature of non-profit corporations and the constraints they must observe if they wish to maintain a tax-exempt status.

non-recourse financing A transaction in which a lender can only seek repayment from the issuer of the financial instrument being tendered.

non-recurring expense An unusual expense in a business, such as a large payment in a lawsuit, clean-up costs in an unexpected environmental accident, or a loss of a plant or mine due to an earthquake, revolution, or other such event.

non-renewable resource A natural resource that cannot be replaced within a reasonable period of time. The most common non-renewable resources are oil, natural gas, coal, uranium, and metal minerals; all of them were formed more than one hundred million years ago. *See also* RENEWABLE RESOURCES.

non-resident tax A federal tax imposed on individuals and corporations not resident in Canada. The normal tax rates prevail for income from employment or carrying on a business in Canada and for 75 percent of the capital gains from the disposal of a property in Canada. Income in the form of dividends, interest, rents, management fees, licences, and royalties are subject to WITHHOLDING TAXES. The withholding-tax rate is 25 percent unless reduced in a bilateral tax treaty with another country; in 1992, Canada offered to lower the withholding-tax rate to 5 percent with countries granting reciprocity to Canada. In addition, corporations are liable for an additional 25 percent tax on after-tax earnings, unless this is reduced by a tax treaty.

non-tariff barrier (NTB) A government measure designed to discourage or block imports at the border. As tariff rates have declined in importance, non-tariff barriers have become a more important protectionist device. The Tokyo Round of the GENERAL AGREEMENT ON TARIFFS AND TRADE, completed in 1979, reduced non-tariff barriers to some extent, and the Uruguay Round could lead to further constraints on their use. Examples of non-tariff barriers include quotas or other quantitative restrictions on imports; government regulations and technical standards written to accommodate domestic producers but to exclude imports (for example, restrictive food and drug laws, or engineering, environmental, and safety standards); government purchasing policies that favour domestic producers; agricultural subsidies and marketing arrangements; the tying of foreign aid, so that recipients have to use the aid money in the donor country; administrative requirements such as customs fees and procedures or domestic-content requirements; and subsidies to encourage import substitution, or to underwrite exports. *See also* NEO-MERCANTILISM.

non-tradeable goods and services Local goods and services that are not exposed to international competition. Examples include local telephone services, most retail trade, products that, due to their weight or volume, are not economical to transport long distances, and health care.

non-voting shares Common shares in a corporation that do not include the right to vote, but share, with voting common shares, the right to dividends. Non-voting shares are not widely used. Their main purpose is to enable a company to raise additional equity capital, while allowing the existing owners of the firm to retain their control. For investors, such shares have less appeal, since they offer the investors little say in a firm's affairs and are of no consequence in a takeover bid for a company.

normal profit The minimum profit necessary to attract a firm to produce a good or service. The profit is sufficient to cover fixed and variable costs and to yield an acceptable rate of return.

normative economics The introduction of value judgements into the study of economics. For example, the view that the highest-paid employee of a corporation should earn no more than five times the pay of the lowest-paid employee is a normative judgement. The economic consequences would be subject to analysis of POSITIVE ECONOMICS, which looks objectively at provable facts. Normative economics is said to be concerned with what should be, while positive economics deals with what is.

North American Free Trade Agreement (NAFTA) A free trade agreement between Canada, the United States (including Puerto Rico), and Mexico that is to come into effect on January 1, 1994 and that will eliminate almost all tariffs between the three countries within 10 years, with the remainder on sensitive items to be eliminated by 2008. The agreement was signed on December 17, 1992, following the announcement by the three countries of their intention to negotiate a NAFTA on February 5, 1991. Actual negotiations, at the ministerial level, were launched in Toronto on June 12, 1991. Legislation to implement the agreement was introduced in Parliament on February 25, 1993. In March, 1993, negotiations were started on additional accords dealing with labour standards and the environment that the United States said were necessary to ratify the agreement in that country. Parliament voted for the NAFTA in June, 1993.

The agreement is divided into a preamble and eight parts: The preamble states the commitment of the three countries to expanding trade, improving competitiveness, creating jobs, improving working conditions and living standards, promoting sustainable development and environmental protection and conservation, strengthening environmental laws, protecting basic workers' rights, and preserving the flexibility needed to protect public welfare and other objectives. Part One establishes the objectives of the agreement and sets out definitions; Part Two deals with trade in goods, including national treatment and market access, rules of origin, customs procedures, special provisions for the automotive and clothing and textile sectors, rules for agriculture, provisions for energy and petrochemicals, and emergency or safeguard actions; Part Three deals with technical barriers to trade, such as standards-related measures; Part Four deals with government procurement and disciplines to enforce the government-procurement provisions; Part Five deals with provisions on investment, cross-border trade in services, telecommunications, trade in financial services, competition policy, the role of state enterprises, and provisions for temporary entry of business persons; Part Six deals with intellectual property; Part Seven deals with institutional agreements, including the establishment of a Free Trade Commission to implement the agreement and a secretariat, the dispute settlement system, and the requirements for notification and transparency; and Part Eight deals with exceptions, the entry into force, an accession clause for the addition of new members, and various annexes.

Part One contains two chapters. The first chapter sets out the free-trade area and asserts that it is consistent with Article XXIV of the GENERAL AGREEMENT ON TARIFFS AND TRADE, which permits free-trade areas. The chapter also sets out the general obligations of each of the three countries. These obligations include: eliminating barriers to trade and facilitating the cross-border movement of goods and services; promoting conditions of fair competition; increasing investment opportunities; protecting intellectual property rights; establishing effective procedures to implement, apply, and administer the agreement and to resolve disputes; and laying the foundation for further trilateral, regional, and multilateral co-operation to expand the benefits of the agreement. The first chapter states that NAFTA shall take precedence over other agreements, including GATT, unless otherwise stated, and that the federal governments are responsible for the implementation of the agreement within their territories by provincial and state governments. Chapter Two sets out general definitions used throughout the agreement.

Part Two contains six chapters dealing with trade in goods. Chapter Three sets out the terms of market access, including the principle of NATIONAL TREATMENT and the schedule for tariff elimination. Tariffs will be eliminated in four phases: immediately on entry into force on January 1, 1994; in five annual steps between 1994 and 1998; in 10 annual steps, from 1994 to 2003; and, for a limited number of U.S. goods, in 15 annual steps from 1994 to 2008. The chapter also provides for the acceleration of tariff cuts. Canada and the United States have until January 1, 1996, to eliminate duty remission or drawback provisions for their companies and Mexico until January 1, 2001. Existing quantitive restrictions on imports and exports are to be lifted; an exception is retained for Canadian exports of raw logs and unprocessed fish. The three countries also agree to recognize distinctive alcoholic products — Canadian Whiskey as a distinctive Canadian product, Bourbon and Tennessee Whiskey as distinctive U.S. products, and Tequila

and Mescal as distinctive Mexican products. The three countries also agree not to impose export taxes on trade with one another and, when export restraints are needed due to supply shortages or for natural resource conservation, to do so in a way that shares the burden and does not disrupt normal trading patterns. In addition, a Committee on Trade in Goods is established to oversee market access developments. Annexes define new rules of origin for automotive trade — 62.5 percent North American content for autos and light vehicles and their engines and transmissions and 60 percent for other vehicles and their engines and transmissions — and new rules of origin for clothing and textiles, with the basic rule that clothing must be manufactured from fibre made in North America, with so-called tariff-preference levels for certain volumes of Canadian-made clothing that does not meet the new rules of origin. Chapter Four sets out the general rules of origin, which state that products must be made from North American parts and materials or, if they incorporate parts or materials from outside North America, the final product must be sufficiently transformed to undergo a change to tariff classification. A de minimis rule states that even where a product does not meet the change of tariff classification test it can still meet the North American rules of origin if offshore materials and parts represent no more than 7 percent of the value of the finished goods. Chapter Five sets out the customs procedures under NAFTA, including certification procedures and record-keeping requirements. Chapter Six deals with energy and petrochemicals. Like Chapter Nine of the CANADA-UNITED STATES FREE TRADE AGREEMENT (FTA), this chapter requires that Canada not discriminate against the United States — or Mexico — by imposing a higher price on energy exports than is charged for oil, gas, electricity or other forms of energy in

Canada and that, in the event of shortages, Canada cut back exports proportional to the overall reduction in supply. Mexico reserves the right to restrict foreign participation in upstream oil and gas development; refining and processing of crude oil and natural gas; the foreign trade, storage, distribution and transportation of crude oil, natural gas, and basic petrochemicals; the supply of electricity as a public service; and the exploration, exploitation and processing of raw materials. Chapter Seven, which deals with agriculture, contains separate agreements between Canada and the United States with Mexico. The three countries agree to eliminate all tariffs on agri-food products during the transition period, with an exception for dairy, poultry, egg, and sugar products in the case of Canada-Mexico trade. Mexico eliminates its quotas on wheat and barley and replaces them with tariffs that will be eliminated in 10 years. A Committee on Agricultural Trade will monitor agricultural trade. The three countries also agree to rules and disciplines on sanitary and phytosanitary measures in agriculture, which they agreed should be based on scientific principles and the appropriate protection from risk. A Committee on Sanitary and Phytosanitary Measures is established to work toward equivalent measures in the three countries. Chapter Eight deals with emergency actions, such as temporary import surcharges, in response to a surge in imports. Due to concerns about Mexico's low wages, emergency actions can be based on a threat-of-injury finding rather than on cases of injury as required in the FTA; and the period of relief can be extended beyond the initial three-year period.

Part Three deals with technical barriers to trade. Chapter Nine of NAFTA sets out rules governing the use of standards so that they cannot be used as non-tariff barriers to trade. It also establishes a Committee on Standards-Related Measures to monitor implementation and pursue further developments. Standards are to be non-discriminatory and based on international practice and scientific findings. The goal of the chapter is to make differences in standards between the three countries as non-trade distorting as possible through compatibility, equivalence, and notification and information exchange requirements. The goal is to make standards and technical regulations compatible, which means identical or equivalent in effect. Unlike the FTA, NAFTA requires the three governments to ensure that provincial and state governments, along with non-government standards bodies, comply with the provisions of the chapter. Each country is required to notify the others of plans to adopt or modify a standards-related measure, and the other countries must be given sufficient time to comment. Four standards subcommittees are established: land transportation, including standards for bus and truck drivers, vehicle emissions, vehicle inspections, road signs, locomotives, and the transportation of dangerous goods; telecommunications standards for equipment; automotive safety, fuel efficiency, and other standards; and labelling of clothing and textiles.

Part Four deals with government procurement and the rules under which businesses from NAFTA countries can bid on federal contracts in one another's countries. Chapter Ten continues the threshold of US$25,000 for federal purchases of goods between Canada and the United States and adds for NAFTA a contract threshold of US$50,000 for goods and services, a threshold of US$6.5 million for construction services, and threshold levels for crown corporations in Canada (including Canada Post, Canadian National Railway, Via Rail, the St. Lawrence Seaway Authority, and the National Capital Commission) the threshold for goods and services is US$250,000 and construction services US$8 million. Canada gains access to contracts of the U.S. Corps of Engineers and the market under the U.S. Rural Electrification Act, and to Mexican state companies, including Pemex, the state oil company.

Part Five deals with investment, services, and related matter. Chapter Eleven deals with investment, which includes minority investments, portfolio investments, and property investments, as well as majority-owned or -controlled investments, and covers any investment made by a company incorporated in North America, regardless of the country of origin. This means Japanese or European-controlled subsidiaries incorporated in North America have the same rights as Canada, Mexican, or U.S. companies. The principle of national treatment is underlined. Canada retains its restrictions on foreign ownership in the transportation, telecommunications, social services, and cultural industries, and its right for INVESTMENT CANADA to review takeovers of the largest Canadian companies. Provincial and state governments have two years after NAFTA comes into effect to list their exclusions or provisions not in conformity with NAFTA that they wish to maintain. Limits on foreign ownership are also permitted in the privatization of crown corporations or other state enterprises or the privatization of government functions. Performance requirements on foreign investors, such as export performance, local content, domestic purchasing, and trade balancing, are not permitted. Expropriation of a business or industry by a government is only permitted for a public purpose, on a non-discriminatory basis, and upon payment of prompt and adequate compensation. Canada is not allowed to require U.S. or Mexican subsidiaries to sell any of their shares to Canadians. The chapter also states

that "it is inappropriate to encourage investment by relaxing domestic health, safety, or environmental measures" and the three countries agree not to pursue such practices; if a country does, the other can seek consultations. A number of options are also set out to resolve investment disputes. Chapter Twelve deals with cross-border trade in services, requiring that the three countries extend national treatment and MOST-FAVOURED NATION treatment to each other and not require the establishment of a "local presence" in order to provide a cross-border service, except for legitimate regulatory reasons such as consumer protection. Existing federal measures that do not conform with NAFTA can be maintained, providing they are listed in the agreement; provincial and state governments have two years from the time the agreement comes into effect to list their exclusions. Sensitive sectors can be left unbound; Canada has excluded public law enforcement, correctional services, income security or insurance, social welfare, public education, public training, health, child-care, basic telecommunications services, aboriginal affairs, minority affairs, and some air and maritime transportation services. An annex on professional services sets out procedures to develop mutually acceptable professional standards and criteria for professional services. The chapter also provides for expanded movement of truck and rail services between the three countries and the provision of specialty air services. Chapter Thirteen deals with telecommunications, establishing a process for harmonization of technical standards and providing for conditions of access to allow companies to operate private leased networks for intra-corporate communications and the right to attach terminal devices to the network. Private leased circuits are to be available on a flat-rate pricing basis. Chapter Fourteen deals with financial services, setting out general rules based on national treatment, most-favoured-nation treatment, the right of consumers to purchase financial services on a cross-border basis, and the right to market access through the establishment of a commercial presence. The chapter includes disciplines on regulations by stock exchanges and futures exchanges and assigns the settlement of disputes to the general provisions of NAFTA (under the FTA financial service disputes were to be dealt with by the Department of FINANCE and the U.S. Treasury). A Financial Services Committee is established to pursue further liberalization. A U.S. or Mexican incorporated financial institution owned in Europe or Japan will not qualify for NAFTA treatment in Canada; the United States and Mexico have taken a more liberal approach, based on country of incorporation rather than country of ultimate ownership. Chapter Fifteen deals with competition policy, monopolies, and state enterprises. The FTA commitment to negotiate new rules dealing with anti-dumping and countervailing duties over a five- to seven-year period is dropped. Instead, a Working Party on Trade and Competition is established to examine, among other things, an alternative to anti-dumping procedures in a free-trade area. The chapter sets out disciplines on the activities of monopolies and state enterprises, based on the principle of non-discrimination in the purchase of sale of goods where a monopoly exists. Chapter Sixteen deals with temporary entry of business travellers to pursue business opportunities created by NAFTA. Four categories of travellers are identified: business visitors who engage in business activities set out in Appendix 1603.A.1; traders and investors who carry on substantial trade and investment; intra-company transferees who are employed in a capacity that is managerial or executive, or involves specialized knowledge;

and professionals, as defined in Appendix 1603.D.1, who want to enter another NAFTA country on a temporary basis to provide their professional skills.

Part Six deals with intellectual property. Chapter Seventeen defines standards for copyright, sound recordings, trademarks, patents, semiconductor integrated circuits, trade secrets, geographical indications, and industrial designs. It sets out rules to enforce intellectual property rights. The registration of trademarks will depend on use; patents will be for at least 20 years from the filing of an application or 17 years from the date the patent is granted; an industrial design that is new or original will be protected for at least 10 years. Each country is to ensure an effective system of enforcement.

Part Seven deals with administrative and institutional provisions. Chapter Eighteen requires each country to promptly publish changes in laws, regulations, and other procedures, and to give an opportunity to the other countries to comment on measures that might affect the operation of NAFTA. Chapter Nineteen sets out the review and dispute settlement process in anti-dumping and countervailing-duty disputes. Any of the three countries may seek a panel to determine whether the law was properly applied in imposing an anti-dumping or countervailing duty; all panels will be binational so that if the United States applies a similar penalty against Canadian and Mexican goods, two panels will be established. If a panel finds the law was properly applied, the matter is dropped; if it finds the administrative authority erred on the basis of the same standards that would be applied by a domestic court, it can send the matter back to the administrative authority to correct the error and make a new determination. Changes to existing anti-dumping and countervailing-duty laws will only apply to NAFTA members if they are specifically named in the legislation.

Chapter Twenty establishes the Free Trade Commission as the central institution of NAFTA; it consists of the Minister for International Trade in Canada, the U.S. Trade Representative, and the Secretary of Commerce and Industrial development in Mexico and will meet at least once a year; it is supported by a secretariat, with offices in all three countries. The three countries resolve to try to settle disputes under NAFTA by consultation and co-operation, but if this fails a panel can be established. The panel will be charged with determining whether or not an action is consistent with NAFTA and may also suggest ways to resolve disputes. If the panel finds an action impairs or nullifies the rights or anticipated benefits of a NAFTA member, and the offending country does not withdraw the measure, then the injured country may suspend the application of equivalent benefits until the issue is resolved.

Part Eight deals with other provisions. Chapter Twenty-one incorporates Article II of the GATT, which allows a country to restrict imports for a number of reasons, including the protection of public morals, the protection of human, animal or plant life or health, the products of prison labour, the protection of national treasures, or the conservation of endangered species. In addition, there is a broad exception to allow each country to protect essential security requirements. The chapter also includes an exemption for existing cultural policies in Canada. Chapter Twenty-two deals with final provisions, including an accession clause for new members. All three countries must agree to admit new members, and countries seeking membership will have to negotiate the price of admission by bringing policies in line with those set out in NAFTA.

North Atlantic Treaty Organization (NATO)   A mutual-defence treaty among Canada, the United States, and the nations of Western Europe, signed in 1949. While its primary focus has been on the defence of Western Europe against possible Soviet attack, it was also expected to strengthen political and economic co-operation among its members. Article Two in the treaty is known as the Canadian article. It encouraged economic co-operation among NATO members, and was seen by the Canadian government as a way to reduce Canada's economic dependence on the United States and to reduce the capacity of the United States for unilateral economic policy measures. In a broader forum, such as NATO, Canada hoped to exert a greater influence on U.S. policies than it could in BILATERAL discussions. The article was another expression of Canada's MULTILATERAL approach to economic problems after the Second World War. NATO's headquarters are in Brussels and its members include Belgium, Britain, Canada, Denmark, Germany, Greece, Ireland, Italy, Luxembourg, the Netherlands, Norway, Portugal, Spain, Turkey, and the United States. With the ending of the Cold War, the break-up of the Soviet Union, and the 1990 signing of the Paris Charter for a New Europe in 1990, the future role of NATO is uncertain.

North-South dialogue   The on-going discussions between the rich, industrialized nations of the northern hemisphere, including Canada, and the poor, less-developed countries of the southern hemisphere, over a NEW INTERNATIONAL ECONOMIC ORDER. These discussions were formally organized at the 1975-77 Conference on International Economic Co-operation, but they also take place in the UNITED NATIONS CONFERENCE ON TRADE AND DEVELOPMENT, the INTERNATIONAL MONETARY FUND, the WORLD BANK, and the GENERAL AGREEMENT ON TARIFFS AND TRADE.

North-South Institute A non-profit organization formed in Canada in 1976 to conduct research into international development and aid issues from a Canadian perspective, and to monitor Canadian programs and performance in the field of international co-operation. It has studied Canadian efforts to deal with world food problems and with the debt problems of the less-developed countries, reviewed Canadian trade policies as they affect developing countries, examined the adjustment problems brought on by the NORTH AMERICAN FREE TRADE AGREEMENT, and conducted research into the place and role of women in developing countries. Its current research efforts are focused on international finance, trade and adjustment, human rights and democratic government, and the Canada-Latin America Forum. It also publishes an annual overview of aid and development issues, and does contract research work for agencies such as the CANADIAN INTERNATIONAL DEVELOPMENT AGENCY and the WORLD BANK. It is funded by private foundations, private industry, and government. It is based in Ottawa.

Northern Pipeline Agency A federal agency established in 1978 to implement the Northern Pipeline Act, passed by Parliament in April, 1978. Its establishment followed the September, 1977, Canada-U.S. agreement on the construction of a natural-gas pipeline from Alaska and the Canadian Arctic to U.S. and Canadian markets. The Northern Pipeline Act implemented the terms of the Canadian-U.S. agreement, provided a CERTIFICATE OF PUBLIC CONVENIENCE AND NECESSITY to the pipeline company for the Canadian portions of the project, and contained provisions to ensure energy, industrial, and economic benefits for Canada and to reduce social and environmental damage from the project. The legislation also created the pipeline agency to co-ordinate and supervise pipeline activi-

ties, according to the law, and to act as the single regulatory agency responsible for the project. The regulatory and administrative powers exercised by other government agencies and departments were delegated to it. Construction of the southern legs of the pipeline were completed in 1982, but plans for the northern portion, from Alaska and the Canadian Arctic have been put on indefinite hold due to low prices. As a result, the Calgary office was closed and the agency operates with a skeleton staff out of Ottawa.

Northwest Atlantic Fisheries Organization (NAFO) The 1979 successor to the International Commission for the Northwest Atlantic Fisheries that Canada had signed in 1950. NAFO has its headquarters in Dartmouth, Nova Scotia, and held its first meeting in March, 1979. Its purpose is to supervise the level of fishing in the Northwest Atlantic, to allocate shares of quotas beyond Canada's 200-mile zone, and to adopt and implement fisheries conservation and research programs. Members include Canada, the EUROPEAN COMMUNITY, Japan, Russia, Bulgaria, Cuba, Denmark, Estonia, Iceland, Latvia, Lithuania, Norway, Poland, and Russia. Spain and Portugal are former members. It sets catch quotas or total allowable catches each year, but since 1986 the European Community has set its own quotas, which are bigger and have led to a serious overfishing of cod, flounder, and plaice in the North Atlantic. It has a scientific council that assesses fisheries' stocks and a Fisheries Commission that sets quotas, regulates catching gear and fishing vessels, and conducts inspections.

not-sufficient-funds cheque (nsf) A cheque that a bank refuses to honour and returns to the payee because there are not sufficient funds in the account to pay the cheque. Banks impose a penalty on the person writing the cheque, in the form of a handling fee.

notary A provincially appointed official who can administer oaths, certify copies of documents, take depositions, and carry out other such public responsibilities.

note Evidence of a debt and a promise to pay issued by a borrower, such as a corporation or government agency. Depending on the terms and conditions, notes may be negotiable — that is, they can be sold at a discount to third parties, and they may be payable to the bearer or to the person named in the note.

notes to financial statements Footnotes in a company annual report that need to be read along with the figures presented in the company's INCOME STATEMENT and BALANCE SHEET in order for its financial affairs to be fully understood. These notes include many important details, such as information on company accounting practices, treatment of income from affiliated companies, valuation of fixed assets and goodwill, an explanation of long-term debt, details on the remuneration of officers and directors, intercorporate transactions, information on the company's tax position, details of any lawsuits that might affect the company's profits, treatment of foreign exchange in earnings, stock options, and pension benefits for senior officers, valuation of inventories, and details of the company's capital structure. These notes can sometimes be more important to understanding a company's true financial position or future prospects than the actual financial figures in the annual report. While a firm's auditors are responsible for the numbers in a financial statement, management is responsible for the notes that accompany the financial statement.

nuclear safeguards Measures to prevent the spread of nuclear weapons to states tthat do not already possess them through controls on the export of nuclear-power technology and fuels. The safeguards were devised by the INTERNATIONAL ATOMIC ENERGY AGENCY (IAEA), a United Nations body based in Vienna. Countries using nuclear-power systems are required to file regular, detailed reports to the IAEA, and to allow international inspection of their facilities to ensure that there is no diversion of nuclear materials from civilian to military use. The development of the safeguards followed the signing of the Treaty on the Non-Proliferation of Nuclear Weapons in 1968.

nugget A piece of precious metal, such as gold, usually found in rivers and streams, that has been worn down by water.

nuisance tariff A tariff so low that it provides no appreciable level of protection for domestic industry but does force an importer to provide all the necessary paperwork for customs officials.

nuisance tax A tax that raises little revenue but causes considerable work for those who must pay it. For example, a 1 percent tariff might produce almost no revenue, but importers would still have to go through all the customs paperwork to pay it.

numbered bank account A bank account whose owner is identified by number rather than by name, giving the account a secret identity. Such accounts have been common in Switzerland, where usually only a senior officer of a bank usually knows the identity of the account holders. Because of this facility, Swiss banks have become a favoured haven for hot money, in particular for the funds of criminals, corrupt officials, and politicians who accumulate funds outside their own country in case they have to leave in a hurry some day. Swiss accounts may also be used by Canadians to hide income and wealth and thus evade taxes they should be paying in Canada although the Swiss government and banks have become more willing to provide information on numbered accounts if criminal activity is suspected.

numeraire   The standard against which the prices of other currencies or goods are expressed. For example, the U.S. dollar and SPECIAL DRAWING RIGHTS (SDR) can be used as numeraires for expressing the value of other currencies. The U.S. dollar is the numeraire for many internationally traded commodities. The SDR is used as the numeraire for transaction in the INTERNATIONAL MONETARY FUND, while the EUROPEAN CURRENCY UNIT is the numeraire used within the EUROPEAN MONETARY SYSTEM.

Nunavut   An Inuktitut word for "our land" that was adopted as the name for a new Inuit territory and government in the eastern part of the Northwest Territories (NWT) to be established in 1990. In 1976, the Inuit Tapirisat of Canada, a national Inuit organization, called for the establishment of a new territory in the eastern and central NWT where most Inuit live. But the Inuit and the Dene and Métis, who also had unsettled land claims, could not agree on a division of the NWT and their land claims areas. In 1990, the federal government appointed John Parker, former Commissioner of the NWT, to recommend a single-line boundary between the claims settlement areas of the Inuit and Dene-Métis. The federal government accepted his recommendation, which was presented to all NWT voters for ratification by plebiscite on May 4, 1992. Of those voting, 54 percent supported the proposal, and it was formally adopted by the federal government and the government of the NWT. In the meantime, negotiations between the Inuit, represented by the Tungavik Federation of Nunavut, and the federal government had led to an agreement in principle in 1990 on land claims. It included an agreement by the federal and NWT governments to establish Nunavut "as soon as possible" and for a process, separate from the land claims, to further this process. At the end of 1991, negotiations were completed on outstanding issues on the land claims. The final agreement committed the federal and NWT governments and the Inuit to negotiate a political accord separate from the land claims to deal with the powers, principles of financing, and timing for the establishment of Nunavut. This political accord was initialed by all the parties in April, 1992, and formally signed on October 30, 1992. Inuit ratification of the land-claim settlement agreement was held in November, 1992, and approved by 69 percent of eligible voters (and 85 percent of those who voted). Nunavut will have jurisdictional powers and basic institutions similar to the present NWT and Yukon. There will be an elected legislative assembly, a cabinet, a territorial court, and a Nunavut civil service. In May, 1993, the prime minister signed an agreement on the new territory with Nunavut leaders, paving the way for federal legislation that will permit the Inuit to have a government similar to that of the Yukon and Northwest Territories by 1999.

O

obsolescence The reduction in the useful life of an asset, such as productive machinery or a major consumer product, caused by new technology or a switch in consumer tastes rather than by normal wear and tear. In industry, obsolescence often occurs because a new invention enables a competitor to reduce production costs significantly, even though existing productive facilities are still in good working order. Some consumer-goods industries resort to planned obsolescence, either by making frequent product changes or by building a product so that it does not last for as long as it could. When oil prices rose sharply in the 1970s, much of the production capacity of industry was rendered obsolete because it was energy intensive. Likewise, new environmental standards can also render production facilities obsolescent because they fail to meet the new standards.

occupational health and safety laws Federal and provincial laws designed to reduce the risk of accidents and disease in industry. Federal and most provincial laws require the establishment of workplace safety committees, with employee participation. The laws cover a range of risks, from noise, safeguards over machinery, and safety clothing to control over toxic or dangerous materials.

odd lot The sale or purchase of shares in a small or uneven number. These transactions often command a higher commission because they may be harder to buy or sell than so-called ROUND LOTS of one hundred. The sale of 85 shares or 115 shares is an odd lot; the sale of any multiple of one hundred shares is a round lot.

off balance-sheet financing **1.** The use of leasing by a firm to pay for the use of machinery and equipment instead of investing money to buy it. The cost of leasing is deducted each year from profits as an operating cost. This means the machinery and equipment is not included as a fixed asset on the firm's balance sheet. The advantage to the firm is that it does not have to tie its capital up in costly equipment. **2.** Banking business that does not entail the taking of deposits or the issing of loans. The activities are fee-based, such as trading in DERIVATIVES or supplying LETTERS OF CREDIT.

offer **1.** The price a would-be purchaser is willing to pay for a property. In the real-estate industry, an offer to purchase a house, for example, is usually accompanied by a deposit to show that the offer is serious. If the offer is accepted but the would-be purchaser changes his mind, he loses his deposit. **2.** In stock and bond markets, the lowest price at which a person is willing to sell. *See also* BID.

Office of Native Claims *See* NATIVE CLAIMS.

Office of Privatization and Regulatory Affairs An office established by the federal government in 1986 to manage the privatization of government-owned enterprises where government ownership was no longer necessary for public-policy reasons, and to review and improve federal regulations so that they do not hinder economic development. The office reports to Parliament through the Minister of FINANCE or a Minister of State attached to the Finance Department.

Office of the Auditor-General of Canada *See* AUDITOR-GENERAL

Office of the Commissioner of Official Languages An office established in 1970 to administer the Official Languages Act, legislation that was amended in 1988. The Official Languages Act affirms that English and French are the official languages of Canada and sets out their equal status in all federal institutions. It defines the rights of Canadians with respect to official languages, as well as the responsibility of federal institutions to provide services in English and French; commits the federal government to encouraging and supporting the development of official language minority communities, and to fostering the full

recognition and use of both official languages in Canada; commits the federal government to co-operate with provincial governments to support the development of French- and English-minority communities, and sets out the right of federal employees to work in their preferred official language subject to geographical and other considerations. It also recognizes the importance of preserving and enhancing the use of languages other than French or English. Canadians have the right to be served in either French or English in the National Capital Region of Ottawa and Hull, from the head office of all federal institutions, and for certain services such as customs and immigration-processing at airports and border-crossing points. Canadians also have a right to be served in either French or English in federal institutions across Canada where there is a significant demand for such services or where it is reasonable to provide such services for reasons of public health, safety, and security, or where the nature of the office requires it. The Commissioner of Official Languages is responsible for ensuring that the letter and spirit of the act are known and acts as a linguistic ombudsman, investigating complaints from those who believe their language rights have not been respected, and as a linguistic auditor responsible for ensuring that the federal government complies with the act. The commissioner is also a promoter of language equality. The office is based in Ottawa; there are also regional offices.

Office of the Comptroller-General of Canada *See* COMPTROLLER-GENERAL OF CANADA.

Office of the Superintendent of Financial Institutions A federal agency established in 1987, following the failure of two Canadian banks, to improve the federal supervision of the banking system and banks. In addition, the office supervises insurance, trust, loan, and investment companies, as well as co-operative credit associations, that are chartered, licensed, or regulated by the federal government. The office was the result of a merger of the Department of Insurance and the Office of the Inspector-General of Banks. The deposit-taking institutions sector monitors the solvency and performance of federally regulated banks, trust, loan, and investment companies, and co-operative credit associations through inspectors operating out of regional offices across Canada. The insurance and pensions sector supervises life and property and casualty insurance companies that are federally regulated, and also supervises the solvency of private-sector pension plans to ensure that the funds are available to meet future pension obligations.

official development assistance (ODA) Government financial aid given or lent to less-developed countries; it can also include technical assistance. The purpose of these loans and grants is to promote the economic development and welfare of the recipient countries; it must be either a grant or a concessionary loan containing a grant element of at least 25 percent. ODA consists of financial assistance provided by multilateral institutions such as the WORLD BANK or the INTER-AMERICAN DEVELOPMENT BANK, or by domestic agencies on a bilateral basis, such as the CANADIAN INTERNATIONAL DEVELOPMENT AGENCY. In 1970, the United Nations Development Decade adopted an ODA target of 0.7 percent of the GROSS NATIONAL PRODUCT (GNP) from each developed country, including Canada; the PEARSON COMMISSION made a similar recommendation. In 1970, Canada's aid programs amounted to 0.42 percent of GNP, and the government declared its intention to reach 0.7 percent of GNP by 1975. In 1978, this figure had reached 0.52 percent, its peak. In 1987, in a policy statement on

aid entitled Sharing Our Future, the federal government set the goal of ODA reaching 0.6 percent of GROSS DOMESTIC PRODUCT by 1995 and 0.7 percent by 2000. By 1993, Canadian ODA had fallen to 0.39 percent after the government announced that due to domestic fiscal constraint, Canada's revised ODA target was to achieve 0.7 percent of GNP but with no date specified. ODA flows have also been diluted by the inclusion of the former Soviet Union and Eastern European countries among those qualifying for ODA. The Development Assistance Committee of the ORGANIZATION FOR ECONOMIC CO-OPERATION AND DEVELOPMENT (OECD) publishes an annual report on the ODA contributions of OECD member-countries, including Canada; it is called *Development Co-operation. See also* CANADIAN INTERNATIONAL DEVELOPMENT AGENCY.

offset agreement   An agreement in a government contract, in which the supplier of a major item, such as military aircraft, agrees to carry out industrial work in Canada equivalent to a specific amount of Canadian content, although the actual aircraft or other major equipment to be supplied may be imported from another country. Offset agreements often require some degree of final assembly or subassembly in Canada plus some contracting out of parts and components to Canadian companies. However, the offset purchases may be in totally unrelated fields. If the government wants a certain level of CANADIAN CONTENT out of a large contract, it may negotiate production of certain parts or components in Canada for worldwide distribution, or persuade the supplier to set up an unrelated industrial activity in Canada that meets the desired level of Canadian content. Offset agreements are sought on big contracts because it is felt that Canada should use this government purchasing power to help strengthen its own industrial development, rather than simply pay out the entire sum on imports that benefit the industrial development of other countries.

offshore drilling The drilling for oil or natural gas from drilling platforms erected in Canada's coastal waters. *See also* ATLANTIC ACCORD.

offshore funds Funds placed in banks in other countries or in other assets in other countries so that they are beyond the direct reach of the tax authorities in the investor's home country. Offshore funds are often placed in tax havens.

offshore mineral rights The ownership of mineral-resources rights on the ocean floor along Canada's coastline. The Supreme Court of Canada, in 1967, ruled that the offshore resources along the Pacific coast belonged to the federal government. However, the provinces have been attempting to negotiate full or shared jurisdiction. In 1979, the federal government announced that it would turn over jurisdiction to the provinces. *See also* ATLANTIC ACCORD.

Ohlin, Bertil (1899-1979) The Swedish economist who won the Alfred Nobel Memorial Prize in Economic Sciences in 1977, along with James Meade, for "their pathbreaking contribution to the theory of international trade and international capital movements."

oil policy In 1975, the federal government set the goal of self-reliance, which meant "supplying Canadian energy requirements from domestic resources to the greatest extent practicable." In 1979, the new Progressive Conservative government set the goal of self-sufficiency for Canada by the year 1990, with the elimination of Canada's need for imported oil by then. The NATIONAL ENERGY PROGRAM in 1980 adopted the goal of reducing Canadian oil consumption through

energy efficiency measures and by incentives to switch the natural gas or electricity. Under the emergency oil plan of the INTERNATIONAL ENERGY AGENCY, member countries including Canada are required to hold oil stocks equivalent to at least 90 days of net oil imports. Since 1985, Canada has had no specific policy for oil self-reliance or self-sufficiency, leaving the supply of oil to the functioning of free markets. *See also* WESTERN ACCORD.

oil reserves *See* ESTABLISHED RESERVES, INITIAL ESTABLISHED RESERVES, REMAINING ESTAB-LISHED RESERVES, ULTIMATE POTENTIAL RESERVES.

oil sands Deposits of sand and other rock aggregates that contain a heavy, viscous oil mixture known as crude bitumen. The oil cannot be recovered through oil wells, but has to be mined and then processed to separate the oil from the sand; the resulting product must then be upgraded so that it can be used by refineries as an oil interchangeable with conventional crude oil. Western Canada has enormous potential reserves at Athabasca, Buffalo Head Hills, Cold Lake, Peace River, and Wabasca. But large-scale exploitation depends on the development of an effective and economic IN SITU recovery system.

oilseeds Seeds, grains, or legumes like soybeans and canola that are processed to produce vegetable oils and meal.

Old Age Security Pension Canada's first universal old-age pension, it started in January, 1952, as a $40-a-month pension to all Canadians 70 years old and over who met a 20-year residency test. It replaced the means-tested Old Age Pension which had been introduced in Canada in 1927; a separate Old Age Assistance Act was also passed in 1951 to provide assistance to persons 65 to 69, with the federal and participating provincial governments sharing the costs on a 50:50 basis. In 1965, legislation was introduced to progressively reduce the age of entitlement to 65; this was achieved in 1970. The Old Age Assistance Plan was scrapped, and in 1967, the GUARANTEED INCOME SUPPLEMENT was introduced to provide additional assistance to retired Canadians on an income-tested basis. Until 1972, the Old Age Security pension was funded by earmarked taxes — a portion of the manufacturers' sales tax, the corporate income tax, and the personal income tax. But starting in 1972, it was funded out of general government revenues. Also starting in 1973, the Old Age Security pension was indexed to inflation on a quarterly basis; in the second quarter of 1993, the monthly payment was $381.60 a month. To be eligible, a recipient must have resided in Canada for the 10 consecutive years immediately preceding the date on which the application is approved or have resided in Canada for at least 40 years since the age of 18. Starting in 1992, the federal government introduced a "claw back" provision that in effect taxed back the Old Age Security Pension for pensioners whose net income exceeded $53,215.

oligopoly   A market in which there are only a few large sellers but many buyers, and that is characterized by limited or intermittent price competition. The main forms of competition consist of advertising, packaging, product differentiation, and service. In an oligopolistic industry, each firm is able to calculate the effect of its pricing and production decisions on the other firms. It is possible for tacit collusion to exist in such a situation, possibly through the price leadership exercised by the largest firm. In some oligopolistic industries, the firms may manufacture an identical product, such as steel or petrochemicals, or similar products in which there is considerable product dif-

ferentiation based on styling or packaging, such as in the refrigerator, automobile, and cigarette industries. Oligopolistic firms tend to be large and require significant capital investment to achieve economies of scale. They are therefore difficult to break up. These high start-up costs or the existence of BARRIERS TO ENTRY usually account for the existence of oligopolies. *See also* IMPERFECT COMPETITION, CONCENTRATION RATIOS.

oligopsony   An industry in which there are only a few large buyers and many sellers; this situation therefore allows the buyers to depress the prices that can be earned by the sellers. Examples include big department-store or supermarket chains, which may buy a product, such as women's blouses or bread, from a great many different sellers.

Ontario Economic Council (OEC)   An advisory body created by the Ontario government in 1968, consisting of businesspeople, union leaders, university economists, and other representatives of the community. The council made recommendations to the government, in published reports. It also assigned research projects to economists, out of a research budget allocated to it by the provincial government, who investigated questions that the council believed to be of great importance. The council was abolished in 1985.

Ontario Energy Board   An Ontario regulatory agency whose principal activities are to regulate natural-gas prices and to review Ontario Hydro requests for electricity rate increases. The board was established in 1960 as a successor agency to the Ontario Fuel Board. The board regulates natural-gas utility rates, approves the construction and expropriation of land for natural-gas pipelines wholly within the province, designates gas-storage areas, reviews Ontario Hydro plans for electricity-rate increases if the Minister of Energy so wishes, and reviews other energy-policy questions when requested by the Minister of Energy and the Environment. The board holds public hearings, and is based in Toronto.

Ontario Energy Corporation   A government-owned energy company created by Ontario in 1974 to invest in oil, natural-gas, and other energy projects. It held Ontario's 5 percent interest in Syncrude Canada Limited, a major tar-sands project, which it sold in 1978. Other major investments have included holding a 25 percent ownership stake in Suncor Corporation, an integrated oil company, participating in the Polar Gas natural-gas-pipeline project for the Arctic, and funding by-product-heat projects — for example, the use of by-product heat from nuclear-power plants to heat commercial greenhouses. The original purpose of the corporation was to invest in energy projects anywhere in Canada or elsewhere, to increase the supply of energy in Ontario, to stimulate the exploration for and development of sources of energy, and to encourage and invest in energy-conservation projects. But its role has been sharply reduced. In 1993, it sold its 25 percent stake in Suncor.

Ontario Municipal Board (OMB)   An Ontario government agency made up of officials appointed to supervise the activities of Ontario municipalities. It must approve many municipal actions, such as zoning changes, official plans, subdivision plans, restricted-area by-laws, municipal capital spending, changes in boundaries, and changes in municipal charters. Its decisions can be appealed to the Ontario cabinet.

Ontario Premier's Council on Economic Renewal   An advisory board drawn from the business, labour, scientific, educational, and other communities to advise the Ontario government on actions to accelerate change and restructuring in the Ontario economy. It was originally established as the Premier's Council in 1987 but had its name changed in 1991. Through task forces and special projects, the council pursues strategic issues — such as innovative forms of financial support for businesses, lifelong learning, the organization of the workplace, wealth creation through innovation, and best business practices.

Ontario Securities Commission (OSC)   The principal provincial securities commission in Canada, which regulates the securities industry in the province with the purpose of protecting the investing public. Its responsibilities include the registration and approval of all securities, such as common shares, preferred shares, and bonds, sold to the public; the registration of salespeople, investment counsellors, and others in the securities industry; the maintenance of up-to-date records of INSIDER TRADING and other corporate disclosures; the regulation of the TORONTO STOCK EXCHANGE; the supervision of MUTUAL FUNDS; and the regulation of COMMODITY-FUTURES and DERIVATIVES under the Commodity Futures Act of Ontario. The OSC, which is based in Toronto, was first established in 1928, but has acted as a full-time regulatory agency only since broader securities legislation was passed in 1945.

Ontario White Paper on Tax Reform   A 1969 Ontario government white paper that proposed sweeping changes in the provincial tax system. Its major proposals included a new provincial income-tax system; the use of tax credits to replace various income-maintenance or welfare schemes, leading to a guaranteed annual income; the introduction of a capital-gains tax; the assumption by the province of a greater share of municipal costs, including local school costs currently paid out of property-tax revenues; and the reform of the property-tax system, by introducing MARKET-VALUE ASSESSMENT.

open-cut mine   A mine that is open at the surface, as opposed to a mine that is worked deep underground and that can only be worked by sinking a shaft and operating through a network of underground tunnels.

open economy   An economy in which there is a high inflow and outflow of trade and investment relative to the size of the GROSS DOMESTIC PRODUCT. A smaller economy such as Canada's is more likely to be an open economy, since it lacks the internal market to produce or consume many of the types of goods and services that are needed. Until recently, a large country was less likely to have an open economy, since it was not as dependent on foreign markets or foreign sources of supply. However, with the globalization of the world economy, even the largest economies, such as that of the United States, or the economies of the largest countries, such as China and India, are becoming open economies in order to participate in world trade and investment. The more open its economy, the less freedom a country has to pursue an independent economic policy. Interdependence is the result.

open-end investment company   *See* MUTUAL FUND.

open-market operations   Transactions by the Bank of Canada to influence money supply and interest rates and thus to help implement MONETARY POLICY by buying and selling government securities, such as government bonds and treasury bills. The purpose of these sales and purchases is to alter the level of cash reserves in the banking system, thereby altering the ability of the chartered banks to make loans, to purchase securities, and thus to finance the expansion of the economy. By selling government securities, the Bank of Canada reduces the cash reserves of the banking system, and hence its lending ability, while raising interest rates, thus encouraging Canadians to save rather than spend. Interest rates are raised because the increased supply of government securities reduces their face value, which raises their effective yield. By purchasing government securities from the banking system, the Bank of Canada increases the cash reserves, thereby increasing the lending ability of the chartered banks. It also lowers interest rates and increases money supply by encouraging spending instead of saving. Rates are lowered because the central bank has reduced the supply of outstanding securities, thus raising their face value and lowering their effective yield or interest rate, and because of the effect of the announcement that the bank is entering the market. Open-market operations are one of the most important tools available to the central bank to influence the size of the monetary base.

open mortgage   A MORTGAGE that can be partially or fully paid off at any time without penalty.

open shop   A place of employment in which a union is recognized as the bargaining agent for employees, but where new employees are not forced to join the union.

open skies   Negotiations launched between Canada and the United States in 1990 to improve access by each country's airlines to each other's airports and to increase transborder air transportation services. Cabotage, or the right of each country's airlines to operate domestic services between different cities in the other country, and foreign ownership issues were excluded from the negotiations. The negotiations were intended to update the 1966 Canada-U.S. air agreement, last revised in 1974. Key issues included scheduled passenger services, airport access standards, and dispute resolution. One problem was to increase Canadian access to landing and departure slots at U.S. airports; these are the property of U.S. airlines and therefore cannot be allocated by the U.S. Department of Transportation. The two countries had hoped to reach agreement at the end of 1992 but failed to do so.

opening price   The price at which transactions in a currency, financial security, share, or commodity start at the beginning of trading in a market.

operating company   A company that is actively engaged in the production of goods or services, as opposed to an investment or holding company, which may be incorporated for tax or other purposes to hold and make investments.

operating profit   The after-tax profit from the normal operations of the business, as opposed to an extraordinary gain from an investment or sale of a company-owned asset.

operations research   A mathematical technique used to decide the best of a series of alternative courses of action. It originated in the Second World War as an important tool in military planning, but is now widely used by business and government, with the aid of computers, to help reach difficult solutions where there are a great many factors and considerable information to take into account. The firm or government agency using operations research has to define the criteria to be met — for example, profitability or the greatest possible public access. Typical operations-research applications include finding the best locations for a company's manufacturing and distribution centres; managing inventory; calculating the minimum number of boxcars, trucks, or planes a transportation company needs to meet its schedules; planning the number of runways and unloading gates an airport needs; or estimating the best construction schedule to meet the future needs of an electrical utility.

operator   In an oil or natural gas project, the company in a consortium that has the authority to explore and develop the oil or gas field on behalf of the various partners.

opportunity cost   A method of measuring the benefits sacrificed by taking one course of action instead of another. It is an economic rather than an accounting concept, since it measures the costs of not doing something else, whereas accounting measures the costs of what is actually being done. The opportunity cost of taking action A — say, building a shopping centre — is the sacrifice of the profits that would have been made by taking action B — building an office tower instead. Similarly, the income from renting out a paid-for building should at least equal the opportunity cost of selling the building and using the proceeds to make another investment.

Opportunity cost is an important concept in making investment choices and allocating resources. It does not make sense to use a FACTOR OF PRODUCTION — land, labour, capital, or technology — for a particular purpose, if it yields less than the opportunity cost of using the factor in some other way. Similarly, it doesn't make sense for a worker to take a job in one industry, when he or she could make more money for the same skills and responsibilities in another industry; opportunity cost is therefore an important consideration in setting wages in different industries. Opportunity cost identifies choices that have to be made, since every factor of production can be said to have an alternative use.

optimum   The outcome that represents the best possible trade-off within a set of constraints. Households and firms are assumed to make rational choices and therefore to optimize their behaviour.

opting out   The right of a province not to participate in a federal-provincial shared-cost program; if a province opts out, the federal government reduces its income-tax points in that province so that the province can gain additional income by raising its tax rates. The additional income raised by the province is supposed to match the funds the province would have received from the federal government under the shared-cost program. In 1965, the Established Programs (Interim Arrangements) Act gave all provinces the right to opt out of certain shared-cost programs, and gave them six months to decide; only Quebec exercised the option. The legislation covered hospital insurance, vocational training, and various social-welfare programs, such as payments to the blind and disabled, and payments under the CANADA ASSISTANCE PLAN. The only programs covered under the act now are the allowances for blind and disabled persons and the Canada Assistance Plan.

option   A contract in which the owner of a piece of land, building, block of shares, film script, or some other property, agrees to sell the property to another party for a specified price during a specified period of time if the other party decides to buy it. In return, the buyer of this right or option pays a sum of money, whether the option is exercised or not. The purchaser of an option loses money if he or she doesn't exercise the option, but this is a small price to pay if it turns out that purchasing the property would have been a poor investment. It is a convenient way of obtaining the right to buy something, and hence of considering an investment without having to put up a lot of money all at once. A property developer, for example, may buy options on adjoining pieces of land with the intention of undertaking a major project. However, if the market turns sour or municipal authorities indicate that they will not approve the project, the developer will not exercise the option.

Options also represent a cheaper way of speculating in the stock and commodities markets. Two types of options can be purchased: a CALL option, which gives the purchaser the right to buy shares or a commodity at a fixed price within a specified period of time, and a PUT option, which allows the purchaser of the option the right to sell someone a fixed number of shares at a fixed price within a specified period of time.

order-in-council   *See* GOVERNOR-IN-COUNCIL.

ore   Various types of rock formations containing minerals that can be extracted economically.

Organization for Economic Co-operation and Development (OECD)   An organization of industrial nations, with a permanent staff of officials, established in 1961 to improve trade and investment flows among its members, to help analyze and deal with balance-of-payments and other economic problems, and to co-ordinate foreign-aid policies through a separate DEVELOPMENT ASSISTANCE COMMITTEE (DAC). Its original members were Canada, Germany, Britain, Ireland, France, Austria, Sweden, Iceland, Denmark, Italy, the United States, Norway, the Netherlands, Turkey, Greece, Belgium, Portugal, Spain, Switzerland, and Luxembourg. Since then Japan, Finland, Australia, and New Zealand have become members. Yugoslavia had an associate status but lost this in

1992 with the break-up of the country. In 1993, the OECD announced that Mexico would become its next member, with South Korea likely to follow.

The OECD plays a number of important roles in the world economy. 1. It attempts to harmonize economic policies among member-nations to check inflation, and to achieve better economic growth. 2. It studies common economic-policy problems, such as inflation, manpower training, taxation, and investment incentives, and recommends possible solutions. 3. It prepares its own semiannual forecasts of economic performance, for the OECD as a whole and for individual OECD members, along with policy recommendations. 4. It carries out comparative studies among OECD members, to see how they deal with specific problems, such as worker retraining, regional development, environmental controls, industrial development, or early retirement, or how they compare, for example, in spending on research and development, unemployment insurance, or social assistance. 5. It co-ordinates policies among OECD members — for example, by defining a code for behaviour by MULTINATIONAL CORPORATIONS, by establishing ground rules on export subsidies, by dealing with nuclear-energy policies or with restrictive business practices, or by formulating responses for the industrialized world to the demands of the LESS-DEVELOPED COUNTRIES for a NEW INTERNATIONAL ECONOMIC ORDER.

The finance ministers of OECD countries meet regularly as members of its Economic Policy Committee; there is a ministerial meeting of the OECD each year prior to the GROUP OF SEVEN Summit. Which deals with balance-of-payments problems. Meetings of OECD committees in other policy areas such as science, the environment, social policy, trade policy, manpower training, and industrial development, also bring OECD-nation cabinet ministers togeth-

er. Individual nations in the OECD are represented by officials of ambassadorial rank. Agencies related to the OECD include the INTERNATIONAL ENERGY AGENCY and the Nuclear Energy Agency. OECD headquarters are in Paris.

Organization for European Economic Co-operation An organization of Western European countries formed in 1944 to work with the United States and Canada, which were associate members, to plan the post-war reconstruction of their economies and to administer the EUROPEAN RECOVERY PROGRAM, better known as the Marshall Plan. After U.S. aid was discontinued, the organization continued to promote trade and investment among the member countries. It was replaced in 1960 by the ORGANIZATION FOR ECONOMIC CO-OPERATION AND DEVELOPMENT.

Organization of Arab Petroleum Exporting Countries (OAPEC) An association of the oil-exporting nations in the Arab world, formed in 1968 to co-ordinate economic policies, undertake joint projects, share expertise, and provide training and employment for one another's citizens. Joint projects include the Arab Maritime Petroleum Transportation Company, the Arab Shipbuilding and Repair Company, the Arab Petroleum Investment and Repair Company, the Arab Petroleum Investment Company, and the Arab Petroleum Service Company. Members include Iran, Iraq, Saudi Arabia, Kuwait, the United Arab Emirates, Algeria, Libya, Bahrain, Qatar, Syria, Tunisia, and Egypt.

Organization of Petroleum Exporting Countries (OPEC) A cartel of oil-exporting nations created in 1960 to raise the producing nations' revenues from oil, following the 1959 and 1960 reductions in posted oil prices by big international oil companies. At that time, oil production and pricing was, for the most part, controlled by the major international oil companies. The original members met in Baghdad in September, 1960, to form OPEC: they were Iran, Iraq, Kuwait, Saudi Arabia, and Venezuela.

During the 1960s, although OPEC had little impact on prices, it was expanding its membership to 13 nations, which accounted for 85 percent of world oil exports. In 1968, OPEC issued a statement asserting that the governments of oil states had the right to participate in the ownership of the oil companies operating in their countries, and to set the posted price of oil to ensure that prices kept up with inflation; OPEC members contended that the oil companies should transfer a part of their "excessively high earnings" to the oil-producing states. In its first test of strength in 1970, OPEC raised the posted price of oil and raised its tax rate from 50 percent of the posted price to 55 percent. But the true significance of OPEC's strength became clear in 1973 and 1974, when the posted price of oil was raised almost fourfold and a number of member states moved to acquire ownership of their oil industry from the big multinational oil companies. Since then, OPEC has also taken other steps to strengthen its hand and to increase the benefits of oil and natural-gas reserves for the producer nations. The foreign oil-producing companies have been for the most part nationalized, and OPEC members have sought to increase their economic benefit by moving into refining, petrochemicals production, and the ownership of tanker fleets. OPEC members argue that their oil and gas reserves will not last forever, and that they are therefore entitled to try to use their oil and gas wealth to strengthen and diversify their economies for the benefit of future generations. However, since the early 1980s, OPEC has lost much of its power. A switch to other forms of energy and the emergence of new sources of supply, along with major advances in energy efficiency, led to a glut in world oil supplies in the 1980s and much lower prices as a result. OPEC could regain its power only by sharply curtailing production or if the oil importing countries failed to reduce their dependence on imported oil in the years ahead. The INTERNATIONAL ENERGY AGENCY forecasts that by 2010, nearly 50 percent of oil consumption could come from the Middle East and Venezuela compared with 30 percent in the early 1990's.

OPEC's members today include Algeria, Ecuador, Indonesia, Iran, Iraq, Kuwait, Libya, Nigeria, the Persian Gulf emirates, Saudi Arabia, and Venezuela; Ecuador, however, is contemplating leaving OPEC. OPEC maintains its headquarters in Vienna, where it has a highly trained staff of oil experts. Its members meet regularly to discuss world oil-production trends, to allocate production quotas, and to discuss strategies to increase the benefits OPEC members get from oil production — strategies such as demanding a bigger share of world refining and petrochemical production. In 1976, the OPEC Special Fund was created, with US$800 million dollars in capital, to assist less-developed countries hurt by oil-price increases. *See also* INTERNATIONAL ENERGY AGENCY.

organization theory   The study of decision making in large organizations. While economics portrays firms to be homogeneous profit-maximizing players, organization theory probes the behaviour of large firms and other organizations to determine how decisions are made. The result is that many decisions are seen to be anything but profit-maximizing and may have to do with the history or culture of the organization, its size, and the nature of its organization and decision-making structure.

Ottawa Agreements A series of trade agreements made among Britain and the members of the British Commonwealth at the Imperial Economic Conference held in Ottawa in 1932. The agreements, consisting of 12 bilateral treaties, raised tariffs against the rest of the world and established lower preferential-tariff rates among members of the Commonwealth. Prime Minister R.B. Bennett of Canada was one of the driving forces behind the conference, practising his 1930 election promise to put "Canada first, then the Empire." But he was successful in persuading the British to agree to the scheme in a large part because the United States had made significant increases in its tariffs.

output The goods and services produced in the economy each year.

output gap The difference between the actual output of the economy and the potential output of the economy; it is the level of output consistent over the medium term with stable inflation. When the economy operates below its potential, there is a recessionary gap; when it operates above its potential, there is an inflationary gap.

output-market equilibrium The level of economic activity and the price level that results from the intersection of the aggregate demand curve and the aggregate supply schedule; this also determines the level of employment in the economy. Equilibrium does not necessarily represent full employment or potential output, but it identifies what will happen as a result of certain conditions. Monetary, fiscal, and exchange-rate policy changes can shift the aggregate demand curve, which is why Keynesian economists favour active government budgets to achieve greater output.

outside director A director of a company who is not an officer of the company and has no important holding in the

company. This type of director is usually appointed because he or she is a community figure, a well-known businessperson whose ideas can be used in the company, or a prominent academic.

outstanding shares The preferred or common shares of a corporation that are held by investors. The number of outstanding shares can be increased if a NEW ISSUE is sold to the public. The number can be reduced if a corporation redeems some of its preferred shares or buys back some of its shares from the public, but the total number of shares is limited by a firm's AUTHORIZED CAPITAL, as set out in its charter.

outward orientation A country that opens its markets to the rest of the world and pursues its own prosperity by promoting its exports.

over-the-counter market (OTC) The market for corporate and government bonds and unlisted shares, usually conducted over the telephone or by telex, with prices reached through negotiation. Companies traded over-the-counter are usually too small to be traded on a normal stock exchange. Taken together, the dollar value of trading for bonds and shares in the over-the-counter market is greater than the dollar value of trading for LISTED SHARES on recognized STOCK EXCHANGES. But the greatest proportion of this trading is represented by the BOND MARKET. The over-the-counter market for unlisted shares is quite small, but nonetheless provides an opportunity to develop a market for shares in small and relatively young companies. The Canadian Dealing Network provides daily quotation lists for bonds and unlisted shares.

overburden A mining-industry term that describes the sand, soil, and other surface material covering a mineral deposit.

overdraft   The movement of a person's bank account into a debit position because the cheques written on the account exceed the amount in the account. Canadian banks provide lines of credit for overdrafts in personal accounts.

overhead   *See* FIXED COSTS.

overheating   Economic policies that generate a level of demand in excess of the productive capacity of the economy, and lead to DEMAND-PULL INFLATION.

overproduction   The production of more goods or commodities than can be sold at a break-even or profitable price.

oversaving   A level of saving in the economy that is too high to be profitably reinvested to meet prevailing levels of consumer demand. It can be a sign of an excessively uneven distribution of income, in which low-income families have too little to spend and high-income families far too much. Oversaving is another way of saying that consumer spending is too low, relative to the size of the economy.

oversubscription   The situation that occurs when the total demand for a NEW ISSUE of shares or bonds exceeds the size of the issue. When this happens, all the would-be purchasers are allocated a correspondingly smaller number than they wanted to purchase.

overtime   The number of hours worked in excess of the number set out in a collective agreement or in federal or provincial labour laws. Employees must be paid a higher rate of pay, usually one and a half times the normal hourly rate, for the overtime hours they work. Some contracts call for the payment of two or even three times the normal hourly rate if employees work

on holidays, on Sundays, or over seven consecutive days. If an employer requires a great deal of overtime work, the union will push for an increase in the number of employees. But employers may prefer to build up a high overtime bill, rather than to increase their workforce, since a larger workforce means additional payments for fringe benefits, and problems if business slackens and employees have to be laid off.

ownership   The legal right to possess a piece of property. Ownership is demonstrated in different ways — by the possession of a share certificate indicating ownership of a portion of a company, for example, or by a deed indicating ownership of land and buildings, by a bond indicating ownership of a claim on a company's assets, or by a receipted bill of sale, indicating that a possession has been paid for in full.

pace-setter In labour relations, a union with significant bargaining power, representing a large number of workers, whose wage settlement in a new collective agreement sets a pattern for other unions and employers.

Pacific Basin Economic Council (PBEC) A forum of business leaders established in 1967 by executives from Australia, Canada, Japan, New Zealand, and the United States to promote economic ties in the region. Since then its membership has expanded to include Fiji, South Korea, the Philippines, Taiwan, Hong Kong, Mexico, Peru, Chile, and Malaysia. An international secretariat is based in Hawaii. An international general meeting is held each year — in 1992 it took place in Vancouver — to discuss political, economic, commercial, and trade trends in the region. Canadian participation is organized through the PBEC Canadian Committee, based in Toronto. It promotes public policies to strengthen Canadian trade and economic interests in the Pacific Rim. It also sponsors the Pacific Rim Opportunities Conference to inform Canadian companies of trade and investment opportunities in the Asia-Pacific region.

Pacific Economic Co-operation Conference (PECC) An international non-government organization of business leaders, senior government officials, academics, and other research specialists from 20 Pacific Rim countries, including Canada. Formed in 1980, PECC was established to bring together government officials and politicians with business and academic groups to discuss ways to overcome obstacles to economic growth and development in the region. In 1990, a small secretariat was established in Singapore. Canada was one of the original 12 members. In 1992, the 20 members were: Australia, Brunei Darussalam, Canada, Chile, China, Hong Kong, Indonesia, Japan, South Korea, Malaysia, Mexico, New Zealand, Peru, the Philippines, Russia, Singapore, Chinese Taipei, Thailand, the United States, and the Pacific island nations or South Pacific Forum. PECC has high-level conferences about every 18 months and also working-level task forces and project groups in agriculture, fisheries, human resource development, minerals and energy, the Pacific economic outlook, Pacific island nations, science and technology, telecommunications, transportation and tourism, and trade policy. Since 1985, Canadian participation has been co-ordinated through the Canadian National Committee for Pacific Economic Co-operation. The chair and its 28 members are appointed by the Secretary of State for External Affairs, with the secretariat operated out of the ASIA PACIFIC FOUNDATION in Vancouver. The PACIFIC BASIC ECONOMIC COUNCIL and the PACIFIC TRADE AND DEVELOPMENT CONFERENCE are also non-voting members of the PECC board.

Pacific Trade and Development Conference (PAFTAD)   A forum of economic experts in the university and research communities organized in 1968 to explore the opportunities and challenges presented to the Pacific Rim by the EUROPEAN COMMUNITY and the emergence of Japan as growth leader in the region. PAFTAD organizes regular meetings to analyze research papers. It also publishes research papers and analysis. In 1984, a small secreteriat was established in Australia.

paid-up capital   The money that shareholders have paid for shares in a corporation and that is available for use by the corporation for the growth of the business. Paid-up capital and RETAINED EARNINGS represent the bulk of SHAREHOLDERS' EQUITY in a corporation.

pan   A method of searching for gold and other precious metals in a stream. Rock from the stream bed is washed in a pan to see if it contains gold or other precious metals.

Panarctic Oils Limited   A company formed by a group of Canadian mining companies, oil and gas companies, and the federal government in 1967 to explore for oil and gas in the Arctic region. The consortium was formed on the initiative of Canadians in the oil and gas industry who lacked the capital to sustain the kind of exploration effort needed in the far North. Almost all the other exploration in the northern regions was in the hands of the large, foreign-controlled oil companies. PETRO-CANADA held the federal interest in Panarctic, which amounts to about 45 percent of the voting shares. Panarctic is not a crown corporation; it is a private corporation in which the federal government, through a crown corporation, was the largest single shareholder. When Petro-Canada was privatized in 1991, it retained the federal interest in Panarctic Oils.

panic   A wave of fear in financial and foreign-exchange markets caused by the belief that an economic collapse is imminent. Such fears usually worsen the situation because investors become anxious to sell at any price, thereby causing an even sharper drop in the price of shares, currencies, real estate, and other investments.

paper   A generic term used to describe a wide variety of commercial paper, money-market instruments, and other financial securities.

paper gold   *See* SPECIAL DRAWING RIGHTS.

paper loss   A loss stemming from the decline in value of an asset, such as shares in a company, real estate, or work of art, whose value has not been realized because it has not yet been sold. An investor faced with a paper loss has to decide whether to cut his loss or hope that, by holding on to the asset, it will again go up in value. *See also* PAPER PROFIT.

paper money   Most narrowly defined, the paper currency issued by the CEN-

TRAL BANK of a country. It is usually money because the government says it is and guarantees its use as legal tender. In the past, paper money was backed by gold and other precious metals, but this is not the case today. Paper money can be more broadly defined to include other forms of paper that can be used as money, such as cheques, and certain debt securities, such as CANADA SAVINGS BONDS.

paper profit An increase in the value of an asset, such as shares in a company, real estate, or work of art, that has not been realized. The profit can only be spent when the asset is sold. *See also* PAPER LOSS.

par value **1.** The face value of a bond, preferred share, or other security, that appears on the certificate of ownership. The interest or dividend paid on a bond is a fixed percentage of the par or face value. However, the MARKET VALUE may be quite different, depending on prevailing interest rates and other factors. For example, the market value of a corporate bond with a par or face value of $10,000, and paying 11.5 percent interest, will have a market value of more than $10,000 if the prevailing level of interest rates declines to, say, 9 percent. In the case of a preferred share, the par value represents the dollar amount that a preferred shareholder would receive if the corporation were wound up or liquidated. Most common shares are issued at NO PAR VALUE since the par value bears no relationship to the market price; dividends are not paid as a percentage of the issue price but are tied to profitability of the firm and the number of common shares outstanding. **2.** The official rate of exchange of a currency, expressed in terms of another currency, a weight of gold, or a basket of foreign currencies.

paradox of thrift While saving is usually considered a virtue, John Maynard KEYNES argued that, if everyone tries to save more and consume less when the economy is operating below its full-employment potential, then the economy will decline and consumers will end up with less income and, therefore, less to save. In other words, excessive savings can lead to lower national income unless offset by increased spending by government or increased investment by business. While the economy depends on savings to divert resources from consumption to investment, the problem arises when savings exceed the level of investment planned by business. In such circumstances, the equilibrium level of the economy may decline, leading to a permanently higher level of unemployment and a lower level of national income and savings. In this way, savings can be a vice rather than a virtue.

paradox of value The explanation as to why a necessity of life, such as water, is cheap, while other items of limited usefulness in society, such as diamonds, are worth so much. It is a question that concerned Adam SMITH in his *Wealth of Nations* (1776). Neoclassical economists, such as Alfred MARSHALL, argued that the MARGINAL UTILITY or scarcity of a product is the explanation. Water is plentiful and the utility or satisfaction of an extra ounce of water is low, while the cost of getting an extra ounce is also low. Diamonds, though, are scarce, so the marginal utility or satisfaction from getting one more diamond is high, while the cost of getting an extra diamond is also high. Under MARGINAL-COST pricing, the price of getting that last extra unit of water or diamond determines the price of all water and all diamonds. In other words, the total utility of water versus that of diamonds is not the key consideration.

parent company The company that owns the controlling block of shares in another company, which allows it to control subsidiaries and affiliated companies. A multinational corporation, for example, usually consists of a parent company in one country and wholly owned or controlled subsidiaries in other countries. The policies of the subsidiary companies will be set by the parent company; it will also allocate to its subsidiaries a share of the cost of parent-company activities, such as research and development, corporate planning, and major managerial services.

Pareto optimum The state of equilibrium that exists when no one in society can be made better off without making someone else in society worse off. This concept, which helped to contribute to the idea of GENERAL EQUILIBRIUM, is named after an Italian engineer, Vilfredo Pareto (1848-1923). Pareto was dealing with economic efficiency rather than equity or fairness. The maximum economic welfare of society is reached when, to make one person better off, you have to take something from someone else, and hence make that person worse off.

Pareto's law The belief that nothing can be done to correct income inequality. Vilfredo Pareto (1848-1923), the Italian engineer, believed that there was an inevitable tendency for income to be distributed in the same way in all countries, in spite of special tax, social, or other policies to correct great disparities in income distribution.

pari passu A Latin term that can be defined as "in equal proportion" or "with equal progress." It is used when new shares are issued to assure buyers that the new shares are pari passu or as equal in their right to dividends as existing outstanding shares.

Paris Club A forum of creditor nations, including Canada, that meets with debtor nations to restructure government-to-government loans and export credits of developing countries and former members of the Communist bloc of Eastern Europe and the former Soviet Union. The Paris Club was established in 1965 but became much more active in the aftermath of the THIRD-WORLD DEBT CRISIS in the early 1980s. At the Toronto economic summit in 1988, the GROUP OF SEVEN industrial nations agreed on a menu of options for multi-year debt rescheduling by the poorest developing countries. The menu included the following options: partial debt cancellation, with one-third of the outstanding debt cancelled and the other two-thirds subject to a market rate of interest and a 14-year term with an eight-year grace period; or no cancellation of any debt but consolidation of all debt and rescheduling over a 25-year term with a market rate of interest and a 14-year grace period; or concessional interest rates but no reduction in debt, with the debt rescheduled on a 14-year term with an eight-year grace period, with interest rates reduced from market rates by 50 percent or 350 basis points, whichever is less. The Paris Club is managed by the French Treasury. To reschedule debt, the Paris Club and commercial banks usually require the debtor country to have an economic stabilization plan with the INTERNATIONAL MOMENTARY FUND.

parity 1. Equality. For example, Canadian workers in a particular industry may try to negotiate wage parity with workers in the same industry in the United States. Or workers in one Canadian city may seek wage parity with workers in the same industry or occupation in another Canadian city — for example, teachers in Windsor and Ottawa, or police officers in Calgary and Edmonton, or carpenters in Ontario and Quebec. **2.** A system of pricing. In energy, for example, there is a tendency to price different forms of energy in terms of a common energy equivalent — say, British thermal units. In agriculture, certain farm products may be priced to yield farms an income equal to some level of income in the non-farm economy. **3.** An official exchange rate or par value used in a system of fixed exchange rates as the central rate in pegging a currency. Currencies had to stay within 1 percent either side of parity under the fixed-exchange-rate system of the INTERNATIONAL MONETARY FUND that prevailed until 1971.

Parkinson's law   In fact, a series of laws drawn up by C. Northcote Parkinson (1909-1993), a British political scientist, that, while satirical in tone, expresses some basic problems of modern management and bureaucratic organization. His best-known law is "Work expands so as to fill the time available for its completion." Other of his "laws" include the following: expenditures rise to meet income; expansion means complexity, and complexity, delay; delay is the deadliest form of denial; and the time spent on any item of a committee's agenda will be in inverse proportion to the sum of money involved. See his book, *Parkinson's Law* (Boston, 1957).

partial-equilibrium analysis   A system of economic analysis — say, of a particular industry or sector of the economy — in which one or more variables are changed, with the other variables left unchanged. This form of analysis can be used to determine the effect of tax, price, and other changes on a particular industry, for example. However, the feedback effects are not studied; for example, in analyzing the impact of the change in the number of infants on the baby-food industry, the impact of the increased production, employment, and corporate taxes on the general economy and the feedback effect this

might have on the number of infants is not analyzed. GENERAL-EQUILIBRIUM analysis is used to determine all the effects of a change in one variable throughout the economy, including the resulting changes in other variables.

participating feature   The provision in some preferred shares that allows them to earn additional dividends, in addition to the fixed dividend provided for in the preferred share, and to the capital distributions above the par value of the preferred shares in the event the company is wound up or liquidated.

participation rate   The percentage of the population 15 years of age and older that is in the labour force; in other words, the percentage of Canadians 15 years and older who have jobs or who are looking for jobs. The participation rates for the entire population and for different groups according to age, sex, level of education, and province of residence are published monthly by Statistics Canada in its monthly LABOUR-FORCE SURVEY (publication 71-001). Changes in the participation rate also affect the unemployment rate. For example, if the participation rate of women in the labour force rises faster than the growth in jobs for women, then the unemployment rate will also increase. Likewise, during a recession, the unemployment rate may look less damaging than it really is because some unemployed workers have left the labour force or younger potential workers have decided to stay in school, reducing the participation rate and thereby the size of the labour force.

partnership   An agreement between two or more individuals to contribute capital or other resources to an unincorporated business, and to share in the profits, losses, and debts of the business. While this kind of arrangement is satisfactory for relatively small businesses, it becomes less so as the business, and its debts, grow, since the partners have unlimited liability for the debts of the business. It then makes more sense to establish a LIMITED-LIABILITY COMPANY. *See also* SOLE PROPRIETORSHIP, LIMITED PARTNERSHIP, CORPORATION.

patent   The legal right to ownership of an invention issued, in Canada, under the Patent Act. By granting this right to inventors, society hopes to encourage invention and innovation, and thus hopes to benefit from increased economic efficiency and growth. The benefit to the inventor is that, for a limited period, he or she can have the exclusive or monopoly right to production, charge a royalty for the use and application of the invention by others, or sell such rights to another person. For a corporate inventor, it means that the firm can produce a distinctive product, which other firms are forbidden to duplicate; without such protection, there would be less incentive for corporations to spend money on research and development. In Canada, patent protection is provided to the originator of the invention, although this can lead to conflicting claims. Unauthorized users can be sued. Disputes are adjudicated by the Patent Appeal Board and the FEDERAL COURT OF CANADA. In many other countries, patent rights are granted to the first to file. Exclusive protection under the Patent Act is provided for 20 years from the date the patent is granted.

Patent Co-operation Treaty   An agreement managed by the WORLD INTELLECTUAL PROPERTY ORGANIZATION that allows an applicant for patent protection in one signatory country to be assured of protection in all of the other signatory countries should the patent application be successful in the country in which it is filed. The agreement was signed in 1970, although Canada did not become a contracting party until 1990. The management of the system of international patents is run out of Geneva, in Switzerland. There are now about 50 signatories, including the United States, Japan, and the European Community.

Patent Office   A division of the Bureau of Intellectual Property within the Department of CONSUMER AND CORPORATE AFFAIRS that administers the Patent Act and publishes a weekly abstract of patents granted.

Patented Medicine Prices Review Board   A board established under amendments to the Patent Act in 1987 to monitor and report on, and to regulate, prices charged for patented medicines to ensure that they are not excessive, and to monitor investment in research and development by pharmaceutical companies. The board was established after the federal government extended the exclusive patent protection for patented medicines in return for commitments by the industry to constrain price increases and increase its investment in Canadian-based research and development from 5 percent of sales to 10 percent by 1996. Companies must file data on prices they charge for their products and on their research and development spending. The board can only review prices charged by the pharmaceutical companies to their customers, who usually consist of wholesalers, hospitals, and pharmacies. If the board finds the price of a patented medicine to be excessive, it can remove the patent protection on that product, another patented product, or both, so that a generic producer who manufactures a lower-cost version may manufacture a competing product or products based on the same patents, or the board can order a price rollback. The board, which is based in Ottawa, publishes an annual report to Parliament. Under further amendments to the Patent Act in 1993, which gave pharmaceutical companies further additional patent protection, the powers of the board were strengthened to ensure that the prices of all patented medicines, including the introductory prices of new products, remained reasonable for consumers. The amendments gave the board the power to order price reductions or impose penalties to compensate for past excessive prices and allowed the board to better control introductory prices for new patented medicines. The amendments provided for fines and imprisonment for failure to comply with the board's orders, and gave the board's orders the same force and effect as an order of the FEDERAL COURT OF CANADA. The board tracks patented medicine prices in relation to the CONSUMER PRICE INDEX.

paternalism A situation in which the state or an employer assumes a wide range of responsibilities on behalf of citizens or employees. For example, a highly developed welfare state that takes complete care of health, education, social welfare, pensions, employment, and housing runs the risk of eliminating individual choice and responsibility. Likewise, a corporation that provides a wide range of benefits for employees runs the risk of imposing its choices on individuals.

pawnbroker A provincially licensed moneylender who makes loans on valuable goods left as security. The pawnbroker issues a ticket to the borrower and cannot sell the goods until a certain period of time has elapsed to allow the borrower to repay the loan with interest.

pay-back period A calculation that is made to determine how long it will take a new investment in new machinery or a new project to generate the cash flow to pay back the original investment cost. This is not the same thing as determining the full return

that can be made from the investment over its productive life. However, since investors normally are anxious to recover their original costs as quickly as possible, it is one of several important calculations made in judging any investment proposal.

pay equity Pay equity can consist either of equal pay for equal work or equal pay for work of equal value.

pay-out ratio The proportion of a company's after-tax profits paid out to shareholders in the form of DIVIDENDs.

payment in kind A BARTER-type arrangement in which one person pays for goods and services in other goods and services. While it is illegal to pay wages this way, private tradesmen and others doing extra work outside their normal jobs sometimes arrange for payment in kind to avoid income taxes.

payola Money or gifts paid to people for their help in promoting company products surreptitiously. A record company may make such payments to a radio-station disc jockey, for example, if the disc jockey promotes a certain record or recording store, or a food company may make such payments to a supermarket manager if the manager gives extra shelf space or shows other preference for a particular product.

payroll tax A tax paid by an employer based on total payroll costs and numbers of employees. Examples in Canada include employer contributions for UNEMPLOYMENT INSURANCE, WORKER'S COMPENSATION, and the CANADA PENSION PLAN.

Pearson Commission The Commission on International Development, appointed in 1968 by Robert McNamara, president of the WORLD BANK. It was headed by Lester Pearson, former prime minister of Canada, and included seven other experts from around the world. The commission was asked to study the effectiveness of international programs of development assistance and to recommend improved programs. In 1969, it published its report, *Partners in Development*. It recommended a development strategy for the 1970s, including adoption by the developed countries of an aid commitment equal to 0.7 percent of gross national product, with at least 10 to 20 percent of such aid being channelled through multilateral institutions. It said that aid should not be considered a substitute for foreign direct investment and advocated expanded international trade as means of development.

peg   In a system of fixed exchange rates, the intervention rate or exchange rate at which the BANK OF CANADA would intervene in foreign-exchange markets to keep the Canadian dollar from rising or falling. Normally, there are two pegs: an official selling price and an official buying price. The gap between the two can be a wide band or a narrow band, depending on the degree of currency fluctuation permitted in the system.

penalty clause   A contract clause that makes one of the parties to a contract pay a certain sum of money to the other if the contract obligations are not fulfilled.

penny stock   A stock that sells for less than $1 and that is usually considered a speculative investment. However, some corporate issues of small companies can become high-quality securities.

pension   Payments to persons who are no longer of working age; pensions may also be paid to workers before the age of 65 to encourage early retirement or to workers who are no longer able to work because of some type of disability. There are five basic sources of pension

income for Canadians: 1. The federal OLD AGE SECURITY PENSION, which, since 1951, has been payable to everyone who meets the age and residency requirements. 2. The federal GUARANTEED-INCOME SUPPLEMENT, which, since 1967, is payable to pensioners who have little or no income other than the old-age security pension. 3. The CANADA PENSION PLAN (or QUEBEC PENSION PLAN), which, since 1967, has paid pensions to members of the workforce based on their wages or salaries up to an annual maximum amount, and which requires workers and their employers to pay premiums during their working lives; there are also some benefits for spouses and families. 4. Private pension plans, based on contributions from employers and employees. 5. Annuity income from REGISTERED RETIREMENT SAVINGS PLANS.

In addition, there are special pension benefits, such as pensions for veterans and their widows, and disability pensions paid through provincial workmen's compensation boards. The provincial governments also provide tax credits and supplementary pension income for senior citizens with low retirement incomes. Some pensions also provide free drugs and medical and hospital care, and subsidized housing. Statistics Canada publishes an annual survey, *Pension Plan Coverage in Canada* (publication 71-217).

pension fund   The contributions of employers and employees to a managed fund, which is invested in bonds, mortgages, shares, and other assets, to earn income that will pay for future pension benefits. Pension funds are usually managed by trust companies or other specialized investment experts who, with their vast pool of dollars, represent one of the most important sources of investment capital in the economy; they are leading INSTITUTIONAL INVESTORS. They are subject to federal and provincial regulation to protect beneficiaries and to ensure that the funds are invested mainly in Canada.

pentanes plus A hydrocarbon liquid very similar to oil and used as oil; it is obtained as a by-product in the processing of natural gas.

per capita The division of any output or consumption figure by the population for that year, to obtain output or consumption per individual. Since population is not static, changes in output or consumption by themselves do not give a true picture, on average, of how much growth in output or consumption is due to population change and how much is due to each person producing and consuming more. Per capita GROSS DOMESTIC PRODUCT (GDP) is used as a rough measure of the relative standard of living of different countries; this kind of average may conceal great disparities in income within a country and does not take into account differences in purchasing power in different countries — for example, differences in health care, food, or housing costs. Moreover, an increase in per capita GDP may simply reflect the fact that a larger share of the population is in the labour force and working, rather than an increase in productivity. In some consumer products, such as sugar or milk, production may rise each year although per capita consumption remains static; the growth is due to population increases. Other products may show increased production, due both to population growth and to increasing per capita consumption; wine is a recent example.

per capita tax In a union, the ongoing payment by individual locals to their national or international headquarters or to a provincial or regional labour council or federation.

perfect competition A market in which the laws of supply and demand work to bring about the most efficient allocation of resources and the lowest possible prices and that is characterized by a large number of small firms competing to supply an identical product. Such an economy is supposed to work according to a number of ideal rules: 1. There are large numbers of both buyers and sellers, with no one a large enough buyer or seller to influence prices or supplies. 2. Products are homogeneous or identical, so that the buyer will always buy at the lowest price, thus forcing all suppliers to have the same low price. 3. Buyers and suppliers have perfect knowledge of prices and products throughout the economy. 4. Perfect freedom of entry to and exit from the market exists, so that new suppliers face no barriers if they want to enter the market, while old suppliers are free to leave. 5. It is assumed that there are no transportation or other such costs. 6. There are no profits other than the minimum return to the factors of production necessary to ensure that they remain in the market.

Perfect competition is a concept used by economists in constructing theoretical models of economic systems. It does not exist in the real world, although FREE-MARKET economists see it as the ideal toward which public policy should aim. *See also* CLASSICAL ECONOMICS, NEOCLASSICAL ECONOMICS, IMPERFECT COMPETITION, MONOPOLY, OLIGOPOLY, INVISIBLE HAND.

performance bond A bond posted by a major contractor or supplier of capital equipment to make sure that a project is completed. If deadlines or performance commitments are not met, the bond becomes the property of the customer.

permanent-income theory The theory developed by Milton FRIEDMAN that consumers will maintain a fairly constant pattern of consumption despite changes in their income. It is the amount of income that is consumed each year by a household without any reduction in its actual wealth. This implies that a household will take a long-term view of its consumption, recognizing the need to save in years of high income, or when there's an unusual gain in income, so that it can dip into savings in years when there is less income. This means that the MARGINAL PROPENSITY TO CONSUME will equal the AVERAGE PROPENSITY TO CONSUME.

permit   A certificate that is issued giving the holder permission to do something, such as to export uranium, cut timber, fish or hunt, construct or alter a building, or import live animals. Under a permit granted an oil or natural-gas company by the federal or a provincial government to search for oil and gas, the company must complete a certain dollar-value of work within a specified period of time. In return, it usually has the right to choose up to half the land and to obtain a LEASE without having to bid in an auction. The other half of the land is leased to the highest bidder, or to the same company for payment of an additional fee.

perpetual bond   A bond that has no maturity date on which the borrower is required to repay the principal. In 1936, the government of Canada sold $55 million of a 3 percent perpetual bond. In September, 1966, it issued new certificates, with another 30 years of annual interest coupons. In 1975, it announced that the bonds would mature on September 15, 1996, when the last of the existing interest coupons had been cashed in.

person-year   The period of time worked by a person in one year if he or she was employed full time for an entire year, or the equivalent — for example, three persons each working for four months. Federal government departments have their staffing budgets set out in terms of person-years needed to carry out the departmental responsibilities, leaving the individual departments to decide the details of staffing. The term used to be man-year.

personal income   The income received by individuals from all possible sources. It includes not only wages, salaries, and pensions, but also rents, dividends, interest, welfare payments, profits of personal businesses, and realized capital gains.

personal income tax   A tax levied as a percentage of personal income. It is both a federal and a provincial tax and the tax rate is graduated, rising with the level of a taxpayer's personal taxable income, according to the ability-to-pay principle.

Under the Income Tax Act, income means income from almost all sources, except certain social-assistance payments, gifts up to a certain amount, capital gains from the sale of personal residences, the first $100,000 of capital gains and half the capital gains from investments, and certain other exemptions, including winnings from provincial lotteries. The tax base includes salary and wages, unemployment insurance, interest and dividends, taxable capital gains, alimony payments, pensions, fees, commissions, and scholarships. In calculating taxable income, deductions permitted under the Income Tax Act, such as pension-plan contributions, charitable donations, basic exemptions, and union dues, are subtracted from total or gross income. The resulting figure is taxable income, or the federal tax base for taxpayers in all provinces except Quebec. The federal tax rate is then applied, starting at about 6 percent of taxable income at the bottom of the tax table, and rising to a top rate of 43 percent. In addition, there is a provincial tax rate, ranging in 1978 from 38.5 percent of the federal tax base for Alberta taxpayers, to 58 percent for Newfoundland taxpayers. The combined federal-provincial top rate thus ranges from 60 to 70 percent, depending on the province in which the taxpayer lives.

The federal government's tax-collecting activities are covered under the Fiscal Arrangements Act of 1977. Quebec has its own personal income-tax system. Personal income taxes accounted for about 48 percent of federal budgetary revenues in fiscal 1992-93, compared with 8 percent in the 1939-40 period. In 1972, the income-tax system was overhauled, with the tax base being significantly broadened to include one-half of CAPITAL GAINS, unemployment-insurance benefits, and scholarships. While the personal income tax is a major source of government revenue, it is also an important tool for INCOME REDISTRIBUTION, since it is based on ability to pay, and also for DEMAND MANAGEMENT, since tax increases and tax reductions can significantly affect the level of demand or purchasing power in the economy. The federal personal income tax was introduced in 1917. *See also* CORPORATE INCOME TAX, ROYAL COMMISSION ON TAXATION, TAX EXPENDITURES.

personal income theory of consumption The theory developed by Milton FRIEDMAN that an individual's consumption each year depends on the average level of income in the current and future years and not just on the current year's income. Friedman contended that households preferred a stable pattern of consumption to one that varied from year to year.

personal property Property, aside from REAL ESTATE, owned by an individual. It can include furniture, automobiles, jewellery, clothing, shares and bonds, and works of art.

personnel management The field of management that deals with the hiring, training, promotion, and motivation of employees. Its responsibilities also include the management of fringe benefits, the development of hiring and firing policies, and special needs, such as employee counselling to deal with problems such as alcoholism.

Peter principle The principle attributed to Laurence J. Peter and Raymond Hull, in their book, *The Peter Principle* (New York, 1969), that states that employees tend to rise to their level of incompetence. For example, companies may make their top salesperson the sales manager, even though that person's real skills may be in sales rather than in management, while a poor salesperson who could be a good sales manager probably will never get a chance at the management job.

Petro-Canada A federal crown corporation created in 1975 to help the government to formulate its national energy policies, to increase Canadian energy supplies, to undertake energy research and development and exploration programs that are in the national interest, to give the government a view of oil-industry operating practices and finances, and to increase the Canadian presence in the petroleum industry, which was heavily foreign controlled. Petro-Canada was privatized in 1991 when the company sold a treasury issue of 19.5 percent of its common shares to the public. After it began operating in 1976, Petro-Canada acquired control of two foreign-owned oil companies in Canada, Atlantic Richfield Canada Limited in 1976 and Pacific Petroleums Limited in 1978, as well as a major share of Western Transmission Company. It was handed the government's 45 percent interest in

PANARCTIC OILS LIMITED and 17 percent interest in Syncrude Canada Limited, a major oil-sands plant. In 1981, it acquired the assets of Petrofina Canada Inc. and in 1985, it purchased the downstream operations of Gulf Canada Limited in western Canada, Ontario, the Northwest Territories and the Yukon. In 1987-88, the company increased its stake in West Coast Energy Inc. (formerly WestCoast Transmission), a stake it sold in 1992. Petro-Canada joined in exploration efforts with private oil companies in the Canadian North and Atlantic offshore region, holding 25 percent of the Hibernia oil project off Newfoundland. It also launched a research and development program to devise new energy sources. And in the 1970s, it became an important oil-importing agency for Canadians, negotiating oil-supply arrangements with Mexico and Venezuela. Its head office is in Calgary.

In September, 1979, the federal government appointed a task force to recommend ways in which major assets of Petro-Canada could be returned to the private sector, while the federal government retained the capacity to arrange state-to-state oil sales, to support high-risk exploration in the frontier regions, and to promote energy research and development. In October, 1979, the task force proposed that all of the profitable assets of Petro-Canada be vested in one company, with the federal government taking over its debt, and that the shares be distributed without charge to Canadians. No Canadian would be allowed to own more than 1 percent of the shares and no institutional investor more than 3 percent. A separate company, to be a non-operating company, would be set up as a government-owned entity to make state-to-state deals, to finance frontier development, and to promote research. The report was not adopted. But when it was privatized in 1991, Petro-Canada had become the largest Canadian-controlled oil and gas company and in 1992, had operating revenues of about $4.7 billion. It is Canada's largest oil refiner and has the largest network of gasoline stations.

petrodollars The surplus foreign-currency funds of members of the ORGANIZATION OF PETROLEUM EXPORTING COUNTRIES (OPEC). During the oil boom of the 1970s, some OPEC members, such as Saudi Arabia, Kuwait, and the Persian Gulf emirates, with tiny populations, could not spend a good part of the money they earned from oil. These surplus funds, to a large extent U.S. dollars, were recycled into EUROCURRENCY markets, U.S. government treasury bills, or real-estate and other corporate investments. This recycling helped to offset the huge trade deficits of many industrial nations, caused by sharp increases in the price of oil. Some economists worried about the huge accumulation of these petrodollars, and feared they could become a threat to the international banking system. To a large extent, petrodollars were placed as short-term funds in Eurocurrency markets, with Western banks in turn relending a large volume of these funds in long-term credits to LESS-DEVELOPED COUNTRIES. In this way, the risk of recycling was shifted from the OPEC countries to the Western banks and governments, which ultimately have to assure the soundness of the financial system. Others feared that the oil-rich countries might use their petrodollars to buy large blocks of prime agricultural and resort land in Western nations, or to buy control of major corporations. With the decline of oil prices in the 1980s, concern over petrodollars lessened.

Petroleum Administration Act An act passed by Parliament in June, 1975, permitting the federal government to regulate the price of oil and natural gas and to allocate supplies. It allowed the federal government to have a single price for oil and natural gas within Canada and to set a higher price for export markets. The act was divided into five parts. Part I allowed the NATIONAL ENERGY BOARD to levy an oil-export tax on exporters. Part II allowed the federal government to negotiate a domestic oil price with the producer provinces and, if the negotiations failed, to set the domestic oil price itself. Part III allowed the federal government to negotiate natural-gas prices with the producer provinces, and, should the negotiations fail, to set natural-gas prices itself. Part IV allowed the federal government to operate a cost-compensation program to stabilize the cost of foreign oil used in Eastern Canada and thus to help maintain the single Canadian price below the international price. Part V gave the Minister of ENERGY, MINES AND RESOURCES the power to obtain information from oil and natural-gas producers, to seize documents, and to inspect their premises. It also required the Energy minister to make an annual report on the administration of the act.

Parts of the legislation, namely parts I and III, were made retroactive to January 1, 1974. The domestic price for oil and natural gas, according to the act, should balance the interests of consumers and producers, should protect consumers against price instability, and should encourage the discovery and development of oil and natural gas to achieve self-sufficiency in Canada. In 1978, the act was amended to allow tar-sands oil and heavy oil to be sold in Canada at the international price, with the price being subsidized by a levy imposed on Canadian refineries.

Petroleum Monitoring Agency A federal agency established in 1980 to report semi-annually on the foreign and Canadian ownership and control of the oil and gas industry and on the financial performance and investment spending of both sectors. Its statistics covered upstream (exploration and development) and downstream (refining and distribution) of companies with more than $10 million in sales or assets. Reports detailed revenues according to source, exploration spending, research and development, and some balance sheet information. In 1992, the PMA was wound up as an independent agency, and its responsibilities were transferred to the Petroleum Monitoring and Information Services in the Department of ENERGY, MINES, AND RESOURCES.

petty cash Money kept available in a business or other organization to pay small expenses.

philanthropy The donation by individuals of large amounts of their wealth for charitable, educational, social, or cultural causes.

Phillips curve A graphic representation showing the trade-off between full employment and low inflation. The relationship, the work of British economist A.W. Phillips, showed that, as unemployment declined, the rate of inflation, represented by the rate of increase in money wages, rose. Similarly, as the rate of unemployment rose, the rate of inflation, represented by the rate of increase in money wages, declined. Since 1958, when Phillips first published his work on the unemployment-inflation trade-off, economic policy makers have had less and less success in achieving their goal of a better curve with less inflation and lower unemployment. Instead, unemployment has become more firmly entrenched at higher levels, and some economists question the relevance of the Phillips curve as a tool of economic analysis in the modern mixed economy.

In its 16th annual review in 1979, the ECONOMIC COUNCIL OF CANADA argued that policy makers could no longer treat unemployment and inflation in a framework that assumes a direct trade-off between the two within a steadily growing economy. Inflation, for example, is not caused only by excess demand; other factors include changes in world oil and other commodity prices, exchange-rate fluctuations, excessive wage demands, declining productivity growth, and changes in relative prices. Similarly, insufficient demand is not the only cause of unemployment; other factors include a mismatch of jobs and skills, poor labour-market information and changes in work attitudes, and financial benefits for those who choose not to work.

physical quality-of-life index (PQLI)
An indicator of national economic progress, used as a supplement to per capita GROSS DOMESTIC PRODUCT (GDP) to compare the standard of living of different countries. It takes three physical factors — life expectancy, infant mortality, and the rate of literacy — and averages them together. The measure was devised in 1977 by the Overseas Development Council, a U.S. non-profit agency interested in the problems of the less-developed countries. It shows that a nation may have a low per capita GDP and a high physical quality-of-life index, such as in Sri Lanka. Conversely, a country such as Mexico can have a higher per capita GDP and a lower physical quality-of-life index. A developed country is one that has a PQLI of 90 or more, as well as a per capita income of more than US$14,000. Canada had a PQLI of 99 in 1990, compared with 98 for the United States, 100 for Sweden, Switzerland, Norway, and the Netherlands, and 101 for Japan and Iceland. The 50 low-income countries with an average per capita GDP of US$319 had a 1990 PQLI of 68; the 41 lower middle-income countries with an average per capita GDP of US$941 had a PQLI of 76; the 37 upper middle-income countries with an average per capita GDP of US$2,299 had a PQLI of 83; and the 41 high-income countries with an average per capita GDP of US$14,421 had a PQLI of 97.

Physiocrats   An 18th century school of French economists, led by François Quesnay (1694-1774), that emphasized land as the sole source of wealth or surplus value and, hence, the only factor of production that should be taxed. The physiocrats believed in LAISSEZ-FAIRE economics and in FREE TRADE. Quesnay devised the *tableau économique*, which showed the interdependence of the many different participants in economic life; in some respects, the tableau was an early predecessor to modern INPUT-OUTPUT tables. The Physiocrats were among the first thinkers to attempt to turn economics into a specialized field of study and a science.

picket line   A line of striking union members who stand at the entrances to their place of work; the purpose is to inform the public that a strike is taking place. Picketing workers hope to persuade customers not to do business with the firm, suppliers not to deal with the firm, would-be workers not to enter the place of business, and other unions in the same firm or other firms to support the strike by not crossing the picket line. Picketing is a legal activity so long as it is peaceful and does not interfere with the rights of third parties to use the streets and sidewalks, or the right of the firm to try to continue operating the business. A worker on a picket line is a picket.

piecework   A method of paying wages that depends in part on the number of items produced by each individual worker. While no employer can pay less than the minimum wage, an employer can tie wages above the minimum wage or other base rate to actual production.

pig iron   The cast iron that is produced from a blast furnace, but has yet to be converted into basic steel products, such as steel rods and beams.

Pigou effect   A theoretical concept named after British economist Arthur C. Pigou (1877-1959), who wanted to show that an economy could automatically return to full employment, something that John Maynard KEYNES denied. Pigou argued that unemployment could be cured by letting wage rates fall, which would in turn lead to a drop in prices. This decline in prices would increase the real value of money, thus encouraging people with savings to spend and invest. This increased economic activity, resulting from the increased purchasing power of liquid money, would return the economy to full-employment conditions. Pigou was attempting to show that an economy with flexible wages and prices could return to full employment without government intervention. However, he did not advocate this, preferring instead to increase the money supply and achieve the same results at much less cost to people. Pigou is also well known for his work in WELFARE ECONOMICS, in particular for showing that governments could make comparisons of the effects of different social policies on different income groups in society, and thus determine the utility of those policies. Pigou showed that there could be a case for government intervention, based on the gap between marginal private net product and marginal social net product.

pilot plant   A test plant used to see whether a new production process works, and to improve the production process before a major investment is made in a full-scale production plant. The construction of pilot plants allowed, for example, the oil and engineering companies planning extraction plants for the Alberta tar sands to improve their production processes before huge investments in fully operating plants were made.

pitchblende   A valuable uranium ore that contains a fairly high percentage of uranium oxide and is highly radioactive.

placing   The issuing of new shares or bonds through an investment dealer or bank. In a public issue or placement, the new shares or bonds will be made available to the public. In a PRIVATE PLACEMENT they will be made available only to selected large INSTITUTIONAL INVESTORS. In either case, the planned issue must be approved by a provincial SECURITIES COMMISSION.

placing power   The capacity of an investment dealer or other financial institution to place a new issue of securities with investors. This is an important competitive strength of a financial institution.

planned economy   An economic system in which all the basic decisions on production, prices, investment, employment, and distribution are made by the government, rather than through the price mechanism or market forces. This means the allocation of resources is the function of the state rather than of the mixture of market forces, supply and demand, consumer tastes, profitability, corporate strategies, and government policies and regulations that affect and determine decisions in a MIXED ECONOMY such as Canada's. While it is possible for a planned economy to provide for a fairer distribution of income among its citizens, a mixed economy should yield a higher average standard of living, since it allows more scope for innovation and risk. Communist countries and some less-developed countries have operated planned economies, where central government agencies set economic goals, allocate resources, and set prices. But today, virtually no countries operate centrally planned economies, with both China and the former Soviet Union turning to a mixed economy, in which the market plays a central role. Economic planning is something quite different, since it does not necessarily mean economic decision making by government alone, using its arbitrary powers to allocate resources and decide what should be produced. Economic planning usually means an effort by government, along with other groups in the economy, such as business and labour, to foresee economic problems, to agree on priorities, and to develop policies to ensure full employment and low inflation.

planned obsolescence   Changes, such as design changes, in a product, introduced to persuade consumers to buy a new product — a car or a dress, for example — before the old one has worn out.

planning   l. The activity of government in defining and reaching economic goals. There are many forms of planning, ranging from the rigid and centralized PLANNED ECONOMY of totalitarian states such as the former Soviet Union and the earlier Communist regime in post-1949 China, to the consensus-building role played by the governments of social democracies, such as Sweden, where the government, with business and labour, tries to reach an agreement on key policies such as labour-market and social policies. In a mixed economy, such as that of Canada, there is little overall planning, although the medium-term fiscal plan in annual federal budgets provides some overall parameters for government spending, taxation, borrowing, economic growth, and inflation. The United States has attempted to introduce technology planning to boost

competitiveness through its critical-technologies strategy. Japan engages in another form of consensual planning, producing 10-year "visions" of the direction and goals of Japan, which provide the framework within which countless private- and public-sector decisions are made. Other types of planning have included the INDICATIVE PLANNING of France, where the government at one time set various industrial goals with industry free to co-operate, and receiving various forms of government assistance if it did, and the INDUSTRIAL-STRATEGY planning tried in Canada through the Board of Economic Development in the late 1970s in which various industries and their unions produced joint sector reports containing recommendations on how to improve their efficiency and output. **2.** A normal function of major corporations, which devise five-year plans setting out product, investment, and market plans, and relate these to future financial needs, competition, and profitability. **3.** The determination, by municipalities, of how land is to be used — for example, commercial versus residential construction, the DENSITY of land use, or the location of major roads and expressways.

Planning-Programming-Budgeting System (PPBS)   A system of planning, organizing, and monitoring government spending. It was designed to help government make choices — a new highway instead of a new airport, for example — in situations where profitability is not the determining factor. Introduced in the U.S. government in 1965, it was subsequently adopted by the Canadian government. Spending was to be set out in terms of programs and objectives, and was supposed to allow policy makers to compare alternative programs in terms of costs and benefits. Government officials preparing spending plans were supposed to devise criteria for weighing the benefits generated by their programs; in preparing a spending submission, officials had to set goals, define objectives, and develop planned programs to achieve those objectives. Although it was hoped that PPBS, because it provided a clearer picture of the benefits of different programs, would allow government officials to make better choices among competing programs, the approach has been largely abandoned because it resulted in a loss of control over operating costs and staffing. Federal planners now put much more emphasis on cost control through accounting measures. *See also* ZERO-BASE BUDGETING SYSTEM.

plant   Major capital assets, including mines, smelters, refineries, factories, commercial buildings, power stations, and government buildings.

plant-gate price   The price for natural gas charged by a natural-gas-producing company to a pipeline company. It is the price for gas that has been gathered and processed from surrounding producing wells, so that it is ready for transmission. *See also* CITY-GATE PRICE.

Plaza Accord   An agreement reached in October, 1985, by the GROUP OF FIVE (G-5) finance ministers of the United States, Japan, Germany, France, and Britain at New York City's Plaza Hotel to lower the value of the U.S. dollar through the co-ordinated action of their central banks. Canada and Italy, angry at being excluded, subsequently sought the expansion of the Group of Five (G-5) finance ministers to the Group of Seven (G-7) finance ministers and the G-5 effectively became the G-7 in 1986. *See also* LOUVRE ACCORD.

pluralateralism   Agreements between several states on trade and investment policies. The CANADA-U.S. FREE TRADE AGREEMENT is a bilateral agreement, the NORTH AMERICA FREE TRADE AGREEMENT a trilateral agreement, and the GENERAL AGREEMENT ON TARIFFS AND TRADE a multilateral agreement; a free trade agreement among, say, half a dozen countries would be a pluralateral agreement.

plutocracy   A government or society that is dominated by a relatively small group of wealthy people, and whose policies are designed primarily to protect the interests of the wealthy. It can be argued that the economies of New Brunswick and Newfoundland have found themselves in this situation in the past.

point   A way of measuring the change in the price of a share, bond, or currency. A point is a one-dollar change in the price of a share, a 1 percent change in the par value of a bond, and one one-hundredth of a cent change in the value of the dollar. This means that a share that goes up one dollar has risen a point; a $1,000 bond that goes up $10 has risen a point; and a Canadian dollar that goes from 86.125 to 86.126 U.S. cents has risen a point.

poison pill   A defence tactic adopted by corporations to ward off hostile takeovers by making the takeover more expensive. The poison-pill defence makes a takeover much more expensive — for example, by permitting existing shareholders to acquire additional shares at below market prices and thereby increasing the cost of the acquisition by putting more shares in circulation; by the targeted company itself taking over another company, thus making itself a less attractive or more expensive takeover target; by issuing new preferred shares that give shareholders the right of redemption at a premium price in the event of a takeover; or by amending its by-laws so that an investor attempting to acquire the company would have to acquire all or nearly all of its shares and not just the bare minimum necessary to exercise effective control.

policy 1. An insurance contract in which an insurance company agrees to provide protection against a particular risk, in return for payment of a premium. 2. In a government or corporation, a statement of rules to be followed in dealing with a particular situation or a set of desired objectives, along with an outline of the methods to be used in reaching those objectives. The policy statement provides the goals and operating instructions for public servants, or corporate employees and middle managers.

policy co-ordination Attempts to help ensure that economic measures by the GROUP OF SEVEN (G-7) industrial countries are consistent with the goals of the G-7 to improve the overall level of performance of the global economy. For example, the G-7 countries have co-operated to achieve exchange-rate stability, to resist protectionist forces within their own countries, and to sustain a higher rate of economic growth. This requires co-ordination; for example, if it is agreed there is a need to rebalance exchange rates, then, if some rates are to come down, others, by definition, must increase. In 1993, for example, there was a consensus among G-7 countries to co-operate to strengthen world growth, to seek conclusion of the URUGUAY ROUND of world trade talks, and to assist Russia in its economic reforms. However, the record of policy co-ordination is mixed, with real co-ordination of policies only an occasional reality. The INTERNATIONAL MONETARY FUND monitors the performance of the G-7 economies, the policy mix pursued by each country, and the extent to which policies of individual countries may run counter to the wider needs of the global economy. *See also* PLAZA ACCORD, LOUVRE ACCORD.

policy mix The set of policies used by a government to achieve the economic performance it desires. For example, to control inflation, a government may use a combination of monetary, fiscal, and supply policies. Rarely is one policy alone sufficient to achieve an economic objective, although in the case of Canada's ZERO INFLATION campaign, monetary policy alone was used.

political economy The study of political and economic institutions and models together to achieve a better understanding of how the real world functions since economic systems function within political systems. For example, it is difficult to analyze the role of the corporation in the economy without also understanding the political system in which it functions, and its political influence; the same is true of the role of unions. It is necessary to link the study of political science and economics together to understand, for example, how income and wealth are distributed, how economic priorities are set, what political barriers exist to effective economic management, and what types of competition policies exist.

poll tax A tax that is levied at the same rate on all citizens.

pollution control Laws and regulations to reduce the contaminants that can pollute the air, water, or land. Contaminants such as gases in the air, toxic chemical wastes in the soil or water, or phosphates, mercury, and other metals in water, can endanger human health and the natural ecological balance if they are allowed to build up in large concentrations. Both the federal and provincial governments have laws and regulations to reduce or even eliminate the pollution resulting from industrial, human, and government activity. Pollution is an EXTERNALITY resulting from many forms of industrial production and is often cited as an example of MARKET FAILURE. The costs of pollution clean-up are counted as part of the GROSS DOMESTIC PRODUCT, but a growing number of economists believe that a new form of national economic accounting is needed to reflect the fact that pollution subtracts from national income rather than adding to it.

Ponzi scheme A scheme in which a borrower pays existing creditors by taking on additional borrowing to finance the debt servicing. At some point the scheme collapses because the borrower is unable to borrow enough to service the ever-expanding level of debt. A number of financial companies in Canada have suffered this fate, offering depositors or purchasers of investment certificates above-market interest rates and financing the instruments by selling more certificates or borrowing money. The scheme was named after a Boston promoter, Charles Ponzi, who defrauded many investors in the 1920s through a series of chain letters.

pooling of interest The use of treasury shares by a company to acquire another company. The balance sheet of the acquiring company is then revised to include the retained earnings and assets of the acquired company at book value.

population The total number of inhabitants in a particular city, region, province, country, continent, or the world, or a subgroup of the population — for example, the labour-force population, the school-age population, the urban population. Statistics Canada publishes population data for Canada in a variety of reports, including the census reports for 1991. The UNITED NATIONS POPULATION FUND and the WORLD BANK publish global population estimates, as well as estimates for individual countries. The key factors in determining population levels are birth and death rates and migration. *See also* CENSUS.

population forecast An attempt by demographers to calculate the future population of a community, province, country, or the world, using standard demographic tools such as fertility, mortality, and migration trends. These forecasts are vital to governments and corporations in planning investment and other policies. World population figures, such as those developed by the UNITED NATIONS POPULATION FUND, help policy makers and policy planners to assess future world food, employment, housing, and other needs, as well as calculating future environmental pressures. National forecasts, such as those prepared by the demographers of STATISTICS CANADA, help to determine future housing, education, hospital, and job needs, and, when these projections are broken into different age groups, can determine the outlook for particular industries, such as baby foods or industries serving senior citizens, as well as the outlook for consumer durables resulting from the rate of new household formation. Community projections are useful in determining future water and sewage needs, land use, numbers of classrooms, and homes for senior citizens. Statistics Canada publishes periodic population forecasts for Canada. Its most recent, *Population Projections for Canada, Provinces and Territories, 1989-2011*, was published in 1990 (publication 91-520). The United Nations Population Fund publishes an annual, *State of the World Population*, which projects up to 50 years into the future.

population pyramid A graphic representation of the age distribution of the population. It will not necessarily be in the exact shape of a pyramid; for example, there may be more 10- to 14-year-olds than there are younger age groups. However, there will be far fewer older people at the top of the pyramid, thus illustrating the fact that younger people outnumber older people. Developing countries tend to be fatter at the bottom of the pyramid, reflecting the fact that they have relatively young populations, while industrial countries tend to have a wider bulge as the pyramid moves upwards, reflecting the fact that their populations are getting older.

population trap The inability of a country to achieve an economic growth rate that is greater than the population growth rate. As a result, the country faces a decline in per capita GROSS DOMESTIC PRODUCT.

porcupine A defensive measure by a company to thwart a hostile takeover, consisting of a complicated agreement with its customers, suppliers, or creditors that has the effect of making it difficult for the acquiring company to integrate the acquired company into its own business structure.

port of entry A port, airport, or border-crossing point where customs and immigration officers are stationed to determine whether individuals or imported goods may enter the country.

portable pension The right to future pension benefits, represented by the accumulated pension contributions of an employee and an employer, which can be carried by an employee from one job to another. At present, the only pensions that are truly portable in Canada are the CANADA PENSION PLAN and the QUEBEC PENSION PLAN. Within some industries and within the public sector, there is some portability. However, in most private-industry jobs, an employee who moves from one compa-

ny to another loses his or her right to future pension benefits and his employer's matching pension contributions, unless the benefits have been VESTED, which under federal and most provincial pension laws means at least two years of continuous employment or two years of participation in the pension plan.

portfolio The mix of shares, bonds, and other investments of an individual or INSTITUTIONAL INVESTOR. The make-up of an investment portfolio will depend on the investment objectives of the investor. Some investors put more of an emphasis on income, while others emphasize capital gain. A portfolio emphasizing income growth will typically have more of its assets in bonds and other money-market instruments, while a portfolio that puts more emphasis on capital gains will be more heavily invested in shares of companies. The object of portfolio strategy is to balance risk and reward through diversification. This is one reason for the popularity of MUTUAL FUNDS.

portfolio investment The purchase of shares and bonds for the income they yield or the capital gains they may bring and not for the exercising of ownership or control. For example, foreign portfolio investment in Canada consists of the purchase of government and corporation bonds and the purchase of shares on Canadian stock exchanges. Foreign portfolio investment is reported in the *Quarterly Estimates of the Canadian Balance of International Payments* by Statistics Canada (publication 67-001). Additional information is contained in the monthly report, *Canada's International Transactions in Services* (publication 67-002). *See also* DIRECT INVESTMENT, FOREIGN DIRECT INVESTMENT.

portfolio theory The theory of how risk-averse investors, who want high returns but low risk, select from a variety of investment choices to achieve the optimal balance of risk and return. It is the return of the entire portfolio of diversified investments that is the key concern for an investor and not just some specific component of the portfolio. The return on the portfolio is the weighted average of all the various components of the portfolio. A typical portfolio will balance off high-risk investments against much less risky investments. In the effort to balance risk and reward, a portfolio will pursue a strategy of diversification.

Ports Canada The federal crown corporation responsible for the administration of federal ports in Canada. The Canada Ports Corporation was created in 1983 to replace the National Harbours Board, which had been established in 1936 to administer Canadian ports. Major ports of national significance can be converted to local port corporations, which give local communities autonomy in the management of their ports. Major ports such as those in St. John's, Saint John, Halifax, Quebec, Montreal, Vancouver, and Prince Rupert have local port corporation status. Ports Canada administers other ports across Canada. It is based in Ottawa.

positive economics The practical study of economic relationships that can be confirmed by actual experience and measurement; by quantifying relationships between economic variables — between a change in mortgage interest rates and the rate of housing construction, for example — positive economics can then show policy makers what will happen if a variable, such as mortgage interest rates, is changed. *See also* NORMATIVE ECONOMICS.

positive externalities The improvement in the productivity of workers and plant and equipment in other firms or industries as a result of an investment in a particular firm or industry. This happens when there is a spillover in knowledge or skills to other firms and workers from the firm and workers using the new technology.

possession utility The satisfaction of a consumer in the possession of particular goods or services, and the satisfaction of the seller in the possession of what he received in exchange for particular goods or services.

post-dated cheque A cheque that is dated for future rather than immediate payment.

post-industrial society A society characterized by the production of knowledge or information rather than goods. The term was first used by Daniel Bell, an American sociologist, in the mid-1960s. He saw Western societies shifting more and more into economic and social structures based on the development of new knowledge and the use of this knowledge to achieve technological innovation. The traditional goods-producing industries would shift to the developing countries, while the industrialized world, increasingly dominated by the scientific, technical, and professional classes, moved into a knowledge or information economy. The ECONOMIC COUNCIL OF CANADA, in its 1975 study, *Looking Outward*, studied the implications of the post-industrial society for Canadians.

post-Keynesian economics The school of economic thought that, while accepting the great contributions of John Maynard KEYNES, contends that Keynesian solutions are no longer enough to achieve satisfactory economic performance and to improve general economic welfare. While Keynes believed that the fundamental need in economic management was to maintain an aggregate level of demand in the economy in order to provide full employment and stable prices, he also had reasonable faith that the market system could take over, once the level of demand was sufficient. Post-Keynesian economists believe that the structure of the economy has changed so much in the past 30 years that, not only does the market system by itself no longer work, but it also cannot be made to work. The growth of large corporations and unions, the increasing role of government in meeting consumer needs such as health, education, and housing, and in regulating business activity, the use of non-market institutions such as FARM MARKETING BOARDS in agriculture, and the appearance of resource cartels, have all diminished the role of market forces. As a result, new policies are needed — INCOMES POLICY, for example — to control inflation. The purpose of post-Keynesian economics is to improve the functioning of the modern MIXED ECONOMY.

Potash Corporation of Saskatchewan A crown corporation created in 1976 by the Saskatchewan government to acquire a major interest in the province's potash industry by purchasing or expropriating existing, privately owned potash mines. In August, 1976, the crown corporation acquired its first potash mine for $128.5 million; it has taken over several other potash companies since then. The company was privatized in 1989 when this province sold most of its shares to the public. At the end of 1992, the Saskatchewan government still owned about 11 percent of the shares.

Potash Development Act Legislation passed by the Saskatchewan legislature in January, 1976, authorizing the provincial government to acquire the assets of producing potash mines.

The POTASH CORPORATION OF SASKATCHEWAN was incorporated to act on behalf of the provincial government and to operate mines taken over by the province. The legislation drew official protests from the U.S. government, and was also criticized by the federal government. The United States feared that Saskatchewan would use its ownership to seek monopoly prices for its potash.

potential gross domestic product The output of goods and services in the economy that would occur under conditions of full employment without generating COST-PUSH INFLATION. It is the highest level of real GROSS DOMESTIC PRODUCT growth that can be sustained without causing accelerating inflation, using the existing FACTORS OF PRODUCTION. It was defined by the ECONOMIC COUNCIL OF CANADA as "the output that can be produced with the available capital stock and available labour, given the productivity of both." The gap between potential output and the actual output of goods and services under conditions of high unemployment is known as the production gap. The gap equals the loss to society each year from the failure to achieve full employment. One of the goals of economic policy is to reduce or eliminate this gap.

potential output The highest level of real GROSS DOMESTIC PRODUCT (GDP) sustainable over the medium term with given factors of production without inducing cost-push inflation; it is the level of non-inflationary growth that can be sustained when all productive factors, including labour, are fully employed. Potential output, therefore, is dependent on the supply and quality of factors, such as capital, labour, research and development, and efficiency of markets. It can also be defined as the output that would occur if the labour force were fully employed and labour and capital were used at normal intensity. The trend rate is measured from peak to peak of the BUSINESS CYCLE. THE INTERNATIONAL MONETARY FUND has calculated that the potential growth rate for the Canadian GDP was 4.9 percent in the 1966-73 period, 3.6 percent in 1974-79, 3.5 percent in 1980-87, and 2.8 percent in 1988-92. Of the 2.8 percent potential GDP in the 1988-92 period, 0.9 percent came from capital, 0.8 percent from labour, 0.7 percent from TOTAL FACTOR PRODUCTIVITY, and 0.4 percent from the public sector. Because there is almost always some underemployment of factors, actual output is usually less than potential output though it can be greater at the peak of the BUSINESS CYCLE.

poverty   The absence of sufficient income to obtain either a subsistence standard of living or the basic necessities of life, as defined by the society in which a person lives. Absolute poverty refers to a standard of living so low that a person is not even able to obtain adequate nutrition or shelter. Relative poverty refers to a standard of living in which a person may be able to obtain sufficient nutrition and adequate shelter, but has no income left over for what have become necessities of life — a television set, for example, or a telephone, magazines, and other such items. While absolute poverty may be the inevitable consequence of a poor society, relative poverty may be due to the uneven distribution of income and wealth in an affluent society. According to Statistics Canada, families that spend 56.2 percent or more of their income on the basic necessities of food, shelter, and clothing have low incomes; they have little income left over for discretionary purposes. A person who lives in relative poverty in one country may be considered wealthy in another; for example, a person living in officially defined

poverty in Canada would be considered wealthy in India.

poverty line   The level of income below which a family or individual in Canada is considered to be living in poverty. Statistics Canada publishes periodic calculations of a low-income threshold that many social agencies use as the definition of the poverty line. It is based on a nation-wide survey of family spending habits and living costs and analyzed in an annual *Income Distributions by Size in Canada* (Statistics Canada publication 13-207). Any family that spends 56.2 percent or more of its income on the necessities of food, shelter, and clothing is considered to be at the low-income threshold or in straitened circumstances. According to Statistics Canada, the percentage of families of two or more people living below this level — the poverty line — declined from 18.4 percent in 1967 to 11.3 percent in 1974; in 1977 it rose to 11.9 percent. In the case of single individuals, the percentage living below the poverty line moved from 38.9 percent in 1967 to 37.4 percent in 1974 and 37.9 percent in 1977. In 1991, 16 percent of Canadians lived below this poverty line; this included 18.3 percent of Canadian children under 18, 61.9 percent of single-parent families, and 20 percent of Canadians over the age of 65. Statistics Canada also calculates the low-income deficiency — the gap between average family income and the low-income cut-off. In 1991, it was $6,072, and the cost of raising incomes to average family incomes would have been $13.4 billion. The Canadian Council on Social Development, a non-profit organization also calculates the poverty line as 50 percent of average family income for a family of three, adjusted for the needs of families of different sizes. A third way of calculating the poverty line is to estimate the amount of income necessary to purchase a basic minimum of goods and services that represent the necessities of life. But in calculating the poverty line, it is also important to take into account the value of free goods and services provided directly by the state, such as housing subsidies, dental care, and subsidized child-care.

poverty trap   The predicament those on social assistance find themselves in when their capacity to earn income from employment is less than what they can receive by remaining on social assistance, or when those on social assistance find that any additional money they earn from part-time work is offset by the loss of an equivalent amount of social assistance. This increases the dependency of individuals on social assistance and reduces their future employability by eroding their potential employment skills the longer they are out of the labour force. This is why social-policy analysts are concerned with finding ways to allow social-assistance recipients to keep some of the money gained from working while they are also receiving benefits; this is also an argument for a NEGATIVE INCOME TAX or GUARANTEED-ANNUAL INCOME.

power of attorney   A written authorization by one person designating another person to act on his behalf; the delegated power may be tightly defined for specific purposes and of strictly limited authority, or it may be of a more general nature, enabling, for example, the designated person to have wide decision-making powers. A PROXY is a form of power of attorney, since it authorizes someone else to vote on behalf of a shareholder.

Prairie Economic Conference   An annual conference of the three Prairie premiers held from 1965 to 1972. The meetings dealt with regional problems, including economic and transportation problems. In 1973, the conference was enlarged to include British Columbia and renamed the WESTERN PREMIERS' CONFERENCE.

Prairie Farm Rehabilitation Administration (PFRA)   An important federal program established in 1935, and still operating today, to help Prairie farmers restore their farmlands after the severe drought and soil drifting that hit Alberta, Saskatchewan, and Manitoba in the 1930s. Under the program, more than 100 community pastures have been established on some 2.5 million acres of marginal land. PFRA assistance has also been used to finance major irrigation and water-supply projects, to help farmers find on-farm sources of water supply, and to provide millions of trees that are planted as shelter belts, which prevent soil from being carried away by the wind in periods of dryness. Today, it operates as a branch of AGRICULTURE CANADA, assisting farmers and local communities with soil and water initiatives, irrigation, seedling distribution, and community pastures. It is based in Regina.

Prairie Grain Advance Payments Act   A federal law passed in 1957 that provides interest-free advance payments to Prairie grain producers for farm-stored wheat, oats, and barley, along with financial assistance for grain drying and harvesting.

Prairie provinces   Manitoba, Saskatchewan, and Alberta.

precautionary balances   The amount of money held by individuals or firms to meet uncertainties arising from timing differences between the receipt of income and the payment of bills or to meet unplanned costs such as repairs to an automobile or replacement of an appliance or, in a firm, the breakdown of equipment or the loss of a customer who leaves behind unpaid bills. This was one of the motives identified by

John Maynard KEYNES for holding money.

preclusive buying The purchase of raw materials, parts, or other goods and services, so that a competitor is not able to buy and use them.

predatory practice An activity designed by a firm or firms in an industry to eliminate a competitor; the activities may be costly in the short run but, if successful, may allow the remaining firms to raise their prices and earn higher profits. Examples include a sharp reduction in prices so that the competitor is unable to compete, or the takeover of a supplier who provides parts or components for the competitor. Such activities, when they reduce or are intended to reduce competition, are illegal under the COMPETITION ACT.

predatory pricing An attempt to eliminate or discourage competition by setting prices unreasonably low or by setting them much lower in one part of the country, where competition is feared, than in others. Once competitors have been eliminated or seriously weakened, prices will be raised again. Such attempts to restrict competition are illegal under the COMPETITION ACT.

preferential tariff A tariff that is lower for the imports from some countries than it is for the same imports from other countries. Under the GENERAL AGREEMENT ON TARIFFS AND TRADE, commodities from developing countries are imported into most Western industrial countries at a lower tariff rate than would be imposed on the same imports from other countries. This is the GENERALIZED SYSTEM OF PREFERENCES, which is to be reviewed in 1994. The BRITISH PREFERENTIAL TARIFF, which established lower tariffs on trade among Commonwealth countries, is another example. *See also*

OTTAWA AGREEMENTS. The EUROPEAN COMMUNITY has entered into preferential arrangements with some associate-member states, mainly less-developed countries.

preferred creditor A creditor who has first claim on the assets of a bankrupt firm or deceased individual; his claim must be paid in full, before any of the UNSECURED CREDITORS can receive even partial payment of their claims. Sometimes preferred or secured creditors will take all of the assets, leaving nothing for the unsecured creditors.

preferred share A share in a company that entitles the shareholder to a fixed rate of return on his or her investment. Like the owner of COMMON SHARES, an owner of a corporation's preferred shares is an owner of the company, and, in the event it is wound up, is entitled to a share of the assets equal to the PAR VALUE of the preferred shares, after creditors, including bondholders, have been paid. Preferred shareholders must be paid promised annual dividends before common shareholders can be paid a dividend. If a company cannot pay its preferred shareholders their dividends in a particular year, then common shareholders must be deprived of their dividends as well; in fact, common shareholders cannot receive a dividend until past-due dividends owed to preferred shareholders are paid in full. Preferred shareholders do not usually have a vote at company annual or other meetings, but they may be entitled to vote if their dividend payments are in arrears. Sometimes preferred shares are convertible into common shares. They may also be participating preferred shares; that is, their holders may share in the rising profits of a company along with common shareholders and may get an extra dividend. Some but not all preferred shares are callable; that is, they can be bought back by the issuing company if it so wishes. Preferred shares are traded, just as common shares are, on the stock market.

premiers' conference The annual gathering of provincial premiers that has been held every year since 1960; the idea was suggested by the Quebec government, and the first of these conferences was held in Quebec City. The agenda of these conferences covers many areas of economic concern, such as inflation, unemployment, capital investment, energy policy, pensions securities legislation, provincial purchasing policies, provincial incentives to industry, and tax policy. The premiers also deal with language policy, the constitution, and social and cultural policy. *See also* WESTERN PREMIERS' CONFERENCE, COUNCIL OF MARITIME PREMIERS.

premium **1.** The annual, semi-annual, or monthly payment to keep an insurance policy in force. **2.** The amount by which the market price of a bond or preferred share exceeds its issue price or face value.

premium pay The rate of pay that is paid for overtime, work under unusual conditions, or work on scheduled days off or public holidays. It is higher than the pay scale for straight time; for example, overtime pay is usually one and a half times the pay for straight time.

pre-payment Payment of the principal of a loan before the scheduled date.

present value The value, in today's dollars, of a future inflow of funds in a proposed investment project. It is a calculation used by corporations in assessing investment alternatives in which the future inflow and outflow of funds is discounted to reflect the TIME VALUE OF MONEY. *See also* NET PRESENT VALUE, DISCOUNTED CASH FLOW.

president The top operating officer of a corporation, and usually the chief executive officer as well, which would also make him or her the chief policy maker in the corporation. In some corporations, though, the chairman rather than the president is the chief executive officer.

price The cost of a good or service, expressed in terms of the amount of money that must be exchanged to obtain it. Price rations goods or services to those who want them the most, since an increase in demand will normally lead to an increase in price; a decline in supply will have the same effect. Price is sometimes described as what you must give up to get what you want. The way prices are set and the role they play in allocating resources are two of the most important issues in economics. In the world of PERFECT COMPETITION, prices are set by the laws of supply and demand. However, in a world of IMPERFECT COMPETITION, non-market factors influence prices, such as the ability of a small number of producers to extract higher prices. A price is also information. *See also* OLIGOPOLY, MONOPOLY, BARRIERS TO ENTRY.

price controls Measures by government to prevent or limit increases in the price of all goods or services or particular goods or services. General price controls may be imposed as part of an anti-inflation policy; for examples, *see* WARTIME PRICES AND TRADE BOARD, PRICES AND INCOMES COMMISSION, ANTI-INFLATION BOARD. When controls are applied to a particular good or service, the purpose is to prevent the price from rising excessively. For example, the government regulates local telephone rates to prevent monopoly services from exploiting the public; from the mid-1970s until the early 1980s, the prices of oil and natural gas were controlled so that price increases could be phased and windfall profits prevented. Sometimes prices are controlled — which can mean increased — to make sure that producers earn enough, for example, farm prices set by FARM MARKETING BOARDS. Price controls mean that the state takes over the role of the market in setting prices.

price cutting An attempt by a firm to increase its share of the market by cutting its prices; price cutting may also be necessary for a firm anxious to retain its market share if competitors are cutting their prices. Price cutting can be illegal if it is designed to prevent a would-be competitor from entering the business; *See also* PREDATORY PRICING.

price discrimination The practice by a supplier of charging different prices to different customers for goods of like quality and quantity, when the price differences cannot be justified by cost differences. For example, if a food company changes one chain of food stores a higher price than it changes another chain for a similar quantity of its product. The practice is illegal under the COMPETITION ACT if it injures an otherwise efficient competitor and the supplier is unable to show that the differences in price are based on differences in cost of supply.

price-earnings ratio The ratio obtained by dividing the current market price of a share by its annual earnings per share, a figure obtained from the EARNINGS STATEMENT in the annual or quarterly report of a publicly traded corporation. A share selling at $20 on a stock exchange and having earnings of $2 per share has a price-earnings ratio of 10:1; this indicates that an investor is willing to pay $10 for the ownership of $1 of that company's earnings. If the price-earnings ratio were 12:1, then investors would

be willing to pay $12 for ownership of $1 of the company's earnings. Price-earnings ratios differ for different industries; but a high price-earnings ratio usually indicates that investors are optimistic about a company's future profit growth and are thus willing to pay a high price for ownership of $1 of its earnings today and the right to higher earnings in the future. High future profits would indicate an ability to pay higher dividends in the future.

price effect The impact on the demand for a product as the result of a change in price. If the income of consumers is fixed and the price goes up, then consumers will be able to buy less of the product, or, if they maintain their level of demand for that product, less of something else. Higher prices can also lead to substitution of a cheaper alternative.

price elasticity The effect of a change in price on the demand for a product or on its supply. If a change in price results in a change in demand, then the product is price elastic. If a change in price has little or no effect on demand, then the product is price inelastic. Likewise, a change in price may encourage an increase or decline in supply.

price elasticity of demand The percentage change in the quantity demanded of a good or service divided by the percentage change in its price. When the percentage change in demand is greater than the change in price, the product or service is said to be price elastic; if the change is less, then it is price inelastic.

price-elasticity of supply The percentage change in the quantity supplied divided by the percentage change in its price. When the percentage change in the amount of a good or service supplied is greater than the price change, the supply is said to be price elastic; if the change is less, then the supply is price inelastic.

price fixing A conspiracy by competing firms to charge the same price, usually an excessively high price, to avoid the lower prices and lower profits that might result from price competition. Price fixing is a criminal offence in Canada under the COMPETITION ACT.

price index An INDEX that shows changes in the overall inflation rate or the rate of price change for a particular sector of the economy, with the base year equal to 100. The monthly CONSUMER PRICE INDEX measures the rate of change in a typical basket of consumer goods and services, including housing, food, and health care. It can be broken down into food and non-food items, goods and services, and other components (Statistics Canada publication 62-001). The quarterly GROSS-DOMESTIC-PRODUCT DEFLATOR measures the overall rate of inflation in the economy, including consumer prices, construction prices, import and export prices, and investment prices (Statistics Canada publication 13-001). Statistics Canada publishes a large number of price indexes, in addition to these, including monthly indexes for industrial selling prices (publication 62-011), raw materials price indexes (publication 62-011), construction price statistics (publication 62-007), and the farm input price index (publication 62-004).

price leader A major firm in an industry, usually the largest firm, that has the power to determine the timing and size of price increases for all of the largest firms in an OLIGOPOLISTIC industry. Formal agreement to set prices this way is illegal, but the same results can be obtained if one firm is tacitly recognized as the price leader and the other firms act accordingly. This type of price behaviour avoids price competition, which oligopolistic firms fear because it could reduce their prices and profits without gaining them an extra share of the market. While consumers would be better off, all of the firms would probably be worse off.

price level The general level of prices in the economy, expressed as an INDEX, or a percentage change from a previous year.

price maintenance An attempt by a supplier to pressure a retailer or wholesaler by agreement, threat, or promise to maintain high prices, or to discourage price reductions. It is a civil offence under the COMPETITION ACT. It is also an offence to discriminate against a customer because of his low pricing policy or to induce a supplier to engage in price maintenance. Suppliers or producers who make suggestions regarding resale prices must clearly state that their customers are under no obligation to accept the suggested price.

price maker A large firm that has a major share of a market; its price decisions influence the prices charged by its competitors.

price mechanism See PRICE SYSTEM.

price rigidity The relative insensitivity of the price of a commodity to changes in supply or demand; most frequently, it refers to the failure of prices to drop in the face of increased supply or reduced demand.

price stability A level of price increase that is so small that it protects the long-term purchasing power of the dollar over time. The historic price stability target for Canada has been a 2 percent inflation rate. From 1979 to 1992, consumer prices in Canada rose at an average annual rate of 6.8 percent. Along with FULL EMPLOYMENT, price stability is one of the basic goals of economic policy. *See also* ZERO INFLATION.

price support   Government subsidies or other assistance to maintain the market price of a commodity at a minimum price level. Price supports are most frequently found in the agricultural sector of the economy.

price system   A system in which the allocation of resources, and thereby the production of goods and services, is determined by the prices that consumers are willing to pay and sellers or producers are willing to accept. When the price system functions freely, the LAW OF SUPPLY AND DEMAND is the operating mechanism that sorts out the countless independent desires of consumers and sellers. For example, if the economy needs more computer programmers, the price or wage will go up to attract more people to train for such jobs.

The effective functioning of the price system as an efficient allocator of resources, however, depends on the existence of competitive markets. If competition is imperfect and oligopoly or monopoly power exists, then the price system will fall short of achieving the most efficient allocation of resources even though it may still be superior to any other system. Moreover, there are some goods, so-called PUBLIC GOODS, whose production cannot be based on the law of supply and demand; for example, hospitals have to be built according to need, and not according to a pricing system where access is based on income. Nor does the price system fully take into account so-called EXTERNALITIES, such as pollution. The consumer of a good may pay only part of the cost of cleaning up the pollution caused by the manufacturer of the product; the rest of the cost may be paid for by the public out of public funds so that the price does not represent the true cost. However, a reliance on the price system is one of the fundamental characteristics of a market economy, despite its flaws. The role of prices in allocating resources is also one of the key assumptions of economists.

price taker   A company whose output is relatively small so that the price it pays for parts, raw materials, and labour, or the price it charges for its goods or services, has no effect on the overall level of prices in its particular industry or in the economy. If it charges a higher price than its bigger competitors, they are unlikely to react by raising their prices as well. In practice, a firm that is a price taker has to follow the prices charged by larger competitors or, if it is in a fragmented industry with plentiful but no dominant firms, it has to follow the price set by market forces.

price war   A series of price reductions by competitors, usually of a temporary nature, so that each competitor can retain its market share. Price wars usually occur when there is a surplus of a product that cannot easily be stored. For example, a temporary surplus of gasoline may lead to a price war among competing gas-station chains; when the surplus is gone, prices will return to their normal level.

Prices and Incomes Commission (PIC)   An anti-inflation agency established by the federal government in January, 1969, following the publication of the white paper, *Policies for Price Stability,* in December, 1968. The white paper said that existing economic institutions did not give the government the scope it needed "to resolve the very real conflict which exists at the present time between the objectives of maintaining high-level employment and restoring the price stability that is necessary for sustained economic growth." In its original terms of reference in 1969, the three-man commission was "to inquire into and report upon the causes, processes and consequences of inflation and to inform those making current price and income decisions, the general public and the government on how price stability may best be achieved." A Commons-Senate committee on price stability, incomes, and employment was to be appointed (which it never was), to hold hearings on the commission's reports.

The role of the Prices and Incomes Commission was subsequently enlarged to include the negotiation of a voluntary-restraint agreement by business and labour. Business leaders met at a national conference on price stability in February, 1970, and agreed to limit price increases to amounts clearly less than the increased costs that businesses were experiencing. The commission had full powers under the Inquiries Act to investigate company costs and income, and to recommend action to the government to punish firms disregarding the guideline. The formal restraint agreement expired at the end of 1970. The commission also tried to persuade labour leaders to agree to a 6 percent wage guideline but failed to get labour to co-operate.

The commission was wound up after its final report and accompanying research were published in August, 1972. In its final report, the commission argued that the exercise of economic power by unions and corporations did not emerge as a major cause of Canada's inflation. It put the blame instead on shortcomings in government economic management, holding government responsible, in particular, for allowing the economy to overheat in the late 1960s. It also argued that, while the

existence of monopoly power is an explanation of high prices, it is not an explanation of rising prices. One of the main costs of inflation, the commission said, is that of trying to bring it down once it is decided that the inflation rate is too high. The principal way to cure and prevent inflation is to improve the management of the economy, principally through better use of monetary, fiscal, and supply policies. It said that temporary price and income controls can be helpful in changing public expectations during periods of high inflation, reducing the need for harsh monetary and fiscal restraint; however, the commission argued that it would only work when there was wide public support and the government was determined to enforce the controls, as well as stick to its restrained monetary and fiscal policies. The report rejected the use of voluntary restraint or punitive taxes to secure compliance with voluntary price and income guidelines.

pricing out of the market   The circumstances that exist when a country's or firm's prices are so high that its goods cannot be sold in their normal markets. This can happen when the cost of raw materials increases, when wage settlements are too high, when an exchange rate is overvalued, or when domestic inflation robs a country or firm of its competitiveness against foreign producers.

primary deficit   A federal or provincial budget deficit that excludes debt-servicing costs such as interest payments. Likewise, a primary surplus is a government surplus before deducting the interest.

primary distribution   The sale of a new issue of common or preferred shares, bonds, or other securities. These are securities that have not previously been distributed or issued, and therefore represent new capital. Such an issue must be preceded by a prospectus approved by a provincial SECURITIES COMMIS-SION. *See also* SECONDARY MARKET.

primary industry An industry that produces the raw materials employed in an economy. Its products range from agricultural and fishing-industry products to products, such as oil and gas, minerals, and pulp and paper, that have been subject to only a limited degree of processing. Their conversion into products ready for consumers or for goods used to produce consumer goods is the role of SECONDARY INDUSTRY or TERTIARY INDUSTRY.

primary market The market for the sale of new bonds, preferred shares, and common shares, with the sale being made to various INSTITUTIONAL INVESTORS. The proceeds go to the issuing entity. Subsequent sales of these securities take place on the secondary market.

primary recovery The crude oil that can be recovered from an oil reservoir by natural pressure that moves the oil into the oil wells.

primary-reserve ratio The cash reserves that chartered banks were required, under the BANK ACT, to set aside from deposits before they could make loans and buy securities. The primary reserves consisted of cash balances that the chartered banks had to maintain in the form of notes of, or deposits with, the BANK OF CANADA and on which no interest was earned. The requirements under the 1979 revisions to the Bank Act set the primary-reserve ratio at 10 percent of Canadian-dollar demand deposits, 2 percent of Canadian-dollar notice deposits for the first $500 million, 3 percent of all Canadian-dollar notice deposits above that amount, and 3 percent of foreign-currency deposits used to finance domestic transactions.

The 1992 amendments to the Bank Act abolished the primary reserve ratio, effective July, 1994.

primary deficit surplus The budgetary deficit or surplus that exists before adding in interest costs on government debt. *See also* STRUCTURAL DEFICIT OR SURPLUS.

prime contractor The chief contractor on a major project, who is responsible for its completion. The prime contractor will often use the services of many different subcontractors to carry out and complete the project.

Prime Minister's Office (PMO) The office of experts that advises the prime minister on government policies. It has an important role to play in setting government economic policy, since the priorities and objectives of the government are set and co-ordinated within the cabinet and the PMO. The prime minister's staff usually includes advisers on economic and energy policy. Its members are political appointees for the most part so their responsibilities include the political success of the prime minister and the government. *See also* PRIVY COUNCIL OFFICE.

prime rate The interest rate the chartered banks charge on short-term business loans to their most creditworthy corporate customers. It is also used as a reference point for loans to other customers who are charged so many points above prime, depending on their creditworthiness. It is usually changed in step with changes in the BANK RATE.

principal **1.** The amount of money owed by an individual, corporation, or government, on which interest is paid. A borrower must pay interest while he has the use of the principal and must repay the principal before the loan is considered to be repaid. **2.** The person, firm, or government whose interests are represented by an agent in negotiations with a third party. **3.** The owner of a business.

Principal affair The collapse of the Principal Group of Edmonton, in 1987, that included First Investors Corporation and Associated Investors of Canada. The Principal Group was formed by Edmonton lawyer Donald Cormie to seek investment funds from the public. At the time of bankruptcy, First Investors and Associated Investors owed almost $500 million to 67,000 Canadians, while Principal owed $85 million to 1,100 noteholders. Cormie pleaded guilty to misleading investors in his company's 1985 unaudited annual review; in this review, Cormie had told investors his group had disposed of its real-estate holdings in advance of the 1981 recession when in fact, according to an inquiry headed by Bill Code, real estate continued to be the group's largest single investment and contributed to the group's bankruptcy. In 1991, Cormie agreed to a 10-year cease-trade order by the Alberta Securities Commission. He pleaded guilty the same year to misleading investors under the COMPETITION ACT and was fined $500,000. The auditors of the group were fined $125,000 and suspended for 30 days in 1991 by the Institute of Chartered Accountants of Alberta, and the Alberta Minister of Consumer and Corporate Affairs was relieved of her position after the Code report found her partly responsible for the lack of proper regulation of the companies. While investors in First Investors Corporation and Associated Investors got back 87 cents on the dollar, and noteholders in the Principal Group got 50 cents on the dollar, the collapse cost Alberta taxpayers about $150 million.

principles of taxation The basis for a sound and acceptable tax policy. Adam SMITH, in his *Wealth of Nations* (1776), said that taxes should be levied according to a person's ability to pay, as indicated by income; should be dependable as to the amount and method of payment, and should not depend on arbitrary rulings by officials; should be levied and collected at a time most convenient to taxpayers; and should cost as little as possible to collect. Since then, other considerations have come into play, such as the desirability of using the tax system to redistribute income from the wealthy to the needy, or to stimulate or restrain economic growth in keeping with the goals of MACROECONOMIC POLICY.

private brand A product manufactured by one company and sold under the name of another. For example, most food-store chains arrange with food-processing companies that sell products under their own brand name to manufacture a similar product that is sold under the supermarket's name.

private company A company whose charter of incorporation limits the number of shareholders to 50, whose shares cannot be bought or sold by members of the public, and whose shares cannot be sold by one shareholder to anyone else without the approval of the board of directors and, in some cases, the prior offer of shares to existing shareholders. A private company, if it is federally incorporated, must file a public annual financial return with the Department of CONSUMER AND CORPORATE AFFAIRS if it has gross revenues in excess of $10 million or assets in excess of $5 million. All publicly traded companies have to file.

private enterprise An economic system in which individuals have the right to own private property and to engage in economic activities of their choice to earn a profit. In such a system, private property has limited legal rights; governments, for example, must regulate some business activities and prices, how capital is to be raised, the liabilities of borrowers, the conditions under which trade takes place, and the circumstances under which an investor is barred from acquiring other business enterprises. A private-enterprise economy is one in which market forces and competition play important roles in allocating resources, so that decision making is highly decentralized among countless individual decisions of firms and households. In a MIXED ECONOMY such as Canada's, there are roles for both private enterprise and government in achieving economic goals and adding to economic output.

private family trust   A provision, made under the Income Tax Act at the time the federal government abolished the inheritance tax in 1972, that allowed wealthy Canadians to shelter their investments from taxation for 21 years (until 1993), when they would have been liable for taxes on the increase in the value of the holdings. In 1992, the federal government amended the arrangement so that a trust could defer any tax until the last beneficiary of the trust died. In addition, a trust is allowed to distribute its holdings to beneficiaries at original cost rather than fair market value. The federal government defended its decision in 1992 to allow wealthy families to further defer tax liabilities by arguing that the change was needed to take care of trusts set up for disabled children.

private good   A good or service consumed by an individual or family and purchased from after-tax income, as opposed to a PUBLIC GOOD paid for out of taxes or user fees. Much of the political debate in modern economies is over the ratio of private to public goods: in general, society seems to want more of both so the argument is over how to provide a desired level of public goods and services, while leaving individuals with a desired level of personal disposable income.

private placement   The sale of a new issue of corporate bonds, preferred or common shares, or other securities to INSTITUTIONAL INVESTORS, such as pension funds and insurance companies, or to other major investors, instead of offering the issue for sale to the public. Usually no PROSPECTUS is required, although SECURITIES COMMISSIONS must be informed of the placement.

private property   The legal right of a person or corporation to own and use an economic good. Private property may consist of a building, land, patent, copyright, trademark, work of art, security such as a share or bond, machinery, or other possessions, including personal possessions. Ownership of personal property may be represented by a deed or title, certificate, receipted bill of sale, or simple possession. Private-property rights are both protected and limited by law. Private property is one of the distinguishing characteristics of a private enterprise or market economy.

private savings   Household savings plus business savings. *See also* SAVINGS.

private sector   That part of the economy under private ownership and control. It includes all privately owned corporations, small businesses, farms, professional firms, and individual entrepreneurial activity, and non-commercial organizations such as unions, non-profit corporations, and churches, as well as households. In effect, it represents that part of economic activity accounted for by consumer spending, corporate activity, and financial institutions. It is one of two major sectors in the MIXED ECONOMY, the other being the PUBLIC SECTOR.

privatization The sale of publicly owned corporations, including CROWN CORPORATIONS, to the private sector. Among the federally owned corprations that were privitized in the late 1980s or early 1990s were Canadair Ltd., the de Havilland Aircraft Co., Teleglobe Canada, Air Canada, and Petro-Canada.

Privy Council Office (PCO) The department in the federal government that serves the prime minister. Its senior official is the clerk of the Privy Council, who is also secretary to the cabinet. The main roles of the PCO are to co-ordinate and support the cabinet and its committees, to prepare material for the prime minister, to liaise with government departments and agencies on cabinet matters, to carry out special studies, and to organize the work of interdepartmental committees of government officials. The PCO has operating secretariats serving different cabinet committees, and thus has its own staff of experts, including those who deal with the economy, energy, native affairs, social policy, defence, external affairs, and government operations and organization. It also has a planning group, which deals with the longer-term needs of public policy, and a security, intelligence, and emergency-planning secretariat. A separate FEDERAL-PROVINCIAL RELATIONS OFFICE advises on federal-provincial relations. *See also* PRIME MINISTER'S OFFICE.

pro forma statement A draft financial statement for a new business, showing estimated revenues and expenses, and how various costs and income will be defined so as to give a financial picture of the new enterprise's financial condition, based on various assumptions or contractual commitments. It can also be a future projection of an existing firm's financial statements, to estimate, for example, future CASH FLOW or WORKING CAPITAL.

pro rata The distribution or division of an asset or benefit based on some proportional relationship: for example, the offer of a RIGHTS ISSUE to buy additional shares according to the number of shares already owned by each shareholder in a firm.

probability The possibility of a particular event taking place, based on a scale from 0.0, or impossible, to 1.0, or inevitable.

probable reserves In the mining industry, an identified ore body that hasn't been fully delineated, and for that reason cannot be classified as a proven or positive ore.

probate The procedure under which a court approves a particular WILL as the true and last testament of someone who has died, which, as such, represents his or her final wishes on how the estate is to be distributed among various beneficiaries. The court also confirms the EXECUTOR named in the will. The probate fee is a percentage of the gross value of the estate before deducting liabilities other than mortgages in real estate.

proceeds **1.** The amount of money remaining from a new issue of shares or bonds after the sales costs, including commissions, have been deducted. **2.** The net yield from the sale of a home, farm, business, or other asset, after the cost of selling the asset, such as a real-estate broker's commission and legal fees, have been paid, and any claims against the asset, such as mortgage debt, have been paid off. **3.** The yield from the tax system after the costs of collecting the tax have been deducted.

procurement The purchase of needed goods and services. The term is frequently used to describe government purchasing of goods and services. Government procurement policies can be used as a non-tariff barrier to keep out imports and protect local industries, or as a tool in industrial strategy, to encourage the development of a domestic industry — for example, in areas of new technology — by acting as a launch market.

Procurement Review Board of Canada An independent administrative review panel established in 1989 under the CANADA-UNITED STATES FREE TRADE AGREEMENT (FTA) to ensure "fair and equitable treatment" for Canadian and U.S. suppliers interested in doing business with the federal government. A supplier of goods — services are not included — who believes a federal government body has treated him or her unfairly in the bidding process or the awarding of a contract may file a complaint with the board. Valid complaints must be addressed within 90 days. Goods covered must have an estimated value of $29,000 to $204,000 (adjusted for inflation every two years) at the time of the solicitation; the goods must be "eligible goods" for a government entity covered by the FTA, and the complainant must be a potential supplier. If the board upholds a complaint, it can recommend that the procuring agency re-issue or re-evaluate the tender, or terminate the existing contract and the awarding of the contract to the complainant. It can also award reasonable costs related to the filing and proceeding with the complaint and preparing the bid. In its first four years, the board received 103 valid complaints, and 25 were upheld. In 1992, the federal government announced that the board would be integrated with the CANADIAN INTERNATIONAL TRADE TRIBUNAL and that the bid protest coverage would be extended beyond the areas set out in the FTA to include any undertakings that might flow from the GENERAL AGREEMENT ON TARIFFS AND TRADE, the NORTH AMERICAN FREE TRADE AGREEMENT, the federal government's open bidding system, and the Intergovernmental Agreement on Government Procurement between the federal government and the provinces.

producer Usually a firm but in fact any unit that supplies goods or services in the economy.

producer goods Goods used in the production of other goods — for example, capital goods such as machinery, machine tools, process-control computers, motors, trucks, and freight cars — and other goods or intermediate inputs — such as oil, natural gas, and raw materials — that are used in the production of consumer goods.

producer's surplus The excess profit earned by a producer above the minimum amount the producer would be willing to earn to maintain the same level of production rather than withdrawing from production.

product Any good or service that can be sold.

product differentiation Efforts to make similar or nearly identical products seem different, thereby allowing firms to compete through these product differences rather than through price competition alone. Sometimes product differentiation results from real differences in quality, but frequently the differences result from styling, design, packaging, brand-name identification, model changes, advertising, or service and warranty claims. Many mass-consumer products, from gasoline, toothpaste, and detergents to beer, shampoos, and automobiles, rely heavily on product-differentiation techniques to retain or increase their share of the market through brand loyalty. Such competition is a sign of IMPERFECT COMPETITION; in PERFECT-COMPETITION models, products are assumed to be homogeneous or perfectly interchangeable, so that the consumer makes his choice on the basis of price alone, and is thus able to force down prices. In a world of imperfect competition, the consumer probably pays more than he would in a world of perfect competition. However, at the same time, the consumer has a greater choice of products.

product life cycle The sales cycle of a product from the time it is launched until the time it is succeeded by a new product or declines due to changing consumer tastes. In the first stage of the life of a product, the product launch stage, sales are low and prices relatively high as the producer attempts to develop a market. In the second stage, the period of product growth, the original producer enjoys rising sales and profits but eventually faces competitors who are drawn into the market. In the third stage, the stage of maturity, the size of the market stabilizes and producers compete for market share as consumers buy replacement products. In the final stage, the stage of product decline, the size of the market shrinks as new products are introduced or changing consumer tastes shift demand so that producers withdraw from the market. With the pace of innovation increasing, the product life cycle for many products is shrinking, forcing companies to become more innovative and to get new or improved products to market as fast as they can while simultaneously striving to develop new products.

product life-cycle theory The theory that as products mature, their production shifts from the country in which they originate to countries that can produce at lower costs. In international trade, this means that products originating in industrial countries such as Canada will, as production methods become standardized so that less skilled labour can be employed, eventually be shifted to production sites in developing countries. This is why industrial countries such as Canada have to develop their innovative skills and invest in research and development and worker upgrading to ensure a constant stream of new, high-value goods and services.

product mix The array of products a firm puts on the market. The product mix includes both the range of products a firm offers to appeal to different segments of a market, and the life of different products, based on the PRODUCT LIFE CYCLE, so that the firm always has a mix of different products at various stages of the cycle.

production The use of labour, capital, and ideas to create producer and consumer goods through various refining, processing, manufacturing, and distribution activities.

production function The maximum amount of output of a specific good or service that can be produced by different combinations of the factors of production, such as labour and capital (for example, factories, machinery and equipment, and inventories) at an existing level of technology. The calculation of different production functions allows a firm to determine the most profitable or efficient mix of factors. While more labour can be added, since the marginal productivity of labour is positive, if the level of capital is unchanged, then the marginal productivity of additional units of labour will decline; the same is true for capital — more can be added but if the supply of labour is unchanged, the marginal productivity of capital for a given level of technology will decline. Labour and capital have to be employed in efficient combinations. For example, it is possible to use different combinations of labour and capital in a firm that produces 25,000 men's suits; the firm will try to find the combination of factors that produces the cheapest suit, bearing in mind that it also has to meet the demands of customers, such as delivery deadlines and quality. If the cost of labour rises and the tax system provides incentives for capital investment, then the firm will recalculate its production function, and most likely substitute capital equipment for labour to the extent that it can. Whenever technological change occurs, the production function has to be recalculated.

production gap *See* POTENTIAL GROSS DOMESTIC PRODUCT.

production-possibility boundary A curve showing the maximum amount of goods and services that can be produced if all the available productive resources of the economy are employed. The production possibility boundary permits the calculation of trade-offs by showing the alternative combinations of output that can be achieved in a fully employed economy; for example, it can be used to show the trade-off between producing more military goods and producing more housing.

productivity The output of goods and services in the economy or in an industry from the effective use of various inputs, such as skilled workers, capital equipment, managerial know-how, technological innovation, and entrepreneurial activity, used to produce those goods and services. It is most simply defined as output per worker or output per man-hour. However, TOTAL FACTOR PRODUCTIVITY measures the efficiency with which all factors are employed. Real improvements in standard of living depend on the ability to raise productivity — that is, to increase the physical volume of output for a fixed level of inputs. Wage increases in excess of productivity increases can be inflationary because they are not backed by increases in output. While productivity is most frequently measured in terms of labour output, the role of labour in achieving productivity gains may be quite small. Much of the responsibility rests with management to ensure that technological change takes place, new markets are developed, the workplace is organized to achieve the most efficient level of output, labour-management relations are well managed, programs exist to upgrade the skills of workers, and the level of managerial know-how is constantly improving. In recent years, technological change has been found to be one of the most important sources of productivity improvement, with technological change including both the most advanced capital equipment and the upgrading of worker skills to make the most efficient use of the new technology. International comparisons of productivity are published by the U.S. Bureau of Labour Statistics and the ORGANIZATION FOR ECONOMIC CO-OPERATION AND DEVELOPMENT. Statistics Canada provides detailed measures of Canadian productivity performance in its annual *Aggregate Productivity Measures* (publication 15-204).

productivity of capital stock The ratio of physical output in the economy, an industry, or a firm, to the real value of capital stock, represented by buildings, equipment, and technology. The level of productivity will depend on how the capital stock is organized and used; advances in technology; the level of care, maintenance, and replacement; and the skills of the workers using it.

profit **1.** What is left over for the owners of a business after all expenses have been deducted from the revenues of a firm. Gross profit is the profit before interest, depreciation, corporate income taxes, or extraordinary items such as the write-off of a bad investment, have been deducted, and before minority interests in a firm have been taken into account. Net profit is the final profit of the firm after all deductions have been made; it is the amount of money that is available for distribution to shareholders as DIVIDENDS, or for reinvestment in the firm for business expansion in the form of RETAINED EARNINGS. Profitability for a firm or industry can be measured in several ways: through year-to-year changes in EARNINGS PER SHARE; through net profit as a percent of sales; through net profit as a percent of SHAREHOLDERS' EQUITY; or through net profit as a RATE OF RETURN ON INVESTED CAPITAL. Net profits for individual firms are available from corporate annual and quarterly reports, and for industry as a whole or individual industries from various reports of Statistics Canada. It publishes an annual report, *Corporation Financial Statistics* (publication 61-207) and also *Financial and Taxation Statistics for Enterprises* (publication 61-219P), along with a quarterly report on business financial statistics (publication 61-008). The annual and quarterly figures on GROSS DOMESTIC PRODUCT show pre-tax corporate profits and the share of national income represented by pre-tax profits. **2.** Economists have a number of different ways of treating profits — for example, as the surplus remaining after the returns on various FACTORS OF PRODUCTION or their full OPPORTUNITY COSTS have been deducted, as a reward for innovation and entrepreneurial skills, as a premium or return for risk, as an ECONOMIC RENT or QUASI-RENT, as a monopoly return resulting from a contrived scarcity, or, in the case of KARL MARX, as the surplus value of labour's contribution to production.

profit and loss statement   *See* EARNINGS STATEMENT.

profit centre   Any division within a firm that is clearly identifiable for accounting purposes, that can be held responsible for its activities, and whose goal is to earn the highest possible profit.

profit margin   The profitability of a firm or industry, calculated by taking the after-tax profit as a percentage of sales, shareholders' equity, or invested capital. Profit margins can be calculated for the private sector as a whole or for a single industry, and the results for a particular firm can be measured against industry averages to determine the efficiency of the individual firm.

profit maximization   The attempt to calculate and to reach the most profitable level of output by keeping costs at the lowest possible level per unit of output and setting prices at a level that will attract maximum sales. Under these conditions, output can be increased until the MARGINAL REVENUE from the last unit produced and sold is equal to the MARGINAL COST of producing that unit. So long as marginal revenue is greater than marginal cost, it will always pay to produce more; once marginal cost passes marginal revenue, then extra production will reduce profits. In economic models, it is assumed that firms seek to maximize profits and thus to achieve the most efficient allocation of resources in the economy, but in real life this may not always be the strategy of the individual firm, especially in the short run. For example, in an OLIGOPOLISTIC industry, the existing firms may be satisfied to live with existing market shares, instead of seeking to maximize profits through competition for a bigger market share at the expense of their rivals.

profit motive The instinctive desire that is said to exist among entrepreneurs in a free-market economy for the highest possible profit. This motive is viewed by free-market economists as the engine of economic growth and the source of economic and social progress. Free-market economists contend that every firm seeks to maximize its profits. *See also* INVISIBLE HAND.

profit sharing Any plan under which employees in a firm receive a share in their employer's profits in addition to their regular wages. The profit sharing can be in the form of money or shares in the firm, and is usually based on a percentage of after-tax profits set aside for employees. Profit sharing can be paid out on an annual basis, or can be accumulated as a form of retirement fund or pension, in which case it is treated differently for tax purposes. The proponents of profit-sharing schemes argue that such schemes can lead to better employee motivation and improved productivity in the firm. Union critics say that they prefer to bargain for better and stable wages that form the base for pension and other benefits and for improved working conditions instead of relying on management to decide whether there should be a profit-sharing bonus in a particular year or what the bonus will be.

profit taking The sale of shares to realize the profit from an increase in the value of the shares. Until the shares are sold and the profits received, all the shareholder has as a result of the increase in the value of his shares is a PAPER PROFIT.

program-evaluation and -review technique (PERT) A scientific method of setting completion dates for projects and of ensuring that the completion time is kept as short as possible. In most applications, a computer system is used to keep track of progress; a project is broken down into all of its separate steps, and calculations are made as to which steps can be done independently, which steps must be completed before others can be started or completed, and how much time must be allowed for the delivery of materials or components, skilled workers, and raw materials. From this information it is possible to chart out the sequence of steps and to determine dates for orders, completion dates for individual stages of the project, the time to start hiring workers, and so forth. The computer can keep track of progress, and give management a periodic review to show whether or not a project is likely to meet its targeted completion date, or whether special steps, such as overtime, are needed to reach the completion date on schedule. The technique was developed in 1958 by the U.S. Navy for the Polaris submarine project and was used later in Canada to schedule the construction of Expo 67 in Montreal. *See also* CRITICAL-PATH METHOD.

program trading The use of computers to manage stock-market portfolio trading strategies, with the computer system monitoring stock-market indicators such as the flow or volume of trading, movements in futures and options, and current prices, rather than corporate earnings or changes in economic conditions that trigger the sale or purchase of shares. Program trading can also be used to take advantage of arbitrage possibilities or price spreads between equity prices and stock-market-index futures and options, such as the Standard & Poor 500 Index in the United States. Because of the possibility that program trading can add to market instability, many stock exchanges now have constraints on program trading. Circuit breakers is the name used for various measures introduced to prevent program trading from sending the market into a deep decline, introduced after the 1987 stock-market collapse; these circuit breakers can disconnect the stock and futures market if there is great volatility in prices. On the New York Stock Exchange, a "side car" is put into effect whenever Standard & Poor's rises or falls 12 points, routing program trades into a special computer file that scans for imbalances in buy or sell orders. Regulations also allow the New York Stock Exchange to halt trading for one hour if the Dow Jones Industrial Average falls 250 points and for two hours if it slides an additional 150 points on the same day.

progress payment   A payment to a contractor when part of the work toward the completion of a project has been carried out. When a contract stretches out over many months or longer, it usually includes a provision for various payments to the contractor as various stages of the work are completed.

progressive tax   A tax in which the tax rate increases in line with increases in the tax base; this means that the larger the tax base — for example, the larger a person's taxable income — the greater the percentage collected as tax. Progressive taxes are based on the ABILITY-TO-PAY PRINCIPLE, with the MARGINAL TAX RATE rising as the tax base rises. The best-known progressive tax is the INCOME TAX in which, as a person's taxable income rises, a greater percentage is taxed. A person with a taxable income of, say, $20,000, would pay a low tax rate. But as this person's taxable income rises, so does the rate of tax, so that the taxable income between, say, $35,000 and $40,000, is taxed at a higher rate than the first $20,000, with the rate rising to a top marginal rate on all taxable income over, say, $60,000.

Tax experts point out that the other side of the coin in a progressive-tax system is that tax deductions end up being worth much more to people with high taxable incomes than to those with low taxable incomes. For example, the person who has a taxable income of $40,000 in the above example, and who invests $2,000 in a registered retirement savings plan, will get a bigger tax refund than the person with only $20,000 of taxable income; the $2,000 of savings for the first taxpayer's retirement will have cost him less than it would have cost the second taxpayer to get the same retirement benefit. This means that in determining the progressive nature of an income-tax system, many factors have to be taken into account, such as the marginal-tax-rate schedule itself, the forms of income that are tax exempt or tax deductible, and various incentives that are built into the tax system. *See also* TAX EXPENDITURES.

progressive taxation   Taxation based on the ability to pay.

proletariat   In MARXIST ECONOMICS, the working or wage-earning class. Karl MARX argued that the wages of the working class were held at a subsistence level to allow capitalists to exploit the workers and to accumulate capital. He predicted that the proletariat would someday rebel at this condition, overthrow the capitalists, and establish a socialist society that would represent the next stage in the inevitable evolution of people toward a communist society.

promissory note   A signed promise by a borrower to repay a lender a stated sum of money plus a stated amount of interest by or on a stated date. Promissory notes are also used in commodity futures trading. In some cases, such notes may be negotiable.

promoter   A term, sometimes pejorative, used to describe a person trying to raise capital for a business enterprise by attracting investors. The term is sometimes used to describe those who tout shares in penny mining stocks, or who try to attract private capital into backing a new venture.

promotion **1.** An organized effort to raise new capital or to make a stock-market profit by pushing the sale of a company's shares. **2.** A marketing effort to launch a new product or to strengthen the sales of an existing product through such devices as contests, sponsorship of sports or other events, a special discount sale, or intensive advertising. **3.** An advance in the career of an employee to a higher level of responsibility and pay.

propensity to consume The proportion of disposable income that a person will spend instead of save, at any given level of income; or the proportion of total personal disposable income that all households will spend instead of save. The average propensity to consume is calculated by dividing total spending on goods and services by total personal disposable income. Most people tend to spend a smaller proportion of their incomes as their incomes rise. At the lowest levels of income, people are likely to spend their entire incomes, and perhaps even more than their total incomes. The marginal propensity to consume is the amount of additional income that will be spent instead of saved. It is calculated by dividing the additional spending by additional income. If there is a low propensity to consume, then government measures to stimulate growth through tax cuts may prove to be ineffective; conversely, if there is a high propensity to consume, then tax cuts can stimulate spending in the economy. But economists also have to look at the PROPENSITY TO IMPORT since a high propensity to import may mean that spending from tax cuts leaks out to foreign producers instead of benefiting the domestic economy, as intended.

propensity to import The proportion of a country's national income that is spent on imports instead of domestically produced goods and services. The average propensity to import is calculated by dividing total imports by total national income. The marginal propensity to import measures the proportion of any increase in national income that will be spent on imports. If a country has a high propensity to import, then tax cuts to stimulate consumer spending may have little beneficial impact on the domestic economy.

propensity to save The proportion of disposable income that a person will save instead of spend, at any given level of income, or, at the economy-wide level, the portion of personal disposable income saved by all households. Most people tend to save more as their incomes rise. At the lowest income levels, there is likely to be no saving and perhaps even DISSAVING. The average propensity to save is calculated by dividing total savings by total personal disposable income. The marginal propensity to save is the increase in savings divided by the increase in personal disposable income.

property The legal right to possess and use economic goods and to derive both present and future benefits from such use. There are different types of property: real property, consisting of land and buildings, for example; personal property, consisting of such assets as furniture and a car; or intellectual property, consisting of such things as copyright, patents, and trademarks.

property tax A direct tax levied on the assessed value of land and buildings; the tax is usually expressed as a mill rate or percent of each $1,000 of assessed value. Property tax is within the taxing powers of the provinces under the CONSTITUTION ACT, 1867.

All the provinces have delegated the power to levy a property tax to their municipalities, although two provinces, New Brunswick and Prince Edward Island, also levy a property tax directly on real property. Methods of assessment differ from province to province. In some provinces, assessment is based on MARKET VALUE; in others, it is based on a multitude of assessment rules that have been developed over the years, which, as a result, may lead to similarly valued properties being assessed at quite different amounts. The main criticism levied against property tax is that it is not based on ability to pay.

proportional tax   A flat-rate tax, which collects the same percentage from the taxable asset regardless of its value, or from taxable income whatever its level. Examples would be sales taxes, the mill rates of property taxes, or tariffs.

proprietorship   A business owned and operated by one person — for example, most small shops and many other small businesses.

prorationing   A method of apportioning oil or other mineral production among all of the producers in relation to their reserves when the supply of a resource is greater than the demand for it. Alberta phased out the prorationing of oil production in the 1980s, although it retained the legislative authority for prorationing in case it became necessary in the future. It had started prorationing in the 1950s.

prospect   A property on which minerals have been discovered, but whose exact mineral value has not yet been determined by geological calculation and exploration.

prospector   An individual acting on his own or retained by a mining company or group of investors to search for mineral prospects.

prospectus   A legal document that describes a new issue of COMMON or PREFERRED SHARES or BONDS being issued for sale to the public; the prospectus must meet the disclosure and other requirements of the provincial SECURITIES COMMISSION under whose jurisdiction the new issue is to be made, and must be approved by the securities commission before any of the new shares or bonds can be offered for sale to the public. A "full, true, and plain disclosure of all material facts" in respect of the offering of such securities must be made. These facts include the price to the public of the shares or bonds; the commission being earned by the UNDERWRITER; the use to which the funds being raised are to be put; a financial history of the company, including its dividend record over the past five years; a commentary on the company's financial statements signed by an outside auditor or accountant; names, addresses, and occupations of the company officers plus their total remuneration; details of principal shareholders in the company; a statement of the company's capitalization; information on current legal suits; and other details, along with a certificate signed by the company's chief executive officer, chief financial officer, and two directors, stating that the information is full, true, and plain disclosure, along with a similar statement signed by the UNDERWRITERS.

protectionism   Policies to restrict trade, such as high tariffs, quotas, import licences, and a wide variety of NON-TARIFF BARRIERS, such as government-purchasing policies, health standards, artificial import valuations, or the aggressive use of anti-dumping or other trade-remedy laws. The purpose of all of these measures is to keep out imports and to protect local industries and jobs. Protectionist policies are more difficult to implement with the adoption of increasingly liberal trade rules under the GENERAL AGREEMENT ON TARIFFS AND TRADE — but not impossible. A popular device is to negotiate so-called voluntary quotas with exporters, using political and economic threats to get agreement; under voluntary quotas, exporting nations agree to limit their exports.

Protestant ethic A term applied by the German sociologist, Max Weber, to his thesis that Protestantism, from the 17th century on, gave a particular impetus to the capitalist drive for material success by making a virtue of hard work and thrift to accumulate capital while making the pursuit of profit and the accumulation of wealth respectable activities. Yet there are societies that have had no connection with Protestantism, where communities have worked hard and striven for riches — Japan, Israel, France, Singapore, and South Korea, for example.

provincial gross domestic product by industry An annual report on the performance of key sectors of each province's economy, including manufacturing, mining, construction, retail trade, and government, health, education, and social services. The report, *Provincial Gross Domestic Product by Industry* (publication 15-203) also includes some analytical discussion of provincial economic performance.

provincial savings institution Savings banks operated by the Alberta and Ontario governments. The Province of Ontario Savings Office opened its doors for business in 1922; it pays interest on deposits but does not make consumer loans. The Province of Alberta Treasury Branch began operations in 1938; it provides regular chequing and savings services and makes consumer, business, and agricultural loans and mortgages.

provincial spending power The principal spending powers of the provinces, set out in Section 92 of the CONSTITUTION ACT, 1867. These powers include spending for the management and sale of public lands, including the timber on those lands, for provincial jails, hospitals, municipalities, and local works and undertakings, and for the administration of justice within the province, on matters affecting civil property and civil rights in the province and on all matters of a merely local or private nature within the province. Section 92 also spells out the provincial responsibility for education. Section 95 gives the federal and provincial governments concurrent powers over agriculture and immigration; but federal law prevails if federal and provincial laws conflict. A 1951 amendment to section 94 (A), gives the federal and provincial governments concurrent powers over old-age pensions, but federal pension laws cannot affect provincial pension laws. The provinces are able to spend in a wide range of areas, including social welfare, education, industrial development, environmental protection, highways, trade promotion, agriculture, resource development, telecommunications, hydroelectric power, consumer protection, health care, labour relations, law enforcement, municipal services, and tourism. *See also* PROVINCIAL TAXING POWER, FEDERAL SPENDING POWER, FEDERAL TAXING POWER, SHARED-COST PROGRAM, EQUALIZATION PAYMENTS, TRANSFER PAYMENT.

provincial taxing power The principal taxing powers of the provinces, set out mainly in section 92 of the CONSTITUTION ACT, 1867. Section 92 (2) allows the provinces to levy DIRECT TAXES, such as income taxes, property taxes, mineral, oil, natural-gas, and timber royalties, retail-sales taxes, corporation taxes, and death and succession duties. The tax must be levied within the province to raise revenue for a provincial purpose. Section 92 (9) permits provinces to raise money by regulating shops, saloons, taverns, and auctioneers, and by other licensing activities for provincial, local, or municipal purposes. Section 124 is of minor importance but does permit New Brunswick to raise money by levying lumber-export duties, a right obtained by the province as a condition on entering Confederation. The provinces may also raise money through charges levied for services under various regulatory powers. Provincial taxing powers may be delegated to municipalities; for example, the provinces have given the municipalities the power to levy PROPERTY TAXES.

Although the provinces have wide powers to levy direct taxes, the courts have been careful to restrict the most blatant misuse of such powers. For example, the courts in the late 19th century ruled that harsh British Columbia taxes on Chinese people were *ultra vires* because they were not levied to raise revenue but to drive the Chinese out of the province. The Fathers of Confederation decided not to let the provinces impose INDIRECT TAXES because they wanted to make sure that Canada remained a common market; they feared that the provinces might use indirect taxes to raise trade barriers against one another. Section 121 of the CONSTITUTION ACT, 1867, underlines their intention, by stating that the products of each province are to be admitted duty free to the other provinces, although judicial interpretations subsequently narrowed the meaning of this section to the point where it has little application today.

provision for credit losses   The amount deducted as an expense from income that the management of a bank or other financial institution considers adequate to meet all credit-related losses of the institution.

provision for loan losses   An amount that represents management's expected losses on loans that is deducted as an expense from a bank or other financial institution's income. The book value of specific commercial and retail loans are reduced to represent their estimated realizable value, while general provisions are usually made for an industry sector or region where specific loan losses cannot be calculated. In addition, a country risk provision is made for potential losses on loans to 46 developing countries designated by the OFFICE OF THE SUPERINTENDENT OF FINANCIAL INSTITUTIONS.

proxy   A document signed by a shareholder of a corporation designating another person to vote his or her shares at the annual or other meeting of the corporation. That person does not have to be a shareholder of the company. The management of a corporation solicits the proxies of shareholders who don't plan to attend corporation meetings, or who support management and do not wish to vote their shares. Proxy documents are mailed out before annual and other meetings. However, a shareholder can assign his or her vote to any other person, including critics of management simply by writing that person's name on the proxy document and signing it. A shareholder can also limit the voting rights of management or anyone else named in the proxy statement. Securities legislation in Canada requires that all management motions planned for annual and other meetings be included in proxy statements, and that the statements must be mailed well in advance of the meeting. Under provincial securities laws, rival shareholder groups must also be given access to the shareholder mailing lists, so that they can also solicit proxies from shareholders.

proxy battle   A competition between management and a rival group of shareholders, or between various groups of shareholders, to get control of the proxies of other shareholders so that they can win votes at annual or other corporation meetings. Proxy battles may take place when there is a contest for control of a company, or when a group of shareholders wants to elect a member to the board of directors to represent their interests.

prudent-man rule   The requirement that a trustee, such as a trust-company officer, invest only in securities that a prudent man or woman would buy if he or she were investing for other people for whom he or she felt morally bound to provide. Some provinces and the federal government designate the type of securities that a trustee or fiduciary may buy. *See also* REASONABLE MAN.

Prudential Finance Corporation affair The 1966 collapse and bankruptcy of a financial company, incorporated in Ontario, that subsequently helped lead to a major overhaul of Ontario securities laws. *See also* ATLANTIC ACCEPTANCE AFFAIR. The company, on bankruptcy, had assets of $23.5 million and liabilities of $27 million. The company president was arrested and charged with theft, forgery, and uttering, and the Ontario Securities Commission was ordered by the Ontario attorney-general to investigate the company's affairs. As events proceeded, a number of other companies were placed in receivership, including North American General Insurance Company, the first federally incorporated insurance company to declare bankruptcy since the early 1920s. Reports tabled in the Ontario legislature in 1968 showed that Prudential had been under investigation by the Ontario Securities Commission since 1963, but that no action had been taken.

prudent portfolio approach   An investment strategy set out in the BANK ACT requiring financial institutions to pursue a well-diversified and risk-minimizing strategy. The investment plan is judged on the basis of what a reasonable person would do in similar circumstances.

psychic income   The pleasure or satisfaction that is derived from a job and is a factor in a person's decision to seek or hold a job, even though it may pay less than another job that this same person could get. A person might work for a charitable organization, where pay is lower, because of the satisfaction received from doing a job that clearly helps the less fortunate. A person who enjoys the outdoors or dislikes the regimentation of an assembly line may work as a mail carrier or garbage collector instead of in a factory, even if the pay is lower.

psychological theory of the business cycle   The theory that changes in the business cycle result from business and general public attitudes about the economic outlook. If confidence is high, then consumers will buy and business will invest. If people are pessimistic about the future, even for non-economic reasons, then consumers may hold on to their money and buy less, while business will delay new investment plans. While economists generally do not attach much significance to public attitudes in explaining the business cycle, it is recognized that public attitudes or confidence can affect the overall level of economic activity. The CONFERENCE BOARD OF CANADA publishes measures of consumer and business confidence.

public accounts   The books of account published by the Canadian government once a year, which show in detail how public funds have been spent in the past fiscal year. The accounts list spending, department by department, for the fiscal year ending the previous March 31, and provide other information, including itemization of government assets and liabilities, to give as true a picture as possible of the financial position of the Canadian government and its agencies. Similar reports are published by each of the provincial governments.

Public Accounts Committee   A standing committee of the House of Commons established in the first session of the first Parliament, in 1867, to give members of Parliament the opportunity to review the PUBLIC ACCOUNTS or spending records of the government and to examine the reports of the AUDITOR-GENERAL. The public accounts and report of the auditor-general are automatically referred to the committee: it is the financial watchdog of Parliament. Since 1957, an opposition member has chaired the committee; it also has a research officer.

public company   A company with limited liability whose shares are traded by members of the public through a recognized STOCK EXCHANGE or OVER-THE-COUNTER MARKET. This means that they are subject to regulation by a provincial SECURITIES COMMISSION and by the stock exchanges on which they are listed.

public corporation   *See* CROWN COR-PORATION.

public debt   The outstanding debt of the federal government and its agencies. It consists mainly of bonds, Canada Savings Bonds, and treasury bills held by residents or non-residents; the portion of public debt held by non-residents, and denominated in foreign currencies, is the potentially worrisome part of the public debt, since the interest and principal must usually be repaid in foreign currencies, which have to be earned and which represent debit entries in the country's balance of payments. In the 1991-92 period,

the market debt amounted to $349 billion, of which 45 percent was in bonds, 44 percent in treasury bills, 10 percent in Canada Savings Bonds, and 1 percent in foreign currency debt. The public debt also includes liabilities of the government, principally superannuation or pension obligations, bringing gross public debt to $467 billion in the 1991-92 period. The gross public debt consists of unmatured debt and other liabilities; unmatured debt includes outstanding bonds, treasury bills, and notes, while other liabilities include assistance, insurance, and pension costs. Net debt equals gross debt minus recorded assets. The Department of FINANCE publishes an annual *Debt Operation Report* detailing the size and composition of the public debt. *See also* NATIONAL DEBT.

public finance   The field of economics that studies the economic and social impact of government tax and spending activities. Among the areas it is concerned with are the following: the economic and social impact of various forms of taxation and the total level of taxation, including the impact on individuals, different income groups, regions, industries, and the economy as a whole; government spending, including its control, budgeting, and economic and social impact; debt management; and fiscal relations among different levels of government.

public good   A good provided by government spending or regulation and consumed collectively by members of the community. Examples include roads, parks, public transit, education, museums, and hospitals. *See also* PRIVATE GOOD, FREE GOOD. Economist John Kenneth GALBRAITH has argued that society overproduces private goods, and underproduces public goods. The benefits of private goods are often more immediately evident than the benefits of public goods;

moreover, there are aggressive producers of private goods who are able to stimulate consumer demand through advertising. In contrast, it is harder for the public to voice clearly its demand for public goods. Yet public goods are an essential part of overall consumption and to the quality of life, and generally are goods that the private sector would not provide on its own since the return would not justify the investment.

public housing Housing that is owned and operated by government agencies. Provincial and municipal governments both build and operate public housing. Provincial and municipal housing corporations provide subsidized housing for needy families and individuals, senior citizens, and the handicapped.

public issue Shares or bonds offered for sale to the public for the first time. Such public offers must first be approved by a provincial SECURITIES COMMISSION. See also PRIMARY DISTRIBUTION.

public lending right The right of authors to receive a royalty from a public library for the repeated use of their books. The amount received could be based on the number of times the book is circulated, or it could be based on the number of copies of books held in public libraries. In Canada, the Public Lending Right Commission was established in 1987 and provides an annual payment to authors based on the number of libraries holding the book rather than the number of times the book is borrowed. Authors argue that libraries reduce the potential sale of their books, thereby reducing their potential royalty income from their books' sales, so some kind of payment is justified. Legal recognition of the public lending right exists in a number of countries, including Denmark, Sweden, and Britain.

public-opinion survey A scientific polling of the adult population as a whole, or of specific groups according to age, occupation, sex, income, or region, to obtain opinions on public issues.

Public Policy Forum A non-partisan forum of business, labour, academic, and public service representatives that was organized in 1987 to encourage consensus-building institutions to replace adversarial processes and to improve the way Canada is governed. Based in Ottawa, the forum advocates new institutions and attitudes to develop a sense of common purpose among the public and private sectors, pointing to the way in which public-private consensus has helped elevate countries such as Germany, Switzerland, and Japan to the top of the world competitiveness rankings. The forum has worked with the federal public service to help streamline bureaucracy and make the governmental culture more open, client-focussed, and receptive to working with the private sector. It has also brought large numbers of business and labour leaders to Ottawa to understand how government works, and has helped establish joint labour-management organizations in the electrical and electronics manufacturing industry, the wood products industry, the grocery products industry, and other sectors. The forum is based in Ottawa.

public ownership The ownership and operation by a government of a corporation that produces a good or service. Generally speaking such corporations are established or acquired to advance or protect the public interest, or to undertake an important activity that private enterprise is unwilling or unable to undertake. Examples of publicly owned corporations in Canada include Canadian National Railway, the provincial power utilities, local bus or transit utilities, and the Canadian Broadcasting Corporation. Most but not all government-owned enterprises are CROWN CORPORATIONS.

public relations   Activities designed to cast a firm, industry, individual, or government in a favourable light with the public. Public-relations departments of firms advise clients or employers on how to cast themselves or their activities in a way likely to win favour with the public, how to get publicity, how to provide information to the press and public, and how to deal with elected politicians and government agencies.

public revenue   Total government revenues. Public revenue includes income from taxes, tariffs, fees, and licences, interest on loans, profits of crown corporations, royalties, revenues from the sale of mineral, timber, or other rights, and all other forms of government income.

public sector   The portion of the economy represented by government activities. Governments purchase goods and services, regulate the activities of business corporations, produce goods and services through government-owned enterprises such as crown corporations, operate schools, universities, hospitals, and other institutions, invest in highways, public transit, and other capital projects, and make transfer payments to individuals. Governments also tax individuals and corporations, manage the macroeconomy, and use the tax system to encourage or discourage particular types of investment, savings, and spending.

Public Service Commission of Canada (PSC)   The hiring agency of the federal government. Its role is to hire employees for the federal government, except for crown corporations, and to promote them on the basis of merit rather than political patronage so that Canada has a public service based on competence rather than political favouritism. The commission also has some responsibility for training, including language training, and human-resource planning. The original Civil Service Commission was created in 1908. In 1918, the principle of merit was protected in law with the passage of the Civil Service Act, which gave the commission responsibility for the hiring and classification of government employees and for recommending pay scales. The Civil Service Act of 1961 reaffirmed the merit principle, and also gave employee associations the right to be consulted on pay and on working conditions. The Public Service Employment Act in 1967 again gave the commission responsibility for government hiring based on the merit principle, but with the introduction of collective bargaining in the public service, responsibility for negotiating pay scales and working conditions passed to the TREASURY BOARD. The Secretary of State reports to Parliament for the commission.

Public Service Staff Relations Act   Federal legislation that, since 1967, has given federal employees the right to collective bargaining and the right to strike. The act sets out the conditions under which collective bargaining takes place; these rights are not as broad as those available to industries covered by the CANADA LABOUR CODE. Bargaining is limited to pay scales, hours of work, vacations, and matters related to these. Under the act, bargaining units must indicate whether they want the right to strike if negotiations reach a stalemate, or whether they want arbitration.

Public Service Staff Relations Board   A labour-relations board created in

1967 by the Public Service Staff Relations Act to determine public-service bargaining units, to certify bargaining agents, to handle grievances and other complaints of unfair labour practices, and to supervise collective bargaining in the public service. It includes a pay-research bureau, which collects information on pay and employment conditions in Canada that can be used by both sides in collective bargaining as objective information. The board also administers the application of health and safety requirements under the CANADA LABOUR CODE where it applies to employees in the federal public service.

public utility A corporation, often government owned but sometimes privately owned, that provides an essential good or service to the public, usually under monopoly conditions. Examples include the provincial power companies, telephone companies, cable television, local transit services, and, in some instances, pipelines. Prices charged by public utilities are usually regulated. Provincial hydro companies, for example, may have to get approval for rate increases from provincial energy boards. Some utilities — for example, Bell Canada — are subject to a regulated UTILITY RATE OF RETURN, while others, such as cable operators, have had to get government approval for rate increases; today, cable TV companies are not regulated.

public welfare **1.** Income maintenance and other programs of public support to the needy. **2.** A more general term that refers to the welfare of society as a whole, as opposed to the interests of a special group.

public works Public infrastructure projects provided by government to meet the economic, social, or cultural needs of the nation, province, or community. Examples include airports, harbours, highways, bridges, theatre centres, hospitals, schools, universities, public housing, subways, government office buildings, and research laboratories. While such works are undertaken according to need and the financial resources of government, they can be accelerated during periods of recession, as a countercyclical measure; they provide jobs, boost demand for building materials, and, through the MULTIPLIER effect, generate economic activity throughout the economy. Similarly, during periods of full employment, it may make sense for government to delay public works and thus reduce the level of demand in the economy.

Public Works Canada One of the first government departments to be established at the time of Confederation, it is the principal construction and real-estate manager for the federal government and its agencies. It supervises government construction projects, manages government buildings and other property, arranges the leasing of commercial buildings for the government, and plans future government property needs, including the need for office space.

pump priming Using government spending on public projects to stimulate the economy and to create jobs.

purchase and resale agreements Agreements under which the BANK OF CANADA provides short-term liquidity to a designated group of investment dealers or jobbers. If unable to find financing at the BANK RATE or lower in the market, then dealers can arrange to sell securities to the Bank of Canada with an agreement to repurchase them at a later date. Since 1980, the rate charged by the Bank of Canada has been the Bank Rate. *See also* SPECIAL PURCHASE AND RESALE AGREEMENTS.

purchase fund   A fund established within a company to buy its outstanding preferred shares, bonds, or other debt if the price falls below a level set by the company.

purchasing power   1. Money in the hands of consumers, or credit available to them to purchase goods and services. In times of recession, a government may cut taxes to increase the purchasing power of consumers, and thus raise the level of demand in the economy. In turn, this should lead to increased investment by business, as rising consumer demand pushes industrial production closer to full capacity. Conversely, purchasing power may be curbed during periods of full employment and rising inflation by increasing taxes. **2.** The physical volume of goods and services that a Canadian dollar can buy. As inflation increases, the purchasing power of the dollar — or any other monetary unit — declines.

purchasing-power parity exchange rate The exchange rate between two currencies that equalizes the purchasing powers of the two currencies for a similar basket of goods and services in each country. This method of exchange-rate calculation permits intercountry comparisons of GROSS DOMESTIC PRODUCT and its expenditure component on more relevant terms. The ORGANIZATION FOR ECONOMIC CO-OPERATION AND DEVELOPMENT publishes periodic estimates of purchasing-power parity exchange rates. Various studies have suggested that Canada's purchasing-power parity exchange rate should be about 80 U.S. cents per Canadian dollar. That would mean that US$1,000 would have the same purchasing power as C$1,250.

purchasing power parity theory The theory that exchange rates between two currencies adjust for differences in inflation to achieve equilibrium and reflect their real relative purchasing powers. If the Canadian dollar at 80 U.S. cents would buy the same basket of goods and services as US$1 in the United States, then equilibrium and purchasing-power parity would exist. But if the US$1 buys more in the United States than the 80-cent Canadian dollar buys in Canada, it would make sense for Canadian consumers to convert their Canadian dollars to American dollars and do their shopping in the United States. In theory, the move of Canadian consumers into the U.S. market would, through the additional demand, lead to higher prices in the United States while lowering them in Canada, forcing an adjustment in the Canadian dollar exchange rate until equilibrium or purchasing-power parity had been restored. However, the theory is questionable not only because many goods and services are not tradeable, such as housing and public services, but also because exchange rates are determined in foreign exchange markets through the supply and demand for currencies.

pure interest   The actual rate of interest paid for the use of someone else's capital, after deducting the administrative and paperwork costs of the loan and the premium charged to cover the risk of default or loss. It is a theoretical concept used in economic analysis.

put   A contract that gives the holder the right to sell a specified number of shares, commodities, or financial instruments during a specified period of time at an agreed price, to someone who has agreed that he will buy the shares; in return, the holder of the put pays a fee to the would-be buyer of the shares for the privilege, whether or not he ever exercises the option to sell. Puts may be written for anywhere between 30 days and six months and, like the direct sale and purchase of shares, are arranged through stockbrokers. A person purchasing a put option does so because he expects a decline in the value of the shares, commodities, or financial instruments during the life of the put. *See also* CALL, OPTION, STRADDLE.

pyramid selling   A method of selling in which agents or salespeople pay a fee to participate, and earn money by finding and charging others to participate as salespeople. Salespeople, in addition to paying a hefty fee to participate, are usually also required to purchase a minimum quota of goods even before they have made any sales. Pyramid selling is, generally speaking, a dubious and often fraudulent form of enterprise that employs high-pressure tactics and misleading claims to persuade people to pay money for the privilege of becoming salespeople. Federal and provincial laws restrict such enterprises. For example, Ontario's Pyramidic Sales Repeal Act licenses companies engaged in pyramidal selling, and stipulates that no more than 10 percent of any investment by an individual in a sales plan can be used as a finder's fee or other such benefit for the other participants.

Q theory of investment The theory developed by economist James TOBIN that states that the stock-market value of a company helps determine whether to make new capital investment. Q is the stock-market value of the firm divided by the replacement cost of the capital of the firm, with the replacement cost being the price that would have to be paid to purchase the firm's plant and equipment in the output market. If the firm has a stock-market value of $200 million and the replacement cost of its capital is $150 million, then Q = 1.33. Q shows the cost of acquiring the firm through financial markets as opposed to the cost of purchasing the firm's capital in the output market. When Q is greater than 1, Tobin argued, then capital investment should be high; but when it is less than 1, it should be low, because it is cheaper to buy another company than to make fresh capital investment.

quadrilateral trade ministers (Quad) Periodic meetings of the U.S. Trade Representative, Japan's Minister of International Trade and Industry, the European Community's Commissioner for External Relations, and Canada's Minister of International Trade to discuss world trade issues.

qualifying share A single share or small number of shares owned by a person serving as a director of a corporation. Ownership of at least one share is necessary if a person is to serve as a company director.

quality control The inspection and testing of products off the assembly line to make sure that product standards are being met along with efforts to improve the production process and training of workers to achieve high quality and reduce or eliminate defective products. Almost all firms have quality-control inspectors who systematically examine the firm's production, to ensure that the expected level of quality is being maintained by the firm's employees. *See also* TOTAL QUALITY MANAGEMENT.

quality of life A concept of standard of living that includes material and non-material well-being. Attempts have been made to measure quality of life — through the development of SOCIAL INDICATORS, for example. However, it remains a highly subjective and thus extremely difficult concept to measure. It includes the quality of health, the choice of consumer goods and services, accessibility to education and employment, and the state of the environment. What is known is that, with rising incomes, people are more likely to take non-economic factors into account — by taking leisure time instead of working overtime, for example, or by blocking commercial development to preserve a landscape or create a park. *See also* HUMAN-DEVELOPMENT INDEX.

quantity theory of money and prices A theory that explains the level of prices and pace of economic activity in terms of the relationship between the level of output and the money supply. The level of inflation or prices is directly linked to changes in the supply of money. Although the theory dates back to the CLASSICAL ECONOMISTS and was subsequently elaborated on by Irving Fisher in 1911, it is associated today with Milton FRIEDMAN of the University of Chicago, and the MONETARIST SCHOOL, which argues that the way to control inflation and sustain a high level of economic activity is to control the supply of money.

The theory can be expressed in mathematical terms as the equation of exchange: total supply in the economy, expressed as the total supply of money, multiplied by the velocity of money, equals total demand in the economy, expressed as total physical output or REAL GROSS DOMESTIC PRODUCT (GDP) multiplied by the price level. Where M is the money supply and V the velocity of money, P the average price level and T the real GDP or number of transactions in the economy, $MV = PT$. The velocity of money, which depends on the efficiency of the banking system and on the spending and saving habits of the population, is assumed to be constant in the short run. The level of output in the economy under full-employment conditions is also assumed to be fixed in the short run. Thus, the variables in the short run are the supply of money and the price level. According to the theory, therefore, only increases in money supply will lead to inflation as the economy approaches full employment. Similarly, a decline in the money supply can lead to deflation.

quarterly report 1. A financial statement issued by a public corporation every three months to keep shareholders up to date on its performance. These reports are unaudited and contain mainly EARNINGS STATEMENT rather than BALANCE SHEET information. Timely quarterly reports are required by securities commissions for publicly traded companies. 2. Quarterly statistics under the SYSTEM OF NATIONAL ACCOUNTS — for example, on the GROSS DOMESTIC PRODUCT, BALANCE OF PAYMENTS, and FINANCIAL FLOWS — published by Statistics Canada.

quasi-rent Although rent is normally associated with land and the resources contained on the land, the British economist ALFRED MARSHALL argued that firms also earn a quasi-rent or extra profit on their other factors of production when demand exceeds supply and there is a delay in expanding productive capacity in an industry. Since it takes time to construct new buildings, heavy engineering works, and other productive facilities, there is a period of time during which existing producers can raise prices without affecting demand. This extra profit they earn is a rent they can exact from their customers. It is called a quasi-rent because it should be temporary, ending when productive capacity in the industry has been expanded to meet consumer demand under normal pricing and profit conditions.

Quebec Deposit Insurance Board   A provincial agency responsible for licensing financial institutions (other than banks) that accept deposits, and for insuring customer deposits. It is also a lender of last resort to provincial trust and mortgage-loan companies and caisses populaires. The board may borrow funds in turn from the CANADA DEPOSIT INSURANCE CORPORATION.

Quebec Pension Plan (QPP)   The Quebec equivalent of the CANADA PENSION PLAN, established in 1965. It is fully portable with the Canada Pension Plan and offers similar benefits. Its investment policy differs, however. While Canada Pension Plan funds are lent to the provinces at the rate of interest paid on outstanding government bonds, Quebec Pension Plan funds are deposited with the Quebec Deposit and Investment Fund, and are used to help develop the industrial base of the province. Its main investments are government bonds, but the investment fund also purchases the bonds, shares, and mortgages of Quebec businesses.

Quebec Solidarity Fund   A special investment fund, organized by the Quebec labour movement, and approved by the Quebec legislature in June, 1983. The savings of members of the Fédération des travailleurs et travailleuses du Québec (FTQ) and of the Quebec public were to be used to create, maintain, or protect jobs in Quebec businesses, mainly in the small and medium sector. A purchaser of shares in the fund gets a 20 percent tax credit in Quebec on the amount invested and a similar credit at the federal level. In addition, the shares qualify for invest-

ment in a REGISTERED RETIREMENT SAVINGS PLAN, so an additional tax saving is available. In all enterprises in which an investment is made, employees receive basic economic training to help them understand their company's financial statements. The fund must invest 60 percent of each year's assets in development capital in small and medium businesses, with a limit of 5 percent of its capital in any single business. The fund also places a director on the board of each company in which it invests. In 1991, the fund accounted for 23 percent of venture capital in Canada and 43 percent of Quebec. In 1993, it had 188,000 shareholders and at the end of 1992, about $615 million in assets.

Quebec stock savings plan   An incentive first introduced in the Quebec March, 1979, budget for Quebec taxpayers to invest in the shares of Quebec-based businesses. It was designed to make up for the lack of venture capital and equity financing for Quebec companies and to provide a means of reducing the high level of personal income tax for individuals in the top income trackets. Quebec taxpayers may deduct the adjusted cost of these shares from their taxable income to a maximum of 10 percent of their total income. Total income is the net income amount on a Quebec provincial income tax return minus the capital gains exemption exercised during the year. Taxpayers are allowed to deduct 100 percent of the cost of shares in growth companies with assets of $2 million to $250 million, 75 percent of the cost of shares in medium-size companies with assets between $250 million and $1 billion, 50 percent of the cost of shares in companies with assets between $1 billion and $2.5 billion, and receive no deductions for purchases of shares in companies with assets in excess of $2.5 billion. They can also deduct 150 percent of the cost of shares in regional venture capital corporations.

queuing theory A mathematical technique that is used to help management decide the level of service to provide in a facility where customers or users expect to be treated on a first-come-first-served basis — for example, the number of loading gates at an airport, the number of check-out counters at a supermarket, or the number of turnstiles in a subway station. While a system that did not provide for some queuing during periods of peak use would probably be unjustifiably expensive, queuing theory helps management to find ways to keep queues to a minimum, and to most effectively move people, planes, or ships in a seaway or canal.

quick asset An asset that is readily convertible into cash at roughly its face value or book value, such as a certificate of deposit or bond, accounts receivable, or cash itself. Such assets are listed as CURRENT ASSETS and are usually considered to include all current assets other than inventories.

quick ratio *See* ACID-TEST RATIO.

quiet enjoyment The continuous use and possession of one's property without interruption due to trespass, pollution, noise, or construction that eliminates sunlight or has some other harmful effect.

quota A government regulation to limit the volume of imports, exports, production, or consumption. Quotas may be expressed as a percentage of a base period or as an actual number. Import quotas are often adopted as a protectionist device to protect local industry from foreign competition; sometimes they are imposed directly by the importing country, and sometimes they are negotiated with exporting countries, which impose "voluntary" export quotas. Quotas may also be imposed on the export of a commodity in short supply or on domestic consumption during a shortage. In international trade, the use of quotas is gradually being restricted and controlled through changes in GENERAL AGREEMENT ON TARIFFS AND TRADE rules. Quotas are also imposed by FARM MARKETING BOARDS on the output of farmers, and Canada's SUPPLY-MANAGEMENT SYSTEM for eggs, poultry, and dairy products depends on import quotas on these products. The MULTIFIBRE ARRANGEMENT allows Canada to impose quotas on the import of clothing and textiles from developing countries. Rationing is another form of quota, since it establishes a limit on the amount of consumption.

quotation **1.** The closing price for a share listed on a stock exchange, a commodity on a commodity market, or a bond on a bond market. **2.** During the course of the trading day, the highest bid to buy and the lowest offer to sell. Quotations are published daily in the financial pages of newspapers.

quoted company A company whose shares are traded on a stock exchange or over-the-counter market.

R

RIO Project (Reshaping the International Order Project) A study sponsored, in 1974, by the CLUB OF ROME and the Dutch government to describe "what new international order should be recommended to the world's statesmen and social groups so as to meet, to the extent practically and realistically possible, the urgent needs of today's population and the probable needs of future generations." The study was headed by Jan Tinbergen, a Dutch economist and winner of the Alfred Nobel Memorial Prize for Economic Science, who assembled 21 international experts to devise a new international economic order.

The report, published in 1976, proposed an international treaty, similar to the Treaty of Rome that had established the EUROPEAN COMMUNITY, and modelled on the CHARTER OF ECONOMIC RIGHTS AND DUTIES OF STATES. This framework treaty would lay the legally binding foundation for a new set of international economic relations, and would provide a legal basis for the negotiation of the agreements needed to implement a new international economic order. The report said

that the DEVELOPING COUNTRIES must have full sovereignty over their natural resources. It also developed the concept of "the common heritage of mankind," which it took to include not only the oceans and space, but also minerals, science and technology, the means of production, and other sources of wealth. It proposed specific medium-range (1976-85) and long-range (1985-2000) policies in 9 areas: the international monetary system; income redistribution and financing of development; food production; industrialization, trade, and the international division of labour, energy, and minerals; scientific research and technological development; multinational corporations; the human environment; arms reduction; and ocean management.

raider An investor or investor group making a hostile attempt to acquire control of a company by acquiring a controlling block of shares. Under Canadian securities laws, raiders acquiring more than 5 percent of a company must declare their interest and state their intentions.

raiding   An effort by a union to persuade members of another union to switch ranks and have it certified as their new bargaining agent. Federal and provincial labour laws restrict the rights of one union to raid another to a relatively short period of time, called an open season, each year or in the life of a collective agreement; individual labour federations, such as the CANADIAN LABOUR CONGRESS, impose penalties on affiliated unions that engage in such practices unless there is clear evidence that a union is not serving its members adequately. Raiding, when it does occur, is usually launched by a union that is affiliated with a competing labour federation. A raiding union, to be certified as the new bargaining agent for a group of members, has to be able to show that it speaks for a majority of the workers and can thus have the existing bargaining agent decertified.

rally   A stock-market term indicating a firm recovery and rise in the share or bond prices after a decline.

Rand formula   A clause in a COLLECTIVE AGREEMENT under which the employer agrees to collect union dues or an amount equivalent to union dues from all employees in the bargaining unit, whether or not they are union members, during the life of the collective agreement. The formula is attributed to a 1946 decision by Mr. Justice Ivan C. Rand of the Supreme Court of Canada, during a conflict between the Ford Motor Company and its union, the United Auto Workers. Mr. Justice Rand said that the company had to make a compulsory CHECK-OFF for all employees, but that all members of the bargaining unit did not have to be members of the union. Such an arrangement is sometimes called an agency shop, as opposed to a UNION SHOP. Most collective agreements now have a Rand-type formula, and

some provinces have made the Rand formula compulsory in all collective agreements.

random sample   In market research or other types of surveys, a statistical method of choosing a sample that is representative of the population to be surveyed. The sample is selected by chance, with every member of the targeted population having an equal chance of being selected.

range   High and low prices or bids and offers for shares and bonds during a specified period of time, for example a day or a week.

rate of interest   See INTEREST RATE.

rate of return   A measure of the profitability of a business, it is the net profits of a business divided by the shareholders' equity or capital employed of the business. Profits can be defined in other ways — for example as operating profit, which excludes investment income, or as net of taxes but not depreciation. Capital can be defined to include long-term debt as well as shareholders' equity.

rate of return on invested capital   A measure of the profitability of a company that shows how well the management has used the resources at its disposal. It is calculated by dividing net earnings by the company's INVESTED CAPITAL, which consists of shareholders' equity plus long-term debt. This ratio allows the financial performance of different firms in the same or different industries to be compared.

rating   A measure of the creditworthiness of a private or public sector issuer of bonds or other securities, or of a particular security of a public or private entity by an independent rating agency. In Canada and the United States, borrowers and securities are graded from triple A down to D, which stands for an obligation in default. Ratings matter both because they determine the interest rate a security issuer must pay and because the rating determines the number of eligible buyers of a security. For example, major pension funds may be limited to triple A bonds; this means a borrower with a low rating may be limited to a relatively small market, making it harder to float large issues.

rating agency An independent company established to rate the securities and creditworthiness of public- and private-sector borrowers. There are two Canadian rating agencies: Canadian Bond Rating Service, based in Montreal, and Dominion Bond Rating Service, based in Toronto. The two big U.S. rating agencies, both based in New York, are Moody's Investors Service and Standard & Poor. Rating agencies are hired by borrowers, not lenders. Without a rating from an established rating agency, most governments, government agencies, and corporations would not be able to issue securities.

rational expectations theory The theory, developed in the United States in the 1970s, that individuals and businesses form their expectations in a rational way, so that government economic policies will have much less impact than economic models suggest. For example, if government cuts taxes or increases spending to fight a recession, individuals and firms will assume that these measures will lead to higher prices and taxes in the future, so they will add this expectation to their wage and price demands so that the effort to stimulate the economy fails. At the same time, if government reduces budget deficits, pursues long-term price stability, and withdraws from interventionist policies, then individuals and firms will see the benefits and behave accordingly. The theory pays a great

deal of attention to the issue of inflation, contending that wage demands are based on expectations of future inflation, not current inflation levels. It assumes that wages adjust more quickly than economic models assume because firms and workers are motivated by their own self-interest to obtain the most accurate information on future inflation, since an increase in wages that is too high will price the firm out of the market and lead to layoffs and low profits. Workers and firms will base their expectations on a rational view of future government policies instead of adjusting to the current rate of inflation. This allows governments to achieve price stability and full employment by persuading workers and firms that policies will be sufficiently tight to bring inflation to zero and hold it there. This is a further argument of the neoclassical school that goes beyond MONETARISM in arguing that markets are self-regulating and that government policies are largely ineffective in managing the economy. Not surprisingly, other economists challenge the notion of perfectly rational behaviour as an unrealistic assumption, just as they challenge the notion of PERFECT COMPETITION, contending that this is not the way the real world behaves but an ideal that is unachievable.

rationalization The reorganization of firms in an industry to become more competitive. The process of rationalization usually includes the closure of the least-efficient plants and mergers to achieve ECONOMIES OF SCALE in production through the remaining, most efficient plants, and to achieve sufficient size and cash-flow to support research and development and similar essential corporate activities. Rationalization usually occurs in industries where there are too many competing firms, each too small to achieve the benefits of mass-production techniques and other economies of scale, or to support product innovation and plant modernization. In Canada, it is argued, too many industries have too many producers and too many product lines so that rationalization is necessary so that they can compete against imports and produce distinctive products that are competitively priced for world markets. One explanation for the proliferation of firms in Canada is that many MULTINATIONAL CORPORATIONS have established branch plants here just to serve the Canadian market by assembling many of the products developed and designed within their parent-company operations elsewhere.

rationing The allocation of consumer goods or industrial materials in a time of shortage, to make sure that all essential needs are first met and that allocation does not depend on who can pay the highest price. Rationing may be introduced for a single commodity — say, oil — by having a government agency allocate the oil among refineries and by rating customers so that high priority is given to hospitals and homes, railways, trucking companies, and farmers, and lower priority is given to commercial enterprises and private automobiles. During the Second World War, the WARTIME PRICES AND TRADE BOARD had wide power to allocate scarce raw materials to industry for military and other essential purposes, and to ban the manufacture of certain non-essential consumer goods. The board imposed coupon rationing for meat, tea, coffee, butter, and sugar, for example. Coupons were issued to all Canadians for equal amounts of such necessities, with the coupons being required at the time of purchase. Retailers, in turn, had to turn in coupons to get new supplies. The Department of MUNITIONS AND SUPPLY rationed the sale of automobiles, trucks, tires, gasoline, steel, non-ferrous metals, rubber, chemicals, oil,

coal, wood fuel, and other raw, semi-processed, and processed materials.

raw land Land that has no services, such as water, sewers, or streets, and therefore cannot immediately be used for new housing, commercial buildings, or other such purposes.

raw material A natural or semi-processed material that is used by a manufacturer in the production of a good. For example, lumber is a raw material for a furniture company, iron ore for a steel company, or steel for a manufacturer of rail cars.

raw materials price index An index of prices paid by Canadians to purchase various commodities. A raw material is either a commodity sold for the first time after being extracted or a recycled product, such as scrap metal, that is a substitute for a raw material. About 80 commodities, grouped into seven major categories, are listed in a composite index as part of Statistics Canada's monthly *Industry Price Indexes* (publication 62-001). The seven categories are mineral fuels, vegetable products, animals and animal products, wood, ferrous metals, non-ferrous metals, and non-metallic minerals.

reaction A downturn in stock or bond markets following an upsurge in prices.

real-business-cycle theory The theory that technology shocks rather than demand shocks or policy shocks explain fluctuations in the economy. *See also* KONDRATIEFF WAVE.

real estate Property, such as land and buildings, that is not movable. *See also* CHATTEL.

real-estate board An association of real-estate brokers in a community that supervises the activities of brokers and organizes and oversees co-operative services, such as the MULTIPLE-LISTING SERVICE. Until 1976, when amendments to the Combines Investigation Act extended competition policy to services, real-estate boards also fixed commission rates charged by member brokers on the sale of land and buildings.

real-estate broker A person who buys and sells land and buildings on behalf of buyers and sellers, and who also arranges the leasing of land and buildings.

real gross domestic product The volume of national output after deducting inflation to base-year prices — currently 1986 prices. When growth rates for the economy are discussed, or set out in a federal budget for example, it is the rate of growth in real gross domestic product that matters since it is this figure that shows the real changes as opposed to changes reflecting inflation. Statistics Canada publishes quarterly and annual data in its NATIONAL INCOME AND EXPENDITURE ACCOUNTS (publication 13-001).

real gross domestic product at factor cost A monthly report by Statistics Canada on the output in the economy by a range of goods-producing and service-producing industries, the production by the business sector and the non-business sector, and the volume of industrial production (publication 15-001). Output is measured in 1986 dollars for the total economy, for business sector goods and business sector services, non-business sector goods and non-business sector services, and by agriculture, mining, fishing and forestry, manufacturing, construction, transportation, communication, finance, insurance and real estate, community, business and personal services, wholesale and retail trade, utilities, and government services. The monthly numbers closely track GROSS DOMESTIC PRODUCT and are a good indicator of how well the economy is performing.

real growth The growth of the economy, or a sector of the economy, after the money-value of the increase is deflated by the amount of inflation during the same period. It gives a true picture of the growth in output, as opposed to illusory growth represented simply by inflation. In a given year, nominal growth of the economy could be 6 percent, but after adjusting for inflation of 2.5 percent the real growth would be 3.5 percent. When talking about economic growth, economists mean real growth and not current money-value or nominal growth.

real interest rate The rate of interest after deducting inflation from the nominal rate. This reflects the real return to a lender or the real cost to a borrower. The real interest rate indicates the volume of goods that can be purchased in the future for a given amount of savings today; nominal interest rates measure the amount of money that will be obtained in the future for a given amount of savings today without reference to its future purchasing power. While nominal interest rates are always positive, real interest rates can be negative, as they were in Canada during part of the 1970s.

real return bond A special type of bond first issued by the federal government in November, 1991. The return is linked to changes in the CONSUMER PRICE INDEX. The first issue, of $700 million, was for a 30-year term with a real coupon rate of 4.25 percent plus the rate of inflation measured by the consumer price index.

real wages The actual purchasing power of wages, as opposed to money or nominal wages. If wages are increased 5 percent but inflation also increases 5 percent, then real wages have not changed at all. If wages increased 5 percent but inflation increased 7 percent, then real wages, which translates to purchasing power, have actually declined; similarly, a 5 percent wage increase when inflation is 3 percent means that real wages have increased.

reallocation of resources   In an economy, a change in the way some resources are used. For example, in social policy, government spending could shift from passive measures that simply provide income support to individuals to an active policy that uses the same resources to help train and equip individuals to become gainfully employed. Likewise, a government could reduce overall social spending and divert resources to education and research and development. On a larger scale, government could cut back its overall level of activity, freeing up more resources for the private sector.

realize   To sell an asset in order to receive the gain in its value.

reasonable man   A person who never does anything without first considering the effect of an act or failure to act on other persons; he or she is always aware of the need to consider the welfare of others. In negligence cases, the defendant's behaviour is usually compared with the behaviour one would expect from a reasonable man. *See also* PRUDENT-MAN RULE.

rebate   The return of part of the payment already made for a good or service. Rebates may be offered for high-volume purchases, prompt payment, or other such reasons. Under Canadian law, the same rebate must be offered to all customers in the same circumstances. *See also* DISCOUNT, which is deducted before the account is paid.

receipt   A written document that shows that delivered goods have been received, a service has been rendered, or payment has been made.

receiver   A person either appointed by a court or by a creditor to take temporary charge of a business and operate it, until the business is either liquidated or wound up and the creditors paid off, or until the owners can arrange new financing to pay off creditors. The receiver's job includes making sure that the records of the business are maintained, and making an inventory of the firm's assets. *See also* TRUSTEE.

Receiver-General of Canada   The chief financial officer of the federal government, who receives all revenues of the government and deposits them in the CONSOLIDATED REVENUE FUND. Each government payment, no matter how small, must be authorized by a specific law of Parliament (such as, say, the GUARANTEED-INCOME SUPPLEMENT legislation), or by annual APPROPRIATION ACTS, which authorize cabinet ministers or their deputies to make requisitions for payment to the receiver-general. He or she is usually the Minister of SUPPLY AND SERVICES.

receivership   The status of a firm whose affairs have been put in the hands of a receiver because it is unable to pay its bills and other obligations.

recession   The down side or contraction phase of the business cycle. A recession is technically a period of declining economic activity, characterized by two consecutive quarters showing a reduction in real gross domestic product. The term is more generally used to describe weak economic activity and increased unemployment, even though there may still be slight economic growth. *See also* RECOVERY.

reciprocal-trade agreement An agreement between two nations, giving each other special and equal tariff and other trade concessions, or an agreement among a larger number of nations, giving one another tariff and trade agreements of approximately equal value. The most important reciprocal-trade agreement is the GENERAL AGREEMENT ON TARIFFS AND TRADE (GATT). The CANADA-UNITED STATES FREE TRADE AGREEMENT and the NORTH AMERICAN FREE TRADE AGREEMENT are also reciprocal-trade agreements. Canada has reciprocal-trade agreements with Australia and New Zealand, and the CANADA-UNITED STATES AUTOMOTIVE PRODUCTS AGREEMENT may also be considered a form of reciprocal-trade agreement. Canada and the United States had a reciprocal-trade agreement from 1854 to 1866 that was abrogated by the United States; a new reciprocity agreement was proposed in 1911, but, while it was passed by the U.S. Congress, it was turned down by Canada after a general election that saw the government of Sir Wilfrid Laurier, who had proposed the agreement, defeated by that of Sir Robert Borden. During the 1920s and the 1930s, Canada negotiated reciprocal-trade agreements with many of its trading partners, including Britain and, following passage by the U.S. Congress in 1934 of the Reciprocal Trade Agreements Act, with the United States. After the end of the Second World War, most nations abandoned the negotiation of bilateral reciprocal-trade agreements and focused on the GATT and on regional free-trade or common-market arrangements instead. *See also* OTTAWA AGREEMENTS.

reciprocity The exchange of tariff reductions and other trade concessions by one nation for similar concessions from another. Trade negotiators seek a balance of concessions or equivalence of advantages, so that the value of tariff or other concessions by one country in one area for other countries is roughly equal to the advantages it will gain from concessions by other countries in another area. However, reciprocity can also mean that one country will only grant a right to another country — for example, the right of another country's banks to receive NATIONAL TREATMENT — if the other country grants the identical rights to the first country.

reconstruction A wide series of measures adopted in 1944 and 1945 to convert the Canadian economy to peacetime activities and to ensure high levels of employment and stable prices following the Second World War. The federal government feared that, without major planning and intervention, the economy might return to the GREAT DEPRESSION levels of unemployment that had existed before the Second World War; it also feared that post-war shortages of necessities might lead to severe inflation. In 1944, the federal government embarked on a number of steps to ease the transition from a wartime economy to a peacetime economy. These included the following: creation of federal and federal-provincial planning committees; passage of the Agricultural Prices Support Act and the Fisheries Prices Support Act to control agricultural and fisheries prices; passage of a new NATIONAL HOUSING ACT to stimulate post-war housing construction; establishment of the Export Credits Insurance Corporation (now the EXPORT DEVELOPMENT CORPORATION) to finance export trade; establishment of the Industrial Development Bank (now the FEDERAL BUSINESS DEVELOPMENT BANK) to finance business expansion; establishment of the Department of NATIONAL HEALTH AND WELFARE (now HEALTH AND WELFARE) to improve social welfare for Canadians by implementing such programs as FAMILY ALLOWANCES; establishment of the Department of

Veterans Affairs, to take charge of the re-establishment in civilian life of Canadians who had served in the armed forces, or otherwise to care for them; and the creation of the Department of RECONSTRUCTION, to take charge of post-war programs to convert the economy back to peacetime activities, to stimulate economic growth, and to control prices. The following year, the federal government spelled out a broad program of measures to achieve full employment and stable prices in its WHITE PAPER ON EMPLOYMENT AND INCOME. Its proposals formed the basis for future government fiscal policies and other policies to promote economic growth and employment while maintaining price stability.

Reconstruction, Department of A federal government department created in June, 1944, to take charge of converting Canada's economy from its wartime footing to peacetime activities, while averting a return to the high unemployment of pre-war Canada and ensuring that post-war shortages did not lead to rapid inflation. The responsibilities of the department were as follows: to determine the employment needs of Canadians being demobilized from the armed forces or laid off from war-related industries as the Second World War drew to an end, and to outline the opportunities to provide new jobs for them; to co-ordinate the activities of other government departments and agencies so that the transition to a peacetime economy occurred as smoothly as possible; and to devise plans for industrial development and conversion, public works, housing and urban planning, industrial research and development, and the development of Canada's natural resources.

The department was organized into several divisions. The industrial-reconversion division helped industry to convert plants developed for war purposes to peacetime uses, and to find the most efficient post-war use of pre-war plants, while trying to ensure a normal flow of employment and income. The surplus-war-assets division advised the government on policies to follow in disposing of a huge inventory of war assets, with the War Assets Corporation actually disposing of the assets. The industrial-research division developed a technical- and scientific-information service for industry, promoted research and development activities, including specific projects to help solve particular industrial and development problems, and co-ordinated the government's long-term scientific programs. The NATIONAL RESEARCH COUNCIL was also made responsible to the Minister of Reconstruction. The depreciation-allowances division advised the Minister of National Revenue on the level of incentive depreciation rates that should be granted for specific new capital spending by industry on plant and equipment. The co-ordinator of controls, a division of the department, advised the government on when specific wartime controls could be lifted without causing inflation due to shortages. The public-works division worked with provincial and municipal governments to help plan and carry out needed public-works projects that would create jobs and help improve the country's infrastructure. The natural-resources-development division, working with the provinces, planned hydro-electric, forestry, and mining projects, and the government-assistance programs needed to see that such projects were carried out. The civil-aviation division promoted the use of civil aviation to improve the economic well-being of the country. The liaison division worked with other federal departments, such as Trade and Commerce (now INDUSTRY, SCIENCE AND TECHNOLOGY) and LABOUR, and with provincial planning councils established for reconstruction purposes. The department, renamed Reconstruction and Supply in 1946, was wound up in 1949.

recovery   The up side or expansion phase of the business cycle, reflecting an increase in economic activity as the economy moves out of its recession or trough. It is characterized by increased demand and employment, which sets the stage for increased investment and further increases in economic growth and employment.

recycling   1. The investment of surplus funds, from countries with strong balance-of-payments surpluses, in countries with serious balance-of-payments deficits, or in commercial money markets. For example, the surplus funds or PETRODOLLARS of such oil-rich nations as Saudi Arabia, Kuwait, and the Persian Gulf emirates in the 1970s were recycled through the EUROCURRENCY MARKET into bonds and other securities issued by deficit nations, many of them LESS-DEVELOPED COUNTRIES, into corporate bonds and shares, or into U.S.-government TREASURY BILLS. Similarly, the surplus oil and gas royalty income of Alberta, through its Heritage Savings Trust Fund, was reinvested in bonds and other securities issued by other governments in Canada in the late 1970s and early 1980s. More recently, the huge current-account surplus of Japan has been recycled into Canadian, U.S., and other foreign-debt securities to finance government deficits in these countries. **2.** The reuse of materials after they are no longer needed for their original purpose. For example, old newspapers and other wastepaper products can be converted into new paper products and aluminum soft-drink cans can be recycled into aluminum that can be used again for other purposes.

redeemable bond   A bond, also known as a callable bond, that can be paid off before maturity by the issuer; the reasons for doing so would be either to take advantage of lower interest rates or to eliminate interest costs. Most government and corporate bonds are redeemable.

redeemable preferred share   A preferred share that may be recalled and paid off by the issuing corporation. Most preferred shares are redeemable.

redemption   The paying off of outstanding bonds or other debt securities, usually for cash but sometimes for new securities, by the issuer. This occurs either on the redemption date specified on the bond or other security, or at some earlier date if the bond or other security is redeemable. *See also* REDEEMABLE BOND, REDEEMABLE PREFERRED SHARE.

redemption price   The price at which a bond or other financial security may be called or redeemed by the issuer prior to the date of maturity.

redistribution of income   Measures adopted by the federal or provincial governments to reduce inequalities in income among Canadians. These policies include direct government spending to ensure free education, accessible health care for all regardless of income, adequate housing, a minimum income (through welfare payments, unemployment insurance, or other programs) to purchase the necessities of life, and a progressive INCOME TAX system based on ability to pay. Income is also redistributed regionally through EQUALIZATION PAYMENTS.

reducing balance   The depreciation of an asset by a fixed percentage each year; for example, a $10,000 machine may be depreciated 20 percent a year, so that for the first year it is depreciated by $2,000, the second year by 20 percent of $8,000, or $1,600, and so forth. *See also* STRAIGHT-LINE DE-PRECIATION, ACCELERATED DEPRECIATION.

redundancy   A term used in government and some business enterprises to indicate the elimination of a job because the function is no longer required. It can result from changing technology, from cancellation of a program or product, or from a shift in demand.

re-export   The export of manufactured products or commodities that have been imported, without any significant processing or other transformation. For example, a large proportion of exports from Hong Kong really consist of re-exports in the form of goods that have been imported into Hong Kong from southern China and then shipped from Hong Kong to other countries such as Canada, with perhaps some additional packaging or labelling in Hong Kong.

refinancing   **1.** The issuing of new bonds or other securities by a government or corporation, with the proceeds being used to retire an existing bond or other security. Sometimes the refinancing may be accomplished by exchanging a new security for an outstanding security. *See*, for example, the CONVERSION LOAN OF 1958. The reasons for refinancing may include a reduction in interest costs, if prevailing rates are lower than those of the outstanding securities, or the extension of the maturity of the outstanding debt. Thus refinancing may occur to roll over an existing debt that is maturing or to replace one form of debt, for example, short-term securities, with long-term bonds or PREFERRED SHARES. **2.** In debt restructuring, an extension of the maturity of existing debt, a renegotiation of interest rates, or the provision of additional debt, or some combination of all of these.

reflation   The adoption of expansionary economic policies to increase aggregate demand and thereby stimulate business activity to achieve full employment. This assumes there is an output gap and therefore spare capacity in the economy that can be utilized. Monetarist critics contend that these policies can only lead to an increase in the rate of inflation if the aggregate demand is achieved by an increase in the money supply or to crowding out of business investment if the stimulus is financed by government borrowing. Keynesians respond that the monetarist assumption that markets work efficiently and that therefore there is no output gap is fundamentally wrong.

reforestation   The replanting of harvested forests by the pulp and paper and lumber companies, or by provincial agencies, to ensure future supplies. Reforestation is usually a condition of a timber licence, although provincial governments may subsidize replanting costs.

refusal to deal   A reviewable form of behaviour by the COMPETITION TRIBUNAL where the refusal by a supplier of a good or service to sell to another company may mean that company is substantially affected or precluded from carrying on a business due to its inability to obtain adequate supplies because of insufficient competition among suppliers. The tribunal may issue an order to a supplier or group of suppliers to accept the company as a customer on the usual trade terms.

regional development   Policies to improve economic conditions in parts of a country that suffer from chronically high unemployment and a general economic performance well below that of the country as a whole. Canada has had such policies in varying degrees almost since Confederation, although they have become much more significant since the start of the 1960s. Typical regional development policies include the following: direct government grants to develop INFRASTRUCTURE, such as roads, power plants, water-supply systems, transportation, and industrial parks in slow-growth regions; government grants to companies locating in designated regions; more generous tax rates to corporations investing in slow-growth regions; and government participation, as a minority equity partner or provider of low-cost loans, through provincial development corporations. The federal government also provides EQUALIZATION PAYMENTS to provinces with weaker tax bases. In 1969, a Department of Regional Economic Expansion was created to direct federal regional-development efforts. The department was later merged into a new Department of Regional and Industrial Expansion. But by the start of the 1990s, no department had overall responsibility. Atlantic activities were run out of the ATLANTIC CANADA OPPORTUNITIES AGENCY and western Canada activities out of the Western Diversification Fund. Quebec and Ontario programs were run out of the Department of INDUSTRY, SCIENCE, AND TECHNOLOGY, although a separate Quebec minister is responsible for Quebec projects. The CONSTITUTION ACT, 1982, commits Canada to the goal of regional development and the principle of equalization payments. *See also* Department of REGIONAL ECONOMIC EXPANSION.

regional development bank A bank established by donor and recipient countries to provide market-rate loans for capital and other projects, concessional financing to some recipient countries for certain types of capital projects or programs, and technical assistance. Canada is an investor in the ASIAN DEVELOPMENT BANK, the AFRICAN DEVELOPMENT BANK, the INTER-AMERICAN DEVELOPMENT BANK, the CARIBBEAN DEVELOPMENT BANK, and the EUROPEAN BANK FOR RECONSTRUCTION AND DEVELOPMENT. Canada is also an investor in the WORLD BANK.

regional trading bloc A group of nations organized together in a regional free-trade zone, common market, customs union, or economic and political union whose RULES OF ORIGIN and other regulations setting out the degree of preferential access enjoyed by member countries within the grouping clearly limit access to the market by countries outside the free-trade zone, common market, or other regional grouping. There is some concern that the CANADA-UNITED STATES FREE TRADE AGREEMENT, the NORTH AMERICAN FREE TRADE AGREEMENT, and the EUROPEAN COMMUNITY will force Asian countries to establish a similar grouping and that these blocs, centred in the Americas, Europe, and Asia will each become protectionist, will bring about a decline in world trade and economic growth, and will lead to escalating conflicts in trade and other conflicts between the three regions. There is also concern that many countries, including some of the poorest countries, will find themselves outside any of the blocs. The alternative is a strong multilateral trading system under the GENERAL AGREEMENT ON TARIFFS AND TRADES (GATT) that embraces all GATT members in a non-discriminatory trading system based on the principle of MOST-FAVOURED NATION.

registered home-ownership savings plan (RHOSP) A tax-incentive plan to encourage Canadians to save toward downpayments to buy their own homes. To qualify for the tax advantage, which permits a taxpayer to save and deduct $1,000 a year to a lifetime maximum of $10,000 from taxable income, an individual must be at least 18, not previously have benefited from a RHOSP, and not own nor have a spouse who owns a home. If the proceeds of a RHOSP are invested in a home, they are not taxable — if not, they are. RHOSPs are trusts managed by Canadian trust companies, although the trust companies may authorize other financial institutions, such as banks, credit unions, and caisses populaires, to act as selling agents. An RHOSP is an example of a TAX SHELTER.

registered industrial accountant (RIA) An accountant trained specifically for internal-management accounting rather than for public practice. An RIA is trained to design and operate accounting systems in business and government and to provide management with the information it needs to operate the business or government department. An RIA is an accountant who has met the professional standards of the Society of Management Accountants.

registered representative A stockbroker or other sales representative employed by a securities firm. The employee must be registered with a provincial securities commission in the province of employment. A registered representative who breaks the rules of a provincial securities commission can be fined or lose his or her right to sell securities either for a limited period of time or permanently.

registered retirement investment fund (RRIF) A fund set up by a financial institution or self-directed by an individual to pay out income from capital accumulated up to age 71 in a REGISTERED RETIREMENT SAVINGS PLAN. A minimum amount must be paid out from the RRIF each year, starting at 7.38 percent of the RRIF's assets at age 71, rising to 8.75 percent at age 80, 13.62 percent at age 90, and 20 percent at age 90 or older.

registered retirement savings plan (RRSP) A tax-deferral scheme that encourages Canadians to save for their retirement. Money set aside is not taxed as long as it remains in the plan. Most financial institutions, such as banks, trust companies, life-insurance companies, and even mutual fund companies, offer managed RRSPs, but individuals are also permitted to set up their own self-directed RRSP with a financial institution. Individuals who do not belong to employer pension plans may invest up to 18 percent of the previous year's earned income, up to a specified dollar limit — $12,500 in 1993, rising to $15,500 in 1996. Individuals who are members of REGISTERED PENSION PLANS can also contribute up to 18 percent of the previous year's earned income minus a pension adjustment, which is the combination of the employee and employer contributions to their pension plan. Individuals are also allowed to carry forward for seven years any unused portion of their allowable RRSP investment. No contributions can be made past age 71, and individuals must begin receiving a retirement income from their RRSP by December 31 of the year in which they turn 71. The amount invested each year is deductible from taxable income, with the tax deferred until the purchaser starts to receive benefits on retirement; this will probably be at a lower tax rate, since a person's income will usually be lower on retirement. When holders of RRSPs mature their RRSPs at age 71, they have three options: receive an ANNUITY that pays a regular income based on the accumulated principle; transfer the funds into a REGISTERED RETIREMENT INVESTMENT FUND from which periodic income is received; or receive a lump-sum payment after paying the necessary tax.

registered security A bond, share, or other security that is registered in the name of its owner on the books of a company or government agency, and that can only be transferred to a new owner when the existing owner endorses the bond, share certificate, or other security.

registered trademark   A TRADEMARK registered or recorded in the Trademarks Office of the Bureau of Intellectual Property in the Department of CONSUMER AND CORPORATE AFFAIRS.

registrar   A trust company or other agent designated by a corporation, that oversees the sale and purchase of the corporation's shares. The registrar receives cancelled share certificates from sellers of shares, records, through the corporation's TRANSFER AGENT, the new share certificates in the name of the new owner, makes sure that all shares are accounted for, and makes sure that the number of shares registered tallies with the number that is supposed to be OUTSTANDING.

registration   The filing of a PROSPECTUS or other form of notification for a new issue of shares or bonds or the sale of outstanding securities by a controlling shareholder with a provincial SECURITIES COMMISSION in the province or provinces in which they are to be sold to the public.

registry   A public record of ownership of land, buildings, shipping, shares, bonds, or other major assets, or of certain types of claims against assets, such as mortgages or chattel mortgages. Registries are maintained by municipalities or provinces for land and buildings, by corporations for shareholders and owners of bonds, and by national governments for shipping and aircraft.

regressive tax   A tax whose burden falls more heavily on those with low incomes than on those with high incomes. A retail-sales tax is an example of a regressive tax, since it takes a larger percentage of the total income of a low-income person than of a high-income person.

regular delivery   The requirement that sellers of shares must deliver the shares to their broker by the fifth business day after the sale has been made.

regulation   The control of the behaviour of corporations or individuals by government rules set out under the authority of federal, provincial, and municipal laws and by-laws. Regulations exist for a wide variety of purposes, such as to control monopoly prices, promote fairness such as in employment equity and affirmative action policies, protect health and safety in the workplace or in consumer products, protect the environment, license businesses, protect investors and borrowers, and promote competition.

regulatory agency   A government agency that regulates the behaviour of corporations or of individuals. Examples include the NATIONAL ENERGY BOARD, the CANADIAN RADIO-TELEVISION AND TELECOMMUNICATIONS AGENCY, the NATIONAL TRANSPORTATION AGENCY, the ALBERTA ENERGY RESOURCES CONSERVATION BOARD, and the ONTARIO SECURITIES COMMISSION.

reinsurance   The assumption of part of the risk insured by one insurance company, by a second insurance company, to reduce the risk.

relative-income theory   The theory that the key determinant in wage demands is not the worker's absolute income but changes in income relative to the comparable income of others. For example, if police officers expect to earn, say, 15 percent more than fire fighters, and fire fighters get large wage increases that narrow the gap to, say, 8 percent, then, in their next wage demands, police officers may try to restore the differential.

relative price The price of one product expressed as a percent of the price of another — for example, the price of natural gas per 1,000 British thermal units (BTU) as a percent of the price of electricity for the same 1,000 BTU.

remainder To sell off at a substantially reduced price the surplus stocks of a firm — the remaining copies of a book, for example, or a seasonal line of clothing.

remaining established reserves Oil or natural-gas reserves yet to be recovered, but recoverable under current technology and economic conditions, and proved by drilling, production, or other means, or contiguous recoverable reserves, which are judged to exist because of geological, geophysical, or other information. *See also* ESTABLISHED RESERVES, INITIAL ESTABLISHED RESERVES, and ULTIMATE POTENTIAL RESERVES.

renewable resources Natural resources whose supply can be replaced as they are used. Examples include forests, fisheries, and fur-bearing animals. *See also* NON-RENEWABLE RESOURCE.

rent 1. The amount paid for the use of land and buildings that belong to someone else — the monthly amount paid by a tenant to a landlord, for example. *See also* RENT CONTROL. 2. The surplus return to land, broadly defined as land, buildings, minerals, oil and natural gas, water, forests, fisheries and wildlife, above that required to meet the demands of investors and workers to exploit the land. This surplus can be taxed away without depriving corporations and workers of their normal returns, and is known as ECO-

NOMIC RENT. 3. The rent paid by a person to oneself. If a person lives in his or her own home, the difference between the mortgage interest and other costs, and what could be earned if the house was rented to someone else, is the IMPUTED RENT.

rent control The limitation of rent increases under provincial law. In Canada, rent controls were implemented during the Second World War and, through the provinces, as part of the ANTI-INFLATION BOARD (AIB) program introduced in 1975. Rent controls can range from a freeze on rents or a fixed-percentage rent increase, to an increase related to the cost increases of landlords. Some provinces retained rent controls after the AIB program ended in 1978. In 1993, the provinces with formal rent-control programs were Ontario, Manitoba, Prince Edward Island, and Nova Scotia.

rentier Someone who receives his or her income from shares, bonds, annuities, real-estate rents, trusts, and other such assets. The income consists of dividends, interest, and rent.

reparations The payment of money and goods demanded by victorious nations from defeated nations following a war. In 1919, under the Treaty of Versailles, the victorious allies imposed heavy reparations on Germany, although John Maynard KEYNES warned that the payments would cripple the German economy. After the Second World War, the Allies, with the exception of the Soviet Union, refrained from demanding reparations; however, Germany was required to pay damages to Jewish families who survived the Holocaust.

repatriation The transfer of ownership of local corporations from non-residents to residents or the transfer of capital from abroad for investment at home. When Canadians talk of repatriating their economy, they are talking of reducing foreign ownership of Canadian corporations by buying back ownership from the non-resident owners.

replacement cost   The actual cost of replacing capital equipment and other production facilities, as opposed to the HISTORICAL COST, or the original cost, of acquiring the capital equipment or other facilities.

replacement-cost standard   A method of VALUATION that determines the value of an asset in terms of what it would cost to replace it at today's prices, as opposed to the original cost of the asset. *See also* INFLATION ACCOUNTING.

repossession   The taking back of an item of personal property, such as an automobile, appliance, or article of furniture, by a bank, sales-finance company, acceptance company, or retailer, when the purchaser fails to keep up payments under the terms of a consumer-credit contract.

repudiation   The stated refusal by a borrower to service or repay a debt, or by a party to a contract to live up to the terms of the contract.

resale-price maintenance   An attempt by a supplier of goods for resale to set the final price at which the goods may be sold to consumers, and to cut off any retailer who refuses to abide by the dictated price. This practice is illegal in Canada; it is an offence under the COMPETITION ACT. No supplier of goods is permitted to set the final selling price of a product or to cut off a retailer for selling at a low price; all a supplier may do is publish a suggested retail price. An exception is made if it can be shown that a retailer is regularly using a particular product as a LOSS LEADER, or in BAIT-AND-SWITCH advertising.

rescheduling   The renegotiation by a borrower with creditors of the terms and conditions under which existing loans are to be repaid. The borrower usually continues to pay interest during the renegotiation and the lender or lenders will often charge a fee in return for an extension of the repayment period for the debt. The usual reason for seeking rescheduling is that the borrower is no longer able to service debts according to the original terms. *See also* THIRD-WORLD DEBT CRISIS.

research and development (R&D)   Scientific, engineering, and design activities that result in new or improved products or production processes. Such spending is considered a significant indicator of a country's capacity for innovation, and therefore for economic growth, since growth is tied to a country's ability to generate ideas for knowledge-based innovation. Some economists regard it as a factor of production much like land, labour, or capital, and some analysts believe that it is the single most important source of PRODUCTIVITY growth. Canada has one of the lowest rates of R&D spending, as a percentage of GROSS DOMESTIC PRODUCT, of any of the Western industrial nations. In 1990, Canada spent 1.37 percent of GDP on R&D, compared with 2.88 percent for the United States, 2.80 percent for Japan, 2.81 percent for Germany, 2.86 percent for Switzerland, and 2.76 percent for Sweden. One reason is said to be the high level of foreign ownership of Canadian manufacturing, which means that Canada imports much of its new technology from the parent companies of foreign subsidiaries instead of developing it itself.

R&D includes basic research, usually in a university or government laboratory, where the emphasis is on scientific knowledge and applied research, carried out in a university, government laboratory, or in a corporation, where the focus is on commercial possibilities in the form of new products or new techniques. There is a growing trend, however, for companies in the same industry to co-operate in generic or pre-competitive R&D that advances the state of knowledge of the industry as a whole. The development phase, though, is usually carried out by a corporation; it consists of perfecting the new product or process, engineering and design work, and the creation of a prototype product or process. R&D is costly and, in many industries, such as petrochemicals and aerospace, it can usually only be carried out by large firms, who can afford to invest in R&D that does not pan out and who can also afford to finance a new product or process from its earliest stages to the time it reaches the market. Because of its importance for economic growth and other spillover benefits for society, governments provide tax incentives and direct grants for R&D. R&D does not flow in a straight line from basic research to applied research to commercialization, but operates through feedback between basic and applied research. *See also* INDUSTRIAL POLICY, SCIENTIFIC RESEARCH AND EXPERIMENTAL DEVELOPMENT TAX INCENTIVE.

reservation price   The price below which producers or suppliers will hold their goods or services off the market. The price is influenced by such factors as expectations of future price changes, storage costs, and the need for cash.

reserve appreciation   An increase in oil and gas reserves in a particular pool or reservoir, resulting from additional drilling or the application of improved recovery techniques.

reserve army of the unemployed   The lines of unemployed people at factory gates who, according to Karl MARX, were pointed out to the workers by bosses intent on depressing wages. According to Marx, the workers were told that they had to settle for low wages, or the unemployed would come in and work for less. In today's economy though, employers may have to bid up wages to attract skilled workers.

reserve bid   The minimum price permitted for an item at an auction. It is set by the owner of the goods being sold.

reserve currency   A national currency that is widely accepted and used in financing international trade, is held in the FOREIGN EXCHANGE RESERVES of other countries, and is used in exchange markets by central banks to maintain or influence the exchange rate of their own country's currency. A reserve currency, held in a country's foreign-exchange reserves along with gold and SPECIAL DRAWING RIGHTS, usually constitutes the major component of those reserves. A reserve currency is also the major component of working balances held by banks and corporations heavily engaged in international trade and investment. Through the late 19th century and into the 1920s, the British pound was the principal reserve currency. Starting in the 1930s, the U.S. dollar took on increasing importance as the world's reserve currency, a role that became even more significant after the Second World War. But, by the mid-1970s, the West German mark and the Swiss franc were used as reserve currencies, and in the 1980s the Japanese yen began to play an international role. The EUROPEAN CURRENCY UNIT is also expected to play a reserve-currency role.

reserve requirement   The statutory requirement on chartered banks to hold reserves against certain of their deposit liabilities, with these reserves kept on deposit with the BANK OF CANADA. Under the 1992 amendments to the BANK ACT, this reserve requirement will be phased out by July, 1994. The maintenance of reserves with the Bank of Canada assured a certain degree of liquidity to cover large-scale withdrawals but also put banks at a competitive disadvantage against trust companies, which did not have to maintain reserves. These reserves also provided the Bank of Canada with an important tool in MONETARY POLICY.

residual-rights clause A clause in a collective agreement leaving all matters not covered in the contract to the prerogative of management.

resource allocation The allocation of resources or FACTORS OF PRODUCTION among different uses in the economy. Because of scarcity, there is always competition for resources. The goal in an economy is to allocate resources in the most efficient manner, which is achieved when prices for various goods and services reflect the lowest possible cost in producing and supplying them. The allocation of resources can be affected by government regulations and subsidies or by restrictive or oligopolistic business practices.

Resources for Tomorrow Conference A move in the early 1960s by the federal government to co-ordinate federal and provincial policies on water and land use and on the management of other resources, such as forests. A conference held in Montreal in October, 1961, brought together 700 representatives of federal and provincial governments, industry, universities, and private groups, to discuss 80 papers on agriculture, water resources, regional development, forests, fisheries, wildlife, and outdoor recreation. The federal government proposed a national-resources council to encourage conservation, and to promote regional and intergovernmental co-operation, the creation of a national advisory land- and water-use board, and the holding of further resources

conferences every three to four years. These proposals were not adopted, but the conference led to the creation of the Canadian Council of Resource Ministers; the council was active in co-ordinating federal and provincial activities in the early 1960s, but later played a much less significant role. The ROYAL COMMISSION ON THE ECONOMIC UNION AND DEVELOPMENT PROSPECTS FOR CANADA in its 1985 report called for the restoration of the council or something similar to it.

restitution The return of property to its legal owner, or the compensation for the damage to or loss of such property.

restraint of trade Any form of collusion among producers, or any practice by a single producer that reduces competition. Examples include PRICE FIXING, PRICE DISCRIMINATION, a refusal to sell to certain buyers, and RESALE-PRICE MAINTENANCE. *See also* COMPETITION ACT.

restricted shares Shares that have limited or no voting rights. For example, certain industries in Canada have limits on the proportion of shares that can be foreign-owned, such as broadcasting, cable television, airline, and railway companies, as well as banks, so the number of shares available to non-residents is restricted. *See also* NON-VOTING SHARES.

Restrictive Trade Practices Commission An investigatory commission established in 1952 under the COMBINES INVESTIGATION ACT to investigate and hold hearings on complaints from the Director of Investigation and Research of the BUREAU OF COMPETITION POLICY in the Department of CONSUMER AND CORPORATE AFFAIRS. In 1986, following passage of a new COMPETITION ACT, the Restrictive

Trade Practices Commission was replaced by the COMPETITION TRIBUNAL.

restructuring   1. The reorganization of a company or industry to make it more competitive. In the case of Canada, this often includes greater specialization, which means a smaller range of products, investment in new production or process technology, recapitalization to provide a sounder equity base, retraining of workers to higher skill levels, the shedding of inefficient firms or company divisions, and a greater commitment to research and development. The promise of restructuring is sometimes used by companies seeking to work their way out of bankruptcy. **2.** The reorganization of a company's or country's debts, which usually means replacing short-term debt with long-term debt and can mean replacing one kind of security with another — for example, replacing some debt with equity.

retail banking   Banking services provided to individuals and small businesses, such as taking deposits and paying interest, making loans, including mortgages, and offering various other services and banking products such as cash chequing, safety-deposit boxes, credit cards, mutual funds, and REGISTERED RETIREMENT SAVINGS PLAN units.

retail price   The price charged to consumers. *See also* WHOLESALE PRICE. The CONSUMER PRICE INDEX measures changes in retail prices.

retail trade   The distribution and sale of goods and services to individuals. The retail trade includes department and chain stores, supermarkets, auto dealers, drugstores, independently owned and operated stores, mail-order houses, door-to-door salespeople, co-operatives, and even the person selling jewellery, candles, and leather belts from a street stand. Statistics Canada publishes monthly reports on retail trade in Canada (publication 63-005) based on a survey of 12,000 companies and with details for 16 different types of stores. The 16 sectors include the following: supermarket and grocery stores; all other food stores; drug and patent-medicine stores; shoe stores; men's clothing stores; women's clothing stores; other clothing stores; household furniture and appliance stores; household furnishings stores; motor vehicle and recreational vehicle dealers; gasoline service stations; automotive parts, accessories, and services; general merchandise stores; other semidurable goods stores; other durable goods stores; all other retail stores. The survey deals largely with the sale of goods, not services. Statistics Canada also publishes monthly data on department store sales (publication 63-002). Retail-trade data are an important indicator of consumer spending since retail sales account for about half of total personal consumption. A sustained increase in retail trade is likely to trigger new business investment to meet expanding consumer demand.

retained earnings   The portion of annual after-tax profits left over, after dividends have been paid to shareholders, for reinvestment in the business. Retained earnings are the single most important source of funds for business expansion. A corporation's BALANCE SHEET shows, under SHAREHOLDERS' EQUITY, the value of retained earnings for the year and the accumulated retained earnings for previous years. The role of retained earnings in business expansion helps to explain the steady growth of foreign-controlled enterprises in Canada, even though flows of new FOREIGN DIRECT INVESTMENT into Canada can fluctuate widely from year to year.

retained-earnings statement In a corporation's annual report, a statement showing the accumulated RETAINED EARNINGS of the corporation, along with the dividends paid out and retained earnings for the current year.

retaliation Steps taken by a country in response to what it contends are unfair trading practices by another country. The GENERAL AGREEMENT ON TARIFFS AND TRADE (GATT) permits a member country to take action, such as by raising tariffs on selected items, against another country that fails to implement the finding of a GATT dispute-settlement panel that has been adopted by the GATT council. The CANADA-UNITED STATES FREE TRADE AGREEMENT and the NORTH AMERICAN FREE TRADE AGREEMENT also contain provisions for retaliatory measures. For example, if Canada adopts new cultural policies, to protect its identity or strengthen its cultural industries, that are opposed by the United States, the agreement specifically allows the United States to retaliate. Similarly, if a country in either of these trade agreements adopts measures that a binational or trinational panel finds nullify some benefit, then retaliation in the form of adopting identical measures is permitted.

return on assets A measure of profitability in banking and other deposit-taking financial-service providers. Net income is calculated as a percentage of average total assets during the year.

return on capital employed Net earnings as a percentage of the sum of total debt, deferred income taxes, and shareholders' equity. It is a measure of the productivity of the assets employed.

return on equity After-tax profits, less preferred share dividends, expressed as a percentage of SHAREHOLDERS' EQUITY. See also RATE OF RETURN ON INVESTED CAPITAL, which includes both shareholders' equity and long-term debt.

return on investment The after-tax profits earned on an investment, expressed as a percentage of the original cost of investment or purchase price. See also RATE OF RETURN ON INVESTED CAPITAL.

returns to scale The increase in production that results from additional units of various factors of production, such as labour and machinery. The typical business enterprise is assumed to get a proportionately greater increase in output from the application of additional labour or machinery in the early life of the enterprise, thus achieving increasing returns. After it reaches a certain size, the additional units of the factors of production are said to yield roughly proportionate increases in output, or constant returns. And if the firm grows ever larger in size, it is assumed to yield proportionately smaller gains in output from the application of additional units of the factors of production, resulting in decreasing, or diminishing, returns. There is some disagreement as to whether the ECONOMIES OF SCALE achieved by a large and efficient firm yield to DISECONOMIES OF SCALE if a firm becomes ever larger. It is argued that, beyond a certain size, the increasing bureaucratization and delegation of responsibility in a firm make it harder for management to respond to market changes and to reach decisions. At the same time, some of the world's largest corporations are also among the most successful.

revaluation A deliberate increase in the value of a country's exchange rate, as opposed to DEVALUATION. If, by intervention on foreign-exchange markets, the BANK OF CANADA helps raise the exchange rate of Canada's dollar from 85 U.S. cents to 88 U.S. cents, it is said to have been revalued. However, if the increase occurs simply due to foreign-exchange-market trading, the currency is said to have appreciated. If a country is running a high and persistent BALANCE OF PAYMENTS surplus it may revalue its currency to reduce the cost of imported goods and raise the cost to others of its exports, thus bringing its international transactions into closer balance. By making its exports more expensive and imports cheaper, a country raises its standard of living, since the same volume of goods and services it produces will now buy an additional amount of foreign goods and services.

revenue The total income a business firm or government receives from all sources.

Revenue Canada The federal government department, also called the Department of National Revenue, established in 1927 with two divisions, Customs and Excise, and Taxation. Until then the collection of customs duties, excise taxes, and other taxes had been the responsibility of the Department of FINANCE. Until the First World War, the federal government relied on customs duties, excise taxes, and other INDIRECT TAXES for its revenue. With the war it introduced, in 1916, an excess-profits tax on business and, in 1917, income tax on individuals and businesses. The department has two deputy-ministers, one for customs and excise, the other for taxation; the two report to a single Minister of National Revenue. The Customs and Excise division assesses and collects duties and taxes on imported and domestically produced products and on air travel and investigates complaints by Canadian industry of DUMPING by foreign producers or the subsidization of imported goods that could be subject to COUNTERVAILING DUTIES. The division also prepares cases for the CANADIAN INTERNATIONAL TRADE TRIBUNAL. The taxation division assesses and collects income-tax returns of individuals and corporations under the INCOME TAX ACT, collects provincial personal income taxes for all provinces except for Quebec and provincial corporate income taxes for all provinces but Quebec, Ontario, and Alberta. It also collects premiums for the CANADA PENSION PLAN and for UNEMPLOYMENT INSURANCE.

reverse split The exchange of several shares in a company for a single new share.

reverse takeover The acquisition of a larger corporation by a smaller one. It can also mean the acquisition of control of a parent company by an affiliate or subsidiary or of a public company by a private company.

revolving credit 1. A form of consumer-credit account used by banks and other financial institutions as well as retailers such as department stores, in which credit card-holders are allowed to run purchases up to a predetermined credit limit, and on which card-holders must make a minimum monthly payment, depending on the amount outstanding. Interest is charged on the outstanding monthly balance. 2. In business, a line of credit against which money can be drawn, with minimum monthly repayment.

revolving underwriting facility An arrangement in which a company issues short-term notes that are supported by an undertaking from its bank that should the company find itself unable to issue notes at some pre-determined price, the bank will buy the notes at this price or guarantee that funds will be available through some form of standby credit.

Ricardo, David (1772-1823) A British CLASSICAL economist who had little formal education but was able to retire at the age of 42 after becoming a millionaire by trading in government securities. His most important work was *The Principles of Political Economy and Taxation*, published in 1817, in which he attempted to construct an economic model to explain the distribution of income in society. He was anxious to determine the laws that governed the distribution of economic output among workers, capitalists, and landowners; his analysis led him to the concept of ECONOMIC RENT. He concluded that an iron law of wages meant that wages would remain at a subsistence level since higher wages would lead workers to have more children, adding to the labour force and driving wages down. Landowners, Ricardo argued, would inevitably be the most prosperous members of society because agricultural land was finite, while a rising population and a growing need for food would raise the profits or rent from land. As population expanded, marginal land would be brought into production and despite diminishing returns, if all land must earn the same profit, the most productive land would earn an economic rent. Industrialists would be limited in their profits because the rising cost of food would force up wages and limit profits. Ricardo also helped to develop the concept of COMPARATIVE ADVANTAGE, which is the basis for present-day theories of international trade and specialization; he arrived as well at a theory of value. Value, he argued, was based on the scarcity of a good and the quantity of labour required to obtain it: while scarcity accounted for the value of a limited number of commodities, in most cases value depended on labour.

rigged bid A form of collusion among a group of firms bidding on a public contract. The firms decide ahead of time which one should get the contract and fix the price of their bids so that the chosen firm makes the lowest bid and thus gets the contract. Usually, in such an arrangement, the bids will be arranged so that each of the firms gets its share of the business but at higher levels of profit than if the firms were actively competing with one another. The practice is illegal and is punishable by jail terms and fines. *See also* COMPETITION ACT.

rigged market A market in which prices are manipulated, so that those doing the manipulating can make a windfall profit. For example, commodity speculators who corner the market in a specific commodity can distort prices; similarly, a small group of investors may be able to rig prices of a company's shares on a STOCK EXCHANGE or OVER-THE-COUNTER MARKET.

right of establishment The right accorded to investors or companies from another country to establish and operate a business in a foreign country and to be treated in the same way as citizens of that country. The CANADA-UNITED STATES FREE TRADE AGREEMENT and the NORTH AMERICAN FREE TRADE AGREEMENT both provide the right of establishment to a wide range of service industries.

right of way The legal right of one party to cross through another party's land. This is usually indicated on the title to the land.

right-to-work law A law that makes illegal the negotiation, in a collective agreement, of a UNION SHOP or other arrangement to maintain union membership in a BARGAINING UNIT. The motive behind right-to-work laws is to weaken the power of unions.

rights issue   A method of raising new equity capital. A company planning to issue new shares will issue to all existing shareholders by a certain date the right to purchase new shares at a specified price in proportion to their existing holdings. A shareholder who does not want to exercise the rights can sell the rights on a stock exchange if the shares of the issuing company are already listed. The shares purchased under a rights offering are acquired directly from the issuing company, and no commission has to be paid to a stockbroker.

risk   The danger of a loss or a low yield from an investment; this danger is accepted by an investor, who must operate in an uncertain business environment when weighing all the possible outcomes from an investment. Generally speaking, the greater the risk in an investment, the greater the profit that is demanded if the investment is successful. Thus, a mining company will seek a high profit from a successful discovery to offset the risk of losses from the possibility of unsuccessful exploration efforts. Similarly, an investor in a new apartment building in a growing city will be facing less of a risk in an investment and therefore may be satisfied with a lower rate of return. Financial institutions deal with a number of different types of risk. Credit risk is the possibility that borrowers will be unable to repay their loans. Liquidity risk is the potential demands for cash resulting from commitments to extend credit, the maturity of deposits, and other transactions. Market risk is the possibility of losses in a portfolio from price changes, such as a fall in the price of common shares. Interest-rate risk is the risk of possible losses from interest-rate changes, such as an increase in deposit costs that reduces the return from a fixed-rate mortgage portfolio. Foreign-exchange risk is the possible loss from exchange-rate movements. *See also* HEDGING.

risk arbitrageur   A specialized stock-market trader who simultaneously purchases shares in a company that is a takeover target, since these can be expected to rise, and sells shares in the bidding company, whose shares can be expected to fall. Likewise, risk arbitrageurs may purchase shares in a takeover company if they expect the company bidding will have to offer a higher price.

risk aversion   The reluctance of an investor to take on risk and to seek safety in the most secure investments. Investors dislike risk, so their investment portfolios hold a wide array of investments to spread or reduce risk. Canadians are said to be risk averse, compared with Americans, with critics pointing to the high level of Canadian savings found in insurance and the lack of investment in venture-capital activities.

risk capital   Capital invested in new or small business enterprises, and subject to greater risk than an investment in an established business enterprise. *See also* VENTURE CAPITAL.

risk premium   The additional interest a country or corporation must pay if its level of debt or poor state of finances raises doubts about its capacity to repay. Ratings by rating agencies are one measure of the risk premium. When a country has a high foreign debt due to continuing fiscal deficits, it may be forced to pay a risk premium if it shows no signs of bringing its fiscal position into balance.

risk-reward ratio   The relationship between the degree of risk an investor is willing to make and the size of the reward he can be expected to earn. The greater the risk, the greater the potential reward; likewise, an investment without risk will yield a relatively modest reward.

Robinson, Joan (1903-1983) A British economist who played a key role in developing the theory of monopolistic or IMPERFECT COMPETITION and how prices and production occur in a market of products that are partial substitutes. Her underlying theory was set out in her 1933 book, *The Economics of Imperfect Competition.*

rollback The power of government to ban a price increase and force a supplier to charge an earlier and lower price. Governments sometimes exercise this power by MORAL SUASION or threats. For example, if a corporation with a significant market share raises its prices and refuses to withdraw the price increases in spite of government requests to do so, the government may threaten to lower tariffs on the product, putting price pressure on the offending company, or can refuse to let the corporation's products be used in government-financed projects. Rollback powers may be granted as part of an INCOMES POLICY. *See also* ANTI-INFLATION BOARD.

rolling stock The diesel engines, freight cars, tanker cars, passenger coaches, and other equipment for railways that are used to carry people or goods.

rollover The extension of the maturity of a debt by issuing new bonds or other securities to replace old ones. A great deal of public debt, both domestic and foreign, is managed this way.

round lot The normal unit of trading on a stock exchange. On Canadian stock exchanges it is usually 100 shares or a multiple of 100 — for example, 600, 1,100, 12,500. Blocks of less than 100 are known as ODD LOTS and usually command a higher commission because they have to be organized into round lots for trading purposes.

Rowell-Sirois Report *See* ROYAL COMMISSION ON DOMINION-PROVINCIAL RELATIONS.

Royal Canadian Mint The federal crown corporation responsible for the production of coins used as money in Canada. It was first established in 1901 as the Ottawa Mint, a branch of Britain's Royal Mint. Until 1931, all of its employees were British civil servants. At that point, the Royal Canadian Mint was established, operating as a branch of the Department of FINANCE. In 1969, it became a crown corporation, enabling it not only to maintain its principal role as producer of Canadian coinage, but also to get more actively into the business of issuing commemorative and other coins for commercial purposes, and to seek, on a competitive basis, coinage business from other countries and from private firms. The Royal Canadian Mint produces coins for about 60 countries. In 1989, the Royal Canadian Mint issued 4,000 shares to the Department of SUPPLY AND SERVICES, allowing it to retain earnings for business improvements and to pay dividends to its shareholder. The chief executive of the Royal Canadian Mint is known as the Master of the Mint. The mint is based in Ottawa but also has a Winnipeg plant.

royal commission A study or investigation appointed by a federal or provincial government to look into a particular problem or incident, and headed by an individual or panel of individuals known either for their experience or for their capacity for independent and objective judgement. Royal commissions usually have full power to obtain documents, to summon witnesses, and to hear evidence under oath. They can hire research staffs and legal counsel, commission research studies, and publish their own analysis and research. Royal commissions have played a significant role in exploring federal and provincial issues. Examples include the commissions on Dominion-Provincial Relations, Canada's Economic Prospects, Banking and Finance, Taxation, and Economic Union and Development Prospects for Canada. Royal commissions are also known as commissions of inquiry.

Royal Commission of Inquiry on Constitutional Problems A ROYAL COMMISSION appointed by the Quebec government in February, 1953, to examine fiscal relations between the federal and provincial governments and to demonstrate that the power of direct taxation, including personal income taxes, rested exclusively with the provinces — in spite of section 91 (3) of the CONSTITUTION ACT, 1867, which gave Parliament the power to raise money "by any mode or system of taxation." The commission was headed by Quebec Chief Justice Thomas Tremblay, who produced a five-volume report in 1954 that not only proposed a radical restructuring of Canada, but also advanced a remarkable analysis of the nature and roots of French-Canadian society and the importance of Quebec as the French-Canadian homeland.

The Tremblay Commission took the Quebec conservative-nationalist view that the federal government was the creation of the provinces, who made a compact among themselves; the purpose of the federal government was to establish the framework within which the French and English communities could live their separate lives, side by side, in a single state. The federal government was, in this view, largely an administrative agency that looked after military, technical, and co-ordinating services required by the provinces. It was the responsibility of the provinces to deal with everything that affected people's lives, social and cultural policy, education, municipalities, and family life; indeed, even the notion of a loyalty to Canada was contrary to the spirit of Confederation. Loyalty was to be to the provinces, which, according to this view, represented the real interests of the people. Confederation was simply an administrative arrangement, not the establishment of a new nation. However, the growth of the federal government, through its dominance of income taxes and social security, was undermining the basis of Confederation — in particular, the right of the provinces to be the principal force in the lives of their people.

The Tremblay Commission called for much greater autonomy for the provinces and a return to what it called the spirit of Confederation. It urged that the federal and provincial governments agree on a maximum level or percentage of gross national product that should be allocated to the state, and that this sector then be divided between the federal and provincial governments, according to their responsibilities. The provinces should have all taxes on income, including personal income tax, and estate, gift, and succession taxes. The federal government should have all taxes having to do with the economy, namely corporate income taxes, sales taxes, and tariffs and excise duties and taxes; sales taxes would have to be established on a progressive scale, so as not to hit low-income Canadians too harshly. The commission also proposed that all social programs be under the jurisdiction of the provinces. It proposed that the provinces should be given the right to sell bonds to the BANK OF CANADA and that a permanent committee of federal-provincial conferences be established, along with a council of the provinces; the latter would facilitate co-operation among the provinces and thus eliminate the need for federal programs or intervention. The commission saw little need for EQUALIZATION PAYMENTS to the poorer provinces if the proposals were adopted, with only the MARITIME PROVINCES requiring modest help.

The other provinces, it said, could establish an equalization fund on their own, without federal participation.

Royal Commission on Banking and Finance   A royal commission headed by Chief Justice Dana Porter of the Supreme Court of Ontario. It was appointed in October, 1961, to examine "all aspects of money, banking, credit, and finance," including all existing financial institutions and the BANK OF CANADA, and the laws regulating their activities.

The commission's report was published in April, 1964. It recommended a number of important changes in the banking system, including the following: abolition of the 6 percent interest-rate ceiling on bank loans, so that the banks could play a bigger role in providing consumer credit; disclosure of bank-loan costs; the entry of banks into conventional mortgage financing; legislation to prohibit banks from agreeing to set common interest, chequing, and other customer charges; a ban on banks owning more than 10 percent of the shares of any non-financial business; and a limit on interlocking directorships by bank officers.

Other proposals included the following: government approval for any purchase of Canadian bank shares by foreign interests; the bringing of trust companies, finance companies, credit unions, and other near banks under the authority of the Bank of Canada; the removal of restrictions on personal and business loans by trust and loan companies; regulation of the investment funds of pension plans, including increasing to 25 percent from 15 percent the amount they could invest from their funds in Canadian common shares; amendments to the BANK ACT, so that the government, through an ORDER-IN-COUNCIL, could overrule the central bank on monetary policy; creation of a national securities commission to ensure high standards of regulation across Canada; much tougher stock-exchange rules to protect investors, including higher listing standards, INSIDER-TRADING penalties, full disclosure by corporations and mutual funds, and improved supervision of securities salespeople; new legislation to control takeover bids; government regulations to control mergers between banks and trust companies, or bank takeovers of other financial institutions; and an interest-rate ceiling on all personal loans made by financial institutions, running to 24 percent a year on the first $300, and 12 percent on amounts above $300 and up to $5,000. Many of its recommendations were incorporated into the Bank Act when it was amended in 1967.

Royal Commission on Bilingualism and Biculturalism   A commission appointed in 1963, with André Laurendeau, editor of *Le Devoir*, and Davidson Dunton, president of Carleton University, as co-chairmen, along with eight other members. It was asked to review the status of bilingualism in Canada and to find ways to improve bilingualism and strengthen the bicultural nature of the Canadian federal state.

Altogether, the commission produced six volumes of recommendations. Among them was volume 3, published in 1969, entitled *The Work World*. It called for the use of French as the principal language of work at all levels in Quebec, as an equal language of work in New Brunswick, and as a significant language of work in those parts of Ontario with significant French-speaking populations. In the federal public service, it found that the use of English dominated; it said that the solution was not to emphasize individual bilingualism, but to establish French-language work units.

The commission summarized its findings on the work world this way: "In every area affecting the work world that we have examined, Francophones are at a disadvantage vis-à-vis their Anglophone colleagues. Their incomes are conspicuously lower in Canada as a whole, in the individual provinces, in specific cities, and in specific industries and occupations. There are comparable disparities in educational attainment. In Canada's work position — including industrial and commercial concerns, the federal public service, and the military — Francophones are much less likely than Anglophones to hold top-level positions. Moreover, the Francophones who do hold high positions are very often required to use English as their language of work. Finally, the Francophone share of ownership in industry is disproportionately small, even when the high incidence of Canadian ownership of the country's industry is taken into account."

Royal Commission on Canada's Economic Prospects A ROYAL COMMISSION appointed in 1955 to investigate Canada's economic prospects over the next 25 years. Specifically, the commission was asked to review Canada's long-term economic prospects and the problems of economic development that were likely to occur. These included developments in the supply of raw materials and energy, population growth, prospects for changes in domestic and foreign markets for Canadian producers, trends in productivity and standard of living, and the requirements for industrial and social capital. The commission, headed by Walter Gordon of Toronto, produced its final report in 1958; it also published a large number of separate studies on different sectors of the Canadian economy. The commission took an optimistic view of Canada's future, but called for policies to reduce foreign ownership and control of the economy, and to encourage Canadians to invest in their own country. It said that anti-combines laws should be modified to permit mergers among

Canadian companies, so that they could achieve more efficient production and compete against foreign firms. To prevent foreign control of Canadian banks and insurance companies, which the commission said must remain under Canadian ownership and control because of their central role in the economy, foreign shareholders of such financial institutions should lose their voting rights. The commission called for a program of continued immigration into Canada, even during recessions, because a growing population would encourage new industries to be established in Canada, and thus help to diversify the economy. A growing population, the commission said, offered great hope for "more control over our economic welfare than we have at present."

In calling for policies to increase Canadian ownership in the economy and to direct the activities of foreign-controlled firms, the commission said that Canada should look to foreigners for DEBT CAPITAL for mortgages and bonds but rely on Canadians for EQUITY CAPITAL, which represents ownership in the form of shares. In Canada, it said, "there is concern that as the position of American capital in the dynamic resource and manufacturing sectors becomes even more dominant, our economy will inevitably become more and more integrated with that of the United States. Behind this is the fear that continuing integration might lead to economic domination by the United States and eventually the loss of our political independence."

The commission saw little prospect of major new free-trade moves, and said that Canada should stick with the existing levels of tariffs. It also predicted that a growing proportion of Canada's trade would be with the United States. It was doubtful about the prospects for significantly increasing the processing of mineral resources in Canada before they were exported.

Concerning energy, it said that Canada should extend an oil pipeline to Montreal if the United States was not willing to buy more Canadian oil, and it urged the establishment of a national energy agency to supervise the development, export, import, and consumption of all forms of energy.

The commission called for policies to make Canadian transportation systems pay their way, and policies to help residents of the Atlantic provinces to move to other parts of Canada if local jobs were not available; it encouraged greater urban planning, as more Canadians moved into cities, and warned against overproduction in agriculture. It said that the provinces should help to finance municipal transit systems, and municipalities should boost their own revenues by imposing sewer and motor-vehicle taxes, or be assured of a proportion of provincial motor-vehicle revenues. The commission also endorsed KEYNESIAN ECONOMIC policies of tax cuts and increased government spending to fight recession.

Royal Commission on Dominion-Provincial Relations   A ROYAL COMMISSION appointed in August, 1937, to re-examine "the economic and financial basis of Confederation and of the distribution of legislative powers in the light of the economic and social developments of the last 70 years." The commission was specifically asked to inquire into the constitutional allocation of taxing and spending powers, to review public expenditure and public debts to see whether the existing allocations were equitable, and to review federal grants and subsidies to the provinces. The commission was appointed after the GREAT DEPRESSION of the 1930s had created a financial crisis in several provinces, and revealed confusing differences of opinion over the division of powers and tax responsibilities, which in turn had hampered the introduction of effective policies to deal with

the country's grave economic condition. The five-man commission was originally headed by Newton Rowell, chief justice of the Supreme Court of Ontario; he resigned due to ill health in November, 1938, and was succeeded by Joseph Sirois, professor of constitutional and administrative law at Laval University.

The commission's three-volume report, which included an economic history of Canada from 1867 to 1939, was published in May, 1940. The commission found that changes in the economy and society since Confederation had produced major imbalances that needed correcting. It proposed changes in the federal system so that the provinces would always be assured of sufficient financial resources, regardless of the state of the economy, to carry out social, health, and education policies, while leaving the federal government with the principal taxing powers and the responsibility to see that the provinces had the funds they needed to carry out their obligations. The commission assigned responsibility for unemployment relief, aid to primary industries such as agriculture, and the payment of contributory and non-contributory pensions to the federal government.

In its financial proposals, the commission recommended that the federal government alone levy personal income taxes, corporation taxes, and succession duties. In return, the federal government was to refrain from competing with the provinces in the tax fields left to them; with respect to the natural-resource wealth of the provinces, the federal government would pay over to the province concerned 10 percent of the corporate income derived from the exploitation of natural resources.

To ensure that each province was able to provide a Canadian standard of services, the commission called for an annual national-adjustment grant from the federal government, to enable each province to provide a Canadian standard of services at normal Canadian taxation rates. A finance commission was to be set up to calculate and review such grants every five years. If voters in a province wanted a higher standard of services than those provided through meeting Canadian standards, then a provincial government could raise additional tax revenues to improve the services.

In other areas, the commission recommended the following: concurrent federal and provincial powers to set up farm marketing boards, thus ending constitutional confusions in this area; establishment of a transportation-planning commission, which would enable the federal government and the provinces to solve the country's transportation policies; the holding of federal-provincial conferences at least once a year, along with the creation of a small secretariat to serve the federal-provincial co-operation; and establishment of a social-science research council, to co-ordinate and fund social-science research in Canada. The recommendations of the commission were considered at a federal-provincial conference in June, 1941. However, the opposition of a number of provinces, along with pre-occupation with the war effort, led to the report being shelved.

Royal Commission on Energy A ROYAL COMMISSION appointed in 1957 to investigate a number of energy issues. Headed by business executive Henry Borden, it issued two reports, in 1958 and 1959. Its most important proposal was that Canada adopt a NATIONAL OIL POLICY in which oil from western Canada would supply Canadian markets west of the Ottawa Valley, with the surplus going to the United States, while the oil markets of Quebec and Atlantic Canada would be supplied by imported oil. The commission rejected proposals by independent western

Canadian oil producers that a pipeline be built to Montreal to create a larger market for their oil. The commission also called for the establishment of a NATIONAL ENERGY BOARD to administer the proposed National Oil Policy. The energy board was established in 1959 and the National Oil Policy implemented in 1961. During the oil crises of the 1970s, the federal government extended the oil pipeline to Montreal, but by the start of the 1980s the National Oil Policy was largely abandoned.

Royal Commission on Government Organization A federal ROYAL COMMISSION appointed in 1960 and headed by J. Grant Glassco to review the existing system and structure of government organization. The commission investigated 23 government departments, 21 statutory boards, and 42 crown corporations. From 1962 to 1963 it issued a five-volume report. Its underlying recommendation was that government should "let the managers manage." To introduce more efficiency and flexibility into government, departments should be freed from inappropriate or rigid central control so that they could develop management methods suited to their own needs. However, at the same time, it called for a strengthened Treasury Board to oversee government operations and urged that senior officials rotate from department to department to develop management experience rather than advancing within an individual department. A Bureau of Government Organization was established to implement the recommendations.

Royal Commission on National Passenger Transportation A ROYAL COMMISSION appointed in 1989 to investigate the national integrated intercity passenger transportation system that will be needed to meet the needs of Canadians in the 21st century. In 1992, the commission, chaired by Lou Hyndman of Alberta, issued a four-volume report calling for an end to government controls and regulations and the transition to a self-sustaining passenger transportation system, consisting of cars, buses, planes, trains, and ferries. The infrastructure for the passenger transportation system includes bus terminals, parking lots, airports, railway stations, ferry terminals, roads and bridges, air navigation systems, railway tracks, waterways and canals, road signs and signals, air traffic control systems, dispatch and signal systems for railways, and vessel traffic services for ferries. The commission found that in 1991, bus travel cost 9.5 cents per passenger kilometre, with passengers paying all but 0.4 cents of the cost; car travel cost 17.4 cents, with users paying 15.8 cents and the other 1.6 cents consisting of taxpayer subsidy; air travel cost 21.1 cents per passenger kilometre, with passengers paying 17.3 cents of the costs; ferry service cost 42.5 cents per passenger kilometre and travellers paid 25.1 cents of the costs; and train travel cost 43.9 cents per passenger kilometre, with passengers paying only 10.9 cents of the cost. At 33 cents per passenger kilometre, rail travel was the most heavily subsidized form of passenger transportation. Government programs or subsidies should not favour particular modes of transportation or destinations, the commission said. The transportation system, should be guided by the objectives of safety, protecting the environment, efficiency, and fairness to taxpayers, travellers, and carriers, so that services are provided only where benefits exceed the costs, and levels of service are provided at the lowest possible cost. The commission recommended that each traveller pay the full cost of his or her travel, and travellers, in total, pay the full cost of the passenger transportation system, including those costs related to protecting the environment, safety, and accidents. While the commission made no recommendation on the ownership of other carriers, it called on the federal government to retain the existing limits on foreign ownership and control of airlines. The commission estimated that implementation of its recommendations would save taxpayers $5.3 billion, increase travel costs by $3.9 billion, and bring about $1.4 billion in savings in the total cost of passenger travel. In 1991, Canadians spent $43.1 billion on intercity travel, of which about $5 billion consisted of subsidies.

Royal Commission on Price Spreads and Mass Buying The most sweeping public investigation ever undertaken in Canada into the market power of department and chain stores; the relationship between manufacturers, such as cigarette companies, canners, bakeries, and meat packers, and the farmers and fishermen who supplied them; working conditions in chain and department stores and in manufacturing industries, including sweatshop conditions in the textiles industry; and unfair practices affecting consumers, such as misleading advertising and inaccurate weights and measures. The principal purpose of the inquiry was to determine the causes of "the large spread" between prices paid to farmers and fishermen by industry and the prices charged consumers by department and chain stores. The study originated as a Special Committee of the House of Commons in February, 1934. Trade and Commerce Minister H.H. Stevens was the chairman. The committee became a ROYAL COMMISSION later that year. In November, 1934, Member of Parliament W.W. Kennedy, became chairman, after Stevens resigned following a dispute with Prime Minister R.B. Bennett. The commission's report was tabled in the

House of Commons in April, 1935. It made a number of significant recommendations, including the following: 1. The creation of a Dominion trade and industry commission to enforce the COMBINES INVESTIGATION ACT, to regulate industrial monopolies, to promote competition, to provide leadership on laws dealing with merchandising, to administer new consumer- protection laws, and to provide national protection for investors in securities markets. 2. Much greater protection for workers, including strictly enforced minimum wages, reduction of hours of work, with a uniform 44-hour work week throughout the country, encouragement of trade unions and a greater role for collective agreements among employers and workers, and establishment of a special group in the Department of LABOUR to study industrial relations, to draft model labour laws, and to plan federal-provincial conferences on labour matters. 3. Greater protection for farmers and fishermen in their dealings with food companies, including marketing boards for fruit and vegetable growers, licensing of all food processors, public livestock yards to reduce the powers of the meat packers, and encouragement of co-operatives for fishermen. 4. Increased competition, through amendments to the Combines Investigation Act, and improved protection for investors through amendments to the Companies Act, including much greater financial disclosure and more stringent responsibilities for company directors and stock promoters.

Royal Commission on Publications A ROYAL COMMISSION appointed in September, 1960, under the chairmanship of *Ottawa Journal* publisher Grattan O'Leary, to study the problems and prospects of Canadian magazines in the face of strong foreign competition, including Canadian editions of foreign magazines, and to study ways to strengthen the development of a Canadian identity through genuinely Canadian magazines. The commission, in its report published in June, 1961, called for the removal of tax deductions for advertising by Canadian advertisers in foreign magazines aimed at the Canadian market and a ban on foreign magazines entering Canada, including so-called Canadian editions of foreign magazines, when they contained advertising directed mainly at the Canadian market.

Royal Commission on Taxation A ROYAL COMMISSION in 1962 under the chairmanship of Kenneth Carter to study every aspect of the federal tax system and to recommend reforms, including tax legislation to encourage Canadian ownership of Canadian industry without discouraging the continued inflow of foreign capital. In February, 1967, the six-volume report, containing hundreds of proposals for changes in the tax system, was published. The commission, recognizing the tax system as one of the fundamental tools of economic and social policy, found the existing tax system to be extremely unfair, since too many people in similar circumstances and with similar purchasing power paid quite different amounts of tax. The commission argued that this also contributed to an inefficient allocation of resources, and hence a lower standard of living for Canadians. The commission said that the system should be made much fairer, and that it should also be much better utilized to promote economic growth, to contain inflation, to increase Canadian ownership of the economy, and to achieve other important economic goals.

The fundamental concern of the commission was equity or fairness, with taxation based on the ABILITY-TO-PAY PRINCIPLE. In any conflict between the goals of fairness and economic growth, fairness must prevail.

Carter said: "Preserving and developing the system by scrupulously fair taxes must override all other objectives." To this end, the commission proposed a new, comprehensive tax base, which would include all net gains in purchasing power, or command over goods and services in cash or kind, for tax purposes. Reflecting its "a buck is a buck" philosophy, the commission recommended that capital gains, windfall gains, family allowances, unemployment insurance, and many other forms of income that were then tax exempt be made taxable. "If a man obtains increased command over goods and services for his personal satisfaction we do not believe it matters, from the point of view of taxation, whether he earned it through working, gained it through operating a business, received it because he held property, made it selling property or was given it by a relative."

The commission proposed that all capital gains, including those on personal residences, be taxable, with a lifetime exemption of $25,000 on homes and farms. It called for the abolition of federal estate and gift taxes and recommended that gifts and inheritances be taxed as income — with an exemption for gifts and bequests between spouses and a modest exemption on gifts and inheritances for other individuals. The commission also argued that families should be allowed to file a joint return. Tax deductions for children would be replaced by TAX CREDITS, which would be worth more to lower-income families. The top marginal tax rate would be reduced to 50 percent from 80 percent, but wealthy people would pay more in taxes because of a much more comprehensive tax base.

The commission also proposed major changes in the taxation of corporations, including abolition of the low 21 percent rate for small businesses, and a system of accelerated depreciation allowances for new and small businesses instead. In addition, Canadian shareholders of Canadian corporations would be credited with a 100 percent credit for the corporation taxes paid on their behalf by the corporation, thus giving Canadians an incentive to invest in Canadian shares and reducing the cost of new capital for Canadian companies. The commission recommended that co-operatives and credit unions be taxed, that the existing three-year tax holiday for new mines be abolished, that the depletion allowances for the mining, oil, and natural-gas industries be sharply reduced, and that life-insurance companies be taxed as any other business. It proposed a halt to expense-account living, with ceilings on the amount an individual could claim on travelling and entertainment expenses, and the treatment as taxable income of any expenditure by an individual above the ceiling. The commission proposed that employees be allowed to deduct employment expenses, such as tools and uniforms, and that there be greater tax incentives for individuals to save for their retirement. It called for the abolition of the federal 11 percent manufacturer's sales tax, along with a halt by the federal government to turning over additional shares of the income-tax field to the provinces. If the provinces wanted more tax room, then the federal government should make room by reducing its sales tax. The commission also said that the federal government should assume full control of the corporation income tax. It called for a new tax court to replace the Tax Appeal Board and for a new board of revenue commissioners to take over federal tax collection and administration from the Department of NATIONAL REVENUE.

The proposed changes were calculated to yield more tax revenue from wealthy Canadians and foreign-owned corporations but less from the ordinary taxpayer. The resulting redistribution of income, the commission said, was necessary, "if we are to achieve greater equality of opportunity for all Canadians and make it possible for those with little economic power to attain a decent standard of living."

Royal Commission on the Economic Union and Development Prospects for Canada A ROYAL COMMISSION appointed in 1982 and chaired by Donald Macdonald, a former Minister of FINANCE, to report on "the long-term economic potential, prospects, and challenges facing the Canadian federation and its respective regions, as well as the implications that such prospects and challenges have for Canada's economic and governmental institutions, and for the management of Canada's economic affairs." The chairman and his 12 commissioners were also directed to recommend "the appropriate national goals and policies for economic development" and "the appropriate institutional and constitutional arrangements to promote the liberty and well-being of individual Canadians and the maintenance of a strong competitive economy." In 1985, the commission delivered a massive three-volume, 1,911-page report touching on almost every aspect of Canadian economic and constitutional life, though it is best remembered for its recommendation that Canada negotiate a free trade agreement with the United States. It also published 72 research volumes.

The commission argued that there were four major roles for government: to oversee the evolution of the many social aspects of Canada; to play a central and related role in symbolizing the citizens' sense of national identity; to play a vital role in influencing and directing the course of the national economy; and to speak and act on behalf of the nation in international affairs. The commission, which stressed the importance of restoring productivity growth and expanding employment opportunities, argued that governments should pull back from direct intervention in many areas of economic activity and rely more on market forces. It argued as well that along with a major reform of the role played by government in the economy, there was also a need for major changes to Canada's social assistance programs, education, unemployment insurance, and collective-bargaining arrangements. It urged greater political reforms, stating that "big government requires more democracy, not less." Parliament's ability to hold government to account should be strengthened and the Senate elected; it also called for further measures to strengthen the hand of the electorate and curb the power of government and the bureaucracy. And while the commission saw federal-provincial tensions as "a reflection of healthy competition among conflicting interests," it proposed improved machinery for the conduct of federal-provincial relations. The commission called for the reduction of interprovincial barriers and greater power for legislative bodies to review agreements reached between the federal and provincial governments. It urged Canadians to take a more open attitude toward the rest of the world, pointing to developments in science and technology, investment, trade, finance, and the environment that would force a greater attention to the world developments. Canada, the commission said, should pay greater attention to environmental and population issues, support reform of the multilateral system represented by the United Nations and its agencies, and pursue bilateral and regional initiatives where these are outward-looking.

The commission called on Canada to negotiate a free trade agreement with the United States in order to secure improved access to the U.S. market and to provide a greater defence against U.S. protectionism. A successful agreement would establish a free-trade area rather than a common market or customs union; cover substantially all trade between the two countries; allow some sectors to be excluded; be consistent with the GENERAL AGREEMENT ON TARIFFS AND TRADE; apply to tariffs, contingency protecting such as ANTI-DUMPING, and COUNTERVAILING DUTIES; allow for a longer period for Canada to eliminate tariffs than the United States; neutralize or reduce non-tariff barriers by common procedures and control them by codes of conduct; establish a joint tribunal to decide on and implement the codes of conduct; provide for mutually accept-able transitional adjustment assistance and safeguards measures; include effective dispute-settlement proce-dures on the proper interpretation of the agreement; be guaranteed by national laws; and provide adequate room to encompass provincial and state interests. It also called for the establishment of a Canada-United States Trade Commission to take over from national authorities the handling of anti-dumping, countervailing-duty and other trade-remedy actions. The commission said that Canada should pursue much stronger support for Canadian culture to offset the impact of the free trade agreement. In addi-tion, as part of its international focus, Canada should adopt the foreign-aid target of 0.7 percent of GROSS NATIONAL PRODUCT by 1990 and 1 percent by 2000.

Reviewing Canada's prospects for growth and employment, the commis-sion warned that without major policy changes Canada faced "steady but unspectacular growth" and great diffi-culty in bringing unemployment on a sustainable basis below 6.5 to 8 per-cent. "A long-term employment goal of less than 5 percent is feasible," it said, but "only if Canadians support the necessary changes in policy and structural and institutional factors

that influence the efficient allocation of resources." Warning that Canada's natural resources could no longer guarantee jobs and rising living stan-dards, the commission said Canada needed a "highly adaptive economy." Industrial policy, it said, should emphasize Canada's productivity per-formance and overall competitiveness. Rejecting a targeted industrial strate-gy, the commission said Canada should also reject a "hands off" approach; government should embrace a market-oriented approach, strength-ening Canada's areas of comparative advantage through "incentives for excellence." It called on the federal government to review the tax system to improve the climate for savings and investment; it also proposed changes in Canada's research and development (R&D) incentives, more emphasis on technology diffusion, and increased funding for business schools to improve management education. Other proposals to strengthen the economy included the adoption of a personal consumption tax, a review of the regulatory process, including a 10-year "sunset clause" on major regula-tory activities, revisions to Canadian competition policy, privatization of some crown corporations, and some relaxation of existing restrictions on foreign investment. It said that takeovers of Canadian companies with assets of $50 million should be subject to review, that a code of conduct bc adopted for all firms in Canada with assets of more than $50 million and that each company be required to file an annual return showing its perfor-mance, and that Canadian directors of foreign-controlled companies be required to file an additional return showing how their corporation was promoting the performance objectives set out in the code. The commission called for improved adjustment poli-cies, directed primarily at moving workers from declining industries to growing industries, incentives to industry to create a first-rate transportation and communications network in Canada, and measures to strengthen the economic union. Turning to economic performance, the commission urged structural changes to make 5 percent unemployment feasible, including major reforms to unemployment insurance and the creation of a Transitional Adjustment Assistance Program and a Universal Income Security Program. The commission proposed indexation of financial assets, accounting systems, and tax systems, including capital gains. It also endorsed the temporary use of wage and price controls or tax-based incomes policies to control inflation. To make wages and prices more flexible, the commission called for changes in the COLLECTIVE BARGAINING process and the encouragement of gains-sharing in which employees would share in the profits or revenues of firms. The commission also expressed concern about budget deficits. But, it said, "we do not believe that short-term budgetary problems should be resolved by making large reductions in the resources redistributed through income transfers." There is no "crisis of the welfare state," the commission insisted. Dealing with natural resources and the environment, the commission called for major new approaches in agriculture, forestry, fisheries, energy, and mining. Canada's system of supply-management marketing boards should be phased out and other measures such as increased R&D and expansion of foreign markets adopted for agriculture. Because of a legacy of mismanagement, the forest sector needed a major infusion of public and private investment to replace timber stands. In the case of oil and gas, the commission favoured a move to world prices for oil, deregulation of natural gas, a tax system based on profit rather than output, and a continuation of the

"tilt" in favour of Canadian-owned firms. It called for the establishment of a Council of Resource Ministers to co-ordinate federal and provincial policies along with a renewed Canadian research effort in Canadian resource industries and in environmental management. It called for a strengthening of the regulatory framework to protect the environment as well as the integration of economic and environmental decision-making.

The commission proposed sweeping changes to Canada's social system, based on the Canadian values of equity, security, opportunity, and sharing. An overhaul of unemployment insurance was needed, it said, including experience rating or premiums based on the risk of unemployment, a reduction in the benefit rate to 50 percent of insurable earnings, an increase in the qualifying period to 15 to 20 weeks of work, and elimination of the extended benefit period based on regional unemployment rates. Total savings of at least $4 billion at 1985 rates of unemployment were probable, it said. Much of this saving should be passed on in the form of premium reductions and an equivalent amount raised in corporate and personal tax increases to fund a Transitional Adjustment Assistance Fund to finance a Transitional Adjustment Assistance Program for Canadians who have exhausted unemployment insurance benefits if they were willing to move or to take retraining. The commission endorsed affirmative action and also proposed that equal-employment provisions be legislated. While endorsing government support for the labour movement and collective bargaining, the commission called for a re-examination of Canada's adversarial labour-management relations and greater flexibility for multi-employer and multi-union bargaining. It proposed mandatory health and safety committees in all workplaces and called on the federal and provincial governments to consider a comprehensive social insurance disability plant to deal with the long-term impact of occupational health problems. The commission was highly critical of the current federal-provincial system of financing universities and proposed that federal cash grants go to university students rather than to provincial governments, in the form of an education-expense tax credit or grant. It also called for a national commission to monitor quality and standards in Canada's elementary and secondary schools. In addition, it urged that the federal government provide a wage subsidy for labour-force entrants aged 15 to 18 who lacked vocational training or post-secondary education and, under the Income Tax Act, a Registered Educational Leave Savings Plan to help finance the cost of training. But its most sweeping social reform called for the elimination of the GUARANTEED INCOME SUPPLEMENT, FAMILY ALLOWANCES, child tax credits, spousal exemptions, child exemptions, federal contributions to social assistance payments, and federal social-housing programs, and their replacement by a Universal Income Security Program, which would be a universally available income guarantee, subject to reduction at a relatively low "tax-back" rate for additional earned income. Under its proposals, a two-adult two-child family would receive up to $9,180 a year, which, the commission said, would be supplemented by provincial social assistance, bringing the guaranteed annual income to about $12,500 to $13,500. The commission also proposed sweeping institutional changes in Canada, including greater consultation and oneness in the political system, including an end to budget secrecy. It proposed that a permanent Economic Policy Committee be established in the House of Commons, which would hold annual pre-budget hearings, with testimony from the Department of FINANCE, the BANK OF CANADA, and the TREASURY

BOARD, as well as private sector witnesses. It called for an elected Senate, based on proportional representation by population. It called for clarification of Section 121 of the CONSTITUTION ACT, 1987, to strengthen the freedom of movement of goods, services, capital, and labour across Canada. It also urged the federal and provincial governments to agree on a Code of Economic Conduct to strengthen the Canadian economic union, to be backed up by a new federal-provincial Council of Economic Development Ministers, supported by a federal-provincial Commission on the Economic Union. The commission proposed sweeping changes to regional-development programs, with the federal government ending all explicit and direct regional employment-creation schemes, along with regionally differentiated tax credits and other measures. Funds formerly allocated to these types of programs would be allocated to Regional Economic Development Grants that would be paid to eligible provinces that signed economic and regional-development agreements with the federal government and signed the proposed Code of Economic Conduct to improve the functioning of the Canadian economic union. Overall, the commission said, regional funding would "increase significantly." The commission recommended the establishment of a federal-provincial Tax Structure Committee to improve the functioning of the tax system; a continuation, with some constraints, on Ottawa's ability to launch shared-cost programs; increased intergovernmental delegation; and the establishment of three federal-provincial ministerial councils in the fields of finance, economic development, and social policy. It urged the recognition of Quebec as a distinct society, that consideration be given to aboriginal self-government, and that Canadian cities be given a greater role in national deliberations.

Royal Commission on Transportation A commission appointed in 1959 to investigate transportation problems in Canada, in particular in the railway industry. The original chairman was Mr. Justice Charles McTague, but he was replaced by Mr. Justice Murdoch A. MacPherson.

The report, in three volumes, was published over 1961 and 1962. It called for a significant increase in the freedom of railways to end uneconomic passenger services and to eliminate, over a fifteen-year period, uneconomic branch lines. While it did not call for the abolition of the CROW'S NEST grain rates, it said that the railways should receive extra subsidies to carry out the grain-handling responsibilities imposed on them by Parliament. The commission pointed to the great changes occurring in transportation in Canada — the great growth in air travel and increasing use of highways and pipelines, for example — and said that new public policies would be needed to ensure a competitive environment that worked to the public benefit. It emphasized that the railways could only compete effectively with other carriers if uneconomic responsibilities were eliminated. The commission led eventually to a new National Transportation Act, and the establishment of the CANADIAN TRANSPORT COMMISSION.

royalty A payment for the use or exploitation of someone else's property. Examples include royalties paid to government by oil, natural gas, or mining companies for the right to extract natural resources, and royalties paid to the owners of PATENTS or COPYRIGHTS to use their INTELLECTUAL PROPERTY. Royalties are usually fixed as a percentage of production, sales revenue, or sales. Under section 109 of the CONSTITUTION ACT, 1867, the provinces are empowered to impose royalties on the exploitation of land, forests, minerals, oil, and natural gas.

rule of law The underlying principle governing Canadian society, namely, that the law as passed by elected representatives is supreme, and that everyone, including the different levels of government and all their officials and agents, including the police, must obey the country's laws. The rule of law is intended to protect citizens from the arbitrary exercise of power by government and from the abuse of power by government. It is also equal in its intent, treating powerful and weak alike.

rules of origin The rules that determine what level of tariff, if any, will be imposed on a product imported from one country into another. Both the CANADA-UNITED STATES FREE TRADE AGREEMENT and the NORTH AMERICAN FREE TRADE AGREEMENT (NAFTA) contain strict rules of origin to determine which products shall enter one country from another within the preferential trade grouping duty free. For example, under NAFTA, motor vehicles must have 62.5 percent North American content, while most textiles and clothing must be made from yarns produced within North America. More generally, goods are deemed to be produced in North America, even though they may contain raw materials or components produced outside North America, if the non-North American content is sufficiently transformed within North America to undergo a change in tariff classification. If a good fails to meet the North-American-content test it will still be considered to be North American in origin if the value of non-North American materials comprises no more than 7 percent of the total cost of the good.

runaway inflation Unusually high and rapidly increasing inflation.

SDR   *See* SPECIAL DRAWING RIGHT.

sacrifice ratio   The increase in unemployment that results from policy measures to lower inflation. Various anti-inflation policies can have different sacrifice ratios. For example, an anti-inflation policy implemented through a tightening of monetary policy alone is likely to cause a greater increase in unemployment than an anti-inflation policy that combines monetary tightening with incomes policy and supply-side measures. The sacrifice ratio is calculated by dividing the unemployment gap, or the amount of unemployment in excess of the "natural rate," over a period of time, by the reduction in the inflation rate during the same period.

safeguard   A temporary measure to curb the flow of imports in an industry threatened by a sharp rise in imports — for example, through a temporary increase in tariffs or an import quota. The GENERAL AGREEMENT ON TARIFFS (GATT), the CANADA-UNITED STATES FREE TRADE AGREEMENT, and the NORTH AMERICAN FREE TRADE AGREEMENT all contain provisions permitting safeguards when a domestic industry is threatened with serious injury due to a surge in imports. Under Article XIX of the GATT, a country may adopt safeguard measures if imports are causing actual damage or threatening to damage a domestic industry for no longer than five years. A country whose exports are affected has the right to seek compensating tariff reductions in other areas or, failing that, has the right to retaliate. Canada has been a significant user of Article XIX. About half the safeguard actions are taken against agricultural products and textiles and clothing. Because of the disciplines imposed by GATT in the use of safeguard measures, countries have increasingly resorted to bilateral arrangements outside GATT known as VOLUNTARY RESTRAINT AGREEMENTS, which are also known as orderly marketing arrangements. These consist of undertakings by exporting countries to limit their exports.

safety-deposit box   An area maintained in the vault of a bank or trust-company branch, in which a number of individual drawers are rented out to customers for the safekeeping of securities, jewels, records, and other valuable items. Each drawer needs two keys to be opened: one belonging to the customer and the other to the financial institution.

Saint Lawrence Seaway Authority The crown corporation established in 1954 to construct, maintain, and operate the Canadian sections of the St. Lawrence Seaway, a deep waterway between Montreal and Lake Erie. The authority also co-operated with its U.S. counterpart, the St. Lawrence Seaway Development Corporation, in jointly building, maintaining, and operating international segments of the seaway. The St. Lawrence Seaway opened for commercial use on April 1, 1959. The seaway is funded by tolls levied on ships using its facilities. It consists of two systems: the Montreal to Lake Ontario section with seven locks, five of them owned and operated by the St. Lawrence Seaway Authority and the other two by the United States, and the Welland Canal section, with all eight locks owned and operated by the St. Lawrence Seaway Authority. The authority is based in Ottawa.

salary Compensation paid to an employee each week, fortnight, or month, not directly tied to actual hours worked, as opposed to a WAGE, which is paid according to the number of hours worked. Industrial employees tend to be paid wages, while administrative or white-collar workers are usually paid salaries.

sale and leaseback A technique of business financing, in which a business sells an asset, such as a plant or item of heavy machinery or equipment, to an investor or financial institution, and then promptly leases it back under a long-term agreement. The business gets immediate cash but retains the use of the asset.

sale and repurchase agreement Sales to the chartered banks, at the initiative of the BANK OF CANADA, of short-term securities under an arrangement to repurchase them from the banks on the next business day.

sales-finance company A company that finances installment-credit purchases of durable goods by consumers, farmers, and small business. Goods purchased in this way include cars, trucks, tractors, farm implements, and household appliances. Many retailers sell sales contracts they have signed with consumers to a sales-finance or acceptance company; car dealers, for example, often handle car sales this way, reselling the sales contract to a finance company, which frequently is owned and operated by the automotive manufacturer.

sales tax A tax that is applied when goods or services are sold. It can be applied at many different stages of production and sale. Canada has a GOODS AND SERVICES TAX (GST) that is collected by the federal government at each stage or transaction in the production and sale of goods and services. All the provinces except Alberta have a retail-sales tax. The GST and provincial retail-sales taxes are direct taxes, because they are paid by the consumer and cannot be passed along to anyone else. Sales taxes are considered regressive by some economists, because they take a larger fraction of income from people with lower incomes and a lower fraction from those with higher incomes, when both groups are purchasing the same goods and services. The GST was introduced on January 1, 1991, replacing a manufacturers' sales tax that was introduced in 1924. The first province to bring in a retail-sales tax was Alberta in 1936, but the province dropped the tax the same year, due to protests by Albertans. The city of Montreal collected its own sales tax from 1935 until 1940, when Quebec introduced a province-wide sales tax. Most provinces adopted retail-sales taxes in the 1950s and 1960s. *See also* VALUE-ADDED TAX.

salvage value The amount of money an asset would fetch if it were scrapped.

sample 1. A small portion of ore or rock that is taken to assess the possible mineral content. **2.** A representative segment of a statistical group — the entire population, the labour force, farms, or consumer prices, for example — from which conclusions can be drawn about the entire group.

Samuelson, Paul (b. 1915) An American economist who won the Alfred Nobel Memorial Prize in Economic Science in 1970 "for the scientific work through which he has developed static and dynamic economic theory and actively contributing to raising the level of analysis in economic science." Samuelson is a KEYNESIAN economist.

samurai bond A yen-denominated bond issued in Japan by a foreign borrower that can be purchased by foreigners. *See also* SHOGUN BOND.

sanctions The severing of trade, investment, and other economic relations with another state, to force it to halt a military act; to withdraw from occupied territory; to alter a domestic policy, such as racial discrimination; or to take some other desired step. In 1966, the United Nations adopted trade sanctions on selected products from Rhodesia (now Zimbabwe) because it would not grant majority rule to its black citizens; these sanctions were later widened to a complete embargo on trade and other economic dealings with Rhodesia, until it changed its racial policies. Canada maintains an Area Control List under the Export and Import Permits Act. At the start of 1993, export permits were required for the export of all goods to the following countries on the list: Bosnia-Herzegovina, Croatia, Haiti, Libya, South Africa, and Yugoslavia.

satisficing theory The theory that firms will seek an acceptable level of profits but will not pursue profit maximization. Other priorities, such as increasing its market share, will deter a firm from pursuing profit maximization, in contrast to economic theory that assumes all firms are profit maximizers.

savings Income that is not spent when it is earned but is set aside for the accumulation of wealth that can lead to future consumption. A country's savings consist of household, business, and government savings. The economic growth of a country depends on investment, which depends either on domestic savings or borrowing from the pool of foreign savings. Individuals save either by putting part of their current income into pension plans and insurance policies, by paying off mortgage principal, by investing their money in shares, bonds, mutual funds, and savings certificates, or by holding their money in bank, trust-company, and credit-union savings accounts. Corporations save by retaining part of their profits each year for reinvestment in their own operations or to acquire other companies. Savings provide the funds for capital formation and productive capability for the future. Governments also "save" when they run budget surpluses. But they reduce the private pool of savings when they run deficits; this is not a problem when the economy is in recession or experiencing slow growth, but government deficits during periods of strong economic growth can crowd out private borrowers, forcing up interest rates and making business investment more expensive. There are many different reasons why individuals save; they include acquiring a home or recreation cottage, providing for emergency family needs, and building up a reserve to meet personal needs in old age. The decision to save may be encouraged by higher interest rates or tax incentives, and may be discouraged by high inflation. Savings are also affected by a person's level of income, with the PROPENSITY TO SAVE rising with income. *See also* MARGINAL PROPENSITY TO SAVE. The level of personal savings in the gross domestic product can be calculated by subtracting from personal disposable income, total personal spending on consumer goods and services, interest on consumer debt, and payments to non-residents; the remaining figure is the level of personal savings in the economy. Canada's personal savings rate is the difference between personal disposable income and total personal spending. Total or gross savings in the economy are published quarterly by Statistics Canada in its NATIONAL INCOME AND EXPENDITURE ACCOUNTS (publication 13-001).

savings bond A bond sold to the public in low denominations and through payroll-deduction and other savings plans. *See also* CANADA SAVINGS BOND.

savings rate The percentage of personal disposable income that is saved.

Say's law The assertion that there can never be a shortage of purchasing power because supply creates its own demand. This was a fundamental tenet of economics from the time it was expressed by French businessman Jean Baptiste Say (1767-1832) until it was effectively demolished by JOHN MAYNARD KEYNES in 1936. Say argued that every time something was produced and sold, the equivalent amount of demand was generated in the economy, in wages, rents, profits, and other forms of income. In other words, the cost of producing goods and services created an equivalent amount of income, all of which would be spent. If some people saved their income, others would borrow it for consumption purchases; if they did not, prices would fall until supply and demand were again in balance. As Say saw it, the economic system was self-correcting and would tend to operate at about full employment, though this would mean that, during periods of adjustment, wages would have to fall. Keynes argued that it was possible to have overproduction or a shortage of purchasing power. Left to its own devices, the economic system would restore EQUILIBRIUM, but at a lower level of output and higher level of unemployment. Keynes argued that the government should borrow excess savings and spend them in the economy to restore a full-employment equilibrium.

scab *See* STRIKEBREAKER.

scarcity The condition that exists when we can't satisfy all our wants; it is the normal condition of economic life, with the efficient allocation of resources in a world of scarcity a fundamental challenge of economics. For scarcity to exist, goods and services must be wanted and there must be some difficulty in obtaining all that we want of them. The study of economics is built around the notion of scarcity. The existence of scarcity creates the need for some kind of system — whether free-market forces and the price system, or government planning — to allocate scarce resources. Even though some consumer goods, such as toasters or transistor radios, may appear plentiful, they are still scarce in the sense that there are not enough of them to distribute freely, and those who want toasters or transistor radios have to forgo some other good or service to satisfy their wants. The idea of scarcity is based on the fact that there are limited amounts of human and material resources, and that no combination of these can produce everything that everyone would want.

scenario   A forecast of a likely outcome based on a particular set of assumptions. In determining the likely demand for oil and natural gas for example, the NATIONAL ENERGY BOARD calculates a series of scenarios of supply and demand, based on different assumptions about Canada's future rate of economic and population growth, and future energy prices.

Schedule I bank   A Canadian-owned bank that is defined in the BANK ACT as widely held, with no shareholder having more than 10 percent of the total shares.

Schedule II bank   A foreign-owned bank or a Canadian-owned bank that is defined in the BANK ACT as closely held, with an individual shareholder owning more than 10 percent of the outstanding shares.

Schultz, Theodore (b. 1902)   An American economist who won the Alfred Nobel Memorial Prize in Economics Science in 1979, along with Sir Arthur LEWIS, for "pioneering research into economic development research with particular consideration of the problems of developing countries." Schultz is best known for his work in analyzing the returns from investment in agriculture and for his work in the benefits from investment in education.

Schumpeter, Joseph A. (1883-1950)   An Austrian-born economist who, after teaching economics in Germany, serving briefly as Austria's finance minister in 1919, and running a private Austrian Bank, moved to Harvard University in 1932 to teach economics. Schumpeter's far-reaching insights into the determinants of economic growth are published in a number of books including *Business Cycles* (1939) and *Capitalism, Socialism, and Democracy* (1942). He was one of the first economists to recognize the powerful role played by ideas, knowledge, innovation, and entrepreneurship in driving economic growth. It was the entrepreneur, Schumpeter argued, who played the critical role in economic growth by developing new goods and services, devising new methods of production and delivery, pursuing new markets, exploiting new uses of natural resources, and inventing new workplace practices or forms of business organization. This made the entrepreneur the principle change agent in the economy; without active entrepreneurs, economic progress would come to an end. Schumpeter attributed much less importance to traditional MACROECONOMIC factors in explaining economic growth, attaching innovation resulting from entrepreneurship as the decisive factor. For a variety of reasons, he argued, innovations tended to occur in surges or cycles. See KONDRATIEFF CYCLE. As innovations occur, Schumpeter said, there is a "creative destruction of capital" as old industries disappear and new industries are created. He regarded this as a healthy and necessary adjustment and an essential part of economic progress. Competition, in this sense, is between old and new ways of doing things, and between old and new industries, rather than the price competition found in standard economics. But despite the past success of entrepreneurs in bringing about enormous economic progress, Schumpeter believed that capitalism was doomed and would be replaced by socialism; his argument was that the seeds of capitalism's decline were contained in its very success, that the continuing growth of capitalism would wipe out small farmers and small business, the social institutions that supported the system, and that business enterprises would become large and bureaucratic and stifle entrepreneurship. Schumpeter did not foresee that technology and innovation opportunities would continue to attract entrepreneurs or that new sources of capital, such as VENTURE CAPITAL, would emerge. Schumpeter's contribution to economics was to explain the significance of technological change and innovation in economic growth and the dynamic role played by entrepreneurs as the agents of economic change and economic progress. He underlined the importance of the creative destruction of capital, as represented by old industries, as opposed to the static equilibrium theories pursued by most economists and their failure to understand the role played by ideas, knowledge, and innovation in accounting for economic growth and as essential factors in economic progress.

Science and Technology, Ministry of State for (MOSST)   A policy ministry created in 1971 to advise the government on science policy, including measures to increase basic research, to attain greater application of the research already underway, to increase research and development in private industry, and to negotiate technology-sharing and research and development projects with other countries. In 1990, it was absorbed into the Department of INDUSTRY, SCIENCE AND TECHNOLOGY CANADA, with a junior minister responsible for science.

Science Council of Canada   A scientific advisory body to the federal government, created in 1966 and given greater independence as a crown corporation in 1969. It was abolished by the federal government in 1992. The council had 25 members selected from industry, the universities, and government, who had a special interest in science and technology; the council also had a full-time staff of experts. Its job was to identify areas of scientific opportunity for Canada, to assess Canada's scientific capabilities and weaknesses, and to recommend policies to improve the contribution of science and technology to the Canadian economy and to the well-being of Canadians. The council has carried out major studies on the need for an INDUSTRIAL STRATEGY; the impact of multinational corporations on Canada's research and development efforts; the status of university research; science opportunities in agriculture, forestry, and the North; occupational health; health care; and energy. It has also recommended major science programs in such areas as transportation, telecommunications, water-resource management, and energy. The council was also a pioneer in developing the concept of SUSTAINABLE DEVELOPMENT, with its reports on the CONSERVER SOCIETY. Many of its reports were unpopular with federal cabinet ministers and senior government officials because its findings inevitably highlighted gaps or weaknesses in federal policies.

science policy   Policy to encourage basic and applied research and development. Tools include financial support for graduate students in science and engineering, direct funding to government laboratories and universities, the contracting out of government research projects to universities and private industry, government risk sharing with industry in major industry projects, direct government funding of major basic science projects, and tax incentives and grants to private industry to carry out research and development projects.

scientific research and experimental development tax incentive   Canada's principal tax incentive for research and development. In 1992, it provided a 100 percent deduction of current and capital spending for qualifying research and development spending plus a 20 percent investment tax credit on these expenditures up to 75 percent of federal tax payable. Unused deductions can be carried forward indefinitely and unused investment tax credits can be carried back three years and forward 10 years. For Canadian-controlled private corporations with taxable income not exceeding $200,000 in the previous year, the investment tax credit is raised to 35 percent for the first $2 million of qualifying expenditures. The 35 percent investment tax credit is phased down to the 20 percent level for small Canadian corporations as taxable income reaches $400,000. In addition, there is a refundable tax credit where the investment tax credit exceeds 100 percent of federal tax payable on current expenditures and 40 percent on capital expenditures. Technological advancement is the key determinant of what spending qualifies.

scrip   A certificate that can be exchanged for cash and that is usually issued when a stock dividend or a stock split results in a shareholder being entitled to a fraction of a stock. Scrip is issued in exchange for the fraction of a stock.

seasonal adjustment   A statistical adjustment to take account of unusual seasonal factors, so that statistical series more accurately reflect underlying trends. The main seasonal factors are climatic (affecting the fishing, farming, forest, construction, and energy industries) and institutional (such as the build-up of retail sales at Christmas and Easter). For example, Statistics Canada makes an allowance each summer for the temporary presence of large numbers of students in the labour force, in order to calculate the seasonally adjusted unemployment rate for the summer months. Similarly, a statistical series on prices could be affected by the sharp increase in fresh fruit and vegetable prices each winter.

seasonal industry   An industry that operates for only part of the year. Examples include fruit and vegetable processing, tourism, shipping on the Great Lakes logging in most parts of Canada, fishing, and farming.

seasonal unemployment   Unemployment caused by climatic and other conditions each year and that is predictable in industries such as tourism, forestry, fishing, and Great Lakes shipping, and less predictable than it used to be in others, such as construction. There is also seasonal employment, such as in the retail industry at Christmas.

seasonally adjusted unemployment rate   *See* UNEMPLOYMENT RATE.

seat   The term used for membership in a stock exchange. Membership in an exchange is obtained by purchase of a seat.

second best   An economic outcome that is suboptimal and that falls below the optimal outcome because of market imperfections or externalities.

second mortgage   An additional mortgage put on a property that already has an existing, or first mortgage, against it. The holder of the second mortgage, cannot be paid, in the event of default, until the holder of the first mortgage has been paid. That is why a second mortgage usually commands a higher rate of interest than a first mortgage.

second world   The designation that existed for the Communist countries of Eastern Europe and the former Soviet Union. The Second-World nations played virtually no role in the NORTH-SOUTH DIALOGUE and the debate over a NEW INTERNATIONAL ECONOMIC ORDER; in spite of their relatively high standard of living, they provided little non-military foreign aid to the DEVELOPING COUNTRIES. The First World consisted of the industrial nations and the Third World of the developing countries. The term Fourth World is sometimes used to describe the poorest of the less-developed countries.

secondary distribution   The sale to the public of a large block of company shares that had previously been distributed; this means it is not a new issue. The shares may come from a significant investor who wants to liquidate his holdings, from an institution such as a pension fund, or from the trustees of an estate. The shares may be purchased by an investment dealer or group of dealers, and resold to the public.

secondary industry   A synonym for manufacturing industry.

secondary market   A bond, stock, or other securities market where shares, bonds, or other securities are sold by one investor to another, following the initial issue of the security in a PRIMARY MARKET. This means that an investor and not the issuing entity — a corporation or government — receives the proceeds of the sale.

secondary offering   The offering of a large block of shares that is too large for a sale to a single or small group of investors, by an investor on the market.

secondary recovery   In the oil and gas industry, the use of proven and feasible techniques to obtain production from oil and natural-gas reservoirs in addition to that resulting from the normal pressures in the reservoirs. Common techniques include water flooding and gas or steam injection. *See also* PRIMARY RECOVERY, TERTIARY RECOVERY.

secondary-reserve ratio   The second reserve that had to be maintained by each of the chartered banks under the BANK ACT; the other reserve requirement was the PRIMARY RESERVE RATIO. Under Bank Act amendments proclaimed in 1992, reserve requirements were to be abolished by 1994. With reserve requirements, the BANK OF CANADA could manipulate the country's money supply by altering the secondary-reserve requirements, and thereby increase or reduce the ability of the banking system to make loans or to purchase securities. The secondary reserve consisted of TREASURY BILLS held by the banks, and the day-to-day loans that the banks make to MONEY-MARKET DEALERS.

Secretary of State of Canada   A federal government department originally established in 1867 as the channel of communication between the new Canadian government and the British government. Today its principal functions include federal support for education, promotion of the official-languages program, citizenship programs, and ceremonial events such as Canada Day and royal visits. The department administers payments to the provinces for post-secondary education under the Federal-Provincial Fiscal Arrangements and Federal Post-Secondary Education and Health Contributions Act, guarantees student loans authorized by the provinces, and funds official-language education.

sector   A division or part of the economy that can be studied by itself. Examples include the private and public sectors, the agricultural and non-agricultural sectors, the primary-industry sector, the goods-producing sector, the service-producing sector, the tradeable goods and services sector, the non-tradeable foods and services sector, and specific industries such as steel, textiles, machinery, motor vehicles, computers, and petrochemicals.

Sectoral Advisory Groups on International Trade (SAGITs)   *See* INTERNATIONAL TRADE ADVISORY COMMITTEE.

secular stagnation The belief that, as economies mature, they lose their dynamic capacity for technological innovation, which in turn leads to less investment, reduced aggregate demand, slower growth, and higher unemployment. This view was advanced by U.S. economist Alvin Hansen in 1938 to explain the slowdown in the U.S. and British economies. The U.S., he argued, was experiencing a slowdown in population growth, had settled its remaining frontier lands, had accumulated enormous productive capacity, and, by its emphasis on labour-saving and high technology, had reached the point where corporate profits could no longer find new investment opportunities. This meant that new policies, such as increased public spending, were needed to increase demand and to create jobs. The rapid advances in technology and the vast array of new goods and services they have spawned over the past 40 years show that economies can sustain their dynamism.

secular trend A persistent trend that reflects the effect of long-term forces at work in the economy. It is a term used in statistics to describe a trend in a particular series. Examples include the rising participation rate for women in the labour force, the growth of service-sector jobs in the economy, the growth of real per capita income, and the decline in many commodity or natural-resource prices.

secured loan A loan that is backed by collateral, which is property owned by the person or corporation seeking the loan. The collateral can consist of bonds, insurance policies, shares, real estate, or other assets, which the borrower must relinquish to the lender if he is unable to repay the loan. A secured loan, because it is backed by collateral that reduces the risk, commands a lower rate of interest than an UNSECURED LOAN.

Securities and Exchange Commission The national U.S. regulatory body established in 1934 to regulate and monitor securities markets.

securities commission A provincial body responsible for the administration of a province's SECURITIES LEGISLATION, including the maintenance and disclosure of corporate information, the issuing of a PROSPECTUS, the proper observance of rules on TAKEOVER bids, the registration of securities-industry firms and employees, and the supervision of STOCK EXCHANGES and OVER-THE-COUNTER MARKETS. Each provincial body, usually a commission but sometimes a branch of a government department, meets with its provincial counterparts twice a year to improve the uniformity of laws and regulations and to work out national policies to reduce the paperwork and costs for firms filing a prospectus in more than one province, for example. The most important securities commissions in Canada are in Ontario, Quebec, British Columbia, and Alberta.

securities legislation Provincial laws to regulate the underwriting, distribution, and sale of securities, and to protect the buyers and sellers of securities such as shares, bonds, commodity futures, tax-shelter packages for motion pictures, oil and gas drilling, real estate, mutual funds, and scholarship plans. Such laws, for example, require any corporation planning to sell a new security to the public to file a PROSPECTUS containing complete and true information. Until the prospectus is approved by a provincial SECURITIES COMMISSION, the new security issue cannot be sold to the public. Securities laws also require the registration of all INVESTMENT DEALERS, stockbrokers, INVESTMENT COUNSELLORS, and others who buy and sell securities or investment advice and management. The laws also require the registration of the securities salespeople, analysts, portfolio managers, and other employees of these firms. Securities laws cover the operation of STOCK EXCHANGES and OVER-THE-COUNTER MARKETS, and deal specifically with the manner in which securities can be traded, INSIDER information, PROXIES and proxy solicitation, the full and timely disclosure of financial information, advertising, conflict of interest, and TAKEOVER bids.

While securities regulation is a provincial activity in Canada, as opposed to a federal activity, as in the United States, the provincial securities laws have achieved a degree of uniformity since the Ontario Securities Act was passed in 1966. Agreements among the provinces on securities trading also give the securities industry a national focus.

securitization The sale of a package of loans by a financial institution to other investors, in the form of bonds or other negotiable securities. A bank or trust company, for example, can take a portfolio of mortgages it holds on various properties and package them into a bond issue or other type of investment, such as a mortgage-based mutual fund. The interest from the package or mortgages or other loans provides the interest to the investors in the securitized pool of securities. Residential mortgages, aircraft leases, collateralized consumer loans, credit-card debts, leases, and commercial-real-estate loans are types of debt that can be converted into fixed-income, asset-backed securities.

security 1. A BOND, SHARE, TREASURY BILL, or other financial asset that yields income and can readily be converted into cash by sale on the bond market, a stock exchange, or other financial market. The fact that it can be converted into cash makes it a negotiable instrument. 2. Property pledged as collateral for a loan.

security of supply A consideration in making long-term import arrangements for essential raw materials. The supply must be readily available from a politically stable country that is unlikely to halt supplies suddenly, and it must be obtainable through a militarily secure route. For example, the United States would prefer to obtain its oil and gas imports from Canada and Mexico because they are politically stable, likely to live up to their contracts, and can be defended by U.S. armed forces against military attack by an enemy — as opposed to obtaining its oil from Saudi Arabia, whose supply route to the United States is several thousand miles long, and therefore hard to defend. Both the CANADA-UNITED STATES FREE TRADE AGREEMENT and the NORTH AMERICAN FREE TRADE AGREEMENT contain provisions to provide some element of security of supply for the United States.

seigniorage The profit made by the ROYAL CANADIAN MINT from converting metals into coins and by the BANK OF CANADA from converting paper into currency that has a higher face value than the original metallic or paper content. The money that is produced can be exchanged for goods and services in the economy. One way of calculating seigniorage is to determine the purchasing power of money that is put into circulation in the economy during a given period of time.

seismic exploration The use of geophysical techniques, such as the speed and reflection of sound waves against different types of rock formations on land or on the ocean bottom, to indicate the possible presence of oil, natural gas, or other minerals.

self-dealing A non-ARM'S LENGTH transaction between a financial institution and a major shareholder, officer, or director. In a 1992 amendment, the

BANK ACT introduced the "related party" concept to control self-dealing, which can lead to imprudent loans or other forms of favouritism or abuse. The amendments generally prohibit the financial institution from entering into a transaction with a related party. Related parties include directors and officers of the financial institution or companies in which these individuals may have a substantial interest.

self-employed   People in the labour force who work for themselves. Examples include doctors, some lawyers and accountants, operators of small stores, consultants, and farmers.

self-reliance   The ability of a country to meet a significant proportion of its essential needs out of its resources and skills; it falls short of SELF-SUFFICIEN-CY, but means that the country is not overly dependent on imports to meet an essential need for a particular commodity or technology, or a group of commodities or technologies. For example, in 1977, Canada set a self-reliance target for oil that would limit oil imports to one-third of its refinery needs, or 800,000 barrels a day, whichever was less, by 1985. At the Tokyo economic summit in June, 1979, that target was reduced to 600,000 barrels a day of imports. Provided that an emergency stockpile exists, along with plans that would allow rationing or allocation of supplies, a country that aims for self-reliance instead of self-sufficiency in a key commodity should be able to withstand a temporary loss of imports without undue hardship.

self-sufficiency   The ability of a nation to meet its needs for a single commodity or product, or for a range of essential commodities and products, from its own resources and skills. While many nations would like to be self-sufficient in basic foodstuffs, energy, key technologies, and the most important RAW MATERIALS, this is usually impractical. The alternative is to develop secure sources of supply or to build up emergency stockpiles of key foodstuffs and raw materials. This can be extremely expensive, however. For example, if Canada decided to become self-sufficient in oil and if the world price of oil were $20 a barrel and expected to remain there, then it would not make economic sense to extract Canadian oil that might cost $35 a barrel, especially if no serious shortage or interruption in foreign supply was expected. Even if there was fear of such an eventuality, it might still be cheaper to pursue energy efficiency. In fact, in a world in which the principle of COMPARATIVE ADVANTAGE has been encouraged by the growth of international trade, self-sufficiency has declined and interdependence has increased. Canada has one of the world's best chances to be self-sufficient in grains, energy, forest products, and raw materials, but is at its present stage of development still highly dependent on other nations for technology. *See also* SELF-RELIANCE.

seller's market   A market in which supply is low and demand high, so that sellers are able to demand and get higher prices. It is a market in which the advantage is held by sellers. *See also* BUYER'S MARKET.

selling costs   The costs that are incurred in selling a good or service. These costs include market research, advertising, promotion, salespeople's salaries and commissions, and distribution.

selling group   Investment dealers and others who are brought in by a BANKING GROUP or SYNDICATE — the lead manager — handling a new issue of shares or bonds, to help sell the issue. The members of the selling group report their subscription results and are allocated a share of the total issue. They buy the securities from the banking group at a discount and resell them to their customers. While the banking group is responsible for the sale of the issue, the members of the selling group have no financial liability if the entire issue is not sold.

selling short   The sale, by a speculative investor, of shares or commodity futures that he or she does not own, in the belief that the price will decline so that the investor will be able to buy them back at a lower price and thus replace the shares, pay the stockbroker's commission, and still make a profit. When the short-sale is made, the stockbroker borrows the shares sold from someone else (usually someone who has a MARGIN account with the same broker), while the short-seller must deposit cash with the broker to cover the sale. This cash is used to buy the same number of shares, if and when the price declines, the share certificates being returned to the account from which they were borrowed and the stockbroker collecting his or her commission. What is left over goes to the short-seller; if the shares go up in price, rather than decline, then he has to pay a deficit and thus suffer a loss. Canadian stock exchanges have strict rules governing short-selling. *See also* LONG SELLING.

semifinished goods   Partially manufactured or processed goods that are not yet ready for consumption and cannot be sold in their present condition.

semiskilled worker   A worker who has some job experience in a particular skill, but who has not gone through an apprenticeship or other extended training program. The skills possessed are of less value than those of a SKILLED WORKER. *See also* UNSKILLED WORKER.

senior bond   A corporate bond that has first claim on a corporation's assets and earnings, such as a first-mortgage bond.

senior debt   The debt that has to be paid off before any other claims can be considered.

seniority   The length of service of an employee in a firm, determining his status when it comes to layoffs, callbacks after layoffs, promotions, length of vacation, or early retirement. Most collective agreements give preferential treatment to workers with the greatest seniority. Length of service may not be the only consideration; service as a union officer may also add to an individual's seniority, for example. Thus, when a firm lays off workers, it lays off those with the least seniority first; when it recalls laid-off workers, it recalls those with the greatest seniority first. Seniority was introduced to prevent favouritism or exploitation of workers.

separation rate   The percentage of workers in the labour force or in a firm or industry who quit, who are laid off, or who retire in any defined period of time. It is an important labour-market indicator, since a rising separation rate usually indicates slackening economic activity, and vice versa.

serial bond   A bond issue with staggered maturities so that it is redeemed by a pre-determined amount each year. By the final year, only a small amount of the original loan remains to be paid off. In a serial-bond issue, the shorter maturities may be sold to banks and trust companies, and the longer maturities to individuals and to institutional investors, such as pension funds and insurance companies.

service industry   An industry that produces a SERVICE rather than a tangible good, for which someone will pay money. A growing proportion of Canadians are employed in service industries rather than in goods-producing industries.

services   Intangible consumer or producer goods that are usually consumed at the time they are produced and purchased. The service sector accounts for the largest share of employment and is the source of growing employment. Trade in services is also a growing portion of international trade, though it is much more difficult to measure than merchandise trade. Many service industries are closely linked to goods-producing industries so that a healthy service sector may depend on a healthy manufacturing sector while, at the same time, the competitiveness of the manufacturing sector may be affected by the quality of the service sector. The value of production of services in the Canadian economy is reported by Statistics Canada in its monthly publication, *Gross Domestic Product by Industry* (publication 15-001). Employment in the service sector is reported monthly by Statistics Canada in its publication, *The Labour Force* (publication 71-001). Canada's trade in services is reported in the quarterly Statistics Canada publication, *Canada's Balance of International Payments* (publication 67-001). Additional information is provided in *Canada's International Transactions in Services* (publication 67-203). Statistics Canada publishes additional reports on the service industries. Examples of services include banking and other financial services such as insurance, construction, transportation, communications, education, and health; business and professional services such as accounting, advertising, law, and management consulting; wholesale and retail trade; engineering; entertainment; and personal services such as hairdressers and drycleaners. Sometimes a service industry will produce an economic good that is not altogether intangible — for example, architectural or engineering drawings, accounting statements, or computer print-outs.

settlement date   The date by which a purchaser of shares, bonds, or other securities must pay for the purchase, or by which the seller of shares, bonds, or other securities must deliver the certificates representing the securities he has sold. For most transactions, it is the fifth business day after the transaction itself.

settlement price   In commodity markets, the average price at the conclusion of the day's trading.

settlements   Settlements between central banks to cover balance-of-payments deficits and debts arising from currency interventions. The BANK FOR INTERNATIONAL SETTLEMENTS is a clearing centre for central banks.

severance pay   A payment made to an employee who is fired, or whose job disappears due to automation or a shutdown of a branch or plant of a firm. The amount may be as little as two weeks' pay in the case of dismissal, or as much as a year's pay if the employee has a long record of service with the firm.

severely-indebted low-income countries   The poorest developing countries, with heavy debt burdens. Their debt is owed mainly to governments and international financial institutions, and most of these countries are found in sub-Saharan Africa.

share   Ownership of part of the capital stock of a corporation, as represented by the possession of share certificates registered in the name of the shareholder. When a company is incorporated, it is authorized to issue a maximum number of PREFERRED and COMMON SHARES. The number of shares issued is the number that has actually been sold to investors, while the number outstanding is the number issued minus any shares that have been bought back — or redeemed, in the case of preferred shares — by the corporation. If the corporation has issued the maximum number of shares authorized, it can increase its authorized capital by SUPPLEMENTARY LETTERS PATENT. Shares are bought and sold on STOCK EXCHANGES or on the OVER-THE-COUNTER MARKET through STOCKBROKERS. The ownership of 5 percent of the common shares of a corporation entitles the owner to 5 percent of the issued dividends, 5 percent of the votes at the annual or other meetings, and 5 percent of the net assets if the corporation is wound up. *See also* NON-VOTING SHARES.

share capital   The total number of shares issued by a company.

share register   *See* REGISTRAR.

share split   *See* STOCK SPLIT.

shared-cost program   A program whose costs are shared by more than one level of government. For example, the federal government introduced hospital insurance, medicare, and the Canada Assistance Plan as cost-sharing programs, paying half the costs to those provinces that agreed to participate. Similarly, provincial governments have shared-cost programs with their municipalities — for example, to encourage the construction of transit systems, to build roads, or to provide day care and other social services. Sometimes, shared-cost programs may bring together all three levels of government — for example, in some federal housing and urban-redevelopment programs.

For the senior level of government, such programs are a way of stimulating activity through a lower level of government, where the senior level of government sees a need but cannot act on its own for constitutional or other reasons. Thus, the federal government, by introducing hospital insurance and

medicare programs, was able to push all the provinces into providing universal health care for Canadians; left on their own, the provinces might have taken much longer, but they could not afford to ignore the incentive of federal funding for half the cost. Such funding is also known as a conditional grant, since another level of government offers to pay a grant if certain conditions are met.

The provinces have resented the introduction of shared-cost programs, contending that the federal government has used this device to enter fields that are really under provincial jurisdiction and to alter a province's own choice of spending priorities. The federal government has responded that it has a duty to see that all Canadians, regardless of where they live, have access to a uniform set of basic services, such as health, welfare, housing, and post-secondary education. Section 106 of the Constitution Act, 1867, permits the federal government to spend money for the "Public Service," which it can perhaps use to justify spending in areas of provincial jurisdiction. Today there are many different types of shared-cost programs, including some in which the federal government and only a few of the provinces participate. Examples include tourism development, manpower training, assistance to the blind and disabled, and regional development. *See also* OPTING OUT, UNCONDITIONAL GRANT.

shareholder   The owner of voting or non-voting shares in a corporation; shareholders are entitled to receive dividends and annual and quarterly reports of the corporation's affairs. Most shares traded are voting shares, which entitle the owner to attend annual meetings to elect directors, approve the auditor's report, and question management on the corporation's policies and plans. Owners of voting shares are also entitled to attend special meetings to approve mergers or changes in the corporation's charter. If shareholders cannot attend a corporation meeting, they are entitled to transfer their votes to others by signing PROXY statements.

shareholder of record   A shareholder whose name and ownership of shares are recorded in the company register as of a certain date, and who is thus entitled to receive a dividend that has been declared, or to participate in a RIGHTS ISSUE.

shareholders' equity   The interest of the shareholders in a corporation if all of its liabilities were to be paid off. It is calculated from a corporation's BALANCE SHEET by deducting total liabilities from total assets; what is left over is shareholders' equity. It consists of several items: 1. Capital stock, which is the money raised by the corporation from the sale of its shares. 2. Retained earnings, which are the after-tax profits over the life of the corporation that have not been paid out as dividends to shareholders but have been reinvested in the business instead. 3. Contributed surplus, the funds raised from the sale of shares in excess of the par value or market value of the shares when they were offered for sale. 4. The excess of appraised value of fixed assets over their original cost, an item that appears when a major fixed asset is reappraised and found to be worth much more than its original cost. One way of measuring the profitability of a corporation is to determine its after-tax profits as a percentage of shareholders' equity; its performance can be compared with that of other firms in the same industry or in other industries. If a corporation suffers a loss, the loss is deducted from the retained earnings of the firm, thus reducing the shareholders' equity.

shark repellant   Defensive measures by a company to discourage a hostile takeover, for example by amending its corporate bylaws to require approval, say, by 70 percent of shares instead of the normal 50 percent to approve a takeover.

Sharpe, William (b. 1934)   The American economist who, with Harry MARKOWITZ and Merton MILLER, was awarded the Alfred Nobel Memorial Prize in Economic Sciences in 1990 for "pioneering work in the theory of financial economics."

shell company   A company that is listed on a stock exchange but that has few assets. Shell companies are often sought by entrepreneurs or promoters as a quick way to acquire a stock-market listing for a new enterprise. Another company will buy the shell company, merge the operations, and perhaps even change the name of the listed company.

shift   The scheduled working hours for a group of employees in a firm or government agency. *See also* SPLIT SHIFT.

shift differential   Extra pay for those who work on shifts other than the normal daytime shift. Employees who work, say, from 4 p.m. to midnight, or midnight to 8 a.m., may get an extra 10 percent above the base rate of pay for daytime workers, to compensate for having to work less attractive hours.

shifting   The passing of a tax from the person on whom it is levied to someone else. For example, corporate income taxes and excise taxes are shifted from the businesses and products on which they are levied to customers of these businesses and consumers of their products.

shipping conference   A group of ocean-going shipping companies that sets shipping rates, routes, and schedules for shipping between designated ports. Most countries agree to such price-fixing arrangements to ensure regular service at their ports. Such arrangements have an exemption from the COMPETITION ACT through the Shipping Conferences Exemption Act; rate, route, and schedule information must be filed with the NATIONAL TRANSPORTATION AGENCY. Canadian companies negotiate with shipping companies through the Canadian Shippers Council, an association of 13 trade and commodity groups. Among those most directly concerned are the CANADIAN EXPORT ASSOCIATION, the CANADIAN IMPORTERS ASSOCIATION, and the CANADIAN MANUFACTURERS' ASSOCIATION. Different shipping-conference agreements are negotiated for different shipping routes. *See also* UNITED NATIONS CODE OF CONDUCT ON CONFERENCE SHIPPING.

shogun bond   A bond issued in Japan by a foreign borrower but that is not denominated in the Japanese yen. *See also* SAMURAI BOND.

shop steward   A union member, usually chosen by fellow workers in the same work area, who handles grievances and other union matters for that group of workers. Although this is the lowest elected job in a union, it is also a very important post, because the shop steward handles so many day-to-day issues with management.

short term   A period of time — generally less than two years — during which a firm is unable to alter all of its FACTORS OF PRODUCTION. For example, while a firm may be able to recruit and train new workers in a relatively short period of time — say, four to six months — it may take up to two years to purchase and install new production machinery, or to build a new factory. In the short term, the main way a firm can increase its production is to make more

effective use of its existing factors of production. *See also* LONG TERM, in which all the factors of production, including factory buildings and heavy machinery, can be varied.

short-term bond   A bond that will mature within three years.

short-term debt   Debt that must be repaid within 12 months. Short-term debt typically consists of bank loans, notes payable, and the portion of long-term debt payable in the current year. Short-term debt is included in CURRENT LIABILITIES in a company's BALANCE SHEET.

short-term forecast   An economic forecast that attempts to outline economic performance for the next 12 to 18 months. Statistics Canada publishes a short-term-expectations survey in its *Daily Bulletin* (publication 11-001). This survey is based on an average of the month-ahead expectations of 23 Canadian forecasters on key indicators such as the CONSUMER PRICE INDEX, the UNEMPLOYMENT RATE, GROSS DOMESTIC PRODUCT, and merchandise imports and exports.

short-term interest rate   The rate of interest charged on commercial loans of six months or less. *See also* TREASURY BILLS.

silent partner   A partner who invests in a business enterprise or other investment project, but who does not participate in its management.

Simon, Herbert (b. 1916)   The American economist awarded the Alfred Nobel Memorial Prize in Economic Science in 1978 "for his pioneering research into the decision-making process within economic organizations." Simon has made extensive use of computer simulations and artificial intelligence to understand organizations, the decision-making process, and business psychology. He argued that the assumption in economic theory of a "rational economic man" motivated entirely by the desire for efficiency obtained by maximizing benefits and minimizing costs, was completely unrealistic. Individuals and firms are both constrained by a lack of complete information, by uncertainty about the future, and by other goals. Instead, behaviour is based on experience.

simple interest   Interest calculated as a percentage of the outstanding principal; it does not include a percentage of any previous interest paid on the same outstanding principal. *See also* COMPOUND INTEREST.

Single European Act   *See* EUROPEAN COMMUNITY.

sinking fund   Money set aside by a corporation each year from its earnings to pay off a long-term debt or preferred share issue, or to replace productive assets. Cash in a sinking fund is usually invested in various securities until the money is needed.

sinking-fund debentures   Bonds that contain a sinking-fund clause that requires the corporation to set aside a specified amount of money each year for the eventual redemption of the bonds. The money must be deposited with a trustee, who either redeems a number of bonds each year, or holds and invests the money until the maturity date.

sit-down strike   A strike in which union members refuse to continue working and may also refuse to leave their place of work.

skewed distribution   An unequal distribution of resources in a country — for example, Saudi Arabia's huge surplus of oil and severe shortages of water and agricultural land.

skilled worker   A trained and experienced worker who has completed an apprenticeship or other skill-building education, and who has worked for several years with that skill.

slowdown   A planned reduction by union members of their production or work effort, so as to put pressure on an employer during COLLECTIVE BARGAINING without going on strike, or to force an employer to settle a GRIEVANCE. *See also* WORK TO RULE.

slump   A sustained weakness in economic activity.

small business   A manufacturing firm with fewer than 100 paid employees or a firm with fewer than 50 paid employees in other sectors, according to the Ministry of State for SMALL BUSINESS. It can also be a firm with less than $5 million in annual revenues. In 1990, 97.2 percent of registered businesses in Canada had fewer than 50 employees. If self-employed are included, 52 percent of Canadians working in the private sector were employed in enterprises with fewer than 100 employees and 45 percent with fewer than 50. Businesses with revenues of $5 million or less accounted for 26 percent of business sales. Small business accounts for between 80 and 90 percent of all incorporated businesses in Canada, but for a much smaller percentage of business activity.

Small Business Loans Act   Legislation passed in 1961, and last revised in 1993, to assist new and existing small businesses with revenues of $5 million or less to obtain term loans of up to $250,000 to help finance specified fixed assets — for example, to modernize existing facilities, purchase machinery and equipment, purchase or build premises, and purchase land for premises. The loans are made directly by approved financial institutions to small businesses, with the

Department of INDUSTRY, SCIENCE, AND TECHNOLOGY providing loss-sharing arrangements between the lenders and the federal government when loans cannot be repaid. A 1 percent guarantee fee is levied on lenders, which is passed on to borrowers. Government absorbs 90 percent of loan losses and lenders absorb the other 15 percent. The maximum interest rate that can be charged is the PRIME RATE plus 1.5 percent.

Small Business, Ministry of State for A federal government cabinet post, created in 1976 to assist the Minister of Industry, Trade and Commerce (now INDUSTRY, SCIENCE AND TECHNOLOGY) to aid small business, encourage entrepreneurship, and serve as an advocate within the federal government. The responsibility includes designing and running specific programs to assist small business, assessing the impact of government policies and regulations on small business, representing the interests of small business to other government departments, and disseminating information to small business. With the establishment of Industry, Science and Technology Canada in 1990, the Minister for Small Business and Tourism became a junior minister to the Minister of Industry, Science and Technology.

small open economy An economy participating in the international trading system that, because of its relatively small size, must sell its exports and buy its imports at prices set in world markets. It is too small to influence world prices. Canada is often regarded as a small open economy.

Smith, Adam (1723-1790) The father of political economy and of the CLASSICAL SCHOOL of economics. Smith believed that sustained economic growth offered the best hope for improving the well-being of the people.

In his monumental work published in 1776, *An Inquiry into the Nature and Causes of the Wealth of Nations*, he argued that the greatest rate of economic growth was most likely to be achieved through the free play of market forces in a competitive economy, in which each individual pursued his or her own best interest. It was from this premise that he formulated his notion of the invisible hand: "Every individual, therefore, endeavours ... to employ his capital ... that its produce may be of the greatest value ... He generally, indeed, neither intends to promote the public interest, nor knows how much he is promoting it ... he intends only his own security; ... only his own gain, and he is in this, as in many other cases, led by an invisible hand to promote an end which was no part of his intention ... By pursuing his own interest he frequently promotes that of the society more effectually than when he really intends to promote it."

Smith spelled out the advantages of the DIVISION OF LABOUR in raising productivity and output. He used the example of the pin factory, contending that each worker could only produce a few complete pins by himself each day if the same worker had to carry out every stage in the production process; however, if each worker carried out only one stage in pin production, the output of the same group of workers would be much higher. He also contributed to the concept of COMPARATIVE ADVANTAGE, or specialization by nations in the things they do best, with each nation trading with the others to meet its needs. The skill of the labour force and its concentration on what Smith viewed as productive activities were the keys to wealth creation. Smith viewed law, accounting, and other services as a drag on wealth creation, arguing that they made no contribution. By unleashing man's competitive instincts, Smith said, the vital goal of dynamic economic growth would be achieved automatically. Smith feared the tendency of businesspeople to seek out ways to circumvent competition and join in collusion against the consumer. "People of the same trade seldom meet together even for merriment and diversion, but the conversation ends in a conspiracy against the public, or on some contrivance to raise prices," he wrote. However, Smith believed that government intervention could be worse because it would slow economic growth. But Smith also argued that commercial society based on greed or the pursuit of selfish self-interest had to be tempered by the civilizing effects of law, family, and religion. The role of government, he contended, was to protect property rights, to provide essential public works, such as roads and docks, and to maintain an effective national defence. Competition could best be ensured by maintaining a climate of strong economic growth; this would reduce the motive for collusion among businesspeople. Smith also developed his four principles of taxation. Taxes should be based on the ability to pay, provide certainty, be convenient to pay, and not be excessive.

Smith also formulated the LABOUR THEORY OF VALUE that states that the amount of labour required to produce a good or service is the value of that good or service; prices, however, are set by supply and demand. This concept was taken up by KARL MARX but rejected by ALFRED MARSHALL. Smith is also important because he was the first to attempt to devise a method of measuring changes in the value of national output.

Smithsonian Agreement An agreement, reached in Washington on December 18, 1971, by the GROUP OF TEN (G-10), that officially devalued the U.S. dollar by 11 percent, set out new exchange rates for the other G-10 currencies, including that of Canada, and allowed currencies to float by 2.25 percent on either side of their official rate,

instead of 1 percent, as set out under the INTERNATIONAL MONETARY FUND's rules for fixed exchange rates. The devaluation was less than the United States had sought: for example, it wanted the Canadian dollar pegged above par with the U.S. dollar, but instead, the Canadian dollar was set at 97.5 U.S. cents. In less than a year, new exchange rates were adopted, which led to a further devaluation of the U.S. dollar; eventually, a system of floating exchange rates was adopted. Under the Smithsonian Agreement, the United States also dropped its 10 percent import surcharge and its proposed job-development tax credit, with Canada, the EUROPEAN COMMUNITY, and Japan agreeing to undertake urgent negotiations on outstanding trade issues.

smokestack industry A mature heavy-manufacturing industry such as steel or other metals or the motor-vehicle industry. *See also* HIGH-TECHNOLOGY INDUSTRY.

smuggling Importing goods into a country without declaring them to customs officials in order to escape payment of tariffs, excise taxes, or other duties on them.

social capital The total resources of a society, including its agricultural land, its natural resources, its buildings, the machinery and equipment used to produce goods and services, its public facilities and infrastructure, ranging from roads, hospitals, schools, and airports to museums, art galleries, and theatres, and the skills and talents of its people.

social contract The consensus that exists among members of a society that reflects their mutual dependence and their basic agreement on the nature of their society, its institutions and principles, its goals, and the rights and responsibilities of its citizens. It is this consensus that makes possible the democratic governing and functioning of the society. In modern economic policy, a social contract or compact implies a bargain among various groups in society, such as business, labour, agriculture, and government to restrain wage and price increases to reduce inflation, in return for various social and economic policies that are in the public interest. The term came into wide use in the 18th century after the French political philosopher, Jean-Jacques Rousseau (1712-1778), published his important work, *Le contrat social*, in 1762.

social cost   The full cost to society of economic activities. While consumers will pay the production costs incurred in a business, there may be additional costs that are not included in the price and that must be paid for by the public. Examples include the pollution of the environment and the health-care costs of injured or ill workers. *See also* EXTERNALITIES.

social credit   An economic and political theory originating with a Scottish engineer, Major C.H. Douglas (1879-1972), after the First World War. Douglas argued that the underlying economic problem of society was a lack of purchasing power, which meant that workers could not buy all of the goods and services produced in the economy. He blamed this in large part on the banks that, he said, forced producers to raise their prices to repay the interest on loans they needed to run and expand their businesses. As a solution, he proposed social-credit governments that would aim to increase total purchasing power. Social-credit policies would include easy credit and low interest rates, which would result in lower prices, and social credit, consisting of discounts to retailers and national dividends to all citizens.

A social-credit government headed by William Aberhart was elected in Alberta in 1935, but it lacked the constitutional power to implement social-credit policies; several of its programs were disallowed by the federal government, with the disallowance upheld by the SUPREME COURT OF CANADA and the Judicial Committee of the Privy Council. The Social Credit Party governed Alberta until 1971, but after its early failed efforts abandoned its attempts to introduce social-credit policies and instead offered frugal, conservative government. The Social Credit Party also has governed in British Columbia, but principally as a coalition of interests opposed to the New Democratic Party alternative. In addition, the Social Credit Party has elected members to the federal Parliament, including an active group of members of Parliament from Quebec who were first elected as Creditistes in 1962 and held the balance of power in 1979, when they brought about the defeat of the minority Progressive Conservative government headed by Joe Clark.

social democracy   A political commitment to democracy, democratic institutions, and the participation by the public in the key economic and social decisions affecting the society with a similar commitment to economic reforms for income redistribution, social insurance, and employee participation in the decision-making process of firms and other employers. It is not a commitment to SOCIALISM but to a MIXED ECONOMY, a greater role for workers in economic decisions, and usually some form of tripartism or sharing of decision-making by business, labour, and government. Sweden is an example of a country with a long history of social democracy; in Canada, the New Democratic Party espouses social democracy.

social indicators   Social statistics used to show the social well-being of

Canadians, much like the economic statistics used to indicate economic trends. Examples include statistics on the following: levels of education and literacy; birth and death rates; illness and life expectancy; ownership and standards of housing; the per capita possession of such consumer goods as automobiles, telephones, TV sets, and microwaves; rates of suicide, divorce, and alcoholism; crime rates; the incidence of poverty and income distribution; the state of the environment; and nutrition levels. In recent years, social scientists have begun to use these statistics to analyze social trends and to establish social relationships, which are projects much like the analysis, forecasting, and model-building activities of economists. Social scientists have, for example, attempted to show the relationships that exist between rates of illness and levels of education, between the incidence of child poverty and its subsequent impact on the ability of young people to perform in school, and between rates of alcoholism and rates of urbanization. Statistics Canada publishes social indicators in its quarterly report, Canadian Social Trends (publication 11-008).

social-insurance number (SIN)   A national registry of all Canadians who have ever worked, filled in an income-tax return, or paid CANADA PENSION PLAN premiums. The allocation of numbers began in 1964 as a preliminary step to the introduction of the Canada Pension Plan, but the SIN is more widely used today as a means of identification on income-tax returns, for example, and for receiving various government benefits.

social mobility   The ability of individuals to advance on the basis of ability or merit, rather than through social, political, and economic connections. This means that education, natural talent, and willingness to work should enable anyone to reach the top positions in the economy. While social mobility has improved in Canada, family background, social connections, and the wealth of one's parents may still give one person an advantage over another, regardless of their comparative talents. *See*, for example, *The Vertical Mosaic*, by John Porter (Toronto, 1965).

social overhead   The public facilities needed by private industry to enable it to function. These include sewer and water systems, roads and airports, schools, and manpower-training facilities. Whether or not these costs are fully recovered from business depends on the way the tax system is designed and administered. *See also* INFRASTRUCTURE.

Social Sciences and Humanities Research Council of Canada   A federal granting agency established in 1977 to support research and scholarship in the social sciences, including economics, and the humanities. In the area of the economy, the council supported broad research in applied ethics in business, improving the ability of Canadian managers to respond to global competitiveness, the development of effective science and technology policy for Canada, the participation of women in the economy, and the relationship between education and work. In 1992, the federal government reduced the role of the council by making it a division of the Canada Council, which provides support to the arts, and subsequently reduced its budget.

social security   Various federal, provincial, and municipal programs to ensure that the aged, handicapped, disabled, unemployed, and the working poor have at least a minimum income to enable them to obtain the basic necessities of life, such as food, shelter, and clothing. Programs include the CANADA ASSIS-

TANCE PLAN and related provincial and municipal welfare services, old-age pensions and a guaranteed-income supplement, the CANADA PENSION PLAN, UNEMPLOYMENT INSURANCE, the CHILD BENEFIT, and veterans' assistance. Some of these programs, such as old-age pensions, are universal — that is, they are payable to everyone. Some are based on contributions, such as the CANADA PENSION PLAN and UNEMPLOYMENT INSURANCE. And some are based on need, such as the guaranteed-income supplement for pensioners, the child benefit for families with medium to low incomes, and the provincial and municipal welfare programs for the unemployed and single parents.

social services The various services that are available to the needy, the elderly, the handicapped or disabled, and the unemployed. These include support services, such as the distribution of hot meals and homemaker services so that the elderly can live on their own; crisis intervention, to prevent suicides or to help abused wives or children; group homes, which provide care for troubled teenagers or the mentally retarded; family-planning assistance; rehabilitation services for the disabled or handicapped; and family counselling.

social welfare What is best for society as a whole. This is not something that can be measured or quantified easily, but it may be expressed in terms of desirable goals, such as full employment, a tax system based on ability to pay, the redistribution of income to reduce great disparities in wealth and income, a minimum income for all citizens, a clean environment, a labour market that provides opportunities for individuals to advance on the basis of merit, a high level of public services, and reasonable opportunities to start one's own enterprise and retain a fair share of the wealth that is created. Sometimes goals can be

in conflict — for example, the desire to improve fairness or equity in the tax system, and the desire to improve productivity and increase economic growth. It is the role of political parties to set out the various social-welfare choices, and the responsibility of voters to understand these choices and to make known their preferences. To a large extent, social-welfare goals or choices are a result of an evolving consensus in society.

socialism A political and economic philosophy based on state or collective ownership of all or a large proportion of the means of production. In a socialist state, centralized planning largely displaces market forces in the allocation of resources, and the reduction of great disparities between individuals in wealth and income is a major objective of social and economic policy. It is a system that has developed a wide range of forms in practice, from the sharply reduced role assigned to private initiative and private property in some developing countries, to the complete ownership of the means of production and the absolute system of state planning that existed in Communist countries until their systems broke down in the 1980s. The idea dates back to France in the 1830s. Karl MARX saw socialism as a stage in the evolution of society, following the collapse of CAPITALISM and preceding the arrival of COMMUNISM.

Société générale de financement du Québec, La *See* GENERAL INVESTMENT CORPORATION.

Society of Worldwide Interbank Financial Telecommunications (SWIFT) An international telecommunications network set up to transfer funds between banks in North America, Europe, and Japan. Canadian banks are part of the network, which is run as a co-operative.

soft currency A currency for which there is little demand in foreign-exchange markets, either because it is not freely convertible or because the economy of the country issuing the currency is weak and unstable and the currency does not represent a secure store of value. The currencies of many developing countries are soft currencies; this means that these countries have to obtain HARD CURRENCIES to finance their foreign trade and to repay their international debts.

soft-energy path   An energy policy that seeks to maintain energy that can be supplied within the bounds of renewable forms of energy, such as hydroelectric power, solar energy, wind energy, and geothermal energy, or from forms that are relatively benign from an environmental point of view. It is based on a major commitment to energy efficiency and conservation. The concept is associated with the American energy expert, Amory Lovins. Lovins did a soft-energy-path study, which looked forward to the year 2025, for the Science Council of Canada in 1976. Using projections from ENERGY, MINES AND RESOURCES CANADA, he argued that a soft-energy policy could cut Canadian energy demand in half.

soft goods   Non-durable consumer goods, such as clothing and shoes, that have only a limited life.

soft loan   A form of foreign aid or OFFICIAL DEVELOPMENT ASSISTANCE. A soft loan is a loan made to a DEVELOPING COUNTRY at a low rate of interest or no interest at all, with a long repayment term of, say, 30 to 50 years. Often, such loans may bear no interest in the first years, may require no repayment of principal for, say, the first 10 years, and may be repaid in the SOFT CURRENCY of the borrowing country.

soft market   A market of weak or falling prices when supply is greater than demand.

softwood-lumber dispute   A major trade dispute between Canada and the United States. Softwood lumber includes a wide variety of products, such as boards, planks, timbers, forming materials, flooring, and siding, produced from coniferous species of trees. On December 30, 1986, Canada and the United States signed a memorandum of understanding on softwood lumber in which Canada agreed to impose a 15 percent export tax on softwood-lumber products exported to the United States in order to avoid the imposition of a COUNTERVAILING DUTY by the United States. The agreement stated that the export tax could be reduced or eliminated for a province if that province implemented qualifying replacement measures, such as an increase in STUMPAGE FEES, and if the replacement measures met with U.S. approval. The agreement also required that Canada make regular reports to U.S. authorities on the financial performance of its lumber industry and that Canada notify the United States in advance of any proposed change in federal or provincial forest policy and gain U.S. concurrence in these changes. In addition, the agreement stated that Canada and the provinces would not use the revenues from the 15 percent export tax to help the lumber industry. No notification or other requirements were imposed on the United States or state governments on changes they might make in lumber policy. As a result of the agreement, the U.S. lumber industry withdrew its petition to the U.S. Department of Commerce for an investigation into Canadian lumber practices. At the same time, Canada and the United States informed the GENERAL AGREEMENT ON TARIFFS AND TRADE (GATT) that they had resolved their dispute, so that the work of a GATT dispute-settlement panel was terminated.

As a result of the softwood-lumber agreement, British Columbia and Quebec made changes in their policies, such as raising stumpage fees and taking other steps. The export tax was then eliminated on exports from British Columbia on December 1, 1987; for Quebec it was reduced to 8 percent in 1988 and to 6.2 percent in 1990. The lumber industry in the four Atlantic provinces was exempted from the 15 percent export tax.

The softwood-lumber agreement was included in the CANADA-UNITED STATES FREE TRADE AGREEMENT (FTA), which came into effect on January 1, 1989, with a six-month termination clause. In September, 1991, the Canadian government announced its intention of terminating the softwood-lumber agreement. The Office of the US Trade Representative then initiated an investigation under section 302 of the Trade Act of 1974 and determined that "certain policies and acts" of Canada restricted U.S. commerce. In March, 1992, the U.S. Department of Commerce made a preliminary determination of injury to the U.S. lumber industry, estimating a net subsidy for Canadian lumber producers of 14.48 percent. In its final determination, in May, 1992, the U.S. Department of Commerce ruled that Canadian softwood lumber was still being subsidized, despite concessions by British Columbia and Quebec, at a country-wide rate of 6.51 percent. In July, 1992, the U.S. International Trade Commission determined that the U.S. lumber industry was materially weakened by imports of Canadian softwood lumber into the United States and a countervailing duty of 6.51 percent was applied to imports from Canada. In May, 1993, a dispute panel under the FTA ordered the Commerce Department to recalculate its findings on subsidy but upheld the Commerce finding that Canada's ban on the export of raw logs constituted an unfair subsidy and that a countervailing duty was justified in this particular instant.

soil erosion The loss of agricultural topsoil due to wind or water. In 1935, the federal government created the PRAIRIE FARM REHABILITATION ADMINISTRATION to help western farmers avoid a repetition of the 1930s dustbowls. Measures included planting rows of trees to act as windbreaks, and the construction of irrigation and water-supply systems to help prevent farmlands from drying up.

Soldier Land Settlement A program adopted at the end of the First World War to help veterans obtain farmland in Western Canada.

sole proprietorship A business owned and operated by a single individual. It does not have to be incorporated. The owner is personally responsible for the debts of the business. *See also* PARTNERSHIP, LIMITED PARTNERSHIP, and CORPORATION.

Solow growth model A model developed by economist Robert SOLOW in 1956 to explain the relationship between savings, capital accumulation, and economic growth; the model demonstrated the importance of technological progress in economic growth. Increases in the capital-labour ratio will lead to DIMINISHING RETURNS, Solow argued, but technological progress, such as new production techniques and new products, will lead to capital deepening and increased returns. In other words, output per capita depends on both the capital-labour ratio and technological progress.

Solow, Robert (b. 1924) The American economist awarded the Alfred Nobel Memorial Prize in Economic Science in 1987 "for his contributions to the theory of economic growth." Solow was one of the first economists to understand and demonstrate the critically important role of knowledge and ideas, in the form of technology, as a source of economic growth.

solvency The ability of a firm or government agency to meet its obligations; this usually means that CURRENT ASSETS are greater than CURRENT LIABILITIES on a firm's balance sheet.

sour crude Oil that has a high sulphur content.

sour gas Natural gas with a high sulphur content.

source and disposition of funds statement *See* STATEMENT OF CHANGES IN FINANCIAL POSITION.

sovereign loan A loan by a chartered bank or other financial institution to a foreign government. Banks entered the sovereign-loan market in a significant way in the 1970s, which led to the THIRD-WORLD DEBT CRISIS in 1982. The banks largely withdrew from sovereign lending as a result, confining their lending to project financing, trade financing, and private-sector financing.

sovereign risk The risk that a national government will either fail to honour its loan obligations or that it will be unable to service all of its debt. To protect themselves against such risks, banks may set a ceiling on the amount they lend to a foreign government or to agencies carrying a foreign-government guarantee.

sovereignty-association The establishment of a sovereign or independent Quebec that would exist in an economic association with the rest of Canada in some form of customs union or common market and a shared currency. The movement for sovereigny-association began with the establishment of the Mouvement Souveraineté-Association in 1967 and the Parti Québecois in 1969. It is based on the concept of Quebec as a distinct francophone society with a distinct identity and collective aspirations that has been dominated as a minority by the rest of Canada and as a result has only some of the necessary institutions of nationhood. Supporters of sovereignty-association contend that Quebec was tricked at the time of Confederation into believing it would have a high degree of autonomy and instead found itself in a centralizing federation. This situation cannot be resolved by constitutional change within the existing federation, they argue. Instead, the Quebec government is the only one that Quebecers can really call their own, which is why the Quebec government must have "complete sovereignty." Supporters of sovereignty-association also argue that independence is the natural condition of national communities, pointing to states much smaller than Quebec that are able to associate of their own free will with other states. In February, 1979, the Parti Quebecois spelled the concept out in detail in a document entitled *Among Equals*. The PQ stated that Quebec had the right to self-determination, and, on achieving sovereignty, would negotiate a new economic and monetary relationship with the rest of Canada, negotiating "on the basis of equality between our two nations."

By sovereignty, the Parti Quebecois meant the exclusive right to make all laws, collect all taxes, spend all government moneys, administer justice, and make any foreign agreements it wanted to. Its concept of association included free trade between Canada and Quebec, with no barriers except those needed to protect agricultural production, to support regional economic development, and to maintain preferential buying schemes; specific agreements between Canada and Quebec on railways, shipping, and air transportation, and on offshore mineral rights; an agreement between Canada, Quebec, and the United States on the operation of the St. Lawrence Seaway; a common external tariff imposed by Canada and Quebec on all imports from other countries; a common dollar, controlled by a joint monetary policy; free circulation of money across the Canada-Quebec border without restriction except insofar as foreign-investment rules and regulations of financial institutions might be affected; the sharing between Canada and Quebec of the outstanding federal debt and federal assets; the free movement of people back and forth across what would be an unguarded and unpoliced border; reciprocal recognition of minority-language rights; and separate responsibility for citizenship and immigration.

A government white paper, Quebec-Canada: A New Deal, was tabled in the Quebec National Assembly in November, 1979. According to the white paper, an international treaty would be signed between Quebec and Canada defining the relationship between the two nations and establishing the rules and institutions that would ensure the proper functioning of Quebec-Canada. Four institutions would be established: 1. A community council, to be made up of an equal number of cabinet ministers from Quebec and Canada and chaired alternately by a Canadian and a Québécois; the council would have decision-making powers on matters entrusted to it by the treaty of association. 2. A commission of experts, acting as the secretariat for the community council. 3. A court of justice, made up of an equal number of judges from Quebec and Canada, with exclusive jurisdiction over the interpretation and implementation of the treaty of association 4. A monetary authority, which would be responsible for money-supply and exchange-rate policies for the common currency of Quebec and Canada. The number of seats on this board would be allocated to Quebec and Canada in proportion to the relative size of their economies, but major questions could be referred to the community council.

spare capacity Unused capacity in an industry or the economy. *See also* CAPACITY-UTILIZATION RATE.

Special Drawing Rights (SDRs) A reserve asset created by the INTERNATIONAL MONETARY FUND (IMF) to supplement the use of gold and U.S. dollars in the international monetary system. Sometimes called paper gold, SDRs were adopted by the IMF in 1969 as the new international reserve asset for the settlement of balance-of-payments deficits and to finance international trade between countries. They were first allocated to IMF members in 1970, according to the size of each nation's quota in the IMF. Originally, the value of the SDR was based on the U.S. dollar and gold, but starting in 1974, it was redefined in terms of a weighted basket of 16 major currencies valued at their exchange rate for the U.S. dollar. In 1978, the currencies of Saudi Arabia and Iran were added to the basket, while those of South Africa and Denmark were dropped. The Canadian dollar was one of the currencies in the SDR basket, but in 1981 the number of currencies in the weighted SDR basket was reduced to the five most widely traded currencies: the U.S. dollar (42 percent), German mark (19 percent), Japanese yen (15 percent), British pound (12 percent), and French franc (12 percent). The SDR interest rate is determined weekly as the average of yields on short-term securities in the financial markets of the five basket currencies. The BANK FOR INTERNATIONAL SETTLEMENTS, the INTERNATIONAL DEVELOPMENT ASSOCIATION, and the WORLD BANK use the SDR as a unit of account. Although the IMF expected to make regular new allotments of SDRs after their first issue in the 1970-72 period, the significant growth in the supply of key currencies in the international foreign-exchange reserves of individual countries constrained the issue of additional SDRs. The last issue was in 1981, and at the end of 1992, there were 21.4 billion SDR allocated. In 1993, the IMF indicated a new allocation was needed to meet long-term liquidation needs in the international monetary system and the Interim Committee undertook a study of the matter. In the meantime, the new reserve asset has become an important international standard of value. The DEVELOPING COUNTRIES have repeatedly sought a special additional allocation of SDRs to help them meet their foreign-exchange requirements and expand their imports, but so far the industrial nations have opposed such an allocation on the grounds that it would be inflationary.

special governor-general's warrants Special authorizations by the governor-general to permit the federal government to spend money when Parliament is not sitting or available. Since no money can be spent by the government without specific authorization from Parliament, unless permitted by specific legislation, some emergency procedure has to exist to enable the government to meet its every-day bills, such as payroll, fuel, rents, and other costs, during times when Parliament is prorogued or recessed. Warrants are issued 30 days at a time, must be published within 15 days in the CANADA GAZETTE, and must be presented to Parliament within 15 days of its return, when they are deemed to have been approved (the warrants are included in the ESTIMATES for approval by Parliament in a subsequent APPROPRIATIONS ACT). Warrants had to be obtained through 1979, 1980, and 1981 when the government was run for more than a year on special governor-general's warrants as the country went through two general elections, in 1979 and 1980. To get a special warrant, a cabinet minister must certify that the money is urgently needed for the public good; the president of the TREASURY BOARD must confirm that there is no other place to which this spending may be charged within the government's accounts, and the cabinet must

make an official request to the governor-general.

Special Import Measures Act Federal legislation passed in 1984 to authorize the Canadian Import Tribunal (which, in 1986, merged into the CANADIAN INTERNATIONAL TRADE TRIBUNAL) and REVENUE CANADA to investigate charges of DUMPING by foreign corporations, subsidies by foreign governments to their corporations that led to an unfair competitive advantage in the Canadian market, and complaints by Canadian importers of a surge in imports in a product, and to recommend to the federal government whether anti-dumping duties should be imposed in the case of dumping, countervailing duties in the case of unfair subsidies, and SAFEGUARDS in the case of import surges.

special purchase and resale agreements Purchases of short-term securities by the BANK OF CANADA from designated investment dealers and banks, also known as jobbers, that are resold to the counterparty the next day. The term "special" indicates that the Bank of Canada has complete discretion over their use, in contrast to normal PURCHASE AND RESALE AGREEMENTS, which are arranged within specified limits at the initiative of eligible investment dealers and banks.

special shareholders' meeting A meeting of company shareholders, other than the ANNUAL MEETING, called to discuss company actions, such as a takeover, merger, or change in the company's charter, and to seek approval from shareholders. A special meeting can also be organized by dissatisfied shareholders, if enough of them agree, to review the company's policies or proposed actions with which they disagree, and perhaps to replace the BOARD OF DIRECTORS and senior officers.

specialization The division of various functions or production steps in the manufacture of a particular product among different workers in the same firm, or the division of different goods and services among different firms, regions, or nations. This results in greater output at lower cost, thus increasing the productivity and output of the economic system, and providing a higher STANDARD OF LIVING. Most economies and firms are highly specialized today, and many seek an even further degree of specialization. Specialization is often an incentive to mechanize and automate, although it can also lead to alienation in the workplace if employees find their jobs monotonous; they may no longer be aware of the product they are helping to manufacture, because their work has become so narrow.

Specialization also increases the interdependence of individuals, firms, and nations, since all of them end up producing only a small proportion of the things they consume. For example, an electronics firm may buy all of its components from suppliers, while an automobile manufacturer is dependent on many independent parts makers in producing a car or a truck. Nations also end up depending on other nations for certain products or commodities, while this is even more the case with individuals. The alternative to specialization is to try to be self-sufficient; however, this is a highly inefficient approach. *See also* COMPARATIVE ADVANTAGE.

specialization agreement An agreement between competing firms in the same industry, under which each firm agrees not to manufacture certain product lines. For example, two companies each producing the same two products may each agree to discontinue producing one of the products and to specialize in the production of the other. This gives each firm the opportunity to establish longer and more efficient production runs. This type of agreement must be approved by the COMPETITION TRIBUNAL. To win approval, the agreement must demonstrate efficiency gains that offset any reduction in competition and must demonstrate that the efficiency gains would not be likely to occur in the absence of the agreement.

specialized financing institution A merchant bank subsidiary that banks, trust companies, and life insurance companies were allowed to establish under 1992 reforms to Canadian financial institutions legislation. The merchant bank-type subsidary can provide specialized business management and financing and advisory services, such as organizing mergers and acquisitions. Specialized financing corporations can invest up to $90 million in the equity of another corporation and hold the investment for up to 10 years, making banks, trust companies, and life-insurance companies sources of equity for manufacturing and other businesses. The total book value of all shares held by a financial institution in a specialized financing institution, along with all loans made by the financial institution to it, cannot exceed 5 percent of the value of the financial institution's regulatory capital.

specie Metal coins that can be converted into paper money — for example, Canadian pennies, nickels, dimes, quarters, half-dollars, and dollars.

specific tariff A tariff applied according to the weight or number of units, rather than to the value of the goods. *See also* AD VALOREM TAX.

specific tax A tax levied according to the weight or number of units, rather than as a percentage of the value. *See also* AD VALOREM TAX.

speculation Investment in shares, bonds, commodities, foreign exchange, land, and buildings, not to retain them for income purposes but to sell them again, in as short a period as possible, at a profit or capital gain. Speculators usually assume greater than normal risks because they hope to make large capital gains in a short period of time.

speculative motive   One of the three motives outlined by John Maynard KEYNES to hold money. An individual or firm will hold money in the belief that opportunities exist to make a capital gain, or avoid a capital loss, on bond, stock, or commodity markets.

speculator   An investor who seeks relatively short-term capital gains from stocks, bonds, real estate, or other investments as opposed to a stream of income or long-term capital appreciation. A speculator is a risk taker.

Speech from the Throne   The statement drafted by the prime minister and his or her staff, and approved by the cabinet, that is read by the governor-general to the members of Parliament and senators assembled together in the Senate at the opening of a new session of Parliament. The speech traditionally gives a report on the state of the nation, indicates the concerns and direction of the government, and outlines the main items of legislation to be considered by Parliament in the ensuing months. The reading of the Throne Speech is followed, in the House of Commons, by an eight-day debate of a motion by the government thanking the governor-general for his or her speech. The opposition parties can move amendments criticizing the speech. These are treated as non-confidence amendments; if one were passed, the government would be defeated and a change in government or new election would probably be necessary.

Spending Control Act   Federal legislation proclaimed in 1992 to limit the annual growth in program spending — all federal spending except for interest on the public debt — to an average annual rate of 3 percent for a five-year period from fiscal year 1991-92 to fiscal year 1995-96. Four self-financing programs were excluded: unemployment insurance and federal advances to the Crop Reinsurance Fund, the Agricultural Commodities Stabilization Accounts, and the Gross Revenue Insurance Fund. The act barred increased borrowing or tax increases to make up for any excess spending that might occur. Instead, with limited exceptions, overspending in one program would have to be met by program spending cuts elsewhere. Exceptions were made for emergencies and for net losses from the sale of government assets.

spending power   In the context of Canada's constitution and federal-provincial fiscal arrangements, the power of either level of government to spend money for a particular purpose. *See also* FEDERAL SPENDING POWER, PROVINCIAL SPENDING POWER, TAXING POWER. The spending and taxing powers of a particular level of government largely determine what it can or cannot do, although the power to regulate is also important.

spin-off   1. A new industry or technology resulting from some other activity. Spin-offs are most common in areas of HIGH TECHNOLOGY. For example, defence and space spending have resulted in new industries and products ranging from food products and insulation for clothing to improved computer and communications systems. Similarly, the growth of a major industry, such as computers, motor vehicles, or petrochemicals, will frequently result in the establishment of new firms that develop new applications or become suppliers of parts or of specialized services; often such industries are created by former employees of the major firms in the industry. **2.** A technique employed by a company to split a business activity out from its other operations and proportionately distribute to its shareholders shares in the enterprise.

split The creation of additional common shares in a company by dividing its existing common shares into a larger number — for example, three new shares for every common share held. While a stock split increases the number of shares outstanding, it does not affect each shareholder's proportionate interest in the company. Reasons for stock splits include reducing the share price to make it more accessible to a larger number of investors, and to increase the number of shares in circulation to create a more active trading market for the shares.

split shift The division of a person's workday into two or more segments to meet peak demand for that person's services. Municipal bus and transit drivers, or waiters and waitresses, may, for example, have their working day split into two segments.

spot contract A contract for immediate rather than future delivery of a commodity. Payment must be made at the time of the contract. *See also* FUTURES MARKET.

spot market A market in which foreign exchange or commodities are sold for immediate delivery. *See also* FUTURES MARKET.

spot price The price for the immediate delivery of commodities or foreign exchange. It is today's price, as opposed to the futures price, the price charged for delivery at a time specified in the future.

spread **1.** The difference between prevailing Canadian and U.S. interest rates. **2.** The difference between the interest paid by a financial institution on a depositor's funds and the rate charged to borrowers. **3.** The difference between the BID and ASK prices on a stock exchange or bond or commodities market; the greater the trading activity for a particular share, bond, or commodity, the narrower the spread. **4.** The difference between the selling price of a good or service and the cost of producing it.

stabilization policy Measures to offset fluctuations in the BUSINESS CYCLE, by preventing or limiting an economic downturn or preventing or limiting high inflation. These measures are in addition to BUILT-IN STABILIZERS, and their goal is to stabilize the economy as close to its full-employment level or potential output as possible while also maintaining stable prices. These measures may include changes in FISCAL and MONETARY POLICY and the introduction of an INCOMES POLICY to achieve full employment and stable prices. For example, in periods of rising prices, stabilization measures usually include higher interest rates, higher taxes, reduced government spending, and, perhaps, wage and price controls. Conversely, during an economic slump, stabilization policies could include lower interest rates, tax cuts, and increased government spending. Stabilization policies are difficult to implement because policy makers are always dealing with statistics that reflect what has happened in the past, while having to make decisions on policies that have inevitable time lags or delays before their effects are felt.

stable population A population in which there is no net emigration or immigration, that has reached a constant rate of growth, with the proportion of those in different age groups remaining constant as well. Each family will have no more than 2.11 children, the population replacement rate. *See also* STATIONARY POPULATION.

stable prices The maintenance of price levels in the economy at an almost constant level over a sustained period of time. While some prices may rise sharply, others are expected to decline, thus maintaining a very low average rate of inflation. Some economists believe a long-term inflation rate of 2 percent is attainable with long-term productivity growth and full employment. Others maintain that a more realistic goal is 3.5 to 4 percent over a sustained period of time. Like full employment, stable prices are an objective of economic policy. *See also* ZERO INFLATION.

stages in balance of payments The theory that countries go through various stages of deficit and surplus in their BALANCE OF PAYMENTS as they go through different stages of economic development. In this theory, countries start off as immature debtors, running deficits on their trade balance, their service account, and their current account; they also have negative net foreign income. In the next stage, as mature debtor-borrowers, they move to a surplus in their merchandise trade but continue to have deficits in services and current account and a negative net foreign income. In the next stage, they are both a debtor and lender and repay debt, with a surplus in merchandise trade and in the current account but a deficit in services and a negative net foreign income. The next stage is that of an immature creditor and lender, with a surplus in merchandise trade, service, and current accounts and a positive net foreign income. As a mature creditor, the merchandise trade balance moves into deficit, but the service and current accounts remain positive and the net foreign income is positive.

stagflation The combination of high unemployment, weak economic growth, and high inflation. Most economies expect to suffer either from recession or high inflation, but sometimes, as in the late 1970s and early 1980s, they can suffer from both. Conventional fiscal and monetary policy failed to provide a solution, leading to a move away from KEYNESIAN policies and active governments to the "conservative revolution," which aimed to reduce the role of government through tax cuts, deregulation, and privatization, and promoted a greater reliance on monetary policy and free markets. *See also* MONETARISM, SUPPLY-SIDE ECONOMICS.

stagnation A chronically poor rate of economic performance, resulting in a declining, zero, or much lower-than-potential rate of economic growth, and a static or declining per capita GROSS NATIONAL PRODUCT. Stagnation results from inadequate AGGREGATE DEMAND AND a low rate of technological innovation, and hence an absence of new investment and productivity-boosting opportunities; in less-developed countries, it may arise from a high rate of population growth that outstrips the capacity of the economy to raise per capita income and meet the demand even for necessities, such as food and shelter.

stale-dated cheque A cheque that has been held for longer than six months before being presented to a bank for clearing. Canadian banks will not cash cheques that are older than six months. The holder has to go back to the issuer and have a new cheque written.

stamp tax A method of raising government revenue by requiring the purchase of a stamp to be affixed to cheques, wills, and legal documents, such as those for the sale of a home or other property. Such taxes were once an important source of government revenue; Canada, for example, imposed a stamp tax on bank cheques, patent medicines, perfumes, and wines during the First World War. However, such taxes are rare today.

standard industrial classification (SIC) The United Nations system of industrial classification that divides goods and services into nine basic categories by major industry. They are agriculture, forestry, and fisheries; mining and quarrying; manufacturing; electricity, gas, and water; construction; the wholesale and retail trade, restaurants, and hotels; transport, storage, and communications; finance, insurance, real estate, and business services; and community, social, and personal services.

standard of living A term that combines economic well-being and certain expectations of quality of life. Although there is no consensus on what constitutes a reasonable standard of living, it is based on wants, rather than on needs, that contribute to the welfare or well-being of individuals. Improvement in the standard of living depends on economic factors, such as improvements in productivity or per capita real economic growth, a system of income redistribution through the tax system or direct spending by government, and the availability of public services, such as health, education, transit, and parks, along with non-economic factors, such as protection against unsafe or unpleasant working conditions, opportunities for advancement in work, a clean environment, a low crime rate, freedom of expression, and the RULE OF LAW. Economists often use per capita gross domestic product as a proxy to compare the standard of living of different countries, since the output of goods and services is an important consideration. However, other measures have also been devised, such as SOCIAL INDICATORS, the HUMAN DEVELOPMENT INDEX, and the PHYSICAL QUALITY-OF-LIFE INDEX.

standards Technical specifications that ensure products meet a specified size or safety, quality, or performance level. Standards cover a wide range of products, from food, pharmaceuticals, and chemicals to electrical products, building materials, and automobiles. *See also* CANADIAN STANDARDS ASSOCIATION, INTERNATIONAL STANDARDS ORGANIZATION, TECHNICAL BARRIERS TO TRADE.

Standards Council of Canada A federal agency, created by Parliament in 1970, to achieve voluntary national product standards to protect consumers, increase economic efficiency, improve health and safety, and expand international trade opportunities by working to achieve international standards. The council's efforts deal with the construction, manufacture, production, quality, performance, and safety of buildings, structures, manufactured goods, and other products and components where standards are not set out by law. The council has assigned standards-writing and -testing to other organizations, to produce a comprehensive set of national standards. These organizations include the CANADIAN STANDARDS ASSOCIATION, the Underwriters' Laboratories of Canada, the Canadian Government Specifications Board, the Canadian Gas Association, and the Bureau de normalization du Quebec. The council worked with the METRIC COMMISSION OF CANADA to introduce the metric system. The council is also responsible for determining the policies and procedures that must be followed if other organizations are to be accepted as part of the National Standards System. It maintains an international standardization branch in Mississauga, Ontario, and is responsible for Canadian participation in the INTERNATIONAL STAN-

DARDS ORGANIZATION and the International Electrotechnical Commission. The council is based in Ottawa.

standby arrangement An agreement negotiated by a borrower country and the INTERNATIONAL MONETARY FUND for a line of credit in reserve currencies that can be drawn upon in the event of a future need.

standby control An economic power, passed by Parliament or a provincial legislature, that permits the government or a government agency to take certain actions, should the need arise. For example, the federal government has the power to impose export or import controls on particular goods or commodities in the event of a shortage and to allocate oil supplies during an emergency. The federal and provincial cabinets often have the power to overrule the decisions of regulatory agencies.

staple theory An important theory of Canadian economic growth, according to which Canadian economic development has been based on the exploitation of a succession of staples or commodities, such as fur, fish, lumber, wheat, metal minerals, and oil and gas, for international markets. This exploitation, in turn, has determined the growth of Canadian transportation systems, the location of Canadian cities, and the establishment of commercial and investment networks, including the banking system and the financial centres of Montreal, Toronto, Winnipeg, Calgary, and Vancouver. The staple theory of Canadian economic history was developed by W.A. Mackintosh, Harold INNIS, and Donald Creighton. The staple theory no longer has the consensus of support it once had among Canadian economic historians, but it is nonetheless the most persistent theme in Canada's economic history and has not been succeeded by any other theory of Canadian development.

statement of changes in financial position An important part of a company's ANNUAL REPORT, showing the net changes in WORKING CAPITAL that have occurred between the previous year's BALANCE SHEET and the current year's balance sheet. The statement shows the various sources of company funds, such as funds from company operations, including DEPRECIATION and DEFERRED INCOME TAXES, issues of securities, and the sale of assets, along with the various applications or uses of funds, including dividend payments, the repayment of long-term debt or redemption of preferred shares, long-term investments in other corporations, and investment in new plants, machinery, and equipment. It is sometimes called the Source and Application of Funds Statement.

statement of material facts An alternative to a PROSPECTUS that can be used for a new or secondary offering of shares already listed on a stock exchange.

stationary population A population with a growth rate of zero; the number of births and deaths in the population is the same.

stationary state The idea of a no-growth economy, developed by a number of classical economists such as Thomas MALTHUS, David RICARDO, and John Stuart MILL, who believed that investment opportunities were restricted by society's limited capacity for innovation, and that capitalists would therefore be faced with declining profits under the LAW OF DIMINISHING RETURNS, to the point where they would cease to save and invest. New capital formation would thus fall to zero, while wages would fall to a subsistence level and economic growth would cease. Adam SMITH foresaw the possibility of a stationary state, but thought it too distant a prospect to worry about, while NEOCLASSICAL economists such as Alfred MARSHALL rejected the notion.

statistical error   An adjustment made to reconcile the incompleteness of numerical data, or their failure to balance completely, based on the recognition that information collected by statisticians can never be perfect. For example, statistics on GROSS DOMESTIC PRODUCT and BALANCE OF PAYMENTS normally contain a small "errors and omissions" entry to reflect the incompleteness of the thousands of statistics collected.

statistician   A person who is educated in the science of statistics and who works in this field.

statistics   A specialized branch of science or mathematics that deals with the assembly and classification of numerical information to establish various hypotheses of economic behaviour or future economic performance, based on expectations or probabilities drawn from historical experience. Statistics are collected from individuals, groups, industries, corporations, nations, and other sources, and organized into understandable and usable forms. Sometimes representative groups, individuals, or firms are surveyed, and conclusions for the entire group, population, industry, or nation are inferred from them. Sometimes all individuals, groups, or firms are surveyed, as in a CENSUS. There is a large body of statistical theory that devises new methods of organizing and presenting information. The field of applied statistics, which is concerned with the application of existing statistical methods, can be broken down into many different categories, such as demographics, economic forecasting, and SOCIAL INDICATORS. *See also* SYSTEM OF NATIONAL ACCOUNTS.

Statistics Canada   The central statistical agency of the Canadian govern-ment. It plays a vital role in collecting, analyzing, and publishing a wide range of statistics on almost every aspect of economic and social life in the country. Without this public agency, policy makers, universities, and business firms would lack the essential information they need to review economic and social policies, to make investment plans, to measure social and economic progress, and to pinpoint problems in the economic and social structure. It also conducts a national census every 10 years (the last one being conducted in 1991) as well as a partial census every intervening five years (the next will be conducted in 1996). Many of the statistical series are available on a computer data network, CANSIM. One of the most important agencies of the federal government, it was established in 1918 as the Dominion Bureau of Statistics; its name was changed to Statistics Canada in 1971. It is based in Ottawa. The chief statistician reports to the Minister of INDUSTRY, SCIENCE, AND TECHNOLOGY. *See also* CENSUS, SYSTEM OF NATIONAL ACCOUNTS.

Status of Women Canada   A federal government department established in 1976 to promote equal opportunities for women in the workplace and all other areas of Canadian life. The department grew out of an office established in the PRIVY COUNCIL in 1971. The department does not administer any programs of its own but conducts research to analyze obstacles to the progress of women and works with other federal departments to lower or remove those obstacles. It is based in Ottawa.

status symbol   Any possession that suggests that the owner is affluent or has a special standing in the community. It can range from the ownership of an extremely expensive car, the consumption of rare wines, membership in an exclusive club, wearing expensive or designer clothes, and living in a big house, to acquaintance with someone in high places, or the parenting of a successful child. *See also* CONSPICUOUS CONSUMPTION.

statutory holiday   A holiday that all employees are entitled to, according to federal or provincial law. Employees who have to work on a statutory holiday are legally entitled to extra pay or other time off. Federal examples include Canada Day on July 1, Labour Day on the first Monday in September, and Christmas Day on December 25. Altogether there are nine federal statutory holidays: New Year's Day, Good Friday, Victoria Day, Canada Day, Labour Day, Thanksgiving, Remembrance Day, Christmas Day, and Boxing Day.

steady state   The idealized position of long-term equilibrium in the economy in which all the variables grow at a constant rate.

Stentor Canadian Management Network
An alliance of Canadian telecommunications companies formed in 1992 to take over the management of Canada's national telecommunications network and its North American and international connections. Its members include all the principal provincial phone companies that provide local and long-distance phone service across Canada, as well as TELESAT CANADA. The predecessor, TransCanada Telephone System, was formed in 1931 to provide connecting services between different phone companies; it was renamed Telecom Canada in 1983. The network today manages a national fibre-optics network and satellite services.

step-out well   An oil or gas well that is drilled away from a discovery in order to determine the size of the reservoir.

sterilization   Measures by the BANK OF CANADA or another central bank to neutralize the impact on the domestic economy and its money supply as a result of its intervention in foreign-exchange markets. For example, if the Bank of Canada sells Canadian dollars to halt a rise in the exchange rate of the Canadian dollar, it also increases domestic money supply; to offset this or neutralize the effect, it can take various measures, such as the sale of bonds, to remove the excess liquidity created by its exchange-market interventions.

sterling   A synonym for the British pound.

sterling area   Those countries that hold a significant portion of their foreign-exchange reserves in British pounds, deposited in the British banking system. Although this was a natural enough arrangement for many members of the British Commonwealth and certain Middle East nations in the days when the pound was a strong RESERVE CURRENCY, these sterling balances have, since the late 1950s, become a liability for Britain. Various measures have had to be adopted to protect Britain against a sudden withdrawal of these reserves, or their conversion to other currencies, since this could cause a sharp drop in the exchange rate of the British pound. The existence of these balances has had some effect on the independence of British foreign and trade policy, since foreign holders of these reserves can threaten to reduce them for political reasons or out of disapproval of British economic and trade policies. In recent years, the importance of these sterling balances has declined.

Stigler, George (b. 1911)   The American economist awarded the Alfred Nobel Memorial Prize in Economic Science in 1982 "for his seminal studies of industrial structures, functioning of markets and causes and effects of public regulation." Stigler is a critic of government intervention and would reduce its role in the economy, arguing that measures intended to benefit consumers can often end up benefiting producers instead.

stock 1. An economic magnitude that is measured at some point in time, usually at the end of the year, such as the stock of Canada's housing units, the level of domestic and foreign debt, the assets of pension funds, and the level of capital stock. For many important economic measures, both a flow account and a stock account are produced. The flow measures changes over the year — for example, the increase in the housing stock, the growth in foreign debt, or financial flows from the sale and purchase of financial assets. The stock, on the other hand, measures the consequences of these flows — for example, Canada's net international investment position at the end of the year or Canada's national balance sheet, in the case of financial flows. 2. A synonym for SHARE.

stock dividend The payment by a company of a dividend in the form of additional shares, instead of cash, to its shareholders; the number of shares received is in proportion to each shareholder's existing share of ownership in the company. The benefit of stock dividends to a company is that it does not have to allocate as large a portion of after-tax earnings to the shareholder but can use more of its earnings to finance expansion. The benefit to shareholders is that they are not taxed on the receipt of the extra shares, but instead pay capital-gains tax when the extra shares are sold.

stock exchange An organized market on which COMMON and PREFERRED SHARES and WARRANTS that meet exchange listing requirements can be bought and sold on behalf of investors or for their own account by stockbrokers who own seats on the exchange and meet membership requirements. While the issuing, sale, and purchase of shares is governed by provincial securities commissions, each stock exchange also has its own board of governors to regulate its activities. Each board sets capital and other requirements for member firms, trading rules, and listing requirements for shares traded on the exchange. A stock exchange plays an important role in the economy: it provides a way for companies to raise new equity capital, and it provides a way for investors to use their savings to buy and sell shares and help finance business expansion. The four stock exchanges in Canada, and the dates they started trading, are the MONTREAL STOCK EXCHANGE (1874), the TORONTO STOCK EXCHANGE (1878), the VANCOUVER STOCK EXCHANGE (1907), and the ALBERTA STOCK EXCHANGE (1913).

stock-exchange index An index showing the trend of a representative and significant group of shares traded on a stock exchange. The TORONTO STOCK EXCHANGE publishes its 300 composite index of 300 representative shares, (with 1975 as the base year equal to 1,000 points), its Toronto 35 index, and a separate index each for minerals, golds, oil and gas, forest products, consumer goods, industry, building, transportation, pipelines, utilities, communications, merchandising, financial services, management companies, and biotechnology stocks. The MONTREAL STOCK EXCHANGE publishes a portfolio index, an industrial index, and a composite index, and the VANCOUVER STOCK EXCHANGE publishes a composite index. Statistics Canada also publishes a number of indexes of prices of Canadian shares, including an industrial index, a utilities and services index, and a finance index. Other stock-exchange indexes include the Dow Jones Index, the Standard and Poor indexes, and the New York Stock Exchange indexes.

stock-exchange listing   *See* LISTED STOCK.

stock-exchange member   An individual or firm that owns a seat on a STOCK EXCHANGE and is therefore entitled to buy and sell shares listed on the exchange on its own account or on behalf of others. A stock-exchange member must abide by all the rules of the exchange, including its capital requirements and trading rules.

stock-exchange seat   *See* STOCK-EXCHANGE MEMBER.

stock option   **1.** In a corporation, the right to purchase, under a stock-option plan, a specified number of a company's TREASURY SHARES at a specified price over a specified period of time. Stock options are often given senior officers of a corporation and sometimes, but rarely, extended to all employees. **2.** A contract giving the purchaser the right but not the obligation to buy or sell a specific quantity of a company's shares at a specific price for a stipulated period of time. The right to purchase the shares is a CALL, to sell the shares, a PUT.

stock savings plan   A tax incentive to encourage Canadians to invest in the equity of Canadian businesses. One of the first was the QUEBEC STOCK SAVINGS PLAN, introduced in 1979, that permits tax deductions for investments in new issues of shares of companies whose head office or principal place of business is in Quebec. The amount of the deduction varies with the size of the company, with more generous deductions permitted for investments in small and medium enterprises. The maximum deduction permitted is 10 percent of a Quebec resident's total income minus the capital-gains exemption claimed during the year. Taxpayers can deduct 150 percent of the value of investments in regional venture-capital corporations, 100 percent of an investment in growth corporations with assets between $2 million and $250 million, 75 percent of the investment in companies with assets of $250 million to $1 billion, and 50 percent of an investment in large companies with assets of $1 billion to $2.5 billion; there is no deduction for very large corporations with assets in excess of $2.5 billion. Newfoundland and Nova Scotia also have stock savings plans. Ontario provides a $1,000 tax credit for investments in a labour-sponsored venture-capital fund. Saskatchewan and British Columbia have a 20 percent investment tax credit for investment in labour-sponsored venture-capital funds. Alberta also provides a tax credit for investments in venture-capital corporations. In the 1980s, the federal government also introduced a tax credit for investments in labour-sponsored venture-capital funds. *See* QUEBEC SOLIDARITY FUND.

stock split   The division of each outstanding share of a company into two or more common shares of the company. This does not increase the capitalization of a company, but it does reduce the market price of each share and should improve the marketability of the shares. Companies usually split their shares when the price of each share has become so high that few investors can afford to purchase a BOARD LOT. This reduces the marketability of the company's shares, and not only constrains their potential price increase, but also constrains the company's ability to issue new common shares successfully.

Splitting the shares makes it possible for a company to achieve a wider distribution of ownership of its shares. For example, if the market price of a company's shares reaches $160 and there are 2,000,000 common shares outstanding, a 4 for 1 split would reduce the value of each share to $40 and increase the number of outstanding shares to 8,000,000. Someone who owned 200 of the $160 shares would get new share certificates indicating that he now owned 800 of the new $40 shares. The value of the investment is unchanged, unless the price of the shares rises on a stock exchange, indicating increased demand resulting from the split.

stock yield The yield of a common or preferred share; it is the percentage return of an investor on his shares at the current market price and is calculated by dividing the annual dividend per share by the current market price.

stocks A synonym for INVENTORIES, the raw materials, components, and subassemblies held by a company to maintain a constant or steady flow of production and thereby achieve a high level of efficiency.

stockbroker A member of a STOCK EXCHANGE who buys and sells shares for investors on a stock exchange. For this service, the stockbroker is paid a commission. Stockbrokers also trade in mutual funds, UNLISTED SHARES, and other securities, and provide credit or MARGIN financing for customers.

stockpile A reserve supply of strategic or essential commodities vital to the national defence or economic life of a nation. Commodities stockpiled may include wheat, oil, copper, and scarce metals used in alloys.

Stone, Sir Richard (b. 1913) The British economist awarded the Alfred Nobel Memorial Prize in Economic Science in 1984 "for having made fundamental contributions to the development of systems of national accounts and hence greatly improved the basis for empirical economic analysis."

stop-buy order An order to a stockbroker to buy a specific number of shares of a company once the shares reach a certain price. Once the price is reached, the shares are automatically purchased on a stock exchange. *See also* STOP-LOSS ORDER.

stop-go policies Short-term economic policies that produce alternating spurts of economic growth followed by contraction. The problem is that government policy makers find themselves trying to fine-tune the economy with economic data that may be several months out of date while implementing changes in policy that may take several months before they have any effect, so the margin for error is high.

stop-loss order An order by an owner of shares to a stockholder to sell a certain number of shares once the shares reach a specific price. The shares are then automatically offered for sale on a stock exchange. *See also* STOP-BUY ORDER.

stop payment An order to a bank by someone who has issued a cheque not to honour the cheque when it is presented for payment.

straddle An option or contract giving the purchaser the right to buy or sell a particular number of shares of a company at a specified price for a specified period of time. It is both a PUT and a CALL, although exercising either option may eliminate the opportunity of exercising the other option. A purchaser of a straddle for 1,000 shares of company A at $50 would exercise the right to sell the 1,000 shares if they fell to, say, $40, and to buy the shares and resell them if the price rose to, say, $60.

straight-line method of depreciation *See* DEPRECIATION.

strategic materials Commodities such as oil, copper, and chromium, industrial goods such as certain types of advanced machinery, and new technologies such as powerful supercomputers, that are vital to a nation's military capacity or the functioning of a wartime economy.

street certificate A share certificate that is made out in the name of a stockbroker or investment dealer, instead of in the name of the actual owner. This makes the certificate easier to sell in a hurry.

strike A decision by employees in a BARGAINING UNIT to stop working following the breakdown of COLLECTIVE BARGAINING and the failure of CONCILIATION and MEDIATION to produce an agreement with the employer on a new COLLECTIVE AGREEMENT. A strike is a form of pressure on an employer, who risks losing business and his share of the market; it may also be a way of angering the public and hurting the economy or health of the community if the employer is a government agency, and therefore creating pressure on government to settle. Generally speaking, strikes are only legal after a collective agreement has expired and certain formal steps, including a STRIKE VOTE, have been taken. Sometimes a union will resort to hit-and-run or rotating strikes, so that only a small number of workers are on strike on any particular day. This means that the other workers will be paid, while the employer has to anticipate where the next strike will occur; sometimes this will provoke the employer into a LOCKOUT of employees. A WILDCAT strike is a strike by workers that do not have the support of union leaders, and is illegal because it occurs while a collective agreement is in force or before all the legal steps up to a strike have been followed. Federal and provincial labour laws govern strike procedures in Canada.

strike vote A vote by union members in a bargaining unit, giving the bargaining committee the authority to declare a strike. Under federal and provincial labour laws, a strike vote has to take place a specified number of days before a strike can legally take place.

strikebreaker A person who takes a job with an employer whose regular workers are out on strike or an employee who does not join fellow workers in going out on strike. Federal and most provincial labour laws allow a struck employer to hire other workers for the duration of a strike and to try to keep on operating. However, labour legislation in Quebec, Ontario, Manitoba, and British Columbia bans or restricts the replacement of workers during a strike. A strikebreaker is also known as a scab.

strip bond A bond from which all or most of the interest coupons have been removed. The bond, which includes the principal and whatever coupons remain, trades separately from the strip of interest coupons; both trade at a discount.

strip mine A mine in which the topsoil and other overburden has been cleared away so that the ore can be removed by surface extraction.

strong market A market in which there is an upward pressure on prices of shares, bonds, real estate, or other assets because demand is greater than supply. *See also* SOFT MARKET.

structural-adjustment program A set of policies in a country to remove barriers to the mobility of labour and capital and to shift resources into the tradeables sector of the economy. When the INTERNATIONAL MONETARY FUND (IMF) and WORLD BANK work with developing countries experiencing economic problems they will often insist on a structural-adjustment program in return for assistance; this is also the case with IMF and World Bank aid for the former Communist countries of Eastern Europe and the former Soviet Union, as well as developed countries, such as Britain, that have had to turn to the IMF for assistance. Structural-adjustment policies include measures to improve the use of resources by government; these measures include privatization of state enterprises and the restructuring of publicly owned enterprises; reform of the price system to reduce or eliminate subsidies such as those in the prices charged by state enterprises, or for food and energy prices; the reduction of high tariffs and quotas; reform of the tax system; improved administration of the tax and customs systems; and other measures to strengthen public administration and improve the role of economic incentives. However, the IMF and World Bank also require that countries participating in structural adjustment programs take special steps to look after the poorest members of their societies.

structural deficit or surplus   The deficit in a government budget that remains even when the economy is operating at the peak of the BUSINESS CYCLE or the surplus that exists when the economy is operating at the TROUGH of the business cycle. Budget deficits or surpluses vary with the business cycle; revenues rise as the economy expands, while payments under BUILT-IN STABILIZERS, such as social assistance and unemployment insurance, fall. The deficit remaining at the normal cyclical peak of the business cycle, then, is structural and requires deliberate action if it is to be eliminated. The concept of structural deficit or surplus allows policy makers to distinguish between structural or medium-term fiscal measures, which may require corrective action, and cyclical fluctuations, such as budget deficits, which should be self-correcting as the recovery proceeds. *See also* FULL-EMPLOYMENT BUDGET.

structural inflation   Inflation resulting from institutional arrangements in the economy, rather than from changes in the business cycle. Union rules that restrict the number of new entrants to a trade can, for example, lead to artificial shortages, and thus to higher pay rates for those in the trade. Similarly, government regulations that prevent competition can cause unnecessary increases in air-transportation or long-distance-telephone prices. The ability of unions to get big wage increases from employers during a period of high unemployment may also be a form of structural inflation if the employers are able simply to pass along those wage increases in the form of higher prices and thus maintain their profit margins.

structural policies   Policies to ensure adequate supplies of the FACTORS OF PRODUCTION, such as skilled workers, equity capital, or technological innovations, to allow the economy to become more productive or to enable slow-growth regions or weak industries to become efficient. Measures can range from farm-consolidation programs to make farms larger and hence more efficient, education and manpower programs to ensure an adequate future supply of skilled and professional workers, retraining programs to help workers in ailing industries obtain employment in new industries, changes in financial-services legislation to encourage the productive use of Canadian savings, incentives and policies to help industry develop new technologies and to diffuse; and REGIONAL DEVELOPMENT policies to improve the INFRASTRUCTURE of slow-growth regions and to persuade industries, through grants and other incentives, to locate there.

structural unemployment   Unemployment, usually long-term in nature, caused by significant changes in the economy or an industry that make products, production systems, or skills obsolete. This means that when the economy is operating at its potential level there may still be significant unemployment in some areas or regions. However, monetary and fiscal policy cannot deal with structural unemployment without contributing to a constant rise in the inflation rate. Structural changes can lead to a mismatch between skills possessed by unemployed workers and those needed by industry; likewise the resources of a region, such as tobacco or asbestos, may become obsolete or fall in demand, leading to high unemployment in a region whose economy was based on these resources. Industrial activities, such as clothing, textiles, and footwear manufacturing, that shift to a lower-cost country can also bring about structural unemployment as the skills of workers in those industries may no longer be needed. Structural unemployment is compounded when there may be no economic reason for new industries to move to communities whose industries have become obsolete, and when there is an understandable unwillingness of workers in their 40s and 50s to leave the part of the country they know and seek new employment opportunities in another part of the country. The role of labour-market policies is to help reduce structural unemployment through training programs for new skills, mobility grants that help workers to move to new communities, or various measures that encourage new local industries.

student loan A government-subsidized loan to a full-time student to help pay tuition, living, and other costs incurred while being a student. Under the Canada Student Loan Act, the federal government pays the interest on the loans of full-time students while they are students and for six months afterward, if a provincial government certifies that the student is eligible for such assistance. All the provinces participate except Quebec, which has its own program.

subcontractor A firm or individual hired to carry out one segment of a project. For example, in the construction of an office building, an electrical firm will be hired as a subcontractor to install wiring and lighting and to see to other electrical needs, while a plumbing firm will be hired to install all the necessary plumbing systems and fixtures. The firm responsible for the overall construction is the prime contractor.

sublet The assignment by a tenant of his or her rights under an existing lease to another person or firm. For example, someone who moves out of an apartment before the lease has expired may rent out the apartment to another person for the remainder of the lease period. The original tenant is responsible for making sure that the landlord is paid.

subordinated debenture A DEBENTURE that is ranked below other securities or obligations of the company, and that has a lesser claim to repayment in the event of bankruptcy.

subordinated debt The debt of a company that can only be paid off after the SENIOR and fully secured debt has been repaid.

subsidiary A company that is legally controlled by another company. Many subsidiaries are wholly owned by a parent firm; however, a subsidiary can be controlled by ownership of a simple majority or a large block of voting shares. Many foreign corporations in Canada are wholly owned subsidiaries, but some have a minority of shares owned by Canadians. Under the CANADA-UNITED STATES FREE TRADE AGREEMENT (FTA), Canada is no longer able to require U.S.-owned subsidiaries to sell shares to Canadians. And as a result of the FTA, a number of U.S. companies have purchased the shares held by Canadians in their Canadian-based subsidiaries. Sometimes a company within Canada will establish a wholly owned subsidiary to carry out a different business activity; this also leaves the way open in the future to raise equity capital in the subsidiary by selling off a minority block of shares

Subsidies and Countervailing Measures Code A code of the GENERAL AGREEMENT ON TARIFFS AND TRADE adopted as part of the Tokyo Round of negotiations in 1979. While the code contains no definition of a subsidy, it sets out some general ground rules on how an importing country should conduct hearings to determine whether subsidies the companies in another country receive confer an unfair trade advantage that causes injury to domestic producers, and when COUNTERVAILING DUTIES should be applied to imports. The URUGUAY ROUND prepared to strengthen the subsidies code. Subsidies for defined research and development activities (up to 50 percent of the cost of basic research and 25 percent of the cost of applied research) and for regional development (in areas where unemployment on a three-year average is at least 110 percent of the national average and per capita income is no more than 85 percent of the national average) could not be penalized by U.S. countervailing duties. In addition, there would be new constraints on the use by all other countries of TRADE-REMEDY LAWS.

subsidy A direct or indirect payment or other assistance by government to someone to produce or purchase goods or services. The effect of a government subsidy is to lower the final price of a product or service, which is why subsidies can become an international trade issue. The most common examples are direct payments by government to industry to help finance a large-scale project such as a major oil project, to help fund the costs of developing a new technology, to investigate foreign markets, or to locate an activity in a slow-growth region of the country. Subsidies can consist of grants, low-interest loans, or tax incentives. However, consumers also receive subsidies — for example, through the support Canada provides for rail transportation, which means that the costs of passenger rail travel do not reflect the true cost, through provincial and municipal support for urban transit, and through government subsidies to the performing arts, which reduce box-office prices. However, consumers may also pay a subsidy to a producer by forcing consumers to pay higher prices; in this sense, tariffs are a subsidy for domestic manufacturers, and prices obtained by farm marketing boards may be subsidies for farmers. Another form of subsidy is a government loan at a low interest rate, or a government-guaranteed loan that allows the borrower to obtain funds at a lower rate of interest than he would otherwise pay.

subsistence wage The lowest wage that can be paid to a worker so that he can obtain the basic necessities of life and still be able and willing to work. For some economists, such as Thomas Robert Malthus, this is the long-term wage, since anything higher will attract too many workers and anything lower will attract too few. See also IRON LAW OF WAGES.

substitutes Rival or competing goods that can be interchanged for one another, since they have the same uses or yield similar satisfaction. If the price of product A rises, the demand for product B, if it is a substitute, should rise if its present price is now lower. Tea and coffee are substitutes as hot beverages;

trains, planes, and buses are substitutes in travel; steel, concrete, bricks, and lumber are substitutes in construction, and chicken and beef are substitutes as sources of protein. *See also* COMPLE-MENTARY GOODS.

substitution effect   The change in demand for a product if its price is changed while the prices of other goods remain unchanged; the extent to which demand changes depends, among other things, on whether or not substitutes exist and are readily available. If the price of raspberries goes up while other prices stay the same, it will benefit consumers to substitute a cheaper product — say, strawberries — to hold down living costs. Similarly, if the price of raspberries falls below the price of strawberries, it will pay to switch to raspberries. Thus, the demand for both strawberries and rasp-berries will change, depending upon their relative prices. *See also* INCOME EFFECT. When substitutes exist, the price of one product or service is influenced by the price of the other — for example, increases in railway freight rates may lead shippers to make greater use of trucks, if trucking charges are unchanged.

subvention   A synonym for a government grant or subsidy.

succession duty   A tax on the wealth received by beneficiaries of an estate. Its purposes are to reduce great inequalities of wealth in society by taxing those who inherit significant wealth, and to raise revenue to help cover the costs of government. The federal government withdrew from the this field at the end of 1971, so that the provinces could raise money from this tax. However, all of the provinces have also withdrawn from the field as well.

suggested retail selling price   A price often printed on consumer goods by manufacturers to show the public what they can expect to pay, unless a particular retailer decides to sell the product for less. *See also* RESALE-PRICE MAINTENANCE.

sunk costs   Money invested in unique machinery and equipment, product development, and other activities such as advertising that cannot be recovered or diverted to another use.

sunrise industry   An industry, usually associated with high-technology, that is expected to achieve strong growth in the future and be an important source of new jobs. Examples include semi-conductors and microelectronics, biotechnology, pharmaceuticals, information technologies, telecommunications, new materials, computer software, entertainment, and advanced manufacturing systems. *See also* SUN-SET INDUSTRIES.

sunset industry   An industry that is expected to play a declining role in the economy and has reached the stage where it is shedding jobs and shrinking production capacity, either because of changes in consumer demand or because the activity has shifted to a lower-cost country elsewhere. Examples include clothing, textiles, footwear, consumer electronics, basic steel, and many areas of light manufacturing, from toys and games to metal-bashed auto parts.

supplementary estimates   Requests to Parliament for approval of additional government spending, beyond the amounts requested in the main ESTI-MATES at the start of the FISCAL YEAR. Additional spending needs can result from unanticipated higher costs, a government decision to increase spending under a particular program, or the introduction of new spending programs during the fiscal year. For example, higher than expected unem-ployment can lead to a need for additional unemployment-insurance spending; a decision to accelerate housing construction will mean that more money will have to be allocated to housing programs, and the introduction of, say, a new research and development program will entail new spending. One set of supplementary estimates is presented in the second half of the fiscal year, while another set is presented at the end of the fiscal year.

supplementary letters patent Changes in the charter issued to a company that has been incorporated under federal or provincial law. An application has to be made to the same government department that issued the original charter. A company may want, for example, to increase its AUTHORIZED CAPITAL if it has grown much faster than expected. This can only be done through supplementary letters patent.

supply The quantity of a good available for sale at a particular price. Supply thus depends on price. Supply can be increased until the marginal cost of the product — that is, the cost of producing one more unit — is equal to the existing price. At that point, a price increase will be needed if the supply is to be increased.

supply and demand *See* LAW OF SUPPLY AND DEMAND.

Supply and Services, Department of A federal government department created in 1969 to act as the central purchasing agent of the federal government; provide centralized services to government departments and agencies (for example, printing and publishing, advertising management, and telecommunications systems); provide management-consulting assistance to government departments and agencies; handle payroll, employee-benefit, and pension services for all government employees; maintain all employee records; conduct auditing services; receive all revenue for the gov-

ernment in the CONSOLIDATED REVENUE FUND; and issue all cheques and make all payments on behalf of the government of Canada. In its role as purchasing agent for the federal government, the department is able to impose quality standards and to use its purchasing power to encourage the development of Canadian-designed products, thereby helping the growth of Canadian companies. In 1992, the CANADIAN COMMERCIAL CORPORATION was made the responsibility of the department. The minister is the RECEIVER-GENERAL OF CANADA, the custodian of enemy property during times of war, and responsible to Parliament for the ROYAL CANADIAN MINT and the Crown Assets Disposal Corporation. The Department of Supply and Services is based in Ottawa.

supply curve The relationship between the quantity of a good that producers wish to sell over some period of time and the price of the good.

supply management Measures to allow farm marketing boards to control the production and prices of eggs, poultry, and dairy products by setting quotas for individual farms and restricting the import of competing products from outside Canada. Without the ability to set quotas on imports, the supply-management system could not function. However, under proposals for trade reform in the URUGUAY ROUND of the GENERAL AGREEMENT ON TARIFFS AND TRADE, it has been proposed that agricultural import quotas be abolished and be replaced by tariffs that initially would be extremely high but that would decline over time.

supply schedule (curve) A curve that shows the relationship between market price and the volume of goods that producers are willing to supply at any given price. As prices rise, so will the supply, and vice versa. *See also* DEMAND SCHEDULE (CURVE).

supply shock An unexpected and significant increase or reduction in the availability of an important commodity or a significant technological improvement that causes a change in the amount of output supplied at a given price. For example, the oil shocks in the 1973-1974 period and 1979 that led to sharp increases in oil prices resulted in the obsolescence of production systems that depended on cheap energy, as well as an increase in both inflation and unemployment, or STAGFLATION. Likewise, the glut of oil and grains in the late 1980s led to a sharp decline in the asset value of oil companies and grain farms as well as the collateral pledged for loans, with a consequent impact on banks.

supply-side economics **1.** The belief that changes in macroeconomic policies have their principal impact on supply rather than demand. For example, if taxes are lowered, the savings will be invested in productive ventures, leading to an increase in the supply of goods and services in the economy. As a result, the belief holds, rising incomes will lead to higher tax revenues. Many supply-side economists deny the ability of government to influence economic performance by increasing aggregate demand; instead, they reject the views of KEYNESIAN ECONOMICS and favour a faith in free markets and CLASSICAL ECONOMICS instead. They favour tight limits on the role of labour unions, a reduction in social and unemployment benefits, deregulation and privatization, and a reliance on MONETARISM. **2.** More generally, policies designed to raise the productive capacity of the economy and thereby its long-term productivity growth rate, such as incentives for investment in machinery and equipment, measures to raise the skills or workers, steps to increase competition, or policies to increase the development and diffusion of new technology.

support point The level or point at which a central bank is likely to intervene to maintain an orderly movement in its exchange rate.

suppressed inflation Inflation that cannot make itself felt in the form of higher prices — for example, because of government wage and price controls or some other factor, such as a temporary oversupply of goods and services — but that will appear once controls are lifted or the temporary surplus disappears.

Supreme Court of Canada The court of appeal from all other courts in Canada that deals with criminal, civil, and constitutional cases. The court dates back to 1875. Its decisions are final; there is no appeal. At one point it could be overruled by the Judicial Committee of the Privy Council in Britain until Parliament made the Supreme Court the court of last resort in all cases in 1949. The court has nine judges, the chief one being the chief justice of Canada. Although most of the court's work consists of handling appeals from the decisions of the top courts of appeal in each province, the federal government may seek a Supreme Court opinion or clarification on any part of the CONSTITUTION ACT, 1867, or the CONSTITUTION ACT, 1982, the constitutionality or interpretation of any federal or provincial measure, and any other point of law. It has ruled on a number of constitutional issues, including jurisdiction over offshore mineral rights along the Pacific Coast in 1967, the legality of the federal government's 1975 wage and price controls in 1976, and the federal responsibility for cable television in 1978. In 1990, the Supreme Court ruled that the federal government was to regulate all the privately owned telephone companies that previously had been regulated by the provinces. This paved the way for the federal Telecommunications Act in 1992. Judges are appointed for terms of "good behaviour" but must retire at age 75. They are appointed from judges and lawyers with at least 10 years' good standing in a provincial bar association, and at least three of the judges must be from Quebec. Supreme Court judges are required to live within 40 kilometres of the National Capital Region. The court is based in Ottawa.

surcharge An additional tax or tariff that is added to an existing tax or tariff.

surplus 1. What is left over — for example, the excess of government revenue after its expenditures have been made, the remaining value of goods or services after deducting all costs, the remaining crops after the year's food needs have been met. **2.** The RETAINED EARNINGS of a corporation. **3.** The contributed surplus of a corporation, which arises when a corporation is able to sell new shares above their par or stated value.

surtax An additional tax levied on either the tax base or on taxable income after the normal tax has been levied; it is usually an additional percentage of the normal tax payable. A surtax is sometimes imposed by a government when it wants to adopt a policy of fiscal restraint to curb excess demand in the economy; it can be applied to consumers or corporations, or both.

survey A method of determining public opinion, attitudes, or expectations, by interviewing a representative sample of the population, based on age, sex, education, occupation, and place of residence, and drawing conclusions for the population as a whole from the results. Surveys can play an important role in setting economic policy by revealing consumer expectations, and hence buying plans, or by indicating the confidence of business leaders and their investment intentions. Surveys are widely used by corporations in MARKET RESEARCH.

suspended trading On a stock exchange, a halt to trading in the shares of a particular company. Suspension may occur until significant news, such as a takeover bid or a major mineral find, is announced and widely disseminated, or until details of a takeover bid are clarified, or because a company breaks the rules of the listing stock exchange. As long as trading is suspended, no member of the stock exchange is allowed to handle an order for the shares in another market. Trading is normally resumed when important corporate news has been disseminated and clarified, or when a listed company has dealt with its infraction of the stock exchange's rules to the satisfaction of the exchange.

sustainable development The concept of economic development that fosters forms of economic growth that are consistent with a healthy environment. As defined by the World Commission on Environment and Development in its 1987 report, *Our Common Future*, it is "development that meets the needs of the present without compromising the ability of future generations to meet their own needs." The commission argued that economic growth based on current technologies and practices would put the world's environment at risk, threatening not only the biosphere through global warming and ozone depletion, but also the sustainability of the world's oceans and other water systems, its forests and agricultural lands, and its genetic base now represented by the vast diversity of plant and animal life. Sustainable development deals with environmental planning and management, economic development, which includes new technologies, the global distribution of income, energy efficiency, renewable forms of energy, and the recycling of raw materials, as well as international trade, world population growth, and the well-being of people, including the issue of poverty. The Science Council of Canada, in 1977, developed a similar concept in its report, *The Conserver Society*. It urged Canadians to build concern for the environment into investment decisions by business and government and spending decisions by consumers. *See also* AGENDA 21.

Sustainable Development Commission A new international body proposed by the UNITED NATIONS (UN) CONFERENCE ON ENVIRONMENT AND DEVELOPMENT in Rio de Janeiro in 1992 to act as a watchdog and ensure that governments implemented the pledges they made at the "Earth Summit." Like the UN Human Rights Commission, it would depend on evidence gathered by private environmental groups and on peer pressure and public opinion to shame countries into following policies compatible with sustainable development. It will monitor compliance with AGENDA 21 as well as with new conventions such as those dealing with global warming and the preservation of the world's biological diversity. The commission would also monitor the environmental activities of international agencies such as the WORLD BANK and receive reports from UN agencies. It would have delegates from 53 countries, including Canada, but no enforcement powers. *See also* UNITED NATIONS SUSTAINABLE DEVELOPMENT COMMISSION.

sustained-yield basis A form of forest management in which trees are supposed to be replanted at the same rate as they are cut down.

swaps A transaction in international banking in which one currency is traded for another in order to earn a higher rate of interest.

swap arrangement An arrangement among various nations, through their central banks, to help one another deal with speculative attacks on one of their currencies or to deal with a balance-of-payments problem. Under a swap, country A's central bank will make available to country B's central bank a specified amount of its currency in return for a credit for country B's currency, with the exchange to be reversed later but at the same exchange rate as the initial transaction. Such arrangements have been used a number of times since 1961, with the assistance of the BANK FOR INTERNATIONAL SETTLEMENTS, to help solve balance-of-payments and foreign-exchange problems. Canada was a recipient of such assistance during its 1962 foreign-exchange crisis.

sweat shop A company that pays workers the lowest possible wage, provides them with the barest of benefits as required under law, and works them the longest possible hours, under high pressure and often under unhealthy conditions. Although labour laws provide workers with some protection against unscrupulous employers, through minimum-wage, hours-of-work, vacation-with-pay, and job-safety laws, workers are not always aware of their legal rights. Illegal or legal immigrants may also be afraid to speak up.

sweet crude Oil that is low in sulphur content.

sweetener A feature to make a purchase, lease, or investment more attractive to a would-be buyer, tenant, or investor. For example, a men's clothing shop may offer a free shirt with each new sports jacket purchased; a landlord may offer free or reduced rent for a period of time or may offer to bear the cost of renovations to attract a tenant; or a company trying to raise new EQUITY CAPITAL may make its PREFERRED

SHARES convertible into COMMON SHARES or attach WARRANTS to its common shares.

sweetheart contract   A collective agreement negotiated by an employer with a dishonest union leader that benefits mainly the employer. It can also be a contract or sales agreement, negotiated between a company and a supplier or customer, that is to the detriment of the majority of shareholders but that benefits a particular shareholder or director who has an interest in the supplier or customer with whom the contract or agreement is negotiated.

swing-shift   In a corporation or government agency operating 24 hours a day, the shift that begins in late afternoon and continues until about midnight.

sympathy strike   An illegal strike to show sympathy for another striking union by union members who have a collective agreement in effect with their own employer, and who are not directly involved in the dispute.

syndicalism   An economic system in which each industry is organized into an autonomous syndicate under the control of the workers. These various units or syndicates for all of the country's different industries meet as a federation to plan national policies and priorities, thus eliminating the need for a strong central government. The idea generated some interest in the late 19th and early 20th centuries, mainly in France, where it was promoted by Georges Sorel and Hubert Lagardelle. Italy's Benito Mussolini showed some interest in syndicalism in the 1930s, and interest has been shown in Canada by some of the more radical spokespeople for Quebec unions.

syndicate   **1.** A group of INVESTMENT DEALERS who jointly UNDERWRITE or buy a new issue of shares or bonds on a wholesale basis and resell them to investors at a profit, or who arrange the sale of a large block of an outstanding issue of shares or bonds so as not to disturb the market unduly. Banks may also participate in a syndicate — in a new issue of provincial bonds, for example. **2.** A group of investors who participate together in launching a new business enterprise that has a large start-up cost or a large capital investment.

syndicated loan   A loan to a corporation or government that is shared among a group of banks to share the risk in a particularly large loan. One bank will act as the lead bank.

synergy   A situation in which two or more groups achieve greater total effectiveness by working together than by working separately. Synergy can be a reason for a merger or for a STRATEGIC ALLIANCE between companies; synergy may also be developed between one company and its suppliers or its customers.

synthetic crude oil   Crude oil produced from TAR-SANDS or heavy-oil deposits that is treated in upgrading facilities to reduce its sulphur content and to decrease its viscosity, so that it can be processed by a refinery into gasoline, heating oil, and other products, much like ordinary crude oil.

system of national accounts   A comprehensive series of statistics, developed by STATISTICS CANADA since the end of the Second World War; these statistics, taken together, give a complete, overall view of changes taking place in the economy and provide a comprehensive basis for economic analysis. The system consists of a number of different quarterly and annual statistical reports: 1. The national income and expenditure accounts, which show who produces the GROSS DOMESTIC PRODUCT, and who gets the economic output and how it is spent (publication 13-001). The output of industry is reported monthly in *Gross Domestic Product by Industry* (publication 15-001). Income and expenditure accounts for individual provinces are reported annually (publication 13-213). 2. The balance of international payments that shows trade, investment, travel, and other transactions with non-residents (publication 67-001). The stock of Canada's non-resident assets and liabilities is reported annually in *Canada's International Investment Position* (publication 67-202). 3. Input-output tables, which show the contributions of different industries to economic growth, including the flow of goods and services between different industries, are reported annually in the *Input-Output Structure of the Canadian Economy* (publication 15-201). 4. Financial-flow accounts, which show the movement of funds between savers and borrowers, including the sale and purchase of various financial assets, are reported quarterly (publication 13-014). The stock of assets and liabilities is reported annually in the *National Balance Sheet Accounts* (publication 13-214).

The system of national accounts is one of the most important concepts in modern statistics; without it, economic policy makers would be hard pressed to build economic models and to improve their skills in economic management. The system of national accounts also provides a basis for making comparisons with economic developments in other countries. The Canadian system is similar to the systems used by the ORGANIZATION FOR ECONOMIC CO-OPERATION AND DEVELOPMENT and by the United Nations.

System of National Accounts Analysis A method of presenting and analyzing government spending and revenues in which government is treated as another sector of the economy. This is the system used when comparing government spending and revenues of different countries. Statistics Canada publishes quarterly (publication 13-001) and annual (publication 13-201) reports on national accounts.

systems analysis A management technique, using computer models, to study the range of alternatives and their outcomes for a system, whether the system is a corporation, a local or national economy, an industry, or something much smaller, such as a local river system.

tailings The waste materials produced in the initial processing of a mineral ore. The solid wastes are separated out from the water used in the processing in a body of water known as a tailings pond.

take-home pay The amount of money received by an employee to spend, after an employer has made all the required deductions for income taxes, pension contributions, unemployment insurance, union dues, and various fringe benefits, such as accident, sickness, dental, and disability insurance.

takeover The acquisition of control of one company by another, usually by purchasing enough shares to exercise control. Companies often find it more attractive to grow by taking over other companies than by investing in new productive assets, especially if stock markets are weak, shares undervalued, and the costs of new capital investment high. A company can also increase its share of the market by taking over competitors. There are different types of takeovers. In some cases, known as horizontal takeovers, one company will buy a competitor in the same market. In other cases, known as vertical takeovers, a customer may take over a supplier, or vice versa. There is also another type of takeover, by a holding or management company or a conglomerate, in which unrelated businesses are acquired. Takeovers allow a company to reduce costs, eliminate competition, acquire new technologies or markets, and diversify into new activities.

Takeovers in Canada may be subject to review under the COMPETITION ACT by the COMPETITION TRIBUNAL to see whether they unduly prevent or lessen competition. Foreign companies have found the takeover of Canadian corporations to be a convenient way of establishing themselves in the Canadian market. The takeover of Canadian companies above a certain size by foreign investors requires approval from INVESTMENT CANADA, which must determine whether the takeover brings a "net benefit" to Canadians. The takeover of publicly traded companies must follow rules set down by provincial securities commissions and local stock exchanges. The Department of CONSUMER AND

CORPORATE AFFAIRS publishes data on takeovers in Canada. Takeovers can be financed either by cash or by an exchange of shares, with a shareholder in the acquired company getting new shares from the acquiring company.

takeover bid An offer to existing shareholders of a company to acquire sufficient shares from them in order to gain effective control of the company. In many instances, the offerer will seek to acquire all of the shares of the company. However, an offerer may only want to acquire sufficient shares to exercise control. To protect minority shareholders, the takeover offer must be made to all shareholders and the offerer seeking less than 100 percent of the shares must prorate his or her purchases among all the shareholders tendering stock. To protect themselves against unwelcome takeovers, some companies have erected various defences, including GOLDEN PARACHUTES, POISON PILLS, and SHARK REPELLENTS.

tangible assets The physical assets of a firm or other entity that can be sold and therefore have a money value. They include buildings, machinery, and equipment. *See also* INTANGIBLE ASSETS.

tar sands *See* OIL SANDS.

tariff A tax or duty on imported goods, levied either as a percentage of their value or according to the number of units shipped. An AD VALOREM tariff or duty is one that is levied as a percentage of the value of the goods being imported or exported. Tariffs are INDIRECT TAXES. In the past they were a major source of revenue for governments; today, their main purpose is to protect domestic industries by giving them a competitive advantage over imports, although NON-TARIFF BARRIERS may be more effective in restraining imports. Critics of tariffs contend that they raise prices for consumers, and discourage the most efficient allocation of resources by frustrating the international location of industries according to COMPARATIVE ADVANTAGE. Defenders claim that tariffs are necessary to countries whose industries are not strongly developed, which must protect themselves against the onslaught of goods and services from countries whose industries are much more advanced. Since the GENERAL AGREEMENT ON TARIFFS AND TRADE (GATT) came into being in 1948, and with seven completed rounds of multilateral trade negotiations, tariff levels have declined from an average of 40 percent to an average of 7 percent today. The URUGUAY ROUND proposed to reduce tariff levels by another 30 percent. In Canada, tariffs are levied under the CUSTOMS TARIFF ACT. There are five different classifications: the British preferential tariff for members of the Commonwealth that are not members of the EUROPEAN COMMUNITY; the general preferential tariff on a large number of products from DEVELOPING COUNTRIES and some Eastern European countries (this expires June 30, 1994); the MOST FAVOURED NATION tariff on products originating from GATT members or other countries with which Canada has formal trading relations; the United Kingdom and Ireland tariff for Commonwealth members belonging to the European Community, which is gradually being raised to Most-Favoured-Nation levels; and a general tariff applied to products from countries with which Canada has no formal trading arrangement. Canada also provides preferential duty-free treatment for most products from the Commonwealth Caribbean countries. Under the CANADA-UNITED STATES FREE TRADE AGREEMENT, all tariffs are to be eliminated by January 1, 1998. Under the NORTH AMERICAN FREE TRADE AGREEMENT, most tariffs between Canada and Mexico would be eliminated by January 1, 2004, with tariffs on some sensitive items remaining until 2009. Tariff issues include the following: tariff escalation, a problem especially for Canada, in which tariffs are higher on processed natural resources than they are on raw materials and higher still on finished products, which discourages the processing of natural resources in resource-producing countries; tariff peaks, in which high tariffs are used to protect sensitive industries such as clothing and textiles or food products; nuisance tariffs, where customs duties are less than 5 percent, so that the revenues collected may not even cover the cost of customs processing; and tariff bindings, the failure of countries to fix or bind tariff reductions negotiated in GATT rounds against future increases in these same tariff items. *See also* GENERAL AGREEMENT ON TARIFFS AND TRADE, GENERALIZED SYSTEM OF PREFERENCES, INFANT INDUSTRY.

Tariff Board   A federal board, created in 1931, to carry out inquiries into the effect of imports on particular industries in Canada, and to hear appeals from importers and others on decisions of REVENUE CANADA on the value for duty, tariff classification, and other such matters affecting the level of duty charged on an import. In 1988, its duties were taken over by the CANADIAN INTERNATIONAL TRADE TRIBUNAL.

tariff war   An escalating competition between two or more countries that impose increasingly harsh barriers against the entry of each other's goods as the war heats up. For example, during the Depression of the 1930s, the nations of Europe, the United States, and the British Empire and Commonwealth tried to solve their own unemployment problems by raising tariff barriers against one another's imports. In this way, they

hoped to export their unemployment problems to others. Since the adoption of the GENERAL AGREEMENT ON TARIFFS AND TRADE in 1948, the potential for tariff wars has been sharply curbed. However, countries can still engage in trade wars by using NON-TARIFF BARRIERS and TRADE-REMEDY LAWS.

tariffication   The replacement of non-tariff barriers, such as import quotas and other restrictions, by tariffs. In the URUGUAY ROUND of trade negotiations, officials at the GENERAL AGREEMENT ON TARIFFS AND TRADE have proposed eliminating Canada's import quotas on eggs, dairy products, and poultry, which are a key part of the SUPPLY-MANAGEMENT system, and replacing the quotas with tariffs that at the beginning could be as high as 300 percent. Likewise, quotas under the MULTIFIBRE ARRANGEMENT on clothing and textiles would be replaced by tariffs.

task force   A group of experts appointed to investigate a particular problem, to come up with an analysis, and to make proposals to solve it.

Task Force on Atlantic Fisheries   In January, 1982, the federal government appointed a task force, headed by Michael Kirby, to recommend "how to achieve and maintain a viable Atlantic fishing industry, with due consideration for the overall economic and social development of the Atlantic provinces." In December, 1982, the task force published a two-volume report, *Navigating in Troubled Waters: A New Policy for the Atlantic Fisheries*. The Canadian fishing industry, it said, was "mired in financial crisis, plagued by internal bickering, beset with uncertainty about the future, and divided on how to solve its problems," despite the fact that it possessed one of the world's great natural fisheries-resources bases and sat at the doorstep of the huge U.S. market. The report contained 57 recommendations to restructure the Atlantic-coast fishing industry and raise the incomes of fishermen.

Task Force on Foreign Ownership and the Structure of Canadian Industry   A task force of eight university economists, headed by Professor Melville H. Watkins of the University of Toronto, and appointed by the federal government in March, 1967. Its assignment was to study "the significance — both political and economic — of foreign investment in the development of our country, as well as ways to encourage greater Canadian ownership of our industrial resources while retaining a climate favourable to the inflow of foreign investment, as required for Canada's optimum development."

The task-force report was presented to the government in February, 1968. It proposed a wide range of policies, with the following among them: 1. A new government agency to co-ordinate policies on foreign ownership. It would monitor the activities of foreign-owned corporations in Canada, scrutinize licensing agreements on technology between foreign parents and their Canadian subsidiaries and seek better ways of importing foreign technology, examine international market-sharing arrangements, work with other countries and international agencies to achieve common policies to control multinational corporations, and examine the tax procedures of the Canadian government and multinational firms to make sure that Canada got its proper share of corporate taxes. 2. Publication of increased information on the activities of foreign-controlled firms in Canada. The report proposed amendments to the Canada Corporations Act, to require that all federally incorporated PRIVATE COMPANIES disclose their annual financial results, and to make mandatory replies from foreign-con-

trolled firms to government questionnaires on compliance with the GUIDING PRINCIPLES OF GOOD CORPORATE BEHAVIOUR. 3. A revised competition policy, with amendments to the COMBINES INVESTIGATION ACT (now the COMPETITION ACT) to encourage greater competition in the economy, and to facilitate the RATIONALIZATION of Canadian industry to make it more efficient through mergers. 4. Establishment of the CANADA DEVELOPMENT CORPORATION, to play a major role in encouraging mergers to create stronger Canadian companies, to promote joint ventures with Canadian capital, and to provide a Canadian presence in industries that were for the most part foreign controlled. Other measures to develop an industrial strategy advocated by the report included encouragement of more research and development in Canada, improved business and management education, and better use of CLOSED-END INVESTMENT funds to facilitate Canadian ownership. 5. Special steps to block the EXTRA-TERRITORIAL application of foreign laws to the activities of foreign-controlled firms in Canada. The task force proposed a new government export agency to make sure that sales orders from Communist countries were filled by American-controlled subsidiaries here, in spite of prohibitions against parent firms under the U.S. Trading with the Enemy Act. The export agency would be able to purchase products from the American subsidiary in Canada and export them itself. It would be illegal for the subsidiary to refuse to sell to the government export agency. The task force also wanted laws to prevent the removal of commercial records from Canada as a result of foreign court orders, legislation to bar Canadian compliance with foreign anti-trust rulings, and questionnaires to foreign subsidiaries here to determine the impact of parent-country anti-trust laws on their Canadian operations. 6. Multilateral tariff reductions, to help Canadians get a bigger share of foreign markets and to promote competition in Canada.

Overall, the task force found that, while foreign investment had produced both costs and benefits to the Canadian economy, a new national policy was needed to ensure Canadian economic independence, and to strengthen the country's capacity for autonomous growth.

tax A mandatory payment made by individuals and corporations to government. Taxes are levied on income or wealth or are imposed on goods and services to finance the cost of government services, to redistribute income, and to influence the behaviour of consumers and investors. Until the early part of the 20th century, the purpose of a tax was to enable the government to pay its own bills. Since then, PROGRESSIVE TAXATION has been used to redistribute wealth from the well-off to the needy. With the adoption of KEYNESIAN ECONOMICS, governments began to manipulate tax rates to encourage or to slow down economic growth. A tax can also be used to encourage desired behaviour — for example, the imposition of higher taxes on cars that consume a large amount of gasoline may help the sale of smaller cars that make more efficient use of gasoline, or tax incentives can be used to encourage business investment or research and development. There are basically four kinds of taxes: income taxes on the income of individuals and corporations; payroll taxes paid by employees and employers, including UNEMPLOYMENT INSURANCE and CANADA PENSION PLAN premiums; expenditure or sales taxes, including EXCISE TAXES, the GOODS AND SERVICES TAX, and TARIFFS; and property taxes, levied on buildings and land and, through the CAPITAL-GAINS TAX,

on other assets with deemed realization of capital gains at death. *See* DIRECT TAX, INDIRECT TAX, INCOME TAX, PROPERTY TAX, SALES TAX, TAX EXPENDITURES.

tax avoidance The reduction of a person's tax liability to the lowest possible level through legal means. This is done by utilizing all possible deductions, taking advantage of all possible methods of reporting and assessing income, and using all possible TAX LOOPHOLES. *See also* TAX EVASION.

tax base The amount on which tax rates are levied. In the case of personal income tax, the tax base is a person's income after all permitted exemptions and deductions have been made. In the case of property tax, it is the assessed value of the property. The tax base is income, wealth, or the price of a good or service.

tax-based incomes policy (TIP) A voluntary incomes policy designed to reduce inflationary wage demands, and thereby the inflation rate, by providing tax relief to workers who stay within wage guidelines; employers would also get tax relief in most TIP schemes, depending on satisfactory price or profit-margin performance. At the end of the tax year participating employees would receive a form from their employer entitling them to a tax credit in their personal income tax that year. The goal of TIP is to supplement macroeconomic policy efforts to reduce inflation by rewarding those who hold down wage demands.

tax burden The total tax an individual or corporation must pay, including income taxes, sales taxes, property taxes, excise taxes, and other taxes. The ratio of tax revenues to GROSS DOMESTIC PRODUCT provides one measure of the total tax burden, though comparisons among countries are difficult because the role of government varies from country to country. For example, health care is a public expense in Canada and is financed by taxation; in the United States, it has largely been a private expense although programs for the elderly have become the faster-rising part of the U.S. budget.

tax-collection agreement An agreement under which the federal government collects personal and corporate income taxes on behalf of the provincial governments. The Fiscal Arrangements Act authorizes the federal government to enter into such agreements; it collects personal income taxes on behalf of all the provinces except Quebec, and corporate income taxes on behalf of all the provinces except Quebec, Ontario, and Alberta. The agreements set out the manner in which the provinces will be paid and the conditions they must meet.

Tax Court of Canada A court established in 1983 to adjudicate disputes between Canadian citizens or firms and REVENUE CANADA or other federal departments over tax assessments under the INCOME TAX ACT, pension benefits under the CANADA PENSION PLAN and the OLD AGE SECURITY PENSION, and unemployment benefits under the UNEMPLOYMENT INSURANCE ACT. In addition, the court hears appeals of war veterans and their families concerning benefits under various programs available to veterans and their families. While the court, with up to 18 judges, is based in Ottawa, it conducts its hearings across Canada.

tax credit A credit that is deducted from the income tax that an individual or corporation would otherwise pay. It differs from a TAX DEDUCTION, which is subtracted from a person's or a corporation's total income, thus lowering the taxable income against which income tax is levied. The value of the tax deduction for an individual depends on the level of income. The higher the income, the higher the top marginal rate of tax, and the greater the value of the tax deduction. In the case of a tax credit, however, the value is the same to all recipients, since it is deducted from the actual tax they would otherwise pay. The tax credit is considered a preferable way of extending benefits to individuals since it gives all recipients the same amount of money, while a tax deduction gives a greater benefit to people with high incomes. Moreover, a tax credit can be paid to people whose income is too low to require them to pay taxes, under a system of NEGATIVE INCOME TAX, whereas a tax deduction can only benefit people who have taxable income. *See also* INVESTMENT TAX CREDIT, CHILD BENEFIT.

tax deduction A deduction permitted under the Income Tax Act from a person's or a corporation's income in calculating tax liability. All the deductions permitted an individual, for example, are subtracted from his or her gross income. The resulting figure is taxable income, and it is on this amount that federal and provincial income taxes are levied. The greater the number and amount of a person's tax deductions, the lower the taxable income and the less tax payable. Because Canada's income-tax system is based on the ability-to-pay principle, the income-tax rate is much higher on the top $2,000 of income for someone with a taxable income of $45,000 than it is on someone with a taxable income of $15,000. Similarly, a tax deduction of $2,000 will be worth much more to someone with a taxable income of $45,000 than it will be to someone with a taxable income of $15,000. A TAX CREDIT differs from a tax deduction; a tax deduction is made from taxable income and brings greater benefits to taxpayers in high tax brackets whereas a tax credit is deducted from the amount of tax a person owes and is therefore worth the same to each taxpayer, regardless of income. Canada's tax system provides many deductions for individuals, ranging from pension contributions and a tax-free portion of interest and dividend income to personal education costs and charitable donations. Self-employed people can deduct a wide range of business expenses, and corporations can deduct their operating, interest, and depreciation costs.

tax deferral   A provision in income-tax laws that permits the tax on personal or corporate income to be postponed if the income is spent in certain specified ways. For example, an individual may invest a certain part of his or her income in a pension plan or REGISTERED RETIREMENT SAVINGS PLAN and defer the income tax on the money invested, either until it is collected some time in the future in the form of a pension or until the money is withdrawn from the pension or savings plan. Similarly, DEPRECIATION or CAPITAL-COST-ALLOWANCE provisions allow a corporation to postpone payment of taxes on corporate income if the corporation makes certain types of investments.

tax evasion   The reduction of a person's tax liability to the lowest possible level through illegal means — for example, by failing to report income or by understating income, by falsifying expenses and deductions so that they are overstated, or by claiming false status. It is a deliberate attempt to defraud tax authorities and is punishable by jail sentences and fines under Canadian law.

tax exclusion   The designation of certain types of income as non-taxable under the Income Tax Act. Examples include gifts and bequests, lottery winnings, WORKER'S COMPENSATION payments, free travel passes, discounts, and similar employee benefits, capital gains on personal residences, and dividends from active foreign subsidiaries in tax-treaty countries.

tax expenditure   Tax revenue that the government gives up through a special provision in its tax laws to provide an incentive for someone to do something or to provide some kind of relief for an individual or corporation. The federal Income Tax Act contains many provisions in the form of exemptions, deductions, deferrals of taxes, credits, and exclusions, that reduce the amount of tax revenues that would otherwise be collected. Tax expenditures are an alternative to direct spending by government and are frequently used to pursue government objectives, including economic objectives such as business investment, spending on research and development, and regional development or social objectives such as saving for retirement, encouraging charitable donations, and assisting lower-income and elderly Canadians. However, unlike direct spending, the concessions and incentives that government grants to industry and individuals in the form of tax expenditures are rarely subject to close evaluation by Parliament to determine their effectiveness or fairness. The Department of Finance published its first report on the cost of various tax expenditures in 1979. Examples of tax expenditures include tax incentives for research and development, the tax deferral for money invested in a REGISTERED RETIREMENT SAVINGS PLAN, and the $100,000 lifetime capital-gains exemption. The most recent corporate tax expenditure report was published in 1985, while the most recent personal tax expenditure report was published in 1993. *See also* TAX CREDIT, TAX DEDUCTION, TAX DEFERRAL, TAX EXCLUSION, TAX INCENTIVE, TAX PREFERENCE, TAX SHELTER.

tax haven A country with extremely low tax rates that is used by corporations and wealthy individuals as an address from which to avoid taxes in their own country, where tax rates are much higher. For example, a corporation exporting from Canada to Japan might be able, on paper, to export its products to a subsidiary in a tax haven at a low price and to re-export them from the tax haven to Japan at a high price. It would earn little profit on the transaction in Canada, where it would be subject to normal corporation taxes, and a high profit in the tax-haven country, where it would pay little if any tax. The corporation would retain the use of those profits earned in the tax haven for its own purposes, while the Canadian public would be deprived of important tax revenues. In recent years, such transactions have been made much more difficult, due to a tightening of Canadian tax laws. Examples of tax havens are Bermuda, the Bahamas, the Cayman Islands, and Liechtenstein. *See also* TRANSFER PRICE.

tax incentive A tax measure designed to encourage a particular type of activity. The investment tax credit, for example, is used to encourage business to invest. Fast write-offs may be used to encourage spending on research and development or on anti-pollution devices. A deferral of taxes set aside as savings for retirement under a REGISTERED RETIREMENT SAVINGS PLAN is designed to encourage people to save and invest. Lower tax rates in slow-growth regions can be used to attract investment that would not otherwise go there. Through the use of incentives, the tax system has considerable potential to influence the behaviour of individuals and corporations.

tax incidence The person who eventually pays the tax burden. When a tax is imposed on one person or firm, it may be possible to shift the burden or cost on to someone else. For example, firms can pass along an increase in corporation taxes to consumers, shift it on to their employees by giving smaller wage increases, shift it back to suppliers by paying less for parts or commodities, or shift it on to all of these groups. Workers who find that their income tax has increased may try to shift part of that burden on to consumers by demanding bigger wage increases, which their employer, in turn, passes along by raising prices. Economists argue over who really pays corporate income taxes: the firm on which it is levied, or the consumer, through the prices he or she pays for a firm's goods or services.

tax lien A lien or claim that is held by a government against a person's or a firm's assets to cover unpaid taxes. A lien by a municipal government on a person's real estate for non-payment of property taxes restricts the ability of the owner to sell that property. At some point, the municipality can step in and auction the property to recover the unpaid taxes.

tax loophole A provision in tax law, usually but not always unintended, that permits a person's or a firm's income to go untaxed or to be taxed at a lower rate. Such a loophole may give special and more favourable treatment to a particular group. For example, professionals, such as lawyers and doctors, if they were able to incorporate themselves, could end up paying tax at a much lower rate than ordinary wage and salary earners. *See also* TAX SHELTER.

tax loss 1. A business loss that can be deducted from profits in future years, thus reducing future taxes, or a loss in one branch or subsidiary of a company that can be deducted from the profits of other branches or subsidiaries of the company in calculating the firm's total tax liability. **2.** The sale of shares at a loss to realize a capital loss that can be deducted from capital gains on the sale of other shares, thus reducing the amount of tax that must be paid on the capital gains. An investor, for example, may decide to sell certain shares that are trading below the price he or she paid for them and that are unlikely to show any recovery on the market for some time to come. The investor is able to deduct the capital loss from the capital gains on other shares, for tax purposes, and to use the money for other investments.

tax point One percentage point of basic federal tax payable; this is the amount a province would get if the federal government transfers a personal income tax point to a province. If the federal government plans to transfer two tax points to the provinces to compensate them for taking over the full cost of what had been a shared-cost program, it turns over to each province two percentage points of the federal basic tax collected from the taxpayers of that province. In the case of corporate income tax, it is one percentage point of taxable corporate profits.

tax preference A provision under income-tax laws that permits a lower rate of tax for certain types of income; examples of tax preference would include a low rate of taxation for small-business income, the taxation of only one-half of capital gains, and a low rate of taxation for resource income.

Tax Review Board A federal board that acted as a tribunal to resolve disputes between taxpayers and REVENUE CANADA. It was replaced by the TAX COURT OF CANADA in 1983.

tax sale The seizure and sale of property belonging to an individual or company, to collect unpaid taxes. The sale is by public auction; after the unpaid taxes and interest have been deducted, the remaining proceeds, if any, are turned over to the owner.

tax-sharing The occupancy of the same tax field by two levels of government. For example, both the federal and provincial governments occupy the personal- and corporate-income-tax and sales-tax fields.

tax shelter A provision under the Income Tax Act that is designed to encourage individuals to make certain types of high-risk investments that the government wishes to see take place by providing tax savings. Examples of tax shelters have included investments by Canadians in films, in offshore drilling in the far North, and in certain types of residential rental properties. Tax shelters allow the investor to reduce income-tax liability significantly or to defer a tax liability. However, federal income-tax changes in 1988 eliminated many tax shelters. The tax shelter for investment in Canadian films remains. *See also* FLOW-THROUGH SHARES.

tax shifting The passing of the tax burden along to someone else by the person or firm on whom it is originally levied. For example, it is argued that CORPORATE INCOME TAX on a firm's profits is usually paid by the firm's customers, because a provision for the tax is included in the price that customers pay for the firm's goods or services. Excise taxes on alcohol and cigarettes levied by the federal government are added to the price of these items, so that it is the firm's customers who really pay that tax as well. Similarly, the GOODS AND SERVICES TAX is shifted by manufacturers and retailers on to consumers. However, consumers cannot shift the retail-sales tax they pay on to anyone else.

tax treaty A bilateral treaty between Canada and another country to make sure that the citizens of both get fair and equal treatment on the income they earn in each other's countries, and to avoid double taxation of the same income. The arrangements may include the following: provisions to make sure that a citizen of country A, working in country B, gets credit in country A for the income taxes paid in country B, and vice versa, so that he or she is not taxed twice on the same income; credits in country A for taxes paid in country B on profits earned by a corporation headquartered in country A from subsidiary activities in country B, and vice versa; and recognition that either country has exclusive tax jurisdiction on certain types of income.

taxable benefit   A benefit provided by an employer that must be treated by the employee as income for tax purposes. It can include the personal use of a company car, paid membership in a club, group insurance, dental care, or any such fringe benefit.

taxable income   Income that is subject to tax after all possible deductions and exemptions have been made.

taxation   A compulsory levy imposed by law by a public body for public purposes, such as the raising of revenue to pay for the costs of public services, the redistribution of income, and the regulation of economic activity.

taxing power   The constitutional right of a federal or provincial government to levy a tax. Under the CONSTITUTION ACT, 1867, the FEDERAL TAXING POWER includes all forms of taxation, direct and indirect. The PROVINCIAL TAXING POWER is limited to direct taxes, because the Fathers of Confederation feared that the provinces might use indirect taxes as barriers to interprovincial trade.

technical analysis   The analysis of stocks and commodities by tracking or charting price changes and changes in trading volume in order to forecast future prices.

technical assistance   A form of OFFICIAL DEVELOPMENT ASSISTANCE consisting of technical knowledge and education. It includes sending experts to a less-developed country to help establish a particular facility, such as a power station, and to train the people there to run it. It may also consist of general technical training offered to a less-developed country in, say, agriculture, health care, education, or management; or it may involve helping to establish training centres for young people, or bringing students from foreign countries to Canada or other advanced nations for technical training. Technical assistance was one of the earliest forms of foreign aid, and is still one of the most important forms. A key element of aid from the International Monetary Fund to Russia and other republics of the former Soviet Union consists of technical assistance in establishing central banks, fiscal policy skills, and tax collection systems.

technical barriers to trade   The use of product standards to discourage imports. As a result of the Tokyo Round of the GENERAL AGREEMENT ON TARIFFS AND TRADE (GATT), an Agreement on Technical Barriers to Trade was negotiated to achieve some degree of agreement on product standards for some categories of goods. However, not all GATT members have signed the agreement.

technical rally   A temporary surge in the price of shares generally or of a particular share on a stock exchange; it occurs when the number of would-be buyers exceeds the number of sellers.

technocracy   A movement originating in California in 1919 with William Henry Smith, an engineer who coined the term; it gained attention briefly during the GREAT DEPRESSION of the 1930s. Technocrats argued that, with the advance of science, technology, engineering, and economic planning, scientists and engineers should replace politicians and businesspeople in running society. According to the technocrats, investors and bankers, not consumers, were the main beneficiaries of technological change, because they absorbed the savings from modern machinery in the form of higher profits, instead of passing along the benefits in the form of lower prices and, hence, increased purchasing power. While technocracy was mainly a U.S. movement, chapters were established in many communities in Canada. Since the 1930s, the movement has lost much of its following and appeal, although the term "technocrat" is often used to describe someone who is concerned with technical details as opposed to the big picture.

technological change Advances in technology and knowledge that increase society's output of goods and services. These advances lead to higher productivity and lower average production costs, and are a critical factor in raising a society's standard of living. Technological change can consist of improved products, better manufacturing processes, advances in managerial know-how, new materials, or improved communications and distribution systems. Technological change is also embodied in the education and skills of workers. It is probably the single most important factor behind the economic progress of the 20th century. In agriculture, for example, technological change in the form of chemical fertilizer, improved seeds, advances in farm management, and the introduction of highly mechanized equipment has led to substantially increased production with a significantly smaller farm labour force; moreover, in real terms, farm prices have declined. Rapid advances in aviation and telecommunications have helped create a global economy by shrinking time and distance. Technological progress in the development of information systems, biotechnology, solar and other renewable energy systems, and new materials is expected to drive much of the world's economic progress as we enter the 21st century. Robert SOLOW won the Alfred Nobel Memorial Prize in Economic Science for his work demonstrating the importance of technological change in economic growth. The CANADIAN INSTITUTE FOR ADVANCED RESEARCH is engaged in a major research project demonstrating the central role of ideas and technological change in economic progress, based on the new growth theories of American economist Paul Romer. Much of the capital investment that takes place today results from technological change. Without technological progress, modern economies would lose a critical source of growth, and individuals would see little improvement in their real standard of living.

technological forecasting Various systems used to identify potential technological developments and to assess their impact. This type of forecasting is vital to governments and large corporations, and, in recent years, has emerged as a highly skilled discipline. Techniques include simple extrapolations from existing state-of-the-art knowledge of particular technologies, the so-called DELPHI TECHNIQUE, which brings various experts together in an attempt to develop a consensus, or to engage in highly creative thinking in which a number of possible futures, or scenarios, are drafted. Technologcal forecasting is an important activity in think-tanks and research centres that assemble expert opinions on future trends and developments.

technological sovereignty The ability of a nation to develop the technological capability it needs to ensure its future economic growth; it does not mean self-sufficiency in all technologies but a capability in some. The term was first used by the SCIENCE COUNCIL OF CANADA in its 1976-77 annual report. The council argued that unless Canada developed an international capability in some of the world's new technologies, it would not be able to participate in the new industrial revolution and would have little to sell to the rest of the world to pay for its imports. This would inevitably reduce Canada's political independence, and lower the standard of living of Canadians relative to that of their industrial trading partners. The council's report set out a strategy to achieve technological sovereignty: 1. Increase the demand for Canadian technology within Canada by, for example, having its federal and provincial governments use their purchasing power as customers for Canadian technology. 2. Expand the capacity of Canadian industry to develop new technology. 3. Strengthen the capacity of Canadian firms to absorb new technology. 4. Improve opportunities for Canadian firms to import technology under conditions more favourable to Canada.

technological unemployment Unemployment that results from the introduction of labour-replacing technology, such as robotics or other automated production systems, or other forms of technological change. This kind of unemployment is bound to occur in a healthy economy, and can be countered by retraining programs, to give workers new skills, and expansionary economic policies, to create new jobs. Since technological change results in improved productivity and real economic growth, new employment opportunities should arise. Technological change has eliminated hundreds of thousands of jobs — for example, farm labour, telephone-switchboard operators, payroll clerks, typesetters in newspapers — but a dynamic economy with proper economic policies is able to generate new industries, products, and services, and new technology has created a wide range of new jobs as well, such as computer programmers and systems analysts, as well as changing many jobs, such as those in financial services. At the same time, unions are properly concerned with the fate of their members affected by technological change, and collective agreements and labour laws today usually contain clauses to ease the impact on workers, especially older workers. *See* FREEDMAN REPORT.

technology The accumulated knowledge of mankind and its adaptation of industry, resulting in new products, production processes, and distribution systems. New technology is probably the single most important factor in economic growth, and is credited with much of the improvement in our standard of living since the Industrial Revolution of the late 18th and early 19th centuries.

technology transfer The transfer of knowledge from the nation in which it is developed to other nations where it is used, or from the company which developed it to other companies. Technology transfer has to do with the means by which access to technology is spread, and the terms and costs of its use by others. Technology can be sold — through the sale or licensing of PATENTS, or the sale of operating systems, industrial processes, and the technology itself. It can also be diffused through the direct investment of MULTINATIONAL CORPORATIONS, the transfer of ideas through scientific papers, the movement of people, and technical aid. The transfer of technology can also be negotiated as part of a major contract; for example, Canada's military offset programs have usually included some forms of technology transfer to Canada when major contracts were placed with foreign military suppliers. Technology can also be stolen, which is the reason that protection of INTELLECTUAL PROPERTY is becoming an important issue in international trade negotiations. Canada has relied heavily on the transfer of technology through the entry of multinational corporations into Canada. LESS-DEVELOPED COUNTRIES are demanding better terms for the transfer of Western technology; a United Nations conference was held in 1979 to try to develop a code to regulate technology transfers and improve the access of less-developed countries to modern technology on more favourable terms and this effort is continuing; however, industrial countries are demanding strengthened patent protection in these countries. Developing countries are also seeking the transfer of environmental technologies on favourable terms as the world attempts to address issues such as global warming and depletion of the ozone layer.

technostructure   A term coined by John Kenneth GALBRAITH to describe the professional managers or bureaucrats who run large corporations and government. They are the graduates of business and engineering schools, trained in the scientific method and in the behavioural sciences, who inhabit the top ranks of business and industry around the world, and who, by virtue of their positions, jointly plan the policies and priorities of modern societies. Because of their similarities, Galbraith predicted that this scientific and managerial elite would foster a convergence of values and lifestyles in the various industrial countries. It can be argued that in fact this so-called technostructure in each country is extending to developing countries and represents a

world citizenship, with its members developing more in common with one another than with other citizens in their own countries.

telecommunications   The modern communications network consisting of the telephone and cable-television systems, communications satellites, microwave, and land-lines for voice and computer communications and the broadcasting system. Sometimes called the electronic highway, it is the basis of the knowledge or information society of the future, in which computer terminals, the television set, and the telephone, or some new technology that combines all three, will provide major new communications links between individuals and industries. Telecommunications will enable individuals to draw on libraries and data banks and to work at home, will provide for instantaneous banking and inventory management, and will lead to many new industries and services. With the introduction of the microprocessor, which substantially reduces the cost of computer systems, of fibre optics, which enable much more information to be carried over a telephone line into the home or office, of communications satellites, which can provide low-cost and high-volume transmission of data, and of computer systems that have immediate access to one another, coming developments in communications are expected to make a significant contribution to economic growth. The Supreme Court of Canada determined in 1990 that the federal government has responsibility for telecommunications. *See also* CANADIAN RADIO-TELEVISION AND TELECOMMUNICATIONS COMMISSION, COMMUNICATIONS, TELESAT CANADA.

Telefilm Canada   A federal crown corporation established in 1967 as the Canadian Film Development Corporation; it was renamed Telefilm Canada in

1984. It provides government assistance to help develop the Canadian film, television-production, and video industry and thereby assure a stronger Canadian presence in these cultural industries, including Canadian content for television programming. The corporation also helps negotiate co-production agreements with other countries. Based in Montreal, Telefilm Canada operates a number of funds, including the Canadian Broadcast Program Development Fund, the Feature Film Fund, and the Feature Film Distribution Fund.

Teleglobe Canada   A crown corporation that was responsible for all communications links between Canada and other countries. It provides access to telephone systems in countries around the world, including links by communications satellites and undersea cables. Teleglobe was originally established by Parliament in 1950 as the Canadian Overseas Telecommunications Corporation. It was privatized in 1987, when it was sold to a private-sector telecommunications company.

Telesat Canada   A government-industry corporation created by Parliament in 1969 to establish a commercial communications-satellite service in Canada. It launched Anik 1, its first satellite, in November, 1972, and began to provide commercial service through a system of earth stations in January, 1973. Its shareholders included the federal government and the major telephone companies. In 1992, the government's share was sold to the private sector. It is a member of Stentor, the nationwide association of telephone companies. Its owners are the member companies of STENTOR and SPAR AEROSPACE.

tenants in common   Two or more persons, each with an undivided interest in a parcel of land or a building. That interest may be sold to another party or left to someone else in a will.

This means that, on the death of one of the owners, the survivors do not have an automatic right to the deceased's interest. *See also* JOINT TENANCY.

tender   **1.** A bid made to fill a government contract, setting out price, terms, and conditions that a would-be supplier promises to meet. Most government contracts are awarded after a call for tenders, in which competing firms submit sealed bids by a specified deadline. The bids are all opened at the same time and the contract, unless there are compelling reasons to decide otherwise, will go to the lowest tender bid. It is an offence under the COMPETITION ACT for companies to collude in submitting their bids; see also RIGGED BID. The tender system is also used by corporations planning major investment projects. **2.** The weekly bid by chartered banks and MONEY-MARKET DEALERS to buy federal treasury bills.

tender offer   An offer for the shares of a company by someone interested in gaining control of a company but whose acquisition may be opposed by the existing management of the company. The offered price is typically at a premium above the existing market price, but the offer is for a limited period of time. Securities legislation requires anyone making a tender offer to disclose the intention to the relevant securities commissions and to provide various details.

term deposit receipt   A debt security issued by a bank or trust company for a fixed sum of money, running for a fixed length of time and paying a fixed rate of interest. The rate of interest is higher than that paid on non-chequing or premium-savings accounts, and depends on the term; the longer the term, the higher the interest rate. Term deposits run anywhere from 30 days to six years. The longer the term, the smaller the denomination: minimum term deposits of less than one year are $5,000; one year or longer, $1,000. The interest rate is reduced if the funds are withdrawn prematurely.

term insurance A life-insurance policy that runs for a limited and specified period of time. If a person outlives the term, he or she receives no portion of the premiums that have been paid. The appeal of term insurance is that it covers a limited period when the insurance is most needed, and is usually cheaper than ordinary life insurance. For example, a father with a young family may want to carry a large amount of insurance while the children are young, so that his wife would be able to raise the children in reasonable comfort if he died. But he may calculate that, as he advances in his career, building up savings and investments, he has less need for a large life-insurance policy. Other forms of term insurance include travel insurance and insurance on a mortgage or consumer loan.

term loan A loan for a fixed period of time, usually more than one year, that has to be repaid by the end of that fixed period of time, as opposed to a DEMAND LOAN, which must be repaid whenever the lender calls in the loan for repayment. A term loan usually requires annual or more frequent repayments of principal.

term structure of interest rates The calculation of the expected rate of interest over the life of a bond. An organization planning a bond issue must calculate what rate of interest will be necessary to encourage an investor to hold the bond to maturity, which means that expected future interest rates as well as current interest rates must be taken into account in setting the yield on the bond.

term to maturity The time remaining until a bond or other loan matures and must be repaid.

terminal A transportation or distribution centre. Examples include airports, railway and bus stations, collection points for food shippers, storage facilities, and buyers.

terms of trade An indication of how a nation is faring in international trade. It is the ratio of the price index for merchandise exports to the price index for merchandise imports. A country's terms of trade improve if its export prices rise more than its import prices, since this means that it can buy more imports without having to increase the volume of its exports. Similarly, a country's terms of trade deteriorate if its import prices rise faster than its export prices, since it has to export more to pay for an unchanged volume of imports. This means that a country with high productivity and unique, desired products should rate better in world trade than a country that exports commodities in surplus supply. A country whose terms have improved enjoys a rise in its real income because of its improved purchasing power for imports. This assumes, however, that the price increase of a country's exports is due to improved quality and the development of new products that the rest of the world wants to buy, and not due to an excessive rise in unit labour costs or other factors reflecting declining competitiveness.

As a country that depends heavily on natural-resource exports, Canada saw its terms of trade improve during the mid-1970s when commodity prices soared. However, the long-term trend for commodity prices has been downward and as a result Canada's terms of trade have deteriorated; this means a bushel of wheat, barrel of oil, or tonne of newsprint or copper buys less of a foreign manufactured product today than it did 20 years ago. Countries without any natural resources but with advanced and high-productivity manufacturing, such as Germany and Japan, have seen their terms of trade improve in the past 20 years. Monthly price-index figures for exports and imports are published by Statistics Canada in its *Summary of Canadian International Trade* (publication 65-001).

territorial waters The coastal waters of a state over which it claims complete sovereignty, including the right to determine who shall enter those waters and under what conditions. States used to claim three miles for their shorelines, the range of a cannon shot. Today, most states, including Canada, claim 12 miles. In addition, most states, including Canada, claim a 200-mile fishing or EXCLUSIVE ECONOMIC ZONE.

tertiary industry An industry that uses knowledge or information as its raw material, or a service industry. Examples include computer programming, banking, health care, law, or engineering.

tertiary recovery Additional crude oil that can be recovered from oil and gas reservoirs by newer and more costly recovery techniques — for example, by flooding to increase pressure or by in situ combustion and steam flooding — to create heat and move the oil. With the development of new recovery techniques, some previously unrecoverable pools can be added to reserve calculations.

test market A community or a group of individuals chosen according to age, gender, or other characteristic chosen to try out a proposed new product or service in order to analyze consumer responses before the product or service is fully launched. A test market is used to determine whether a proposed new product or service should be modified or cancelled altogether or to refine proposed nationwide marketing and advertising campaigns.

Textile and Clothing Board A federal board set up in 1969 to investigate complaints from industry and other groups that clothing or textile imports are causing or threatening to cause serious injury to Canadian manufacturers. The board could recommend to the then Minister of INDUSTRY, TRADE, AND COMMERCE that quotas be imposed, or that other steps be taken to protect the industry, or it could decide that a complaint was unjustified. In 1988, it was absorbed by the CANADIAN INTERNATIONAL TRADE TRIBUNAL.

theory of production and distribution The theory of how the incomes of the various FACTORS OF PRODUCTION are determined and how these factors of production are transformed from inputs into outputs. Traditional or CLASSICAL ECONOMIC theory assumes that the incomes of each of the factors of production is determined by the LAW OF SUPPLY AND DEMAND in a market in which the owners of the factors of production attempt to maximize their incomes while firms attempt to maximize their profits. Production will be increased to the point where marginal cost and marginal revenue are equal for each factor of production. Production itself will depend on the level and combinations of factors of production as well as their price and marginal productivity, along with the volume of production demanded at any given price. Other factors, such as technology, will also influence production. In a world of imperfect competition, though, other factors such as the bargaining power of unions and the ability of firms to extract economic rent or monopoly profits must also be taken into account.

theory of the firm The study of how and why firms behave as they do; in particular, how they combine labour and capital, decide what to produce and at what volumes, and set the prices at which they sell their products. Economic theory has assumed that firms are profit maximizers, so that firms produce to the point where marginal cost and marginal revenue are equal. However, this theory worked better in a world of small firms that were owner-operated. Today, with the growth of large-scale organizations where there is little connection between the ownership and control of the firm, some economists question whether firms are profit maximizers or whether they are driven by other objectives, such as raising market share or reaching growth targets in sales and production.

thermal power   Electricity generated by power stations that burn oil, natural gas, and coal. Thermal power is a major source of greenhouse gases that contribute to global warming.

thin market   A market in which either the supply or demand for a commodity or security is so small that even a modest change in supply or demand can cause a large increase or decline in price. For example, if most of the shares of a company are held by a few individuals or institutions, then any unusual sale or purchase of the shares will lead to a big change in price. A thin market is a market with either few buyers or few sellers, or both.

Third Option   A foreign economic policy strategy, announced by the federal government in October, 1972, to reduce Canada's economic dependence on the United States. It came in the aftermath of 1971 U.S. policies that hurt the Canadian economy, from resulting Canadian worries that its economy was becoming too closely tied to the U.S. economy. The government policy paper noted the strong north-south pull of the United States and Canadian economies, and worried that growing interdependence would "impose an unmanageable strain on the concept of a separate Canadian identity, if not on the elements of Canadian independence." It set out three options for Canada: 1. Maintain more or less the existing relationship with the United States, which would mean few policy changes. 2. Move deliberately toward closer integration with the United States. 3. Pursue a comprehensive, long-term strategy to develop and strengthen the Canadian economy and other aspects of Canadian national life, and thus reduce Canada's vulnerability to sudden changes in U.S. policies or to the danger of eventual absorption by the United States.

The government chose the third option, which meant supplementing Canada's economic relationship with the United States by developing greater economic and commercial ties with the EUROPEAN COMMUNITY and with Japan. This option, the government's policy paper said, would "lessen the vulnerability of the Canadian economy to external factors, including, in particular, the impact of the United States and, in the process, strengthen our capacity to advance basic Canadian goals and develop a more confident sense of national identity." It said that to create a stronger, and hence less vulnerable, economic base would require "the specialization and rationalization of production and the emergence of strong Canadian-controlled firms," and that this in turn might "have to entail a somewhat greater measure of government involvement than has been the case in the past." One of the results of the Third Option was the negotiation of the FRAMEWORK AGREEMENT FOR COMMERCIAL AND ECONOMIC CO-OPERATION between Canada and the European Communities. The Third-Option policy was spelled out in a special edition of the Department of External Affairs publication called *International Perspectives*.

third-party insurance   *See* LIABILITY INSURANCE.

third world   Those nations that see themselves as members of neither the developed Western, capitalist world, nor of the former Communist world of Eastern Europe and the former Soviet Union. The third world consists of the DEVELOPING COUNTRIES, most of whom have per capita incomes below US2,500. Many of its members include countries that have gained their independence since the end of the Second World War. It includes many of the nations of Asia, Africa, Latin America, and the Middle East. Third-world nations have been the driving force behind the quest for a NEW INTERNATIONAL ECONOMIC ORDER. However, because the income gap between developing nations is growing, with some, such as Mexico, Malaysia, Argentina, and South Korea, showing rapid economic growth, and others, such as Bangladesh, Pakistan, India, and many central-African states, showing extremely low per capita incomes, some economists now divide the developing world into the third-world nations, which are making steady gains in per capita income and have good prospects for growth, and the FOURTH WORLD nations, which have abysmally low per capita incomes of $200 or less, few resources, and poor prospects for growth. One separating line between the third and fourth worlds is per capita income of $200. The third- and fourth-world nations are the South in the North-South dialogue.

third-world debt crisis   The debt crisis in DEVELOPING COUNTRIES that emerged in August, 1982, when the Mexican government announced it could not meet its debt-servicing obligations. The Mexican announcement was followed by similar announcements by other developing countries that they too were unable to meet their debt-ser-

vicing obligations. While the debt levels being accumulated from the mid-1970s were not sustainable, and resulted in part from aggressive lending by the banks of the industrial countries seeking to expand their asset base, the debt crisis was triggered by a sharp rise in world interest rates originating in the United States, the resulting global recession, and the related decline in world commodity prices that generated much of the foreign exchange with which developing countries serviced their foreign debts. In Latin America, from 1981 to 1983, real interest rates were running above 20 percent. However, domestic factors were also important, with economic mismanagement in many developing countries contributing to high inflation, an inefficient allocation of resources, and huge budget deficits. One result was capital flight, as billions of dollars were transferred by individuals and firms from developing countries to the relative stability of investments in the industrial countries. But the debt crisis not only threatened the economies of the developing countries, it also threatened the financial viability of the banking system in the industrial countries, including Canada. The developing countries did not default on their loans but, instead, continued to try to service them even though this inflicted great pain within their own countries; this was especially true in Africa. For this reason, the indebted developing countries referred to the 1980s as a lost decade. One consequence was that while the indebted developing countries serviced their existing debts, there was no inflow of new lending. As a result, there was a net flow of funds from the developing countries to the industrial countries, the reverse of what would have been expected considering the different stages of development. From 1974 to 1981, Latin America received a net inflow of US$91 billion from the industrial world; however, from 1982 to 1990, there was a net outflow of US$224 billion from Latin America to the industrial world. For several years, no concerted effort was made to address the debt issue. However, with the crisis mounting, the BAKER PLAN was outlined in late 1985 by the United States; it provided only modest assistance and emphasized instead the need for the developing countries to adopt pro-market policies such as an end to subsidies, balanced budgets, the reduction of trade barriers, deregulation, and privatization. This yielded only modest relief. The Toronto GROUP OF SEVEN summit in 1988 adopted more liberal guidelines to deal with the debt problems of the poorest countries, whose debts were mainly to foreign governments. In 1989, the United States unveiled the BRADY PLAN, which provided the means for debt relief and the restructuring of outstanding debt held by the commercial banks.

In its 1992-93 report and publication of its annual *World Debt Tables*, the WORLD BANK reported that by 1992 the debt crisis was "largely over for commercial banks and many (though not all) of their middle-income borrowers." However, at the same time, it said, "external viability remains elusive for many low- and lower-middle-income developing countries, most of whose debt is owed to official creditors." The World Bank said additional debt forgiveness was necessary for many of them to reduce their "unsustainable debt burdens." The key lesson of the debt crisis is that the mobilization of domestic resources and sound economic policies must accompany foreign borrowing, the World Bank said. In Canada, the Superintendent of Financial Institutions required that a minimum 35 percent provision for loan losses be maintained for aggregate exposures to 46 developing countries that have had difficulty in servicing all or part of their foreign debts to commercial banks. Third World debt held by the six major Canadian banks

peaked at $25.2 billion in 1986. By 1992, this had been reduced to $7.7 billion, and $2.7 billion after provisions.

threshold reserves   The necessary level of proven or established reserves of oil, natural gas, or other mineral resources, before investments will be made to extract and exploit them. Without this level of reserves, financiers would be unwilling to lend funds, since they could not reasonably be assured of getting their money back. The threshold level depends, among other things, on distance to market. For example, even small oil and gas reservoirs can be exploited if they are close to existing pipeline and gathering systems. However, the threshold level for oil or gas in the far North or off the coast of Labrador/Newfoundland is much higher, since the costs of installing gathering and distribution systems, such as a major new pipeline, have to be justified.

throughput   The volume of raw materials processed by a refinery or smelter or distributed through a pipeline in a given period of time.

tied aid   Foreign aid to a developing country that attaches conditions to the way in which the soft loan or grant is to be spent. The most common condition is that all or a fixed portion of the aid must be spent in the donor country. The fact that aid is tied and, as such, creates jobs in the donor country, as well as eliminating any adverse balance-of-payments effect, is often used by governments of donor countries to justify aid expenditures to their own taxpayers. However, it means that recipient countries must use the aid in ways that do not necessarily conform to their needs, or that may force them to acquire goods and services that are more expensive than or inferior to those available elsewhere. Most bilateral-aid programs contain some tied-aid requirement, though in recent years, donor nations have been reducing such conditions. An increasing portion of foreign aid is now handled by multilateral institutions such as the WORLD BANK and its affiliated agencies, or through regional development banks and the UNITED NATIONS.

tied selling   The requirement by a supplier that a customer, such as a retailer, acquires a second product as a condition of being granted a supply of the first product, or that the customer refrain from selling, in conjunction with the tying product, another product not manufactured by that supplier — for example, the requirement by the manufacturer of a photocopier that the customer use only paper or toner supplied by the manufacturer. It is a reviewable practice by the COMPETITION TRIBUNAL, which can issue an order prohibiting the practice. Tied selling may be permitted where there is a unique technological relationship between products.

tight money   The condition that exists when a restrictive MONETARY POLICY is being pursued. Interest rates are high and credit is hard to obtain.

time and motion study   The systematic study of the amount of time necessary for an employee under normal conditions to perform a particular task. This kind of study helps to establish standards for performance, to calculate production schedules, to determine labour costs, and to analyze how to speed up ways a job is done. These studies are a normal part of a firm's efforts to improve PRODUCTIVITY in workplaces, based on the principles of TAYLORISM or mass production, in which every task in the production process is reduced to its simplest requirements.

time deposit   A bank deposit with a fixed maturity date. Time deposits usually pay a higher rate of interest.

time lag   In economic policy, the length of time it takes a change in economic policy to take effect. There is always a delay between the time government changes a policy and the time the economy responds, which policy makers have to take into account. For example, the government may want to spur economic growth through a tax cut for individuals, hoping that this will eventually increase consumer spending and cause business, in turn, to invest in productive facilities or to increase housing construction. However, first the money from the tax cut has to get into consumer pockets, and consumers have then to decide whether to spend or save their extra income. Even when consumers decide to spend, this may not have an immediate impact on production. Business inventories may be high, and these will have to be run down first. Only then will there be an impact on production, and, assuming business believes that the higher level of demand can be sustained, and provided it is operating its factories near or at capacity, only then will important job-creating investment decisions be made. Experience with time lags and the limitations of economic FINE-TUNING shows how hard it is for a government to achieve quick changes in economic behaviour.

time preference   An individual's preference for consumption now instead of consumption in the future. This preference will differ for individuals depending on their tastes, levels of income, age, expectations of future income, and other such factors. It supposes that each individual can, in effect, set his or her own interest rate, which is his time preference. The amount of money required to pay an individual for delaying consumption of goods and services worth $1,000 for, say, a year, expressed as a percentage of that $1,000, is the individual's time preference, or the personal interest rate he or she has set as the price for delayed consumption. If that interest rate is higher than existing interest rates in the economy, then that individual is more likely to postpone consumption. The concept is an important element in interest-rate theories and in the analysis of saving and investment. It recognizes that individuals who postpone consumption must be paid for doing so with increased future consumption. However, how much extra depends on the individual.

time series   A series of particular economic statistics taken at enough different points in time, with seasonal fluctuations removed, to show whether or not there is a particular economic trend. This can then be used to make forecasts about the future. For example, monthly statistics of non-food items in the CONSUMER PRICE INDEX for, say, 12 to 16 months, may show a definite upward or downward pattern. Similarly, the same statistics over a period of years would show the kind of inflation rate that is "normal," though not necessarily acceptable.

time value of money   A concept used in investment analysis, according to which a specific amount of money in the hand at present is worth more than the same amount of money in the future, because money available now can be invested and earn a return. Thus $100 invested today at 10 percent would be worth $110 a year from now, and worth more than $100 received a year from now.

timely disclosure   The requirement, by securities commissions and stock exchanges, that corporations act swiftly to disclose to the public any news that may have a favourable or unfavourable effect on the price of their shares.

Examples could include takeover bids, mineral discoveries, an unexpected loss, or the firing of the chief executive officer. Timely disclosure means that ordinary shareholders should have the same information on which to base buy/sell decisions as company insiders.

Tinbergen, Jan (b. 1903)   The Dutch economist who won the Alfred Nobel Memorial Prize in Economic Science in 1969, the first year it was awarded, along with Ragnar FRISCH, "for having developed and applied dynamic models for the analysis of economic processes."

tip   An amount of money, usually a small percentage of the cost of the service rendered, given voluntarily to a person performing a service. For example, diners in a restaurant normally leave a tip of 10 to 15 percent of the cost of their meal, after deducting taxes. Tips constitute an important part of the income of some workers, such as restaurant employees, cab drivers, and hotel doormen. Tax authorities make some allowance for tips when reviewing the income-tax returns of such workers.

title   Evidence, in the form of a document, that proves a person's ownership of land and buildings. A title shows the history of changes in the ownership of a particular property and indicates whether there are any tax or other claims against the property. When a property is purchased, a title search is undertaken to make sure that the person selling the property is the actual owner and to determine what claims, if any, there are against the property. Generally speaking, titles are registered in provincial registry offices, though in some large cities, the municipality may maintain the office. Different provinces or parts of provinces have different methods of registration. Western Canada and northern Ontario have a land-title system, in which the state guarantees the title, and the person conducting the search has only to look at the most recent record. Southern Ontario and the Maritimes use a land-registry system, in which the state does not guarantee the system and the lawyer making the search has to check back in time and personally guarantee the title.

Tobin, James (b. 1918) The American economist awarded the Alfred Nobel Memorial Prize in Economic Science in 1981 "for his analysis of financial markets and their relation to expenditure decisions, employment, production, and prices." A liberal Keynesian economist, Tobin has studied extensively the role of fiscal and monetary policy in affecting investment decisions. *See also* Q THEORY OF INVESTMENT, KEYNESION ECONOMICS.

toll The charge made to use an expressway, bridge, canal, tunnel, or ferry. The term is sometimes used to describe long-distance telephone rates. Tolls were once widely used to finance public projects, an example of the USER-PAY PRINCIPLE OF TAXATION. They are also a source of revenue once construction costs have been recovered. Although tolls fell into disuse many years ago, they are now reappearing as an option in the financing of highways and other projects at a time when governments have less discretionary revenue.

tombstone An advertisement placed as a matter of record following a share or bond issue that sets out the price and the amount raised and identifies the members of the syndicate that managed the issue.

Toronto Futures Exchange A futures exchange set up as a division of the TORONTO STOCK EXCHANGE in 1980 and inaugurated as a separate corporate entity in January, 1984. It operates

under the jurisdiction of the Commodity Futures Act of Ontario, which is administered by the ONTARIO SECURITIES COMMISSION. The principal products traded are DERIVATIVES: the Toronto 35 Index Future, the Toronto 35 Index Option, and the Silver Option. Clearing of contracts is carried out by TRANS CANADA OPTIONS INC., which is the clearing corporation for Canadian derivative products. In 1990, the TORONTO STOCK EXCHANGE introduced Toronto 35 Index Participation Units, or TIPS. The TIPS represent units of a trust that holds weighted quantities of the 35 stocks included in the index.

Toronto Stock Exchange (TSE) Canada's principal stock exchange, both in terms of volume of shares traded and value of shares traded. It originated in 1852 with a group of businessmen in Toronto who traded shares for 30 minutes each day. It was incorporated in 1878, and has grown since then to the point where, today, it has more than 125 seats, or members. For a time, there were two stock exchanges in Toronto: in 1899, the Toronto Stock and Mining Exchange was established as a second exchange to provide a market for speculative mining shares. It was replaced by the Standard Stock and Mining Exchange in 1908. But in 1934, the Standard merged with the TSE. The TSE is governed by a board of governors, chosen from member firms, who operate the exchange and have the responsibility to see that TSE rules are followed, so that the investing public is protected.

Toronto Stock Exchange indexes The principal index is the Toronto 300 composite index, representing the share prices of 300 major corporations traded on the TORONTO STOCK EXCHANGE. There is also the Toronto 35 index, along with separate indexes for 15 major industrial groups in the composite index. The base year is 1975 and equals 1,000, so that if the TSE index is at 3450, it means prices are 3.45 times the 1975 levels. The 15 major industrial groups are metals and minerals; gold; oil and gas; paper and forest products; real estate and construction; consumer products; industrial products; transportation; pipelines; utilities; communications; merchandising; financial services; management companies; and biotechnology.

Toronto Summit The summit of the GROUP OF SEVEN (G-7) leaders, held in Toronto in June, 1988. Its principal accomplishment was the adoption of a plan for debt relief for the poorest DEVELOPING COUNTRIES, especially those of Sub-Saharan Africa. Options included concessional interest rates, longer repayment periods, or a partial reduction of debt-servicing obligations during a debt-consolidation period. The G-7 leaders called on the PARIS CLUB to work out the technical arrangements by the end of 1988.

tort A civil offence against another person for which damages can be sought; it does not include the breaking of a contract, which is a separate matter. Examples include the following: all forms of negligence or damages caused by a person's failure to take reasonable care in driving, maintaining a building, or manufacturing a product; nuisance, a form of negligence that prevents a person from having continuous enjoyment of his or her land, due to fumes, smoke, or erosion caused by a neighbour; and libel and slander, which may damage a person's reputation and, hence, the ability to earn a livelihood. A tort is a civil wrong for which damages can be sought to compensate for the damages or injuries a person has suffered. The term covers a wide field of legal actions, ranging from suits against manufacturers for faulty products, and neighbours whose activi-

ties cause pollution, to suits against municipal authorities who fail to keep sidewalks repaired, and newspapers that publish false information about a person's character.

total cost All of the costs of production in a firm, consisting of both variable costs and fixed costs. A firm will cease production if it cannot recover its total costs.

Total Quality Management (TQM) A business strategy focused on customer satisfaction, which becomes the responsibility of all parts of the organization and of all of its employees. It covers product quality, service quality, management quality, and quality in everything the company does. TQM has significant implications for the way a business functions. It requires more emphasis on employee training and education, the recognition of employee contributions, and opening the channels of communication in an organization. As well, it means a greater sharing with employees of management responsibility, including the use of the team approach in the organization along with greater employee involvement and empowerment. It also means setting quantifiable and measurable standards for implementation, letting the customer define quality, and moving from top-down management to team systems.

total revenue All of the revenue of a firm from all sources, including the sale of goods or services, investment income, royalty income, and revenue from the sale of assets.

total utility The sum of all the satisfaction an individual receives from consuming any given quantity of goods or services, or the sum of the utilities of all members of society added together. Some economists argue that it is possible to use the tax system to increase maximum total utility. Since each extra dollar of income is said to bring less satisfaction to a person, a dollar taxed away from a wealthy person and redistributed to a poor person will add to the total utility, or satisfaction, of society. *See also* UTILITY.

trade The exchange of goods and services for money. Foreign trade consists of exchanges of goods and services for money between Canadians and non-residents. *See also* COUNTERTRADE.

trade agreement An agreement to reduce trade barriers or to formalize trade arrangements between countries. The world's most comprehensive trade agreement is the GENERAL AGREEMENT ON TARIFFS AND TRADE (GATT). It is a multilateral trade agreement seeking the widest possible membership of nations prepared to accept GATT obligations and is based on the principles of non-discrimination and MOST-FAVOURED NATION. However, smaller groups of nations may integrate their economies on a regional basis, establishing preferential arrangements that discriminate against non-members. These arrangements include the following: a free-trade area in which members eliminate tariffs and other barriers between themselves but maintain their own tariff and other arrangements with the rest of the world; a customs union, in which members, in addition to free trade among themselves, adopt a common trade policy toward the rest of the world, including a common external tariff; a common market, which extends beyond a customs union to include the free movement of capital and labour as well as goods and services within the trade bloc; and complete economic union, which includes a common currency, co-ordinated fiscal and monetary policy, a uniform competition policy, and other harmonized policies. The EUROPEAN COMMUNITY began as a common market, moved to a customs union, and with the 1992 MAASTRICHT TREATY was headed for full economic union and a form of political union. The CANADA-UNITED STATES FREE TRADE AGREEMENT and the NORTH AMERICAN FREE TRADE AGREEMENT both establish free-trade areas, though some experts believe they will eventually lead to a common market, with a common external tariff, and a system of exchange rates in which the Canadian and Mexican currencies are pegged to the U.S. dollar.

trade association An association of companies in the same industry that advances the interests of the industry in a variety of ways. These can include representations to government on proposed legislation or existing policies, the collection of industry-wide statistics and other information for the publication of trade directories, the organization of seminars, conventions, and educational activities, general public-relations work on behalf of the industry, and the organization of overseas trade missions. The COMPETITION ACT makes it a criminal offence for members of an association to discuss prices or to engage in any kind of activity that restrains trade or "unduly" affects competition. Examples of trade associations include the CANADIAN MANUFACTURERS' ASSOCIATION, the Canadian Grocery Product Manufacturers' Association, the CANADIAN BANKERS' ASSOCIATION, and the CANADIAN PULP AND PAPER ASSOCIATION.

trade barrier Any government policy that restricts the free movement of goods and services between countries. The best-known barriers are tariffs and quotas. However, there are many NON-TARIFF BARRIERS to trade as well, such as health and safety regulations written in such a way as to exclude imports or to restrict imports, excessive delays in the processing of import paperwork, government-purchasing preferences in favour of domestic producers, and subsidies to domestic producers. Trade barriers can also exist within a country between different regions. For example, the Fathers of Confederation intended Canada to be a single market, but individual provinces may favour local companies in awarding contracts, or may employ other devices, such as farm marketing boards, to keep out the products of other provinces. *See also* INTER-PROVINCIAL BARRIERS TO TRADE.

trade bloc A group of two or more countries that agree to increase trade among themselves through reciprocal trade preferences that they do not grant to countries outside their bloc. A trade bloc can take the form of a free-trade area, a COMMON MARKET, or a CUSTOMS UNION. Some experts fear that the world may divide into three regional trade blocs — Europe, North America, and Asia — if there is a worldwide return to PROTECTIONISM. The NORTH AMERICAN FREE TRADE AGREEMENT can be seen as producing a North American trade bloc. The alternative to a world of trade blocs is a well-functioning global or multilateral trading system based on the GENERAL AGREEMENT ON TARIFFS AND TRADE, in which nations around the world have equal access to one another's markets based on the principles of non-discrimination and MOST-FAVOURED NATION.

trade-creation effect The beneficial effect of lowering or eliminating international trade barriers. A reduction or elimination of trade barriers should lead to increased trade and an increase in economic activity, which in turn creates larger markets for commerce. Proponents of the CANADA-UNITED STATES FREE TRADE AGREEMENT and the NORTH AMERICAN FREE TRADE AGREEMENT argue that while

these trade arrangements may lead to TRADE DIVERSION that takes away exports from other countries, the overall effect will be a more prosperous North American market that should benefit exporters from outside the free-trade area as well.

trade credit The credit that a manufacturer or other supplier extends to his customers.

trade cycle *See* BUSINESS CYCLE.

trade deficit The situation that exists when the value of a country's merchandise imports is greater than the value of its merchandise exports. Sometimes the trade deficit is calculated on the value of both goods and services traded. Canada may have a TRADE SURPLUS with some countries but a trade deficit in its total trade with all countries, or vice versa. Monthly figures on Canada's merchandise trade are published by Statistics Canada (publication 65-001). *See also* BALANCE OF PAYMENTS, CURRENT ACCOUNT.

trade diversion One consequence of a free-trade area, common market, or customs union, in which goods formerly imported from a low-cost producer are now obtained from a different, higher-cost producer within the trading group. While trade increases among members within the trading group, non-members may lose export sales, so that the world economy is no better off.

trade embargo The cut-off of trade to a country, in a bid to change its policies. In the 1930s, the League of Nations tried to halt Italy's invasion of Ethiopia by cutting off its access to oil. The United States, under its Trading with the Enemy Act, has blocked trade with Cuba to try to force Cuba to pay compensation for U.S. subsidiaries it nationalized, and to curb its support for political insurgency in Latin America and Africa. Members of the United Nations, including Canada, banned trade with Rhodesia (now Zimbabwe) to force its white-minority government to recognize the political rights of its black majority. The Arab nations of the Middle East have banned trade with companies that have close contacts with Israel or that have Jewish owners, in an attempt to punish those who deal with or support Israel. Members of the NORTH ATLANTIC TREATY ORGANIZATION withheld strategic materials and military technology from the former Soviet Union and its satellites and other nations of the Communist world. Under the Export and Import Control Act, Canada required export permits for all shipments of goods to Bosnia-Herzegovina, Croatia, Haiti, Libya, and Yugoslavia at the start of 1993. *See also* BOYCOTT.

trade fair   A fair or exhibition organized by government or industry and held to bring together buyers and sellers in a particular industry, such as aerospace, machinery, or computer systems, or to promote the products and services of a particular country, such as a Canadian trade fair in Mexico. They are important commercial events, allowing producers to display their latest wares and buyers to see a wide range of products all under the same roof.

trade liberalization   Measures to reduce barriers to trade. The principal vehicle has been the GENERAL AGREEMENT ON TARIFFS AND TRADE that, since 1948, has succeeded in sharply reducing tariffs around the world. The emphasis in trade negotiations has shifted in recent years to the reduction of non-tariff barriers, such as quotas or the use of product standards to discriminate against imports; the establishment of clearer rules for the use of trade disciplines such as SAFEGUARDS, ANTI-DUMPING laws, and COUNTERVAILING DUTIES; to the strengthening of codes on subsidies and government procurement; to rules in new areas such as INTELLECTUAL PROPERTY and TRADE-RELATED INVESTMENT MEASURES; and to the extension of trade rules to trade in services.

trade mission   A visit by a group of businesspeople and government officials to another country or countries, usually to sell goods and services, but sometimes to buy. Trade missions are organized by both the federal and provincial governments to blitz foreign markets and to increase exports or to attract foreign investment. They can consist of representatives of a group of companies in the same industry, or of a variety of companies, all interested in the same country or countries. Buying missions are organized by the Japanese government, which wants to increase imports and defuse international criticism of its large trade surplus. The purpose of the Japanese missions is to persuade producers in Canada that selling to the Japanese market is not as difficult as they think.

trade-related investment measures (TRIMS)   Conditions imposed on foreign investors by a host country that affect trade. Examples of conditions that host countries may impose on foreign investors include requirements that the foreign investor use local suppliers of goods and services to achieve high levels of domestic content, export a certain percentage of production, transfer technology from the parent company, conduct research and development, use local management, and make some shares in the domestic subsidiary available to local investors. Not all of these affect trade, but the requirement that local suppliers be used instead of importing parts and components from another country, and the requirement that the foreign subsidiary export a certain percentage of production, do affect international trade. The URUGUAY ROUND of the GENERAL AGREEMENT ON TARIFFS AND TRADE included negotiations on trade-related investment measures. Both the CANADA-UNITED STATES FREE TRADE AGREEMENT (FTA) and the NORTH AMERICAN FREE TRADE AGREEMENT (NAFTA) contain provisions restricting the power of domestic governments to impose conditions on foreign investors. As a result, Canada cannot impose specified "performance requirements" on U.S. or Mexican companies to achieve specified export levels, minimum domestic content, preferences for domestic sourcing, trade balancing, or technology transfer or undertake world product mandates. Nor can Canada require that a U.S.- or Mexican-owned subsidiary in Canada make any of its shares available to Canadians. However, INVESTMENT CANADA may still be able to impose research and development commitments from U.S. or Mexican companies buying up Canadian-owned companies. The FTA and NAFTA ensures NATIONAL TREATMENT and currency exchange and remittance. NAFTA also provides for a dispute settlement mechanism to resolve investment disputes.

trade-remedy laws Laws applied by a country to penalize or curb imports. The most common trade-remedy laws are those dealing with DUMPING or those imposing COUNTERVAILING DUTIES to offset allegedly unfair subsidies. While the GENERAL AGREEMENT ON TARIFFS AND TRADE (GATT) provides for anti-dumping and countervailing duties, there is concern over the way individual countries, notably the United States, actually implement trade laws, leading to charges that the process itself is unfair. U.S. trade legislation contains a number of trade-remedy provisions. The section 201 clause of the 1974 Trade Act, as amended, provides a wide range of possible relief to a domestic industry where increased imports are a substantial cause of serious injury or a threat of serious injury. The section 301 clause of the 1974 Trade Act, as amended, allows the U.S. government to unilaterally impose trade penalties on another country if the United States, on its own, determines that another country is violating a trade agreement or engaging in what the United States decides are unfair trade practices. The Omnibus Trade Act of 1988 included a "Super 301" provision that gave the U.S. administration even greater unilateral scope to impose trade penalties on other countries, including a requirement of mandatory action where another country was found by the United States to deny U.S. companies rights under existing trade agreements, or where a measure of another country is "unjustifiable and burdens or restricts United States commerce." The section also gave the U.S. administration the discretionary authority to take sweeping action against any country that adopts a policy that the United States, for its own reasons, declares to be "unreasonable." Examples of unreasonable measures included the denial of market opportunities to U.S. companies, policies by another country to target an industry for export growth, or the denial to U.S. corporations of the right to make investments in another country. However, the most sweeping authority was a provision that said that any action by another country, even if it was not in violation of the international rights of the United States, could be deemed by the U.S. government to be "otherwise unfair and inequitable." Super 301 expired under a sunset clause in 1990, but in 1993, members of the U.S. Congress moved to reinstate it. Section 701 provides the basis for U.S. countervailing duties and Section 731 for anti-dumping duties. Section 337 allows the United States to retaliate against what it sees as unfair trade practices, such as patent or trademark infringements, and Section 332 allows the United States to investigate any trade irritant. The alternative to the unilateral use of domestic trade-remedy laws is a strengthening of the dispute-settlement mechanism of the GATT, which adjudicates disputes on the basis of GATT rights and obligations of member states, which these states cannot change unilaterally, rather than on the basis of domestic trade laws that can be changed unilaterally by a member state. The CANADA-UNITED STATES FREE TRADE AGREEMENT (FTA) and the NORTH AMERICAN FREE TRADE AGREEMENT (NAFTA) both contain provisions for settling disputes arising over the application of trade-remedy laws. However, the role of binational or trinational panels is restricted to determining whether due process was followed in applying the trade-remedy law. Both the FTA and NAFTA leave untouched the ability of a member country to unilaterally alter its trade-remedy laws, aside from requirements of notification, the right of consultation, and the right of other countries in the trade agreement to adopt mirror legislation.

trade sanctions   Measures to limit or bar either imports or exports. Trade sanctions are sometimes used as a way of exerting pressure on another country to change its policies, such as sanctions to pressure South Africa to end its policies of racial discrimination or to pressure Libya to halt its support of terrorist groups.

trade surplus   The situation that exists when the value of a country's merchandise exports is greater than the value of its merchandise imports. Sometimes the trade surplus is calculated on the value of both goods and services traded. Canada may have a TRADE DEFICIT with some countries but a trade surplus in its total trade

with all countries, or vice versa. Monthly figures on Canada's trade are published by Statistics Canada (publication 65-001). *See also* BALANCE OF PAYMENTS, CURRENT ACCOUNT.

trade union   *See* UNION.

trade-weighted exchange rate   The average of the various exchange rates of one country against the currencies of its major trading partners, weighted according to the amount of trade conducted with each of those trading partners.

tradeable goods and services   The part of the economy that is directly engaged in international competition. Most manufacturing would fall into this category, along with some services such as engineering, insurance, and tourism. Other parts of the economy, such as health, education, and retail trade, are not directly exposed to international competition.

trademark   A particular word, logo, symbol, or other device, used by a corporation to identify its product or service to consumers. It is used in advertising and promotions, marked on company products or packaging, and used in corporate identification — on letterheads and buildings, for example. Because of its unique character, it is of value to its owner and is protected under law. No one else can use a trademark registered with the Department of CONSUMER AND CORPORATE AFFAIRS; if they do, they can be sued for infringement. Widespread acceptance by consumers of a trademark can sometimes make it extremely difficult for others to enter an industry. In this sense, a trademark can increase the market power of a corporation.

trader   1. An investor who buys and sells shares or other securities and options on an on-going basis with the goal of making quick profits. **2.** An employee of a stockbroker who carries out buy and sell orders on behalf of the firm and its customers.

trading limit   The maximum amount of a commodity that anyone can purchase in a single day, or the maximum amount of a futures position that can be held by any one individual.

transaction costs   The costs incurred in acquiring goods or services. Examples can include the costs of getting approval for a construction project, the costs of arranging a loan or of raising equity capital, or the costs in locating employees, suppliers, or customers and reaching agreement with them.

transaction demand for money   One of the three reasons given by John Maynard KEYNES as to why individuals and firms hold money, it is the money an individual or firm holds to meet on-going expenditures that occur between the times when new money, such as salaries or sales revenues, is received. For a firm it is the money necessary to pay employee salaries, suppliers, and other on-going costs, while for the individual it includes daily living costs. The amount of money held and thereby not invested depends on a number of factors, including the volume of transactions to be financed and the level of interest forgone by not investing. *See also* SPECULATIVE MOTIVE, PRECAUTIONARY BALANCE.

Trans Canada Options Inc.   The clearance and guarantee network for trading futures and options in Canada. Members include member firms in the TORONTO, MONTREAL, and VANCOUVER STOCK EXCHANGES, the TORONTO FUTURES MARKET, and the international options market division of the Montreal Stock Exchange. Trans Canada Options also links foreign investors with the Canadian exchanges and Canadian

investors with the international network of exchanges where futures and options are traded.

transfer   A change in ownership of land, buildings, mineral rights, previously issued bonds and stocks, or other such assets. A transfer deed is a document that shows that the transfer has taken place. In an economic sense, transfers are not investments, since they are only a change in the ownership of existing capital and not the creation of additional real capital. A transfer may be subject to a tax — for example, to a land-transfer tax when real estate is sold.

transfer agent   The trust company appointed by a publicly traded corporation to maintain up-to-date lists of the names and addresses of shareholders and the number of shares each shareholder owns, to issue and cancel share certificates, and to distribute dividend cheques and income-tax statements on dividend income.

transfer payment   A payment by a government to an individual, a business, a farmer, or another level of government. Examples of transfer payments range from old-age pensions and social welfare to business and farm subsidies, federal payments to provinces to help finance social welfare or health care, and similar payments by provincial governments to municipalities. These payments do not add anything to the GROSS DOMESTIC PRODUCT, since they do not represent payments for goods or services produced by the recipient. They represent a form of income redistribution and are financed from the income produced by others.

transfer price   The price charged within a MULTINATIONAL CORPORATION or large industrial enterprise for goods or services shipped from one affiliate or subsidiary, or the parent company, to another affiliate or subsidiary. Transfer prices are a major concern to tax authorities because they can be artificial prices, quite different from those that would be charged if the corporate affiliates were separate and unrelated firms operating at arm's length; this means it is not always easy to allocate taxable profits within a highly integrated multinational corporation. The ability to manipulate prices in this way gives a corporation considerable scope in allocating profits on such transactions to the country with the lowest tax rate. For example, a multinational corporation with a Canadian subsidiary using parts from another subsidiary, say, in Malaysia, could ship the parts from Malaysia to another subsidiary of the company in a TAX HAVEN — say, Bermuda — where taxes are extremely low, and reship the parts to Canada from Bermuda. The parts could be shipped from Malaysia at a barely break-even price, thus depriving Malaysian tax authorities of tax revenues from corporate profits, with the Bermuda subsidiary reselling them to Canada at a very high price, thus capturing the profit in Bermuda, where it will be virtually untaxed. In this way, the parent company has minimized its taxes by its transfer-pricing policy. In recent years, these practices have become much harder to carry out, because Canadian, U.S., and other taxing authorities have adopted tougher rules on transfer pricing; they have also limited the ability to avoid taxes by shifting international profits into tax havens. Corporate affiliates are supposed to deal with one another on an ARM'S LENGTH basis. Because the transfer price may be manipulated to affect where taxes are actually paid, tax authorities may correct the allocation of profits among the different members of a multinational corporate group in order to eliminate the effect of transfer-price manipulation. Nonetheless, there are still opportunities through transfer pricing to inflate profits in countries with low tax rates and to minimize them in countries with high tax rates.

transmission mechanism   The process through which changes in MONETARY and FISCAL POLICY influence AGGREGATE DEMAND in the economy. Changes in tax policy, government spending, or money supply can affect aggregate demand in various ways. For example, consumers may rush out and spend any extra money they get, driving up demand and, at some point, triggering new investment. Or households can save additional money, ultimately driving down interest rates, which also encourages investment and leads to additional demand.

transnational corporation   See MULTINATIONAL CORPORATION.

transparency   The openness of a country's policies to viewing and scrutiny by other countries. In trade policy, the goal is to make a country's trade rules, investment policies, government-procurement procedures, and other business practices visible and open to others.

Transport, Department of   Also known as Transport Canada, this is the federal government department responsible for all aspects of national transportation policy as set out by Parliament — for example, in the various National Transportation Acts passed since 1967. The most recent version went into effect in 1988. The ministry, which was established in 1936 by merging the Department of Railways and Canals, the Department of Marine and Fisheries, and the civil aviation branch of the Department of National Defence, has a central policy-planning group that advises the Minister of Transport, and four operating groups that carry out transport policy. These are as follows: 1. The Marine Group, whose responsibilities include the Canadian Coast Guard, Ports Canada, and the St. Lawrence Seaway. 2. The Airports Authority Group, which is responsible for more than 200 airports across Canada. 3. The Aviation Group, which is responsible for airline services and aviation safety. 4. The Surface Group, which is responsible for railways, interprovincial truck and bus transportation, motor-vehicle safety standards, and the transportation of hazardous goods, as well as the federal interest in rail and rapid-transit research. The ministry is responsible for a major crown corporation, the Canadian National Railways Company. The Minister of Transport reports to Parliament for the NATIONAL TRANS-PORTATION AGENCY, PORTS CANA-DA, and the ST. LAWRENCE SEAWAY AUTHORITY.

traveller's cheque A cheque easily usable as money, issued by a company established for that purpose or by a bank. A person buying traveller's cheques signs them once when acquiring them and again when they are cashed; this establishes a means of identification when the cheque is cashed. The appeal of the cheques is that they are safer to carry than money; if stolen or lost, they can be readily replaced at no loss to the traveller. And, since they can be denominated in the currency of the country visited, the traveller avoids problems of foreign-exchange conversion during a trip. The issuing company or bank makes a profit by earning interest on the money paid for the cheques between the time they are issued and the time they are cashed.

treasury bill A short-term government security, issued for a term of three months, six months, or one year, and held mainly by large INSTITU-TIONAL INVESTORS. Treasury bills represent an important source of funds for the federal government; some provinces, such as Ontario, also issue them. Federal treasury bills are issued in denominations of $1,000, $5,000, $10,000, $25,000, $100,000, and $1 million. They do not pay interest; they are sold below their face or par value but mature at their par value. The difference between the issue price of the treasury bill, which is less than its par value, and the par value is, in effect, the interest rate paid and is taxed as interest income.

Treasury bills are sold by auction each week by the BANK OF CANADA to the highest bidder. Only the chartered banks and 10 MONEY-MARKET DEALERS, along with some other INVESTMENT DEALERS who make occasional bids, are allowed to bid. They, in turn, resell the treasury bills to large institutional investors and corporations looking for a place to put short-term cash. The amount offered by the Bank of Canada in a particular week may equal the amount maturing, or may be greater or less. This depends on the bank's DEBT MANAGE-MENT policy, and the federal government's cash requirements.

Treasury bills account for almost 15 percent of the national debt. Before the First World War, Canadian treasury bills payable in sterling were sold in British and European financial markets. With the outbreak of the war, the federal government turned to the Canadian banking system to raise funds through the sale of treasury bills. But the treasury-bill market did not become important until after the Bank of Canada began operating in 1935. At the end of the 1991-92 fiscal year, non-residents held about 15 percent of outstanding Canadian treasury bills.

Treasury Board Both a committee of the federal cabinet and a department of the government, it is the manager of the government's spending, hiring, collective-bargaining, and administrative activities. It consists of two arms, the Treasury Board Secretariat and the COMPTROLLER-GENERAL OF CANADA. It is responsible for all personnel policies in the public service, financial-management policies and procedures, spending controls, the analysis of long-term spending trends, the allocation of government resources among competing departments and agencies, and implementation of bilingualism programs within the government. Each year, the cabinet sets out the priorities of the government, based on an overall level of spending for the entire federal government, known as the fiscal framework. Individual departments must then submit their proposed spending plans in line with these priorities. The Treasury Board Committee of Cabinet — consisting of the minister responsible for the Treasury Board (known as the President of the Treasury Board), the Minister of FINANCE, and four other cabinet ministers — then scrutinizes the submissions of individual departments, cutting or adding to programs, depending on the government's priorities.

The Treasury Board Secretariat's branches include the following: the administrative policy branch, which is responsible for efficiency in government operations and effectiveness in the delivery of government programs; the personnel-policy branch, which develops programs and policies for the management of the public-service workforce, including policy on standards, job classifications, pay, and pensions, along with co-ordinating government human-resource planning, the implementation of employment equity, and training programs; the program branch, which has the responsibility of recommending to cabinet the allocation of government resources and ensuring that government programs are implemented and achieve their intended goals, as well as managing the annual multiyear planning and ESTIMATES exercise within the fiscal framework; the staff-relations branch, which is responsible for labour relations within the federal government, including negotiating collective agreements, dealing with discipline issues, managing strikes, and representing the government in labour disputes before the Public Service Staff Relations Board or the courts; and the official-languages branch, which audits and evaluates both the implementation of the government's official-languages policy and its effectiveness.

The Treasury Board has existed as a committee of cabinet since Confederation. In 1869, it was made a statutory committee, the only one there is, with the Minister of Finance as chair and his or her department carrying out the staff work. It was not until almost a century later, in 1966, that the Treasury Board was made into a separate government department, following the recommendation of the ROYAL COMMISSION ON GOVERNMENT ORGANIZATION. The Finance department's role is to manage the economy, while that of the Treasury Board is to manage the government and make sure that its priorities and policies are being implemented. Provincial governments follow similar procedures in implementing their policies, allocating resources, managing staff, and setting procedures to monitor spending, and some have established their own treasury boards.

treasury shares Company shares that are authorized but have not been issued to the public or shares that were previously issued but have been reacquired by the company. When a company is incorporated, its charter sets out its capitalization, which describes the number of shares it may issue. A publicly traded company rarely issues the total number of shares authorized; the treasury shares are those that have yet to be issued. They can be sold to the public, offered to owners of another company, instead of cash, in a takeover bid, or sold to employees of a firm in an employee stock-purchase plan. Treasury shares are not considered to be an asset of the company.

Treaty of Rome The treaty signed by six nations of Western Europe (France, West Germany, Italy, Belgium, the Netherlands, and Luxembourg) in 1957, creating the EUROPEAN COMMUNITY (EC). The common market came into effect on January 1, 1958. The treaty set out the objectives of the EC and the procedures under which the community would evolve into a full-fledged economic and political unit. The goals of the treaty were to achieve the completely free movement of goods, services, labour, and capital among the community's members, and to establish a common external tariff in dealings with the rest of the world, along with a common policy on mergers and other business practices, a common agricultural policy, a common transportation policy, and a regional development policy to aid the depressed areas of the community. The treaty also dealt with the political evolution of the EC, creating a Council of Ministers that deals with policy, an EC Commission, which is the central bureaucracy of the community, a European Parliament, and a court of justice. The common external tariff was achieved by July, 1968; the free movement of labour by 1969; and the election of a European Parliament in 1979. The treaty also envisaged the gradual evolution of a common monetary system; a step in that direction was made in 1979 with the implementation of the EUROPEAN MONETARY SYSTEM. *See also* SINGLE EUROPEAN ACT, MAASTRICHT TREATY.

Tremblay Report *See* ROYAL COMMISSION OF INQUIRY ON CONSTITUTIONAL PROBLEMS.

trial balance An accounting exercise to determine the accuracy of a company's or an organization's books of account, or ledger. All the debit and credit balances are added; total credits should equal total debits. It is a routine part of every audit.

trickle down The notion that if the wealthiest groups in society prosper, or are helped to prosper by lower taxes, then ultimately all groups in society will benefit. As the wealthy become wealthier, the notion goes, they will spend more, with this spending ultimately benefiting even the poorest members of society.

trilateralism The relationship, based on shared economic and security interests and political values, among the United States, Canada, the European Community, and Japan; the term came into use in the 1970s. The leaders of this trilateral group meet at the annual GROUP OF SEVEN economic summit, and are all members of the ORGANIZATION FOR ECONOMIC CO-OPERATION AND DEVELOPMENT. Some analysts believe the world will divide into three trade and currency blocs, each one centred on one of the trilateral members. There is also a privately funded Trilateral Commission, headquartered in New York, that researches and debates common issues and expounds the virtues and interests of international capitalism. It consists of about 200 private citizens, some of whom are from Canada.

tripartism A formal process in which government, business, and labour collectively set goals and policies and collaborate in implementing them. This process can apply to the major areas of economic and social policy or can be confined to a specific area such as labour-market policy and training. A tripartite approach to managing the Canadian economy was proposed by the federal government after the introduction of mandatory price and income controls in 1975. The government's proposal envisaged formal consultation with business, labour, and other groups to reach a consensus on economic goals and priorities, and implied acceptance by these groups of a share of responsibility in helping to implement the consensus. Under tripartism, business, labour, and other groups would share responsibility with the government for the performance of the economy. In May, 1976, the Canadian Labour Congress adopted a new manifesto, in which it endorsed a form of tripartism that would give unions a much larger voice in setting national policy, including business investment decisions and monetary and fiscal policy. In October, 1976, the government published a working paper, *The Way Ahead: A Framework for Discussion*, that drew back from the idea of formal consultation and put more emphasis on strengthening market forces in the economy and on improving labour-management relations. When Canada emerged from anti-inflation controls at the end of 1978, the idea of tripartite management of the economy had been dropped by the government, in favour of a much less structured form of consultation with business, labour, and other groups. One criticism of tripartism was that it undermined the democratic process by reducing the role of elected representatives, giving power to business and labour leaders who were not accountable to the public, and by necessarily excluding other groups. However, a tripartite approach has been adopted in the CANADIAN LABOUR FORCE DEVELOPMENT BOARD.

trough The low point in the BUSINESS CYCLE. It is the turning point between a period of economic decline and the beginning of economic recovery.

truncation The state of an economy in which industry is largely under for-

eign control, and consequently fails to carry out a number of its usual functions. This results in lower growth, employment, and trade than if the industry were domestically controlled. Many of the essential functions of individual firms, such as research and development, industrial design, marketing, investment planning, and corporate finance and strategy, are performed by their foreign parents rather than by the subsidiaries in a country such as Canada. This means that domestic skills will not be fully developed and that fewer of the spin-off industries that result from these skills and activities will be created.

The term was used in the 1972 federal government report, FOREIGN DIRECT INVESTMENT IN CANADA. The report said: "Truncated subsidiary operations usually lack the capacity and opportunity over time to develop the full range of activities normally associated with a mature business enterprise." The term describes a BRANCH-PLANT ECONOMY, in which subsidiaries are unable to initiate new products or develop new markets, while the country as a whole becomes overly dependent on foreign technology, know-how, and decisions. Too many of the conditions necessary for businesses to pursue their own commercial objectives are absent because they are located in the foreign parent companies.

trust Money or other property that is held by one person, often a TRUST COMPANY, for the benefit of another person or persons. These assets are administered according to the terms of the trust agreement. Each province has a trustee act, which regulates the kinds of investments that can be made by the TRUSTEES of a trust fund. The investments must be of high quality and must yield a reasonable income. Approved investments include federal, provincial, and municipal bonds and debentures, bonds, debentures, and preferred and common shares of blue-chip Canadian companies, debt securities issued by loan or acceptance companies, and the bonds and debentures of stable foreign countries and international institutions. *See also* PRUDENT-MAN RULE.

Trust Companies Association of Canada The association that represents Canada's trust companies. It was established in 1952 and, in 1993, represented 48 trust companies and their trust and loan affiliates and subsidiaries. It has two divisions: the industry sector, which deals with all levels of government on policy and regulatory issues affecting the industry, and the educational sector, which provides training programs for industry employees. It is based in Toronto.

trust company A financial institution that operates under either federal or provincial legislation. Federally incorporated trust companies operate under the Trust and Loan Companies Act, proclaimed in 1992, that closely parallels the new BANK ACT, proclaimed in the same year. A trust company can engage in all of the same activities as a CHARTERED BANK, either directly or through a subsidiary, and, like a bank, operates through a network of branches. There is one important difference: a trust company, unlike a bank, does not have access to the BANK OF CANADA as a lender of last resort. As a financial intermediary, a trust company can accept deposits from the public, make mortgage, consumer, and business loans, sell savings certificates known as GUARANTEED-INVESTMENT CERTIFICATES, issue and administer credit cards, sell REGISTERED RETIREMENT SAVINGS PLAN units, manage and sell MUTUAL FUNDS, provide portfolio and money-management services and investment counselling, engage in

real-estate brokerage as well as real-estate management and development, distribute some insurance products, deal in gold, silver, and foreign exchange, and act as a trustee. A trust company can also own a securities dealer and engage in corporate underwriting. Customer deposits are protected through the CANADA DEPOSIT INSURANCE CORPORATION or its Quebec equivalent. A trust company must also set aside counterpart funds, similar to bank reserves, to protect depositors and holders of its GUARANTEED-INVESTMENT CERTIFICATES. In its fiduciary role, a trust company administers estates, pension plans, trusts, and agency contracts. The degree of decision-making power is set out in an agreement between a trust company and a customer. However, legislation also controls the types of investments that can be made, generally restricting investments to first mortgages, government bonds, blue-chip stocks, corporate bonds, and similarly secure assets, based on the PRUDENT PORTFOLIO APPROACH.

A trust company also acts as a financial agent for corporations and municipalities, as a transfer agent and registrar for new stock and bond issues, and as a trustee for a new bond issue. Under federal legislation, all direct or indirect acquisitions of shares in a trust company in excess of 10 percent must be approved by the Minister of FINANCE. Five years after the annual meeting at which a trust company's equity reaches $750 million, at least 35 percent of its shares must be held by independent shareholders and the company must be listed on a Canadian stock exchange. Companies that already had $750 million in equity when the act came into effect in 1992 had five years to comply. Non-compliance can lead to a freezing of the company's total asset size. However, widely held financial institutions that own a trust company can seek an exemption from the 35 percent rule. The act also prohibits the sale of more than 10 percent of the voting shares of a trust company to any individual non-resident or more than 25 percent of the trust company's shares in total to all non-residents; but this does not apply to foreign-controlled trust companies that existed before the legislation. Nor does it apply to U.S. and Mexican non-residents under the CANADA-UNITED STATES FREE TRADE AGREEMENT and the NORTH AMERICAN FREE TRADE AGREEMENT. The federal and provincial governments are barred from owning shares in a trust company. The Trust and Loan Companies Act also sets out strict rules on the management of trust companies, including provisions to deal with SELF-DEALING and the role of outside directors. The legislation also limits the proportion of loans and investments in real estate that may be held by a trust company.

trustee 1. A person or company, often a trust company, managing money or property for the benefit of others. The role and investment policies of trustees are regulated by the trustees acts of the different provinces. 2. In bankruptcy, an administrator appointed by a court to manage the affairs of an insolvent company and to distribute the remaining assets to eligible creditors. 3. In union administration, the person appointed by the union to take over and manage the affairs of a local that has fallen into corrupt hands, or an official appointed by a federal or provincial government to manage an entire union that has been found to be operated illegally. 4. For bondholders, a company, usually a trust company, appointed by the company issuing the bonds to keep a watch on assets pledged as security for the bond or to ensure that other conditions, such as regular payments to a SINKING FUND, are made on time.

turnkey project The delivery of a completed project, which a contractor is able to turn over to the purchaser ready for use — in other words, one in which the purchaser has simply to turn the key in the door. Turnkey projects have become an important part of international trade. A consortium of companies operating through a contractor can export an airport, factory, subway system, refinery, or power station to another country, and can both provide the capital equipment and supervise construction and installation.

turnover The number of times a particular item is replaced in a business or in the entire economy in a specified period of time — for example, the number of times in a year that labour in a plant or inventory in a store has to be replaced. If a company has 1,000 employees, and 150 of them leave and have to be replaced during a year, the company has a turnover rate of 15 percent. Such a calculation can be extended to the economy at large. In Canada's case, there is a large flow of workers in and out of jobs, and Canada is said to have a high labour-turnover rate.

two-tier gold price A 1968 agreement that helped to sever the historic link between gold and the world monetary system. The agreement, made in Stockholm among the central banks of the United States, Britain, West Germany, Switzerland, Italy, the Netherlands, and Belgium, and the INTERNATIONAL MONETARY FUND and the BANK FOR INTERNATIONAL SETTLEMENTS, effectively froze the gold in the official reserves of individual nations. The need for action arose because the world price of gold had risen well above the official U.S. price of $35 an ounce, leading some foreign holders of U.S. dollars to cash their U.S. dollars in for gold, and either to hoard it or to sell it at a profit on world gold markets. Action was taken to prevent a huge loss by the

United States of its gold reserves, a development that could have precipitated an international monetary crisis.

Under the agreement, two gold markets were established. One, the official gold market, would continue to price gold at $35 an ounce in transactions between central banks and international monetary institutions; the other, the free market, would operate at supply and demand prices, with gold seeking its own level. Central banks agreed neither to sell nor to buy gold on the free market, nor to acquire gold from one another to replace gold already sold on the market. Canada gave its support to the agreement. At the same time, the nations participating in the agreement reaffirmed that, in the future, world reserves would be increased through the use of SPECIAL DRAWING RIGHTS, or paper gold. The need for such an agreement came to an end in 1971, when the United States announced that it would no longer allow foreign central banks or international institutions to convert their holdings of U.S. dollars into gold. Early in 1976, the members of the GROUP OF TEN, including Canada, announced that they would not engage in gold purchases, following the Jamaica Agreement; they agreed that the International Monetary Fund would sell part of its gold holdings at world prices and would use the proceeds to help the DEVELOPING COUNTRIES to cope with their balance-of-payments problems.

tying contract A contract in which a company forces another company or an individual, who wishes to buy some of its products or services or lease its property, to buy other of its goods and services as well or to deal exclusively in its goods and services. This kind of arrangement is common in franchise-type contracts where, for example, someone operating a gasoline station may also be required to deal only in the tires, batteries, and other products supplied by the oil company that has leased the gasoline station. Similarly, a television or movie-production company may compel a television network or theatre chain to buy other of its programs or films, if the network or chain wants to buy particular programs or films. In some instances, these arrangements can be overturned by the COMPETITION TRIBUNAL. *See* TIED SALES.

ultimate potential reserves An estimate of the total crude-oil or natural-gas reserves that will have been developed in an area by the time that all exploration and development activity has been completed; it takes into account the geological prospects of the area, as well as anticipated technology and economic conditions, including future prices. Ultimate potential reserves include the oil or natural gas produced to date, the REMAINING ESTABLISHED RESERVES recoverable under current technology and anticipated economic conditions, and future additions, from extensions and revisions to existing pools and from the discovery of new pools.

ultra vires A law, regulation, or action by a government that is unconstitutional under the CONSTITUTION ACT, 1867, and CONSTITUTION ACT, 1982. Both federal and provincial claims to authority have been supported or rejected by the Supreme Court of Canada. Early efforts by British Columbia in the 1930s to establish farm marketing boards were declared ultra vires and so were laws passed by Parliament in 1935 to establish a system of unemployment insurance, minimum wages, hours of work, and producer marketing boards. *See also* FEDERAL SPENDING POWER, FEDERAL TAXING POWER, PROVINCIAL SPENDING POWER, PROVINCIAL TAXING POWER.

unaudited report A financial report whose accuracy has not been confirmed by outside auditors. It is normally an interim report, such as a quarterly report to shareholders.

unconditional grant A grant by the federal government to a province, or by a provincial government to a municipality, with no strings attached to the way the money is spent. *See*, for example, EQUALIZATION PAYMENTS.

undercapitalized A business firm that lacks the financial resources to seize commercial opportunities, through investment and marketing, for example. The term often refers specifically to an inadequate EQUITY base. The size of a company's equity base determines how much it can or should borrow in the form of DEBT capital.

underconsumption theory The theory advanced by CLASSICAL and NEOCLASSICAL ECONOMISTS that overproduction and therefore underconsumption were impossible. Under conditions of PERFECT COMPETITION — homogeneous products, large numbers of buyers and sellers, full knowledge of market conditions, and easy mobility of producers in and out of the market — the system would automatically adjust and return to full-employment conditions. *See also* SAY'S LAW. The theory was demolished by John Maynard KEYNES. *See also* KEYNESIAN ECONOMICS, BUSINESS CYCLE.

underground economy The part of the economy that is not reported and therefore is not included in the GROSS DOMESTIC PRODUCT (GDP). The underground economy, sometimes referred to as the informal economy, the black economy, or the parallel economy, consists of both criminal activities, such as prostitution, drug trafficking, and gambling, and activities by individuals and small businesses who want to evade tax payments and therefore under-report or fail to report all their business activities. Activities include BARTER transactions, in which people trade goods and services, with no money changing hands. Different estimates of the size of Canada's underground economy vary from 5 percent to 20 percent of GDP.

undersubscribed A new issue of bonds or shares whose total sales fall short of the planned size of the issue, as opposed to oversubscribed, where total demand is in excess of the planned issue.

underwriting The raising of capital for a corporation or government by investment dealers who purchase a new share or bond issue from the issuer and resell it to other investors. The issuer gets the price paid by the underwriters; the underwriters make a profit on the difference between what they pay the issuer and what they receive when they resell the issue.

unemployment The inability to find a paying job at the minimum wage or higher. Unemployment represents a loss to the economy, as well as to unemployed individuals, since it represents an underutilization of resources and therefore lost output. An individual is considered to be unemployed if at least 15 years old, without a job, and available for work and seeking a job. Unemployment can be caused by a lack of demand, and hence growth, in the economy; this kind of unemployment can be addressed by fiscal and monetary policies to increase demand. Unemployment can also be structural in nature — when those without jobs lack the skills that are in demand, lack knowledge about the jobs that exist, or live in areas suffering from chronic unemployment and are unable to move to areas where there are jobs. This type of unemployment can only be addressed through manpower-training programs, improved labour-market operations, and special measures to aid slow-growth areas. A third type of unemployment is technological unemployment, caused by the introduction of technological change. It can be dealt with by manpower retraining and by policies that encourage economic growth. Finally, there is frictional unemployment, the unemployment that always exists because there are always some people in the midst of changing jobs, just entering the labour force, or who are affected by seasonal factors, such as the winter closing of the St. Lawrence Seaway or the reduction in forest-industry activities during the winter. Statistics Canada provides monthly information on the state of employment and unemployment in its LABOUR-FORCE SURVEY (publication 71-001).

unemployment insurance A government-sponsored program of insurance to provide workers who lose their jobs with an assured source of income for a limited period of time while they search for a new job or enroll in a retraining program. Employers and employees pay premiums to cover the cost of the program, with employers paying seven-twelfths and employees five-twelfths of the costs. Since 1990, total program costs, including costs of training unemployed workers under the unemployment insurance system, have been borne fully by the premiums of employers and employees. Unemployment insurance was introduced in Canada in 1935, but the original legislation was declared ULTRA VIRES, or unconstitutional, by the Supreme Court of Canada and the Privy Council in Britain, who said it invaded provincial jurisdiction. After a constitutional amendment, a new law was passed by Parliament in 1940 that came into effect in July, 1941, covering mainly BLUE-COLLAR WORKERS. The legislation was significantly amended in 1971, extending compulsory coverage to all members of the labour force, adding maternity benefits, and increasing the duration and amount of benefits, while reducing the amount of work needed to qualify. Since 1978, the scope of benefits has been progressively reduced, in the belief that they had become a disincentive to work. In 1986, a federal commission headed by Montreal businessman Claude Forget recommended that the unemployment-insurance program be overhauled and limited to providing temporary assistance to workers between jobs. The commission also recommended that extended seasonal benefits and training support be eliminated, and that benefits be restricted to those with a minimum of 350 hours of insurable earnings. Benefits would be payable for a maximum of 50 weeks, after a two-week waiting period, for up to two-thirds of insurable earnings. The Forget commission argued that job creation and long-term income-maintenance benefits should not be a part of the unemployment-insurance system but should be funded separately. Its findings were not adopted by the government, but other steps were taken to reduce benefits. In 1992, the federal government announced that workers who voluntarily quit their jobs, except in cases of well-documented harassment by an employer or if a spouse was relocated to another community by an employer, would lose their entitlement to unemployment-insurance benefits. Maximum benefits were also reduced in 1993 to 57 percent of insurable earnings or $424.65 a week, from 60 percent of insurable earnings, or $447.00 a week. In addition, a growing portion of employer and employee premiums has been shifted to job-training programs. *See* CANADA EMPLOYMENT AND IMMIGRATION COMMISSION. Unemployment insurance is an important BUILT-IN STABILIZER in the economy; it cushions the impact of a recession because it automatically ensures that unemployed persons still retain some purchasing power. Statistics Canada publishes a monthly report detailing numbers of beneficiaries, total disbursements, number of claims or applications, average weekly benefits, weeks of benefits, and other data by province and major census metropolitan areas (publication 73-001). In 1992, just over $19 billion was paid in benefits.

Unemployment Insurance Commission (UIC) A federal agency created in 1941 to administer Canada's UNEMPLOYMENT INSURANCE program. It became part of the CANADA EMPLOYMENT AND IMMIGRATION COMMISSION in 1976, when the UIC and the Department of Manpower and Immigration were merged.

unemployment rate The percentage of persons in the labour force who are unemployed. The labour force consists of all Canadians 15 years of age and older who are either employed or who want to work and are looking for work. The unemployed are those who want to work and are available for work and who are actually looking for work or who have a job that will not start until a later date. There are two measures in the monthly Statistics Canada LABOUR-FORCE SURVEY (publication 71-001): the actual unemployment rate, which is the percentage of people unemployed; and the seasonally adjusted unemployment rate, which shows the percentage of people unemployed after making allowances, based on past experience, for such seasonal fluctuations as the entry of large numbers of students into the labour force for part-time jobs during the summer months, or the loss of jobs in the forest, fishing, and construction industries during the winter months. The seasonally adjusted rate is used to show underlying trends in unemployment and employment. The survey also publishes a three-month moving average, which is also useful in tracking underlying trends.

unfair business practice Any business practice designed to mislead the consumer or to take advantage of consumer ignorance or ill health. Examples include false claims about the quality, standards, and performance of products or services, excessive prices or phony discounts, and high-pressure sales tactics. Federal and provincial consumer-protection laws now make many unfair business practices illegal. *See* COMPETITION ACT.

unfair competition Any practice by a business corporation to restrict or reduce competition. Examples include cut-throat competition to drive someone else out of business, false or misleading advertising, price discrimination, and

tying arrangements. Such practices are, for the most part, illegal. The principal legislation is the COMPETITION ACT.

unfair labour practice Any practice of management or unions designed to prevent free certification of workers in the union of their choice, or to interfere in free collective bargaining. Federal and provincial labour laws set out conditions to prevent such practices. Employers, for example, are not allowed to interfere with or participate in a union, or to take any action against employees who attempt to organize a union or who are active in union affairs. Employers are also forbidden to require an employee to sign an undertaking, as a condition of employment, that he or she will not join a union. Unions are not allowed to strike during the life of a collective agreement, except under narrow and tightly defined conditions, nor are they permitted to intimidate people into joining a union or switching their support to another union. *See also* CANADA LABOUR CODE.

unfair trading practice The dumping or subsidizing of exports or the use of non-tariff barriers to prevent imports.

unfavourable balance of trade *See* TRADE DEFICIT.

unincorporated business A business enterprise, usually an owner-operated business or a partnership — for example, small stores, restaurants and dry cleaners, and small landlords. It is not necessary to incorporate to operate a small business but registration is required by provincial governments.

union A recognized organization of workers joined together to improve members' wages, working conditions, retirement pensions, paid vacations, fringe benefits, and other interests. Unions were formed to offset the lop-sided power of employers to set wage rates and working conditions. Unions existed before Confederation, a number of them affiliates of U.S. unions. The Toronto Trades Assembly, formed in 1871, was the first local labour council; the first national congress of labour unions, the Canadian Labour Union, was formed in 1873. Unions first gained legal recognition in an act of Parliament passed in 1872.

In 1990, 34.7 percent of Canadian workers belonged to trade unions; the highest level was in Newfoundland, where 55.1 percent of workers belonged to unions, while the lowest level was in Alberta, where 26.6 percent of workers were union members. Each year Statistics Canada, under the Corporations and Labour Unions Relations Act, publishes a report on union membership, finances, and other details (publication 71-202). However, the statistics understate the influence of unions. Unions have an impact on everyone's wages and working conditions because non-union companies tend to follow unionized salary and benefit agreements. Unions also help to shape government laws on vacations with pay, minimum wages, hours of work, occupational health and safety, rights to severance pay, advance notice of layoffs due to technological change, and training. Unions also play a role in campaigning for social policies, such as improved pensions and health care.

Most unions in Canada are either national or international. They are made up of hundreds of locals, which represent workers in individual firms or government organizations. The locals' main responsibility is to represent members in collective bargaining, with the locals doing the actual bargaining, and the union head office providing bargaining assistance and, if need be, strike pay. Unions in federally controlled industries, such as banks, railways, the federal public service, and the airlines, are subject to the CANADA LABOUR CODE; those under provincial jurisdiction, and they are the majority,

are subject to provincial labour laws. Details of union membership are published annually by the federal Department of LABOUR, in the publication *Labour Organization in Canada*. In addition, Statistics Canada publishes an annual survey, *Canada's Unionized Workers* (publication 71-214), as well as an annual report on the activities of unions (publication 71-202). *See also* LABOUR COUNCIL, COLLECTIVE BARGAINING, CERTIFICATION, BARGAINING UNIT, CANADIAN LABOUR CONGRESS, CANADIAN FEDERATION OF LABOUR, CONFEDERATION OF NATIONAL TRADE UNIONS.

union label   Some kind of mark, design, or tag on a product to let the consumer know that it was made by union members. It may also consist of the initials of a union on a letter if the letter has been typed by a union member, or a decal on a bus or cab, if the driver belongs to a union.

union security   Any provision in labour law or a collective agreement that protects a union against loss of members or loss of dues. An example would be compulsory CHECK-OFF of dues by the employer to provide a union with necessary funds, thus saving the union the costs of collecting money from members. Another example is the UNION SHOP, which ensures that everyone joining a company must join the union. Employers are compelled by law to collect dues on behalf of a union. *See also* RAND FORMULA.

union shop   A place of work where all employees in a bargaining unit, other than management, must be members of the union (or pay union dues?), and where all new employees, other than management, must join the union after a specified period of time. New employees don't have to be union members when they are hired, but must join the union after they are hired; the union shop is distinguished from a CLOSED SHOP, where new employees must be union members before they can be hired. In Canada, most places of work represented by unions are union shops.

unit cost The total cost of a single product or service. It is calculated by dividing total costs — FIXED and VARIABLE — by the number of units produced. The term "average cost" is also used.

unit labour costs A measure of competitiveness, calculated by dividing the total wage bill, including fringe benefits, by the total number of units of a good or service produced. It can be expressed as an index and used in comparison with other countries to see whether Canada is remaining competitive in its costs or is pricing itself out of international markets. A rise in unit labour costs is not necessarily due to higher wages and fringe benefits. For instance, if production declines but the workforce remains the same, then unit labour costs will automatically increase, even if wages are frozen. When unit labour costs are compared in a common currency, say the U.S. dollar, then changes may reflect exchange-rate changes rather than wage changes. Unit labour costs are an important economic indicator, which shows the combined effects of changes in compensation and PRODUCTIVITY on the costs of production and, hence, on the rate of inflation. Unit labour costs for a particular industry, listed in Statistics Canada's CENSUS OF MANUFACTURES, can be calculated by dividing the total VALUE-ADDED of the industry by the total payroll costs. Changes in unit labour costs can also help to indicate productivity changes in an industry; for example, if unit labour costs increase less than increases in compensation, then the difference is accounted for by productivity improvements. Statistics Canada publishes an annual report on unit labour costs, *Aggregate Productivity Measures* (publication 15-204).

United Nations (UN) A family of global organizations conceived in the final days of the Second World War to establish a new international order based on the peaceful resolution of disputes between states, international cooperation to promote economic, social, and cultural progress, universal respect for human rights and fundamental freedoms, and the strengthening of friendly relations between countries. The UN acts as a centre for harmonizing the actions of nations to achieve these and other common goals. The UN Charter was drawn up by 50 nations, including Canada, at the UN Conference on International Organization that met in San Francisco from April 25 to June 26, 1945, when the charter was signed. The UN officially came into existence on October 24, 1945, when the charter had been ratified by a majority of signatories, including the United States, the Soviet Union, China, France, and Britain. Canada did not officially join until November 9, 1945, two days after Mexico. The UN Charter is based on fundamental human rights, including the equality of men and women, the rule of law in international affairs, and the promotion of social and economic progress and better living standards. Membership in the UN is open to all nations that accept the obligations of the UN Charter. At the beginning of 1993 it had 181 members.

The UN system has six principal institutions. The first is the General Assembly, in which every UN member state has one vote; decisions on key issues such as those on peace and security require a two-thirds majority while other questions require a simple majority. The General Assembly is the principal forum of the UN and it has sweeping powers to discuss and make recommendations on any issue falling within the scope of the UN Charter, except when the same matter is being discussed by the Security Council. It can initiate studies and make recommendations in a wide variety of areas, including international collaboration in economic, social, cultural, educational, and health fields. It also approves the UN budget and apportions contributions among UN members. In addition, the General Assembly elects the non-permanent members of the Security Council, members of the Economic and Social Council, the elected members of the Trusteeship Council, the judges of the International Court of Justice (jointly with the Security Council) and, on the recommendation of the Security Council, the secretary-general of the UN. With a large agenda each year, the UN General Assembly delegates much of its work to seven Main Committees, including the Second Committee, which deals with economic and financial matters.

The second key institution in the UN is the Security Council, which has the main responsibility for world peace and security. The council has 15 members — five permanent members (China, Britain, France, Russia, and the United States) and 10 members elected for two-year terms by the General Assembly. Decisions on substantive matters require nine votes, including the concurring votes of all five permanent members. In addition to dealing with peace and security issues, the Security Council also recommends to the General Assembly the appointment of the secretary-general.

The third UN institution, the Economic and Social Council, co-ordinates the economic and social work of the UN and its large family of specialized agencies and institutions. It has 54 members, who serve for three-year terms. The council serves as a forum for the discussion of international social and economic issues, makes or initiates studies or reports, promotes respect for and observance of human

rights, calls international conferences and prepares draft conventions for submission to the General Assembly, co-ordinates activities of specialized UN-affiliated agencies, and consults with non-governmental organizations. The council has six functional commissions that deal with statistics, population, social development, human rights, the status of women, and narcotic drugs. It has five regional commissions for Africa, Asia and Pacific, Europe, Latin America and the Caribbean, and Western Asia, and six standing committees dealing with natural resources, transnational corporations, human settlements, negotiations with intergovernmental agencies, negotiations with non-governmental organizations, and program and co-ordination.

The fourth UN institution is the Trusteeship Council, which supervises the administration of trust territories; the only remaining trust territory is the Trust Territory of the Pacific Islands, administered by the United States. The others, mainly in Africa or the Pacific, have either become independent countries or joined neighbouring states.

The fifth UN institution is the International Court of Justice, based in The Hague, Netherlands. Its statute is an important part of the UN Charter. All members of the UN can refer cases to the court and both the General Assembly and the Security Council can seek an advisory opinion from the court. The court's jurisdiction covers all cases that member states refer to it along with all matters arising out of the UN Charter or UN treaties and conventions in force. The court has 15 judges elected by the General Assembly and the Security Council.

The sixth UN institution is the Secretariat, headed by the secretary-general, who is appointed by the General Assembly on the recommendation of the Security Council. The Secretariat is the administrative arm of the UN and is responsible for carrying out the programs and policies of the UN. The UN has about 25,000 employees around the world and operates on a budget of about US$2 billion. *See also* INTERNATIONAL COVENANT ON ECONOMIC, SOCIAL, AND CULTURAL RIGHTS.

United Nations Centre for Human Settlements (HABITAT) A UNITED NATIONS (UN) agency established in 1978 following a recommendation from the UN Conference on Human Settlements, held in Vancouver in 1976. Based in Nairobi, Kenya, it co-ordinates UN activities dealing with human settlements. Its main functions are technical co-operation, research, training, and the dissemination of information. It works with DEVELOPING COUNTRIES to deal with major problem areas such as the large-scale growth of cities in the developing world, and national settlement policies. It deals with urban and regional planning, housing and infrastructure development, the upgrading of urban slums, low-cost building technologies, technologies for urban and rural water supply and sanitation systems, and the development and strengthening of government institutions. In 1988, the General Assembly of the UN adopted the Global Strategy for Shelter to the Year 2000, a strategy in which governments pursue ways to encourage people to provide and improve their own shelter rather than having governments provide all the necessary shelter.

United Nations Children's Fund (UNICEF) A UNITED NATIONS (UN) organization devoted to improving the well-being of mothers and children. It concentrates on areas such as basic nutrition and primary health care, education, pre-natal and child-raising education, water supply and sanitation, and shelter. It was started in 1946 as

the UN International Children's Emergency Fund, or UNICEF, to meet the emergency needs of children in post-war Europe and China. In 1953, it became the UN Children's Fund, responsible for developing programs of long-range benefit to children in DEVELOPING COUNTRIES so that they can achieve their full potential. In 1959, the UN General Assembly adopted the Declaration of the Rights of the Child. UNICEF was awarded the Nobel Peace Prize in 1965. The UN marked 1979 as the International Year of the Child, and UNICEF was responsible for co-ordinating follow-up actions. UNICEF provides funds to train health and sanitation workers, nutritionists, child-welfare workers, and others who deal with the well-being of children. It also delivers technical supplies, equipment, and other assistance to improve the well-being of mothers and children, including equipment and medicines for health clinics and pumps and other equipment to deliver clean water. UNICEF has put significant emphasis on immunization and oral rehydration as low-cost means of protecting the health of children.

United Nations Code of Conduct on Conference Shipping An international agreement devised within the UNITED NATIONS CONFERENCE ON TRADE AND DEVELOPMENT (UNCTAD) in 1979 to give DEVELOPING COUNTRIES the opportunity to obtain a share of the shipping of imports and exports in and out of their ports, and thus to break the monopoly enjoyed by shipping companies operating through shipping conferences. Under the 40-40-20 formula devised by UNCTAD, each of two trading partners would be entitled to 40 percent of the shipping, with the other 20 percent up for grabs. Canada has not signed the code, also known as the Liner Code, because it has no MERCHANT MARINE of its own.

United Nations Commission on International Trade Law (UNCITRAL)   A body established by the UNITED NATIONS in 1966, with representation from 36 countries, including Canada, to negotiate international conventions to facilitate international trade and commerce. It has developed a number of conventions in areas such as arbitration, international payments (including a legal guide on electronic funds transfers), international sale of goods, and international legislation on shipping. Its conventions include the Convention on the Limitation Period in the International Sale of Goods (1974), the Convention on the Carriage of Goods by Sea (1978), the Convention on Contracts for the International Sale of Goods (1980), the Convention on International Bills of Exchange and International Promissory Notes (1988), and the Convention on the Liability of Operators of Transport Terminals in International Trade (1989). UNCITRAL has published various rules and a model law on arbitration and a legal guide for the drawing up of international contracts for the construction of industrial works.

United Nations Commission on Sustainable Development   A UNITED NATIONS (UN) agency established following the 1992 UNITED NATIONS CONFERENCE ON ENVIRONMENT AND DEVELOPMENT to follow up on implementation of AGENDA 21, the action plan adopted by government leaders at the UN environmental conference. The commission reports to the UN through the UN Economic and Social Council.

United Nations Commission on Transnational Corporations   A UNITED NATIONS (UN) body established in 1974 to help the world body deal with MULTINATIONAL (transnational) corporations. The 48-member commission acts as a UN forum to examine issues relating to multinationals; promotes the exchange of views of governments, business, unions, and other groups; helps individual countries to set policies dealing with multinationals; conducts inquiries into the activities of multinationals, and publishes studies and reports; assists the UN in its efforts to develop a code of conduct for multinationals; and recommends priorities and programs for the UN's Centre on Transnational Corporations, which began operation in 1975 and is a research and policy advisory body with its own staff. The commission also supports the work of an Intergovernmental Working Group of Experts on International Standards of Accounting and Reporting. The UN Commission on Transnational Corporations reports to the UN Economic and Social Council. The commission is an advisory body to the council. In 1993, the Centre on Transnational Corporations was merged into UNITED NATIONS CONFERENCE ON TRADE AND DEVELOPMENT in Geneva.

United Nations Conference on Environment and Development (UNCED)   A 12-day conference held in Rio de Janeiro, Brazil, in June, 1992, (informally called the "Earth Summit") and attended by the leaders of more than 120 countries, including Canada, with almost 180 nations represented altogether. The conference adopted by consensus three major agreements and more than 150 nations signed two major conventions. The three agreements included the Rio Declaration, AGENDA 21, and a Statement on Forest Principles. The two major conventions were the Framework Convention on Climate Change and the Biological Diversity Convention. The Rio Declaration affirms the fundamental principles guiding human behaviour toward the environment and sets out the rights and responsibilities of nations, communities, and individuals toward the environment. It contains 27 broad principles and emphasizes protecting the environment as part of economic development, safeguarding the ecological systems of other nations, and giving priority to the needs of the developing countries. Agenda 21 is an ambitious set of more than 100 programs that set out an ambitious plan of action as the world moves toward the 21st century. The document sets out the social and economic aspects of SUSTAINABLE DEVELOPMENT, such as strategies to reduce poverty, improve human health, and stabilize world population growth, as well as programs for a large list of environmental problems. Agenda 21 is not legally binding and did not include specific commitments of aid from the industrial countries, as the developing countries had sought. The Statement on Forest Principles is a legally non-binding agreement that urges an accelerated program of reforestation, afforestation, and conservation. The Framework Convention on Climate Change sets out the general goal of stabilizing concentrations of greenhouse gases, such as carbon dioxide, to avert global warming. Few specific targets or measures are included, although the industrial nations, including Canada, agreed on the desirability of holding emission levels in the year 2000 to their 1990 levels. The convention did, however, set up a mechanism to decide on stronger measures at a future date if needed. The Biological Diversity Convention, which is legally binding, requires signatory countries such as Canada to adopt rules to make inventories of plants and wildlife, conserve biological resources, and protect endangered species. It also imposes a legal responsibility on individual countries for the practices of their corporations in other countries, and proposes technical support, research sharing, and compensation for developing countries for the extraction of genetic materials; the United States refused to sign the biological convention. The conference recognized that the Agenda 21 proposals will require significant financial resources, but left open how its goals would be achieved. It was recognized that funding would have to come both from polluters, through various charges and tradeable permits, and through increased development assistance. The Earth Summit also called on the UNITED NATIONS to create a high-level Commision on Sustainable Development to monitor progress in implementing Agenda 21. The secretary-general of the Rio conference was a Canadian, Maurice Strong.

United Nations Conference on the Law of the Sea (UNCLOS) A series of UNITED NATIONS (UN) conferences, dating back to 1958, that has attempted to establish an international body of law on the rights of states in coastal waters, the limits of coastal waters, the conservation of fisheries, and the ownership of sea-bed oil, natural gas, and minerals. UNCLOS I, held in Geneva in 1958, reached agreements on sea law to deal with fishing and conservation practices, the territorial sea, the continental shelf, the high seas, and the settlement of disputes. In 1970, the UN General Assembly declared the sea bed and ocean floor, and the resources beneath them, to be "beyond the limits of national jurisdiction" and to be the "common heritage of mankind," and initiated new discussions to develop further the law of the sea. UNCLOS III negotiations began in Caracas, Venezuela, in 1974 and continued through 1982. A new Convention on the Law of the Sea was adopted by a Conference on the Law of the Sea and has since been adopted by most UN members, including Canada, but not by the United States. Under the convention, coastal states have sovereignty over their territorial sea for up to 12 nautical miles in breadth but foreign vessels would have the right of "innocent passage"; coastal states would have sovereign rights in a 200-nautical-mile exclusive economic zone with respect to natural resources and certain other economic activities such as fisheries, along with jurisdiction over marine-science research and environmental protection; an International Sea-Bed Authority was to be established to regulate mineral exploration and exploitation in the international sea bed, either through its own mining operations through its own operating arm, the Enterprise, or by contracting with private or state ventures; states were to settle any disputes through an International Tribunal for the Law of the Sea. On June 1, 1977, Canada declared a 200-nautical-mile fishing zone.

United Nations Conference on Trade and Development (UNCTAD)   A UNITED NATIONS organization established in December, 1964, to promote the economic interests of the DEVELOPING COUNTRIES, especially trade-related development issues, and to make international systems and institutions more supportive of the economic development goals of the developing countries. In 1964, the first of eight major assemblies was held to discuss trade, foreign aid, and other concerns such as the stabilization of commodity prices. Since then, seven other assemblies have been held: UNCTAD II (1968), UNCTAD III (1972), UNCTAD IV (1976), UNCTAD V (1979), UNCTAD VI (1983), UNCTAD VII (1987), and UNCTAD VIII (1992). While UNCTAD has adopted radical positions in the past, insisting on sweeping concessions from the industrial countries, UNCTAD VIII resulted in an agreement on market-oriented economic policies and political pluralism. UNCTAD played a key role in bringing forward the GENERALIZED SYSTEM OF PREFERENCES and in developing a maritime shipping code. UNCTAD has also placed high priority on helping the least-developed countries and on international-aid targets. UNCTAD maintains a secretariat in Geneva, the site of its

first conference. In addition to the LESS-DEVELOPED COUNTRIES, it includes 24 DEVELOPED COUNTRIES (Canada is one of them) and 12 former Communist countries. At UNCTAD, the less-developed nations meet in caucus as the GROUP OF SEVENTY-SEVEN (their number at UNCTAD in 1964; it is now about 170). Among the group's aims are better trade terms with the industrial world, including preferential-tariff treatment; the stabilization and strengthening of international commodity markets and greater participation by developing countries in the processing of resources; the renegotiation of international debt; the strengthening of developing-country export capacities through improved terms of technology transfer, greater flows of foreign aid, increased support from multilateral financing institutions, and increased foreign investment; new issues of SPECIAL DRAWING RIGHTS to help members solve balance-of-payments problems; special support for the world's 42 least-developed and poorest countries; and access to world shipping on better terms. Much of the debate over the NEW INTERNATIONAL ECONOMIC ORDER has taken place within UNCTAD. Its executive body, the Trade and Development Board, meets annually in Geneva.

United Nations Convention on Biodiversity   A treaty signed at the UNITED NATIONS CONFERENCE ON ENVIRONMENT AND DEVELOPMENT in 1992 to protect the world's endangered plant and animal species and the areas they inhabit. Many of the species are critical for the development of new drugs, pest-resistant crops, and other genetic advances. Individual countries are to develop their own strategies to protect their biological diversity, with the industrial countries helping to finance the cost of these programs in the DEVELOPING COUNTRIES. The convention sets out rules determining how pharmaceutical and other companies will access unique species of plants and animals, with the developing countries entitled to receive a share of the profits from any products developed from these species.

United Nations Development Program (UNDP)   A UNITED NATIONS (UN) organization that provides technical and financial assistance to DEVELOPING COUNTRIES. Created in 1965 by the merging of the UN Special Fund and the UN Expanded Program of Technical Assistance, it is the most important international source of technical assistance for developing countries. Some 80 percent of its country program funds go to countries with a per capita income of US$750 or less. It also administers a number of special funds, including the UN Capital Development Fund, the Special Measures Fund for Least Developed Countries, the UN Fund for Science and Technology for Development, and the UN Development Fund for Women. UNDP is financed by annual voluntary subscriptions from UN members, including Canada. It is one of the world's principal multilateral foreign-aid programs. It also publishes the HUMAN DEVELOPMENT INDEX and a *Human Development Report*.

United Nations Economic Commissions   Five UNITED NATIONS (UN) commissions established to monitor the local and regional economies and to promote growth and development in different regions of the world. The UN Economic Commission for Africa is based in Addis Ababa, Ethiopia; the UN Economic Commission for Europe, which is also responsible for Canada and the United States, is based in Geneva; the UN Economic Commission for Latin America and the Caribbean is based in Santiago, Chile; the UN Economic Commission for Asia and Pacific is based in Bangkok, Thailand; and the

UN Economic and Social Commission for Western Asia is based in Amman, Jordan.

United Nations Educational, Scientific and Cultural Organization (UNESCO)   A UNITED NATIONS (UN) institution established in 1946 to promote international co-operation through education, science, culture, and communications. Based in Paris, UNESCO helps countries formulate literacy programs and train teachers and educational planners and administrators. Through education and training programs, UNESCO is also helping developing countries increase their scientific and technological manpower. Its cultural programs include the conservation and preservation of the world's cultural heritage, the stimulation of artistic creativity, and the study and development of cultures. Its communications activities include measures to encourage the development of news media in developing countries.

United Nations Environment Program (UNEP)   A UNITED NATIONS agency that helps to co-ordinate a number of programs to protect the earth's environment, gather information on the state of the environment, and alert national governments to environmental problems. It operates Earthwatch, the environmental monitoring and assessment arm of the UN. It improves early-warning indicators of significant environmental changes, improves the planning and co-ordination of monitoring at the global and regional level, produces assessments of environmental problems, and promotes the development of environmental statistics and environmental reporting. Its activities also include the Global Environment Monitoring System, the International Register of Potentially Toxic Chemicals, and a worldwide data network, Infoterra. In 1975, it established the Environment and Industry Office, which works with industry, governments, and non-government organizations to develop environmentally sound forms of industrial development. UNEP plays an important role in negotiating international agreements, such as the Montreal Protocol of 1987 to help arrest the depletion of the world's ozone layer, and the Basel Convention of 1989, which provides controls on the international movement and disposal of hazardous wastes. It was created following the UN Conference on Human Environment, which took place in Stockholm in 1972. The program's headquarters are in Nairobi, Kenya. Canada is a member of its governing council and is a contributor to the UN Environment Fund.

United Nations Framework Convention on Climate Change A treaty signed at the UNITED NATIONS CONFERENCE ON ENVIRONMENT AND DEVELOPMENT in 1992 to limit future emissions of greenhouse gases. Under the convention, the industrial nations are to limit their emissions of greenhouse gases and make public reports on their progress, though no targets are set. The industrial countries are to provide the DEVELOPING COUNTRIES with funding and technology to help curb their emissions of greenhouse gases as they industrialize and grow. Due to the vagueness of the convention, future negotiations will take place to reach a more precise agreement.

United Nations Industrial Development Organization (UNIDO) A UNITED NATIONS (UN) body established in 1966 to assist in the industrial development of DEVELOPING COUNTRIES; it became a specialized agency of the UN in 1986. Based in Vienna, Austria, it assists developing countries in accelerating their industrialization, provides technical assistance for industrial development, and facilitates the transfer of technology from industrial to develop-

ing countries. In 1988, it established the International Centre for Science and High Technology at Trieste to improve training opportunities for developing-country scientists.

United Nations Monetary and Financial Conference *See* BRETTON WOODS AGREEMENT.

United Nations Population Fund (UNFPA) A UNITED NATIONS (UN) body that is today the world's largest international source of funding for population-and family-planning programs in DEVELOPING COUNTRIES. It helps educate family-planning workers and funds family-planning campaigns and clinics. It also helps developing countries design, administer, and implement family-planning programs. The UN established a Population Commission in 1947 to deal with demographic questions. In 1967, the UN established a Trust Fund for Population Activities; it was renamed the UN Fund for Population Activities in 1969, and renamed the UN Population Fund in 1987. The concern of UN members with population issues was reflected in the World Population Conference held in 1974, which adopted a World Population Plan of Action, and by the International Conference on Population held in 1984. UNFPA publishes an annual report on world population projections, along with long-term demographic projections, on a country-by-country basis.

United Nations Relief and Rehabilitation Administration (UNRRA) The first multilateral-aid program of the United Nations, financed by Canada, the United States, and Britain to provide emergency relief, such as food and medical supplies, to western Europe as the Allied armies advanced toward Germany. Although Canada was the third largest contributor to UNRRA after it was created in November, 1943, Canada was kept off the central committee by its other members (Britain, the United States, the Soviet Union, and China) until 1945. UNRRA was wound up in 1947.

universal bank A bank that provides both commercial and investment banking services.

universal payment A social-security payment that is made to all citizens regardless of need. For example, all Canadians 65 and over are paid a federal OLD AGE SECURITY PENSION. To some extent, these payments are taxed back from Canadians with higher incomes, but not 100 percent. Critics argue that social assistance should go only to those who really need it, and that it should be possible to do much more to reduce poverty without raising total social-assistance costs. For example, Canada's universal system of FAMILY ALLOWANCES was replaced by the income-related CHILD BENEFIT. Advocates of universal payments contend that they are valuable because they eliminate demeaning means tests, in which social workers and government officials question individuals about their income and assets before deciding whether a person should get such assistance. *See also* GUARANTEED ANNUAL INCOME.

Universal Postal Union (UPU) A UNITED NATIONS (UN) agency that helps to facilitate the international movement of mail through various reciprocal arrangements. Its congress meets once every five years. The agency, which is located in Berne, Switzerland, was founded in 1874. It became an agency of the League of Nations in 1920, and of the UN in 1948. Canada has been a member since 1878.

universality The availability of a government program to all, regardless of need. For example, the CANADA HEALTH ACT states that health care should be available to all Canadians. Similarly, the federal OLD-AGE SECURITY PENSION is paid to all Canadians.

unlisted share A share that is not listed on a stock exchange but is traded in an OVER-THE-COUNTER MARKET.

unload The sale of a significant holding of a share, bond, currency, or commodity on the market despite a low price simply in order to dispose of the asset. Unloading usually takes place because the investor believes prices will fall even further, so it makes sense to get out sooner rather than later.

unofficial strike *See* ILLEGAL STRIKE.

unsecured creditor A creditor who has lent money to a firm, individual, or other entity without obtaining collateral for protection against possible default. In a BANKRUPTCY, the unsecured creditor is the last to be paid and, in most cases, receives little or no repayment, since assets are inadequate to cover all liabilities.

unsecured loan A loan that is not backed by collateral. As a result, the lender charges a higher rate of interest, reflecting the greater risk, than would be charged on a SECURED LOAN.

unskilled worker A worker, such as a labourer, filing clerk, or messenger, who is able to perform simple tasks but who has no special training or skills earned through an apprenticeship or other program.

upstream The exploration and development activities of an oil company up to and including the extraction of oil from producing wells. *See also* DOWNSTREAM.

urban population As defined in the 1971 census, all Canadians living in incorporated cities, towns, and villages with a population of 1,000 or more or in incorporated communities of 1,000 or more, having a population density of at least 1,000 per square mile (386 per square kilometre). People living on the fringes of cities, towns, and villages are also considered urban, provided they meet the same population and density criteria. *See also* METROPOLITAN AREA. The percentage of urban population has grown significantly as Canada has industrialized.

urban renewal   The redevelopment of downtown areas to reinvigorate city centres. Although Canadian cities have not experienced the decline of downtown areas experienced in U.S. cities, there nonetheless has been a need to revive and rebuild commercial space and housing. Urban-renewal projects may include land assembly for shopping-office complexes, new cultural centres, convention centres, transportation terminals, and high-density housing. Properly planned, urban redevelopment can provide an incentive for other property owners to undertake new projects or to rehabilitate existing buildings and increase local assessment — and thus, property-tax revenues for municipalities as well.

urban sprawl   The unplanned spread of low-density housing, shopping centres, industry, and service facilities. It represents a poor use of land around cities and builds up high future servicing costs. For example, it is expensive to offer adequate public transportation to people living in widely scattered subdivisions, since distances are long and passenger volumes low. Similarly, sewer, water, and other services have to be carried long distances to serve relatively small numbers of people. Planners also object to urban sprawl because such areas offer few cultural, recreational, and other facilities to enhance the quality of life.

urbanization   The movement of people from rural communities to cities and towns. Urbanization means different types of jobs, land use, consumer demands, transportation needs, lifestyles, industry, and political and social values. *See also* URBAN POPULATION, METROPOLITAN AREA.

Uruguay Round   A round of multilateral trade negotiations launched under the GENERAL AGREEMENT ON TARIFFS AND TRADE (GATT) at a ministerial meeting in Punta del Este in Uruguay in September, 1986. The goals were the most ambitious ever undertaken for any set of GATT negotiations, including, as well as a one-third cut in tariffs, the inclusion of agriculture under GATT disciplines; the elimination of the MULTI-FIBRE ARRANGEMENT and the inclusion of clothing and textiles under GATT; the extension of GATT to include services, intellectual property, and trade-related-investment measures; an expanded subsidies code; major improvements to the dispute-settlement mechanism; a new GATT function of conducting and publishing studies of trade practices of member countries; and the creation of a new world trade body, the Multilateral Trade Organization. A total of 105 nations participated in the 1986 launch of the Uruguay Round, including 96 who were members of GATT. The Punta del Este declaration set out the objectives. Two negotiating groups were established, the Group of Negotiations in Goods and the Group of Negotiations in Services. Some 14 negotiating groups were established under the Group of Negotiations in Goods, including agriculture, subsidies, tropical products, textiles and clothing, tariffs, and intellectual property. The Group of Negotiations in Goods and the Group of Negotiations in Services reported to the Trade Negotiations Committee. An additional body, the Surveillance Body, was established as part of the Uruguay Round; its job was to monitor the "standstill and rollback" commitments made by GATT members as part of the Punta del Este declaration. In the declaration, GATT members promised not to introduce new trade barriers during the negotiations and to roll back measures found to be contrary to GATT. The goal was to complete the negotiations by the end of 1990, with a midterm-review ministerial meeting held in Montreal in December, 1988. However, the 1990 deadline was not met. In December, 1991, the staff of the GATT, headed by its managing director, Arthur Dunkel, put together a proposed compromise agreement, based on areas of agreement that had been reached and, where they had not, by GATT staff.

In what became known as the Dunkel package, four different types of measures were proposed: market-opening measures, such as tariff reductions, with the average level of tariffs cut by 30 percent and some tariff schedules eliminated altogether; measures to strengthen the rules of GATT, such as modest new constraints on the application of anti-dumping rules, a much expanded subsidies code, and the inclusion of agriculture and clothing and textiles within GATT; with tariffs replacing import quotas. measures to include new sectors not previously covered, such as trade in services, intellectual-property protection, and trade-related investment measures; and measures for institutional reform, such as a much improved dispute-settlement system and the creation of a new Multilateral Trade Organization. The proposed new rules on farm trade included commitments to reduce domestic support for agriculture and to shift support from payments related to production to direct income support for farmers; a gradual reduction in the level of border control on agricultural imports, with quotas, such as those used in Canada's SUPPLY MANAGEMENT system, being replaced by tariffs; commitments to reduce national budgetary expenditures on subsidized agricultural exports as well as to reduce the actual volume of subsidized exports; and agreements to reach a sounder scientific basis for regulations related to animal and plant health and safety. The proposed subsidies code included definitions of the kinds of government support for research and development and for regional development that would not be subject to countervailing duties, and introduced new measures to give GATT a stronger role in resolving disputes over subsidies and constraining the application of national countervailing duty applications. The services package included a body of general rules, a package of initial liberalization commitments by individual GATT members, and a number of special conditions or exceptions related to individual services; Canada, for example, could exempt cultural industries. Services range from banking, insurance, and tourism to consulting, telecommunications, accounting, film and video, and the provision of labour. The intellectual-property provisions provided protection for patents, copyright, trademarks, integrated-circuit layouts, trade secrets, geographical indications, and appellations of origin, as well as a system of dispute settlement. The institutional reforms included a streamlined dispute-settlement system, with clearer deadlines, a more automatic process, and much improved implementation of panel decisions, along with the trade-policy-review mechanism for individual countries that was launched in 1989 (at the end of 1992 Canada had been reviewed twice), and the creation of the Multilateral Trade Organization as a more powerful world trade body, which subsumed GATT and various codes established under the Tokyo Round, and took under its wing new agreements on services, intellectual property, and trade-related investment measures, along with an integrated dispute-settlement system. The goal in 1993 was to conclude negotiations so that the Uruguay Round measures could take effect on January 1, 1995.

United States International Trade Administration (ITA)   The branch of the U.S. Department of Commerce that investigates complaints of dumping and subsidized imports for the U.S. government and determines the level of anti-dumping or countervailing duty to be applied if injury or the threat of injury is found. Under the U.S. system, the ITA makes a preliminary finding of an anti-dumping or countervailing duty action. The U.S. INTERNATIONAL TRADE COMMISSION (ITC) then makes a preliminary finding on injury. If there is a preliminary injury finding, the ITA then makes a final determination on the anti-dumping or counter-vailing duty to be applied and the ITC then conducts a hearing to make a final determination on injury. If the ITC makes a final injury determination, then the anti-dumping- or countervail-ing-duty determination of the ITA goes into effect.

United States International Trade Com-mission (ITC)   A U.S. trade agency created in 1974 to determine whether or not injury or the threat of injury to U.S. industry exists in anti-dumping and countervailing cases. *See also* U.S. INTERNATIONAL TRADE ADMINIS-TRATION. The ITC also conducts inves-tigations into trade issues and the impact of changes in U.S. trade policy on U.S. industry. For example, the ITC con-ducted studies on the economic impact in the United States of the CANADA-UNITED STATES FREE TRADE AGREE-MENT and the NORTH AMERICAN FREE TRADE AGREEMENT.

United States Trade Representative (USTR)   The senior U.S. official responsible for U.S. trade negotiations and the administration of U.S. trade laws. The USTR is a member of the cabi-net and is designated as an ambassador. The Office of the U.S. Trade Representa-tive is a branch of the Executive Office of the President.

user-pay principle of taxation   The imposition of a tax, toll, or other levy on the user of a particular government service, usually to recover all or part of the costs of providing the service. For example, Canadians who travel by air pay a tax when they buy their tickets to help cover the cost of operating air-ports. Tolls are often imposed on bridges, ferries, and tunnels, and some-times on highways. Fees are charged to enter campsites and parks, while gov-ernment subsidies may be eliminated or reduced on rail travel, all with the pur-pose of charging the user all or a larger part of the cost of providing the service.

usury   A rate of interest in excess of that set by law, or in excess of a com-mon standard of what is acceptable in a community. Medieval and Islamic thinkers argued that any rate of inter-est constituted usury. There are some legal limits on interest rates in Canada: federal legislation sets out a "criminal interest rate," which is an annual inter-est rate in excess of 60 percent of the credit advanced.

utilitarianism   A political-economic philosophy that asserts that the basic role of government is to achieve the greatest happiness for the greatest number. It seeks to maximize the total utility of the community, which it sees as the sum of individual utilities. Its best-known advocate was Jeremy Ben-tham, who saw self-interest as the prime human motivator, and the pur-suit of happiness as the prime human concern.

utility   The satisfaction that comes from consumption of various goods and services. The utility or value of particular goods or services depends on the extent to which they can fill consumer wants; this utility is reflected in the price a consumer is willing to pay for a particular good or service. The consumer is assumed to rank his preference for goods and services in terms of the utility derived from them. *See also* MARGINAL UTILITY, LAW OF DIMINISHING MARGINAL UTILITY.

utility rate of return   The maximum profit rate that may be earned by a monopoly company operating as a utility. The rate is usually set as a percent of invested capital; the prices charged by a utility (a telephone company, for example) for its different services are set by a regulating agency (in the case of Bell Canada, the CANADIAN RADIO-TELEVISION AND TELECOMMUNICATIONS COMMISSION) in the context of the potential profit that would result from any changes in those prices. A utility's profit has to be set high enough so that it can attract investment capital; it has to be regulated so that it does not use its monopoly position to earn excessive profit. The regulated rate of return is usually slightly above the prevailing rate of interest earned on government and corporate bonds.

utility theory of value   The theory that calculates the value of goods and services according to their ability to satisfy human wants in some order of preference. Assuming a certain level of income, the theory then attempts to provide a basis for calculating consumer demand in a particular period.

utopia   A vision of a perfect or ideal society. Many different thinkers have described their particular utopias; models of utopian vision would include Plato's *Republic*, Francis Bacon's *New Atlantis*, Sir Thomas More's *Utopia*, Edward Bellamy's *Looking Backward*, and Karl Marx's ideal of dictatorship by the proletariat.

uttering   The use of a forged document in the knowledge that it is forged, with the purpose of obtaining some benefit. For example, cashing a cheque with a forged signature or altered amount, or using a forged or stolen bond certificate as collateral to obtain a loan.

vacancy rate A statistic showing the availability of apartments and other rental accommodation, published semi-annually by CANADA MORTGAGE AND HOUSING CORPORATION (CMHC). It is based on a survey by CMHC of rental accommodation with three or more units available for rent. Separate vacancy rates are published for 26 different metropolitan regions in Canada. If the rate is low, say less than 1 percent, then the market is tight and there will be upward pressure on rents. A vacancy rate of 3 percent is said to be needed by tenants to give them bargaining power with landlords over rent increases and other terms of a lease. At that level, tenants should be reasonably confident of finding alternative accommodation, if they are unable to negotiate a satisfactory lease with their existing landlord.

vacation-with-pay legislation Federal or provincial laws that entitle workers to annual vacations; the length of the vacation is normally related to the period of time spent working for a particular employer during the year. In most parts of Canada, paid vacations required by law are equivalent to 4 per-cent of an employee's earnings. Vacation-with-pay legislation was first introduced in Canada in 1944, when Ontario passed such a law. Federal vacation-with-pay legislation was passed by Parliament in 1958. Through collective bargaining, many Canadians today have annual vacations that exceed the legal minimum. Most large employers grant an extra week or weeks of vacation after a specified number of years of continuous employment.

valuation **1.** The assessment of property to establish a value for tax purposes — for example, to determine the value of paintings or antiques for CAPITAL-GAINS TAX on death, or the assessment of real estate for municipal tax purposes. **2.** The appraisal of property for insurance purposes by qualified experts.

valuation day The base date for the calculation of CAPITAL GAINS for tax purposes. It is December 22, 1971, for Canadian common and preferred shares listed on Canadian stock exchanges, foreign shares listed on

Canadian stock exchanges, publicly traded but unlisted Canadian shares, rights, and warrants, and some convertible bonds. It is December 31, 1971, for all other assets subject to the tax, such as bonds, antiques, real estate, art collections, and shares in private companies. Capital gains on all assets except personal residences and on assets worth less than $1,000 are subject to tax. On death, the capital gain is deemed to have been realized, even though the asset may not be sold, and the estate is taxed for the relevant amount.

value   The quantity of one product or service that will be given or accepted in exchange for another. It is therefore a measure of the economic significance of a particular good or service. This value in exchange depends on the scarcity of the good or service and the extent to which it is desired. Some of the first economists such as Adam SMITH and David RICARDO believed value represented the amount of labour used to produce a good or service. Later, economists argued that the utility or satisfaction resulting from the consumption of a particular good or service was the source of its value. Today, however, value is seen as the outcome of both supply and demand.

value-added   The difference between an industry's total revenue and the costs of the materials, parts, and services it has purchased from others. The goal in a modern economy is to increase value-added through highly specialized products based on technology, marketing, and other skills. Value-added measures the value that the industry has added to the raw materials, parts, and services it has used in producing goods and services. For example, if a company buys $100 of raw materials, processes it, and resells it for $150, then the value-added is $50. However, if the same company uses that $100 of raw

materials to make specialized products that it can sell for $300, then the value-added is $200. The value-added is the money that an industry pays on wages and salaries, taxes, dividends, and interest or the money that it reinvests. It is a vital figure in assessing the importance of different industries in the economy. GROSS DOMESTIC PRODUCT is the nation's total value-added in a given period. Statistics Canada also publishes a breakdown of value-added figures for all major manufacturing industries (publication 31-203). It defines value-added as the value of production minus the value of materials, parts, and energy used in production.

value-added tax (VAT)   An INDIRECT TAX, similar to a sales tax, but levied only on the contribution that each firm in the production-distribution process adds to a product. The tax is levied at each point of sale; it is levied on the selling price of the good or service after deducting the cost of goods and services used in its production. Everybody in the production-distribution process, from the manufacturer of original components, through to the final retailer of the product, is required to pay a value-added tax on the value added to the product. For example, if a lumber company buys logs from a logging company for $50 and converts the logs into planks that are sold for $100, then the lumber company has added $50 in value and is taxed on the $50. If a furniture company buys the $100 of planks and uses them to make a table that sells for $400, then another $300 of value has been added and that is the amount taxed. This is how the value-added tax is passed along through each stage of production and distribution. It is a REGRESSIVE TAX, in that the person with a low income pays a larger proportion of his income than a wealthy person pays to consume the same product. The entire burden of the tax is shifted to the ultimate consumer, who pays the tax as part of the price of the product he purchases. It is the system of indirect taxation used throughout the EUROPEAN COMMUNITY. Canada introduced a form of value-added tax with its GOODS AND SERVICES TAX.

value of the Canadian dollar   The exchange rate of the Canadian dollar, expressed in terms of a key international currency. Initially, this was the British pound; after 1910, the key currency became the U.S. dollar. The value of the Canadian dollar indicates its purchasing power in foreign markets for goods and services, including travel. Conversely, it also indicates the purchasing power of foreigners when buying Canadian goods and services. Since the end of the First World War, the Canadian dollar has fluctuated widely in value. In 1920, it fell to 82 U.S. cents, but by 1922 it had recovered to 98.73 U.S. cents. When Canada returned to the GOLD STANDARD, from July, 1926, to January, 1929, the Canadian dollar was close to par with the U.S. dollar. However, the GREAT DEPRESSION pushed the Canadian dollar down. After Britain went off the gold standard, in September, 1931, the Canadian dollar went down to 80.5 U.S. cents, in December, 1931. The Canadian dollar recovered during the Depression, trading at one point as high as 103.6 U.S. cents. With the outbreak of the Second World War, Canada established the FOREIGN EXCHANGE CONTROL BOARD, which fixed the value of the Canadian dollar at a buying rate of 110 U.S. cents and a selling rate of 111 U.S. cents. In July, 1946, although controls were retained, the buying and selling rates of the Canadian dollar were reduced to 100 U.S. cents and 100.5 U.S. cents. In September, 1949, when the British devalued the pound by 30.5 percent, Canada revalued the dollar to a buying rate of 110 U.S. cents and a selling rate of 110.5 U.S. cents.

In October, 1950, the fixed exchange rate was abandoned and the Canadian dollar was allowed to float in foreign-exchange markets. The Foreign Exchange Control Act was repealed by Parliament in 1952. For the next decade, the Canadian dollar was at or near parity with the U.S. dollar, but in May, 1962, it was pegged at 92.5 U.S. cents, staying at this rate until May, 1970, when it was unpegged again. Since then it has floated, as high as 104 U.S. cents in 1974, and as low as 69.13 U.S. cents in 1986.

Vancouver Stock Exchange (VSE)   A stock exchange created in 1907 that has been in business ever since. It maintains three boards: one for resource and development companies, one for industrial companies, and one for listings of JUNIOR COMPANIES for the VANCOUVER CURB EXCHANGE. It is considered to be an exchange for smaller, higher-risk companies, although a number of Canadian blue-chip companies are listed there as well.

variable cost   A cost that varies with production. Examples include the costs of raw materials, parts, and labour directly involved in the production process. If production falls, fewer of these variable inputs are employed; however, if production rises, more of these variable inputs are used so that variable costs rise. *See also* FIXED COSTS.

variable interest rate   An interest rate that varies directly with changes in the PRIME RATE charged by the banks. If the prime rate rises, so does the rate on loans paying a variable rate of interest, and vice versa. Many small-business, corporate, and personal demand loans have a variable rate of interest that changes as the prime rate changes.

variance   1. The difference between actual spending by a business firm or a department of the firm and the amount actually budgeted for the same period. **2.** A measure of risk on the return of an asset. It is calculated as the squared sum of deviations from the average return; each deviation is weighted by the probability of occurence of that particular rate of return.

vein   In mining, an ore that has moved up from some deeper underground source to fill a crack or fault in a rock formation.

velocity of circulation   The number of times a unit of money changes hands within a given period of time. The velocity of money is the ratio of GROSS DOMESTIC PRODUCT (GDP) to the total money stock. To calculate the amount of GDP that has to be supported by each $1 of money supply, divide the GDP by the M-1 money supply. The resulting number indicates the number of times each $1 of M-1 has to circulate in a year to support the economy at current levels. A high velocity of circulation means that people are holding on to their money for a short period of time because the economy is expanding. The speed or velocity with which money changes hands is also based on the sophistication of financial markets; a highly specialized financial system is able to attract savings and to invest them quickly into new activities or assets. Changing technology, such as electronic banking and computer communications, along with changing tastes, lifestyles, and expectations, also influence the velocity of circulation. The rate of turnover, generally, rises during periods of growth and declines during a recession.

venture capital   Capital available for new or small-business enterprises that is invested at greater-than-normal business risk, since the business enterprises may not succeed. Venture capital usually consists of EQUITY CAPITAL

and may be provided by financial firms specializing in such investments or by private investors who seek out high-risk opportunities because of the rewards these can bring if they are successful. Venture capitalists tend to seek a high rate of return and a payback on their investment after five years. The Canadian venture capital industry has formed the Associaton of Canadian Venture Capital Companies, based in Toronto.

vertical integration   The control by a single firm of successive stages of the production and distribution process. Companies seek to vertically integrate because this gives them greater command over costs, can bring about certain ECONOMIES OF SCALE, and should increase profits. Examples of vertical integration would include the following: an oil company that engages in exploration and development, operates pipelines, refines its oil into gasoline, fuel oil, and other products, and then sells its product through gasoline stations and home-heating-oil distributorships to the public; a steel company that owns iron-ore mines, basic steel-producing facilities, and manufacturing operations that produce finished steel products; an aluminum company that mines bauxite, processes aluminum ingots, and manufactures aluminum products; and a supermarket chain that also owns food-processing companies and farms. Firms can pursue a strategy of backward integration, by purchasing companies that have been its suppliers, or a strategy of forward integration, by purchasing companies that formerly were its customers.

vesting   Attributing a specified amount of money in a pension plan to a particular individual participating in the plan. This sum of money forms the basis for the individual's future pension. For example, an employee who participates in a company pension plan has vested his or her contributions and those of the employer, and has; in the case of most provinces and industries under federal jurisdiction, accrued interest. If an employee changes jobs before retirement age, though, the only amount that belongs to the employee is his or her own accumulated contribution, plus the accrued interest, unless the employee has been a member of the pension plan for at least two years. After two years of service, these contributions plus those of the employer are vested. In some provinces, though, vesting terms are much higher — five years in Alberta, for example. Advocates of pension reform argue that the loss of future pension benefits when people change jobs reduces labour mobility, and gives employers an unfair hold over employees who would like to move to another job but cannot afford to give up future pension benefits. *See also* PORTABLE PENSION.

Via Rail Canada   A crown corporation established in 1977 to operate all passenger rail services in Canada. Initially a subsidiary of Canadian National Railways, in 1978 it became a separate crown corporation. It is financed directly by the federal government through the Ministry of TRANSPORT. Its head office is in Montreal.

visibles   Merchandise exports and imports, as opposed to INVISIBLES, such as interest, dividend, and travel payments. Both visible and invisible items of trade are considered in the CURRENT ACCOUNT of a country's BALANCE OF PAYMENTS. The visible balance of trade is simply another name for the merchandise balance of trade.

vital statistics   Basic statistics of a population; they include birth, death, marriage, divorce, and death rates, and other statistics on disease and health. Statistics Canada has actual vital statis-

tics dating back to 1921 and estimates for earlier periods. Publications on births, deaths, marriages, and divorces are published as supplements to its vital statistics series (publication 82-003). Vital statistics are used by demographers in making population forecasts.

volatile market   A market in which prices move up and down in an irregular or erratic fashion.

volume   The number of shares traded during a specified period — for example, in a trading day. A pickup in the volume of trading in the shares of a particular company is a signal that investors are paying increased attention to the company.

volume discount   A discount in price given to someone who purchases in larger-than-normal quantities. These discounts are common in the retailing industry; large chains are able to negotiate lower prices than small independently owned and operated stores. Volume discounts are legal so long as the same discount is available to everyone who wishes to buy the same volume of goods.

voluntary arbitration   A method of resolving differences between an employer and a union in negotiations for a new contract; both parties voluntarily agree to send the outstanding issues to arbitration, and to accept the results. *See also* COMPULSORY ARBITRATION.

voluntary export restraint (VER)   An agreement by an exporting country to limit its exports to another country. VERs are usually entered into when the exporting country is threatened with trade restrictions by the importing country. VERs represent a form of managed trade and are a circumvention of the rules of the GENERAL AGREEMENT ON TARIFFS AND TRADE

(GATT). Importing countries seeking VOLUNTARY RESTRAINT AGREE-MENTS often do so because the GATT disciplines on the use of SAFEGUARDS to curb an upsurge in imports have been significantly tightened. From September, 1984, to March, 1992, Canada agreed to limit its steel exports to the United States. During this period, the United States forced Canada to establish the Canadian Steel Producers' Association, in 1986, to monitor Canadian Steel exports.

voluntary restraint agreement (VRA)
See VOLUNTARY EXPORT RESTRAINT.

Von Hayek, Friedrich August (1899-1992) The Austrian economist who won the Alfred Nobel Memorial Prize in Economic Science in 1974 with Gunnar MYRDAL for their "pioneering work in the theory of money and economic fluctuations and for their penetrating analysis of the interdependence of economic, social and institutional phenomena."

voting shares Common shares in a corporation that entitle their owner to vote at ANNUAL and SPECIAL MEETINGS. Each common share usually carries one vote; the owner of such shares can delegate votes to others by exercising PROXY. PREFERRED SHARES generally do not carry a vote, but if the company fails to pay a dividend on time, the owners of preferred shares may get voting rights. The owners of voting shares control the company; they elect the board of directors, which in turn is responsible for selecting the senior officers of the company and for supervising the policies, investments, and operations of the company. If the shareholders are dissatisfied with the way the company is being run, they can vote out the directors and install new directors. If a sufficient number agree, the shareholders of a company can also call a special meeting of shareholders to examine the company's affairs and policies and to seek remedies.

wage The amount of money earned by an individual during a work week, calculated by multiplying the number of hours worked by a fixed hourly rate of pay. Statistics Canada publishes detailed wage information in its monthly *Employment, Earnings, and Hours* (publication 72-002).

wage and price guidelines Proposals by government that business and labour help to fight inflation by voluntarily holding wage and price increases below a specified ceiling or in line with some specified standard, such as price increases not exceeding cost increases, or wage increases no greater than productivity increases plus some allowance for inflation. Experience in Canada and other countries shows that, while such guidelines may work for a short period of time, they can lead to mandatory controls. While there may be initial support for guidelines, there is usually a call for penalties or rollback powers if the guidelines are broken by major corporations or unions. Without some means of enforcement, public support for the guidelines can quickly disappear. Wage and price guidelines are one form of INCOMES POLICY. *See also* PRICE CONTROLS, PRICES AND INCOMES COMMISSION, ANTI-INFLATION BOARD, WARTIME PRICES AND TRADE BOARD.

wage-cost-push inflation Inflation resulting from wage increases that are not the result of a tight demand for labour due to full employment and overheating of the economy.

wage differential The difference in wage rates paid to different groups of workers. Differences can be based on different levels of skills, education, and responsibilities, differences in bargaining power of workers, such as union versus non-union workers, differences in the productivity of various industries, differences based on gender, or differences in living costs in different parts of the country. Wage differentials can be an important market signal to encourage mobility from low-wage sectors to high-wage sectors. However, changes in the actual wage differentials between different occupations and professions can also lead to wage-driven inflation as workers seek to restore differentials.

wage drift   The tendency for total wages to exceed basic wage rates set out in a collective agreement. This excess pay consists of overtime, special bonuses for productivity, and other incentives. The difference between the basic wage rate and what an employee gets is the wage drift. Since it is the total purchasing power in the economy that affects inflation rates, the existence of wage drift can undermine a policy of wage restraint.

wage-fund theory   The theory that the funds available to pay wages to workers are fixed by the level of savings or capital in society, and that wage increases can therefore only occur if there is a reduction in the number of workers or an increase in the level of savings. According to this theory, developed by JOHN STUART MILL and other CLASSICAL ECONOMISTS, the amount of money available for wages does not come from the sale of goods and services but from a pool of capital in the economy that depends on the rate of savings. In many respects, the wage-fund theory was a restatement of the subsistence theory of wages. *See also* the MARGINAL PRODUCTIVITY THEORY OF WAGES.

wage leadership   The influence that powerful unions can have on the general level of wage settlements in the economy by seeking and gaining a larger-than-average increase, or by refraining from seeking such an increase and settling for something more modest.

wage-price spiral   The inflation that occurs when employers grant significant wage increases and pass along the increased costs to consumers in the form of higher prices; they expect the government to keep the overall level of demand in the economy sufficiently high so that the more expensive products can be sold. Higher prices, in turn, lead to fresh demands for higher wages, which again are passed along to consumers in the form of higher prices; in this way the process repeats itself again and again, with wages and prices increasing by bigger steps each rung of the way up the inflation ladder. *See* COST-PUSH INFLATION. Some economists, such as John Kenneth GALBRAITH, argue that the wage-price spiral is a characteristic of economies dominated by large unions and corporations, since their power is such that, even during a recession, they can continue to increase wages and prices. Galbraith has used this argument to justify permanent controls on the wages and prices of large unions and big business. MONETARISTS argue that a wage-price spiral would not be possible if the government refused to finance the inflation, by holding down the growth in MONEY SUPPLY to the long-term real growth rate of the economy.

wage rate   The basic rate of pay for an employee for a specified period of work, such as an hour or a week. In addition to the basic wage rate, an employee may get extra pay based on output or a commission based on sales. Overtime wage rates are higher than basic wage rates: usually one and a half times the basic wage rate. Statistics Canada publishes a monthly report, *Employment, Earnings and Hours*, that sets out industry wage rates for a variety of industries and communities across Canada (publication 72-002). The Department of LABOUR also publishes information on wage settlements across Canada.

wage restraints   The restriction of wage increases within a specified limit, as part of a policy to help control COST-PUSH INFLATION. The restraint can be voluntary, with unions agreeing to some kind of wage ceiling; it may also consist of guidelines, with government policies to help enforce compliance, or of mandatory controls or a wage freeze.

wage settlements Monthly statistics published by the federal Department of LABOUR showing the average annual rate of pay increase in collective agreements covering 500 or more workers. The pay rate used is the base wage rate for the lowest-paid job classification consisting of a significant number of workers in a bargaining unit. All industries except construction are monitored. The statistics do not include COLA CLAUSES or the value of fringe benefits, but they do provide the single most important indicator of basic wage trends. Statistics are produced for all industries, for the public- and private-sector settlements, and by region. The Labour Canada monthly report is *The Wage Settlements Bulletin*.

walkout An illegal work stoppage, in which workers walk off the job in protest over some grievance, even though they are not legally allowed to do so when a collective agreement is in force.

Wall Street The financial heart of the United States, and the world's single most important financial market, located at the lower end of Manhattan Island in New York City. In a small concentrated area are located the New York and American stock exchanges, commodity exchanges, and the major stockbrokers, investment bankers, insurance companies, and trust companies. The name is also a synonym for U.S. capitalism. The Canadian equivalent is BAY STREET in downtown Toronto. In an earlier era, it was St. James Street in downtown Montreal.

Walras, Leon (1834-1910) A Swiss economist who is credited with being the father of mathematical economics, he wrote a mathematical equation to show that the total value of goods demanded in society always equals the total goods supplied, as well as showing how a change in the supply and demand for one good would effect all others. His mathematical model helped advance the study of GENERAL EQUILIBRIUM analysis. He was also one of the first economists to explain DIMINISHING MARGINAL UTILITY.

wants The need or desire for goods or services that are not free. A consumer may have the purchasing power to acquire a particular good or service, but only by not acquiring something else. The economic measures of wants is the willingness and ability of consumers to purchase desired goods or services.

War Exchange Conservation Act Federal legislation passed in December, 1940, allowing the Canadian government to clamp tight controls on imports in order to conserve foreign exchange, mainly U.S. dollars, for essential war needs. The legislation prohibited imports from hard-currency or non-sterling countries of non-essential items such as cigarettes and cigars, wines and spirits, fiction magazines and comics, perfume, china, glass, silverware, electrical appliances, sporting goods, cameras, toys, jewellery, private automobiles, and clothing. The legislation also restricted, through a system of licensing, imports such as tobacco, commercial vehicles, lumber products, and petroleum products. At the same time, imports from Britain were encouraged by means of a sweeping tariff cut, while exports to the United States and other hard-currency countries were encouraged by tax incentives.

warrant The right to buy common shares of a corporation at a specified price up to some specified future date when that right expires. Warrants are issued in two ways: 1. A stock-purchase warrant may be attached to a corporate bond or to preferred shares as a SWEETENER, to induce investors to accept a lower rate of interest on a bond or to pay a higher price for a preferred share. These warrants may be traded on a STOCK EXCHANGE or on the OVER-THE-COUNTER MARKET. 2. A warrant may automatically go with the common shares of some companies, and gives existing shareholders the right to buy a new issue of common shares in proportion to their existing holdings. This is a subscription warrant or right and can also be traded, if the holder does not want to exercise his warrant.

warranty A form of protection for consumers against unsatisfactory merchandise. The federal Sale of Goods Act gives consumers an implied warranty on whatever they buy; it says that a product must be fit for its purpose and be of merchantable quality, and that the person who sold it must be the legal owner. If these conditions are not met, the consumer is legally entitled to a refund or replacement. Some manufacturers also offer an expressed warranty, which comes with the product and gives certain guarantees on replacement, repairs, and durability. These warranties sometimes include a statement that consumers, by possession of the printed warranty, waive their rights to the implied warranty under the Sale of Goods Act. However, a number of provinces have passed laws stating that consumers cannot waive their rights of implied warranty; therefore, whether a product comes with an expressed warranty or not, consumers still have recourse because of the implied warranty under federal law.

Wartime Prices and Trade Board The principal agency created by the federal government in September, 1939, with the outbreak of the Second World War, to control prices and rents and to ensure adequate supplies and the equitable distribution of food, clothing, housing, and other necessities, through rationing, direct orders on production, or a ban on the production of certain goods. The board consisted of five senior civil servants, who supervised a broad array of subsidiary boards and commissions. A system of selective and usually temporary price controls existed until 1941, when a price ceiling or maximum price was set for all goods for the remainder of the war. Prices could not be increased above the level that prevailed in a base period from September 15 to October 11, 1941. Wage controls were introduced at the same time (*See also* WARTIME WAGES CONTROL ORDER.). Price increases were only granted when real financial need on an overall corporate basis could be shown.

The main problems the board had to deal with were to ensure that product quality was maintained and that black-market activities were thwarted. In 1942, the board banned the establishment of new businesses and new lines of business, except by permit. Prices for "new products" that appeared after 1941 were determined by board officials. Rent controls prevailed through most of the war for residential and commercial space, and special rules had to be introduced to protect tenants against eviction, from having to pay more than one month's rent in advance, from having to rent or buy furniture at artificial prices, or from having to make special payments as a condition of getting a lease. The board introduced a system of RATIONING to ensure the fair distribution of meat, tea, coffee, butter, sugar, and gasoline, administering the system through 600 local ration boards and the national Ration Administration. The board also used its power to order the production of certain essential products, such as some items of clothing, when industrial output was too low. The board was dissolved in 1951, its activities having been gradually phased out after the end of the Second World War.

Wartime Wages Control Order   A system of wage controls introduced during the Second World War to help prevent high inflation. The government followed a voluntary program until October, 1941, when a wage ceiling was imposed at the same time as across-the-board price controls (*see also* WARTIME PRICES AND TRADE BOARD). Wage rates were frozen at the wage level as of November 15, 1941, but cost-of-living adjustments were permitted. The program was administered by the National War Labour Board and regional war labour boards, which was advised by committees of employers and union leaders. The various boards could adjust wage rates to remove any "gross inequality or gross injustice." In December, 1943, cost-of-living bonuses were abolished and employers were forbidden to raise any individual's wage rate, except in cases of promotion or demotion, without approval from the Department of Labour, which took over administration from the War Labour Boards. The wage-control program was phased out after the Second World War.

wash sale   An attempt to manipulate the stock market through fictitious sales in which no change of ownership occurs. By increasing market activity in a particular share, stock-market manipulators can attract new buyers and raise the value of the shares they own. In transactions known as wash sales, manipulators create the impression of hectic activity by buying and selling shares to themselves. Such activities are illegal in Canada.

wasting asset   An asset with a declining life that becomes less valuable over time until it is finally exhausted. Oil and natural gas wells, mines, and timber stands are examples of wasting assets. In a BALANCE SHEET, wasting assets are usually listed under FIXED ASSETS. See also DEPLETION ALLOWANCE.

watered stock   The issue of new shares of a company below their asset value. This dilutes the value of existing shares, and so is unfair to existing shareholders. Although this practice was once not uncommon, it is now illegal in Canada.

Watkins Report   *See* TASK FORCE ON FOREIGN OWNERSHIP AND THE STRUCTURE OF CANADIAN INDUSTRY.

ways and means motion   A motion introduced at the end of the Minister of FINANCE's BUDGET SPEECH, moving that the budget measures be implemented. It is the motion, or set of motions, that is debated during the budget debate and voted on at the end of the debate. The Finance minister then introduces legislation, usually amendments to existing tax laws, to implement his or her specific tax and other changes. This legislation is then debated by the members of Parliament and senators and passed by Parliament. Parliament also debates supply motions, which are motions dealing with the spending of money.

weak market   A market in which there are more sellers than buyers and in which prices are falling.

wealth   The total of accumulated investments by an individual or a country that have a market value. This means that they can be sold. Under this definition, wealth includes not only tangible possessions, such as real estate, antiques, and shares and bonds, but also intangible assets, such as special skills or knowledge that can be used to generate income. Wealth is different from income. Wealth represents a stock of assets that can be used to generate income; the greater the wealth a person has at his or her disposal, the greater the income that person can generate. A person who does not inherit wealth, or acquire wealth in the form of skills and knowledge, has less chance of generating income and accumulating assets surplus to daily living needs. National wealth includes the wealth of all individuals and the public assets, such as resources, crown lands, and public buildings. Statistics Canada publishes an annual report on the wealth of Canadians in its NATIONAL BALANCE-SHEET ACCOUNTS (publication 13-214).

wealth distribution   The way in which the ownership of wealth is distributed among the various members of society. The usual approach is to show how much wealth is owned by each 20 percent of society. While statistics for Canada are sketchy, in Western societies generally there tends to be much greater inequality in the distribution of wealth than in the distribution of income. Inequalities in the distribution of wealth give some Canadians much greater command over resources than other Canadians have. Inequalities of wealth also help to explain great disparities in income. In the absence of offsetting tax policies, inequalities in the distribution of wealth may increase over time, due to inheritance and capital gains. Hence, taxes such as CAPITAL-GAINS TAXES, ESTATE TAXES, GIFT TAXES, and SUCCESSION DUTIES are devices to reduce huge concentrations of wealth and power. While Statistics Canada publishes an annual survey on *Income Distributions by Size in Canada* (publication 13-207), it has published no comparable data on wealth distribution.

wealth tax   A tax that is levied upon what a person owns, rather than what he receives as income. Estate and gift taxes and succession duties are forms of wealth tax. In recent years, there has been a growing interest in a wealth tax or capital levy, the argument being that, if the tax system is truly to be based on the ABILITY-TO-PAY PRINCIPLE, then

a person's wealth should also be taken into account. The taxation of CAPITAL GAINS at death, based on deemed realization, is one form of wealth tax.

wear and tear   An accounting term used to describe the gradual decline in value of an asset, such as a machine or truck, that results from its normal use. *See* DEPRECIATION.

weighted average   A method of averaging used in statistics to take into account the relative importance of the different numbers being averaged. Each of the numbers to be averaged is multiplied by another number called a weight, which represents its relative importance. The results are then added, to yield the weighted average. The technique is used, for example, in calculating the CONSUMER PRICE INDEX, where, for example, an increase in the cost of food is given a much larger weight than an increase in the cost of personal recreation, since food is a much bigger portion of the typical consumer's shopping basket. *See also* TRADE-WEIGHTED EXCHANGE RATE.

welfare   Public support for the needy, disadvantaged, and handicapped. It includes INCOME-MAINTENANCE PROGRAMS, subsidized housing, free medical and dental care, veterans' allowances, nursing-home care, and assistance for Native peoples.

welfare economics   The branch of economics that deals with economic performance in terms of ethical standards or social values. It does not accept the outcome of market forces as the only choice facing a society; instead, it intervenes against market forces or seeks to redirect them to achieve desired outcomes. These may include reducing disparities in wealth and income, the adoption of the goal of SUSTAINABLE DEVELOPMENT, the improvement of job opportunities and career advancement for women and minorities, offsetting the harmful side effects of market forces, such as the spread of MONOPOLIES, or more generally seeking ways to improve the well-being of the ordinary citizen. In welfare economics, the just society is one in which human welfare is maximized. Welfare economics is also concerned with the social costs of economic activity — of occupational disease and pollution, for example. The problem is that different citizens have different ideas on what constitutes their welfare. As a result, economists are still divided over the best way to measure the maximization of welfare. The PARETO OPTIMUM defined an increase in total welfare as a situation in which some people were able to be made better off without anybody else being made worse off.

welfare state　A society that uses the power of the state to ensure at least a minimum standard of living for all of its citizens by redistributing income. Most democratic societies operate some kind of welfare state. The government, through pensions, income-maintenance programs, subsidized housing, universal medical care, free education, unemployment insurance, progressive taxation, aid for marginal farmers, and other such measures, tries to make sure that every citizen is able to enjoy a share in the wealth and output of society. Canada's welfare state was largely developed after the Second World War and was largely in place by the start of the 1970s.

wellhead price　The price of oil as it comes from the well at the producer end of the distribution system. It is the price established from a delivery point in the oil-production system. The price paid for oil elsewhere in the country or in foreign markets is the wellhead price plus pipeline distribution costs to the destination point. *See also* CITY-GATE PRICE.

Western Accord　An agreement signed on March 28, 1985, by the federal, Alberta, British Columbia, and Saskatchewan governments to deregulate oil and gas markets, to remove or phase out a number of federal oil and gas industry taxes and charges, and to set new rules for federal oil and gas policy in western Canada. The agreement, when fully implemented, also meant a significant transfer of resources from the federal government to the oil and gas industry. The agreement effectively dismantled the NATIONAL ENERGY PROGRAM. In addition to shifting from a regulated framework for oil and gas prices to a market-sensitive system, the accord eliminated the Petroleum and Gas Revenue Tax, the Petroleum Compensation Charge, and the Canadian Ownership Special Charge. The role of the NATIONAL ENERGY BOARD was also reduced in regulating short-term oil exports and allocation crude among eastern Canada refineries, while the role of the ALBERTA PETROLEUM MARKETING COMMISSION was also reduced (it would no longer act as the selling agent for oil belonging to the oil companies in Alberta). The producing provinces retained their power to control production of oil and gas, to ensure good conservation practices, or in the event of market constraints, to "ensure equitable sharing of production." If supplies of oil or petroleum products to Canadian consumers are "significantly jeopardized," the accord said the federal government, after consultation with the western provinces, will "restrict exports to the extent it considers necessary to ensure adequate supplies to Canadians." Likewise, in the event of a strong increase in international oil prices, with potential negative effects in Canada, the federal government, after consulting with the western provinces, "will take appropriate measures to protect Canadian interests." The Petroleum Incentives Program, which provided exploration and development subsidies that favoured Canadian-controlled companies, was to be ended a year after the signing of the accord. The federal government agreed that in future, "tax-based incentives designed to stimulate investment in Canada's oil and gas industry shall be of general application to the industry without discrimination as to location of activity in question or as to ownership and control." The four governments agreed that the net benefit from changes resulting from the Western Accord would "flow through to the industry." At the same time, the accord said, the phase out of federal oil and gas industry taxes and charges was necessary to "enhance the producing industry's capability to reinvest in the development of new oil and gas resources for all Canadians. Canadian security of supply requires that a high level of reinvestment occur. The federal and provincial governments expect such reinvestment will occur and will pursue an active program of monitoring industry reinvestment to ensure that Canada's energy security objectives are realized."

Western Economic Diversification Canada A federal department that was established in 1988 to promote the development of western Canada's economy. Launched with a $1.2 billion fund, the department provides grants or subsidies to western Canadian companies to develop new products, services, and technologies, to replace imports with local production, and to improve productivity and exports. The fund also supports other programs, such as soil conservation, biotechnology research for agriculture, the development of new markets for western Canadian coal, the funding of forestry research, the development of a strategy for tourism, the support for cultural industries such as film production and book publishing, and measures to increase container activity in West Coast ports and to improve the grain-transportation sys-

tem. It is based in Edmonton.

Western Economic Opportunities Conference (WEOC) A conference of the federal government and the four western provinces of British Columbia, Alberta, Saskatchewan, and Manitoba, planned to stimulate and broaden the economic and industrial base of western Canada, held in July, 1973, in Calgary. The federal government published background papers on industrial and trade development, capital financing and financial institutions, mineral-resource development, agriculture, transportation, and regional development opportunities. For their part, the western premiers published four position papers, on economic and industrial development opportunities, transportation, agriculture, and regional financial institutions. The western provinces sought decentralized offices for the then Department of Regional Economic Expansion, increased federal purchasing in western Canada, selective tariff changes, more funding for industrial development in western Canada, increased agricultural development, the right for provincial governments to own shares in chartered banks, federal funding for certain railway fixed costs so that freight rates could be reduced, improved port facilities at Prince Rupert, British Columbia, and Churchill, Manitoba, and increased efforts to promote the development of petrochemicals, steel, and transportation-equipment industries in western Canada, thus diversifying its industrial base. The federal government agreed to a greater decentralization of its regional development offices, more government purchasing from suppliers in western Canada, the release to the provincial governments of previously confidential information on freight rates, amendments to the BANK ACT to permit the provinces to be shareholders in chartered banks, additional funding for northern transportation, and financing to improve port facilities at Prince Rupert.

Western Grain Stabilization Plan   A form of federal assistance to provide Prairie grain producers with protection against drops in income due to poor conditions in international markets, sharp rises in production costs, and other developments beyond the control of farmers or governments. Under the plan, participating farmers and the federal government contributed to the Western Grain Stabilization Fund. The farmers' levy was 2 percent of sales, to a maximum of $25,000 a year. Support was paid to prevent the net cash flow — the difference between production costs and sales revenues — from falling below the average of the five previous years. The last payment under the program was made in January, 1991.

Western Premiers' Conference   An annual conference of the premiers of Manitoba, Saskatchewan, Alberta, and British Columbia, to discuss common economic, social, and other problems. The four premiers seek out a common ground for representation to the federal government in such matters as freight rates, tariffs, and grain handling. They also examine ways in which they can co-ordinate their policies with one another. The four western premiers have been holding such an annual conference since 1973; prior to that, the three Prairie premiers met usually through the PRAIRIE ECONOMIC CONFERENCE.

western provinces   Manitoba, Saskatchewan, Alberta, and British Columbia.

wheat pool   A system of country and terminal grain elevators co-operatively owned by farmers. The major pools are the Saskatchewan Wheat Pool, which has branched out to operate fertilizer, seed, and various other business activities, the Alberta Wheat Pool, Manitoba Pool Elevators, and the United Grain Growers.

white-collar crime   Crime committed by fraud or deceit, as distinguished from violent crime. Such crime is called white-collar crime because much of it takes place in the business world. It can range from embezzlement within a corporation and stock manipulation, to fraudulent bankruptcy, the use of forged documents to obtain credit or possession of property, TAX EVASION, and so-called computer crimes.

white-collar workers   A general term used to describe those who work in offices or in other areas where the principle activities are the handling of paper and dealing in information-related activities, as opposed to BLUE-COLLAR WORKERS, who work directly in the production of goods.

white knight   An investor who rescues a corporation from an unfriendly takeover by acquiring a large enough position to prevent a hostile investor from acquiring sufficient shares to gain control.

white paper   A statement of government intentions or policies. It may also include draft legislation. White papers are often used by a government to declare its policies and to get public reaction before the government presents final legislation to Parliament or to a provincial legislature. Publication of draft legislation in a white paper enables a government to spot possible flaws or unintended results and thus present better legislation to Parliament. *See also* GREEN PAPER, ROYAL COMMISSION, TASK FORCE.

White Paper on Employment and Income   A federal blueprint for post-war conversion of the Canadian economy to a peacetime footing under conditions of full employment and stable prices; the white paper was presented to Parliament by the Minister of RECONSTRUCTION in April, 1945. It was a statement of the objectives and plans of the Department of Reconstruction, and proposed to combine the demobilization of the armed forces and the winding up of the war industry with the task of rebuilding the Canadian economy, without reverting to the depressed economic conditions of the 1930s. The white paper calculated that 900,000 more jobs would be needed than existed in 1939, with a growth of 60,000 a year after that. It put primary emphasis on policies to boost private industry, stimulate housing construction, modernize agriculture, and increase consumer spending. The government said that it would seek a reciprocal reduction in world trade barriers, plus international agreements to promote stability in international food and raw-materials markets, which would help boost exports.

To increase private investment and convert wartime industries to peacetime uses, taxes were to be cut and interest rates held at a low level. Special lending programs for business and agriculture were also expected to help. Housing construction was expected to surge, since housing construction had been far too low for the previous 15 years. Consumer spending was to be encouraged through income-maintenance programs, such as unemployment insurance and family allowances, and through subsidies to farmers and fishermen to support farm and fishery prices. The government indicated that it was ready to introduce contributory old-age pensions and national health insurance, as soon as agreement could be reached with the provinces. The white paper emphasized that public-investment spending could become a permanent method of creating jobs in post-war Canada, and proposed two immediate steps: 1. the advance planning of a shelf of necessary or desirable projects that could be carried out when jobs were needed; and 2. a federal-provincial spending policy, to develop Canada's hydro-electric, forestry, and mining industries. The white paper also called for a significant increase in research and development, to raise the technical level of Canadian industry.

Other measures proposed to increase Canada's post-war economic performance included increased spending on labour mobility and retraining. The government, through the white paper, also promised a relaxation of wartime controls on prices, supplies, foreign exchange, and other restrictions, as soon as they could be lifted without triggering inflation. Most important, the white paper made it clear that the lesson of the DEPRESSION had been learned; it adopted KEYNESIAN ECONOMICS and promised that, when unemployment threatened, the government would run budgetary deficits and increase the national debt so that employment and income goals could be achieved. Conversely, the white paper said, in times of full employment and high levels of income, budget plans would call for a surplus.

White Paper on Foreign Policy   A federal white paper published in June, 1970, after a two-year review of Canadian foreign-policy interests. Six major themes were emphasized: sovereignty and independence; peace and security; social justice; quality of life; a harmonious natural environment; and economic growth. The three top priorities, the white paper said, were policies related to economic growth, social justice, and quality of life, with much more emphasis than in the past on a foreign policy that would improve Canadian economic performance. This meant stronger efforts to increase Canadian trade, and to keep up to date "on such key matters as discoveries in science and technology, management of energies and resources, significant trends in world trade and finance, policies of major trading countries and blocs, and activities of multinational corporations."

Greater emphasis on social justice meant that Canada would increase its foreign aid, while the priority placed on quality of life meant that Canada would play a larger role in international environmental-protection activities, increase its cultural exchanges, and pay more attention to such matters as curbing the international flow of drugs and finding more effective measures to combat terrorism. There was no direct discussion of Canada-U.S. relations in the white paper, but the discussion of sovereignty and independence was assumed to include the need to strengthen a Canadian identity, distinct from that of the United States. The white paper consisted of six booklets on policies concerning Europe, Latin America, the Pacific, the United Nations, international development, and a general booklet entitled *Foreign Policy for Canadians*. *See also* THIRD OPTION.

wholesale banking   The banking business that is conducted between banks and other financial institutions and major corporations. *See also* RETAIL BANKING.

wholesale price   The price paid by a middleman or wholesaler, who buys goods in large quantities from domestic or foreign manufacturers and resells them in smaller quantities to retailers.

wholesale trade   Trade conducted by distribution or supplier companies that serve retailers and non-retailer markets such as institutions and industrial and commercial users. Statistics Canada publishes a monthly report on wholesale trade (publication 63-008). It provides sales, inventory, and other information on nine wholesale groups: food, beverage, dairy, and tobacco products; apparel and dry goods; household goods; motor vehicles, parts, and accessories; metals, hardware, plumbing and heating equipment, and supplies; lumber and building materials; farm machinery, equipment, and supplies; other machinery, equipment, and supplies; and other products. *See also* RETAIL TRADE.

wholesaler   A middleman who buys products from importers, manufacturers, and other wholesalers and resells them to retailers, other wholesalers, industrial and commercial users, and foreign markets, thus playing an indispensable role in the production-distribution system. The existence of an active wholesaler network means that manufacturers do not have to maintain their own distribution systems.

wholly owned subsidiary   A subsidiary that is 100 percent owned by a parent company. *See also* SUBSIDIARY.

widely held   A company that has no dominant or controlling shareholder, with ownership of its shares spread among a large number of different owners. Under the BANK ACT, the seven Schedule I banks, Canada's largest, must be widely held, which means that no shareholder may own more than 10 percent of the outstanding shares.

wildcat   Exploration drilling that is undertaken without any useful knowledge of what may be found in the rock formation being drilled.

wildcat strike   An illegal strike that takes place without the approval of union leaders — and perhaps even over their objections — and without observance of the various steps leading up to a legal strike. A wildcat strike may reflect the anger of union members at the bargaining stance of management, but sometimes it can be a signal from union members to their own leadership that they do not like the way that union affairs are being handled. Most wildcat strikes last only for a few hours or days.

will   A legal document made by an individual, setting out the ways in which assets shall be disposed of after death and naming someone, an executor, who is to make sure that the terms of the will are carried out and to administer the estate. When a person dies without making a will — dies, in other words, INTESTATE — a court must appoint someone to administer the estate and to dispose of the assets according to procedures set out in provincial laws. Before the terms of a will can be carried out, it must go through PROBATE, to ensure it represents the last will and testament of the individual.

windfall profit A sudden and unexpected increase in profits or in the value of land, natural resources, and other assets. The gain is not due to anything the owner of the business or asset has done; it is caused by the actions of other people. For example, oil companies in Canada were faced with the prospect of a windfall gain on their Canadian oil-resources reserves when the ORGANIZATION OF PETRO-LEUM EXPORTING COUNTRIES quadrupled the world price of oil in the 1973-1974 period. They did not receive the full windfall gain, however, because the provincial governments sharply increased their royalty charges, while the federal government delayed the introduction of world prices in Canada. A person who owns a piece of land along a subway route, especially if it is nearby a subway station, may enjoy a windfall profit on the sale of the land. Economists and policy makers question whether the owner should be entitled to the full benefit of a windfall gain. *See also* ECONOMIC RENT, QUASI-RENT.

Windfall Mines and Oils affair A July, 1964, scandal on the Toronto Stock Exchange (TSE) that resulted in significant changes in Ontario securities legislation, and similar changes subsequently in other provinces. The principal shareholders of Windfall Mines and Oils Limited, Mrs. Viola MacMillan and her husband, George MacMillan, made misleading statements about allegedly rich

copper finds where none existed. Rumours sent the price of Windfall spiralling, while Mrs. MacMillan sold all of her family's shares and sold short shares she did not own. The stock moved from 56 cents to $6.50; when Windfall issued a subsequent statement saying that there was no ore, it fell to 35 cents.

The TSE and the Ontario Securities Commission were both sharply criticized in a judicial inquiry, which reported in October, 1965. Previously, a director of the Ontario Securities Commission had been forced to resign. The report said that the MacMillans had deliberately misled the public, while making a personal profit of $1,455,928. The report placed full blame on the TSE for permitting trading to continue when it should have been stopped, and called for a ban on the PRIMARY DISTRIBUTION of shares on the TSE, a strengthening of the Ontario Securities Commission, and the creation of a national body to regulate stock exchanges in Canada. The TSE fined a member firm $1,000 for accommodating trading in the sale of Windfall shares and reprimanded two others. Subsequently, the TSE took a number of other steps to reassure the public, introducing tighter policies for stockbroker firms, higher educational requirements for floor traders, a suspension and delisting policy for inactive oil and mining companies with less than $25,000 in net liquid assets, and tougher rules to deal with deceptive practices by stockbrokers and to bar WASH SALES. In 1966, a new Ontario Securities Act was passed, requiring monthly publication of INSIDER REPORTS, fuller disclosure in company annual reports, including year-to-year comparative statistics and a statement of SOURCE AND DISPOSITION OF FUNDS, new rules on takeover bids, changes in prospectus requirements to give investors more information, and improved shareholder PROXY forms, giving shareholders more information on how management intended to use the proxies. Mr. and Mrs. MacMillan and John Campbell, a securities-commission official, were charged. Mrs. MacMillan was convicted of wash trading and sentenced to nine months in jail in 1968, but was released on probation after nine weeks. She and her husband, along with Mr. Campbell, were acquitted on fraud charges.

winding up   The legal process of dissolving an incorporated or limited company.

Winnipeg Commodity Exchange (WCE) The only agricultural commodities exchange in Canada. The main items traded are canola, flaxseed, domestic feed barley and wheat, rye, and oats.

The exchange was founded in 1887 and, for a period before World War Two, it was the world's most important grain exchange; since then, the centre of the grain trade has shifted to Chicago. In 1972, it changed its name from Winnipeg Grain and Produce Exchange to Winnipeg Commodity Exchange, reflecting its ambitions as a commodities exchange and futures market, although futures had been traded at the exchange since 1904. Its policies are set out and administered by a board of governors elected from its more than 300 member brokers and more than 100 associate companies, such as grain shippers and merchants, from around the world.

Winnipeg General Strike   A general strike called in Winnipeg in 1919 by the One Big Union (OBU), a federation of unions in Western Canada. The OBU was a radical labour federation that drew many of its ideas from the British labour movement; it believed in the inevitability of class struggle and in the need for workers to advance their demands through direct action. The general strike was sparked when the building and metals trades went on a city-wide strike, after their employers had refused to grant wage increases or to recognize their union. The Winnipeg Trades and Labour Council sought the advice of the OBU, which called a general strike among all

unions in Winnipeg until union demands for recognition, wage increases, and the reinstatement of all striking workers were met. Confrontation quickly developed, as city officials feared that the OBU would attempt to seize control. The leaders of the union were arrested on charges of inciting a revolution. However, the strike was subsequently called off, after the employers agreed to collective bargaining and the government threatened to take even tougher steps to deal with the union.

The strike began on May 1, 1919, with sympathy strikes running until June 26, 1919. The most serious disturbance came on June 21, when one striker was killed and 30 other persons, including 16 policemen, were injured, after the Riot Act was read by the mayor of Winnipeg. Troops armed with machine guns were also brought into the city after crowds got out of control.

winter-works program   A federal program, launched in the winter of 1958-1959, to create winter jobs by paying half the payroll costs of a municipality, its contractors, or subcontractors, on approved municipal projects. The program was ended in fiscal year 1963-1964. *See also* MUNICIPAL DEVELOPMENT AND LOAN FUND.

withholding tax   1. A tax deducted at source. The best example is the income tax collected by employers from the pay cheques of their employees and forwarded to the appropriate tax authorities. **2.** A tax levied by the federal government on interest and dividend payments, pensions, royalties, and other payments to non-residents; the tax is imposed on the recipient of the interest and dividend payments. The tax rate is 25 percent but, in most instances, is reduced to 15 percent on portfolio investment and 10 percent on direct investment as part of a tax treaty; this means, for example, that non-residents receive 85 percent of the dividends and interest that they earn on their Canadian investments. The withholding tax can be altered to help achieve economic-policy goals. For example, since June 1975, the federal government has suspended the withholding tax on interest payments on new long-term corporate bonds sold to non-residents to make it easier for Canadian corporations to borrow abroad. There is also an exemption for interest on government bonds.

work in progress   A term used in accounting to describe products that are at some uncompleted stage of production during the accounting period. The items are usually included with INVENTORIES in a company's BALANCE SHEET.

work permit   A permit issued by the CANADA EMPLOYMENT AND IMMIGRATION COMMISSION that allows a non-resident to take a temporary job in Canada. Anyone who is neither a Canadian citizen nor a landed immigrant has to get a work permit. The permit states the name of the employer, describes the job, indicates the location of the job, and gives an expiry date; generally speaking, the maximum length of a work permit is one year, but it can be renewed. Canada has had a formal system of work permits since 1973. There are some exemptions, such as foreign diplomats and news correspondents and members of the clergy. Under the CANADA-UNITED STATES FREE TRADE AGREEMENT and the NORTH AMERICAN FREE TRADE AGREEMENT, professionals and other service-industry workers in each of the countries has certain rights to work in each of the other countries.

work sharing   **1.** A reduction in the work week of all employees in a firm, to prevent the loss of jobs when there is insufficient business to keep everyone fully employed. A firm may, for example, put all of its employees on a three-day week, so as to spread the work around and avoid layoffs. **2.** The shar-

ing of the same job by two or more people who alternate periods of work. For example, two mothers raising young children could alternate each week to perform the same job.

work to rule   A tactic by a union to slow work down that stops short of bringing work to a complete halt. Workers do this by following, to the smallest detail, every work rule laid down by management. This, for example, could involve more shutdowns of machinery to check parts and much more time than usual spent checking out the safety of equipment before it is turned on, or workers simply following every step in a labour contract meticulously. By using such tactics, union members are able to frustrate management and to reduce production or service sharply, yet still continue to earn their full pay.

work week   The average number of hours worked in a week by non-government employees. STATISTICS CANADA collects information every month from all employers of 20 or more people on the number of persons employed, full- or part-time, and the number of hours worked by each person. In addition to government employees, members of religious organizations, farm workers, fishermen, hospital workers, teachers, professors, and health and welfare workers are excluded. Hours worked include paid holidays, vacations, and overtime. Short-term change can indicate whether economic activity is picking up or slowing down; in a recovery, for example, there will be more overtime and part-time workers will put in longer hours. In the long run, the figures show a decline in the average work week. In 1952, the average manufacturing work week was 43.15 hours; by 1992 it was 38.3 hours. Statistics Canada publishes the monthly report, *Employment, Earnings and Hours* (publication 72-002).

worker participation A role for employees in the decision-making process of a firm. With the introduction of TOTAL QUALITY MANAGEMENT and QUALITY CIRCLES, and other forms of workplace restructuring resulting from new systems of technology, workers are getting to play a greater role in the decision-making process. However, Canadian companies reject European-style systems where employees by law have a specified number of seats on a board of directors or where work councils are established within companies, with employer and employee representation, to exchange information and to reach decisions affecting production and product quality. *See also* INDUSTRIAL DEMOCRACY.

worker's compensation A form of income support for workers and their families in the event of injury or death on the job. Help is also provided in the form of medical and rehabilitation assistance. The cost of worker's-compensation assistance is borne by employers, who are assessed according to the degree of risk in their industry.

The programs are run by the provincial governments, and date back to 1915, when Ontario became the first province to introduce legislation. Until then, injured workers and their families had to sue employers for financial compensation for injuries or disease caused by an employer's negligence. This meant that many workers never received compensation because they could not afford the costs of going to court; if they could, they might have to wait several years for a settlement.

Under worker's-compensation laws, workers cannot sue their employers but are assured of compensation for themselves and their families. Benefits range from up to 75 percent of average weekly earnings (with some adjustment for inflation) in cases of complete disability, to much less for partial disability, depending on the nature of the

handicap. More than 90 percent of Canadian workers are covered by worker's compensation. Worker's-compensation boards administer the funds, and determine which workers qualify for assistance and how much they shall get.

working capital The funds available for carrying on the activities of a business after an allowance is made for bills that have to be paid within the year. Working capital is calculated by deducting the current liabilities from the current assets of a firm, and indicates a company's ability to pay its short-term debts. The excess of current assets is the working capital. Different industries have different working-capital requirements; those with rapid turnover have less need than those in, say, the capital-goods industry, where turnover may be slow.

working conditions The environment in which a person works; federal and provincial labour laws and collective-bargaining agreements play a large role in defining working conditions. The concerns range from job safety and health hazards to lunch and rest breaks, hours of work, vacations with pay, and the physical environment of the workplace.

working control Owning sufficient voting shares of a company to exercise control over its management and policies. Working control is usually 51 per cent but, in a major corporation, with widely held ownership of its shares, working control can be much less than 51 percent.

Working Party Three (WP3) A small but important committee of officials from central banks and finance ministries of key members of the ORGANIZATION FOR ECONOMIC CO-OPERATION AND DEVELOPMENT (OECD), that analyzes short-term BALANCE-OF-PAYMENTS problems on a regular basis. The group, which was formed in 1961 when the United States realized that it had to do something about its emerging balance-of-payments problems, reports to the Economic Policy Committee of the OECD, a committee of finance ministers from OECD countries. The members of WP3 include Canada, Britain, France, Germany, Italy, Japan, the Netherlands, Sweden, Switzerland, and the United States. *See also* GROUP OF TEN.

working poor People who work full time but who do not earn enough to keep themselves above the POVERTY LINE. The 1973 federal Working Paper on Social Security in Canada proposed a number of measures to boost the income of the working poor. The one measure that was adopted was the boost in the family allowance, from an average of $7.21 per child to $20 per child. Since then the family allowance was reinforced with a child tax credit for lower-income families, and in 1993, the system was replaced by a CHILD BENEFIT, which eliminated the family allowance and targeted the entire benefit to lower-income families. When the GOODS AND SERVICES TAX was introduced on January 1, 1991, a refundable tax was paid to lower-income families. Governments have also tried to help the working poor by designing the income-tax system so that low-income Canadians do not have to pay.

World Bank A group of institutions established to promote long-term economic growth and to reduce poverty in DEVELOPING COUNTRIES. Affiliated with the UNITED NATIONS, the World Bank, or International Bank for Reconstruction and Development, was conceived at the July, 1944, UNITED NATIONS MONETARY AND FINANCIAL CONFERENCE, held in Bretton Woods, New Hampshire. It was expected that many countries would lack the necessary foreign exchange for reconstruction and development following the Second World War and would not be sufficiently creditworthy to raise all the funds they needed through commercial borrowing. With an equity base from the share capital provided by countries (countries pay in only a small portion of the value of their shares with the rest "on call" should the bank be unable to pay its creditors) in proportion to the size of their economies, the World Bank borrows in world financial markets and relends the money to qualifying borrowers. With its triple A credit rating, the World Bank is able to borrow more cheaply than its borrowing member countries and to relend at a floating rate determined by its own cost of borrowing, which means at attractive interest rates. The World Bank opened for business on June 25, 1946. Canada was one of the original shareholders. Before a country can become a member of the World Bank, it must be a member of the INTERNATIONAL MONETARY FUND. Both institutions are based in Washington.

The World Bank provides both project loans and, since 1980, loans to support institutional and policy reforms, such as adjustment to trade liberalization or the adoption of market-based pricing. While much of the bank's early lending was to countries devastated by war, such as Germany and Japan, today its lending is focused on the developing countries and financing projects there that contribute to economic growth and poverty reduction. Projects include irrigation, roads, power plants, schools, water and sewage systems, and ports, as well as funding of financial institutions to fund economic development, such as risk capital for new enterprises, along with funding for health and education programs, technical training, and research and development. Since the late 1980s, the World Bank has played an important role in assisting the former Communist countries of Eastern Europe and Russia and the other republics of the former Soviet Union to rebuild their economies and make the transition to market economies. Loan decisions are approved by the World Bank's Board of Executive Directors and are supposed to be based on economic rather than political criteria, although the United States has used its voting power to block loans to countries with which it has disputes. The World Bank, whose fiscal year runs from July 1 to June 30, has made a profit in every year since 1947; in 1992, it reported a profit of US$1.7 billion, and only 2.1 percent of its loans were overdue by more than six months. The bank does not reschedule its loans. The World Bank gets policy direction from the DEVELOPMENT COMMITTEE, a committee of 22 finance ministers representative of the World Bank's membership of 167 countries. In its 1988 capital increase, Canada contributed three percent.

In 1956, a separate World Bank institution, the International Finance Corporation (IFC), was spun off to promote private enterprise in developing countries. It does this by making equity investments in developing-country enterprises and by helping to tap additional loan and equity financing in international markets. It is the largest single source of private-sector financing in developing countries; it can buy up to 35 percent of the equity of a company, but it is never the single largest shareholder and does not participate in management. The IFC also helps finance the creation of new companies as well as funding the expansion of companies. It also participates in the development of investment banks, venture-capital companies, and insurance companies in the developing world. The IFC raises its capital on world financial markets. Canada is a shareholder.

Another World Bank affiliate, the International Development Association (IDA), was established in 1960 to help finance development in the world's poorest countries. Qualifying countries have per capita incomes of less than US$765. In 1992, some 58 countries out of IDA's 144 members qualified as borrowers.

IDA provides interest-free credits to qualified borrowers, with credits extended for 35 to 40 years, with a grace period of 10 years during which no principal has to be repaid. Because IDA charges no interest, it cannot be funded by commercial borrowing. Instead, donor countries provide a replenishment every three years; 34 countries contributed to the 10th replenishment, providing about US$18 billion, including about US$720 million from Canada, covering the 1993-96 period. Much of the IDA lending is for economic adjustment as poor countries struggle to adjust to a market-based world economy. IDA funding helps finance public-sector reform, such as reforming public enterprises, making social services more accessible to the poor, providing water, electricity, transportation and telecommunications systems, agriculture development, urban development, and strengthening public finances. IDA accounts for 25 percent of all World Bank lending. IDA credits are interest-free and are repaid over a 35- to 40-year period.

A third World Bank affiliate, the Multilateral Investment Guarantee Agency (MIGA) was established in 1988 to encourage the flow of foreign direct investment to developing countries. It does this by insuring investments against non-commercial risks or political risks and by providing promotional and other advisory help to developing countries anxious to attract foreign investment. MIGA insures against currency inconvertibility, expropriation, war and civil disturbance, and breach of contract. The current insurance limit is US$50 million per project. Canada is a member. The World Bank, since 1965, has also operated the International Centre for the Settlement of Investment Disputes where a foreign government is a party to a dispute. The World Bank also administers the GLOBAL ENVIRONMENT FACILITY, which was established in 1990 on a three-year pilot basis to administer a US$1.3 billion fund to help developing countries to contribute to the solution of global environmental problems. Canada contributed US$20 million or 2 percent. Funding is available to developing-country projects to reduce global warming, protect international waters, preserve biological diversity, and prevent further depletion of the ozone layer.

World Economic Conference   An international conference held in London from June 12-27, 1933, in an attempt to halt the world depression and end the protectionist trade and banking policies that were only making a grave economic situation worse. The draft agenda proposed the restoration of the gold standard, along with tariff reductions and other forms of international economic co-operation. The conference followed British, French, and U.S. discussions, and was organized under the League of Nations as the International Conference on Monetary and Economic Questions. The conference attracted leaders from all over the world, including Prime Minister R.B. Bennett of Canada.

The conference was dealt a death blow by U.S. President Franklin Roosevelt, who vetoed a conference plan to stabilize major international currencies, even though all of his senior aides supported it. With the U.S. rejection of the plan for currency stabilization being read as a signal that the United States was not prepared to exercise international economic leadership, the conference lost its momentum. It failed to reach any agreement of importance on international trade or currency arrangements that would have ended the BEGGAR-THY-NEIGHBOUR POLICIES of many countries, which were making the Depression worse and preventing economic recovery. Following the collapse of the conference, the various trade and currency blocs reverted to their former practices.

World Food Conference   A UNITED NATIONS conference held in Rome, in November, 1974, to draft a set of policies to increase world food supplies and improve distribution systems, so as to avert future famines and end malnutrition in the DEVELOPING COUNTRIES. The conference was held against a backdrop of regional crop failures between 1972 and 1974, sharply rising food prices, and fears of future shortages. Canada was one of the participants. Some 20 policies were adopted, and two new bodies, the WORLD FOOD COUNCIL and the INTERNATIONAL FUND FOR AGRICULTURAL DEVELOPMENT, were created as a result.

World Food Council   A UNITED NATIONS (UN) body created in 1974, following the WORLD FOOD CONFERENCE, that brings together agriculture and development ministers from 36 countries, including Canada, to review the world food situation and discuss initiatives to solve problems of world food production and security, as well as to monitor food-aid programs, in order to eliminate hunger and malnutrition. According to the council, the number of hungry and malnourished people in the world is approaching 600 million, with nutritional diseases a major cause of suffering and death. In the view of the council, hunger is largely an economic issue that has more to do with poverty than food scarcity. It has attempted to persuade the DEVELOPING COUNTRIES to allocate more of their development resources to agriculture and established an International Emergency Food Reserve in 1980, which is administered by the World Food Program, a separate UN initiative launched in 1961. It was instrumental in the establishment of the INTERNATIONAL FUND FOR AGRICULTURAL DEVELOPMENT (IFAD) in 1977, which was launched with US$1 billion and has since been replenished several times. In 1980, it facilitated the Food Aid Convention, which established 7.6 million tons as the absolute minimum annual level of food aid required by food-deficient countries; that same year it promoted with other UN agencies the creation of a food-credit facility at the INTERNATIONAL MONETARY FUND to help countries finance food imports in times of emergency or natural disaster. The council works closely with the FOOD AND AGRICULTURE ORGANIZATION. The IFAD lends money, mainly on highly concessional terms, to raise agricultural production. It is based in Rome.

World Health Organization (WHO) A UNITED NATIONS agency, established in 1948 and based in Geneva, whose mandate is to improve health conditions worldwide and to raise health standards. In 1977, it adopted its "Health for All by the Year 2000" as its priority goal. The strategy, based on primary health care, has eight key elements: public education on health problems; adequate food supply and nutrition; safe water and sanitation; maternal and child health care, including family planning; immunization against major infectious diseases; prevention and control of local diseases; appropriate treatment of common diseases and injuries; and provision of essential drugs. Its specific activities include measures to prevent the spread of disease, emergency help to deal with health problems in areas struck by natural disasters, the establishment of safe and uniform standards for drugs, health research, the collection of statistics, and the improvement of health-care services in DEVELOPING COUNTRIES. The agency also supports a variety of research programs into tropical diseases and co-ordinates global education and research into acquired immune deficiency syndrome, or AIDS. Canada is an active member.

World Intellectual Property Organization (WIPO) A specialized UNITED NATIONS agency created in 1974 to protect patents, copyrights, trademarks, and other forms of INTELLECTUAL PROPERTY through international agreements and conventions. WIPO has its origins in the 1883 Paris Convention for the Protection of Intellectual Property and the 1886 Berne Convention for the Protection of Literary and Artistic Works. The convention establishing WIPO was signed in 1967 and came into effect in 1979. WIPO promotes the wider acceptance of existing intellectual-property treaties and the negotiation of new ones where needed. It also helps DEVELOPING COUNTRIES implement intellectual-property protection and attempts to establish uniform worldwide standards of protection for the owners of intellectual property. Canada is a member. The agency is based in Geneva.

World Meteorological Organization (WMO) A UNITED NATIONS organization established to co-ordinate and improve international knowledge of world meteorological, geophysical, and hydrological systems. It is also playing a key role in monitoring global warming. The origins of the WMO date back to 1873, when the International Meteorological Organization was established; it was succeeded in 1939 by an intergovernmental World Meteorological Organization. The current convention was drafted in 1947 and came into effect in 1950. It has established networks of meteorological and hydrological observation stations around the world to gather, co-ordinate, and exchange information. It has established World Weather watch, to track weather patterns by combining data from earth observation stations and from space-based systems. It also manages the World Climate Program, which was established following the World Climate Conference in 1979, to monitor global warming and determine the extent to which climate changes were due to human activity, as opposed to natural causes. In 1989, the

Global Atmosphere Watch was established as an early warning system on greenhouse gases, changes in the world's ozone layer, and acid and toxic rains. It is based in Geneva. Canada has been a member since 1951.

world oil price   *See* INTERNATIONAL OIL PRICE.

write down   The reduction in the value of an asset in a company's balance sheet to reflect the real loss in value of the asset. For example, if a company takes over another company that ends up losing money, at some point its value will be reduced on the acquiring company's own books.

write off   The removal of an asset from a company's balance sheet to reflect the fact that the asset is of no value.

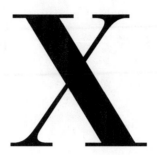

X-efficiency The efficiency with which a firm is managed — in other words, how well it acquires and uses the various FACTORS OF PRODUCTION. A firm that operates at maximum X-efficiency is one that is operating at its minimum costs. However, if it is protected from competition through monopoly, high tariffs, or subsidies, it is less likely to operate at maximum X-efficiency. Large bureaucratic firms are also less likely to achieve maximum X-efficiency due to their inflexibility.

yardstick A standard used in making comparisons or in assessing performance. For example, a yardstick for desirable economic growth might be the average annual rate of economic growth for the previous decade. Productivity increases can be used as a yardstick against which to measure the inflation potential of wage increases.

year-end audit The annual review of a firm's or an organization's financial records — including its BALANCE SHEET and EARNINGS STATEMENT — that is conducted by outside auditors to verify the firm's or organization's accuracy.

yield The annual return on an investment. It is expressed as a percentage of the cost of the investment. A $1,000 investment in a bond that pays $95 in annual interest has a yield of 9.5 percent; the same $1,000 investment in a common share that pays $37.50 in dividends has an annual yield of 3.75 percent. Fixed-interest bonds can only be sold to other investors during a period of rising interest rates if the price of the bond falls; this permits the yield to keep pace with rising interest rates. A $100 bond yielding 5 per-

cent might have to fall to, say, just under $67 if interest rates rose to 7.5 percent; $5 is 7.5 percent of $67. In a period of falling interest rates, bond prices will rise.

yield curve The graphical presentation of the interest rates according to the term to maturity. For example, while short-term interest rates may decline sharply, rates may become progressively higher for medium and long-term rates, reflecting market uncertainty or expectations about future economic developments such as the rate of inflation. Short-term rates tend to be lower than long-term rates. But if the yield curve slopes upward sharply, this usually suggests that financial markets expect inflation to trend to higher rates, even if inflation is currently low.

yield to maturity The total yield of a bond, including both the interest received on the bond's market value plus the amount of principal that will be received when the bond matures. This is an important concept when a bond is selling below or above its FACE VALUE.

zero-base budgeting system A system of budget planning that forces an evaluation of all spending within government and corporate departments. All budgets are assumed to start from a base of zero, which means every existing program has to be justified; this is in contrast to normal planning where it is assumed that existing programs will be maintained and the main issue will be the percentage increase in funding available for those programs. This forces officials each year to justify continued spending on a relatively unimportant, on-going program instead of shifting the resources to a new and more important program.

zero coupon bond A bond that has no coupon attached and that does not pay an annual rate of interest. Instead, the buyer receives the face value of the bond on maturity, having purchased it at a discount. The discount is the imputed rate of interest.

zero population growth (ZPG) A population-growth rate of zero; the number of births and deaths in the population are equal. It means that each couple should have no more than 2.11 children, since some children will die early in life or will not have children when they grow up.

zero-sum game A conflict game in which one participant can only gain at the expense of another; the sum of gains and losses adds to zero for every possible move. The situation is used in game theory to simulate conflicts between companies over markets, between nations over resources, or between Ottawa and the provinces over tax dollars. In a market with little growth, such as the market for sugar, one sugar company can only increase its sales at the expense of other sugar companies.

zoning A planning tool used by municipal governments to control the type of development that takes place in different parts of the community. A community will zone some areas for industry, others for commerce, others for high-density housing, and still other areas for single-family housing.

Zoning rules designate both the kinds of use permitted on a particular piece of land and the DENSITY of that activity. Zoning plans are usually drafted as by-laws. Since municipalities are creatures of the provinces, provincial governments have a veto over zoning decisions of municipal councils. Spot-rezoning refers to an exemption in the zoning for a particular piece of land.